International Agency, Distribution and Licensing Agreements

To my wife Anastasia without whose encouragement
this book would not have been written

Foreign chapters contributed by

Australia
Cheng Lim
Mallesons Stephen Jaques

Cyprus
Panayiotis Neocleous
Andreas Neocleous & Co

Czech Republic
Jan Kotík, Lukáš Vondryska and Martin Bourgeault
Dewey Ballantine

Hong Kong
Rob McCallough
Masons

Hungary
Dr Tamás Gödölle
Bogsch & Partners

Japan
Keiji Matsumoto
Mori Hamada & Matsumoto

Poland
Krystyna Szczepanowska with the assistance of Daniel Hasik
IP Department, Linklaters

Romania
Gelu Maravela
Musat & Associates

Singapore
Vemala Rajamanickam
Allen & Gledhill

United States
Mark Uhrynuk
Mayer Brown Rowe and Maw

Other titles by Richard Christou available from Sweet and Maxwell:

Drafting Commercial Agreements 2nd edition—0 421 654 104
Boilerplate: Practical Clauses 3rd edition—0 421 782 803

International Agency, Distribution and Licensing Agreements

Fourth edition

Written and edited by

Richard Christou
Solicitor (M.A. Cantab.)

London
Sweet & Maxwell
2003

Fourth Edition 2003

Richard Christou has asserted his right under the Copyright, Designs and Patents Act 1988 to be identified as the author of this work.

Published in 2003 by
Sweet & Maxwell Ltd of
100 Avenue Road, Swiss Cottage,
London NW3 3PF
Computerset by YHT Ltd, London
Printed and bound in Great Britain by MPG Books Ltd, Bodmin, Cornwall

No natural forests were destroyed to make this product;
only farmed timber was used and replanted

A CIP catalogue record for this book is available from the British Library

ISBN 0 421 791 101

Contents

Preface to the First Edition

The purpose of this book is to provide a practical guide to the negotiation and drafting of international agency, distribution and manufacturing agreements for the supply of goods. The book is structured around five main precedents covering agency, distribution outside the EEC, distribution inside the EEC, selective distribution systems, and manufacturing licences. The precedents on agency, selective distribution and manufacturing cover areas both inside and outside the EEC, by means of alternative clauses where necessary. Also, the chapter on selective distribution contains detailed provisions on technical support, warranties, spares and after-sales service, which can be used in any distribution agreement relating to technically complex goods, inside or outside the EEC.

Additional chapters then cover generally applicable clauses, and auxiliary agreements relating to software, escrow and consultancy. Although this book is intended primarily for the lawyer practising in the areas of international commercial law, it will also prove of interest to those with commercial negotiating responsibility for such agreements. If it is important for lawyers to understand the commercial requirements of their clients, it is also equally important for their clients to have some idea of the legal framework within which they have to work. Although written by an English lawyer, this book is not intended only for English lawyers, and it can be of particular help to lawyers practising outside the EEC who are called upon to deal with agreements affecting the EEC.

No apology is made for the fact that this book has a reasonably high proportion of its contents devoted to the impact of EEC competition law on such agreements. The Common Market now covers twelve of the states of Western Europe, and it is no longer possible for businessmen, or their legal advisers, to proceed with such agreements without understanding the opportunities and pitfalls to which EEC competition law gives rise.

The plan of the book is to provide a precedent for each clause followed by a commentary drawing attention to the relevant legal and commercial aspects of its drafting, application and use. When using this book for the first time it is suggested that Chapter 1 be read initially, followed by the chapter for which it is desired to draft an agreement. Not until the chapters have been read, so that the implications of the clauses can be fully considered, should drafting begin. It is not possible in these types of agreements to provide blanket precedents which are applicable in every case without intelligent adaptation and selection. The form of the book permits the selection of desired clauses and the draftsman should not hesitate to mix and match clauses from the various chapters as required, once their significance has been understood from a study of the relevant commentary.

As initial assistance, Appendix 1 gives references to sets of clauses that would be suitable in many cases for specimen agreements on the subjects covered by this book.

In each chapter there is an introductory section which gives both commercial and legal background to the agreement concerned. In the commentary as well, emphasis is placed on the commercial environment in which these agreements are implemented. No draftsman can produce a satisfactory agreement of this type or advise properly on its anticipated and desired effects unless he understands its commercial as well as its legal significance.

Appendices 2, 3 and 4 are specifically referred to in the text, and should be consulted as necessary. The remaining Appendices contain full texts of relevant EEC legislation.

It cannot be overemphasised when dealing with agreements affected by EEC law that it is not enough to have a bare knowledge of its provisions. Although the relevant provisions are quoted in the commentary in the chapters concerned, it is useful to read the whole text of any piece of this legislation, when considering drafting an agreement affected by it, with particular reference to the lengthy preambles setting out the purposes of the Regulations. Both the EEC Commission and the European Court interpret EEC competition law very much by reference to its intended purpose, and do not rely, to the same degree as a lawyer versed in the common law would, on the strict interpretation of the wording of statutes.

The quotation from the cases, in the commentary and the printing of the texts of the legislation, are intended to enable the draftsman to get the feel of this method of interpretation, and understand how the Commission and the Court react, in the light of this interpretation, to the particular economic and commercial effects generated by the provisions of the agreements that come before them for consideration.

R Christou
London
May 1986

Preface to the Fourth Edition

Since the 3rd Edition of this book appeared in 1996 the world has changed drastically both economically and politically. In 1996 one looked forward to a period of growth and stability. In 2003, overheated Stock Markets have collapsed, the world has been shaken by political changes, war and the prospect of terrorism, and most of the major economies, far from looking forward to growth, are now more likely to be in danger from deflation.

Nevertheless, in this changing economical and political scene the importance of trading relationships which deliver real value remains undiminished. Because of this, use of agency, distribution and licensing agreements to trade across national boundaries is of increasing importance, particularly given the enlargement of the European Union (by a further ten states in May 2004) which will create a single market covering Western and most of Central Europe.

So far as the subject matter of this book is concerned, the major area for new developments is that of competition law. The whole framework of European and UK competition law has been drastically changed; the first through legislation providing for the direct application of Arts 81 and 82 of the EC Treaty by the Courts and Competition Authorities of the European Union Member States, and the second by the passing of the Competition Act 1998 and the Enterprise Act 2002 which have repealed the old framework for competition and control of monopolies and mergers, that was in force in the UK for the last 50 years, and replaced it with a system based on the principles of EC Competition Law.

In this new and difficult environment, robust, clear and comprehensive agreements, a real understanding of the commercial principles on which they are based and a sound grasp of the impact of competition law is more vital than ever. I have thus taken the opportunity in this 4th edition not only to update the text and precedents to take account of general developments in applicable laws, but also substantially to revise the text and some of the precedents to deal with these major issues.

The changes in competition law described above, with their emphasis on assessing the competitive effects of any agreement not in relation to its terms but by its impact on the market, has necessitated a new approach to the core chapters of this book, namely Chapters 5, 6 and 8. I have also taken the opportunity, given the complexity of the subject, to add a number of flow charts to guide the reader through the current position on the application of

UK and EU competition law in relation to commercial agreements.

Another major area of development has been in relation to the Agency Directive (Counsel Directive 86/653) which has now been the subject of many important decisions in the UK Courts. It has therefore been possible to re-write Chapter 3 with considerably more authority as to the way in which the Agency Directive is to be interpreted.

Finally, given the increased importance of international trade with the new accession countries for EU membership in 2004, besides updating the current international chapters I have also included further chapters dealing with the law as it stands in the Czech Republic, Cyprus, Hungary, Poland and Romania.

The other major development that has taken place since the last edition of this book has been the extent to which legal sources are now available over the internet. Rather than the reproduction of lengthy appendices containing relevant legislation I have therefore taken the opportunity to remove much of the appendices containing material which is readily available over the Internet and to use the space for further text and commentary on the precedents. Thus, unlike previous editions, the appendices are kept to an absolute minimum. However the reader's attention is drawn to Appendix 4 which sets out a list of relevant websites on which the legislation referred to in this book can be found.

The law in this book is in general stated as that in force at the end of April 2004.

R Christou
London
July 2003

Table of Cases

Table of Statutes

Table of Statutory Instruments

Table of European and International Legislation

Conventions

Treaties

Regulations

DIRECTIVES

Decision

Recommendation

Table of Foreign Legislation

Czech Republic

Denmark

Finland

France

Germany

Greece

Hong Kong

Singapore

Spain

Sweden

Switzerland

USA

Miscellaneous

Chapter 1

Definitions and Interpretations

Contents

1.1 How to use this book

The following chapters contain precedents covering specifically the business relationships of agency, distributorship, manufacture under licence and consultancy. There are, however, certain common elements which all of these agreements require, and it has been felt most useful to deal with these in a preliminary chapter, reference then being made to the various specimen clauses as required for each precedent. **1–01**

In this chapter there are also precedents for use in the areas of confidentiality and restrictions on competition. The precedents here are more elaborate than those used in the later chapters to cover these subjects. They may therefore be used (subject to the comments in later chapters about restrictions under various legal systems) in substitution, where it is felt that the circumstances warrant a tighter and more comprehensive clause. **1–02**

It is not necessarily intended that each of the precedents in the following chapters should be supplemented by all of the specimen clauses in this chapter. Commercial pressures may well dictate that some of them are not acceptable in specific cases, and there will always be instances where the desire of the clients for a short and relatively informal agreement outweighs the desire of the draftsman to cover every legal eventuality. **1–03**

1–04 The numbering system used in this book ensures that each clause in the book has a unique number. This enables cross-referencing to be used with the aim of shortening the precedents by cutting out repetitive matter. In each chapter (other than this one) the first section (*e.g.* 2.1 or 3.1) is an introductory section so that the precedent proper starts at the second section (*e.g.* 2.2 or 3.2). This means that when drafting an agreement under any chapter, the first section of the precedent can consist of the definitions to be chosen from Chapter 1.2. After that the numbering in the precedent can be used as the actual numbering in the agreement, and all cross references will agree. There is also one numbered section at the end of each precedent headed "Interpretation and Signature" which can be used to contain all the clauses from Chapter 1, as sequentially numbered subclauses, that it is wished to include, and which do not fall within the definition section.

1–05 The same method has been used for numbering schedules. In each precedent the schedules are properly numbered, and it will only be necessary to include any schedule text as provided in the precedent or as prompted by the definitions in 1.2 into the relevant schedule for the precedent. For this reason the schedule numbers in Chapter 1.2 are left blank to be filled in as appropriate by the draftsman for the particular precedent he is dealing with.

1–06 With regard to the parties, the term "Principal" is used throughout these precedents to cover the principal in agency or distribution situations, the licensor in licence agreements (with the exception of Chapter 8, where the term "Licensor" is used), and the employer in a consultancy agreement. The terms "Agent", "Consultant", "Licensee" and "Distributor" are used in the chapters to designate the appropriate relationships. For the purposes of simplicity the precedents in Chapter 1 refer to the "Distributor" in all cases, unless a particular clause is only for a certain type of agreement, in which case the appropriate definition is used. Thus in some cases it will be necessary to substitute the term "Distributor" with "Agent" (Chapters 2 and 3), "Licensee" (Chapters 7 and 8) or "Consultant" (Chapter 9).

1–07 The provision actually setting out details of the parties will be an unnumbered section at the head of the agreement, giving their full names, defining the one as the Principal and the other as the Agent, Distributor, Licensee or Consultant as appropriate, and giving both parties' principal place of business or registered office, as the case may be, for the purposes of serving notice.

1–08 A typical heading would be as follows:

THIS AGREEMENT is made between

[ ] whose [registered office] [principal place of business] is at [ ] (the "Principal")

and[ ] whose [registered office] [principal place of business] is at [ ] (the "Distributor")

The dating and signature clause of the agreement, which is likewise intended to be unnumbered, and, strictly, should be printed after the schedules, at the very end of the agreement, is set out in Chapter 1.12.2.

1.2 Definitions

1.2.1 The products

1.2.1(a) The Products shall mean the products [equipment and spare parts] listed in [Pt * of] Sch. * [in the form and to the specifications listed in Pt * of Sch. *] [in the packaging detailed in Pt * of Sch. *]. **1–09**

OR

1.2.1(b) The Products shall mean the range of [dietetic] products listed in Sch. 1 hereto [which Schedule may from time to time be amended by the addition or deletion of products by mutual agreement recorded in writing]

OR

1.2.1(c) The Products shall mean all those [cosmetic and skin care] products from time to time manufactured and sold by the Principal under the Trade Mark.

OR

1.2.1(d) The Products shall mean those [confectionery] products listed in Sch. * which list shall automatically be varied by the deletion therefrom of any such product which the Principal ceases to manufacture and by the addition thereto [automatically] [at the request of the Principal] [at the request of the Distributor] of any new product in the [confectionery] field which the Principal puts on the market outside the Territory:

Provided that:

such new product can legally be sold in the Territory (whether or not subject to the prior obtaining of any consent permission or licence) or can be altered so that it can be so sold; and, if so required:

such new product is so altered; and/or

the said consent permission or licence is obtained;

in both cases at the expense of the [Distributor] [Principal] prior to its addition to the said list.

The four versions of the definition of the products to be covered by the agreement are largely all usable in any of the agreements in the following chapters. The main problem to be addressed is the question of variations to the definition during the life of the agreement, either because a need is perceived for a new product in the market concerned, or because the principal chooses to withdraw a particular product from the market. The product examples in the square brackets are for illustration only, and should be adapted to the relevant product range. **1–10**

Version (a) is fixed and detailed, although of course the parties can choose **1–11** to amend it by agreement if they both so wish, even though no provision to this effect is included. This type of definition is perhaps best suited to manufacturing agreements, or to agreements covering the distribution of technically sophisticated products or pharmaceuticals.

1–12 Version (b) is slightly looser, with its reference to a product range, but its specific addition of the provision relating to amendment by mutual agreement, while it records the intention of the parties at least to consider variation, actually imposes no greater legal obligations than the first version.

1–13 Version (c) is perhaps best suited to agency agreements where the agent is intended to handle the whole product range of the principal irrespective of its alterations from time to time. It is also useful in distribution arrangements where the product line is a large one, with a strong family approach produced by the use of a well-known trade mark which is more important than the individual items of the line. These may well change frequently in response to changing consumer taste, or even to seasonal requirements. Food and drink, and cosmetic product lines are areas where this often occurs.

1–14 Version (c) gives the advantage of total flexibility. The principal is free to drop an item without notice, and the distributor is free to take up a new item in the same way. This does, however, have implications for the distributor, which must be accepted. If he has an obligation imposed upon him elsewhere in the agreement to stock the whole range of the product line from time to time existing, he will then have to take up new items whether he likes it or not.

1–15 Version (d) recognises the need to amend the schedule in a disciplined way, and the problems that may be encountered in adapting a new product to a particular market. The principal is protected when he ceases to manufacture an item. New items may be added, and the different phrases in square brackets indicate the possible ways in which this could occur.

1–16 Reformulations to take account of preservatives or colouring ingredients that are permitted in a particular territory is an area often encountered in foods, cosmetics and pharmaceuticals. Technical changes (*e.g.* from 220 to 110 volts working for electrical equipment) to make products suitable for the territory are another. Once again not only adaptations but also the obtaining of consents to market may be necessary. These matters are covered in the proviso, as well as the question of who pays for them.

1.2.2 The territory

1–17 1.2.2(a) The Territory shall mean the countries [geographic areas] [states] listed in Sch. *

OR

1.2.2(b) The Territory shall mean the states listed in sched * PROVIDED THAT:

(i) if there is any change to the geographical boundaries of one of the said states whether by way of expansion or contraction and such change has been recognised (pursuant to the principles of international law) either *de jure* or *de facto* by the government of the Principal's state of [incorporation] [residence] all references to the said state shall (from the date upon which such change is so recognised) be deemed to be references to such state with its boundaries as so changed; and

(ii) if one of the said states should cease to exist as a political entity and such change has been recognised (pursuant to the principles of international law) either *de jure* or *de facto* by the government of the Principal's state of [incorporation] [residence]) it shall (from the date upon which such change is so recognised) be deemed to have been deleted from Sch. * unless it has been replaced by a successor state occupying substantially the same geographical boundaries, in which case all references to the said state shall thereupon be deemed to be references to the said successor state.

OR

1.2.2(c) "The Territory" shall mean the Member States of the European Union [as constituted at the date of this Agreement.] [for the time being. For the avoidance of doubt if a state shall cease to be a Member State or shall become a Member State of the European Union it shall thereupon cease to be or become, respectively, part of the Territory.] [Notwithstanding the foregoing if [*Ruritania*] which is not currently a member of the European Union shall after the date of this Agreement become a Member State of the European Union the Territory shall be so defined as to exclude [*Ruritania*].]

Again the most important matter to be considered is changes to the extent of the territory during the life of the agreement. It is not normal to have a specific provision that the territory be changed at the option of one party, nor even by mutual agreement. If the parties do come to such an agreement it is usually recorded by a formal variation of the original document. The more difficult point is when changes occur for political reasons, during the course of the agreement, which make the territory different to that which the parties originally contemplated.

1–18 Version (a) lists countries, states or geographic areas by name. This is a simple clause which is appropriate for parts of the world where one can assume sufficient political stability for there to be no changes in the boundaries or the political constitution of the areas in question during the lifetime of the agreement.

1–19 However, the events of the last ten years both in Eastern Europe and the former Soviet Union have shown that this is by no means always the case. Version (b) is an attempt to deal with areas of instability.

1–20 For the purposes of trading, it is normally political boundaries that define a territory rather than physical ones. The boundaries of a state can change, even to the extent of it disappearing entirely, either by legal means, or because of conquest. Similarly new states can be formed out of old ones either by militant separatist movements or peacefully by mutual agreement. The parties to agency, distribution and licensing agreements have to recognise these changes since, whatever their views as to the legality or desirability of such changes, they have an obvious impact on the ability of the parties to discharge their obligations under the agreement. Some changes may make this simply more difficult or inappropriate, but many of the changes concerned may make it impossible.

1–21 Examples of such events are the separation of Bangladesh from Pakistan, the occupation of Northern Cyprus by Turkey, the splitting of Czechoslovakia into two new republics and German Reunification. More extreme problems, but of the same type, occurred with the break up of the Soviet Union and the emergence of independent states from various parts of Yugoslavia as a result of separatist movements. The absorption of Hong Kong into the People's Republic of China in 1997 is a further example of such an event, although the special legal status that has been granted to the former Crown Colony is such that any agreement containing Hong Kong as part of the territory covered should deal specifically with the issues raised by its special status (see Chapter 14).

1–22 The proviso (i) of version (b) refers to the recognition of the change in geographical boundaries of a state. The proviso can be limited only to those cases where the change has taken place legally in accordance with international law (*e.g.* by a treaty ceding part of the territory of one state to another to settle a boundary dispute) and is therefore recognised as having occurred *de jure*. Alternatively, one can take a pragmatic view, and include as well those cases where the change has taken place illegally (*i.e.* by military conquest) but is sufficiently permanent that it is recognised as having occurred *de facto*, irrespective of the legality or morality of what has happened. Proviso (i) takes the position that both *de jure* and *de facto* situations should be covered, since even in the case of a *de facto* situation both parties will be unable to implement the agreement, without taking account of the change that has occurred.

1–23 Since views on legality differ in the international community, proviso (i) limits recognition of boundary changes to those which the government of the principal's state has accepted, whether on a *de jure* or a *de facto* basis, since the principal may well find it hard to take a different view to that of his government as to the status of the boundary change. However, if desired, some more general international standard may used, such as recognition by the EU, or the United Nations, but in many cases such recognition takes a long time to occur, and it is more sensible for the parties to face up to the change and deal with it as soon as possible.

1–24 Under the operation of proviso (i), where an agreement covered the territory of the German Federal Republic, the change in its boundaries after absorption of the German Democratic Republic on German Reunification would automatically have been taken into account. Similarly where an agreement covered the territory of Yugoslavia, under proviso (i) it would now apply only to the rump Yugoslavia left after the separation of the various new states. Again, the Turkish occupation of Northern Cyprus and the separation of Bangladesh from Pakistan, would, under proviso (i), result in a diminution of the geographical territory under an agreement applying to the Republic of Cyprus or the state of Pakistan, respectively.

Proviso (ii) of version (b) deals with the disappearance of a state in its entirety, and follows the same approach to *de jure* and *de facto* recognition as the first limb. However, proviso (ii) is limited in its operation. If a state ceases to exist, as in the case of the German Democratic Republic for example, it will simply be taken out of the list. However, where, as in the case of Czechoslovakia, a state ceases to exist because its geographic territory becomes divided amongst a number of new political entities, the agreement would no longer cover any of the relevant geographical area, and new agreements would have to be struck for the new successor states, in this case the Czech and Slovak Republics. It is only where there is one successor state covering the whole of the previous state's territory (*e.g.* where a colony becomes independent) that the successor state would be covered. Other political permutations, and in particular the appearance of new states, as in Yugoslavia or the former Soviet Union, are too complicated to cover, and are best dealt with by cancellation and renegotiation in the light of the changed circumstances. **1–25**

Finally, it should be noted that neither proviso takes account of changes which are neither recognised *de jure*, nor at least sufficiently permanent to be recognised *de facto*. In such cases of instability, the better course is to rely upon a force majeure clause (see cl.1.7). **1–26**

Version (c) is one relating to a federation or other grouping of states or countries. The obvious example of this is the European Union. In cases where the territory is not the European Union as a whole, (and, given its current and potential future extent, agreements covering the whole of the European Union are becoming increasingly unlikely) it may still be necessary to define the European Union for other purposes relating to territory in the agreement (*e.g.* rights to export or prohibitions on export outside the European Union). In this case the clause can be adapted for this purpose. **1–27**

Following the advent of the Treaty of European Union of 1993 (the Maastricht Treaty) the old terminology of the European Economic Community or the EEC has become obsolete, and a number of new terms have now appeared. The European Economic Community (EEC) was originally one of three separate European communities, the others being the European Coal and Steel Community (ECSC) and the European Atomic Energy Community (EURATOM). In 1993, the members of these three communities were regarded as members of the new European Union which came into force under the Maastricht Treaty. The legislative basis for this Union was the three original treaties, which were somewhat modified by the Maastricht Treaty, and the Maastricht Treaty itself. The three former treaties dealt with economic aspects of the Union. The EEC Treaty in particular was amended by the Maastricht Treaty to include a section on common economic and monetary policy, and its name was changed to the European Community (EC) Treaty. The Maastricht Treaty overlaid on the three treaties common foreign and security policies for the Union and a regime for co-operation in justice and home affairs. **1–28**

So far as the ECSC and EURATOM Treaties are concerned, the former **1–29** expired on July 23, 2002. Competition cases previously dealt with under that treaty in relation to coal and steel are now dealt with under the general competition law rules of the EC Treaty. The EURATOM Treaty remains in existence, but contains no reference to competition law.

1–30 Opinion is divided as to whether one should now refer to the European Union or the European Community. Most people suggest that the term European Union should be used when dealing with the Member States' activities in the areas covered specifically by the Treaty of Maastricht (such as common foreign policy initiatives) while the term European Community, or the "Community", could be used when considering the economic activities of the Member States derived from the provisions of the old EEC (now European Community) Treaty.

1–31 So far as the old references to EEC law were concerned (for instance EEC competition law) it is still correct to refer to EC law since the provisions regulating that law are contained not in the Maastricht Treaty but in the EC Treaty. Thus, as they are adopted under the EC Treaty, directives will continue to be called EC Directives, and the Commission in Brussels will continue to call itself the Commission of the European Communities (since it still deals with both of the original communities still remaining, in so far as they now have a separate existence, and acts under the EC Treaty). However, the EC Council has renamed itself the Council of the European Union since it acts both under the EC Treaty and the Maastricht Treaty.

1–32 Given the above changes in terminology, and the emphasis in this book on legal and economic rather than political activity, references will largely be to the European Community, conveniently abbreviated to EC, and to European Community law, abbreviated to EC law, or EC competition law, where appropriate. Any references to the European Union will be abbreviated to EU.

1–33 Following the conclusion of the signature of the Treaty of Nice in 2001, its subsequent ratification in 2002, and its coming into force on February 1, 2003, the stage is set for further enlargement of the European Union. The related Protocol on Enlargement and its attached Declarations provided for a potential enlargement from 15 up to 27 Member States, although the actual number of new Member States will not be known until the completion of all of the accession negotiations with each accession state. The potential accession states are: Poland, Romania, Czech Republic, Hungary, Bulgaria, Slovakia, Lithuania, Latvia, Slovenia, Estonia, Cyprus and Malta. At the Copenhagen Summit in October 2002, it was agreed that negotiations should now proceed to finalise treaties for the accession of all of these states, except Bulgaria and Romania, with effective date of May 1, 2004, in time for the European Parliament elections in June 2004. Discussions with Bulgaria and Romania continue, as currently some concern over the rate of their economic progress has caused the Member States to conclude they are not yet ready for accession. Turkey also hopes to start accession negotiations in the near future, perhaps as early as 2005, but as yet no formal commitment to such negotiations has been forthcoming from the European Union.

1–34 The Treaty of Nice envisaged a gradual enlargement of the Union over the period 2004 to 2009, depending upon the progress and success of each accession negotiation. The pace of the accession negotiations has been quicker than anticipated, but the Treaty does not require amendment since its provisions come into force (as regards the European Parliament) from 2004 and otherwise from 2005. The Treaty deals principally with the changes needed to the various European Union institutions required to enable them to continue to work efficiently when the increasing number of Member States with diverse interests complicates representation and decision making. It builds upon, but also amends, the provisions of the Treaty of Amsterdam, 1999, which covered similar issues, particularly by the extension of the principle of qualified majority voting. It also facilitates the establishment of enhanced cooperation among Member States, as originally provided for under the Treaty of Amsterdam.

Given the process of enlargement, it is more important than ever to **1–35** decide, when drafting definitions of the European Union, whether it is appropriate to freeze the definition at the current number of Member States, or perhaps at some future but intermediate stage of the enlargement, or to allow the definition to change in line with the gradual enlargement of the Union. Everything will depend upon the circumstances in which and the purpose for which the definition is to be used, but the matter must be considered and a decision taken. In many cases, the wisest course will be to freeze the definition at the current number, or some future stage of the enlargement, and to increase the definition to cover further enlargement by a contract amendment, if the parties can agree that this is appropriate. Version (c) above shows some of the ways in which these issues can be dealt with. If the phrase in the first set of square brackets is used, the definition is frozen at a point in time. Subsequent additions or withdrawals do not change the definition and the material in the next two sets of square brackets would not be used at all. If one requires a fluctuating definition, the material in the second rather than the first set of square brackets should be used. Finally, if a fluctuating definition is adopted, particularly given the somewhat uncertain nature of the current accession process, it may be necessary to exclude one or more potential accession states, in the event that they do become Member States at some time in the future; for instance, because they are already part of the Territory covered in an agreement with another distributor or licensee. In this case, the sentence in the third set of square brackets, suitably adapted, should be added as well.

Besides the formal enlargements of the EU, there have been a growing **1–36** number of association agreements (known as "Europe Agreements") entered into in the last ten years between the EU and various interested states. These agreements are a preparatory step to full membership of the EU. The signatory state, in order to prepare for membership, must remove obstacles to trade with the EU, such as tariff barriers and quotas, and harmonise regulatory legislation particularly in the area of competition law, state aid, public procurement, intellectual property and the transfer of capital. Particularly in regard to competition law, the signatory state will adopt provisions analogous to Arts 81 and 82 of the EC Treaty. This means that, in effect, EC competition law is now being applied over an increasing and very large area of the continent of Europe. For instance in June 1995, a conference took place in Hungary, between the Commission and representatives from Hungary, Bulgaria, the Czech Republic, the Slovak Republic, Poland and Romania, to discuss competition law and its possible harmonisation across Central Europe.

1–37 Europe Agreements were signed with the twelve current potential accession states and Croatia. Signature of an agreement like a Europe Agreement is a prerequisite for full membership of the EU, and was, for instance, the path followed by Spain and Portugal, and latterly by the twelve current potential accession states. Agreements similar to Europe Agreements have also been entered into with Turkey (Customs Union Agreement), Russia, Moldava and Ukraine (Partnership and Cooperation Agreements), Albania (Trade and Economic Cooperation Agreement) and with Tunisia and Israel (Euro-Mediterranean Association Agreements).

1–38 Lastly, mention should be made of the European Economic Area (EEA) which extended the EC single market in goods and services, and thus provisions of the EC Treaty, such as those relating to competition, public procurement and free movement of goods, to five of the Member States of the European Free Trade Association (EFTA), namely Austria, Finland, Iceland, Norway, Sweden and Liechtenstein. Although Austria, Finland and Sweden have joined the EU, the EEA does still retain its significance in trading relations between the EU and Norway, Iceland and Liechtenstein.

1–39 1.2.3 *The Trade Mark* The Trade Mark shall mean those registered trade marks [and trade and brand names] set out in Sch. *.

The phrase in square brackets covers unregistered names which should be listed in so far as they are used in the sale of the products.

1–40 1.2.4 *The Patents* The Patents shall mean those patents listed in Sch. *.

It is normal to list precisely both trade marks and patents, in the schedule, and cover any change by a formal variation to the original agreement.

1–41 1.2.5 *Connected Person* Connected Person shall be defined in accordance with the Companies Act 1985, s.346.

1.2.6 *Director* Director shall be defined in accordance with the Companies Act 1985, s.741 and shall include a "shadow director" as defined in that section.

1.2.7 *Holding and Subsidiary Company* Holding Company and Subsidiary Company shall be defined in accordance with the Companies Act 1985, ss.736, 736A and 736B.

1.2.8 *The Group* The Group shall mean the group of companies composed of the Principal, its Holding Company (if any) and all Subsidiary Companies of the Principal and of the Principal's Holding Company (if any).

Definitions 1.2.5 to 1.2.8 are the ones generally accepted in the UK which are used to define groups of companies, and the persons who control them. These definitions will be used later in connection with the clauses relating to confidentiality (cl.1.4) and restrictions on competition (cl.1.5).

Where English law applies it is sufficient to use cll.1.2.5, 1.2.6 and 1.2.7 as printed. Where the proper law of the agreement is not English law, and or where the parties are not familiar with the English Companies Act, it is better to reproduce the relevant sections from the statute suitably adapted. **1–42**

It should be noted that the Companies Act 1985, s.736 was amended—widening the definition of "subsidiary" to include more concepts of control than just share ownership—by the Companies Act 1989, s.144, which substituted a new s.736 and added new ss.736A and 736B. Those who find the new version of s.736 too wide may continue to use the old one by incorporating its provisions verbatim in the definition section. **1–43**

> 1.2.9 *Competing Activity* Competing Activity shall mean any business trade or occupation the same as, or similar to, or in conflict or in competition with any business trade or occupation [relating to or carried on in respect of the Products] [carried on by any company within the Group]. **1–44**

The first phrase in square brackets gives what is probably the most commercially acceptable version of the clause. The second version may in some cases be applicable, for instance, if a consultant or agent with a very wide brief is employed to cover all of the group business, but, quite apart from commercial acceptability, a clause of this width is likely in many jurisdictions to be regarded as unenforceable as an unreasonable restriction on competition.

> 1.2.10 *The Information* The Information shall mean all communications and all information whether written visual or oral and all other material supplied to or obtained by the Distributor from any company in the Group during the continuance of this Agreement and all information recommendations or advice given to any company in the Group by the Distributor in pursuance of its duties under this Agreement and shall without limitation of the foregoing include any information from whatever source supplied to or obtained by the Distributor concerning the trade secrets customers business associations and transactions financial arrangements and technical or commercial affairs of the Group whether or not related to the Products. **1–45**

This is a wide definition of information upon which obligations of confidentiality can later be imposed. It is sufficiently wide that it will also encompass the definitions of knowhow set out below. It is however necessary to define knowhow separately as obligations additional to those of confidentiality are imposed in relation to it under the manufacturing agreements in which the term is used.

Restrictions on use and disclosure of confidential information which relates to group companies other than the principal, and not to the products, do not give rise to the problems on restraint of trade in the way that restrictions on competition do when applied to group company businesses **1–46** unrelated to the products. However, where the information is a report generated by a consultant in pursuance of duties under the agreement some problems may arise. These are discussed under Chapter 1.4.

1.2.11 The knowhow

1–47 1.2.11(a) The Knowhow shall mean all patentable and non-patentable inventions discoveries improvements processes and copyright works (including without limitation computer programs) and designs (whether or not registered or registrable) listed in Sch. *.

OR

1.2.11(b) The Knowhow shall mean:

1.2.11.1 A complete file containing:

details of all manufacturing processes and formulae [reasonably] necessary [to enable the Licensee] to manufacture the Products; and

a list and specifications of all plant and machinery and all quality control and other facilities [reasonably] necessary [to enable the Licensee] to manufacture pack store transport market and sell the Products; and

1.2.11.2 Technical assistance and training [reasonably] necessary to transfer [to the Licensee] the Principal's experience and methods in the field of manufacturing quality control and development of the Products; and

1.2.11.3 Commercial assistance and training in the transfer of marketing and sales knowhow; and

[1.2.11.4 All improvements additional experience and development in the foregoing matters relating to the Products generated by the Principal during the continuance of this Agreement.]

OR

1.2.11(c) The Knowhow shall mean the following details in relation to each of the Products:

quantitative composition
manufacturing procedure
specification of finished product
method of analysis of finished product
specifications of raw materials
methods of analysis of raw materials
data on stability of preparations
indication/dosage
description of performance
animal tests
clinical tests
data on toxicology

OR

1.2.11(d) The Knowhow shall mean:

1.2.11.1 Production drawings of subassemblies as manufactured by the Principal for the Products;

1.2.11.2 Layout and other documents for manufacturing assembling and testing the Products;

1.2.11.3 Purchasing specifications for components for the Products;

1.2.11.4 Test specifications for manufactured items;

1.2.11.5 Documents relating to installation, maintenance, factory operating, data testing and training;

1.2.11.6 Drawings specifications and information for the manufacture or procurement of all production tools gauges inspection equipment and accessories required for the manufacture of the Products;

1.2.11.7 Specifications of machine tools and accessories required for the manufacture of the Products together with written advice on their ordering selection and procurement;

1.2.11.8 Technical assistance and training in the implementation of all the foregoing in accordance with the detailed programme set out in Sch. *.

Knowhow is defined under manufacturing agreements basically for two purposes. The first is so that an obligation can be imposed upon the principal to transfer it to the licensee. The second is to impose obligations of confidentiality in relation to it upon the licensee. From the point of view of both parties these two requirements generate different ways of looking at the definition.

If confidentiality is considered, the principal wishes to define it as widely **1–48** as possible, to make sure it is all caught, while the licensee wishes to circumscribe the definition to enable him to comply with his non-disclosure obligations in relation to a defined set of information. If transmission is considered, the licensee wishes to obtain not only all the knowhow in possession of the principal that has anything to do with the products, but also to be sure that what he gets is sufficient to enable him to produce the products. He will thus wish to have a general definition that catches as much as possible. The principal is concerned in this case to make sure that he does not have an open-ended obligation imposed upon him, which may go on for a very long time, and require him to reduce to transmittable form experience that resides only in the heads of his staff. He will prefer to have a defined list of documents only.

Version (a) of the definition provides for the listing method. If this is **1–49** combined with the very wide definition of information in 1.2.10 it will satisfy the requirements of the principal for certainty of the knowhow he has to disclose and wide cover for confidentiality.

1–50 Version (b) is one which is far more open-ended, and thus satisfies the aspirations of a demanding, and perhaps not technically very well qualified, licensee. The key to its operation is the inclusion of the phrase "necessary to manufacture ... the Products" in 1.2.11.1 by which each specified class of information to be transferred is qualified. This means that the obligation is imposed upon the principal to transfer whatever information is needed to manufacture the products.

1–51 The word "necessary" has to be interpreted in an absolute sense as "that in the absence of which it is not possible to manufacture the products". It does not mean merely information which it would be more convenient for the licensee to have, but which he could develop on his own, basing his work on information transferred to him by the principal. An example here would be detailed working drawings to set up the licensee's production line. It would save the licensee time and money if he had them, but he could make them himself from general design drawings and product specifications, or pay an expert to do so for him. However, without the general design drawings and product specifications he would not know what to make. The former are convenient, the latter necessary. If the licensee requires more than the bare minimum of necessary information, then he must either include the word "reasonably" where indicated in the square brackets or else specify what is required.

1–52 It should also be noted that what is necessary is not (without specific provision) interpreted in relation to the licensee himself, personally. Thus, in the absence of special provisions, a less technically sophisticated licensee could not claim more information was "necessary" for him, than for a licensee with technical experience in that line of products. This can be remedied by making the qualifying phrase relate to the licensee by adding the phrase in square brackets "to enable the Licensee" as indicated. The principal could well prefer the alternative of a phrase like "to enable a person skilled in the art of manufacturing items similar to the Products".

1–53 In 1.2.11.2 of version (b) inclusion of the word "necessary" here means that the principal would have to carry out as much training as needed to put the licensee in a position to manufacture the products. The inclusion of the phrase in square brackets "to the Licensee" strengthens this. However, the inclusion of the word "reasonably" as indicated in square brackets would in this clause work to cut down the amount of training the principal would have to do.

1–54 The theme of open-endedness is continued in 1.2.11.3 of version (b), with no particular limitations on the amount of training to be given.

1–55 Lastly, 1.2.11.4 imposes the same obligations upon the principal in relation to all improvements to the products generated in the life of the agreement. This is a very serious open-ended obligation, not only because the amount of work to be undertaken cannot be quantified when the agreement is signed, but because of the perennial argument between licensors and licensees as to when a modification ceases to be an improvement of an existing product, and becomes a new product in its own right subject to a new agreement. The importance of this is that even though there may have been a down-payment to cover the transfer of initial knowhow, the transfer relating to improvements will have to be funded, in the absence of specific provisions, out of running royalties. In extreme cases, the royalties can be entirely eaten away by the costs of continued training and transfer of knowhow in improvements.

It is unfortunate for licensors that most developing countries which have legislation controlling transfer of technology usually permit only one lump sum payment, control the level of royalty permitted, and require to be imposed on the licensor an obligation to transfer improvements during the life of the agreement. India, for instance, imposes these kinds of requirements. The only safeguard for the licensor is to specify the amount of training which is covered by the lump sum, and (where and in so far as this is permitted by control of technology transfer legislation) specify a scale of charges for any additional training that the licensee requires, either for improvements, or because of lack of technical sophistication. **1–56**

The last two versions attempt to find a compromise between the rather extreme positions of the first two versions. They are intended respectively for a cosmetic or pharmaceutical product, and for an electronic or mechanical product of reasonable complexity. The compromise is effected by a rather detailed listing of classes of items to be transferred, while avoiding the qualification of classes of information by use of the "necessary" phrases as discussed in relation to version (b). Version (d) is also concerned to specify the training programme that will be provided by means of a schedule, which could, if required, include the scale charges for additional training outside the agreed initial programme. In both of the last two versions, no obligation to transfer improvements is imposed, but can of course be added if required. **1–57**

1.3 Interpretation

1.3.1 *Headings* The headings used in this Agreement are included for convenience only and are not to be used in construing or interpreting this Agreement. **1–58**

1.3.2 *Legislation* Any reference in this Agreement to any statute decree law statutory instrument or other regulation having the force of law shall be deemed to include any lawful modifications thereto or re-enactments thereof made after the date of signature of this Agreement. **1–59**

1.3.3 *References* In this Agreement: **1–60**

1.3.3.1 any reference to the plural shall include the singular and any reference to the singular shall include the plural;

1.3.3.2 any reference to one gender shall include all genders;

1.3.3.3 any reference to a person shall include natural persons and partnerships firms and other such unincorporated bodies and companies and corporate bodies and all other legal persons of whatever kind and however constituted;

1.3.3.4 any reference to a clause or a schedule shall (unless otherwise specifically provided) be to a clause or schedule of this Agreement;

1.3.3.5 any reference in a schedule to a paragraph shall unless otherwise specifically provided mean a reference to a paragraph of that schedule.

The precedents in cll.1.3.1 to 1.3.3 are the standard interpretation provisions which are usual in commercial agreements of this type. Some of them may be irrelevant in particular cases but their use does need to be considered in each case as the specific agreement is being drafted. Clauses 1.3.3.4 and 1.3.3.5 are especially recommended as they cut down the repetitious use of "hereof", "hereto", "of this Agreement" and so on, after clause, schedule and paragraph references in the agreement. The precedents in this book assume that these two clauses will always be included.

1–61 1.3.4 *Order of Precedence* In the event of an inconsistency between any of the clauses, schedules and specifications or other documentation incorporated in this Agreement by reference the inconsistency shall be resolved by giving the clauses the schedules and such specifications and documentation the following order of precedence:

1.3.4.1 The clauses (including any amendment thereto made under cl.1.8.2).

1.3.4.2 The schedules (including any amendment thereto made under cl.1.8.2).

1.3.4.3 The provisions of any specification or other document incorporated herein by reference.

This is a useful provision where one is dealing with a complicated agreement in which reference is made to technical specifications or other documents (such as standard conditions of sale) which are not reproduced in the agreement itself. The provision also clarifies the situation where such specifications or documents are reproduced in schedules to the main agreement. An instance where this sort of problem, with inconsistencies between the main agreement and schedules, can arise is where a technical standard of some length, which is published separately, is itself attached to the agreement as a schedule for ease of reference.

1–62 1.3.5 *Proper Law* The construction performance and validity of this Agreement shall in all respects be governed by the laws of [England].

This clause specifies the system of law which will be applied in the event of the need to interpret any provision of the agreement or to settle a dispute as to the obligations arising under it and their performance.

1–63 The choice of the proper law in the agreements covered in this book first of all depends upon the commercial balance of power between the two parties, the stronger often insisting upon his local system of law as the proper law for the agreement. This presents problems for the other party, who may well be unaware of the obligations and liabilities thus imposed upon him. One solution is for this party to instruct local lawyers to advise him upon the terms of the proposed agreement, and the effect upon it of the proper law that is chosen. Throughout this book reference is made to the need to consult local lawyers. Appendix 1 sets out a questionnaire which indicates some of the areas that should in general be covered. It can be used in whole or in part or adapted as required, remembering that legal advice is expensive, and it is not cost-effective to ask for any that is not strictly relevant to the particular agreement.

In cases where consulting local lawyers is difficult or expensive, or where **1–64** the proper law of the other party is unacceptable, the other solution is to propose the law of some neutral third country with which both parties are reasonably familiar, and which is broadly acceptable to both of them because of that country's international reputation for neutrality and the impartial administration of justice. Countries often chosen in this way are Switzerland, the Scandinavian countries, particularly Sweden, and sometimes France and England.

There are two major problems with choice of law clauses in international **1–65** agreements. The first is the question of whether a tribunal will apply the system of law specified by the parties or choose some other system. The second is the issue of overriding local law.

So far as the first problem is concerned, outside the European Union, **1–66** there are no international conventions which assist in the matter, except for the United Nations Convention for the International Sale of Goods 1980 (known as the Vienna Convention). The UK is not a party to this convention. In general, most principles of international law will require the tribunal to apply the system of law which is most directly connected with the parties in question. Possible systems of law to apply would be that of the place where a party is domiciled, the law of the place where the contract was made or the law of the place where it was to be performed. Another possibility, for instance in the case of immovable property, would be the place where the subject matter of the dispute was situated. It should however be remembered that the question of where a party is domiciled or where a contract is made is itself partly a question of law, and the tribunal has to take a decision as to what system of law to apply to decide that question in the first place. In this case, it will again refer to the principles of its own system of private international law for guidance.

A choice of law clause clearly stating which law to apply is likely to be **1–67** applied by the tribunal, but the tribunal has no obligation to do so. Again the question of which law to apply is decided by the tribunal's own system of private international law, and the choice of law clause is only one factor to be taken into account. For instance choice of law clauses may not be permitted under the local law governing the tribunal, or may require some special formality (which has been omitted) before they can become effective. However, all things being equal, the tribunal will more likely respect the choice of law clause than not.

The second problem usually arises when, for whatever reason, the tri- **1–68** bunal that has jurisdiction is situated either in the state where one of the parties is domiciled, or else in the state where the contractual obligation is to be performed. As to the first possibility, if the party so domiciled can adduce some mandatory provision of the local law which but for the choice of law clause he could rely on for his benefit (ie consumer protection legislation or the right to compensation on termination of an agency agreement or a contract of employment) then the relevant provision of the local law will be applied by the tribunal to override (either wholly or *pro tanto*) the choice of law clause as amounting to an ineffective attempt to exclude the mandatory provisions of the local law. As to the second possibility, this would arise where the tribunal having jurisdiction was situated in the state where the disputed obligation was to be performed, and the performance of the contract, although legal under the system of law to be applied according to the choice of law clause, was illegal under the law of the place of performance. In this case, the tribunal would be forced to apply the law of the place of performance in preference to that specified in the choice of law clause. In this connection, it is sometimes also said that a tribunal can refuse to apply a system of law simply on grounds of public policy, but this rather vague principle is seldom invoked.

1–69 The principle of overriding local law does not always operate as described above. There are cases in which an express clause imposing another system of law will win out. However, these cases would appear to be limited to instances where both of the parties to the dispute are present within the jurisdiction applying the system of law imposed by the clause, even if one of them is also operating in the jurisdiction where the contract is to be performed, and goes to a local tribunal claiming overriding provisions of the law of the place of performance.

1–70 In *Shell International Petroleum Co Ltd v Coral Oil Co Ltd (No.1)* [1999] 1 Lloyd's Rep., QBD Commercial Court, both parties entered into contracts governed by English law with a clause requiring disputes under contracts to be submitted to arbitration. Coral was an English company, but managed from the Lebanon. The performance of the contract was to take place in the Lebanon. Shell lawfully terminated the contacts by giving due notice. However Coral refused to accept the termination and claimed that in performing the contracts, it had acted as Shell's agent in the Lebanon and therefore was entitled to compensation for termination of an agency agreement without cause as provided under Lebanese law. Shell applied for declarations and injunctions preventing Coral from bringing proceedings in Lebanon. The issue was whether Coral was entitled to pursue a claim for compensation under the provisions of Lebanese law.

1–71 The court granted the relief sought by Shell. Coral's claim depended on the prior existence of the contracts between the parties. The intention of the parties was that any dispute was to be governed by English law and referred to arbitration. Shell could not be said to have abandoned its rights under the contracts by starting this action to prevent proceedings being brought in Lebanon contrary to the terms of the original contracts. This was not a case where proceedings had already been started in the Lebanon and Shell had allowed them to proceed for some time: no proceedings had yet been started. There were strong reasons for granting an injunction. It would hold the parties to their agreement. A Lebanese court would be required to apply a provision of Lebanese law which was contrary to the parties' intentions in the contracts and the court should exercise its discretion to enable the intentions of the parties to be put into effect.

A further example of this approach, although admittedly relating to states within the European Union, discussed in Chapter 3.10, can be seen in *IFR Ltd v Federal Trade SpA* ([2001] WL 1677001 (judgment date September 19, 2001, QBD, 2000 folio 1393). **1–72**

Within the European Union the situation is much clearer. The Rome Convention of 1980 on the Law Applicable to Contractual Obligations generally states that the parties may choose which system of law is to govern their contract, (Art.3) but that where an applicable local system of law contains mandatory provisions (*i.e.* provisions which expressly or by implication apply notwithstanding the choice of some other system of law) those provision apply and override the choice of law clause (Art.7). In the absence of an express choice of law clause, the applicable law is the law with which the contract is most closely connected. It is assumed, unless proved otherwise, that the law most closely connected is that of the state where the party who is obliged to perform the basic underlying purpose of the contract ("characteristic performance") has its seat. For instance in a contract for the sale of goods, characteristic performance would be regarded as the obligation to deliver the goods, and the applicable law would therefore be where the seller had its seat of business. The UK is a signatory to the Convention, and implemented it by the Contracts (Applicable Law) Act 1990. **1–73**

The most common areas of overriding with agency and distribution agreements are the controls upon registration and implementation of such agreements, the mandatory imposition upon the principal, particularly in agency agreements, of the obligation to pay compensation for unjustified termination (even where the agreement expires only by effluxion of time and is not renewed) and legislation controlling the transfer of technology. References to all of these areas are discussed in detail as they arise in the consideration of the various precedents later in this book. **1–74**

So far as English law is concerned, leaving aside the effect of EC Directives, the problem of mandatory application of particular rules of law, in relation to the type of contracts covered in this book, is largely confined to the application of the Unfair Contract Terms Act 1977 (UCTA), which, *inter alia*, regulates the use of various types of exclusion of liability in certain classes of business contracts, either by prohibiting their use altogether, or requiring that the exclusion conform to a standard of reasonableness set out in s.11 of the Act. International agreements, which are largely the concern of this book, are in most cases excluded from the operation of UCTA. **1–75**

Section 27(1) of UCTA provides that ss.2–7 (so far as England, Wales and Northern Ireland are concerned) and ss.16–21 (so far as Scotland is concerned) shall not apply to contracts which are governed by the law of any part of the UK only because the parties inserted an express governing law clause to that effect. This provision thus prevents the relevant sections from having any effect on contracts which, apart from such a governing law **1–76** clause, would, under the general provisions of conflict of laws prevailing under private international law as applied in the UK, be governed by a foreign proper law. On the other hand, a contract which, under such conflict of laws provisions, would be governed by the laws of any part of the UK, except for the fact that the parties inserted a governing law clause specifying a foreign proper law, may still be caught by UCTA. Section 27(2), permits the court or the arbitrator a discretion to ignore the governing law clause if it appears that it has been included only for the purpose of evading the provisions of UCTA.

1–77 By implication all other contracts with a foreign element are exempt. A contract genuinely governed by a foreign proper law is obviously exempt (whether or not it contains a foreign proper law clause), whether so specifically stated in UCTA or not. Also exempt would be a contract which could or should have been governed by one of the systems of law in the UK, where s.27(2) does not apply, and the parties have chosen a foreign proper law for a genuine reason other than evasion of UCTA (*e.g.* because the other party was a foreigner who insisted on using the law of his own jurisdiction as the governing law of the contract). The conclusion seems to be that where one wishes UCTA not to apply, one should, where possible, by observing the relevant conflict of law rules, create a contract genuinely governed by a foreign proper law, so that there is no need for an express choice of law clause which can be attacked or negated under s.27(2).

1–78 Section 26(1) of UCTA provides that "the limits imposed by this Act on the extent to which a person may exclude or restrict liability by reference to a contract term" do not apply to international contracts for the supply of goods. Such contracts, even if *prima facie* caught under s.27, will be exempt under s.26 of UCTA, if they fulfil its rather strict requirements. Although there is no exemption for a contract which consists exclusively of the international supply of services, a mixed contract (*e.g.* supply and installation, or supply and supervision of installation, of plant abroad) will come under s.26. Therefore in such cases, where it is desired that UCTA not apply, one method is to draft one contract for both goods and services, and not two separate contracts for each element.

1–79 International distribution agreements will also fall under s.26 since they are pure agreements for the sale of goods, and thus fall within the Sale of Goods Act 1979 (see s.1(3) of that Act). An arrangement where an agent works on a commission with a consignment stock, is obviously not an agreement for the sale of goods, but is a contract under or in pursuance of which *possession* of goods passes (UCTA, s.26(3)(a)) and would also be caught. Contracts with commission agents, indenting agents and canvassers and consultants will not be caught under s.26, as no goods pass between them and their principal. They merely collect orders and pass them back to their principal who fulfils the orders direct. Their contract is not one *under* which possession or ownership of goods passes. Nor, it is submitted, can it properly be regarded as one in *pursuance* of which possession or ownership passes either.

1–80 The various licences of intellectual property and knowhow dealt with in this book will fall outside of the ambit of UCTA, whether they are international contracts or not. Schedule 1 of UCTA provides that the provisions of UCTA which could otherwise be relevant (ss.2–4 and 7) do not apply, under the law of England and Wales or of Northern Ireland, *inter alia*, to "any contract *so far as it relates* to the creation, or transfer of any right or interest in any patent, trade mark, copyright, registered design, technical or commercial information or other intellectual property..." which can be taken to cover licences of intellectual property or knowhow. The same effect is achieved in relation to Scotland by the narrow drafting of s.15(2) of UCTA which states that "ss.16–18 of this Act apply to any contract *only to the extent that* the contract relates" to the matters listed in s.15(2)(a) to (e), which cover the supply of goods and services, a contract of service or apprenticeship, occupier's liability and the grant of rights over land which do not amount to an estate or interest. Clearly these matters do not include a licence of intellectual property rights.

Where the contract in question is made up partly of a licence of intellectual property and partly of obligations relating to the supply of goods or services, it would appear that those aspects of the contract, which are not comprised within the provisions relating to the licence, would be governed by UCTA, under all of the systems of law in force in the UK. This conclusion can be drawn from the use of the words "so far as [the contract] relates ..." in Sch.1, which applies to the systems of law in the UK other than in Scotland, and the use of the words "*only to the extent that* the contract relates" which applies to Scotland.

An obvious example of this would be a patent licence covering a product **1–81** to be manufactured by the licensee combined with an agreement for the sale (by the licensor to the licensee) of essential materials or components to be used by the licensee in its manufacture. Here (supposing the contract were governed by English law, for instance) UCTA would not apply (pursuant to Sch.1) to the provisions relating to the licence, but Pt I of UCTA would apply in relation to the provisions of the agreement governing the sale of the goods. Thus, for instance, s.6 of UCTA would apply to prevent the licensor contracting out of the obligation to pass a good title to the goods sold to the licensee, but no provision in UCTA would prevent the licensor from excluding his liability in the event he did not have a good title to the patent which was licensed, or if a third party started infringement proceedings against the licensee, and contested the validity of the licensed patent. Similarly, in the case of a knowhow licence for the manufacture of a product, the licensor could exclude liability in the event that the knowhow was in some way defective or insufficient to enable to the licensor to manufacture the product in question, but if there was an additional obligation in the agreement to supply essential raw materials for that manufacture ss.6 and 7 of UCTA would apply to prevent the licensor contracting out of liability for defects in the materials supplied, except to the extent that the relevant exclusion clause passed the reasonableness test under s.11 of UCTA.

There has been some discussion of this issue, in relation to the develop- **1–82** ment, supply and licensing of software, in the recent cases of *Saphena*

Computing Ltd v Allied Collection Agencies Ltd [1995] F.S.R. 616, CA; *The Salvage Association v Cap Financial Services Ltd* [1995] F.S.R. 654; *St Albans City and District Council v International Computers Ltd* (reported at first instance [1995] F.S.R. 686 and at [1996] 4 All E.R., CA; and *Holman Group Ltd v Sherwood International Group Ltd* (QBD (T & CC)) Judgment date: April 12, 2000, considered in Masons Computer Law Reports March 2001). The judgments in these cases would support the conclusions reached in the preceding paragraph, and the drawing of a line between the provisions relating to the licence of intellectual property and the provisions relating to the supply of goods and services. However, it must be admitted that this line is not easy to draw, and that these cases do not give a great deal of help in where to draw it. The situation is particularly complicated, as can be seen from the subject-matter of the disputes in these cases, in relation to a licence of software. The whole issue is thus discussed in more detail in Chapter 11 which relates to software licences.

1–83 If one considers the distribution, consultancy and agency agreements covered by this book on the basis that UCTA does apply to them, for instance because they are local arrangements with both parties resident in the UK and covering a territory within the UK, so that neither s.26 nor s.27 would have any application, the result is in fact that UCTA still has very little effect.

1–84 Part I of UCTA applies to contracts under the Laws of England and Wales or of Northern Ireland. Section 2 regulates exclusion of liability, in all business contracts, for death or personal injury (s.2(1)) or other damage (s.2(2)) suffered by one party to a contract and caused by the negligence of the other. Section 3 regulates the exclusion of liability for breach of contract, but, where business to business contracts are concerned, only where the party seeking to avoid liability is dealing on its written standard terms of contract. Sections 4 and 5 relate only to consumer transactions, and ss.6 and 7 cover exclusion of certain warranties (*e.g.* of title and fitness for purpose) on the sale or other supply of goods in both business to business and consumer contracts.

1–85 Most of the agreements entered into in the field covered by this book are not likely to be between natural persons, so that s.2(1) can have no application, and even where it does, exclusion of such liability is not generally a feature of these contracts, and certainly not of the precedents in this book. Although s.2(2) can clearly apply in contracts between legal entities, once again the types of contracts with which this book is concerned rarely seek to limit or exclude such liability. Even where they do, UCTA permits this to the extent that it is reasonable under s.11. Section 3 may well have no application, since such agreements are often negotiated rather than entered into on standard terms. In any event, even where standard terms are used, the limitations of liability are likely only to be those which would in most cases be considered reasonable under s.3, such as the exclusion of liability in the event of *force majeure*, or the limitation of liability to exclude loss of revenue or profit, or of consequential or indirect loss. Sections 4 and 5 have no application to the types of contracts this book is concerned with, and ss.6

and 7 can have application only in relation to such contracts which include the sale or supply of goods. Even here, in business to business relationships, a reasonable exclusion of liability is permitted by UCTA in most areas other than as to good title, which is not, in most cases, a contentious issue between the parties (see *Watford Electronics Ltd v Sanderson CFL Ltd* [2001] 1 All E.R. (Comm) 696, CA.) In conclusion, the most likely area for consideration of UCTA is thus in the drafting of standard conditions of sale for the supply of goods under a distribution agreement where neither s.26 nor s.27 operates to avoid its application (see, for instance, the discussion in Chapter 4.26).

Where the law of Scotland is concerned, the analysis of the provisions of Pt II of UCTA would reach the same conclusions as those set out in relation to Pt I above. **1–86**

Finally, it should be noted that, under s.8, UCTA also regulates exclusion of liability for pre-contract misrepresentations. The situation is more complicated here, and the issue is discussed in relation to whole agreement clauses, which is where it most usually arises, in Chapter 1.8. **1–87**

Allied to the problem of pre-eminent local law is the practical problem of enforcing rights under the agreement. In most cases the party against whom proceedings are being instituted will have assets only in his country of residence, rather than in the country of residence of the other. Thus, even if the plaintiff obtains judgment in the courts of his own country, he will still have to look for some sort of reciprocal arrangement with the courts of the country in which the defendant is resident, if he is to enforce that judgment locally against the defendant's assets situated there. Where a specific treaty does not exist for reciprocal enforcement of foreign judgments, this necessitates trying the action again before the local courts. Apart from the added expense, the local courts are quite likely to take cognisance of any adverse rights in favour of the defendant arising under the local law, irrespective of the proper law clause. **1–88**

In many cases this problem is specifically recognised and dealt with in the clauses relating to the resolution of disputes (see cll.1.6.1 and 1.6.2). **1–89**

1.4 Confidentiality clauses

1.4.1 The parties agree that all rights to the Information (other than those specifically granted to the Licensee by this Agreement) are reserved to the Principal and the Licensee shall use the Information only for the purpose (hereinafter called the "Purpose") [of exploiting its rights and fulfilling its obligations under this Agreement (including without limitation the manufacture marketing and sale of the Products)]. **1–90**

The confidentiality clauses set out in 1.4 are deliberately of an extensive and detailed character. They are unlikely to be suited to the usual types of agency and distribution agreements, except where technically sophisticated and vital information is being disclosed. It will be recalled that the definition of Information in cl.1.2.10 not only covers commercial and marketing information but also includes knowhow as defined in cl.1.2.11 and this makes these clauses suitable for the imposition of obligations upon a licensee who has technically sophisticated manufacturing information transferred to him under a manufacturing arrangement. The clauses would also be suitable where there is a large software element in the information transferred.

1–91 The first clause, cl.1.4.1, imposes the primary obligation of use only for permitted purposes. The phrases in square brackets are indicative only but would suit the manufacturing agreements covered in Chapters 7 and 8, and should be adapted as necessary to specify the purpose for which the information can be used.

1–92 1.4.2 The Licensee shall not use the Information except in connection with the Purpose to benefit itself or others and will not communicate Information to others except as specifically permitted by this Agreement in connection with the Purpose or if expressly authorised prior to its disclosure so to do in any instance by the Principal.

The prohibition on an unauthorised disclosure is the other prohibition required to safeguard confidential information. In practice, the areas where the licensee is likely to have to disclose information other than to employees within its operation, are to subcontractors who carry on manufacturing or packing operations, (see cll.7.6 and 7.19 and 8.6 and 8.19) and to the various authorities who are required to grant licences for the manufacture and sale of the products in the territory (see cll.7.15 and 8.15).

1–93 1.4.3 The Licensee undertakes that Information will be made available in confidence only to such of its employees and subcontractors as need to know the same for the Purpose and that such employees are bound by their contracts of employment and such subcontractors are bound by confidentiality undertakings identical to cl.1.4 not to use or disclose the Information transmitted to them by the Licensee.

It is normal to attempt to limit disclosure of information to a need to know basis even within the permitted classes of third parties. Most contracts of employment actually contain clauses requiring employees not to disclose confidential information that they have access to in the course of their employment, and, in most jurisdictions, even in the absence of express terms, implied terms to this effect are held to exist under the general law relating to contracts of employment. Thus, this obligation is not an onerous or unusual one. Similarly it is usual to bind subcontractors by confidentiality obligations if they are given confidential information relating to the subcontract and its performance.

1–94 1.4.4 The Licensee undertakes at its own expense to enforce the obligations of confidentiality imposed upon its employees and subcontractors in accordance with cl.1.4.3 in so far as they relate to a disclosure of Information by such employees or subcontractors.

Since there is no privity of contract between the principal and the employees and subcontractors of the licensee, it is necessary either to insert a provision like this clause, or else to require that, prior to disclosure to them, the employees and subcontractors enter into a confidentiality agreement direct with the licensee which he can then enforce in the event of wrongful use or disclosure. This is more usual where technically vital information is disclosed for very limited purposes, particularly subcontract manufacture. Understandably the licensee is usually reluctant to involve his subcontractors and employees in such complicated arrangements, particularly where employees are concerned. Certainly in the usual type of manufacturing arrangement covered by Chapters 7 and 8 it is unlikely that such direct undertakings would be acceptable or necessary in most cases.

Where they are to be used, however, cl.1.4 together with the relevant **1–95** provisions from the definitions in Chapter 1.2 could be adapted. It is however necessary in these cases, in jurisdictions where the concept exists, to decide if consideration is necessary to make the direct agreement enforceable, and, if so, whether it exists or whether, if the law of the jurisdiction permits, execution as a deed under seal is an acceptable alternative. The consideration may simply be the agreement to disclose the confidential information to the licensee, but it is more usually found in such cases in the grant of permission from the principal for the employment by the licensee of the employee or subcontractor on the particular project involving the use of the confidential information. Another possibility is the grant by the licensor of permission for the information in question to be disclosed to the employee or subcontractor concerned.

1.4.5 The Licensee agrees that Information shall not be copied or reproduced by **1–96** it without the express permission of the Principal except for such copies as may be reasonably required for the Purpose by the Licensee.

Although the general law of copyright nearly all over the world would cover this point, it never does any harm to include this provision specifically. The return of copies of the information and of the original information in material form is dealt with in the termination provisions of the precedents in the following chapters (see for instance Chapter 7.17 below).

1.4.6 The Licensee undertakes [to prevent] [to exercise its best endeavours to **1–97** prevent], [to exercise the same procedures and safeguards as used in connection with its own confidential information for the purpose of preventing] the disclosure of the Information and the access of unauthorised persons to the Information.

The three versions in square brackets are listed in descending order of severity. The absolute obligation to prevent disclosure would make the licensee an absolute insurer against the possibility of disclosure, whether or not inadvertent, or made by an employee in contravention of the licensee's instructions. Most licensees refuse this obligation on the grounds that it is impossible to police. The second version would require the licensee to institute in all probability special procedures to ensure compliance, and should be considered where the licensee is perhaps not used to holding sensitive information. Again, however, the obligation is heavy, and would not be fulfilled merely because the licensee has some system in force for safeguarding information. He would be obliged to consider whether that system were in fact the best that he could institute, and, if not, to improve it. The last version is the least severe and merely requires the licensee to treat the information as carefully as he treats his own sensitive information. Where one is dealing with large concerns used to safeguarding their proprietary information of a technical nature it is unlikely that they will easily agree to any further obligation than this.

1–98 1.4.7 The Licensee shall in the discharge of its obligations under cl.1.4.6 arrange proper [and secure] storage for Information in the form of documents papers computer disks magnetic tapes or in any other material form.

The inclusion of the phrase in square brackets goes to the point of absolute insurance discussed under cl.1.4.6.

1–99 1.4.8 The obligations imposed under cll.1.4.1 to 1.4.6 inclusive shall not apply to Information if the same:

1.4.8.1 was in the public domain at the time it was disclosed or thereafter shall fall into the public domain except through the default of the Licensee its employees agents or subcontractors; or

The public domain exclusion is not only generally recognised as a fair one (because otherwise as a result of his contract the licensee would be in a worse position with regard to the information than the public at large) but also because in most jurisdictions it is recognised that obligations of confidentiality cannot be imposed upon the use and disclosure of publicly available information. In basic terms, and in one way or another depending upon the jurisdiction, this is regarded as generally anti-competitive or in restraint of trade.

1.4.8.2 was known to and recorded by the Licensee prior to its disclosure to the Licensee by the Principal; or

The same considerations apply to this exception as to cl.1.4.8.1.

1.4.8.3 was disclosed after the express prior authorisation of the Principal; or

This exception is really for the avoidance of doubt only.

1.4.8.4 becomes known to the Licensee from a source other than the Principal without breach of this Agreement by the Licensee; or

This is really another version of the public domain exception. There are instances in which it can be said that information, although known to more than the two parties, and transmitted in certain cases by third parties without restrictions of confidentiality, are known at large to some extent, but not sufficiently to be within the public domain. This clause covers this situation.

> 1.4.8.5 was independently developed by the Licensee [without the benefit of any of the Information] [by employees of the Licensee who had no access to any of the Information]; or

The independent development exception is often insisted upon by licensees, particularly by licensees which are large companies or members of groups of companies, where there are independent centres of activity which do not generally have detailed contact with each other. Thus, at one factory one division of the licensee may be undertaking manufacture under licence of a product in a field which is the subject of research at a laboratory of the licensee in another location. In principle it is unfair, and probably unrealistic, to bind a licensee with these sort of operations so that he should be restricted in the use of the independent development. The problem in all of these cases is to prove that the development was independent, and made without the aid of the information disclosed by the principal. The first phrase in square brackets shows the basic intent, but theoretically could be used so that the independent development could be carried out in the same operation and by the same employees who had access to the information of the principal. It is true that the licensee might have a difficult time convincing the court that such employees had not made use of the information to guide the independent development, but the possibility is there. It is therefore more usual to use the second phrase in square brackets which makes the true intent of the provision rather clearer, and makes it somewhat more difficult for the licensee to rely upon the provision. He will in this case have to prove definitely that there was no access to the principal's information by the employees carrying out the independent development, if he wishes to rely on it.

> 1.4.8.6 is disclosed [five years] from the time of receipt thereof.

It is always a question as to whether confidentiality restrictions should be subject to a time limit. Quite apart from the problems of restriction under Art.81 of the EC Treaty once the licence agreement has expired (see Chapter 8) there is the question of the need for such long restrictions and the possibility of policing them. Again, in many fields, there is the tendency for technical information to become obsolete with the passing of time. It can sometimes be the situation that after a period of years not only can the parties find difficulty in any longer identifying the information that was transmitted in the first case, and regarded as confidential, but even if they can, they no longer consider it of any use. Commercial information, as it becomes older, also tends to become obsolete as markets and the businesses involved in them change. Thus, although it is not always appropriate, thought should be given to the imposition of time limits. Time limits can either run from the date of the agreement, or from the date of disclosure. The former has the merit of simplicity, but means that if there is a continuing stream of disclosure, covering training and improvements, and market information, the items disclosed later will have a shorter period of protection than may be desirable. The precedents in this book deal more often with continuing relationships where, despite the difficulty of policing, the time limit should rather run from the date of disclosure, with obsolete information falling away, and new information becoming subject to the restrictions as it is disclosed.

1–100 1.4.9 If only a portion of the Information falls within any one of the exceptions under cl.1.4.8 the remainder shall continue to be subject to the prohibitions and restrictions of cl.1.4.

This clause is necessary to preserve situations where only a part of the information falls within the exceptions to the confidentiality obligations. It has a particular application where a product is put upon the market. Although the design of the product will come within the public domain, so that others may (subject to any other industrial or intellectual property rights) make it if they will, there may well be valuable process manufacturing information which makes it very much easier or cheaper to manufacture the product concerned. If this is the case, the principal and the licensee will still have confidential information about how to make the product, which will give them a competitive advantage over third party manufacturers.

1–101 A fictitious example but one very much on the point would be the tube of toothpaste. Once one sees a tube of toothpaste on the market, the idea and the design of dispensing paste in tubes by squeezing them seems very obvious, and of itself can (if one leaves aside questions of patent and design rights) be used by anybody. However, the licensee and the originator of the idea also know that the easy way to fill the tubes is not through the nozzle, but through the open bottom, which is then sealed off. This fact is not obvious by inspection, but any third party who tries to make tubes of toothpaste without this knowledge is in for a difficult time, and the originator should quite fairly continue to keep this information confidential even after he has started to market tubes of toothpaste.

1–102 1.4.10 No licence or conveyance of any rights to the Licensee under any discoveries inventions or patents or to use the Information other than for the Purpose is granted or implied by the transmission of the Information to the Licensee under this Agreement.

This is a provision for the avoidance of doubt, and should be inserted even in areas where there is a manufacturing licence involved. This is equivalent to a field of use restriction for the purposes of EC law, and care should be taken over this point, which is discussed in Chapter 8.2.

1.4.11 Notwithstanding anything contained elsewhere in this Agreement, the provisions of this clause shall survive the termination or expiry of this Agreement. **1–103**

Care should be taken to ensure that, even if a time limit is imposed, the confidentiality obligations survive the termination of the Agreement.

1.5 Competing activity clauses

1.5.1 The Agent shall not knowingly be directly or indirectly engaged or interested in any capacity (including without limitation through a Connected Person) in any Competing Activity [in the Territory] during the period of this Agreement provided that: **1–104**

> where the Agent is interested in stocks shares or debentures where they are listed or quoted on a stock exchange and the company that issued them carries on or is the Holding Company of a company that carries on any Competing Activity the Agent may hold not more than [five] per cent in nominal value or number of a class of the stocks shares or debentures so listed or quoted;

and provided further that:

> (for the avoidance of doubt) neither the Agent nor a Connected Person may be interested either directly or indirectly in any unlisted or unquoted company which carries on any Competing Activity.

Restrictions upon competing activities are always a sensitive area. This clause coupled with the definition of competing activity in 1.2.9 and the associated definitions is again deliberately broad and onerous. This clause uses the defined term Agent because in most cases this is the situation where such an onerous clause is most likely to be acceptable, both legally and commercially. EC law is not normally concerned with such a provision in an agency agreement, restricting competing activity during the continuance of the Agreement, as Art.81 does not in the vast majority of cases apply to agency agreements (see Chapter 5.1.1.3.11). However, EC law would have application to a licensing agreement or a distribution agreement. The provision could also be used in the area of consultancy agreements (see Chapter 9).

In areas where EC law does not apply, there may of course be local laws to contend with, but generally this clause would be regarded as an enforceable clause in most jurisdictions, particularly common law ones. Most jurisdictions see it as reasonable that competing activities should not be permitted during the existence of an exclusive agency distributorship or licensing arrangement, although with such width it is unlikely to be acceptable to a licensee or a distributor. It is normal to limit the operation of the clause to competing activity within the territory, but it could be extended wider in appropriate cases. **1–105**

1.5.2(a) Upon the termination [(other than by reason of a breach by the Principal]) or expiry of this Agreement the Agent shall not engage for a period of [one year] in the [Territory] in a Competing Activity. **1–106**

OR

> 1.5.2(b) Upon the termination [(other than by reason of acceptance by the Agent of a repudiatory breach by the Principal]) or expiry of this Agreement the Agent shall not engage directly or indirectly for a period of [two] years in the Territory in any business activity which relates to goods of the same kind as the Products [and which competes with sales of the Products].

Clause 1.5.2 presents greater difficulties. If one takes into consideration common law, most civil jurisdictions, and, indeed Art.81, such a covenant is usually considered in restraint of trade, contrary to public policy, and *prima facie* void.

1–107 In legal proceedings this presumption of invalidity can, in some cases (including most common law jurisdictions), be rebutted by proof that the restraint is reasonable, but the restraint must be reasonable in the interests of both contracting parties, and also in the interests of the public. The onus of proving reasonableness between the parties lies on the person in whose favour the covenant is made, and the onus of proving that the covenant tends to be against the public interest lies on the person granting the covenant. Somewhat similar ideas would govern the consideration of exemption for such arrangements under Art.81(3) (see Chapter 5.18).

1–108 The continuing restraint must, in common law jurisdictions, be no wider than is reasonably necessary to protect the interest of the person in whose favour it is made. The existence of some proprietary interest to be protected must first be proved, and it must then be shown to the court that the restraint, as regards its area and time of operation and the business it is designed to protect, is not too wide. The interests that the courts normally have in mind as worthy of such protection are either trade secrets or good will.

1–109 The suggested restraint to the territory for a period of one year is deliberately conservative for this reason. The extent and the time period that is reasonable has to depend on the facts of each case, but, as a practical guide, the clause should always impose the bare minimum restraint that the principal feels he can live with.

1–110 Restrictive covenants in contracts of employment are looked at very severely as the need to protect the mobility of labour, and the freedom of the employee to work where he will, are regarded as of overwhelming importance. In the types of arrangements covered by this book, the considerations may be rather less severe, but the courts are still likely to take a narrow view of the restraints that can justifiably be imposed.

1–111 Mere bans on competing activity after the end of the agreement are unlikely to be enforceable in the case of licensees or distributors, in any jurisdiction, except as they arise indirectly, by an enforceable provision not to make use of confidential information, disclosed during the course of the agreement, after termination (see cl.1.4.11 and the discussion in Chapter 5.18). This information could relate not only to technical, but also to marketing matters, and thus to customer listings and mailing lists. The case of the agent, who is more akin to an employee, is slightly different, and it is likely that cl.1.5.2 stands some chance of being enforced in the case of an agent. With regard to agents, the position is now regulated to some extent under EC law by the Council Directive 653/1986 on the Coordination of the Laws of the Member States relating to self-employed commercial agents (discussed in detail in Chapter 3). Article 20 of the Directive permits such restraint of trade clauses if they are for not more than two years after termination of the agreement, and relate only to the territory or the group of customers and the territory, entrusted to the agent, and, in either case, only to the relevant type of products covered by the agreement. Version (b) above is a clause which would comply with the Directive. The third phrase in square brackets is not required by the Directive but should be inserted, as the Directive is without prejudice to any stricter prohibitions on covenants in restraint of trade in the local law of the relevant Member States. Despite the Directive, therefore, all the points above must still be considered, particularly the length of the restraint, and some reasonable restriction to activities which do in fact compete.

So far as the use of the first phrase in square brackets is concerned, an **1–112** earlier decision of the High Court in relation to a restrictive covenant in a contract of employment held that where a covenant is expressed to take effect after termination of the contract "howsoever caused" or "irrespective of the cause or manner of termination" there is an argument that the restraint is void because the wording is sufficiently wide to cover a termination by reason of a breach of contract by the employer. (*D v M* [1996] I.R.L.R. 192.) There seemed no reason why the principles in this case, although concerned with employment law, should not apply to restrictive covenants in other relationships, such as those of agency or distributorship. Hence the use of such phrases as the one in square brackets was suggested. However, the case was soon overruled by the Court of Appeal in *Rock Refrigeration Ltd v Jones* [1997] 1 All E.R. 1. The Court held that it was not necessarily the case that a covenant which purported to restrict an employee's conduct after termination of the contract "howsoever occasioned" was unreasonable and therefore unenforceable. Where the employer was in repudiatory breach due to unlawful termination of the contract the covenant became unenforceable only on acceptance of the breach by the employee. However, the contract remained binding, unless and until the employer committed a repudiatory breach which was accepted as such by the employee. Applying this case, the phrase is not necessary, but, drafting in the interests of certainty, its insertion still seems harmless and desirable.

1.5.3 The Agent shall not during a period of [one year] after the termination **1–113** [(other than by reason of acceptance by the Agent of a repudiatory breach by the Principal] or expiry of this Agreement solicit orders for items which compete directly or indirectly with the Products from persons [whether] inside [or outside] the Territory who were during the continuance of this Agreement serviced by the Agent as customers of the Principal for the Products.

Following the comments upon cl.1.5.2 which would all apply to this clause, this precedent is given for those situations connected with agency where a non-solicitation clause is desired to be inserted directly. A non-solicitation clause in this form stands more chance of being enforceable than the wider cl.1.5.2. In accordance with the discussion of the Directive above, this clause would have to be limited to the territory by the deletion of the phrases in the second and third set of square brackets, in order to comply with Art.20 of the Directive, where applicable.

1.6 Disputes

1.6.1 Arbitration

1–114 1.6.1(a) Any question or difference which may arise concerning the construction meaning or effect of this Agreement or concerning the rights and liabilities of the parties hereunder or any other matter arising out of or in connection with this Agreement shall be referred to a single arbitrator in London to be agreed between the parties. Failing such agreement within thirty days of the request by one party to the other that a matter be referred to arbitration in accordance with this clause such reference shall be to an arbitrator appointed by the President for the time being of the London Chamber of Commerce. The decision of such arbitrator shall be final and binding upon the parties. Any reference under this clause shall be deemed to be a reference to arbitration within the meaning of the Arbitration Act 1996.

OR

1.6.1(b) Any dispute or claim arising out of this Agreement shall be finally settled by arbitration in [Japan] pursuant the rules of [the Japanese Commercial Arbitration Association] by which each party agrees to be bound.

OR

1.6.1(c) Any dispute or claim arising out of this Agreement shall be referred to and resolved by the International Chamber of Commerce ("ICC") in Paris in accordance with the ICC Conciliation and Arbitration Rules. [The ICC shall decide which system of law shall be applied in relation to the dispute].

Arbitration clauses and their usefulness are tied up to a great extent with the considerations already discussed, in relation to the difficulty of enforcing rights under a law other than that of the country of the party against whom enforcement is sought (see cl.1.3.5). In many cases arbitration awards are easier to enforce than judgments obtained from a court, given the large number of states which have become signatories to the 1958 New York Convention on the Recognition and Enforcement of Foreign Arbitral Awards. Where this Convention does not apply, and in the absence of a relevant bilateral treaty, arbitration awards cannot be implemented (if the party against whom they are made refuses to comply with them) without what amounts to the retrial of the case in the local courts to obtain a court order under which the award can be enforced. It should be noted that this situation is no different in the EC. There is no special provision of EC law which helps with the enforcement of arbitration awards between Member States. Within the European Union, the Brussels and Lugano Conventions and Chapter III of the Brussels Regulation (discussed below under cl.1.6.3) do not provide for the recognition of arbitral awards, but only court judgments (see for instance Art.1(2)(d) of the Brussels Regulation).

The three versions give fairly common types of clauses. Version (c) is of a type often favoured in commercial arbitrations of an international character. The last sentence, in square brackets, is also sometimes used to get over the problem where neither party can agree to the proper law which should govern the agreement. **1–115**

The main problem relating to arbitration clauses, in any jurisdiction, is the relationship, under the local law of the state where the arbitration is conducted, between the process of arbitration and the court. This resolves itself into three basic questions. How far can parties to a contract set up their own private tribunal to resolve disputes under the contract, outside the jurisdiction of the court? How far can the courts intervene in the process of arbitration to regulate the conduct of the arbitration (procedural questions) and to overturn the arbitrator's award (substantive questions of law and/or fact)? Will the court assist in the enforcement of the award, and, if so, how? **1–116**

The answers to these questions depend upon the particular provisions of the local law, and this is one of the questions that should be addressed to a local lawyer, if one is considering detailed arbitration provisions in an agreement. **1–117**

1.6.2 Expert

> If any dispute arises between the parties with respect to [the amount of commission due to the agent under cl. *] [whether the Products comply with the specification set out in Sch. *] [whether the distributor has sold sufficient of the Products to meet the minimum sales targets set out in sched *] then such dispute shall at the instance of either party be referred to a person agreed between the parties, or, in default of such agreement within twenty-one days of notice from either party to the other calling upon the other so to agree, to a person chosen, on the application of either party by [the President for the time being of the London Chamber of Commerce]. Such person shall act as an expert and not as an arbitrator, and the decision of such person shall be final and binding upon the parties. The costs of such expert shall be [borne equally by the parties] [borne by the parties in such proportions as the expert in his discretion shall decide]. **1–118**

In any relationship there may be disputes between the parties as to questions of fact, which have no particular legal issues bound up with them. Such questions are often settled by appointing a third party to decide them, who is usually known as an expert. Unlike an arbitrator, his decision can, and usually is, provided to be final and binding upon the parties. Since the expert is called upon to decide questions of fact only, such clauses are enforceable without any need to consider any rules of public policy against ouster of the jurisdiction of the courts. This means that neither party would (in the absence of agreement from the other) be able either to try the relevant issue in court, or, in most situations, to appeal to the court if dissatisfied with the expert's decision. The only possibility of such an appeal, and this irrespective of any wording in the clause to the contrary, would be where the expert acted fraudulently or in bad faith, or if there were a manifest error on the face of the award. The clause set out above is a typical expert clause, showing some of the situations where an expert might be used, and providing for a method of appointing an expert if the parties cannot themselves agree upon whom to appoint.

1.6.3 Courts

1–119 1.6.3(a) The parties agree to submit to the [exclusive] [non-exclusive] jurisdiction of the [English] courts.

OR

1.6.3(b) Any legal proceedings instituted against the Distributor by the Principal shall be brought in the courts of the Distributor's country of domicile and any legal proceedings against the Principal by the Distributor shall be brought in the courts of the Principal's country of domicile and for the purposes of such proceedings the law governing this Agreement and such proceedings shall in each case be deemed to be the law of the country in which the relevant proceedings have been instituted in accordance with this clause. For the purpose of proceedings brought against it by the other party under this clause each party agrees to submit to the jurisdiction of the courts of the other party's country of domicile.

Neither an arbitration clause nor an expert clause removes the need for a proper law clause, and for a clause deciding which courts shall have jurisdiction in the case of legal disputes. In the very restricted circumstances in which an appeal to the courts can lie against the award of an arbitrator, or the situation where one wishes to contest the decision of an expert on grounds of bad faith or fraudulent behaviour of the other party, a resort to the courts may be necessary. The proper law clause may be necessary to decide whether the arbitration clause or the expert clause itself is valid, or the way in which it should be operated. Arbitration or expert clauses do not remove all possibility of resort to the courts, they only circumscribe it. Of course, there are many circumstances in which the parties may prefer an agreement in which there is no arbitration or expert provision at all, and in which the only regulation of disputes is to be either by informal agreement, and negotiation, or resort to the courts.

1–120 Version (a) is a simple clause giving jurisdiction to one court. A common mistake when using such clauses in the UK is to use the term "UK Law". UK law as such does not exist. There are of course a number of systems of law in force in the UK and one of these systems should always be individually specified, namely England and Wales, or Northern Ireland, or Scotland.

Version (b) is a more complicated one. It can sometimes be used to compromise where the parties cannot agree on a proper law and a court, but it is also useful in international situations generally. If the defendant is always on his home ground this means that if judgment is obtained it will be from the court in the jurisdiction where the defendant has his assets, thus removing the problem of enforcing a foreign judgment. Also, since the defendant is on his home ground, he is more confident as to what his rights are under his own law, the proceedings will be in his own language, he can use the type of legal representatives that he is familiar with, his witnesses will not have far to travel, and generally his costs will be less than those of the plaintiff. **1–121**

This means that both parties are unlikely to raise claims as plaintiffs unless they really feel a genuine grievance, and think their claim is likely to result in a judgment in their favour. Since claims of this nature are the ones which the other party is most likely to want to settle, and frivolous claims are deterred, this sort of clause has the merit of cutting down litigation. It also means that neither party can be forced, against his will, to the expense of foreign litigation by the other party. Thus this type of clause gives some certainty to both parties that the costs of litigation can be controlled, and that the other is unlikely to institute legal proceedings against them lightly. **1–122**

In the version shown here there is reference to the courts of each party's domicile, but in practice it is probably better to state the name of the country, and specify the court concerned in more detail in each case, perhaps by referring to the district court of the town where each party's principal offices are. It should also be remembered that in countries with a federal constitution, at the very least reference to the state in which the party is resident must be made; reference to country of domicile is not enough. **1–123**

Finally, if the second version is used the proper law clause (cl.1.3.5) should not be included. **1–124**

The use of the term "non-exclusive" in version (a) means that the dispute can certainly be dealt with by the courts of one named forum but that if, under the rules of any system of private international law, a party can find another forum, then he is not precluded from litigating there as well. This is a useful provision to add where the parties may have assets in a number of jurisdictions. **1–125**

Incidentally, deleting "non-exclusive", or even using the term "exclusive" may not always achieve the desired effect of limitation to one jurisdiction. Similarly, although the language of version (b) is mandatory in conferring jurisdiction on a named forum, it should not be assumed that this will always be effective. **1–126**

First there is the question of whether the named tribunal in the named jurisdiction will recognise the clause and accept jurisdiction over the case at all. In the absence of some applicable treaty, the clause itself is not necessarily conclusive on the issue. It is true that where, on the basis of the rules of private international law relating to conflict of laws which apply in that jurisdiction, the tribunal should entertain the proceedings it will almost certainly do so, even in the absence of a specific jurisdiction clause.

1–127 However, these principles are usually applied in the absence of contracts with express clauses dealing with jurisdiction. Where such clauses exist, the court is more than likely to enforce the original intention of the parties (even if one has later had a change of heart) by accepting jurisdiction (and if necessary rejecting a contention that it is *forum non conveniens*) or issuing an antisuit injunction to prevent a party bringing concurrent proceedings in another jurisdiction.

1–128 In *Aggeliki Charis Compania Maritima SA v Pagnan SpA (The Angelic Grace)* [1995] 1 Lloyd's Rep. 87, CA, an injunction was sought to restrain a party from bringing proceedings in an Italian court in breach of an English arbitration agreement. The Court of Appeal granted the injunction and stated that English courts should feel no diffidence in granting such an injunction, provided that it was sought promptly and before the foreign proceedings were too far advanced. There was no difference in principle between an injunction to restrain proceedings in breach of an arbitration clause and one to restrain breach of an exclusive jurisdiction clause.

1–129 Similarly in *Shell International Petroleum Co Ltd v Coral Oil Co Ltd (No.1)* [1999] 1 Lloyd's Rep., QBD Commercial Court (discussed in detail at Chapter 1.3.5 above) and *IFR Ltd v Federal Trade SpA* (discussed in detail in Chapter 3.10) the presence of express clauses was decisive.

1–130 Nevertheless, it must not be forgotten that the effect of the jurisdiction clause is persuasive rather than mandatory. In the last analysis, the court will feel free to ignore the clause if the interests of justice are best served by doing so. Thus, the court can accept or refuse jurisdiction whether or not there is a clause conferring jurisdiction upon it. It can also refuse to recognise a clause conferring jurisdiction upon another tribunal.

1–131 The underlying principles governing the rejection or acceptance of jurisdiction by a tribunal can be seen in the application of the concepts of *forum conveniens* and *forum non conveniens*. *Forum conveniens* is the forum with which the claim has the most substantial connection (see *Spiliada Maritime Corp v Cansulex Ltd (The Spiliada)* [1987] 1 A.C. 460, HL and *Connelly v RTZ Corp Plc (No.1)* [1996] 1 All E.R. 500, CA). The other side of the coin is the concept of *forum non conveniens*, where a party to pending litigation petitions the tribunal not to hear the case on the grounds that it is not the *forum conveniens*. The court will consider itself *forum non conveniens* if it is "satisfied that there was some other tribunal, having competent jurisdiction in which the case might be tried more suitably for the interests of all the parties and for the ends of justice" (see *Connelly v RTZ Corp Plc (No.2)* [1998] A.C. 854, HL, which followed the old case of *Sim v Robinow* (1892) 19 R. 665).

1–132 Where the court rejects a petition that it is *forum non conveniens* and accepts jurisdiction, it will in appropriate circumstances issue an antisuit injunction to prevent the petitioning party bringing concurrent proceedings in another jurisdiction.

1–133 Thus, the English courts are not obliged to respect a clause conferring exclusive jurisdiction on a foreign court, but have a discretion as to whether or not to grant a stay of any proceedings brought before them. The court will consider whether the parties are within the jurisdiction of the court, and, if so, whether the interests of justice would be best served by allowing the English action to proceed or by granting a stay to allow the foreign action to proceed in its stead (see *The Eleftheria* [1969] 2 W.L.R. 1073). In most situations, the court will grant a stay of the English proceedings, but this is not always so. For instance, in *Evans Marshall & Co Ltd v Bertola* [1973] All E.R. 992, an extreme case, with very special circumstances, the English Court ignored a clause conferring exclusive jurisdiction on a Spanish court (Spain not then being a member of the EU) because the substance of the claim related to England, the witnesses and one of the two defendants were English, and one of the claims related to conspiracy between the defendants. In addition the Spanish courts were notorious for the slowness of their proceedings and would not help the plaintiffs by granting interim relief to make up for this.

Both versions of this clause should be used with care when one or both parties are resident in Member States of the EC or the EEA. Here, special rules apply. **1–134**

The Council Regulation on the Jurisdiction and the Recognition and Enforcement of Judgments in Civil and Commercial Matters (44/20/01) came into effect on March 1, 2002. The Regulation is directly applicable, with no need for implementing legislation, and binds all of the Member States of the European Union with the exception of Denmark, which exercised the special rights granted to it on accession, and refused to participate. The regulation replaces the Brussels Convention on Jurisdiction and Enforcement of Judgments in Civil and Commercial Matters of 1968 (as amended). However, the Convention still applies as against defendants domiciled in Denmark and to cases brought before the courts in Denmark. The Lugano Convention of 1988 which extended the principles of the Brussels Convention to the EFTA countries is still in force and has application in Norway and Switzerland, and also (at least pending its accession to the EU) to Poland. (See *Insured Financial Structures Ltd v Elektrocieplownia Tychy SA* [2003] EWCA Civ 110, CA.) So far as the UK is concerned the Brussels Convention was implemented through the Civil Jurisdiction and Judgments Act 1982. **1–135**

So far as the Brussels Convention is concerned, the general rule for commercial disputes is that a defendant is sued in the Member State where it is domiciled, although a plaintiff may choose instead to sue in the Member State where the main obligation under the contract is to be performed. Consumers have special treatment, in that they can bring proceedings as plaintiffs in the Member State where they are domiciled, provided they were invited to contract, or advertising took place, in the state in which they were domiciled, and they concluded the relevant contract in that state. **1–136**

However, these general rules can be displaced by the intention of the parties. Under Art.17 of the Brussels Convention, "If the parties, one or more of whom is domiciled in a Contracting State, have agreed that a court **1–137** or the courts of a Contracting State are to have jurisdiction to settle any disputes which have arisen or which may arise in connection with a particular legal relationship, that court or those courts shall have exclusive jurisdiction..."

1–138 The Regulation follows the same principles as, but has clarified and updated, the Convention in the light of experience since it first came into force. Article 2 sets out the basic principle that persons domiciled in a Member State shall, whatever their nationality, be sued in that state. If a defendant is not domiciled in any Member State then jurisdiction is decided by the relevant rules of private international law in force in the state where application to the courts is being made, and the Regulation in effect has no application (Art.4). Articles 5, 6 and 7 specify certain exceptions to the basic principle in Art.2. So far as contracts are concerned, Art.5(1)(a) provides that a person domiciled in a Member State may be sued in another Member State if the place of performance of the relevant contractual obligation is in that other state. Where a contract is for the sale of goods or the performance of services, the place of performance, unless otherwise agreed, is where the goods are to be delivered or the services to be performed.

1–139 Articles 15 to 17 provide mandatory protection for consumers. A consumer can sue in the state where the consumer is domiciled or in the state where the other party is domiciled (Art.16(1)), and the other party may only sue the consumer in the state where the consumer is domiciled (Art.16(2)). The consumer's rights cannot be waived except by an agreement entered into after the dispute has arisen, or in a case where, at the time the contract was concluded, the consumer and the other party were both domiciled or habitually resident in the same Member State, and they then agreed that the courts of that Member State should have jurisdiction.

1–140 Article 22 provides for certain mandatory rules of jurisdiction: immovable property—where situated; corporate law issues relating to companies or other legal persons or associations of natural or legal persons—where the organisation has its seat; validity of entries in public registers—where registered; validity of registration of intellectual property—where registered; enforcement of judgments—where judgment is to be enforced.)

1–141 Article 23 provides the same exception for jurisdiction clauses as Art.17 of the Convention. However, it is more flexible in that (unlike the Convention) it specifically permits a clause which confers non-exclusive jurisdiction. One of the most difficult problems under the Convention was the status of clauses which either did not specify whether the jurisdiction was or was not exclusive or expressly provided for non-exclusive jurisdiction (see *Meath v Glacetal* [1979] 1 C.M.L.R. 52, *Kurz v Stella Musical Veranstaltungs GmbH* [1992] All E.R. 630, *Continental Bank NA v Aeolos Cia Navieria SA* [1994] 2 All E.R. 540 and *Insured Financial Structures Ltd v Elektrocieplownia Tychy SA* [2003] EWCA Civ 110, CA). (It should be remembered that in those cases where the Convention, or the Lugano Convention, still applies, the conferring of non-exclusive jurisdiction is better avoided, and the exclusive jurisdiction alternative for version (a) above should be used accordingly.)

1–142 These issues no longer arise where the Regulation applies. Here, the parties are free to specify exclusive or non-exclusive jurisdiction as they prefer. Presumably if the jurisdiction is specified as non-exclusive then the Regulation itself will provide the rules for deciding the other Member States in which proceedings can be brought.

The Article states that: "If the parties, one or more of whom is domiciled in a Member State have agreed that a court or the courts of a Member State are to have jurisdiction to settle any disputes which have arisen or which may arise in connection with a particular legal relationship, that court or those courts shall have jurisdiction. Such jurisdiction shall be exclusive unless the parties have agreed otherwise. Such an agreement conferring jurisdiction shall be either (a) in writing or evidenced in writing or (b) in a form which accords with practices which the parties have established between themselves or (c) in international trade or commerce, in a form which accords with a usage of which the parties are or ought to have been aware and which in such trade or commerce is widely known to and regularly observed by parties to contracts of the type involved in the particular trade or commerce in question." **1–143**

It should be noted that the way in which this provision is drafted has the result that a jurisdiction clause which uses neither the word "exclusive" nor the word "non-exclusive" will have the effect of conferring exclusive jurisdiction. **1–144**

However, Art.23(5) provides that jurisdiction clauses are subject to and cannot override the mandatory provisions of the Regulation, namely Art.13 (certain insurance contracts), 17 (consumer contracts discussed above) 21 (employment contracts) and 22 (mandatory specified proceedings discussed above). **1–145**

The Regulation also goes some way to making jurisdiction clauses enforceable on a global scale. Article 23(3) provides that: "Where [a jurisdiction clause relating to one Member State] is concluded by parties, none of whom is domiciled in a Member State, the courts of other Member States shall have no jurisdiction over their disputes unless the court or courts chosen have declined." To this extent, the Regulation forces courts of Member States to honour jurisdiction clauses inserted in agreements where all the parties are outside the European Union. **1–146**

Finally, it should be noted that under Art.24, apart from jurisdiction derived from other provisions of the Regulation, if a defendant chooses to enter an appearance other than for the purpose of contesting jurisdiction, the court in question will have jurisdiction unless another court has exclusive jurisdiction pursuant to an agreement under Art.22. **1–147**

Version (b) is also of somewhat doubtful application where the Brussels or the Lugano Conventions still apply. Following *Meath v Glacetal* above, would lead to the conclusion that such a clause does not fall within Art.17, and that the parties would be left to rely on the general rules of jurisdiction under the Conventions. However, looking at the *Continental Bank* case above, it does seem that Art.17 can apply where only one party submits to the jurisdiction of a particular court, and the other party is left free to sue in any jurisdiction permitted under the Conventions. An extension of this **1–148** decision to a situation like version (b), where each party submits to the exclusive jurisdiction of a different court does not seem logically impossible, if the *Continental Bank* case correctly construed Art.17. Nevertheless, the prudent course would be not to use version (b) where the Conventions apply. Of course, these arguments would no longer apply to the Brussels Regulation. Here each party can specify exclusive or non-exclusive jurisdiction, and, whatever the exact status of the jurisdiction conferred in relation to each party under version (b), there seems no reason why the Regulation should not apply it.

1–149 There is little that can be done by way of contractual provisions to deal with the issue of enforcing court judgments or orders once obtained. Outside of the European Union, except where bilateral treaties exist, a court is only obliged to recognise a foreign judgment if and to the extent required by its national law. In general, the courts of most states will recognise a judgment by a foreign court if it is final and conclusive, is not contrary to public policy of the state where it is to be enforced, does not have on the face of it a mistake of law or fact, and is either for the payment of a debt or for a fixed and ascertained sum of money by way of damages.

Within the European Union, Chapter III of the Brussels Regulation provides that judgments by the courts of one Member State are to be recognised and freely enforced in the other Member States, without any special procedure being required (Art.32). The Brussels and Lugano Conventions, so far as still applicable, have broadly the same provisions. It should however be noted that no recognition is provided for arbitral awards either under the Regulation (see Art.1(2)(d)) or the Conventions.

1–150 1.6.4 *Waiver* The failure of a party to insist in any one or more instances upon the performance of any provisions of this Agreement shall not be construed as a waiver or relinquishment of that party's rights to future performance of such provision and the other party's obligation in respect of such future performance shall continue in full force and effect.

This is one version of a clause commonly met with, to ensure that forbearance in any particular instance is not to the prejudice of the party exercising it. This is particularly useful in international agreements, where, with the parties far away from each other, there may otherwise be a dispute as to whether the party trying to enforce his rights has actually waived his rights in respect of acts of the other party or simply did not know of them.

1–151 1.6.5 *Severability* In the event that any one or more of the provisions contained in this Agreement shall for any reason be held to be unenforceable illegal or otherwise invalid in any respect under the law governing this Agreement or its performance, such unenforceability illegality or invalidity shall not affect any other provisions of this Agreement and this Agreement shall then be construed as if such unenforceable illegal or invalid provisions had never been contained herein.

The situation with regard to the severability of provisions which are objectionable under a particular system of law varies in some cases according to the jurisdiction. This clause may be no more than for the avoidance of doubt in some jurisdictions, but its presence is in any event useful as a precaution.

1.6.6 *Compliance with laws* In the performance of this Agreement both parties shall comply with all laws rules regulations decrees and other ordinances issued by any governmental or other state authority relating to the subject matter of this Agreement and the performance by the parties hereto of their obligations hereunder. **1–152**

This clause can be used in cases where it is required to emphasise the duty on both parties to comply with relevant laws. Its use would require the reconsideration of the particular provisions imposing this liability on the party to the agreement other than the principal shown in the following chapters (see, *e.g.* Chapter 2.3.4).

1.6.7 *Power of attorney* The Distributor hereby irrevocably appoints the Principal to be his attorney in his name and on his behalf to execute and do any instrument or thing and generally to use his name for the purpose of giving to the Principal (or its nominee or assignee) the full benefit of the provisions of cll. ****, and in favour of any third party a certificate in writing (accompanied by a certified copy of this Agreement) signed by any authorised signatory of the Principal (in the presence of and witnessed by a Notary Public) that any instrument or act falls within the authority hereby conferred shall be conclusive evidence that such is the case. **1–153**

This clause is useful in situations where the principal needs some document executed by the other party to the agreement to perfect rights he has under the agreement. One of the most likely areas is where there is an obligation to assign to the principal a licence of some sort to market the products (see, *e.g.* Chapter 4.17.6) or a trade mark registration, that should belong to the principal, which has been wrongfully registered by the other party. The other party may refuse to sign the necessary documentation and then the principal can do it on his behalf.

In some countries the use of powers of attorney is regulated by provisions relating to formalities of execution. These can include execution under seal, legalising, witness by a notary public, and sometimes the preparation of a certified translation into the local language of the territory where it is to have effect. There can also be formalities connected with registration and stamping in the territory where the power is to be used. In these cases such a clause is not likely to be held to confer a valid and exercisable power of attorney. If this is the case, then, if it is felt essential to have such a power, a separate instrument should be executed in accordance with the local law's requirements. **1–154**

1.7 Force majeure

1.7 *Force majeure* Neither party shall be liable to the other for any failure to perform or delay in performance of its obligations hereunder [other than an **1–155** obligation to pay monies] caused by (i) Act of God (ii) outbreak of hostilities, riot, civil disturbance, acts of terrorism (iii) the act of any government or authority (including, revocation of any licence or consent) (iv) fire, explosion, flood, fog or bad weather [(v) default of suppliers or subcontractors] (vi) theft, malicious damage, strike, lockout or industrial action of any kind (vii) any cause or circumstance whatsoever beyond its reasonable control.

This clause gives both parties a release from liability in the event of failure to perform obligations through circumstances beyond their reasonable control. Some *force majeure* clauses incorporate a more extended list of events, and in particular cases the parties, or the draftsman, may feel more comfortable for including them, but this short-form clause really performs as well in most cases. The specific inclusion of industrial disputes is necessary because it may be held that such matters are within the control of the party concerned, since it is presumably his conduct that caused them in the first place, or prevents them from being settled.

1–156 The phrase in square brackets relating to the payment of monies is inserted mainly to enable the principal to terminate the agreement for failure to pay by the other party. In the case of such a failure, the principal may well consider that he is not interested in excuses, however valid.

1–157 The phrase in square brackets relating to default of suppliers and subcontractors is more of a problem. In its absence, the clause would operate so that such a default would have to be considered on its merits, bearing in mind the reason for the failure, whether the party seeking to rely on the failure was himself at fault, and whether an alternative supplier could be found in time. If there were no *force majeure* clause at all, the party concerned would be liable even though it was a third party who had defaulted, and whatever the reason for the default. The inclusion of the wording in square brackets would probably excuse the party concerned, whatever the reason for the third party default, unless it were caused by a deliberate act or omission of the party concerned, such as a failure to provide information needed before the supplier could begin manufacture.

1–158 In the absence of this clause the general legal rules governing such matters under the proper law of the agreement would apply. It should be noted that the term "*force majeure*" itself has no precise definition in common law jurisdictions. It has been said in the English courts that for an event to be one of *force majeure* it must be outside the control of the parties to the contract, and must cause some physical or material restraint (*Hackney Borough Council v Dore* [1922] 1 K.B. 431). It has been held to include strikes in progress but not bad weather (*Matsoukis v Priestman* [1915] 1 K.B. 681). Thus clauses which merely excuse the parties for failure to perform "due to *force majeure*" should be avoided in common law jurisdictions.

1–159 *Force majeure* is really a concept derived from the Napoleonic Civil Code of France, and most Western European jurisdictions with civil codes use the term in one translation or another. However, the definition and the consequences are not the same in all civil codes, and thus even in these jurisdictions it is better to use a clause of the type suggested above.

1–160 Whether one looks at the common law doctrines of frustration or the civil code concept of *force majeure*, the basic principle is that there are circumstances in which a party should be excused from his obligations under the contract if it is impossible (legally or physically) to perform them, and the impossibility has arisen because of events outside the control of the parties, which have occurred after the contract was entered into, and which were usually unforeseen by the parties at the date the contract was entered into.

Although originally the common law recognised no such excuse for per- **1–161** formance, in the absence of an express provision giving such an excuse, the English courts began to mitigate the harshness of the rule by holding that supervening illegality or disappearance of the subject matter of the contract were sufficient to excuse failure to perform (*Taylor v Caldwell* (1863) 3 B & S 826). Today the English courts consider that "Frustration occurs whenever the law recognises that without default of either party a contractual obligation has become incapable of being performed because the circumstances in which performance is called 'for would render it a thing radically different from that which was undertaken by the contract' (Lord Radcliffe in *Davis Contractors Ltd v Fareham UDC* [1956] A.C. 696).

Lord Radcliffe's statement is in fact not that much unlike most of the civil **1–162** code provisions relating to *force majeure*. Most of these jurisdictions treat force majeure in much the same way. The events have to be such that it is legally or physically impossible to perform the contract. There has to be no fault or negligence imputed to the party relying on *force majeure*. The events have to be of an irresistible character, and the party concerned must have done everything in his power to perform his obligations. The requirement as to foreseeability varies. France, for instance, requires it, but not all jurisdictions do. Many jurisdictions consider the default of a supplier or subcontractor to be an event of *force majeure*. France does not.

In all jurisdictions the results of *force majeure* are roughly the same. The **1–163** contract is terminated and there is an equitable right to readjust the past to prevent one party taking advantage of the termination to benefit either from work done and not paid for or payments made in advance. This is normally achieved by special provisions in the code, or the application of a general principle of unjust enrichment. In the absence of statutory provisions the common law merely holds that the contract is at an end, and loss lies where it falls. However, the same results are arrived at in common law jurisdictions through legislation, for instance, in the UK, the Law Reform (Frustrated Contracts) Act 1943.

There are two other matters that arise under the general situation of **1–164** impossibility of performance. One of these is the existence of circumstances, unknown to the parties at the time the contract was entered into, which subsequently come to light, and whose discovery shows that the contract cannot be performed. In most jurisdictions such matters fall within the province of the law relating to mutual mistake.

The other is a class of events which arise subsequent to the formation of **1–165** the contract and which, although they do not make it impossible to perform the contract, make it much more onerous for a party to perform than he had ever contemplated as being within the degree of risk he had thought he was running when he entered into the contract. Although, in some jurisdictions, some of these events may be classified as *force majeure*, and, in common law jurisdictions, if their effect is extremely severe, the contract may be held to be frustrated, in general they are treated in civil code jurisdictions under a concept of "hardship" which is separate from, although similar to, *force majeure*. In common law jurisdictions there is no such principle. Either the contract is frustrated, or it must be performed, whatever economic loss the party affected by the event may suffer.

1–166 The clause as drafted here would not of itself in most cases excuse a party simply because the contract becomes more difficult or expensive to be performed, provided that it can still be performed. The drafting of a clause that would have that effect is possible but in practice is often hard to justify commercially.

1–167 Most hardship cases are concerned with the question of increased cost of performance, or of extension of time to overcome unforeseen difficulties. Thus, in the sort of agreements that this book is concerned with, the most likely problem areas for the principal are in the supply of goods to his distributor (where he has specific delivery and price obligations) or unforeseen difficulties in adapting a product to make it saleable (or sometimes even function) in the territory concerned. The other party to the agreement is less likely to take on obligations relating to such matters in the first place. It is therefore really more practical, and more acceptable commercially, to attack specific problem areas by putting in such things as price adjustment clauses, clauses allowing the principal to pass on cost increases, or new taxes, and to provide that in the event of certain difficulties (*e.g.* adaptation of the product proving particularly difficult) extensions of time will be allowed, and charges made on a time and material basis to the other party for work to be done (which will encourage the other party to terminate if things get too expensive). It could also be provided that the principal should (in the event of such difficulties) have the option to terminate the arrangement without compensation to the other party. This course may not always be possible under the prevailing local law, in which case the other types of hardship clauses must be used.

1–168 The law relating to hardship, in the absence of a clause varies widely. France, Spain and Belgium, for instance, do not recognise the concept, while West Germany, Italy and Switzerland do. Switzerland serves as a good example of the way the doctrine is applied. Swiss law recognises the concept both through certain limited provisions in its commercial code, and also by the build up of precedents in certain cases based either on good faith principles, or the general power that the Swiss courts have, under art 1 of the Civil Code, to fill in gaps in the law and freely to imply into contracts any terms necessary to give them efficacy. The events which trigger the application of these principles must be general catastrophes, often but not exclusively of an economic nature, which are unforeseeable, occur without fault on the part of the individual relying on them, and produce a degree of risk, far beyond that anticipated when the contract was entered into, which is likely to cause the economic ruin of the party affected. Possible events that could trigger the clause are hyper-inflation or violent fluctuations in exchange rates. The doctrine is usually applied only in long-term contracts. The court can terminate the contract if the party suffering the hardship requests it, or can renegotiate the contract, at the request of both parties.

Another area where the problems of *force majeure* and hardship arise is in **1–169**
the compliance with formalities relating to import and export licences and quotas. In general the agreement should provide for the buying party to obtain the import licence, and the selling party to obtain the export licence. In each case the obligation is then placed upon the party most easily able to discharge it. This is the effect of selling FOB (see Chapter 4.26). Similarly, an FOB sale will make it the responsibility of the selling party to comply with export quotas, and the buying party with import quotas. Sales Ex Works impose all of the obligations on the buying party and sales Delivered Warehouse on the selling party. A sale CIF leaves the obligations split. The selling party must have an export licence to load the goods and ship them. He can unload them at the destination without the need to obtain any other licence. The import licence is produced as part of the procedure for clearance through customs, which on a sale CIF is the responsibility of the buying party.

In some cases these obligations are varied because of the need to obtain **1–170**
exchange control permission to open a letter of credit or make a payment in advance before the goods can be shipped. In this case, whatever the shipment terms, the buying party will have to obtain most of the permissions necessary to import the goods into his country if he is to get the necessary exchange control permission to set up the letter of credit or make the payment.

If the contract is silent about what happens if a licence cannot be obtained **1–171**
or a quota is exceeded, it is likely that the party who is obliged to obtain or comply with it will be held liable to the other if he fails to do so (*Congimex Companhia General de Comercia Importadora e Exportadora Sarl v Tradax Export SA* [1983] 1 Lloyd's Rep. 250, CA). He will be in breach of an obligation and only an express clause excusing him for failure to perform for reasons beyond his control will excuse him. Even then such a clause will protect him only provided that the failure is not in some way his own fault (*Maritime National Fish Ltd v Ocean Trawlers Ltd* [1935] A.C. 524) and that he can show he has taken all reasonable steps and used due diligence to ensure that the relevant licence was obtained or kept in force, or that the relevant quota was not exceeded (*Charles H Windschuegl Ltd v Pickering & Co Ltd* [1950] Lloyd's Rep. 89. If a quota is subsequently imposed and renders the contract incapable of performance then there could very well be upheld a claim that the contract was frustrated or that *force majeure* provisions in the relevant proper law applied, provided that, in jurisdictions where lack of foreseeability is a requirement, the imposition was not foreseen at the time the contract was entered into. The same would be true for the imposition of an import or export ban subsequent to the formation of the contract or the subsequent imposition of a licensing system with which the parties could not comply. In any case, in practice, the inclusion of the

force majeure clause would provide a relief from liability (see also Case C3/74 *Einfuhr und Vorratsstelle fur Getreide und Futtermittel v Pfutlenreuter (Wilhelm)* [1974] E.C.R. 589, ECJ).

1.8 Whole agreement

1.8.1 Whole agreement clause

1–172 1.8.1(a) This Agreement sets forth and shall constitute the entire agreement between both the parties with respect to the subject matter hereof and shall supersede any and all promises representations warranties or other statements whether written or oral made by or on behalf of one party to the other of any nature whatsoever or contained in any leaflet brochure or other document given by one party to the other concerning such subject matter.

OR

1.8.1(b) This Agreement (including the documents and instruments referred to herein) supersedes all prior representations, arrangements, understandings and agreements between the Parties (whether written or oral) relating to the subject matter hereof and sets forth the entire complete and exclusive agreement and understanding between the parties hereto relating to the subject matter hereof.

1.8.1.1 Each party warrants to the other that it has not relied on any representation, arrangement, understanding or agreement (whether written or oral) not expressly set out or referred to in this Agreement.

1.8.1.2 Without prejudice to the generality of the foregoing, save as expressly provided in this Agreement, (a) the Principal gives no promise, warranty, undertaking or representation to the Distributor, (b) the Principal shall be under no liability in respect of the transactions contemplated by, and the subject matter of, this Agreement and (c) all other warranties express or implied by law legislation or otherwise howsoever are hereby expressly excluded.

1.8.1.3 Each party further agrees and undertakes to the other that no breach of this agreement shall entitle it to rescind this Agreement, and that its remedies for any breach of this Agreement shall be solely for breach of contract, which remedies shall be subject to and in accordance with the provisions of this Agreement.

1.8.1.4 No provision contained in this clause, or elsewhere in this Agreement, shall operate so as to exclude any liability of one of the parties in respect of a fraudulent misrepresentation made by that party to the other, or to restrict or exclude any remedy which the other party may have in respect of such misrepresentation.

Whole agreement clauses are designed to give both parties certainty in that they can now refer to the terms of the agreement in confidence that the other party cannot bring up a particular representation, perhaps made in correspondence, or orally in pre-agreement negotiations, which can overturn the express terms of the agreement. Version (a) is a relatively simple clause, which would in general be suitable for most international agreements. Version (b), which is discussed in detail below, is a more complex clause designed to deal with certain decisions in this area in the English courts.

It is sometimes said that such clauses are unfair because they allow a party to make extravagant claims and representations without incurring any legal liability for them, even though they may have been a material inducement to the other party to enter into the contract. However, the alternative to this would be to require legal scrutiny and drafting of all the pre-agreement correspondence and other documents, and, theoretically, minuting and legal scrutiny of the proceedings of all meetings at which oral representations are made. In fact, commercial negotiations cannot be carried on in this fashion, and few businessmen would welcome the constant monitoring by their legal advisers that would be required if their every word had to be carefully chosen for its legal effect. **1–173**

Most commercial negotiations are carried on by parties who understand their interests and are capable of protecting themselves, or retaining advisers to protect themselves, by ensuring that all relevant representations and warranties are included in the final agreement. While whole agreement clauses may not be suitable for consumer transactions, there is every reason and inducement for both sides to include them in commercial arrangements. **1–174**

The exclusion of liability for pre-contract misrepresentations, which can be obtained through the use of a whole agreement clause, is to a certain extent regulated by the Unfair Contract Terms Act 1977 (UCTA), which has already been discussed generally in relation to the agreements covered by this book in Chapter 1.3.5. Section 8 of UCTA amends the Misrepresentation Act 1967, and the Misrepresentation (Northern Ireland) Act 1967, to provide that no exclusion of pre-contract misrepresentations is permitted, under the 1967 Acts, unless the exclusion satisfies the reasonableness test under s.11 of UCTA. Prior to this amendment, the 1967 Acts provided that such an exclusion was of no effect except to the extent that the court or arbitrator in question allowed reliance upon it as being fair and reasonable in the circumstances of the case. Thus the effect of s 8 has been to replace a general determination as to reasonableness by the tribunal with the reasonableness test laid down by UCTA for all other exclusion clauses. **1–175**

This section is of the very widest application. It is not limited, as are ss.2–7 of UCTA, either by s.1 to business to business and consumer transactions, or by the exception of the operation of those sections from the classes of contracts set out in Sch.1 to UCTA. The ambit of s.8 is thus defined purely by the 1967 Acts, and they apply to all contracts of any nature, whether business to business, or entered into with a consumer, or non-business transactions between private individuals. Subject, then, to the extent, if any, to which the conflict of laws provisions of ss.26 and 27 of UCTA apply, the 1967 Acts, as amended, would appear to regulate all of the contracts dealt with in this book, if they are governed by one of the systems of law in force in the UK. **1–176**

That this is the correct view can be seen by analysis of the precise wording of ss.26(1) and 27(2). Section 26(1) refers to the "limits imposed by this Act" **1–177** and states that they do not apply to contracts for the international supply of goods as defined in s.26(3). The anti-avoidance provision in s.27(2) states "this Act has effect notwithstanding . . .". Both of these reference include s 8. So far as s.26(1) is concerned, s.8 is clearly one of the "limits imposed by this Act". So far as s 27(2) is concerned, the wide reference to "this Act" would also include s.8. The 1967 Acts themselves are obviously not caught by either of these references.

1–178 On this view, it is not correct to take the position that s.8 has amended the 1967 Acts, and it is thus the extent of the application of the 1967 Acts, rather than ss.26 and 27 of UCTA, which determines the issue. The proper way to approach the matter is to regard s.8 as the operative provision. Thus the extent to which it can be regarded as having amended the 1967 Acts in relation to contracts to which UCTA can apply is regulated by the operation of ss.26(1) and 27(2).

1–179 On this basis s 8 is to be treated in the same way as the other provisions of UCTA. It would not apply to international contracts for the supply of goods, but attempts to avoid it in other contracts would be regulated by s.27(2).

That this is correct can be shown by looking at the way the draftsman has dealt with s.27(1).

1–180 Section 27(1) applies where the parties choose as the proper law of a contract one of the systems of law in the UK, and, apart from that choice, the contract would be governed by the law of some other country outside the UK. In this case, s.27(1) states that ss.2–7 and 16–21, as relevant, do not operate as part of the proper law. Thus s.27(1) does not refer, as do ss.26(1) and 27(2) to " this Act" (which phrase must as discussed above include s.8), but only to specific sections, not including s.8. All of the other sections not mentioned in s.27(1) in some way relate to or modify the sections which are mentioned. The only exception to this is s.8, which stands on its own as a section independent of ss.2–7 and 16–21, inserted for the sole purpose of modifying the 1967 Acts.

1–181 One presumes that the draftsman must have intended to use this different language. His omission of s.8 from the application of s.27(1) shows that he regarded s.8 as the operative provision which achieved this regulation, rather than the 1967 Acts which that section amended. If this were not so, there would have been no reason to exclude s.8 from the operation of s.27(1) and he would have used the phrase "this Act" as he did in ss.26(1) and 27(2). The conclusions which can be drawn from this are as follows:

- First, s.27(1) has no application in relation to s.8 at all, so that anywhere a UK system of law is specified in a clause of law clause s.8 will always have effect.
- Second, s.8 would not apply in respect of a contract for the international supply of goods falling within s.26.
- Third, all contracts with a choice of law clause not specifying one of the systems of law in the UK (other than those for the international

supply of goods) would, so far as the application s.8 is concerned, be regulated by s.27(2).

These conclusions give rise to two rather curious results.

First, a contract for the international supply of goods will not be regulated by s.8 even though it is governed by one of the systems of law in force in the UK. However, since the 1967 Acts themselves are part of the systems of law in force in the UK they would presumably apply to the contract but in their unamended form. If this is the case, then the tribunal would be left to decide whether the clause was fair and reasonable, in all the circumstances of the case, using the wording of the 1967 Acts, prior to amendment by s.8. (It is of course questionable whether, for any practical purposes, the decision that the tribunal would come to would be any different to what it would have been if the reasonableness test under s.11 of UCTA had applied.) **1–182**

Second, the anti-avoidance provisions of s.27(2) will operate so as to apply s.8 to clauses excluding liability for pre-contract misrepresentation, unless they are contained in contracts for the international supply of goods, or the choice of foreign proper law is for a "genuine" reason. Thus, in contracts for the international supply of goods, express choice of a foreign proper law can be used to avoid the application of the 1967 Acts, unless (at least as far as the EC is concerned) an argument can be raised that the 1967 Acts are mandatory legislation within the meaning of Art.7 of the Rome Convention (see Chapter 1.3.5), which seems unlikely. **1–183**

The above conclusions can be applied to various classes of contracts as follows: **1–184**

- First, contracts for the international supply of goods covered by s.26 can never be regulated by s.8, whether or not there is an express choice of law clause, and, if there is, no matter what system of law it specifies.
- Second, contracts for the international supply of goods covered by s.26 governed by one of the systems of law in the UK will be subject to the 1967 Acts in their unamended form.
- Third, contracts for the international supply of goods covered by s.26 containing a choice of law clause specifying a foreign law will not be subject to the 1967 Acts in their unamended form, or as amended by s.8, even if, in the absence of the clause, the contract would have been governed by one of the systems of law in force in the UK (*i.e.* the anti-avoidance provisions of s.27(2) cannot apply).
- Fourth, contracts not covered by s.26 which contain an express choice of law clause imposing one of the systems of UK law would be governed by s.8 in all cases.
- Fifth, contracts not covered by s.26 which contain an express choice of law clause imposing a foreign proper law would avoid the whole of UCTA (including s.8) only if the choice of law clause survived the anti-

avoidance provisions of s.27(2); however, if it did so survive then, *ipso facto*, the 1967 Acts (in their unamended form) would have no application either.

- Sixth, where contracts not covered by s.26 contain no choice of law clause, it would depend upon the usual conflict of laws principles as to whether one of the systems of UK law applied. If one of them did, then s.8 would apply.

1–185 There have a been a number of decisions in the English courts on the reasonableness of whole agreement clauses, where they are subject to UCTA. In general, where the parties are of equal bargaining power, and have been properly advised, whole agreement clauses are treated as being reasonable in business to business contracts (see *W Photoprint Ltd v Forward Trust Group Ltd* (1993) 12 Tr. L.R. 146, QBD). This seems to be the line followed by the Court of Appeal in a number of recent cases (see *WRM Group Ltd v Wood* [1998] C.L.C. 189, CA; *EA Grimstead & Son Ltd v McGarrigan*, [1998–99] Info. T.L.R. 384, CA; *The Inntrepreneur Pub Co (GL) v East Crown Ltd* [2000] 2 Lloyd's Rep. 611; *Watford Electronics Ltd v Sanderson CFL Ltd* [2001] EWCA Civ 317, CA and *Granville Oils and Chemicals Ltd v Davies Turner & Co Ltd*, unreported, April 15, 2003).

1–186 However, it has also been held that where a pre-contract representation was the vital factor which induced a party to enter into the contract, exclusion of liability for such a representation by a general whole agreement clause in a set of standard conditions was unreasonable under s 11 of UCTA, and that the only type of exclusion which would have been reasonable was one which referred specifically to the representation in question (see *St Marylebone Property Co Ltd v Payne* [1994] 45 E.G. 156; *Lease Management Services Ltd v Purnell Secretarial Services Ltd* [1994] C.C.L.R. 127; *Sovereign Finance Ltd v Silver Crest Furniture Ltd* [1997] C.C.L.R. 76, QBD; *Danka Rentals Ltd v Xi Software Ltd*, (1998) 17 Tr. L.R. 74 QBD; *Pegler Ltd v Wang (UK) Ltd* [2000] B.L.R. 218, QBD and *Messer UK Ltd v Bacardi-Martini Beverages Ltd* [2002] EWCA Civ 549, CA).

1–187 There are two other decisions on the question of the more general type of whole agreement clause. The first (*Alman and Benson v Associated Newspapers Ltd*, unreported, June 20, 1980, Browne-Wilkinson J.) held that a whole agreement clause which stated only that the agreement "sets forth the entire agreement and understanding of the parties" is not sufficient to exclude a claim for rescission or damages based upon a pre-contractual misrepresentation, although there was no reason why appropriate wording could not have been added which would have had this effect. The second (*Witter Ltd v TBP Industries Ltd*, [1996] 2 All E.R. 573, Jacob J.) held that a whole agreement clause could not preclude the plaintiff from seeking rescission or claiming damages on a tortious basis, in addition to his right to claim damages for breach of contract, unless the clause contained express provision to this effect.

1–188 In the second case, the learned judge went on further to consider the effect of the clause more generally. In his opinion (contrary to the remarks of Browne-Wilkinson J.) merely stating that a party has not relied on pre-contract negotiations was not sufficient to exclude liability; the clause would have to go further and expressly exclude any remedy, other than breach of contract, in respect of any untrue statement in reliance upon which the other party had entered into the contract. He also remarked that, in any event, in his view, the clause failed to satisfy the reasonableness test under s.8 of UCTA because it was so wide that it excluded fraudulent misrepresentation which was clearly unreasonable.

There has been considerable discussion as to the effect of these two cases, and, in particular, as to the validity of the *obiter dicta* in Jacob J.'s judgment in *Witter*. However, it is current practice to take these two cases into account when drafting whole agreement clauses subject to English law. On this basis, simple clauses like version (a) above are no longer regarded as appropriate under English law. Version (b) above is thus offered as a whole agreement clause which deals with these issues. **1–189**

1.8.2 Variation

1.8.2 This Agreement may not be released discharged supplemented interpreted amended varied or modified in any manner except by an instrument in writing signed by a duly authorised officer or representative of each of the parties hereto. **1–190**

This clause serves much the same purpose as cl.1.8.1, but this time for representations and discussions (oral and written) which occur after the agreement has been executed. Again in the interests of certainty there should be a formal, controlled process for changing the terms of the agreement. It should not be allowed to occur without the minds of both parties being drawn to the change proposed and due consideration to its effects being given, both from a legal and a commercial point of view.

1.8.3 Prior agreements

1.8.3 This Agreement hereby cancels all prior agreements between the parties (if any) relating to the Products and also cancels and nullifies all rights (if any) of either party arising against the other by virtue of all or any of the said prior agreements. **1–191**

Finally, where there have been one or more prior agreements between the parties relating to the same subject matter, these should not be allowed to run on concurrently, and any rights arising out of them should be subsumed into the new agreement, once again in the interests of certainty. If nothing else, this prevents a party to the negotiations holding up his sleeve some right which he imagines he will continue to enjoy under a prior arrangement, perhaps forgotten by the other party. He will have to bring out the matter into the open for a proper commercial and legal resolution or else his right, even if it does exist, will be lost through the operation of this clause.

1–192 Of course, before incorporating any of the clauses under Chapter 1.8, the draftsman should make sure that the party he represents understands their full effect, and that all necessary warranties representations and prior rights are preserved by specific provisions elsewhere in the new arrangement.

1.9 No joint venture or partnership

1–193 Nothing in this Agreement shall create a partnership or joint venture between the parties hereto and save as expressly provided in this Agreement neither party shall enter into or have authority to enter into any engagement or make any representation or warranty on behalf of or pledge the credit of or otherwise bind or oblige the other party hereto.

This clause is a general one ensuring that in so far as possible one party cannot enter into obligations on behalf of the other. In practice such clauses run up against problems of ostensible authority. This is discussed in more detail in Chapter 2.3.6 and 2.3.7 in relation to agency agreements.

1.10 Third party rights under contracts

1–194 1.10(a) No term of this Agreement is intended for the benefit of any third party, and the parties do not intend that any term of this Agreement should be enforceable by a third party either under the Contracts (Rights of Third Parties) Act 1999 or otherwise.

OR

1.10(b) The parties intend that [this clause] [cl. *] shall be enforceable by [ABC Limited] [their employees servants or agents] [any person who carries out work on the contract site] pursuant to and in accordance with the Contracts (Rights of Third Parties) Act 1999.

The basic principle is that a contract generates rights and obligations only between the parties to the contract. Although the contract may purport to confer a benefit on a third party, that third party cannot enforce it against the contracting parties (*Scruttons Ltd v Midland Silicones Ltd* [1962] A.C. 1, HL). Similarly, where the contract attempts to impose an obligation on a third party, the contracting parties cannot enforce it against the third party even if he has notice of it. (*Port Line Ltd v Ben Line Steamers Ltd* [1958] 2 Q.B. 146.)

1–195 This position in the UK has been changed to some extent by the Contracts (Rights of Third Parties) Act 1999. Section 1(1) of the Act states that "subject to the provisions of the Act, a person who is not a party to a contract (a "third party") may in his own right enforce a term of the contract if—(a) the contract expressly provides that he may, or (b) subject to subsection (2), the term purports to confer a benefit on him. Section 1(2) states that s.1(1)(b) does not apply if "on a proper construction of the contract" it appears that the parties did not intend the term to be enforceable by the third party. Section 1(3) requires that the third party be expressly identified in the contract by name, as a member of a class or as answering to a particular description but need not be in existence when the contract is entered into. Section 1(4) provides that no right is conferred on the third party to enforce a term of a contract otherwise than subject to and in accordance with any other relevant terms of the contract. Section 1(5) affords the third party all the remedies in enforcing his rights which he would have had if he had been a party to the contract. Section 1(6) provides that where a term of a contract excludes or limits liability in relation to any matter, references in the Act to the third party enforcing the term shall be construed as references to his availing himself of the exclusion or limitation.

Version (a) sets out a simple blanket exclusion of all third party rights **1–196** under a contract. This should probably be the default position for agency, licensing and distribution agreements which are essentially two party agreements, that rarely, if ever, are intended to confer any benefit upon third parties. If the parties intend to confer rights on third parties in any particular situation, this should only be done expressly, in respect of each individual and each term, as a conscious act, after assessing all of the consequences.

Version (b) would be suitable to attach to a term of the agreement, **1–197** whether or not conferring a benefit on a third party, which it is intended that one or more third parties should be able to enforce. Note that the three phrases in square brackets give examples of the different possibilities set out in s.1(3) of the Act for the nomination of the third party. In commercial contracts, the conferring of benefits on classes of persons, as in this precedent is likely in most cases to be for the purpose of allowing them the benefit of indemnity or exclusion clauses affording them relief from claims in tort by the promisee for negligent performance of their duties. Under the common law, such exclusion or indemnity clauses would have benefited their employer only. (*Scruttons Ltd v Midland Silicones Ltd* [1962] A.C. 1, HL).

Where version (b) is used it is also possible to include version (a) (with the **1–198** addition at the beginning of a phrase such as "Save where expressly provided otherwise [in this agreement][in cl. *]" if there are a number of provisions which could are for the benefit of, or could be enforced by, third parties, and it is intended only to provide that some of those provisions (but not all of them) are to be enforceable by the relevant third parties.

1.11 Notices and other communications

1.11.1 Any notice and any permission consent licence approval or other **1–199** authorisation to be served upon or given or communicated to one party hereto by the other (in this clause called a "communication") shall be in the form of a document in writing including without limitation a telex or cable [but not a facsimile or an electronic mail message].

1.11.2 All communications shall be made to the Principal at the following address or to the following telex number:

Address:
Telex number:
For the attention of:

And to the Distributor at the following address or the following telex number:

Address:
Telex number:
For the attention of:

1.11.3 All communications shall be delivered by hand during normal business hours or sent by cable or telex or sent by registered post (where possible by airmail).

1.11.4 A communication shall have effect for the purposes of this Agreement and shall be deemed to have been received by the party to whom it was made:

1.11.4.1 if delivered by hand upon receipt by the relevant person for whose attention it should be addressed under cl.1.11.2 or upon receipt by any other person then upon the premises at the relevant address who reasonably appears to be authorised to receive post or other messages on behalf of the relevant party; and

1.11.4.2 if sent by telex upon the transmission of the communication to the relevant telex number and the receipt by the transmitting telex machine of an answer back code showing that the telex message has been received properly by the telex machine to which it was transmitted; and

1.11.4.3 if sent by cable [seventy-two hours] after the text of the cable has been given to the relevant telegraph company or other authority for transmission unless before the expiry of that period an advice of inability to deliver is received by the party making the communication; and

1.11.4.4 if sent by registered post [seven days] after the date upon the registration receipt provided by the relevant postal authority.

1.11.5 Each party shall be obliged to send a notice to the other (in accordance with this clause) of any change in the details for it recorded in cl.1.10.2 which details shall then be deemed to have been amended accordingly.

This clause goes in some detail into the service of notices or other communications. Although much shorter clauses are available, this has the advantage of certainty and regulating the form and manner of all important communications between the parties, as well as specifying when they are deemed to be received and to take effect. The method of delivery by hand is very often useful, particularly on account of the extensive international courier services that are now available. Telex is a useful medium, in some parts of the world (although in most cases it is now obsolescent if not obsolete), where both parties have it, because, apart from the fact that there have been a number of judicial decisions about its legal efficacy, one knows when the message sent has been received, because the receiving machine sends an answer-back code to confirm this. The provisions relating to cables and registered post are in line with usual practice.

Wherever possible, legally important notices should be delivered by hand or telex, while the more usual commercial matters can be dealt with by registered post. The more technically advanced forms of data transmission, such as facsimile machines, and electronic mail, have been omitted from a general clause, but two parties who both have particular compatible facilities of this kind could well specify them in a particular instance. If so, the necessity to be sure that the transmission of the message has occurred and that it has been received should be borne in mind, and the draftsman should provide exactly what will be deemed proof of receipt, and when the communication will have effect, in each case. **1–200**

1.12 Authority to execute

1.12 Each individual executing this Agreement on behalf of a party hereto represents and warrants that he has been fully empowered to execute this Agreement and that all necessary action to authorise the execution of this Agreement has been taken. **1–201**

This clause theoretically would permit an action against the individual concerned for breach of warranty of authority. In practice questions of the ability to meet any award of damages would make proceedings unlikely. The real use of this clause is to concentrate the minds of the individuals signing to make sure that the relevant authorities are obtained. In case of doubt it is preferable to require some proof of authority to sign, such as a power of attorney, or a certified copy of a board or shareholders resolution.

1.13 Stamp duty and execution clauses

1.13.1 The Distributor shall be responsible for the presentation of this Agreement to the relevant fiscal and other authorities of the Territory for the purposes of assessment and stamping in accordance with the laws of the Territory relating to stamp duty upon documents of the same nature as this Agreement. The Distributor shall effect such presentation as soon as possible after the signing hereof and shall be responsible for the timely presentation stamping and payment of stamp duty in accordance with such laws. [Upon proof of payment the Principal will reimburse the Distributor with [ ] per cent of the stamp duty paid.] The Distributor shall be responsible for [the balance of] the stamp duty all other relevant costs expenses and disbursements (if any) and also for any penalties payable by reason of failure to comply with time limits for presentation or payment or other requirements laid down by the said laws. **1–202**

1.13.2 SIGNED on [ ] by the duly authorised signatories of the parties hereto

For and on behalf of the Principal

For and on behalf of the Distributor

Formalities of execution and stamping are normally governed by the proper law of the agreement. According to the general principles of private international law, an English court will regard a contract as valid in regard to these matters of form, if it complies with the formalities of either the proper law of the contract, or the law of the place where the contract was made.

1–203 Obviously, where a local law requires registration or other formalities such as stamping in order for the agreement to have legal effect, it will be necessary to comply with these requirements, even if the local law is neither the law of the place where the contract was made, nor the proper law. If the agreement does not have legal effect under the local law such matters as receiving exchange control permission for payments or the granting of import licences for the product will not take place.

1–204 Stamp duty is a not uncommon requirement, although such agreements do not need stamping under stamp duty law in the UK, and, where this is the case a clause like 1.12.1 may be added to the agreement, adapted as necessary depending upon how the stamp duty will be borne. It is usually easier for the local representative to deal with this, since he is equally interested in the enforceability of the agreement, and in a better position to achieve it, however the cost is finally to be borne.

1–205 The agreements in this book do not in most jurisdictions require any formalities for execution either by way of sealing or witnessing. A simple clause in the form of 1.13.2 will usually suffice, together with the signatures of the parties (if natural persons) or their authorised representatives.

Chapter 2

Agency Agreements Outside the EC

Contents

2.1 Commercial and legal background

This chapter is concerned with those agreements which in the strictest sense **2–01** are called agency agreements. The agent is instrumental in the conclusion of the contract between his principal and the customer, either because he introduces the two parties to each other, or because he actually negotiates and concludes the contract between them, acting by virtue of the powers to bind the principal which the principal has delegated to him. However, the agent himself has no liabilities under this contract nor is he a party to it. The "del credere" agent is a partial exception to this rule in that he undertakes to indemnify his principal if the customers whom he finds fail to pay his principal (other than by reason of the principal's default) under the contracts concluded on behalf of the principal by the agent. The agent who acts for an undisclosed principal can also be regarded as an exception in that the customer can choose between holding the agent, or, in the event that he is eventually identified, the principal, as bound under the contract. It should be noted that an agent acting for an unnamed principal, but who has disclosed that he is acting as an agent, but not on whose behalf, does not fall within this rule.

2–02 It is useful to distinguish certain other trading relationships to which the term agency is often loosely applied. Forwarding agents act merely to arrange and facilitate the carriage and export of goods between the seller and the buyer. Similarly, clearing agents act in the country of importation of goods, usually, but not always, on the part of the buyer, for the purpose of clearing imported goods off the ship or aircraft, through customs, and, often, delivering them to warehouse as well. In both cases these types of agents may have the power to act for their "principal" in specific matters, like entering into a contract for the carriage of goods, or signing customs declarations on his behalf, but in most cases they will act as independent contractors, supplying their services to the person for whom they act in return for a fee.

2–03 Mention should also be made of the "confirming house". This acts in a variety of ways, and it may fulfil the role of a del credere agent, or simply an agent in the true sense of the word. However, it often acts as principal in relation to a supplier (buying goods from the supplier in its own right), and at the same time and in relation to the same goods as agent for the customer who has commissioned it to procure those goods. Thus the confirming house will ultimately expect to be indemnified for its liabilities under the contract with the supplier, and for its customer to take over and pay for the goods. Confirming houses often operate as forwarding or clearing agents as well.

2–04 EC law impacts on agency agreements in a variety of ways. In some instances competition law under Art.81 or 82 of the Treaty of Rome may be involved, and, in all cases, where the agent carries on activities within a Member State of the EC, the relationship between principal and agent will be regulated by the Council Directive 653/86 of December 18, 1986 on the Coordination of the laws of the Member States relating to self-employed Commercial Agents.

2–05 However, this chapter is concerned with an agency agreement which is suitable for use where the agent carries on his activities in a territory outside of the EU, and thus the issues raised by EC law and the various systems of law in force in the UK have no relevance. The Directive is analysed in Chapter 3, in relation to a precedent which deals with the various problems raised by the Directive and which suggests alternative approaches to deal with those problems. The effect of EC and UK competition law on agency agreements will be discussed in Chapter 5, where a comparison between the way agency and distribution agreements are treated under EC and UK competition law will be provided as the best way of explaining the relevant issues.

2–06 For this reason, the precedent in this chapter takes its form on the basis of an agency agreement governed by agreement between the parties, without the concept of an overriding system of law, such as the Directive, or some competition law regime, which constrains the form of the agreement. This basic precedent would thus be suitable for a system of law, such as that in most states in the US, which does not regulate the agency relationship, or for agency contracts subject to one of the systems of UK law but where the agent is acting outside the EC. Most systems of overriding law outside the

EC (such as those in South American Countries or the Middle East) do not prescribe particular terms of the agency agreement, but are more concerned with providing the agent with compensation on termination. The precedent does not therefore deal with clauses covering these systems of law, but their impact is discussed in the course of the chapter where relevant.

Finally, it should be noted that the precedent in this chapter deals with an **2–07** agency agreement relating to the supply of goods. Agency agreements for the supply of services alone are not very common, although services (such as maintenance) might well be supplied together with products, and thus become the subject of an agency agreement. This precedent could be adapted for use in relation to the supply of general services, by redefining "Products" as the relevant services, and then making any necessary consequential amendments, but it is important to remember that many types of agents in the service industries (for instance in travel, advertising or financial services of one sort or another) carry on business in particular ways either because of trade custom, applicable general law or special regulatory regimes, which would require that a specialised agreement be used. Such agreements are outside the scope of this book.

2.2 Appointment of agent

2.2.1 Appointment

2.2.1(a) [Subject to cl.2.3.8] the Principal hereby appoints the Agent to be the **2–08** [exclusive] [non-exclusive] agent of the Principal in the Territory for the marketing and the promotion of the sale of the Products to customers resident or carrying on business in the Territory and for the soliciting from such customers and transmission to the Principal of requests for quotations or orders for the Products.

OR

2.2.1(b) [Subject to cl.2.3.8] the Principal hereby appoints the Agent to act as its [exclusive] [non-exclusive] agent in the Territory to negotiate and to enter into contracts on behalf of the Principal for sale of the Products with customers in the Territory. [The Agent shall make deliveries of the Products to fulfil these contracts out of the stock of Products provided by the Principal and held by the Agent in terms of Sch.4.]

These clauses define the scope of the agent's authority. The first version provides for a canvassing or indenting agent, who will solicit enquiries for the products in the territory. He will transmit them back to the principal, who will then decide whether to accept the particular enquiries, and upon what terms. The agent in these cases may or may not have a power to communicate to customers details of the terms and prices on which the principal will do business, and depending on the exact scope of his duties will take a more or less active part in the negotiation and conclusion of the contracts resulting from the enquiries. He will not, however, actually conclude the contracts on behalf of the principal in the territory.

2–09 The second version appoints an agent with power to negotiate and conclude contracts in the territory on behalf of his principal. The second part of the clause, if included, will enable the agent to have a stock of the products, which will belong to the principal, and which the agent will hold as bailee at his own risk, to enable him to satisfy the contracts that he negotiates. Such an arrangement is often known as factoring, and the agent as a factor. It can also be a useful device where the principal wishes to assist a would-be distributor who cannot afford to finance a large inventory, whose financial position is not strong enough to warrant selling the stock of products to him on credit, and who has no other security to cover his debt. Under English law this relationship is to some extent governed by the Factors Act 1889.

2–10 Whether one chooses a selling agent, a factor, or a canvassing agent depends primarily upon commercial considerations as to the best way to serve a particular market, and the extent to which trust can be placed in the potential agent. However, the choice made will decide the question of whether the principal is regarded as carrying on business in the territory concerned. Where the principal is dealing with a canvassing agent the contracts are normally concluded in the country of residence of the principal, as it is the principal who takes the lead in the negotiations and finally accepts the order concerned. In this situation it is almost impossible for the principal to be regarded as carrying on a trade or business in the territory. The same is also normally true where an agent actually concludes the contract in the territory on behalf of the principal. However, the use of a factor nearly always gives rise to the contention that the principal has got a permanent establishment in the territory so that he is required to pay tax in the territory on the profits arising from the business he transacts through the factor in the territory. Before deciding which form of agency to use in a particular country, especially if a factoring arrangement is required, the local revenue laws should be studied carefully. There is also the question as to whether the arrangements will require the principal to go through other formalities, such as registration of a branch office, or obtaining permission to trade in the territory concerned.

2–11 It should be noted that in both versions of the clause the agent can be appointed on an exclusive or non-exclusive basis. In both versions the introductory phrase in square brackets should be added where the appointment is on an exclusive basis but the principal wants to reserve the right to deal direct in certain circumstances. This right is detailed in cl.2.3.8.

2.2.2 Term of agreement

2.2.2 This Agreement shall run [for a period of [three] years from [ ] and thereafter] unless or until terminated by either party giving to the other not less than [six] months prior notice in writing [such notice to expire at the end of the said period of [three] years or at any time thereafter].

Most agency agreements tend to run for an initial fixed period, and thereafter to be determinable by a reasonable period of notice, on the basis that the agent will not be encouraged to devote time and attention to promoting the products unless he sees the certainty of an initial term long enough to produce sufficient commission to reward his initial efforts.

2.3 Responsibilities of agent

2.3.1 Due diligence

> 2.3.1 During the period of this Agreement the Agent shall serve the Principal as agent on the terms of this Agreement with all due and proper diligence (acting dutifully and in good faith) observe all instructions given by the Principal as to its activities under this Agreement act in the Principal's interests and use its best endeavours to increase the sale of the Products in the Territory and to improve the goodwill of the Principal in the Territory. **2–12**

This general clause usually serves as no more than a statement of intent, and good faith on behalf of the agent. However, in circumstances where the agent is felt by the principal to be performing unsatisfactorily, but without there being any definite breach of the agreement to which the principal can point to justify termination, this clause can be referred to. The reference to improvement of the principal's goodwill is appropriate here since the agent acts on behalf of the principal. It is the principal who has the primary relationship with customers in the territory, and thus the customer-base and the goodwill in it belongs to the principal and not to the agent. There is some question as to the definition of the term "best endeavours" and the extent of the obligation it imposes (see *Davis Ltd v Tooth & Co Ltd* [1937] 4 All E.R. 118, for a form of words which was held to be equivalent to this term—"to devote the principal part of their energies ... to pushing the sale" was held to mean "to do the best it could to sell as much as could be sold".) This term seems to impose a higher standard than reasonable endeavours, although not necessarily an obligation to do everything possible, regardless of whether or not it is practicable. Looking at *Davis Ltd v Tooth & Co Ltd*, there also seems to be a suggestion that what is practicable is judged subjectively by reference to the particular entity undertaking the obligation.

2–13 The same approach was taken in *Midland Land Reclamation Ltd v Warren Energy Ltd*. This case in the Queens Bench Division (Official Referees Business) heard by Judge Bowsher, QC, is unreported. Judgment was given on January 20, 1997. The facts of the case are complicated, but amongst the issues was a discussion of best endeavours obligations. The learned judge stated that a best endeavours provision is sufficiently certain to be enforceable and relied on *Walford v Miles* [1992] A.C. 128 at 138C for this proposition.

2–14 He held that "best endeavours" imposes a duty to do what can reasonably be done in the circumstances, and the standard of that reasonableness is that of a reasonable and prudent board of directors acting properly in the interests of their company (see *Terrell v Mabie Todd & Co* 69 R.P.C. 234). He also quoted *Sheffield District Railway v Great Central Railway* (1911) 27 T.L.R. 451—"Best endeavours means what it says—it does not mean second best endeavours". He rejected the argument that a "best endeavours obligation is the next best thing to an absolute obligation or guarantee". In his view "To be satisfied of a breach of a best endeavours clause. . . . I would wish to hear evidence that in the light of the knowledge available at the time of the alleged default the party alleged to be in default was culpable".

2–15 Looking at these cases there is clearly some confusion over the exact standard of diligence to be required of "best endeavours" as opposed to "reasonable endeavours". The judgment in *Midland Land* can be read as support for the proposition that there is no difference between the two, despite the fact that traditional wisdom holds that "reasonable endeavours" imposes a lower standard. Those who hope to impose the higher standard will always use "best endeavours", on the basis that this gives them at least a peg on which to hang their arguments in the event of dispute. For those wishing to accept only the lesser standard, use of "reasonable endeavours" will provide some comfort, but not too much.

2–16 In both cases, it is better, where possible, to specify the standard to which specific obligations are to be discharged in more detail, even if a catch-all phrase is also used. For instance, take the obligation to pay money (or at least a significant sum) to bring a particular result about. The use of "reasonable endeavours" has traditionally been supposed to exclude this, and "best endeavours" to impose it. However, given the cases above it is certainly unclear whether "best endeavours" actually imposes this obligation (and if so to what extent—*i.e.* payment of a reasonable sum, or any sum however large that is required irrespective of the resources of the payor) or whether "reasonable endeavours" does not. In these circumstances it is best to make clear the extent (if any) of any liability to pay sums of money to bring about the desired result.

2.3.2 Proper facilities

2–17 2.3.2 The Agent shall maintain and provide at its own expense and to the reasonable satisfaction of the Principal such offices and other premises administration facilities and marketing organisation as may be necessary for the efficient and effective performance of its obligations under this Agreement.

This clause is not so important at the commencement of the relationship, when the agent has been just approved by the principal and presumably has satisfactory arrangements and facilities. It is very useful later on in the term of the agreement when the principal wishes to ensure that the agent continues to display his initial level of commitment to the agency.

2.3.3 Market intelligence

2.3.3 The Agent shall pass on promptly to the Principal all information useful for the business of the Principal including that relating to marketing sales prospects product reliability competitor activity and unauthorised use by third parties of the Principal's trade marks patents or other intellectual or industrial property rights. The Agent shall (without prejudice to the generality of the foregoing) send to the Principal a written report on the first day of each calendar month covering any items which have arisen in the previous month relevant to the matters covered by this clause. Such a report shall also include an estimate by the Agent of likely orders for the Products during the coming two months. **2–18**

Market intelligence should be provided on a regular basis by the agent in the terms of this clause.

2.3.4 Compliance with local law

2.3.4 The Agent shall comply with all laws and regulations for the time being in force in the Territory which affect in any way the Agent's activities therein and indemnify the Principal in full against any and all costs claims expenses demands and proceedings incurred by or levied against the Principal resulting from any contravention by the Agent of such laws and regulations. **2–19**

Clauses such as this should not be regarded in most cases as providing a realistic indemnity which will permit the principal to sit back and let the agent take all the responsibility for these matters. In many cases the agent will not have sufficient financial resources to pay a large sum by way of compensation. However, the clause does act to focus the agent's mind on these problems, and, to this extent, help to prevent them arising. In the event that the agent is later found to have acted so that a contravention of the laws of the territory has resulted, its presence in the agreement may help to demonstrate the good faith of the principal and to prevent the principal being found to be an accessory to, or liable for, the agent's default.

2.3.5 Confidentiality

2.3.5 The Agent shall keep strictly confidential not disclose to any third party and use only for the purposes of this Agreement all information relating to the Products (whether technical or commercial) and to the affairs and business of the Principal and its subsidiary or associated companies, whether such information is disclosed to the Agent by the Principal or otherwise obtained by the Agent as a result of its association with the Principal. Without prejudice to the generality of the foregoing where the Agent is a company within a group of companies and or its activities in pursuance of this Agreement are carried out through a branch office or other local establishment in the Territory, the said information shall not without the prior consent of the Principal be disclosed to other companies within such group and or to any employees of the Agent who are not employed at the said branch office or local establishment. For the avoidance of doubt this provision shall survive the expiry or termination (for whatsoever cause) of this Agreement. **2–20**

This form of confidentiality clause is most suited to agency situations where the agent is not likely to be given detailed technical knowledge. It is particularly suitable where the agent belongs to a multinational group of companies. In these situations it is often the case that the principal is cooperating with one member of the group in one country, and wishes to appoint that member as its agent there, while, in another area, it is competing with other members of the group. In these cases it is important to prevent the flow of information from one member of the group to another.

2.3.6 No authority to bind principal

2–21 2.3.6 Save as and if specifically provided elsewhere in this Agreement or otherwise expressly authorised by the Principal the Agent shall not without the Principal's prior express approval incur any liabilities on behalf of the Principal nor pledge the credit of the Principal nor make any representations nor give any warranty on behalf of the Principal. The Agent has no authority to and shall not take part in any dispute or institute or defend any proceedings or settle or attempt to settle or make any admission concerning any dispute proceedings or other claim relating to the Products or any contract concerning the Products or relating to the affairs of the Principal generally. The Agent will immediately inform the Principal of any of the foregoing and will act in relation thereto only upon and in accordance with the instructions of the Principal but so that the Principal will indemnify the Agent against any costs expenses or liabilities incurred by the Agent by reason of the Agent so acting other than against any of the same incurred by reason of the agent's own negligence or default.

This is a standard type of clause for restricting the actual authority of the agent to bind the principal. Again, it is often of most use to establish the basis of the relationship between principal and agent, and to draw the agent's attention to the necessity to be careful in these areas. It is unfortunately the case that in most common law jurisdictions, at any rate, third parties who deal with the agent can often take advantage of the doctrine of ostensible authority (*i.e.* that the agent was put by the principal in such a position that he looked to third parties as if he had the authority of the principal to bind the principal) to hold the principal to undertakings the agent has made on his behalf. Of course, breach of this clause would, whatever the third party's position, give the principal a right to compensation from the agent. However, this right is limited by the financial strength of the agent. This area is particularly of concern when the agent is a factor, and some of the problems relating to this are dealt with in cl.2.3.7 and in Chapter 2.14.

2.3.7 Notification of agency status

2–22 2.3.7 The Agent will cause to be printed an express statement that it acts only as [indenting agent] [canvassing agent] [selling agent] for the Principal on all letterheads invoices leaflets brochures or other documents issued by it on or in which it refers to the Products or the Principal. The Agent shall also affix a clearly visible plaque containing such statement at the Agent's registered office and at any other place of business of the Agent. Such statement shall likewise appear in all advertisements published by the Agent in which the Products or the Principal are mentioned. The Agent shall not expressly or by implication in any negotiations relating to the Products or otherwise describe itself as acting in any capacity for or on behalf of or in relation to the affairs of the Principal other than in accordance with such statement.

This clause will oblige the agent to give sufficient publicity to the capacity in which he acts for the principal so that the problem of ostensible authority referred to above should be largely overcome (in the absence of bad faith by the agent) if the agent properly observes the clause and the principal polices it properly.

2.3.8 Limits of exclusivity

2.3.8 The Principal will refer to the Agent all requests for quotations on Pro- **2–23**
ducts intended for sale in the Territory except that if for any reason (including without limitation a conflict of interest in which the Agent becomes involved) the Principal in its entire discretion considers it inappropriate for the Agent to act in respect of any transaction or for any period the Principal retains the right in respect of such transaction or during such period to appoint another Agent to act for the Principal and or to negotiate with and effect relevant sales direct with customers. In all such cases the Principal will advise the Agent of the actions it has taken and will pay to the Agent his commission (if any) upon such sales in accordance with the relevant provisions of Sch.3.

This clause is appropriate only where the agent has been appointed on an otherwise exclusive basis, but, in these cases, it is important to deal with situations in which there is a conflict of interest (perhaps as a result of the agent belonging to a multinational group—see cl.2.3.5) or where there are certain large customers (for instance state corporations or government departments) with which the principal wishes to continue to deal direct on certain occasions. The agent may well resist such a wide discretion, and it may be necessary to specify the classes of customers or the situations where the principal can operate direct in more detail. An alternative commonly used is to merely provide that the agent will receive reduced commission or no commission at all on direct sales in the territory made by the principal. This possibility is also discussed in Chapter 2.13.

2.3.9 Not to act outside territory

2.3.9 The Agent shall not without the prior consent of the Principal market or **2–24**
promote the Products outside the Territory during the continuance of this Agreement nor during the continuance of this Agreement [and for a period of [two] years after its termination] market or promote nor assist or advise in the marketing or promotion of any products which would or could compete or in any way interfere with the sale of the Products inside the Territory.

2.3.10 Restrictions on negotiating terms

2–25 2.3.10 The Agent shall (unless otherwise agreed) notify the Principal promptly of all requests for tenders and other prospective business and shall in all cases market and promote [and solicit requests for quotations and orders for] [and negotiate and contract on behalf of the Principal for] the sale of the Products only at the prices and only upon the terms established and notified from time to time by the Principal to the Agent.

Clauses 2.3.9 and 2.3.10 (other than the second phrase in square brackets) are sufficient to define and restrict the activities of a canvassing or indenting agent who does not have the ability to conclude contracts on behalf of his principal. The second phrase in square brackets in cl.2.3.10 should be substituted for the first such phrase to cover the case of an agent who, whether or not he acts as a factor, concludes contracts on behalf of his principal.

2–26 The phrase in square brackets in cl.2.3.9 imposes a period of non-competition after the termination of the agreement. This is often commercially sensible. Of course any such provision, and its reasonableness, particularly in relation to its length of time, has to be tested for enforceability under the proper law of the agreement. Where English law applies, a period of one or two years is likely to be considered reasonable, but longer periods should be avoided unless there are very special circumstances which it is felt could be used to justify the unusual length. It should be noted that although such clauses are *prima facie* likely to be enforceable in the case of agents, because they are a legitimate means for the principal to protect the good will he has in the customer base in the agent's territory (see Chapter 2.3.1), the position is different with distributors (see Chapter 4.3.6).

2.3.11 Sales as a factor

2–27 2.3.11 All sales of the Products negotiated by the Agent shall be for use or consumption by persons within the Territory and shall be made upon the prices terms and conditions from time to time notified by the Principal to the Agent.

In cases where the agent is a factor or acts generally to negotiate sales of the Products this clause should be added in addition to cll.2.3.9 and 2.3.10].

2.3.12 Collection of principal's moneys

2–28 2.3.12 Where the Agent has been given authority (other than in terms of Sch.4) to collect any sums of money on behalf of the Principal the Agent shall promptly upon such collection remit them to the Principal by cheque in the currency in which they were collected to the Principal's registered office or as otherwise from time to time notified by the Principal. Such payment shall be made in full without any deduction whatsoever other than withholding taxes or sales or value added taxes which the Agent is obliged by the law of the Territory to deduct therefrom together with any commission due under cl.2.4.7 to the Agent in respect of the transaction to which the sum collected relates.

2.3.13 Separate bank account

2.3.13 Pending remittance all cash cheques drafts or other negotiable instruments relating to the sums referred to in cl.2.3.12 shall be held on trust for the Principal by the Agent and if pending remittance or in order to collect and or remit the same it is necessary for the Agent to pay the said cash cheques drafts or other negotiable instruments into a bank account the Agent shall pay the same into a separate bank account designated as a trust account in the name of the Agent as trustee for the Principal. **2–29**

Clauses 2.3.12 and 2.3.13 cover the situation where an agent (who is not a factor) collects money on behalf of his principal. The requirements to hold sums collected as trustee and to pay them into a separate trust bank account are to facilitate the recovery of these sums by the principal in the event of the insolvency of the agent. The sums which he holds in the capacity of trustee do not form part of his property which can be taken for the benefit of his creditors generally. The separate bank account, if the provision is observed by the agent, avoids the difficulty of tracing sums which he has misappropriated or paid with his own funds into a mixed bank account. Although the principles relating to tracing of trust moneys would, under English law at any rate, allow the principal to follow them into the mixed bank account, the practical difficulties involved in analysing the transactions and showing that the moneys have been paid into the account, and when, and what has happened to them, make the chances of recovery in this situation very unlikely.

2.3.14 Del credere guarantee

2.3.14 Subject to the prior consent of the Agent either generally or in relation to any specific transaction the Agent shall guarantee to the Principal the due performance by any customer or customers of contracts that they have entered into with the Principal as a result of the Agent's activities under this Agreement. Such guarantee shall be by way of separate agreement in writing between the Principal and the Agent in a form to be agreed but which shall in any event provide that the Agent is not to be liable thereunder in the event of a refusal to perform by the customer or customers which is caused by any default of the Principal. **2–30**

This clause covers the obligations of a del credere agent in a general form. In some cases it may be necessary to include a specific form of guarantee as a clause within the contract itself, or to execute a general guarantee agreement at the same time as the agency agreement. The detailed agreement enables any local formalities of execution or particular wordings to be complied with, so that the agent cannot later declare the guarantee to be unenforceable under the law in the territory, or the law governing the agreement. In some cases, all that is required is for the agent to endorse bills of exchange or other negotiable instruments received from his customers before passing them on to the principal. In this way the agent normally becomes liable on them in the event of a default by the customer who originally drew them. Finally, care should as a matter of course be taken in all guarantee arrangements to ensure that the agent is not released by any waiver or variation by the principal of his rights under the original contract with the customer. Where guarantees are not drafted to cover this point, such variation or waiver usually releases the guarantor under the general law, and this is certainly the case under English law.

2.4 Responsibilities of principal

2.4.1 Sales literature, documentation and information

2–31 2.4.1 The Principal shall supply to the Agent free of charge a reasonable quantity of sales literature.

It is normal for the principal to undertake this obligation in regard to sales literature. Agents are normally neither permitted nor required to print their own sales literature, nor to contribute towards the expenses of its provision.

2.4.2 Samples

2–32 2.4.2(a) The terms and conditions for the supply of any necessary models or samples relating to the Products shall in each case be the subject of special agreement between the Principal and the Agent.

OR

2.4.2(b) The Principal will supply samples of the Products to the Agent upon request and subject to reasonable notice upon the following terms:

2.4.2.1 The Principal's commitment in respect of each Product shall (subject to cl.2.4.2.4) be to supply samples of that Product for a period (the "Sample Period") of [three years] commencing on the date that it was first shipped by the Principal to customers in the Territory as a result of the activities of the Agent.

2.4.2.2 The Principal shall supply such samples free of charge and shall ship them to the Territory on FOB terms (in accordance with the current edition of Incoterms) consigned to the Agent.

2.4.2.3 All duties costs charges and expenses (including without limitation customs and excise duties) after supply FOB as aforesaid shall be borne by [the Agent] [the Principal].

2.4.2.4 At no time shall the Principal be under an obligation to supply to the Agent a quantity of a Product as samples to the extent that the quantity requested by the Agent together with all quantities of samples of that Product supplied by the Principal to the Agent between the date of commencement of the relevant Sample Period and the date of the relevant request by the Agent exceeds [ten] per cent of the quantity of that Product shipped by the Principal to customers in the Territory between those two dates.

2.4.2.5 The samples shall remain the property of the Principal (and the Agent shall hold them as bailee for the Principal at the Agent's risk) until their disposal in accordance with cl.2.4.2.6.

2.4.2.6 The Agent shall dispose of all such samples of the Products supplied to it under this clause by the Principal free of charge to customers or potential customers of the Products in the Territory for the sole purpose of promoting the sale of the relevant Products in the Territory.

The situation with samples varies considerably depending on the nature of the Products. Where the Products are expensive capital equipment version (a) of cl.2.4.2 is preferable. In the case of consumer goods it is often necessary for the agent to provide a considerable number of free samples to support his campaign to promote the products and version (b) is designed to cover such matters.

Where the agent acts as factor and sells stock under Chapter 2.14 or purely as a sales agent under cl.2.3.10 the principal is free in most cases to impose what terms he likes on the agent as regards with whom, and the prices, terms and conditions upon which, he negotiates the sales of the products (see Chapter 4 for the different position with distributors and Chapter 5 for the effect of EC law on the subject). If he sells samples to the agent he will often be unable to control the prices and terms of their disposal by the agent, whether he expressly permits the agent to sell them on or even if he requires them to be given away as free samples. Clauses 2.4.2.5 and 2.4.2.6 should provide sufficient protection when samples are given to the Agent free of charge. Where samples are to be sold to and sold on by the agent it is preferable to use a factoring relationship and adapt Chapter 2.14 to cover the situation. **2–33**

The question of who would be liable and to what extent for damage caused by defects in the samples is a difficult one. Although in theory it would be possible to require the agent to take total responsibility as between the agent and the principal, and to indemnify the principal for any third party claims made direct against the principal, this is neither just, nor practical, given in most cases the financial resources of the agent. In practice the principal should be sufficiently covered by product liability insurance for any such claims made either by the agent, as a result of claims for negligent manufacture made against him by third parties to whom he has given the samples, or made directly against the principal by such third parties. It is therefore wisest to leave the matter to insurance and the general law and not seek to prescribe for the various possibilities in the agreement. **2–34**

2.4.3 Direct quotation in territory

2–35 2.4.3 The Principal shall not submit offers or quotations nor enter into any negotiations nor effect sales or disposals to any person in the Territory without the Agent's consent [except in the circumstances provided for in cl.2.3.8] and [subject to that exception] refer all such offers quotations or tenders to the Agent.

This is a standard type of clause that would be used in situations where the agent was appointed on an exclusive basis. The phrases in square brackets are of course only to be used if cl.2.3.8 is included.

2.4.4 Responsibility for agent's expenses

2–36 2.4.4 The Principal shall pay to the Agent such expenses as are specifically and reasonably incurred at the request of the Principal and will also consider partially supporting any specific market research projects in the Territory that the Agent suggests it is desirable to undertake [PROVIDED THAT [the Agent shall be responsible for] [for the avoidance of doubt the Principal shall indemnify the Agent against] all costs and expenses associated with the storage, insurance, handling and delivery to customers of the stock of the Products provided by the Principal and held by the Agent in terms of Sch.4]

Although the agent would normally be expected to fund all expenses out of commission there will be situations when the principal will require the agent to undertake particular activities which the agent would not undertake without such compensation. However, it is also the case that an enterprising agent would undertake marketing activities on his own account and the final part of the clause keeps open the possibility of partial funding from the principal as an incentive to carry out these activities.

2–37 The proviso to the clause, in square brackets, is only appropriate where the Agent acts as a factor and holds a stock of the products pursuant to Sch.4. Within the square brackets there is the further choice of whether the factor should be responsible for all of the costs associated with handling, insurance, storing and delivering the products to customers, or whether the Principal should bear these. It would be quite usual for the principal to bear the costs of getting the goods to the agent's warehouse (including transport, insurance and customs duties) but for the agent then to bear the cost of storing the goods in the territory (often a factor will act for a number of principals and have warehouse facilities where all of their goods are stored), insuring them and the cost of delivery in territory to customers. This division can be simply provided for in this precedent. Since cl.2.14.1 states that the principal will deliver the goods at its cost to the agent's warehouse), it is only necessary to adopt the option stating that the agent rather than the principal is responsible for the costs and expenses after delivery to the agent's warehouse.

2–38 Where the agent is required to bear these costs and expenses, this will be taken into account in setting the level of commission, and the agent will have to defray such costs and expenses out of commission. However, the agent may be permitted to recover delivery charges direct from the customers or to deduct them, in addition to commission, from the invoice sums collected. Schedule 4 provides for some options to cover this point in cl.2.14.6.

2.4.5 Advertising

> 2.4.5 The Principal may in its absolute discretion carry out advertising or publicity activities in the Territory but the Agent shall not be entitled to carry out such activities upon its own initiative without the prior consent of the Principal irrespective of whether the Principal decides to contribute towards the cost of the same or not. **2–39**

The balance of this clause is in favour of the principal in the sense that it is most usual for agents to be closely supervised in such activities even though they are expected to take part in those sponsored by their principal. Not only does the principal usually bear the cost of most of these activities, but unsupervised promotion or advertising by agents can, in some cases, lead either to extravagant and unjustified claims being made for the products, or to their being given an image and market position which the principal would regard as undesirable.

2.4.6 Acceptance of orders

> 2.4.6 The Principal shall not be obliged to accept any order tender or request submitted by the Agent in the course of its activities in the Territory and shall accept the same only at its absolute discretion and only on such terms and conditions as it may consider appropriate and shall supply all Products thereunder direct to customers in the Territory. [The Principal shall at the date of despatch of any Products to such customers send a copy of the relevant invoice to the Agent, by way of notification of delivery of such Products]. **2–40**

Clause 2.4.6 is not necessary where the agent acts as a factor or selling agent as then cl.2.3.10 provides the principal with sufficient protection.

2.4.7 Payment of commission

> 2.4.7 The Principal shall pay commission to the Agent in accordance with Sch.3. **2–41**

Clause 2.4.7 would be appropriate for a selling agent who is not a factor or for a canvassing or indenting agent. The remuneration of an agent in so far as he acts as a factor is dealt with under Chapter 2.14.

2.5 Industrial property rights

2–42 2.5.1 The Agent shall not use or permit to be used by any person under its control any of the patents trade marks or trade or brand names registered designs or any other industrial or intellectual property rights owned or controlled by the Principal without the prior written consent of the Principal.

2–43 2.5.2 The Agent shall not register any patents trade marks trade or brand names registered designs or other industrial or intellectual property rights covering products or processes owned devised or manufactured by or on behalf of the Principal without the prior written consent of the Principal.

2–44 2.5.3 The Agent agrees to send the Principal prior to the use of any such trade marks or trade or brand names a sample of each letterhead invoice price list label packing material sign brochure and all other advertising material displaying such trade mark or trade or brand name and only to use items of such printed materials the proofs for which have received in each case the express and specific prior written approval of the Principal.

2–45 2.5.4 Upon termination of this Agreement for any reason the Agent shall immediately cease to use all such trade marks or trade or brand names in any manner whatsoever (including without limitation on stationery or vehicles) for which consent was granted and shall return to the Principal or otherwise dispose of at the Principal's direction free of any charge all printed matter displaying such trade marks or trade or brand names in the Agent's possession.

It is important to control the use of trade marks by the agent, to prevent their being used in such a way that registrations are invalidated, or the principal's property rights in them are affected. It is also necessary to ensure that the agent himself gains no interest in any intellectual or industrial property rights belonging to the principal. The reference to products with a lower case "p" in cl.2.5.2 is intentional in order to widen the scope of the clause. Clause 2.5.4 is the usual provision necessary to prevent the agent passing himself off as still connected with the principal and his products once the agreement is terminated.

2.6 Non-assignment by agent

2–46 This Agreement shall not be assigned or transferred by the Agent without the prior consent of the Principal.

This clause is necessary as in most cases the agent has been chosen by the principal for his personal abilities. The case of transfer of ownership or control of a limited company acting as agent is dealt with under cl.2.7.1.5.

2.7 Termination of agreement

2.7.1 Notwithstanding the provisions of cl.2.2 the Principal may by notice to the Agent terminate this Agreement immediately upon the happening of any one of the following events: **2–47**

2.7.1.1 If the Agent shall become bankrupt or be wound-up or make any arrangement or composition with its creditors;

2.7.1.2 If the Agent shall attempt or purport to assign or transfer this Agreement in breach of cl.2.6;

2.7.1.3 If the Agent's ability to carry out its obligations hereunder is prevented or substantially interfered with for any reason whatsoever (whether or not within the control of the Agent) including without limitation by reason of any regulation law decree or any act of state or other action of a government or (where the Agent is a natural person) by reason of ill-health, disability or death;

2.7.1.4 If the Agent shall commit any breach of any of its obligations hereunder (other than cl.2.6) and (where such breach is capable of remedy) fail to remedy such breach within [thirty] days of receipt of the Principal's notice specifying such breach;

2.7.1.5 If the Agent shall become resident outside the Territory or (being a company) shall change its place of registration or have its ownership or control altered without the prior consent of the Principal.

2.7.2 Termination of this Agreement shall not affect the rights and liabilities of either party subsisting at the date of termination. **2–48**

2.7.3 Termination of this Agreement whether under cll.2.2 or 2.7 [or expiry of this Agreement by effluxion of time] shall not entitle the Agent to any compensation, indemnity, damages or other payment in respect of such termination [or expiry] [except to the extent that the governing law of this Agreement provides for the same]. **2–49**

This clause contains the events in which termination of the agreement would be desirable from the point of view of the principal. The cure-period in cl.2.7.1.4 is often extended to 60 days. The additional phrases in the first two sets of square brackets in cl.2.7.3 are necessary where the agreement is only for a fixed term and terminates at the end of it without the need for notice to be served.

Using cl.2.7.3 without the final set of square brackets would, so far as the contract is concerned, bar the agent from any compensatory payments in respect of termination, but this is not always effective. The provisions of the local law in the state where the agent carries on his activities, or the governing law of the agreement, may well provide for such payments and override the contractual provisions. In this case, one would be better advised to add the third set of square brackets, which does at least provide some possibility of limitation to amounts prescribed by law. **2–50**

2–51 The position as far as the EC is concerned has now been changed by the Directive to harmonise all Member States' laws so as to provide for compensation. This is discussed in Chapter 3. In many countries outside the EC, the local law will also override this provision. This is usually so even if there is a proper law clause specifying the exclusive application to the agreement of English law, or some other proper law which does not provide for mandatory compensation. Although distribution arrangements are sometimes subject to local laws regarding compensation on termination, this is true to a much greater extent for agency agreements. French law, for instance protects agents but not distributors. The laws of some states (for instance most South American countries) do not make a distinction between agents and distributors, but generally protect all local representatives. It is impossible to be exhaustive: for instance, Switzerland, and most Middle Eastern countries protect agents but not necessarily distributors. In general (leaving aside the UK, since it is now subject to the Directive under EC law) countries deriving their legal systems from the common law (such as the USA, Canada, Australia) do not have such compensation provisions.

2–52 In most countries where compensation is granted it is often the case that an aggrieved agent who has not been compensated has the right to seek an order preventing the importation of the principal's goods into his country through another agent. Very often in these countries there is an official agency register, in which each agent is required to register his agreement before he can act under it. Once registered, no other agent can act for the principal until the old agent has deregistered, and the new agent registered in his place. One of the grounds of refusal to deregister is of course unjustified termination without compensation. An example of this is found in the law of the Lebanon, the United Arab Emirates and Iran.

2–53 The provisions of such laws normally grant compensation calculated on a number of years' purchase of the annual commissions paid to the agent under the agreement. Sometimes commissions are averaged over the period of the agreement and sometimes over the period of the last few years prior to termination. Justified termination is normally exempt from compensation, but the local courts normally refuse to recognise as justifying termination anything less than flagrant breach of the agreement usually amounting to some form of dishonesty or gross neglect. Mere failure to pursue sales energetically is unlikely to be accepted as a just cause. Nor is the fact that the agreement has expired by effluxion of time.

2–54 One strategy to adopt where compensation is to be paid is to attempt to adduce evidence of low sales in the period to be looked at. These would normally result in low commissions and therefore in low compensation. This is particularly useful if compensation is calculated by reference to the last few years of the agency when, presumably, dissatisfaction has arisen because of a low level of activity by the agent. This is not always successful (even where calculation on this basis is provided for under the law concerned) as the agent is likely to raise matters like failure by the principal to supply sufficient products or supply of defective products which not only meant demand was not satisfied or was reduced, but that the agent should also be compensated for commissions not earned as a result of the principal's defaults in relation to the products.

Such disputes are usually dealt with by negotiation rather than litigation or arbitration. A common result is a promise to pay the old agent a small percentage on sales generated by the new agent in the first few years of the new arrangements. Care should be taken to ensure that such arrangements are legally binding under the local law. A practical way this can be achieved (if one is not carrying out these negotiations in the territory) is to have the settlement agreement notarised by a public notary and legalised by the local consulate of the agent's country. It would then, in practice, be difficult for the agent to raise the dispute again in the courts of his home country. **2–55**

2.8 Good business practice

See cl.9.14. **2–56**

2.9 Disclosure and registration

See cl.9.15. The contents of cll.9.14 and 9.15 should be reproduced here, replacing the terms "Company" and "Consultant" with "Principal" and "Agent" respectively. **2–57**

2.10 Interpretation clauses and signature

2.11 Schedule 1—the products

2.12 Schedule 2—the territory

Clauses 2.10 to 2.12 should be reproduced as required from Chapter 1. **2–58**

2.13 Schedule 3—the commission

2.13.1(a) In respect of every order for the Products obtained by the Agent during the continuation of this Agreement the Agent shall be paid by way of remuneration commission on the net invoice price before any value added or sales taxes or other taxes or duties [FOB port of shipment] [Ex Works of the Principal], at a rate to be agreed not later than the time when the order is given or if the order is preceded by a tender not later than the time when such tender is submitted. In fixing the rate of commission the parties shall take into account (*inter alia*) the following factors: **2–59**

2.13.1.1 the efforts expended by the Agent and their effectiveness;

2.13.1.2 the value of the order to the Principal; and

2.13.1.3 the degree of competition experienced in marketing the Products in the Territory.

OR

2.13.1(b) During the continuance of this Agreement the Agent shall be paid a commission at the relevant percentage or percentages set out below upon the net invoice price before any value added or sales taxes or other taxes or duties ([FOB port of shipment] [Ex works of the Principal]) of all Products sold to customers in the Territory [whether] from orders received by the Principal through the Agent or otherwise, pursuant to cl.2.3.8:

Product	Percentage

OR

2.13.1(c) During the continuance of this Agreement the Agent shall be paid a commission at the relevant percentage or percentages set out below upon the net invoice price before any value added or sales taxes or other taxes or duties ([FOB port of shipment] [Ex works of the Principal]) of all Products sold to customers in the Territory under orders received from the Agent:

Product	Percentage

In the event that the Principal makes sales of the Products to customers in the Territory pursuant to cl.2.3.8, the Principal shall [reserve for the Agent such commission (if any) as the Principal considers appropriate in all the circumstances] [not be required to pay any commission to the Agent] [pay commission to the Agent at the rate of*].

Version (a) applies where the products are capital equipment, or at any rate large one-off orders. It is equally appropriate whether the agency appointment is exclusive or non-exclusive. Where the products are consumer or bulk consumption goods that are ordered frequently and in large quantities as part of a running set of standard transactions version (b) is more appropriate. If the words in square brackets are omitted, the clause would be suitable for a nonexclusive appointment. With the words in square brackets included the agent's exclusivity is protected even if the principal does deal direct pursuant to cl.2.3.8. Version (c) shows an alternative way of dealing with cl.2.3.8 under an exclusive appointment. The various suggestions in square brackets at the end of 2.13.1 in version (c) merely give an idea of what the parties can negotiate in varying circumstances.

2–60 It should be noticed that commission is stated be payable on the net invoice price before VAT or sales taxes. The fixing of the net invoice price at FOB means that in effect the agent also receives commission on some delivery costs as well. Setting the price on an Ex Works basis avoids this.

2–61 2.13.2 Commission shall become due and payable to the Agent as soon as the Principal has received the full order price from its customers. Where the order provides for payment by instalments a proportionate part of the commission shall become due and payable to the Agent (as soon as such instalments are received by the Principal) equivalent to the proportion which such instalments form of the order price except that where the Principal is required under the terms of such order to provide bonds or other securities for such instalments no proportionate part of such commission shall become due and payable to the Agent unless and until such bonds or other securities are released to the Principal.

The provisions of this clause protect the principal against having to pay commission out on bad debts, or in instances where even though payment has been made an outstanding bond (usually a warranty or a performance bond) is later called. Agents occasionally ask that the commission should still be payable if the bond has been called because of a default of the principal.

2.13.3 After termination of this Agreement the Agent shall be entitled to receive commission at the relevant aforesaid rates on all orders accepted from such customers up to the date of such termination [and (after such termination) only in respect of orders placed in fulfilment of a minimum purchase commitment legally binding upon any such customer contained in a long term agreement negotiated between the Principal and any such customer by the Agent up to such minimum quantity only] provided that [in both cases] payment is received from the relevant customers for the said orders. **2–62**

2.13.4 Where the Principal is obliged to pay commission to an agent previously appointed in respect of the Products, under an agreement (now terminated or expired) which contains a provision equivalent to cl.2.13.3, on any order in respect of which the Agent would (except for this clause) be entitled to commission under this Agreement, then, notwithstanding any other provisions of this Agreement to the contrary, the Agent shall not be entitled to any commission on that order.

The first part of cl.2.13.3 is a usual provision on termination. The second part in square brackets is a possible alternative for situations where the agent has laid the foundations for long-term sales of the products and it is not just that the principal should be able to reap the reward of these labours by terminating the agreement, even by notice. This is particularly appropriate in countries where the law does not provide for compensation on unjustified termination of the agreement. Clause 2.13.4 should always be used if there was a previous agents in the territory who is entitled to post-termination commission under a provision in his contract equivalent to cl.2.13.3. This will avoid payment of double commission, one to the old agent and one to the current agent.

2.13.5 Any commissions paid to the Agent by the Principal hereunder shall represent the Agent's sole remuneration for its activities within the Territory and unless otherwise agreed the Agent shall not be entitled to reimbursement by the Principal in respect of any out-of-pocket or other expenses incurred by the Agent in connection with its duties hereunder all of which expenses shall be for the sole account of the Agent. **2–63**

It is usual for the agent not to receive expenses on top of commission. In some cases however, part of the commission received is expressed to be receivable by way of an allowance for advertising expenditure, on condition that the agent expends at least that or some multiple of that amount on advertising the products in the territory. Such an advertising budget provision is however more usual in the case of a distributor (see Chapter 4).

2–64 2.13.6 Unless otherwise agreed the currency of payment of commission payable to the Agent in respect of each order shall be the same currency as the currency of payment of the price of that order and payment shall (subject to the granting of any necessary exchange control or other governmental permission) be made by [cheque sent to the Agent's registered office] [by telegraphic transfer to a bank account nominated by the Agent].

This provision normally protects the principal against exchange rate fluctuations as he will have just received from the customer a supply of the relevant currency before having to pay out the agent's commission. The payment is also made conditional upon governmental permissions to prevent the principal being held liable for a failure to receive such permission.

2–65 2.13.7 The commission payable by the Principal hereunder is stated on a gross basis and all withholding taxes levies or other deductions of any kind in respect of such commission which are the responsibility of the Principal shall be deducted from the commission by the Principal and be for the account of the Agent.

The most usual deduction from commission is some form of withholding tax, and in the absence of this sort of provision it can fall to the account of the principal.

2.14 Schedule 4—stock of the products

2–66 2.14.1 The Principal will (at the cost of the Principal) deliver to the Agent's warehouse a stock of the Products (which shall remain the property of the Principal) of a quantity and value to be decided by the Principal from time to time. The Principal will make up such stock (periodically at a frequency to be decided by the Principal) to the then current quantity and value fixed by the Principal. The Agent shall have no right of action against the Principal for any delay or failure by the Principal to deliver initially or subsequently make up such stock to any particular quantity or value or at all.

2–67 2.14.2 The parties hereby declare and agree that the Agent is acting in a fiduciary relationship to the Principal in regard to all transactions and other matters covered by or arising out of this Agreement and that in particular, but without prejudice to the generality of the foregoing:

2.14.2.1 The Agent holds all stocks of the Products from time to time in its possession as bailee for the Principal. The Agent shall handle and store all such stocks under appropriate conditions and with due care and attention. In particular the Agent shall store such stocks in a way that they are identified as the property of the Principal.

2.14.2.2 The Agent hereby acknowledges the Principal as the true owner of such stocks.

2.14.2.3 The Agent holds as trustee for the Principal all moneys and all book debts which arise from and in respect of sales or other disposals negotiated by the Agent for such stocks in respect of which it has not yet made a remittance to the Principal in accordance with cl.2.14.6 [provided that the Agent shall be permitted and is hereby given authority to act as agent for the Principal to factor on behalf of the Principal all the aforesaid book debts in the usual manner in which such factoring transactions are conducted and (for the avoidance of doubt) the proceeds of such factoring or any rights to such proceeds which have not been paid over to the Agent at any time shall be held in trust for the Principal in the same way as the book debts from which the said proceeds and the said rights arise].

2.14.2.4 If the Agent is obliged to issue invoices in respect of sales of the Products which include charges for value added or sales tax or other taxes or duties ("taxation amounts"), the Agent shall be responsible for the collection of all taxation amounts from the relevant customer and their due payment to the relevant fiscal authority on behalf of the Principal. For the avoidance of doubt pending such remittance the Agent shall treat all taxation amounts as moneys received under cl.2.14.2.3. and shall hold the same as trustee for the Principal in accordance with the terms of cl.2.14.2.3.

2.14.2.5. The Agent shall promptly pay all taxation amounts to the relevant fiscal authority in accordance with the procedures and within the time limits prescribed by applicable law. The Agent shall indemnify the Principal for any failure to perform its obligations under this clause, including without limitation for any penalties or fines which the Principal is required to pay to the relevant fiscal authority because of such default.

2.14.2.6 Any insurance, transport or other handling costs and expenses ("delivery charges") related to the delivery of consignments of the Products from the Agent's warehouse to customers shall be the responsibility of the Agent but the Agent shall be entitled to charge delivery charges to and recover the same from such customers by way of an invoice issued in the Agent's name (acting as principal) and entirely separate from the invoice issued by the Agent on behalf of the Principal in relation to the relevant consignment of the Products. The Agent shall not be entitled to any commission in respect of delivery charges and shall be responsible (to the entire exclusion of the Principal) for the collection and payment of any value added tax or sales tax or other taxes or duties payable in respect of delivery charges.

2.14.3 The Agent will insure (and keep insured throughout the time it continues **2–68**
to hold such stock) all such stock held by it to its full value against all risks. The Agent undertakes to notify the relevant insurers as to the Principal's interest in such stock to endorse this interest on the relevant insurance policy and to hold any proceeds of such insurance policy on trust for the Principal to the extent of the Principal's interest. The Agent will on request produce a copy of the relevant policy of insurance and the receipt for the current premium.

2.14.4 In consideration of its service to the Principal the Agent shall receive by **2–69**
way of remuneration that percentage of the various net invoice prices (before any taxation amounts and (for the avoidance of doubt) before any delivery charges) at which the Products are sold by the Agent on behalf of the Principal shown below:

Product	Percentage

[or at such higher percentage as may from time to time be notified by the Principal to the Agent]

2–70 2.14.5 The Agent will keep full books of account and all relevant supporting vouchers showing all transactions relating to the Products negotiated or effected by the Agent under this Agreement including without limitation the collection of all taxation amounts and their remittance to the relevant fiscal authority.

2–71 2.14.6 The Agent will remit to the Principal [sixty days] after the last business day in each week an amount equal to the net invoice value of the Products delivered to purchasers during that week less taxation amounts and (for the avoidance of doubt) delivery charges and less such amount as the Agent is permitted to deduct in accordance with cl.2.14.4 irrespective of whether the Agent has itself received payment in respect of such Products at the time of remittance and pending such remittance will not mix any moneys in respect of such Products received (including taxation amounts) [either direct] from the purchasers [or from debt factors (as the proceeds of the factoring on behalf of the Principal of book debts arising from sales of the products negotiated by the Agent)] in any bank account which is not solely designated as an agency account relating to monies held in trust for the Principal by the Agent.

2–72 2.14.7 The Agent will supply from time to time upon the written request of the Principal the reports returns and other information relating to the performance of its obligations under this Schedule and to contracts for the sale of the Products negotiated by it as follows:

2.14.7.1 Not more than fourteen days after the end of each week a statement showing the transactions effected during that week in relation to the Products as recorded in the Agent's accounts kept in accordance with cl.2.14.5;

2.14.7.2 Not more than fourteen days after the end of each week a statement by customer showing the Products sold during that week together with copies of all relevant invoices showing separately units sold and their sales value;

2.14.7.3 Not more than fourteen days after the end of each month a statement certified by [a director or other authorised officer of] the Agent stating opening and closing stocks for the month in question and showing total unit sales of the Products during that month together with a record of any receipts of deliveries of the Products during that month from the Principal such monthly statement to be accompanied by a statement of the kind referred to in cl.2.14.7.1 but showing the position at the end of the relevant month.

2.14.7.4 Not more than fourteen days after the date of each payment of a taxation amount to the relevant fiscal authority all relevant details thereof including without limitation copies of all documents sent to the relevant fiscal authority in respect of such payment together with a copy of the invoices in respect of which such payment has been made.

2–73 2.14.8 The Agent will allow the authorised officers of the Principal or any authorised representative upon reasonable notice during working hours to inspect and count the stock of the Products and to inspect verify and take copies of the accounts and vouchers kept by the Agent in accordance with cl.2.14.5.

2–74 2.14.9 Upon termination of this Agreement for whatever cause or at any time previous to such termination the Agent shall upon request at the expense of the

Principal immediately return to the Principal or to a nominee of the Principal or on the direction of the Principal otherwise dispose of all stocks of the Products held by the Agent under this schedule. If there is any deficiency in the stock of the Products discovered as a result of such request or of an inspection and count in terms of cl.2.14.8 either because of loss or theft or damage or because of deterioration due to incorrect storage or handling by the Agent such deficiency shall be deemed to have been stock sold by the Agent on the date of such discovery under the terms of this Agreement and the Agent shall account to the Principal for it in accordance with cl.2.14.6.

2.14.10 Samples of Products covered by cl.2.4.2 shall not form part of the stock **2–75**
of Products governed by this Schedule.

This schedule provides for the arrangement covering the consignment stock that the selling agent, acting also as factor, would hold on behalf of his principal. It is important to realise that in many jurisdictions (see particularly the EC and the EEA as discussed in Chapter 3.14 in relation to the Brussels Convention and Regulation) the setting up of a factor with consignment stock is sufficient to constitute the principal as doing business in the territory in which the agent is acting. This can obviously render the principal liable to taxation in that territory and also to the jurisdiction of the local courts should a dispute arise with any third parties who are dissatisfied with goods purchased from the factor.

The amount and value of the stock are normally left to the discretion of **2–76**
the principal, and it is important that the agent should not be able to claim lost commission on the ground that the principal has failed to deliver stock so that all demand for the products has not been satisfied.

Clause 2.14.2 sets out the basis on which the stocks are to be held, and is **2–77**
vital if the stocks, and their proceeds of sale are not to be considered part of the general assets of the agent and so, for instance, fall to the receiver or liquidator or trustee in bankruptcy in the case of the agent's insolvency. It is necessary to make the clause cover the proceeds of sale and book debts because where a factor disposes of goods which are in his possession with the consent of his principal, he passes a good title to a third party, even if the principal has directed him not to dispose of the goods at that moment, provided that the third party is unaware of the situation and takes for value (Factors Act 1889, s.2).

The existence of the trust should make it possible for the principal to trace **2–78**
proceeds of sale into a mixed bank account, but it is preferable to ensure that they have been kept in a trust account separately to ensure ease of recovery and identification (see cl.2.3.12). The possibility of the agent factoring book debts is discussed below.

Given the prevalence of sales and value added taxes today, it is necessary **2–79**
to deal with the issue of how these are collected and paid. Since the agent is acting on behalf of the principal, the collection and remittance of such taxes is the primary responsibility of the principal. However, where the agent collects invoice proceeds on behalf of the principal, the only practical method of dealing with the obligation is for the agent to collect and pay

these sums on behalf of the principal as well. In some jurisdictions more detailed provisions may be necessary, but the current drafts set out in general what is required. The fact that the agent holds the tax collected as trustee for the principal is of course necessary because in the event of the agent's insolvency the principal will still have to account for the tax collected out of his own pocket. An indemnity in case the agent defaults on the obligation is also desirable protection.

2–80 Clause 2.14.2.6 provides for the agent to bear any charges relating to delivery of the goods from his warehouse to customers, but gives him the chance to recover the costs from the relevant customers on his own account. In this respect he is not acting in any way as agent for the principal.

2–81 If the agent is not sufficiently strong financially it is wisest to require that he insures the products so that he is in a position to compensate the principal in the event of their destruction. In some cases it is easier for the principal to insure because most blanket assets all risks policies provide cover (usually on the basis of an annual declaration) for all goods in the ownership of the insured in a designated area (*e.g.* the UK) even if they are not on premises owned by the insured. Under these policies the principal usually has an insurable interest even if risk in the goods is with the factor.

2–82 A factor is normally remunerated by way of commission which he deducts from the invoice sums received before remitting them to the principal. The phrase in square brackets in cl.2.14.4 would cover the case where the principal wished to run special promotions and the agent complained that the drop in selling prices reduced his actual return under the factoring arrangement.

2–83 Clause 2.14.5 provides the necessary obligations for the Agent to keep records for purposes of monitoring by and accounting the principal.

2–84 The payment terms of cl.2.14.6 can be based on the premise that the agent will factor, on behalf of the principal, invoices generated by the sale of the Products and that the debt factor will take responsibility for bad debts. Since the agent is obliged to remit the net invoice value to the principal (*i.e.* the full value before allowing for the debt factor's discount) the debt factor's discount for this arrangement in effect has to come out of the agent's margin allowed under cl.2.14.4.

2–85 The result of this clause is that, to the extent the debt factor does not bear the risk of bad debts, the agent does, since he is obliged to remit to the principal even if he has not collected the sums due under the relevant invoice. Clauses 2.14.2.4 and 2.14.2.5 achieve the same result in relation to taxation amounts, since these must be paid even if not collected (unless, presumably, the fiscal authorities accept that they need not be paid under some exemption relating to bad debts). Similarly, cl.2.14.2.6 has this effect since, if the agent cannot collect delivery charges from the customer, he will have to bear them.

2–86 The agent is in all these circumstances in effect being put into something more onerous than the position of a del credere agent. This is not uncommon for factors who, after all, go out and find the customers that they contract with, without any reference to or approval from the principal. It is also very common for factors expressly to take on the responsibility of a del credere agent.

This position causes some problems in the EC when deciding whether or not an agency agreement is subject to Art.81 of the EC Treaty. (See Chapters 5.1.1.3.11 and 5.1.1.3.15) The discussion of the way this schedule should be adapted to avoid the agreement becoming a "non-genuine agency agreement" and hence subject potentially to Art 81 is discussed in particular in Chapter 5.1.1.3.15 and an alternative version of this schedule which should achieve this objective is set out in Chapter 3.14. **2–87**

If the arrangement is to work properly the agent will need to make full and proper returns of sales and collection of their proceeds. This is provided for in cl.2.14.7. The form of reporting here ties in with the remittance arrangements in cl.2.14.4. **2–88**

In many cases the closest supervision is required to ensure that the terms of the agreement relating to the safekeeping of the stock and the proper application of the proceeds of sale are being adhered to by the agent, particularly in the early stages of a new relationship. It cannot be overemphasised that, in an insolvency situation, if the agent has not kept stock and the proceeds of its sale properly separated, whatever the actual legal rights available to the principal, they are difficult to apply in practice. The principal should make full use of his rights of inspection, if necessary appointing a consultant in the territory (see Chapter 9) in the initial stages of the arrangement. Clause 2.14.8 makes provision for these matters. **2–89**

Since the stock is at the risk of the agent cl.2.14.9 provides that he must make up all deficiencies on the termination of the agreement, or on any prior stock-take. The principal must also be free to uplift the stock at any time, either because of the termination of the agreement or because of impending insolvency. **2–90**

Where the principal wants to encourage the factor to give free samples he can also designate a particular delivery of the products as falling under cl.2.4.2 (provision of samples) rather than increase the percentages in respect of a particular lot of the products under the phrase in square brackets at the end of cl.2.14.4. Clause 2.14.10 expressly provided that such samples are not part of the stock. **2–91**

Chapter 3

Agency Agreements Inside the EC

Contents

3.1 Commercial and legal background

3–01 This chapter is concerned with agency agreements which are affected by EC law, and thus applies in general to agency contracts where the agent carries on his activities in one of the Member States of the EC. Agency agreements are largely unaffected by competition law, and the limited effect that it has is thus better considered as part of a discussion of the impact of competition law on vertical agreements in general. Chapter 5 deals with this general discussion in relation to both EC and UK competition law and also considers the effect of EC and UK competition law on agency agreements. This chapter concentrates on the extent to which the relationship between the principal and the agent is regulated by the Council Directive 653/86 of December 18, 1986 on the Coordination of the laws of the Member States relating to self-employed Commercial Agents. This Directive exerts a measure of harmonisation on the terms of agency agreements. The Directive lays down certain mandatory rights and obligations of both principal and agent, provides for the way in which the agent is to be remunerated, provides for the way in which the agency agreement can be terminated, and for the payment of compensation to the agent upon termination in certain circumstances, and also restricts the extent to which the agent can be bound by a non-competition clause after termination. The Directive is in general modelled upon the laws of Member States (civil law jurisdictions, in particular Germany and France) which gave considerably more protection to agents than the UK did. In passing the Directive the Council felt it appropriate to be guided by the principles of Art.136 of the EC Treaty in relation to harmonisation measures, and to ensure that harmonisation should be implemented so as to bring all Member States up to the highest standard, rather than harmonising downwards to the lowest common denominator. This required considerable change in the way agency agreements are treated under the systems of law in force in the various parts of the UK (namely England and Wales, Northern Ireland, and Scotland—occasionally collectively referred to in this chapter as "UK law" for the sake of convenience). Under UK law, prior to the implementation of the Directive, such agreements were regarded as private arrangements almost entirely regulated by agreement between the parties upon the general basis of the relevant laws of contract. Other Member States, such as Ireland, and to a lesser extent Italy, had the same problems.

3–02 The Directive, like all Council directives, was not directly applicable within Member States but required enabling legislation in each state to achieve its effect. However, it provided for quite generous transitional periods to cushion the shock. Leaving aside the UK, Ireland and Italy, it came into force from January 1, 1990, but only in relation to agreements concluded after that date. As far as agreements in existence on January 1, 1990 were concerned, these were to be brought under the Directive by no later than January 1, 1994. The UK and Ireland had a dispensation which permitted them to implement the Directive from January 1, 1994, but from this date the implementation had to apply to both new and existing agreements. Italy was permitted to delay the bringing into force of the provisions relating to compensation on termination (Art.17 of the Directive) for new agreements until January 1, 1993. Thus by January 1, 1994 the Directive should have been fully implemented for both new and existing agreements in all of the then Member States of the EC, and also within the EEA. So far as states which have become members of the EC after that date (namely Austria, Finland and Sweden) their relevant treaties of accession apply this legislation to agency agreements, on and from the date of accession. Since it was felt that the economic situation of the new members was entirely compatible with that of the other Member States very few transitional arrangements were provided for in the treaties of accession. The new members were thus required to adopt, effective as from the date of accession, all national enabling legislation necessary to implement Community directives and regulations in existence at the date of their accession, unless a specific derogation was granted. There was no such derogation provided for in the case of the Directive.

3–03 Since the states in the current round of accession negotiations (Poland, Czech Republic, Hungary, Slovakia, Lithuania, Latvia, Slovenia, Estonia, Cyprus and Malta) will not all finalise their treaties of accession until some time in early 2004 (deadline May 1, 2004), it is not certain how this particular issue will be treated, but it is likely that the same line will be taken as for Austria, Finland and Sweden, and that the new accession states will be required to implement the Agency Directive, without a derogation for transitional purposes, with effect from the date of accession. However, the exact situation (which may be different for different accession states depending on their economic situation) can only be ascertained once the relevant accession treaties have been executed.

Attached as Appendix 2 can be found the results of a questionnaire which was sent to local lawyers in each Member State of the EC and the EEA (other than the UK), which summarises (as of April 2003) the current state of implementation of the Directive in each of those states. **3–04**

Within the UK the Directive was implemented by Statutory Instrument. So far as England, Wales and Scotland are concerned (Great Britain) the enabling instrument is the Commercial Agents (Council Directive) Regulations 1993 (SI 1993/3053). (Mention should also be made of SI 1993/3173 which corrected an error in SI 1993/3053, by adding the words "indemnity or" after the opening word of the first line of reg.17 and The Commercial Agents (Council Directive) (Amendment) Regulations 1998 (SI 1998/2868) which brought the jurisdictional provisions of the original regulations in line with the provisions of the Directive, and corrected a further error in reg.17(2) by substituting the word "contract" for "contact".) The Directive was implemented for Northern Ireland by a separate set of regulations, the Commercial Agents (Council Directive) Regulations (Northern Ireland) 1993 (Statutory Rules for Northern Ireland SI 1993/483), with similar provisions. The Northern Ireland Regulations were also amended by further Regulations corresponding to SI 1993/3173 and SI 1998/2868. In this chapter, however, references to the Regulations should be understood as references to SI 1993/3053 as amended. **3–05**

The Regulations have reproduced the wording of the Directive very closely. Additionally, they provide a definition of the term "secondary agent" as used in the Directive, and legislate to some extent for the effect of the Regulations on agency agreements governed by foreign systems of law (see SI 1998/2868). **3–06**

Council Directives are not of themselves intended to be legislation and are not generally drafted with the attention to detail and the need to avoid ambiguity and inconsistency which is required in a piece of legislation. Their purpose is to provide a set of guidelines on a particular legal issue. The spirit of those guidelines can then be implemented in detail by the legislature of each Member State in a way which best conforms to the idiosyncrasies of that Member State's legal system. In the past, Directives were implemented in this way in the UK. However, at the time of the implementation of the Directive in 1993, there had been a number of instances where the Commission had successfully contended before the European Court of Justice that the then current UK approach had resulted in defective implementing legislation and incomplete adoption of Directives. For instance, in *Dr Sophie Redmond Stichting v Bartol* [1992] I.R.L.R. 366 ECJ, the European **3–07**

Court decided that reg.2 of the Transfer of Undertakings (Protection of Employment) Regulations 1981 (SI 1981/1794) had incorrectly implemented the EC Acquired Rights Directive 187/77. This required correction by the UK through the passing of amending provisions under the Trade Union Reform and Employment Rights Act, 1993.

3–08 Where there has been a sufficiently serious failure to implement a Directive, and hence a sufficiently serious breach of EC law, the offending governments can attract not only criticism but also, in some, though not all, circumstances, liability to those who have suffered as a result of this failure.

3–09 The leading cases in this area can be found in the European Court of Justice rulings in *Francovich v Italian Republic* [1991] ECR 1–5357; C-91/92 *Faccini Dori v Recreb Srl* Case [1995] All E.R. (EC) 1; joined cases C-46/93 and C-48/93 *Brasserie du Pecheur SA v Federal Republic of Germany* and *R. v Secretary of State for Transport, ex p Factortame Ltd* [1996] 1 C.M.L.R. 889; Case C-92/93 *R. v HM Treasury Ex p. British Telecom plc* [1996] All E.R. (EC) 411; Case C-192/94 *El Corte Ingles SA v Cristina Blazques Rivero* [1997] C.C.L.R. 1; Case C-194/94 *CIA Security International SA v Signalson SA and Securitel SPRL* [1996] All E.R. (EC) 557; and Case 5/94 *R. v Minister of Agriculture, Fisheries and Food Ex p. Hedley Lomas (Ireland) Ltd* [1996] 3 W.L.R. 787.

3–10 More recent examples of this approach can be found in cases relating to EC Commission proceedings for failure to implement the Council Directive 9/96 on the legal protection of databases (Case C370/99 *Commission v Ireland* [2001] E.C.D.R. 9 and Case C348/99 *Commission v Luxembourg* [2000] E.C.D.R. 437) and in respect of France's violation of Arts 28 and 30 of the EC Treaty by its ban on British beef imports (Case C1/00 *Commission v France* [2002] 1 C.M.L.R. 22.)

3–11 *Rechberger v Austria* [2000] 2 C.M.L.R. 1, ECJ was a recent example of enforcement of individual rights against states who fail to implement directives, where damages were payable to an individual by the state of Austria because of its failure to implement the Council Directive 314/90 on Package travel, Package holidays and Package tours.

3–12 The whole question of such individual rights was usefully discussed, and the authorities analysed, in *R. v Durham CC Ex p. Huddleston* [2000] 1 W.L.R. 1484, CA. Durham maintained that the wording of the Planning and Compensation Act 1991 prevented them from properly applying Council Directive 337/85 on the assessment of the effects of certain public and private projects on the environment. If the Directive had been in force Huddleston would have been able to contest the validity of planning permission (properly granted under the 1991 Act) for a certain mining project. Huddleston contended that he was entitled as an individual to enforce the Directive against the state, and to require an environmental impact survey of the effect of the project on surrounding areas, including his own house. The appeal was allowed. The authorities showed that, where a Member State had failed to implement a Directive, an individual with rights arising from the Directive was entitled to assert those rights against it. Thus Durham's impotence in the face of the state's failure to implement the Directive gave rise to Huddleston's entitlement to insist that the state should give effect to the meaning of the Directive and confer upon Durham the powers which it should have had if the Directive had been properly implemented.

The weight of these decisions caused a more cautious approach to implementation in the UK, with a tendency to reproduce the wording in the Directive, and to leave any ambiguities or inconsistencies to be sorted out by the courts. It is perhaps to be regretted that this course was followed, since the Directive does have some difficult provisions which would have benefited from clarification and translation into language familiar to British lawyers.

This more careful approach to implementation is still with us today, although familiarity with EC legislation and judicial principles has to some extent ameliorated the strictly literal approach that prevailed in the case of the Directive. This can be seen, for example in the current proposals for implementation of the Council Directive on Certain Aspects of the Sale of Consumer Goods and Associated Guarantees (44/99). **3–13**

In regard to formalities surrounding the creation of agency agreements, the Directive is very flexible. Article 13(2) provides that any Member State may legislate that agency agreements are not enforceable unless they are evidenced in writing but it does not make this a mandatory requirement. In the UK oral agency agreements were usually enforceable, and the UK has not altered this position in the Regulations. Certain other states have taken up the option (*e.g.* Greece and Portugal, but the latter only for exclusive agreements). However, in all Member States (whether or not the local law provides for only agency agreements evidenced in writing to be enforceable) Art.13(1) of the Directive requires the implementation of provisions enabling each party to an agency agreement to require the other to provide him with a document setting out the terms of their agreement, including any terms subsequently agreed. **3–14**

The reconciliation between the apparently conflicting terms of Arts 13(1) and 13(2) depends upon the fact that Art.13(2) takes precedence over Art.13(1). Article 13(2) states that, *notwithstanding Art.13(1)*, a Member State may provide that an agency contract shall not be valid unless evidenced in writing. Thus, when dealing with oral agency agreements, Member States must provide for entitlement to the written statement (Art.13(1) "waiver is not permitted . . .") unless (Art.13(2) "Notwithstanding paragraph 1. . .") they choose to provide that oral agency agreements are not enforceable at all. Where a Member State chooses to make oral agreements unenforceable, Art.13(1) would then have no application in relation to them, because such agreements would not be capable of existence in the first place under the laws of the relevant Member State. Thus Member States, who do not recognise oral agency agreements, are not put in the position of having to implement Art.13(1) in such a way that a party to a wholly oral agreement could cure its lack of enforceability by relying on that implementation of Art.13(1) to require the other party to reduce it to writing. On the other hand, the fact that a Member State's local law permits oral agency agreements, would not excuse it from implementing the right to a written statement under Art.13(1). **3–15**

3–16 In a Member State where only agreements evidenced in writing are enforceable, Art.13(1) must still be implemented. This is arguably necessary, either because the agreement may be evidenced by a series of documents that could be usefully summarised, or because the precise wording of Art.13(2) does not seem to require that all of the terms of the agreement be reduced to writing. Where an agreement is mainly written, but partly oral, a requirement to provide a written statement so that the oral terms are also clearly evidenced seems sensible. Nevertheless, in practical terms, Art.13(1) is clearly of most use for those Member States which permit oral agency agreements to be enforceable.

3–17 When considering the drafting of agency agreements subject to the Directive, it is important to remember that it is designed so that enabling legislation (in each Member State) has an overriding effect which prevents derogation under contract from its provisions. It does not provide for criminal sanctions if provisions contrary to the Directive are inserted in a new agency agreement. Those provisions will merely be overridden by the relevant enabling legislation and be of no effect. Similarly, existing agreements, through the overriding legislation, were automatically conformed to the Directive from the date they were covered by it, namely January 1, 1994. For this reason it was not legally necessary to amend existing agency agreements to conform to the Directive. Relevant enabling legislation in effect did this automatically. Although the relevance of transitional issues has long passed for all existing Member States, the same issues, with the same consequences, will arise once the new accession states become members of the EU, and should be borne in mind accordingly.

3–18 Subject to the need (in some Member States) to have a written agreement, the parties, in reliance on the relevant enabling legislation, could leave most of the pertinent provisions of their agreement to be governed by the relevant proper law. However, in practice the spelling out of the parties' rights and obligations in accordance with the Directive under the terms of this precedent is much to be preferred for the purposes of clarity and the avoidance of misunderstanding. This is desirable both in the case of new agreements, and also in relation to the modification of existing agreements, to bring them into line with the Directive. The precedent in this chapter thus takes the text of the agency agreement in Chapter 2, and adapts it where necessary to conform expressly to the Directive, on the basis that this precedent is offered as an agreement governed by English law, and entered into with an agent who carries on his activities either in the UK or in some other Member State of the EC.

3–19 It is worth emphasising that the Directive applies not only to selling agents, but also to purchasing agents (see Art.1(2)). The precedent in Chapter 2, and the amendments to it set out in this chapter, deal with selling agents (which are much more common than purchasing agents). However, the precedent could be used for a purchasing agent, with some adaptation, principally in connection with the grant of the agent's authority.

3.2 Appointment of agent

3.2.1 Appointment

See Chapter 2.2.1. 3–20

The relevant clauses from the precedent in Chapter 2 are perfectly applicable under the Directive. The Directive leaves entirely open the question of whether an appointment can be exclusive or non-exclusive, and even envisages that there may be an appointment not only by reference to a geographical territory but by reference to a special group of customers. The type of appointment, however, does affect the question of the agent's right to remuneration. This will be discussed below.

The question of whether the form of appointment under version (a) of cl.2.2.1 (marketing, promoting and soliciting orders for transmission to the principal) or version (b) (authority to negotiate and conclude contracts) would be caught by the Directive is not an easy one, and, unfortunately as always, will depend upon the facts of each case. 3–21

As far as the Directive is concerned, it applies to "commercial agents" who are defined as "a self-employed intermediary who has continuing authority to negotiate the sale or purchase of goods on behalf of another person, hereinafter called the principal, or to negotiate and conclude such transactions on behalf of and in the name of the principal" (Art.1(2)). 3–22

This definition contains three essential elements. First, the commercial agent must act **on behalf of another person** (the "principal"), not for himself. Second, he must have authority to **negotiate and/or conclude contracts** on behalf of that person. Third that authority must be a **continuing authority**. 3–23

Since the agent must act on behalf of another person, this requirement rules out of scope of the Directive, and the Regulations, a distributor who buys from a "principal" then resells to a third party. The point is obvious but was first dealt with by the Court of Appeal in *AMB Imballaggi Plastici Srl v Pacflex Ltd* [1999] 2 All E.R (Comm) 249. Gibson L.J. said: "The plain implication of the language of the Directive and of the Regulations is that if the sale or purchase of goods is negotiated by the intermediary in its own interest rather than on behalf of the principal, the intermediary is not a commercial agent. The paradigm example of an intermediary so negotiating is as a distributor purchasing goods from the manufacturer but re-selling the goods for a profit on the mark-up". 3–24

In this case there was discussion as to the extent to which the fact that the remuneration was by way of a mark-up was determinative of the status of Pacflex as a distributor rather than an agent. However, it seems clear from the later decision of *Mercantile International Group plc v Chuan Soon Huat Industrial Group plc* [2002] 1 All E.R. (Comm) 788, CA, that the presence of mark-up is only one factor to be taken into account and not necessarily the determinative one. Rix L.J. said: 3–25

"[Counsel for the Respondent] relied on the weight which was [in *AMB v Pacflex*] accorded to the mark-up factor. In my judgment, however, that is to mistake the real significance of that decision. It was a finding of the trial judge, assisted no doubt by the mark-up factor, that the basis upon which the parties did business was that of sale and resale. There was, as both Waller and Peter Gibson LJJ stressed, nothing to indicate that Pacflex had any authority, or even purported to have any authority, to enter into contracts as an agent on behalf of AMB. The combination of those two circumstances, which were entirely consistent with one another, made any attempt to find a relationship of principal and agent an impossible one ... [*Ex p. White, re Nevill* (1871) L.R. 6 Ch. App. 397] shows that such an arrangement [*i.e.* remuneration by way of mark-up] is not inconsistent with agency. It is true that the arrangement in that case was spelled out in terms, which is not the case here. Even so, the effect is the same, and any inference that might in other circumstances have been drawn from the mark-up, as perhaps it was in *Pacflex*, is here overwhelmed by the underlying documentation."

3–26 It should be noted that Waller, LJ, who gave the main judgment in *Pacflex*, was one of the other two judges who heard the case in the Court of Appeal and that he stated he agreed with Rix, L.J.'s judgment.

3–27 Second, it can be seen that the presence of the element of "negotiation" is essential if the agent is to fall within the scope of the Directive. Conclusion is optional. The concept of "conclude" is simple. Here the agent actually enters into the contract on behalf of the principal and thus creates the legal relationship between the principal and the third party in accordance with the well-understood principles of agency law. However, the definition of "negotiation" is more difficult.

3–28 When deciding whether version (a) or (b) will fall within the scope of the Directive, the issue is whether, in either case, the agent engages in "negotiation". In version (b) the word "negotiate" is used, together with the word "conclude". The use of the full wording from the Directive is alone likely to be very persuasive, without further discussion about the definition of "negotiation", and the principal will have to show very clearly that, despite the use of the word, in fact the relationship was such that the agent carried on no activities which could possibly be described as negotiation. It must also be admitted that the use of the word "negotiate" together with the word "conclude" will make this task more difficult, since if an agent concludes a transaction, except in extraordinary cases (such as *Parks v Esso* discussed below), it is relatively easy for him to claim that he also had some part in negotiating it.

3–29 However, version (a) does not use the word "negotiate" but simply describes the activities the agent is to undertake. It then becomes relevant to ask precisely what is the definition of "negotiation" and whether any or all of those activities fall within it, thus bringing the agent above the "negotiating threshold" and within the scope of the Directive. Indeed, the question of whether any particular representative or agency relationship is above or below the negotiating threshold, can be usefully approached in the same way.

Assistance on the definition of negotiation has recently come from the decision of the Court of Appeal in *Parks v Esso Petroleum Ltd* [2000] E.C.C. 45. This was an appeal from the decision of Sir Richard Scott, V.C., at first instance, reported at [1999] 1 C.M.L.R. 455. Parks operated a petrol station for Esso under an agreement in which he was described as acting as an "agent" for Esso. He did not own the petrol station (occupying it under a bare licence from Esso) nor did he own the fuel (title to which passed directly from Esso to the relevant motorist as fuel was purchased and paid for). He fell into various disputes with Esso and his agreement was terminated. He claimed, *inter alia*, that he was a commercial agent within the definition of the Regulations and therefore entitled under reg.17 to compensation for termination without cause. **3–30**

At first instance, the Vice-Chancellor considered that, if Parks were to be regarded as a commercial agent within the scope of the Regulations, he would have to show that he either negotiated or negotiated and concluded contracts on behalf of Esso. It was common ground that Parks concluded such contracts, at the latest when a motorist paid for fuel he had purchased. The question was whether Parks took any part in negotiating such contracts, and whether such negotiation was a necessary element if he were to claim the benefit of the Regulations. **3–31**

The Vice-Chancellor found that negotiation was a necessary element and that it was absent in this case. He said: **3–32**

> "If the word 'negotiated' is given its ordinary English meaning, I feel myself quite unable to avoid the conclusion that the plaintiff is not a commercial agent. He does not negotiate the sale of motor fuel. The price at which motor fuel is sold is fixed by the principal. He concludes the sale as agent, but he does not negotiate it in any sense at all. [Counsel for Mr Parks] submitted, in effect, that I should ignore the word 'negotiate' in the definition of commercial agent. Otherwise, he said, the definition would exclude individuals such as the plaintiff from the benefit intended to be conferred by the regulations and would not accord with the purposive construction required by European law of European instruments.
>
> [Counsel for Mr Parks] found for me a copy of the Directive that the regulations were made in order to implement. It is Council Directive 86/653. But that Directive, too, in its English translation, and I have seen no other, uses the word 'negotiate' in exactly the same context as is to be found in the English regulations. There is no assistance for [counsel] in the content of the Council Directive.
>
> In the absence of any material which justifies ignoring the inclusion in the regulations definition, and for that matter in the text of the Directive, of the word 'negotiate', I can see no reason why I should depart from the ordinary meaning of the language used. Accordingly, I conclude that the plaintiff is not a commercial agent as defined in the regulations and they do not apply to him."

3–33 Parks appealed against this finding. The Court of Appeal dismissed the appeal. In general the Court affirmed the decision at first instance, but parts of the judgment are useful (if not necessarily conclusive, since they must to some extent be regarded as *obiter*) in deciding just how far the agent must go to get above the negotiating threshold. In delivering his judgment, Morritt L.J. made the following relevant points:

> "[Counsel for Parks] makes, in effect, five points.
>
> First, he submits that the normal meaning of the word 'negotiate' in English does not require any element of bargaining but encompasses brought about the sale, effected or facilitated the sale, arranged for the sale to happen. He relied on the second definition of the word 'negotiate' in the Oxford English Dictionary which is as follows: '2. trans. To deal with, manage, or conduct (a matter, affair, *etc.*, requiring some skill or consideration)'.
>
> Secondly, he submits that the provision, 'enabling or requiring the agent to operate credit accounts at his own risk', indicates that the agent was required to do more than merely bring about a transaction. Indeed he was required to exercise some discretion or choice.
>
> Thirdly, reliance in the written argument was placed on the Commission's explanatory memorandum in respect of the first draft of the Directive. This indicated that: 'It is for the principal alone to decide, for example, whether and on what terms a commercial transaction is to be entered into and performed. In this respect therefore the agent's independence is limited'.
>
> Fourthly, he relied on the fact that in the German version the verb is 'vermitteln' as opposed to 'verhandein', the former connoting 'to bring about, facilitate, procure', whereas the latter connotes also 'bargaining'.
>
> Fifthly, he relied on cases decided under the German Commercial Code to indicate that in Germany one in the position of Mr Parks would be regarded as a commercial agent and, as the Commission had pointed out, German law is relevant to the construction of the Directive.
>
> I will deal with these submissions in reverse order. First, I do not think that the decisions of the German courts on which counsel relied are of any assistance. They were decided in the period 1964 to 1986. The German Commercial Code was altered in 1989 in anticipation of the promulgation of the Directive. Thus they are not decisions on the definition contained in the Directive and imported into the regulations, which alone is the Community concept for the construction of which they might be of help. In any event, as the provisions of Article 2(1) demonstrate individual Member States are permitted to make their own provision for the exclusion of those whose activities were thought to be secondary. This facility was taken up in the Schedule to the regulations to which I have referred. Accordingly, the decisions on the application of a different provision of German law which has not been incorporated into a concept of Community law are, in my view, of no help.
>
> The current provision of German law is contained in Article 84 of the

German Commercial Code. That provides: (1) A commercial agent is a person who as an independent businessman is regularly entrusted with the negotiation of business deals for another principal or with transacting them on behalf of the latter. A person is independent if he is essentially able to shape his activities freely and to determine his own hours of work. (2) A person, who, without being independent in the sense of (1), is regularly entrusted with the negotiation of business deals for a principal or with transacting them on his behalf, is deemed an employee. (3) The principal may also be a commercial agent.

Counsel for Mr Parks relies on the fact that the German word which has been translated as 'negotiation' is 'vermitteln', not 'verhandein'. He relies on the fact that the former appears in Cassels English/German dictionary in the sense of 'bring about, facilitate, secure or procure', whereas only the latter also includes 'barter away'. He contends that this choice in the German text indicates that the word 'negotiate' is used in a wider sense than bargain. For my part I do not think this exercise provides any help over and above that already provided by the Oxford English Dictionary. In the passage from the latter work I have already quoted, the meaning of 'negotiate' appears to me to be essentially the same as the word chosen in the German text.

I do not think that the third point, which appeared in the written argument but was not referred to in the oral argument, assists one way or another. Nor do I think that the fact that the risk of non-payment is imposed on the agent assists in the determination of the meaning of the word 'negotiate'. The definition points to the authority 'to negotiate the sale ... or to negotiate and conclude the sale'. Decisions on how to pay for petrol bought at the pump are either unilateral on the part of the motorist or follow the completion of the sale. In so far as the site operator has a discretion in the method of payment, and it is limited to those approved by Esso, it does not in my view indicate any process of negotiation of the sale itself, merely the mechanics for its completion in the minority of cases.

So I return to the one short point which arises on the appeal. Did Mr Parks negotiate and conclude the sale of the petrol owned by Esso to those who attended his forecourt? I take the normal meaning of the word from the Oxford English Dictionary definition relied on by Mr Parks. This definition does not require a process of bargaining in the sense of invitation to treat, offer, counter-offer and finally acceptance, more colloquially known as a haggle. But equally it does require more than the self-service by the customer followed by payment in the shop of the price shown on the pump, which is how the system operates nowadays.

In my view the motorist would be astonished to be told when he inserted the nozzle of the pipe into the top of his petrol tank that he was 'negotiating' with the site operator.

In my view it is quite plain that there is no process of negotiation involved. To revert to the Oxford English Dictionary definition Mr Parks relied on, Mr Parks did not 'deal with, manage or conduct' the sale of petrol to his customers, for he took no part in the customer's choice and self-service. In so far as the definition indicates the need for skill or consideration Mr Parks provided none.

Further, the provisions of the Schedule, in particular those which distinguish between sales individually negotiated and those which depend on the customer's self-selection, show beyond doubt that the regulations are not intended to apply to one in the position of Mr Parks. The point is a short one. I agree with the Vice-Chancellor and would dismiss this appeal."

3–34 The factual situation in *Parks v Esso* very clearly falls below the negotiating threshold. Parks had no real contact with the customer (except to accept payment) nor any influence over what the customer chose to purchase. The Court reached its decision on two separate principles, both of which reinforced the other.

3–35 The first was the dictionary definition of "negotiation". Morritt L.J. was satisfied that this definition does not require that the agent has actually to bargain with the customer in the sense of setting the prices terms or conditions for the transaction (the "haggle"), but the agent must "deal with, manage or conduct" the transaction, and this "indicates the need for skill or consideration" on the part of the agent.

3–36 The second was that para.4(c) of the Schedule to the Regulations specifies as one indication that a relationship should be treated as a "secondary agency", and not as a commercial agency within the scope of the Regulations, that it is one where "customers normally select goods for themselves and merely place their orders through the agent". This was obviously the situation in Parks' case. The Schedule is discussed below in more detail, but it should be remembered that whilst the first finding is one which has a general impact on the definition of "negotiate" for the purposes of EC law, and could theoretically be overturned by a ruling of the European Court, the second relates to a purely domestic provision, since, as discussed below, the Directive allows Member States an option to define and then exclude secondary agents from the scope of the Directive by the operation of local law alone.

3–37 Given the approach in *Parks v Esso*, and unless and until the European Commission or the European Court of Justice lay down further guidelines, it seems that the negotiating threshold is set low, and that the only real requirement on the agent is that he take an active rather than a passive role in relation to the transaction. Parks took a passive role in the sense that he did nothing to find customers, assist them in their choice or persuade them of the desirability of purchasing his principal's goods. He had no dealings with the customers until they had made their own choice and came to pay. On the other hand, an agent who goes out and finds customers for his principle, persuades them that a transaction would be in their interest, gives them some advice about it, or perhaps measures up or makes estimates, and then forwards the completed documentation to his principal to accept or reject the order, would seem to be "conducting the transaction" with some "care and skill" even if he was working from fixed prices, terms and conditions and there was no "haggle". Thus a person who "negotiates" in the sense described in *Parks v Esso* will fall within the definition of commercial agent whether or not he also concludes on behalf of his principal the transaction that he has "negotiated".

Given the above, and although the matter can only be a question of fact to be decided in each case, it seems likely that version (a) will also fall within the scope of the Directive, since the agent takes an active role in finding customers, marketing to them, soliciting for orders and then forwarding those orders to the principle. **3–38**

Another way of stating the problem is to ask whether the agent or representative is a mere order taker. As a matter of public policy, and looking at the law in force in Member States where commercial agents are protected, in general the concept of a mere order taker is likely to be applied very restrictively. In many industries the commercial agent does no more than solicit for and process orders and could be seen as no more than an order taker, falling below the negotiating threshold. Nevertheless, if this class of commercial agent were not protected the Directive would fail in much of its purpose. **3–39**

Although in the UK, the special exclusion under para.4(c) of the Schedule to the Regulations will allow the court to focus on the question of whether the agent is an order taker for a customer who self-selects, this issue is not necessarily germane in other jurisdictions. However, even in the UK, given the exact facts in *Parks v Esso*, it is likely that many agents who superficially appear to be order takers will come above the negotiating threshold because they play some sort of an active role in finding the customer and influencing his choice. The sort of order taker who would not be covered (other than in the precise facts of *Parks v Esso*) can perhaps best be exemplified in a catalogue showroom run by a representative. Catalogues are on display to people who come into the shop. They look through the books, and make their choice, and then go to a desk where their order is processed, and either concluded (as in the case of *Parks v Esso*) or forwarded to the producer or distributor for fulfilment. Going on *Parks v Esso*, it seems likely that a representative who also employed staff who assisted customers in making their choice from the catalogues and advised them about which products to buy would actually come above the negotiating threshold. The dividing line is obviously a very fine one. Another possibility (and one contemplated in the UK in para.4(a) of the Schedule to the Regulations, is where the principal distributes a catalogue direct to potential customers and the representative then calls on them and takes any orders that they have decided to place after looking through the catalogue. It should also be noted that para.5 of the Schedule to the Regulations states that mail order catalogue agents for consumer goods are presumed to be outside the Regulations unless proof to the contrary is forthcoming. **3–40**

Finally, it is necessary to consider the status of representatives who do not even act as order takers, but engage in various forms of sales promotion, such as staging exhibitions, giving demonstrations or distributing samples or **3–41** other promotional material. Looking at the principles set out above, it will be seen that active involvement in bringing about a specific transaction is necessary, otherwise it will not be possible to say that the representative is negotiating the transaction in the sense described in *Parks v Esso*. Such representatives must fall below the negotiating threshold since, not being concerned with any specific transaction, they have *ipso facto* no negotiating role at all.

3–42 Thus, such representatives (whether or not designated as agents in any formal agreement) are not only not agents in the legal sense at all, but also not commercial agents falling within the scope of the Directive. It is better practice expressly to designate them as representatives or marketing consultants, rather than agents. Agreements covering such relationships are discussed in Chapter 9.

3–43 Third, the commercial agent must have "continuing authority" to act on behalf of the principal. The use of this phrase appears to mean that where an agent was engaged in relation to one transaction only, the Directive would not apply. It could only apply where the agent is appointed with authority to deal with multiple transactions during the period of the agency agreement. A question would arise if a principal used the same agent on an ad hoc basis for a number of one-off transactions. Here it is possible that, if this were done regularly, eventually an agency agreement with continuing authority, covered by the Directive, might arise through a course of dealing. One way of avoiding this might be to make sure that each ad hoc appointment was made under a written arrangement clearly stating that no continuing authority was granted, and that grant of one ad hoc authority in relation to a particular transaction conferred no right on the agent to be appointed in respect of future transactions.

3–44 In *AMB Imballaggi Plastici Srl v Pacflex Ltd* [1999] 2 All E.R. (Comm) 249, CA, the Court stated that continuing authority was a necessary element, but the facts of the case were such that it was assumed to be present without the need to consider a precise definition. However, parts of the decision in *Mercantile International Group plc v Chuan Soon Huat Industrial Group plc* [2002] 1 All E.R. (Comm) 788, support the approach described above. In this case the parties had had a relationship stretching back to 1985, which had been recorded in a series of different agreements and were also in part purely oral. Rix L.J. said:

> "I do not see how either the purchasers or CSH could argue that these decades of contracts did not evidence binding contracts, negotiated by and through the agency of MIG on behalf of its principal CSH. MIG was undoubtedly authorised to make such contracts, did make them, and made them expressly as agents for and on behalf of its principal, CSH. Moreover, CSH knew that MIG was making such contracts, [and] received the confirmations of them . . . In those circumstances, CSH never interfered to complain that MIG was purporting to act as its agent, making contracts in its name and on its behalf, while not being authorised to do so. On the contrary it clearly permitted and encouraged MIG to

hold itself out as its agent for the purpose of negotiations and making sales in its name. I would therefore conclude, in agreement with the judge, that MIG had continuing authority to negotiate the sale of goods on behalf of CSH, its principal..."

In addition to the three essential points in the definition of commercial agent considered above, the nature of the definition automatically excludes some types of agreements that might otherwise be called agency agreements either as a matter of law or commercial practice. **3–45**

The first limitation on the scope of the Directive is that it requires that the agent be concerned with contracts for the "sale or purchase of goods". Thus agency relationships concerned exclusively with contracts for the supply of services are outside the scope of the Directive. The Directive does not define "goods", but (according to the DTI, in the Draft Guidance Notes referred to below) "the term 'goods' is used without definition in Art.23 of the EC Treaty (and elsewhere) in relation to the free movement of goods and has the same meaning here. It is to be distinguished from the free movement of services and capital and, of course, land, which by definition cannot move freely. It is thought that the definition of 'goods' in s.61 of the Sale of Goods Act 1979 ('goods' includes all personal chattels other than things in action and money, and in Scotland all corporeal moveables except money...)" will provide useful guidance. **3–46**

The definition of "goods" for the purposes of the EC Public Procurement Directives, which is now implemented in the UK, under reg.2 of the Public Supply Contracts Regulations 1995 (SI 1995/201) is also of some assistance since an EC law definition of goods for one EC Directive is at least persuasive for the interpretation of the same term in another. It reads: "goods" includes electricity, substances, growing crops and things attached to or forming part of the land which are agreed to be severed before the purchase or hire under the supply contract and any ship, aircraft or vehicle. It should also be noted that in *Tamarind International Ltd v Eastern Natural Gas (Retail) Ltd* [2000] Eu L.R. 708, (discussed below) it was assumed with very little argument that the Regulations *prima facie* applied in relation to an agency for the sale of natural gas. **3–47**

Agency arrangements for software products are not that common. However, where they do occur, the agent is likely (at least under the law in the UK) to be regarded as dealing in goods if he acts as agent for the sale or supply of physical media on which the software is recorded (*e.g.* shrink-wrapped software supplied on discs), or he deals in the supply of systems combining hardware and software. The matter is discussed in detail in Chapter 11.1.3. **3–48**

Where the agent deals with mixed contracts for the supply of both goods and services, there is no guidance as to the extent of the Directive's application. One possible common sense rule could be to hold that where the agency agreement relates to the supply of goods with provision of ancillary services (*e.g.* contracts for the supply of plant and machinery together with a contract for installation or for maintenance) the Directive should apply to **3–49** the relationship. However, if the agreement truly relates to contracts for the supply of services, and the provision of the products is merely ancillary, (*e.g.* a maintenance contract including the supply of spare parts) the Directive should not apply. Another approach, which would lead to almost the same result would be to look at the issue from the question of value. If more than half the value of the mixed contract is for the supply of goods, then it is to be regarded as a contract for the supply of goods, and, if not, then as a contract for the supply of services. This is again an argument by analogy from the Public Procurement Directive, where a similar approach is taken to decide whether the regimes relating to the supply of goods or of services should apply to a particular procurement (see, for instance, reg.2 of the Public Supply Contracts Regulations 1991 (SI 1991/755) as amended by reg.33 of the Public Services Contracts Regulations 1993 (SI 1993/322) and now consolidated in the Public Supply Contracts Regulations 1995 (SI 1995/201)).

3–50 Where an agent deals both in contracts purely for the supply of goods and purely for the supply of services, it is arguable that the provisions of the Directive would apply only in relation to the contracts for the supply of goods, and ignore those relating to the supply of services. However, unless contracts for the supply of services are very much in the minority, rather than cope with the confusion of using a single agency agreement for all contracts, it is probably advisable to draft two separate agency agreements, one (governed by the Directive) covering contracts for the supply of goods), and one (outside the terms of the Directive) covering contracts for the supply of services. So far as the principal is concerned, the most compelling reason to adopt this approach is to make sure that the various provisions of the Directive relating to commission and compensation on termination do not apply to the contracts for the supply of services negotiated, or negotiated and concluded, by the agent.

3–51 Finally, it should be noted that although the Directive does not apply to agents for the supply of services, this is not the end of the matter. The Regulations have followed the Directive strictly in this respect so that under UK law agents for the supply of services are outside the scope of the Regulations. However, some Member States already had protection covering at least some agents for the supply of services, and others have extended their local implementation to cover such agents. For instance the Dutch implementation of the Directive also covers agents for the supply of services, except insurance agents who are covered by special legislation (further, but not exhaustive, information on this issue is contained in Appendix 2). Furthermore, there is a civil law principle of application by analogy, where a court will take a piece of legislation which applies to a particular situation or relationship and then extend the scope of that legislation by applying the principles contained in it to similar situations or relationships even though they do not fall within the express ambit of the legislation in question. Although there is no known instance of this, it would not be impossible for a court in a civil law jurisdiction to apply the local implementation of the Directive by analogy to an agency relationship for the supply of services. Taking all this into account, when considering appointing an agent for the supply of services, who is to operate in any Member State of the EC other than the UK, enquiry should be made of a local lawyer to check whether there are any local law provisions regulating such agency relationships. This should be done even if the choice of law clause specifies UK law, since the local law provisions may well have an overriding effect (see the discussion after Chapter 3.10 to 3.12).

Since this precedent follows the precedent in Chapter 2, it is drafted to **3–52** cover agency relationships for the supply of goods, and not services. It would however be possible largely to use the existing precedent for the supply of general services, simply by redefining the "Products" as the relevant services. However, not only are agency agreements solely for the supply of services (as opposed to services ancillary to products sold by the service provider, such as support or maintenance) quite rare, but in many cases (*e.g.* travel agents or financial services agents) there is special legislation regulating the relationship and requiring specially drafted agreements to deal with them. Such arrangements are outside the scope of this book.

The second limitation on the scope of the Directive relates to the type of **3–53** agency arrangement concerned. The definition in Art.1(2) of the Directive ("a self-employed intermediary who has continuing authority to negotiate the sale or purchase of goods on behalf of another person, hereinafter called the principal, or to negotiate and conclude such transactions on behalf of and in the name of the principal") does not apply to all of the types of agents referred to in Chapter 2.1. The definition would include a del credere agent, but not an agent concluding transactions on behalf of an undisclosed principal, since, in this case, the agent is clearly not negotiating and concluding the transaction "in the name of the principal". A confirming house would not fall within the definition. Although the confirming house has a right to be indemnified by the "principal" who has commissioned the purchase of the goods, the contract of purchase is concluded between the seller and the confirming house. The confirming house has not acted as agent in the conclusion of any contract between the "principal" and the seller. The Directive also specifically excludes (see Arts 1(3) and 2) directors and officers of companies in relation to their companies, members of partnerships in relation to their fellow partners, receivers, managers, liquidators or trustees in bankruptcy, unpaid commercial agents, the UK government purchasing body known as the Crown Agents for Overseas Governments and Administrations regulated under the Crown Agents Act 1979, commercial agents acting on commodity markets or exchanges, and, if an individual Member State so wishes, "those persons whose activities as commercial agents are considered secondary by the law of that Member State". Such persons are usually referred to in the UK, not quite correctly, as "secondary agents".

The exclusion of secondary agents is thus an optional matter to be **3–54** determined by each Member State. The UK decided to exclude persons whose activities as commercial agents were considered secondary, and the Regulations provide for this in Arts 2(3) and (4). Schedule 2 sets out a detailed set of principles for deciding whether the activities as commercial agent should be regarded as secondary. The Schedule (para.2) defines the primary purpose of the type of agency relationship which the Directive is intended to cover and states (para.1) "where it may reasonably be taken that the primary purpose of the arrangement with [the agent's] principal is other than that described in para.2, then the 'activities of a person as commercial agent are to be considered secondary'. Paragraph 3 then lists a number of factors, if these are present they are 'indications' that the arrangement falls within para.2 so that the agent is covered by the Directive. If these are absent, this is an 'indication to the contrary'. Paragraph 4 lists 'indications' that an arrangement does not fall within para.2 with the result that the agent is not covered by the Directive. The drafting is rather complicated, and the Guidance Notes on the Regulation issued by the DTI are not very helpful on this point, and, indeed, by implication from the judgment in *Tamarind International Ltd v Eastern Natural Gas (Retail) Ltd* [2000] Eu L.R. 708, discussed below, are probably wrong.

3–55 The Directive itself provides no guidelines, definition or preamble relating to secondary agents. Under these circumstances a submission for a ruling to the European Court as to the definition of "secondary agent" would not be possible, and the decisions of courts in the UK on the interpretation of the Schedule must therefore be final (see for instance, by way of example of the operation of this principle in another context) the European Court decision in Case C-346/93 *Kleinwort Benson Ltd v City of Glasgow District Council* [1995] All E.R. (E.C.) 514).

3–56 Some specific guidelines can be discovered in the schedule, even without a consideration of its terms as a whole. First, an agent who normally carries on business in another capacity (*e.g.* a distributor), and carries on agency activities as a "sideline", is likely to be a secondary agent. Paragraph 3(c) states that an agent who "devotes substantially the whole of his time to representative activities (whether for one principal or a number of principals whose interests are not conflicting)" is likely to fall within para.2. Thus in the opposite case, presumably, he would not. Certainly such agents who act mostly in another capacity are excluded from the scope of the legislation implementing the Directive in France).

3–57 Second, describing the relationship as one of "commercial agency" is indicative of the fact that it is not a secondary agency (see para.3(e)). This means that it is particularly important not to use the description in an agreement unless one is describing an agency relationship which is clearly governed by the Regulations. For instance, consultants or marketing representatives who are arguably below the "negotiating threshold" discussed above should never be misdescribed as "agents", still less as "commercial agents".

3–58 Third, persons who act as "order takers" only, where the customers select goods for themselves and the orders are forwarded to the principal by the agent for acceptance, are likely to be secondary agents (see para.4(c)). This would confirm the opinion expressed above that such persons could well fall below the "negotiating threshold", and thus outside the Directive, in any event.

Finally, para.5 states that mail order catalogue agents for consumer goods and consumer credit agents are presumed to be secondary agents unless the contrary is established. Reference should be made to Appendix 2 for the way secondary agents are dealt with in other Member States. **3–59**

Some guidance as to the construction of the Schedule can be found in *AMB Imballaggi Plastici Srl v Pacflex Ltd* [1999] 2 All E.R (Comm) 249, CA and *Tamarind International Ltd v Eastern Natural Gas (Retail) Ltd* [2000] Eu L.R. 708, QBD (Comm Ct). **3–60**

The Schedule was heavily criticised by Waller L.J. in *AMB v Pacflex.* However, it must be remembered that his remarks are *obiter*, as the case was decided on the grounds that Pacflex was not an agent but a distributor. In his view the Schedule had gone beyond the exclusion relating to secondary agents that was permitted by Art.2(3) of the Directive. He said: **3–61**

> "I am quite bewildered as to what is the proper construction of the Regulations and the Schedule. Article 2(3) of the Directive seems to allow a Member State to disapply the Directive where the ***activities*** [emphasis added] of the agent as agent are secondary, as compared with the rest of the agent's business ... The Schedule then seems to contemplate an assessment not of the activities of the agent as 'a commercial agent' as compared with his other business, but an assessment of ***the agent's arrangement with a principal.*** [emphasis added] That this was probably unintentional is confirmed by the Guidance Notes issued by the Department of Trade and Industry which include this paragraph in relation to the Schedule: The comparison to be made is between the agent's activities as a commercial agent and his other activities and not the relationship with the principal ... Paragraph 1 of the Schedule refers to a primary purpose 'other than as set out in paragraph 2'. But paragraph 2 does not set out a purpose: it describes aspects of the arrangement with a particular principal ... Paragraphs 3 and 4 suggest pointers are being supplied as to whether an arrangement is within paragraph 2, but provide no assistance as to what is being compared with what for the purpose of deciding what might be secondary as compared with what might be primary, nor any assistance as to whether other factors are excluded ..."

Morison J., also considered the Schedule in *Tamarind v Eastern Natural Gas*, which decided, *inter alia*, the question of whether an agent who was selling natural gas supply contracts on behalf of a gas and electricity utility company was a secondary agent. Since he had to construe the Schedule in order to reach a decision his remarks, unlike those of Waller L.J., are not *obiter*. In addition it is clear from the reports of the case, and the details of Morison J.'s judgment, that he had the benefit of much more argument by counsel on both sides with regard to the interpretation of the Schedule and also was taken through the *travaux preparatoires*, and many of the consultative documents, relating to the passing of the Directive and its implementation in the UK. All of this information does not appear to have been available to the Court in *AMB v Pacflex*, and this is understandable given that the **3–62** question of secondary agency was not central to that case in the way that it was in *Tamarind*.

3–63 Thus, for the time being, and absent any adverse decision in the Court of Appeal, the approach in *Tamarind*, and not the approach in *AMB v Pacflex*, should be taken as the correct one. The judgment in *Tamarind* is useful not only for its general points on the construction of the Schedule, but also because it gives some support for the conclusions as to the operation of the Schedule expressed above, and for its analysis of the particular provisions in the Schedule which were relevant to the facts of the case itself.

3–64 Morison J. cautioned that the Schedule should not be so widely interpreted as to frustrate the primary purpose of the Directive, but did not find that Parliament had in fact exceeded the exclusionary powers granted to it under Art.2(2). Nor does he appear to have considered the Schedule particularly difficult of construction. He said:

> "Article 2(2) permits Member States to derogate from the protection which the Directive is intended to confer on commercial agents. Such a derogation must not substantially frustrate the purpose of the Directive itself and thus in practice remove the protection that the provisions of the Directive are intended to guarantee. [see *Barbara Bellone v Yokohama SpA* (1998) E.C.R. 1–2205 and in particular the Advocate *General's* Opinion paragraph 30]...
>
> there is no yardstick in the common law which measures and defines those agents whose activities are secondary and those whose activities are not...
>
> The UK's original thoughts on this issue were that [where] the agent was wholly or mainly engaged in activities other than acting as a commercial agent he was to be regarded as outwith the provisions of the Regulations. In other words, the question whether an agent's activities were to be regarded as secondary was to be answered by looking at all the agent's activities and determining whether the agent was preponderantly acting as a commercial agent. This approach was described in argument, I think not unhelpfully, as the horizontal approach."

3–65 It can be seen that Waller L.J. regarded this "horizontal approach" as the correct one, and this explains why he considered that the Schedule as currently drafted had gone outside the scope permitted under Art.2(2). In his view the Schedule wrongly focused on the relationship between principal and agent rather than on the activities of the agent. Morison J., with the benefit of the extensive argument and his perusal of all the relevant documents appears to have had no such difficulty. He continued:

> "...the extract from Hansard shows that between publication of the draft in 1990 and the final version in 1993, there had been further consultations, which resulted in major amendments. There should, I think, be no *a priori* assumption that the Regulations, as enacted, adopted a horizontal approach. To identify the core or essential activities of an agent might

involve examining the relationship between the agent and principal: the 'vertical' approach.

What Parliament has done is to ask the court to inquire into the primary purpose of the agency agreement. That purpose is to be judged by reference to criteria specified in paragraph 2 by using and applying the indicators in paragraphs 3 and 4. In other words the Court is invited to look at the nature of the commercial bargain between the principal and agent ... by adopting this approach Parliament has properly reflected the purpose of the Directive. What the Directive is aimed at is the protection of agents by giving them a share of the goodwill which they have generated for the principal..."

It can be seen that this approach, applied to the Schedule, answers Waller L.J.'s question as to why para.1 refers to a primary purpose, while, in his view, para.2, apparently, does not do so. In order to explain the approach, it is necessary to start from the wording of Art.2(2) of the Directive. This refers to persons "whose activities ***as commercial agents*** are considered secondary". Thus the Directive does not refer to any other activities the agent may be engaged in. Instead, it invites the Member States to look at activities in the field of commercial agency and then to specify (if so desired) upon the basis of criteria to be set by that Member State (see the use of the word "considered" which enables each Member State to apply its own criteria) that certain classes of that activity are secondary. **3–66**

The legislation in the UK follows this approach. Paragraph 1 looks at "the activities of a person as commercial agent" and provides that those activities are to be considered secondary if the primary purpose of the arrangement with the principal is other than that set out in para.2. This should be understood as saying that even though a person carries on activities as a commercial agent, if those activities are incidental to, but not the primary purpose of, the arrangement with the principal, then they will be regarded as secondary and outwith the Regulations. **3–67**

It is now possible to look at para.2 and consider just what the "primary purpose" described in that paragraph really is. **3–68**

Paragraphs 2(a) and (b) start by setting the scene, as it were. The principal's business is the sale or purchase of goods of a particular kind (2(a)). Those goods are normally sold through transactions "individually negotiated and concluded on a commercial basis" (2(b)(i)). Procuring a transaction on one occasion is "likely to lead to further transactions in those goods with that customer on future occasions, or to transactions in those goods with other customers in the same geographical area or among the same group of customers" (2(b)(ii)). **3–69**

Paragraph 2 then concludes by saying that when these circumstances prevail, ("accordingly") "it is in the commercial interests of the principal in developing a market in those goods to appoint a representative to such customers with a view to the representative devoting effort, skill and expenditure from its own resources to that end". Here we find the primary purpose of the arrangement. The principal's products are of the type, and **3–70** normally sold in such a way, that there is the potential to develop a market for them (with repeat business) in a particular area or with a particular customer base. Thus the purpose of the arrangement is to appoint a representative who will devote himself to developing that market for the principal. Another way to put this is that the primary purpose of the arrangement is for the representative to generate goodwill for the principal in the relevant market for the relevant products, and this thinking can be seen in some of Morison J.'s statements in *Tamarind*:

> "Whilst it is true that most people who switched to Eastern did so because of price it would be unfair to say, as Mr Stadlen suggested, that the contracts sold themselves as the customers were being given a free lunch. Statistics do not bear this out, as only a relatively small proportion of the population were prepared to switch . . .
>
> The agents were contractually obliged to establish profitable long term relationships based upon mutual trust and understanding [the Code of Conduct]. They were allocated an area on an exclusive basis and could and did change to a different area with Eastern's agreement. The gas contracts were devised by Eastern and were not negotiable and it was Eastern's hope if not expectation that once an Eastern customer always an Eastern customer. That is why their image or brand was so important . . .
>
> I am therefore satisfied that the agency arrangements in this case fall within the Regulations. I am fortified in this view because it seems to me that in this case Eastern have received a substantial measure of future goodwill. The further transactions referred to in paragraph 2(b)(ii) do not, I think, have to be negotiated by the agent. Having marketed the gas, apparently successfully, Eastern may derive long-term benefits from their agents' efforts in developing the gas market . . ."

3–71 The last point to be made is in relation to the so-called vertical and horizontal approaches. It can be seen that on the above analysis, the emphasis is almost entirely upon the vertical approach. The question of whether the agent also carries out other activities either on his own behalf, or for the principal, or for third parties, does not seem particularly relevant. Looking at para.3(c), which at first sight does seem to apply the horizontal approach, there are two possibilities. It may be that this is a "fossil" left over from the earlier drafting when the horizontal approach was to be preferred. However, more correctly, it should really be seen as based on the assumption that, where the principal has entered into an arrangement with an agent who does not devote substantially the whole of his time to representative activities, this is at least an indication that the primary purpose of the arrangement is unlikely to be representative activity of the type falling with in para.2.

3–72 It may perhaps be asked whether the horizontal or the vertical approach is the correct reflection of the original provision in the Directive. The answer must be that, just as the exclusion itself is optional, to be adopted or not on the decision of each Member State, so are the criteria for deciding whether the activities as a commercial agent are or are not secondary. The wording of Art.2(2) of the Directive is not prescriptive in this respect, so that either a horizontal or a vertical approach would seem within its scope, depending upon the decision of each Member State, providing that, in either case, as Morison J. stated in *Tamarind* the exclusion does not go so far as to "remove the protection that the provisions of the Directive are intended to guarantee".

The last question as to the limitation of the scope of the Directive is whether it applies only to natural persons or to legal entities as well. The Directive starts off by referring to the commercial agent as a "self employed intermediary" (Art.1(1)), and throughout uses "he" or "his" when referring to the agent. There are also cases where the provisions (such as those relating to the death or retirement of the agent) have application only to a natural person. Notwithstanding this, the purpose of the Directive could so easily be frustrated if principals could avoid its provisions by requiring their agents to incorporate, it is hard to see how this can be a correct interpretation within the scope of the Directive. The Guidance Notes on the Regulation from the DTI state that the Directive (and hence the Regulations) cover legal entities. ("The expression 'self-employed' is derived from Arts 43, 47 and 48 of the EC Treaty (which deal with freedom of establishment and freedom to provide services) and is consistent with Community law, to be understood as including, for example, companies as well as self-employed individuals".) Earlier drafts to the Guidance Notes explained this issue in more detail. Draft 8/2 stated that the distinction [in Arts 42 and 57] is drawn between economic independence (whether as a natural or legal person) and the position of workers, which is governed by Art.48. It does not in any way imply that a commercial agent can only be an individual. In community terminology, even insurance companies are described as 'self-employed' (see Directive 239/73). Additional support for this contention can be found in the fact that the Crown Agents (a statutory body) are specifically excluded from the scope of the Directive. This would have been unnecessary if the Directive applied only to natural persons. **3–73**

The fact that, like the Directive, the Regulations only use personal pronouns causes no problem, because, under the Interpretation Act 1978, the use of any gender-related pronouns in legislation embraces all other such pronouns, so that within the reference to "he" or "his" is also included reference to "she", "her", "it" and "its", and so on. **3–74**

3.2.2 Term of agreement

3.2.2(a) This Agreement shall run [for a period of [three] years from [ ] [and thereafter unless or until terminated by either party giving to the other not less than [three] months prior notice in writing [such notice to expire at the end of the said period of [three] years or at any time thereafter]. **3–75**

[Such notice may be served so as to expire on any day of a month] [Such notice shall be served so as to expire only on the last day of a month]

OR

3.2.2(b) This Agreement shall run [for a period of [ ] years from [ ] and thereafter] unless or until terminated by either party giving to the other prior notice in writing of not less than the relevant period indicated below:

3.2.2.1 During the first year of this Agreement, one month's notice.

3.2.2.2 During the second year of this Agreement, two months' notice.

3.2.2.3 During the third and any subsequent year of this Agreement, three months' notice.

[Such notice may be served so as to expire on any day of a month] [Such notice shall be served so as to expire only on the last day of a month]

Articles 14 and 15 of the Directive envisage fixed and indefinite period agreements. The former expire by effluxion of time, the latter are terminable by notice (Art.15(1)). If a fixed period agreement continues to be performed by both parties after expiry of the fixed period, it is converted to an indefinite period agreement terminable by notice (Art.14). A mandatory period of notice of one month is set (Art.15(2)) for the first year, two months for the second and three months for the third and subsequent years. Member States have the option (Art.15(3)) to extend the mandatory period on the same formula up to six months for the sixth and subsequent years, but the Regulations have not adopted this option (see reg.15(2), (for the position on the other Member States see Appendix 2). The parties may agree on longer notice periods, but, if so, the period of notice to be observed by the Principal must not be shorter than that to be observed by the agent (see Art.15(4)). Unless otherwise agreed by the parties, the notice must expire at the end of a calendar month (Art.15(5)). It should be noted that where a fixed term agreement becomes converted under Art.14 into an agreement with an indefinite term terminable by notice under Art.15, the calculation to determine the mandatory notice period is based upon the length of time for which the agreement has been running from the beginning of the fixed term, not from the time the agreement was converted to one with an indefinite term.

3–76 Version (a) of this clause would comply strictly with the terms of the Regulations and the Directive either for a fixed term contract, expiring automatically by effluxion of time, if only the first part is used, or for a contract with an initial fixed term, thereafter determinable by notice, if the additional phrase in square brackets commencing "and hereafter ..." is also used, provided that where the fixed term is for three years or less, the number of months' notice to be given is (for the sake of simplicity in drafting) always specified as three (to comply with Art.15(2)), even though this would be more than required if notice of termination were served soon after the expiry of a fixed term period of less than three years.

3–77 Version (b) (without the inclusion of the first phrase in square brackets) likewise complies with the Regulations and the Directive in relation to a contract for an indefinite term, determinable only by notice. It would be possible use version (b) to cut down the required notice period to the bare minimum in the case of a contract with a fixed initial term of less than three years by adding the first phrase in square brackets so as to include an initial fixed term followed by the sliding scale. If the fixed term were for one year, cl.3.2.2.1 would be omitted and so on.

These provisions of the Directive are straightforward and easy to apply. **3–78** Hence judicial decisions on their interpretation have not so far proved necessary in the UK. The equivalent provision of the Regulations (reg.15) was applied by a Scottish Court to give an agent who received commission on the sale of bakery products a right to a three month notice of termination of his agency contract, even though there was no written provision to that effect (*King v T Tunnock Ltd* [1996] S.C.L.R. 742, Sh Ct).

There has been some discussion of the remedy available to an agent who **3–79** is given no notice or short notice of termination in violation of reg.15 and then chooses to treat such purported termination as a repudiation which he accepts, thereby terminating the contract. Under English law the remedy is likely to be damages for breach of contract measured by reference to the amount of commission that would have been earned during the period of due notice. Under Scottish law, the matter is not free from doubt, but may give rise to a right to compensation as if the agreement had not been terminated. The issue is discussed at length in *Roy v M R Pearlman Ltd* [1999] 2 C.M.L.R. 1155.

3.3 Responsibilities of the agent

3.3.1 Due diligence

3.3.1 During the period of this Agreement the Agent shall serve the Principal as **3–80** agent on the terms of this Agreement with all due and proper diligence (acting dutifully and in good faith) observe all reasonable instructions given by the Principal as to its activities under this Agreement act in the Principal's interests and use its best endeavours to increase the sale of the Products and improve the good will of the Principal in the Territory.

This general clause complies with Art.3 of the Directive. There has been some question as to whether a clause of this nature can impose stricter obligations upon the agent than ones to "act dutifully and in good faith". The clause above goes further than this with its imposition of a best endeavours obligation. Article 5 of the Directive makes Art.3(1) mandatory, in that it states that "the parties must not derogate from the provisions of Articles 3 and 4". However, the imposition of stricter obligations, or of obligations in addition to the obligations imposed by Art.3, is not a derogation from that Art.3, and thus not in breach of Art.5.

3.3.2 Proper facilities

3–81 See cl.2.3.2.

3.3.3 Market intelligence

3–82 3.3.3 The Agent shall pass on promptly to the Principal all information useful for the business of the Principal including that relating to marketing sales prospects product reliability competitor activity and unauthorised use by third parties of the Principal's trade marks patents or other intellectual or industrial property rights. The Agent shall (without prejudice to the generality of the foregoing) send to the Principal a written report on the first day of each calendar month covering any items which have arisen in the previous month relevant to the matters covered by this clause. Such a report shall also include an estimate by the Agent of likely orders for the Products during the coming two months.

The provisions of this clause conform with the obligation provided for in Art.3(2)(b) of the Directive for the agent to "communicate to the principal all the necessary information available to him".

3.3.4 Compliance with local law

3–83 See cl.2.3.4.

3.3.5 Confidentiality

3–84 See cl.2.3.5.

3.3.6 No authority to bind principal

3–85 See cl.2.3.6.

Clause 3.3.6 which attempts, together with cl.3.3.7, to restrict and exclude the power of the agent to bind the principal, is particularly important in EC and EEA Member States, given the application to these states of the Council Regulation on the Jurisdiction and the Recognition and Enforcement of Judgments in Civil and Commercial Matters (44/2001) (which has replaced the Brussels Convention) (see Chapter 1.3.5 and 1.6.3.) Normally the convention required and the Regulation now requires a defendant to be sued in the courts of the contracting state in which he is domiciled. Exceptionally, however, where there is a contract dispute arising out of the operations of a "branch, agency or establishment" the defendant may be sued in the contracting state in which that branch, agency or establishment carried on activities or (if different) in which it was registered. (See Art.5 of the Convention (now Art.5 of the Regulation) and the European Court of Justice decisions in Case C-439/93 *Lloyd's Register of Shipping v Société Campenon Bernard* [1995] All E.R. (EC) 531 and Case C-420/97 *Leathertex Divisione Sintetici SpA v Bodetex BVBA* [1999] 2 All E.R. (Comm) 769.) Clearly, an agent who can bind his principal will, under Art.5, lay the principal open to action, in the courts of the contracting state in which the agent is registered or carries on business, by the third party with whom the contract has been concluded.

3.3.7 Notification of agency status

See cl.2.3.7. **3–86**

3.3.8 Limits on exclusivity

See cl.2.3.8. **3–87**

3.3.9 Not to act outside territory

> 3.3.9 The Agent shall not without the prior consent of the Principal market or promote the Products outside the Territory during the continuance of the Agreement nor during the continuance of this Agreement [and for a period of two years after its termination] market or promote nor assist or advise in the marketing or promotion of any products which would or could compete or in any way interfere with the sale of the Products inside the Territory. **3–88**

3.3.10 Restriction on negotiating terms

> 3.3.10 The Agent shall (unless otherwise agreed) notify the Principal promptly of all requests for tenders and other prospective business and shall in all cases market and promote [and solicit requests for quotations and orders for] [and negotiate and contract on behalf of the Principal for] the sale of the Products only at the prices and only upon the terms established and notified from time to time by the Principal to the Agent. **3–89**

These clauses are compatible with the Directive. The agent has a general duty to look after the principal's interests during the agreement (see Art.3(1)) and obey reasonable instructions (see Art.3(2)(c)). This will clearly include doing business on the terms the principal describes, not handling competing goods, and not doing business outside his assigned territory. The phrase in square brackets in cl.3.3.9 imposes a period of non-competition after the termination of the agreement. The Directive (Art.20) permits a provision along these lines, provided the term of the obligation is not more than two years. Of course any such provision, and its reasonableness, particularly in relation to its length of time, has also to be tested for enforceability under the proper law of the agreement (see Art.20(1)(c)). For the position in each of the Member States reference should be made to Appendix 2.

3.3.11 Sales as a factor

3–90 See cl.2.3.11.

3.3.12 Collection of principal's monies

3–91 See cl.2.3.12.

3.3.13 Separate bank account

3–92 See cl.2.3.13.

3.3.14 Del credere guarantee

3–93 See cl.2.3.14.

3.4 Responsibilities of the principal

3.4.1 Sales literature, documentation and information

3–94 3.4.1 The Principal shall supply to the Agent free of charge a reasonable quantity of sales literature all necessary documentation relating to the Products and all information which is necessary to perform his duties to the Principal hereunder.

The provisions in this clause relating to documentation and information are required by Art.4(2)(a) and (b) of the Directive. Quite what "necessary documentation" means is unclear, particularly as the requirement to provide information would seem to cover technical or commercial details which the agent needs to know about the Products in order to sell them. Presumably, sales literature, price lists, standard form contracts, technical manuals and the like are one such class of documents. Another would be contractual documents relating to shipment of the products if the agent for some reason required them, and finally, possibly, any documents which the agent needed to establish himself as registered with local regulatory authorities to act "as agent" in relation to the products. It is probably advisable to tack on to the phrase a list of documentation and information that the Principal intends to supply so as to provide some specificity. However, since the parties cannot derogate from these provisions (Art.5) the list should be a non-exhaustive one beginning with the words "including without limitation ...". In this way, the use of a list cannot be regarded as cutting down the rights of the agent by defining those rights more narrowly than the general wording in the Directive.

3.4.2 Samples

See cl.2.4.2. **3–95**

3.4.3 Direct quotation in territory

See cl.2.4.3. **3–96**

3.4.4 Responsibility for agent's expenses

See cl.2.4.4. **3–97**

3.4.5 Advertising

See cl.2.4.5. **3–98**

3.4.6 Acceptance of orders

> 3.4.6 The Principal shall not be obliged to accept any order tender or request submitted by the Agent in the course of its activities in the Territory and shall accept the same only at its absolute discretion and only on such terms and conditions as it may consider appropriate and shall supply all Products thereunder direct to customers in the Territory. The Principal shall at the end of each month notify the Agent of all orders for the Products procured by the Agent which it has accepted or refused during that month. The Principal shall also (within seven days of the same occurring) notify the Agent of any such order accepted by the Principal which the Principal has failed to execute in accordance with its terms. **3–99**

This clause is of course only appropriate where the agent has no power to conclude orders on behalf of the principal (see Chapter 2.4.6). The first sentence of this clause is compatible with the Directive. There is a duty to pay commission on orders which are not executed because of the default of the principal (see Art.11(1) of the Directive), but this does not go so far as to impose on the principal any duty to accept orders tendered to him by the agent. The second and third sentence comply with the mandatory provisions of Arts 4(2)(b) and 4(3) of the Directive. The Directive actually requires notification "within a reasonable period"; the suggested time limits of one month and seven days would seem reasonable in most cases, but others could obviously be agreed or the phrase "within a reasonable period" used instead.

3.4.7 Payment of commission

3–100 See cl.2.4.7.

3.4.8 Sales forecasts

3–101 3.4.8 The Principal shall notify the Agent within a reasonable period of time once he anticipates that the volume of sales of the Products in the Territory will be significantly lower than that which the Agent could normally have expected.

This clause complies with Art.4(2)(b) of the Directive. The drafting is vague, copying the wording of the Directive exactly, and is probably better left so. The only way to tighten up the drafting would be to refer to the provision of sales forecasts by the principal and impose an obligation either to update these on a rolling basis (say quarterly or monthly) or to notify the agent when the principal anticipates they will not be met. Clause 3.3.3 imposes a similar obligation on the agent to notify the principal.

3.4.9 Duty to act in good faith

3–102 3.4.9 In discharging his obligations to the Agent the Principal shall act dutifully and in good faith.

This clause is required by Art.4(1), and reciprocates the agent's duties to the principal under Art.3(1) (see cl.3.3.1).

3–103 The inclusion of an obligation on the principal to act in good faith is a major change in the law of agency as understood in common law countries. The agent has always stood in a fiduciary relationship to the principal, and thus has always had at least some of the obligations towards his principal contained within a general duty to act in good faith. However, the duty of the principal at common law has always been to act in accordance with the express (and, if any, implied) terms of the contract he has entered into with the agent. The general obligation to act in good faith, as opposed to observing the terms of the relevant contract, is not a concept normally applicable to the law of contract as understood in common law jurisdictions. It is however very common and well understood in the civil law jurisdictions upon whose legislation the Directive is based (see Chapter 3.1). This change in the relationship between principal and agent has important implications which have not to date been fully assimilated by principals and agents within the UK. This will be discussed below, with special reference to termination, under Chapter 3.7.

3.5 Industrial property rights

See cl.2.5. **3–104**

3.6 Non-assignment by agent

See cl.2.6. **3–105**

3.7 Termination of agreement

3.7.1 Notwithstanding the provisions of cl.3.2 the Principal may by notice to the Agent terminate this Agreement immediately upon the happening of any one of the following events: **3–106**

3.7.1.1 If the Agent shall become bankrupt or be wound up or make any arrangement or composition with its creditors;

3.7.1.2 If the Agent shall attempt or purport to assign or transfer this Agreement in breach of cl.3.6;

3.7.1.3 If the Agent's ability to carry out its obligations hereunder is prevented or substantially interfered with for any reason whatsoever (whether or not within the control of the Agent) including without limitation by reason of any regulation law decree or any act of state or other action of a government;

3.7.1.4 If the Agent shall commit any material breach of its obligations hereunder (other than cl 3.6) and (where such breach is capable of remedy) fail to remedy such breach within thirty days of receipt of the Principal's notice specifying such breach; and

3.7.1.5 If the Agent shall become resident outside the Territory or (being a company) shall change its place of registration or have its ownership or control altered without the prior consent of the Principal.

3.7.2 Termination of this Agreement shall not affect the rights and liabilities of either party subsisting at the date of termination. **3–107**

3.7.3(a) Termination of this Agreement whether under cll.3.2 or 3.7 [or expiry of this Agreement by effluxion of time] shall not entitle the Agent to any compensation, indemnity, damages or other payment in respect of such termination [or expiry] [except to the extent that the governing law of this Agreement provides for the same]. **3–108**

OR

3.7.3(b) Termination of this Agreement whether under cll.3.2 or 3.7 [or expiry of this Agreement by effluxion of time] shall not entitle the Agent to any compensation, indemnity, damages or other payment in respect of such termination [or expiry] except that if the Agent is a commercial agent to whom the Commercial Agents (Council Directive) Regulations 1993 (SI 1993/3053) apply, then in the circumstances of a termination in respect of which the Agent is entitled to either compensation or indemnity under Art.17(1) of the said Regulations, then, pursuant to Art.17(2) of the said Regulations, and subject to and in accordance with the provisions of the said Regulations, the Agent and the Principal agree that the Agent shall be entitled to [an indemnity in terms of Art.17(3)(4) and (5)] [to compensation in terms of Art.17(6) and (7)] of the said Regulations.

OR

3.7.3(c) The parties acknowledge that the Agent is a commercial agent to whom the Commercial Agents (Council Directive) Regulations 1993 (SI 1993/3053) apply, and hereby agree that in the circumstances of a termination in respect of which the Agent is entitled to compensation or indemnity under Art.17(1) of the said Regulations, then, pursuant to Art.17(2) of the said Regulations, and subject to and in accordance with the provisions of the said Regulations, the Agent shall be entitled to [an indemnity in terms of Art.17(3)(4) and (5)] [to compensation in terms of Art.17(6) and (7)] of the said Regulations.

OR

3.7.3(d) Termination of this Agreement whether under cll.3.2 or 3.7 [or expiry of this Agreement by effluxion of time] shall not entitle the Agent to any compensation, indemnity, damages or other payment in respect of such termination [or expiry] except that the parties acknowledge that the Agent is a commercial agent to whom the Commercial Agents (Council Directive) Regulations 1993 (SI 1993/3053) apply, and hereby agree that in the circumstances of a termination in respect of which the Agent is entitled to compensation or indemnity under Art.17(1) of the said Regulations, then, pursuant to Art.17(2) of the said Regulations, and subject to and in accordance with the provisions of the said Regulations, the Agent shall be entitled to [an indemnity in terms of Art.17(3)(4) and (5)] [to compensation in terms of Art.17(6) and (7)] of the said Regulations.

This clause contains the events in which termination of the agreement would be desirable from the point of view of the principal. A combination of Arts 15 and 16 of the Directive restrict termination without notice to some extent. Article 15(2) prescribes that the parties may not agree on periods of notice shorter than those prescribed therein. Article 16, however, does permit immediate termination where, under the law of the relevant Member State, provision is made for immediate termination because of (a) the failure of one party to carry out all or part of its obligations or (b) where exceptional circumstances arise. Clauses 3.7.1, 3.7.1.2, 3.7.1.3, and cl.3.7.1.4, appear to be covered by (a) above and cl.3.7.1.1 by (b). Clause 3.7.1.5 causes more difficulty. It is not clear that any of the events there automatically result in failure to carry out the agent's obligations, nor whether they are exceptional circumstances which result in termination of the agreement under law (the Regulations, for instance, refer to "any enactment or rule of law which provides for the immediate termination of the agency contract" (see reg.16). One partial way around the problem would be to draft an express obligation that the agent may not change his residence and terminate under (a) if this is breached. Such a method could not apply to a limited company in relation to change of control unless the obligation were to be imposed on its shareholders as parties to the agreement.

Finally, with regard to termination without notice for failure to perform, it should be remembered that only such termination as is permitted under the general law of the Member State concerned is covered by Art.16. This means that, in most cases, as under English law, a substantial breach or failure would be required to justify immediate termination. Thus there is little point in drafting in a great many detailed obligations and providing that each one of them is of the essence. This being so, cl.3.7.1.4 refers only to material breaches. In any event, the principal's obligation to act in good faith (see cl.3.4.9) would probably mean that an attempt to terminate the agreement on a technicality (however strict the wording of the clause) would put the principal in material breach of his obligations and give rise to a cause of action for the agent. For instance, if a sales target were imposed upon the agent, and the principal terminated the agreement for failure to fulfil the target, even if the obligation to fulfil the target was stated to be of the essence, the principal would still be bound to act in good faith. He could not terminate the agreement if there was a good reason, outside the agent's control, for failure to fulfil the target, even if the agreement did not contain a force majeure clause excusing performance in those circumstances. Further, he could not terminate the agreement if the agent had materially fulfilled the target, but missed it by a trivial amount. **3–109**

In this connection, the cases of *Duffen v Frabo SpA (No.1)*, [1999] E.C.C. 58, CA, and *Duffen v Frabo (No.2)* [2000] E.C.C. 61, Central London CC, support the contention (in line with the ordinary provisions of contract law) that the right to terminate an agency contract without notice is available to a principal only in the event of a material breach by the agent. Otherwise, such a termination amounts to an unlawful repudiation of the contract which the agent is free to accept so as to bring the contract to an end to enable him to claim under the Regulations. **3–110**

In *Duffen v Frabo (No.2)* HH Hallgarten, Q.C. said: "But can it be said that the claimant's conduct ... was repudiatory or, more precisely, that such represented breaches which were so serious as to be incapable of remedy, *i.e.* were irremediable? In this regard it has to be remembered that the Agreement contained its own code covering termination, set out in cll.6.2.1 and 6.4, and in my view each of these breaches or apparent breaches was capable of being remedied, and thus the claimant cannot, as at the date when he purported to terminate the Agreement, be regarded as being in repudiation". **3–111**

The way in which the various Member States treat the requirement to justify immediate terminations are detailed in Appendix 2, but broadly, they all cover material breach, *force majeure* or impossibility of performance and, in most cases, insolvency. **3–112**

The Directive provides for the alternative remedies of either indemnity or compensation upon termination of the agency agreement, and clearly version (a) of cl.3.7.3. is not incompatible with this scheme. Indemnity or compensation is payable when the agency relationship terminates or expires by effluxion of time, for whatever reason, subject to the exceptions listed in **3–113**

Art.18 (discussed below). They should thus be looked at almost exactly like compensation under unfair dismissal or redundancy legislation, rather than as provisions whose purpose is to penalise the principal for an unlawful termination.

3–114 There was considerable discussion in the UK as to whether the remedy of compensation applied when an agency agreement expired by effluxion of time. Although the situation has clarified as to the status of the remedies of indemnity and compensation, even as late as 1999, in *Whitehead v Jenks & Cattell Engineering Ltd* [1999] Eu L.R. 827, it was still held, on an interlocutory hearing, that, although the Deputy Judge at an Order 14 hearing had considered that Art.17 applied in the event of an expiry by effluxion of time, there was an arguable case that this was not so.

3–115 The more recent Scottish case of *Frape v Emreco Ltd* [2002] S.L.T 271, was decided upon the basis that compensation was payable upon expiry by effluxion of time. Given Morland J.'s statement in *Ingmar GB Limited v Eaton Leonard Inc.* [2001] Eu L.R. 755, QBD, discussed below, that he regarded himself as bound by Scottish decisions on the Regulations, since Parliament had clearly intended that the regime in the Regulations should be applied uniformly throughout the UK, this case settled the matter for English courts as well. Lord McEwan said:

> "I am firmly of the opinion that I am compelled by authority and by the need to give commercial sense and effect to the regulations to interpret them in a way that will allow the pursuer compensation. This means, as I have said, giving a wide purposive meaning to the word 'termination' ... In the present case that means, and I so decide, that the word is habile to cover contracts which expire through the effluxion of time. In common sense it seems to me that such an interpretation does no serious violence to the word 'termination'. Apart from the broad general principles laid down by the European cases, which have to be treated with great respect, the authority of *Whitehead* is eloquent and persuasive of the proper way forward. I am impressed by the carefully worded decision of the deputy judge and adopt it and follow it. I cannot improve on her analysis on p 11 of the copy supplied. In so doing I consider I am following the 'purposive' approach laid down by Lord Oliver in *Litster*"

3–116 The latest English case, *Tigana Limited v Decoro Limited* [2003] E.W.H.C. 23 QBD, in which judgment was given on February 3, 2003, by Davis J. has followed *Frape*. After a detailed analysis of the construction of the Directive and the Regulations the learned judge concluded:

> "In my judgment, therefore, all the intrinsic indications are that the phrase 'termination of the agency contract' in Regulation 17 extends to agency contracts which have expired by effluxion of time. But if there be adopted what is called a purposive approach to construction—and after all the court is positively required to seek to construe the Agency Regulations to accord with the Directive—then that conclusion is confirmed,"

The Commission originally agreed to the incorporation of alternative remedies on the basis that all of the Member States could not agree on one remedy. Article 17(6) requires the Commission to submit a report to the Council on the operation of Art.17, for the purpose of assessing the practical consequences of the two options, and to decide if one option or the other is more advantageous to the agent. If necessary, after enquiry, Art.17(6) requires the Commission to submit a proposal to the Council to amend the Directive in this respect. The Commission sought information from interested parties during 1995 and delivered its Report on the Application of Article 17 of the Council Directive on the Coordination of the Laws of the Member States relating to Self-Employed Commercial Agents (86/653/EEC) on July 23, 1996 (COM(96) 364). The Report shows, as does the research of Appendix 2, that there is more disparity and confusion about the implementation of the Directive than might appear at first sight. The Report concluded that currently there was very little jurisprudence concerning the Directive, and it appeared there was a need for clarification of Art.17, but that any more far-reaching conclusions were premature, so that no change in the Directive was suggested. The Report contains much useful information, and, if read in conjunction with the survey in Appendix 2, provides a very complete picture of the status of the application of the Directive within the EC prior to its enlargement in May 2004. It will be referred to in the rest of this chapter from time to time as the "Commission Report". **3–117**

As stated above, the Directive provides two possible remedies, indemnity or compensation. Article 17(1) states that each of the Member States shall "take measures necessary to ensure that the commercial agent...is indemnified in accordance with paragraph 2, or compensated in accordance with paragraph 3". Initially most commentators in the UK read this provision as meaning that, when implementing the Directive, each Member State had to choose to implement either indemnity under Art.17(2) or compensation under Art.17(3). All of the Member States except the UK have interpreted Art.17(1) this way, and opted either for compensation or indemnity. Consequently when the time came for implementation in the UK the DTI were inundated with representations from various interest groups as to which alternative should be chosen. The DTI finally, and to many people's surprise, chose a very elegant way out of resolving the situation. They did not interpret Art.17(1) as requiring them to decide which alternative the agent should have available to him in the UK and then to implement that alternative by legislation. Instead, they interpreted Art.17 as requiring (or at least permitting) them merely to ensure that the agent always had available one or the other alternative, but leaving the choice of which alternative to the parties when they negotiated the specific agency agreement in each case. It must be said, elegant though this solution may be, many commentators have questioned whether this is yet another instance of the UK failing to implement a Directive properly. Only time, and reference to the European Court, will tell whether this is so. However, the Commission Report does not take the view that the UK has failed to implement the Directive properly, nor, currently has there been any legal challenge as to this method of implementing Art.17. **3–118**

3–119 The DTI's solution is implemented by reg.17(1). Regulation 17(2) then provides that, unless the parties choose otherwise, the agent shall be compensated rather than indemnified. Thus within the UK the use of version (a) of cl.3.7.3 would result in the agent becoming entitled to compensation rather than indemnity.

3–120 The question of alternative remedies under reg.17 was considered in the Scottish Case of *Hardie Polymers Ltd v Polymerland Ltd* [2002] S.C.L.R. 64, Outer House. Hardie sought compensation in accordance with reg.17 for the termination of a commercial agency agreement without cause, but after due notice. Polymerland argued that the agreement, properly interpreted, provided for indemnity rather than compensation and the words "compensation after termination" in cl.10 of the agency agreement meant no more than "termination payment". Hardie argued that the default remedy was compensation in terms of reg.17(2) and that this remedy would be rendered unavailable if indemnity was determined to be the intention of the agreement. The Court held that notwithstanding the use of the word "compensation" there was sufficient clarity to conclude that the intention of the agreement was the remedy of indemnity, and that Hardie consequently were excluded from claiming compensation. The approach of the court in this case shows the importance of clear drafting to ensure that there is no dispute as to which of the two remedies is to be applied. On the other hand it also shows that in appropriate cases the mere use of the word "compensation" is not sufficient to give rise to the particular right of compensation under reg.17.

3–121 Given this discussion, it is necessary to be more specific in drafting termination clauses in agreements which are governed by one of the systems of law in force in the UK. Versions (b) (c) and (d) of cl.3.7.3 deal with this issue. Version (b) is drafted from the point of view of the principal, so that the fact that compensation is only payable in those cases where the Regulations actually provide for it is stated explicitly. The drafting of version (b) is such that it does not actually acknowledge that the agent is covered by the Regulations at all. Thus in the event of a claim for compensation the agent has to get over the initial hurdle of showing that he is a commercial agent entitled to protection in the first place. Version (c) is drafted from the point of view of the agent, so that both parties acknowledge from the outset that he is entitled to the benefit of the Regulations in respect of a relevant termination. Version (c), given that it favours the agent, is also silent on the circumstances in which the agent is not entitled to compensation on termination, leaving this to be dealt with by the Regulations themselves. Of course, a compromise position would be to take the first part of version (b) and combine it with version (c). This is set out as version (d). It should be noted that each version specifies either compensation or indemnity as required. This is not strictly required by Art.17(2) since silence will be taken to mean that the parties opt for compensation. Thus, in this sense, as stated above, version (a) would still comply with the Regulations and result in compensation for the agent in the case of an applicable termination. However, it is much better to spell matters out as in versions (b) (c) or (d) to avoid the confusion that the parties suffered in *Hardie Polymers Ltd v Polymerland Ltd.*

Article 18 provides for exceptions to the agent's entitlement to a remedy, broadly where the termination or failure to renew is caused by a default or voluntary act of the agent. First, the agent is not entitled to a remedy where the principal has terminated because of a default of the agent which would, under the relevant governing law, entitle him to terminate the agreement immediately. Second, no remedy is available where the agent has voluntarily resigned his agency (*i.e.* he has not done so because of any breach of the agreement by the principal), *unless* (if a natural person) the occasion of termination was the retirement of the agent due to age, infirmity or ill health. Finally, Art.18 provides that where the agent has, with the agreement of the principal, assigned the agency to another person, he is not entitled to a remedy, presumably because the assignee will have paid the agent for the assignment of the agency. **3–122**

The entitlement to compensation or indemnity is also triggered by the death of the agent (Art.17(4)). Where the agent is not a natural person, there is no suggestion that the liquidation of a company is equivalent to death and therefore attracts compensation. On the contrary, liquidation would be one of the events where immediate termination of the agreement without compensation was justified under general law (see cl.3.7.1.1). **3–123**

When the agent is a limited company, with a sole, or at most, a few shareholders, who actually run the business, the question arises as to whether compensation or indemnity is also payable in the event that the company ceases to act as agent because these individuals die or retire by reason of age, infirmity or ill health. Neither the Directive nor the Regulations provide that this is the case. Given the usual strict interpretation of legislation in the common law jurisdictions, it seems unlikely that such an argument would prevail in the UK in regard to a claim brought under the Regulations. However, this is not to say that a court in some civil law jurisdiction might not proceed by analogy with the relevant local implementation of the Directive to provide a remedy in this case, since the spirit of the Directive would suggest that if a sole trader or a partnership should receive indemnity or compensation in these circumstances it seems hard that he or they should be deprived of a remedy just because of the fact of incorporation. **3–124**

In all cases, the agent loses the right to compensation or indemnity if "within one year following the termination of the [agency] contract he has not notified the principal that he intends pursuing his entitlement" (Art.17(5)). The wording in the Regulations (reg.17(9)) is identical. There is no indication that service of a writ is required, nor is the form of notice prescribed. In theory any form of notice (including an oral one) should suffice. This issue was considered in *Hackett v Advanced Medical Computer Systems Ltd* [1999] C.L.C 160, QBD, where the agent's solicitor sent a letter stating his client's intention to claim compensation. The court said that in applying the Regulations unnecessary formality should be avoided. It was not necessary to give precise details of the particular regulation under which **3–125** he was applying. It was enough to indicate an intention to pursue a claim, and the solicitor's letter was adequate to do this.

3–126 However, for evidentiary purposes, a notice in writing, with some proof of actual receipt, should be served. It is not necessary to follow the procedure and form set out in the notice clause (if any) in the agency agreement, (since the agreement has expired, and the clause can have no further effect), unless there is an express survival provision keeping the notice clause in force after termination of the contract. For safety's sake, the form and procedure of any notice clause could well be followed, but care should be taken with provisions in the clause which deem receipt to have occurred in circumstances where actual receipt has not taken place. First of all it is unclear that a deemed receipt would satisfy the wording of Art.17(5) or reg.17(9), given the use of the word "notified" in both provisions. Second, unless the notice clause has survived the termination of the agreement and is still in force, the deeming provisions will have no legal effect. Finally, the provision covers a notice served "within one year following the termination" of the agency agreement. It is unclear whether a notice served before the termination of the agreement, perhaps in anticipation of a threatened termination, would fall within the clause. Therefore, even where the agent has already notified the principal of his intention to claim in the event that termination actually occurs, a formal notification should also be made after the termination has occurred.

3–127 It should be noted that although there can be no derogation from the agent's rights to damages or compensation under the agency agreement, such derogation is permitted after its termination (Art.19). This allows the parties to arrive at a negotiated and legally binding settlement (after termination of the relationship, but not before in *anticipation* of termination) at something less than what may be the agent's full rights (if he went to law).

3–128 The drafting of cl.3.7.3. now needs to be considered in the light of these provisions of the Directive. Immediate termination under 3.7 does not give rise to a right to a remedy under the Directive, but both termination by notice (except where the agent resigns or passes on the agreement to a third party as described above), and expiry by effluxion of time, do. Clause 3.7.3 therefore complies with the Directive. Version (a) makes no reference to the circumstances under which the Directive provides for compensation or indemnity. This is left to the operation of the relevant local law. However, should one wish to choose indemnity rather than compensation, following the discussion below, versions (b) (c) or (d) should be used as appropriate.

3–129 The details of the remedy of indemnity are set out in Art.17(2). This provides for an indemnity upon termination of the agency relationship if, and to the extent that, the agent has brought new customers or significantly increased the volume of business for the principal, the principal continues to derive "substantial benefits from such customers", and the payment of the indemnity is equitable in all the circumstances. The indemnity is capped at one year's purchase of the average annual remuneration of the agent over the past five years or over the life of the agency agreement, if shorter. There are thus three key conditions to the payment of an indemnity-generation of new customers and/or new business by agent, continued enjoyment by the principal of substantial benefits from those new customers and/or that new business and equity.

The remedy of indemnity is copied from the German Civil Code, consequently the method of calculation used in Germany provides valuable guidance. The Commission Report regards this method as the correct one to be used, and explains it in detail. Although the Nordic countries and Austria have now tended to follow the German method, this is not the case in other Member States and there are some wide disparities. The position in each of the Member States is set out in Appendix 2. However, it must be said that a careful reading of Art.17(2) supports the use of the German method, and for this reason, an explanation of it is set out below. Reference should be made to the Commission Report for a detailed worked example which the Commission clearly hoped Member States would follow in the future. **3–130**

The German calculation works as follows: one must first separate out, from old customers and the existing level of business, the new customers and the increased level of business from old customers which the agent has generated in his time acting for the principal. One must then look forward and decide what sort of benefit the principal will continue to derive in the future from the new customers and the increased business from old customers (see Art.17(2)(a) para.1). If it is "substantial", one then goes on to quantify how long those benefits will last, and the rate at which the benefits will decrease as customers move away ("migration"). With these parameters in place, a volume of business for the principal into the future can be calculated, and then the indemnity *prima facie* to be paid to the agent will, in practice, be the commission that he would have earned on this business, less a discount for accelerated payment in a lump sum. This figure is then adjusted (although this rarely happens in practice) to take account of any surrounding circumstances that would make it "equitable" (*i.e.* fair) that he receive more or less than this (see reg.17(2)(a) para.2). **3–131**

One such circumstance which (under Art.17(2)(a) para.2) Member States had the option as to whether or not to specify, was the "application or otherwise of a restraint of trade clause within the meaning of Article 20". This point seems to go either to mitigation or to the value of the benefit enjoyed by the principal once the agreement has been terminated. So far as mitigation goes, it could be argued that if the agent is prevented from working in whole or in part by such a clause it is clearly "equitable" that he receive an enhanced indemnity because of this. If he is not so prevented then he will have greater opportunity to make a living elsewhere, and thus, perhaps, it may be equitable, in the particular circumstances of the case, that the payment under the indemnity be reduced. So far as valuation of the benefit enjoyed by the principal is concerned, this will be enhanced if there is a non-compete clause, since the agent will be unable to compete with his former principal, and diminished if there is no such clause and the principal is vulnerable to competition. **3–132**

The UK has not chosen to include this option in the Regulations. However, the fact that the Directive contemplates this as a situation where **3–133** an enhanced or reduced indemnity may be payable does suggest that (irrespective of any express provision in the Regulations), where the agent has found another agency, or was free to have done so but made no attempt to look for one, it could well be argued that it would be equitable to reduce the indemnity. The situation in regard to taking account of such clauses in other Member States is set out in Appendix 2.

3–134 Once the amount of the indemnity has been calculated as above, then it is subject to the cap, (Art.17(2)(b)) and cut off at the cap if it is higher. It is important to realise that the formula in Art.17(2)(b) does not act as a formula for calculating the amount paid to the agent. This is done as described above under Art.17(2)(a). The formula is only used for calculating the cap itself. The cap takes account of all forms of payment, not just commission, and it is based on all customers, not just new customers or those whose business has increased. Because of this, awards in Germany rarely reach the cap unless the agent has generated all or nearly all of the customers.

3–135 As the alternative to this indemnity, under Art.17(3) the agent can seek compensation for the damage he suffers as a result of the termination of his relations with the principal. Such damage is particularly deemed to occur in circumstances where "the termination deprives him of the commission which proper performance of the agency contract would have procured him, while at the same time the principal enjoys substantial benefits following such termination out of the agent's activities prior to such termination", and/or where the agent is not able (by the time of termination) to amortise the costs and expenses that he incurred for the performance of the agency agreement on the principal's advice during the period of the agency agreement. In this connection it is important that the principal insert a clause like cl.3.4.4 so that the principal can have some control over the way these expenses build up over the course of the agreement, to ensure that he is not met with an excessive bill for unamortised expenditure upon termination of the relationship.

3–136 Compensation has been adopted only by France, the UK, Iceland and Ireland. The Directive included the remedy, because compensation has long been the remedy available to agents under local French law. It is important to realise that the term "compensation" has a special meaning in French law, and is the subject of a great deal of jurisprudence. The remedy of compensation considers the "damage" the agent suffers as a result of the "termination of his relations with the principal". The term "damage" should not be interpreted as "damages for breach of contract" but as "loss". For this reason compensation is payable, like the indemnity, whether the agency agreement has been terminated because of a breach by the principal, or by due service of notice as provided under the agreement. Contrary to what some commentators suggested in the past, it is payable in the event that a fixed term contract expires and is not renewed.

3–137 The agent is compensated because he has lost the agency through no fault of his own, not because the principal is necessarily in breach of the agreement by terminating or refusing to renew it. The remedy of compensation is not subject to any cap, and, subject to the fact that the agent will not be able to recover twice for the same loss, a concurrent claim would also lie to recover damages for any breach of contract committed by the agent. This analysis is based purely on an examination of the wording of Art.17(3), but it is borne out by an examination of the way compensation is calculated in France. Since this remedy was available in France before the implementation of the Directive, and the Directive gives no guidelines on how to calculate compensation, the courts have simply continued to follow the previous guidelines and decisions.

Awards are calculated as between one to two years' gross remuneration based on the average of the last three years. Normal awards are for two years but courts retain a discretion to award less (not usually below one year) where the principal shows the agent's loss was in fact less. The courts will also award more if the agent shows his loss was greater because of age or length of service. **3–138**

The payment is seen as representing the cost to any successor of purchasing the agency agreement, based on its goodwill value, or as compensating the agent for the period of time it would take the agent to reconstitute the client base he has lost. Compensation is for the loss crystallised at the moment of termination. Future developments are not taken into account, such as the principal ceasing to trade, or the agent continuing to work with the same clients or developments in the market place. The fact that termination has arisen because of the expiry by effluxion of time of a fixed term contract is also irrelevant; compensation is still payable in the same amount. Further, the agent is not required to mitigate his loss. **3–139**

Additionally a claim can be raised for damages at law for premature termination of the contract, the award being calculated by identifying the period during which the contract would have continued (if not prematurely terminated) and then awarding an amount equal to the commission earned in the identical period in the previous year, or the average of the amount received in that period in the two previous years, whichever is the higher. **3–140**

It is not really possible to say that one remedy is to be preferred over the other, since everything depends upon the circumstances of the particular relationship, the way in which termination has occurred, and whether one is advising the principal or the agent. However, the two remedies do have significant differences. The indemnity can be characterised as a more restrictive remedy than compensation. **3–141**

Entitlement to the indemnity arises only if the three key conditions described above are satisfied, and it is subject to a cap. On the other hand, the agent is entitled to compensation on a general basis for loss he suffers merely because the agency relationship has ceased, and there is no cap on the amount that may be claimed. The instances for which the agent may be compensated under Art.17(3), are particular examples, but do not limit the generality of the right to compensation under the first paragraph of Art.17(3). In this sense, even though the element of "substantial benefit" is present in the remedy of compensation, it is not a limiting factor in the same sense as the key condition of "substantial benefit" found in the remedy of indemnity. **3–142**

3–143 The remedy of indemnity examines the state of the agent's activities at the date of termination, uses this data to calculate what benefits the principal will enjoy in the future as a result of these activities and then gives the agent a fair share of those benefits. On the other hand, the remedy of compensation looks not at what the principal has gained, but what the agent has lost because of termination of the relationship. It is true that one factor which can be taken into account is the lost commission that the agent would have received upon business the principal will enjoy in the future because of the agent's activities. However, this factor is not a key condition to entitlement as it is for an indemnity. It is quite possible that there may, in fact, be no benefits accruing to the principal, but this will not deprive the agent of compensation for loss actually suffered (*e.g.* unamortised expenditure), or, for the loss of future business and new customers (which will now never materialise) which he could have reasonably hoped to achieve if the relationship had continued.

3–144 On the basis of the above discussion, it would seem as if the items for which the agent will receive payment under the remedy of indemnity are only a subset of the items for which a claim can be made under the remedy of compensation. Given this, together with the cap and the need to fulfil the three key conditions under the remedy of indemnity, *prima facie* indemnity appears to be the remedy which favours the principal, and compensation the remedy which favours the agent. There is, however, one significant issue which remains to be discussed.

3–145 Article 17(2)(c) and reg.17(5) state that "the grant of an indemnity shall not prevent the commercial agent from seeking damages". In this phrase the word "damages" is to be interpreted as damages awarded at law for breach of contract. Thus, to the extent that the indemnity does not compensate the agent for damage suffered for breach of contract, a claim for damages will lie in addition to the claim for indemnity, (subject to no double recovery), and the cap on the indemnity will have no application in relation to the claim for damages.

3–146 Leaving aside simple situations like a claim for commission due but not paid to the agent on termination, under Art.4(1) the principal has an obligation to act towards the agent in good faith. Arguably, a termination of the agency agreement in bad faith (whether for an immaterial breach, by service of contractual notice or failure to renew an expired fixed term agreement) could be a breach of that obligation for which the agent could claim damages, in addition to the indemnity. Another ground for a claim in damages would be misrepresentation in relation to unamortised expenditure where it was incurred upon the advice of the principal. It could be persuasively argued in many cases that the agent only incurred the expenditure on the basis of an express or implied representation from the principal that the agency agreement would last long enough for the expenditure to be recovered.

3–147 If these arguments are correct, there would in practice in such a case be little difference between the two remedies. The agent could not only look forward (under the indemnity) to be compensated for future business which the principal actually enjoys as a result of his activities, but he could also look backward (under the claim for termination in bad faith) to claim unamortised expenditure and then also forward again (subject to no double recovery) to claim loss of anticipated future profits.

The arguments about termination in bad faith as stated above have not yet been approved by any court in the UK. (It is however noteworthy that the facts in *Duffen v Frabo SpA (No.1)*, [1999] E.C.C. 58, CA and *Duffen v Frabo SpA (No.2)* [2000] E.C.C. 61, Central London CC, came at least close to a possible breach of good faith on the part of the principal, but the point was never taken by the agent, nor considered by the courts.) However, there are some indications from other jurisdictions that this may be well founded. **3–148**

In Germany, the legislation provides for the concurrent remedies (although there can be no double recovery) of an indemnity (capped as under the Directive) on a no fault basis (s.89b of the Commercial Code) together with a claim (where applicable) for damages for breach of contract, (s.89a of the Commercial Code). This claim for damages can include a claim for loss of profits or for the fact that an agreement has been terminated by the principal prematurely in an unlawful manner (*e.g.* without giving proper notice). It can also include a claim for damages in relation to express or implied misrepresentation by the principal which has caused the agent to incur expenditure which has not been recovered at the time the relationship is terminated. There is also the possibility (though only in extreme and quite special cases) that damages could lie in addition to the indemnity where the termination can be demonstrably shown to be in bad faith. One possibility is where, although the agreement is terminable by notice, or for a fixed term, the principal has expressly or by implication represented to the agent that he will continue the agreement and not terminate it in accordance with its terms, and the agent has acted in reliance on this to his detriment. The situation is similar in other Member States and is set out in detail in Appendix 2. In particular the situation in Portugal and Spain supports the arguments set out above. On looking at these cases through the eyes of a common law lawyer, it is clear that, quite apart from questions of breach of good faith, a UK court could well provide concurrent remedies to that of indemnity relying on the legal principles relating to misrepresentation or equitable estoppel. This is the practice in Australia (see Chapter 13.2.8). **3–149**

The particular point of termination in bad faith is also considered in France. Increased compensation may be awarded to the agent if the court considers that the termination was "abusive", for instance if the agent can show that there was some element of malice or unfairness in the circumstances of the termination. **3–150**

The practice in France will be unlikely to help increase an award of compensation under the Regulations, since UK law rarely provides for penal damages, as opposed to compensatory awards, and is unlikely to do so in this case. Nevertheless, where parties subject to the Regulations have chosen indemnity as the remedy, the French practice could certainly reinforce a claim for damages caused by the termination in breach of the obligation of good faith (abusive) to the extent that the loss suffered was not recovered because of the cap on the indemnity. **3–151**

3–152 As an example of a similar line of legal reasoning, most of the law in the US which protects employees from unfair dismissal is based upon the concept that a termination (short of retirement age) without cause is a breach of the duty of good faith which an employer owes to an employee under the contract of employment. The employee is entitled to compensation for the loss of his employment caused by the breach of that duty of good faith. This concept has also been applied under some of the US Sales Representative Laws which are discussed in detail in Chapter 17.

3–153 In all of the EC except the UK, the question of the difference between the remedy of indemnity and the remedy of compensation is largely an academic one. The Member States have all chosen one remedy or the other, and that is an end of the matter. The only possible relevance in these circumstances is the question of forum shopping, which may in some cases enable the agent to pick a jurisdiction where the remedy he prefers will be available. This is discussed in more detail under Chapter 3.10 to 3.12.

3–154 Within the UK however, it is vital to understand the differences between the two remedies, since the parties are free to choose one or the other under their contract. Unfortunately, the law in the UK, given the relatively recent implementation date of the Regulations, was slow to develop, since both of the remedies, indemnity and compensation, were based on concepts foreign to the common law. There is now, however, substantial guidance from judicial decisions as to the way these remedies should be applied, and the amounts payable under them calculated.

3–155 The questions relating to the implementation of Art.17 under reg.17 have now been considered in a number of cases before the UK courts. Many of them have come before the Scottish courts, but it appears that by and large the English courts will feel bound by the findings of Scottish Courts of an appropriate relevant seniority given that the Regulations apply to the UK as a whole, and it would be undesirable for different interpretations to prevail in different parts of the UK. An authoritative expression on this point can be seen in Morland J.'s statement in *Ingmar GB Limited v Eaton Leonard Inc.* [2001] Eu L.R. 755, QBD:

> "In my judgment in so far as the Court of Session interpreted the purpose of the Regulations and enunciated principles of law I am and should be bound by the decision of the Inner House as a first instance judge. The Regulations expressly 'govern the relations between commercial agents and their principals and. . .apply in relation to the activities of commercial agents in Great Britain'. Separate and identical regulations apply to Northern Ireland. Clearly it would be undesirable that different principles of law were applied in relation to compensation in England and Wales from Scotland."

3–156 The first case to consider the Regulations was *Page v Combined Shipping and Trading Ltd* [1997] 3 All E.R. 656, CA. This case related to interlocutory proceedings and it was not necessary for the Court to make any real determinations as to the effect of the Directive and Regulations. However, the

Court in general accepted that there was at least "a good arguable case" that the Directive and hence the Regulations introduced a new regime which "not only provides for compensation for the lawful termination of the agency contract but lays down its own measure of compensation" (*per* Millet L.J.).

The next case to consider the Regulations was *Duncan Moore v Piretta PTA Limited* [1998] E.C.C. 392, QBD, where Mitting J., considered the Regulations in general and the remedy of indemnity in particular. To date this is the only case to have considered in detail the remedy of indemnity. First, he laid down the following basic principle as to the interpretation of the Regulations which has, with one or two minor exceptions, been followed in all subsequent cases on the Regulations: **3–157**

> "The duty of an English court in construing the regulations is to give effect to the manifest purpose of the Directive under which the regulations are made. So much is clear from the judgment of the House of Lords in *Litster v Forth Dry Dock Company Ltd* [1990] 1 AC 546. ... I therefore look to the preamble to the Directive to ascertain its purpose....It is apparent from the preamble that the primary purpose of the Directive is the harmonisation of community law by requiring all Member States to introduce rights and duties similar to those already subsisting in at least two of the Member States of the Community, Germany and France.... Consistent with the purpose of achieving harmony between Member States, it is in my judgment permissible to look into the law and practice of the country in which the relevant right, in this case the right to indemnity, originated, namely Germany; and to do so for the purpose of construing the English regulations and to use them as a guide to their application. The practice in other countries where the rights appear to be new, for example Italy, seem to me to be of less assistance."

In this case, the learned judge then applied the principles followed under German law to the remedy of indemnity under reg.17. The case is useful for its careful analysis of the remedy of indemnity and as a model of the way in which calculation of the amount payable under this remedy should be made. The case is also helpful in deciding certain other points in relation both to the application of the remedy of indemnity and the construction of the Regulations in general. **3–158**

First, the Regulations do to some extent have a retrospective effect. Mitting J. held: **3–159**

> "Regulation 23(1) applies the regulations to contracts, whenever made, which are in existence on 1 January 1994....There is nothing in the words of Regulation 17 to limit the indemnity to customers brought in after 1 January 1994; nor does Regulation 23(2) have that effect because no rights or liabilities in relation to an indemnity had accrued before 1 January 1994. Nor are the regulations truly retrospective, as they would be if, for example, they had provided that on a termination of an agency agreement before 1 January 1994 the agent was entitled to an indemnity.

The regulations provide for an indemnity on termination after 1 January 1994 by reference to facts which in part will have occurred before that date. That is not an unusual concept in an analogous context, that of employment law ... The new right for commercial agents seems to me to be of that kind. It is not in my judgment repugnant to the presumption that legislation, domestic or European, should not be construed so as to have retrospective effect."

3–160 Second, he held that the Directive and the Regulations would apply to the whole period of an unbroken agency relationship, even if it was covered by a number of agency agreements. ("In my judgment the phrase 'the agency contract' means simply 'the agency'. The word 'contract' after 'agency' [in reg.17(1)] adds nothing.... The plaintiff was retained under an unbroken series of contracts...By reason of my construction of the regulations and the Directive, the plaintiff is entitled to an indemnity calculated by reference to his activities during the whole of his agency...").

3–161 Third, the learned judge held that in assessing the amount paid under an indemnity, no account should be taken of extraneous factors such as the duty to mitigate, or, indeed, the fact that the agent had mitigated his loss. "My task is not to assess a loss to the agent but to determine the extent of his indemnity by reference to principles laid down in the regulations". He did however qualify this statement by adding: "Equitable principles might require there to be taken into account such part of the goodwill as the agent was able to exploit for himself or for the benefit of another principal".

3–162 This last point clearly goes to the question (discussed above) of what impact the presence or absence of a non-compete clause has on the equitable part of the assessment of indemnity. The impression to be gained from this passage is that Mitting J. would have been prepared to consider this impact in appropriate cases even though the Regulations have not adopted the option under the Directive of specifying that this impact should be taken into account. There would seem nothing to prevent this in the wording of the Regulations, since the requirement to apply an equitable assessment should clearly take into account all pertinent factors, including where relevant in relation to non-compete clauses.

3–163 The next case to consider the Regulations was *Duffen v Frabo SpA (No.1)* [1999] E.C.C. 58, CA. This case was chiefly concerned with the application of a clause in an agency agreement which provided for the payment of a specific sum of £100,000 by the principal to the agent in the event of premature termination of the agency agreement. The Court held that this clause was unenforceable as a penalty clause, However, they also held that the existence of the clause, and the finding that it was unenforceable, could not prevent the plaintiff claiming for compensation under reg.17. The appropriate remedy was obviously compensation rather than indemnity because the agreement itself, relying on the penalty clause had made no mention of the agent's rights (if any) under reg.17. The Court remitted the case to the Central London County Court for assessment of the amount of compensation to be paid. The finding in these proceedings will be discussed below.

The next consideration of the Regulations was in a Scottish Case, *Roy v MR Pearlman Ltd* [1999] S.C. 459, Outer House. This case considered the remedies available to an agent who was given short notice of termination in contravention of reg.15 and the rights of such an agent to post-termination commission under reg.8. These issues are discussed elsewhere in this Chapter. However, the principal importance of the case is in its approach to calculation of the amount payable under reg.17 in relation to the remedy of compensation. **3–164**

Hamilton L.J. accepted that the remedy of compensation was based upon pre-existing French law and practice. He followed the general principles laid down in *Moore v Piretta* as to the interpretation of the Regulations, and therefore held that French law and practice should be used to assist in calculating the amount payable under the remedy. He said that it was not necessary: **3–165**

> "to have the content of such law and practice spoken to formally by experts ... French law and practice is not being invoked because an issue in this court requires to be determined in accordance with French law but because, in the context of a directive which provides for a remedy drawn from French legal experience, assistance towards a harmonised approach may be obtained by having regard to the longer experience of the French courts in applying that remedy. That is more in the nature of a comparative law exercise, for the purposes of which a Scottish court is entitled to have direct regard to sources of foreign law."

The calculation of compensation was next considered in the Central London County Court case of *Duffen v Frabo SpA* (No.2) [2000] 1 Lloyd's Rep. 180. After considering the cases, the Directive, the Regulations and the arguments, Hallgarten J. accepted that the remedy of compensation was founded on French law, that it was payable in the event of termination of the agency relationship without cause, and that Regulation "was not meant to duplicate what was otherwise recoverable at common law". He stated that "the application of the Regulations entails abandonment of at least some common law principles", but while he found French law and practice helpful up to a point, he was only prepared to go so far. "It is one thing to be told and to acknowledge that under French law, events after termination have no bearing on the compensation to be awarded; it is quite another to be asked to go on and to award as a matter of routine two years commission, which is said to be the standard award granted by the French courts, albeit this standard award is itself subject to exceptions". **3–166**

His approach to calculation does not seem expressly to have taken account of the basic principle of French law, that the compensation payment should be looked at as a payment of an amount equal to the value of the goodwill that the agent has generated for the principal by his activities. He began by considering closely the provisions of reg.17(7)(a), while admitting that it was not determinative, since compensation remained at large under reg.17(7). He said **3–167**

> "it is instructive to see how tightly this deeming provision has been drawn. As I read it, one has to ask first what commission might have accrued to the agent in the normal course of events and then to ask to what extent depriving the agent of his commission nonetheless gives to the principal substantial benefits linked to the agent's activities, *i.e.* his activities prior to termination? In other words, the deeming provision only comes into play to the extent that the defendants can be said to have benefited from the claimant's prior efforts, and in relation to any customer procured by the claimant for the defendants there would probably be two benefits, namely (i) the very existence of that customer for future business and (ii) the defendants' ability to continue to deal with that customer without any longer having to bear the burden of paying a retainer or commission to the claimant. In many cases, I believe that this would result in a handsome payment to an agent . . ."

3–168 Although not in so many words, this approach is leading the learned judge to consider in effect whether the agent did generate any goodwill for the principal. His finding was that "in the present case, since the claimant did not introduce one new customer to the defendants and was less than successful in nurturing existing customers, had regulation 17(7)(a) been the claimant's exclusive remedy, the compensation would in my view have been nominal and derisory". In other words the agent had done nothing to create any goodwill.

3–169 The learned judge concluded by stating that in his view the right approach was to look at the earnings which might have accrued to the claimant "without taking into account particular common law concepts of avoided loss, mitigation, etc." He also considered that the earnings should be calculated on a net rather than a gross basis (*i.e.* after deducting the expenses of the agency). "It is one thing to disregard what the agent was able to do or in fact did upon and in consequence of termination; it is quite another artificially to inflate what would have been the true benefit to the agent had the agency continued".

3–170 Given the agent's poor performance, the facts of the case were that not only did the principal enjoy no increased business from the agent's activities, but the agency itself was loss-making, in that the commission earned by the agent did not cover his expenses. Thus, in these circumstances, whether one looks at it from the point of view of the valuation of the goodwill which the agent created for the principal or the value of the agency to the agent if it had been continued, the answer is the same. The agency was worth nothing.

3–171 This was not, however, the end of the story. The principal had agreed to pay the agent a retainer for a fixed period up to July 31, 1998, and the learned judge held that this was a simple contractual obligation (and not an unenforceable penalty) which the principal could not avoid by premature termination of the agreement. The principal was therefore obliged to pay the retainer for the remainder of the period of the agreement, despite the agent's poor performance.

3–172 The last case, although interesting and persuasive, is only a county court decision, and thus of less value as an authoritative precedent. The next decision to deal with the issue of compensation was a more authoritative one. This was the decision on appeal in the Scottish case of *King v T Tunnock Ltd* [2001] E.C.C. 6, Extra Division. In this decision the Court continued to apply the French law and practice in calculating compensation claims, and did so much more closely than Hallgarten J. did in *Duffen v Frabo SpA* (*No.2*), although it is unlikely that their Lordships would have come to a different conclusion on the peculiar facts of *Duffen* (*viz.* a loss-making agency).

The opinion of the Court is a closely argued analysis of the two remedies of indemnity and compensation (in this case compensation was being sought). The basis of the opinion is that the remedy of indemnity is based on pre-existing German law, the remedy of compensation is based on pre-existing French law, and that purposive construction of the Directive, and hence the Regulations, requires the Court to pay close attention to and to have considerable respect for the relevant pre-existing system of law. To this extent the basic principles do not differ from *Duncan Moore v Piretta PTA Limited* [1998] E.C.C. 392, QBD and *Roy v MR Pearlman Ltd* [1999] S.C. 459, Outer House. However, the argument and the authorities (including French authorities) before the Court enabled their Lordships to consider the matter in much more detail. **3–173**

Their Lordships first proceeded by construction of the relevant provisions of reg.17 and a comparison between the provisions for compensation and indemnity: **3–174**

> "The only requirement [for compensation] is damage through the termination of the agent's relation with his principal. Reference to the termination of the relationship with the principal is important. There is no equivalent provision regarding indemnity. Indemnity can arise if the agency is terminated and the principal continues to gain through the agent's efforts. Thus one has to pay regard particularly to commercial factors such as commission lost to quantify the indemnity. However, compensation is payable upon rupture of the relationship with the principal. At that point of time the value of the lost agency must be ascertained and there is simply no reference to the actual course of events to be expected after the termination. Indemnity hinges upon the principal continuing in business and exploiting the agent's connection."

Their Lordships approached the matter with a different emphasis to that of Hallgarten J. in *Duffen v Frabo SpA (No.2)*. He accepted that reg.17(6) provided the primary remedy, but he considered that reg.17((7) virtually governed the way in which compensation should be determined under reg.17(6). Their Lordships, however, unlike Hallgarten J., held that it was in fact reg.17(6) that was determinative, and that reg.17(7) merely specified two instances (out of many possible instances) when compensation would be payable. This is an important issue, since to follow Hallgarten J. would be to approximate the remedy of compensation much more closely to the **3–175** remedy of indemnity. Their Lordships considered this to be an incorrect approach:

> "Unless reg 17 (7) represents a restriction or qualification of 17 (6) it is not necessary for the agent to project his actual prospective loss. All he needs to prove is that after termination he had lost the value of an agency asset which, prior to the termination, existed. ... Under reg 17 (7) damage is deemed to occur 'particularly' when termination takes place in various defined circumstances. Now the sheriff and the sheriff principal construe reg 17 (7) as meaning in effect that damage will be deemed to occur 'only when the specified circumstances apply' or at least 'in particular' when these circumstances apply. It must be observed that if the intention had been to provide that compensation should be paid when reg.17(7)(a) or (b) apply then it would have been much easier to say that rather than to employ the circuitous draftsmanship occurring in reg.17(6) and 17(7). In any event the deemed damage is said to occur not 'only' in certain circumstances but 'particularly' in certain circumstances. The meaning of the word 'particularly' received careful consideration in the debate before us. We agree with the view that 'particularly' is used in its normal meaning of 'especially noted' or 'more than others'. It has to be observed that in the French text the word used is 'notamment' which is defined as meaning 'notably' or 'among others'...
>
> However, once one were to accept that reg.17(7) does not set out the exclusive circumstances giving rise to compensation, the only guidance that is left as to what other circumstances might give rise to compensation are the governing provisions of reg.17(6). If it can be shown that damage has been done to the agency relationship then compensation will arise and the remaining question is the level of that compensation...
>
> The vital difference between indemnity provisions and the compensation provisions is that indemnity requires that the principal should continue his business. If the principal does not continue in business after the termination the requirements of reg.17(3) cannot be satisfied. In the case of compensation there is no prerequisite to entitlement that the principal continues in business. Thus compensation may arise where (as in this case) the principal shuts down the relevant part of his business..."

3–176 So far the opinion was based mostly on the construction of reg.17. However, in support of these findings their Lordships considered the position under French law, relying in part on the text book by Dalloz, *Repertoire Droit Commercial* (2nd ed., 1996). They concluded: "It seems clear from the material produced that the French courts will regard compensation as being reparation for the loss of the value of the terminated agency agreement. The agent gets a reward for the value of the agency he has built up and which he suddenly loses."

3–177 They considered the method of calculation for compensation set out under French law in *Repertoire Droit Commercial*, s.3, at para.87. referring to the calculation of compensation for a commercial agent whose agency has been terminated. As translated this says: "The compensation or indemnity due on termination of the contract is customarily calculated either on the last two years of the proper or normal performance of the contract or on the last three years (taking the annual average of the commissions in these years and multiplying them by two) ... without taking into account events subsequent to the termination of the contract; what is lost is part of the market on the day the contract ended—the damage to the agent as suffered at that moment (accordingly the cessation of business by the principal is of little relevance). The mode of fixing the compensatory indemnity is reparation for damage and prejudice suffered (by the agent) is therefore based on the commissions earned during the last years of the proper performance of the contract. This is, effectively, the only certain element without any element of supposition for measuring the incorporeal value lost by the agent".

Their Lordships also noted that the Commission Report "also confirms what the other authorities set forth, namely that compensation in France is customarily paid on the basis of two years' purchase of gross commission, although the court always has an ultimate discretion to deviate from that standard". Here it should be remembered that Hallgarten J. and the lower courts in *King v Tunnock* considered that any calculation should be on net rather than gross commissions. **3–178**

Their Lordships concluded: "It is obvious, in our view, that on the basis of their own terms reg.17(6) and reg.17(7) provide for a different basis of making compensation than our traditional common law approach. However, as stated, the regulation does fit in well with the French approach to such compensation. ... Thus the French conclusion that mitigation of loss by the agent is not a factor when compensation is approached as we have described, is in our view persuasive. The directive and regulations, as presented, seem to harmonise with the French approach and given their terms, and the general objective of achieving harmonisation, we see no justification for construing the regulations as being radically different from the French approach". **3–179**

It remained only to fix an appropriate level of compensation. Their Lordships noted that "even in France the two year rule is only a benchmark and can be varied at the discretion of the judge". However, the general practice under French law was relevant and "entitled to some respect". Their Lordships went on to consider the practicality of the French approach: **3–180**

> "The French law obviously considers that there is some merit in finding a clear and practical basis for determining a fair level of loss. We equally consider that given the particular type of loss we are dealing with a broad approach is both inevitable and a practical requirement of the law."

It is at this point important to correct the misapprehension that in this case their Lordships then went on to suggest that a tariff approach should be adopted, which would exactly follow that of the French courts. As an appeal court they had limited evidence available to them. They knew that two years **3–181** commission amounted to £27,144, because this had been calculated, though not awarded, by the lower courts. The appellant was asking them to award this compensation in reliance upon the practice of the French courts. In fact they approached the matter by asking whether, in the light of what little evidence they had available to them, £27,144 seemed a reasonable valuation for the agency. They found that in the circumstances of the particular case it was, and were also fortified in their decision by the fact it was likely the French courts would have calculated the compensation in this case in the same way. However, they did not preclude other methods of calculation, or the taking of other circumstances into account in appropriate cases. Indeed, they also made the point that although in France two years commission is customarily awarded, even there the court will also take account of particular circumstances which require this amount to be varied:

> "... In the present case the sum of two years' gross past commission was found by the sheriff to amount to £27,144. The pursuer had operated the agency since 1962. His father had worked the agency for many years before him, so that when looked at along with the annual commissions which were generated by the agency, it is likely that the pursuer's business enjoyed considerable goodwill ... we are of the view that there may well be cases where compensation for loss for the damage to an agent caused by termination of an agency contract will raise narrower issues ... This is a case where we can conclude, even on the limited information that is available, that the agent would have expected to receive a capital sum representing at least the total for the last two years of his earnings to be paid before he would voluntarily have given up his agency. We are reassured that under French law compensation of two years' commission would be regarded as a standard compensation for loss of an agency, so that it is difficult to believe that in the present case such compensation could be other than reasonable."

3–182 The next case was an English case, *Barret McKenzie v Escada (UK) Ltd* [2001] E.C.C. 50, QBD, in which Bowers J. was asked by counsel for the agent, relying largely on *King v Tunnock*, to apply the French "tariff" of two years commission. Bowers J. refused to do this, stating

> "... the claimant is arguing that, first of all, this compensation is outside any common law concept, and that I accept. One is not assessing damages for the loss of the future prospects of the agency and it is not a question of mitigation of loss, as has been mentioned already. It is, I think, almost agreed that what here is being compensated for as 'entitlement' is in the nature of a quasi-proprietary right. It is the loss of the value of the agency to the agent which is being compensated for, and the precise moment at which that valuation takes place is at or about immediately on termination, as if the agency had not been terminated. All that, it seems to me, is virtually uncontested and accepted. It is accepted also that the reflection of the French law is not disputed.

What is hotly disputed is the fact that in the last paragraph the Court of Session took the view that, given the particular type of loss concerned, a broad approach was inevitable and a practical requirement of the law, and in fixing the level of compensation the approach of the French courts of using two year purchase of gross commission as a benchmark was entitled to respect, and in those circumstances that is what the Court of Session did.

That part of it is hotly contested because much of the other reasoning on valuation appeared to be coming to a different conclusion and it was only towards the end of the judgment that Lord Caplan appears to take what can only be described as the 'broad brush' approach rather than valuing the loss of the asset which in fact had ceased to exist."

Bowers J. thus refused to accept any tariff system for calculation, or to hear any evidence as to the way French courts dealt with exceptional circumstances. He preferred the approach adopted by Hallgarten J. in *Duffen v Frabo SpA*, which required the court to make an assessment of the value of the agency on the specific facts of each case, whilst applying the generally accepted principles (derived ultimately from French law) upon which the remedy was based. In particular he adopted Hallgarten J.'s remarks that he would find it "offensive" to calculate commission and award compensation on a gross rather than a net basis, despite the fact that this was the French practice. **3–183**

It should be noted that Davis J. found nothing particularly offensive in the possibility of calculating on the basis of gross commissions in *Tigana Ltd v Decoro Ltd*, although he actually used net commissions in that case. He said: **3–184**

"It seems clear that the Directive contemplates that goodwill established by an agent for the benefit of the principal can be treated, as it were, as a quasi-proprietary right in which the agent is taken to have a share and of which he is divested on termination. It would not necessarily be commercially unusual, for example, for the price for the sale of the goodwill of an agency (if assignable) to be calculated by reference to gross earnings."

Looking at *King v Tunnock*, as discussed above, there does seem to have been some misapprehension as to the basis on which the Court was proceeding. The opinion does not attempt to consider the valuation of the agency agreement until the end of the opinion, and it is hard to see that the Court is "leading up" to any particular approach, and then changed its mind. Although their Lordships approved of the French practice, they made their minds up on what evidence they had available, and used the French practice more as a cross-check than a guideline. The conclusion of the Court can thus be summarised as (i) £27,144 did not seem a large sum of money for an agency that had been in existence for over thirty years (ii) this sum, representing two years' commission, would probably have been awarded by a French court, and (iii) this practice "reassured" the Court in their finding that such an amount represented a reasonable valuation. **3–185**

3–186 It is also true that Lord McEwan heavily criticised the judgment in *Barret v Escada* in *Frape v Emreco Ltd* [2002] S.L.T 271. He said: "Whatever else this case shows it is plain that the deputy judge was most reluctant to interpret the regulations in the way the European Court would have wished. It is obvious that the opinion has not been revised and it contains a number of blatant errors. I therefore have to disregard it".

3–187 It is submitted, however, that not a great deal really divides the three cases of *Duffen v Frabo SpA (No.2), Barret v Escada*, and *King v Tunnock* except that their Lordships had, in the last case, more regard to a long-established practice in a foreign court, dealing with equivalent legislation, in order to reassure themselves that they were acting reasonably.

3–188 *Ingmar GB Ltd v Eaton Leonard Inc* [2001] Eu L.R. 755, QBD, was decided six months after the previous case in July 2001, and here the court took a not dissimilar view of the way to assess compensation under the Regulations.

3–189 In effect Morland J. approved of and considered himself bound by the principles set down in *King v Tunnock*, but took care to point out that in that case the "two year tariff" was only a guideline and not a rule of law:

> "Although I consider myself bound by the Court of Session on matters of law, where the Court was giving guidelines as to appropriate methods of calculating or assessing compensation, I must remember that they are guidelines not rules of law. However, in my judgment unless the guideline is inappropriate on the facts and circumstances of the particular case, the guideline should be followed. If a principal and an agent, whether in a litigation situation or not, know the likely method by which the Courts will assess compensation on termination, that must ease the resolution of disputes and be in the overall public and commercial interest within the Community. My paramount consideration in assessing the compensation remedy having regard to the facts and circumstances of this case must be to achieve the purpose of the Regulations derived from the Council Directive. If it is appropriate to follow the Court of Session's guidelines, so much the better…
>
> In my judgment Lord Caplan was laying down not a principle of law but a guideline that in many cases the two-year purchase of average gross commission may be appropriate … In *King v Tunnock* the facts were far removed from the present case … [in the present case] The defendants were the manufacturers of sophisticated products including specialist equipment costing up to and beyond £100,000 designed for a limited but high quality market, the aircraft and automotive industries. An agent selling such products had to have engineering training and experience and expert knowledge of the qualities and performance of the defendants' products so as to be able to sell to the limited potential customer base which would also be expert and knowledgeable. The annual average gross commission received by the claimants for three years preceding 6 September 1996 was £105,810.98…

... the written evidence of Professor Ferrier which was before me [stated]:

> 'The amount of compensation, because it represents the counterpart of the loss suffered by the agent, must be evaluated solely by the judges ... In calculating the level of compensation, the judges usually fix the level of compensation to two years of gross, that is without deduction for the expenses to the agent of making the sales, commissions calculated on the basis of an average of the three previous years. This calculation is considered to be simply a practice and not a custom. The courts are very careful to exclude any notion of tariff when calculating the level of compensation.'

In my judgment on the facts of the present case to apply the French customary method of calculation of compensation based upon two years of gross average commission of the previous three years would result in an injustice to the defendants and an excessive windfall to the claimants way above the value of the agency on 7 September 1996 and therefore would be inappropriate. I entirely agree with the dicta of Judge Hallgarten Q.C. in *Dufen v Frabo SpA I*, when he said: ... 'the regulation is after all framed so as to provide compensation and not to provide a windfall ...'

In this case the average gross commission for the previous three years was £105,810.98. Using a two-year purchase, the assessment of compensation would be £211,621.98 which in my judgment would be excessive and result in a considerable degree of windfall.

Taking into account the following factors: the length of time of the agency, approaching 8 years, the inevitable lack of profitability in the early years, the high degree of engineering and sales expertise required and put into the agency in obtaining, nurturing and developing the customer base, and the degree of profitability of the agency at the time of its rupture, in my judgment a fairer and more realistic result is achieved by aggregating Mr Craig's [the owner and motivating force of Tigana and thus in reality the person doing the real work of the agency] remuneration and pension with the Management Charge, which in effect was Mrs Leese's [the employee of Tigana in charge of administration] take although paid to Ingmar Ltd. In this case that method will achieve the purpose of the Regulations ... I consider it fair to use the years 1993, 1994 and 1995 but not 1996 because it is not representative ... I therefore award compensation under Regulation 17 of £183,600."

Once again, this case can be seen to be broadly in line with all of the preceding ones, and seems to have drawn the right conclusions as to the status of *King v Tunnock*. That case is a powerful analysis of reg.17, and sets out many principles of law, but it does not set out a tariff for calculation. Nor, indeed, do the French courts regard their practice as a tariff. There is nothing in the Regulations, the Directive, or French law and practice, which would lead one to the conclusion that compensation should not in the particular circumstances of each case be calculated in the way that the **3–190** particular courts chose to do so. Indeed, this decision seems one which could easily have been reached by a French court. What all of these cases show, however, are agreement on the underlying principles (based on French law) for the application of a right to a type of compensation new to the common law (a "foreign animal" in the words of Bowers J.). It is still up to the Courts, just as it is in France, to calculate that compensation in accordance with the facts of each case. The French practice is only a guideline, although clearly a stronger one in France than it is likely to become in the UK. An agent in the UK would, on the basis of these cases, be well advised to come before the Court with cogent proof of the value of his agency if he hopes to get substantial compensation.

3–191 The latest English case to consider the issue is *Tigana Limited v Decoro Limited.* Davis J. considered the previous cases and rejected the "tariff" approach. He concluded:

> "In my judgment . . . I am not bound to seek to apply what is said to be French law and practice, and I am not bound to apply a 'two year tariff' (albeit subject . . . to a discretion to depart from it) in this case. There is no 'tariff' applicable under English law, in my judgment, for the purposes of determining compensation under Regulation 17. Nor, in my view, is an English court, where the agency contract is governed by English law, bound to enquire into French (or any other Member State) law. Rather, in my view, the court has to make its assessment of the compensation (if any) to be paid under Regulation 17 having regard to the 'balance sheet' of relevant considerations, by reference to the circumstances of each case."

3–192 The learned judge then went on to set out the considerations which he considered were appropriate in the circumstances of the particular case:

> "The question then is: what are the factors to be taken into account in making the assessment and in deciding what compensation (if any) to award? I would venture to suggest that the following factors are likely to feature or to require consideration in such cases. I would not for one moment seek to offer this as an exhaustive list: further, some may not in fact feature at all in some cases; yet further, the weight (if any) to be given to each of such factors will vary from case to case. But at least the following can, I think, be identified:
>
> 1. The period of the agency, as provided for in the contract.
> 2. The period for which the agency in fact lasted up to termination.
> 3. The terms and conditions attaching to the agency as provided in the agency contract.
> 4. The nature and history of the agency and of the particular market involved.
> 5. The matters specifically mentioned in Regulation 17(7)(a) and (b).
> 6. The nature of the client base and of the kind of contracts anticipated to be placed (for example, "one-off" or repeat).

7. Whether the principal has appointed the agent as its exclusive or non-exclusive agent.
8. The extent to which the agent has bound himself during the agency to act exclusively for the principal and the extent to which the agent is free to act for others (and whether in the same field of goods or services or not).
9. The extent to which the principal retains after termination of the agency benefit (for example, by way of enhanced trade connection or goodwill) from the activities of the agent during the agency.
10. The extent to which an agent is free, after termination, to have dealings with customers with whom he dealt during the agency (A restraint of trade clause will be a relevant consideration in this context).

[NB. *In the case of compensation there is nothing in the Directive relating to the impact of non-compete clauses as there is in relation to indemnity (see the discussion above on Mitting J.'s observations in* Duncan Moore v Piretta PTA Limited) *but it seems even more appropriate to take the impact of a non-compete clause into account in relation to assessment of compensation which is based upon a valuation of the goodwill of the agency business.*]

11. Whether there are any payments under Regulation 8 (or other Regulations) which ought to be taken into account.
12. The manner in which the agency contract is ended: for example by notice given by the principal; or by notice given by the agent; or by effluxion of time; or as the case may be.

[NB. *Here, there may be a hint of the concept of an abusive termination as discussed above. Otherwise, it does not seem correct to refer to expiry by effluxion of time as a factor to be taken into account, particularly given the learned judge's earlier remarks in the same case to the effect that the Directive and the Regulations clearly provided for compensation in this circumstance.*]

13. The extent to which the principal and agent respectively have financially contributed to the goodwill accruing during the period of agency.
14. The extent to which there may have been loss caused by any relevant breach of contract or duty.

[NB. *Here we see the possibility of recovering damages for breach of contract in addition to the compensation provided for under the Regulations and perhaps even a hint as to the possibility of compensation for breach of the duty of good faith.*]

I have come to the conclusion that the compensation to be awarded to Tigana should be assessed by reference to the net remuneration of Tigana in the period of its agency [from the end of 28th October 1998 to 31st

December 1999]. In making that assessment, I have also asked myself, by way of a check, whether such an award is fair and proportionate: if it seemed to be prima facie to be too high (or too low) I would have reconsidered the weight I had been minded to give to the various factors."

3–193 So far as any current difference between the approach of the Scottish and English courts to this question, it can, perhaps, be fairly said, that the Scottish court will tend to apply the two year guideline as a default or fall-back position, unless there is evidence that a different valuation should be placed on the agency agreement. The English courts will require more evidence as to the actual value of the agency agreement and will proceed first from the facts of each case, without having any particular regard for the French guideline. To the extent that this approach produces differing treatment of agents in Scotland and the rest of the UK (and it is by no means certain that it will) then it is for the European Court, the House of Lords or Parliament to intervene.

3–194 These UK authorities support the conclusions set out above as to the application of the two remedies in the UK. The authorities also give some assistance as to which remedy to choose in the circumstances of any particular case.

3–195 First, there are two important issues which need to be considered when trying to decide between the two remedies. The first is the question of the burden of proof. In both cases the burden of proof rests with the agent, but the matters requiring proof are different in each case. Under the remedy of indemnity, the agent has to show the generation of new customers and/or new business by the agent, continued enjoyment by the principal of substantial benefits from those new customers and/or that new business, and that it is equitable that the agent receive a share of those benefits. Under the remedy of compensation the agent has to prove "the damage he suffers as a result of the termination of his relations with his principal". He will also, in situations where he wishes to rely on those provisions, need to deal with the matters in reg.17(7)(a), (substantial benefit to the principal) and 17(7)(b) (unamortised expenditure). The broad difference between the burden of proof in the two remedies is thus that under indemnity the agent must prove the benefit to the principal, while under compensation he must prove his own loss.

3–196 Second is the question of the meaning of "substantial benefit". In relation to the remedy of compensation, this definition is not vital, since it only refers to particular instances where compensation is payable, but it is a key condition of the application of the indemnity. Its use in the context of the indemnity would seem to mean that if only a trivial benefit is enjoyed, the agent gets no indemnity at all, rather than merely a small indemnity of a size commensurate with the benefit. The temptation, at least in relation to the remedy indemnity and given the spirit of the legislation, may be to construe "substantial" very loosely, so that where the principal enjoys any benefit at all (except one so trivial it amounted in practice to no benefit) the criterion of substantiality would be satisfied, and the third key condition of equity would operate to provide a commensurate payment.

The vexed question of the duty to mitigate under either of the remedies has now been laid to rest. It is clear from the authorities that, in line with their brethren in the rest of the EU, judges in the UK will not consider the duty to mitigate, or indeed, the actual avoidance of any loss, when calculating the amount to be paid under either of the remedies. **3–197**

Davis J. discussed these issues in regard to the remedy of compensation in *Tigana Ltd v Decoro Ltd* as follows: **3–198**

> "It is clear that the 'damage' suffered by a commercial agent as a result of the termination of the agency (Regulation 17(6)) is—generally speaking (and breach of contract cases aside)—to be regarded as a putative loss and not simply (by common law standards) actual loss. This is shown by the exclusion of principles of mitigation and applicability of the compensation provisions to termination on death or retirement. Clearly one important element, as the recitals to the Directive show, is to avoid a principal being unjustly enriched by retaining for itself without payment the entirety of the benefit of goodwill to which the activities of the agent during the agency have contributed. But another element (which finds both reflection and emphasis in Regulation 17(7)(a)) is to compensate the agent for the loss of a beneficial agency contract. One can perhaps there see some analogy with redundancy payments in an employment context: although the analogy cannot be pushed too far, since the policy considerations behind redundancy payments for employees are rather different."

The only point in relation to mitigation that might remain is most likely to appear in relation to the remedy of indemnity. The third requirement of that remedy is to consider whether it is "equitable" to increase or decrease the calculated amount by reference to any other considerations. Thus in *Duncan Moore v Piretta PTA Limited* [1998] E.C.C. 392, QBD, Mitting J. thought "Equitable principles might require there to be taken into account such part of the goodwill [of the terminated agency] as the agent was able to exploit for himself or for the benefit of another principal". However this is not really the application of a concept of mitigation. As discussed previously, it really looks at the question of non-competition post termination of the agency agreement. Even here any such benefit enjoyed by the agent should presumably not be taken into account if there is no non-competition clause in effect following the termination of the agreement, and, even if there is one, the assessment of the benefit, and hence any diminution in the indemnity payable, should be limited to the period when the non-compete clause takes effect (see the discussion in relation to Chapter 3.3.9.). **3–199**

The issue of non-competition also has a bearing in relation to the remedy of compensation. Given that compensation is based on the value of the agency at termination, the agency will presumably be of less value if there is no non-compete clause binding the agent. It also seems possible that, at least in the UK, the court might take account, in this regard, of any evidence as to the agent's actual activities after the termination and up to the date of the **3–200** trial, if he has actually entered into competition with his old principal (see the discussion of this possibility above in relation to *Tigana Ltd v Decoro Ltd).*

3–201 From all of the foregoing, it is possible to make some recommendations as to when to choose the remedy of compensation and when that of indemnity. When acting for a principal, it is probably better to specify the remedy of indemnity. First, it is more difficult for the agent to show entitlement to an indemnity, given the need to fulfil the three key conditions. Second, if an indemnity is payable, at least it will be on the basis that the principal should enjoy future substantial benefits from which he can recoup the payment of the indemnity to the agent. Third, the payment is subject to the cap. Fourth, the possibility of a parallel claim in damages is difficult for the agent to mount unless the principal is obviously in breach of contract (for instance by failure to pay commissions or by a premature unlawful termination); claims for misrepresentation or termination in bad faith (despite the giving of due notice) are more difficult to bring home. Fifth, the presence of the cap means that the maximum amount at risk when the agent dies or retires due to age, infirmity or ill-health, can be capped, so that it is relatively easy for the principal to cover some or all of his potential liability by building up provisions in his accounts and/or taking out keyman insurance on the agent in question.

3–202 When acting for the agent, it is better to choose the remedy of compensation. The remedy of indemnity must be unattractive to the agent for exactly the same reasons it is attractive to the principal. First, the agent has to prove his entitlement to the remedy under the three key conditions. Second, the presence of the cap formula does not help the agent. He has to prove what he is entitled to, which may be less than the cap but can never be more, and the presence of the formula in the remedy does not really help him to do this. It may provide a bargaining benchmark, but it relates in fact only to calculation of the cap, not to calculation of the payment under the indemnity. Further, the parallel claim for damages may be hard to mount, or not available at all, particularly when the agent needs it most at the time of retirement due to age, infirmity or ill-health.

3–203 On the other hand, under the remedy of compensation, the agent only to has to prove his loss, and he can claim this without worrying about a cap. It is not essential that the principal enjoy a substantial benefit from the agent's activities, so that proof in this matter and the definition of "substantial" are of much less importance. Thus it is certainly no harder for the agent to prove his loss than it is for him to prove the entitlement to an indemnity under the three key conditions. Additionally, when seeking compensation, all of the ancillary claims, which may be hard to raise together with the claim for indemnity, under the parallel claim for damages, will simply form part of the "loss" for which the agent can prove. In particular, the question of whether the termination was or was not in bad faith may well be irrelevant. Based on the French practice, although it is now questionable as to the extent that this will be followed in the UK, awards under compensation are usually considerably higher than those under indemnity in German courts, for the reasons discussed above.

3.8 Good business practice

See cl.9.14. 3–204

3.9 Disclosure and registration

See cl.9.15. The contents of cll.9.14 and 9.15 should be reproduced here, replacing the terms "Company" and "Consultant" with "Principal" and "Agent" respectively. 3–205

3.10 Interpretation clauses and signature

3.11 Schedule 1—the products

3.12 Schedule 2—the territory

Clauses 3.10 to 3.12 should be reproduced as required from Chapter 1. 3–206
There is however a specific issue in relation to governing law and jurisdiction clauses in relation to the Regulations which must be considered here.

In their original form, the Regulations applied only "in relation to the 3–207
activities of commercial agents in Great Britain", (see reg.1(2)). However, reg.1(3) also provided that (even though the agent is carrying on his activities in Great Britain) the Regulations will not apply if the proper law of the contract is expressed to be the proper law of another Member State. This was simply intended to mean that the implementation of the Directive in the relevant local law would apply to protect the agent instead of the Regulations. Both of these situations would have the same result whether the principal was also resident in the UK or not. This may seem of academic interest, but of course there are various options in the Directive, which have not been taken up in the Regulations, but may well have been implemented in another Member State. In this case, if one of the parties finds one or more of these options to its liking, it would be possible to invoke them by choosing the relevant proper law.

If an agent were carrying on his activities outside the UK, then the 3–208
Regulations could not apply, even if there were an express proper law clause in the contract specifying one of the systems of UK law as the proper law.

If the agent were carrying on his activities outside the EC, then the 3–209
relevant system of law in the UK would apply (subject to any overriding local law, see Chapter 2.7) and the Regulations and hence the Directive would be irrelevant, although, for the sake of clarity, the parties could insert an express term excluding the operation of the Regulations. Alternatively, the Regulations could, if the parties agreed, be imposed in substance as a matter of contract, possibly by way of an incorporation by reference.

3–210 However, as originally drafted, this left uncovered the situation where the agent is carrying on his activities in another Member State of the EC and yet one of the systems of UK law governs the agency agreement. By definition the Regulations would not apply (he is not carrying on his activities in the UK). The EC Commission considered that this left a possible loophole in that an agent carrying on activities outside the UK under an agreement governed by one of the systems of law in the UK might not be able to seek a remedy under the local implementation of the Directive in the Member State where he was carrying on his activities, and yet would have no remedy in the UK because the Regulations did not apply to him.

3–211 It was always arguable that the local law of the Member State in which he was carrying on his activities would provide him with a remedy under that Member State's implementation of the Directive, since the Directive is mandatory legislation, within the meaning of Arts 3 and 7 of the Rome Convention of 1980 on the Law Applicable to Contractual Obligations. This is certainly the view taken in the Commission Report. Further, by way of example, the implementations of the Directive in Germany, the Netherlands and Italy are expressly stated to be mandatory in this way. This would oblige the agent's local court to apply the foreign implementation of the Directive to the agency agreement (see Chapter 1.3.5.)

3–212 This approach can be seen in the European Court cases: Case C215/97 *Bellone v Yokohama SpA* [1998] E.C.R. I–2191, Case C456/98 *Centrosteel Srl v Adipol GmbH* [2000] 3 C.M.L.R. 711 and Case C485/01 *Caprini v Conservatore del registro delle imprese di Trento* judgment of November 21, 2002. In the first two cases, the Court held that Italian legislation, which required that no agency agreement was valid unless it was duly entered in a commercial register, could not be used to claim that an unregistered agreement was invalid so as to prevent an agent claiming under the Italian implementation of the Directive. In the third case, the court held that the requirement that an agent be registered in this way was not illegal under EC law provided that the registration was used for local administrative purposes and not to avoid the legal protection available to agents under the Directive. This position is also supported by the European Court decision in Case C381/98 *Ingmar GB Ltd v Eaton Leonard Technologies Inc* [2001] All E.R. (EC) 57 discussed below.

3–213 Nevertheless the UK was required to put the matter to rest beyond doubt. Thus amending regulations were enacted (The Commercial Agents (Council Directive) (Amendment Regulations 1998 (SI 1998/2868) which renumbered the original Art.1(3) as 1(3)(a) and introduced a new Art.1(3)(b) which provided that:

> "(whether or not it would otherwise be required to do so) [a court or tribunal] shall apply these regulations where the law of another member State corresponding to these regulations enables the parties to agree that the agency contract is to be governed by the law of a different member State and the parties have agreed that it is to be governed by the law of England and Wales or Scotland."

Similar amendments were made to the Northern Ireland Regulations. Thus where an agent carries on activities in a Member State other than the UK, the parties may agree to govern the agency agreement by one of the systems of law in the UK, provided that the local law where the agent carries on his activities does not forbid this. In this case, the court in the UK is obliged to apply the Regulations even though the agent does not carry on activities within the UK. Not all Member States would permit this. For instance, Portuguese law does not permit the application of a foreign law to an agency agreement unless the foreign law is more favourable to the agent. **3–214**

The effect of the 1998 Regulations was discussed in *IFR Limited v Federal Trade SPA* ([2001] WL 1677001 (judgment of September 19, 2001, QBD, 2000 folio 1393). Federal carried on business (allegedly as an agent in Italy), under an agreement where the governing law and jurisdiction clause provided for English law, with disputes to be heard before the High Court. Federal claimed that the clause was void because it derogated from its rights to compensation under the Directive. At the time the agreement was entered into the unamended 1993 Regulations did not apply the UK implementation of the Directive to agents who carried on activities abroad. On this basis Federal should have been entitled to bring proceedings in Italy under the Italian implementation of the Directive. However, by the time agreement expired, on June 30, 2000, and the proceedings in England were commenced, the 1998 Regulations had come into force. **3–215**

The Court stated: **3–216**

> "... the derogation argument is confronted by at least one insurmountable problem. The duty to indemnify the agent arises under Article 17 'after termination of the agency contract'. The duty not to derogate from the Article 17 duty operates under Article 19 'before the agency contract expires'. The Commercial Agents (Council Directive) (Amendment) Regulations 1998 came into effect on 16th December 1998 ... The powers of the English court ... to apply the Directive [when the agreement is governed by English law, but the Agent carries on business outside the UK] are therefore not confined to agency contracts which are entered into on or after 16th December 1998, but extend to proceedings which came before the court on or after that date, even if they relate to a contract already existing on that date. Accordingly, even if the English law and jurisdiction clause would have prevented enforcement of Article 17 against IFR up to that date, it then ceased to do so and any derogation had therefore ceased by the time the 1998 Agreement had expired."

The final question to be decided is what happens if the principal is resident outside the EU and applies his local system of law to govern the agency agreement. If the agent carries on his activities within a Member State of the EU, does the relevant local implementation of the Directive override the foreign law clause as a mandatory provision and apply the Directive against the apparent intention of the parties. In Case C381/98 *Ingmar GB Ltd v* **3–217**

Eaton Leonard Technologies Inc [2001] All E.R. (EC) 57 the European Court decided that the Directive was just such a mandatory provision.

3–218 The agent was incorporated in and carried on its activities in the UK. The Principal was a US company carrying on business in California. The law of the state of California governed the agency agreement. The agent claimed to take advantage of the Regulation, to seek compensation on termination, on the basis that it was carrying on business in the UK, and that the Regulation therefore applied as an overriding, mandatory provision under the EC Treaty. The proceedings were commenced in England and referred by the Court of Appeal to the European Court for a finding on the issue. The Court held that that Arts 17 and 18 of the Directive had to be applied in situations where the commercial agent carried on his activity in a Member State despite the fact that the principal may be established outside the Community. The aims and objectives behind the Directive, particularly Arts 17 to 19, were to protect commercial agents in the event of termination of the contract and although Member States had a discretion to choose indemnification or compensation as the means of protection, the regime established by the Directive was mandatory in nature. Furthermore, since the Directive also aimed to protect freedom of establishment and undistorted competition in the internal market, it was essential that Arts 17 to 19 were observed throughout the Community to ensure Community legal order.

3–219 It can be seen that the conclusion of the court logically follows from the fact that the Directive is a harmonising measure. If the Directive is to achieve its purpose, then it can do so only if each local implementation is in fact an overriding measure as between agents carrying on business in the relevant jurisdiction and their principals, whether the principals are resident in any state of the EC, or outside it, and whether the governing law is that of one of the EU Member States or not. In this sense the decision of the Court is still keeps the Directive in compliance with the powers delegated to the Council under the EC Treaty. The Directive is not being applied outside the territory of the EC.

3–220 In his opinion addressed to the Court, the Advocate-General put the matter in this way: "Thus the geographical basis which distinguishes Community law, according to the very terms of the Treaty, leads me to believe that the existence of an element of connection with Community territory in a legal relationship, even if it is contractual, is such as to justify the application of the norm of Community law in question. That analysis in no way amounts to attributing an extraterritorial effect to the provisions of the Directive, contrary to Eaton's submission".

3–221 The judgment of the Court confirmed this approach: "The purpose served by the provisions in question requires that they be applied where the situation is closely connected with the Community, in particular where the commercial agent carries on his activity in the territory of a Member State, irrespective of the law by which the parties intended the contract to be governed".

3–222 As stated above, there could be circumstances in which it might benefit a principal or an agent to engage in "forum shopping". It can be seen from the discussions in various sections of this chapter, that there are a number of areas where the Directive allows certain options in the way Member States can implement it. There are five main areas: secondary agents (Art.2(2)), agent's entitlement to commission when others deal with his customers or in his territory (Art.2(2)), whether agency contracts must be in writing (Art.13(1)), compulsory periods of notice for the fourth year of the contract onwards, and whether the agent is to receive an indemnity or compensation on termination (Art.17(1)). Given the possibilities of forum shopping discussed below, it is always prudent to obtain local advice on the way the Directive has been implemented in relation to these issues in the Member State in which the agent is carrying on his activities, whatever system of law the choice of law clause in the agreement specifies. Some examples of these differences (but not an exhaustive list) are set out in the next paragraph (full details are set out in Appendix 2.)

France, Germany, Spain and the UK exclude secondary agents, for instance, but Portugal, Greece, Italy, Denmark and the Netherlands do not. Portugal, Italy, UK and Spain have taken the option to apply Art.7(2) only to exclusive agreements, but France, Greece, the Netherlands, Denmark and Germany have not. Greece and Portugal require agency agreements to be evidenced in writing pursuant to Art.13(2), but in the case of Portugal, this applies only to exclusive agreements. Spain, Italy, Germany, Denmark, Greece and (unless the contract otherwise provides) the Netherlands have adopted the minimum notice requirement for the fourth year onwards. In most of the Member States the agent is entitled to an indemnity on termination, but France has chosen compensation, and, as discussed above, in Chapter 3.7, the UK has adopted both options and left it to the parties to choose. **3–223**

It is possible to use the provisions of the Rome and Brussels Conventions and the Council Regulation on the Jurisdiction and the Recognition and Enforcement of Judgments in Civil and Commercial Matters (44/2001) (known as the Brussels Regulation) (all discussed in Chapter 1.6.3) to "forum shop" to a limited extent to enable usually the agent, but sometimes the principal, to choose a jurisdiction in which the implementation of the Directive contains the option he prefers in relation to one or more of the issues listed above. For instance, France has chosen compensation as the remedy on termination, but Germany has chosen indemnity. If the agent is in France, the principal in Germany, and the agreement is subject to German law, the agent will have a choice. He can either pursue the principal in Germany, (under Art.2 of the Brussels Regulation), accepting German law, and obtain an indemnity, or he can attempt to bring an action in France (under Art.5 of the Brussels Regulation) relying on the overriding nature of the French implementation of the Directive to displace the choice of German law by relying on Art.7 of the Rome Convention. Under the principle of first seisure (Art.21 of the Brussels Regulation) if the agent has successfully commenced his action in France, the principal will not be able to contest the jurisdiction of the French court nor bring an action himself in relation to the same issues in the German courts. **3–224**

3–225 This question of forum shopping is particularly interesting in the area of secondary agency and the requirement for an agreement to be in writing. An agreement which may not be covered by the Directive, or not enforceable at all, in the Member State of one of the parties may thus be covered or enforceable in the Member State of the other party. For instance, if the principal is in Netherlands (agreement not required to be in writing) and the agent is in Greece (agreement must be in writing), the agent might be able to enforce his rights under the Directive by suing the principal in the Netherlands under Art.2 of the Brussels Regulation. His difficulty here will be that, since there can, by definition, be no express choice of law clause, he will have to use the general principles of private international law to show that Dutch Law is applicable to the contract. This is difficult where the Rome Convention applies since the primary rule is that the governing law is the place of establishment of the party performing the characteristic obligations, which in the case of agency is the law of the agent's place of establishment (see Art.4.1 and 4.2 of the Rome Convention) but there are some exceptions to this rule (see Art.4.5). If he can establish Dutch law, he should succeed in his action, because the implementation of the Directive in the Netherlands does not have the restriction that it applies only to an agent carrying out his activities in the Netherlands. The same problems apply in the case of secondary agents, although here matters could be further complicated by a written agreement, which, at least in theory, could have an express choice of law clause in it.

3–226 The discussion above is all on the basis that the agent is carrying out his activities in only one jurisdiction. It is of course possible for an agent to be appointed in respect of more than one country, and this could obviously include cases where the agent is appointed both in respect of one or more Member States of the EC and also of a state outside the EC. In this case, the preferred route would be to enter into one separate agreement for each state. In this way, whatever the choice of law clause is in each agreement, and whatever the overriding effect of each of the relevant systems of local law, each agreement will at least have only to contend with the interplay of the chosen proper law and one system of local law.

3.13 Schedule 3—the commission

3–227 3.13.1(a) In respect of every order for the Products obtained by the Agent during the continuation of this Agreement the Agent shall be paid by way of remuneration commission upon the net invoice price before any value added or sales taxes or other taxes or duties [FOB port of shipment] [Ex Works of the Principal] at a rate to be agreed not later than the time when the order is given or if the order is preceded by a tender not later than the time when such tender is submitted. In fixing the rate of commission the parties shall take into account (inter alia) the following factors:

3.13.1.1 the efforts expended by the Agent and their effectiveness;

3.13.1.2 the value of the order to the Principal; and

3.13.1.3 the degree of competition experienced in marketing the Products in the Territory.

OR

3.13.1(b) During the continuance of this Agreement the Agent shall be paid a commission at the relevant percentage or percentages set out below upon the net invoice price before any value added or sales taxes or other taxes or duties [FOB port of shipment] [Ex Works of the Principal] of all Products sold to customers in the Territory whether] from orders received by the Principal through the Agent, or otherwise, pursuant to cl.2.3.8:

Product	Percentage

OR

3.13.1(c) During the continuance of this Agreement the Agent shall be paid a commission at the relevant percentage or percentages set out below upon the net invoice price before any value added or sales taxes or other taxes or duties [FOB port of shipment] [Ex Works of the Principal] of all Products sold to customers in the Territory under orders received from the Agent:

Product	Percentage

In the event that the Principal makes sales of the Products to customers in the Territory pursuant to cl.3.3.8, the Principal shall pay commission to the Agent at [one quarter of] the rate provided under cl.3.13.1(c).

Article 6 of the Directive provides that the agent's remuneration is to be agreed between the parties (subject to any overriding provisions about minimum levels of remuneration for agents in the governing law of the Member State concerned—there are none under the systems of law in force in the UK) and, in the absence of agreement, to be in accordance with customary practice (if there is any relevant practice) or else what is reasonable in all the circumstances. To the extent that remuneration "varies with the number or value of the business transactions" it is deemed to be "commission", and then Arts 7 to 12 of the Directive have application. These articles deal in detail with what transactions the agent is entitled to claim commission on, when the commission must be paid, and the agent's right to details of the transactions on which his commission is earned.

Obviously the remuneration under the three versions above would fall **3–228** within the definition of commission, and, as they are agreed between the parties, comply with Art.6. Under version (a), if no agreement were reached the agent would have recourse to the courts and rely on the provisions in the Directive about customary or reasonable levels of remuneration. However, the real problem arises in relation to the classes of transaction upon which commission must be paid. Article 7(1) provides that commission is to be paid on transactions concluded as a result of the agent's actions, and also on transactions concluded with customers whom the agent has previously acquired for transactions of the same kind. This provision applies regardless of whether the appointment is on an exclusive or non-exclusive basis. Additionally Member States have a choice of specifying a right for the agent to commission either on all transactions with customers belonging to a specific area or group with which he has been entrusted, or on all transactions with customers belonging to a specific area or group for which he has exclusivity (Art.7(2)). The Regulations (reg.7(2)) have adopted the latter alternative. (Full details of the position in other Member States are set out in Appendix 2.)

3–229 The application of Art.7 has different implications for exclusive and nonexclusive agency agreements. Versions (a), (b) and (c) above are compliant with Art.7 and appropriate for exclusive agency agreements. Version (a) should be used where the principal did not reserve the right to deal direct. Where the principal has reserved the right to deal direct under cl.3.3.8 version (b) should be used if the principal is happy for the agent to get the same commission in both cases where the agent has generated the order and where the principal has dealt direct. Version (c) should be used where the principal has reserved the right to deal direct but wants to pay the agent a lower rate of commission in cases where the principal has dealt directly.

3–230 The question of differential rates of commission causes problems. Do Arts 7 to 12 of the Directive permit differential rates? Since commission is to be agreed between the parties under Art.6, there seems to be nothing to stop them agreeing a lower level for direct sales, than for sales through the agent, subject to any local law of a Member State controlling this. Certainly there is no such control under English law. There is one further argument which reinforces the contention that differential rates of commission can be agreed. If the parties had not agreed rates under Art.6(1), then they would be thrown back in each case to deciding what was customary or reasonable on the facts of each case. It is well known that in many trades the custom is for the commission on orders placed direct with the principal to be less (often a half or a quarter) of the commission on orders placed through the agent. This reflects the fact that the agent incurs less or no cost of selling where the principal deals direct. It can also be shown, in the absence of any trade custom, that, for precisely this reason, where the order is not placed through the agent, it is reasonable that his remuneration be at a level which reflects his contractual rights (*i.e.* exclusivity or "ownership" of the customer) but also reflects the reduction or absence of his activity (and the reduction in his selling costs) in generating the order in question. If, then, custom and reason would provide differential commission rates in these circumstances, it is hard to see why an agreement between the parties could not produce the same effect.

3–231 One proviso must be made here. This argument would not permit the differential level for the commission in these cases to be set at zero or at so low a level that it is effectively non-existent. This would amount to expressly contracting out altogether from the right to receive commission in respect of the relevant class of transaction. The argument as to whether this is possible is looked at below.

3–232 Some commentators have suggested that, given the level of commission can be set by agreement, it should be possible not only to agree different rates for different classes of transactions, but also to require the agent completely to contract out of his right to commission in the circumstances where the principle deals direct (see under Art.7(1)(b)) or his right to receive commission on certain orders after his termination (see Art.8). A further argument used to advance this suggestion is that while the Directive states that the parties may not "derogate ... to the detriment of the commercial agent" from certain parts of Arts 10, 11 and 12 (relating to rights as to when commission is due and payable), there is no such provision in relation to Arts 7, 8 and 9, which deal with the classes of transaction upon which commission is payable.

This view does not seem to be correct for a number of reasons. At the most basic level, such an interpretation would render Arts 8 and 9 nugatory, and frustrate one of the major purposes of the Directive. EC legislation is normally interpreted purposively by the European Court, rather than on a strict interpretation of the wording as in the case of a common law statute. Even if it could be shown that the drafting of the Directive was defective, the European Court would go back to interpret the Directive in the light of the general intentions expressed in the preamble. The Directive is a measure to harmonise the regulation of commercial agency throughout the EC. This would include the circumstances in which commission is payable to commercial agents. If Arts 8 and 9 were applicable only where the parties so agreed, the Directive would fail to achieve harmonisation in an area of major importance to commercial agents. It seems very unlikely that such an interpretation would prevail. **3–233**

In any event, an examination of the drafting of the Directive does not really support this contention, although there are clearly some areas where the wording could have been made clearer. Article 1 states that "The harmonisation measures prescribed by the Directive *shall* apply to the laws ... of the Member States ..." and Art.22 imposes on Member States the obligation to "bring into force the provisions necessary to comply with this Directive ...". Articles 7 and 8 are written in the imperative and state that "A commercial agent *shall* be entitled to commission ..." on the various classes of transactions listed in them. Thus, applying Arts 1 and 22 to, *inter alia*, Arts 7 and 8, the Member States must enact legislation which ensures that agents are entitled to commission in the relevant circumstances laid down in those Articles. The Regulations certainly do this by copying the wording of the relevant Articles, and retaining their wording in the imperative (see regs 7 and 8). On this reasoning Arts 7 and 8 are mandatory, without any need for a specific provision stating that this is in fact the case. **3–234**

What of the references to agreement in Art.6(1)? It is true Art.6(1) talks about agreement, but this is in a negative way ("In the absence of agreement ... the commercial agent shall be entitled to ... the remuneration ... customarily allowed ... or reasonable remuneration ..."). Further, Art.6(3) states that Arts 7–12 shall not apply if the agent is not remunerated by way of commission. This implies that where the parties have agreed under Art.6(1) that the agent will receive commission, Arts 7–12 *will* apply. The **3–235** wording of Arts 6(1) and 6(3) make it possible to reconcile the element of agreement in Art.6 with the mandatory nature of Arts 7 and 8 in two ways:

3–236 The first situation to consider is where the parties have dealt expressly in the agreement with certain of the classes of transactions in Arts 7, 8 and 9, but remained silent on others. In this case, the parties have agreed that the agent will be remunerated in respect of certain classes of transactions by way of commission, so that, by implication from Art.6(3), Arts 7 and 8 will apply in their entirety. Thus, the agent will then be entitled to commission on all of the classes of transactions covered by Arts 7 and 8, even if the parties have remained silent about some of them. The only effect of their silence is that no rate has been agreed for commission in respect of the transactions which have not been mentioned in the agreement. Here Art.6(1), "in the absence of any agreement as to remuneration ..." in respect of the omitted classes of transactions, will entitle the agent to the commission which is "customary" or "reasonable" within the applicable provisions of Art.6(1).

3–237 The second situation to consider is where the agreement states expressly that the agent is entitled to commission only on certain classes of transactions, and also expressly excludes his right in respect of other such classes. On the reasoning in the previous paragraph, Arts 7 and 8 still apply in their entirety, by implication from Art.6(3). The only remaining problem is to deal with the wording relating to agreement in Art.6(1). Here, if the parties have expressly excluded the right to commission in respect of certain classes of transactions, there has clearly been no agreement as to remuneration in respect of them. Again, the only effect of this will be, as in the previous paragraph, to trigger the provisions of Art.6(1) which provide that, "in the absence of any agreement", the agent then becomes entitled to customary or reasonable commission on the excluded classes of transactions.

3–238 The last remaining question to answer here is why the Directive contains provisions apparently confirming the mandatory nature of some articles, but fails to apply such provisions to all of the Articles in the Directive, and in particular fails to do so for Arts 7 and 8. It is important to realise that the Directive does not classify articles as either mandatory or non-mandatory. Instead the term used is normally a prohibition against "derogation". The Directive has provisions (see Arts 5, 10(4), 11(3), 12(3), and 19) which state that the parties may not "derogate", or in some cases "may not derogate to the detriment of the commercial agent", in relation to Arts 3, 4, 10(2), 10(3), 11(1), 12(1), 12(2) 17 and 18. Articles 15(2)and 15(3) (which provide for the periods of notice required to terminate an agency agreement of indefinite duration) do not use the "derogation" wording. However, based on the same principle, the articles contain provisions stating that the parties may not agree shorter periods of notice. However, Arts 6, 7, 8, 9, 10(1), 14, 15(1), 15(4), 15(6), 16 and 20 use mandatory language (in most cases the word "shall") but no provisions prohibiting derogation. The answer would seem to lie in the difference in the nature of the two classes of Articles.

3–239 The first class, to which the confirmatory provisions are applied, sets a minimum standard. Paradoxically, the presence of this "mandatory" wording actually allows for some flexibility in the implementation of these provisions. The parties cannot agree contractual terms and conditions which fall below this standard (*i.e.* "derogate" from it) or, as it is stated in most cases, they cannot agree such terms and conditions if they adversely affect (*i.e.* are "to the detriment of") the *commercial agent*. However, there is nothing to prevent the parties agreeing terms which impose a higher standard, or which fall below the standard set to the detriment of the *principal*. For instance, the duties towards one another imposed on the agent and the principal by Arts 3 and 4 respectively are the minimum requirement. Article 5 requires that the parties not derogate from these duties and obligations, but they are thus left at liberty to agree additional and/or more stringent duties and obligations if they so wish. Similarly, Arts 17 and 18 set minimum standards for compensation or indemnity of the agent upon termination of the relationship with the principal. Article 19 prevents the principal from forcing the agent to accept less than these minimum standards, but there is nothing to prevent the parties agreeing more generous terms for compensation or indemnity (*e.g.* no cap on the indemnity) if the agent has sufficient bargaining power to impose them on the principal.

The second class of articles, which are "mandatory", but have no confirmatory provisions, do not set minimum standards which leave some scope for upward revision by agreement. They deal with absolutes which require implementation as they are worded with no change either by way of improvement or derogation. A good example of this is Arts 14, 15(4) and 15(6) which are clearly mandatory. Their inclusion in the Directive would make no sense otherwise. Similarly, Arts 7 and 8 set down that the agent is entitled to commission in respect of the stated transactions. Any question of the parties stipulating differing, albeit higher, standards is irrelevant here. **3–240**

It will be noticed that Art.13 has not been referred to above. Article 13(1) states that each party "shall be entitled" to a signed written statement from the other setting out the main terms of the agency agreement between them. Its final sentence reads "Waiver of this right shall not be permitted". This wording is unlike any of the other confirmatory provisions, and is applied to a provision which does not set a minimum standard, but appears to be an absolute requirement to be implemented as worded. On the arguments set out above, Art.13 should be capable of mandatory application without the need for this sentence, just like Arts 7 and 8. Does the use of this sentence in Art.13(1), thus throw doubt on the above interpretations? There are a number of arguments that it does not. **3–241**

First, directives are drafted loosely, and interpreted purposively rather than strictly. Thus, the fact that one provision is stated to be mandatory when this is not really necessary should not be regarded as of sufficient weight to overthrow the interpretations set out above and based on a detailed analysis of the whole of the Directive. Second, in any event, it is at least a plausible argument that this last sentence is directed to the Member States who are given the task of implementing the Directive, rather than to the parties to a commercial agency relationship themselves. On this interpretation, the last sentence of Art.13(1) would then be understood as a direction to Member States that they could not preclude a party to an oral **3–242** agency agreement from requiring the written statement, simply because they disapproved of oral agency agreements. Their only solution would be, pursuant to Art.13(2), to pass (or have already passed) legislation to make oral agency agreements unenforceable. On this analysis, the last sentence of Art.13(1) ceases to cause any problems of construction in relation to the mandatory and confirmatory provisions discussed above (see the more detailed discussion of Art.13 in Chapter 3.1). It should be noted that the Regulations do not appear to interpret the last sentence of Art.13(1) as in the second argument above, since they enact this sentence as reg.13(2) ("Any purported waiver of the right referred to in paragraph 1 shall be void"). Here, whatever the true status of the sentence in Art.13(1), reg.13(2) is clearly a direction to the parties to the agreement.

3–243 Some help on all of these issues can be gained by looking at other Member States' implementations of the Directive. They seem to provide support for the contentions outlined above.

3–244 For instance, in the case of France, the implementation of the Directive (Loi 91–593) is a fairly faithful translation of the Directive, and the retains the structure of a number of Articles in the imperative (usually following the pattern of "the agent shall have the right ...") followed by a final clause which consolidates all of the provisions that the Directive states are mandatory. This Article (16) again follows the pattern of the Directive in providing two classes of mandatory articles—those where any contractual variation is not permitted and those where no derogation to the prejudice of the agent is permitted. This Article does not mention the articles equivalent to Arts 6, 7 and 8 of the Directive.

3–245 French practice (although there are no specific provisions to this affecting the Law) permits commission on direct sales to be at a lower rate, and permits the inclusion within the agreement of a list of customers with whom the principal may contract without paying commission (see, *e.g. Société Domaines Maisons et Chateaux Sarl v GIE Laurent Perrier Diffusion* [2001] E.C.C. 43, Court of Appeal, Paris: "Although a commercial agency agreement may include a special clause limiting the agent's right to commission to contracts concluded by him himself, there was no stipulation of that kind in the present case as the agreement merely fixed the appellant company's remuneration by reference to orders 'originating from the customers assigned to the agent', but without requiring those orders to be recorded and received by the agent himself").

3–246 This is broadly consistent with the principles set out above, particularly since France permits commissions to be paid on direct dealing within a territory or group of customers entrusted to the agent on a non-exclusive basis, so that the list can be looked at as an exception to the grant of the group in the first place, (see the discussion of the correct form of grant in the next paragraph) rather than a waiver of the right to commission in the case of direct dealing. No derogation from the entitlement to commission under Arts 7 and 8 appears to be permitted under the implementations in Germany, Italy, and Spain. In the Netherlands, the position is not entirely clear as regards Art.7, but derogation from Art.8 is expressly prohibited.

However, it must be said that Belgium divides the provisions of the Directive into "mandatory" and "supplementary" provisions. The former are the ones containing the "derogation" language, the latter are all the others, such as Arts 7 and 8, which can be excluded by agreement. The present writer does not consider this view to be correct, but again, interpretation from the European Court will be necessary to clarify the issue. **3–247**

From the above, it follows that Arts 7 and 8 create serious issues for a principal who wishes to avoid paying commission when dealing direct. The best way of avoiding the problems is to restrict the grant of the agency agreement so that the particular customers with whom the principal wishes to deal direct are never part of the agent's customers at all. This is effective whether or not the grant is on an exclusive basis. If, as a question of fact, customers have never been acquired by the agent, problems under Art.7(1) cannot arise, and careful drafting should avoid problems under Art.7(2). For instance, a grant of an agency in respect of "all retail outlets in the city of ... other than department stores" avoids department stores as a group of customers, nor has there been a grant of a geographical territory. On the other hand a grant of an agency "for the city of ... provided that the agent is not authorised to canvass or seek orders from department stores", looks more like a grant of a geographical area, and should not be used, in order to avoid any unnecessary problems with whether or not the principal is entitled to exclude the department stores under Art.7(2). **3–248**

Where the grant is a non-exclusive one, the question of dealing direct in fact causes more problems. Here the effect of Art.7(1) means that the agent is entitled, firstly, to commission on transactions concluded through him, but also (despite the non-exclusive nature of the grant) on direct transactions with customers he has previously acquired. Direct dealing with customers he has not acquired does not normally give rise to a right to commission, but care needs to be taken with Art.7(2) in this connection. Where Member States have adopted the second alternative, based on exclusivity, as the UK has, there is no problem, but the first alternative will in many cases turn a non-exclusive grant into an exclusive one if, as is very common, a territory, or a class of customers is specified in the agency grant. In Member States that have chosen this alternative, the only type of non-exclusive grant that would appear to be possible would be something like "XYZ Ltd is hereby appointed as non-exclusive agent for the sale of the Products ..." specifying neither territory nor customers. Obviously, this will cause problems for undertakings that have a network of agents—at least some of whom are exclusive—in that this type of non-exclusive agent can in theory find orders anywhere, including the territory of another exclusive agent, and cannot be restrained, thus putting the principal in danger of paying double commission. Where networks of agreements are in force, it seems as if the most practical way is either to have them all on a non-exclusive basis granted in such a way that Art.7(2) can never apply, or else to grant them all on an exclusive basis, and take the consequences in terms of commission if the principal decides to deal direct. However, non-exclusive agreements can also cause problems under Art.7(1) in relation to transac- **3–249** tions not put through the agent, but which are with customers he has previously acquired. What happens if the transaction is not made direct by the principal, but by another non-exclusive agent also entitled to operate in the same territory? It would seem that both agents would be entitled to commission, the first because he had previously acquired the customer, the second because he had concluded the transaction. Once again the Directive seems to be driving operators of networks of agencies down the road of using exclusive agreements with defined territories to avoid such problems although it is of course true that the territories can be quite small and do not have to relate to the whole of a Member State. Given all the above, a version (d) can now be drafted for a non-exclusive agency appointment, in which cl.3.3.8 would not be used, and which conforms to the Directive:

> 3.13.1(d) During the continuance of this agreement the Agent shall be paid a commission at the relevant percentage or percentages set out below upon the net invoice price before any value added or sales taxes or other taxes or duties [FOB port of shipment] [Ex Works of the Principal] of all Products sold in the Territory either from orders received by the Principal through the Agent, or from orders received by the Principal from customers whom the Agent has previously acquired for the Principal as customers for the Products whether or not such orders were received by the Principal through the Agent [PROVIDED THAT (i) where such orders were not received by the Principal through the Agent or (ii) where the Agent transmits to the Principal such an order from a customer previously acquired by another agent appointed by the Principal in respect of the Products under an agreement that is in force at the time the relevant order is transmitted THEN in either case the relevant percentage shall be reduced by [one half]:
>
> Product Percentage

This version will suffice with no difficulty where the local Member State has not opted for the first alternative in Art.7(2). If it has so opted, this version will avoid Art.7(2) problems only if the grant is not specific as to customers or territory. Version (d), can, of course, also be adapted to cover the idea of agreement to commission on the basis of an ad hoc arrangement in respect of each order as in version 3.13.1.(a) above. The phrase in square brackets provides (i) for differential commission rates on orders not received through the agent, and (ii) for avoidance of double payment of commission where a number of non-exclusive agents are operating in the same customer base.

3–250 The operation of Arts 6 and 7 of the Directive, and some guidance on the question of the mandatory nature of Art.7 can be obtained from the European Court Case of *Kontogeorgas v Kartonpak AE* [1997] 1 C.M.L.R. 1093.

3–251 The Greek Court of first instance submitted to the European Court the following questions for a ruling:

> "(1) Where a commercial agent is responsible for a specific geographical area, is he entitled to commission on transactions entered into without his involvement at any stage and irrespective of whether he himself had found the customers in question, or is he so entitled only on transactions concluded in his area of activity as a result of his intervention and with

customers which he himself has found; and (2) What is the meaning to be attached to the term 'customer belonging' to that area? In particular, where the customer is a company whose seat is located in a different place from that in which its business and trading activities are carried on, does the word 'belonging' refer to the company's seat or to the place in which its commercial activity is carried on."

The Advocate-General in his opinion said "what is laid down in Article 7(2) goes beyond that provided for in Article 7(1) and accordingly conclusion of a contract following the involvement of the agent does not, under the abovementioned Article 7(2), constitute the precondition for entitlement to commission. Moreover, if that condition had to be met in the cases provided for in Article 7(2), then the existence of that paragraph would be unnecessary". The Court agreed with this approach in their judgment and found that: "the first indent of Article 7(2) of the Directive must be interpreted as meaning that, where a commercial agent is responsible for a geographical area, he is entitled to commission on transactions concluded with customers belonging to that area, even if they were concluded without any action on his part". **3–252**

So far as the second question was concerned, again following the opinion of the Advocate-General, but this time going somewhat farther, the Court found that: **3–253**

"...the meaning of the term 'customer belonging to that area' must be determined, where the customer is a legal person, by the place where the latter actually carries on its commercial activities. Where a company carries on its commercial activity in various places, or where the agent operates in several areas, other factors may be taken into account to determine the centre of gravity of the transaction effected, in particular the place where negotiations with the agent took place or should, in the normal course of events, have taken place, the place where the goods were delivered and the place where the establishment which placed the order is located."

The guidelines provided here are useful, and it is submitted, very much in line with a common sense approach and a purposive interpretation of the Directive. **3–254**

The question of the mandatory nature of Art.7 of the Directive can be gathered from some comments of the Court on the approach that Kartonpak took to avoid its agent's claim under Art.7(2). The Court commented as follows: **3–255**

"Kartonpak considers, however, that Article 7 of the Directive must be read in conjunction with Article 6, which leaves it to the parties to the contract to specify what remuneration the commercial agent will receive. Since exclusivity is not mandatory in law, it would be incomprehensible if the agent were entitled to commission for all sales made in his area. It should be noted, on this point, that [emphasis added] ***Article 6 of the Directive concerns an agent's rate of remuneration and not, in contra-distinction to Article 7, transactions on which commission is payable. The matters covered by those two provisions are consequently not the same.***"

3–256 Although this comment is not as clear as one would wish, it can at least be taken to mean that while Art.6 allows the parties to fix the agent's commission by agreement, once it has been so agreed, it must be applied to all the transactions covered by Art.7. Although Art.8 was not mentioned in the judgment, presumably the same reasoning would apply as between Art.6 and Art.8.

3–257 In *Ingmar GB Limited v Eaton Leonard Inc* [2001] Eu L.R. 755, QBD, Morland J. took a rather different view. He said: "It should be noted that there is no non-derogation article equivalent to Article 19 applicable to Articles 7 and 8. In my judgment the absence of such a specific non-derogation article means that commercial agents and principals may derogate contractually from Articles 7 and 8 but only so far as they do not thwart the purpose of the Council Directive". It is noteworthy that *Kontogeorgas v Kartonpak AE* was not cited in this case, although it was decided some four years before, and it is not clear as to the basis upon which the learned judge came to the conclusion that he did in regard to the two articles. The point does not seem to have been argued before him. Nor is it clear from his remarks how he conceived that one could derogate from these two articles "without thwarting the purpose of the Directive".

3–258 In *Kontogeorgas v Kartonpak AE*, it was not necessary to consider the actual impact of an agreement as to differing rates of commission for different classes of transactions, because there was no such agreement. Thus, the nub of the judgment on this point is that the possibility of the agreement of rates of commission under Art.6 has no bearing on the application of those rates (once agreed) under Arts 7 and 8. Agreement can fix the rates, but (once fixed) application is mandatory.

3–259 There is some basis for a further contention (see the highlighted words in the quotation from the judgment set out above) that only one such rate can be fixed for the agent under Art.6. This is because the judgment speaks of "rate of remuneration" in the singular. If this were so, it would mean that a uniform rate (once agreed) would be applied on a mandatory basis to all transactions caught under Arts 7 and 8. This interpretation would prevent differing (albeit fair and reasonable) rates being set for different classes of customers or transactions as contended for under the argument set out above.

3–260 This further contention seems hard to support. First, the particular issue was never before the Court, since no rates for different classes of transactions were agreed between Kartonpak and Kontogeorgas. Second, there appears to be nothing in the letter or spirit of the Directive to prevent the agreement to such differing rates, provided they are at a customary level, or, at the least, fair and reasonable, and thus in line with the express provisions of Art.6.

Leaving aside this further point, it is at least clear that the Court considered Arts 7 and 8 to be of mandatory application despite the lack of specific provision that the parties could not derogate from them. This fortifies the arguments set out above on the classification of mandatory and non-mandatory provisions of the Directive. **3–261**

On the other hand, Morland J.'s approach would seem to suggest that Arts 7 and 8 are not mandatory. However, it is hard to see the practical application of his further statement that derogation is permitted only in so far as it would not frustrate the purposes of the Directive. It is submitted that the only practical ways to derogate from those articles is either not to grant the agent rights in respect of certain classes of customers, transactions, or geographical areas in the first place or to agree varying rates of commission. As argued above, the first approach is not a derogation from Arts 7 and 8 as the excluded customers, transactions or areas were never part of the agreement in the first place. So far as the second is concerned, this (as *Kontogeorgas v Kartonpak* shows) is more properly approached by way of agreement of a commission rate as permitted by Art.6. It has nothing to do with derogation from Arts 7 and 8. **3–262**

The only possibility of reconciling the two cases seems to be first to hold that Arts 7 and 8 are mandatory, and then to consider that the derogation proposed by Morland J. actually comes about through the agreement of differing rates of commission under Art.6. His statement that such "derogation" must not frustrate the purposes of the Directive would then apply (as set out in the argument above) to prevent an agreement to a *de minimis* commission for certain transactions which would thus render one or more of the provisions of Arts 7 and 8 ineffective. **3–263**

However, Morland J.'s remarks are *obiter*, while those of the European Court in *Kartonpak* were central to the judgment, in that its concept of the difference between Art.6 and Arts.7 and 8 was what caused the Court to reject Kartonpak's arguments in relation to the first question before it. In any event, it must be said that the European Court does not have the same concept of *obiter dicta* that prevails in the common law, and thus its pronouncements carry more weight even if they are not considered central to its judgment. **3–264**

On the present state of the law, and given the analysis of the two cases set out above, it appears at least likely that a court in the UK would accept the possibility of varying rates of commission being agreed under Art.6, but then apply those rates as a mandatory requirement in the circumstances contemplated in Arts 7 and 8. This enables a practical (rather than, it must be admitted, a theoretically sound) reconciliation of the two cases. In the absence of further judicial guidance, it is submitted, that, currently, although not free from doubt, this is the best view of the state of the law in this complex area. **3–265**

3.13.2 Commission shall become due and payable to the Agent in accordance with cl.3.13.1 as soon as the Principal has received the full order price in respect of the relevant order from its customers. Where the order provides for payment by **3–266** instalments a proportionate part of the Commission shall become due and payable to the Agent (as soon as such instalments are received by the Principal) equivalent to the proportion which such instalments form of the order price except that where the Principal is required under the terms of such order to provide bonds or other securities for such instalments no proportionate part of such commission shall become due and payable to the Agent unless and until such bonds or other securities are released to the Principal PROVIDED (i) where and to the extent that an order is not executed the agent shall nevertheless be entitled to commission in accordance with cl.3.13.1 unless the order is not executed due to a reason for which the principal was not to blame (ii) that where the agent is entitled under proviso (i) to commission on an order such commission shall become due upon the date or dates upon which, but for the default of the Principal, the customer who placed the relevant order would have been obliged to make the relevant payment or payments to the Principal in respect of that order (iii) where the agent is not entitled under proviso (i) to commission on an order and the Principal has already paid all or any part of commission to the Agent the same shall forthwith be refunded to the Principal by the Agent and (iv) in the event of the agent failing to refund commission pursuant to proviso (iii) the Principal may set-off or deduct an amount equal to such commission from any other commission or any other sum then or at any time thereafter owing to the Agent by the Principal. For the purposes of this clause an order shall be deemed to be "executed" to the extent that the Principal has delivered goods in accordance with the relevant order and the third party customer has accepted such goods and paid for them in full.

The Directive contains provisions as to when commission is due and payable (Arts 10 and 11). Unfortunately Art.10 is not a model of clarity. Article 10(1) specifies that commission is due as soon as either the principal executed or should have executed the transaction, or the customer executed the transaction, and Art.10(2) specifies that commission is due at the latest when the customer executes his part of the transaction, or when he should have done, if the principal had complied with his contractual obligations. Article 10(4) then provides that there can be no derogation from 10(2) to the disadvantage of the agent, but is silent about derogation from 10(1). In most transactions covered by agency agreements for the supply of goods, execution by the principal means delivery of the goods, and execution by the third party means payment for them in full. Article 10(2) thus in effect provides that once the customer has paid, commission must be due, irrespective of whether the principal has at that time delivered or not. Hence, the only sense to be made of Art.10(1), which could of course provide for an earlier due date, such as delivery by the principal, seems to be that the provisions of Art.10(1) are more favourable options for the agent which can be adopted by agreement between the parties.

3–267 Most principals will wish for commission to be due when the customer has paid. Clause 3.13.2 provides for this, and, on the above argument, does not seem inconsistent with Art.10(2) of the Directive. Since the preamble to Art.10(1) talks about commission becoming due "as soon as and to the extent that ..." the contract is executed, the provisions in cl.3.13.2 about payment by instalments and retentions would also seem to be compatible with the Directive.

3–268 The final problem to be faced is in relation to contracts that are not executed. Although this term is not defined in the Directive or the Regulations, a contract for the supply of goods would, based upon the discussion above, seem to be "executed" when the principal has delivered all of the goods in accordance with the contract and the third party customer has accepted delivery and paid for them in full. This is dealt with in the proviso to the clause. Article 11(1) states that the right to commission, once it arises (*i.e.* under Art.7), cannot be extinguished unless, and then only to the extent that, the concluded contract is not executed and the reason for non-execution is not a default of the principal. Clearly if the customer is in breach either through refusing to pay in full, or by not accepting delivery, or there is an event of *force majeure*, the contract is not executed and the right to commission is extinguished. However, where the principal is in breach, and this is the reason for the failure to execute the contract, the principal remains liable to pay commission, and cannot contract out of that liability (Art.11(3)). Looking at the conditional language in Art.10(1)(b) and (2), it appears that commission on such contracts becomes due either when the principal should have performed his part, or when the customer should have performed his part (on the supposition that the principal had actually performed rather than been in breach). Applying the arguments above, it would seem that the latest that could be provided for such commission to fall due is when the customer should have performed. As an example, let us suppose that the principal should have delivered goods at the end of July, but did not do so, and the payment should be made at the end of the month following that in which delivery should have been made, then the commission would become due at the end of August.

Article 11(2) also provides that any commission already paid in respect of contracts which have not been executed due to a reason for which the principal is not to blame must be refunded. It is worth putting such a provision expressly into cl.3.13.2. The clause works on the basis that commission (except for the case covered by the proviso) is due and payable only when the third party has paid the principal in full. This means that, in most cases where a contract is not executed, the third party will never have paid the principal and the commission in respect of the order will never have been paid. **3–269**

However, in some cases a part payment may have been made. If the contract provides for payment by instalments or deposit, and some payment has been made, under cl.3.13.2 the principal would already have paid a proportionate part of the commission to the agent, and this part should be refunded. The Directive is silent upon the issue of whether the agent has to refund commission only if the principal has refunded the part payment or deposit to the customer. Thus, in circumstances where the contract entitles the principal to keep the part payment, because the fact that the contract is not executed is not the principal's fault the clause, since it does not deal with this situation expressly, would still require the agent to return the part payment of commission. Of course, if the part payment is refunded because the contract was not executed due to the principal's fault, not only would the agent keep commission already paid, but he would also be entitled to the **3–270** balance of commission due, under Art.10(2). The last point on return of commission is to note that the presence in the preamble to Art.11(1) of the words "to the extent that" means that where an order provides for delivery of separate consignments (each paid for at the latest on or after delivery) the concept of execution of the order is applied separately in relation to each consignment. Thus Art.11 has no application to a consignment delivered and paid for, even if there is no execution of later consignments. This is catered for by the inclusion in the clause of the words "to the extent that" in provision (i) and in the definition of "execution".

3–271 Finally, the clause also, in addition, provides for a right of set-off against future commission if the agent fails to repay any commission paid under these circumstances. Such a right does not appear to be in contravention of the Directive or the Regulations.

3–272 3.13.3 After termination of this Agreement the Agent shall be entitled to commission as aforesaid (a) on orders for the Products accepted by the Principal after such termination if the said order was mainly attributable to the Agent's efforts during the period covered by this Agreement and if they were accepted within a period of [six months] after the termination of this Agreement or (b) if the said orders reached the Principal or the Agent before the termination of this Agreement PROVIDED THAT (i) if upon the termination of this Agreement a new agent has been appointed by the Principal for the Products the Agent shall be entitled only to such proportion of the aforesaid commission as is equitable in the circumstances, the balance being paid to the new agent by the Principal as aforesaid, (ii) that, in the event that the Principal has already paid the whole of the commission in respect of such an order to the Agent any part of that commission to which the Agent is not entitled by reason of the operation of proviso (i) shall be refunded to the Principal by the Agent and (iii) in the event that the Agent does not repay any commission required to be refunded to the Principal pursuant to proviso (ii) the Principal may set-off or deduct an amount equal to such commission from any other commission or any other sum then or at any time thereafter owing to the Agent by the Principal.

3.14.4 Where the Principal is obliged to pay commission to an agent previously appointed in respect of the Products, under an Agreement (now terminated or expired) which contains a provision equivalent to cl.3.13.3, on any order in respect of which the Agent would (except for this clause) be entitled to commission at the rate specified in cl.3.13.1, then notwithstanding any other provision of this Agreement to the contrary, the Agent shall only be entitled to receive the balance of such commission remaining after payment by the Principal of the proportion due under that provision to the old agent.

This clause complies with Arts 8 and 9 of the Directive. It should be noted that Art.8(1)(b) talks about transactions which are entered into within a reasonable time of the termination of the relevant agency agreement. The period of six months seems broadly reasonable for most types of goods, but it may need adjusting depending upon the circumstances of the case. Alternatively, the phrase, "within a reasonable period of time after the termination of this Agreement" could be substituted, leaving the discussion of exactly which orders are to be subject to post-termination commission to be held after termination if they arise. (It should be noted that under Italian law, commission on all such post-termination orders is payable to the agent, irrespective of when received, and that no cut-off by way of time limit can be imposed under the Directive.) It seems from *Ingmar GB Limited v Eaton Leonard Inc* [2001] Eu L.R. 755, QBD, that the court will consider the circumstances of each case to decide the length of the "reasonable period". Thus it should be possible for the court to ignore the specification of a particular period in the agreement, if it feels that it is too short. However, the fact that the agent agreed to the period when signing the agreement will make it more difficult for him to contend that the period is nevertheless unreasonable. In that case, where in fact no period was specified, the Court held that commission was recoverable under reg.8 in respect of a particular transaction because, "although the transaction was entered into 21 months after the agency was terminated it was 'within a reasonable period' having regard to the nature of the agency, the product and the customer base".

Davis J. considered the operation of art.8(a) in *Tigana Ltd v Decoro Ltd* **3–273**
and calculated post-termination commission as follows:

> "The essential task, therefore, under Regulation 8(a) is to identify those transactions (if any) concluded after [the agency ended] where (a) the transaction was 'mainly attributable' to Tigana's efforts during the period of the Sales Agreement *and* (b) the transaction was entered into within a 'reasonable period' after 31st December 1999 [when the agency ended]. The overall task, therefore, is one of judgment and assessment (but not of discretion) by reference to the facts of the case. It is to be noted, however, that the provisions of Regulation 8(a) are conjunctive and cumulative: the transaction concluded is to be mainly attributable to the agent's efforts during the period of the agency contract *and* if the transaction is entered into within a reasonable period after the agency contract terminated. Thus the second part of Regulation 8(a) delimits the first part. What is a reasonable period in this case? I have come to the conclusion it is nine months. I so conclude for essentially the following reasons:
>
> 1. By October 2000 Mr Feltham-White [the new agent] had become established as Decoro's agent in place of Mr Coleman [the owner of Tigana].
> 2. Up to October 2000, Mr Feltham-White's activities had been confined to consolidating and administrating the customers introduced by Mr Coleman: by then, he had become familiar with existing customers and thereafter he also started to introduce some new custom himself.
> 3. By October 2000, there had been (or were about to be) High Point, and other trade fairs, where new Decoro models were displayed. Repeat orders for 1999 models were thus tending to disappear.
> 4. The significance of Mr Coleman's erstwhile involvement with Decoro would by October 2000 be likely substantially to have diminished in the eyes of even his most loyal supporters.

5. For the purposes of Regulation 8(a), nine months seems to me to be a fair reflection, in the circumstances, both of the nature of Tigana's agency and of the actual period of such agency.

Accordingly, while I think that a proportion of the orders placed up to the end of 2000 (and, perhaps, even in the first part of 2001) could be said still to be mainly attributable to Mr Coleman's efforts, in my judgment nine months is to be determined as the reasonable period for the purposes of Regulation 8(a)."

3–274 Where a principal thinks it is likely that agents will come and go frequently in a particular territory, it is important to ensure that all of the agreements contain cl.3.13.3. Where one is dealing with a network of non-exclusive agents who can deal freely across the relevant territory, it is also important that all such agreements should contain version (d) of cl.3.13.1 together with the phrase in square brackets in that clause, to take care of conflicts between concurrently appointed agents, to the extent reasonably practicable. In all cases, exclusive or non-exclusive, cl.3.13.4 must be included so as to require the agent to share his commission with another agent whose agreement has been terminated. This provision is the other side of the right to the entitlement to post-termination commission in cl.3.13.3. Both provisions are obviously necessary as a standard term in all the principal's agency agreements, past current and future, if the principal is not to have conflicts between current and terminated agents over such commission.

3–275 **3.13.4** See cl.2.13.5.

3–276 **3.13.5** See cl.2.13.6.

3–277 **3.13.6** See cl.2.13.7.

3–278 3.13.7 The Principal shall supply the Agent with a statement of all commissions due hereunder not later than the last day of the month following the quarter in which such commissions have become due. Such statement shall set out the main components used in calculating the amount of such commission. The Agent shall, upon request, be entitled to all the information (including without limitation n extract from the Principal's books of account) which is available to the Principal and which the Agent needs in order to check the amount of such commission due to the Agent.

This provision complies with Art.12 of the Directive.

3.14 Schedule 4—stock of the products

3–279 3.14.1 The Principal will (at the cost of the Principal) deliver to the Agent's warehouse a stock of the Products (which shall remain the property of the Principal) of a quantity and value to be decided by the Principal from time to time. The Principal will make up such stock (periodically at a frequency to be decided by the Principal) to the then current quantity and value fixed by the Principal. The Agent shall have no right of action against the Principal for any delay or failure by the Principal to deliver initially or subsequently make up such stock to any particular quantity or value or at all.

3.14.2 The parties hereby declare and agree that the Agent is acting in a fiduciary relationship to the Principal in regard to all transactions and other matters covered by or arising out of this Agreement and that in particular, but without prejudice to the generality of the foregoing: **3–280**

3.14.2.1 The Agent holds all stocks of the Products from time to time in its possession as bailee for the Principal. The Agent shall handle and store all such stocks under appropriate conditions and with due care and attention. In particular the Agent shall store such stocks in a way that they are identified as the property of the Principal.

3.14.2.2 The Agent hereby acknowledges the Principal as the true owner of such stocks.

3.14.2.3 The Agent holds as trustee for the Principal all moneys and all book debts which arise from or in respect of sales or other disposals negotiated and concluded by the Agent on behalf of the Principal for such stocks in respect of which it has not yet made a remittance to the Principal in accordance with cl.3.14.6.

3.14.2.4 If the Agent is obliged to issue invoices in respect of sales of the Products which include charges for value added or sales tax or other taxes or duties ("taxation amounts"), the Agent shall (subject to cl.2.14.2.6) be responsible for the collection of all taxation amounts from the relevant customer and their due payment to the relevant fiscal authority on behalf of the Principal. For the avoidance of doubt pending such remittance the Agent shall treat all taxation amounts as moneys received under cl.3.14.2.3 and shall hold the same as trustee for the Principal in accordance with the terms of cl.3.14.2.3.

3.14.2.5 The Agent shall promptly pay all taxation amounts collected by it to the relevant fiscal authority in accordance with the procedures and within the time limits prescribed by applicable law. The Agent shall indemnify the Principal for any failure (due to the Agent's own fault) to perform its obligations under this clause, including without limitation any penalties or fines which the Principal is required to pay to the relevant fiscal authority because of such default.

3.14.2.6 The Principal shall be solely responsible to the entire exclusion of the agent (i) for satisfying the requirements of any fiscal authority which requires to be paid a taxation amount which the Agent has (despite the exercise of due diligence) been unable to collect or unable to collect on time (an "uncollected taxation amount") and (ii) for the initiation of litigation to recover from a customer any unpaid sums of whatsoever nature.

3.14.2.7 The Agent shall include any insurance, transport or other handling costs and expenses ("delivery charges") paid by the Agent in relation to the delivery of consignments of the Products from the Agent's warehouse to customers in the invoice issued by the Agent on behalf of the Principal in relation to the relevant consignment of the Products. The Agent shall not be entitled to any commission in respect of such delivery charges but when accounting to the Principal in respect of the relevant invoice pursuant to cl.3.14.6 may deduct the relevant delivery charges from the relevant sum remitted to the Principal. Where the Agent has (despite the exercise of due diligence) not been able to collect delivery charges ("uncollected delivery charges") from a customer the Principal shall promptly reimburse them to the Agent.

3.14.2.8 To the extent that the Agent is subsequently able to collect an uncollected taxation amount (in respect of which the Principal has made an equivalent payment to the relevant fiscal authority) or uncollected delivery charges (in respect of which the Principal has made reimbursement to the Agent) from a customer, the Agent shall remit the same to the Principal in accordance with cl.3.14.6. For the avoidance of doubt pending such remittance the Agent shall treat all sums received in respect of such uncollected taxation amounts and uncollected delivery charges as moneys received under cl.3.14.2.3. and shall hold the same as trustee for the Principal in accordance with the terms of cl.3.14.2.3.

3–281 3.14.3 The Agent will at the cost of the Principal insure (and keep insured throughout the time it continues to hold such stock) all such stock held by it to its full value against all risks. The Agent undertakes to notify the relevant insurers as to the Principal's interest in such stock to endorse this interest on the relevant insurance policy and to hold any proceeds of such insurance policy on trust for the Principal to the extent of the Principal's interest. The Agent will on request produce a copy of the relevant policy of insurance and the receipt for the current premium.

3–282 3.14.4 In consideration of its service to the Principal the Agent shall receive by way of remuneration that percentage of the various net invoice prices (before any taxation amounts and delivery charges) at which the Products are sold by the Agent on behalf of the Principal shown below:

Product	Percentage

[or at such higher percentage as may from time to time be notified by the Principal to the Agent]

The parties acknowledge and agree that the levels of percentages set out under this clause include and take account of any costs relating to the stocks of the Products held by the Agent under this clause and to the performance of the Agent's obligations under this clause (including without limitation in relation to the storage and handling of the Products in the Agent's warehouse) to the extent that the same are not provided to be specifically reimbursed to the Agent in accordance with the terms of this schedule.

3–283 3.14.5 The Agent will keep full books of account and all relevant supporting vouchers showing all transactions relating to the Products negotiated or effected by the Agent under this Agreement including without limitation the collection of all taxation amounts and their remittance to the relevant fiscal authority.

3–284 3.14.6 The Agent will use its best endeavours (other than the initiation of litigation) to collect in accordance with the Principal's prescribed payment terms all invoice amounts due and owing from customers (including taxation amounts and delivery charges) and (to the extent so collected) to remit to the Principal [sixty days] after the last business day in each week an amount equal to the net invoice value of the Products delivered to purchasers during that week less taxation amounts and delivery charges and less such amount as the Agent is permitted to deduct in accordance with cl.3.14.4 and pending such remittance will not mix any moneys in respect of such Products received from the purchasers in any bank account which is not solely designated as an agency account relating to moneys held in trust for the Principal by the Agent.

3.14.7 The Agent will supply from time to time upon the written request of the Principal the reports returns and other information relating to the performance of its obligations under this Schedule and to contracts for the sale of the Products negotiated by it as follows: **3–285**

3.14.7.1 Not more than fourteen days after the end of each week a statement showing the transactions effected during that week in relation to the Products as recorded in the Agent's accounts kept in accordance with cl.2.14.5;

3.14.7.2 Not more than fourteen days after the end of each week a statement by customer showing the Products sold during that week together with copies of all relevant invoices showing separately units sold and their sales value;

3.14.7.3 Not more than fourteen days after the end of each month a statement certified by [a director or other authorised officer of] the Agent stating opening and closing stocks for the month in question and showing total unit sales of the Products during that month together with a record of any receipts of deliveries of the Products during that month from the Principal such monthly statement to be accompanied by a statement of the kind referred to in cl.3.14.7.1 but showing the position at the end of the relevant month.

3.14.7.4 Not more than fourteen days after the date of each payment of a taxation amount to the relevant fiscal authority all relevant details thereof including without limitation copies of all documents sent to the relevant fiscal authority in respect of such payment together with a copy of the invoices in respect of which such payment has been made.

3.14.8 The Agent will allow the authorised officers of the Principal or any authorised representative upon reasonable notice during working hours to inspect and count the stock of the Products and to inspect verify and take copies of the accounts and vouchers kept by the Agent in accordance with cl.2.14.5. **3–286**

3.14.9 Upon termination of this Agreement for whatever cause or at any time previous to such termination the Agent shall upon request at the expense of the Principal immediately return to the Principal or to a nominee of the Principal or on the direction of the Principal otherwise dispose of all stocks of the Products held by the Agent under this schedule. If there is any deficiency in the stock of the Products discovered as a result of such request or of an inspection and count in terms of cl.3.14.8 because of loss or theft or damage or because of deterioration due to incorrect storage or handling such deficiency (to the extent that it is due to the fault of the Agent) shall be deemed to have been stock sold by the Agent on the date of such discovery under the terms of this Agreement and the Agent shall account to the Principal for it in accordance with cl.3.14.6. **3–287**

3.14.10 Samples of Products covered by cl.3.4.2 shall not form part of the stock of Products governed by this Schedule. **3–288**

There is nothing in the Directive which would prevent an agent holding consignment stock, which is the property of the principal, on behalf of the principal. However, its presence where the state in which the factor carries on business or is registered is one of the contracting states to the Brussels Convention (see Chapter 2.3.6) will almost certainly render the principal liable to the jurisdiction of the local courts of that state, in the event of a dispute with a purchaser of the goods supplied by the factor.

3–289 It should also be noted that care must be taken with the details of such arrangements when considering the impact of EC competition law on the agency agreement. This matter is discussed, together with some suggestions for drafting to avoid Art.81(1), in Chapter 5.1.1.3.15. The basic principle is that the agent should not bear any of the costs relating to the handling storage or sale of the consignment stock and that he should bear no risk in connection with the stock, its storage or sale, or in relation to the collection of payment for the stock, except to the extent that such risk arises due to his own fault. The draft of the schedule set out above should be read in conjunction with the commentary in Chapter 2.14, but the key difference between the terms of this schedule and of Sch.2.14, is that the agent does not bear any of these costs or risks.

Chapter 4

Distribution Agreements Outside the EC

Contents

4.1 Commercial and legal background

In this chapter we shall be concerned with distributors. A distributor, unlike an agent, purchases products from the principal for his own account, takes title to the products purchased and then resells them to his customers in his territory. Thus no contractual relationship is created between the principal and the ultimate customers. Instead there are separate sets of contracts— **4–01** those between the principal and the distributor, and those between the distributor and his customers. The distributor takes his remuneration from the margin between the prices at which he purchases the products and the price at which he sells them on. Since the distributor is an independent contractor he assumes far more risk, and can look to his principal for far less indemnification than an agent can. In particular he normally assumes the risk of bad debts on the sales he makes, and often assumes obligations in relation to warranty claims, maintenance, and advertising expenditure. In return for the greater assumption of obligations and risk, the distributor normally enjoys more freedom than an agent in the way that he deals with the products in the territory, and a higher rate of remuneration.

4–02 However, the relationship between principal and distributor can be adjusted by contract in many cases, so that the two parties can allocate the obligations between them as is commercially appropriate in the particular relationship. On the one hand the actions of the distributor can be so circumscribed, and his indemnities so wide, that he approaches the position of an agent. On the other, the principal can assume obligations to such an extent that the relationship begins to approach that of a joint venture.

4–03 When a principal chooses the particular relationship that he requires he thus has a range of options open to him. He can start with the maximum control, involvement and risk, by opening a branch office in the territory. The desirability of this is determined by a number of factors. The formalities involved in setting up trade in a foreign country are often complicated and difficult for people who are not familiar with them. Quite apart from having to comply with requirements that may be burdensome (for instance in France where one sets up a trading branch office it is usually necessary to file the complete worldwide accounts of the legal entity of which the branch is a part), the registration may open the way for local taxation authorities to levy tax on all or part of the profits of the legal entity of which the branch forms part. Some, but not all of these problems may be resolved by setting up a local subsidiary, but here the procedures are often lengthy and in some cases a local subsidiary wholly owned or controlled by aliens is not permitted.

4–04 In addition, the question of transfer taxes has become an increasing problem in international trade. The Revenue authorities of the territory from which goods are exported to the branch or subsidiary will want to be sure that products and services (and indeed licences of intellectual property) are sold and transferred at arms-length market rate prices. If the transfer prices are too low, profit (and hence potential tax revenue) is being shifted out of their territory to the territory where the branch or subsidiary operates. On the other hand the Revenue authorities having jurisdiction over the branch or subsidiary will want to be sure that transfer prices are not too high, for fear of excessive profit being retained in the home territory, from which the grant or supply comes, to the detriment of their tax revenues. This is a complex area requiring competent international accounting and financial advice if problems are to be avoided in one territory or the other.

4–05 The decision to set up a local operation thus has to be made after weighing up the considerable level of investment in time and money required, the availability of expertise to run the operation, difficulties in practice in controlling foreign operations closely enough, unfavourable overhead structures caused by the degree of centralised control necessary, and the fact that the local employees lack incentive to operate in an entrepreneurial role.

Although a good incentive or bonus scheme, coupled with a system of decentralised management on the basis of local profit centres, can go a long way towards overcoming some of these drawbacks, exporters often prefer to consider a joint venture with a local company, which will undertake some of the investment and some of the risks, and provide the necessary local knowledge. The joint venture can take two forms, either a loose association on the basis of a partnership or consortium, or else a special company can be incorporated for the purposes of the joint venture and the parties to the venture can participate through shareholdings in the joint venture company. Many countries encourage such joint venture local companies, but in some countries (*e.g.* Malaysia) on the basis that the local partner is the majority shareholder. **4–06**

The looser and more informal consortium enables the parties to regulate their relationship easily through contract, but it does have the drawback that each of the parties is (as regards the outside world) jointly and severally liable for the acts of the partnership or consortium, and the acts of the one member (often the local partner) fully bind all the parties, even if they have not agreed to or are not aware of the act in question. Further, the liability of each member is unlimited. This creates risks where the two parties to the arrangement are in different countries, and close control and liaison is not easy. **4–07**

The joint venture company has the merit of limiting the liability of the participants according to their shareholdings, and also solves the problem of joint and several liability by interposing the joint venture company as a screen between the members of the venture and the outside world. However, the joint venture now has a greater degree of formality, and it may be less easy for a dissatisfied member to withdraw from the relationship. Also, where the joint venture company is not substantial, third parties may be unwilling to contract with it, because of the limited liability factor, unless a guarantee is given by the shareholders, which defeats the object of the limited liability company. **4–08**

Thus many exporters prefer to make use of the relationship with a distributor. The distributor is an independent contractor, and thus does not bind the principal by his acts. Subject to anything to the contrary in the distributorship agreement, no partnership or joint venture is created, and the principal is not regarded as carrying on a trade or business in the territory. Thus the risk of unwanted contractual obligations, the need to register, and the possibility of local taxation are all avoided. In return for the distributor undertaking most of the work and risk in the relationship, the distributor naturally receives greater rewards, and this should, in turn, stimulate his activity as an entrepreneur. **4–09**

4–10 This chapter is concerned with distribution agreements outside the area of the EC, and the agreement is one which is best suited for large volume sales of the ordinary types of consumer goods. Distribution agreements within the EC are subject to special rules. General distribution agreements will be considered in relation to EC law in Chapter 5. Chapter 6 is concerned with selective distribution arrangements for the purpose of setting up networks of authorised distributors with particular reference to high technology and luxury products. Selective distribution agreements also have special rules applicable to them under EC law, and this aspect is considered in detail in Chapter 6.

4–11 Since EC competition law only deals with anti-competitive agreements to the extent that they affect trade between Member States, in past years it would theoretically have been possible to use this precedent, without consideration of EC competition law, but of course taking account of local competition law, in circumstances where both the parties were resident in one Member State and their agreement had no effect on trade outside that Member State. With the increasing progress towards a single market in the EU, the EC Commission and the European Court have become much more likely to find an effect (or at least a potential effect) on trade between Member States even in these circumstances. Furthermore, most Member States have been encouraged by the Commission, during the last decade, to adopt competition law regimes which closely correspond to EC competition law, although some local differences still remain.

4–12 Competition law in the UK has followed this path, and was radically changed by the Competition Act 1998, which repealed the Restrictive Trade Practices Act 1976, the Resale Prices Act 1976 (see s.1) and the Competition Act 1980 (see s.17), replacing these statutes with a new regime based very closely on EC competition law.

4–13 It would now be most unwise to draft a distribution agreement for implementation only in any one Member State of the EU without taking into account both EC competition law and the national competition law of the relevant Member State. Furthermore, given the likely similarities between the two regimes, the agreement would probably have to take much the same form even if the parties were certain that there was no effect on trade between Member States.

4–14 As stated above all of these issues will be dealt with in relation to EC competition law in Chapters 5 and 6. At the same time it is most convenient to discuss the impact of the new UK regime in those chapters, in order to compare and contrast it with the EC regime, and to discuss how the two regimes will interact in the future.

The precedent in this chapter thus proceeds on the basis that it should not be used anywhere in the EU including the UK, even if the parties consider there is no effect on trade between Member States.

4–15 Of course, nothing discussed above would prevent a principal based in one of the Member States, including the UK, from entering into an agreement in this form with a distributor outside the EU (subject to certain caveats around the possibility of reimportation of goods sold by the distributor into the EU – see the discussion in Chapter 5.5.2) and applying the national law of the relevant Member State as the governing law of the agreement.

4.2 Licence

4.2 The Principal hereby grants the Distributor [an exclusive] [a non exclusive] licence to distribute and sell the Products under the Trade Mark in the Territory during the continuance of this Agreement. **4–16**

The basic grant of the distributorship can be on an exclusive or non-exclusive basis. Apart from the EC most areas of the world have no special legislation relating to exclusive as opposed to non-exclusive distributorships although in the countries where registration of the local representative is required there can by definition only be one distributor for a particular product. It is questionable whether in the absence of an express provision to the contrary the grant of an exclusive licence to a distributor would prevent the principal from setting up a local manufacturing operation in the territory. The best view seems to be that although local manufacture itself would not breach the exclusivity, the principal would commit a breach once he, himself, or through a local manufacturer, began to distribute and sell the products in the territory. Some authorities consider that the use of the word "sole" as opposed to "exclusive" would permit the principal to distribute himself within the territory, but not to permit any third party to distribute. However, given the varying interpretations in different jurisdictions, if it is intended that the principal should himself be able to supply into the territory of an exclusive distributor, then express provision should be made for this, and also as to whether or not the distributor should in some way be compensated for direct sales, for instance by receiving a commission on an agency basis.

It is advisable to grant the distributor the right to sell under any relevant trade marks. As discussed below it is better to grant rights to use trade marks on a strictly controlled basis, than to leave the distributor to use them informally, and thus, perhaps, depending on the law of the territory, build up rights in them adverse to those of his principal. **4–17**

4.3 General undertakings by distributor

4.3.1 Due diligence

4.3.1 The Distributor shall during the continuance of this Agreement diligently and faithfully serve the Principal as its distributor in the Territory and shall use its best endeavours to improve the good will of the Principal in the Territory and to further and increase the sale of the Products in the Territory. **4–18**

A general provision to this effect is useful for the same reasons as discussed in Chapter 2.1. The reference to the duty to improve the principal's good will is less appropriate to a distributor than an agent, given that the distributor has the primary relationship with the customers in the territory, since he contracts directly with these customers in his own right. Nevertheless there is still an issue surrounding the goodwill of the principal in relation to the products sold, particularly if the products are sold under an internationally recognised trade mark or brand name, and the inclusion of this provision is at least helpful in this respect.

4.3.2 No interference with sales of products

4–19 4.3.2 The Distributor shall not do anything that may prevent the sale or interfere with the development of sales of the Products in the Territory.

Although this provision is aimed basically at preventing dealing with competing goods, it is also a useful clause to have available in termination negotiations to ensure that during any period of notice, or in the situation where the distributorship is non-exclusive, the distributor does not actively obstruct or cause harm to the market for the products in the territory.

4.3.3 Conforming to local legislation

4–20 4.3.3 The Distributor will ensure that it conforms with all legislation rules regulations and statutory requirements existing in the Territory from time to time in relation to the Products.

This provision puts the responsibility for such things as conforming to labelling requirements, or permitted ingredients, or licensing or safety legislation, on to the distributor. In practice, since the distributor is not a manufacturer he must make sure that the principal is aware of all such requirements as are in force from time to time, and ensure that the principal manufactures the products in conformity with them.

4.3.4 Proper storage of products

4–21 4.3.4 The Distributor undertakes to store the Products under conditions that will prevent deterioration and also (on the instructions of the Principal) to store particular Products under such special conditions as may be appropriate to their requirements. Where the Distributor is responsible for clearing goods through customs and other import formalities into the Territory it shall exercise its best endeavours to ensure that such clearance is carried out as quickly as possible and that pending such clearance the goods are stored as aforesaid. The Distributor agrees to allow the Principal or its authorised representative to inspect the Products when in storage under the control of the Distributor from time to time upon reasonable notice.

Proper storage of the products is vital, particularly in countries where extremes of temperature and humidity prevail which are not normally encountered in the principal's country of manufacture. This is particularly important in the area of edible goods, or machinery that requires protection from the weather. Many sensitive products in fact spoil through incorrect storage or simple delay while awaiting customs clearance. The distributor should at least undertake to try to carry out clearance, which will usually be his responsibility, as quickly as possible. The right to inspect in storage should also be reserved, although this will often be done through a consultant (see Chapter 9).

The principal should be concerned in this area not purely for lost sales, but also and more importantly for the loss of good will if products which have deteriorated in storage are later put on the market. **4–22**

4.3.5 Purchase targets

4.3.5 The Distributor undertakes to achieve targets in relation to the Products in accordance with Sch.4. **4–23**

Where the distributor is put in the position of exclusivity, and normally with an initial fixed period to his agreement, it is reasonable that he should be asked to achieve certain minimum targets at least in the fixed period of the agreement. These targets can be either for purchases from the principal or for sales by the distributor in the territory. In the case of a distributorship purchase targets are easier to monitor, and more realistic, in that, if the distributor wishes, it is possible for him to take extra stock to fulfil his targets even if sales are not going well at that particular time. Since the principal makes his money by selling to the distributor this should not be of too much concern to him. The matter is dealt with in detail, together with appropriate safeguard provisions, in Chapter 4.24.

4.3.6 Non-competition clause

4.3.6 The Distributor undertakes during the continuance of this Agreement [and for a period of [one year] thereafter] without the Principal's prior written consent not to manufacture or sell in or import into the Territory any goods competitive with the Products and not to be interested directly or indirectly in any such manufacture sale or importation. This provision shall not apply to those goods (if any) listed in Sch.5. **4–24**

The schedule is set out in Chapter 4.25. Although non-competition clauses are as usual in distributorship as in agency agreements, particularly exclusive ones, it often occurs that a distributor who is sufficiently successful to be chosen by the principal to represent him already has experience in the particular type of product concerned and may wish to handle, or have contractual obligations to go on handling, competing products that he already distributes. Rather than exclude competing activity altogether, it is preferable to reach an understanding by detailing and thus limiting the competing products to the special cases really in issue. The schedule can always be enlarged by subsequent agreement if commercial pressures make this necessary. So far as the phrase in square brackets is concerned, a post termination ban on competition in the case of a distributor is often problematic. It may very well be unenforceable under local legislation concerning restraint of trade. Reference should be made to the discussion in Chapter 1.2.9 and Chapter 1.5. However, within the UK (leaving aside the questions of competition law discussed in Chapter 5) such a wide clause is unlikely to be enforceable, as an unreasonable restraint of trade. The situation is probably the same even for a clause on the non-solicitation of customers. The customers are the customers of the distributor, not of the principal, and the good will in the customer base belongs rather to the distributor than to the principal (see Chapter 4.1). The principal will therefore find it hard, if not impossible to show that he has a legitimate good will interest in the customer base serviced by the distributor which he is entitled to protect by a non-competition clause (See Chapter 4.1). Thus, a post termination ban on competition, even if it were limited to non-solicitation of existing customers, would become a mere naked restraint on competition, and hence unenforceable. The only possible post termination restraint would be against using confidential information acquired from the distributor (see Chapter 4.18).

4.3.7 No copying of products

4–25 4.3.7 The Distributor undertakes not to copy produce make modify or manufacture or assist any other party to copy produce make modify or manufacture the Products or any part thereof for use sale or any other purpose.

This type of provision is common enough in distribution agreements, since the distributor often has more technical information about the products (perhaps for purposes of registration or for maintenance or servicing) and also more opportunity to analyse or dismantle the products than other manufacturers. In general the provision is enforceable and backed up by the various intellectual and industrial property rights that the principal presumably has in relation to the products in the territory.

4–26 The problems in the area of the supply of spare parts dealt with in the House of Lords decision in *British Leyland Motor Co Ltd v Armstrong Patents Co Ltd* [1986] A.C. 577 have now largely been settled in the UK by the Copyright, Designs and Patents Act 1988.

4–27 In that case, the court affirmed the then current general principle of the law of copyright that "The indirect copying of a purely functional object which was not patentable...nor was of a registrable design...was nevertheless capable of being a breach of the copyright in the mechanical drawing of the object if it was apparent to a non-expert that the object was a copy of the drawing". This case concerned the copy and manufacture by the defendants of an exhaust pipe to be sold as a spare part for replacing exhaust pipes on cars which had been designed and manufactured (including the original exhaust pipes) by the plaintiffs. However, it was also held that "the manufacturer of an article such as a motor vehicle or other consumer durable could not by the exercise of copyright preclude the user of the article from access to a free market for spares necessary to maintain it in good working order". A purchaser of such an article had a right to keep it repaired and maintained, and the vendor was not entitled to derogate from or interfere with that right by asserting its copyright in spare parts to prevent third parties manufacturing and putting on the market spare parts which the purchaser could obtain to satisfy his requirements. In the words of Lord Templeman "Every owner of a car has a right to repair it. That right would be useless if suppliers of spare parts were not entitled to anticipate the need for repair". This decision is thus one of the instances of the principle referred to generally as "non-derogation from grant".

This case brought to an end a series of similar cases in which it had been sought to maintain that copyright could be used to prevent the copying of spare parts by means of reverse engineering. **4–28**

As far as the UK is concerned the case was rendered irrelevant rather than overturned by the legislation (effective from August 1, 1989) concerning the unregistered design right set out in the Copyright, Designs and Patents Act 1988. First of all, s.51 of the Act removes the protection of the principle quoted in *British Leyland* relating to copying from drawings by making the article to which the drawing relates. It is now no longer an infringement of copyright in a design document or model to make an article (unless it is an artistic work) to that design or in accordance with that model. Nor is it an indirect infringement of such design or model if one makes a copy of an article already lawfully made to that design or model. By itself, and in the absence of patent protection, or misuse of confidential information, this provision provides a charter for third party manufacturers of spare parts. **4–29**

However, s.213 of the Act replaces the protection taken away by s.51, by creating an unregistered design right. This is a new intellectual property right in "the design of any aspect of the shape or configuration (whether internal or external) of the whole or any substantial part of an article". The right has most of the features of copyright, but it lasts for only fifteen years from the time when the design was recorded in a document, or an article made to the design (whichever first occurs), but this period can be shortened in practice since protection ceases ten years after articles to the design were first put on the market anywhere in the world (see s 216 of the Act). In effect this allows for up to a five-year lead-time to production, and ten years for commercial exploitation. **4–30**

The right can be assigned or licensed (ss.222 and 225). During the last five years of the term licences of right are available on terms to be agreed, or, in default of agreement, to be settled by the Comptroller-General of Patents, Designs and Trade Marks (s.237 of the Act). **4–31**

The right obviously applies to spare parts, except in so far as they have an **4–32** artistic or decorative aspect to them, which may be protectable either through copyright as an artistic work, or by reference to their aesthetic appeal under the Registered Designs Act 1949. However, s.213 contains two significant exclusions to unregistered designs which can be protected. These relate to the "features of shape or configuration of an article which (i) enable the article to be connected to, or placed in around or against another article so that either article may perform its function, or (ii) are dependent upon the appearance of another article of which the article is intended by the designer to form an integral part". These so-called "must fit" exceptions have obvious applications to the unique aspects of the design of spare parts. In practice, they remove any protection (if one excludes the possibility of patents and registered designs) from the copying of aspects of spare parts which have to be copied if they are to fit into the relevant equipment and perform their proper function. Other aspects of spare parts which it may be desirable, but not essential, to copy will of course still be protected, but the protection is in practice not very great given the licence of right provision, which will start to become available just when the market for spare parts for any particular product is likely to be of greatest interest to third party manufacturers (*i.e.* when it has had a reasonable period of time on the market and become a mature established product).

4–33 A recent example of the application of the new unregistered design right can be seen in the case of *Baby Dan AS v Brevi SRL* [1999] F.S.R. 377, Ch D.

4–34 This type of design protection is not uncommon within different Member States of the EU, and in many other countries of the world (see USA, Japan, Taiwan and Singapore), although provisions differ as to whether registration is necessary to obtain protection. The need and procedure for registration should be considered if one is looking at claiming protection in any particular territory. Where the right is not protected by registration there is still a tendency for the demarcation line between registered and unregistered designs to become blurred.

4–35 The EC law on designs has progressed along similar lines to the law set out in the 1988 Act. Again, in the area of spare parts, (or "component parts of complex products" as the Commission refers to them) the emphasis has been on the need to avoid giving protection which would overly restrict the ability of third party manufacturers to make and supply spare parts.

4–36 Council Directive 71/98 on the legal protection of designs dealt with measures to harmonise the protection of registered designs under the laws of the various Member States. Article 16 states the provisions of the Directive "shall be without prejudice to any provisions of Community law or the law of the Member State concerned relating to unregistered design rights, trade marks or other distinctive signs, patents and utility models, typefaces, civil liability or unfair competition".

4–37 Article 3(2) of the Directive provides that a registered design can only be protected "to the extent that it is new [and has] an individual character". So far as spare parts are concerned, Art.3(3) provides that a design applied to or incorporated in a product which constitutes a component part of a complex product shall "only be considered to be new and to have individual character, if the component part, once it has been incorporated into a complex product remains visible during the normal use of the latter and, to the extent that the visible features of the component part fulfil in themselves the requirements as to novelty and individual character".

The Directive also provides in Art.7 (but again only in relation to registered designs) similar provisions to those in the 1988 Act which removed protection for spare parts under the unregistered design right. Article 7.1 provides that "A design right shall not subsist in features of appearance of a product which are solely dictated by its technical function". Article 7.2 deals with the "must-fit" exception by providing that a "design right shall not subsist in features or appearance of a product which must necessarily be reproduced in their exact form and dimensions in order to permit the product in which the design is incorporated or to which it is applied to be mechanically connected to or placed in, around or against another product so that either product may perform its function". **4–38**

The Directive, which actually required little amendment of the existing UK legislation was implemented in the UK by The Registered Design Regulations 2001 (SI 2000/3949), which amended the Registered Designs Act 1949 accordingly. **4–39**

So far as the UK is concerned, the Directive has created changes in the law relating to registered designs but left the unregistered design right under the 1988 Act unaffected. Its effect, so far as registered design rights are concerned is to remove their protection in relation to a spare part except to the extent that its visible features, when the part has been installed as part of a complex product, have the necessary attributes of novelty and individual character. However, whatever rights of protection the spare part enjoys under the unregistered design right remain unaffected. Given the must-fit exceptions, this in practice provides very little additional protection except for non-essential features that could not be the subject of a registered design (presumably in most cases because they are not visible when the part is installed). **4–40**

Council Directive 6/2002 has brought into existence a Community Design Right, pertaining to both registered and unregistered designs. The substantive provisions of the Directive are aligned with Directive 71/98. The Directive has provisions identical to Arts 3(2), 3(3) and 7 of Directive 71/98 (see Arts 2 and 9). It was implemented (so far as registration of a Community Design was concerned in the UK by the Registered Designs Regulations 2003 (SI 2003/550). **4–41**

The Directive applies to both registered and unregistered design rights, but at present does not apply to spare parts at all, as the application of the Directive to components of complex products is suspended until the Commission has finalised its general policy (often referred to as a "repair clause") for such items. **4–42**

The current position under the legislation in force in the UK, in conformance with the two EC Directives, is thus that spare parts have no protection under the Community Design, that they can only take advantage **4–43** of the UK registered design right if they have some aesthetic features not connected with their function, which are still visible when they are installed, and that their protection under the UK unregistered design right is severely limited by the "must fit" exception.

4–44 The result of Directive 6/2002, once fully implemented, would mean that spare parts in general would not be able to take advantage of protection under a registered or unregistered Community Design Right, unless their visible features, after installation, had the necessary aesthetic attributes. This would, so far as motor vehicles were concerned, leave only external body parts with protection under the Community Design. Internal spare parts would cease to have any design protection under the Directive, either registered or unregistered.

4–45 The Commission has also stated that when it finally makes its proposal on the repair clause, the relevant provisions will also necessarily amend Directive 71/98, presumably by extending its effect to unregistered designs, since the purpose of the repair clause will be to harmonise the law relating to the supply of spare parts throughout the Community.

4–46 When the situation is finally resolved, there will obviously be an impact on the current position in the UK, as the unregistered UK design right under the 1988 Act will require amendment. The effect will be that, as under the Community Design, spare parts will cease to enjoy any design right protection at all except in relation to their aesthetic features (as defined in terms of novelty and individual character) and only in so far as these features are still visible when incorporated in the relevant complex product.

4–47 Turning from the position within the EC, the principles in *British Leyland* are still applicable in those common law jurisdictions outside the UK, which continue to apply the old law in force prior to the 1988 Act, equivalent to the Copyright Act 1956. However, their application is strictly limited in scope to cases of genuine repair.

4–48 This approach can be seen in the Privy Council decision in the Hong Kong case of *Canon Kabushiki Kaisha v Green Cartridge Co (Hong Kong) Ltd* [1997] A.C. 728, PC (HK). It was held that a company infringing a copyright in drawings for replacement toner cartridges for printers was not entitled to continue to manufacture or refurbish the cartridges under the spare parts exception. The manufacture or refurbishment of a toner cartridge was not the sort of repair that a person who bought an item would assume he could do for himself without infringing the manufacturer's rights. The cartridge itself was a consumable item that the owner of the machine would replace when exhausted, returning the empty cartridge for recycling. Further, when a cartridge was replaced nothing in the machine would need to be repaired.

4–49 Hoffman L.J. further stated that the decision in *British Leyland* was founded on unfairness to the customer and abuse of monopoly power. On the facts of this case, the competition argument was far less compelling. Customers probably took account of the cost of replacing cartridges when selecting a machine, and there was competition as between the manufacturers of replacement cartridges and those who refilled existing cartridges, such that it could not be said without proof that Canon's use of its intellectual property rights had allowed it to obtain a dominant position in the market, much less to abuse that position.

Another example is the decision in *Creative Technology Ltd v Aztech Systems Pte Ltd* [1997] F.S.R. 491. The Court of Appeal in Singapore, where the law on copyright is still basically similar to that in the UK prior to the 1988 Act, considered the application of *British Leyland* to copyright in software. Although not dismissing entirely the application of the principle of non-derogation from grant, it held that this could not extend, as contended in that case, to the act of disassembly or reverse engineering for the purpose of creating a competing product. **4–50**

It should be remembered that at the time of the judgments in *British Leyland*, competition law in the UK (under the Restrictive Trade Practices Act 1976) did not contain a principle analogous to abuse of a dominant position under Art.82 of the EC Treaty. The Court of Appeal (reported at [1984] 3 C.M.L.R. 102) found as a fact that British Leyland were not in a dominant position for the purposes of Art.82 (then 86) and that, even if they were, the mere exercise of their copyright to prevent third party manufacture was not an abuse of that position, under the then current EC law authorities. Thus, if the perceived evil was to be remedied it had to be approached through the common law principles relating to unreasonable restraint of trade and non-derogation from grant. **4–51**

It is however clear from the remarks in the two cases cited above, that the common law approach in the House of Lords decision in *British Leyland* has certain similarities to the way the European Court and the EC Commission apply the concept of abuse of a dominant position under Art.82 in cases of refusal to supply, or to grant a third party licence for the manufacture of, spare parts. (Compare for instance, Lord Hoffman's statement in *Canon* : "the decision in *British Leyland* was founded on unfairness to the customer and abuse of monopoly power", and the European Court cases: *Volvo AB v Erik Veng (UK) Ltd* [1989] 4 C.M.L.R. 122 and *Consorzio Italiano Delia Componentistica Di Ricambio Per Autoveicoli and Maxicar v Regie Nationale Des Usines Renault* [1989] 4 C.M.L.R. 265; and *Ransburg-Gema AG v Electrostatic Plant Systems Ltd* [1989] 2 C.M.L.R. 712, ChD.) This type of abuse of a dominant position under EC law is discussed in detail in Chapter 6.24.15). **4–52**

This view of the case is particularly important given that (since the decision in *British Leyland*) competition law in the UK has been brought into line with EC competition law by the Competition Act 1998 (see the detailed discussion in Chapter 5.1.2) The Chapter II prohibition of the Competition Act 1998 (corresponding to Art.82 but without the need for an effect on trade between Member States, provided trade within the UK is affected) now enables the same concept of abuse of a dominant position to be applied directly in the UK. The cases, decisions and principles of EC competition law (such as the cases cited above) are to be applied in the UK in deciding cases under the Chapter II Prohibition (s.60 of the Act). This issue is discussed in more detail both in relation to Art.82 and the Chapter II **4–53** prohibition in Chapter 6.24.15. However, the conclusion must be that *British Leyland* has not only been rendered irrelevant by the 1988 Act, but also to some extent unnecessary by the importation into UK law of the concept of abuse of a dominant position.

4–54 Further assistance in this matter, and a clear statement of the principles involved can be found in the Court of Appeal decision in *Biotrading & Financing OY v Biohit Ltd* [1998] F.S.R. 109, CA, which examined the issue not in the context of Arts 81 or 82, but in the context of free movement of goods. Here the defendants copied a design belonging to the plaintiffs, by working off drawings belonging to the plaintiff, in order to manufacture a competing product. The manufacture took place in Finland, but the plaintiffs attempted to assert their rights under the 1988 Act in the UK to prevent importation into the UK of the allegedly infringing product. The defendants raised one of the so-called "Euro defences" claiming that to prevent the importation by raising the alleged infringement would contravene the provisions of the EC Treaty providing for free movement of goods (see Arts 28 and 30) on grounds that were not "justified" within the meaning of Art.30 (see Chapter 5.1.1.4). The Court rejected this defence, just as it had been rejected in the Court of Appeal decision in *British Leyland*, and held that *British Leyland* was still good law. The success of the so-called Euro defence turned upon the issue of "justification". The European Court cases (see those cited above) showed that acting to protect one's intellectual property rights was not of itself an abuse of a dominant position unless an additional anti-competitive motive was present. Where no such motive was present the plaintiffs were "justified" in raising the issue of infringement to prevent the importation of the infringing goods into the UK.

4–55 The final question is whether, given the advances in both UK and EC competition law, the principle of non-derogation from grant, as set out in *British Leyland*, has become entirely obsolete, even if it is still good law. So far as the effect of the 1988 Act is concerned, although this rendered the principle irrelevant in relation to design rights, it can still apply in relation to copyright in general, or other types of intellectual property, such as patents.

4–56 Second, although the approximation of EC and UK competition law by the 1998 Act has imported the concept of abuse of a dominant position into UK law, there is still a place, if a somewhat limited one, for the remedy provided by the invocation of the principle of non-derogation from grant.

4–57 On one view the remedy arising from the principle of non-derogation from grant, is more limited than those arising from the concept of abuse of a dominant position. Non-derogation from grant opens up a certain possibility of self-help, but it can only be used as a means of defence, unlike the remedies arising from abuse of a dominant position which provide a means both of attack and defence. If the purchaser of the equipment is in a position to repair the item in question, he can do so and ignore any contravention of the supplier's intellectual property rights. If the supplier objects, and brings an action for infringement, he will be met by the defence that he cannot derogate from his grant. On the other hand, if the purchaser requires spare parts or technical information, to be supplied to him by the supplier, to enable the purchaser to carry out the repair, then the purchaser must bring proceedings himself. To borrow Lord Denning's words (see *Central London Property Trust v High Trees House* [1947] K.B. 130 and *Combe v Combe* [1951] 2 K.B. 215, CA in relation to the defence of equitable estoppel) the principle of non-derogation from grant can act only as a "shield" and not also as a "sword".

The concept of abuse of a dominant position acts not only as a shield but also as a sword. It can provide a defence for the purchaser, just as the concept of non-derogation from grant. However, it can also be used to enable the purchaser, in appropriate circumstances, to compel the supplier to provide the spare parts or information required. **4–58**

On this comparison, the principle of non-derogation from grant appears to have been eclipsed by the concept of abuse of a dominant position. There is, however, still one advantage, where self-help is possible, to the use of the concept of non-derogation from grant. It is not necessary to go into the question of whether the supplier is in a dominant position in order to raise the defence. Thus the threshold set to invoke the defence of non-derogation is lower than that set for abuse of a dominant position. **4–59**

Support for the propositions set out above can be found in the case *Saphena Computing Ltd v Allied Collection Agencies Ltd*, [1995] F.S.R. 616, where the English Court of Appeal considered the matter in relation to copyright in and licences of software. However, once again, the application of the principle is tightly restricted to the act of repair. **4–60**

The Court of Appeal came to the conclusion that the principle of non-derogation from grant does allow a somewhat limited right to repair software if bugs are discovered. However, this right is qualified to the extent that in many cases, possessing only the object code for the program in question, it will not be possible for the licensee to repair the software, since access to the source code is normally required. If at the time the bug is discovered the licensee happens to have the source code in its possession it is entitled to use the source code for this purpose. However, it has no right to require the licensor to facilitate repair by delivering a copy of the source code to it, or by allowing it to retain the source code beyond the period of acceptance testing so that it continues to be available if bugs appear in the future. If such bugs do appear then the remedy against the licensor would be in damages for supplying a product which was not fit for purpose, until the expiry of the period of limitation. **4–61**

Given the current situation as described above the question can be put as to whether in the case of a distributor the principal will be able to act to prevent him copying or assisting in the copying of spare parts, to the extent that they are unprotected by any intellectual property rights, purely by means of an express provision in the distributorship contract like cl.4.3.7. Again, given the current status of the *British Leyland* case, it seems even more likely that a court could extend the principle in the *British Leyland* case to hold that such a provision in the agreement was as a matter of public policy unreasonably in restraint of trade so that the rights of consumers to obtain spare parts for the purposes of repair could not be indirectly fettered **4–62** by the contractual provision.

4–63 In any event, since the current UK and EC legislation would (subject to intellectual property rights other than designs) permit third parties not bound by the contract to provide such spare parts in competition with the distributor and the principal, it might well be best for the principal to recognise the commercial realities and grant the distributor a licence to manufacture spare parts, or provide them to him at a price and on terms which makes copying unattractive. The contractual provisions for the supply of spare parts are set out in Chapter 6.24.13 and 6.24.14.

4.3.8 Patent and trade mark notices

4–64 4.3.8 The Distributor shall leave in position and not cover or erase any notices or other marks (including without limitation details of patents or notices that a trade mark design or copyright relating to the Products is owned by the Principal or a third party) which the Principal may place on or affix to the Products.

This clause is useful, and in some jurisdictions essential, to ensure that the distributor cannot lay claim to ownership of or licences under the principal's relevant intellectual property.

4.3.9 Shipment inspection reports

4–65 4.3.9 The Distributor shall send to the Principal an inspection report on each shipment of the Products received by the Distributor as well as such other information on the quality and performance of the Products as may from time to time be reasonably required of the Distributor by the Principal.

This clause is a useful provision to enable the principal to monitor the state of the Products, which can act as a supplement to actual inspection.

4.3.10 Indemnity

4–66 4.3.10 The Distributor undertakes that it will indemnify the Principal against all proceedings costs liabilities injury loss or damage arising out of the breach or negligent performance or failure in performance by the Distributor of the terms of this Agreement.

This general indemnity need not necessarily be expressly inserted, given the normal rights to compensation arising on breach of contract under the general law, but it serves first of all the purpose of reminding the distributor of his responsibilities, and also its express terms should enable the principal to be compensated for damages which might under the law generally applicable be held to be too remote for recovery.

4.4 Enquiries

4.4 The Principal shall during the continuance of this Agreement refer all enquiries received by it for sale of the Products in the Territory to the Distributor. The Distributor shall during the continuance of this Agreement refer to the Principal all enquiries it receives for the Products for sale outside or export from the Territory [other than in the case of Products sold within the Territory (1) as ship's or aircraft's stores for use sale or consumption on such ship or aircraft outside the Territory or (2) for final resale in a duty-free shop in the Territory]. **4–67**

4.5 Non-export clause

4.5 During the continuance of this Agreement the Distributor shall not sell outside or export or assist in or be a party to the export of the Products from the Territory unless the prior consent of the Principal has been obtained [provided that this clause shall not prevent the sale of the Products by the Distributor as ship's or aircraft's stores or for duty-free shops in terms of cl.4.4]. **4–68**

Clauses 4.4 and 4.5 need to be read together, and provide the usual restrictions on both the principal and the distributor in relation to supply inside and outside the territory respectively. The additions of the phrases in square brackets are a reminder not to overlook ship and aircraft stores and duty-free sales, which could be an important part of a distributor's trade if he were dealing in products such as alcoholic drinks in a small territory. It is also true, however, that in many cases duty-free shops are regarded as a separate operation which are sometimes dealt with by one organisation for more than one country. In such cases, it should be remembered to exclude duty-free sales from the agreement entirely, so as to permit the principal to supply to his duty free distributor for these purposes without breaching his obligations to his main distributor for the territory.

Some agreements impose a specific obligation upon the principal not to sell the products within the territory. Although this can of course be inserted if required, the fact that the agreement is on an exclusive basis is usually regarded as sufficient. A related provision is one requiring the principal to exercise his rights under any other distributorship agreements that he may have, or his intellectual and industrial property rights relating to the products or their trade marks, to prevent third parties importing into the distributor's territory and thus indirectly breaching the exclusivity provision. However, in most cases, although in practice a principal is likely to attempt to settle matters, particularly where the two parties involved are both his distributors, an express provision would (if it were to be effective) have to bind the principal in the ultimate to take legal proceedings to prevent the importation complained of. Quite apart from any legislation relating to a particular territory which might prevent his exercising his rights in this way it is highly undesirable from a commercial point of view that the principal be required against his will, at the behest of the distributor, to go to the expense of legal proceedings of which the outcome may be uncertain, and which **4–69** would presumably cause irreparable damage to relationships between the principal and the party against whom they were taken.

4.6 Supply of the products

4.6.1 Exclusive purchase

4–70 4.6.1 The Distributor shall purchase all its requirements for the Products ready packaged from the Principal.

This clause places an obligation on the distributor to purchase exclusively from the principal, and not, for instance, from another distributor or a licensed manufacturer who may be able to supply the products at a sufficiently lower price to make the transaction worthwhile.

4.6.2 Terms and conditions

4–71 4.6.2 The parties hereto agree that orders placed by the Distributor with the Principal under cl.4.6.1 or for any other items shall be on the terms set out in Sch.6.

For the details of the schedule see Chapter 4.26. It is in the interest of both parties that they clearly understand the terms upon which the products are sold to the distributor. It is of course possible to provide simply that the standard conditions from time to time prevailing of either the distributor or the principal shall apply to all such transactions, but the setting out of the agreed set in a schedule avoids all uncertainty as to which set should apply. In common law jurisdictions such a clause prevents one of the parties raising the question of the "battle of the forms" (see *Butler Machine Tool Co Ltd v Ex-Cell-O Machine Corp (England) Ltd* [1979] 1 W.L.R. 401, *BRS v Arthur V Crutchley Ltd* [1968] 1 All E.R. 811, *Sauter Automation Ltd v HC Goodman (Mechanical Services) Ltd* (1986) 34 Build. L.R. 81, Ch D; *Chichester Joinery Ltd* v *John Mowlem & Co plc* (1987) 42 Build. L.R. 100; *G Percy Trentham* v *Archital Luxfer* [1993] 1 Lloyd's Rep. 25, CA; *Nissan UK Ltd v Nissan Motor Manufacturing (UK) Ltd* (1995) 12 Building Law Monthly Issue 5, CA; *Hitchins (Hatfield) Ltd v H Butterfield Ltd*, (1995) 12 Building Law Monthly Issue 7, CA; *Jarvis Interiors Ltd v Galliard Homes Ltd* [2000] C.L.C. 411, CA; and *Lafarge Plasterboard Ltd v Fritz Peters & Co KG* [2000] 2 Lloyd's Rep. 689, QBD).

4–72 In some other jurisdictions (such as Germany or Switzerland) which give the courts wider powers under commercial codes it will also prevent the court placing its own terms on any contract where the actual terms and conditions to apply have not been clearly specified, and conflicting standard forms have been used by each side. Recent cases in the UK appear to have moved somewhat closer to this position, in that an inconclusive "battle of the forms" may still be found to have created a contract, but to which neither set of standard conditions applies (see *Lidl UK GmbH v Hertford Foods Ltd* [2001] EWCA Civ 938, CA).

4.6.3 "Most favoured nation" clause

4.6.3 The Principal undertakes that the price charged by it to the Distributor under this Agreement for any Product is the lowest price charged at that time (at the same volume and upon the same terms and conditions, including as to delivery) to any export customer of the Principal for that Product and should at any time this not be the case or cease to be the case then the Principal shall immediately adjust the relevant price charged hereunder to the Distributor to achieve compliance with this undertaking and such adjustment shall apply to any orders of the Distributor at the time placed with the Principal but not yet shipped. **4–73**

This "most favoured nation" clause, as it is sometimes called, is obviously unwelcome to principals, and is likely to be included only where the distributor has very much the upper hand in the negotiations. In certain jurisdictions, for instance the USA, where one is dealing with distribution arrangements within different areas in the same territory, arbitrary and discriminatory differences in prices charged to two distributors in the same position for the same products are regarded as a breach of the anti-trust laws, as are discounts related solely to volume, without any justification of volume-related cost savings.

4.6.4 Modifications and improvements

4.6.4 The Principal reserves the right to improve or modify the Products without prior notice [provided that details of any modification affecting [form fit function or maintenance] [or] [any permissions consents or licences obtained by the Distributor pursuant to cl.4.15.2] shall be notified to the Distributor in which event the Distributor may vary or cancel any orders placed for the Products prior to the receipt of such notification except to the extent that these orders can be met by the supply of Products which do not incorporate the improvement or modification notified hereunder. Variation or cancellation hereunder shall be effected by the Distributor notifying the Principal thereof within fourteen days of receipt by the Distributor of the relevant notification of the relevant improvement or modification. The Distributor's rights of cancellation under this clause shall be its sole remedy in the event of any improvement or modification being made to a Product, and in particular, but without limitation, no compensation or damages for breach of contract shall be payable to the Distributor by reason of such improvement or modification.] **4–74**

This provision gives the right to the principal to vary products as required in the light, for instance, of changes in technology for manufacturing, cost reduction, or non-availability of components, or ingredients. All of the provisions, from the proviso in the second line where the first set of square brackets opens, are designed as optional in situations where the principal does not require, or it is not practical for him to have, an absolute right to change the products.

4–75 The concept of "form fit and function" is well-known in the supply of mechanical or electrical or electronic products, particularly in government procurement arrangements, where often these matters alone are required to be invariable. For instance, in the area of instruments for use in military vehicles, the so-called black box specification is often used, where the dimensions of the box, and the input and output requirements alone are specified. With the development of semiconductor technology this has in some cases resulted in "black-boxes" staying the same size, but instead of being filled with valves, now being largely empty because of the much smaller size of semiconductors.

4–76 The area of permission consents and licences is more likely to be affected with products which are edible or pharmaceutical, when a change in formulation has been made.

4–77 The optional part of the clause, where it is to be used, thus needs to be adapted slightly depending on the exact nature of the products in each case.

4.7 Distributor's records

4–78 4.7 The Distributor shall keep accounts together with supporting vouchers (including without limitation copies of invoices and other relevant papers showing all orders for the supply of the Products by the Principal to the Distributor and by the Distributor to its customers) and shall allow the Principal or its authorised representative (at all reasonable times whether this Agreement be terminated or not) to inspect audit and copy the same for the purpose of checking any information given by the Distributor to the Principal or of obtaining any information or data relevant to the operation of cl.4.17.2 or of any other of the obligations to be performed by the Distributor under this Agreement.

This right of audit is necessary for the proper operation of the buy-back option for Products in favour of the principal upon the termination of the agreement (cl.4.17.2). It is also useful to insert generally to check on other matters, such as whether the distributor has been exporting outside the territory or not observing any agreed and enforceable pricing policy. It is also a useful provision to enable the principal to deal with the tracing of any products with manufacturing defects that may have been sold on by the distributor, particularly if the principal has to implement a general product recall in the territory.

4.8 Advertising and merchandising

4–79 4.8.1(a) All advertising and sales promotional material shall be provided by the Principal to the Distributor free of charge. The Principal shall carry on and be responsible for the entire cost of all advertising for the Products in the Territory. The Principal will from time to time make contributions as agreed between the parties for incentive schemes for dealers and the Distributor's sales staff to promote sales of the Products.

OR

4.8.1(b) The cost of all advertising and sales promotion activities shall unless otherwise decided be borne by the Distributor

OR

4.8.1(c) The Distributor shall notify to and agree with the Principal not later than the end of [October] in each year an advertising and sales promotion programme for the Products for the next year. This programme may be varied by the Distributor in the light of current market conditions during the course of the relevant year but the Distributor shall spend on each such programme not less than an amount equal to [five] per cent of the actual proceeds of sale of the Products received by it in the preceding year. Expenditure by the Distributor in fulfilment of any of its obligations under any other clause of this Agreement (including without limitation expenses of registering any Products under cl.4.15) and compensation of any sort credited by the Distributor to its customers for the return of any Products other than Products which the Principal is required to replace as defective in accordance with its warranty obligations under Sch.4 shall not be reckoned as part of the aforesaid amount.

The different versions of this clause above impose obligations for advertising within the territory respectively on the principal and the distributor. Versions (b) or (c) imposing the obligation on the distributor are more likely to be used. Version (c) is used in cases where a detailed programme is required. Here, the percentage of expenditure obviously depends upon the nature of the products and whether initial introduction expenses are being incurred, or a continuing presence in the market maintained. An expenditure in the region of 5 per cent is not untypical. It is in the principal's interest to raise the sum as high as possible, since it is coming out of the distributor's margin, and going to increase sales of the products in the territory. Care should be taken as to the items of expenditure which the distributor is allowed to count as discharging his obligations. The most likely bone of contention is in the area of product returns which are accepted and paid for by the distributor from his wholesaler customers, not because the products are defective, but only because they are slow-moving, or sales have fallen, or he wishes to persuade wholesalers to take on new lines.

4.8.2 All advertisements point of sale promotion merchandising and publicity material for the Products issued by the Distributor shall be subject before issue to the prior approval of the Principal. **4–80**

4.8.3 All sales promotion activities carried on by the Distributor for the Products of whatever nature must receive the prior approval of the Principal which reserves the right to veto the same entirely at its discretion. **4–81**

Clauses 4.8.2 and 4.8.3 should be included even if the distributor has no obligations to carry out advertising and promotion activities, and should apply, as they are written, even if the distributor carries out these activities voluntarily and at his own expense. The principal will have his own worldwide programmes for these matters and will not wish the distributor to carry on activities which conflict with the particular image and market position he has planned for the products.

4–82 4.8.4 The cost of all merchandising returns from customers relating to the Products shall (unless otherwise agreed in writing or in respect of Products which the Principal is obliged to replace as defective in accordance with its warranty obligations under Sch.4), be borne by the Distributor.

If version (c) of cl.4.8.1 is used it could be argued that this clause is not strictly necessary. It should nevertheless be included for the avoidance of doubt, and should certainly be inserted if one of the other versions of cl.4.8.1. is used.

4.9 Sales and marketing policies

4–83 4.9.1 The Distributor shall conform to the general sales and marketing policies philosophies and principles of the Principal and the Principal reserves the right to issue directions from time to time to the Distributor to ensure such conformity.

This is a useful general clause, which is unlikely to be enforced on most occasions, but provides a catch-all in the event that in some unforeseen way the distributor sells the products or carries on ancillary activities in a manner that the principal disapproves of, but is not caught by cl.4.8. It is impossible to foresee all of the possible ways that a distributor will wish to act in response to market forces in the territory, and such clauses are therefore necessary to safeguard the principal's position.

4–84 4.9.2 Selling prices for the sale of the Products in the Territory by the Distributor shall be established and revised from time to time by the mutual agreement of the Principal and the Distributor.

This clause should be treated with care. The question of setting selling prices in the territory can cause problems. In many territories it is illegal for the principal to set minimum resale prices for the distributor. This is generally the case in all of the Member States of the EU, including the UK, and also the position under EC Competition law. The law in relation to these jurisdictions is discussed in Chapter 5.9.2.

4–85 Similar legislation is in force in many other countries (*e.g.* Australia). In countries where the local law permits, a provision can be inserted either as the clause above, or a more specific one detailing the prices at which the distributor is to resell, or the percentage selling margin that he is to be allowed to mark up each product on resale.

4–86 4.9.3 The Distributor undertakes not to alter treat or otherwise deal with any of the Products (or their packaging) or to present any such Products for sale in a group package without in both cases obtaining the prior written consent of the Principal.

This clause continues the imposition of restrictions to ensure that the products are sold in accordance with the principal's marketing policies. One of the easiest ways of sales promotion, often to the detriment of the image of the products, is for the distributor to repackage two or more unrelated products in a group package and sell them off at a discount. For the reasons discussed above it is difficult in many cases to forbid the sale at a discount, but the sale in a group package, which is often the most damaging part of the transaction for the products' image, can be forbidden.

> 4.9.4 The Distributor undertakes not to apply the Trade Mark to any item not one of the Products nor to distribute or sell any such items with the Trade Mark so applied or to engage in any other practice or activity likely to mislead potential purchasers into believing that an item is one of the Products when in fact it is not. **4–87**

This clause prevents the distributor taking advantage of the reputation of the principal and his trade marks in an unjustified manner. In England the common law remedy in relation to passing off, and some provisions of the Trade Descriptions Acts, prohibiting the false or misleading description of goods offered for sale, also prevent such practices.

4.10 Stock of the products

> 4.10 The Distributor shall at all times during the continuance of this Agreement carry at least [three months] stock of the Products so that all orders received by the Distributor can be supplied without undue delay. The Distributor shall supply such reports as to stock levels and movements as the Principal may from time to time request. **4–88**

This clause is a general provision but in appropriate cases it may be necessary to give more precise details of stocking levels to be observed. There is also the question as to whether the distributor should be required (as a condition of obtaining any of the products covered by the agreement) to purchase and carry a stock of every item in a range of products so that he can offer a complete choice to customers. The practice of requiring such stocking is known as full-line forcing. Requirements as to the supply and stocking of spare parts are also dealt with in Chapter 6.24.10 and 6.24.11.

4.11 Distributor's staff

> 4.11 The Distributor shall maintain during the continuance of this Agreement sufficient staff to sell distribute and promote the sale of the Products throughout the Territory and perform in a timely and satisfactory manner the Distributor's obligations under this Agreement and in particular shall create and maintain a sales force of sufficient size from time to time to fulfil the Distributor's obligations under this Agreement in relation to the sale and marketing of the Products. **4–89**

This clause is a general imposition of staffing and marketing obligations, but in relation to technically sophisticated products more precise provisions are desirable (see Chapter 6.24).

4.12 Monthly reports

4–90 4.12 The Distributor shall send to the Principal by the thirtieth day following the end of each calendar month during the continuance of this Agreement a report of sales made of the Products in the Territory during that month together with such other marketing and other information in relation to the operation of the Agreement as the Principal may reasonably require. Forms for these reports will be supplied by the Principal.

This clause ensures that the principal is kept properly abreast of the market situation in the territory. Many distributors are reluctant or do not have the resources to spend the time on completing such reports. It is a material help to the distributor, and a great aid in getting such reports produced, if the principal supplies free of charge a standardised report form which can be filled in with a minimum of effort and prompts the distributor to report succinctly on the matters required.

4.13 Industrial property rights

4–91 4.13.1 It is agreed that all rights to the Trade Mark are and shall remain the exclusive property of the Principal. The Distributor shall at the expense of the Principal enter into such agreements with the Principal (including but without limitation registered user agreements) and shall execute such documents and carry out such actions as may be necessary to protect such rights of the Principal in the Territory.

4–92 4.13.2 The Trade Mark shall not be used in any manner liable to invalidate the registration thereof and the right to use the Trade Mark in connection with the appropriate Products is only granted to the extent that the Principal is able to do so without endangering the validity of the registration.

4–93 4.13.3 The Distributor shall (in so far as it becomes aware thereof) notify the Principal of any unauthorised use in the Territory of the Trade Mark or of any other intellectual or industrial property rights in the control or ownership of the Principal. At the request and cost of the Principal the Distributor shall take part in or give assistance in respect of any legal proceedings and execute any documents and do any things reasonably necessary to protect the Principal's intellectual and industrial property rights (including without limitation the Trade Mark) in the Territory.

Although the distributor is entitled to sell products carrying the trade mark in the territory, he should not thereby become entitled to any rights in the trade mark. In some countries, it is not possible for a local distributor to import goods bearing a trade mark of which he is not registered as the owner or user (*e.g.* Brazil). In these circumstances it is necessary to enter into some form of registered user agreement, whereby the distributor has proper rights to use the mark, but the capacity in which he uses it is clearly seen not to be that of an owner.

If such agreements are not entered into and registered on the local trade mark register, the distributor may in time by use of the mark build up rights in it which will (if the mark is unregistered) entitle him to register himself as its owner in the territory, or, in some cases (where the mark is registered but the local law demands some sale of the goods under the mark by the owner of the mark in order for the registration to become effective) enable him to attack the principal's registration irrespective of the fact that the principal originally authorised him to distribute under the mark. **4–94**

It should be noted that the concept of registered user agreements has been abolished in the UK by the Trade Marks Act 1994, but still exists in some other jurisdictions. The need for such an agreement should therefore be considered with a local lawyer in the relevant territory. The whole question of trade mark licences and registered user agreements is discussed in Chapter 12. **4–95**

4.14 No joint venture or partnership

See cl.1.9. **4–96**

The parties can also include (suitably adapted) the more formal provisions of cll.2.3.6 and 2.3.7 in relation to avoiding the problems of ostensible authority, if they feel that the circumstances warrant it.

4.15 Commencement and term of agreement

> 4.15.1 This Agreement shall (subject to earlier termination as herein provided) commence upon [the date of signature hereof] and continue in force for an initial period of [three years] and thereafter shall continue unless and until terminated by not less than [six months] notice given by one party to the other such notice not to be given prior to the expiry of the said period. **4–97**

With a distributorship it is highly unlikely that there will not be an initial fixed term. Compared to an agent, a distributor has to invest much more of his own resources in creating a market for the products in the territory, and to take much more risk, in that he will have to purchase stocks of the products and then create the demand to make them sell. Particularly where the products have not been sold in the territory before, he will require the initial period to assure himself that he will have sufficient time not only to create a market, but also to get back his investment. For similar reasons, most distributors will wish to have an exclusive arrangement, to ensure that another seller in their territory will not profit by their activity and be able to make sales at a lower price because he has no need to recover marketing expenses.

4–98 4.15.2 The Distributor shall obtain at its own expense all necessary permissions consents and licences (including but without limitation those required to be given by any government department or any body constituted under the law of the Territory for licensing or other regulatory purposes relating to the Products) to enable the Distributor to market distribute and sell the Products in the Territory and to ensure the full and legal operation of this Agreement.

It is usual for the distributor to be required to carry out all the formalities necessary to enable the agreement to be put into effect in the territory. First of all there may be the necessity to register the agreement with local exchange control or financial authorities, to enable the distributor to import products and remit the payments for them abroad. In many countries, where foreign exchange in hard currencies is scarce, quotas or other limitations may be applied, either to the agreement itself, or by way of the requirement to obtain an import licence for every shipment of the products into the territory.

4–99 The other important area relates to permission to market the goods. Many types of goods are subject to this regulation. Areas to watch particularly are pharmaceuticals, cosmetics and dietary products such as slimming goods and vitamins. In most countries there are restrictions on their marketing without first having them licensed by health or medical authorities. Details are required of ingredients, claims made for the products, and in some cases results of clinical tests.

4–100 In these products and in food products generally there are in most countries lists of permitted and banned ingredients and additives, particularly in the areas of colouring and preservatives, and usually requirements as to the labelling of products and the declaration of formulae and other matters on the labels. Advertising can also be restricted in regard to the claims which can be made for the product either in advertisements generally or on the label itself. EC regulations, particularly in labelling, container sizes, and permitted ingredients, have to a large extent harmonised these requirements in the different Member States of the EC.

4–101 Other products which require care are electrical and electronic products. Consumer goods of this type are subject to safety requirements in most countries. Telecommunications and radio and television transmitters and receivers, and sometimes even other electronic products such as computers (for example in the USA), are usually subject to regulation by the local telecommunications authority or a government department or statutory authority having special responsibility in communications matters. Examples of bodies with wide powers in all of these areas are the USA licensing authority, the Federal Communications Commission, usually known as the FCC, and the UK licensing authority, the British Approvals Board for Telecommunications, usually known as the BABT (for a further discussion of the role of consultants in these matters see Chapter 9).

4–102 4.15.3 If the said permissions consents and licences are not obtained and fully operative within a period of [six months] from the aforesaid date of commencement the Principal shall thereafter have the option to terminate this Agreement immediately by notice to the Distributor. The said option shall cease if (prior to its exercise) the aforesaid permissions consents and licences have in fact been obtained and are fully operative even though this has been achieved outside the said period of [six months].

In most cases the distributor will not be able to start the necessary procedures to obtain approval until the agreement has been signed and he is properly constituted as the distributor for the products in the territory. The question then arises as to whether the fixed period of the agreement should run from the date the licences are obtained and marketing can begin, or from the date of the agreement, so that the time necessary to obtain the licences eats into the fixed period. The former way of dealing with things is more satisfactory for the distributor, given the time that is often needed to obtain consents. The latter, of course, is preferred by the principal as it gives the distributor an incentive to carry out the procedure to obtain consent quickly, and get on with selling the products.

There is also the problem that, irrespective of the start date for the period, while the agreement is in force, the distributor will usually have the sole rights during the fixed period to market the products in the territory, so that if he, through ill luck, or his own default, does not obtain the necessary permission, the hands of the principal are tied unless he terminates the agreement. In the absence of a special provision the principal would have to rely on breach of a general "due diligence" provision which is often hard to prove in such situations. It may also be the case that, unknown to the principal, there is something about the distributor which means that in fact he will never be granted the licence. For instance, the licensing authority may require him to have certain technical facilities or staff with particular qualifications and he may be unable or unwilling to obtain these. In all of these situations, the principal will wish to try another distributor who may be more diligent or better qualified. Clause 4.15.3 enables him to do this without argument after a reasonable period of time. **4–103**

4.15.4 The Distributor shall not be entitled to any compensation on the termination of this Agreement by reason of any of any of the provisions of cll.4.15 or 4.16 [including but without limitation by reason of expiry by effluxion of time]. **4–104**

The phrase in square brackets is applicable only to a distributorship agreement which has only a fixed term.

Compulsory compensation upon termination of an agency agreement has already been discussed in Chapter 2.7. As stated there, distributors are less likely to receive compensation under overriding provisions of the law of the territory than agents are, but there are still many countries where compensation for a distributor can be obtained even in the event of expiry of the agreement by effluxion of time or after proper notice. Where local laws make reference to the calculation of compensation, this is usually on the basis of net profits rather than commission but otherwise the points made in Chapter 2.7 still apply. **4–105**

Distributors are also more concerned than agents are in the case where the **4–106** principal fails to ship them products or ships them defective products. Not only does the distributor lose the market, but he also suffers unrecovered overheads while the organisation he has set up to market the products stands idle. The liability of the principal to the distributor for defective products under warranty arrangements is considered in Chapter 4.26 (Sch.6). However, the very fact that defective products are supplied may cause the distributor to lose his market for the products generally, and cause him to terminate the agreement for what he regards as a breach of its terms by the principal. Thus unjustified termination can occur not only because of a premature termination by the principal, but also through a termination by the distributor because of some action (such as shipping defective products) which causes the distributor to regard himself as entitled to treat the agreement as terminated because of the principal's breach.

4–107 Where the local law does not provide for compulsory compensation on a particular basis, the ordinary law relating to compensation for breach of contract would govern the situation in these cases of unjustified termination. The question then arises as to what extent the distributor is allowed to recover from the principal not only for the expenses caused by the premature termination such as those involved in winding up the organisation, but also for loss of profits.

4–108 On general principles, the future period which can be looked at for lost profits can only be the unexpired portion of the fixed term, if relevant, or the period of notice which should have been given by the principal to terminate the agreement. It therefore seems reasonable that where the agreement is terminable by notice, the distributor would be unlikely to recover by way of compensation more than the profits he should have made during the notice period. In addition claims could be made by the distributor for any period prior to the actual date of termination in which the principal was under an obligation to supply and failed to do so, or caused a loss of market.

4–109 This right to compensation for lost profits is, in the absence of a compensation provision in the local law, also tied up with the question of the principal's liability to supply products to the distributor at all.

4–110 If the event causing the termination of the agreement also causes the principal to be unable to supply, and is an event beyond his reasonable control, any clause excusing him from failure to supply because of circumstances beyond his control would apply to relieve him of liability. Even if the agreement had not been terminated he would have had no liability to supply, and the question of lost profits cannot therefore arise.

4–111 On the other hand, there may be no requirement under the agreement for the principal to supply at all, since the agreement may well state that the principal is under no duty to accept orders placed on him by the distributor, except at his discretion. If this type of provision holds, there can be no question of compensation for loss of sales on an unjustified termination, because it can be argued that the original agreement never gave the distributor the right to have goods supplied to him, other than at the principal's discretion. The principal might, then, be in breach of any exclusivity provision if he tried to set up another distributor or to supply into the territory himself, during the remainder of the fixed term of the notice period, as relevant, but in the absence of an exclusivity provision, or if he were pulling out of the territory or going out of that line of business, the distributor would have no rights that he could complain had been breached, and could receive no compensation for lost profits.

It is true that many courts would be inclined to read an implied term into the agreement that the principal was not to refuse to supply on grounds that amounted to bad faith, or without reasonable cause. However, if the express provision in the agreement were drafted clearly enough, there would be no room for such an implication. In some countries (see for instance, the UK statute, the Unfair Contract Terms Act 1977, s.3, although this section only applies to consumer sales and transactions where a party relies on his written standard terms, and the Act in general does not apply to international sales of goods) it is not permitted unreasonably to draft an exclusion clause which excuses a party from failure to perform that which he has undertaken by contract to perform. However, where the contract is circumscribed so that the liability to perform is never taken on in the first place, this sort of provision is often drafted around. For instance, a provision stating that the principal would accept all orders, but would not be liable for failure to supply goods under them for any reason, would be caught, but one which said the principal was under no obligation at all to accept orders, would not be. The various possibilities relating to acceptance of orders are discussed in Chapter 4.26 (Sch.6). The other area of compensation for unjustified termination, in jurisdictions where the basis of compensation is not laid down, is any additional expenses for winding up the operation, caused by the principal's unjustified termination. Expenses can presumably be recovered generally where a fixed term agreement is terminated during the fixed term, at least where the fixed term is not nearly over, because the distributor would be justified in saying that without that premature termination he would not have had to wind up his operation. Where the termination is under an agreement where a fairly short period of notice is available to terminate it, it could be argued that the expenses in winding up the operation would have had to be borne if notice had been given. Thus the fact that notice was not given had only accelerated the bearing of expenses which would have been borne anyway. The only exception would be expenses specially incurred because no notice has been given—*e.g.* payments in lieu of notice to employees, which could have been avoided by giving them notice of termination of employment, if the distributor had himself been given notice so that he knew in advance what would happen. **4–112**

4.16 Termination

4.16 Without prejudice to any right or remedy the Principal may have against the Distributor for breach or non-performance of this Agreement the Principal shall have the right summarily to terminate this Agreement: **4–113**

4.16.1 On the Distributor committing [a breach of any of its provisions (other than cl.4.3.5)] [a material breach of this agreement other than a breach of cl.4.3.5] providing that (where the breach is capable of rectification) the Distributor has been advised in writing of the breach and has not rectified it within [twenty-one] days of receipt of such advice.

The inclusion of the phrase in the first set of square brackets means that the distributor cannot complain that a particular provision is not a substantial term of the agreement so that its breach is not a sufficiently serious matter to justify termination of the agreement. In practice, it is unlikely, however, to be in the interest of either party to claim termination for a breach that is not substantial, and it is common to use the phrase in the second set of square brackets instead. The cure-period is a usual provision, and the exclusion of breach of the provision relating to targets is necessary because of the special nature of this obligation which requires that breach of it be dealt with separately.

4–114 4.16.2 On the Distributor failing to achieve a target under cl.4.3.5 unless such failure was caused by a default of the Principal or by reason of Act of God, fire explosion war riot civil commotion or governmental decree or legislation.

Obligations upon the distributor to meet specified targets are usually found in exclusive agreements. In these cases, there is no other outlet in the territory for the sale of the products if the principal is not satisfied with the distributor's efforts, but poor sales performance does not of itself give rise to a clear breach of any other kind (not even necessarily of a due diligence provision) for which the agreement can be terminated.

4–115 An alternative possibility to termination for unjustified failure to reach a target is to provide that the exclusivity provision shall lapse and either the principal may supply direct into the territory himself (which is presumably not very satisfactory or a distributor would not have been appointed in the first place) or the principal may have the right to appoint an additional distributor. However, the practical use of this power is doubtful. The reasons that made it appropriate for the original arrangement to be exclusive (either the nature of the products or the market in the territory) will presumably still apply in most cases so that a second distributor is in fact unlikely to be found who will be willing to take on an arrangement where the existing distributor goes on selling in the territory. Thus it is usually best to provide that failure to meet targets in exclusive arrangements is a ground for termination by the principal, so that a new distributor can be appointed.

4–116 4.16.3 If the Distributor shall have any distress or execution levied upon its goods or effects.

4.16.4 On the commencement of the winding up or bankruptcy of the Distributor or on the appointment of a receiver of the distributor's assets or on the Distributor ceasing to do business at any time for thirty consecutive days (other than for annual holidays).

Clauses 4.16.3 and 4.16.4 are the usual provisions for termination on insolvency. The final part of cl.4.16.4 is again a usual provision, but in many countries (*e.g.* France) it is customary for businesses to shut completely for a period for annual holidays and this should be provided for.

4.16.5 On the Distributor for any reason of whatsoever nature (other than a default of the Principal) being substantially prevented from performing or becoming unable to perform its obligations hereunder. **4–117**

This provision is one which might in other circumstances justify a party for failure to perform. However, the harsh commercial facts of life are that if the distributor cannot, for whatever reason, go on distributing, the principal must find another distributor or lose the market. However, in circumstances where there is a general disaster affecting the territory as a whole the distributor is unlikely to be replaced, as no other distributor is likely to be found, and the agreement may very well subsist, albeit in limbo, until the state of emergency is over.

4.16.6 On the Distributor assigning or attempting to assign this Agreement without the prior written consent of the Principal. **4–118**

4.16.7 If control of the Distributor shall pass from the present shareholders or owners or controllers to other persons whom the Principal shall in its absolute discretion regard as unsuitable.

Because of the personal nature of the distribution arrangements, the principal is wise to reserve the right to terminate on quite a wide basis if the "personality" of the distributor changes in a way of which the principal does not approve.

4.17 Effect of termination

4.17.1 Upon termination of this Agreement from any cause whatsoever (including but without limitation expiry by effluxion of time) the Distributor shall at the request of the Principal promptly return to the Principal all documentation of any nature whatsoever in his possession or control relating to the Products or to the Principal and to the activities of the Distributor in relation to the Products or the Principal (other than correspondence between the Distributor and the Principal which does not relate to technical matters). **4–119**

This clause is widely drafted, and in practice it is unlikely that the principal will be able to make certain that the distributor has totally complied with it. It is however very useful where the principal wants the return of specific items of documentation that he knows the distributor has in his possession.

4.17.2 Upon such termination the Distributor if so required by the Principal shall sell back to the Principal, at the prices set out below, the following classes of Products (which shall in all cases exclude Products covered by cl.4.17.3) purchased by the Distributor from the Principal hereunder and remaining unsold: **4–120**

4.17.2.1 Products invoiced within twelve months of the termination date of this Agreement—landed cost (including customs duties) into Distributor's warehouse;

4.17.2.2 Products invoiced more than twelve but less than twenty-four months from the termination date of this Agreement—[sixty] per cent of landed cost (including customs duties) into the Distributor's warehouse;

4.17.3 Upon such termination Products invoiced more than twenty-four months before the said termination date and Products (irrespective of when invoiced) which are unmerchantable obsolete illegal damaged deteriorated defective or otherwise unfit for sale or (where any Product has a shelf-life) with more than half of their shelf-life expired shall be destroyed forthwith by the Distributor in the presence of the Principal or the authorised representative of the Principal at the expense of the Distributor and without making any charge upon the Principal.

The most vexed question on the termination of a distribution agreement is the disposal of the distributor's stock. On the one hand the principal will not want to leave him with a substantial stock of the products, or with defective products, which he may choose to sell off at distress prices and ruin the reputation of the product or the market for the product. On the other hand he will not want to be obliged to take back excess and often obsolete inventory. Clauses 4.17.2 and 4.17.3 attempt to achieve rough justice between both sides. It is important to note, however, that cl.4.17.2 is only an option in favour of the principal. If he chooses not to exercise it the distributor will be left to do as he likes with stock in his hands unless it is covered by cl.4.17.3.

4–121 4.17.4 Upon such termination the Distributor shall have no further rights to use the Trade Mark in any way whatsoever and in particular but without prejudice to the generality of the foregoing shall cease to use the Trade Mark on its letterheads packaging vehicle liveries or elsewhere and shall at the request of the Principal sell any stocks of the Products not disposed of under the previous sub cll. of 4.17 in packaging which bears neither the Trade Mark nor the name of the Principal.

It is important to ensure that, if the distributor is left with any products which he does not sell off to the principal or destroy, the principal should have the right to require that he dispose of them in packaging which does not bear the principal's trade mark. This prevents any distress disposal, or the disposal of defective products, affecting the reputation of the principal's trade mark. However, in most cases the principal will only leave the product with the distributor if not concerned as to how it is disposed of by the distributor. The truth is that in most cases, the old distributor tends to have the whip-hand. Whatever the provisions of the contract, most principals who care for the reputation of their product tend to reach an amicable accommodation, usually involving the transfer of all stock, whether or not defective or obsolete, to the new distributor, in return for a global payment by the principal. The new distributor can then arrange with the principal what is to be destroyed, and what can be sold. Provisions like cll.4.17.3 and

4.17.4 tend to be used more as a fall-back position, and to assist in the bargaining that takes place in the termination negotiations.

4.17.5 Upon such termination the Distributor shall (if so required) supply the Principal with a list of the Distributor's customers for the Products. **4–122**

This is of material assistance to any new distributor, and something for which most principals can and should ask. However, it must be said that most distributors will resist such a provision and that a court is unlikely to imply it into the agreement in the absence of such an express provision (*Accumulator Industries Ltd v CA Vandervell & Co* [1912] R.F.C. 391.) In the absence of an express provision, the Distributor will regard the customers in the territory as his customers, and the good will he has built up with them as his good will, not the good will of the principal. There may obviously be certain instances of termination where the distributor intends to go on doing business in the same product area, perhaps with products now obtained from a competitor of his old principal. In such cases, he will clearly not wish to have the principal undermine the distributor's good will by soliciting the customers direct.

4.17.6 Upon such termination the Distributor shall (if legally possible) assign to the Principal free of charge all permissions consents and licences (if any) relating to the marketing and or distribution and or sale of the Products and execute all documents and do all things necessary to ensure that the Principal shall enjoy the benefit of the said permissions consents and licences after the said termination to the entire exclusion of the Distributor. **4–123**

The licences that have been obtained by the distributor in order to commence marketing of the products in the territory are vital for the continuation under the new distribution arrangements. In some cases they are not just licences relating to the products, but are permissions to the distributor personally to market them. All documentation relating to licences should be handed over to the principal on termination, but the licences personal to the distributor cause a problem. Either the old distributor will have to assign them to the principal or to the new distributor, or the new distributor will have to go through the process of obtaining these approvals all over again. In some cases such personal licences are not assignable, under the local law relating to them, but this provision is useful to catch those cases where assignment is both necessary and possible. In its absence distributors have been known to hold principals to ransom by refusing to assign such licences.

4.18 Confidentiality

The clause in Chapter 2.3.5 may be adapted or the clauses in Chapter 1.4 **4–124**
can be used if a longer form is desired. In most cases the short form is sufficient for distribution agreements not dealing with extensive technical information.

4.19 Transmission of rights

4–125 4.19 This Agreement and the benefit of the rights granted to the Distributor by this Agreement shall be personal to the Distributor who shall not without the prior consent of the Principal mortgage or charge the same to any third party nor subcontract or assign the same or part with any of its rights or obligations hereunder save that the foregoing shall not prevent the Distributor from factoring or mortgaging or in any way creating a charge or security over Products the title in which shall have passed to it or over book-debts created by the sale of such Products.

This is a longer form of the non-assignment clause which is more suitable for a distributor than that for an agent set out in Chapter 2.6.

4.20 Interpretation clauses and signature

4.21 Schedule 1—the products

4.22 Schedule 2—the territory

4.23 Schedule 3—the trade mark

4–126 Clauses 4.20 to 4.23 should be reproduced as required from Chapter 1.

4.24 Schedule 4—purchase targets

4–127 4.24 The Distributor undertakes (subject to prior termination in accordance with cl.4.15) to achieve during each consecutive period of twelve months of the currency of this Agreement (the first such period to commence upon the date of commencement of this Agreement) the following minimum targets for purchases from the Principal for the Products during the relevant period as follows:

Period	Target

Provided that the quantity for all periods thereafter shall be set by the mutual agreement of the parties hereto as a result of reviews to be completed not later than three calendar months prior to the commencement of the relevant period;

AND

Provided further that if the parties are unable to reach mutual agreement as to the fixing of any minimum quantity as aforesaid [then no further target shall be set and the Principal shall have the right to amend cl.4.2 to a non-exclusive licence, but the Distributor shall not be regarded as in any way in breach of this Agreement nor shall any of its rights hereunder be prejudiced or removed save as provided in relation to the said cl.4.2] [then the Distributor shall be regarded as in breach of this Agreement under cl.4.16.1].

The provisions of this schedule provide the necessary targets which should be applied in an exclusive distribution arrangement. They are purchase targets not sales targets for the reasons discussed in Chapter 4.3.5. It is not usually practicable to set targets beyond the first few years of the agreement at the time it is signed. Very often, where there is a reasonably short fixed period, say up to three years, targets are set for only this period, reliance being placed on general powers to terminate the agreement after this period by notice, under the due diligence provisions, if the sales performance is not satisfactory. Again the alternative has been given at the end of the clause, in the event that mutual agreement as to targets cannot be reached, of either turning the agreement into a non-exclusive one (which is not always practicable—see Chapter 4.16.2) or of terminating it. The latter alternative tends to concentrate the minds of the parties, and ensure that except in cases where there is a fundamental incompatibility, agreement is reached.

The imposition of purchase targets should be treated with care. Their **4–128** purpose should not really be to force the distributor to purchase excess product which he does not need, cannot sell, and probably cannot pay for. The only result of this is the build up of excessive and obsolete inventory which the principal will have to deal with if the agreement is eventually terminated either for breach of the minimum purchase obligations or because the distributor has become insolvent. The real use of these targets is to give the distributor an incentive to perform, and to give the principal a lever (through the threat of termination if the distributor does not) to encourage performance. Also, as a last resort, failure to meet the purchase targets can be used as a reason to terminate an unsatisfactory distributor, or to turn an unsatisfactory exclusive distributor into a non-exclusive distributor to give the principal or another trader a chance to sell in the territory.

4.25 Schedule 5—competing goods

See Chapter 4.3.6. **4–129**

4.26 Schedule 6—terms of supply of principal

4.26.1 In this Schedule the term "goods" means the Products and any other items which the Principal may from time to time sell to the Distributor. **4–130**

For the sake of convenience the schedule applies not only to the products but also to anything else that the principal may sell to the distributor, for instance advertising materials.

4.26.2 Terms of supply of the Principal to the Distributor shall be as follows: **4–131**

4.26.2.1 Prices to the Distributor for any of the goods shall be at the Principal's relevant export prices for the Territory as from time to time prevailing.

A pricing provision of this nature is usual to allow the principal to increase prices as necessary. In some cases price lists are annexed to the agreements, and provisions for price escalation are included, but this is not usual for most types of distribution agreements.

4–132 4.26.2.2 The acceptance of orders for the goods shall be at the entire discretion of the Principal [but orders will normally be accepted subject to availability of the goods]. [In the event of a shortage of supply of any of the goods, the Principal reserves the right to supply only part of such orders, and, if necessary, to operate a quota system to share out available quantities of such goods [(in such proportion as the principal in its entire discretion shall determine)] [in fair and equitable proportions] between all of its customers who place orders for such goods.]

For the effect of this provision upon the question of compensation for unjustified termination see Chapter 4.15.4. In order to put the principal in the best position, although perhaps not a commercially tenable one, it would be necessary to omit the phrase in square brackets in the first sentence. The sentence in the second set of square brackets is not strictly necessary, but can be useful. It is also a help in areas subject to various competition law regimes to combat allegations by the distributor of unjustified refusal to supply or of abuse of monopoly power. Where this is the reason for its inclusion, the phrase in the second set of square brackets in that sentence ("in fair and equitable proportions") should be used, not the phrase in the first set. This will avoid the charge of discriminatory or abusive conduct in determining how the quota system is to be operated.

4–133 4.26.2.3 Delivery dates or periods specified in orders accepted by the Principal are firm provided that the Principal is in possession of all information and documents necessary to permit the Principal to proceed to fill such order in a timely manner and without interruption.

This is a normal precaution to prevent unjustified complaints for delay in delivery.

4–134 4.26.2.4 The Principal shall be under no liability for delays in delivery or performance or failures to deliver or perform because of circumstances of whatsoever nature beyond its reasonable control.

This is a clause, of the type usually called "*force majeure*" providing for excusable delays in delivery. The nature and application of these types of clauses is discussed in Chapter 1.7 and an alternative, longer form precedent is provided.

4–135 4.26.2.5(a) In case of delay or failure other than in circumstances where cl.4.26.2.4 applies the Principal shall reimburse the Distributor in respect of any loss or damage suffered by the Distributor by reason of such delay or failure up to a maximum of [0.25] per cent of the order price of the Products in delay for each [week] from the due date of delivery or performance under the relevant order until the actual date of delivery or performance provided that the Principal's total liability for such delay or failure shall not exceed [five] per cent of the order price of the Products in delay and that such sum shall be paid to the Distributor by the Principal upon proof of such loss or damage as liquidated and ascertained damages in full and final satisfaction for all liabilities of the Principal to the Distributor arising from such delay or failure.

OR

4.26.2.5(b) All dates for delivery of the goods are given in good faith but are only estimates and the Principal shall not be liable for any failure to deliver on any date so given [or at all].

Version (a) is a standard liquidated damages clause. Such clauses, although on the face of them appearing as penalties, in fact are to be set at a level that they can in good faith be regarded as a genuine pre-estimate of the damage suffered for late delivery. Then, the last part of the clause acts as a safeguard and limitation to the principal of the amount of compensation he has to pay. Such clauses are not common in distribution agreements for large volumes of goods. They tend to be more appropriate in arrangements covering one-off purchases often of capital goods. The alternative is to use version (b) of the clause which does not impose a fixed delivery date on the principal at all. The last phrase of version (b) in square brackets is somewhat severe. If it is used, consideration should first be given as to its legality under any relevant legislation affecting exclusion of liability (see discussion at Chapter 4.15.4). Where version (b) is used, cl.4.26.2.3 is conflicting and unnecessary and should be deleted.

4.26.2.6 The established export prices for the goods shall include delivery [Ex Works] [FOB port of shipment] [CIF] [C&F] (as defined in the edition of Incoterms from time to time current). Property and risk in the goods shall pass to the Distributor when delivered in accordance with this paragraph. **4–136**

This clause incorporates the provisions of Incoterms, which are the general terms for delivery used in international trade, which are published by the International Chamber of Commerce, based in Paris. These terms are widely recognised, and it is useful to have them as part of the contract. The latest edition of Incoterms was published in 2000, and details can readily be obtained from the Incoterms web site. Most distribution arrangements seem to rely on shipment Ex Works or FOB, but CIF or C&F named ports are also used. DDP (Delivery Duty Paid) is not often used in distribution arrangements, as the idea of the principal clearing goods and being responsible for compliance with the importation formalities in the territory goes against the philosophy of distribution agreements, and the responsibilities which they generally impose on the distributor.

4.26.2.7 All charges after delivery as in cl.4.26.2.6 together with the cost of all relevant [export and] import documentation and customs duty (if any) shall be for the account of and shall be paid by the Distributor. **4–137**

This is a clarification of Incoterms which is not strictly necessary, but which serves to make the point to the distributor. The words in square brackets are appropriate only for Ex Works delivery.

4–138 4.26.2.8 Payment for the goods shall be made by the Distributor to the Principal [thirty days] after delivery or upon such other terms as may be negotiated from time to time in writing by the Principal and the Distributor. Payment shall be made to the Principal in [sterling] (or in such other currency as the Principal may request) in [London] in full free of all charges deductions and withholding taxes.

The payment clause envisages that most distributors will receive credit terms. This is a question which has to be considered every time a distributor is appointed, and also from time to time during the relationship with a distributor. In each case one has to consider what is a safe risk not only for the length of the period for payment, but also for the maximum amount outstanding at any one time. Although it is possible to insure export debts in some cases this is not always the answer. One alternative is payment cash against documents (CAD) at sight. The documents of title to the goods (usually bill of lading or airway bill are sent through the principal's local banker to his correspondent banker in the territory with instructions to hand over the documents to the distributor upon payment of the order price for the goods concerned. This ensures that the distributor cannot get hold of the goods until he has paid for them, but, unlike a letter of credit, does not require him to pay for the goods before they arrive in the territory.

4–139 The fact that under a letter of credit the payment is usually made upon shipment, when the documents are presented by the seller to the buyer's bank, rather than on arrival in the territory, and the expensive and cumbersome nature of the procedure, makes letters of credit less than popular with purchasers. It does, however, have the advantage for the seller that he knows, once the credit has been set up (provided it is irrevocable and confirmed) that he can go ahead and ship the goods without fear that in the meantime the buyer will try to cancel the contract or become insolvent. It is thus often the case that where one sells CAD an initial payment of part of the price is required when the order is placed. The other advantage of the letter of credit (although this is one of the reasons it can be so expensive for the buyer) is that the buyer always automatically takes the risk of exchange rate fluctuations if the credit is opened in the local currency of the seller.

4–140 4.26.2.9 The Principal undertakes that all consignments of the Products delivered hereunder shall be of [merchantable] [satisfactory] quality, fit for all the purposes for which they are commonly supplied, of sound and safe materials and workmanship, conforming to the agreed performance specifications set out or referred to in Sch.1, and in any event shall not fall below the standards applied by the Principal to consignments of the Products manufactured by it for supply to customers other than the Distributor. The Distributor shall have the right to reject all consignments not conforming with this paragraph and the Principal undertakes to indemnify the Distributor for all loss or damage suffered by the Distributor as a result of claims by third parties by reason of the Distributor failing to meet contractual obligations following such rejection. Risk and property in any consignment so rejected shall pass back to the Principal upon leaving the Distributor's warehouse for its return to the Principal.

This warranty clause is a very strict one, but in fact it really only summarises the obligations of the principal who supplies defective products as they stand under the general law in most jurisdictions. Where one is dealing with pharmaceuticals, and cosmetics, and consumer goods generally, the greatest problem for the principal is not claims made by the distributor, but claims made direct by the ultimate consumers which cannot be barred by provisions in the distribution agreement, and should be covered by the principal's product liability insurance. Nor is it feasible in most cases to expect the commercial arrangements to be so much to the advantage of the distributor that he will agree to indemnify the principal for this liability. Furthermore it is unlikely that he will be financially strong enough to bear significant product liability claims, or, in the current state of the product liability insurance market, afford premiums for high amounts of insurance cover. In appropriate cases this warranty can be replaced by a more limited guarantee, particularly where the distributor assumes technical responsibilities relating to servicing guarantees and maintenance. These are discussed in Chapter 6.24 (see particularly Chapter 6.24.15).

In regard to the precise wording of the warranty, it should be noted that **4–141** the term "merchantable quality" as used in the UK in the Sale of Goods Act 1979 has now been replaced by a new standard of "satisfactory quality" by s.1 of the Sale and Supply of Goods Act 1994. This standard is therefore an appropriate one to use instead of or in addition to the old standard of "merchantable quality" where the distribution agreement is governed by one of the systems of law in force in the UK. The phrase "fitness for all the purposes for which they are commonly supplied" is actually copied (*mutatis mutandis*) from s.1 of the 1994 Act, and is one of the criteria by which "satisfactory quality" is now to be judged.

4.26.3 The terms of this Schedule shall prevail over any terms or conditions of **4–142** purchase of the Distributor set out in correspondence purchase orders or any other documents to the entire exclusion of the latter.

This is a necessary clarifying provision, to ensure that later exchanges of documentation and the general laws relating to the formation of contracts do not result in these conditions being superseded.

Chapter 5

Distribution Agreements Inside the EC

Contents

5.1 Commercial and legal background

When dealing with distribution agreements within the EU, the most **5–01** important issue to consider is the impact of competition law. In general, either under EC law itself or the national laws of the Member States, the relationship of principal and distributor is largely left to be regulated by the intention and agreement of the parties. Apart from some states which require registration formalities on the creation of a distributorship, and regulatory laws relating to the quality, specifications or composition of the products and services covered by the distribution agreement, the one great exception is in the area of competition law. This should be understood in its widest sense, covering not only EC competition law and the various competition regimes existing in each of the Member States, but also related issues such as resale price maintenance, refusal to supply and unfair trading practices. The somewhat lengthy preamble to this chapter thus deals in detail with these issues, since it is not possible to draft a distribution agreement for use within the EU without a proper understanding of them.

5.1.1 EC competition law

5–02 EC competition law applies within the EU and also within what remains of the EEA (Iceland, Norway and Lichtenstein), and with the extension of the EU due to take place in 2004, (see Chapter 1.2.2) this regime will now cover one of the major industrial groupings in the world, with a population greater than that of the United States.

5–03 Given the extent of the area to which the regime will soon apply, radical changes in the way EC Competition law is enforced will apply from May 1, 2004 to coincide with the latest enlargement of the EU. These new measures will also affect the interaction between the local competition law, and national competition authorities, in each Member State, with EC Competition law and the EC Commission.

5–04 Changes in procedure and enforcement have not altered the basic principles of EC Competition law which are still enshrined in Arts 28 (formerly 30), 30 (formerly 36), 81 (formerly 85) and 82 (formerly 86) of the EC Treaty. The renumbering of these articles was effected by the Treaty of Amsterdam in 1999. For convenience, throughout this chapter, and the remainder of this book, reference will be made to these articles as renumbered, even though in some quotations from legislation, decisions or judgments the old numbers will have been used in the originals. Articles 28 and 30 deal with the free movement of goods and services required to create a true single market. They are therefore concerned to prohibit unilateral practices which partition the common market and destroy its unity. Article 81 deals with anti-competitive arrangements between undertakings which affect trade between Member States. Article 82 deals with an abuse by an undertaking or group of undertakings of a dominant position in a substantial part of the common market, which affects trade between Member States.

5.1.1.1 The old regulatory framework for Articles 81 and 82

Currently Regulation 17/62 of the EU Council provides the framework for the EC Commission's powers of enforcement and implementation of Arts 81 and 82. The framework deals with the Commission's powers to investigate possible breaches of the articles (either on its own initiative or as a result of a third party complaint), the Commission's powers to decide if a breach has occurred and to exact fines in appropriate cases. In the case of Art.81, the framework also provides the basis for the procedures relating to negative clearance (*i.e.* seeking a declaration from the Commission that Art.81 does not apply at all to a particular transaction) and relating to applications for exemption (permitted under discretionary powers provided for under Art.81(3), and delegated to the Commission by the Council under Reg.17/62, which can be exercised if the Commission considers that despite its restrictive aspects the arrangement is in the public interest). Commission Regulation 3385/94 sets out the procedural guidelines for notifications for negative clearance under Art.81 and applications for exemption under Art.81(3). **5–05**

Notification under Art.81(3) has one important consequence in relation to fines. Article 15(5) of Reg.17/62 states that fines "shall not be imposed in respect of acts taking place after notification to the Commission and before its Decision in application of Article 81(3) ...". **5–06**

5.1.1.2 The new regulatory framework for Articles 81 and 82

The old regulatory framework is to be replaced with effect from May 1, 2004 by a new Council Regulation (already published on December 16, 2002 as 1/2003) which repeals Reg.17/62 in its entirety, except for transitional provisions. Article 34.1 of Reg.1/2003 provides that pending applications under Reg.17/62 will lapse if they have not been dealt with by the effective date of May 1, 2004. However, Art.34.2 provides that any procedural steps already taken under Reg.17/62 will continue to have effect. This means that where a decision on negative clearance has already been made, under Reg.17/62, it continues in effect for the purpose of the new framework. Similarly, where the grant of an exemption has already been made under Reg.17/62, it continues unaffected by the new Regulation. This applies not only to individual exemptions but also to block exemptions issued by the Commission through Regulations made pursuant to Reg.17/62. However, in this case, since all exemptions are granted for a fixed period of time, once the period has expired, it will not be possible, in the case of individual exemptions, to renew the relevant exemption by further application to the Commission, and the new Reg.1/2003 will therefore apply to the agreement or arrangement in question. However, although block exemptions are also time limited, there is nothing in the new framework to prevent the Commission extending existing block exemptions under relevant existing delegations of authority under **5–07** existing Council Regulations or to issue new block exemptions if the Council sees fit so to empower it by further Council Regulations.

5–08 Article 33 of Reg.1/2003, empowers the Commission to issue appropriate detailed implementing provisions in the same way that Reg.17/62 did. The preamble to Reg.1/2003 explains the purpose and rationale for the new framework. The relevant extract reads as follows:

> "In order to establish a system which ensures that competition in the common market is not distorted, Articles 81 and 82 of the Treaty must be applied effectively and uniformly in the Community ... [Reg.17/62] has allowed a Community competition policy to develop that has helped to disseminate a competition culture within the Community. In the light of experience, however, [Reg.17/62] should now be replaced by legislation designed to meet the challenges of an integrated market and a future enlargement of the Community. (Recital 1) ... account must be taken ... of the need to ensure effective supervision, on the one hand, and to simplify administration to the greatest possible extent on the other ... (Recital 2)...The centralised scheme set up by [Reg.17/62] no longer secures a balance between these objectives. It hampers application of the Community competition rules by the courts and competition authorities of the Member States, and the system of notification it involves prevents the Commission from concentrating its resources on curbing the most serious infringements. It also imposes considerable cost on undertakings. (Recital 3)...The present system should therefore be replaced by a directly applicable exception system in which the competition authorities and courts of the Member States have the power to apply not only Article 81(1) and Article 82 of the Treaty ... but also Article 81(3) ... (Recital 4) ... In order to ensure that Community competition rules are applied effectively, the competition authorities of Member States should be associated more closely with their application. To this end they should be empowered to apply Community law (Recital 6). National courts have an essential part to play in applying the Community competition rules. When deciding disputes between private individuals, they protect the subjective rights under Community law, for example by awarding damages to the victims of infringements ... They should therefore be allowed to apply Article 81 and 82 of the Treaty in full ... (Recital 7) ... The principles laid down in Article 81 and 82 of the Treaty, as they have been applied by [Reg.17/62] have given a central role to the Community bodies. This central role should be retained, while associating the Member States more closely with the application of the Community competition rules. In accordance with the principles of subsidiarity and proportionality as set out in Article 5 of the Treaty, this Regulation does not go beyond what is necessary in order to achieve its objective, which is to allow the Community competition rules to be applied effectively. (Recital 34.)"

5–09 Article 1.1 of Reg.1/2003 provides that agreements decisions and concerted practices caught by Art.81(1) which do not satisfy the conditions of

Art.81(3) for the provision of an exemption shall be prohibited, "no prior decision to that effect being required". Article 1.2 provides that where such agreements, decisions and concerted practices do fulfil the conditions of Art.81(3) they shall not be prohibited "no prior decision to that effect being required". Finally, Art.1.3 provides that abuse of a dominant position under Art.82 is prohibited "no prior decision to that effect being necessary". Article 2 deals with the burden of proof. The burden of proving an infringement of Art.81(1) or Art.82 rests with the party or authority alleging the infringement. The undertaking or association of undertakings claiming the benefit of Art.81(3) bears the burden of proving that the conditions of that paragraph are fulfilled.

Regulation 1/2003, has not affected the powers of the Commission to **5–10** continue to deal with cases under Arts 81 and 82. Article 4 provides that the Commission continues to have powers to deal with individual cases under Art.82 in accordance with the procedures set out in the regulation. These powers are set out in Arts 7 to 10. It can conduct its own investigations into and make findings in relation to infringements of Art.81(1) and 82, and to impose "behavioural or structural remedies to bring the infringement effectively to an end" (Art.7). Article 8 allows it to adopt interim measures, and Art.9 to take binding commitments from infringing undertakings which agree to implement measures "to meet the concerns expressed by the Commission in its preliminary assessment" of the relevant infringement. Article 10, preserves the right of the Commission, acting on its own initiative, to find, "where the Community public interest relating to the application" of Arts 81 or 82 so requires in any individual case, either that the relevant article is inapplicable, or, in the case of Art.81, that the relevant arrangement should be exempted under Art.81(3).

Articles 17 to 22 set out the Commission's new powers to investigate **5–11** potential breaches of Arts 81 and 82, and to require national competition authorities to assist in such investigations. These powers are wider than those under Reg.17/62, and include the right to search domestic premises if it is reasonably suspected that business records relevant to the investigation are being kept there. Articles 23 and 24 deal with the fines and penalties which the Commission can exact for breach of Arts 81 or 82 or for refusal to cooperate in an investigation. Articles 25 and 26 provide for limitation periods in relation to the penalties detailed under Arts 23 and 24. Under Art.25, these are three years in the case of infringements of provisions concerning requests for information, and five years in the case of all other infringements (*i.e.* infringement of the prohibitions in Arts 81(1) and 82). Time runs from the date the infringement is committed, or, if it is a continuing infringement, from the date it ceases. Where the Commission has made a decision pursuant to Arts 23 or 24 (*e.g.* set a fine for an infringement of Art.81(1)) time runs from the day the decision becomes final, and the limitation runs for a period of five years. A further decision varying the original decision or refusing an application for variation, and any action by the Commission or a Member State acting on the request of the Commission to enforce payment of the penalty or fine, starts time running afresh.

5–12 The extent of fines for infringement of Art.81 or 82 is limited to 10 per cent of the total turnover of the relevant undertaking in the preceding business year. The word "total" should be noted. This means that worldwide turnover of the undertaking is used in the calculation, and not just the turnover relating to the arrangement that has infringed Art.81 or 82. Given the flexible definition of the term "undertaking", it may well be that in some cases where groups of companies are involved, the limit will apply to group turnover if it can be shown that the offending conduct was driven out of the group headquarters.

5–13 Articles 27 and 28 provide for the conduct of hearings before the Commission for the parties, complainants and other interested parties.

5–14 Finally it should be noted that Art.29.1 continues the existing powers of the Commission to withdraw the benefit of block exemptions in individual cases where it considers that the exempted arrangement "has certain effects which are incompatible with Article 81(3)".

5–15 Article 5 confers powers on the competition authorities of the Member States to apply Arts 81 or 82 in individual cases. For this purpose they can, acting on their own initiative or on a complaint, require that an infringement be brought to an end, order interim measures, accept commitments to cease or modify infringing behaviour, and impose fines and penalties as provided for under their national law. They may also decide not to act if on the basis of information in their possession the conditions for prohibition are not met. Article 6 merely confers upon national courts the power to apply Arts 81 and 82.

5–16 As with Art.29.1, so Art.29.2 confers a similar power on national competition law authorities to withdraw the benefit of a block exemption in an individual case where the effects incompatible with Art.81(3) are manifested in the territory of the Member State or "in a part thereof which has all the characteristics of a geographic market".

5–17 Articles 11 to 16 deal with the cooperation between the Commission and national competition law authorities and national courts. The thrust of these Articles is to ensure so far as possible the uniform application of EC Competition law by emphasising its precedence over national law, and by providing for a free flow of information relating to the implementation of Arts 81 and 82 by and between all interested parties. Art.11.1 states the principle that the "Commission and the competition authorities of the Member States shall apply the Community competition rules in close cooperation". Article 11.2 requires the Commission to send "the most important documents it has collected with a view to applying [its powers granted under] Arts 7,8,9,10 and 29(1)". Under Art.11.3 the national competition authorities have the duty to inform the Commission "in writing before or without delay after commencing the first formal investigative measure" in a case under Art.81 or 82. They may also inform other national competition authorities. Article 11.4 requires a national authority to inform the Commission not later than thirty days before it reaches a decision in a case under Art.81 or 82, together with a summary of the case and the envisaged decision. The information supplied may be made available to other national authorities by the Commission, and national authorities may also exchange such information among themselves. Article 11 emphasises the central role of the Commission both as clearing house and control mechanism for ensuring conformity between the decisions of the various national competition authorities. It must however be asked, given the volume of decisions that will presumably occur under the new framework, whether the Commission will in reality be able to attend in detail to the flow of information that will arise.

Article 12 provides for a freer exchange of information, in that the Commission and the national competition authorities are empowered to provide one another with, and use in evidence, any matter of fact or law, including confidential information, for the purpose of applying Arts 81 and 82. Information exchanged can only be used for the purpose of applying Art.81 or 82 and "in respect of the subject-matter for which it was collected by the transmitting authority" (*i.e.* not in respect of a different investigation). "However, where national competition law is applied in the same case and in parallel to Community competition law and does not lead to a different outcome, information exchanged under Art.12 may also be used for the application of national competition law". **5–18**

So far as investigations are concerned, it should be noted that Reg.1/2003 confers no power on national competition authorities to make investigations themselves on their own initiative. If the investigation takes place within the Member State of the relevant national competition authority, then national law will prescribe the extent of its investigatory powers. As discussed above Art.22 requires national competition authorities to carry out national investigations to assist the Commission in a Community investigation, if the Commission so requires. The national investigation must be carried out in accordance with the relevant national law. If a national competition authority wants to carry on investigations outside the Member State in which it is empowered to act, it can only do so by requesting that the national competition authority in the foreign Member State carry out the investigation on its behalf and transmit the results to it. Article 22.1 empowers, but does not compel, national competition law authorities to assist in such cases on the request of their foreign colleagues from other Member States. **5–19**

One problem with the new framework is to decide which competition law authority should deal with a particular case. Art.13 provides a kind of priority, in that where two or more national competition authorities are acting in respect of the same matter, the fact that one authority is dealing with the issue is sufficient grounds for the others to suspend proceedings or reject the complaint. The Commission may also suspend proceedings or reject a complaint if a national authority is dealing with the case. Finally where the Commission or a national authority has received a complaint which has already been dealt with by another competition authority, it may reject it. It should be noted that Art.13 provides a power to suspend or reject, but such suspension or rejection is not compulsory. Thus Art.13 still leaves open the possibility of concurrent investigations in more than one Member State. However, Art.11.6 preserves the Commission's rights of **5–20** precedence as the central controlling authority on competition matters. If the Commission initiates proceedings itself, the national competition authorities are relieved of their competence to apply Arts 81 or 82 in relation to that case. The only proviso is that where a national competition authority is already acting on a case, the Commission will not take over the proceedings without first consulting with that authority.

5–21 In a further effort to ensure uniform application of the EC Competition rules, Art.14 of Reg.1/2003 continues the role of the Advisory Committee on Restrictive Practices and Dominant Positions. This Committee is made up of representatives of all the national competition authorities, and the Commission is obliged to consult it before exercising its powers under Reg.1/2003 (Art.14.1) and to "take the utmost account of the opinion delivered by the Advisory Committee" (Art.14.5). The Committee can also discuss cases being handled by a national competition authority, either at the request of another national authority or of the Commission. It cannot issue an opinion on such cases. It can also discuss general issues of Community competition law (Art.14.7).

5–22 Article 15 provides coordination of the activities of the Commission and national courts. The courts may ask the Commission to give them information or an opinion on the application of Community competition rules (Art.15.1). Member States must send copies of relevant judgements of their national courts to the Commission (Art.15.2). Under the so-called *amicus curiae* provision of Art.15.3, national competition law authorities are entitled to make written submissions to their national courts on competition cases, and, if the court permits, to attend and make oral submissions. The Commission has similar powers in relation to the national courts of all of the Member States. For the purpose of making these submissions, the relevant competition authority may request the relevant court to provide any documents necessary for the assessment of the case.

5–23 Finally, Art.16 provides for uniform application of Community competition law. National courts are in the widest sense bound under the EC Treaty by the decisions of the European Court of Justice in relation to the interpretation of EC law, including EC competition rules. Article 16.1 applies the same rule to Commission decisions. A national court cannot take a decision under Art.81 or 82 which runs counter to a decision already taken by the Commission. Nor can they give decisions which would conflict with a decision contemplated by the Commission in proceedings it has initiated. To that effect the national court may consider whether it is necessary to stay its proceedings. Article 16.2 deals with national competition authorities, and provides that in making decisions which are already the subject of a Commission decision, they cannot take decisions which would run counter to the decision adopted by the Commission. Once again, Art.16 preserves the preeminence of the Commission over national competition authorities and national courts. Article 10 of Reg.1/2003 will ensure that in appropriate cases Commission decisions will continue to provide precedents for the decisions of national competition law authorities and national courts. Given the way the new framework will operate these decisions will presumably be far fewer than before and concern important, and, in many cases novel, issues, covering areas not previously considered. The only question perhaps to be considered here is the relative status of a judgment of the European Court and of a Commission Decision. The former can overrule the latter. This general principle is confirmed in relation to Arts 81 and 82 by Art.31 of Reg.1/2003. Presumably, national authorities and courts will, in the case of any conflict, or perceived conflict, between a judgment of the European Court and a decision of the Commission, be obliged to follow the former, or to suspend proceedings whilst seeking a ruling of the European Court in order to resolve the conflict.

The power of the Commission to provide confidential guidance appears still to exist, although not specifically dealt with in the Articles of Reg.1/2003. However, it appears that it will be less easily forthcoming than before. Recital 38 of the preamble states: "Where cases give rise to genuine uncertainty because they present novel or unresolved questions for the application of these rules, individual undertakings may wish to seek informal guidance from the Commission. This Regulation is without prejudice to the ability of the Commission to issue such informal guidance". There is also nothing in Reg.1/2003 which would prevent or amend the Commission practice of issuing general notices, announcements and guidelines dealing with the way in which it proposes to deal with various aspects of the implementation and enforcement of Arts 81 and 82. These provide valuable general guidance and certainly contribute to a more uniform application of EC Competition law, although there is nothing in Reg.1/2003 which would oblige national competition law authorities or national courts to apply such general guidance, since it does not have the force of law in the way that a decision under Reg.1/2003 does. **5–24**

The Commission has published a statement (IP/02/1739) and a Memorandum (MEMO/02/268) which explains more of the thinking behind the new framework. However, the essence of the changes are the abolition of the notification procedure and the making of Art.81(3) directly applicable. The first change "puts more responsibility in the hands of the companies who will need to ensure themselves that their agreements do not restrict competition, and, in case that they do, that these restrictions qualify under Art.81(3)". The second change "allows joint enforcement of the rules governing restrictive practices by the Commission, the national competition authorities and the national courts". The reform is now possible since over the last forty years "a great number of individual decisions have been made applying the exemption criteria of Article 81(3). National competition authorities and national courts are therefore well aware of the conditions under which the benefit of Article 81(3) can be granted". Further, in any event, "a system of notification is no longer workable as the EU prepares to take in ten new Member States". The Commission and the national competition authorities will put in place a network of competition authorities (the European Competition Network) which provides for greater cooperation and for "an allocation of cases according to the principle of the best-placed authority". The Commission as "guardian of the Treaty" has a **5–25** "special responsibility in the network". Finally over the next year the Commission will issue "a number of notices explaining or clarifying how certain concepts must be understood with a view to provide general guidance and legal certainty for business".

5–26 The new framework has attracted considerable discussion and controversy. The system under Reg.17/62 of notification, together with the concept of provisional immunity from fines once notification was made, although expensive, cumbersome and time-consuming, did provide legal certainty. Undertakings will now have to decide the matters, previously settled by the Commission upon notification, by themselves. This will require the use of experts, both of lawyers to decide the applicability of past decisions, judgments and guidance, and of economists to define the relevant market and gauge the economic impact of the particular arrangement or activity. The only test of the correctness of those assessments will be an investigation at some time in the future and a finding by the Commission or the relevant national competition law authority, or a judgment of the relevant national court, or, in the last resort, of the European Court.

5–27 Since there is no system for notification to the Commission of individual agreements for an individual exemption under Art.81(3) (as provided for by Reg.17/62) there is no longer any concept of provisional immunity upon notification. If an undertaking has made a wrong assessment of its position under Art.81(1) or Art.81(3) (or indeed of its position under Art.82) then its liability for payment of fines will arise from the date it implements the procedure in question, not the date upon which it discovers (as a result of the decision of a competent competition authority or competent court) that its assessment was mistaken.

5–28 The only comfort for undertakings can be found in the precise wording of Art.23.2 of Reg.1/2003. This provides that the Commission can impose fines for the infringement of Art.81 or 82, but only where the undertaking concerned has infringed the relevant Article "intentionally or negligently". (In this connection see also the plea of want of autonomy discussed below in relation to Case T-387/94 *Asia Motor France SA v Commission* [1996] ECR II-961.)

5–29 This shows how important it is for the undertaking to make a reasoned and fully documented assessment of the impact of the relevant arrangement or practice and to show how it has come to the conclusion that there is no infringement or, in relevant cases, that such infringement is exempt under Art.81(3). Except in truly reprehensible cases, such a course should prove that there was no intention to infringe. The real question is not whether the assessment was made in good faith but whether it was made negligently. Here the best recourse is to rely on competent third party professional advice. Even if that advice is itself incorrect or negligently given, the undertaking receiving that advice should be in a good position to prove that it discharged its responsibility not to act negligently by appointing properly qualified professional advisers. Other mitigating circumstances would be prompt and full cooperation in any investigation and an immediate termination of the conduct in question once a decision of infringement was made.

Needless to say, where the so-called "hardcore restrictions" (discussed below) are concerned—such as export bans, price fixing, market sharing or resale price maintenance, a plea by the undertaking concerned that it made its assessment without negligence and in good faith will be almost impossible to sustain. The Commission, and, indeed, all national courts and competition authorities, consider that the illegality of these restrictions has been publicised so widely (in decisions, judgments, notices and the wording of relevant block exemptions) that no undertaking can maintain with credibility that it did not know such practices were for all practical purposes illegal. **5–30**

The other problem to consider is that, with the implementation of direct applicability, national competition law authorities, national courts and professional advisers will find it considerably more difficult to apply EC competition law consistently across the enlarged European Union, particularly since, for obvious reasons, the decisions of the national competition authority or national courts of one Member State are not binding on the competition authorities and national courts of other Member States. It would be unfortunate if some Member States developed different customs and practices in the application of EC competition law rules. This could lead to forum shopping, and also, in the case of arrangements or practices spanning several Member States, the possibility that what was lawful in one state would be found unlawful in another. Although the cooperation, advisory and information exchange provisions in Reg.1/2003, and the supervisory and pre-eminent role of the Commission, will go some way towards dealing with this issue, there will clearly be problems, at least in the initial stages. **5–31**

The main problem is likely to be the extent to which a competition authority, court or practitioner in one Member State should take cognisance of the decisions and judgments of national authorities and courts in other Member States—not because these are binding, but in order to attain as close as possible to uniform application. Quite apart from the difficulties of finding the resources to cope with such a large volume of precedents in many different languages, even if the Commission acts as a clearing house and *amicus curiae*, it will inevitably be the case that differences of opinion will arise and that the Commission will be unlikely to be able to resolve them all expeditiously. If these problems are not solved by the application of sufficient resource and flexibility, fragmentation into separate jurisdictions all of which apply the EC Competition rules slightly differently seems very likely. Some comments on these problems and on the role of the national courts in enforcing Arts 81 and 82 can be found in a speech by Mr Mario Monti (Commissioner for Competition Policy, European Commission) given in June 2001 (SPEECH/01/258). **5–32**

When considering the applicability of Arts 81 and 82, in particular the possibility of exemption under Art.81(3) or presence or absence of a dominant position under Art.82, the most important issue is the definition of the relevant market, both for the purpose of establishing the relevant market share of the enterprise in question and also to decide what market its **5–33** conduct is or is not capable of affecting. The two most important cases relating to this definition are *United Brands & Co v EC Commission* [1979] 1 C.M.L.R. 429, and *Nederlandsche Banden-Industrie Michelin NV v EC Commission* [1985] 1 C.M.L.R. 282.

5–34 A market is primarily defined by reference to two parameters—the product market and geographic market. Occasionally (for instance off-peak electricity supply or travel out of rush hour or in school holidays) there may also be a third market parameter relating to time.

5–35 The first case laid down the principle that the opportunities for competition must be considered first of all in relation to the particular features of the product. The Court held that bananas represented a market of their own, separate from all other fruit, in that they had particular characteristics (very nourishing, soft, easy to eat and without stones or pips) which made them particularly suitable for infants, old people and invalids in a way distinct from all other fruit. So far as the geographic market was concerned the Court referred to a clearly defined geographic area in which the product is marketed and where the conditions of competition are sufficiently homogeneous for the effect of the economic power of the undertaking concerned to be able to be evaluated. In order to ascertain the question of whether the conditions of competition were sufficiently homogenous the Court referred primarily to transport costs, taking the view that where such costs do not in fact stand in the way of the distribution of the product they are a factor which contributes to making the relevant market a single market.

5–36 In the second case, the market in question was considered to be for new replacement tyres for lorries, buses and other heavy vehicles. Consideration was given in detail to the way the relevant product market should be defined. The principle laid down was that the context of the market must be judged "comprising the totality of the products which, with respect to their characteristics, are particularly suitable for satisfying constant need and are only to a limited extent interchangeable with other products".

5–37 These cases and many others were recently considered, and the general conclusions reaffirmed and amplified in Case T-65/96 *Kish Glass & Co Ltd v Commission [2000] 5 C.M.L.R. 229* and *Case T-25/99 Roberts v Commission* [2001] 5 C.M.L.R. 21. *Kish* has since been the subject of an appeal to the European Court on procedural grounds ([2002] 4 C.M.L.R. 16) but this is unlikely to change the substantive findings of the Court of First Instance.

5–38 Reference should also be made to the Commission Notice on the Definition of Relevant Markets published in 1997. This document sets out in detail the principles adopted by the Commission in ascertaining the relevant market and discusses the case law and Commission decisions, up to the date of the Notice, on which those principles are based.

5.1.1.3 The substantive principles—Article 81

Having discussed the framework of enforcement, it is appropriate to consider the basic substantive principles of EC Competition law, and then to understand how they apply in relation to the agreements dealt with in this book. **5–39**

Since this book concerns agreements between undertakings, in most cases the relevant article for consideration under EC competition law is Art.81. However, in certain instances, where the principal enjoys a dominant position, Art.82 may become relevant. The applicability of Art.82 is discussed throughout this book, and in particular in this chapter and Chapter 8, as relevant, but it is necessary, as a preliminary point, to consider in detail the operation and application of Art.81. The operative part of Art.81(1) reads as follows: **5–40**

> "The following shall be prohibited as incompatible with the Common Market: all ***agreements*** between ***undertakings***, ***decisions by associations of undertakings***, and ***concerted practices*** which ***may affect trade between Member States*** and which have as their ***object or effect the prevention, restriction or distortion of competition*** within the Common Market..."

Article 81(2) provides that any agreements or decisions prohibited pursuant to Art.81(1) shall be automatically void. **5–41**

However, Art.81(3) provides for exemption of any agreement or category of agreements, decision or category of decisions and any concerted practice or category of concerted practices, which contributes to improving production or distribution of goods or promoting technical or economic progress while allowing consumers a fair share of the resulting benefit. These criteria are subject to two provisos. First, the agreement must not impose any restrictions on competition other than those which are indispensable to the attainment of these objectives. Second, and in any event, the restrictions imposed must not afford the undertakings concerned the possibility of eliminating competition in respect of a substantial part of the products in question. **5–42**

The use of the word "category" enables the exemption not just of individual arrangements but also of classes of arrangements. This is the basis upon which the various general exemptions (block exemptions) discussed in this chapter and elsewhere in this book have been brought in. Clearly, as discussed below, the wording of Art.81(3) also allows individual exemption on a case by case basis. **5–43**

The anticompetitive agreement must bring public benefit that outweighs its anticompetitive effect. This necessitates a value judgment, balancing the negative effect on competition against the positive benefit to the public. However, in any event, the agreement must not (i) impose more restrictions than are absolutely necessary to achieve the intended benefit and/or (ii) be capable of creating a substantial anticompetitive effect. The presence of **5–44** these two requirements thus creates certain boundary conditions within which the value judgment must be made. First, no restriction can be imposed unless it is indispensable to achieve the object of the agreement and thus the resultant benefit. Thus, each restriction must be tested against this criterion, and any restrictions other than those indispensable to achieve that object must be eliminated. The value judgment then consists in weighing the positive benefits created by the remaining restrictions against their negative effect on competition. The wording of point (ii) means however, that at a certain level of restriction the anticompetitive effect will become so great ("... eliminating competition in a substantial part ...") that no potential benefit will be able to outweigh it. This is very likely to occur when the undertaking imposing the restriction is in a dominant position, even if the imposition of the restriction does not itself amount to an abuse of that dominant position in terms of Art.82.

5–45 In considering the impact of Art.81, each of the words or phrases highlighted in the extract above require separate definition and discussion. Following this, it will then be necessary to deal with the requirement that an effect on trade between Member States or on competition be "appreciable" if Art.81(1) is to apply at all, taking into account that the doctrine of "cumulative effect" can result in its application even to arrangements which when looked at in isolation appear insignificant. It will then be possible to discuss the status under Art.81(1) of the various relationships dealt with in this chapter, bearing in mind that Art.81(1) applies to arrangements between two or more undertakings and not to unilateral action on the part of one undertaking alone. The relationships considered are: concentrative joint ventures, agency, cooperative joint ventures, subcontracting, and distribution.

5–46 *5.1.1.3.1 Definition of "undertaking"* The first issue is the definition of the term "undertaking". The definition was recently discussed, and the previous case law summarised, by the European Court in Case C-218/00 *Cisal di Battistello Venanzio & Co SAS v Istituto Nazionale per l'Assicurazione contro gli Infortuni sul Lavoro* [2002] 4 C.M.L.R. 24. Here the Court stated: "According to settled case law, ... the concept of an undertaking in competition law covers any entity engaged in economic activity, regardless of the legal status of the entity or the way in which it is financed ... In that regard it has also consistently been held that any activity consisting in offering goods and services on a given market is an economic activity". The Court held that in this case INAIL (which managed Italy's compulsory social security scheme for insurance against accidents at work) could not be an undertaking because it fulfilled an exclusively social function (*i.e.* the provision of a form of state social security). However, it can be seen that once the factor of economic activity is present the form of the entity undertaking it is immaterial. The article thus applies to all forms of legal entities, partnerships, trusts, unincorporated associations and natural persons, provided that they carry on an economic activity.

5–47 It should be noted that final consumers are not regarded as undertakings, since in their capacity as consumers they do not engage in economic activity. Thus an agreement between one undertaking and one or more consumers cannot fall under Art.81. Of course, this concept has no application to Art.82, where the abuse by an undertaking of a dominant position will in many cases have a direct effect on consumers.

5.1.1.3.2 Definition of "agreement" Article 81 covers first of all "agreements between undertakings". One of the recent cases to discuss this definition was Case T-41/96 *Bayer AG v Commission* [2000] E.C.R. I-03383, the Court held that the essence of an "agreement" within the context of Art.81(1) is to be found in "a concurrence of wills between economic operators on the implementation of a policy, the pursuit of an objective, or the adoption of a given line of conduct on the market" The Court further confirmed that: **5–48**

> "As regards the form in which that common intention is expressed, it is sufficient for a stipulation to be the expression of the parties' intention to behave on the market in accordance with its terms, without its having to constitute a valid and binding contract under national law. It follows that the concept of an agreement within the meaning of Article 81(1) of the Treaty centres around the existence of a concurrence of wills between at least two parties, the form in which it is manifested being unimportant so long as it constitutes the faithful expression of the parties' intention."

It can be seen that oral or written agreements would be covered, as would also the so-called "gentlemen's agreements" which are binding morally, but not in law. **5–49**

One limitation on the application of Art.81 derives from the concept of "agreement" as discussed above. There can be no agreement in the case of unilateral conduct, where one party imposes its will on the other without that other's consent. **5–50**

In *Bayer AG v Commission*, a principal adopted a new policy toward all of its distributors, by imposing a quota system. The purpose of the system was to limit supplies so that distributors would find it difficult to supply both their domestic market and to export outside their territory. Bayer's intention was to use the quota system to prevent or reduce parallel trade in a pharmaceutical product, by way of exports from France and Spain (low price markets) to the UK (a high price market) which were causing losses in its UK operation. **5–51**

The Commission considered this to be an anti-competitive agreement caught by Art.81. In the Commission's view, the "agreement" came about because the distributors had tacitly accepted the quota system and hence the export ban by continuing to do business with the principal after the adoption of the new policy. However Bayer had never discussed the question of an export ban with the distributors, or asked them to limit export orders. It did not penalise any distributor that it found had exported product. Nor did it increase the quota of any distributor to reward it for not exporting. It **5–52** simply cut down on the level of parallel imports by providing less product to the parallel exporters. Furthermore, the distributors themselves continued to export, and resorted to various stratagems to increase the quota that Bayer allocated to them, so as to increase the quantity of exports that they could make.

5–53 The Court held that: "... the Commission cannot hold that apparently unilateral conduct on the part of a manufacturer, adopted in the context of the contractual relations which he maintains with his dealers, in reality forms the basis of an agreement between undertakings within the meaning of Article 81(1) of the Treaty if it does not establish the existence of an acquiescence by the other partners, express or implied, in the attitude adopted by the manufacturer".

5–54 However, the Court went on to say that:

> "a distinction should be drawn between cases in which an undertaking has adopted a genuinely unilateral measure, and thus without the express or implied participation of another undertaking, and those in which the unilateral character of the measure is merely apparent. Whilst the former do not fall within Article 81(1) of the Treaty, the latter must be regarded as revealing an agreement between undertakings and may therefore fall within the scope of that article. That is the case, in particular, with practices and measures in restraint of competition which, though apparently adopted unilaterally by the manufacturer in the context of its contractual relations with its dealers, nevertheless receive at least the tacit acquiescence of those dealers."

5–55 The Court concluded:

> "the right of a manufacturer faced, as in this case, with an event harmful to his interests, to adopt the solution which seems to him to be the best is qualified by the Treaty provisions on competition only to the extent that he must comply with the prohibitions referred to in Articles 81 and 82. Accordingly, provided he does so without abusing a dominant position, and there is no concurrence of wills between him and his wholesalers, a manufacturer may adopt the supply policy which he considers necessary, even if, by the very nature of its aim, for example, to hinder parallel imports, the implementation of that policy may entail restrictions on competition and affect trade between Member States."

5–56 The plea that there is no agreement can also be based on an allegation that one or more of the parties was forced into the agreement against their will. This is sometimes called the plea of "want of autonomy". Such a plea was put forward, but without success, in the European Court of First Instance in Case T-387/94 *Asia Motor France SA v* Commission [1996] E.C.R. II-961. Here five French importers of Japanese cars were accused, by third party dealers, of operating a cartel. The five companies pleaded that they were operating within the framework of a government policy which strictly limited importation of Japanese cars into France.

The Commission, and, subsequently the Court, refused to accept this plea. It was accepted that if the infringing conduct had been brought about by outside pressure from a national authority in a Member State, then Art.81 could not apply. However, such a plea of want of autonomy was unlikely to succeed "in the absence of any binding regulatory provision imposing the conduct at issue . . . [unless] it appears on the basis of objective, relevant and consistent evidence that that conduct was unilaterally imposed upon them by national authorities through the exercise of irresistible pressures such as, for example, the threat to adopt State measures likely to cause them to sustain substantial losses". **5–57**

5.1.1.3.3 Definition of "decisions of associations of undertakings" The concept of decisions of associations of undertakings relates principally to arrangements entered into by trade associations which their members then agree to observe, or which they must agree to observe as a condition of admission to membership. Such decisions usually result in a trade association setting out standard terms, conditions and prices upon which its members will provide products or services. An early example of this is the Commission Decision *Re Gas Water Heaters* [1973] C.M.L.R. (RP) D231, discussed in Chapter 6.1. **5–58**

A more recent example is the Decision of the Commission *Re Federatie van Nederlandse Kraanverhuurbedrijeven/Stichting Certificatie Kraanverhuurbedrijf*, Commission Decision [1995] O.J. L312, which is discussed further below, and was approved by the European Court of First Instance (Joined Cases T-213/95 and T-18/96 [1998] 4 C.M.L.R. 259). FNK was a crane-hire equipment operators' trade association, and SCK was a standards body which certified the safety of cranes. The Commission received a complaint that FNK would not admit operators whose cranes had not been certified by SCK, and that it fixed hire rates for its members. It was claimed that SCK was an independent standards body acting in the interests of public safety. The Commission found that in fact SCK was not independent from FNK and was a voluntary standards organisation, not set up by statute. In any event, the Commission held that the fact that SCK was a certification institution, recognised by Dutch law, and complying with pertinent European Standards did not prevent Art.81 from being applicable, nor did the fact that SCK rules are recognised by Dutch law. **5–59**

5.1.1.3.4 Definition of "concerted practice" The concept of "concerted practice" was recently considered by the European Court of First Instance in the Joined Cases T-202/98 and T-207/98 *Tate & Lyle plc v Commission, British Sugar plc v Commission* and *Napier Brown & Co Ltd v Commission* [2001] 5 C.M.L.R. 22. **5–60**

The Community sugar scheme is designed to protect and support the production of sugar within the Community. It sets a minimum price at which a Community producer can always sell his sugar to the public authorities and a threshold price at which sugar not subject to quotas can be **5–61** imported from non-member countries. The guaranteed minimum price only applies to national production quotas allocated to each Member State by the Council. The Member States can then divide these quotas up between their national producers as they see fit. British Sugar produces sugar from sugar beet grown in the UK, and the entire British sugar quota was allocated to it. Tate & Lyle imported all of its cane sugar for processing from countries outside the EU. Thus it had no benefit from the guaranteed minimum price, but suffered the imposition of the threshold price on imports designed to protect domestic production. Tate & Lyle thus suffered from a clear structural disadvantage compared to British Sugar and British Sugar was in a dominant position on the market for sugar in the UK. British Sugar and Tate & Lyle between them supplied nearly all of the requirements for industrial and retail sugar in the UK. Napier Brown was a sugar merchant active in the UK.

5–62 Napier Brown originally complained that in 1984 to 1986 British Sugar was abusing its dominant position by engaging in a price war which led to abnormally low prices on the industrial and retail sugar markets. The issue went through several stages, including investigation by the Commission, and a decision that British Sugar had abused its dominant position, which resulted in a fine and the giving of some commitments by British Sugar not to engage in predatory pricing in future.

5–63 In 1986 a meeting took place between British Sugar, Tate & Lyle and Napier Brown at which British Sugar announced the end of the price war. That meeting was followed by some further 18 meetings up to 1990 in relation to industrial sugar (which also included representatives of other UK sugar merchants) at which British Sugar gave information to all participants as to its future prices. It also distributed a list to the other participants of its prices for industrial sugar in relation to purchase volumes. In addition British Sugar and Tate & Lyle met on eight occasions up to 1990 to discuss retail sugar prices and British Sugar gave Tate & Lyle its price table on three occasions, once five days before and once two days before their official release into circulation.

5–64 In 1998 the Commission, after further investigations and statements of objection issued a decision (Decision 210/99) fining British Sugar ECU 39.6m, Tate & Lyle ECU 7m and Napier Brown ECU 1.8m for infringing Art.81(1).

5–65 The three applicants appealed to the Court on the grounds, *inter alia*, that, although they admitted the meetings took place, the Commission had failed to show that any agreement as to price-fixing had taken place at them, or that the meetings and the parties' subsequent conduct constituted a concerted practice. British Sugar merely informed the other participants of its future pricing intentions and they merely listened. The Court found that the Commission was right, on the facts of the case, to take the view that the purpose of the meetings was to restrict competition by the coordination of pricing policies. The fact that only one of the participants revealed its intentions was not sufficient to exclude the possibility of an agreement or a concerted practice. The Court said: "Each economic operator must determine independently the policy which he intends to adopt on the common market ... The requirement of independence ... does however strictly preclude any direct or indirect contact between such operators the object or effect whereof is either to influence the conduct on the market of the actual or potential competitor or to disclose to such a competitor the course of conduct which they themselves have decided to adopt or contemplate adopting on the market".

The Court went on to approve the previous decision in *Rhone-Poulenc v Commission* Case T-1/89 [1991] E.C.R. II-867 in which meetings, at which information about prices was exchanged among competitors, amounted to a concerted practice, as each participant would not only attend the meeting with the aim of eliminating advance uncertainty about the future conduct of its competitors, but each undertaking would also not fail to take into account, directly or indirectly, the information obtained from its competitors in order to determine the policy it intended to pursue on the market. "This Court considers that that conclusion also applies where, as in this case, the participation of one or more undertakings in meetings with an anti-competitive purpose is limited to the mere receipt of information concerning the future of their market competitors ... By participating at one of those meetings each participant knew that during the following meetings its most important competitor, the leader in the industry concerned, would reveal its future price intentions". **5–66**

This case shows very well the difference between an agreement and a concerted practice. The participants in the meetings made no agreement as to fixing prices. However, the information given to them by British Sugar enabled them to determine their own pricing policy in the knowledge of how the dominant undertaking in their industry would set its own prices. The concerted practice thus consisted in a number of undertakings attending meetings on a regular basis for the purpose of learning information from a competitor which they would take into account when determining their own conduct on the market. **5–67**

5.1.1.3.5 Requirement for an effect on trade between Member States The EC Treaty is concerned to create a common market, thus the basic purpose of all of its provisions, including Arts 81 and 82, is to promote trade between Member States. This is why Arts 81 and 82 requires not just that there be an effect on competition, but also upon trade between Member States. If there is no such effect, then any effect on competition is a matter for the relevant national competition authority, and not for the Commission, and Arts 81 and 82 have no application. **5–68**

However, the precise wording of Art.81(1) ("may have an effect") means that an infringement of Art.81(1) occurs not just when there is an actual effect on trade between Member States but also when the circumstances are such that there could be such an effect at some time in the future. Thus the use of the word "may" brings in two types of effect—actual and potential. Furthermore, under the single market which has been in force in the EC since 1992, all agreements are to be presumed to have an actual (or at the **5–69** very least potential) effect on trade between Member States, unless the parties can definitively prove to the contrary. Thus, it is almost impossible for the parties to claim that their agreement is not caught by Art.81, because it has no effect on trade between Member States.

5–70 However, when a competition authority asserts that the arrangement has such potential effect, this assertion cannot be based on mere speculation. The joined cases *Tate & Lyle plc v Commission, British Sugar plc v Commission* and *Napier Brown & Co. Ltd v Commission*, discussed above in more detail in relation to the concept of "concerted practice" also considered the question of the actual or potential effect of the information disseminated by British Sugar to its competitors. The Court reviewed the existing authorities and again affirmed that "for an agreement between undertakings or a concerted practice to be capable of affecting trade between Member States, it must be possible to foresee with a sufficient degree of probability and on the basis of objective factors of law or fact that it may have an influence, direct or indirect, actual or potential, on the pattern of trade between Member States ... It is not necessary that the conduct in question should in fact have substantially affected trade between Member States. It is sufficient to establish that the conduct is capable of having such an effect".

5–71 It is a common assumption that, because an arrangement only relates to one Member State, it can have no actual or potential effect on trade between Member States. This is not correct, and there are a number of cases which illustrate this.

5–72 For instance, at the simplest level, if a principal and a distributor both situated in one Member State, enter into a distribution agreement and the distributor undertakes not to handle competing goods, it is clear that there is at least a potential effect on trade between Member States because producers of competing goods outside of the relevant Member State will not be able to sell their goods in that state through that distributor.

5–73 In the European Court case Case C-234/89 *Delimitis v Henninger Brau AG* [1992] C.M.L.R. 210, there was an exclusive purchasing arrangement between a café in Frankfurt and a local brewery. The European Court held that the effect of this agreement was that the café owner could not purchase beer from other sources, including sources in other Member States. Whether or not the café owner wanted to do this was irrelevant. The agreement had a potential effect on trade between Member States.

5–74 There are however more subtle applications of the principle that agreements apparently relating only to one Member State can nevertheless affect trade between Member States.

5–75 In the Decision of the Commission *Re Federatie van Nederlandse Kraanverhuurbedrijeven/Stichting Certificatie Kraanverhuurbedrijf*, discussed above in relation to decisions of undertakings, FNK and SCK also disputed the applicability of Art.81 on the surprising ground that "mobile cranes are by their nature not meant to be transported" so that there could be no effect on cross-border trade. The Commission found that this was factually incorrect, and that, even if the participants in FNK did not at present engage in intra-Community activities, the potential for them to do so was clearly present. Moreover, two of the complainants were from Belgium, which showed that such trade was a genuine possibility.

The decision was appealed to the European Court by both SCK and FNK. (Joined Cases T-213/95 and T-18/96 [1998] 4 C.M.L.R. 259) The Court of First Instance upheld the Commission's Decision. It stated: **5–76**

> "The applicants are wrong in contending that inter-State trade cannot be affected ... simply because in the mobile crane-hire sector any trade between Member states is precluded. It is common ground that mobile cranes have an operating radius of roughly 50 kilometres. Inter-state trade can therefore be developed in the frontier regions of the Netherlands. It should be borne in mind that practices restricting competition which extend over the whole territory of a Member State have, by their very nature, the effect of reinforcing compartmentalisation of national markets."

In Case C-266/93 *Bundeskartellamt v Volkswagen AG/VAG Leasing GmbH*, [1996] 4 C.M.L.R. 478, discussed below in relation to agency agreements, the arrangements which infringed Art.81(1) applied to the whole of the German market. The Court stated that "practices which restrict the whole territory of a Member State, by their very nature, have the effect of reinforcing the compartmentalisation of markets on a national basis thereby obstructing the economic interpenetration which the Treaty is designed to bring about". **5–77**

In the joined cases *Tate & Lyle plc v Commission, British Sugar plc v Commission* and *Napier Brown & Co. Ltd v Commission*, discussed above, the Court said: "the fact that a cartel relates only to the marketing of products in a single Member State is not sufficient to exclude the possibility that trade between Member States might be affected. Since the market concerned is susceptible to imports the members of a national price cartel can retain their market share only if they defend themselves against foreign imports. In the present case it is undisputed that the sugar market in Great Britain is susceptible to imports". **5–78**

5.1.1.3.6 Requirement for an effect on competition Obviously, if the arrangement has no effect on competition, then there can be no infringement of Art.81(1), even if the arrangement does in some way have an actual or potential effect on trade between Member States. However, the very broad wording of Art.81 means that most arrangements within the EC which have an actual or potential effect on trade between Member States can at least be scrutinised by the Commission to see if they affect competition. **5–79**

As will be seen from the cases discussed below, just as in the case of trade between Member States, the effect on competition does not have to be actual. A potential effect will suffice (see Joined Cases T-77/92 and T-66/92 *Parker Pen Ltd v Commission* and *Herlitz AG v Commission* [1994] E.C.R. II-549). Furthermore, as will also be seen from those cases, once an anticompetitive object is established, the finding of a potential effect on compe- **5–80** tition follows almost automatically, and is much easier to make than the corresponding finding on potential effect on trade between Member States. (See the joined cases *Tate & Lyle plc v Commission, British Sugar plc v Commission* and *Napier Brown & Co. Ltd v Commission*, where the Court stated: "Once the anti-competitive purpose ... has been established, it is no longer necessary to verify whether the agreement also had any effect on the market". This should be compared with the dicta relating to potential effect on trade between Member States in the same cases referred to in Chapter 5.1.1.3.5., where a more analytical approach is required.)

5–81 Thus, the Commission will almost always automatically hold that where an anticompetitive object has been established, even where there is no actual effect at present, it could produce such an effect in future. This results in a finding that a potential effect on competition exists. Such findings by the Commission, even though the parties may regard them as speculative, are unlikely to be overturned by the European Court unless they are patently unreasonable (see the Commission Decision in *Re Vacuum Interrupters Ltd* [1977] 1 C.M.L.R. 340)

5–82 The question of actual and potential effect on competition was considered further in the European Court case Case C-7/95 *John Deere Ltd v Commission* [1998] 5 C.M.L.R. 311. This case concerned a system for the exchange of information between manufacturers of agricultural vehicles operating in the UK, which enabled them to identify sales of individual competitors as well as information on dealer sales and imports of own products. The Commission found the system contravened Art.81(1) and refused an exemption under Art.81(3).

5–83 John Deere appealed to the Court of First Instance and then to the European Court. One of the issues raised was the fact that the Commission had been unable to establish that the system produced an actual anti-competitive effect. The Court said:

> "According to the settled case law of the Court, in order to determine whether an agreement is to be considered to be prohibited by reason of the distortion of competition which is its effect, the competition in question should be assessed within the actual context in which it would occur in the absence of the agreement in dispute. Article 81(1) does not restrict such an assessment to actual effects alone; it must also take account of the agreement's potential effects on competition ..." The Court concluded on this point that: "the Court of First Instance must be considered to have concluded correctly that the information exchange system reduces or removes the degree of uncertainty as to the operation of the market and that the system is therefore ***liable*** [emphasis supplied] to have an adverse influence on competition between manufacturers."

5–84 The wording of Art.81(1) catches arrangements which have as their "*object or effect* the prevention, restriction or distortion of competition". This means that the parties can be caught in two ways. Their conduct may have the potential or actual effect of preventing, restricting or distorting competition, and in this case it is irrelevant whether they intended this or not (see *Société Technique Miniere Machinenbau Ulm* ECJ [1966] E.C.R. 235.) On the other hand, their conduct may have the object of preventing restricting or distorting competition, in which case they will not be able to escape by claiming that it had no actual effect, since a potential effect will inevitably be found to result from their anticompetitive object.

The Decision of the Commission *Re Bay-O-Nox* (Commission Decision [1990] O.J. L21), gives some guidance as to the interpretation of the word "object" in Art 81(1). In this decision, the Commission judges the motive for the behaviour in question not by what the parties say it was, but by what a reasonable man looking at the conduct of the parties would conclude that it was. **5–85**

The Commission considered a contractual provision imposed by Bayer AG to provide a discount to customers for its animal feed products and additives, who were prepared to use the goods for their own purposes as opposed to resale. Bayer claimed that this was a legitimate restriction to impose in a selective distribution system. The Commission rejected this argument saying that "selective distribution must in particular include freedom to trade within the network of authorised firms. Such freedom is not allowed in the case in point". It should be noted that Bayer at the same time imposed an unrealistically high price on goods purchased for resale, with the avowed intention of preventing resale to unauthorised users. **5–86**

Bayer also contended that the practice was necessary to prevent customers who were not properly trained in the use of the products from misusing them or mixing them with inferior quality substitutes and reselling them. Thus its purpose in imposing the own-use requirement was not anti-competitive. The Commission rejected this argument as well, and found that the requirement contravened Art.81(1) as it had the object of restricting competition. The Commission said: "The term 'object' has an objective meaning in this context. It does not matter what the intention subjectively pursued by the parties was. It was directly evident from its wording that the own-use requirement was a ban on trading". **5–87**

The interaction between the principles of "object" and "effect" is shown up well in the two appeals against the Decision of the Commission *Re Parker Pen, Parker Pen Ltd v Commission* and *Herlitz AG v Commission.* Parker and Herlitz claimed that although a distribution agreement contained a clause banning exports, this had been included unintentionally and that, in any event it had not been implemented since some distributors had ignored it and exported outside their territories. The Court refused to agree, and upheld the Commission Decision imposing fines on Parker and Herlitz. First, on the facts it did not find that the clause had been inserted unintentionally. Second, even if it had been inserted unintentionally, a clause prohibiting exports by its very nature constitutes a restriction on competition. The fact that it had not been implemented by some distributors did not prove it had had no effect, since such clauses, by their very existence could create a 'visual and psychological effect' which contributed to a partitioning of the market. The fact that a clause, which is intended to affect competition, **5–88** has not been implemented does not excuse it under Art.81(1).

5–89 This case thus shows how difficult it is to escape from the broad wording of "object or effect". First of all the applicants stated that they did not intend to ban exports because the clause had been put in the agreement by mistake. One of the reasons why the Commission would not accept this contention, was the definition it gives the term "object". Since the clause prohibited exports and it was inserted in the agreement, it was certainly reasonable to presume that the intention of the parties was to ban exports. However, even if the parties had been able to displace the Commission's presumption as to the "object" of the clause, they still could not escape problems under the second limb of the provision, namely "effect". A clause banning exports always has, if not an actual effect, a potential effect on competition. The very existence of the clause created this potential effect. The fact some distributors had not been deterred was no defence, since others in the past might have been deterred,(which if proved would have amounted to an actual effect) and perhaps others in the future would be (a potential effect).

5–90 Thus, the wording of the phrase, "object or effect" generates a matrix of possibilities:

- anticompetitive object + actual anticompetitive effect
- anticompetitive object + potential anticompetitive effect
- no anticompetitive object + actual anticompetitive effect
- no anticompetitive object + potential anticompetitive effect
- no anticompetitive object + no potential AND no actual anticompetitive effect

It is only under the last possibility that no infringement of Art.81 can occur. The matrix does not include a line for "anticompetitive object + no actual AND no potential anticompetitive effect" since, as discussed above, once an anticompetitive object is established a finding of potential anticompetitive effect in practice follows automatically.

5–91 *5.1.1.3.7 The concept of "appreciable effect"* Article 81 does not apply where the impact of the arrangement on trade between Member States or on competition is not appreciable. This principle of "appreciable effect" has been settled in numerous court judgments (see for instance *Bagnasco v Banco Popolare di Novana* [1999] 1 E.C.R. 135). From time to time the Commission has set out notices stating the criteria it will apply in deciding the question of "appreciable effect". This has been done in a series of Notices on Agreements of Minor Importance. The latest was issued in 2001 (O.J. C368/13 dated December 22, 2001).

5–92 The current Notice deals mainly with the question of appreciable effect in relation to competition. It states that agreements between actual or potential competitors do not have an appreciable effect on competition if the combined market share of the parties does not exceed 10 per cent on any of the relevant markets affected by the agreement. The definition of actual or potential competitors is set out in the Commission Notice "Guidelines on the applicability of Article 81 of the EC Treaty to Horizontal Cooperation Agreements" (O.J. C 3 January 6, 2001). Agreements made between parties who are not actual or potential competitors are held not to have appreciable effect on competition if the combined market share of the parties on the relevant market does not exceed 15 per cent. Where is it uncertain whether the agreement is between competitors or non-competitors, the 10 per cent threshold applies. Where the relevant market is covered by parallel networks of agreements (*e.g.* a number of selective distribution networks) entered into by different suppliers or distributors which have a cumulative foreclosure effect on competition, individual suppliers or distributors with a market share not exceeding 5 per cent are in general assumed not to contribute significantly to the cumulative foreclosure. A cumulative foreclosure effect is unlikely to exist if less than 30 per cent of the relevant market is covered by parallel networks of agreements having a similar effect. The concept of cumulative effect is discussed in Chapter 5.1.1.3.8.

The Notice states that the thresholds relating to appreciable effect on competition have no application in the event that the agreements contain the usual hardcore restrictions. For horizontal agreements between actual or potential competitors these are restrictions which directly or indirectly, in isolation or in combination with other factors under the control of the parties, have as their object: the fixing of prices for sales to third parties, limitation of output or sales and the allocation of markets or customers. These restrictions are among those specifically prohibited under Art.81(1). So far as agreements between non-competitors are concerned, since the latest version of the Notice was issued after Reg.2790/99 (the Vertical Restraints Block Exemption discussed in detail below in Chapter 5.2), the Commission has adopted the same hardcore restrictions as contained in that regulation. **5–93**

Here it should be noted that although that Regulation applies these restrictions and their exceptions to vertical agreements, the Notice deals with agreements between undertakings which are not competitors. Given the wide definition of "actual and potential competitor" in the Guidelines on Horizontal Cooperation Agreements mentioned above, this in practice means much the same thing. Indeed, the hardcore restrictions relating to agreements between non-competitors make little sense in relation to a horizontal agreement. This is also borne out by the fact that the Notice also states that, where the agreement is between competitors who operate for the purposes of the agreement at different levels of the production or distribution chain, (*i.e.* a vertical agreement between competitors) all of the hardcore restrictions relating to non-competitors are also prohibited. Presumably, in the event of a horizontal agreement that was not between actual or potential competitors, the restrictions relating to non-competitors would apply so far as they were relevant, and the restrictions which the Notice prohibits in relation to agreements between competitors would **5–94** generally be unlikely to be part of such a horizontal agreement and would, even if they were also present in the agreement, be considered by the Commission as having no appreciable effect on competition, in any event, given that the horizontal agreement was not between competitors. In any particular case where there was in fact such an appreciable effect, these provisions would be dealt with in the light of the specific prohibitions in Art.81(1) itself, with some (although slight) possibility of exemption under Art.81(3). The hardcore restrictions relating to agreements between noncompetitors (being identical with the provisions of Art.4 of reg.2790/99) are as follows: restrictions which directly or indirectly (in isolation or with other factors under the parties' control) have (a) the object of resale price maintenance (but not maximum resale price maintenance or recommended resale prices) or (b) restrictions on resale by the buyer or (c) the restriction of active or passive sales to end users by the retail members of a selective distribution system, without prejudice to the possibility of prohibiting a member of the system from operating out of an unauthorised place of establishment or (d) the restriction of cross-supplies between distributors within a selective distribution system, including between distributors operating at different levels of trade or (e) a restriction by the supplier of components to an original equipment manufacturer of the sale by that manufacturer to third parties of such components as spare parts.

5–95 However notwithstanding the general prohibition on resale by the buyer under (b) above, certain restrictions on resale by the buyer are permitted, namely (i) a restriction on active sales into the exclusive territory or customer group reserved to the supplier or allocated by the supplier to another buyer, where such restriction does not limit sales by the customers of the buyer, (ii) a restriction of sales to end users by a buyer operating as a wholesaler (iii) the restriction of sales to unauthorised distributors by the members of a selective distribution system and (iv) a restriction of the buyer's ability to sell components supplied for the purposes of incorporation (*i.e.* original equipment manufacture), to customers who would use them to manufacture the same type of goods as those produced by the supplier.

5–96 A discussion of these provisions and their impact on vertical agreements can be found under Chapter 5.2 as part of the discussion on the effect of Art.4 of Reg.2790/99.

5–97 The Notice deals mainly with the issue of an appreciable effect on competition. Paragraph 3 of Part I of the Notice, however, also mentions the issue of an appreciable effect on trade between Member States. Agreements can never fall under Art.81 if they do not have an appreciable effect on trade between Member States. The Notice makes no attempt to quantify the concept of appreciable effect on trade between Member States, but acknowledges that agreements between small and medium sized undertakings "are rarely if ever capable of appreciably affecting trade between Member States". Small and medium sized undertakings are defined in the Annex to Commission Recommendation 280/96 (O.J. L 107 April 30, 1996) as undertakings which have fewer than 250 employees and have either an annual turnover not exceeding €40m or an annual balance sheet total not exceeding €27m. This recommendation will be revised. It is envisaged that the turnover threshold will be increased to €50m and the balance sheet threshold to €43m. Paragraph 3 makes no mention of hardcore restrictions. These are only relevant in relation to the effect on competition. Thus if the arrangement has no appreciable effect on trade between Member States, it can contain hardcore restrictions, since Art.81 has no application in the first place. Of course, such restrictions will probably infringe local competition law in the Member State concerned.

The concept of appreciable effect cuts across the concepts of actual and potential effect. Where there is an actual effect it is always, at least in theory, possible to decide whether this actual effect is also appreciable. However, how is it possible to decide whether a potential effect is appreciable? This involves two judgments as to the future—first how likely is it that there will be an effect, and then how likely is it that that effect will be appreciable. It can be seen that, so far as the effect on competition is concerned, in a sense the Notice on Agreements of Minor Importance conflates the two issues. **5–98**

If an agreement falls within the scope of the Notice, then, except in extraordinary circumstances, the Commission holds there will be no appreciable effect on competition. This has two consequences. First the Commission will not concern itself with assessing whether or not there is an actual effect on competition. Second, it has no need to consider whether there is a potential effect on competition. This is because, in both cases, it has already decided that any such effect, even if found, and whether actual or potential, cannot be appreciable. **5–99**

On the other hand, by excluding the hardcore restrictions such as price fixing or sharing markets from the scope of the Notice, the Commission has already made a decision that the effect of any such restriction on competition will always be appreciable, because otherwise it would not have excluded the relevant restriction from the Notice. Even if, in such a case, no actual effect can be found (whether or not appreciable) this makes no difference since it is always relatively easy (as in the *Re Parker Pen* Decision) to posit a potential effect, and this, by definition, will always be appreciable, because the Commission has already decided that it will be so. **5–100**

Thus in practice, by the application of these principles, the Commission has laid down a set of rules covering at least some of the circumstances in which it will or will not hold that a potential effect on competition is appreciable. **5–101**

This is the explanation of the cases which hold that where there is an arrangement with an anticompetitive object, the Commission does not have to show that there was an actual anticompetitive effect and in practice a finding of a potential anticompetitive effect is made automatically. The anticompetitive objective will already have been found to be present by the application of the objective standard of the reasonable man, irrespective of any other explanation given by the undertakings concerned. If they can take advantage of the Notice on Agreements of Minor Importance, then whether actual or potential the effect will not be appreciable. Where the undertakings fall outside the Notice because the arrangement amounts to a hardcore **5–102** restriction, or their combined market share is too large, the possibility of a potential effect will be easy to find (in fact already assumed to exist in the case of a hardcore restriction) and that effect will by definition always be substantial.

5–103 The European Court of First Instance commented on this issue in the Joined Cases *Tate & Lyle plc v Commission, British Sugar plc v Commission* and *Napier Brown & Co. Ltd v Commission*:

> "It is clear from case-law that, for the purposes of applying Article 81(1) of the Treaty, there is no need to take account of the concrete effects of an agreement when it is apparent, as in this case, that it has as its object the prevention restriction or distortion of competition within the common market. Therefore once the anticompetitive nature of the purpose of the meetings has been established, it is no longer necessary to verify whether the agreement also had any effects on the market."

5–104 In this passage the Court finds it unnecessary to consider whether the meetings "***had*** any effects" on competition (*i.e.* whether there was an ***actual*** effect on competition) once an anticompetitive object has been established. This approach is also in keeping with the wording of Art.81(1) itself, which prohibits arrangements which have an anticompetitive "object" ***or*** "effect". An arrangement may satisfy both requirements but either one is sufficient.

5–105 So far as the effect on trade between Member States is concerned, the wording of Art.81 does not require any demonstration of an actual effect (note the use of the words "may affect trade ..."). However, there is some question as to whether the potential affect must be appreciable or whether any potential effect at all, however slight is sufficient. Reading the text of the Notice on Agreements of Minor Importance, it seems as if the Commission accepts that the effect on trade must be appreciable, if Art.81(1) is to apply. Otherwise it would not have excluded the actions of small and medium sized enterprises from Art.81 on the basis that they could not have an appreciable effect on trade, even if they implemented hardcore restraints.

5–106 The text of the current Notice is clear on this point, but the relevant decisions of the European Court are less so.

5–107 In *Tate & Lyle plc v Commission, British Sugar plc v Commission* and *Napier Brown & Co. Ltd v Commission* the Court also went on to comment, in response to another argument from the applicants, that it was irrelevant that the Commission had not been able to demonstrate that the effect on trade between Member States was appreciable:

> "It is accepted case law that the Commission is not required to demonstrate that an agreement or concerted practice ***has*** an appreciable effect ... All that is required [by Art.81] is that anti-competitive agreements and concerted practices should be ***capable of having an effect*** on trade between Member States."

5–108 The Court relied on the judgment in Case T-7/89 *Hercules Chemicals v*

Commission [1991] E.C.R. II-01711 where the Court stated in relation to the same issue:

> "Contrary to the applicant's assertions, the Commission was not required to demonstrate that its participation in an agreement and a concerted practice ***has had*** an appreciable effect on trade between Member States. All that is required by Article 81(1) of the EC Treaty is that anti-competitive agreements and concerted practices should be ***capable of having an effect*** on trade between Member States. In this regard, it must be concluded that the restrictions on competition found to exist ***were likely to distort trade patterns from the course which they would otherwise have followed...*** It follows that the Commission has established to the requisite legal standard ... that the infringement in which the applicant participated was ***apt to affect*** trade between Member States, and it was not necessary for it to demonstrate that the applicant' s individual participation ***affected*** trade between Member States."

Although the wording is not as clear as might be wished, study of the two passages, particularly by reference to the words and phrases highlighted here for emphasis, shows that the Courts are contrasting first of all actual with potential effect. (See the use of the word "has" in the first passage and "has had" and "affected" in the second passage.) The Commission thus had no need to show an actual appreciable effect. Thus, the contrast seems to be not between an appreciable and an insignificant effect, but between an actual effect and a potential effect (see the remaining highlighted phrases and in the first passage particularly the word "capable", and, in the second passage the words "capable" "likely" and "apt"). **5–109**

The question of whether that potential effect also has to be appreciable is not stated specifically, but would this would seem to be the case. This can be deduced first because the passages both contrast the concept of potential effect with the concept of actual appreciable effect, and the correctness of the comparison would require that (albeit implicitly) the potential effect should likewise be appreciable. Second, on a reading of the facts of the two cases and the judgments in general, there was no doubt of the existence of the anticompetitive object and effect of the practices concerned. Also in both cases, but particularly in *Hercules*, there was, in any event, and irrespective of the points being made in the passages quoted, a demonstrated actual appreciable effect on trade between Member States. Any potential effect, in addition to the actual effect that had occurred, likewise could not have been other than appreciable. **5–110**

The other point to note in this connection was that in *Hercules* one of the issues raised (the case concerned a price and quota fixing cartel in the polypropylene chemical manufacturing industry with many members) was that the contribution of Hercules itself, even if did take part in the cartel was not great enough appreciably to effect trade between Member States. Here the Court commented: "the infringement in which the applicant participated was ***apt to affect*** trade between Member States, and it was not necessary for **5–111** [the Commission] to demonstrate that the applicant's individual participation ***affected*** trade between Member States". The use of the words emphasised in this quotation goes to support the contention that the distinction being made is between an actual and a potential effect rather than between an appreciable and an insignificant effect.

5–112 This analysis is also supported by another part of the judgment in *British Sugar* (quoted in Chapter 5.1.1.3.5) when the Court was considering whether an actual as well as a potential effect on trade between Member States was required. The passage states: "It is not necessary that the conduct in question should in fact ***have substantially affected*** trade between Member States. It is sufficient to establish that the conduct is ***capable of having such*** an effect". The use of the words emphasised in the quotation show that, at least in this passage, the Court was of the view that the potential effect on trade between Member States must also be substantial.

5–113 In conclusion, it can be seen that, whether dealing with the effect on competition or the effect on trade, the potential effect is always more important. Even if there is no appreciable actual effect, or, indeed, no actual effect at all, this is not fatal to a claim that infringement of Art.81(1) has occurred, although it may make it more difficult to prove. The real question in such cases is whether it is possible to make a case for a potential effect which is also appreciable.

5–114 *5.1.1.3.8. The concept of "cumulative effect"* The concept of appreciable effect can be modified in appropriate circumstances by the concept of cumulative effect. It may be that an individual agreement looked at in isolation appears to have no appreciable effect (actual or potential), but what of the cumulative effect where many such agreements entered into by one or more suppliers exist in a relevant market?

5–115 *Delimitis v Henninger Brau* deals not only with actual or potential effect, but shows how the concept of cumulative effect also applies. In this case there was an exclusive purchasing arrangement between a cafe in Frankfurt and a German brewery. The European Court held that the effect of this agreement was that the cafe owner could not purchase beer from other sources, including sources in other Member States. Whether or not the cafe owner wanted to do this was irrelevant. The agreement had a potential effect on trade between Member States. The agreement on its own was insignificant, but it was common practice in Germany to enter into such agreements, and their cumulative effect was significant. Thus the question of whether any particular agreement, such as this, was caught by Art.81, depended, according to the Court, upon whether there was genuine difficulty for suppliers in other Member States to get access to the German market, and the extent to which "the agreements entered into by [Henninger] contributed to the cumulative effect produced in that respect by the totality of the similar contracts found on that market".

5–116 This case requires some explanation. In applying these principles, one does not compare all of the agreements in the relevant market and look at their cumulative effect as a whole even though they have been entered into by different suppliers. Instead, it is necessary to aggregate each supplier's set of agreements into a network. First one considers the cumulative effect of all of the networks on the relevant market. If this cumulative effect produces an appreciable effect on competition, and on trade between Member States, it is then necessary to consider the network under which the agreement complained of has been concluded. If the contribution of that network to the cumulative effect of all the networks is appreciable, then all of the agreements in that network, including the agreement complained of, contravene Art.81(1), even if the individual effect of each such agreement is not appreciable.

This principle in *De Limitis* was more clearly explained by the Commission in its decision *Re Scottish and Newcastle plc* (O.J. L/186, July 19, 1999). "Beer supply agreements entered into by breweries whose contribution to the cumulative effect is insignificant do not therefore fall under the prohibition under Art 81(1). Therefore in assessing the extent of the contribution made by the brewery in question, in this case, S&N, the brewer's total tied network ... must be assessed". In other words it is the network that "must make a significant contribution to the sealing-off effect brought about by the totality of the brewers' tying agreements ...". **5–117**

The same approach can be found in the European Court of First Instance judgments of June 8, 1995 in the German ice cream cases Case T-7/93 *Scholler Lebensmittel GmbH & Co KG v Commission* and *Langnese-Iglo v Commission* [1995] E.C.R. II-1713 where the Court said: "Where there is a network of similar agreements concluded by the same producer, the assessment of the effects of that network on competition applies to all the individual agreements making up the network". These cases were further discussed on appeal to the European Court (reported at [1999] All E.R. (EC) 616). **5–118**

Some refinements on the concept of cumulative effect can be found in the European Court judgment in *Neste Markkinointi Oy v Yotuuli Ky* [2001] 4 C.M.L.R. 27. The defendants had raised a Euro-defence by claiming that an exclusive purchasing agreement by which they were bound was contrary to Art.81(1), in that it could not take advantage of the then current block exemption for exclusive purchasing agreements (Reg.84/83) because it was a contract concluded with an indefinite duration, in that it continued unless and until terminated by one year's notice. The plaintiffs claimed that even if that agreement fell outside the block exemption, very few of the plaintiffs' agreements were terminable by notice, and that most of them were for fixed periods of time, enjoying the exemption under the block exemption. Therefore when considering the cumulative effect of agreements in the plaintiffs' network, a distinction should be made between those which were for a fixed period and those which were terminable by notice. The Court agreed with this approach: **5–119**

> "a notice period of one year is one which can give reasonable protection to the economic and legal interests of each of the parties to the contract and limit the restrictive effect of the contract ... In those circumstances where the contracts which may be terminated upon one year's notice at

any time represent only a very small proportion of all the exclusive purchasing agreements entered into by a particular supplier, they must be regarded as making no significant contribution to the cumulative effect, for the purposes of the judgment in *De Limitis* and therefore as not being caught by the prohibition [in Art.81(1)]. The fact of subdividing exceptionally a supplier's network is not arbitrary nor does it undermine the principle of legal certainty ... [it] results from a factual assessment of the position held by the operator on the relevant market, the aim of the assessment being, on the basis of an objective criterion of particular relevance ... to limit the number of cases in which a supplier's contracts are declared void to those which together contribute significantly to the cumulative effect of sealing the market."

5–120 *5.1.1.3.9 The requirement for two or more undertakings* However, despite the width of Art.81, there is one important restriction on its application. In order for Art.81 to apply at all the arrangement must be between two or more independent undertakings. The relevant test as to what constitutes an independent undertaking is whether it has economic autonomy or is part of a group subject to central control. Where there is no economic autonomy a parent and a subsidiary have been considered one undertaking and so has a group of companies. The European Court of Justice decisions which laid down these principles are *Beguelin Import Co v G L Import-Export SA* [1972] C.M.L.R. 81; *Commercial Solvents v European Commission* [1974] E.C.R. 223; and *Centrafarm BV v Sterling Drug Inc* [1974] 2 C.M.L.R. 480.

5–121 The principle was reaffirmed by the European Court in *Viho Europe BV v Commission* [1997] All E.R. (EC) 163. This again concerned Parker Pens. Parker had now rearranged its distribution network in the EU so that it carried out its activities through a number of wholly-owned subsidiaries. Parker prohibited each subsidiary from supplying Parker Pens to customers in Member States other than the one in which that subsidiary was established. The appellant complained that this practice was contrary to Art.81. The Court noted that Parker and its wholly-owned subsidiaries formed a single economic unit within which the subsidiaries did not enjoy real autonomy in determining their course of action, but carried out the instructions issued to them by their parent company. In those circumstances, although Parker was dividing national markets within the EC between its subsidiaries, Art.81(1) could not apply, even if there was a competitive effect on third parties, since Parker was a single economic unit, and its conduct could not amount to an agreement or arrangement between undertakings pursuant to Art.81. Thus the complaint failed. However, such unilateral conduct could, of course, amount, in an appropriate case, to an abuse of a dominant position under Art.82.

5–122 Similar reasoning can be found in the Commission Decision *Re Systemform GmbH* (O.J. L47 February 18, 1997) here Novapost was appointed as distributor for Systemform with a contract territory, and an obligation against active selling outside that territory was imposed. Novapost, in breach of that obligation appointed Novalliance to sell actively outside the contract territory. When Systemform attempted to prevent supplies reaching Novalliance from Novapost, Novapost complained that Systemform was illegally enforcing an export ban on Novapost. The Commission refused to accept this contention. Novapost and Novalliance were both majority-owned subsidiaries of Eurinvest. Thus they were regarded as a single entity, and Systemform was within its rights to prevent Novapost breaching the prohibition against active selling by means of another subsidiary within the same group.

The principle in *Viho* is subject to the qualification that the subsidiaries in fact have no autonomy. There have been situations in which it has been held that if a subsidiary or a branch in fact acts without the control of the parent, in an independent manner, then Art.81 can apply to arrangements between a parent and its branch or subsidiary (see *BMW Belgium v EC Commission* [1980] 1 C.M.L.R. 370). **5–123**

Thus it follows that where integration leads to a true merger with the disappearance of the legal entity or business of one of the parties so that the businesses become concentrated in the hands of the other, there can be no infringement of Art.81(1) (see the Decision of the Commission *Re SHV/Chevron* [1975] 1 C.M.L.R. D68). **5–124**

It is thus open to any company to decide that it will organise its agency and distribution affairs within the EC by means of a network of branches or subsidiary companies which it controls. These could either be new entities set up specially for the purpose, or the network could be created by the acquisition of suitable existing local businesses (perhaps ones previously acting as distributors) which, after merger with the acquiring organisation, would cease to be separate entities to which Art.81 could have application. **5–125**

Horizontal agreements which result in the creation of a new entity (albeit economic rather than legal) can fall under this class of relationships. A true horizontal grouping will result where two or more undertakings surrender control of a particular business activity, such as the marketing of a particular product line in a defined area, to a joint management body, which really controls their relevant activities and assets, so that the original participants become no more than passive investors. Once this situation becomes properly established the undertakings which set it up will cease to exist as separate economic entities for the purposes of Art.81, at least in relation to the particular business carried on under the grouping arrangement, so that Art.81 can no longer apply (see the Commission Decisions *Re de Laval/Stork* [1977] O.J. L215/11; *Re IMI/Heilman* [1978] 3 C.M.L.R. 44; and *Re Peroxygen Cartel* [1985] 1 C.M.L.R. 481). **5–126**

5.1.1.3.10 EC merger control and joint ventures After the passing of the Council Merger Control Regulation (Reg.4064/89), the Commission has distinguished between "concentrative" and "cooperative" joint ventures. An arrangement of the type described above, would be regarded as a concentrative joint venture as only one undertaking survives the fusion of the parties' interests in the particular area of business concerned. However, if **5–127** the entities setting up the joint venture continue to be interested in the business activity carried on by the joint venture it will be regarded as a cooperative joint venture. This is merely a horizontal agreement between two independent undertakings who continue to exist and carry on or be interested in the relevant business carried on by the joint venture. In this case, the agreements setting up such a joint venture will fall under Art.81.

5–128 The Merger Regulation (Reg.4064/89—the "Regulation") was amended by Council Regulation 1310/97, (the "Amending Regulation") which came into effect on March 1, 1998. The Commission has currently tabled a draft Council Regulation (the "draft Regulation") consolidating and further amending the two current Regulations. The draft Regulation concentrates mainly on procedural and jurisdictional amendments, but also takes the opportunity to clarify some of the substantive provisions of the current Regulations and to update them by the inclusion of advances in the Commission's thinking embodied in Notices, and the effect of various Commission decisions and judgments of the European Court that have appeared since 1997. The Commission intends that the draft Regulation should come into effect on May 1, 2004, coincident with the start date of Reg.1/2003, discussed above, and the enlargement of the EU by the accession of the further ten new Member States.

5–129 The Regulation applies in relation to concentrative joint ventures where the parties create a joint venture "performing on a lasting basis all the functions of an autonomous economic entity". This is known as a "full function" joint venture. Prior to passing of the amending Regulation a "full function" joint venture could only be regarded as a concentration, controlled by the Regulation, if it did not give rise to coordination of competitive behaviour of the parties amongst themselves or between them and the joint venture. This could only occur where the parties setting up the full function joint venture allowed the joint venture to run its own affairs independently with no interference from them in its decision-making, so that they acted only as passive investors.

5–130 Thus, prior to the passing of the amending Regulation, concentrative joint ventures which did not amount to the creation of a full function joint venture ("partial-function" operations) and concentrative full function joint ventures giving rise to coordination of competitive behaviour (*i.e.* where the participants controlled the decision-making of the joint venture) were outside the Regulation, and were both regarded merely as horizontal cooperation agreements to be considered under Art.81. Following the passing of the amending Regulation all full function joint ventures (irrespective of the issue of decision-making) are now considered to be concentrations falling with the Regulation so that only the partial function operations will continue to be dealt with under Art.81.

5–131 In 1994 the Commission published a Notice on the distinction between concentrative and cooperative joint ventures and a Notice on the notion of a concentration, which latter was superseded by a further notice on the same subject issued in 1998. These Notices are useful guides to the application of the Regulation, but the first has to be read with some caution in the light of the changes to the way full function joint ventures are now dealt with after the passing of the amending Regulation.

The 1994 Notice omits the previous requirement that a full function joint venture must be "economically independent" of its parents. Where one or more of the parents is in a market which is upstream or downstream from that of the joint venture and where it is envisaged that the venture will rely substantially on sales to or purchases from such parent(s), the revised Notice calls into question the "full function" character of the venture, rather than its "independence". Exceptionally, such substantial reliance may last for an initial start-up period, which should normally not exceed three years, depending on the market in question. However, this is a departure from the five-year benchmark established in earlier case law. **5–132**

The requirement of "lasting basis" is flexibly defined in para.16 of the revised Notice. Normally, where the joint venture is full function, it is assumed that it would have the requisite durability. Likewise, terms for the dissolution of the venture or the withdrawal of parents in the event of deadlock should not affect the long lasting character of the venture. If the venture states a definite duration, it must be sufficiently long to effect a lasting change in the structure of the undertakings concerned. This may depend upon the volatility of the sector concerned. The revised Notice cites *Re British Airways/TAT*, Commission Decision of November 27, 1992 for this proposition. In this case, the Commission concluded that a joint venture in the airline sector was concentrative despite the venture's stated maximum duration of six and a half years. **5–133**

However, the amending Regulation introduced one additional distinction in relation to full function joint ventures. In general all concentrations are appraised under the Regulation as to whether they "create or strengthen a dominant position as a result of which effective competition would be substantially impeded in the common market or a substantial part of it" (Art.2(2)). Thus all full function joint ventures will now be appraised on this basis. However, where a joint venture "has as its object or effect the coordination of the competitive behaviour of undertakings that remain independent", the Commission must use two criteria for appraisal. The first, under Art.2(2), is the creation or strengthening of a dominant position and the second, under Art.2(3), is the relevant coordination of competitive behaviour "which shall be appraised in accordance with the criteria of Art 81(1) and (3) of the EC Treaty with a view to establishing whether or not the operation is compatible with the common market". It is important to realise that this second appraisal does not take place under Art.81. It is merely that the criteria which would have been used under Art.81 are to apply to the appraisal made under the Regulation. Thus, with the one exception of the additional appraisal criterion, the Regulation now applies to the full function joint venture which has as its object or effect the coordination of competitive behaviour. The position as described above is in essence unchanged in the draft Regulation. **5–134**

This widening of the scope of the Regulation to include all full function joint ventures is desirable for two reasons. **5–135**

5–136 First, clearance following notification under the Regulation is given on a once and for all basis. This provides more certainty than either the old regulatory framework under Reg.17/62 or the new framework under Reg.1/2003. Under Reg.17/62, it was possible to apply for exemption under Art.81(3), but exemption was only granted for a defined period of time, usually five years, after which the parties, if they wished to continue to operate the arrangement, had to apply for a further period of exemption, with no certainty that it would be granted. Under Reg.1/2003, the parties can no longer apply to the Commission at all, and have to make their own assessment of exemption under Art.81(3). However, here, although no fixed time limit can apply, they are in practice under a duty to review matters from time to time to assure themselves that Art.81(3) still applies to exempt the arrangement.

5–137 Second, once a concentration falls to be dealt with under the Regulation, local competition authorities in individual Member States cease to have jurisdiction, and a clearance under the Regulation is all that is required. This was not the case with an application under Reg.17/62 in relation Art.81(3), where local authorities also had parallel jurisdiction to consider the transaction under local competition law. Under Reg.1/2003, since Art.81 now has direct applicability, national authorities will now be able to apply not only local competition law but EC competition law as well. Thus the "one stop shop" approach under the Regulation is clearly easier for businessmen and their advisers to deal with, so that the extension of this approach to more joint ventures must be welcome.

5–138 Any concentration is, however, only subject to the Regulation (with all the benefits of the "one stop shop"), if it has what the Regulation calls a "Community dimension". This in general means the Regulation only applies to very large cross-border transactions within the EC. In practice many full function joint ventures do not have a Community dimension and thus fall outside the Regulation. Under the amending Regulation, there are currently two sets of criteria. Satisfaction of either set is sufficient to give rise to the community dimension. This situation is not changed by the draft Regulation.

5–139 The first set of criteria provides that the Community dimension will exist where the combined aggregate worldwide turnover of all the parties to the transaction (measured on a group basis, where a relevant party is part of a group of companies) exceeds €5,000m, and the aggregate EC turnover of at least two of the parties (taken individually) exceeds €250m. However, even in this case, the Regulation does not apply if two thirds of the European Community turnover of each party arises in the same Member State. The second provides that the community dimension will exist where (a) the combined aggregate worldwide turnover of all the parties to the transaction (measured on a group basis, where a relevant party is part of a group of companies) exceeds €2,500m, (b) in each of at least three Member States, the aggregate turnover of all the undertakings concerned is more than €100m, (c) in each of at least three of the Member States included for the purpose of point (b), the aggregate turnover of each of at least two of the undertakings is more than €25m, and (c) the aggregate EC turnover of each of at least two of the undertakings concerned is more than €100m. Again, even if these criteria are satisfied, the Regulation does not apply if two thirds of the EC turnover of each party arises in the same Member State.

Article 5 of the Regulation contains rules for the calculation of turnover, **5–140** and the Commission published two Notices in 1994, one dealing with the notion of undertakings concerned and the other with calculation of turnover, which are helpful explanations of these rules.

Where the Regulation applies, approval to the transaction must be sought **5–141** in advance from the Commission (on pain of large fines for failure to do so) in accordance with the Regulation and with Commission Regulation 447/98 which lays down procedural rules for applications and the way they are to be dealt with. These rules are to be subject to substantial change under the draft Regulation, and in due course, coincident with the implementation of the Council Regulation, the Commission will issue a further Regulation to replace Commission Regulation 447/98.

No concentration caught by the Regulation can be implemented prior to **5–142** Commission clearance under the Regulation. Where the Commission decides that, on the application of the criteria discussed above, the concentration is not compatible with the common market, it will either refuse clearance or, in cases where this is practicable, it will discuss with the parties variations to the terms of the transaction which would satisfy its concerns. It will then clear the transaction on the basis that the agreed variations are implemented.

If a merger or acquisition is regarded as a concentration, but it does not **5–143** have a Community dimension, then the Regulation cannot apply. In these circumstances, it is questionable whether the European Commission has any jurisdiction at all. Article 81 does not apply to a concentrative merger or acquisition. The only possible ground of jurisdiction is the old principle in *Commission v Continental Can* [1973] C.M.L.R. 199, which states that where an enterprise already has a dominant position in a market, a transaction which strengthens that dominant position (*e.g.* an acquisition which will give that enterprise a still larger market share) is itself an abuse of a dominant position under Art.82.

If these special circumstances do not apply, then the Commission will **5–144** have no jurisdiction over the concentrative acquisition or merger, and the relevant competition law authorities of the Member States involved will have jurisdiction instead. There is no possibility of overlap between the Commission and the competition law authorities in the Member States, because where the Regulation applies the local authorities have no jurisdiction, although where the interests of one Member State are particularly affected, the Commission can, under the Regulation, refer aspects of the transaction to the relevant authority for consultation and comment.

The case of the full function joint venture is different. If it falls outside the **5–145** Regulation, it will nevertheless be subject to Art.81. There will always be some kind of continuing agreement or arrangement between the shareholders or partners in the joint venture entity, (even if only the memorandum and articles setting up and regulating a legal entity that has been chosen as the vehicle for the joint venture) that will survive the transaction creating the entity, have a continuing effect and therefore be subject to scrutiny under Art.81. The issue then will be the extent to which these continuing arrangements provide for coordination between competitors, or have some other anticompetitive effect, and, if so, whether they are covered by a block exemption or are otherwise capable of exemption under Art.81(3).

5–146 So far as cooperative or partial-function joint ventures are concerned, these can only be the subject of consideration by the Commission under Art.81, since by definition they are not concentrations within the ambit of the Regulation in any event.

5–147 In both these cases, the competition law considerations usual for exemption under Art.81(3) will all apply, as will any applicable block exemptions in areas, such as research and development, which are generally understood by the Commission not to affect competition (see Commission Regulations 2658/2000 (specialisation agreements); 2659/2000 (research and development agreements) and 240/1996 (technology transfer block exemption). In 1993 the Commission published a Notice on Assessment of Cooperative Joint Ventures under Article 81, which contained some helpful guidelines. This Notice was updated and reissued in 2001 (O.J. C 3, January 6, 2001). Of course, from May 1, 2004, the cooperative or partial-function joint ventures will in the first instance have to be dealt with by the joint venture partners under the new framework of Council Regulation 1/2003. This means that they will have to assess the compatibility of their joint venture with Art.81, and the applicability of any relevant block exemptions, without the benefit of a notification to the Commission in cases of doubt. Here the reissued Notice should prove of great assistance.

5–148 The above discussion has assumed that a company wishes to organise its distribution network on a purely internal basis, by setting up a group of subsidiaries and/or branches, perhaps with the aid of horizontal arrangements which (by merger or acquisition) result in the creation of concentrative joint ventures. The alternative is to consider the involvement of, and cooperation with, third parties. This may entail the use of agents, distributors, subcontractors or cooperative joint ventures. As will be seen in the following discussion, all such alternatives require consideration in the light of the impact of Art.81.

5–149 *5.1.1.3.11 The status of agency relationships under Article 81* The next possibility apart from integration into a group is the appointment of agents. What the Commission now describes as a "genuine agency agreement" is not caught by Art.81. It is irrelevant whether the agency agreement is exclusive or not. The principles on which agency agreements are excepted from Art.81 were originally set out in the Commission Announcement on Exclusive Agency Contracts Made with Commercial Agents dated December 24, 1962.

5–150 From time to time the Commission has attempted to revise the 1962

Notice to take account of the developments in its thinking in the light of decided cases. In 1990, the Commission issued a draft Notice on Commercial Agency Agreements, but the draft was complicated, and some of the points it made were of doubtful legal validity. In any event, it aroused considerable opposition from industry, and appears to have been dropped. However, with the issuing of its Guidelines on Vertical Restraints (O.J. C 291/01 October 13, 2000), discussed in detail in chapter 5.2 below, the Commission finally communicated its current view on the status of agents in relation to Art.81, which supersedes the 1962 Notice.

A "non-genuine agency agreement" is subject to scrutiny under Art.81, **5–151** but in this case the rest of the Guidelines and the Commission Regulation 2790/99 on the application of Art.81(3) of the Treaty to categories of vertical agreements and concerted practices also apply (see Art.1(g) of the Regulation). This regulation, known generally as the block exemption for vertical agreements, is also discussed in detail in Chapter 5.2. In effect this means that the agent should be treated as "an independent dealer who must remain free in determining his marketing strategy" (Guidelines para.15). The consequences of this are discussed below (see Chapter 5.1.1.3.15.)

The Guidelines (Pt II.2 paras 12 to 20) state that an agency agreement **5–152** exists where there is a legal or physical person who is invested with power to negotiate or negotiate and conclude contracts for the supply of goods or services in the name of and/or on behalf of another person. (Here it should be noted that although the Guidelines are to be read in conjunction with the Council Directive on Commercial Agents (653/86), that Directive only applies to agents who act in the supply of goods, while the Guidelines and the block exemption for vertical agreements apply to vertical agreements for both goods and services.)

The factors which determine whether an agency agreement is genuine or **5–153** non-genuine are set out in para.16 of the Guidelines. If the agency relates to goods, property in the contract goods must not vest in the agent. If the agency relates to services, the agent must not himself supply the contract services. These preliminary requirements go to the heart of the relationship. If the relevant condition is not fulfilled, the relationship is unlikely to be one of agency at all as it is usually understood in law, but more likely that of a distributor (in the case of goods) or perhaps of a franchisee (in the case of services).

However, para.16 goes on to state that, if the relevant one of these pre- **5–154** liminary requirements is satisfied, the determining factor will be whether or not the agent bears financial and commercial risk on transactions negotiated or negotiated and concluded on behalf of his principal. The question of assumption of risk is to be assessed on the facts and the economic reality of each case. It has nothing to do with the legal form of the relationship. In general the Commission consider that Art.81 is not applicable if risk is not undertaken in the following areas: contributing to costs of supply and transport or sales promotion; holding stocks of goods at the agent's risk (other than the risk of loss or destruction through the agent's negligence); running sales, after sales or warranty services at the agent's expense; making market specific investments (such as petrol tank storage in the case of petrol retailing or specific software to sell insurance policies in the case of insurance agents); assuming third party product liability (unless the liability arose because of the agent's own negligence); assuming responsibility for the customer's nonperformance of the contract (with the exception of the loss of the agent's commission).

5–155 In connection with this last point it should be noted that while the 1962 Notice specifically permitted the agent to assume the *del credere* liability on the customers he found for the principal, the Guidelines make no specific mention of this liability. Since the agent assumes this liability under a separate arrangement for a separate commission or fee, then the best way is to regard the *del credere* guarantee as a separate relationship outside the agency agreement. The agency agreement is unaffected by Art.81, and, although the *del credere* agreement falls to be considered under Art.81, unless it contains additional terms not usually found in a *del credere* agreement, there should be nothing anticompetitive in it which would infringe Art.81.

5–156 If the agency agreement does not fall within the scope of Art.81(1), then all the obligations imposed on the agent in relation to the contracts concluded and/or negotiated on behalf of the principal fall outside Art.81(1). The following obligations imposed on the agent will generally be considered to be an inherent part of an agency agreement, as they are essential if the principal is to assume the risks on the transactions and to be in a position to determine the commercial strategy: restrictions on the products or services covered by the agency agreement, on the agent's territory, on the customers entrusted to the agent and on the prices at which products and services are to be supplied under the concluded contracts.

5–157 Again the grant of an exclusive agency contract will not infringe Art.81(1). Neither will the imposition on the agent of non-compete clauses unless this leads to a foreclosure of the market for agency services (see below.)

5–158 Despite all of the foregoing an agency agreement may still fall within Art.81 if by means of it a horizontal agreement or concerted practice is implemented. One example of this would be a reciprocal grant of exclusive agencies between competitors. This would clearly implement a market sharing and or product allocation arrangement depending on the terms of the reciprocal agreements.

5–159 Finally, so far as foreclosure of the market for agency services is concerned, it should be noted that although agency agreements in general fall outside Art.81, a principal may, perhaps, by means of a network of exclusive agencies coupled with non-compete clauses, manage to prevent competitors from entering a market, because all the suitable agents are tied to him under exclusive agreements preventing them from handling competitive products. In these cases there is nothing to prevent the Commission taking action against the principal under Art.82 of the EC Treaty if the principal is an undertaking in a dominant position in the relevant market (see *Suiker Unie v EC Commission*, [1976] 1 C.M.L.R. 295). However, as discussed above in the

Guidelines, such practices can also be caught under Art.81 by the application of the principle of cumulative effect.

Besides the principles relating to allocation of risk set out in the Guidelines, there are also certain European Court and Commission decisions which have looked at other situations where the agent is considered to be sufficiently independent of his principal that the relationship between them can be looked at under Art.81. The basic test to be applied is whether the agent is truly economically dependent upon his principal. If not, the agent is regarded as an independent dealer. This economic independence can arise in two ways. First, the agent can carry on other activities than agency, such as distribution, the manufacture and sale of his own products, or the sale of his own services. Second, the agent can act for a number of principals. Set out below is a summary and analysis of the case law in this area. **5–160**

In the Decision of the Commission *Re Pittsburgh Corning Europe* [1973] C.M.L.R. D2, the so-called representative was held to be an independent undertaking because, although it acted in part as a true agent most of its business came from the manufacture of its own products and from its activities as a distributor. The same principal was applied in the European Court Decision of *Suiker Unie v EC Commission* [1976] 1 C.M.L.R. 295, the so-called "Sugar Cartel" case, in which agents acted for each other but also traded in their own account as principals.

In the Decision of the Commission *Re International Federation of Association Football (FIFA)*, Commission Decision [1992] O.J. L326, the status of a travel agent was considered. '90 Tour Italia SpA was entrusted by FIFA with the exclusive rights for the supply of stadium entrance tickets for the 1990 World Cup held in Italy for the purpose of putting together package tours for the purpose of seeing matches played at the World Cup. A Belgian travel agent wishing to put together package tours for this purpose could not obtain tickets because of the exclusive agreement with '90 Tour Italia SpA. **5–161**

The Commission relied on Case 36/74 *Walrave v Union Cycliste International* [1975] 1 C.M.L.R. 320 and Case C-41/90 *Hofner v Elser/Macrotron* [1993] 4 C.M.L.R. 306 to hold that any entity which carries on activities of a commercial nature (regardless of its legal form) is an undertaking for the purposes of Art.81(1). FIFA qualified as an undertaking since although the World Cup was a major sporting event it also included activity of an economic nature, particularly the sale of tickets for matches, the sale of souvenirs and the sale of broadcasting and advertising rights. **5–162**

So far as Tour Italia was concerned, FIFA contended that it was purely an agent, entrusted with a particular function by FIFA in relation to the sale of tickets for package holidays, and therefore not a separate undertaking from FIFA. The Commission rejected this argument. Tour Italia not only dealt with the tickets, it also provided the whole package holiday, which was sold on prices and conditions set by Tour Italia. It had to acquire a number of tickets on its own resources and take the risk of them not being sold. These other activities and acceptance of such a high degree of risk in relation to failure to sell tickets meant that Tour Italia was not merely an agent (and **5–163** may not have been an agent at all, even in relation to the sale of the stadium tickets) so that it was a separate undertaking from FIFA.

5–164 Under the circumstances, the Commission found that the exclusive nature of the relationship between FIFA and Tour Italia was restrictive of competition. The Block Exemption for Exclusive Distribution Agreements (Reg.83/83) had no application since it applied only to the supply of goods not services. Furthermore, in any event, even if goods had been involved, it would have had no application because customers could obtain tickets only as part of package tours from the exclusive' distributor and had no alternative source of supply.

5–165 The Commission found that the arrangements contravened Art.81, but did not impose fines because this was the first Decision of such a nature in connection with a sporting event, but it reserved the right to do so in the future now that it had clarified the position.

5–166 In the Decision of the Commission *Re Eirpage*, Commission Decision [1991] O.J. L306, the Commission considered a joint venture in the telecommunications area for direct connection pager services in Ireland. The relevant point here is that Eirpage did not sell the paging service itself, but through a network of independent, non-exclusive agents, remunerated by commission based on the number of subscribers they recruited for Eirpage. Eirpage would pass enquiries for its paging service on to the agents. The agents all sold paging equipment, and, indeed many of them were also manufacturers or distributors of particular brands of paging equipment. Some of them even had their own brand of operator assisted paging services which they supplied to other customers. The Commission took the view that while the relationship between Eirpage and the agents was clearly one of agency, the agents acted in other capacities as well and were clearly undertakings independent from Eirpage (as opposed to mere auxiliaries), thus Art.81(3) applied to the agency agreements. The Commission required certain amendments to the agreements which promoted competition.

5–167 First, the agent could be required to promote Eirpage's service as a first option only where the prospective customer was derived from a sales lead supplied by Eirpage. If that service was unsuitable for the customer the agent could then promote his own or another service. In all other cases, the agent was free as to which service to promote. Second, an obligation of "loyalty in all matters" to Eirpage was considered too restrictive, and in conflict with the agent's other activities. It was reduced to an obligation to follow Eirpage's instruction, only in issues which concerned Eirpage's business. Third, there was a general duty to bring to Eirpage's attention marketing information which was likely to benefit Eirpage in marketing its services. This obligation could not be reconciled with the agent's existing or possible activities in competition with Eirpage and so was deleted. Fourth, a three year post-termination ban to prevent the agent from soliciting Eirpage customers was deleted. Finally, agents who also supplied interconnected paging services, and therefore were direct competitors of Eirpage should not be permitted as agents; further, if an existing agent chose to offer such services in the future, he should be obliged to resign the agency.

In the European Court of Justice decision in the *Flemish Travel Agents* case (*Vlaamse Reiseburos v Commission* [1987] 4 C.M.L.R. 213), the Court held that a travel agent, although acting as a true agent, does so for such a large number of tour operators and transport suppliers that the agent has no real economic dependency upon any one of the principals that he acts for. The Court ruled that a term in various agreements between the agent and some of his principals which prevented the agent from offering discounts or bonuses to customers out of his own commission (in a sense a kind of price fixing) was in contravention of Art.81(1). **5–168**

The same logic is also implicit in a Decision of the Commission relating to the fixing of tariffs for the use of their services by the trade association acting for Italian Customs Agents (*Re Consilio Nazionale degli Spedizionieri Doganali/Associazione Italiana dei Corrieri Aeri Internazionali*, Commission Decision [1993] O.J. L203). Here, the question was whether the agent's trade association (CNSD) was an "association of undertakings engaged in economic activity" for the purposes of Art.81 so that its conduct in fixing tariffs could be called into question under Art.81(1). The Commission held that the customs agents were undertakings engaged in an economic activity. Although the question was more concerned with whether a person engaged in a liberal profession can be said to engage in an economic activity, it was taken for granted that the agents were economically independent undertakings. One assumes that this was on the basis of the fact that they acted for a large number of principals, often only in respect of a single transaction, as in *Vlaamse Reiseburos*. **5–169**

Each of the above cases does turn upon its particular facts, and a number of points can be made in relation to each one. In the cases concerning agents who carry on other activities it cannot be always assumed that the carrying on of a subsidiary activity (*e.g.* an agent who occasionally acts as a distributor) will always render the agent economically independent from his principal. **5–170**

For instance in the 1987 Decision of the Commission *Re Austin Rover Group/Unipart*, the Commission decided that Unipart was economically dependent upon Austin Rover, for whom it acted as agent for the supply of certain categories of its spare parts, even though it also acted as distributor for Austin Rover in respect of other categories. In part, the reasoning behind the case may have been influenced by the fact that Unipart was a division of Austin Rover which had been sold off, so that Unipart was still clearly very dependent upon Austin Rover for its continued survival. Further, in the *Vlaamse Reiseburos* case, the agents acted for very many principals. It cannot be assumed that an agent who made a living acting for a small number of principals would be treated in the same way. **5–171**

The most recent cases on the status of agents have focused on practices in the motor vehicle trade. Many manufacturers use distribution networks composed partly of agents, partly of distributors and partly of undertakings which perform, in different areas of activity, the functions of agents and of distributors. In addition, the term "agent" is often loosely or incorrectly applied to undertakings in these networks. The Commission has taken **5–172** advantage of a detailed analysis of these situations to hold that the agreements between manufacturers and many so-called agents are in fact subject to scrutiny under Art.81.

5–173 In *Bundeskartellamt v Volkswagen AG/VAG Leasing GmbH* the leasing company was a subsidiary of Volkswagen which had exclusive agency arrangements with dealers in Volkswagen's selective distribution network, and was therefore held by the Commission to have an unfair advantage over dealers and independent leasing companies in the leasing of Volkswagen cars. The Court noted that the leasing arrangements were an adjunct to the selective distribution network which was itself in contravention of Art.81(1) but exempted under Reg.1237/85. This regulation did not, however, exempt the exclusive agency agreements.

5–174 Here the agents were clearly undertakings independent of Volkswagen, since their main business was as dealers in Volkswagen's vehicles. The agency agreements themselves could thus be considered under Art.81 and clearly contravened Art.81(1). The object, or at least the effect, of the exclusive agency agreements was to restrict competition in the provision of leasing services. They applied to the whole of the German market and "practices which restrict the whole territory of a Member State by their very nature have the effect of reinforcing the compartmentalisation of markets on a national basis, thereby obstructing the economic interpenetration the Treaty is designed to bring about". A similar case is about to be tried in relation to the Mercedes Benz distribution network. By its decision of October 10, 2001 *Re Mercedes Benz* (COMP/36.246) the Commission fined DaimlerChrysler AG over €71m in respect of measures adopted by the company to impede parallel trade in cars (by instructing its German distributors and agents not to sell outside Germany, and requiring them to obtain a 15 per cent advance payment from foreign customers), to restrict its agents or distributors from the sale of passenger motor vehicles to independent leasing companies as stock, and to restrict the grant of discounts in Belgium. The Commission decided that the arrangements between the company and its agents could be examined under Art.81 because the agents undertook considerable financial risks, and could therefore be regarded as independent dealers. The Company has filed an application (Case T-352/01 filed on December 20, 2001) for annulment of the Decision with the European Court of First Instance partly on the grounds that the Commission was wrong in law to regard its network of agents as independent dealers. This part of the application relies upon the usual ground that a true agent is regarded as one undertaking with its principal, so that restrictions imposed on the agent are restrictions imposed by the principal for its own protection in contracts entered into by the principal and only negotiated by the agent. When issued the judgment should provide further useful material on the application of Art.81 to agency agreements.

5–175 It will be noted that the agency cases (other than *Mercedes Benz*) which were decided after the coming into force of the Council Directive on the Coordination of the laws of the Member States relating to self-employed Commercial Agents 86/653 of December 18, 1986 discussed in Chapter 3 (namely *FIFA, Eirpage, CNSD* and *Volkswagen*) related to the provision of services, so the problem of the application of this Directive to such relationships has not been considered. However, it can be seen, particularly from *Eirpage*, that the Commission's view of this type of agency relationship does not sit easily with the provisions of the Directive, particularly with the obligations of the agent to look after his principal's affairs in good faith. It is arguable that agents of the type referred to in *CNSD* would have fallen outside the Directive (even if they had dealt in goods) since they were engaged in ad hoc transactions and did not have the "continuing authority" to act on behalf of their principal which is a requirement for the application of the Directive. It should be noted that, in the UK at least, the types of agents discussed in all of the cases other than *CNSD* would (if they were supplying goods) probably fall within the definition of secondary agents (see in particular para.3(c) of Sch.2 of the Commercial Agents (Council Directive) Regulations 1993 (SI 1993/3053) and thus be unaffected by the Directive.

There is one final point to be considered—the relationship between the agency cases discussed above and the principles laid down in the Guidelines. **5–176**

The Guidelines are concerned to distinguish between a "genuine agency agreement" and a "non-genuine agency agreement". In a genuine agency agreement "the selling or purchasing function forms part of the principal's activities, despite the fact that the agent is a separate undertaking. The principal thus bears the related financial and commercial risks and the agent does not exercise an independent economic activity in relation to the activities for which he has been appointed as agent by the principal" (para.15). **5–177**

These statements are tantamount to saying that, since the principal acts through the agent, any restrictions which he imposes on the agent are really unilateral decisions on the part of the principal as to with which customers, in which territory and upon what prices terms and conditions he wishes to trade. In this sense there is no agreement between the principal and the agent which can be scrutinised under Art.81. It may be that those restrictions will result in turning away business which the agent could, in their absence have negotiated or negotiated and concluded for his principal. However, except to the extent that he will make less commission, the agent is not prejudiced by and should have no say in determining the principal's policy, as he does not have to cover costs or risks relating specifically to the agency, such as disposing of stocks on which he has taken the inventory risk, or amortising the cost of market-specific investments which can only be used in the agency activities. **5–178**

The Guidelines thus use the analysis of the allocation of the risk to decide whether the agent is carrying on an independent economic activity. If so, then the principal does not act through the agent, but acts by way of an agreement with the agent, which can be scrutinised under Art.81. Only two of the cases discussed above approach the issue in this way. *Re Mercedes Benz*, the latest case, and a Commission Decision, clearly sets out this type of thinking. The other case where this approach appears at least partially is **5–179** the Commission Decision *Re International Federation of Association Football (FIFA)*. The other cases appear to fall into three different categories, not really dealt with under the Guidelines.

5–180 The first category is where an undertaking acts for the same principal as both agent and independent dealer. It is fairly easy to see how, taken as a whole, and on the criterion of assumption of risk, as described in the Guidelines, the relationship can become a non-genuine agency agreement. This was the line taken in *Re Austin Rover Group/Unipart* and *Bundeskartellamt v Volkswagen AG/VAG Leasing GmbH*.

5–181 The second category is where an undertaking acts as agent for one party but as an independent dealer either because it manufactures and sells it own products or else acts as a distributor for a third party. Here, the very existence of the dual role appears to the decisive factor which rendered the agent really independent of the principal. *Re Pittsburgh Corning Europe, Suiker Unie v EC Commission* and *Re Eirpage* fall within this category.

5–182 The third category deals with agents who act for very many principals. Here the reasoning appears to be that the lack of reliance on any one principal renders the agent independent from them all. *Consilio Nazionale degli Spedizionieri Doganali/Associazione Italiana dei Corrieri Aeri Internazionali* and *Vlaamse Reiseburos v Commission* fall within this class.

5–183 Although it is possible to reconcile the Guidelines with the first category of cases above, in that, taken as a whole, the relationship is one in which the agent carries on an independent economic activity, this is not so easy for the second and third categories.

5–184 The reasoning why undertakings in the second category are regarded as independent dealers seems closer to that underlying the concept of secondary agency as mentioned in the Commercial Agents Directive (653/86) where secondary agents (as defined by Member States under local implementations of the Directive) can be excluded from the scope of the Directive. However, under the Guidelines, analysis is confined to the relevant agreement between principal and agent and does not take account of other activities carried on by the agent independently of that relationship, either on its own or with third parties.

5–185 So far as the decisions in the third category are concerned, the reasoning is far less clear. First the Guidelines state that they apply whether the agent acts for one or several principals (para.13). Thus the somewhat doubtful attempts to distinguish between agents acting for one or several principals (and to apply Art.81(1) to the latter but not the former) which characterised the draft Notice of 1990 have been abandoned. It could be argued that although they apply where the agent acts for several principals (*i.e.* only a few but more than one) they do not apply where the agent acts for very many principals. However, if the classification of the relationship between each principal and the agent is to be considered in isolation from any other relationships the agent may have, what does it matter how many principals the agent has, even if they are as numerous as in the case of a travel agent? Each relationship should be considered separately under the Guidelines to see how risk has been allocated.

The only possible way to reconcile the rationale of the cases in category three with the principle of the allocation of risk in the Guidelines is to consider that an agent acting for very many principals does in fact take some risk on the contracts he negotiates and/or concludes for his very many principals, perhaps by block buying of tickets or allocations in advance of sales (as in *FIFA*) or by incurring other risks such as market specific investment or sales promotional expenditure. However, although *FIFA* considered this issue, *Vlaamse Reisburos* did not. **5–186**

In general, the reconciliation of these earlier cases and decisions with the Guidelines is not complete, and this difficulty is a typical example of the problems caused when the thinking of the Commission and the European Court changes over time in response to particular competitive situations. This is particularly obvious if one compares the 1962 Notice with the Guidelines. Although the former does deal with the issue of risk, there is much more emphasis than in the Guidelines on the lack of independence which an agent ("an auxiliary") must have in relation to his principal. This emphasis on independence, or the lack of it, does seem to have coloured the judgments and decisions in the earlier cases. **5–187**

In these instances, it may well be that it is not possible to draw broad principles from pragmatic decisions on the facts of particular cases. All that can be said in this regard is that since all Commission Notices are without prejudice to the decisions of the European Court, there is no reason why the principles set out in these Cases (if not the Decisions) should not survive the Guidelines. **5–188**

Thus, when considering the status of an agency relationship, it can be approached by analysing that relationship in isolation, under the Guidelines, to see if it is genuine or non-genuine on the criterion of the allocation of risk, or it can be approached under the case law to decide whether the agent is really independent of the principal, because he also acts in his own right as an independent dealer for himself or for third parties, and not just as a mere auxiliary of his principal. **5–189**

This discussion emphasises once again the need to consider all the circumstances of the case, both factual and legal, when deciding on the impact of competition law upon a particular agreement. Here, it is not enough to consider the status of an agency agreement from the point of view of the Guidelines. Any impact from the principles derived from relevant case law must be considered as well. **5–190**

5.1.1.3.12 The status of joint ventures under Article 81 Once one goes beyond the concept of the agency agreement the relationships move towards greater independence and thus Art.81 comes into application as a matter of course. **5–191**

The relationship of the cooperative joint venture must be distinguished from that of distributor for the purposes of EC law, as there are different exemptions under Art.81(3) which apply to each of these relationships. **5–192**

As stated above, cooperative joint ventures are nothing more than agreements between two or more undertakings all of which retain their **5–193** independence. These are therefore always potentially the subject of a Decision under Art.81. Where the Commission was prepared to exempt certain joint ventures under Art.81(3) there seem to be two general principles.

5–194 The first principle is that small and medium-sized enterprises are treated more leniently, since it is felt that they need to be able to cooperate together to withstand their larger competitors (which promotes competition) and also because such joint ventures by their nature do not affect large market-shares (see, for instance, *Re Compagnie International des Wagons-Lits de Tourisme/Volkswagen AG* [1988] O.J. L300, where, by a Notice, the Commission approved the merger of two car-rental businesses to achieve an effective European-wide competitive operation).

5–195 These principles are now embodied in two block exemptions relating to specialisation agreements (Reg.2658/2000) and to research and development agreements (Reg.2659/2000) both of which came into force on January 1, 2001. Both regulations operate on the principle that cooperation between undertakings which do not enjoy a large aggregate share of the relevant market does not have an appreciable effect on competition. The regulations are accompanied by the Guidelines on the applicability of Article 81 of the EC Treaty to Horizontal Cooperation Agreements (O.J. C 3 January 6, 2001) which explain not only their operation but also the Commission's approach to horizontal cooperation in other areas than specialisation and research and development. There is no list of permitted terms (white list) nor is there a "grey list" of terms which are dealt with through the short form non-opposition notification procedure. There is however a black list dealing with the usual hardcore restrictions—price fixing, output limitation, allocation of markets or customers, limitation on passive selling outside an assigned territory.

5–196 Specialisation agreements deal with circumstances where two or more undertakings have surplus production capacity. An agreement may be reached to close down some of the capacity, leaving one or more undertakings with a fully-loaded facility, from which the requirements of all the undertakings will then be supplied at the lowest possible unit cost. An alternative form of specialisation would be an agreement that two or more of the undertakings concerned will each specialise in the production of one or more particular products, with reciprocal supply obligations, so that all undertakings will obtain either from their own or one of the others' facilities all of the different items that they require. Again the aim is to restrict the production of particular items to one or more facilities to ensure that those facilities are fully loaded.

5–197 Such agreements have obvious implications for infringement of Art.81, but the Commission considers that their benefits outweigh their effect on competition provided that the aggregate market share of all the undertakings concerned in such an agreement does not exceed 20 per cent of the relevant market. The exemption permits the parties to enter into both cross-supply and unilateral supply or outsourcing arrangements. Exclusive supply and purchasing obligations are permitted, and the undertakings concerned may set production amounts and production capacities and volumes. Where there is a production joint venture that also carries on distribution, the parties may agree the prices at which the joint venture is to sell to its customers.

The exemption for cooperative research and development agreements is even more generous. Where the parties are competitors or potential competitors, the agreement is exempt if together they do not hold more than 25 per cent of the relevant market. This is defined as the market of existing products with which the product to be developed will compete. If the parties are not competitors, there is no initial threshold at all. Instead they may continue their cooperation through into production and sale, until the new product gains (though their combined activities) a 25 per cent share on the relevant market. (At this stage, of course, if the parties consider that the criteria under Art.81(3) continue to apply in all the circumstances of the case, there is nothing to prevent them continuing with the joint venture even though the block exemption no longer applies). If the cooperation extends to production, then the parties may fix production targets, and if to distribution as well, then sales targets and sales prices may also be set. **5–198**

Finally, the new accompanying Guidelines on the applicability of Art.81 of the EC Treaty to Horizontal Cooperation Agreements emphasise that there is no presumption that a cooperation agreement is illegal just because it falls outside the block exemptions. The Guidelines contain explanation and examples to aid self-assessment, some comment and analysis of the block exemptions and a discussion of horizontal cooperation agreements outside the exemptions, particularly joint selling, joint purchasing and joint marketing agreements. The line taken by the Commission is that such arrangements are either outside Art.81(1) or should have the benefit of exemption under Art.81(3) where they enable enterprises with a low market share to cooperate so as to provide more effective competition against undertakings already present in the market with a large market share or even a dominant position. It should not be forgotten that such arrangements can certainly take advantage of the Commission Notice on Agreements of Minor Importance 2001, and the Notice should always be the first consideration in deciding whether such arrangements do or do not fall foul of Art.81. **5–199**

The Commission generally takes a very different line where it is dealing with larger-sized organisations as can be seen for instance in its Decision in 1980, *Re Floral GmbH* [1980] 2 C.M.L.R. 285. **5–200**

However, it does view favourably initial moves to enable even large firms to get into a position to supply on a particular market (because increasing the number of entrants promotes competition) provided that once entry has been achieved, there is no further restriction on activities in the market. This can be seen clearly in relation to research and development contracts. This is the reason why the block exemption Reg.2659/2000 promotes cooperation in research and development provided the parties concerned do not have too great a market share. Furthermore, even where the combined market share is large, the Commission has in the past been prepared in certain cases to **5–201** grant individual exemption, outside the block exemption, to such arrangements provided they do not spill over and control the fruits of the development in relation to production and marketing in a restrictive manner.

5–202 A good example here is the Commission Decision *Re Continental Gummi-Werke AG/Compagnie Generale des Establissements Michelin/Michelin et cie* [1988] O.J. L305, which related to the development of a new type of wheel and tyre, but left the collaborators free to exploit the developed product in competition; in fact the product was intended to be an industry standard and licensable to all comers.

5–203 However, in some industries it is research and development which provides the competitive edge, and then the very arrangement on research will be regarded as restrictive of competition (see *Re Henkel/Colgate* [1972] O.J. L14/14). There is also sometimes the opposite effect where the investment needed is so great that no enterprise could reasonably be expected to make it unless there were controls beyond the research and development stage on into production and marketing. Here such restrictions have been exempted on the grounds that without them the joint venture would never have come into existence at all (see *Re GEC/Weir* [1977] O.J. L327/26 and *Re Brown Boveri AG/NGK Insulators Ltd* [1988] O.J. L301).

5–204 Finally, mention should be made of the EC vehicle available (since July 1, 1989) for certain types of cross-border joint ventures, where the participants are located across at least two Member States. This is known as the European Economic Interest Grouping, which is in effect a separate legal entity, but gives its members the liabilities they would have under an unlimited partnership. The concept of the EEIG was established under the Council Regulation 2137/85. The Regulation makes it clear that although the formation of EEIGs and cooperation through them is to be encouraged, an EEIG is still subject to Art.81 and will, in appropriate cases, require consideration under Art.81(1) and (3). The EEIG is intended as a vehicle for partial-function joint ventures which do not have as their primary aim the making of a profit. Thus joint ventures for the purposes of research and development or specialisation are particularly suitable for the EEIG where the necessary cross-border element exists.

5–205 *5.1.1.3.13 The status of subcontracting under Article 81* Subcontracting is in some ways only another form of joint venture, and the Commission wishes to encourage it because, again, it is primarily the small and medium-sized firms which act as subcontractors (see the Commission Notice on Sub-Contracting Agreements of 1968).

5–206 The types of subcontracting arrangements which the Commission regards as not caught by Art.81 are now set out in its 1978 Notice on Sub-Contracting Agreements. Patents and knowhow may be licensed to the subcontractor to enable him to perform the contract. Restrictions may be imposed by the contractor limiting the use of such industrial property to the purposes of the contract, prohibiting their disclosure to third parties, and prohibiting supply to third parties of the goods to be supplied under the subcontract with the aid of the patents and knowhow.

There are some additional restrictions which may also be imposed. The obligations may be placed upon the subcontractor to apply the contractor's trade marks only on goods to be supplied under the subcontract. The subcontractor can be obliged to grant back licences on improvements and variations, on the licensed patents and knowhow, generated by him in the course of performance of the subcontract. Such a licence must be non-exclusive, unless the improvements cannot be used apart from the original inventions. However, no restrictions can be imposed on the knowhow and industrial property rights generated by the subcontractor, or known to him already, or in the public domain at the time they were communicated to him by the contractor. **5–207**

Subcontracting is by its nature a one-off type of relationship, where the subcontractor is performing for the contractor a designated task relating to a particular main contract. Such a relationship is not one which is normally of much use for a continuing relationship for the distribution and sale of goods, except in the case where the distributor, who also has a licence to manufacture the products he distributes, subcontracts their manufacture, while himself concentrates on distribution. This possibility is dealt with in Chapter 8.19. Subcontracting can also be used in discharging a distributor's obligations for after sales service (see Chapter 6.24.12). **5–208**

This leads away from the more general forms of joint ventures (of use perhaps in setting up the conditions necessary for entry into a market), the joint cooperation between small and medium-sized enterprises, and the more specialised subcontracting relationships, to the relationship of the principal with a true distributor, where the parties are most in an arm's length situation. **5–209**

5.1.1.3.14 The status of distributors under Article 81 The Commission distinguishes between the relationship of agent and distributor on the basis of assumption of risk,(see the Guidelines on Vertical Restraints discussed above in Chapter 5.1.1.3.11). The Commission is not concerned with the wording of the agreement but will apply the criterion of the assumption of risk in each case and make its decision on the facts (see the Commission Decisions *Re Pittsburgh Corning Europe* and *Re Mercedes Benz* above). **5–210**

The true distributor purchases goods from the principal, takes title to and risk in them, takes the inventory risk (*i.e.* that he will be unable to find purchasers for them or that they will suffer damage or destruction) and takes the credit risk in relation to sales he makes (*i.e.* the loss by way of a bad debt if his purchasers do not pay him), and, finally, takes the responsibility to his customers for dealing with defective goods that he has sold them. (This last responsibility exists as a matter of contract between the distributor and his customers, irrespective of the extent, if any, to which the distributor has backed off this liability under a warranty agreement between him and his principal.) He sets his own selling and marketing policies and derives his remuneration from the turn he makes by selling product at a higher price than he purchased it. **5–211**

Here reference should be made to the discussion of the definition of **5–212** distributor in Chapter 3.2.1 particularly in relation to the cases of *AMB Imballaggi Plastici Srl v Pacflex Ltd* [1999] 2 All E.R (Comm) 249 and *Mercantile International Group plc v Chuan Soon Huat Industrial Group plc* [2002] 1 All E.R. (Comm) 788, CA.

5–213 From the principles set out above it can be seen that an agent who acts as a factor is unlikely to be considered to have assumed the risk necessary to make him be regarded as a distributor, since the stocks that he deals with belong to the principal, and the only risk he takes in relation to them is that of a normal bailee for reward (*i.e.* to keep them safely).

5–214 A problem arises in cases where a principal obliges the same undertaking to operate purely as an agent, in areas where the principal wishes to control the agent's selling policy, without falling foul of Art.81, but permits it to operate as a distributor in other areas where restriction of the selling policy is not of any concern. Here, the whole of the relationship will be caught by Art.81, (see the Commission Decision *Re Pittsburgh Corning Europe* and the European Court judgment *Bundeskartellamt v Volkswagen AG/VAG Leasing GmbH*, and the discussion in Chapter 5.1.1.3.11).

5–215 Thus, in general, the relation of distributor and principal is caught under Art.81, and this gives rise to the necessity either to draft the agreement in such a way that it will not contravene the provisions of Art.81(1), or to draft it in such a way that it will be exempt under Art.81(3).

5–216 Article 81 will *prima facie* have application because of three aspects, one or more of which are usually of relevance in any distribution agreement. The first is the appointment of a distributor on an exclusive basis, the second the restriction of the activities of the distributor to a particular territory, the third the restriction on the distributor not to handle competing products. The other area which will always give rise to problems under Art.81 is that of restrictions on trading terms, in particular resale price maintenance, and confining the distributor's right to supply to certain classes of outlets only. In the clauses to be considered in this chapter these are therefore the areas which have particularly to be borne in mind.

5–217 *5.1.1.3.15 Treatment of non-genuine agency agreements under Article 81* The Guidelines on Vertical Restraints envisage numerous types of risk and different possibilities for their allocation between agent and principal. From a commercial point of view this results in a certain spectrum of relationships, with the genuine agent at one end and the true distributor at the other. However, so far as the Commission is concerned, "the agency agreement is considered genuine . . . if the agent does not bear any, or bears only insignificant, risks . . . In the opposite situation the agency agreement is considered a non-genuine agency agreement . . ." (para.15). "Where the agent incurs one or more of the above risks or costs, then Art.81(1) may apply as with any other vertical agreement" (para.17). This suggests that so far as the application of Art.81 is concerned the situation is for all practical purposes binary—no application to a genuine agency agreement and application in the case of a non-genuine agency agreement, even though the latter classification can comprise many different allocations of risk between the agent and the principal.

There are thus in this area, three relevant relationships for the purpose of EC competition law: a genuine agency agreement, a non-genuine agency agreement and a distributor agreement. Each of these are different forms of vertical relationship, but only the first is not caught by Art.81. It is also important to emphasise that a non-genuine agency agreement is still an agency agreement, rather than a distribution agreement under another name. **5–218**

For instance, a financial services agency could impose no risks on the agent in relation to contracts negotiated on behalf of the principal, but still fall within Art.81 because the agent undertook market specific investment in software. On the other hand an agent negotiating contracts on behalf of his principal for the sale of consumer goods to wholesalers could fall within Art.81(1), because he undertook responsibility for product liability claims or for nonperformance by customers he had found, even though he made no market specific investment at all. **5–219**

Some assistance with the way Art.81 is applied to non-genuine agency agreements can be found in para.48 of the Guidelines: **5–220**

> "In the case of agency agreements, the principal normally establishes the sales price as the agent does not become the owner of the goods. However, where an agency agreement falls within Art.81(1) . . . an obligation restricting the agent from sharing his commission, fixed or variable, with the customer would be a hardcore restriction under art 4(a) of the Block Exemption Regulation. The agent should thus be left free to lower the effective price by the customer without reducing the income for the principal"

This passage would suggest that Art.81(1) causes no problem where the principal sets the prices, terms and conditions on which the agent is to negotiate or negotiate and conclude contracts. The principal is merely setting the parameters for the agent's mandate to act on his behalf. (After all, if the mandate is merely to negotiate, the principal could always reject any proffered orders whose prices terms or conditions he found unacceptable.) Problems with Art.81 will occur when the principal tries to restrict the way in which the agent goes about discharging his mandate. Since the agent is characterised as an "independent dealer", then, just as in the case with a true distributor, restrictions on the territory in which the agent can act, on dealing with competing goods and services, on the types of customers he can approach and any restrictions on inducements he can offer to customers to enter into contracts (provided they do not violate the mandate) are all vertical restraints which can be scrutinised under Art.81(1) in the same way as under a distribution agreement. As para.15 of the Guidelines puts it, in this case the agent should be treated as "an independent dealer who must remain free in determining his marketing strategy". **5–221**

As vertical restraints, these restrictions will be subject to the applicable principles set out in the Guidelines, and, where Reg.2790//99 applies, will be exempt under that regulation unless they amount to hardcore restrictions. **5–222**

5–223 The result of this analysis appears to be that in most cases, once the agency agreement (for whatever reason) is non-genuine in terms of the Guidelines, the principal should proceed in all respects as if he were dealing with a distributor, except in regard to the agent's mandate as to the prices terms and conditions upon which he can negotiate or negotiate and conclude transactions on behalf of the principal.

5–224 Even here, a certain caution is necessary. If the mandate is set up in such a way that it amounts to an indirect hardcore restriction, there would still be a violation of Art.81. For instance, if the principal requires the agent to conclude contracts for fulfilment outside his territory at less favourable prices than contracts for fulfilment inside his territory, the policy could amount to an indirect partitioning of the market for the agent's activities which would contravene Art.81(1). It was precisely this practice which caused the Commission to find a violation of Art.81(1) in the agency agreements in *Re Mercedes Benz*.

5–225 In general, the conclusion must be that the principal would be better advised to appoint a true distributor, wherever this is commercially feasible, off-load all of the risk relating to the relationship, and deal with Art.81 problems as they arise. The only case when this might not be appropriate is where the cost of the products or the complexity of the services concerned is so high that a distributorship is impractical. Here, it may be necessary to enter into a non-genuine agency agreement. For instance, if the contract goods were high value capital equipment sold one at a time, and the agent could not sell without market specific investment, or without providing after sales service at his own cost, the principal should enter into an agency agreement which would appear very much like a distribution agreement (and which would have to take care not to infringe Art.81(1)), except that the representative would not take title to the goods sold, and the contract for their supply would be concluded between the principal and the third party customer. This relationship has all the characteristics of a distributorship except that the "distributor" does not bear any inventory risk or cost.

5–226 A similar approach can be seen in a distribution agreement where the distributor is allowed to hold stock on a consignment basis. He does not take title to the stock, or take the inventory risk (because in effect the stock is held for sale or return), but in all other respects he acts as an independent dealer.

5–227 These examples show that, while a non-genuine agency agreement and a distribution agreement are different legal concepts, there are circumstances where, from a commercial point of view, there is little to distinguish them.

5–228 The precedent in Chapter 3 deals with a standard agency agreement, and provided its terms are adhered to, there is nothing in it which would constitute a non-genuine agency agreement within the definition of the Guidelines, although of course the parties could agree other terms, outside the agreement itself, either expressly or tacitly, which would turn the whole relationship into a non-genuine agency agreement. In this respect care should be taken with the following clauses:

- **cl.3.3.2 (proper facilities)**—this is permissible under the Guidelines as it does not include market-specific investment.; "general investments in for instance premises and personnel are not material to this assessment" (para.15); care should be taken that the principal does not in fact require market specific investments either relying on the general wording in this clause or in a side agreement.
- **cl.3.4.2 (samples)**—the principal should take care not to charge for samples. Version (b) makes this explicit, but version (a) leaves the possibility open.
- **cl.3.4.4 (responsibility for agent's expenses)**—this clause is acceptable as drafted.
- **cl.3.4.5 (advertising)**—is acceptable as drafted since the agent has no responsibility to assume advertising or sales promotion expenses.
- **Sch.4 (stocks of the products)**—this schedule imposes no risks in the stocks of the products held by the agent other than in relation to the usual duty of a bailee to look after the goods with reasonable care (cl.3.14.2.1) and the duty to insure the goods at the agent's expense (cl.3.14.3); this latter obligation should not cause the agency agreement to become non-genuine, first because in most cases it will not be a significant assumption of cost, and second because it is only one of the ways in which the agent assumes the risk of holding the goods as bailee.

It should be noted that some of the provisions in the agency precedent in Chapter 2, particulary Sch.4, would cause any agreement, using these provisions in the EC, to become a non-genuine agency agreement.

5.1.1.4 Articles 28 and 30 and the free movement of goods

Articles 28 and 30 deal with the general principle, of paramount importance, under the EC Treaty, that goods and services must be allowed to flow freely around the common market, across national borders of the various Member States, without undue hindrance. This is the basis underlying the foundation of the common market under the Treaty of Rome and, even before that, of the European Coal and Steel Community. Any artificial barriers to trade between Member States partition the market and frustrate the creation of the single market. **5–229**

The EC Treaty attacks conduct partitioning the market in two ways. First it prohibits undertakings engaged in commercial activity from implementing anticompetitive arrangements under Art.81, and from activity amounting to abuse of a dominant position under Art.82, which would, *inter alia*, partition the common market. Second, it lays down a general prohibition in Art.28 against "quantitative restrictions on imports and all measures having equivalent effect". This is addressed not just to undertakings but also to the **5–230** governments of Member States. Its main aim has been to promote the removal of all barriers to trade between Member States created by national laws and regulatory regimes. However, Art.30 permits certain exceptions to this prohibition, and both Member States and commercial undertakings have, on occasion, taken the opportunity to further partisan interests, at the expense of the single market, by invoking one or more of those exceptions in particular cases. The Commission and the European Court are assiduous in attacking all such attempts where, in the words of Art.30 they "constitute a means of arbitrary discrimination or a disguised restriction on trade between Member States".

5–231 In the area of vertical agreements, suppliers have often had resort to Art.30 to attempt to partition the common market, without resorting to the imposition on their buyers of contractual restrictions on export which would infringe Art.81(1) without the possibility of exemption.

5–232 Suppliers commonly resort to three lines of attack under Art.30. The first relates to intellectual property rights, the second to repackaging of products and the third to exploiting national differences in more general regulatory regimes, which still depend upon local implementation in each Member State, rather than a completely uniform application across all Member States of the EC.

5–233 *5.1.1.4.1. Partitioning the market through intellectual property rights*

Here the most important issue to consider is to what extent intellectual property rights can be used to partition the EC, by the prevention of parallel imports from other areas within the EC, and thus reinforce the possibility of confining the activity of distributors to their allocated territories without the need to impose a contractual ban on exports and thus infringe Art.81(1).

5–234 The key to the problem of parallel imports is the wording of Arts 28 and 30 of the EC Treaty. Article 28 provides broadly that there shall be no restrictions imposed upon the free movement of goods across borders between Member States of the EC so that the EC actually exists as a unified common market. Article 30 derogates from the general prohibitions of Art.28 by permitting certain closely defined impediments to cross-border trade. In particular Art.30 provides that Art.28 "shall not preclude prohibitions or restrictions on imports, exports or goods in transit justified on the grounds of ... the protection of industrial and commercial property. Such prohibitions or restrictions shall not however constitute a disguised restriction on trade between Member States".

5–235 The question is thus to what extent the Treaty can prevent the holder of intellectual property rights exercising against third parties the rights which the relevant national legal system permits him to exercise by virtue of his holding those rights. It is only by virtue of the exercise of those rights that the principal can attack third parties who are not parties to any of the distribution agreements within his network, so as to prevent them acquiring goods in one country, and exporting them to another, thus upsetting the territorial exclusivity in his arrangements. It is also the only way (if it be at all possible) that he can impose upon his distributors the absolute ban on cross-border trade which he cannot impose in the distribution agreement without contravening Art.81 and losing the benefit of the exemption granted under Reg.2790/99.

The first case where the European Court grappled with the problem came from the area of patents. In *Parke Davis & Co v Probel* [1968] C.M.L.R. 47 Parke Davis of Detroit held patents in Holland for an antibiotic. Probel imported the drug from Italy into Holland. In Italy no patents for drugs or antibiotics were granted, and the drug was made in Italy by a third party with no connection with or permission from Parke Davis. Parke Davis relied on an infringement of its Dutch patent, by the importation from Italy without its consent, as grounds for an injunction to stop the imports. The case was referred from the Dutch Court to the European Court for advice on the effect of Arts 30, 81 and 82 on the right of Parke Davis to be granted an injunction. **5–236**

The Court held that Parke Davis was not contravening these Articles by its attempt to prevent the free flow of the drug from Italy to Holland. Article 30 permits the prohibition of such imports in so far as it is necessary for the existence of the industrial property in question. The Court cautioned that the exercise of particular industrial property rights, as opposed to their existence, could in some cases contravene Arts 28 and 30. It was clear however that on the facts, if the import from Italy had been permitted, the Dutch patent would be rendered worthless. Going one step further it is also clear that Art.28 could not prevent the enforcement of a national industrial property right in another Member State of the EC against a naked infringer who happened to operate in that Member State, and to import into the territory in question. **5–237**

The distinction between exercise and existence was a difficult one, particularly in relation to a patent which is nothing more than a right to stop other people using a patented process or making a patented invention. In such a case it is often difficult to distinguish the existence from the exercise. **5–238**

The Court in this case also held that Art.81 had no application as there was no two party arrangement; and that the mere fact that a patent is held, and national law is invoked to protect it, does not of itself constitute an abuse of a dominant position under Art.82. There must be some actual abuse which distorts competition. However, if the right is exercised in a repressive or discriminatory way then Art.82 may be invoked (*Belgian Radio and Television v Fonior and SABAM* [1974] 2 C.M.L.R. 238, where there was an oppressive exercise of copyright held by a performing rights society). In this sense it should be noticed that the *Renault* and *Volvo* cases, discussed in Chapter 6.24.15, are not a demonstration of a new principle of law by the European Court, but are really only instances of the distinction between exercise and existence, which goes right back to *Parke Davis*, coupled with dicta on when the exercise is abusive in relation to control by a manufacturer of the market in spare parts for his product. **5–239**

The next case concerned trade marks. In *Sirena Srl v Eda Srl* [1971] 2 C.M.L.R. 260 it was clear that the Court felt that trade marks were somehow less important or worthwhile rights than patents, and their thinking **5–240** appears to have been influenced by this to some extent. The Court said that trade marks were often used as a mere prop for advertising and that they were the sort of industrial property most likely to partition the EC. In the case an Italian firm (Sirena) took an assignment of a trade mark for a face cream from a US firm. In 1970 the US firm licensed a German manufacturer under the same trade mark. Eda imported the German product into Italy, and was sued by Sirena for infringement of the Italian trade mark. The Court held that the original assignment, in 1937, amounted to an agreement under Art.81, which was still continuing in its effects of restraining the free flow of goods, and hence unenforceable. Therefore the plaintiff had no enforceable right to the Italian trade mark and could not prevent the import of infringing goods from another Member State.

5–241 This decision seems a hard one to accept unless upon the ground that trade marks are not so worthy of protection as patents, and that therefore the property rights in a trade mark are put lower than the need not to avoid partitioning the market. In the words of Art.30 their protection is not "justified".

5–242 The next case, *Deutsche Grammophon GmbH v Metro SB Grossmarkte GmbH & Co KG* [1971] C.M.L.R. 631 concerned copyright. Here, Metro had a French subsidiary that purchased records from DG for sale in France at a low price. Metro reimported those records into Germany and sold them cheaply through its outlets. DG attempted to use German copyright law to prevent the importation. Although DG was entitled to a remedy under German law, the Court prevented them from exercising it on the grounds that its exercise would contravene Art.30. The same principles have been followed in a series of copyright cases and Decisions involving performing rights societies. The most often cited of these is *Musik-Vertrieb Membran GmbH v GEMA* [1981] 2 C.M.L.R. 44.

5–243 The following case was concerned with trade marks, and this applied the ideas in *Sirena v Eda*. In *Van Zuylen Freres v HAG AC* [1974] 2 C.M.L.R. 127 HAG had registered the trade mark HAG for coffee in Germany and (through a subsidiary) in Belgium. During the Second World War, the Belgian subsidiary's assets, including the trade mark, were sequestrated and subsequently assigned to the plaintiffs. The plaintiff now tried to use its Belgian mark to stop the import of coffee from Germany, bearing the German mark. The Sirena case could not apply exactly, as there was no prior agreement between the two parties or their predecessors in title to the marks, and the separation of the marks had occurred involuntarily. Nevertheless the two trade marks had a common origin and the Court therefore held that enforcement of the rights of one owner against the goods bearing the mark of the other owner could not be justified under Art.30.

5–244 The treatment of trade marks can be contrasted with the treatment of patents in the next two cases one of which concerned trade marks and the other patents. They were heard by the European Court together. *Centrafarm BV v Winthrop BV* and *Centrafarm BV v Stirling Drug Co Inc* [1974] 2 C.M.L.R. 480. In the first case Winthrop attempted by the exercise of trade mark rights to prevent the importation into Holland of drugs originating from its UK subsidiary. Again it was not permitted to do this under Art.30. In the second case Centrafarm attempted the same importation from the UK into Holland of drugs manufactured in the UK by Stirling's UK subsidiary. Stirling had patents in both the UK and Holland, and tried to prevent the import by exercising its Dutch patent rights. Here the Court refused again to permit this, but in its judgment it laid down a much more logical way of dealing with patents.

The Court first of all decided what was, in terms of EC law, the right which a patentee could exercise, and then decided if Centrafarm had infringed that right. The right was "the exclusive right to use an invention to manufacture industrial products and put them into circulation for the first time". The right was therefore defined, as far as the EC went, by reference to priority in time and not to territorial exclusivity in a particular area of the EC. The principle of exhaustion of rights was thus applied by the Court in relation to patents looking at the EC as one indivisible market. **5–245**

The Court arrived at this principle as follows. Under Art.30, all restrictions on trade between Member States which have been prohibited by the preceding articles are exempted only if they are "justified" for the protection of industrial property rights. Therefore a restriction cannot be exempted merely because it is necessary for such protection. It must be justified as well in the light of the purpose of the EC Treaty, and this involves a value judgment of the Court—industrial property rights versus free movement of goods. Then the second part of Art.30 gives the guidelines as to when such protection will not be justified—"when it constitutes a means of arbitrary discrimination or a disguised restriction on trade between Member States". Thus the Court is really saying by its definition for EC purposes of the patentee's rights, what rights arising under national law it is prepared to protect and how far it is prepared to allow national law to have effect, bearing in mind the supremacy of the EC Treaty. The Court then went on to say that "where the product has been put on the market in a legal manner, in the Member State from which it has been imported, by the patentee or with his consent, particularly in the case of a proprietor of parallel patents, then a derogation from the principle of the free movement of goods is not justified". Thus the Court avoided any conflict between the exercise and the existence of rights in the terms of the *Parke Davis* case and the wording of Art.30. **5–246**

There was now no doubt that patents under common ownership or control could not be used to split up the market by preventing imports between Member States. Once the patentee puts the goods on the market in one Member State, or authorises someone else to do so, he cannot by the existence of parallel patents in another state prevent their importation into that other state. However, the principle based on the right of the patentee, to be first to put the patented goods into circulation, still allows him to proceed against a naked infringer, and thus leaves the *Parke Davis* judgment intact. In addition, the Court stated categorically that where parallel patents in two states are in different ownership and the original proprietors are legally and economically independent as well, then the holders of those patents can **5–247** exercise their rights to prevent the importation into their respective states of goods manufactured under the other's patent.

5–248 In *Merck & Co Inc v Stephar BV* [1981] 3 C.M.L.R. 463 one point was clarified that had remained obscure after *Parke Davis* and the two *Centrafarm* cases. The previous cases left open the question of whether the exhaustion of rights doctrine could apply only if the product was first put upon the market with the consent of the owner of the right in a Member State where he owned rights which existed to be exhausted. This was because *Parke Davis* concerned action by a naked infringer and the *Centrafarm* cases situations where a licensee under a patent authorised by the holder of the parallel patent had first put the product on the market.

5–249 Here a product was put on the market with the consent of the patentee in Italy (where there was no patent protection available to him) and the Court held that even though he had put the goods on the market in a country where he had no patent rights he had nevertheless in effect exhausted his rights under the patents he did have in other Member States. Since he had chosen to market his products in a state which did not give him patent protection he had to take the consequences, and could not exercise his rights under a patent in another Member State to prevent import of those goods from Italy. Thus the Court saw the important aspect of the doctrine of exhaustion of rights as whether the product had been put on the market with the consent of the owner of the rights, not whether rights existed in the area of the EC in which they were first put on the market. This is a decision which one feels is really only common sense, even if, with respect, it ignores some logical inconsistencies. However, the fact that Art.30 permits the Court to make a value judgment as to what protection is justified, allows it to reach such a conclusion on policy grounds, in the light of the purpose of the Article, without difficulty.

5–250 This case was extended and applied to copyright in Case C-341/87 *EMI Electrola GmbH v Patricia im-und Export Verwaltungsgesellschaft* [1989] 2 C.M.L.R. 413, ECJ. Here it was confirmed that, even if the infringing copy were first put on the market by a third party in a Member State where the relevant intellectual property right had lapsed its import into a state where corresponding rights still subsisted could be prevented, provided the infringing copy had not been put on the market by the third party in the state where rights had lapsed with the consent of the proprietor of the relevant rights.

5–251 The situation at this stage was that patents, copyright and trade marks seemed to have been all approximated but that there were indications that the common origin doctrine might be applied more rigorously in the case of trade marks, and, even that similar trade marks without any common origin might be held to constitute cases of parallel trade marks which could not be enforced against each other to prevent the free flow of goods. If this were so then patents would arguably be treated more favourably than trade marks.

5–252 In the case of *EMI Records Ltd v CBS United Kingdom Ltd* [1976] 2 C.M.L.R. 235, some of these fears were laid to rest. The case concerned a trade mark with a common origin. The mark Colombia was owned worldwide by CBS, the US firm. CBS assigned all the Western European registrations to EMI. EMI now wanted to exercise its trade mark rights to prevent importations into the EC of records from the US bearing the Colombia mark, even though these records had been lawfully put into circulation by CBS. CBS resisted on the grounds of the common origin doctrine as set out in *Van Zuylen v HAG*. The Court ruled firstly that the doctrine of common origin did not apply where the exercise of the rights did not affect trade between Member States. This was the case here, as the exercise of the rights was aimed at stopping importation into the EC as a whole.

A further useful point was that the Court appeared to overrule *Sirena v* **5–253**
Eda in that it declined to hold that the original assignment between CBS and EMI constituted a continuing infringement of Art.81, since, for there to be such an infringement, there would have to be continuing concerted practice between the parties to implement the restrictive effects envisaged by the original agreement. This was not possible where "the said effects do not exceed those flowing from the agreement". This means that once the original agreement has served its purpose—the assignment of the mark—it cannot infringe Art.81 if it is then forgotten by the parties and they do not continue actively to implement any of its provisions, or in some other way carry on a concerted practice or course of conduct, which is based upon the existence of the agreement, and which restricts competition.

The case of trade marks was further clarified with the decision in *Terrapin* **5–254**
(Overseas) Ltd v Terranova Industrie CA Kapferer & Co [1976] 2 C.M.L.R. 482. The two firms were respectively English and German. There was no connection between them. They were both in the building trade, but Terrapin supplied portable buildings, and Terranova supplied building materials. Terrapin attempted to register its mark in Germany, and Terranova opposed this on the grounds that it was confusingly similar to Terranova's mark. In the ensuing proceedings in the German courts, Terrapin appealed against this opposition, and the German Courts formulated the following question for the European Court:

> "Is it compatible with the EC Treaty rules of free movement of goods (Arts 28 and 30) that a firm, relying on its trade mark and its commercial name established in Member State A, opposes the import of similar products manufactured by a firm established in Member State B, whenever these products have been given, in B, a trade mark which is likely to be confused with trade marks protected in A, provided there exists no legal or economic link between the two firms and provided the two trade marks have been created separately?"

The Court ruled that it was compatible, and therefore one of the greatest **5–255**
concerns relating to trade marks under EC law was removed. Apart from the question of the doctrine of common origin, patents, trade marks and copyright all now seemed to be treated in approximately the same way. (The current position on the doctrine of common origin is discussed below.) It

should also be noted that the Court warned that if an owner did not defend his trade mark rights with equal strictness against infringers of all nationalities then he could be found to have exercised an arbitrary discrimination or a disguised restriction within Art.30.

5–256 Again, applying the principle that trade marks represent a "worst case" in the treatment of industrial property rights, it is likely that *EMI v CBS* would apply to patents and copyright in so far as it held that Art.28 is irrelevant to the movement of goods in and out of the EC as a whole. Where there is no connection between the two patent holders there is no problem; and the concept of common origin (even if it were to apply to patents) is not applicable.

5–257 One caveat (which applies to all types of industrial property rights) should, however, be made to the judgment in *EMI v CBS*. Article 81 may apply to an agreement between traders inside and outside the EC if the effect of that agreement is to isolate the EC from outside imports, or prevent some kind of imports into the EC at all. This could affect the state of competition within the EC. EMI did not have any concern about this because there was no agreement in force with CBS at the time it wished to enforce its rights, but the danger is obviously there in appropriate cases, and the Court made this clear. If the outside party also has subsidiaries within the EC, which could market its products if imported, then such an isolation could well affect trade between Member States as well.

5–258 For instance, in *Bureau Européen des Unions de Consommateurs v Commission*, European CFI Case T-37/92, the Court stated that it is *prima facie* not impossible that the agreement whose objective is to restrict imports from a non-member country into only one of the Member States, falls within the scope of Art.81(1) or Art.82. The arrangements in question (agreements between the Society of Motor Manufacturers and Traders of the UK and the Japanese Automobile Manufacturers Association), restricted the import of Japanese cars to the UK only. However, they were by their very nature liable to impair the functioning of the common market. The arrangements restricted imports into the Community even though they only affected the territory of one Member State. They were liable to interfere with the natural movement of trade, and thus affect trade between Member States and reinforce the compartmentalisation of markets on a national basis. Under the application of the "effects" doctrine the Commission could claim jurisdiction in such a case even if both the parties who actually made the arrangement were outside the EC, provided they had subsidiaries inside.

5–259 If Art.81 did not apply, but the Commission still wished to attack the exercise of industrial property rights to prevent imports from outside the EC into the EC, then the rights of the licensee would have to be redefined, in terms of Art.30, to the right to put upon the market for the first time anywhere in the world and not just within the EC. This would seem an extension which goes beyond Art.30 and also beyond the intention of the Community Patent Convention which aims at treating the EC as if it were one indivisible state. This view has been supported by the case of *Polydor Records Ltd v Harlequin Record Shops Ltd* [1982] 1 C.M.L.R. 677 in which the owner of a copyright in the UK tried to prevent the importation of records from Portugal (not then a member of the EC) which infringed that right.

At that time there was in a force a special free-trade agreement between the EC and the state of Portugal which had as its aim the liberalisation of trade between the EC and Portugal. Although the relevant wording of the trade agreement was not exactly the same as Art.30 it was similar. The Court said that there was a distinction between the purposes of the free-trade treaty and the EC Treaty. The latter "seeks to create a single market reproducing as closely as possible the conditions of a domestic market". The former sought only to liberalise certain aspects of trade between the EC and Portugal. **5–260**

The relevant provisions thus had to be interpreted in the light of the particular purposes for which they were intended. "It follows that in the context of the Agreement [with Portugal] restrictions on trade in goods may be considered justified on the grounds of protection of industrial and commercial property in a situation in which their justification would not be possible within the community". If one considers the purpose of the EC Treaty in this light, it seems very unlikely, except in special circumstances clearly affecting cross-border trade within the EC, that Art.28 can be taken to prevent restrictions on imports from outside the EC into a Member State. **5–261**

This conclusion has been confirmed by the trade mark cases discussed below which confined the concept of exhaustion of rights to exhaustion within the Community (see Case C-355/96 *Silhouette International Schmied GmbH & Co. KG v Hartlauer Handelsgesellschaft mbH* [1998] E.C.R. I-04799; Joined Cases C-414/99 to C-416/99 *Zino Davidoff SA v A & G Imports Ltd* and *Levi Strauss & Co. v Tesco Stores Ltd* [2001] E.C.R. I-08691; Case C-244/00 *Van Doren v Lifestyle & Sportswear Handelgesellschaft GmbH* [2003] E.T.H.R. 4. **5–262**

In the early 1980s the emphasis shifted to the area of design rights, packaging, and get-up, which enjoy varied protection under the national laws of various Member States, and had not been the object of any EC-wide harmonisation exercise. The principles evolved under the previous cases relating to patents, copyright and trade marks are relied upon in these "design" cases and, in some cases, elaborated upon. **5–263**

In *Industrie Diensten Groep BV v JA Beele Handelmaatschappij BV* [1982] 3 C.M.L.R. 102 a Dutch court granted an injunction (under a Dutch law which prevented the marketing of copies of another's products which amounted to "slavish imitations") to a Dutch company against a German company to prevent the importation into Holland of goods manufactured in Germany which were "slavish imitations" of goods manufactured in Sweden and marketed for many years in Holland by the Dutch company. Patents relating to the product had long expired and there was no other industrial property right that either of the parties could rely on, by way of copyright or registered design. Thus both parties lawfully put their goods on the market in different Member States of the EC, and the only obstacle the Dutch Company could raise to the import of the German company's goods was the **5–264**

Dutch law against "slavish imitations". The European Court was asked if this law was contrary to Arts 28 and 30, as an unjustified restriction on the free movement of goods.

5–265 The Court pointed out that there had been no EC regulations to harmonise the laws of different Member States concerning "slavish imitation", and therefore the question could be considered specifically only in the light of the Dutch law, which is, subject to Arts 28 and 30, prepared to prevent the import of products lawfully marketed in another Member State. The Court held that in principle this law contravened Art.28 but that (following *Re Cassis de Dijon* [1979] 3 C.M.L.R. 494 and *EC Commission v Ireland* [1982] 1 C.M.L.R. 706) if there were no community rules relating to a particular method of marketing a product: "Obstacles to movement within the Community resulting from disparities between national laws must be accepted in so far as such laws applying without discrimination to both domestic and imported products may be justified as being necessary in order to satisfy mandatory requirements relating in particular to the protection of consumers and fairness in commercial transactions".

5–266 The Court found nothing to suggest that the law discriminated against imported products, and also found that it protected the general interests of consumers by preventing confusion between competing products. It was clear that in this case there was no compelling reason for the products to be identical, so that the marketing of the slavish imitation was causing needless confusion which was not justified on technical economic or commercial grounds. Thus there was no reason why the national law should not protect the rights of the Dutch company (which had been marketing its products for some time), in order to prevent confusion to consumers.

5–267 Again the Court made a value judgment under Art.30, and found that the relevant national law granted rights to the Dutch company the exercise of which to prevent the free flow of goods was "justified" in the interests of fair trading and consumer protection. It is possible to see that a similar result would occur if in the UK one were to invoke the common law rights relating to passing off to prevent the import of copied products. The unregistered design right in the UK, would now have similar considerations applied to it, and it could well be similar in its operation to the Dutch law against "slavish imitations".

5–268 This case should be contrasted with *Danske Supermarked A/S v Smerco A/S* [1981] 3 C.M.L.R. 590 in which the copied products were legally put on the market in the UK with the consent of a Danish undertaking which then tried to stop their importation into Denmark under a national fair trading law. The Court held here that if the goods had been put on the market in the UK with the consent of the Danish firm, then their mere importation into Denmark could never amount to unfair trading of which the Danish firm could complain. The element of consent is what distinguishes this case from *Diensten*. The approach of the Court was very similar to that in its parallel industrial property rights cases and in particular to *Merck v Stephar* discussed above.

5–269 In *Keurkoop BV v Nancy Keen Gifts BV* [1983] 2 C.M.L.R. 47 the European Court considered Art.30 in relation to registered designs. The design for a ladies' handbag was registered by Nancy Keen under the Benelux Uniform Law on Designs. Nancy Keen was not the author of the design, but obtained the exclusive right to the design by reason of being the first to register it in Benelux Territory. The bag was in fact manufactured in Taiwan. Nancy Keen imported the bag via a company in Switzerland. Keurkoop started selling in Holland, by mail order, a bag obtained direct from Taiwan which was virtually identical in design with Nancy Keen's bag. Nancy Keen instituted proceedings in the Dutch courts and obtained an injunction preventing Keurkoop from selling bags "having an appearance identical to, or displaying only minor differences from that of the design" registered by Nancy Kean. The Dutch Court of Appeal referred to the European Court for a preliminary ruling on the question of whether the rights granted by the Benelux Uniform Law on Designs fell within Art.28 or 81 of the EC Treaty.

The Court held that the protection of designs comes within the protection of industrial and commercial property within the meaning of Art.30 inasmuch as its aim is to define exclusive rights which are the distinguishing characteristic of industrial and commercial property. In the absence of any Community regulation or harmonisation of national laws, the rules of free movement of goods under Art.28 do not prevent the operation of a national law like the Benelux Uniform Law on Designs, which grants the exclusive rights in the Benelux territory to the first person to register the design, even though that person is not the author, and the only grounds for objection to registration by persons other than the author are basically lack of novelty in the design. **5–270**

The Court observed that "the protection ... established by Article 30 would be rendered meaningless if a person other than the owner of the right to a design in a Member State could be allowed to market in that state a product which is identical in appearance to the protected design". **5–271**

The following quotations from the judgment neatly summarise the position of the Court with regard to industrial property rights under Art.30, and the protection of industrial property generally under EC law: **5–272**

> "Article 30 is thus intended to emphasise that the reconciliation between the requirements of the free movement of goods and the respect to which industrial and commercial property rights are entitled must be achieved in such a way that protection is ensured for the legitimate exercise, in the form of prohibitions on imports which are 'justified' within the meaning of that Article, of the rights conferred by national legislation, but is refused, on the other hand, in respect of any improper exercise of the same rights which is of such a nature as to maintain or establish artificial partitions within the EC. The exercise of industrial and commercial property rights must consequently be restricted as far as is necessary for that reconciliation. This protection does not extend to opposition of the importation into a Member State of product which has been lawfully marketed in another Member State by or with the consent of the pro-

prietor of the rights himself, or a person legally or economically dependent on him. Nor may the proprietor of an exclusive right rely on his right if the prohibition on importation or marketing ... could be connected with an agreement or practice in restraint of competition contrary to ... Article 81. Although a right to a design, as a legal entity does not as such fall within ... Article 81 the exercise of that right may be subject to the prohibitions contained in the Treaty when it is the purpose, the means or the result of an agreement, decision or concerted practice.

It follows that the proprietor of a right to a design acquired under the legislation of a Member State may oppose the importation of products from another Member State which are identical in appearance to the design which has been filed provided that the products in question have not been put into circulation in the other Member State by or with the consent of the proprietor of the right or a person legally or economically dependent on him, that as between the natural or legal persons in question there is no kind of agreement or concerted practice in restraint of competition, and, finally, that the respective rights of the proprietors of the right to the design in the various Member States were created independently of one another."

5–273 The UK industrial property right of design copyright has also been the subject of decisions in this area. British Leyland attempted to stop parallel imports by means of its ownership of design copyright and copyright in spare parts for its motor vehicles. In *British Leyland Motor Corporation Ltd v TI Silencers Ltd* [1979] F.S.R. 591, Ch D, the defendant claimed that BL was exercising its rights in design copyright contrary to Art.30 to impede the flow of goods in and out of the UK. The English court applied EC law directly, and held that on the facts BL were neither in contravention of Art.30, nor were they in contravention of Art.82 given their policy of freely granting licences on a non-discriminatory basis. The court was particularly concerned to stress that BL treated all infringers in the same way, always offering a licence to copy on non-discriminatory terms, before proceeding to litigation if the offer was refused. This decision has now to be reconsidered in the light of restrictions on rights of manufacturer to control the market in spare parts for his products (see Chapter 4.3.7 and Chapter 6.24.15) but the basic principles still seem to stand as regards the application of Art.30.

5–274 In Case C-19/84 *Pharmon BV v Hoechst AG* [1985] 3 C.M.L.R. 775, there was serious further consideration of the concept of "justification" under Art.30. Here Hoechst attempted to use their patent rights to stop the importation into the UK of a drug which was being lawfully manufactured and put on the market in Holland. The Court held that Hoechst should be granted an injunction because the manufacture and marketing in Holland had not occurred as a result of their free consent, but because they had been forced by legislation to grant a compulsory licence of right. The fact that they were enjoying a royalty under that licence made no difference to their lack of consent. The matter was summed up by the advocate general in his opinion to the Court when he stated that obstacles under Art.30 could be regarded as "justified only where the patent proprietor's consent [to the putting of the patented product on the market] is lacking".

Pharmon was followed in *Thetford Corporation v FIAMMA SpA* [1988] 3 C.M.L.R. 549. That case concerned a patent which was valid under UK legislation, despite prior publication of a specification, only because the specification had been published more than fifty years ago. Thus this type of patent was peculiar to English law. The Court relied on *Pharmon* to uphold the patent, stating that "where national law normally provides for an injunction [to prevent infringement of a patent] that measure is justified under Art 30". **5–275**

Case 434/85 *Allen & Hanbury's Ltd v Generics (UK) Ltd* [1988] 1 C.M.L.R. 70, ECJ, makes the same point as *Pharmon*, but the other way around. Here, the patentee was subject to a licence of right in the UK, and he still sought to rely on his patent to prevent the import of infringing products from Holland. The Court held that a patent subject to a licence of right changes its nature from a right to prevent others putting the patented goods on the market in the relevant territory to a right to receive a reasonable reward for the exploitation of the patent in the relevant territory. Under the circumstances of the licence of right, anyone could manufacture the product in the UK, subject to payment of a royalty. Importers should be put on the same footing as local manufacturers, ie they should be able to import provided they take a licence of right and pay the relevant royalties. On this basis, provided the importer paid the relevant royalty as he was willing to do in this case, there was no "justification" for protection against infringing imports under Art.30, since, because of the licence of right, the patentee had lost the right to prevent infringement anyway. *Allen & Hanbury* was applied and approved in *Generics (UK) Ltd v Smith Kline & French Laboratories Ltd* [1990] 1 C.M.L.R. 14. **5–276**

The question of consent has been subject to some rather delicate distinctions in the area of copyright and performing rights law. In the European Court decision of *Warner Bros Ltd and Metronome Video ApS v Christiansen* [1990] 3 C.M.L.R. 684 the copyright owner of a film sold video cassettes freely in the UK and allowed them to be rented out. He had given no consent to rental of his film in Denmark, and the law of Denmark prohibited such an act without his consent. Christiansen lawfully bought a copy of the film in the UK, lawfully imported it into Denmark and then proposed to rent it out for viewing in Denmark. The Court held that since there could be no rental under the law of Denmark without the consent of the copyright owner, the fact that he had given his consent to the sale and rental of his film in the UK only did not prevent him from withholding his consent to rental in Denmark. (He could not of course prevent someone buying a copy of his film in the UK and importing it into Denmark.) The consideration that the Court gave to the question of "justification" is again consistent with previous cases. It was said, "this is not a question of tempering the principle laid down under Art 30—and hence the rights of whoever imports cassettes—with the question of a public interest such as safeguarding the rights of the cinematographic industry" as it was only **5–277** necessary to reconcile the importer's claim to unrestricted use of what he had lawfully bought in the EC, with the copyright owner's rights to restrict him in that use under the law of Denmark.

5–278 Although it may not at first seem so, these cases discussed above have an effect on the common origin doctrine as applied to trade marks in the *Hag* case, and this issue was discussed in relation to trade marks by the German Appeals Court in *Re Cafe Hag* [1989] 3 C.M.L.R. 154. The facts were basically the same as in the original case, except that the defendant was a successor in title to the original plaintiff, and the plaintiff was the original defendant. In his opinion in *Pharmon* the Advocate-General had indicated his concern with the application of the common origin doctrine in the 1974 *Hag* case, and also cast some doubts on the remarks about common origin in *Nancy Kean*. The reason is that there seems to be little difference in principle between an appropriation of an intellectual property right in one territory by the sequestrator of enemy property and the watering down of the exclusive nature of an intellectual property right by forcing the grant of a compulsory licence. In both cases the state has taken away the owner's rights. This goes to the root of the doctrine, as expressed in *Pharmon*, that the exercise of an intellectual property right to prevent parallel imports is "justified" when the imports were put on the market without the consent of the proprietor. Certainly, in the 1974 *Hag* case, there was no consent to the putting on the market, despite the common origin of the mark. In the current case, the German court decided the matter in the light of *Pharmon*. It held that only the proprietor can affix his trade mark to a product, and that a "third party" cannot do so without his consent. It was thus choosing the consent doctrine of *Pharmon* over the common origin doctrine of *Hag*, its reasoning being that the sequestration broke any connection or consent between the two enterprises, which were not related (partly because the Belgian Hag company had sold its interest to a third party Swiss company) even in the "widest" sense. Thus, imports by the Belgian operation into Germany bearing the Hag mark infringed the German proprietor's exclusive right to affix his mark to products sold in Germany, and such imports were therefore prevented. The German court's reasoning for not applying the 1974 *Hag* case, despite its somewhat unclear distinction between the current facts and those of 1974, seems to be a policy decision, which regards consent as more important than common origin. It criticised the "terse judgment" in *Hag* with "similarity of origin being given a central position, one formulated in a way which is undoubtedly unfortunate".

5–279 The case was referred to the European Court as Case C-10/89 *SA CNL-Sucal NV v Hag AG* [1991] F.S.R. 99. The Court reaffirmed that the doctrine of exhaustion of rights applied to trade marks as well as other intellectual property. In this sense "common origin" is no longer a real issue as a separate doctrine applying to trade marks. The Court reaffirmed that "according to settled case law, Art.30 allows exceptions to the fundamental principle of freedom of movement in the common market of goods covered by an intellectual property right only in so far as such exceptions are justified for safeguarding the rights which are the specific subject matter of that property; and consequently, an owner of an industrial and commercial right protected by the law of a Member State cannot rely on that law in order to prevent the importation or marketing of a protected product which was lawfully sold in the market of another Member State either by the owner of the right with his consent, or by a person connected with him by ties of legal or economic dependence."

The Court stated that trade mark rights constitute an essential element of **5–280** the system of undistorted competition which the EC Treaty aims to establish and maintain. "The specific subject-matter of a trade mark right is to grant the owner the right to use the mark for the first marketing of a product and thereby to protect him against competitors who would like to abuse the position and reputation of the mark by selling products to which the mark has been improperly affixed."

The Court, reversing its own 1974 ruling, now held that the 1944 **5–281** sequestration did indeed break the unity of the mark and destroyed its common origin, that consequently there were now two entirely separate marks, the Belgian mark and the German mark, which happened to be identical or similar to each other, that each mark now enjoyed full protection in its own territory, that marketing by CNL in Belgium was not with the consent (derived from common origin) of Hag and therefore did not exhaust Hag's rights, that therefore Hag was entitled to use German trade mark law to prevent the parallel importation of CNL's coffee if it used the "Hag" mark.

It will be recalled that in this case the separation of the two trade mark **5–282** registrations took place involuntarily. In the most recent case on this subject, *IHT Internationale Heiztechnik GmbH v Ideal Standard GmbH* [1995] F.S.R. 59, the ECJ held that the doctrine of common origin has no application even if the separation took place voluntarily (*i.e.* by an assignment).

The Court held that trade marks are territorial in nature, and that each **5–283** national trade mark should be regarded as a separate mark independent of all the others. Thus, the principle established in *Hag No. 2* applied even where two trade marks in different Member States (originally owned by one person) became owned by two independent persons by reason of a voluntary assignment. The underlying principle of the exhaustion of rights in relation to trade marks, is "unitary control". The function of a trade mark is to guarantee that all goods bearing a particular trade mark have been produced under the control of a single undertaking. The origin which a trade mark is intended to guarantee is not defined by reference to the manufacturer but by reference to the control of manufacture.

The reasoning in the case shows the distinction between the concept of **5–284** exhaustion of rights by putting the goods on the market, and the concept of common origin. The court accepted that by the assignment, the assignor of the trade mark gave an implicit permission to the assignee to be the first to put goods bearing the trade mark on the market in the area covered by the assignment (France), but this consent was not the relevant consent for application of the doctrine of exhaustion of rights. For the concept of exhaustion of rights to apply the owner in the importing state must (directly or indirectly) be able to control the quality of the products to which the trade mark is affixed in the exporting state (*i.e.* he must own that registration of the mark as well, and either affix the mark to the goods when manufactured in the exporting state himself, or someone else must do so as his licensee).

5–285 Since the assignment split the control over the manufacture of the products to which the marks in the two states were to be affixed, the doctrine of exhaustion of rights could not apply, and the concept of common origin was irrelevant.

5–286 It is now possible to summarise the treatment of industrial property rights for EC competition law purposes. The two keys to the problem are the concepts of "consent" and "abuse". The basic right of the holder is to put the goods to which his industrial property right relates upon the market somewhere within the EC (whether or not in an area where his rights exist under national law) for the first time. Once he has done this (or it has been done with his consent, or by a person legally or economically dependent on him) his rights are exhausted and he can no longer use his industrial property rights to prevent the movement of those goods within the EC. He can use his rights against an infringer, who has put goods on the market (for the first time), without lawful authority. He will have this right even if the infringing goods are first put on the market in a state where he has no intellectual property rights, but, of course, in this case, his only remedy will be to prevent imports into states where he does own relevant intellectual property rights. The above deals with the question of "existence".

5–287 It is clear from the cases, however, that the holder of intellectual property rights can exercise them only if that exercise is "justified" under Art.30. This involves a value judgment. This principle was implicit from the time of the *Parke Davis* case, and became quite clear in the *Diensten*, and *Nancy Kean* cases and has been reaffirmed in *Volvo AB v Erik Veng (UK) Ltd* [1989] 4 C.M.L.R. 122; *Consorzio Italiano Della Componentistica Di Ricambio Per Autoveicoli and Maxicar v Regie Nationale Des Usines Renault* [1989] 4 C.M.L.R. 265; and in Case T-76/89 *Independent Television Publications Ltd v Commission (Magill TV Guide Ltd intervening)* [1991] 4 C.M.L.R. 745), which was confirmed by the ECJ [1995] All E.R. (EC) 416. These cases are discussed in detail in Chapter 6.24.15 in relation to the question of liability under Art.82 for refusal to grant a licence of an intellectual property right.

5–288 Nevertheless, once the rightholder has shown that a putting of goods on the market has not exhausted his rights because of the absence of the necessary element of his consent, to deny him the exercise of his right to prevent the putting of those goods on the market would mean that his right would effectively cease to exist. Therefore, once the proprietor has shown his lack of consent as described above, it is clear that exercise of his right will be permitted unless that exercise can clearly be shown to be abusive. *Ideal Standard*, for instance, contains *dicta* that if an assignment of a trade mark were for the purpose of giving effect to an underlying anti-competitive agreement it would be void under Art.81. However, the Court stated that this rule could not be applied mechanically to every assignment, but only after a thorough analysis of the facts in each case. Further, *Renault* and *Volvo* lead us to conclude that the weight of evidence needed to prove that there is an abuse is considerable and that the burden of proof in a practical sense will rest with the side attempting to claim that the rights should not be exercised. *Magill* caused some commentators to consider that the climate had changed and that it would now be far easier to classify a refusal to grant a licence as an abuse. In fact this has not occurred. As discussed in Chapter 6.24.15, *Magill* turned on some very special facts, and has not been widely applied.

A slight variation on the theme of consent and abuse can be seen in the First Council Directive (104/89) on the approximation of the laws of the Member States relating to trade marks. Article 7(1) provides that once the proprietor has put goods on the market in the EC with his trade mark affixed he cannot use his trade mark rights to prevent further commercialisation of those goods unless (Art.7(2)) there exist "legitimate reasons ... especially where the condition of the goods is changed or impaired after they have been so put on the market". This is discussed in more detail in relation to the repackaging cases (see Chapter 5.1.1.4.3), but the provision in the Directive is in fact only another instance of justification under Art.30. Cases relating to the First Trade Mark Directive, discussed below, and relating to repackaging discussed in Chapter 5.1.1.4.3, approach Art.7(2) on the basis that there is no difference in principle between the application of that provision and of the concept of justification under Art.30. **5–289**

It should also be noted that Council Directive 71/98 on the legal protection of designs (which provides for harmonisation of registered design rights amongst EU Member States) and Council Directive 6/2002 which has brought into existence a Community Design Right (covering both registered and unregistered designs) have equivalent provisions to Art.7(1) of Directive 104/89 (Arts 15 and 24 respectively) which relate to exhaustion of rights for both Member States' registered designs and the registered and unregistered community design. These Directives are discussed in more detail in Chapter 4.3.7. **5–290**

The latest cases on parallel imports and exhaustion of rights once again focus upon the importance of the value judgment of the court when deciding what protection is justified under Art.30. **5–291**

In Case C-317/91 *Deutsche Renault AG v Audi AG* [1995] F.S.R. 738, Audi owned German registrations for the mark Quattro in respect of four wheel drive cars. Renault's German subsidiary introduced onto the German market a four wheel drive car called the Espace Quadra and applied to remove the Quattro mark from the Register, on the grounds that its presence and the provisions for its protection under German law impeded the importation of the Espace Quadra into Germany and was therefore an abuse under Arts 28 and 30 of the EC Treaty. **5–292**

The matter was referred to the European Court. The Court applied *Keurkoop BV v Nancy Keen Gifts BV*, *Volvo AB v Erik Veng (UK) Ltd*, *Thetford v Fiamma SA*, *Centrafarm BV v Winthrop* and *SA CNL-SUCAL NV v HAG GF AG (HAG No.2)*. **5–293**

The Court held that the conditions for the protection of a mark such as Quattro were, subject to the requirement for "justified" protection under **5–294**

Art.30, a matter for national law. A manufacturer from another Member State was not precluded under German law from claiming the protection granted, nor did the protection vary according to whether or not the goods bearing the mark were of national or foreign origin. Accordingly, the national provisions did not represent either arbitrary discrimination or a disguised restriction on intra Community trade within the terms of Art.30. The adoption of criteria for a finding of confusion were a matter for national law, subject to Art.30. Finally, there was nothing to suggest that the German court's interpretation of the concept of confusion differed depending on whether the proprietor of the mark was German or from another Member State. There was, therefore, no abuse of Arts 28 or 30.

5–295 In *British Sky Broadcasting Group Ltd v Lyons (David)* [1995] F.S.R. 357, Ch D, Sky applied for summary judgment in respect of Lyons's unauthorised importation and sale of decoders (in alleged breach of s.298 of the Copyright, Designs and Patents Act 1988 which prohibits the import into the UK of devices that provide unauthorised access to broadcasts) which enabled purchasers to receive Sky's programmes without authorisation. Lyons contended, *inter alia*, that s.298 of the 1988 Act amounted to a quantitative restriction on imports, which are prohibited by the EC Treaty Arts 28 and 30, because the section only applied to transmission from the UK. Sky contended that s.298 was justified under Art.30 in respect of protection of industrial and commercial property.

5–296 The Court granted summary judgment and dismissed the Euro-defence. There are two principles to be applied in interpreting Art.30. First it is for national legislature to determine the conditions and procedures for the protection of a right such as a transmission right, and secondly they must not constitute a means of arbitrary discrimination or a disguised restriction on trade between Member States. Since s.298 applied to everyone and was not different in kind or effect to national conditions for obtaining rights such as copyright, it did not amount to illegal discrimination or a disguised restriction on trade between Member States.

5–297 In the Joined Cases C-267/95 and C-268/95 *Merck Sharp & Dohme Ltd v Primecrown Ltd* and *Beecham Group plc v Europharm of Worthing Ltd* [1996] E.C.R. I-062852 a novel argument was raised as to grounds on which the use of patent rights to prevent parallel imports could be justified.

5–298 Merck and Beecham claimed that they had an ethical (and indeed perhaps even a legal) duty to patients in Spain and Portugal to supply them with their pharmaceutical products, but the local legislation in those states fixed the prices at which those products could be sold so low that a substantial trade was carried on in the export of those products to other areas of the EU. This resulted in loss of revenue and profits for pharmaceutical companies which eroded the economic value of their patents and made it harder to fund sufficient research and development activity for new pharmaceutical products.

5–299 There are two strands to this argument. The first is that, if the alleged ethical or even legal duty to put the products on the market in Spain and Portugal could be proved, then Merck and Beecham could not be said to have consented to putting their products on the market in those states. In this case, the exception to the rule in *Merck v Stephar* set down in *Pharmon v Hoechst* [1985] E.C.R. 2281 would apply. The second strand is that, irrespective of the question of consent, Merck and Beecham were "justified" in terms of Art.30 in using their patents to prevent parallel imports because of the adverse economic effects that they suffered as a result of the state pricing policy in Spain and Portugal.

So far as the first strand was concerned, the Court accepted that if such a legal obligation could be shown to exist this would mean that "the patentee cannot be deemed, within the meaning of the ruling in *Merck v Stephar*, to have given his consent to the marketing of the products concerned. He is therefore entitled to oppose importation and marketing of those products in the State where they are protected. It is for the patentee to prove the existence of such a legal obligation, before the national court from which an order prohibiting imports is sought". It must be said that on the facts of this case, the Court could not see that such a legal obligation existed. **5–300**

However, in the absence of a specific legal obligation, the Court refused to accept any argument based on ethical or moral obligations. The Court stated that "such considerations were, at any rate in the present context, difficult to apprehend and distinguish from commercial considerations. Such ethical obligations cannot, therefore, be the basis for derogating from the rule on free movement of goods laid down in *Merck v Stephar*". **5–301**

The Court also refused to accept that the economic effects created by price controls "justified" the prevention of parallel imports. The Court stated: "this circumstance cannot justify a derogation from the principle of free movement of goods. It is well settled that distortions caused by different price legislation in a Member State must be remedied by measures taken by the Community authorities and not by the adoption by another Member State of measures incompatible with the rules on free movement of goods". **5–302**

The next case to be heard, *Parfums Christian Dior SA and Parfums Christian Dior BV v Evora BV* [1997] E.C.R. I-06013 was an elaboration on the question of exhaustion of trade mark rights under Directive 104/89. **5–303**

Evora operated a chain of chemists" shops. They were not appointed within Dior's selective distribution system, but they sold Dior products in the Netherlands obtained by means of parallel imports. Dior did not attempt to contest the legality of selling these products but when Evora advertised them for sale as part of a Christmas promotion Dior claimed that the advertising did not correspond to the luxurious and prestigious image of the Dior trade marks, and brought proceedings for infringement of those marks and to prevent the continuation of such catalogue advertising. Dior also claimed that the advertising carried out by Evora infringed its copyright. **5–304**

The Court ruled that when exhaustion of rights occurred under Art.7, this exhaustion was total, so that all of the rights under Art.5 were exhausted at the same time, including the right to control the use of the trade mark by third parties in relation to the goods which had been put on the market. "Thus the reseller of goods, in respect of which trade mark rights have been **5–305** exhausted under art 7 is also free to make use of the trade mark in order to bring to the public's attention the further commercialisation of those goods".

5–306 The Court then turned to Dior's assertion that the advertising was prejudicial to the "mental condition" of the goods—that is their luxury status and allure. The Court accepted that Art.7(2) did give a right in some instances to challenge the use of the mark, but that a balance had to be struck in all cases between the right of the proprietor to prevent advertising or other treatment of his products or their packaging which was prejudicial to the mark and the right of the third party reseller to sell the products concerned and advertise them in the way that was customary in his particular trade.

5–307 The Court considered that where the reseller used methods of advertising customary in his trade even if they were not the same as those used by the trade mark owner himself, the trade mark owner could not object unless he could show that, "given the specific circumstances of the case, the use of the trade mark in the reseller's advertising seriously damages the reputation of the trade mark". Of course in any specific case, it would be for the national court to decide this question on the facts of the case.

5–308 Finally, so far as the question of copyright was concerned, the Court stated, after an analysis of the case law that: "it is sufficient to hold that, in circumstances such as those in point in the main proceedings, the protection conferred by copyright as regards the reproduction of protected works in a reseller's advertising may not, in any event, be broader than that which is conferred on a trade mark owner in the same circumstances".

5–309 Case C-355/96 *Silhouette International Schmied GmbH & Co. KG v Hartlauer Handelsgesellschaft mbH* E.C.R. [1998] I-04799 was concerned with the application of the concepts of exhaustion of rights in relation to trade marks, but this time with the question of the concept of international exhaustion of rights, when products are put on the market for the first time outside the EC.

5–310 Silhouette produces spectacles in the higher price ranges. It markets them worldwide under the trade mark "Silhouette", registered in Austria and most countries of the world. Hartlauer was a distributor of low price spectacles. Silhouette refused to supply it because it considered distribution of its products by Hartlauer would be harmful to its image as a manufacturer of top-quality fashion spectacles. Silhouette sold 21,000 out-of-fashion spectacle frames to a Bulgarian company, Union Trading. Hartlauer subsequently obtained the spectacles from Union Trading and reimported them into Austria and sold them there. Silhouette brought an action for interim relief seeking an injunction restraining Hartlauer from offering spectacles or spectacle frames for sale in Austria under its trade mark.

5–311 Silhouette claimed that it had not exhausted its trade mark rights, because Art.5 of Directive 104/89 provides that rights are exhausted only when the products have been put on the market in the EEA by the proprietor or with his consent. Since Silhouette had not consented to Hartlauer's reimportation into the EC, its rights could not therefore have been exhausted.

However, the Austrian courts had applied, before the passing of Directive 104/89, a concept of the international exhaustion of trade mark rights. Under this principle, if the products had been put on the market anywhere in the world by or with the consent of the trade mark owner, then the trade mark owner's rights in relation to those products would have been exhausted. If the Austrian Court continued to apply the principle of international exhaustion of trade marks, Silhouette would not be able to proceed against Hartlauer. **5–312**

The Austrian Courts referred the matter to the European Court for a ruling as to whether the Austrian rules providing for international exhaustion of rights in a trade mark were contrary to Art.7 of the Directive. **5–313**

The Court held that, on a true construction, Art.7 only provided for the exhaustion of trade mark rights in respect of goods put on the market by the proprietor or with his consent in the EC. **5–314**

Article 7 did not apply to international exhaustion of rights. Moreover, the article was prescriptive in that it prevented Member States applying any other principle in relation to exhaustion of trade mark rights under local law. The Court stated: **5–315**

> "The Directive cannot be interpreted as leaving it open to the Member States to provide in their domestic law for exhaustion of the rights conferred by a trade mark in respect of products put on the market in non-member countries. This, moreover, is the only interpretation which is fully capable of ensuring that the purpose of the Directive is achieved, namely to safeguard the functioning of the internal market. A situation in which some Member States could provide for international exhaustion while others provided for Community exhaustion only would inevitably give rise to barriers to the free movement of goods and the freedom to provide services."

A similar decision on similar facts was reached in Case C-173/98 *Sebago v Maison Dubois* [1999] E.C.R. I-4103.

The same principles on international exhaustion of rights were applied to copyright under the Copyright Directive (Reg.250/91) in Case T-198/98 *Micro Leader Business v Commission* [2000] 4 C.M.L.R. 886 in relation to the supply of software. MLB, supplied wholesale office and computer equipment which included computer software products manufactured by an American company, MC. MLB imported copies of the French language version of MC's Canadian software into France. The software was identical to the product sold in France by MC's subsidiary, MF, but lower in price. MF took steps to prevent the sale of any French language versions of the Canadian product to anyone other than an approved MF distributor thus effectively preventing MLB from importing copies of the Canadian software. MLB made a complaint to the European Commission, contending that the activities of MF and MC breached the EC Treaty (Art.81 and Art.253). **5–316**

The Commission dismissed the complaint. MLB then instituted pro- **5–317** ceedings in the European Court seeking annulment of the Commission's decision. MLB contended that MC and MF were engaged in concerted practices designed to keep prices on the French market high, and that MC and MF had abused their dominant position in the French market by fixing prices at an artificially high level.

5–318 The Court held that the Commission had been correct in their conclusion that MC and MF could not have been guilty of concerted practices since they formed a single economic entity and that by virtue of Directive 250/91, rights of distribution into the EC had not been exhausted following sale of a software package into Canada and therefore unauthorised importation of the Canadian product into France did amount to an unlawful infringement of MC's copyright.

5–319 The Commission's conclusion that the prohibition in question amounted to lawful enforcement of copyright pursuant to Directive 250/91 and that there had been insufficient evidence provided to substantiate the assertion of abuse of dominant market position in France was, however, flawed. Although normally enforcement under copyright was lawful, such enforcement could amount to abuse in exceptional circumstances. The Court referred to Case T-76/89 *Independent Television Publications Ltd v Commission (Magill TV Guide Ltd intervening)*, [1991] 4 C.M.L.R. 745 (see the discussion of this case in Chapter 6.24.15). Evidence had been provided of alleged abusive conduct and such evidence should not have been dismissed out of hand without an investigation into whether the conduct complained of had been abusive in line with the findings in *Magill.*

5–320 Joined Cases C-414/99 to C-416/99 *Zino Davidoff SA v A & G Imports Ltd* and *Levi Strauss & Co. v Tesco Stores Ltd* [2001] E.C.R. I-08691 also dealt with the interpretation of Art.7 of the Directive 104/89, and were a reference to the European Court from the High Court in the UK. The facts and questions to be determined were similar in both cases, and thus reference will be made only to the case relating to Levi Jeans.

5–321 Levi Strauss manufactured and sold jeans products to distributors outside the EEA. These products found their way into the UK and were there sold by various distributors. Levi Jeans were, in particular, sold by Tesco, one of the leading supermarket chains in the United Kingdom, and Costco, a wholesaler and retailer of clothes. They obtained jeans originally sold by Levi's or on its behalf, from traders who imported them from authorised retailers outside the EEA in the US, Mexico and Canada. The contracts pursuant to which they acquired those products contained no restrictive covenants to the effect that the goods were, or were not, to be sold in a particular territory.

5–322 Levis claimed that the import and sale of Levi jeans by the defendants constituted an infringement of their trade mark rights. They stated that in the United States and Canada they had informed their authorised retailers, both in writing and orally, of guidelines including a "no-wholesale" stipulation, by virtue of which the goods could be sold only to end purchasers. In their written order acknowledgement forms they reserved the right, which they exercised several times, to cease supplying their products to a retailer violating that prohibition. In Mexico, they told their authorised wholesalers not to sell for export. Tesco and Costco pointed out that they were not bound by any contractual restriction. Levis, they argued, had not attempted to impose or give notice of any restriction to run with the goods, nor had they reserved any rights in any way. In their submission, therefore, the operator buying the jeans in question was entitled freely to dispose of them.

The Court held that following the decisions in Case C-355/96 *Silhouette International v Schmied* [1998] E.C.R. I-4799 and Case C-173/98 *Sebago v Maison Dubois* [1999] E.C.R. I-4103 it was clear law that Arts 5 and 7 of the Directive provided only for exhaustion of Community rights. "The effect of the Directive is therefore to allow the proprietor to market his products outside that area without exhausting his rights within the EEA". The real question at issue in this case was to lay down the criteria by which to "determine the circumstances in which the proprietor of a trade mark may be regarded as having consented, directly or indirectly, to the importation and marketing within the EEA by third parties who currently own them, of products bearing that trade mark, which have been placed on the market outside the EEA by the proprietor of the mark or with his consent". **5–323**

This amounted to deciding whether there had to be express consent to such marketing within the EEA or whether such consent could also be implied. After analysing the legislation and the case law, the Court held that: **5–324**

> "It follows that consent must be expressed positively and that the factors taken into consideration in finding implied consent must unequivocally demonstrate that the trade mark proprietor has renounced any intention to enforce his exclusive rights. It follows that it is for the trader alleging consent to prove it and not for the trade mark proprietor to demonstrate its absence. Consequently, implied consent to the marketing within the EEA of goods put on the market outside that area cannot be inferred from the mere silence of the trade mark proprietor. Likewise, implied consent cannot be inferred from the fact that a trade mark proprietor has not communicated his opposition to marketing within the EEA or from the fact that the goods do not carry any warning that it is prohibited to place them on the market within the EEA. Finally, such consent cannot be inferred from the fact that the trade mark proprietor transferred ownership of the goods bearing the mark without imposing contractual reservations or from the fact that, according to the law governing the contract, the property right transferred includes, in the absence of such reservations, an unlimited right of resale or, at the very least, a right to market the goods subsequently within the EEA. A rule of national law which proceeded upon the mere silence of the trade mark proprietor would not recognise implied consent but rather deemed consent. This would not meet the need for consent positively expressed required by Community law."

The Court also held that national rules on the enforceability of sales restrictions against third parties had no relevance, nor did the fact that the **5–325** importer of the infringing goods did not know that the trade mark proprietor objected to their being put on the market in the EEA.

5–326 The way in which the passage quoted above from *Davidoff* should be interpreted has recently been considered by the European Court in Case C-244/00 *Van Doren v Lifestyle & Sportswear* Handelgesellschaft *GmbH* [2003] E.T.M.R. 44.

5–327 In its judgment, the Court summarised the facts as follows:

> "Stussy Inc., a company established in Irvine (United States) is the proprietor of the word and device mark 'Stüssy', which is registered in respect of clothing. Goods bearing this trade mark are marketed worldwide. They have no particular characteristic which would enable them to be recognised as having been allocated to a specific sales territory. Van Doren has exclusive distribution rights in respect of Stussy Inc.'s products in Germany. Stussy Inc. authorised the claimant to bring legal proceedings in its own name to obtain injunctions against, and claim damages from, third parties for infringement of the trade mark.
>
> According to Van Doren there is in each country of the European Economic Area ('EEA') only one exclusive distributor and general importer for 'Stüssy' articles and that distributor is contractually bound not to sell the goods to intermediaries for resale outside his contractual territory. Lifestyle markets in Germany 'Stüssy' articles which it has not acquired from Van Doren. Van Doren brought proceedings against Lifestyle claiming that the articles distributed by Lifestyle were products which had originally been put on the market in the United States, and that their distribution in the Federal Republic of Germany and other Member States had not been authorised by the trade mark proprietor."

5–328 After proceedings at first instance in Germany, with judgment in favour of Van Doren, Lifestyle appealed to the *Bundesgerichtshof* (the German appeal court). That Court considered that the existence of the conditions for exhaustion of the trade mark right, which is a defence under the German trade mark legislation, must in principle be proved by the defendant, according to the general principle of German law that each party to proceedings must prove the existence of the conditions for application of the rule on which he relies. However, it was concerned as to the impact of Arts 28 and 30 of the EC Treaty on this rule, and referred the issue to the European Court for clarification.

5–329 The European Court noted the *Bundesgerichtshof's* concerns as follows:

> "However, the referring court took the view that if the burden of proof is imposed on the third party against whom a trade mark proprietor has brought proceedings, there is a risk that a dealer unconnected with the proprietor could be prohibited from marketing products bearing that mark even where the products have been put on the market in the EEA with the consent of the proprietor. In general, a dealer will be readily able to show from whom he has purchased goods but he will not be able to

make his suppliers reveal the previous supplier or identify other links in the distribution chain. Moreover, even if he were able to trace the distribution channel back to the trade mark proprietor and to show that the goods were put on the market in the EEA with the consent of that proprietor, his supply source would be liable to dry up immediately.

Under those circumstances there is a risk that the trade mark proprietor will use the trade mark to partition national markets. The court therefore raises the question whether Art 28 requires provision for an exception to the general rule [under German law] that the full burden of proving the factual conditions for exhaustion of the right conferred by a trade mark lies with the third party."

After considering the legislation and the case law, the Court confirmed their effect in the following terms: **5–330**

"The effect of the Directive is therefore to limit exhaustion of the rights conferred on the proprietor of a trade mark to cases where goods have been put on the market in the EEA and to allow the proprietor to market his products outside that area without exhausting his rights within the EEA. By making it clear that the placing of goods on the market outside the EEA does not exhaust the proprietor's right to oppose the importation of those goods without his consent, the Community legislature has allowed the proprietor of the trade mark to control the initial marketing in the EEA of goods bearing the mark."

The real issue, when considering these exhaustion of rights cases, is that there are two matters which are relevant. The first is the question of where the goods were first put on the market by or with the consent of the proprietor. If this was within the EEA, then his rights are exhausted. However, if the goods were first put on the market outside the EEA, then the second question arises. Did he import, or consent to the import, of the goods into the EEA? Only if this question is answered in the affirmative will his rights be exhausted. In *Van Doren*, it was necessary to answer both these questions and this was why the Court distinguished the case from the earlier decisions: **5–331**

"It must be observed that there are differences between *Zino Davidoff* and *Levi Strauss* and the present case. In the former cases, in which the Court had to consider the way in which the trade mark proprietor's consent to marketing in the EEA is expressed and proved, it was common ground that the goods at issue had been marketed outside the EEA by the trade mark proprietor or with his consent and then imported and marketed in the EEA by third parties. In paragraphs 46, 54 and 58 of *Zino Davidoff and Levi Strauss* the Court held that, ***in such circumstances*** [emphasis added], the consent of a trade mark proprietor to marketing within the EEA cannot be presumed, that it must be express or implied and that it is for the trader who relies on that consent to prove it.

In the present case, the dispute in the main proceedings turns primarily on whether goods were placed on the market for the first time within or outside the EEA. Such a situation raises the question *inter alia* of the burden of proving where the trade-marked goods were first put on the market in cases of dispute on that point."

5–332 It can be seen that there are two separate matters which require proof in these cases:

- Where the goods were first put on the market.
- Were they put on the market in the EEA with the trade mark proprietor's consent.

Of course if it can be shown that the goods were first put on the market in the EEA then the second point follows automatically. The Court then ruled upon the questions raised by the *Bundesgerichtshof* as follows:

> "The answer to the question referred should therefore be that a rule of evidence according to which exhaustion of the trade mark right constitutes a plea in defence for a third party against whom the trade mark proprietor brings an action, so that the conditions for such exhaustion must, as a rule, be proved by the third party who relies on it, is consistent with Community law and, in particular, with Articles 5 and 7 of the Directive.
>
> However, the requirements deriving from the protection of the free movement of goods, enshrined, *inter alia*, in Articles 28 EC and 30 EC may mean that this rule of evidence needs to be qualified.
>
> Accordingly, where a third party succeeds in establishing that there is a real risk of partitioning of national markets if he himself bears that burden of proof, particularly where the trade mark proprietor markets his products in the EEA using an exclusive distribution system, it is for the proprietor of the trade mark to establish that the products were initially placed on the market outside the EEA by him or with his consent. If such evidence is adduced, it is for the third party to prove the consent of the trade mark proprietor to subsequent marketing of the products in the EEA."

5–333 Up to the decision in *Davidoff*, the situation seemed fairly clear, in that the concept of exhaustion of rights had been expressed as having application only within the EC, so that international exhaustion of rights was irrelevant. The attack on this position through the approach to the question of consent is subtle. If the manufacturer puts the goods on the market outside the EC but somehow consents in advance to their being put on the market within the EC, his rights will be exhausted as soon as importation takes place. *Davidoff* seems, on a straightforward reading of the judgment to hold that the importer must prove the manufacturer so consented and that, although consent may be express or implied, mere silence can never be deemed to be consent.

Van Doren has affirmed *Davidoff* but added a gloss to it. As a general rule a defendant in a trade mark (and, presumably, any other intellectual property right) infringement action must prove all of the facts necessary to establish his defence. In general this rule is compatible with Community law. However, an infringer may be able to claim protection under Art.28 from revealing his sources of supply in order to prove where the goods were first put on the market, if he can show that revealing those sources would allow the trade mark proprietor to cut off sources of parallel imports within the EEA. **5–334**

Where the protection of Art.28 is claimed, it will be for the trade mark proprietor to show where he first put the goods upon the market. If he can show that this was outside the EEA, then the burden of proof reverts under the rules in *Silhouette* and *Davidoff* to the infringer to prove that those goods then first came into the EEA with the trade mark proprietor's consent. **5–335**

The situation as to burden of proof is now much clearer, even if the actual circumstances in which an infringer can claim the protection of Art.28 are likely to be somewhat vague and subject to the discretion of the court, under the usual practice of deciding what is "justified" in the particular circumstances. **5–336**

However, the position does now present some problems for the trade mark proprietor. How is it possible for him to prove where goods where first put on the market, and thus, in appropriate cases, to shift the burden of proof to the infringer? The situation is relatively easy where the goods have some unique characteristics or formulation and it can be shown that such goods are never first put on the market in the EEA, but always sold in specific territories outside the EEA. However, where the goods themselves have no unique characteristics, as was the case in *Van Doren*, the only solution seems to lie in the use of labelling or other forms of identification such as serial or batch numbering. **5–337**

This possibility was contemplated in Case C-349/95 *Loendersloot v George Ballantine & Son Ltd* [1997] E.C.R. I-06227, discussed in Chapter 5.1.1.4.3, and was also considered in *Van Doren*. The *Bundesgerichtshof* suggested that such marking could be a solution in appropriate cases, and the European Court discussed this. It is, however, fair to say that the European Court did not specifically approve the measure and the advocate-general was somewhat critical of the idea in his submission to the Court. The Court stated: **5–338**

> "It [the *Bundesgerichtshof*] considers that a possible solution might be to impose that burden on the third party [*i.e.* of proving that the products were put on the market in the EEA by the trade mark proprietor or with his consent] only if the manufacturer has first used such means as can reasonably be expected of him to distinguish, by affixing signs, goods which have been put on the market in the EEA by him or with his consent from goods which have been put on the market outside the EEA. Where it appears that the trade mark proprietor consistently acts in such a way, the third party is required to prove that the conditions for exhaustion are satisfied, if, prima facie, the goods could have been first put on the market only outside the EEA."

5–339 At least in the current state of the law, manufacturers of generic goods would be well advised to mark them in order at least to assist in determining where they were first put on the market, and also to be resolute and consistent in pursuing unauthorised importation into the EEA as an infringement whenever it actually occurs and they become aware of it, so that no tacit consent to such imports can be said to have been given.

5–340 *5.1.1.4.2 Partitioning the market through general regulatory issues* The above discussion has focused upon the use of industrial property rights to prevent parallel imports. Attempts have been made to use other methods such as local regulations relating to consumer protection, or limitations on the way in which warranty service is provided. These issues are discussed in relation to selective distribution agreements in Chapter 6.24.14.

5–341 The general principles in this area in relation to Arts 28 and 30 were laid down in the European Court Case C-120/78 *Rewe-Zentral AG v Bundesmonopolverwaltung fur Branntwein* [1979] 3 C.M.L.R. 494 more commonly known as the *Cassis de Dijon* case. The case concerned the refusal by the German Spirits Monopoly to permit the import into Germany of a certain French liqueur (Cassis de Dijon) because of its insufficient alcoholic strength.

5–342 The Court held that as there were no common rules yet in force regulating the manufacture and sale of alcohol it was for Member States to control these matters in their own countries and so the interruption of free movement of goods must be accepted in order to ensure fiscal control, the maintenance of health standards, commercial fairness and consumer protection. However, the Court also held that the imposition of a rule laying down a minimum content of alcohol in one Member State infringed Art.28 of the EC Treaty. Provided the goods were clearly labeled so that consumers were not misled, there was no reason relating to the criteria otherwise laid down in the judgment which could justify such national regulations.

5–343 The general principle under Art.28 was that it should be possible for goods made and sold in one Member State to be sold freely in another. In other words, just as in the case of the use of intellectual property rights to restrict parallel imports, the Court was exercising a value judgment under Art.30, in relation to the national regulatory regime, and found that there were no reasons which in terms of Art.30 justified the restriction which it imposed on minimum alcohol content. Although there is now a common regime across the EC relating to the sale and manufacture of alcohol, the principle still holds good in relation to other regulatory matters where no such general regime exists.

5–344 Another example, again relating to alcohol, but of more general application, was *Re Criminal Proceedings Against Karl Prantl* [1985] 2 C.M.L.R. 238. Prantl was prosecuted under a German law which made it an offence to sell in Germany any wine in a particular shape of bottle (called Bocksbeutel) unless it had been produced in certain districts in Germany, which had traditionally used that bottle. Prantl imported from Italy, and sold in Germany, Italian wine bottled in bottles which were virtually identical in shape to the Bocksbeutel. The Italian bottles were likewise traditionally used in certain areas of Italy for bottling Italian wines. The German courts held that Prantl had breached the German law, but submitted to the European Court the question of whether the law was in contravention of the rules of free movement of goods under Arts 28 and 30 of the EC Treaty.

The Court held that although it was established in many cases that where **5–345**
the Commission had produced EC regulations covering such matters they should take precedence over national laws incompatible with them, in this case, there were no such regulations, even though the wine industry had been largely covered by EC Regulations. There was no doubt that this law impeded the free movement of goods, and that it did not fall within the *Cassis de Dijon* principles. It was a measure which discriminated against imported products, since only producers in that particular area of Germany could market wine in the Bocksbeutel in Germany. Foreign producers like the Italians who traditionally used the Bocksbeutel shape for their bottles would not be able to import into Germany without changing their packaging for exports which would increase their costs, make things generally more difficult, and put them at a disadvantage in selling their products in Germany.

Regulation 355/79, regulating the wine industry, states that the purpose of **5–346**
any rules relating to description and presentation should be to make such descriptions and presentations sufficiently clear and accurate to enable the buyer to form an opinion of the products, but that the information given should take account of different customs and traditional practices in Member States. The German law had failed to take account of the traditional practices of the Italian Bocksbeutel users, and an exclusive right to use a certain type of wine bottle granted to nationals of one state by national law could not be used to bar the importation of products in the same or similar shape bottles produced in accordance with a fair and traditional practice in another Member State. The argument that the German law prevented consumer confusion was not accepted because the EC Commission had already put out comprehensive requirements as to the labelling of wine bottles to prevent confusion.

As regards Art.30 the fact that a penal sanction was imposed by the law **5–347**
did not justify the protection of the law on grounds of public policy under Art.30, nor could the law be justified under Art.30 as the protection of an industrial or commercial property right on the grounds that the bottle is used traditionally by national producers, if identical or similar bottles are used in another Member State in accordance with a fair and traditional practice for marketing wines produced in that state.

Following the principles in *Cassis de Dijon*, it can be seen that manu- **5–348**
facturers who wish to limit parallel imports by reference to national regulatory regimes have to find some ground which "justifies" that restriction within the meaning of Art.30. The most common grounds relied on are product safety or the need to ensure that consumers are not misled.

For instance, in *Re Herbicides,* Commission Decision [1993] O.J. L272, **5–349**
the Commission investigated exclusive distribution arrangements for her-

bicides. The suppliers found a novel way to restrict parallel imports into Germany by the use of product registrations. The supplier formulated a product, under its trade name, for Germany, and then registered that product under this particular formula, as required by law, in Germany. Only products registered with that precise formula could be sold in Germany. It then supplied its German distributor with products under its trade mark to that formula. Products supplied under its trade mark to other Member States were then manufactured using a different formula, which meant that if those products were imported into Germany they could not be sold, because the formula used in their manufacture was different to the formula that had been registered. The Commission found that the differences in formula for different territories did not appear to have been caused by specific German requirements, and that the formula used in France could have been registered in Germany. The Commission held that the practices described gave absolute territorial protection to the German distributor, and therefore contravened Art.81.

5–350 It is similarly instructive to consider the series of cases relating to marketing authorisations for pharmaceuticals for human use.

5–351 The primary community legislation in this area is Council Directive 65/65, although over the years it has been heavily amended. Article 3 initially provided that no proprietary medicinal product could be placed on the market in a Member State unless a prior authorisation had been issued by the competent authority of that Member State. Article 1(1) of Directive 65/65 defines a proprietary medicinal product as "any ready-prepared medicinal product placed on the market under a special name and in a special pack". Article 4 lists the information and documents which must accompany an application for a marketing authorisation. Article 5 of Directive 65/65 provides that a marketing authorisation "shall be refused if, after verification of the particulars and documents listed in Article 4, it proves that the proprietary medicinal product is harmful in the normal conditions of use, or that its therapeutic efficacy is lacking or is insufficiently substantiated by the applicant, or that its qualitative and quantitative composition is not as declared. Authorisation shall likewise be refused if the particulars and documents submitted in support of the application do not comply with Article 4".

5–352 Article 4.8 of the Directive, as amended by Council Directive 21/87, established an "abridged" procedure which, subject to certain conditions, relieved the manufacturers of medicinal products which are essentially similar to medicinal products already authorised from having to provide the results of pharmacological and toxicological tests and of clinical trials, thus saving the time and expense necessary to assemble such data, and avoiding the repetition of tests on humans or animals where these are not absolutely necessary. This abridged procedure is designed to facilitate the marketing of so-called generic products.

5–353 A generic medicinal product is a copy of an innovative medicinal product whose formula can be reproduced by other manufacturers, the copy being sold under the same description at a price generally lower than the innovative product. In such a case, since the entry into force of Directive 21/87, an applicant for a marketing authorisation for a generic medicinal product may refer to the results in the file relating to the original innovative proprietary medicinal product, either with the consent of the holder of the marketing authorisation for the innovative product, or otherwise if a period of six to ten years has elapsed since the first marketing of the original proprietary product in the Community (data exclusivity period).

It can be seen that this article provides a certain protection for the manufacturer of the innovative product in that the manufacturer of the generic product cannot get access to the file supporting the authorisation for the innovative product without the consent of the innovative manufacturer until the data exclusivity period has expired. This gives the innovative manufacturer a head start in exploiting his product, before generic manufacturers can use the abridged procedure to get on the market easily and quickly. **5–354**

As originally constituted this regulatory regime was not completely harmonised on a community-wide basis, and the reconciliation of each national regulatory system with the requirements for free movement of goods under Art.28 had to be reconciled by the use of the principles of "justification" under Art.30 in accordance with the principles laid down in *Cassis de Dijon*. **5–355**

However, on January 1, 1995 a new Community system of marketing authorisations came into force following the adoption of Council Directive 39/93 amending Directives 65/65, 318/75 and 7319/75 in respect of medicinal products and Council Regulation 2309/93 laying down Community procedures for the authorisation and supervision of medicinal products for human and veterinary use. It established two new procedures: a decentralised procedure providing for the mutual recognition of marketing authorisations; and a centralised procedure providing for a Community marketing authorisation issued by the European Agency for the Evaluation of Medicinal Products; a marketing authorisation issued by that Agency is valid throughout the Community. **5–356**

Prior to January 1, 1995, manufacturers attempted in general to persuade courts to interpret the possibilities of the lack of harmonisation in the regulatory regime restrictively, so as to limit parallel imports, while parallel importers, of course, argued for the most flexible interpretation. In fact, the chronological progression of the cases shows a continual extension in favour of parallel imports. **5–357**

In Case C-104/75 *Officer Van Justitie v de Peijper* [1976] E.C.R. 613 the European Court set out the general principles applicable in the absence of a community wide harmonised regulatory scheme. Centrafarm purchased Valium manufactured in the UK by Hoffman-La Roche and marketed it in Holland. Hoffman-La Roche's Dutch distributor marketed in the Netherlands Valium which had also been manufactured by Hoffman-La Roche. The Dutch Valium sold at a much higher price than the UK Valium. There was a Dutch marketing authorisation for the Valium put on the market in the Netherlands by the Dutch importer and a UK marketing authorisation for the Valium, put on the market in the UK, which Centrafarm had pur- **5–358** chased there. On the basis of their national legislation the Netherlands authorities wished to prevent Centrafarm from marketing the Valium imported from the UK, because it was impossible for the parallel importer (i) to provide the authorities with the full file relating to the quality, efficacy and safety of the medicinal product—a file which the importer authorised by the manufacturer had, however, already submitted to the same authorities in order to obtain the marketing authorisation for that product—and (ii) to obtain from the manufacturer the supervisory records relating to each batch.

5–359 The Court held that "these requirements were unnecessarily restrictive and therefore could not be justified in terms of Art.30". If the UK and the Dutch Valium were the same (since they were both manufactured to the same formula by Hoffman-La Roche, albeit in different countries) then the UK Valium could take advantage of the Dutch marketing authorisation once it was imported into the Netherlands. The manufacturer or his duly appointed importer would have to show that there were several variants of the product, each with a different therapeutic effect, before there would be any justification for treating the variants as different products requiring different marketing authorisations.

5–360 This judgment gave rise to a Commission communication on parallel imports of proprietary medicinal products for which marketing authorisations have already been granted ([1980] O.J. L143/8). In that communication the Commission accepted that importing Member States may check that a proprietary medicinal product that has been imported in parallel is in fact covered by the marketing authorisation already granted. For that purpose the competent authorities may require the parallel importer to supply certain information readily accessible to him, for example the name and permanent address of the person responsible for placing the product on the market in the Member State concerned, and any other information useful for the marketing of the proprietary medicinal product in question, such as its composition, therapeutic indications, side effects and specimens.

5–361 It also stated that where the competent authorities have at their disposal all the information submitted by an authorised importer or by the manufacturer, submitted when a previous application for a marketing authorisation for the same product was made, they are entitled to require the manufacturer, or his duly appointed importer, to state whether several variants of the same medicinal product have been manufactured and whether those variants show that there are differences having a notable therapeutic effect which would justify treating those variants as different medicinal products.

5–362 That communication was not binding, and in fact the Commission never proceeded finally to embody it in a Directive, but the principles laid down in *de Peijper*, of course continued to have effect. Additionally, Germany, the Netherlands, the United Kingdom and Denmark instituted a simplified registration procedure, based on the principles of that communication, for medicinal products imported in parallel.

5–363 Case C-201/94 *R. v The Medicines Control Agency Ex p. Smith & Nephew*

Pharmaceuticals Ltd and *Primecrown Ltd v The Medicines Control Agency* [1996] E.C.R. I-5819 followed and extended the principles in *de Peijper*.

Smith & Nephew manufactured and marketed Ditropan in the UK under licence from the US company Marion Merrell Dow (hereinafter "MMD"). The MCA granted a marketing authorisation for Ditropan to Smith & Nephew in 1991. In 1993 Primecrown applied for an authorisation under the Medicines Control Agency's ("MCA") parallel import authorisation procedure (known somewhat cryptically as MAL 2 (PI)) for the purpose of importing and selling, in the UK, Ditropan manufactured and marketed in Belgium by MMD's Belgian subsidiary (hereinafter "MMD Belgium") pursuant to a Belgian marketing authorisation. **5–364**

The pharmaceutical assessor appointed by the MCA concluded that the Belgian Ditropan was identical in formulation to Smith & Nephew's Ditropan, and the MCA granted the authorisation sought by Primecrown.It subsequently withdrew the authorisation when it discovered that MMD Belgium and Smith & Nephew were not connected companies, and that the only link was they were both licensed by MMD in the USA. Thus, unlike *de Peijper*, the UK and Belgian Ditropan were not produced by the same manufacturer. **5–365**

The Court concluded that the requirement of MAL 2 (PI) that the parallel import had to be manufactured by the same entity, or at least by connected entities, was too restrictive in terms of the principles laid down in *de Peijper* and in terms of Art.28. Nor did it matter that the licensor was in this case situated outside the EC. The decisive factor was whether the two products, although not identical in all respects, were manufactured according to the same formulation and using the same active ingredient and also had the same therapeutic effects. This was all that the MCA were entitled to lay down as a requirement, in this respect, for granting a licence under MAL 2(PI). If this requirement were fulfilled, the MCA must treat the parallel import product as being covered by the marketing authorisation for the local UK product "unless there are countervailing considerations relating to the effective protection of the life and health of humans". (*i.e.* a "justification" for not doing so in terms of Art.30). **5–366**

However, if the parallel import did not satisfy those criteria, the relevant national authority had no choice but to go through the full procedure provided for under Directive 65/65 and to require all of the information necessary to justify the grant of a full marketing authorisation within the termas of that Directive. **5–367**

This case also deals with the application of the abridged procedure. Smith & Nephew complained that the MCA had used the details in their file for the full UK authorisation to grant the parallel import licence to Primecrown. They saw this as an abuse of the abridged procedure in Art.4.8 since the file was accessed before the expiry of the data exclusivity period. The Court laid down that a parallel import does not fall within the definition of a generic product covered by the abridged procedure. Thus the safeguards in the abridged procedure had no relevance. The issue was whether Smith & Nephew could claim that restricting access to their file was justified under **5–368**

Art.30. The Court held that this restriction was not justified. Nothing in Art.30 covered the case, and the Council had already decided what protection it would give to innovative companies in relation to generic products. There was no justification for extending this protection to parallel imports.

5–369 In Case C-94/98 *R. v The Licensing Authority established by the Medicines Act 1968 (represented by the Medicines Control Agency) Ex p. Rhône-Poulenc Rorer Ltd and May & Baker Ltd* E.C.R. [1999] I-08789, which again related to periods before January 1, 1995, the Court considered an extension of this principle.

5–370 In 1989 and 1993, M & B, a member of a group of companies which operate in the research-based pharmaceutical industry, obtained marketing authorisations issued by the MCA covering various forms of tablets and capsules of the product called "Zimovane", which is used for the treatment of insomnia. M & B appointed RPR as its agent to manufacture and market that product. RPR developed a new version of Zimovane. It contains the same active ingredients and has the same therapeutic effect as the old version, but is manufactured by a different manufacturing process and using different excipients which provide a particular benefit to public health compared with the old version of Zimovane. Thus, strictly speaking old and new Zimovane were different products.

5–371 RPR obtained a licence for new Zimovane from the MCA and, upon its request, the licence for old Zimovane was withdrawn. Accordingly, RPR then marketed only new Zimovane in the UK, but continued to market old Zimovane in the other Member States, under the relevant local licences. Before the authorisations relating to old Zimovane were revoked, parallel import licences for that version were granted to several companies, in accordance with MAL 2 (PI). When the parent authorisation upon which they depended was revoked by the MCA, they lapsed under para.12 of MAL 2 (PI). However, the MCA decided to treat the parallel import licences as still valid, those licences then being appended to the marketing authorisation issued for new Zimovane. The MCA also issued three new parallel import licences for the old version of Zimovane, and also appended them to the primary authorisation for new Zimovane.

5–372 M & B and RPR lodged applications for judicial review of the MCA's decisions claiming that, in the absence of any subsisting primary marketing authorisations for the old version of Zimovane in the UK, imports of that version into the UK were not parallel imports, so it was contrary both to the legislation applicable in the UK (*i.e.* MAL 2 (PI) and to Community law (ie the principles in *de Peijper* and *Smith & Nephew*) to treat them as such.

5–373 In its decision, the Court extended the principle in *Smith & Nephew*. In that case, the product which was the subject of the parallel importation was identical in both the state of export and the state of import, and primary authorisations were current in both states. Here it was arguable that, since old Zimovane and new Zimovane were not identical products, there was now no primary authorisation for old Zimovane in the state of importation on which parallel importers of old Zimovane could rely.

5–374 However, the Court held that, provided old Zimovane and new Zimovane had the same active ingredients and the same therapeutic effect and that the different excipients used in the two versions did not cause any additional risk to health, the MCA was entitled to treat the two products as equivalents, since they were both manufactured and put on the market by the same undertaking. The local regulatory authority under Directive 65/65 (*i.e.* the MCA) was the competent authority to decide these questions of fact.

Since the MCA had so decided, it was within its authority to treat the authorisation for old Zimovane (in the exporting Member State) and the authorisation for new Zimovane (in the UK) as in effect authorisations for the same product. It could therefore continue to extend the benefit of the parallel import authorisation procedure under MAL 2 (PI) to the imports into the UK of the old Zimovane, just as if an authorisation for the old Zimovane was still in force in the UK. A contrary interpretation of MAL 2 (PI) would not have been justified under Art.30, and would therefore have been contrary to the basic principle laid down in *de Peijper*. **5–375**

In Case C-172/00 *Ferring Arzneimittel GmbH v Eurim-Pharm Arzneimittel GmbH* [2003] E.T.M.R. 9, the Court held that Art.28 precluded national legislation whereby a licence holder's withdrawal of marketing authorisation automatically invalidated a parallel import licence. This was so even where there was a new version of the medicinal product on the market of the relevant Member State. However, such a rule was subject to restrictions preventing the parallel importer continuing to rely on the withdrawn licence, which would be justified under Art.30 where there was a risk to public health arising out of the coexistence of the two versions on the same market. Whether there was such a risk was a matter on which the court could not pronounce, and must be decided by the national authority. However, it was conceivable that Ferring's concerns as to risks were valid, since it was necessary to keep the old product refrigerated while this was unnecessary for the new product, and the risk of confusion might arise even with appropriate labelling. **5–376**

This case goes much further than *May & Baker*, because in that case there was at least an equivalent primary authorisation in force in the state of importation, covering new Zimovane. **5–377**

The Court explained that where a marketing authorisation of reference was withdrawn at the request of its holder for reasons other than the protection of public health (*e.g.* in order to put a new variant of the product on the market) there did not appear to be any grounds justifying the automatic cessation of the validity of the parallel import licence. First, the withdrawal of a marketing authorisation of reference did not mean in itself that the quality, efficacy and non-toxicity of the old version—which continued to be lawfully marketed in the Member State of exportation under the marketing authorisation issued in that state—was called into question. Second, *pharmacovigilance* (*i.e.* the monitoring of pharmaceutical products to ensure their compliance with health and safety requirements) satisfying Directive 319/75 could ordinarily be guaranteed for medicinal products that were the subject of parallel imports through cooperation with the national authorities of the other Member States by means of access to the documents and data **5–378** produced by the manufacturer or other companies in the same group relating to the old version in the Member States in which that version was still marketed on the basis of a marketing authorisation still in force.

5–379 The next case, Case C-433/00 *Aventis Pharma Deutschland GmbH v Kohlpharma GmbH and MTK Pharma Vertriebs-GmbH* [2002] E.T.M.R. 54 dealt with the new harmonised regime in force since January 1, 1995. It shows how the principles set out in the repackaging cases (see Chapter 5.1.1.4.3) and the authorisation cases can overlap. It is possible to obtain a central marketing authorisation for pharmaceutical products under Council Regulation 2309/93. This authorisation applies to any state in the EC, but its terms are precise and cover not just the product itself but also the various labels and forms of packaging under which it can be marketed. Where the product is to be sold in more than one package, specific approval for each package has to be obtained and this approval is then valid throughout the EC.

5–380 Aventis manufactured the medicinal product "Insuman" under a central marketing authorisations for packs containing ten cartridges of 3 ml, and for packs containing five cartridges of 3 ml. It markets Insuman in Germany in packs of ten cartridges and in France in packs of five cartridges. Kohlpharma and MTK imported Insuman from France in packs of five cartridges and repackaged it in packs of ten with German labelling for marketing in Germany. These packs of ten thus complied with the central authorisation obtained by Aventis in respect of their packs of ten units with German labelling. Aventis claimed that this repackaging was not necessary because instead of repackaging, it was sufficient to bundle two packs of five together and stick a German label over them. Since the repackaging was not necessary to market the product in Germany, it was an infringement of Aventis's trade mark rights in terms of the repackaging cases.

5–381 The European Court disagreed with Aventis. The Court said "the detailed and specific requirements regarding the packaging of the medicinal products which are the subject of a central marketing authorisation, which are intended to prevent consumers from being misled and thereby to protect public health, preclude the bundling of the packages of those medicinal products". In other words marketing must take place in one of the authorised packages or not at all. The question for the national court to answer was whether it was possible to sell the products in Germany in their original French packages but with a German label. If that was either illegal or impracticable then it would be "objectively necessary" for the parallel importers to repackage the products in the German packaging in order that the imported product could gain effective access to the market in Germany.

5–382 Joined Cases C-15/01 and C-113/01 *Paranova Läkemedel AB* and *Paranova Oy* are currently before the European Court. The issues in these cases are the same as in *Ferring* and it would seem the same answers would be returned by the Court to the Swedish and Finnish courts as were given in *Ferring* to the German court.

5–383 The Opinion of Advocate General Jacobs delivered to the Court on December 12, 2002 contains a helpful summary and commentary on the whole course of the pharmaceutical authorisation cases, and the principles behind them, as discussed above. Much of the commentary in this section is based upon his opinion. The Opinion concludes with a discussion of *Ferring*:

> "The Court made it clear in *Ferring* that ... the question of the existence and the reality of the risk [to the health and life of humans] is a matter which is primarily for the competent authorities of the Member State of import to determine, and the mere assertion by the holder of the marketing authorisation for the new and old versions that there is such a risk is not sufficient to justify prohibition of the importation of the old version. The determination by the competent authority of the existence and reality of the risk must in my view be substantiated: the mere assertion would not be sufficient if the authority could not demonstrate that that concern was justified.
>
> In my view the combined effect of the abovementioned *pharmacovigilance* requirements (See Directive 2001/83/EC of the European Parliament and of the Council of 6 November 2001 on the Community code relating to medicinal products for human use, [2001] O.J. L 311, p. 67) is such that it would be only in exceptional cases that the competent authority of the Member State into which a medicinal product was imported in circumstances such as those of the present case could prohibit such imports on the ground that it could not ensure *pharmacovigilance*."

5.1.1.4.3 Partitioning the market through prohibition of repackaging The repackaging cases combine the principles discussed in relation to intellectual property rights and regulatory regimes. Where a reseller of parallel imports has to repackage or relabel products in order to comply with a regulatory regime in force in the state of importation, can the manufacturer oppose the repackaging, and therefore the importation, on the grounds that his trade mark rights are infringed when the reseller reaffixes his trade mark to the new package? In other words is the opposition (which amounts to an indirect ban on exports) prohibited under Art.28 or justified under Art.30. **5–384**

Hoffmann La Roche & Co AG v Centrafarm VPE GmbH [1978] 3 C.M.L.R. 217 and *Centrafarm BV v American Home Products Corporation* [1978] E.C.R. 1823 were the first cases on the subject of repackaging. In both cases Centrafarm purchased goods in one country which had a trade mark lawfully affixed to them. In one case it then imported the goods into another country, and repackaged them, affixing another trade mark. In the other, it repackaged them into a bulk pack and reaffixed the same trade mark. In both cases it had no right to deal with the trade mark it affixed, and the owner brought actions to stop its use in this way. Centrafarm relied on the doctrine of the exhaustion of rights, but in both cases the court said that in principle the doctrine could not apply here because Centrafarm, having no rights in the trade mark which it had affixed, was in the position of an unauthorised infringer. **5–385**

However, the Court cautioned that although in theory such rights could be enforced, Art.30 would prevent their enforcement if the motive behind their enforcement (as opposed to their objective effect) was not to protect **5–386** the trade mark but to prevent parallel imports by means of a disguised restriction on trade. Once again the concept appears to be that national rights can only be enforced under Art.30 to the extent that this is "justified" in terms of that Article.

5–387 A third repackaging case was heard in Holland, *Hoechst AG* v *Centrafarm BV* [1980] 1 C.M.L.R. 650, in which Centrafarm claimed that they had to repackage Hoechst products imported by them into Holland, in order to comply with Dutch labelling regulations, and to insert into the package an instruction leaflet in Dutch. Therefore, they had no choice but to disturb the package and replace it with another on which they affixed the Hoechst trade mark. As in previous cases Hoechst tried to use its Dutch trade mark to prevent Centrafarm affixing the Hoechst mark to the package. Hoechst succeeded as its primary intention was held to be to prevent unauthorised use of its trade mark. The fact that this incidentally contributed to a partitioning of the EC by preventing the parallel import of Hoechst products from Germany to Holland was held to be irrelevant. Once again Centrafarm was in the position of a naked infringer putting products on the market for the first time under a trade mark to which it had no right. Again the situation might have been different if it could have been shown that it was Hoechst's true aim to stop parallel imports.

5–388 In *Pfizer v Eurim* [1982] 1 C.M.L.R. 406 the repackager did not disturb the original blister packed product, but enclosed it in an outer package, through which the original package and the trade mark of Pfizer were visible. In these circumstances, where there was no disturbance of the package, and no reaffixing of the trade mark, the Court held that protection of the trade mark under Art.30, to the extent of preventing this activity, was not justified. The trade mark was meant in part to reassure customers as to the quality of the product, and since the original package was clearly not tampered with, the trade mark still performed that purpose in this case. Irrespective of whether the trade mark owner was intending to protect his rights, or to partition the market, the Court felt that in these precise circumstances the objective fact that the exercise of the rights would partition the market was sufficient, and it was not necessary to consider the intention of the owner in relation to their exercise.

5–389 In a further case between Hoffmann-La Roche and Centrafarm in the German Federal Supreme Court ([1984] 2 C.M.L.R. 561) the Federal Supreme Court applied the repackaging decisions of the European Court and ruled that if the trade mark owner has packaged the product in one Member State in a particular size and in another Member State in another pack size, thus making it more difficult for importation of products in the one pack size into the Member State where the products are sold in the other pack size, then the trade mark owner can resist the repackaging into appropriate pack sizes for the territory of importation, and the affixing of the trade mark owner's mark on the new packaging provided that the prevention was intended not to partition the market but to protect the trade mark. The right to resist was also subject to the proviso that the differences in packaging sizes were not adopted for the purpose of making cross border trade difficult, but for genuine reasons connected with servicing the market for which each of the packages was originally intended.

The repackaging cases also made it clear that the exercise of rights under a trade mark in accordance with Art.30 does not mean, purely because its owner has a dominant position in the goods to which it relates, that that exercise will be regarded as an abuse of that dominant position, provided that the exercise is "justified" in terms of Art.30.

The most recent European Court cases on repackaging are Joined Cases **5–390** C-427/93 and C-436/93 *Bristol-Myers Squibb v Paranova A/S* and Joined Cases C-71/94, C-72/94 and C-73/94 *Eurim-Pharm Arzneimittel GmbH v Beiersdorf*, all reported at [1996] C.E.C. 716) and Case C-232/94 *MPA Pharma GmbH v Rhone Poulenc Pharma GmbH* [1996] E.C.R. I-03671.

In *Bristol-Myers* (a case brought partly to decide the scope of Art.7 of the **5–391** Directive 104/89, discussed above), the Court accepted the principles in *Hoffman-La Roche* that the trade mark owner could resist the repackaging unless the effect of his use of the trade mark rights was not to protect his mark, but artificially to partition the market. The Court however stated that where the producer packages in different methods or different sizes for different territories, such that the method and size of package prevents exports from one territory to another, the repackager must be allowed to repackage in such a way that importation is possible. However, the producer would be entitled to resist any repackaging which went beyond what was necessary to achieve this purpose. The Court also accepted the principle in *Hoffman-La Roche* that the producer could resist packaging which adversely affected the product, but stated that this requirement should be construed narrowly and could not be invoked too lightly. The Court also affirmed the principles in *Hoffman-La Roche* that the repackager must include a statement on the package that repackaging had taken place, but held that this statement did not have to declare that the repackaging had taken place without the producer's consent. The Court also accepted that the producer had the right to resist if the repackaging did not "appropriately present" the product (*e.g.* it was defective, of poor quality or untidy) and that the repackager must give the producer notice of the intention to repackage and supply him with a sample so that he could ascertain this.

In the other cases listed above, the Court gave further details and **5–392** guidelines as to the kind of repackaging that the producer could or could not resist, depending upon the particular circumstances of each case. However, the most complete statement of those guidelines appears in Case C-232/94 *MPA Pharma GmbH v Rhône-Poulenc Pharma GmbH* [1996] E.C.R. I-03671).

Rhône-Poulenc marketed "Orudis retard" in Germany as a remedy for rheumatism, in packets of 20, 50 and 100 tablets contained in blister packs, thereby complying with the standard sizes recommended by various professional and commercial groups and by the German sickness insurance institutions. In Spain, Orudis retard was sold only in packets of 20 tablets, by a sister company of Rhône-Poulenc. Pharma imported Orudis retard in parallel from Spain, and marketed it in Germany. In order to obtain packages of 50 tablets, it repackaged the product in new external packaging designed by itself, in which it placed the blister packs taken from various original Spanish packets.

5–393 The new external packaging contained statements that MPA was the importer and responsible pharmaceutical firm, that Rhone-Poulenc was the manufacturer and that MPA had repackaged the products to comply with German regulations. MPA also inserted in the packet user information which it drew up itself. Rhône-Poulenc regarded the marketing of the repackaged product as an infringement of the trade mark "Orudis", and applied for an injunction against Pharma.

5–394 First, the Court confirmed that the approach under Art.7 of Directive 104/89 and the approach under Art.30 of the EC Treaty was identical. The Court said: "those two provisions, which pursue the same result, must be interpreted in the same way". The Court continued:

> "In answering the question whether a trade mark owner's exclusive rights include the power to oppose the use of the trade mark by a third party after the product has been repackaged, account must be taken of the essential function of the trade mark, which is to guarantee to the consumer or end user the identity of the trade-marked product's origin by enabling him to distinguish it without any risk of confusion from products of different origin. That guarantee of origin means that the consumer or end user can be certain that a trade-marked product offered to him has not been subject at a previous stage of marketing to interference by a third person, without the authorization of the trade mark owner, in such a way as to affect the original condition of the product.
>
> Therefore, the right conferred upon the trade mark owner to oppose any use of the trade mark which is liable to impair the guarantee of origin so understood forms part of the specific subject-matter of the trade mark right, the protection of which may justify derogation from the fundamental principle of the free movement of goods."

5–395 The Court took the opportunity to summarise the previous case law on the subject and to clarify it by setting out the following guidelines:

- The trade mark owner cannot oppose the repackaging of the product in new external packaging when the packet size used by the owner in the Member State where the importer purchased the product cannot be marketed in the Member State of importation by reason, in particular, of a rule authorizing packaging only of a certain size or a national practice to the same effect.

- Where, in accordance with the rules and practices in force in the Member State of importation, the trade mark owner uses many different sizes of packaging in that state, the finding that one of those sizes is also marketed in the Member State of exportation is not enough to justify the conclusion that repackaging is unnecessary.

- The owner may oppose the repackaging of the product in new external packaging where the importer is able to achieve packaging which may be marketed in the Member State of importation by, for example, affixing to the original external or inner packaging new labels.
- The trade mark owner may oppose any repackaging involving a risk of the product inside the package being exposed to tampering or to influences affecting its original condition. As regards pharmaceutical products, repackaging must be regarded as having been carried out in circumstances not capable of affecting the original condition of the product where, for example, the trade mark owner has placed the product on the market in double packaging and the repackaging affects only the external layer, leaving the inner packaging intact, or where the repackaging is carried out under the supervision of a public authority in order to ensure that the product remains intact.
- The mere removal of blister packs from their original external packaging and their insertion with one or more original packages into new external packaging or their insertion into another original package cannot affect the original condition of the product inside the packaging.
- As for an operation consisting in the addition to the packaging of new user instructions or information in the language of the Member State of importation, there is nothing to suggest that the original condition of the product inside the packaging is directly affected thereby.
- The possibility of the importer providing certain additional information should not be excluded, however, provided that information does not contradict the information provided by the trade mark owner in the Member State of importation.
- Since it is in the trade mark owner's interest that the consumer or end user should not be led to believe that the owner is responsible for the repackaging, an indication must be given of who repackaged the product, clearly shown on the external packaging of the repackaged product. It is, however, not necessary to require that the further express statement be made on the packaging that the repackaging was carried out without the authorisation of the trade mark owner, since such a statement could be taken to imply, that the repackaged product is not entirely legitimate.
- A clear indication may be required on the external packaging as to who manufactured the product, since it may indeed be in the manufacturer's interest that the consumer or end user should not be led to believe that the importer is the owner of the trade mark, and that the product was manufactured under his supervision.
- There remains the possibility that the reputation of the trade mark, and thus of its owner, may nevertheless suffer from an inappropriate

presentation of the repackaged product. In such a case, the trade mark owner has a legitimate interest, related to the specific subject-matter of the trade mark right, in being able to oppose the marketing of the product. In assessing whether the presentation of the repackaged product is liable to damage the reputation of the trade mark, account must be taken of the nature of the product and the market for which it is intended. In the case of pharmaceutical products, the requirements to be met by the presentation of a repackaged pharmaceutical product vary according to whether the product is sold to hospitals or, through pharmacies, to consumers. In the former case, the products are administered to patients by professionals, for whom the presentation of the product is of little importance. In the latter case, the presentation of the product is of greater importance for the consumer.

- Finally, the trade mark owner must be given advance notice of the repackaged product being put on sale. The owner may also require the importer to supply him with a specimen of the repackaged product before it goes on sale, to enable him to check that the repackaging is not carried out in such a way as directly or indirectly to affect the original condition of the product and that the presentation after repackaging is not such as to damage the reputation of the trade mark. Similarly, such a requirement affords the trade mark owner a better possibility of protecting himself against counterfeiting.

5–396 Case C-352/95 *Phytheron International SA v Jean Bourdon SA* [1997] E.C.R. I-01729) again concerned Art.7 of Directive 104/89, the product at issue was manufactured in Turkey, where Schering, a company incorporated under German law and belonging to the German Hoechst group, had it manufactured by another subsidiary before importing it into Germany. Hoechst held the relevant trade mark in both France and Germany. Bourdon imported the product from Germany into France. French law required that the product could not be imported into France without the addition of certain information on its packaging. This could be dealt with by applying an extra label. Schering opposed such repackaging as an unjustified interference with its trade mark rights. It relied, as grounds for the contention that its rights had not been exhausted, partly on the place of manufacture and partly on the fact that manufacture and importation into Germany had been carried out by another subsidiary.

5–397 The Court held that Art.7 applied where the owner of the trade mark in the state of import and the owner of the mark in the state of export are the same or where, even if they are different persons, they are economically linked, for example as subsidiaries of the same group as in the case of Hoechst here. The Court also stated that it was of no importance for the application of Art.7 whether or not the product protected by the mark was manufactured in a non-member country. Once the product was imported into the EC, the trade mark owner's rights were exhausted. This was the case whether the importation was carried out by the trade mark owner, or another company in the same group as the owner.

In any event, the Court held, based on the principles set out in the repackaging cases, that the mere addition on the label of information could not constitute a legitimate reason, within the meaning of Art.7(2) of Directive 104/89, to oppose such repackaging, provided that the label so altered did not omit important information or give inaccurate information and its presentation was not liable to damage the reputation of the trade mark and that of its owner. **5–398**

Case C-349/95 *Loendersloot v George Ballantine & Son Ltd* [1997] E.C.R. I-06227) dealt with repackaging of a non-pharmaceutical product, whisky, and, here the Court held that somewhat different rules should apply given the nature of the product. **5–399**

Ballantine produced and marketed whisky in bottles to which it affixed labels bearing its trade marks. Those marks also appeared on the packaging of the bottles. In addition, Ballantine also printed identification numbers on the labels, and, in some cases, also printed the name of the importer into a particular territory, and/or the word "pure" on the label. **5–400**

Loendersloot was a transport and warehousing firm. Its customers included traders who engaged in parallel imports. Loendersloot removed the existing label from the whisky bottles in order to remove the identification numbers, and, in certain cases, the name of the importer and the word "pure". It would then reaffix labels bearing the original trade marks, but without these additional items. It did this in respect of the identification numbers to prevent the manufacturer tracing and cutting off sources of parallel imports, and in respect of the word "pure" and the declaration of the importer, because this was not permitted under the local regulations of certain states into which the whisky then went as a parallel import. **5–401**

Ballantine brought proceedings against Loendersloot in the Netherlands seeking an order restraining Loendersloot from this activity. After reaching the appeal courts in the Netherlands, the matter was submitted to the European Court for a ruling. **5–402**

The Court observed that the task of the national courts, who have to assess whether the relabelling is necessary in order to prevent artificial partitioning of the markets between Member States, is different in cases such as that in the current proceedings and cases concerning the repackaging of pharmaceutical products. "In the latter the national courts must consider whether circumstances in the markets of their own States make repackaging objectively necessary. In the present case, on the other hand, the national court must assess whether the relabelling is necessary to protect the sources of supply of the parallel trade and to enable the products to be marketed on the various markets of the Member States for which they are intended". **5–403**

Ballantine contended that the removal of the identification numbers was unnecessary to enable the products in question to be marketed on the markets of the various Member States in accordance with the rules in force there. The court accepted this and agreed that it was often necessary for producers to put batch numbers on their products to comply with Council **5–404**

Directive 89/396 on indications or marks identifying the lot to which a foodstuff belongs or to facilitate product recalls.

5–405 If the identification numbers had the sole purpose of identifying the flow of products to prevent parallel imports, and there was no legitimate reason for their existence, then presumably the trade mark owner would not be justified under Art.28 of the EC Treaty or Art.7(2) of Directive 104/89 in resisting the relabelling required to remove them. As the Court said above, the question was whether such relabelling would then be necessary to protect the sources of supply for parallel importers. In this case, it presumably would be.

5–406 The problem would occur if the identification numbers were in fact necessary to comply with Community law, or to facilitate product recall, but were also in fact used by the trade mark owner to trace and prevent parallel imports. In this case, the Court considered that the remedy of the parallel importer lay in competition law rather than under Art.7.

5–407 This is not a very satisfactory answer. It should be remembered that unless the supplier is in a dominant position unilateral actions to cut down or prevent parallel imports are not a breach of EC competition law. This was held in *Bayer AG v Commission* which related to a refusal to supply (see the discussion in Chapter 5.27). *A fortiori* this principle should apply to the action of a manufacturer who prints identification numbers on his labelling for legitimate reasons and then also uses them in order to trace and prevent parallel imports. In the absence of a dominant position, it would seem that the parallel importer would be left without a remedy, since, according to the Court, the manufacturer would be "justified" under Art.30 or have a legitimate reason under Art.7.2 for opposing the removal of the labels.

5–408 Finally, in this context, it should also be remembered that there is a growing body of opinion that products should be marked in order to trace their movement into and around the EC, so that it can be shown where they were first put on the market for the purposes of helping discharge the burden of proof in relation to exhaustion of rights (see *Van Doren v Lifestyle & Sportswear Handelgesellschaft GmbH* discussed in Chapter 5.5.3.)

5–409 All of this would suggest that, except in the case of demonstrated abuse of a dominant position, the parallel importer should not be entitled to relabel solely to remove identification marks.

So far as the removal of the word "pure" and the importer's name from the labels, and in certain cases substituting the parallel importer's name, was concerned, if the labelling laws of the country of importation required this, the relabelling would be necessary and Ballantine and others could not oppose it under Art.7(2).

5–410 The Court pointed out that there were certain restrictions to the right to relabel even in these circumstances:

> "However, the person carrying out the relabelling must use means which make parallel trade feasible while causing as little prejudice as possible to the specific subject-matter of the trade mark right. Thus if the statements on the original labels comply with the rules on labelling in force in the

> Member State of destination, but those rules require additional information to be given, it is not necessary to remove and reaffix or replace the original labels, since the mere application to the bottles in question of a sticker with the additional information may suffice."

The Court then turned to the requirement of the Court's case law as regards repackaging of pharmaceutical products, that a person who repackages products must inform the trade mark owner of the repackaging, must supply him, on demand, with a specimen of the repackaged product, and must state on the repackaged product the person responsible for the repackaging. "The rules in the pharmaceutical cases do not apply in their totality given the nature of the products in the current proceedings. Having regard to the nature of the action of the person carrying out the relabelling, the interests of the trade mark owner, and in particular his need to combat counterfeiting, are given sufficient weight if that person gives him prior notice that the relabelled products are to be put on sale". **5–411**

Microsoft Corp v Computer Future Distribution Ltd [1998] E.T.M.R. 597, Ch D also related to a case of removal of labels with distinguishing marks on them. It was not a true repackaging case as no substitute labels were affixed. The case is thus a combination of the law on exhaustion of trade mark rights (rather like *Silhouette*) and repackaging. **5–412**

Microsoft applied for summary judgment against CFD claiming injunctive relief for trade mark and copyright infringement and passing off in respect of CFD's sale of Microsoft's software. CFD had removed the outer packaging from various software products of Microsoft, which had contained restrictions on the resale of the software outside USA and Canada and certificates of authentication. Some of the software's outer packaging which CFD had removed had made clear that the software was only authorised for sale to educational and non profit making establishments. In some cases, CFD had sold a collection of Microsoft's software as a package but included only one of its end user licence agreements instead of including one for each item of software. Microsoft claimed that CFD had infringed its trade marks by using identical signs, namely the Microsoft trade marks, in respect of identical goods without consent. Microsoft claimed it had legitimate reasons for opposing the manner in which CFD had dealt with the software, under Directive 104/89 Art.7 and s.12(2) of the Trade Marks Act 1994, even if an international exhaustion defence was available to CFD, as CFD's actions had diminished Microsoft's trade marks as an indication of authenticity and quality. CFD argued that it had not relabelled or repackaged the goods, but had simply delabelled them, which CFD claimed was not an activity involving any relevant alteration to the condition of the goods after they had been put on the market by Microsoft. CFD submitted that this was a matter which gave rise to a triable issue. **5–413**

The Court granted summary judgment and held that with respect to trade mark infringement, CFD had deliberately destroyed Microsoft's outer packaging to facilitate sales of the software in a manner which Microsoft had not authorised. Removing the packaging facilitated the tampering with **5–414** the contents of the original products. CFD's contention that Microsoft could have no legitimate reasons for opposing CFD's manner of trading was one which did not give rise to a triable issue and Microsoft had established trade mark infringement. With respect to copyright, by supplying the products in the manner complained of, CFD was purportedly authorising those it supplied to use and copy software without Microsoft's consent. Microsoft had not consented to the importation of software products intended for the North American market by the wording of the documentation within the packs. Microsoft had also made out its case under passing off because CFD had sold software which it falsely represented as licensed for use by Microsoft. That was conduct which was likely to be damaging to Microsoft's goodwill and reputation. Whilst it was arguable that Microsoft had knowingly delayed in enforcing its rights, such conduct was not equivalent to consent by Microsoft to CFD's conduct. Nor was there any evidence to suggest that Microsoft had waived any of its rights against CFD or was estopped from enforcing them.

5–415 Case C-379/97 *Pharmacia & Upjohn SA v Paranova A/S* [1999] E.C.R. I-06927 relates to a situation where it was alleged that repackaging was necessary because the same product was sold under different trade marks in different Member States, for entirely legitimate reasons relating to a previous trade mark settlement between Upjohn and a third party.

5–416 Upjohn Group marketed clindamycin, using the trade mark "Dalacin" in Denmark, Germany and Spain, the trade mark "Dalacine" in France and the trade mark "Dalacin C" in the other Member States. Paranova purchased clindamycin in France, packaged under the trade mark "Dalacine", and repackaged and marketed it in Denmark under the trade mark "Dalacin". It also purchased in Greece clindamycin packaged under the trade mark "Dalacin C", and repackaged and marketed it in Denmark under the trade mark "Dalacin".

5–417 Upjohn sought an injunction in the Danish courts on the grounds that Paranova's replacement of one trade mark by another constituted an infringement of Upjohn's trade-mark rights under Danish law and that Community law did not preclude such an injunction in view of the fact that there were objective grounds (*i.e.* the settlement agreement) justifying the use of different trade marks in different Member States where the pharmaceutical products in question are to be marketed.

5–418 Paranova's primary argument was that the different marks used in Greece, France and Denmark constituted in reality the same trade mark, with the result that the trade-mark rights of the Upjohn Group in all the versions of the trade mark had been exhausted under Art.7 of the First Council Directive on Trade Marks as soon as product was put on the market under any one version of the trade mark. It also contended that Upjohn's purpose in using the different versions of the one trade mark was to create an artificial partitioning of the markets contrary to Community law. The matter was referred to the European Court.

5–419 The Court considered that the question to be answered in these cases was "whether the circumstances prevailing at the time of marketing made it objectively necessary to replace the original trade mark by the trade mark used in the importing Member State in order that the product in question could be placed on the market in that State by the parallel importer". This was for the national court to decide.

However, the Court offered some guidelines: 5–420

> "This condition of necessity is satisfied if, in a specific case, the prohibition imposed on the importer against replacing the trade mark hinders effective access to the markets of the importing Member State. That would be the case if the rules or practices in the importing Member State prevent the product in question from being marketed in that State under its trade mark in the exporting Member State. This is so where a rule for the protection of consumers prohibits the use, in the importing Member State, of the trade mark used in the exporting Member State on the ground that it is liable to mislead consumers. In contrast, the condition of necessity will not be satisfied if replacement of the trade mark is explicable solely by the parallel importer's attempt to secure a commercial advantage."

This case is important in that it effectively held that all of the variant trade 5–421 marks were one trade mark for the purpose of exhaustion of rights and gave no importance to the issue of the settlement agreement. In this last connection it should be observed that if Upjohn were obliged to honour the settlement agreement by using different versions of the trade marks, it seems reasonable that the parallel importer should do the same. Thus the presence of the settlement agreement would seem rather to justify the repackaging than to create a reason why it should not be permitted. In fact, it seems as if the Court took this point tacitly, by concentrating on the question of the potential use of the variant trade marks to partition the market, which, it seems to have concluded, was Upjohn's primary purpose.

The real issue in this case, is thus when the repackaging is necessary and 5–422 when it is only for the purpose of securing a "commercial advantage". The Court did not give a great deal of guidance on this issue, presumably leaving it to the national court to decide on the facts of each case.

However, this question was considered further in the latest of the 5–423 repackaging cases, Case C-443/99 *Merck, Sharp & Dohme GmbH v Paranova Pharmazeutika Handels GmbH* ([2002] E.C.R. I-03703). This case again concerned the interpretation of Art.7(2) of Directive 104/89 on Trade Marks, and related to the marketing in Austria of pharmaceutical products which were manufactured by the Merck group and were the subject of parallel importation by Paranova from Spain.

Paranova had obtained approval from the Austrian authorities to market 5–424 the products in Austria, under a parallel import licence. Paranova complied in all respects with the guidelines laid down in the repackaging cases, except in one respect. It wanted to repackage the imported products in new packaging with German language information on them. There was no regulatory requirement under the authorisation to repackage the products in order to change the contents of the containers, since they were sold in both Austria and Spain with the same number of units in each package. Thus sticking an extra label on the existing packaging would have been sufficient to provide the German language information required.

5–425 The reason for the repackaging was that Paranova (and the Austrian authorities) believed attaching labels would have had an appreciable influence on the sale of the pharmaceutical products, "because relabelled foreign packs engendered reactions of mistrust and rejection from both pharmacists and consumers". Merck contended that since the repackaging was not legally necessary, and an extra sticker would have sufficed, the repackaging was an unlawful interference with its trade mark rights.

5–426 The issue in the case was whether opposition to repackaging which was not otherwise legally necessary was justified within the meaning of Art.7(2), if over-stickering (although adequate to comply with local law) would jeopardise the marketability of the product. The Austrian court found as fact that such over-stickering would be likely to jeopardise the marketability of the product.

5–427 The Court gave the following guidance to the national court:

> "The trade mark proprietor may oppose the repackaging if it is based solely on the parallel importer's attempt to secure a commercial advantage. However, there may exist on a market, or on a substantial part of it, such strong resistance from a significant proportion of consumers to relabelled pharmaceutical products that there must be held to be a hindrance to effective market access. In those circumstances, repackaging of the pharmaceutical products would not be explicable solely by the attempt to secure a commercial advantage. The purpose would be to achieve effective market access. It is for the national court to determine whether that is the case."

5–428 Although the issue is left for the national court to determine the inference to be drawn from this decision is that relabelling should be used in preference to repackaging and that any repackager should have to pass a stiff test before a national court ought to be satisfied that such repackaging is necessary to make sales practicable as opposed to merely providing a commercial advantage to make them easier.

A further instance of the distinction drawn in this case between repackaging and relabelling, and a useful discussion of the current state of the law, can be found in *Glaxo Group Ltd v Dowelhurst Ltd* [2003] EWHC 100, Ch D.

5.1.2 Competition law in the UK

5–429 It is now necessary to consider the new competition law regime brought into effect in the UK by the Competition Act 1998, and the way in which it interacts with EC Competition law, particularly as a result of the operation of the new EC regulatory framework under Reg.1/2003.

This regime broadly speaking came into force on March 1, 2000, although there are complex transitional provisions in force which relate to agreements made prior to that date and already then enjoying exemption under the Restrictive Trade Practices Act 1976. Transitional provisions are set out in s.74 and Part V of Sch.1 to the Act. The Office of Fair Trading has in addition published a guidance paper "Transitional Arrangements" (OFT 406) explaining and commenting upon those transitional provisions. **5–430**

Part I of the Act creates two basic prohibitions. The "Chapter I Prohibition" (see s.2) deals with anti-competitive agreements or concerted practices (referred to generally in this section as "agreements") between undertakings or anti-competitive decisions made by associations of undertakings. The "Chapter II Prohibition" (see s.18) deals with abuse of a dominant position by an undertaking or undertakings. The Chapter II Prohibition is subject under s.19 to a number of defined exclusions mainly in relation monopolies and mergers (see Sch.1 to the Act) which are now dealt with under the Enterprise Act 2002, and a number of more general exclusions set out in Sch.3 to the Act. Schedule 3 also gives the Secretary of State power to provide that the Chapter II prohibition does not apply in certain circumstances. These exclusions and powers go somewhat further in limiting the operation of the Chapter II Prohibition than is the case with the equivalent provision under Art.82 of the EC Treaty, where no power of exemption or exclusion is provided. **5–431**

The Chapter I Prohibition is closely modelled on Art.81, and the Chapter II Prohibition on Art.82 of the EC Treaty. The only substantial difference between the wording of the Prohibitions and that of Art.82 is that the former confine the effect of the relevant activity to trade within the UK. The UK regime is obviously not concerned with the effect on trade with other Member States of the EU (which is the province of the EC Treaty) or with the effect on international trade in general. **5–432**

Breach of the Chapter I or the Chapter II Prohibition is punished by fines (see ss.36–38). In addition, where there is a breach of the Chapter I Prohibition, the agreement or decision concerned is void, as is the case under Art.81 (see s.2(4)). Third parties who are affected by such breaches were not in the first place given a specific right to seek compensation under the Act, but this right has now been conferred by s.18 of the Enterprise Act 2002 (which inserts a new s.47A to this effect into the 1998 Act). Section 47A allows individuals who have suffered damage as a result of a breach of either the Chapter I or II Prohibition or of Art.81 or 82 to bring an action before the Competition Tribunal claiming civil damages from the infringing undertaking. It should be noted that such damages (unlike in US anti-trust cases) contain no element of penalty but are calculated on the usual common law basis in respect of actions for breach of statutory duty. A similar right to bring civil actions on the part of consumers suffering such loss has been conferred under s.19 of the 2002 Act, which inserts a new s.47B to this effect into the 1998 Act. **5–433**

5.1.2.1 The regulatory framework

5–434 The Director General of the Office of Fair Trading is primarily responsible for enforcing the new regime. He is provided under the Part III of the Act with significantly strengthened powers to investigate potential breaches of the two Prohibitions, and to make decisions, based on his investigations, that undertakings have in fact breached a Prohibition. In these circumstances he has powers to direct the undertakings to change or end the agreements or conduct in question (see ss.32–35) and to impose civil penalties for such breaches in the form of fines (see ss.36–37). The directions and any fines imposed are enforceable by a court order on the application of the Director General (see s.38). The Director General can act either on his own initiative or at the instance of affected third parties.

5–435 The Act sets up a new Competition Commission (see s.45) to which (or rather to a division of which known as the Competition Appeals Tribunal) appeals can be made against the decisions or directions made or fines imposed by the Director General (see s.48). These appeals can be made by undertakings to whom the decisions or directions apply or upon whom the fines have been imposed (see s.6). Interested third parties can appeal against decisions or directions made by the Director General, but not in relation to fines imposed by him (see s.47). Appeal lies from the Commission (with leave) to the Court of Appeal (for matters in England and Wales) to the Court of Sessions (for matter in Scotland) and to the Court of Appeal of Northern Ireland (for matters in Northern Ireland). Appeal lies on a point of law and for a review of the level of fines (see s.49).

5–436 So far as the Chapter I Prohibition is concerned, the Director General is granted powers to exempt agreements on an individual basis, in the same way that the EC Commission can under Art.81(3) (see ss.4 and 5). Section 9 sets out the grounds upon which an exemption can be granted. These are basically the same as those set out in Art.81(3). Similarly the Secretary of State, acting on the recommendation of the Director General, is empowered to exempt by Order certain categories of agreements from the Chapter I Prohibition (see s.6). This type of exemption is identical to the block exemptions enacted by the Commission under Regulations made pursuant to Art.81(3) and to the EU Council Regulation 17/62. These exemptions are also referred to under the Act as block exemptions.

5–437 There are provisions in the Act (ss.39 and 40) which give the Secretary of State power to exempt by statutory instrument undertakings which have entered into "small agreements" (other than price fixing agreements) from the penalties (under s.36(1)) for breach of the Chapter I Prohibition, and similarly to grant immunity to undertakings whose conduct falls within the prescribed definition of "minor significance" in relation to penalties (under s.36(2)) for breach of the Chapter II Prohibition. (These powers have now been exercised by the passing of The Competition Act 1998 (Small Agreements and Conduct of Minor Significance) Regulations 2000 (SI 2000/262).

5–438 Section 36 provides that the Director General may impose the penalties for breach of a Prohibition only if he is satisfied that the undertaking in question acted intentionally or negligently (s.36(3)). In any event (see ss.36(4) and (5)) no penalty may be exacted if the Director General is satisfied that the undertaking acted on the reasonable assumption that s.39 or s.40 (as relevant) gave it immunity from s.36.

Undertakings can take advantage of this limited immunity as of right, on the basis of their own assessment, without reference to the Director-General. However, he can withdraw the immunity in any case where, after investigation, he is satisfied that the relevant conduct is likely to give rise to a breach of the relevant Prohibition. Nevertheless, no penalty can be imposed for the period before the withdrawal of the immunity, and the withdrawal must be by means of a written notice which gives the undertaking sufficient time to secure that there is no further breach of the relevant prohibition (see ss.39(4)–(8) and ss.40(4)–(8)). **5–439**

Any party to an arrangement which might infringe the Chapter I Prohibition can notify the arrangement to the Director General (see s.12) either for confidential guidance (see s.13) or a firm decision (see s.14) as to whether the agreement in question does breach the Chapter I Prohibition. The application under s.14 can also request an individual exemption if the Director General finds the arrangement in question infringes the Chapter I Prohibition. This mirrors the old procedure for notification to the Commission under Reg.17/62, and has survived the changes in the EC regulatory framework brought about by Reg.1/2003. It should be noted that, just as in the case of Reg.17/62, notification of an arrangement provides provisional immunity from fines from the date of notification until the date of the relevant decision (see s.14(4).) The Director General is normally unable to reopen proceedings once guidance has been given or a decision made, unless the situation changes or he has not been given the full facts of the case. (see ss.15 and 16). However, it is important to note that where the Director General reassesses the situation and withdraws a decision or guidance, penalties cannot normally be exacted in respect of the period prior to the notification of withdrawal. However, retroactive penalties may be exacted where the reason for the reassessment was that information, provided by a party to the agreement, on which the original guidance or decision was based was "incomplete false or misleading in a material particular" (see ss.15(5) and 16(5)). **5–440**

Similar provisions apply to undertakings which seek decisions or guidance as to whether their conduct might constitute a breach of the Chapter II Prohibition against abuse of a dominant position (see ss.20–24). **5–441**

Since the EC Commission and the European Court have found that in many cases trade between Member States may be affected even where both parties are within the same Member State, many agreements will therefore be caught both by Art.81(1) and the Chapter I Prohibition. Similarly, it is possible that an undertaking in a dominant position in the UK could affect trade between Member States through an abuse of that dominant position, or, indeed, enjoy a dominant position (and abuse it) in more than one Member State (including the UK). In this case there could be a breach both **5–442** of Art.82(1) and the Chapter II Prohibition. The Act is based so closely upon EC Competition law that in practice the real issue is not that of different approaches, but which of the two authorities has jurisdiction in any case affecting both trade within the UK and between Member States, or whether both authorities exercise that jurisdiction concurrently. The interaction between the European and UK Competition regimes has recently been considered and radically readdressed by EC legislation (see Reg.1/2003) which gives a new role to the national competition authorities of each Member State in enforcing and administering Art.82. This regulation is discussed in detail in Chapter 5.1.1.2.

5.1.2.2 Substantive principles

5–443 However, quite apart from these new developments, the Act itself contains a number of harmonising provisions which ensure that the UK regime closely follows EC Competition law precedents, practices and principles.

5–444 First, s.10 of the Act applies the concept of what are described as "parallel exemptions" to agreements between undertakings which would otherwise breach the Chapter I Prohibition.

5–445 Section 10(1) provides that, where an agreement affects not only trade within the UK but also trade between Member States, it is exempt from the Chapter I Prohibition if it is exempt from Art.81(1) by virtue either of a Commission or Council Regulation (*i.e.* a block exemption) or of an individual exemption granted by the Commission pursuant to Art.81(3). Included within the scope of such individual exemptions are both those granted expressly, and those arising through the expiry of the relevant opposition period set out in an application made under one of the block exemptions containing a provision for short-form notification and exemption under a non-opposition procedure. Such an exemption is termed a "parallel exemption" (s.10(3)).

5–446 Section 10(2) provides for a further type of parallel exemption in that "an agreement is also exempt from the Chapter I Prohibition if it does not affect trade between Member States but otherwise falls within a category which is exempt from Art.81(1) under" one of the block exemptions described above. In other words, it is an agreement which could have taken advantage of the relevant block exemption but for the fact it did not affect trade between Member States.

5–447 It should be noted that the definition of "Regulation" is confined to true regulations adopted by the EC Commission or the EC Council (see s.10(10)) and that parties would not be able to take advantage, under the concept of Parallel Exemption, of Commission Notices and Announcements, such as that on Agreements of Minor Importance, or Subcontracting.

5–448 There is no concept of parallel exemption to apply to breaches of the Chapter II Prohibition, since it would have been inconsistent with the purpose of Art.82 (to prevent abuse of a dominant position) to include in the EC Treaty a provision equivalent to Art.81(3), which would effectively then permit the Council or the Commission to condone such abuses.

The last, and most significant provision, which applies to the whole of the new regime in general, and in particular to both the Chapter I and Chapter II Prohibition, requires that the Director General, and all courts and tribunals concerned with the new regime, operate the new regime on the basis of principles that are consistent with EC competition law. Section 60 states: **5–449**

"(1) The purpose of this section is to ensure that so far as is possible (having regard to any relevant differences between the provisions concerned) questions arising under [Part I] in relation to competition within the United Kingdom are dealt with in a manner which is consistent with the treatment of corresponding questions arising in Community Law in relation to competition within the Community.

(2) At any time when the court determines a question arising under [Part I] it must act (so far as is compatible with the provisions of [Part I] and whether or not it would otherwise be required to do so) with a view to securing that there is no inconsistency between:

(a) the principles applied and decision reached by the court in determining that question; and
(b) the principles laid down by the [EC Treaty] and the European Court and any relevant decision of that Court as applicable at that time in determining any corresponding question arising in Community Law.

(3) The court must in addition have regard to any relevant decision or statement of the Commission.

(4) subsections (2) and (3) also apply to (a) the Director [General of Fair Trading], and (b) any person acting on behalf of the Director [General of Fair Trading] in connection with any matter arising under [Part I].

(5) In subsections (2) and (3) 'court' means any court or tribunal.

(6) In subsections (2)(b) and (3) 'decision' includes a decision as to:

(a) the interpretation of any provision of Community law;
(b) the civil liability of an undertaking for harm caused by an infringement of Community law."

This provision is clearly the strongest possible guarantee that the principles of EC competition law will be applied within the UK regime even if it does not go quite so far as to incorporate the whole body of EC competition law within the UK regime. The provisions of ss.60(2) and (3) would enable regard to be had not only to European Court and Commission Decisions, but also (see the use of the word "statement" in s.60(3)) to Commission Notices and Announcements. For instance, it would seem highly likely that the Commission Guidelines on Vertical Restraints in so far as they relate to **5–450** the status of agency agreements under Art.81, together with the relevant European Court judgments and Commission Decisions, would be applied to exclude most agency agreements from the ambit of the Chapter I Prohibition (see the detailed discussion on agency agreements in Chapter 5.1.1.3.11).

5–451 Regulation 1/2003 also deals with the relationship between EC and national competition rules. Article 3 provides that where the national courts or competition authorities apply national competition law they must also apply Art.81 or 82 as relevant as well. The application of national competition law must not lead to the prohibition of arrangements which affect trade between Member States but do not infringe Art.81(1) or fulfill the conditions for exemption in Art.81(3) including by way of any applicable block exemption. However, Member States are not precluded under the Regulation from adopting and applying stricter national laws which prohibit or sanction unilateral conduct engaged in by undertakings. This provision relates to certain national laws in various Member States dealing with issues like abusive behaviour toward an economically dependent undertaking, even where the abuser is not in a dominant position. Lastly, the article does not apply when Member States apply national merger control law or when they apply provisions of national law which predominantly pursue an objective different from that pursued by Art.81 and 82 (*e.g.* dealing with unfair trading practices, whether contractual or unilateral).

5–452 It can be seen that s.60 of the Competition Act, and the principles set out in s.10 relating to parallel exemptions covers the requirements of Art.3.

5–453 Under s.52 of the Act, the Director General is required to publish general advice and information about the application of the Chapter I and the Chapter II Prohibitions and their enforcement. This may, in particular, include "advice (or information) about the factors which the Director will take into account in considering whether, and if so how, to exercise a power conferred upon him by the Act". Such information and advice can be supplemented and updated from time to time. This has a resulted in a series of very useful guidelines upon the operation of the Act. These are all freely available for reading and downloading from the UK web-site of the Office of Fair Trading and should be consulted as a matter of course by practitioners who have to deal with the Act in any way.

5–454 One of the most important of these guidelines is "The Chapter I Prohibition" (OFT 401). Besides explaining in considerable detail the operation of the Chapter I Prohibition, it also deals with the concept of "Appreciable Effect". This concept is equivalent to the principle set out in the EC Commission Notice on Agreements of Minor Importance 2001 (discussed in Chapter 5.1.1.3.7) but it is more generous. The Director General takes the view that an agreement will generally have no appreciable effect on competition if the parties' combined share of the relevant market does not exceed 25 per cent, although there may be circumstances in which this is not the case. Indeed in some cases a combined market share of more than 25 per cent might still be acceptable considering the content of the agreement and the structure of the relevant market. However, an agreement which fixes prices, shares markets, imposes minimum resale prices or is one of a network of similar agreements which have a cumulative effect are generally regarded as having an appreciable effect even where the combined market share is less than 25 per cent. The definition of the relevant market is crucial for the application of the concept of appreciable significance, and in this connection reference should be made the guidelines "Market Definition" (OFT 403) and "Assessment of Market Power" (OFT 415).

5.1.2.3 Mergers and concentrative and cooperative joint ventures

So far as such matters do not fall within the jurisdiction of the EC Commission under the Merger Regulation (see Chapter 5.1.1.3.10), they are now dealt with in the UK under the Enterprise Act 2002 which repealed the Fair Trading Act 1973, in so far as it still remained in force after the passing of the Competition Act 1998. The new regime is set out in Pt 3 of the Enterprise Act. The Director General is required to investigate a completed or prospective "relevant merger situation". This is defined in two ways. Section 23(1) provides for a situation where two or more enterprises have ceased to be distinct enterprises and the value of the turnover in the United Kingdom of the enterprise being taken over exceeds £70 million. Section 23(2) provides for a situation where two or more enterprises have ceased to be distinct enterprises, and as a result of the merger any person achieves a market share in the UK (or a substantial part thereof) of 25 per cent or more in the sale or purchase of any goods or services. **5–455**

It can be seen that, as discussed in Chapter 5.1.1.3.10, this concept of two or more enterprises ceasing to be a distinct entity easily covers the concept of a concentrative joint venture, and that given the relatively low thresholds, many more concentrative joint ventures will fall to be examined under the UK merger regime than they will under the equivalent EC regime. There is however no concept equivalent to the full-function or partial-function joint venture. Either the joint venture results in two or more enterprises ceasing to be distinct entities or it does not. Thus, in this case, there is a much cleaner line drawn between the joint venture which is a concentration and the joint venture that amounts to a horizontal cooperation. **5–456**

The decision as to whether or not to approve the relevant merger situation depends upon an assessment of "relevant customer benefits". These are defined in s.30. A "relevant customer" is a customer of any person carrying on an enterprise which, in the creation of the relevant merger situation concerned, has ceased to be, (or as the case may be) will cease to be, a distinct enterprise. The term includes customers of such customers and any other customers further down the supply chain. Benefits for these relevant customers consist of lower prices, higher quality or greater choice of goods or services or greater innovation, provided that such benefits come about because of the merger and are unlikely to have come about if the merger had not taken place. **5–457**

In regard to the operation of the Act, the Office of Fair Trading has **5–458** produced some helpful guidelines. Reference should be made to OFT 508—"Overview of the Enterprise Act" and OFT 506 which is a draft paper for Guidelines on the Substantive Assessment of Mergers, which is due to be finalised later in 2003.

5–459 Once again, as under EC Competition law, joint ventures which only amount to horizontal cooperation agreements will be dealt with under the Competition Act 1998, in relation to the Chapter I Prohibition. Reference should be made here to three publications from the Office of Fair Trading OFT 401 ("The Major Provisions of the Competition Act 1998"), OFT 401 ("The Chapter I Prohibition) and OFT 416 (Exclusions for Mergers and Ancillary Restrictions") which explains how mergers are dealt with outside of the 1998 Act. Here the possibility of the application under s.10 of the Act of the parallel exemptions under Commission Regulations 2658/2000 (specialisation agreements) and 2659/2000 (research and development agreements, should be considered, but it should also be remembered that, as set out in the OFT Guidelines "The Chapter I Prohibition", in ss.218 to 222 (OFT 401), if the parties to the joint venture have a combined market share of less than 25 per cent, their arrangement will escape scrutiny under the Chapter I prohibition as not having an appreciable effect, except in the case of the usual hardcore restrictions price fixing, market sharing, minimum resale prices, and networks of agreements having a cumulative effect. Thus the parallel exemptions are in practice of little value.

5–460 There are in fact two areas where they can assist. First, the 25 per cent threshold is not an absolute one. Thus, in circumstances in which the OFT might be tempted to hold that parties with a lower market share actually had an appreciable effect on competition then the Regulations could be used as parallel exemptions. Second, there is no initial market share test under Reg.2659/2000 for research and development agreements between non-competitors. Thus, if it were possible for the OFT to claim that a pair of non-competitors engaged in joint research and development somehow had a joint market share in excess of 25 per cent (although this seems unlikely) the more generous provisions of Reg.2659/2000 could again be called in aid.

5.1.2.4 Cooperation between the EC and UK competition authorities

5–461 Regulation 1/2003, discussed in Chapter 5.1.1.2 sets out the new regulatory framework for direct applicability of Art.81 and 82 by the Member States of the EU. Article 35 of the Regulation requires the Member States to designate the competition authority or authorities responsible for the application of Art.82 in such a way that the provisions of the Regulation are effectively complied with. Article 35 envisages a distribution of functions among various authorities and tribunals in the way that best serves the particular legal regime in each Member State. In the UK it is likely that the regime provided for UK competition law will also be applied for the enforcement of Arts.81 and 82. The Director General of the Office of Fair Trading will be the primary competition authority, with the system of appeals from his decisions lying first to the Competition Commission Appeal Tribunals (see s.48 of the 1998 Act) and thence to the specified courts of appeal. The High Court, The Court of Appeal and the House of Lords will have the powers laid down by Art.6 of the Regulation to apply Art.82 directly.

5.1.3 Practical guidelines on competition law analysis

The preceding sections of Chapter 5.1 have set out in detail the various competition law issues which impact upon the distribution, agency and licensing agreements entered into within the EC. These will be supplemented by detailed commentary in relation to selective distribution agreements (Chapter 6) and Manufacturing Agreements (Chapter 8). However, at this point it is useful to set some guidelines for the way in which to approach the assessment of all of these agreements under the two competition law regimes, with particular reference to the distribution agreement discussed in this chapter. **5–462**

A competition law assessment can no longer be approached in a formalistic way, by trying to fit the various clauses of an agreement into some kind of exemption or to draft them in such a way that they fall outside the scope of a particular prohibition. This was never really possible with EC competition law, and has ceased to be the case with UK competition law once the new regime under the Competition Act 1998 was adopted. **5–463**

It is thus necessary to consider the nature and characteristics of the parties to a relationship, the terms and conditions governing that relationship, and the surrounding environment (both legal, factual and economic) in which that relationship is carried on. The approach is thus necessarily a holistic one, based upon an assessment of all of the relevant circumstances, and not limited to the analysis of the agreement alone, still less of particular provisions contained in it. What may be a perfectly acceptable provision in one agreement, may equally be completely unacceptable in another agreement where the circumstances differ. **5–464**

Although they should not be used in a formalistic sense, on the basis that their application will produce definitive answers applicable in all cases, the flow charts set out in Appendix 3, can be used as frameworks for, and to assist in, this analysis. Additionally, so far as possible, the commentary on each of the clauses in the precedents in these chapters will indicate the extent to, and the conditions and circumstances under which, the particular clause is or is not acceptable under the two competition law regimes. **5–465**

It should also be noted that under UK competition law, the situation with regard to vertical restraints has been vastly simplified by the Vertical Restraints Order (discussed in Chapter 5.2). Absent resale price maintenance, which has always been a particular concern of the Office of Fair Trading, no vertical agreement for the purchase sale or resale of goods or services will be scrutinised unless one of the parties to it is in a dominant position. The issues will then revolve around whether or not the restraints in that agreement amount to an abuse of that dominant position. **5–466**

5–467 Finally, the preliminary sections in the Guidelines on Vertical Restraints, already referred to above, and discussed in detail in the rest of this chapter, provide some valuable insights as to the way in which vertical agreements are analysed by the Commission for the purposes of EC competition law. Section VI.1 (the framework of analysis) is particularly useful in this respect.

5–468 The Commission emphasises here that, if a vertical agreement falls outside the block exemption, there is no presumption that it is illegal. The situation depends upon the facts of the case. The Commission consistently takes the view that in general vertical restraints are not only less harmful than horizontal restraints but considers that in at least certain cases they may even promote competition (*e.g.* where it is necessary to grant a distributor exclusivity in order to persuade him to take on and bring to market a product that he would otherwise be reluctant to deal with). The determining factor will, however, in most cases be the market power of the undertaking imposing the vertical restraint. This power can have two effects harmful to competition. The first is the stifling of intra-brand competition, if the undertaking imposing the restraint has foreclosed the market (by the exercise of its market power) with a network of agreements containing similar restraints. The second is the extent to which that market power is so great that inter-brand competition is weak or non-existent as well.

5–469 In s.1.1 the Commission begins by considering the negative effects of vertical restraints (foreclosure of markets, reduction of inter-brand competition, reduction of intra-brand competition and creation of obstacles to market integration.) It shows how vertical restraints can conveniently be considered in various groupings—single branding (*i.e.* the buyer is induced to buy from one supplier); limited distribution (*i.e.* the supplier restricts number of distributors); resale price maintenance; and market partitioning (*i.e.* buyer is restricted in where he sources or buys a particular product) (see paras 106–114). In s.1.2 it then describes the positive effects of vertical restraints (promoting non-price competition, improved quality of service and improved efficiency).

5–470 Section 1.3 lays down the general rules for evaluation of vertical restraints. Competition concerns usually arise only where there is insufficient inter-brand competition. That is: "... if there exists a certain degree of market power ... the power to raise prices above the competitive level and, at least in the short term, to obtain supra-normal profits ..." (para.119(1)). Thus vertical restraints that reduce inter-brand competition are more harmful than those which reduce intra-brand competition. For example, if one manufacturer imposes resale price maintenance on a distributor in an attempt to enjoy supra-normal profits, and there are powerful competitors on the market, inter-brand competition will provide consumers with substitutable products at lower prices. In the end the price-fixing manufacturer will simply lose sales and be forced to give up the practice.

5–471 A summary of the Commission's guidelines here is as follows:

- The limited distribution restraints significantly restrict consumer choice.

- Exclusive dealing arrangements are worse than non-exclusive as they tend to foreclose the market to competitors.
- Restraints on non-branded goods are generally less harmful than those affecting branded goods.
- A combination of vertical restraints aggravates their negative effects.
- Negative effects are also aggravated where several suppliers and their buyers organise their trade in a similar way ("parallel networks" with "cumulative effects").
- Vertical restraints linked to opening up new geographic or product markets in general do not restrict competition.

Section 1.4 sets out the methodology of analysis. The relevant factors for **5–472** assessment under Art.81(1) (which emphasise the holistic approach) are:

- market position of the supplier;
- market position of competitors;
- market position of the buyer;
- entry barriers (how easy is it for undertakings outside the market to enter and compete);
- maturity of the market (negative effects more likely than in a new dynamic market);
- level of trade (vertical restraints more harmful at resale than wholesale level in general);
- nature of the product;
- other factors (anything else relevant to the case, particularly—cumulative effect of similar agreements; regulatory environment; and duration of agreement imposing restraints).

Section VI.2 then proceeds to analyse specific vertical restraints by reference **5–473** to the classification into groups described above. The details of this analysis are applied as relevant throughout this chapter to the various clauses of the precedent and in Chapter 6 to the precedent relating to selective distribution.

5.2 Licence

5.2.1 The Principal hereby grants the Distributor a licence during the con- **5–474** tinuance of this Agreement to distribute and sell the Products under the Trade Mark in accordance with and subject to the terms of this Agreement

5.2.2 The Principal undertakes that during the continuance of this Agreement it **5–475** will not appoint in the Territory any other distributor or reseller of the Products nor directly supply any of the Products to distributors, resellers or users located within the Territory.

Clause 5.2.1. in isolation is a simple non-exclusive grant of a distributorship. Its use in combination with cl.5.2.2 creates an exclusive distributorship. However, if the intention is to create a non-exclusive distributorship, for the avoidance of doubt it is best to add in the word "non-exclusive" before the word "licence" in the second line of cl.5.2.1.

5–476 It should be noted that (unlike cl.4.2) the grant of the distributorship is not made in respect of a particular territory. This is because the notion of a territory must not be used to restrict the possibility of sales outside that territory to the extent required by EC competition law. A licence only to sell within a defined territory is at least in contradiction with later provisions of this precedent which provide for sales outside the territory in certain circumstances (see Chapters 5.3.8, 5.4 and 5.5), and, at worst, could be construed as an indirect restriction aimed at preventing such sales. Hence the licence to sell is limited not by reference to the Territory but by reference to the provisions of the agreement in general. The concept of territory is thus mainly used in the precedent in relation to the provision of exclusivity of appointment in favour of the distributor (achieved by cl.5.2.2) and in relation to the imposition of certain obligations concerning the distributor's activities within the territory, and of those restrictions (permitted by EC competition law) on the distributor's activities outside the territory.

5–477 Although all exclusive distribution arrangements are *prima facie* caught by Art.81, the Commission has long recognised that the existence of the exclusive distribution agreement linked to a particular territory is too deep-rooted, for sound commercial reasons, to abolish. Distributors are not prepared to assume the risk and investment in making a market unless they are safeguarded from either the principal or competing distributors taking advantage of their marketing activities, and taking away from the distributor sales of the products for which he has created the demand by his own efforts.

5–478 The Commission originally passed a block exemption (Reg.67/67) in 1967 to cover certain classes of exclusive distribution agreements. This was replaced in 1983 by two block exemptions, one covering exclusive distribution (Reg.83/83) and one covering exclusive purchasing (Reg.84/83).

5–479 Both of these regulations were replaced by the much wider block exemption for vertical agreements and concerted practices: Commission Regulation 2790/99 which came into force on June 1, 2000 and expires on May 31, 2010. The Regulation is accompanied by a set of Guidelines on Vertical Restraints [2000] O.J. C291/1, sections of which have already been discussed earlier in this chapter. The Guidelines are freely available over the internet from the Commission's Europa web-site.

5–480 The Guidelines confirm that agency agreements, agreements of minor importance and agreements between small and medium-sized enterprises fall outside Art.81 and hence except in special circumstances, or where hardcore restrictions are present, are not usually the subject of the block exemption. The Guidelines then deal with vertical agreements which are covered by the block exemption and those vertical agreements which fall outside it.

Part VI of the Guidelines explains the Commission's general approach to vertical agreements, and this has been discussed in Chapter 5.1.3 above. The section also summarises the approach to the application of the Block Exemption as follows: **5–481**

- First, does Art.81(1) apply at all?
  - — is this an agreement between two undertakings (*i.e.* is this a parent/subsidiary or principal/agent relationship);
  - — is there an actual or potential effect on trade between Member States;
  - — is there an actual or potential effect on competition;
  - — does the Commission Notice of 2001 on Agreements of Minor Importance have any application?
- Second, if Art.81(1) does apply, are there any hardcore restrictions present:
  - — if so, the new block exemption cannot apply and it will be hard, if not impossible, to make a case out for exemption under Art.81(3)
  - — if not, the deciding factor is the market share of the relevant undertaking on the relevant market:
    - — if 30 per cent or less, then the block exemption will apply
    - — if over 30 per cent, then consideration should be given as to whether on the facts of the case, the agreement is exempt under Art.81(3).

It should be remembered that under the framework set out in Reg.1/2003, all of this assessment must be carried out by the parties themselves without the possibility of notification under the old procedure (Reg.17/62) to the Commission to obtain individual exemption under Art.81(3). However, in difficult or novel cases, it should be possible to obtain confidential (albeit nonbinding) guidance from the Commission. **5–482**

Having dealt with the general issues and principles related to vertical agreements and vertical restraints, it is now possible to consider the block exemption itself in detail. **5–483**

The block exemption replaced the expiring block exemptions on exclusive distribution (Reg.83/83), exclusive purchasing (Reg.84/83) and franchising (Reg.4087/88). The Technology Transfer Block Exemption (Reg.240/96) and the block exemption under Commission Regulation 1400/2002 of July 31, 2002 on the application of Article 81(3) of the Treaty to categories of vertical agreements and concerted practices in the motor vehicle sector (which replaced the previous Commission Regulations (123/85 and 1475/95 on the same subject) remain in force and outside the Regulation (see **5–484**

Art.2.5). The Commission was empowered to pass the Regulation by Council Regulation 19/65 as amended by Council Regulations 1215/99 and 1216/99.

5–485 Article 2.1 of the Regulation defines vertical agreements as agreements or concerted practices between two or more undertakings *each* operating for the purposes of the agreement at a different level of the production or distribution chain, relating to conditions under which parties purchase, sell or resell goods or services. An example of such an agreement would be a distribution agreement between a manufacturer and a reseller, or between a wholesaler and a retailer. If there were three parties to the agreement, it would have to be an arrangement such as one between a manufacturer, wholesaler and retailer. One between, for instance, a manufacturer and two resellers or between a wholesaler and two retailers would not qualify.

5–486 Here it should be emphasised that, while Regs.83/83 and 84/83 only applied to distribution and supply agreements for goods, Reg.2790/99 applies to vertical agreements for both goods and services. This is obviously necessary as the regulation also now applies to franchise agreements.

5–487 Article 2.1 further provides that conditions contained in vertical agreements, to the extent that they constitute restrictions on competition falling with the scope of Art.81(1) are declared exempt pursuant to Art.81(3). Such conditions are referred to as Vertical Restraints.

5–488 Article 2.2 provides that vertical agreements between an association of undertakings and its members or between such an association and its suppliers are also exempt provided each individual member is a retailer of goods and no individual member, together with its connected undertakings, has a total annual turnover in excess of 50m Euros. It should be noted that this exemption only covers the vertical agreements which create, in effect, a purchasing club so that small retailers can take advantages of volume discounts associated with bulk buying. The horizontal agreements between such members or decisions adopted by their association can still be scrutinised under Art.81 unless another exemption applies.

5–489 Article 2.3 permits provisions in a vertical agreement for the assignment or use of intellectual property rights, provided that the licence or assignment is not the primary objective of the agreement, that the intellectual property directly relates to the use, sale or resale of goods or services by the buyer or its customers, and that no restrictions are imposed on the use of the intellectual property which would have the same object or effect as vertical restraints which are not exempt under the Regulation. An example of such an arrangement would be a licence of intellectual property to a distributor to enable him to modify or service products he had bought from a manufacturer for resale.

5–490 Article 2.4 exempts vertical agreements between competitors provided that the arrangement is not reciprocal, and either (a) the buyer's total annual turnover does not exceed €100m, or (b) the supplier is a manufacturer and distributor of goods, while the buyer is a distributor and not manufacturing goods which compete with the contract goods or (c) the supplier is a provider of services at several levels of trade while the buyer does not provide competing services at the level of trade where it purchases the contract services. Except as set out above all other vertical agreements between competing undertakings cannot take the benefit of the regulation.

Article 3 provides that the exemptions granted by Art.1 only apply to vertical agreements where, in the case of agreements containing exclusive supply obligations, the buyer's market share does not exceed 30 per cent of the market where it purchases the contract goods or services, and, in all other cases, the supplier's market share does not exceed 30 per cent of the market on which it sells the contract goods or services. (An exclusive supply obligation means any direct or indirect obligation causing the supplier to sell the goods or services specified in the agreement only to one buyer inside the EC for the purposes of a specific use or for resale (Art.1(c)). **5–491**

Article 9 contains detailed provisions for calculating market share, but once again it will be necessary to consult the 1997 Commission Notice on the Definition of the Relevant Market. Certain provisions in the Regulation require the calculation of turnover. Article 10 lays down the rules for this. **5–492**

Article 4 deals with certain general exclusions. Vertical agreements cannot take advantage of exemption under the regulation if, directly or indirectly (in isolation or with other factors under the parties' control), they impose: **5–493**

(a) resale price maintenance (but not maximum resale price maintenance or recommended resale prices); or

(b) restrictions on resale by the buyer; or

(c) the restriction of active or passive sales to end users by the retail members of a selective distribution system, without prejudice to the possibility of prohibiting a member of the system from operating out of an unauthorised place of establishment; or

(d) the restriction of cross-supplies between distributors within a selective distribution system, including between distributors operating at different levels of trade; or

(e) a restriction agreed between the supplier of components to an original equipment manufacturer of the sale, by that supplier, of such components as spare parts to third parties not entrusted by the manufacturer with the repair or servicing of its manufactured products.

However notwithstanding the general prohibition on resale by the buyer under (b) above, certain restrictions on resale by the buyer are permitted, namely: **5–494**

(i) a restriction on active sales into the exclusive territory or customer group reserved to the supplier or allocated by the supplier to another buyer, where such restriction does not limit sales by the customers of the buyer;

(ii) a restriction of sales to end users by a buyer operating as a wholesaler;

(iii) the restriction of sales to unauthorised distributors by the members of a selective distribution system; and

(iv) a restriction of the buyer's ability to sell components supplied for the purposes of incorporation (*i.e.* original equipment manufacture), to customers who would use them to manufacture the same type of goods as those produced by the supplier.

5–495 Article 5(a) contains a specific black list. There is no exemption for non-compete clauses imposed during the life of a vertical agreement if they are either of an indefinite duration, or for a period in excess of five years, except where such clauses cover restrictions on competing goods or services supplied during the occupancy of tied premises. Article 5(b) provides that there is no exemption for a non-compete clause after termination of the vertical agreement unless it is for a period of one year or less, covers only competing goods or services, is limited to the land or premises from which the buyer operated during the contract period and is indispensable to protect transferred knowhow. The article states that this provision is without prejudice to the possibility of the imposition of an indefinite period of confidentiality to protect knowhow which is not in the public domain. Article 5(c) provides that the benefit of the regulation does not apply to any direct or indirect obligation imposed on members of a selective distribution system not to sell the brands of particular competing suppliers.

5–496 The Commission may withdraw the benefit of the exemption under Art.6, in any individual case where it finds facts which are incompatible with the conditions in Art.81(3). This may particularly be the case where parallel networks with similar vertical restraints have a cumulative effect on the relevant market. Article 7 permits a national competition authority to withdraw the benefit of the exemption in its Member State if the effect described in Art.6 occurs therein or in a distinct geographic market therein. Article 8 permits the Commission (by regulation and on six months notice) to withdraw the benefit of the regulation from any market where parallel networks of similar vertical restraints cover more than 50 per cent of that market.

5–497 The difference between Art.4 and Art.5 is important. If a vertical agreement contains an Art.4 restriction (hardcore restriction) it cannot take advantage of exemption under the regulation at all. If it only contains an Art.5 restriction, then the restriction itself is not exempt under the regulation, but this does not prevent the exemption of the rest of the agreement under the Regulation if it would otherwise qualify.

5–498 Lastly it should be noted that even before the passing of Art.6 of the Regulation the Commission always looked at the true facts of the situation rather than the letter of the agreement. Even under previous block exemptions the Commission could withdraw the benefit of the relevant regulation and undertake a special investigation if it was convinced that in fact the products were not subject to efficient competition within the territory. In Case T-7/93 *Scholler Lebensmittel GmbH & Co KG v Commission* and *Langnese-Iglo v Commission* [1995] E.C.R. II-1713, the European Court of First Instance considered a Commission Decision where the benefit of Reg.83/83 was withdrawn by the Commission, and the right of withdrawal was contested by the complainants.

Ice cream manufacturers often supply a freezer free of charge to ice cream retailers, but only on the condition that they will use the freezer exclusively for that manufacturer's products ("freezer exclusivity"). These arrangements were originally considered by the Commission to fall under the Block Exemption for exclusive purchasing agreements (Reg.84/83), since they lasted for a short time and were, in any event terminable by notice, so that other manufacturers could persuade the retailer to change his allegiance and sell their brands instead. It therefore issued a letter of comfort to the manufacturers concerned. **5–499**

However, after complaints from third parties it changed its mind, and decided that, despite the comfort letter it would withdraw exemption under Art.14 of the block exemption. It also issued an order prohibiting the manufacturers from entering into such exclusive arrangements in the future. The European Court of First Instance dismissed the manufacturer's complaint that the Commission could not retract the comfort letter. It was entitled to do so if further facts came to light. It upheld the Commission's Decision that the agreements were in contravention of Art.81, and rejected a contention that the Commission was wrong to issue a Decision which covered such agreements collectively, without considering each agreement with each retailer on an individual basis. However, it did accept that the Commission had no power under Reg.17/62 to issue a prohibition on the manufacturers entering into such agreements in the future. The Commission would have to assess such agreements if and when they were entered into. This decision was later confirmed on appeal to the European Court (Case C279/95 [1999] All E.R. (EC) 616). **5–500**

A similar conclusion was reached by the Commission in relation to freezer exclusivity practices by Unilever in Ireland (see Commission Statement IP/98/242 dated March 11, 1998). After a complaint in 1993, the Commission agreed with Unilever certain changes to its freezer contracts, offering retailers the option to buy the freezer cabinet from Unilever on hire purchase, so that they could then buy and display competing brands of ice cream. The Commission withdrew its complaint, but reviewed the situation in 1997. It found on carrying out further market research that in fact retailers did not take up the option to purchase freezer cabinets and Unilever's dominant position in the Irish market for ice cream products meant that its competitors were effectively foreclosed from the market because of its freezer exclusivity practice. Accordingly in a decision in 1998 the Commission found the freezer exclusivity provision in Unilever's agreements with retailers infringed Art.81 and that, because of its market share in Ireland (85 per cent), the practice of imposing such a condition in its agreements also amounted to an abuse of a dominant position under Art.82. **5–501**

5–502 Although Reg.2790/99 is imported into UK competition law as a parallel exemption under s.10 of the Competition Act 1998, it has in fact been rendered unnecessary by the passing of The Competition Act 1998 (Land and Vertical Agreements Exclusion) Order 2000 (SI 2000/310), passed pursuant to s.50 of the Act. The Order reproduces the definition of vertical agreement (*i.e.* vertical agreements for the purchase sale or resale of goods or services) from the Regulation, including the provision allowing ancillary licences of intellectual property rights. Article 2 provides that the Chapter I Prohibition shall not apply to an agreement to the extent that it is a vertical agreement. However, Art.3 provides that Art.2 does not apply where the vertical agreement, "directly or indirectly, in isolation or in combination with other factors under the control of the parties has the object or effect of restricting the buyer's ability to determine its sale price, without prejudice to the possibility of the supplier imposing maximum sale prices or recommending a sale price provided that these do not amount to a fixed or minimum sale price as a result of pressure from, or incentives offered by, any of the parties." Article 3 follows Art.4 of the Regulation, except that the Regulation only deals with arrangements which have the object of fixing prices, whilst Art.3 of the Order covers arrangements which have both the object and the effect.

5–503 The Order is thus far more generous than the Regulation. However, two points should be remembered here. First, Art.3 of Reg.1/2003 requires national competition authorities to apply Arts 81 or 82 whenever they are also applying national competition law, if the arrangements not only affect trade within the relevant Member State, but also affect trade between Member States. Given the discussion above about the possibility of a potential affect on trade between Member States in the current unified status of the common market, it is highly likely that, except in very special circumstances, the Order will have little practical effect. There will not be many instances in which trade within the UK is (actually or potentially) affected, without also finding at least a potential effect on trade between Member States. Second, even where the Order does have a practical effect, it does not apply to the Chapter II Prohibition, so the imposition in an agreement of restrictive terms other than resale price maintenance will be caught if the imposing undertaking is in a dominant position.

5–504 The issues relating to the grant of exclusivity under a distribution agreement within the EC, can therefore be briefly summed up as follows:

- UK competition law:
  - — will not consider the grant of exclusivity under the Chapter I Prohibition;
  - — will consider the grant of exclusivity under the Chapter II Prohibition if the grantor is in a dominant position;
  - — does not regard the mere grant of exclusivity as an abuse of a dominant position unless coupled with other conduct which was considered abusive (such as some kind of market foreclosure, the

achievement of supra-normal profits or refusal to supply without an objective reason).

- Under EC competition law:
  - the grant of exclusivity raises no problems if the market share of the grantor does not exceed the 30 per cent threshold even if combined with other non-hardcore vertical restraints;
  - where the market share of the grantor exceeds the 30 per cent threshold, the grant of exclusivity can be scrutinised under Art.81, and depending on the facts of the case may infringe Art.81(1) or be exempt under Art.81(3);
  - where the grantor is in a dominant position, then the grant of exclusivity which produces appreciable anti-competitive effects is far less likely to be exempt under Art.81(3) unless the grantor can point to an objective justification (see the Commission Guidelines para.135).

Section 2.2 (paras 161 to 177) of the Commission Guidelines considers in detail the status of a grant of exclusivity under EC competition law. Here the Commission is mainly concerned with the possibility of the reduction of intra-brand competition and market partitioning which facilitates price discrimination. This possibility is increased if the grant of exclusivity is coupled (as it usually is) with non-compete clauses of various kinds. (see para.161). The Commission admits that exclusive distribution may lead to efficiencies, particularly where "investments by the distributors are required to protect or build up the brand image. In general the case for efficiencies is strongest for new products, complex products, for products whose qualities are difficult to judge before consumption (so-called experience products) or of which the qualities are difficult to judge even after consumption (so-called credence products). In addition exclusive distribution may lead to savings in logistics costs ..." (para.165). **5–505**

However, the Commission's conclusion is that "the market position of the supplier and his competitors is of major importance, as the loss of intra-brand competition can only be problematic if inter-brand competition is limited ... Above the 30 per cent market share threshold there may be a risk of significant reduction of intra-brand competition. In order to be exemptable, the loss of intra-brand competition needs to be balanced with real efficiencies" (para.163). **5–506**

5.3 General undertakings by distributor

5.3.1 Due diligence

See cl.4.3.1. **5–507**

5.3.2 No interference with sales of products

5–508 5.3.2 The Distributor shall not [during the continuance of this Agreement] do anything that may prevent the sale or interfere with the development of sales of the Products in the Territory. [The obligations imposed by this clause shall continue until the expiry of a period of [five years] from [the date of signature of this Agreement] [the Effective Date] provided that if this Agreement is terminated for any cause whatsoever prior to the expiry of such period then upon such termination such obligations shall cease immediately.]

As discussed in Chapter 4.3.2, this clause is partly aimed at preventing sales of competing products, although there may be other circumstances in which it can be invoked. As such it will fall within the class of non-compete clauses discussed in part in Chapter 5.3.5 and in more detail in Chapter 5.3.6. The same detailed issues relating to non-compete clauses, discussed in those sections, would apply to this clause. In particular the principles for the use of the various possibilities set out in square brackets are the same as those discussed in relation to the possibilities set out under Chapter 5.3.6 in relation to cl.5.3.6.

5–509 This clause, like the other non-compete clauses discussed in Chapter 5.3.6 does not in general cause a problem under UK competition law. A detailed discussion of the treatment of non-compete clauses under UK competition law can be found in that section.

5.3.3 Conforming to local legislation

5–510 See cl.4.3.3.

5.3.4 Proper storage

5–511 See cl.4.3.4.

5.3.5 Purchase targets

5–512 5.3.5 The Distributor undertakes to achieve targets in relation to the Products in accordance with Sch.4 hereto.

Regulation 83/83 permitted the imposition of minimum purchase quantities as provided in this clause (see Art.2(3)), but the position is no longer so simple. In principle the imposition of minimum purchase obligations is viewed as a specific instance of "quantity forcing" which is one component of what the Commission calls the "single branding group" of vertical restraints. The single branding group of vertical restraints is discussed in detail in Chapter 5.3.6.

5–513 Where Reg.2790/99 prima facie applies to the distribution agreement, because the supplier's market share does not exceed 30 per cent, and there are no hardcore restrictions forbidden by Art.4, the treatment of a minimum purchase obligation depends upon its status in relation to the definition of "non-compete obligation" set out in Art.1 of the regulation. This definition reads in part "... any direct or ***indirect*** [emphasis added] obligation on the buyer to purchase from the supplier or another undertaking designated by the supplier more than 80 per cent of the buyer's total purchases of the contract goods or services and their substitutes on the relevant market, calculated on the basis of its purchases in the preceding calendar year". Obviously, if a minimum purchase obligation is set sufficiently high it could create an indirect obligation on the distributor to buy 80 per cent or more of the relevant goods only from the designated supplier, because he would not be free to buy from other suppliers of competing goods until the minimum purchase obligation had been fulfilled.

It is up to the parties to decide, on the basis of the current circumstances **5–514** and likely future projections, whether the purchasing quantity obligations are set at such a level that the 80 per cent threshold is currently exceeded or likely to be so exceeded at some future time during the period covered by the clause. Note that the Commission states (para.58 of the Guidelines) that "Where for the year preceding the conclusion of the contract no relevant purchasing data for the buyer are available, the buyer's best estimate of his annual total requirements may be used". The wording of Art.1(b) of Reg.2790/99 ("... in the preceding calendar year") means that the parties must also keep the issue under review at the beginning of each year of the agreement, in case their original estimates were incorrect, and it then appears that, due to an unforeseen change in demand, there is likely to be a breach of the 80 per cent threshold in the coming year.

If on the basis of these estimates, the minimum purchase obligation does **5–515** not cause a breach of the 80 per cent threshold, then it will not be regarded as a non-compete clause within the Art.1 definition. It is still a vertical restraint, but will be exempted by the general provisions of Art.2 of the regulation.

If, on the same basis, it breaches the 80 per cent threshold, it then falls **5–516** within the definition of "non-compete clause" in Art.1. Here, the parties have two choices. First they can draft the clause in accordance with the special conditions set out in Art.5(a), which, if complied with, permit a non-compete clause to be exempted under the Regulation. These conditions, which apply to all types of single branding restrictions are discussed in Chapter 5.3.6. If the parties do not wish to comply with those conditions, but still wish to keep the obligation, the remainder of the agreement can still benefit from exemption under Reg.2790/99, since the non-compete clauses are Art.5 restrictions not Art.4(hardcore) restrictions. However, in this case, they would then have to be satisfied that, in the special circumstances of the case, the clause qualified for exemption under Art.81(3).

If Reg.2790/99 does not apply because the principal's market share is **5–517** greater than 30 per cent, then the minimum purchase obligation will simply fall to be considered under Art.81, just like any other vertical restraint in the agreement. As usual everything will depend on the circumstances of the case, but the 80 per cent threshold will not be relevant. The higher the minimum purchase obligation the more likely it will be that the clause will infringe Art.81(1), and the less likely that it will be exempt under Art.81(3). Given that the supplier's market share will be at least 30 per cent, problems will usually arise well before the 80 per cent threshold is reached. Here, in most cases, the real issue will be the extent to which the supplier has foreclosed the market to other suppliers by imposing minimum purchase obligations on a number of distributors. The problem of cumulative foreclosure effect in relation non-compete clauses is discussed in Chapter 5.3.6 with reference to the general position under single branding obligations.

5–518 Quantity forcing does not in general cause a problem under UK competition law. A detailed discussion of the treatment of non-compete clauses under UK competition law can be found in Chapter 5.3.6.

5.3.6 Non-competition clause

5–519 5.3.6 The Distributor undertakes [during the continuance of this Agreement] not to manufacture or sell in the Territory any goods competitive with the Products nor to be interested directly or indirectly in the importation into the Territory of any such goods without the Principal's prior written consent. This provision shall not apply to those goods (if any) listed in sched 5. [The obligations imposed by this clause shall continue until the expiry of a period of [five years] from [the date of signature of this agreement] [the Effective Date] provided that if this Agreement is terminated for any cause whatsoever prior to the expiry of such period then upon such termination such obligations shall cease immediately.]

The full definition of a non-compete obligation in Art.1 of Reg.2790/99 reads: "any direct or indirect obligation causing the buyer not to manufacture, purchase sell or resell goods or services which compete with the contract goods or services, or any direct or indirect obligation on the buyer to purchase from the supplier or another undertaking designated by the supplier more than 80 per cent of the buyer's total purchases of the contract goods or services and their substitutes on the relevant market, calculated on the basis of the value of its purchases in the preceding calendar year". The wording is very precise. The first limb refers to "any direct or indirect obligation" the second to any direct or indirect obligation ***on the buyer***". Thus the first limb can refer not only to obligations undertaken by the buyer but also obligations undertaken by the supplier. This allows the first limb to catch not only non-compete obligations binding the buyer but also obligations on the part of the supplier to provide inducements (*e.g.* loyalty rebates or fidelity discounts) to the buyer to purchase only or predominantly from the supplier. Together all such obligations and inducements are grouped by the Commission in what it terms the "single branding group" of vertical restraints.

5–520 Obviously a non-compete clause of the nature set out in the precedent falls within the single branding group of vertical restraints.

In the Commission Guidelines on Vertical Restraints paras 106–108, the single branding group is defined as: "... those agreements which have as their main element that the buyer is induced to concentrate his orders for a particular type of product with one supplier. This component can be found amongst others in non-compete and quantity forcing on the buyer, where an obligation or incentive scheme agreed between the supplier and the buyer makes the latter purchase his requirements for a particular product and its substitutes only or mainly from one supplier. The same component can be found in tying ...". These clauses prevent other suppliers selling to the affected buyers, thus leading to foreclosure of the market, make market shares more rigid, eliminate inter-brand competition amongst retailers (as they will only handle the brand covered by the obligations or inducements), and, in the case of tied products will probably cause the buyer to pay a higher price than he would otherwise do. Although suppliers may compete to obtain single branding contracts, the benefit of this initial competition is diluted the longer the duration of the contracts. **5–521**

Article 5 of Reg.2790/99 provides that no exemption shall be given *inter alia)* to any "direct or indirect non-compete obligation the duration of which is indefinite or which exceeds five years". The use of the words "direct or indirect" would appear otiose here as the definition of "non-compete obligation" in Art.1 already deals with direct or indirect obligations. If it is anything more than mere surplusage, the double use of the words could presumably be intended to make the ambit of Art.5 as wide as possible. **5–522**

This clause is therefore permissible under Reg.2790/99, just as any other single branding vertical restriction would be provided that it complies with the requirements of Art.5. The same is true of cl.5.3.2 (no interference with sales of the products) cl.5.3.5 (minimum purchase targets) and cl.5.6.1. (obligation to obtain supplies of the products only from the principal). **5–523**

In most distribution agreements, such clauses have no special provision in them as to the duration of the obligation they impose. Thus, they endure for the life of the agreement and then fall away. If this approach is taken, then such clauses, when inserted in a distribution agreement which continues unless and until terminated by notice, will be deemed to be of an indefinite length. Article 5 expressly provides that "A non-compete obligation which is tacitly renewable beyond a period of five years is to be deemed to have been concluded for an indefinite period" (see the discussion of this issue in *Neste Markkinointi Oy v Yotuuli Ky*). **5–524**

In order to take advantage of the exemption, one possibility is to enter into a distribution agreement with a fixed term of five years or less. If this is the case, then, in the clause above, and in cl.5.3.2, the phrase in the first set of square brackets should be used and not the longer sentence in the second set of square brackets. Here, the relevant clauses would be for a fixed term of five years or less depending upon the term chosen for the agreement. Upon expiry, the parties could, if they so chose, renew or enter into a new agreement, upon terms mutually agreed, which yet again contained non-compete obligations and was for a further fixed term of up to five years. This is not a "tacit" renewal, but one which depends upon the mutual express **5–525** agreement of the parties. If the market share of the supplier still does not exceed 30 per cent upon renewal or upon execution of the new agreement, then it will still be possible to take advantage of Reg.2790/99.

5–526 Indeed this approach is contemplated by the Commission. "However non-compete obligations are covered [by Reg.2790/99] when their duration is limited to five years or less, or when renewal beyond five years requires explicit consent of both parties and no obstacles exist that hinder the buyer from effectively terminating the non-compete obligation at the end of the five year period. If, for instance, the agreement provides for a five year non-compete obligation and the supplier provides a loan to the buyer, the repayment of that loan should not hinder the buyer from effectively terminating the non-compete obligation at the end of the five year period; the repayment needs to be structured in equal or decreasing instalments and should not increase over time". (Commission Guidelines on Vertical Restraints para.58) Presumably this qualification would also apply where a non-compete clause (or the agreement in which it is contained has expired by effluxion of time) but there were obstacles (as described in the Guidelines) which would force the buyer to accept another fixed term contract (again with non-compete clauses in it) upon its expiry.

5–527 Where the parties do not wish to enter into an agreement for a fixed term, the alternative would seem to be expressly to limit the operation of the clause in question to a period of no more than five years from the date of signature of the agreement, or, if later, from the date the agreement (and hence the non-compete obligation) enters into force—the "Effective Date". The drafting for this eventuality is set out in the second set of square brackets in the clause above and in cl.5.3.2.

5–528 Such a provision could also be added in respect of cl.5.3.5 and cl.5.6.1. However, in the case of cl.5.3.5, minimum purchase targets are usually set down as a legally binding obligation for the first few years of the distribution agreement only. After this further targets (if any) are usually set by mutual consent. This is provided for in Sch.4. This approach would satisfy the Commission's requirement that the renewal of the obligation be by express rather than by tacit consent.

5–529 So far as cl.5.6.1 is concerned, the only approach is as for cl.5.3.6, so that either the agreement is for five years or less, or a provision limiting the clause to five years or less is expressly inserted along the lines of the provision suggested for cl.5.3.6.

5–530 One possibility, where the agreement has an initial fixed term and is thereafter terminable by notice, is to make the duration of the non-compete obligations equal to the fixed term. If either party is not happy with the operation of the agreement once the non-compete clauses drop away he can always terminate the relationship by due notice.

5–531 The difficulty with this approach is that it could be argued the principal always holds the threat of termination and appointment of another distributor over the buyer and that this means in practice the buyer will continue to observe the non-compete obligations as a result of an express or tacit threat from the principal. Perhaps such a situation could be described as an obstacle which hinders the buyer from effectively terminating the non-compete obligation. However, except if there has been an express threat, it could be argued that termination should not be an issue where the buyer has no economic ties, such as the loan described above, which would prejudice him in the event the agreement was terminated. Further, given that this is a case where, by definition, the principal has a 30 per cent market share or less, the distributor should be able to find an alternative source of supply and to carry on business if the principal terminates the agreement. This analysis is, however, subject to the rule (discussed in Chapter 6) that where a selective distribution network is concerned, the principal cannot terminate only one distributor without cause; here he must wind up the whole network.

There is support for the contention that termination, or the potential (even if tacit) threat of termination, could give rise to the stated problem, in a statement made by the Commission in relation to an investigation into the practices of Checkpoint Technologies Ltd, an Israeli company, on the Finnish market (see Commission Statement IP/02/521 April 9, 2002). The Commission was concerned that Checkpoint had told some of its distributors and resellers that if they handled competing software products they would no longer be supplied with Checkpoint's software products. Checkpoint was one of the main operators on the world market in the sale of firewall and virtual private network (VPN) software which prevented hacking and provided encryption facilities for public networks. The Commission were concerned that such threats, given Checkpoint's market power, were having a negative foreclosure effect on the market for firewall/VPN software. Checkpoint agreed with the Commission that it would not place undue or unacceptable pressure upon distributors and resellers regarding their independent decision to handle competing products and it would confirm to them by letter that they were free to do so. Checkpoint also undertook to ensure its staff understood the implications of EC Competition law and the requirement to observe it properly. The Commission withdrew its objections on this basis. **5–532**

The Checkpoint case shows that a principal may have some difficulty in terminating a distribution agreement because he is not happy with the situation once non-compete obligations have fallen away. However, the extent of Checkpoint's market share was a significant factor in the case, which does not, in any event, seem to have an application in relation to the question of removal of exclusivity as opposed to termination. **5–533**

Given the above analysis, the best approach to non-compete restrictions is either to provide that the agreement containing them runs for a fixed term of five years or less, or, if this is not commercially acceptable, that the restrictions themselves run for five years or less, and that, upon their expiry, the agreement automatically becomes non-exclusive. It cannot be said that in these circumstances any threat exists as both parties understand what will happen from the outset. **5–534**

There is one exception to the five year rule. This relates to sales from tied premises, such as petrol stations or public houses or restaurants. The five **5–535** year limitation does not apply where "the contract goods or services are sold by the buyer from premises and land owned by the supplier or leased by the supplier from third parties not connected with the buyer, provided that the duration of the non-compete obligation does not exceed the period of occupancy of the premises and land by the buyer" (Art.5(a) of Reg.2790/99).

5–536 Finally it should be noted that under transitional provisions the Commission has stated (see para.90 of the Guidelines) that "Agreements of suppliers with a market share not exceeding 30 per cent who signed with their buyers non-compete agreements with a duration exceeding five years are covered by the Block Exemption Regulation if on 1 January 2002 the non-compete agreements have no more than five years to run".

5–537 Of course it is always open to the parties to proceed on the basis that their particular non-compete clause does not comply with the conditions in Art.5(a), but that, in the particular circumstances of the case, Art.81(3) will apply to exempt it. If they are confident on this issue, and there are no hardcore restrictions present, the rest of the agreement can then take advantage of exemption under Reg.2790/99. This approach is discussed in more detail in relation to minimum purchase obligations in Chapter 5.3.5.

5–538 Where Reg.2790/99 does not apply because the supplier's market share is greater than 30 per cent, the Commission has set out guidelines to help undertakings determine whether any agreement or network of agreements having a cumulative effect and containing single branding group restrictions actually infringes Art.81(1) in any relevant market. This requires an economic analysis of the facts in each case. It should always be remembered that there are three possibilities as the result of any such analysis—no infringement under Art.81(1), infringement under Art.81(1) but exemption under Art.81(3) or infringement under Art.81(1) and no exemption under Art.81(3).

5–539 The methodology for this analysis is set out in section 2.1 of the Guidelines on Vertical Restraints (paras 138–160.) "The market position of the supplier is of main importance … In general this type of obligation is imposed by the supplier and the supplier has similar agreements with other buyers" (para.140). "It is not only the market position of the supplier that is of importance but also the extent to and the duration for which he applies a non-compete obligation. The higher his tied market share, *i.e.* the part of his market share sold under a single branding obligation, the more significant foreclosure is likely to be. Similarly the longer the duration of the non-compete obligation, the more significant the foreclosure is likely to be (para.141). The Commission considers that provided an undertaking is not in a dominant position, non-compete obligations of less than one year in general should not have an appreciable effect on competition (*i.e.* no infringement under Art.81(1)) while those of over five years probably would (*i.e.* infringement under Art.81(1) but no exemption under Art.81(3) likely). For obligations between one and five years, there has to be a proper balancing of the pro- and anti-competitive effects, such as positive efficiencies in distribution and consequent cost savings for consumers against reduced inter-brand competition due to foreclosure (infringement under Art.81(1) but possible exemption under Art.81(3)). (para.141).

In this context it is worth noting para.158 of the Guidelines: "Below the level of dominance the combination of non-compete with exclusive distribution may also justify the non-compete obligation lasting the full length of the agreement. In the latter case, the non-compete obligation is likely to improve the distribution efforts of the exclusive distributor in his territory (see also para.161–177)". This statement supports the contention set out above, in relation to agreements covered by Reg.2790/99, that a provision converting an exclusive distributorship to a non-exclusive distributorship, upon termination of non-compete obligations, should not cause problems under Reg.2790/99. In addition, where the supplier's market share is less than 30 per cent and Reg.2790/99 applies, then, even though the non-compete clause itself is not exempt under Art.5(a) because it runs for longer than five years, in many situations the same argument would apply to provide for individual exemption of such a clause under Art.81(3) where it is was coterminous with a grant of an exclusive distributorship which ran for more than five years or was of indeterminate length. **5–540**

Finally, the situation is clear with regard to undertakings in a dominant position. "Where an undertaking is dominant, or becoming dominant as a consequence of the vertical agreement, a vertical restraint that has appreciable anticompetitive effects can in principle not be exempted" (para.135). The Commission further states: "Dominant companies may not impose non-compete obligations on their buyers unless they can objectively justify such commercial practices within the context of Article 82" (para.141). **5–541**

A good example of the Commission approach to this issue can be seen in the "freezer exclusivity" cases discussed above (see *Scholler Lebensmittel GmbH & Co KG v Commission* and *Langnese-Iglo v Commission* and the Commission Statement IP/98/242 dated March 11, 1998 relating to Unilever's freezer exclusivity arrangements in Ireland). **5–542**

The question of the foreclosure or cumulative foreclosure effect of networks of supply agreements each containing non-compete clauses is also important. (Reference should be made here to the discussion on the concept of cumulative effect in Chapter 5.1.1.3; see *Delimitis v Henninger Brau; Re Scottish and Newcastle plc; Scholler Lebensmittel GmbH & Co KG v Commission* and *Langnese-Iglo v Commission;* and *Neste Markkinointi Oy v Yotuuli Ky*). The Commission states in para.142 of the Guidelines that "foreclosure may however occur ... when a number of major suppliers enter into non-compete contracts with a significant number of buyers ... (cumulative effect situation) ... if individually these suppliers are covered by the Block Exemption Regulation a withdrawal of the block exemption may be necessary ... a tied market share of 5 per cent is not considered in general to contribute significantly to a cumulative foreclosure effect". (Note the similar statement in para.II.8 of the Commission Notice on Agreements of Minor Importance".) **5–543**

The Commission comments in para.146 on circumstances when the foreclosure effects (particularly cumulative foreclosure effects) may arise. It states that: **5–544**

- The effects are less likely to occur with "intermediate products" (*i.e.* raw materials, semi-finished or semi-processed ingredients, components or sub-assemblies).
- The effects are more likely to occur with final products (*i.e.* finished products intended for end use in their existing form).
- where intermediate products are concerned a foreclosure effect is unlikely so long as less than 50 per cent of the market is tied.
- Where the agreement concerns supply of a final product, foreclosure is less likely at the wholesale level of trade (para.147).
- Foreclosure for final products is most likely to occur at the retail level of trade (para.148) and this is also the level at which the cumulative foreclosure effect for final products is most likely to arise (para.149).
- In either case, a cumulative foreclosure effect is unlikely to arise if all suppliers have market shares below 30 per cent and the total tied market share is less than 40 per cent. In this case, withdrawal of the block exemption is unlikely (para.149).
- When not all companies have market shares below 30 per cent but none is dominant a cumulative foreclosure effect is in either case unlikely to arise if the total tied market share is below 30 per cent (para.149). (Note the similar statement in para.II.8 of the Notice on Agreements of Minor Importance).

5–545 The position under UK competition law, if applicable, is very simple. Non-compete obligations are not mentioned in The Competition Act 1998 (Land and Vertical Agreements) Order 2000 (SI 2000/310), so that the Chapter I Prohibition has no relevance. Thus single branding group restrictions of the type discussed in cll.5.3.2, 5.3.5, 5.3.6 and 5.6.1 are lawful unless the supplier is in a dominant position on the relevant market in the UK or a substantial part of the UK. It is then likely that the Office of Fair Trading will follow the Commission practice in relation to single branding group restrictions imposed by suppliers in a dominant position. In this case, the Commission regards such an imposition as an abuse unless the undertaking concerned can "objectively justify such commercial practice within the context of Art.82" (para.141).

5.3.7 No copying of products

5–546 5.3.7 The Distributor undertakes not to copy produce make modify or manufacture or assist any other party to copy produce make or manufacture the Products or any part thereof for use sale or any other purpose.

This would appear to be permissible at first sight as it is not a restriction arising in truth out of the agreement, but merely a statement of the rights which the principal has by reason of his ownership in the intellectual and industrial property relating to the products, which he could exercise in any case. Such a clause is, however, a vertical restraint to the extent it prevents copying and similar activities in relation to products, or parts thereof, not protected by intellectual property rights, which can be carried out without the use of know how transmitted to the distributor by the principal. Given the current position on design rights (see Chapter 4.3.7) this has particular application to spare parts. In this case the clause would amount to an indirect non-compete clause and should be amended accordingly (see Chapter 5.3.6) if it is designed to take advantage of the exemption under Reg.2790/99.

The use of industrial property rights to control the free flow of spare parts **5–547**
is discussed in Chapter 6.24.15. Also discussed is whether too tight control of a market in spare parts by the manufacturer of the products for which they are required in fact constitutes an abuse of a dominant position under Art.81.

In any event, given this situation, it may be better to omit this clause (certainly where Reg.2790/99 does not apply) leaving the principal to rely on any relevant intellectual property rights to prevent copying.

5.3.8 Patent and trade mark notices

5.3.8.1 [Save as provided in cl.5.3.8.2] [T]he Distributor shall leave in position **5–548**
and not cover or erase any notices or other marks (including without limitation details of patents or notices that a trade mark design or copyright relating to the Products is owned by the Principal or a third party) which the Principal may place on or affix to the Products or their packaging. The Distributor shall not interfere with the packaging of the Products nor present any Products for sale in a group package.

[5.3.8.2 In order to make any sale of the Products (not prohibited by the pro- **5–549**
visions of cll.5.5.1 and 5.5.2) outside the Territory into any other Member State of the European Community (a "permitted export") the Distributor shall be entitled to carry out the following activities in relation to any quantity of the Products which is to be the subject of a permitted export, to the extent that such activities are necessary to effect that permitted export:

- (i) Fixing together two or more packages without disturbing the original packaging, so that the combined packages are sold to end-users as a single unit ("bundling");
- (ii) repackaging in new internal or external packaging ("internal repackaging" and "external repackaging" respectively and together "repackaging"); and
- (iii) affixing additional labels to original external or internal packaging ("internal relabelling" and "external relabelling" respectively and together "relabelling")

For the avoidance of doubt:

- (a) The Distributor shall carry out relabelling rather than bundling or repackaging if this is sufficient to carry out a permitted export.
- (b) The Distributor shall carry out bundling together with relabelling

rather than repackaging if this is sufficient to carry out a permitted export.

(c) Where relabelling is necessary to carry out a permitted export, this shall be external relabelling rather than internal relabelling if external relabelling is sufficient to carry out the permitted export.

(d) Where repackaging is necessary to carry out a permitted export, this shall be external repackaging rather than internal repackaging if external repackaging is sufficient to achieve the permitted purpose.

The permission granted by this clause is subject to the following conditions:

5.3.8.2.1 The Distributor shall not effect any relabelling or repackaging which will damage the reputation of the Trade Mark.

5.3.8.2.2 The Distributor shall not effect any repackaging involving a risk of the product inside the package being exposed to tampering or to influences affecting its original condition; for the avoidance of doubt it is agreed that no such risk will arise:

5.3.8.2.2.1 where repackaging is carried out under the supervision of a public authority in order to ensure that the original condition of the relevant Product has not been directly or indirectly affected; or

5.3.8.2.2.2 where blister packs are removed from the original external package and inserted intact into another external package (whether new or original).

5.3.8.2.3 Any relabelling or repackaging effected by the Distributor pursuant to this clause may include the addition of a translation into the language of the Member State of importation of the user instructions or information provided by the Principal; the Distributor may also include additional information provided such information does not contradict any information provided by the Principal in the state of importation.

5.3.8.2.4 Where the Distributor effects relabelling or repackaging it shall clearly set out on the external package of the relevant Product:

5.3.8.2.4.1 its name and the address of its principal place of business;

5.3.8.2.4.2 that it was responsible for the relabelling or repackaging;

5.3.8.2.4.3 unless already present and visible, the name and principal place of business of the manufacturer of the product, and if different, the name and principal place of business of the trade mark owner; and

5.3.8.2.4.4 unless still present and visible any patent, design or copyright notices, and any notices relating to manufacture of the products under licence [and any other markings numbering or notices] on the original packaging;

Provided that where (except for the need to comply with this clause) the original external package would have been retained the Distributor shall set out the relevant items using relabelling.

5.3.8.2.5 Whenever as the result of any bundling relabelling or repackaging carried out by the Distributor any representation of the Trade Mark (the "old representation") affixed by the manufacturer or the trade mark proprietor to the relevant Products or their original packaging has been obliterated, removed or rendered no longer visible, (including without limitation by reason of the removal of the original external packaging for the purposes of external repackaging), the Distributor shall affix a new representation, where reasonably possible in or close to the original position of the old representation, or else in some other suitable position. The Principal hereby grants the Distributor a licence under the Trade Mark to carry out the activities referred to in this clause.

5.3.8.2.6 The Distributor shall provide the Principal with a specimen of the bundled relabelled or repackaged product not less than thirty days before it goes on sale, to enable the Principal to check:

5.3.8.2.6.1 that the bundling, relabelling or repackaging is necessary to achieve the relevant permitted export;

5.3.8.2.6.2 that the bundling, relabelling or repackaging has not been carried out in such a way as directly or indirectly to affect the original condition of the relevant Product; and

5.3.8.2.6.3 that the presentation after bundling, relabelling or repackaging is not such as to damage the reputation of the trade mark.]

The problems with this clause are caused by the so-called repackaging cases discussed in Chapter 5.1.1.4.3. To the extent that cl.5.3.8.1 used in isolation prevents the distributor removing and reaffixing or adding extra labels to the products, or interfering with the packaging, it will prevent him repackaging or relabelling even if this is necessary in order for him to export product to, and put it on the market in, another Member State.

Of course, if the product is of a kind which can be exported freely across borders without any need for repackaging or relabelling then none of the issues to be discussed in this section would arise, and it would be possible to use cl.5.3.8.1. alone and renumber it as cl.5.3.8. **5–550**

The repackaging cases (subject to certain conditions) do not permit the manufacturer to exercise his trade mark rights in such a way as to interfere with trade between Member States by preventing repackaging necessary for such export sales (usually described as parallel imports). If the manufacturer cannot use his trade mark rights to prevent third parties engaging in repackaging necessary for parallel imports, is it possible for him to use contractual provisions to prevent his distributor engaging in such activities? **5–551**

The question is thus whether, and to what extent, cl.5.3.8.1 amounts to the imposition of an indirect prohibition on exports by the distributor. First, such a clause cannot prevent all parallel imports even where repackaging is necessary. The distributor can always sell to a third party (whether or not situated in the Member State of importation) who, not fettered by the contractual restriction and taking advantage of the principles in the repackaging cases, can carry out any necessary repackaging itself. However, the clause will prevent the distributor himself from carrying out parallel imports and selling to end-users in another Member State. Further, the relevant regulatory regime in the other Member State may not just forbid sale to end-users without compliance with local packaging requirements, but also prevent even such sales into that state made to a wholesaler or other reseller (who could then carry out the repackaging and sell to end-users). In this case, the clause effectively bars the distributor from making any export **5–552** sales at all into that other state.

5–553 This provision is not dealt with specifically in Reg.2790/99, although it was a permitted restriction under its predecessor Reg.83/83 (Art.2(3)(c)), but, on the analysis set out above (and depending upon the products distributed under the agreement), it will amount to an indirect prohibition on exports in relation to products and Member States where repackaging is necessary before a parallel import can be placed on the market there. Having established this ground rule, it is necessary to determine the consequences, first if Reg.2790/99 applies and second if it does not.

5–554 So far as Reg.2790/99 is concerned, the issue is whether this clause is a hardcore restriction forbidden under Art.4(b), in that it indirectly prevents sales outside the distributor's territory where such sales cannot be made without repackaging.

5–555 It is true that, if the clause were regarded as an indirect restriction on active sales alone, then it would be acceptable in so far as it complied with the conditions set out in the first exception to Art.4(b), since that exception permits the prohibition of active sales even if no repackaging is necessary. However, this exception does not permit the prohibition of all active sales outside the territory, but only those made into territories reserved to the principal or his other distributors (see Chapter 5.5). Therefore, if cl.5.3.8.1 applies to all areas of the EC both within and outside the distributor's territory, it will, at least in some cases, not be possible to take advantage of the exception since the clause will indirectly prohibit active sales to all areas of the EC not just into the reserved territories.

5–556 In cases where all of the EC outside the distributor's territory has legitimately been reserved for the principal or his other distributors (see the discussion on this point in Chapter 5.5) then it will be possible to take advantage of the first exception to Art.4(b), so far as active sales are concerned.

5–557 The next question is whether the prohibition on repackaging prevents the distributor making passive sales for export outside his territory? On the above analysis the answer must be in the negative, since any intending parallel importer could always buy and repackage himself, even if, for regulatory reasons, he had to carry out the repackaging before it left the Member State from which it was to be exported. Passive sales to end-users are never an issue, because, even though repackaging were required to achieve this, the second exception to Art.4(b) permits a prohibition on wholesalers selling to end-users, which would be applicable in the case of this distribution agreement which is not designed to cover retail sales.

5–558 If this is correct, then in the event of passive sales outside the territory, the distributor could supply the order, but would not be permitted to repackage the goods in order to satisfy local regulations in the state of importation. This repackaging would have to be carried out by the importer.

5–559 Where Reg.2790/99 does not apply, then the above analysis indicates that cl.5.3.8.1 would always be regarded as a vertical restraint, since it will always be an indirect restriction on some types of export sales unless the product concerned did not require repackaging in order to be put on the market anywhere in the EC. Where repackaging was required, if the parties wished to keep this clause, then they would have to convince themselves that it was exempt under Art.81(3). Given that it is an indirect prohibition on exports it seems unlikely that this would be possible.

The situation can thus be summed up as follows: **5–560**

- If the products can be sold anywhere in the EC in the same packaging, it is safe to use cl.5.3.8.1 alone.
- Where Reg.2790/99 applies, if the goods do require repackaging for sale outside the distributor's territory:
  - — if the whole of the EC outside the distributor's territory is legitimately reserved to the principal or allocated to his other distributors, then it is safe to use cl.5.3.8.1 alone;
  - — if there are areas outside the distributor's territory not reserved to the principal or allocated to his distributors and the goods cannot be sold in those areas without repackaging, then cl.5.3.8.1 cannot be used alone as it will become a hardcore restriction as it indirectly prevents active sales into those areas, even if not passive ones.
- Where Reg.2790/99 does not apply, if the goods do require repackaging for sale outside the distributor's territory then the clause will always be a vertical restraint, and, subject to the possibility of exemption under Art.81(3), will infringe Art.81(1).

Given the situation described so far, where the products do require repackaging for export and no exemption is possible under Reg.2790/99, one possible response is not to include cl.5.3.8.1 at all, and for the principal simply to rely first upon the provisions of the agreement which prevent active sales into reserved territories, and only as a last resort upon whatever powers he still has to prevent repackaging under Art.30 if the distributor in any particular case goes beyond what rights the repackaging cases afford him. **5–561**

However, since third parties can take advantage of the repackaging cases and he cannot control their conduct by contract in any event, it must be asked why the principal should be particularly concerned about restricting the powers of the distributor to repackage, even in those circumstances where this is possible because Reg.2790/99 applies. **5–562**

In fact it could be advantageous for the principal to permit the distributor to carry out repackaging on the basis that at least the principal would know who was carrying out the repackaging and would have some control (to the extent permitted by community law) over the way the repackaging was carried out. Furthermore, cl.5.3.8.1 does not only cover repackaging where this is necessary for export, but also many other types of tampering with the products which the principal can legally prohibit except to the extent that their prohibition indirectly prevents repackaging permitted under the repackaging cases. **5–563**

5–564 Thus, the best course of action is to retain cl.5.3.8.1 to ensure that no unauthorised tampering with the products or their packaging occurs, but to exclude from cl.5.3.8.1 repackaging where necessary for export to areas of the EC outside the distributor's territory and regulate such repackaging in terms of cl.5.3.8.2. Clause 5.3.8.2 is based upon the guidelines set out in the repackaging cases. If cl.5.3.8.2 is used, then of course the set of square brackets in cl.5.3.8.1 should also be included.

5–565 The whole basis of the clause is to ensure that bundling relabelling or repackaging is kept to the minimum necessary to enable the permitted export to take place. Given the dicta in the repackaging cases it is better not to attempt to define what is "necessary". It appears that the term does go beyond compliance with legal and regulatory requirements. If buying practices in the state of importation are such that for all practical purposes users will not purchase the product unless it is bundled, relabeled or repackaged in a certain way, then "necessary" would extend to actions required to satisfy those buying practices. However, what is "necessary" does stop short of what would just make sales easier. The bundling relabelling or repackaging is not justified just to obtain a commercial advantage. Unfortunately, it is not possible to define all of these variables with sufficient precision to cover all possible eventualities. From the point of view both of the distributor and the principal it is better to remain with the concept of "necessary" and to judge each particular instance of bundling, relabelling or repackaging by this simple yardstick.

5–566 Leaving apart the problems raised by the repackaging cases, cl.5.3.8.1 also causes more general problems in relation to anticompetitive activities. If the markings protected by the clause are simply trade mark and patent notices and details of the name and address of the manufacturer of the products, this should cause no additional problems. However, if they also contain special markings such as serial or batch numbers or details of the name and address of the distributor to whom they have been sold, there may be an anticompetitive motive in putting such details on the packaging—namely to trace the origin of parallel imports.

5–567 The affixing of such markings, and the imposition of an obligation not to remove them, at the very least raises some questions as to infringement of Art.81(1). Manufacturers often adduce other reasons for such markings, for example the need to record batch numbers for product safety purposes (*e.g.* product recalls) and this is acceptable to the Commission. However, the Commission will not easily accept that health and safety concerns are genuine unless a proper case is put forward, and there is no evidence of the use of the markings which is inconsistent with this information. (see Case T-49/95 *Van Megen Sports Group BV v Commission* [1997] 4 C.M.L.R. 843 and Case C-349/95 *Loendersloot v George Ballantine & Son Ltd* [1997] ECR I-06227) and the Commission statements in the Guidelines on Vertical Restraints condemning the monitoring of resale prices (para.47) and of exports (para.49); but contrast the discussion about legitimate uses of marking to determine where products were first put on the market in the recent decision of *Van Doren v Lifestyle & Sportswear Handelgesellschaf* considered in Chapter 5.1.1.4.1.)

It will be noted that cl.5.3.8.2.7 contains the phrase "and any other markings numbering or notices" in square brackets. If this phrase is inserted it will cover the batch numbers and other such markings referred to in the above cases. Where there is no defensible reason for such markings then not only is this phrase best omitted, but it would be better if such markings were not present in the first place. **5–568**

5.3.9 Shipment inspection reports

See cl.4.3.9. **5–569**

5.3.10 Indemnity for breach

See cl.4.3.10. **5–570**

5.4 Enquiries

> 5.4 The Distributor shall during the continuance of this Agreement refer to the Principal all enquiries it receives for the Products for sale or ultimate delivery outside the EC. **5–571**

It is sometimes considered that this type of restriction is possible to enable at least some control over the activities of the distributor outside the EC, since in many cases there is no probability that trade between Member States will be affected by such a provision. If there is no such actual or potential effect Art.81 has no application and exemption under Reg.2790/99 is irrelevant. There is some limited support for this view, depending upon all the circumstances of the case, but unless such a provision is of particular commercial importance to the parties, it is better to omit it rather than to try to decide whether, on the facts of the particular case, it is anti-competitive under EC competition law rules (see *EMI v CBS*, *Polydor v Harlequin* and *Javico International* and *Javico AG v Yves Saint Laurent Parfums SA* discussed in Chapter 5.5.2).

It should be noted that a similar clause imposing an obligation on the distributor to refer enquiries for areas within the EC, but outside his territory, will be regarded as an indirect ban on exports infringing Art.81(1) even if the principal also assumes a reciprocal obligation to refer to the distributor any enquiries received by the principal from customers within the territory (Case T-176/95 *Accinauto SA v Commission* [2000] 4 C.M.L.R. 67) and Case T-175/95 *BASF v Commission* [2000] 4 C.M.L.R. 33). **5–572**

Accinauto SA was a Belgian company distributing the BASF group's motor vehicle refinishing paints in Belgium and Luxembourg. Accinauto undertook to "pass on" to BASF any customer enquiries coming from **5–573** outside the contract territory. The Commission considered that the phrase "pass on customer enquiries" must be understood to mean that the party to whom the enquiries are "passed on" takes the place of the party doing the "passing on". As a result, Accinauto was prohibited from deciding independently whether to supply customers based outside Belgium or Luxembourg. It was BASF which decided whether and on what conditions Accinauto, BASF or a third party might respond to those orders. The Commission fined BASF €2.7m and Accinauto €10,000 for operating a disguised prohibition on passive export sales.

5–574 Accinauto appealed to the Court to annul the Commission Decision so far as it concerned Accinauto, maintaining that the expression "pass on customer enquiries" referred solely to the passing on of information allowing BASF the better to plan its distribution organisation and commercial strategy, and fulfil its obligation to supply the market on an equitable basis in the event of difficulties in supply. Also the obligation only related to enquiries from customers not to orders. Thus there was nothing in the agreement which required BASF's consent to sales outside the territory.

5–575 The Court, approaching this in exactly the way any Civil law jurisdiction court would, considered the following factors to be of importance—the wording of the clause, the scope of the other clauses in the contract which related to the authorised dealer's obligation under that clause, and the factual and legal circumstances surrounding the conclusion and implementation of the agreement which enabled its purpose to be elucidated.

5–576 The Court considered that it was irrelevant that the passing-on obligation applied only to enquiries, rather than orders. "If a negative response were given to an enquiry passed on in pursuance of the clause, there would be no point in the customer placing an order with Accinauto. The fact that the authorised dealer was obliged to pass on enquiries which precede orders does not support the conclusion that he retains his freedom of decision in full and is not subject to any restriction as regards satisfying the orders".

5–577 The Court found that the clause could not relate simply to the supply of marketing information:

> "The Court therefore finds that the passing-on obligations by providing for reciprocal notification of specific supply enquiries, are different in kind from the obligations to provide information.
>
> Secondly, the passing on obligation forms part of a clause which contains a ban on active exports outside the territory. It follows that the interpretation contended for by the applicant, whereby the term 'pass on' simply means 'inform' the other party of the existence of the supply enquiries, cannot be accepted.
>
> The Court therefore finds that the applicant's explanations concerning the purpose of the passing-on obligation in Article 2(2) of the 1982 agreement are not such as to invalidate the Commission's contention that that clause contains a disguised prohibition on passive export sales without prior authorisation.
>
> Moreover, the history of the agreement offers an explanation for the

ambiguous terms in which the parties drafted the clause complained of and for the disguised nature of the export ban which it contains. The parties were sufficiently aware, through their earlier experience, of the fact that an express export ban is contrary to Community competition law. Nevertheless, they clearly expressed their intention to make enquiries from outside the contract territory subject to a specific system of recording which enabled the manufacturer to influence the dealer's conduct with respect to exports, should this prove to be necessary."

The conclusions on "passing on" clauses relating to enquiries from outside the EC are therefore as follows. If the clause has an actual or potential effect on trade between Member States as a matter of fact (within the criteria set down in *Javico*) then it will infringe Art.81 (1) because it will amount to an indirect ban on cross border sales within the EC. In this respect such a clause is no different to the one imposed on Accinauto by BASF. In both cases, the clause amounts to an indirect ban on passive sales across borders. In terms of Reg.2790/99, it would therefore be a hardcore restriction falling under Art.4(b) (because it covered passive sales and not active sales) and rendering the agreement which contained it ineligible for exemption. If the facts of the case were such that the clause had no actual or potential effect on trade between Member States then there would, of course, be no infringement of Art.81(1). **5–578**

So far as UK competition law is concerned, the Chapter I Prohibition would have no application to a "passing on clause", whether it related to areas inside or outside the EC. The effect of the Chapter I Prohibition is excluded by the Vertical Restraints Order except in relation to resale price maintenance, which has nothing to do with this clause. Where the undertaking concerned is in a dominant position, the Chapter II Prohibition would only have application if it could be shown that the clause affected trade within the UK. This is of course more likely to happen if the passing on clause covered areas within rather than outside the EC. **5–579**

This is in any event largely academic. In the case of a clause covering areas inside the EC, EC competition law rules would also apply in parallel, and Art.81 could be applied directly under Reg.1/2003 by the Office of Fair Trading. Where the clause related to areas outside the EC, showing an effect on trade within the UK would in practice still mean that EC competition law rules applied in parallel. If the prohibition actually or potentially prevents product coming into the UK, then it will also almost certainly prevent the possibility of export to other Member States of any product which (but for the clause) would have come into the UK. This must produce at least a potential effect on trade between Member States. **5–580**

5.5 Extra-territorial activities

5.5.1 Sales activities inside the EC

5–581 5.5.1.1 The Distributor shall not during the continuance of this Agreement carry on the following activities in any area within the EC which is outside the Territory in respect of (a) any territory (a "reserved territory") or (b) any customer group (a "reserved customer group") which has in the case of either (a) or (b) been reserved exclusively to the Principal or allocated exclusively by the Principal to another distributor:

5.5.1.1.1 actively approach individual customers in a reserved territory or a reserved customer group for orders for the Products (including without limitation by way of direct mail or personal visits); or

5.5.1.1.2 actively approach a reserved customer group or a specific group of customers in a reserved territory through advertisements in media or other promotions specifically targeted at that reserved customer group or at customers in that reserved territory; or

5.5.1.1.3 open branches for the sale of the Products in a reserved territory, or establish a distribution outlet or warehouse for the Products in a reserved territory.

5–582 5.5.1.2 Notwithstanding the provisions of this clause, the Distributor shall be entitled to carry out general advertising or promotions in media or on the internet that reaches customers in a reserved territory or a reserved customer group provided that such advertising and promotion is primarily intended to reach customers (including without limitation customers in the Territory) who are outside any reserved territory and do not form part of any reserved customer group ("general customers") and that such advertising and promotion is a reasonable way to reach such general customers.

5–595 5.5.1.3 The reserved territories and the reserved customer groups in existence at the date of this agreement are set out in Sch.6. Upon a territory becoming or ceasing to be a reserved territory or upon a group of customers becoming or ceasing to be a reserved customer group, the Principal shall notify the Distributor of this occurrence and thereupon Sch.6 shall be deemed to have been amended accordingly.

5–583 These restrictions are drafted as a result of a consideration of Art.4(b) of Reg.2790/99 and paras 49–52 of the Guidelines on Vertical Restraints. Article 4(b) forbids "the restriction of the territory into which, or of the customers to whom, the buyer may sell the goods or services, except the restriction of active sales into the exclusive territory or to an exclusive customer group reserved to the supplier or allocated by the supplier to another buyer, where such a restriction does not limit sales by the customers of the buyer. The Guidelines give further details as to the interpretation of this provision, which have been taken into account in drafting the above clause.

5–584 This provision differs considerably from the restriction permitted by

Reg.83/83 (Art.2(2)(c)) which permitted a complete ban on active sales outside the distributor's territory. This provision is more closely modelled on the provisions of the Technology Transfer Block Exemption (Reg.240/96). The result is that the distributor is free to carry out active selling in areas and to customers which fall outside his own territory provided that they are not territories or customer groups reserved to the principal or allocated to other distributors on an exclusive basis. It is not entirely clear when these territories or customer groups have to be reserved or allocated. If they are specified at the time the agreement is entered into there would seem to be no issue, but what if a further territory is allocated or reserved after the date of the agreement? Can the distributor complain?

From a contractual point of view, the provisions of cl.5.5.3 should deal with the issue. So far as Art.4(b) of the regulation is concerned, the wording is sufficiently wide that it would appear to permit allocation after the date an agreement is entered into, and there is nothing in the Guidelines upon this subject. Indeed, although the wording is somewhat different under Reg.240/96, and relates only to reserved territories, there is again nothing in the wording of that regulation that would prevent changes in reserved territories after the date of the agreement. **5–585**

Subsequent reservation of territories or customer groups where the distributor has not commenced active selling at the time of reservation should present no problems. However, what happens where the principal subsequently wishes to make such a reservation, but the distributor has (without breach of contract) already commenced active sales activities in that territory or customer group? If the strict terms of the clause were all that were involved, the distributor would presumably have to cease such active selling. However, an argument could be mounted that the clause as drafted is thus to a certain extent an indirect prohibition on active selling which is not permitted by the exceptions to Art.4(b), since, at the time selling takes place the territory or customer group is not reserved or allocated. **5–586**

A pragmatic solution to this problem, which avoids the difficulty of interpreting Art.4(b), would be for the principal to reserve at the outset of the agreement all of the territories in which he considers that he either has an interest then or is likely to have an interest in the future. It is not possible to bring future territories or customer groups within the provision relating to allocation to another buyer, since, in the instance under discussion, at the time the agreement is entered into no such buyer actually exists (see the use of the word "allocated" rather than "reserved" or some other phrase such as "intended to be allocated".) However, this should not prevent the principal reserving such territory for himself, even if he is not active in the territory at the date of reservation, and even if he intends to exploit it in the future by the grant of a distribution agreement. One word of caution. The principal should, so far as possible, have a genuine commercial interest in the areas which he reserves, even if this is a potential interest for future trading rather than actual activity at the time of reservation. An automatic reservation of the whole of the EC outside the relevant distributor's territory without cogent commercial justification seems to go too far. Even if this complies **5–587** with Art.4(b), in appropriate cases the Commission, or a national competition law authority, could withdraw the benefit of the vertical restraints block exemption under Art.6 or 7, for effects incompatible with Art.81(3).

5–588 Finally, it should be noted that in the Guidelines the Commission have taken the opportunity to grapple with the question of whether general advertising or sales over the internet which, without any specific intent so to do, reach into reserved territories or reserved customer groups should be regarded as active or passive selling. The Guidelines consider both such activities amount to passive selling, and the clause has been drafted to reflect this.

5–589 The provisions in this clause relate to the partial prohibition of active sales. However, if customers outside the territory wish to purchase from the distributor, and seek him out, he must be free to supply them, even if the customers concerned are located in the territory of another distributor or of the principal himself.

5–590 The reasoning behind this is that, if there are extreme price differentials between two territories, in the EC, and if there are no restrictions on cross-border trade, the ordinary laws of supply and demand will cause customers from the territory where products are more expensive to seek out supplies from the less expensive territory, thus equalising prices in the two territories towards the lower end of the differential, and promoting the idea of a unified common market at similar prices for the same goods. Nevertheless, the distributor is not to create an artificial demand for such cross-border flows, by his own activities. It is generally more beneficial for consumers in each territory if they each have a distributor who is concentrating on serving the needs of his own territory properly.

5–591 The restrictions described above fall within the group restraints known in the Guidelines as "market partitioning" and of course are usually found together with the grant of an exclusive distributorship, this grant amounting to a restraint which falls within the "limited distribution" group of restraints. Where the restrictions on active sales, (as dealt with in the precedent above), are concerned, it would be unwise to assume that if Reg.2790/99 did not apply (because the supplier's market share exceeded the 30 per cent threshold) that the clause could be included as drafted in reliance on exemption under Art.81(3). In section VI.2.2 of the Guidelines, the Commission discusses exclusive distribution which, as pointed out above, usually contains both limited distribution and market partitioning restraints. "Above the 30 per cent market share threshold there may be a risk of significant reduction of intra-brand competition. In order to be exemptable the loss of intra-brand competition needs to be balanced with real efficiencies". Again, in para.180 (in a discussion of market partitioning by customer allocation in the context of selective distribution) the Commission states "... above the 30 per cent market share threshold ... exclusive customer allocation is unlikely to be exemptable unless there are clear and substantial efficiency effects".

5–592 In any case, the above discussion, whether within or outside Reg.2790/99 relates to limitations on active sales not passive sales. It is of course a contravention of Art.81(1) to introduce absolute cross-border bans on the sale of goods within the EU, and such bans rarely benefit from exemption under Art.81(3). There are however two circumstances where this exemption is normally available. The first is under the specific provisions of the Technology Transfer Block Exemption—Reg.240/96, and these are discussed in Chapter 8. The second can be found in para.10 of the Guidelines which reads as follows:

> "... vertical restraints linked to opening up new product or geographic markets in general do not restrict competition. This rule holds irrespective of the market share of the company for two years after the first putting on the market of the product. It applies to all non-hardcore vertical restraints and, in the case of a new geographic market, to restrictions on active and passive sales imposed on the direct buyers of the supplier located in other markets to intermediaries in the new market. In the case of genuine testing of a new product in a limited territory or with a limited customer group, the distributors appointed to sell the new product on the test market can be restricted in their active selling outside the test market for a maximum period of one year without being caught by Art.81(1)."

These guidelines will only have application in limited cases, but are clearly very useful where they do apply. The conclusions to be drawn are as follows: **5–593**

- The precedent above (a non-hardcore restraint) could still be used even if the supplier's market share exceeds the 30 per cent threshold provided it is used—
  - — in the case of a new product; or
  - — in the case of a new geographic market (for a new or existing product); and
  - — in either case, for a limited period of two years after the ***first*** putting on the market of the product; and
- In the case of a genuine test market for a new product a further restraint can be imposed on the reseller to prevent passive and active sales outside the test customer group or territory, for a maximum period of one year.
- In the case of penetration of a new geographic market a further restraint can be imposed on the direct buyers of the supplier located in other markets, for a maximum period of two years, which prevents—
  - — active or passive sales to intermediaries in that new geographic market

Nevertheless, leaving aside the exceptions described above, in general direct and indirect export bans are one of the Commission's main concerns in relation to its competition investigations, and undertakings which imple- **5–594** ment such restraints without the protection of exemption under Art.81(3) routinely suffer large fines.

5–595 Although these principles have been well known and part of the established competition law of the EC almost since its inception, firms still impose export bans on their distributors with monotonous regularity. Sometimes this seems to occur through ignorance or negligence (see Case C-277/87 *Sandoz v Commission* [1990] E.C.R. I-45 and Case C279/87 *Tipp-Ex v Commission* [1990] E.C.R. I-261.) and then, although this is no excuse, fines are relatively light. More deliberate infringement incurs heavier penalties. In *Re Bayer AG*, Commission Decision [1990] O.J. L21 a fine of 500,000 ECU was imposed. In *Re Toshiba*, Commission Decision [1991] O.J. L287, Toshiba was fined 2m ECU for operating a system of export bans, both in its standard conditions (for a period of time) and through concerted practices in other cases. In setting the level of the fine, the Commission took into account, on the one hand the seriousness of the offence, and, on the other, the facts that Toshiba had cooperated with them, and had now instituted a full EC compliance programme in their operations.

5–596 In Case T-49/95 *Van Megen Sports Group BV v Commission* the European Court of First Instance upheld the Commission's decision to impose flat rate fines on a manufacturer of sportswear and all its distributors, for systematic reporting and investigation of parallel imports, marking of products to identify origin of parallel imports and suspension of supplies to specific markets to prevent actual or potential parallel imports.

5–597 In the Commission Decision *Re Systemform GmbH* (OJ L47 February 18, 1997), Systemform imposed prohibitions on distributors selling to customers whose head office was situated outside the contract territory and imposed obligations on distributors to forward to Systemform all enquiries coming from customers situated outside the contract territory or who were known to intend to export goods out of the contract territory. The clauses were prefaced by the statement "in any event and unless such an obligation is prohibited by any national or supranational law applicable in the contract territory, [the distributor] shall not ..." the Commission gave this short shrift. The apparent qualification did not change the intention or effect of the restrictive clause, since it merely stated the legal position under EC competition law, that restrictions of the type imposed were void under Art.81(1). The inclusion of the clause had the intention of prohibiting exports. If there was no such intention there was no need to impose the prohibition at all. In addition the qualification was unlikely to change the effect the restriction would have on a distributor unless he was unusually familiar with EC law.

5–598 In *Volkswagen AG v Commission*, the European Court of First Instance approved the Commission Decision (Commission Statement IP/00/725) to fine the company heavily for entering into agreements with its subsidiaries and dealers in Italy to prohibit or restrict sales in Italy to final consumers in other Member States. The Commission set the fine at 102 million ECUs and the Court reduced it to 90 million ECUs. The fine reflected the seriousness of the case. Volkswagen was a large group and in implementing the export ban it ignored the extensive case law on the subject.

The Commission is more lenient with smaller entities. In its decision *Re Editions Nathan* (Commission Statement IP/00/713) it fined a producer of educational material and school textbooks, together with its Belgian distributor, for preventing sales outside their own exclusive territories and restricting the distributor's freedom to set prices and commercial conditions of sale. The Commission took account of the fact that the agreements had only been operated in France and Belgium, that the companies had cooperated actively during the investigation, and that the Belgian distributor was a family company. Nathan was fined €60,000 and the distributor €1,000. **5–599**

Again in its Decision *Re Triumph Motor Cycles* (Commission Statement IP/00/1014), where Triumph prevented its Benelux dealers selling to UK customers, the scale and duration of the infringement were small, there was a limited impact on the market, and Triumph cooperated actively in the investigation, and undertook to remove the export ban. Under the circumstances, the Commission closed the case without imposing a fine. **5–600**

Car manufacturers have continued to attract large fines for export bans. In its decision *Re Opel Nederland BV* (Commission Statement IP/00/1028) the Commission fined Opel €43 million for obstructing exports of new cars to end users outside the Netherlands from September 1996 to January 1998. Opel gave dealers direct instructions not to export, required dealers to sell the majority of cars through their franchise to customers in the Netherlands and operated a large number of bonus campaigns which provided that no bonus would be paid if dealers sold cars to end consumers from abroad. The fine was lower than that imposed on Volkswagen because the Commission considered not that the infringement was less severe, but that it had been carried out for a shorter time and with less rigour. **5–601**

Shortly after, in its Decision *Re J C Bamford Group* (Commission Statement IP/00/1526) the Commission fined Bamfords (the large UK manufacturers of construction, farm and industrial handling equipment) €39.6 million for putting in place distribution agreements and other practices which had the effect of severely restricting out of territory sales, as well as interfering with the freedom to set resale prices. These restrictions had been in effect since 1988. The fine reflected the duration and gravity of the offence, which was first ascertained after a "dawn raid" on the company premises in 1996. As Competition Commissioner Mr Mario Monti commented: "It is shocking that important companies present in all Member States still jeopardise the most fundamental principles of the internal market . . ." **5–602**

The Commission actions against car manufacturers continued with its Decision *Re Mercedes Benz* (Commission Statement IP/01/1394) in which it fined the company €71,825,000 for measures adopted to impede parallel trade in cars and limit competition in the leasing and sale of motor vehicles. The company told its dealers and agents in Germany not to sell cars to end users outside Germany, required them in any event, if they did so, to demand a 15 per cent deposit (which was not required for German customers), limited sales of cars in Spain and Germany to independent leasing **5–603** companies by preventing them buying unless they had already found a customer (this meant they could not buy for stock to take advantage of rebates on volume purchases). It also participated in a price fixing arrangement in Belgium. The company denied these findings, contested the level of the fine, and has appealed to the European Court.

5–604 The latest Commission Decision in this area is against Nintendo and its seven European distributors (Commission Statement IP/02/1584) for attempting to restrict parallel imports of Nintendo computer games software. Each distributor was obliged to prevent parallel trade from its territory. Under the leadership of Nintendo the companies collaborated intensively to find the source of any parallel trade. Traders who allowed parallel shipments were boycotted or punished by being given smaller shipments. The conduct was carried on for seven years and resulted in very high price differentials between various Member States. The Commission set the total fines for all parties at €167.8 million, but Nintendo was fined €148 million from this amount to reflect its size in the market, that it was the driving force behind the infringement and that it continued its conduct even after it knew the investigation was going on.

5–605 It can be seen that case law in relation to export bans has reached a stage where undertakings engaging in any type of direct or indirect export ban do so at their peril. Given the new approach to direct application of Art.81 under Reg.1/2003. It is more important than ever that undertakings understand what constitutes an export ban and make sure that they do not engage in any conduct which directly or indirectly contributes to such a ban or impedes parallel imports without legal justification.

5–606 The Commission is keen to encourage undertakings to cooperate with it in its investigations, and even to come forward and reveal secret arrangements to which they are a party and from which they might wish to withdraw, if they could do so without penalty. It therefore encourages those who are, in any instance, the first to come forward, by offering them exemption or significant reduction from fines that would otherwise be due on their activities. (See Commission Notice on Fines ([1996] O.J. C207) subsequently replaced by the 2002 Notice [2002] O.J. C45/3. At the same time it is increasing the severity of its fines for deliberate infringements. In *Re Cement Cartel,* Commission Decision [1994] O.J. L343, the Commission fined 42 members of a cartel relating to the production and supply of cement a total of 248m ECU, as a penalty for price fixing and market sharing activities. This is still the largest collective fine ever imposed.

5.5.2 Sales activities outside the EC

5–607 5.5.2 The Distributor shall not sell during the continuance of this agreement the Products outside the EC [except into areas from which it is reasonably likely that reimportation of the Products into the EC would occur].

This provision is occasionally inserted, since it is regarded as not affecting cross-border trade within the EC, and there is some support for the Commission's acceptance of such provisions from Decisions relating to selective distribution agreements (see Chapter 6.22.3 particularly *Re Junghans*, and *EMI v CBS,* and *Polydor v Harlequin* discussed in Chapter 5.1.1.4.1). However, everything depends upon the circumstances of the individual agreement under consideration.

The phrase in square brackets can probably be safely omitted unless one is aware of a particular circumstance relating to the products (or products of a similar nature) where there is an actual appreciable trade from an area outside the EC to a point within the EC from which supplies are then distributed across borders within the EC between Member States, or else the circumstances are such that there is at least an appreciable potential for such trade. **5–608**

The European Court judgment in Case C-306/96 *Javico International and Javico AG v Yves St Laurent Parfums SA* [1998] 5 C.M.L.R. 172 dealt with these issues but not very helpfully. Javico was a German company which entered into distribution agreements with YSL to distribute its products in Russia, Ukraine and Slovenia. The agreements required Javico to sell the products only in the assigned territories, and not to re-export them. YSL discovered Javico selling products destined for the contract territories in Member States of the EU and terminated the agreements, suing for damages in the French courts. YSL's complaint was upheld at first instance, and Javico appealed, contending that the obligations in the agreement were void under Art.81(2). The French court of appeal applied for a ruling on the issue to the European Court. The Court held that where the principal and the distributor are both located in Member States, the distribution relates to a territory outside the EU and the distributor is prohibited from selling the contracted products outside of the relevant territory to any other country, including Member States of the EU, then, if that prohibition has an appreciable effect on competition within the Community and is liable to have an appreciable effect on trade between Member States, it will infringe Art.81(1). However, since this all depends upon the facts of each case, it is for the national court to decide the issue. **5–609**

This is not a very helpful judgment, but the Court did give some pointers as to the way to assess the facts. The first factor is the position and importance of the parties on the market for the product. Such agreements (given that they prevent sales to all countries outside the territory) do not have the object of affecting competition in the EC, but of making the distributor concentrate on the target market. However, it is necessary to consider whether, whatever their object, the agreements have the effect of preventing restricting or distorting competition. The stronger the position of YSL (*e.g.* if the relevant market in the EC is an oligopoly or YSL actually enjoys a large market share or even a dominant position) the more likely there will be only limited competition in the EC, and thus the more effect a source of the contract products from outside the EC would have. There is then the consideration of price differentials. Unless the price of the contract products on the target market is appreciably less than in the EC there will be **5–610** no point to reimporting them. Even if the price differential is present, it will be of no effect if it is eroded by the cost of transport and customs duties when the goods are first exported to the target market and then reimported to the EC. Finally, trade between Member States cannot be appreciably effected if the products intended for the markets outside the Community account for only a very small percentage of the total market for those products in the territory of the common market.

5–611 It should be noted that *Javico* deals with a special case, where the principal and the distributor were both resident in the EC, but the territory was outside the EC. Where the principal attempts to prevent imports from outside the EC not by imposing contractual obligations, but by exercising trade mark or patent rights, the legal position relates to the effect of the doctrine of exhaustion of rights within the EC and the impact of Arts 28 and 30 of the Treaty or of Arts 5 and 7 of The First Council Directive (104/89) on the approximation of the laws of the Member States relating to trade marks. The relevant legal principles are discussed in detail in Chapter 5.1.1.4.1. However, the following cases discussed in that section are of particular relevance: *Silhouette v Hartlauer, Levi Strauss & Co. v Tesco* and *Van Doren v Lifestyle & Sportswear Handelgesellschaft.* Reference should also be made to *EMI v CBS* and *Bureau Europeen des Unions de Consomateurs v Commission* discussed in Chapter 5.1.1.4.1 in relation to agreements, with parties outside the EC, which affect trade within it.

5.5.3 Identical obligations on other distributors

5–612 5.5.3 The Principal shall impose on any other distributor or agent appointed by it for areas of the EC outside the Territory obligations identical to those imposed upon the Distributor under cll.5.4 and 5.5 including cl.5.5.3.

This type of clause can cause problems within the operation of Reg.2790/99. As the clause stands, it is probably in order, since it does not bind the principal to impose any restriction which is not permitted by the Regulation. However, the effect of the network of identical distribution agreements thus created, and the way in which they are in practice operated, can affect competition within the EC, and can indirectly cause a partitioning of the market into separate territories to a greater extent than the Commission considers desirable.

5–613 In this connection reference should be made to discussion on the application of the concept of cumulative effect both in Chapter 5.1.1.3.8, and in the Commission Guidelines on Vertical Restraints (paras 146 to 149), discussed above in Chapter 5.3.6 in relation to non-compete obligations. Here attention is particularly drawn to the importance of the issue of foreclosure where the supplier imposing restraints has a market share over the 30 per cent threshold and cannot take advantage of the Vertical Restraints Block Exemption.

5–614 Apart from the Commission's general power to look at the facts of every case to see if the situation is anti-competitive, Reg.2790/99 contains specific provisions to ensure that vertical agreements are not used, as disguised means of preventing competition, to a greater extent than specifically permitted by the Regulation.

The Regulation thus as a general rule does not apply to vertical agreements between competing undertakings (Art.2.4). The Commission has in some cases, however, granted a special exemption to such arrangements under Art.81(3) (see *Re Phillips International BV/John Fluke Manufacturing Inc*, discussed above). The provision even catches the situation where one or both of the parties entering into the reciprocal arrangements is not itself a competitor but an undertaking "connected" with that party is a competitor (Art.11) **5–615**

However, Art.2.4 does permit competing undertakings to enter into a non-reciprocal vertical agreement, provided that the turnover of the buyer is less than €100m (Art.2.4(a)), or the supplier is a manufacturer and distributor of goods while the buyer is a distributor not manufacturing goods competing with the contract goods (Art.2.4(b)), or the supplier is a provider of services at several levels of trade while the buyer does not provide competing services at the level of trade where it purchases the contract services (Art.2.4(c)). Thus the possibility of specialisation where a small enterprise is involved is preserved. The benefit of the "low turnover" provision is retained even if the figure is exceeded, provided that the excess in any two financial years of the agreement is not more than 10 per cent (Art.10.2). It should be remembered that the inclusion of connected undertakings applies not only to the body of Art.2.4, to determine the extent of the exclusion from the benefit of Reg.2790/99, but also the exemptions to this exclusion set out in Arts.2.4(a) (b) and (c). Thus, in arriving at the total turnover of €100m mentioned in Art.2.4(a), it is necessary to include the turnover of any "connected" parties (excluding inter-trading), so that groups of companies which are of any size at all are unlikely to benefit from the provision (Art.10.1), and, in determining the applicability of Art.2.4(b) and (c), not only the actual entities acting as supplier and buyer must qualify for the exemption but also any connected undertakings of the buyer and supplier (art 11.1). **5–616**

The exemption under the Regulation may be withdrawn by the Commission (Art.6) or by one of the Member States in relation to its geographic area (Art.7) where, even if the agreement could otherwise take advantage of the Regulation, in any particular case that vertical agreement has effects incompatible with Art.81(3) and in particular where access to the relevant market or competition therein is significantly restricted by the cumulative effect of parallel networks of similar vertical restraints implemented by competing suppliers or buyers. Although the provision is clearly of the widest application, the latter phrase is concerned particularly with selective distribution networks (see Chapter 6). **5–617**

5.6 Supply of the products

5.6.1 Exclusive purchase

5–618 5.6.1 The Distributor shall purchase all its requirements for the Products ready packaged from the Principal.

Under the original block exemption for exclusive distribution agreements (Reg.67/67) it was not possible to impose an obligation on the distributor to obtain the products only from the principal. He was entitled to obtain the goods from any source within the EC, such as another distributor or wholesaler. This is still the case with selective distribution arrangements (see Chapter 6.7.1 and 6.8.1), but Reg.83/83 permitted the imposition of this obligation for the first time.

5–619 The current Reg.2790/99 does not deal with this issue expressly, but this type of obligation is regarded as one of the "single branding group" of restraints which is always potentially restrictive of competition as a kind of indirect non-competition clause. The issue of the legality of such exclusive purchase obligations is considered in the discussion on the "single branding group" of vertical restraints in Chapter 5.3.6. This clause should not be inserted without a detailed consideration of its legality in the light of that discussion as applied to the particular circumstances of the case.

5–620 It is also important in this context to consider the issue of tying which is another of the single branding group of vertical restraints discussed in the Commission Guidelines on Vertical Restraints (see section 2.7 paras 215–224).

5–621 Under Reg.2790/99 tying is permitted where the market share of the supplier on both the market of the tied product and the market of the tying product does not exceed 30 per cent. It may be combined with other non-hardcore vertical restraints such as non-compete or quantity forcing in respect of the tying product or exclusive purchasing (see the Guidelines para.218). Even where the 30 per cent threshold is exceeded, para.222 states that the question of a possible exemption under Art.81(3) arises as long as the tying company is not dominant. Tying obligations may help to produce efficiencies arising from joint production or joint distribution. However, para.224 states that Art.81(3) is unlikely to provide assistance where no efficiencies result from tying or where such efficiencies are not passed on to consumers.

5–622 There are a number of cases relating to the "tying" of distributors which are relevant in this context. In the so-called "ice cream" cases (see *Scholler Lebensmittel GmbH & Co KG v Commission* and *Langnese-Iglo v Commission*) ice cream manufacturers supplied a freezer free of charge to ice cream retailers, but only on the condition that they would use the freezer exclusively for that manufacturer's products ("freezer exclusivity"). The Commission finally decided that freezer exclusivity raises a significant barrier to entry in the ice cream market, and appreciably affects competition, and trade between Member States, since once a retailer has become tied to one manufacturer by freezer exclusivity, other manufacturers may not be able to get a second freezer in the premises. The Unilever Group was involved in a similar issue in Ireland (Commission Statement of March 10, 1995 on Unilever Group). However, additionally in *Unilever*, the manufacturer recovered the cost of the freezer by "inclusive pricing" (*i.e.* as part of the sale price of the ice-cream, but he charged this price even in cases where the retailer did not have a freezer supplied by Unilever. After discussion with the Commission, Unilever removed this inclusive pricing arrangement but reserved its rights to contend that its arrangements for supply of a tied freezer were legal.

The Commission reviewed Unilever's position in 1997 and concluded (see Commission statement IP/98/242 dated March 11, 1998) that Unilever's dominant position in the Irish market for ice cream products meant that its competitors were effectively foreclosed from the market because of its freezer exclusivity practice. Accordingly the Commission found the freezer exclusivity provision in Unilever's agreements with retailers infringed Art.81 and that, because of its market share in Ireland (85 per cent), the practice of imposing such a condition in its agreements also amounted to an abuse of a dominant position under Art.82. **5–623**

Apart from the contractual question, where the supplier imposes the tying obligation, either directly under a contract or unilaterally as a sales policy (*i.e.* a refusal to supply product A unless product B is also purchased), then this is no more than a special instance of a unilateral refusal to supply. This refusal is not subject to scrutiny under Art.81, so that in the absence of a dominant position, EC competition law will have no application. This principles is discussed in Chapter 5.1.1.3.2 in relation to *Bayer AG v Commission* and refusal to supply is considered in more detail in Chapter 5.27. **5–624**

However, if the supplier is in a dominant position, that unilateral tying policy will almost always constitute an abuse of that dominant position under Art.82 (see the Commission's comment in the Guidelines on Vertical Restraints at para.215: "If tying is not objectively justified by the nature of the products or commercial usage, such practice may constitute an abuse under Art.82"). There are two leading cases which deal with this issue, and upon which the Commission's approach is based. **5–625**

In the Decision of the Commission *Re Hilti* [1991] 2 E.C.R. 1439, the Commission held that Hilti was in a dominant position for the supply of power actuated nail guns, and that a requirement that distributors for those goods also supply Hilti's nails and cartridge strips for use in those guns was an abuse of a dominant position. Hilti attempted to justify the tie on the grounds of safety for users, but this was completely rejected by the Commission. **5–626**

A similar decision was made in Case C-333/94 *Tetra Pak International SA v Commission* [1996] ECR I-5951, where Tetra Pak tied the undertakings which rented its packaging machines to using only cartons and packaging material supplied by Tetra Pak. Here the European Court said that if Tetra Pak was so concerned about safety it could satisfy those concerns by giving **5–627** the users of its machinery a specification for the cartons and packaging material which should be used, and then leave them free to buy from any supplier who could satisfy that specification.

5.6.2 Terms and conditions

5–628 5.6.2 The parties hereto agree that orders placed by the Distributor with the Principal under cl.5.6.1 or for any other items shall be on the terms set out in Sch.6.

5.6.3 "Most favoured nation" clause

5–629 5.6.3 The Principal undertakes that the price charged by it to the Distributor under this agreement for any Product is the lowest price charged at that time to any export customer of the Principal for that Product (at the same volume and upon the same terms and conditions, including as to delivery), and should at any time this not be the case or cease to be the case then the Principal shall immediately adjust the relevant price charged hereunder to the Distributor to achieve compliance with this undertaking and such adjustment shall apply to any orders of the Distributor at the time placed with the Principal but not yet shipped.

Problems can arise with the application of clauses like 5.6.2 and 5.6.3 under EC law, where a supplier chooses to charge different prices to distributors in different countries within the EC. As a rule this is unilateral conduct, and, since the agreement in each case between the distributor and the principal is not of itself the cause of the distortion of competition, Art.81 will not apply to the individual distribution agreements.

5–630 It is the overall policy of the principal as between his different distributors which causes the problem. Article 82 of the EC Treaty can apply in two ways to this situation where the principal has enough of a market share to have a dominant position in the relevant products. First of all Art.82(a) prohibits "unfair prices". Thus if prices in any area are excessively high, or are excessively low in order to drive out competitors, the prices charged by the principal to one or more distributors will be regarded as unfair.

5–631 In most cases where Art.82(c) has been invoked there have been different prices charged in respect of different Member States. In order for Art.82(c) to apply the dominant principal must apply "dissimilar conditions to equivalent transactions" and there must as a consequence be some effect upon competition. In practice, provided the first requirement is fulfilled the Commission and the Court tends to assume the existence of the second.

5–632 Such a provision as this clause would, if inserted in all the distribution agreements of the network, and if adhered to in practice, prevent this charge being made. However, the principal may well claim that he is justified in charging different prices in different territories because in each territory he charges what the market will bear, having regard to the spending power of the customers in that territory. This was the argument put forward in *United Brands & Co v EC Commission* [1979] 1 C.M.L.R. 429. The Court did not state that a dominant supplier was never justified in charging what the market would bear (*i.e.* setting his price according to the laws of supply and demand) but said that he could do this only in territories where he, as opposed to the local distributor, took "the risk of the market". This, presumably, means where the supplier was himself supplying direct on the market in question rather than through an independent third party distributor.

United Brands sold to almost all its distributors FOB Rotterdam, and left **5–633** them to sell on in the territories for which they were distributors, at whatever prices they chose. However the FOB Rotterdam prices were set at different levels depending on how high the distributors could charge in each territory, and still retain a large share of the market. The distributor took the risk of the market, and United Brands simply took a profit. In these circumstances the Court held that United Brands could not differentiate between prices for different territories unless there were some definite factors which justified this.

The Court basically had in mind the idea of costs in each territory plus a **5–634** "fair profit" as being the formula to arrive at the price for each territory. The difficulty is in the definition of allowable costs. Obvious items are costs of production, transport, marketing, promotion, advertising and VAT. The Court also seemed willing to let the principal take into account the various characteristics of the relevant local market, to the extent that the principal is himself involved in expense there. Under this heading would come the need to respond to lower prices of competition and at least to a limited extent aligning prices to the cost of living in the territory concerned.

Under Art.82(a) the problem is more abstruse as excessive pricing is of **5–635** itself considered to be an abuse of a dominant position, irrespective of the effect upon competition. Thus the Court here only had to ask itself if the supplier was reaping profits which he would not have been able to obtain if there had been normal and efficient competition prevailing. Thus Art.82(a) has become a weapon to protect consumers against excessive pricing as an evil in its own right.

The Court sought to establish a relationship between what it called the **5–636** "economic value" of the product and the price charged for it. If the price is far in excess of the "economic value" then an abuse will exist. Once again the basic method suggested was to compare production costs against sales price and see if the difference produced an excessive profit margin (*i.e.* one which is much greater than that competitors are making and or more than would be obtainable if there were free competition).

However there are alternative methods of deciding whether a price is **5–637** excessive. One very strong piece of evidence is the existence of price differentials, in different territories, for what on the surface appear to be similar transactions. Comparisons with competitors' prices for equivalent transactions are also useful. The problem is to ensure that first of all any comparison is between two situations which are truly the same, so that any differentials justified by market conditions are removed, and then to establish exactly what costs can be justifiably included in the make-up of the cost price of the product.

5–638 Lastly, in regard to the application of Art.82, it should be noted that a dominant position can be found in many cases, where one would not ordinarily think that one existed, by a narrow definition of the market in which the dominant position is held to exist. In many jurisdictions the competition authority has great freedom to define the market to which it applies its competition law, so that by a narrow definition many suppliers are found to be in a dominant position for the products which are the object of the investigation. This is certainly the situation with the Commission. In the *United Brands* case, for example, the relevant market was defined to be bananas, rather than fruit in general.

5–639 An important decision under Art.82 in relation to discounts and pricing practices, which is also useful for showing how the European Court approaches the definition of the relevant market, was made in the case of in *Nederlandsche Banden-Industrie Michelin NV v Commission* [1985] 1 C.M.L.R. 282. The question of abuse of a dominant position under Art.82 was considered exhaustively in relation to the market for new replacement tyres for lorries, buses and other heavy vehicles. Consideration was given in detail to the way the relevant market should be defined, and the determination of whether the undertaking concerned had a dominant position in it. It was held that temporary trading at a loss is not necessarily inconsistent with a dominant position, nor was charging only reasonable prices. These matters went to the question of abuse of the dominant position, not whether the dominant position existed.

5–640 The case was particularly concerned with discounts allowed by Michelin to its dealers in Holland. It was held that a quantity discount which is measured solely on the basis of volume purchased is not an abuse. Michelin also worked a sales target discount system which rewarded the dealer with higher levels of discount as sales targets, set at the beginning of each year, were progressively exceeded. There was no exclusivity qualification for the discount, either to compel the dealer to purchase exclusively from Michelin, or to punish him with the loss of the discount if he bought elsewhere. This distinguished the case from the earlier cases where fidelity discounts which rewarded exclusive buying (but did not impose an obligation to buy exclusively) were held an abuse of a dominant position.

5–641 However, the Court observed that the tendency of the sales target system was to put pressure on dealers only to buy from Michelin, particularly towards the end of the year if sales were not doing too well. This tended to encourage customers not to obtain supplies from other manufacturers, whatever their needs, in case they:

> "run the risk of losses which the other manufacturers could not easily make good by means of the discounts which they were able to offer. Its network of commercial representatives enabled Michelin to remind dealers of this situation at any time so as to induce them to place orders with it."

5–642 Thus this system was an abuse of a dominant position even though it was not an exclusive arrangement, since it hindered other competitors from breaking into the market, and limited the dealers' choice of suppliers. The position of dependence in which dealers find themselves and which is created by the discount system in question constituted an abuse of a dominant position.

Article 81 can in some cases raise a problem in the area of differential pricing. The point was made in the Commission Decision *Re The Distillers Company Ltd* [1978] 1 C.M.L.R. 400. Distiller's UK wholesalers were refused various allowances and rebates if they exported Distiller's products (mainly whisky and gin) to other EC countries. Thus the wholesalers paid nearly twice as much for products that they exported compared to those they sold in the UK. Distillers had previously imposed an export ban under its conditions of sale, but had withdrawn this when asked to do so by the Commission. The Commission held that each agreement itself imposed differential pricing, to what were equivalent transactions, with the aim of restricting exports from the UK to other Member States of the EC. Each distribution agreement was itself therefore in contravention of Art.81, since the discriminatory practice was imposed under each agreement, rather than by Distiller's unilateral actions as part of a general pricing policy which it was able to enforce by reason of a dominant position. **5–643**

Currently, such a provision would be considered an indirect ban on exports which constituted a hardcore restriction in terms of Art.4(b) of Reg.2790/EC. It can be seen that the situation in the *Distillers* Decision was completely different to that in *Bayer AG v Commission* discussed in Chapter 5.1.1.3.2. There the refusal to supply, which indirectly hindered exports, was not part of an agreement, and Bayer's distributors had not expressly or tacitly agreed to it. In *Distillers* each distributor expressly agreed to the two tier pricing system by signing the agreement in which it was incorporated. **5–644**

The *Distillers* Decision was confirmed in the later European Court case *The Distillers Company Ltd v EC Commission* [1980] 3 C.M.L.R. 121, and a subsequent Commission Notice *Re Distillers Company plc* [1983] 3 C.M.L.R. 173. However, in relation to the events covered by the Notice, Distillers imposed differential pricing on sales to their distributors of Johnny Walker Red Label Whisky upon the reintroduction of the product to the UK. After it had been discontinued in the UK it had continued to be sold in the EC. A higher price for export sales was thus created. The Commission permitted this for a transitional period, while Red Label was reintroduced into the UK, but said that the differential would have to be gradually eliminated. This Notice is interesting in that it underlines the Commission's relative forbearance in relation to anticompetitive practices which support the introduction of a new product, or develop a new market, provided that the practices do not last for longer than necessary to establish the product on the market (see also para.10 of the Guidelines on Vertical Restraints.) **5–645**

When granting exemption under Art.81(3), the Commission stated "The Commission has consistently condemned all attempts to hinder the right to engage in parallel trade between Member States. The Commission could not therefore accept a dual pricing system which has as its object or effect the **5–646** partitioning of markets within the EC". Exceptional circumstances existed in connection with large scale introduction of Red Label because it was temporarily withdrawn from the UK, and "the reintroduction of a well-known brand at UK price levels could encourage parallel transactions to an extent which might disrupt the manufacturer's existing distribution network elsewhere in the EC".

5–647 Thus this method of attacking differential prices works without the need for there to be a dominant position to be considered under Art.82. This has to be contrasted with *United Brands* where there was only one price per dealer, and no dealer made any agreement with United Brands as to price differentials, which were imposed unilaterally by United Brands. An agreement upon one price, even if unfair, will not normally cause the distribution agreement to contravene Art.81, even if there are different prices charged to third parties with which it can be compared. The remedy only lies under Art.82 if the principal is in fact in a dominant position.

5–648 The question of differential pricing was considered again in *Akzo v Commission* [1991] 1 E.C.R. 3359. Here the question related to differential pricing which was instituted for the purpose of driving a competitor out of business ("predatory pricing"). Akzo offered the customers of a competitor prices lower than those which it offered to its own customers. The European Court of Justice held that where an undertaking is in a dominant position it will be an abuse under Art.82 to supply products at prices below their marginal cost (*i.e.* below the variable (direct) cost element of those products, and completely ignoring overheads (indirect costs)). This is because, even on a marginal costing basis, the products are being sold at a loss, and the undertaking can have no purpose in making such a loss except to attack its competitors and to gain market share. However, when a product is sold below total cost (*i.e.* variable cost plus overheads) there may be good business reasons to selling on this basis since, if the price is above marginal cost then at least a contribution to overheads is obtained. In these cases, the question of abuse depends upon intention. Is the purpose of the price cutting in order to simply obtain more business, or is it predatory? In the latter case, an abuse occurs. Thus the test for predatory pricing is partly an objective one (in the obvious case of sale below variable cost) but also partly subjective (in the case of sale below total cost). The principles in *Akzo* were applied by the Commission in the Commission Decision of *Re Tetra Pak II* [1992] O.J. L72/1 in a case where Tetra Pak had abused its dominant position by, *inter alia*, selling below marginal cost in Italy. The Decision was upheld by the European Court in Te*tra Pak International SA v Commission*.

5–649 Finally, in the Guidelines, the Commission mentions (para.152) the so-called "English Clause", where the buyer is required to report to the supplier any better offer from a third party and give the supplier the opportunity to match it. This is a common feature of preferred as supposed to exclusive supplier agreements, where the competitive tension between the supplier and the buyer mean that the supplier wants to be sure of providing the goods or services but the buyer wants to be sure that the price at which they are supplied is competitive. The Commission regards English clauses as another type of non-compete or quantity forcing clause which would be subject to all of the principles relating to non-compete clauses discussed in Chapter 5.3.6, including the applicability of Art.5(a) of Reg.2790/99. The Commission concludes that Art.82 "specifically prevents dominant companies from applying English clauses or fidelity rebate schemes".

In the UK, only the Chapter II Prohibition can have application in relation to excessive pricing, unless the excessive pricing is coupled with some form of resale price maintenance which would not permit the application of the Vertical Restraints Order to exclude the operation of the Chapter I Prohibition. **5–650**

The approach of the Office of Fair Trading to excessive, predatory and discriminatory pricing is set out in the OFT Guidelines "Assessment of Individual Agreements and Conduct" sections 2 to 4. By and large the approach is the same as that of the Commission, and the OFT relies upon some of the cases mentioned above in setting its approach. However, when dealing with the question of excessive pricing, the OFT appears to go somewhat further in relation to what (like the Commission) it calls "supra-normal profits". **5–651**

In section 2.6, it suggests that prices can yield supra-normal profits where they return a profit in excess of the undertaking's weighted average cost of capital. Sections 2.7 to 2.11, however, set out some exceptions to this general principle, if such a return can be achieved without any anticompetitive action – for instance in response to shortages of supply or increased demand, or by reason of increased efficiency or successful innovation. (See sections 2.7 to 2.13). **5–652**

An alternative yardstick for measuring supra-normal profits is set out in section 2.16. This looks at the stand-alone costs of the activity in question, and considers that, if revenues significantly and consistently exceed those costs, this may indicate that excessive prices have been charged. This approach is similar to that adopted by the Court in the *United Brands* case discussed above. **5–653**

In any event supra-normal profits are just one factor in assessing abuse of a dominant position ("It is unlikely, however, that the Director General would conclude that an undertaking was abusing a dominant position solely on the evidence of supra-normal profitability"—section 2.15.) **5–654**

5.6.4 Modification and improvements

See cl.4.6.4. **5–655**

5.7 Distributor's records

See cl.4.7. **5–656**

5.8 Advertising and merchandising

5–657 See cl.4.8.

Regulation 83/83 permitted the imposition upon the distributor of advertising, sales promotion and marketing responsibilities and expenditure. There is nothing in the current Reg.2970/99 to prevent this. The following should however be added as cl.5.8.5.

5–658 5.8.5 Nothing in this clause or elsewhere in this Agreement shall entitle the Principal to pay regard to or monitor the prices at which the Distributor sells the Products.

It is wise to include this clause for agreements within the EC to prevent restrictions on prices being imposed in a disguised way as marketing policy directions or through approval of advertising copy (see the Commission Guidelines on Vertical Restraints—para.47). It should however be remembered that this clause is useful only as a reminder to the parties of the way they should conduct their operations, and to enable the distributor to resist any attempts at monitoring. If the supplier institutes a monitoring procedure and the distributor acquiesces in it, this will amount to an agreement which infringes Art.81(1) (see Case T-176/95 *Accinauto SA v Commission* [2000] 4 C.M.L.R. 67) and Case T-175/95 *BASF v Commission* [2000] 4 C.M.L.R. 33)

5–659 For further discussion on this issue see Chapter 6.9.6 and Chapter 8.9.6.

5.9 Sales and marketing policies

5–660 5.9.1 Selling prices for the sale of the Products by the Distributor shall be established and revised from time to time by the Distributor

It should be noted that unlike the corresponding provision in cl.4.9.2 there is no mention of the distributor's territory. This is to ensure that permitted exports outside that territory are also covered by this clause (see the discussion on the question of specifying the distributor's territory in Chapter 5.2.)

5–661 Article 4(a) of Reg.2790/99, and indeed Art.81(1) in general, does not permit any form of resale price maintenance. The Commission rarely if ever granted an individual exemption to such clauses under Art.81(3), and it is unlikely that in the current climate the parties to any agreement containing such a clause would be able to convince themselves that Art.81(3) applied (see the Commission Guidelines on Vertical Restraints para.46 *et seq*).

5–662 Article 4(a) applies only to resale price maintenance (that is the imposition of fixed or minimum prices). Strictly speaking it permits recommended sale prices or the imposition of a maximum sale price. However, such recommended or maximum prices must not "amount to a fixed or minimum sale price as a result of pressure from, or incentives offered by, any of the parties". Paragraph 47 of the Guidelines discusses in detail just how such indirect pressures or incentives may arise, and refers in particular to:

- agreements which fix the distributor's margin or the maximum level of discount that the distributor can grant from a prescribed price level;
- making grant of rebates or reimbursement of promotional rebates conditional on observance of a given price level;
- delay or suspension of deliveries or termination of contracts in relation to observance of a given price level.

The Commission also points out that such direct or indirect means of fixing prices can be made more efficient if linked with a price monitoring system to identify price cutting distributors. Finally, the printing of a recommended resale price on a package or the supplier obliging the buyer to apply a "most-favoured customer clause" may amount to such indirect means. **5–663**

Where the Block Exemption on Vertical Restraints does not apply because the supplier's market share exceeds the 30 per cent threshold even the practice of recommending resale prices or imposing a maximum price may infringe Art.81(1). Although the Commission does not expressly state that this will always be the case, the Guidelines on Vertical Restraints comment: "The stronger the market position of the supplier, the higher the risk that a maximum resale price or a recommended resale price leads to a more or less uniform application of that price level ... under such circumstances the practice ... may infringe Art.81(1) ..." (para.227). **5–664**

The same rules apply, although they are explained slightly differently, in the UK under the Competition Act.1998. **5–665**

Any agreement imposing minimum resale prices can be examined under the Chapter I Prohibition, if imposed by way of an agreement, and, in any event, under the Chapter II Prohibition where the undertaking imposing the same is in a dominant position (see ss.2 and 18 of the Competition Act 1998, and The Competition Act 1998 (Land and Vertical Agreements Exclusion) Order (SI 2000/310)—the "Vertical Restraints Order"). **5–666**

The Vertical Restraints Order excludes from the Chapter I Prohibition all vertical agreements, (Art.3) but provides (Art.4) that: "Article 3 shall not apply where the vertical agreement, directly or indirectly, in isolation or in combination with other factors under the control of the parties has the object or effect of restricting the buyer's ability to determine its sale price, without prejudice to the possibility of the supplier imposing a maximum sale price or recommending a sale price, provided that these do not amount to a fixed or minimum sale price as a result of pressure from, or incentives offered by, any of the parties". **5–667**

First of all this means that any vertical agreement, such as this distribution agreement, can be scrutinised under the Chapter I Prohibition, if it is caught by Art.4. Further, since the Vertical Restraints Order does not apply to the Chapter II Prohibition, any imposition of resale prices (fixed, mini- **5–668** mum, maximum or recommended) by an undertaking in a dominant position (whether by agreement or not) can be investigated by the OFT to see if it constitutes an abuse of that dominant position.

5–669 The OFT has stated that it considers the imposition of minimum resale prices will always result in an infringement of the Chapter I Prohibition, where imposed by agreement, and of the Chapter II Prohibition, in any event, where imposed by a dominant undertaking. Helpful guidance on this issue is given in the Guidelines issued by the Office of Fair Trading ("OFT"): "Vertical Agreements and Restraints", OFT 419, and "Assessment of Individual Agreements and Conduct", OFT 414, (see particularly paras 6.8 and 6.9) which are readily available from the OFT web site.)

5–670 The situation is less clear with regard to the setting of recommended resale prices or the setting of maximum resale prices. The question revolves around the application of the phrase in Art.4, "except where such a maximum or recommended price results, in practice, in a fixed or minimum price because of pressure from, or any incentives offered by, any of the undertakings involved". Presumably it is up to the OFT to decide in the first instance whether any such pressure or incentives exist. If they do, the benefit of the Vertical Restraints Order will be lost, and, since the imposition of the maximum or recommended price thus, by definition, amounts to the imposition of, probably, a fixed, or perhaps a minimum, price, the OFT will, in accordance with its policy, regard this as an infringement of the Chapter I Prohibition (see Guideline OFT 419, p.12 for some examples of pressure or indirect incentives.) Since the wording of the proviso in Art.4 is identical to the wording of the proviso to Art.4(a) of Reg.2790/99, not only will the OFT pay attention to the issues raised in the Commission Guidelines, but it is also not surprising that the OFT Guidelines have strong similarities to the Commission Guidelines on the same issues (see paras 46 *et seq*. of the latter.)

5–671 However, whatever the situation under the Chapter I Prohibition and the Vertical Restraints Order, imposition of recommended or maximum prices can still be examined under the Chapter II Prohibition, where the undertaking imposing them is in a dominant position. Here it seems reasonable that the OFT will follow the same principles as those described by the Commission in the Guidelines paras 225 to 228 where the market share of the supplier is greater than 30 per cent. This should mean that setting of maximum or recommended resale prices would, even in the absence of "pressures" or "incentives" aimed at setting fixed or minimum prices, be likely to be regarded as an infringement of the Chapter II Prohibition (see also OFT 414 para.6.9).

5–672 Thus the conclusion must be that, in general in the absence of other restrictive conditions or arrangements, and provided that the principal is not in a dominant position, a restriction as to maximum resale prices, or the recommending of resale prices, in a distribution agreement would be enforceable under the current law in the UK.

5–673 The question of refusal to supply is also linked with resale price maintenance. Suppose the principal imposed a restriction preventing the distributor from supplying outlets that were likely to or had sold the products at cut-prices. Forbidding sales to discount warehouses or supermarkets is an example of this. The old Resale Prices Act 1976, specifically provided not only that such a restriction was illegal but also prevented the principal from refusing to supply or withholding supplies from the distributor, and from requiring the distributor to withhold supplies from an outlet, on these grounds. The question of refusal to supply is now much more problematic under both EC and UK competition law. This issue is discussed in section 5.26.

5.9.2 The Distributor undertakes not to alter, adapt [combine, mix, dilute, adulterate] or otherwise modify or change any of the Products without obtaining the prior written consent of the Principal. **5–674**

5.9.3 The Distributor undertakes not to apply the Trade Mark to any item not one of the Products nor to distribute or sell any such items with the Trade Mark so applied or engage in any other practice or activity likely to mislead potential purchasers into believing that an item is one of the Products when in fact it is not. **5–675**

Unlike the corresponding clauses in Chapter 4 these clauses have been modified to ensure that they do not deal with the issue of repackaging or relabelling. Clause 5.3.8 now deals with these issues exclusively, taking into account the principles set out in the repackaging cases discussed in Chapter 5.1.1.4.3.

As drafted neither clause causes problems. The activities prohibited here are clearly unauthorised (and have nothing to do with relabelling or repackaging). There is nothing in EC competition law, in general, or in the repackaging cases in particular, which prevents the imposition of the prohibitions contained in these clauses. **5–676**

Clause 5.9.2 deals with unauthorised tampering with the products themselves, rather than their packaging. The phrases in square brackets are more appropriate to products in liquid or powder form, but would not be necessary where the product was an item of equipment, for instance a computer or a camera. Clause 5.9.3 deals with conduct which is unlawful in the sense that it attempts to deceive purchasers by passing off other unauthorised products as the principal's products. **5–677**

5.10 Stock of the products

5.10.1 The Distributor shall at all times during the continuance of this Agreement carry at least [three months] stock of the Products so that all orders received by the Distributor can be supplied without undue delay and shall supply such reports as to stock levels and movements as the Principal may from time to time request. **5–678**

5.10.2 The Distributor shall carry the full range of items comprised in the Products so that at all times customers may be able to inspect and to purchase the full range of the Products manufactured by the Principal. **5–679**

The Commission Guidelines on Vertical Restraints do not discuss the imposition of the obligation to keep proper stocks and to purchase the full range of the products Where Reg.2790/99 applies such an obligation would in any event cause no problems in most cases. The only danger might arise under Art.5(a). If an unreasonably high level of stocking were imposed, or if, in relation to full-line forcing, the whole product line was very extensive and each product type was very costly, the distributor might be precluded from handling competing products because he could not afford the inventory cost or perhaps the cost of additional premises in which to handle them. In this case, the clause might could constitute an indirect non-compete clause, and, if it is still wished to impose it, the considerations set out in Chapter 5.3.6 in relation to non-compete clauses must be borne in mind.

5–680 If the Regulation did not apply, then it would seem likely that the benefits to consumers of keeping proper stocks of a full product range would in most cases justify an exemption under Art.81(3), but again the issue relating to indirect non-compete clauses should be borne in mind. The imposition of full-line forcing is most usually found as a feature of selective distribution systems. This issue is discussed in Chapter 6.22.5.

5–681 In the UK, full-line forcing as a feature of vertical agreements is regarded as a common business practice and is not prohibited unless it leads to a significant reduction in competition. (See the OFT Guidelines: "Assessment of Individual Agreements and Conduct", OFT 414 p.19 para.6.7) Maintaining adequate stocks of the products to satisfy demand would cause no problems under the Chapter I Prohibition and would seem to be an objective justification for the imposition of the obligation if the principal were in a dominant position and the Chapter II Prohibition applied.

5.11 Distributor's staff

5–682 See cl.4.11.

Nothing in Reg.2790/99 would prevent the imposition of the obligations to have a properly trained staff and to provide customer services such as maintenance and guarantee services. The provision cited above is a general one, and the matter is dealt with in more detail in Chapter 6.22.2 in relation to selective distribution agreements where the provision is of most importance.

5–683 In general, even if an agreement falls outside Reg.2790/99, there appears to be nothing in the Guidelines condemning such a provision. However, where the supplier has a very large market share, and certainly if in a dominant position, such a provision if applied too strictly, and without objective justification, might result in an indirect quantitative restriction, if only a few distributors could afford to comply with the unnecessarily high standard required. The same issues would arise under UK competition law when the supplier was in a dominant position.

5.12 Monthly reports

See cl.4.12. 5–684

Apart from the issues relating to the possibility of using these reports for unlawful monitoring of the distributor's activities, neither UK nor EC competition law lays down requirements in relation to these clauses. The question of monitoring of course breaks down into that of the information asked for and the use to which it is put. It is better, unless absolutely necessary, not to require information in a form which could be used to trace parallel imports or resale prices.

5.13 Industrial property rights

5.13.1—see cl.4.13.1. **5–685**

5.13.2—see cl.4.13.2.

5.13.3—see cl.4.13.3.

There appears to be nothing in Reg.2790/99 or the Guidelines on Vertical Restraints that would cause particular problems with these clauses. Nor is it readily apparent why such clauses should infringe Art.81(1) in any event. The Guidelines deal at length with licences or assignments of intellectual property which are ancillary to the main purpose of the vertical agreement (*i.e.* the supply of goods or services). Obligations not to infringe the supplier's intellectual property are contemplated (see paras 39 to 41) and, at least in relation to franchisees, obligations on the franchisee to inform of infringements, and to take action or assist the franchisor in taking action against the infringer. There seems no reason why these obligations should not also be imposed on a distributor.

The one problem area is that of no-challenge clauses. The view of the Commission on no-challenge clauses or delimitation agreements is that they are restrictive of competition and can be considered under Art.81. This is discussed particularly in relation to licence agreements (where the problem is more acute) in Chapter 8.13.4. The *Maize Seed Case* (discussed in detail in Chapter 8.2) held that a settlement of legal proceedings relating to industrial property rights can also be considered for the same reasons under Art.81. **5–686**

The same view is taken of such clauses in distribution agreements. This can be seen in many Commission Decisions, but perhaps the best example is the European Court case of *BAT Cigaretten-Fabriken GmbH v EC Commission* [1985] 2 C.M.L.R. 470. BAT, carrying on business in Germany, and a firm called Segers carrying on business in Holland, both traded in tobacco products. BAT had registered in Germany for such products a mark which it did not use (Dorcet). Seger also registered in Germany his mark for tobacco products (Toltecs Special). BAT started opposition proceedings on the **5–687** grounds that Toltecs was confusingly similar to Dorcet. Seger did not want litigation with a large company, and so he agreed with BAT to restrict to certain classes of tobacco products only any imports into Germany bearing his mark. Even though BAT's mark was dormant, and after a certain time could have been contested by Segers asking for it to be struck off for non-use, Seger made no attempt to contest the mark, but chose to enter into the agreement and also agreed not to raise any objections to Dorcet or any further registration of that or a similar mark by BAT. The Commission fined BAT for operating an agreement which in effect partitioned the market between Seger and BAT.

5–688 They regarded the agreement as a delimitation agreement coupled with a no-challenge clause which was designed to protect BAT's mark even after the period of protection under German law for a dormant mark (five years from registration) had expired.

5–689 Although the Court recognised the usefulness of delimitation agreements to settle disputes or confusion over the parties' respective spheres of application, the application of Art.81 could not be excluded if such agreements were also for the purpose of market sharing or restricting competition (see *Grundig v Consten* [1966] C.M.L.R. 418). The Court said of the agreement between BAT and Segers that "the analysis of the agreement showed that all the obligations and disadvantages which it contains are against Segers' interests" particularly restrictions to use the mark on certain products, restrictions on advertising, and the no-challenge clause, which continued to have effect even after a challenge could lawfully have been made by Segers.

5–690 This case has recently been considered in *World Wide Fund for Nature (formerly World Wildlife Fund) v World Wrestling Federation Entertainment Inc.* [2002] U.K.C.L.R. 388, CA.

5–691 In its 22nd Report on Competition Policy for 1992, the Commission further considered the question of delimitation and non-use clauses in relation to trade marks in the market for bananas, and held that such clauses could not only contravene Art.81, but could, where imposed by an undertaking in a dominant position, also be an abuse of Art.82. The Commission proceeded against Chiquita Europe in relation to its conduct towards Fyffes plc. In the past Fyffes Group Ltd had been a subsidiary of Chiquita and had sold bananas in the UK under the Fyffes brand. At the same time Chiquita had sold bananas in Europe under the Fyffes brand. In 1986 Chiquita sold Fyffes Group Ltd to Fyffes plc. The transaction included a trade mark licence giving Fyffes exclusive use of the mark Fyffes in the UK for three years, but at the same time prohibiting it from using the mark Fyffes for the sale of fresh fruit and bananas outside the UK until 2006. After the expiry of the three year period Chiquita no longer used the Fyffes mark, although it still had registrations in its name, outside the UK, but relied on the agreement to prevent Fyffes using the mark in Continental Europe. It also brought infringement proceedings against Fyffes in reliance on its own registrations of the Fyffes mark.

5–692 The Commission considered that Chiquita had infringed both Arts 81 and

82. The non-use clause prevented Fyffes from selling its products EC wide under a strong brand name. To the extent it applied after the initial term of three years it could no longer be said to be a legitimate protection of Chiquita's continental goodwill. Thus the clause infringed Art.81. Further the clause had the effect of protecting Chiquita's dominant position in Continental Europe, so that by imposing the clause and relying on it, Chiquita was also in contravention of Art.82. The fact that Chiquita had its own registrations of the Fyffes mark did not help matters. In fact, since Chiquita had partitioned the mark between itself and Fyffes, it would not be allowed under Art.28 to rely on its trade mark registrations in other Member States to oppose the importation of bananas which had lawfully been put on the market by Fyffes in another Member State. Chiquita had therefore abused its dominant position by relying on its registrations of the marks in legal proceedings brought against Fyffes to prevent it selling bananas under the mark in Continental Europe. This was all the more so because Chiquita itself no longer used the Fyffes mark.

The principles in the delimitation cases discussed above will survive the **5–693** expiry of the "common origin doctrine" discussed in Chapter 5.1.1.4.1. In particular, *IHT Internationale Heiztechnik GmbH v Ideal Standard GmbH* can be distinguished from the delimitation cases since in the former there was no element of a continuing agreement which could be considered under Art.81 after the assignment which partitioned the mark had taken effect (see *EMI Records Ltd v CBS United Kingdom Ltd)*. In addition, *Chiquita* is also to be distinguished in that Art.82 did not apply in the common origin cases, as none of the enterprises concerned were in a dominant position.

5.14 No joint venture or partnership

See cl.1.9. **5–694**

5.15 Commencement and term of agreement

See cl.4.15. **5–695**

5.16 Termination

See cl.4.16. **5–696**

It should also be noted that within the EC, distributors have no general right to compensation upon termination under EC law, although some Member States (*e.g.* Belgium) do provide such a right under local law, which has an overriding effect (see Chapter 2.7 and the discussion after Chapters 3.10 to 3.12.)

5.17 Effect of termination

5–697 See cl.4.17.

A problem arises under this clause as to whether the obligations imposed upon the distributor to sell back stocks of the products to the principal upon termination contravene Art.81. In principle it would seem that such a clause must restrict competition because the distributor is not permitted to do as he likes with his own property.

5–698 A case in which a similar but not identical situation was considered was *Société de Vente de Ciments et Betons de l'Ouest SA v Kerpen & Kerpen GmbH & Co KG* [1985] 1 C.M.L.R. 511 where the European Court held that:

> "clauses in contracts of sale restricting the buyer's freedom to use the goods supplied in accordance with his own economic interests are restrictions on competition within the meaning of Article 81 ... A contract which imposes upon the buyer an obligation to use the goods supplied for his own needs, not to resell the goods in a specified area and to consult the seller before soliciting business in another specified area has as its object the prevention of competition..."

Although this case is not precisely on the point it does seem to cover, with a very small extension, the type of clause used in the precedent.

5–699 The first question is whether Reg.2790/99 applies to exempt such a clause. In order to bring this clause within the hardcore restrictions set out in Art.4 it would have to be regarded as an indirect restriction on the ability of the buyer to determine its sale price, because it has to sell back to the principal at a fixed price (see Art.4(a)) or as being a restriction of territory into which, or of the customers to whom, the buyer may sell the contract goods, because the goods in question must be sold back to the principal (Art.4(b)). The Commission Guidelines on Vertical Restraints discuss Art.4(a) and (b) at paras 46 to 49. The commentary makes it hard to fit this clause under Art.4(a), but the commentary on Art.4(b) (para.49) does deal with indirect means of enforcing sales restrictions, and this clause could fall within that guidance. If this were to be the case, then any agreement containing such a clause could not take advantage of the Regulation, and it would then be up to the parties to decide if the clause (together with the rest of the agreement) was exempt under Art.81(3). It is, however, likely that if the rest of the agreement would have been exempt under Reg.2970/99 except for the presence of this clause as a hardcore restriction, the agreement would be exempt under Art.81(3) anyway because the clause itself, relating only to a restricted stock of the products upon termination of the agreement is unlikely to have an appreciable effect either on competition or on trade between Member States.

5–700 The most likely part of the Regulation which would catch this clause is, however, Art.5(b) which covers "any direct or indirect obligation causing the buyer, after termination of the agreement, not to ... sell or resell goods ..." Although this provision is primarily aimed at post-termination non-compete clauses, the wording is very wide and would seem to catch the circumstance where, after termination, the distributor can no longer sell the stock of goods, that he has left, as he wishes, because he is obliged to sell them back to the principal. If this is correct, then the clause itself will not be exempted under Reg.2790/99, but the rest of the agreement can still take advantage of the regulation. It would then be necessary to consider simply whether, in the light of all the circumstances, such a clause would be exempt under Art.81(3), or, as discussed above, outside Art.81(1) altogether for lack of appreciable effect.

Under UK Competition law, unless the clause amounts to an indirect **5–701** form of resale price maintenance, caught by Art.4 of the Vertical Restraints Order, that Order will still apply to exempt the agreement from the operation of the Chapter I Prohibition in any event. The same arguments on the question of resale price maintenance apply as in the above discussion relating to the analogous provision in Art.4(a) of Reg.2790/99.

Given the serious consequences if this clause is found to be a hardcore **5–702** restriction, consideration should always be given to whether in truth the principal is really so concerned about buying back stock at the end of the arrangement. Wherever possible it is better to drop such a provision entirely. One other solution is to insert a provision declaring that the principal will (subject to mutual agreement) buy back the stock as provided in the precedent. This would set up a framework within which the parties could agree to the disposal of the stock, but the inclusion of the element of the requirement for mutual consent should prevent the contravention of Art.81 and fall outside the provisions of Arts 4 and 5 of Reg.2790/99 and Art.4 of the Vertical Restraints Order.

A final possibility is to amend the clause, as set out in cl.4.17, so that it **5–703** does not apply to all stock, but only to stock which is damaged or deteriorated or with its shelf-life *completely* expired. In this case, the argument could be made with some force that the distributor should not put such product on the market, and that either the force of the clause was such that, under the circumstances of the particular case, it had no appreciable effect on trade between Member States and/or upon competition, or that, if it did, consumer protection justified exemption under Art.81(3). If this course is adopted, it is vital that the principal assures himself that the motivation behind such a clause is the health and safety of consumers, or, perhaps, genuine concern for his reputation, or for the feasibility of providing proper after-sales service and guarantee cover if such stock is sold, and not a desire to prevent a distributor selling stock at a deep discount in the market upon termination of the agreement and causing pricing problems for the principal or the new distributor in the future.

5.18 Confidentiality

5–704 See cl.4.18.

The question of the rights of the principal to require the distributor to keep knowhow confidential after the termination of a knowhow licence is dealt with in Chapter 7.18. It should be mentioned that Art.5(b) of Reg.2790/99 permits post-termination non-compete clauses in limited circumstances and for a period not exceeding one year.

5–705 However, such a clause is only permitted if it is necessary to protect knowhow transferred by the supplier to the distributor. Nevertheless, the restrictions in Art.5(b) are expressed to be without prejudice to the "possibility of imposing a restriction which is unlimited in time on the use and disclosure of knowhow which has not entered the public domain". Thus knowhow can be protected in two ways—first by a restricted post-termination non-competition clause (since if the buyer cannot compete, by definition he cannot use the knowhow); and second by a conventional confidentiality undertaking which can be of indefinite duration provided the knowhow does not enter the public domain.

5–706 On this basis, there seems no clear reason why a post-termination non-compete clause of the type described here would not be exempt under Art.81(3) in the case of imposition by a supplier whose market share exceeded the 30 per cent threshold. In any event, even if the status of such a clause is unclear, there should be no reason why a pure confidentiality obligation imposed to protect knowhow would infringe Art.81(1).

5–707 So far as UK competition law is concerned, the imposition of a simple confidentiality clause could be imposed without consideration of the Chapter I Prohibition, and also, except in cases which approached an unjustified refusal to grant a licence (see Chapter 6.24.15) without consideration of the Chapter II Prohibition. Even a post-termination non-compete clause unconnected with the protection of knowhow could be imposed without consideration of the Chapter I Prohibition (although it could well be an abuse of a dominant position under the Chapter II Prohibition) but in this case, care would have to be taken to assess the impact of the common law doctrines which render void an unreasonable restraint of trade.

5–708 In general, post-termination non-compete clauses are rare in ordinary distribution agreements, and this precedent therefore does not contain one. In view of the limited scope permitted under Art.5(b), such a clause is of little value in any event.

5.19 Transmission of rights

5–709 See cl.4.19.

5.20 Interpretation clauses and signature

The appropriate clauses should be selected from Chapter 1 as required. **5–710**

5.21 Schedule 1—the products

5.22 Schedule 2—the territory

5.23 Schedule 3—the trade mark

Clauses 5.20 to 5.23 should be reproduced as required from Chapter 1. **5–711**

5.24 Schedule 4—purchase targets

4.24 The Distributor undertakes (subject to prior termination in accordance with cl.4.15) to achieve during [each consecutive period] [the first five consecutive periods] of twelve months of the currency of this Agreement (the first such period to commence upon the [date of signature of this Agreement] [Effective Date]) the following minimum targets for purchases from the Principal for the Products during the relevant period as follows: **5–712**

Period	Target

[Provided that the quantity for all periods thereafter shall be set by the mutual agreement of the parties hereto as a result of reviews to be completed not later than thirty days after the commencement of the relevant period.]

This clause deals with the issues concerning non-compete clauses discussed in Chapter 5.3.6. It either provides for quantity forcing for the duration of the agreement if the agreement lasts for five years or less (use the first phrase in square brackets) or for a quantity forcing obligation of a lesser duration than the length of the agreement (use the second set of square brackets). Given that the Commission has no objection to an expressly agreed renewal of a non-compete obligation, there would seem to be no objection to the addition of the sentence in the third set of square brackets where the quantity forcing does not extend for the duration of the agreement. Unlike the equivalent provision in Chapter 4.24, the review must take place after the conclusion of the previous period, since the parties may need to assess by reference to the previous year whether the 80 per cent threshold will be exceeded in the current year.

5.25 Schedule 5—competing goods

5–713 See cl.4.25.

5.26 Schedule 6—Reserved territories and reserved customers

5.27 Schedule 7—terms of supply of principal

5–714 See cl.4.26.

Although in general the terms and conditions set out here are suitable for use within the EC there are a few special issues which need to be considered in relation to competition.

5–715 The first is the question of refusal to supply. In general terms an undertaking is free to refuse to supply its products under EC competition law, (see *Bayer AG v Commission*), provided this is a unilateral act and not somehow part of an agreement that can be scrutinised under Art.81. However, *Bayer* draws a fine line between unilateral imposition and tacit agreement. The way in which Art.81 can apply in these situations is when the seller threatens to withhold supplies if the buyer does not observe resale price maintenance, the buyer complies in order to obtain supplies, and is then "rewarded" by being given supplies. At this stage at least a tacit agreement (and perhaps an express one) has arisen along the lines of the supplier agreeing to continue supplies and the buyer in return agreeing to apply resale price maintenance. This is clearly an agreement contravening Art.81 and a hardcore restriction under Art.4(a) of Reg.2790/99. It is relatively easy to find such an arrangement where there is a distribution agreement in existence which contains a provision allowing the principal to accept orders only at his discretion, without the need to show an objective reason for such refusal. Such an arrangement is even more likely to be found where the agreement also contains a provision for recommended or maximum resale prices, and/or provisions which directly or indirectly affect the ability of the distributor to obtain supplies of equivalent products elsewhere, such as non-compete or quantity forcing clauses, or fidelity rebates or discounts.

5–716 However, whatever the position under Art.81(1) an undertaking which is in a dominant position cannot refuse to supply its products without an objectively justifiable reason (*Commercial Solvents v Commission* [1974] E.C.R. 223 and *United Brands v Commission* [1978] E.C.R. 207). One such justifiable reason is that the would-be purchaser cannot pay for the goods (*Leyland DAF Ltd v Automotive Products plc* [1994] 1 B.C.L.C. 245, CA).

5–717 Refusal to supply can shade into a quota system to be used in times of shortage of supply. A quota system would not of itself contravene Art.81, even if the quotas were shared out upon some subjective basis which favoured some customers at the expense of the others. However, again, an undertaking in a dominant position has to be careful as to the way in which it applies a quota system. It is in most cases preferable that an objective system is put in place, relying for example upon a proportionate scaling back of all orders placed, perhaps with a minimum order quantity. Favouring traditional customers was at one time permitted under Art.82 (see *BP v Commission* [1978] E.C.R. 1513), but this is probably not now the case.

In Case T-65/89 *BPB Industries plc v Commission* [1993] 5 C.M.L.R. 32 the plaintiff was a manufacturer of both plasterboard and plaster. It was in a dominant position, for the purposes of Art.82, in the market for plaster but not for plaster board. In a time of shortage for plaster, the plaintiff laid down a system of loyalty payments and (in effect) quotas which favoured those of its customers who had bought plasterboard only from it and not from its competitors. The Court held that though it is open to an undertaking in a dominant position, and it is also a matter of normal commercial policy, in times of shortage, to lay down criteria for according priority in meeting orders, those criteria must be objective and must not be discriminatory in any way; they must be objectively justified and observe the rules of fair competition between traders. Favouring "loyal" customers was discriminatory treatment which amounted to an abuse of a dominant position under Art.82. This was so even if the practice lasted for a short time and customers who were not "loyal" were not greatly disadvantaged. In any event the Commission had taken these aspects of the case into account when setting the level of fines. **5–718**

It is not possible to distinguish *BPB Industries* from *BP v Commission* on the grounds that the former case represented a tying together of the sales of two products. The loyal customers had purchased the plasterboard from BPB previously, before they knew that there would be a shortage of plaster. It could of course be argued that such a quota system would reinforce the purchases of BPB's plasterboard in future, since customers would realise that, in any further shortage of plaster, they would be favoured if they had bought BPB's plasterboard, but this point seems not to have been considered. The principle of the case turns simply upon the difference between a quota system set up on subjective criteria (an abuse) and one set up on objective criteria (not an abuse). **5–719**

Finally, it is necessary to consider the question of promotional assistance and discounts as an element of pricing. It has always been the case that it is a contravention of Art.82 for a firm in a dominant position to provide loyalty rebates or turnover related discounts (*Michelin v Commission* [1983] E.C.R. 3461), but by and large such activities are not a contravention of Art.81 unless they are used to reinforce a practice which contravenes Art.81 (see the Commission Decision *Re The Distillers Company Ltd* [1978] 1 C.M.L.R. 400). **5–720**

Another Decision in this area is the Decision of the Commission in *Re Gosme/Martell*, Commission Decision [1991] O.J. L185. There the Commission considered a scheme of promotional assistance and discounts in respect of goods purchased by a distributor, which excluded goods pur- **5–721** chased by the distributor for resale by export out of his designated territory. The Commission said that any prohibition on exports was inherently liable to affect trade between Member States, and that any practice or agreement making them less profitable was also liable to do so. Given that Martell was a large undertaking with a significant market share, the effect on trade was likely to be appreciable. The Commission therefore held that the arrangements contravened Art.81. A fine of 300,000 ECU was levied on the principal for operating this system.

5–722 Michelin has recently been fined again by the Commission (€19.76m) for abusing a dominant position in replacement tyres for heavy vehicles in France during most of the last decade. The Commission concluded that Michelin's system of quantitative rebates, bonuses and other commercial practices illegally tied dealers and foreclosed the French market to other manufacturers. (See Commission Statement IP/01/873 dated June 20, 2001.)

5–723 Under UK competition law the same principles on refusal to supply, as described above in relation to Art.81 and Reg.2790/99, will apply in respect of the Chapter I Prohibition and the Vertical Restraints Order, as the provisions of Art.4(a) of the Order are substantially the same as those of Art.4(a) of the Regulations. Of course, if the supplier is in a dominant position, in the UK, then all consideration of the terms of the agreement or the surrounding arrangement would be largely irrelevant, since, as will be seen below, the refusal to supply without objective justification, would be an abuse of that dominant position under the Chapter II Prohibition.

5–724 It should be noted that the OFT considers one of the indirect ways in which the principal could force the distributor to adhere to minimum prices (and hence infringe the Chapter I Prohibition) is by "intimidation, delay or suspension of deliveries and contract termination in relation to the observance of a certain price level" (OFT 419 p.12). However, OFT 419 relied upon the draft form of the Guidelines (published in September 1999) and was in any case published before the judgment in *Bayer* was handed down.

5–725 The issue of refusal to supply in a larger sense (*i.e.* where no agreement is involved) is always susceptible of scrutiny under the Chapter II Prohibition, but of course the Chapter I Prohibition is irrelevant. It is always necessary to consider whether the undertaking refusing to supply is in a dominant position in the market in question. ("The Director-General [of the OFT] takes the view that refusal to supply an existing customer by a dominant undertaking can be an abuse if no objective justification for the behaviour can be provided ... In some limited circumstances refusal to supply a new customer might be an abuse." See OFT 414 p.24 et *et seq.*)

5–726 Under the Resale Prices Act 1976 (repealed by s.1 of the Competition Act 1998) one of the grounds upon which a refusal to supply was justified was where the purchasing outlet had sold the products in question, or similar products, as "loss leaders" within the last twelve months. There is no equivalent concept in relation to Art.81 under EC competition law. The OFT still recognises the concept of "loss leaders" in relation to predatory pricing (See OFT 414 p.12, where it defines loss leading as the sale of products below average variable cost in order to increase sales of complementary products.) However, there is no indication whether a refusal to supply because of prior loss leading activity is an "objective justification" for refusal to supply. Moreover, the OFT does not seem averse to the concept of loss leading *per se*, but only where it amounts to predatory pricing. This will not be the case "unless it was clear that the real intention was to eliminate a competitor" (*ibid.*) Given the above and the wording in Art.4 of the Vertical Restraints Order, it can only be submitted that a clause preventing the Distributor selling products as loss leaders would cause the agreement to fall outside the Vertical Restraints Order, thus giving rise to a potential infringement of the Chapter I Prohibition.

Of course, depending on the facts, there may be cases where "loss leading" can be regarded as an "objective justification" for refusal to supply. Where this is present, presumably the OFT could hold that there had been no infringement of the Chapter I, or, in appropriate cases, of the Chapter II, Prohibition. Examples of objective justification for refusal to supply are given as poor creditwothiness or temporary shortage of supply (OFT 414 p.24 para.7.1). **5–727**

However, this cannot be exhaustive. For instance, if one wished to dispose of stock in obsolete packaging, it would be reasonable to impose a condition that it be sold off only as distress stock or through market traders because it was undesirable to continue to have old packaging visible in other outlets conflicting with a new design of packaging now generally available. This conflict would of course be regarded as detrimental to plans for promoting and marketing the product in its new get-up. Similarly one could envisage circumstances in which sale as a loss leader might afford an objective justification for refusal to supply, or in which a contractual prohibition on resale as a loss leader might not be found to be an infringement of the Chapter I Prohibition. Perhaps it could be claimed that resale as a loss leader would be detrimental to the reputation of the product, or that it would detract from the service the customer could expect, either to assist his choice in purchasing the product, or in relation to after-sales service. **5–728**

Chapter 6

Selective Distribution for Technical and Luxury Products

Contents

6.1 Commercial and legal background

Manufacturers are often not content for the goods that they sell to be **6–01**
distributed in a haphazard manner. They often wish to influence the way

and the terms and conditions on which they pass through the chain of distribution and reach the customer. The problem arises mainly in the areas of luxury consumer goods, particularly perfumes and cosmetics, white goods (basically washing machines, dishwashers and similar products), brown goods (hi-fi equipment, radio and television and video recorders), and motor vehicles. It can also apply to any technically sophisticated product whether or not intended primarily for consumer use, such as personal computers for business or professional purposes.

6–02 The control in all these cases is usually maintained by selective distribution systems. As a rule the manufacturer will set out certain criteria with which he wishes the persons who handle his goods to comply, and will arrange that only such people can have the opportunity to handle his goods.

6–03 In some cases, the control is imposed early on, in that the manufacturer exercises discrimination in the choice of the distributors or wholesalers who buy directly from him and then makes them pass similar criteria, appropriately adapted, down to the retailers who in turn buy from them. Sometimes the manufacturer is content to exercise relatively little discrimination in the choice of wholesalers or initial distributors and to confine himself to specifying particular classes of retailers to whom his goods may be sold by the middlemen.

6–04 A classical example of a fully evolved system would be a manufacturer who appoints an exclusive distributor for each of a number of separate countries, and permits that distributor to sell only to approved wholesalers, who each have a defined portion of their distributor's territory in which to operate. The wholesalers in turn would be permitted to sell only to approved retailers who would each in turn serve a defined part of the wholesaler's subterritory. No one would be permitted to sell outside the particular territory allotted to him, nor to obtain the relevant products other than from his designated supplier. Prices would be controlled at all levels, and horizontal and reverse sales within the system would be forbidden. Criteria for approval would range from technical expertise, suitable staff and premises, and willingness to advertise, to the need to restrict the number of outlets to that which could operate profitably at the various levels of distribution in the various territories.

6–05 The object of the manufacturer in setting up such a system could vary from the desire to have an efficient and economic distribution system, which provided good service, particularly in the after-sales area, to ultimate users, to the desire to keep up prices. Such systems are sometimes set up collectively by trading associations, as well as singly by individual manufacturers. There is also no reason why someone at a lower point in the chain, such as a sole distributor, should not set up on his own initiative a selective distribution system for the steps in the chain of distribution below him.

6–06 The system in its classical form as described above does in fact fall foul not only of Art.81, but also of the competition laws in most states in the EC, and outside. This is basically because of its price control provisions and its restrictions on the sources of supply and rights of resale of each member of the system, and its restriction of the number of members in the system.

6.1.1 Selective distribution networks under EC competition law

With regard to EC law, most selective distribution systems which contravened Art.81(1) were not able, because of the extent of the restrictions that were present, (particularly the restriction on not supplying goods outside of the network other than, in the case of retailers, to end users), to take advantage of Reg.83/83 (the old block exemption covering exclusive distribution agreements) or Reg.84/83 (the old block exemption covering exclusive purchasing agreements) to obtain exemption for each agreement within the system individually as a series of separate distribution agreements. This meant that, under the old regulatory framework for EC competition law (see Chapter 5.1.1.1) each selective distribution network had to be the subject of a specific exemption by the Commission under the individual procedure pursuant to Art.81(3). **6–07**

The treatment of selective distribution networks under EC competition law has thus evolved over the years through a series of Commission Decisions (supplemented by judgments of the European Court to cover doubtful or disputed points), without, in all cases except the motor vehicle sector, the benefit of a relevant block exemption. The motor vehicle sector is now covered by the block exemption under Commission Regulation 1400/2002/EC of July 31, 2002 on the application of Article 81(3) of the Treaty to categories of vertical agreements and concerted practices in the motor vehicle sector (which replaced the previous Commission Regulations (123/85 followed by 1475/95) on the same subject). This block exemption continues to apply despite, and is unaffected by, the more general block exemption for vertical agreements (Reg.2790/99) discussed in detail in Chapter 5.2. It is discussed and analysed in detail in Chapter 6.26. Its provisions are specific to the motor vehicle sector, but because of the particular competition concerns which the Commission has in relation to this sector, the regulation probably represents a good example of the strictest approach the Commission would follow in considering provisions likely to be exempt under Art.81(3) where Reg.2790/99 does not apply. However, the principles and the precedent discussed in this chapter are of more general application. **6–08**

Currently, the Commission treats all the other types of selective distribution agreements as just another type of vertical agreement. Thus Reg.2790/99 covers all selective distribution networks (with the exception of those covered by Reg.1400/2002 in the motor vehicle sector) in general terms, like any other vertical agreements. However, the Commission has taken into account previous relevant Decisions and case law, in framing both the regulation and the Commission Guidelines on Vertical Restraints (discussed generally throughout Chapter 5 in relation to distribution agreements). Regulation 2790/99 thus prohibits certain restraints often found in selective distribution agreements which the Commission considers to have too great an anticompetitive effect. The Guidelines have sections dealing specifically with selective distribution networks, which in part sum **6–09** up previous Decisions and case law, and in part set out the current Commission stance towards selective distribution networks.

6–10 This stance has become more negative in recent years because of increasing concern over the cumulative effect of many selective distribution networks existing side by side in particular markets and product sectors (see Chapter 5.1.1.3.8 for a discussion on the concept of cumulative effect).

6–11 Set out below are a selection of Commission Decisions and European Court cases which show how these institutions have treated the more obvious forms of restrictive practices which can operate under the name of selective distribution systems.

6–12 In *Re Gas Water-Heaters* [1973] C.M.L.R. D241, three Belgian manufacturers and two importers of gas water heaters agreed collectively on standard conditions of sale, terms of payment and conditions, and after-sales service. They agreed to supply only certain classes of dealers, and to give them certain discounts including, in some cases, an aggregated rebate discount. The Commission refused to sanction the arrangement on the grounds that it prevented the supply to other dealers such as large shops, chain stores and so on. Furthermore other dealers would find it hard to break into the market given that the dealers supplied under the agreements enjoyed such advantageous discounts. In addition the aggregated rebate discount was disallowed because it discouraged the dealers who enjoyed it from obtaining supplies from elsewhere than the parties to the agreement. For this reason the Commission stated that aggregated rebate discounts would always be a contravention of Art.81(1).

6–13 In *Re AEG-Telefunken AG* [1982] O.J. L117/82 which was affirmed in the European Court Decision in *AEG-Telefunken AG v Commission* [1984] 3 C.M.L.R. 325 the Commission imposed fines on AEG who, although they had notified their selective distribution arrangements, and obtained an exemption, had in fact applied them in such a way that dealers who cut prices could not get to become members of the network. This was the first time the Commission had fined the operator of a selective distribution system not for the terms which it imposed, but for the manner in which those terms were actually applied.

6–14 As discussed below, the Commission gave its original exemption to the BMW selective distribution network because it recognised the benefits of efficiency and after-sales service generated by the arrangements for the consumer. However, in common with all other approved networks the original arrangements, approved in relation to BMW Germany, did not include bans on cross-border trade, but required the trade to be confined to consumers and members of the network. BMW (Belgium) set up a similar arrangement whereby its dealers in Belgium were to sell only to other members of the network or to ultimate consumers, anywhere in the EC. Thus cross-border trade was still preserved.

6–15 In 1975 prices of BMW cars were lower in Belgium than in other areas of the EC and cross-border trade with Belgium became advantageous. Indeed some exports even found their way to dealers who were not in the network. BMW Belgium, acting in fact against the wishes of its parent, reminded all its dealers not to sell outside the network. The dealers themselves went further, and through their consultative council told all dealers not to sell outside Belgium. BMW Germany attempted to correct this, but before it could do so, the Commission moved against the Belgian company and the Belgian dealers. It decided that they had contravened Art.81(1) in that the circular and Decision of the council amounted to an arrangement between the dealers and the Belgian company prohibiting exports.

BMW Belgium appealed to the European Court (see [1980] 1 C.M.L.R. 370). Before the Court it was argued that the terms of the circulars were only intended to stop dealing outside the network, but the Court rejected this argument, as not, on the face of it, correct. It therefore upheld the Commission's Decision on the contravention of Art.81(1). **6–16**

The Commission has continued to scrutinise the BMW selective distribution system over the years. In *BMW v ALD Auto-Leasing*, Case C-70/93 [1995] E.C.R. I-3439, BMW sent a circular telling BMW's dealers not to supply to leasing companies which supplied vehicles for customers outside the relevant dealer's territory. BMW did this because dealers had complained that they had to service free of charge such vehicles supplied into their territory by such leasing companies, and yet they had not had the benefit of any profit from the sale of the vehicle in the first place. **6–17**

The European Court held that the circular was sent "in the context of the contractual relations between BMW and its dealers", so that it formed "part of a set of continuous business relations governed by a general agreement drawn up in advance" and was therefore subject to Art.81. The provision clearly had an appreciable effect on trade between Member States. There was nothing in Reg.123/1985 (the block exemption then covering selective distribution in the motor vehicle trade) which would help BMW in this instance, so the restriction would be caught by Art.81(1). **6–18**

In *Re Association Pharmaceutique Belge*, Commission Decision [1990] O.J. L18, the Commission considered a registration scheme for pharmaceutical products. The APB tested and registered products on behalf of Belgian pharmacists. No pharmacist would sell pharmaceutical products which had not been so tested and registered. The APB concluded agreements with manufacturers whereby it tested and registered their pharmaceutical products so as to enable them to be sold in Belgium through pharmacies. Originally, the APB required manufacturers who contracted with it to undertake not to sell pharmaceutical products except through pharmacies (in practice this meant not through discount stores and supermarkets). The Commission held that this established a system of exclusive distribution limited to pharmacies. It required the APB to amend the agreements with the manufacturers so that they were free to sell products registered with the APB to outlets other than pharmacies, provided that in this case they did not bear the APB stamp. It did not object to selective distribution networks creating their own control system and seal of quality. Since competition between different types of outlets for pharmaceutical products is often on grounds of price rather than quality, the restriction of competition resulting from the exclusion from the registration system was **6–19** not appreciable.

6–20 In Case T-19/91 *Société d'Hygiéne Dermatologique de Vichy v Commission* [1992] E.C.R. II-415, the European Court of First Instance upheld a Commission Decision that a selective distribution system which allowed only dispensing chemists to sell the relevant skin-care products infringed Art.81(1) and would not be granted an exemption under Art.81(3). The requirement did not apply to the technical qualifications of trained sales staff, (*i.e.* that they should have a pharmacist's diploma), which would have been an objective qualitative criterion, but to the type of outlet. The Commission and the Court were not convinced by Vichy's arguments as to why it was necessary to sell through a pharmacy, with a dispensing chemist, rather than through any outlet with one or more of the sales staff holding a pharmacist's diploma.

6–21 Since Vichy could not demonstrate a qualitative reason for sale through a pharmacy, the requirement was in fact a quota, since it restricted the potential number of outlets (who could have employed sales staff with a pharmacist's diploma) without a reason based upon an objective qualitative criterion. Furthermore "the effects on competition were accentuated by the fact that, by reason of the intake quota and constraints of professional ethics imposed on dispensing chemists in most of the Member States concerned, it was well known that competition between dispensing chemists was restricted".

6–22 The Commission Decision *Ford New Holland Ltd*, Commission Decision [1993] O.J. L20, first of all clarifies that Reg.123/1985 did not apply to selective distribution for agricultural vehicles (in this case, tractors). Ford New Holland (currently a subsidiary of Fiat, and previously owned by the Ford Motor Company) had notified the agreements on which its system was based, but neglected to tell the Commission that it was operating a policy of discouraging parallel imports because of significant price differentials for tractors between different Member States. It used a variety of means to attack such imports. It established systems for the identification of parallel imports using vehicle registration documents that were made available by the UK government for statistical purposes. It encouraged dealers to report parallel imports, and even die-stamped a secret number on tractors for the purpose of identification, and inspected tractors on farms to check their origin. Ford sent letters to various dealers telling them parallel imports were undesirable, threatened to cancel the dealership of offending dealers, made discounts conditional upon registration within the contract territory or upon purchase for own use, refused warranty service for parallel imports and used safety regulations as a pretext for preventing exports.

6–23 The Commission held that Ford New Holland's actions had the object and effect of preventing trade between Member States. There was no justification for it seeking to deny the benefits of free trade to prospective purchasers of its products situated in a state in which the domestic price of its products was higher.

6–24 Exemption under Art.81(3) was not possible as Ford New Holland had not disclosed all of the relevant facts. However, a fine would not be imposed since the Commission had to some extent tolerated Ford New Holland's claims to be covered by Reg.123/1985 even after much of its investigation had been completed, which led the company to think tracing and prevention of sales to unauthorised dealers was legitimate. Also many of the practices related to the past and had now ceased. Finally the current owners (Fiat) accepted that the company's conduct amounted to an infringement and were taking vigorous steps to avoid a repetition.

Selective distribution networks and practices in the motor vehicle sector continue to occupy the Commission as can be seen by the more recent cases and Decisions discussed in Chapter 5: Case C-266/93 *Bundeskartellamt v Volkswagen AG/VAG Leasing GmbH*, [1996] 4 C.M.L.R. 478; *Volkswagen AG v Commission* [2000] 5 C.M.L.R. 853; *Re Triumph Motor Cycles* (Commission Statement IP/00/1014); *Re Opel Nederland BV* (Commission Statement IP/00/1028); *Re J C Bamford Group* (Commission Statement IP/00/1526); *Re Mercedes Benz* (COMP/36.246 of October 10, 2001), currently under appeal to the European Court. **6–25**

The most recent area to receive severe scrutiny (also discussed in Chapter 5) was that of computer games software, in the Commission Decision against Nintendo and its seven European distributors (Commission Statement IP/02/1584). **6–26**

It can thus be seen that selective distribution systems have received considerable scrutiny under EC law. This chapter deals with a precedent which follows the principles set down in various Commission Decisions and European Court cases on restrictions and provisions for selective distribution systems operating in the EC, as summed up and, to some extent, amended or supplemented by the special provisions of Reg.2790/99 and the further commentary set out in the relevant parts of the Commission Guidelines on Vertical Restraints. **6–27**

Although it is possible to draft the arrangements for such a system in a way that should make it fall outside Art.81 entirely, this will so dilute the "selective" nature of the system that practical commercial considerations will dictate further restrictions which, except in the rare cases discussed in this chapter, will have to be considered in the light of the applicability of Reg.2790/99. Where the regulation does not apply, the principles in the Guidelines will have to be considered so that the parties can determine, under the new regulatory framework, (see Chapter 5.1.1.2) whether the agreement can take advantage of exemption under Art.81(3). **6–28**

The purpose of the precedent in this chapter, coupled with a discussion in detail of the cases, the regulation and the Guidelines, is to enable the draftsman to identify the areas where the regulation applies and those where, if it does not, exemption under Art.81(3) should or should not be applicable. In this connection it is vital to adopt the holistic approach to the analysis discussed in Chapter 5.1.3, looking at the parties to a relationship, the terms and conditions governing that relationship, and the surrounding environment (both legal, factual and economic) in which that relationship is carried on. **6–29**

6.1.2 Selective distribution under the local laws of EC Member States

6–30 As discussed in Chapter 5.1.1.3.5, the advent of the single European market has made it almost impossible to claim that a selective distribution system, which is limited purely to one Member State, has no effect on cross-border trade within the EC, so that Art.81 has no application. Just as with ordinary exclusive distribution agreements there is always the potential for effect on trade between Member States (see the Commission Decision *Re BMW* discussed in Chapter 6.18.1 and the European Court case *Salonia v Poidomani* discussed in Chapter 6.22.3).

6–31 In any event, whether such selective distribution systems operate in one or more Member States, it is obviously necessary to examine in detail the local laws relating to anti-competitive practices, resale price maintenance and refusal to supply. It is therefore useful at this stage to examine briefly some of the local laws on competition in Member States within the EC for examples of the way they operate in relation to local arrangements, and how the local law can interact with the EC law on competition.

6–32 The new competition regime in force in the UK, under the Competition Act 1998, closely approximates that of the EC (see Chapter 5.1.2). However, the Competition Act 1998 (Land and Vertical Agreements Exclusion) Order 2000 (SI 2000/310) excludes all vertical agreements from the Chapter I Prohibition, including selective distribution agreements, unless they contain the hardcore restrictions relating to resale price maintenance (see Chapter 5.2). This means that so far as the UK regime itself is concerned, in most cases the only problem will be the impact of the Chapter II Prohibition if the party setting up the selective distribution network is in a dominant position.

6–33 The one note of caution relates to Art.7 of the Order, which permits the Director General of the Office of Fair Trading to withdraw the benefit of the Order in relation to any vertical agreement if he considers that a vertical agreement will, if not excluded, infringe the Chapter I Prohibition and he would not be likely to grant an unconditional individual exemption under the Competition Act. (see para.5 of OFT 419: Vertical Agreements and Restraints, and see also Competition Act 1998 Sch.1)). This will not occur unless a party has significant market power (in practice usually over 25 per cent—see OFT 419 para.1.11) or a network of similar agreements exists in the relevant market (*i.e.* in this case a number of selective distribution networks, not a number of selective distribution agreements in one network—see para.5.1 of OFT 419 and Chapter 5.1.1.3.8 for a discussion on this concept of cumulative effect).

6–34 Thus, in most cases, if the parties avoid the obvious traps in relation to setting pricing policy, the selective distribution network should cause no problems under UK competition law, even though such a network also entails a refusal to supply parties who are not members of it. For a discussion on resale price maintenance reference should be made to Chapter 5.9 and for refusal to supply to Chapter 5.27.

6–35 Where considering the Chapter I or the Chapter II Prohibition in relation to selective distribution networks, the greatest concern of the Director General relates to cumulative effect. In particular such networks can lead to foreclosure of the market to retailers, depending on the qualification criteria for appointment to the network. The OFT guidelines make a number of points:

- "If a manufacturer imposed an absolute restriction on the number of retailers the effect would be likely to be more significant than if it set objective standards for all its retailers to meet. However such objective standards may still prevent entry by new innovative retail operations and the Director General might become concerned if standards were clearly designed to favour existing retailers over new entrants" (para.6.15 OFT 414—"Assessment of Individual Agreements and Conduct.")
- "The key factor is likely to be the market power of the manufacturer, or manufacturers imposing the restraints. The size of any networks will also be important; even where a manufacturer has a relatively small market share the network of agreements [ie a number of selective distribution networks in this case] may cover a high percentage of the market. In situations where a network of agreements exists, the Director General may wish to withdraw the benefits [of the Order] . . ." (para.6.16 of OFT 414)
- "A further consideration in assessing the market power of the manufacturers is likely to be the strength of their brands . . . Retailers may find it difficult to establish themselves if they are unable to stock certain leading brands." (para.6.17 OFT 414)
- "Selective distribution . . . reduces the number of competing retailers in a particular product, reducing the intensity of retail competition in that product [intra-brand competition]. This can lead to higher retail margins and less innovation in retailing and distribution". (para.6.20 OFT 414)

Germany's anti-cartel and unfair trading provisions (Act Against Restraints **6–36** of Competition) does permit selective distribution systems, but requires that enterprises which have a dominant position in a market should not abuse it by discriminating between purchasers for their products. Selection of outlets by their suitability to handle the products in question is permitted, and even a quota system for the number of dealers, if general market conditions require it. Aggrieved persons (*i.e.* dealers who have been excluded from the system or refused supply) do not complain to an investigatory body like the Office of Fair Trading but take direct legal proceedings in court against the exclusion, and can recover damages, or obtain an order for supply.

(Case C-41/96 *VAG-Handlerbeirat eV v SYD-Consult* [1997] C.E.C. 1226 **6–37** is a European Court decision which shows some of the possibilities of interaction between local and EC competition law, in this case in relation to the local German regime.

6–38 VAG, the German association of concessionaires approved by Volkswagen AG, (VW), for the sale of its vehicles in Germany, brought unfair competition proceedings against SYD. SYD sold in Germany new VW vehicles purchased in Italy from approved VW concessionaires and reimported into Germany. Since the sale prices in Italy were considerably lower than those charged in Germany, SYD was able to offer the vehicles to its German customers at a considerably lower price than those charged by approved German VW concessionaires.

6–39 Within the EU, VW had set up a selective distribution system enjoying exemption under Reg.123/85 and VAG alleged that SYD obtained new vehicles covered by that system by taking advantage of a breach of contract by Italian concessionaires. VAG alleged that practice constituted the securing by SYD of an unfair competitive advantage contrary to the German law on unfair competition, "the UWG".

6–40 In proceedings before the Hamburg Regional Court SYD objected to the proceedings on the basis that VW's selective distribution system was not "impervious". For the purposes of German law, the word "impervious" means exclusive or closed to outsiders. SYD argued that the German case law that VAG was relying on held that a selective distribution system is binding on the parties and enforceable against third parties, under the UWG, only if it is absolutely impervious, in which case a third party who has succeeded in obtaining products covered by the system is presumed to have taken advantage of a breach of contract by an approved distributor, and can be proceeded against accordingly.

6–41 It was common ground that VAG's system was not impervious, but VAG contended that the principle of unrestricted and uniform application of EC law precluded the application of the German case law imposing the requirement that the system be impervious.

6–42 The national court referred this question to the European Court for a preliminary ruling. The Court ruled that neither Art.81(3) nor Reg.123/85 could be interpreted as precluding the application of national case law on unfair competition under which a selective distribution system, even if enjoying exemption under those provisions, was not enforceable against third parties unless it was impervious. The imperviousness of a selective distribution system was not a condition for its validity under EC law. It followed that a selective distribution system which was not impervious and could not, under national case law on unfair competition, be enforced against third parties, might still be valid under Art.81. In any event Reg.123/85 concerned only contractual relations between suppliers and their approved distributors and could not affect the rights and obligations of third parties.

6–43 Holland has a similar type of law permitting selective distribution systems, but controlling their abuse.

6–44 In France, the law makes an unjustified refusal to sell both a civil and a criminal offence. However, both exclusive dealing arrangements, and requests for supply of an abnormal character are given as justifications for refusal. The latter ground can be used to justify selective distribution systems where the qualifications for entry are related to matters like the capability of the purchaser and the suitability of its premises and resources for handling the types of product concerned. This especially applies to luxury goods.

In France, as well, there have been a number of cases in which motor traders have tried to enforce Reg.123/85 in the local courts directly against third party parallel importers. These cases have all held that Reg.123/85 could not be interpreted as prohibiting a trader (who was outside the official distribution network for a given make of a motor vehicle and was not an authorised intermediary within the meaning of Reg.123/85 Art.3(11)) from acquiring new vehicles of that make by way of parallel imports, and from importing them into France (see Case C-226/94 *Grand Garage Albigeois SA v Garage Massol SARL* [1996] E.C.R. I-651, Case C-309/94 *Nissan France SA v Dupasquier* [1996] C.E.C. 503 and Case C-128/95 *Fontaine SA v Aqueducs Automobiles SARL* [1997] 5 C.M.L.R. 39). **6–45**

In recent years there has been a growing tendency towards greater harmonisation in the practical application of the various national laws of Member States and of EC competition law. It has thus increasingly been the case that national law of Member States is being overridden in proceedings brought in national courts by one party trying to claim that the system is a contravention of EC law, and therefore invalid, even if permitted by national laws on competition. This tendency has of course culminated in the new regulatory framework for EC competition law with the direct application of Arts.81 and 82 by national competition law authorities and national courts under Reg.1/2003 (see Chapter 5.1.1.2) **6–46**

Since the Commission and the European Court often find that even what look like operations confined to one Member State do affect cross-border trade, and therefore fall under their jurisdiction through the operation of Arts.28 and 30, 81 or 82 of the EC Treaty (see Chapter 5.1.1.3.5), there is thus a tendency to reinforce and harshen local competition laws, where they exist, and to introduce concepts of control of anti-competitive practices where they are weak or non-existent. This means that increasingly EC law now in practice sets the minimum standards for control of anti-competitive activity throughout the EC (see Art.3 of Reg.1/2003) However, there is nothing under Reg.1/2003 which prevents the local competition law of a Member State applying stricter laws (Art.3.2) or laws that predominantly pursue an objective different to that pursued by Arts.81 and 82 (Art.3.3). **6–47**

This approach can be seen in various cases and Decisions. In the Commission Decisions relating to the French and Dutch tobacco industry distribution arrangements (see p.159 of the 10th Report on Competition Policy, *Re SEITA* (1980) and *Re SSI* [1982] O.J. L232/82 respectively) the arrangements were found to be anti-competitive, since the French arrangements impeded foreigners from distributing within France, and the price controls in Holland operated to the detriment of importers and in favour of nationals. In the European Court case of *Commission v Italian Republic* [1983] 2 C.M.L.R. 255, relating to state price control in the Italian **6–48** tobacco distribution market, the Commission unsuccessfully argued that the facts proved the effect of the national arrangements on cross-border trade, but the Court accepted the principle of the argument that, if such an effect had been present, there would have been a restriction on competition. In the European Court case of *Salonia v Poidomani* (see Chapter 6.22.3) a system of selective distribution for newspapers and periodicals within Italy was set up under local law which allowed only Italian nationals to become members. (Competition law in Italy was at that time relatively weak, and there were in general little obstacles there to local selective distribution systems.) The Court again accepted the argument as to anti-competitive effect in theory, and remitted the case to the Italian court to apply the theory to the facts.

6–49 The most instructive set of cases on this subject is the Perfume cases. Retail outlets complained to their national court in France, Belgium and Holland for refusal by manufacturers of luxury perfume and other beauty products to include them in selective distribution systems for those products, claiming that there had been a contravention of the relevant national laws against unjustified refusal to supply. The manufacturers complained against included Guerlain, Rochas, Lanvin, Lancome, Nina Ricci and L'Oreal. In these cases the Commission had given informal clearance by letters to the selective distribution arrangements under Art.81 (see Chapter 6.18.1). The manufacturers relied on the letters to excuse them from a claim that the arrangements contravened Art.81(1). The European Court gave a series of similar decisions in 1979 and 1980 (see, as the best example, *L'Oreal NV & L'Oreal SA v De Nieuwe AMCK PVBA* [1981] 2 C.M.L.R. 235). It held that the letters were purely administrative arrangements, and the national courts, although they should take them into account, could not be prevented by them from directly applying Art.81 to the facts of each case as they knew them. The Court went on to say that if the national courts felt that internal competition law was contravened by the selection arrangements then there was once again no reason why the Commission's letters should bar them from coming to this conclusion. Since internal competition law could be stricter than Art.81, the letter of the Commission had even less relevance in this case.

6.1.3 Selective distribution agreements in territories outside the EC

6–50 Where one is dealing with countries outside the EC an examination of the relevant local laws must of course be undertaken. Countries where particular care has to be taken are the USA, with its extensive anti-trust legislation, and other common law countries such as Australia and Canada which apply similar rules. No selective distribution system should be set up without detailed enquiry as to the effect upon its operation of national competition laws in the various territories where it is to be operated.

6.1.4 The basis and applicability of the precedent

As it stands the precedent concentrates on EC competition law, and would be acceptable for use within the EC for distribution agreements affecting cross-border trade between Member States. The Commission Decisions in *Yves St Laurent Parfums SA*, Commission Decision [1992] O.J. L12, and *Parfums Givenchy SA* Commission Decision [1992] O.J. L236 set out a useful summary of the Commission's thinking on selective distribution agreements in the area of luxury up-market goods such as high fashion perfumes. There are summaries in these Decisions of the terms and conditions in the Yves St Laurent and Givenchy selective distribution agreements and a commentary upon their acceptability or otherwise. The Commission Decision in *Grundig AG* Commission Decision [1994] O.J. L20 provides a further summary of the Commission's thinking in the area of selective distribution agreements for technical products. These three Decisions are worth reading in detail for anyone who intends to draft a selective distribution agreement in this area of the market. Together with *Re IBM PC* [1984] 2 C.M.L.R. 342, they are used as the basis for the precedent, which has also been adapted to conform to the special requirements of Reg.2790/99 in relation to selective distribution agreements. **6–51**

It is important to note that Reg.2790/99 does not prescribe a set of acceptable terms and conditions for selective distribution agreements, any more than it does for other vertical agreements. It simply specifies certain hardcore restrictions under Art.4 and certain anticompetitive clauses under Art.5 which have particular application to selective distribution agreements. If these provisions (along with the general hardcore restrictions and other specific anticompetitive clauses) are avoided, the other vertical restraints usually found in selective distribution agreements will be exempted under Reg.2790/99, when it applies to the agreement in general. Thus the earlier case law is still valid and relevant, first to understand the underlying concepts and principles relating to selective distribution under EC competition law, and second for assistance (along with the Guidelines) in framing an agreement which should be exempt under Art.81(3) where Reg.2790/99 does not apply. **6–52**

This precedent will also broadly be acceptable for the different national laws of the Member States, particularly the UK, but a detailed survey of local law should always be made. So far as countries outside the EC are concerned, the level of control of anti-competitive activities imposed by EC law is sufficiently high that the agreement is likely to be acceptable in most countries, and should certainly serve as a good basis to work from for adaptation to local laws. The real question would probably be in many areas, whether the local law permits greater restrictions on competition than those imposed by the precedent particularly in the area of more subjective judgment as to qualification for entry into the network, resale price maintenance, and territorial restrictions. **6–53**

6.2 Scope and purpose

6.2.1 Definition of network

6–54 6.2.1 The Products manufactured by the Principal are marketed distributed and sold in the EC through a network of distributors and retailers authorised and appointed for this purpose (the "Network" "Authorised Distributors" and "Authorised Retailers" respectively).

6.2.2 Authorised distributors

6–55 6.2.2 Each Authorised Distributor fulfils the qualifications and has undertaken the obligations set out in Sch.2 ("Distributor Requirements") and has undertaken the distribution of the Products in respect of the territory allocated to it [on an exclusive basis] pursuant to an agreement made with the Principal in identical terms to this Agreement ("Authorised Distributor Agreement").

6.2.3 Authorised retailers

6–56 6.2.3 Each Authorised Retailer fulfils the qualifications and has undertaken the obligations set out in Sch.3 ("Retailer Requirements") under an agreement made with the Principal in the form set out in Sch.5 ("Retailer Agreement").

6.2.4 Purpose

6–57 6.2.4 The Distributor wishes to be appointed an Authorised Distributor and the Principal wishes to appoint the Distributor as such upon the terms of this Agreement.

This section sets out the basic nature of the system. In this example there are two tiers of distribution. The level of Authorised Distributor could either consist of true wholesalers, who each have an area of a particular Member State, and then distribute to the Authorised Retailers, who operate the retail outlets for the Products, or each Authorised Distributor could have an exclusive distribution arrangement for the whole of a Member State of the EC and exercise more overall control and give more assistance to the Authorised Retailers in that state as a whole. In the latter case one would expect to see the Authorised Retailers undertaking a higher level of responsibility for servicing and maintenance in the area of technical products, because it would not be practical for one centrally based distributor to cope with all this. The technical support provisions in Sch.4 (Chapter 6.24 below) of the precedent are based on the assumption that the distributor will carry out most of the technical aspects of the arrangements, leaving the Authorised Retailers with less responsibility. This division of responsibility is reflected in the precedent for the Authorised Retailer Agreement in Sch.5

(Chapter 6.25 below). The precise division of responsibility will have to be decided in every case and Schs.4 and 5 adjusted accordingly.

A single-tier system is also possible, but tends to be used more in luxury and non-technical goods, where the manufacturer can deal directly with Authorised Retailers, because the product is not complicated, and not a great deal of back-up is necessary. In this case, the basis of the arrangements should be the Authorised Retailer Agreement set out in Sch.5, which will be drafted under the consideration that it will always be executed between the principal and each retailer, with no wholesaler in between. In this case care should be taken to consider the provisions of the main agreement in the precedent and to decide if any of those provisions are appropriate to the particular situation and therefore need to be included. **6–58**

6.3 Appointment of distributor as authorised distributor

6.3.1 The Principal hereby appoints the Distributor as an Authorised Distributor of the Products and hereby grants the Distributor (pursuant to such appointment) a licence to market distribute and sell the Products under the Trade Mark in accordance with and subject to the terms of this Agreement. **6–59**

[6.3.2 The Principal undertakes that during the continuance of this Agreement it will not appoint in the Territory any other distributor or reseller of the Products (other than Authorised Retailers) [nor directly supply any of the Products to distributors, resellers, retailers (whether or not Authorised Retailers) or end users located within the Territory]]. **6–60**

This clause is the grant of the distributorship to the distributor.

The key difference between selective and exclusive distribution is that, in selective distribution, the restriction on resale is not a restriction on active selling to a territory but a restriction on any sales to non-authorised distributors, leaving only appointed dealers and (so far as retailers are concerned) final customers as possible buyers (see the Guidelines (para.184). However, there is no reason why a principal cannot confer exclusivity of *appointment* in relation to a particular territory upon an authorised member of a selective distribution network (see, for instance, the Guidelines para.53: "Selective distribution may be combined with exclusive distribution provided that active and passive selling is not restricted"). The situation with regard to restrictions on resale by authorised members of the system is, however, completely different to that permitted by Reg.2790/99 in respect of exclusive distribution agreements which do not form part of a selective distribution system. This issue is discussed in Chapter 6.7. **6–61**

However, the grant of an exclusive appointment, since only one undertaking can be appointed in respect of each exclusive territory, does impose, if not an actual quota system, at least some quantitative restrictions on the number of potential appointees. The exact status of quantitative restrictions under selective distribution systems, in relation to Reg.2790/99 and art 81, are discussed in Chapter 6.18.1 and 6.22. In general such restrictions (and **6–62** therefore exclusive appointments) are permitted under Reg.2790/99 (see paras.185 and 186 of the Guidelines).

6–63 Where the appointments are made on an exclusive basis, and cl.6.3.2 is used, then it is also appropriate to add the phrase in square brackets in cl.6.2.2, referring to the appointment of the other members of the network on an exclusive basis as well. Attention should also be given to the phrase in square brackets in cl.6.3.2. Although there are detailed provisions in Reg.2790/99 relating to cross-supplies between distributors in a selective distribution system, even if operating at different levels of trade, (Art.4(e)) and a requirement that retailers must be free to sell actively or passively to all end users (Art.4(c)) there are no such requirements in relation to the manufacturer or the principal setting up the selective distribution network. Thus, if commercially desirable, the imposition of the restriction in square brackets would be exempted under Reg.2790/99, and, except in extraordinary cases, presumably also exempt under Art.81(3) where the regulation did not apply.

6.4 Distributor requirements

6–64 6.4.1 The Distributor warrants that at the date of [signature] [on or before the date of commencement] of this Agreement it [complies] [will comply] with and [satisfies] [will satisfy] the Distributor Requirements set out in Pt 1 of Sch.2.

The alternatives in the second set of square brackets cater for a distributor who has not yet set up his operation in such a way as to fulfil all the necessary qualifications, but is willing to do so once he has signed an agreement. This type of provision is not likely to be very common.

6–65 The criteria in Pt 1 are descriptions of the type of business and facilities the distributor has to have if he is to qualify as an Authorised Distributor.

6–66 6.4.2 The Distributor accepts and undertakes to perform the Distributor Requirements set out in Pt 2 of Sch.2.

The criteria in Pt 2 are specific obligations in relation to the way he conducts his business that the distributor must undertake if the principal is to appoint him.

6–67 6.4.3 The Distributor undertakes to continue to comply with and or perform as the case may be all of the Distributor Requirements for so long as this Agreement continues in force.

This imposes the obligation on the distributor to act in the way required of an Authorised Distributor throughout the term of the agreement.

6.5 General undertakings by Distributor

6.5.1 Due diligence

See cl.4.3.1. 6–68

6.5.2 Not to interfere with sale of the products

See cl.5.3.2. 6–69

This clause amounts (as discussed in Chapter 5.3.2) to a non-compete clause. Exactly the same considerations apply to non-compete clauses in selective distribution agreements as they do in other distribution agreements. There are also some added issues to be considered in selective distribution agreements. Reference should be made to the discussion under Chapter 6.5.5 below.

6.5.3 To conform to local legislation

See cl.4.3.3. 6–70

6.5.4 Proper storage for products

See cl.4.3.4.

6.5.5 Non-competition clause

See cl.5.3.6. 6–71

All of the considerations relating to non-compete clauses discussed in Chapter 5.3.6 apply in the case of selective distribution agreements. In addition Art.5(c) of Reg.2790/99 states that no exemption is available under the regulation to "any direct or indirect obligation causing the members of a selective distribution system not to sell the brands of particular competing companies". The Guidelines comment on this provision as follows in para.61:

> "The Block Exemption Regulation covers the combination of selective distribution with a non-compete obligation, obliging the distributor not to resell competing brands in general ... The objective of the exclusion of this obligation [not to sell the brands of particular competing companies]

is to avoid a situation whereby a number of suppliers using the same selective distribution outlets prevent one specific competitor or certain specific competitors from using these outlets to distribute their products (foreclosure of a competing supplier which would be a form of collective boycott). (An example of indirect measures having such exclusionary effects can be found in Commission Decision 92/428/EEC in Case No IV/33.542—*Parfum Givenchy* (OJ L 236 August 19th 1992, p11).)"

6–72 It should be remembered that (unlike the hardcore restrictions in Art.4) the presence of this obligation would not prevent the rest of the agreement taking the benefit of exemption under Reg.2790/99. However, the parties would have to convince themselves that particular reasons existed why this obligation should be exempt under Art.81(3) in the case of their agreement. *A fortiori*, where Reg.2790/99 does not apply because the market share of the supplier is over 30 per cent, it is almost impossible to see how such an obligation would fall within Art.81(3), because the market power of the supplier coupled with such a restriction would create a significant foreclosure effect.

6.5.6 No copying of products

6–73 See cl.5.3.7.

The discussion on this issue in Chapters 4.3.7 and 5.3.7 applies equally to selective distribution agreements. However, in this case, where dealing with products requiring the supply of spare parts, which the distributor has undertaken to provide as part of his duties in relation to maintenance and servicing of the products covered by the selective distribution network, it is particularly important to take note of the matters covered in Chapter 6.24.15 below relating to this issue.

6.5.7 Patent and trade mark notices on the products

6–74 See cl.5.3.8.

The general discussion in Chapter 5.3.8 applies equally to selective distribution agreements but with even more force. Clauses 5.3.8.1 and 5.3.8.2 should either be applied in their entirety, where the products are of a kind which require bundling, relabelling or repackaging when sold in a Member State outside that where the relevant distributor is located, or else the clause should be entirely omitted, and reliance be placed upon the general principles set out in the repackaging cases (see Chapter 5.1.1.4.3) to the extent repackaging actually takes place.

6–75 As will be seen in the discussion in Chapter 6.7 below, it is a requirement that each authorised member of the network be free to sell to any other member of the network but can be restricted from selling outside that network to unauthorised dealers. Any prohibition on bundling, repackaging and relabelling which effectively prevents the goods flowing freely around the selective distribution network will amount to an indirect ban on such sales, and thus be regarded as a hardcore restriction under Art.4(b) of Reg.2790/99, which does not fall under any of the permitted exceptions listed in Art.4(b).

Given the requirement for the free flow of goods around the system, it is probably necessary to permit each distributor not only to bundle, relabel or repackage any goods he sells to another member of the system, but also to bundle, relabel or repackage any goods he buys from another member of the system. This being the case, the first few lines of cl.5.3.8 should be redrafted as follows: **6–76**

> In order to make any sale of the Products (not prohibited by the provisions of cl.6.7.2) (a "permitted sale") the Distributor shall be entitled to carry out the following activities in relation to any quantity of the Products which is to be the subject of a permitted sale, to the extent that such activities are necessary to effect that permitted sale: . . .

The references in cl.5.3.8 to "permitted export" should then all be replaced with references to "permitted sale".

6.5.8 Inspection reports

See cl.4.3.9. **6–77**

6.5.9 Indemnity for breach

See cl.4.3.10. **6–78**

6.6 Enquiries

> 6.6 The Distributor shall during the continuance of this Agreement refer to the Principal all enquiries it receives for the Products for sale or ultimate delivery outside the EC [and all enquiries from any potential purchaser in the EC to whom the Distributor is prohibited from selling pursuant to cl.6.7.2 except where such potential purchaser is a consumer or end-user or the relevant enquiry relates to an application to join the Network in circumstances where the Distributor is able to appoint the enquirer as an Authorised Retailer pursuant to cl.6.18.1]. **6–79**

The treatment of enquiries in Chapter 5.4 above is not quite applicable to a selective distribution network. Although the discussion still has some relevance, this clause now has to be considered in the light of the different restrictions on sales set out in cll.6.7.1 and 6.7.2. If every member of the network is required only to sell to authorised members of the network (and perhaps to end-users) within the EC, but can otherwise be prohibited from making sales, either inside or outside the EC, then a clause requiring reference of enquiries outside the EC to the principal could have no effect on permitted trade within the EC. Authorised members of the network can only obtain supplies from each other or the principal (cl.6.8.1) and cannot sell to unauthorised members nor buy from them. Further sales to end-users outside the EC, even if permitted, could not affect trade between Member States, because (by definition) products the subject of such sales have not been purchased for resale but for use.

6–80 There thus seems no reason not to impose such a clause in the context of a selective distribution network.

6–81 The clause can also be extended (by the portion in square brackets) to cover enquiries from unauthorised dealers within the EC which the distributor is not permitted to supply. Care should be taken in cases where the distributor can appoint either retailers (as in the case of this agreement) or, sometimes, wholesalers as well, to ensure enquiries to join the network need not be passed on if the distributor can deal with them himself. So far as end-users are concerned, even if the distributor is prohibited from supplying them directly, (see the phrase in square brackets in cl.6.7.1) it makes more sense to allow the distributor to handle their enquiries by passing them on to a convenient authorised retailer.

6.7 Sales activities

6–82 6.7.1 The Distributor shall be free to sell the Products to any Authorised Retailer and Authorised Distributor [and any consumer or end-user] anywhere in the EC whether inside or outside the Territory.

6–83 6.7.2 The Distributor shall not sell the Products outside or inside the EC except as provided in cl.6.7.1.

It will be seen, as the decisions and cases on selective distribution are discussed later in the chapter, that no system was likely to be approved under Art.81(3) unless it provided for free movement of the products between any two members of the system (including reverse and horizontal sales). Article 4 of Reg.2790/99 now contains certain hardcore restrictions together with some specific exceptions which apply to selective distribution systems and summarise the previous case law:

6–84 A selective distribution system is defined by Art.1(d) of the regulation as "a distribution system where the supplier undertakes to sell the contract goods or services, either directly or indirectly, only to distributors selected on the basis of specific criteria and where those distributors undertake not to sell such goods or services to unauthorised distributors".

6–85 The restriction on sales to unauthorised distributors by the members of a selective distribution system, set out in cl.6.7.2, is permitted by the third exception to the hardcore restriction on reselling prohibited by Art.4(b) (see Guidelines para.52).

A restriction on buyers operating at the wholesale level of trade from selling to end-users (whether or not the buyer is part of a selective distribution system) is permitted by the second exception to Art.4(b) (see Guidelines para.52). The words in square brackets in cl.6.7.1 can therefore be omitted except in the case of an authorised retailer, and the overall prohibition, in cl.6.7.2. of sales other than as permitted in cl.6.7.1 will impose a restriction on wholesalers selling to end users. **6–86**

Article 4(c) prohibits as a hardcore restriction the restriction of active or passive sales to end users by members of a selective distribution system who operate at the retail level of trade, without prejudice to the possibility of prohibiting a member of the system from operating out of an unauthorised place of establishment. As stated above, Art.4(c) has no application where the authorised distributor is not a retailer. In the case of a retailer, the words in square brackets must be included in cl.6.7.1. **6–87**

The Guidelines (para.53) comment that Art.4(c) covers both active and passive sales and that "end users" covers both professional end users or final consumers. They add "Selective distribution may be combined with exclusive distribution provided that active and passive selling is not restricted". This general statement must be understood to apply to active and passive selling by members of the network to each and other, by retail members (since Art.4(c) only deals with retailers) to end-users, given the previous provision relating to restrictions on wholesalers selling to end users. **6–88**

The Guidelines (para.54) confirm, pursuant to the proviso to Art.4(c), that restrictions can be placed on the dealer's ability to determine the location of his business premises. Selected dealers may be prevented from running their business from different premises or from opening a new outlet in a different location. If the dealer's outlet is mobile (shop on wheels) an area may be defined outside which the mobile outlet cannot be operated. **6–89**

Although the wording of para.54 is not completely clear, it appears from its context not to apply just to retailers. Paragraph 54 starts off "In addition". It is also noteworthy that the proviso to Art.4(c) merely speaks of "a member of the system" while the body of the article refers to "members operating ... at the retail level ...". The first phrase would cover all members including wholesalers and other distributors, and contrasts with the second which can clearly only apply to retailers. It should be noted that although Art.4(c) uses the words "unauthorised place of establishment" the Guidelines in para.54 clearly relate this not to a place of establishment which does not meet the proper criteria under the selective distribution agreement, but simply a location which is not permitted by the principal. The power of the principal to require the dealer to operate from certain premises (a "location clause") is thus another type of vertical restriction which is exempted by the operation of the regulation. **6–90**

On the above analysis it is possible to impose a location clause on any member of the selective distribution system not just retailers, and for such a clause to enjoy exemption under Reg.2790/99 because it is not a hardcore restriction. This appears logical for four reasons. **6–91**

First, a location clause does not prevent a distributor or wholesaler from **6–92** selling to other members of the system either actively or passively. In any event, it is hard to see how a location clause would act as a real impediment to sales except at the retail level. However, distributor/wholesalers can be directly prohibited from selling to end users under the second exception to Art.4(b) anyway, and Art.4(c) expressly permits a location clause in relation to retailers.

6–93 Second, the wording of the proviso to Art.4(c) supports this conclusion. There is a careful distinction between members of the system and members of the system who operate at the retail level. The proviso only makes sense if a location clause is generally permissible under Reg.2790/99 (in relation to "members of the system"), and the legislator wanted to make clear that even though he was requiring that retailers must be permitted to make active and passive sales to any end users, they could still be bound by a location clause even if it might be argued that it impeded active sales. In other words without the proviso the main part of Art.4(c) might have been taken to contradict the general principle that a location clause was permissible.

6–94 Third, location clauses were permitted under the old block exemptions for selective distribution in the motor vehicle sector (Reg.123/85, renewed as Reg.1475/95), even though the Commission was always particularly concerned about competition in this sector. *A fortiori* a location clause should be exempt under the less strict provisions of Reg.2790/99.

6–95 Fourth, there seems no logic in permitting a location clause at the retail level where it could arguably have some impact on active sales and yet banning it at wholesale level where the impact is much less, if any at all.

6–96 Article 4(d) prohibits the restriction of cross-supplies between distributors within a selective distribution system, including between distributors operating at different levels of trade (*i.e.* including both wholesalers and retailers). The combined effect of cll.6.7.1 and 6.7.2 permit such cross-supplies. The Guidelines comment (para.55) that the prohibition covers passive as well as active selling. "This means that selective distribution cannot be combined with vertical restraints aimed at forcing distributors to purchase the contract products exclusively from a given source, for instance exclusive purchasing. It also means that within a selective distribution network no restrictions can be imposed on appointed wholesalers as regards their sales of products to appointed retailers".

6–97 It should be noted that there are no provisions restricting active or passive selling outside the Territory analogous to the provisions in cl 5.5.2 which relate to exclusive distribution agreements. The relevance of the territory is, as discussed, in Chapter 6.3 above, and emphasised in para.53, only for exclusivity of appointment.

6–98 The following summary of the special provisions in Art.4 relating to selective distribution systems shows why this is the case:

- First, Art.4(d) prohibits restrictions on active or passive selling to other members of the selective distribution system.
- Second, Art.4(c) prohibits restrictions on active or passive selling by

retailers to end users, subject to the requirement to sell from authorised premises.

- Third, the second exception to Art.4(b) permits the prohibition of active or passive sales by wholesalers to end users.
- Fourth, the prohibition of active or passive sales to unauthorised distributors is permitted by the third exception to Art.4(b).

Given these provisions there is now no requirement for, or, indeed, possibility of, any further prohibitions on active sales outside the territory, under the first exception to Art.4(b), as applied in the case of general distribution agreements by cl.5.5.2. The four provisions above cover both active and passive sales by reference to the identity of the buyers rather than geographical location as in the case of exclusive distribution agreements. This difference is recognised by the Guidelines (para.184): **6–99**

> "Another difference [of selective distribution] with exclusive distribution is that the restriction on resale is not a restriction on active selling to a territory but a restriction on any sales to non-authorised distributors, leaving only appointed dealers and final customers as possible buyers."

6.7.3 Notwithstanding the provisions of cll.6.7.1 and 6.7.3, the Distributor shall be entitled to carry out general advertising or promotions in media or on the internet that reach potential purchasers to whom the Distributor is prohibited from selling the Products pursuant to cl.6.7.2 ("unauthorised purchasers") provided that such advertising and promotion is primarily intended to reach potential purchasers to whom the Distributor is authorised to sell the Products pursuant to cl.6.7.1 ("authorised customers") and that such advertising and promotion is a reasonable way to reach authorised customers. **6–100**

This clause is the counterpart of cl.5.5.2. It may seem somewhat excessive, given the restrictions on supply that are imposed in a selective distribution system, but it can do no harm, and the Commission Guidelines do mention that dealers should be "free to advertise and sell with the help of the Internet" (para.53) so there seems no harm in including this provision.

6.7.4 The Distributor shall at its own entire discretion determine the prices at which and (except as specifically provided in this Agreement) the terms and conditions on which it sells the Products. **6–101**

Another vital element, that shows in all of the decisions and cases on any aspect of EC competition law, is that there should be no resale price control imposed by the arrangements. (See Chapter 5.9) This principle is applied with particular emphasis by the Commission in selective distribution systems, both to express and disguised restrictions, since such systems are one of the best means for imposing price controls, unless special care is taken to prevent this. As usual the express provision will not save the system if there are disguised restrictions (see *AEG-Telefunken* discussed above) but it at least acts as a statement of intention.

6.8 Supply of the products

6.8.1 Purchase within network

6–102 6.8.1 The Distributor shall purchase all its requirements for the Products either from the Principal or from any other Distributor or Authorised Retailer in the Network within the EC.

This is the other aspect of free movement of goods in the system. If the members are stated to be free to sell to each other, each agreement must also permit the relevant member to buy from the other members (see Art.4(d) of Reg.2790/99 and the discussion in relation to cll.6.7.1 and 6.7.2). It should be noted that this freedom extends to reverse and horizontal sales at all levels of the system. Thus, for instance, retailers can sell to each other or even to wholesalers, if this is economically advantageous.

6.8.2 Terms and conditions of supply

6–103 See cl.4.6.2.

The terms and conditions are to be found reproduced in Chapter 4.26 which can either be set out under cl.6.8.2 or in an additional schedule as Sch.6, if preferred. It should be noted that where this precedent relates to technically sophisticated products and Sch.4 (Chapter 6.24) is used cl.4.26.2.9 (warranty clause from principal to distributor) should be omitted. This point is discussed in Chapter 6.24.

6–104 Consideration should also be given to cl.4.26.2.2 (no obligation on principal to accept orders) and the discussion of its effect upon compensation for unjustified termination in Chapter 4.15.4. Consideration of the discussion on refusal to supply in Chapter 5.27 reinforced by the statements on this subject in the *Re IBM PC* and *Re SABA (No.2)* Decisions, which are discussed below (Chapter 6.13.10), would lead to the conclusion that the principal or supplier under a selective distribution system should insert a provision allowing him to refrain from supplying goods only where he is prevented from doing so for reasons beyond his control or he is out of stock. Otherwise the right to refuse to supply orders could be regarded as a disguised restriction to keep members of the system from implementing sales policies which (for the purposes of restriction of competition) the supplier of the goods wished to prevent. Given the prohibition of indirect hardcore restrictions in Art.4 of Reg.2790/99, this is particularly important if it is intended to rely on exemption under that regulation.

6–105 The first sentence of cl.4.26.2.2 should therefore be replaced by a provision as follows:

The Principal shall accept all orders for the Products from the Distributor and supply the same (subject to the provisions of these terms and conditions) unless and then only for so long as the Principal is out of stock.

The second sentence of cl.3.26.2.2 referring to the implementation of a quota system should always be added, and the basis for apportioning shares should always be "fair and equitable proportions", not the discretion of the principal.

6.9 Records, inspection and policing

6.9.1 The Distributor shall retain for at least one year duplicate copies of all invoices relating to sales of the Products by it, recording the date of purchase and the name and address of the purchaser, and [the serial number and] the description of the relevant Products. **6–106**

6.9.2 The Distributor shall retain for at least one year duplicate copies of all purchase orders for the Products placed by it on the Principal or any other person, recording the date of purchase and the name and address of the seller, and [the serial number and] the description of the relevant Products. **6–107**

6.9.3 The Distributor shall in addition to the specific requirements of cll.6.9.1 and 6.9.2 keep all relevant accounts together with supporting vouchers (including without limitation copies of invoices) and other relevant papers relating to the business carried on by it in the Products under this Agreement. **6–108**

6.9.4 The Distributor shall upon reasonable notice supply at any time to the Principal, from these records, details of persons who have sold to it and bought from it Products during the preceding twelve months, including names and addresses and the description [and serial number] of the relevant Products for each transaction. **6–109**

This provision as to the supply of customer and product information was permitted by the Commission in *Re IBM PC* (discussed below) so that IBM could contact customers direct for purposes of product modification or recall to deal with general product defects or safety problems if any ever arose.

6.9.5(a) The Principal shall have the right at any time upon reasonable notice to inspect all of the records referred to in this clause for the purpose of verifying the accuracy of any information given to it by the Distributor under cl.6.9.4 and otherwise for verifying that the distributor is in compliance with its obligations under this Agreement. **6–110**

OR

6.9.5(b) The Principal shall have the right at any time upon reasonable notice to appoint an independent firm of chartered accountants (the "auditor") to audit and inspect all of the records referred to in this clause for the purpose of verifying the accuracy of any information given to it by the distributor under cl.6.9.4 and otherwise for verifying that the Distributor is in compliance with its obligations under this Agreement provided that the auditor shall not disclose to the Principal details of the records concerned which shall remain confidential between the auditor and the Distributor and the auditor shall issue a certificate either stating that the information given under cl.6.9.4 is correct and or that the Distributor is in compliance with its obligations under this Agreement as aforesaid, or stating that this is not the case and specifying details of the inaccuracies and or the lack of compliance as the case may be.

6–111 6.9.6 Nothing in this clause or elsewhere in this Agreement shall entitle the Principal to pay regard to or monitor the prices at which the Distributor sells the Products.

Policing or verification provisions are obviously necessary to ensure that each member of the system is carrying out his obligations properly, and in particular is not selling outside the system's rules. The Commission's attitude to policing provisions is governed not by the nature of the policing provision itself, but how it is used in practice. This is demonstrated in a number of contrasting decisions.

6–112 In *Hasselblad (GB) Ltd v EC Commission* [1984] 1 C.M.L.R. 559 the European Court considered the Commission Decision imposing fines on the Hasselblad selective distribution network. The Court confirmed that Hasselblad's policy of attempting to prevent sole distributors from exporting out of their territory into other Member States of the EC was contrary to Art.81(1). This was so even though the agreements themselves did not impose express prohibitions. Policing measures aimed at tracing through serial numbers sales which violated this policy, exchange within the system of price lists and terms of business, discrimination against parallel imports as regards after-sales service, and exhortations by Hasselblad to its distributors not to engage in parallel imports, were all alleged by the Commission as evidence of a concerted practice within Art.81.

6–113 The Commission Decision *Ford New Holland Ltd*, detailed above, also describes the extensive abuse of a policing system.

6–114 However in *Re SABA (No.2)* [1984] 1 C.M.L.R. 677 the Commission pointed out that policing provisions "provided they do not exceed the requirements of a proper surveillance ... are simply the corollary of the principal undertaking which they seek to underpin and have the same status in law". Thus the policing obligation cannot *per se* contravene Art.81(1), but it will do so if the obligation the observance of which it is intended to police contravenes Art.81(1). This principle was also adopted in Commission Decisions in *Yves St Laurent Parfums SA, Parfums Givenchy SA* and *Grundig AG*.

6–115 Version (b) of cl.6.9.5 seeks to demonstrate that the principal cannot abuse his policing powers, because an impartial third party carries out the policing and merely tells the principal if the distributor is or is not breaking the rules. Whether version (a) or (b) is used cl.6.9.6 should be added as a precautionary measure, although once again it will not help the principal if, in practice, he ignores it.

6–116 It can be said that in recent years the Commission has become more suspicious of provisions permitting monitoring (see the discussion in

Chapters 5.3.8, 5.8.5 and 5.9.1 above and consider the following cases discussed in those sections: Case T-49/95 *Van Megen Sports Group BV v Commission* [1997] 4 C.M.L.R. 843); Case C-349/95 *Loendersloot v George Ballantine & Son Ltd* [1997] E.C.R. I-06227); Case T-176/95 *Accinauto SA v Commission* [2000] 4 C.M.L.R. 67) and Case T-175/95 *BASF v Commission* [2000] 4 C.M.L.R. 33. Also see the Commission statements in the Guidelines condemning the monitoring of resale prices (para.47) and of exports (para.49). However, contrast the discussion on the legitimate uses of batch numbering and other identification marks in Case C-244/00 *Van Doren v Lifestyle & Sportswear* Handelgesellschaft *GmbH* Judgment of April 8, 2003 detailed in Chapter 5.1.1.4.1)

6.10 Monthly reports

See cl.4.12 and the discussion on monitoring in Chapter 5.12 and Chapter 6.9.6. **6–117**

6.11 Industrial property rights

See cl.5.13. **6–118**

6.12 Commencement and term of agreement

6.12.1 This Agreement shall commence on [the date of signature hereof] [*] and shall continue unless and until terminated in accordance with cll.6.12.2, 6.12.3, 6.12.5 or 6.13. **6–119**

6.12.2 The Principal may terminate this Agreement at any time by not less than twelve months' notice provided that at the same time the Principal serves notice of the same length upon all Authorised Distributors and Authorised Retailers in the Network in order to terminate all Authorised Distributor Agreements and all Authorised Retailer Agreements with the intention of disbanding and terminating the activities of the Network. **6–120**

6.12.3 The Distributor may terminate this Agreement at any time by six months' notice to the Principal. **6–121**

6.12.4 Permissions licences and consents—

See cl.4.15.2. **6–122**

6.12.5 Termination for failure to obtain permissions licences and consents—

6–123 See cl.4.15.3.

6.12.6 No compensation on termination

6–124 See cl.4.15.4.

6.13 Termination

6–125 6.13 Without prejudice to any right or remedy the Principal may have against the Distributor for breach or non-performance of this Agreement the Principal shall (subject to cll.6.13.9 and 6.13.10) have the right summarily to terminate this Agreement:

6.13.1 On breach other than of cl.6.13.2

6–126 See cl.4.16.1.

6.13.2 On the Distributor ceasing to comply with any of the Distributor Requirements provided that (where the breach is remediable) the Principal shall have given to the Distributor notice of such failure and the Distributor shall have failed to remedy the breach complained of within [thirty] days of the receipt of such notice [or (if such breach is not reasonably remediable within such time limit) shall have failed to take active continuing and effective means to commence the remedying thereof];

6.13.3 On distress and execution—

6–127 See cl.4.16.3.

6.13.4 On insolvency—

6–128 See cl.4.16.4.

6.13.5 On failure to perform—

6–129 See cl.4.16.5.

6.13.6 On assignment without permission—

See cl.4.16.6. 6–130

6.13.7 On change of control—

See cl.4.16.7. 6–131

6.13.8 On the Distributor committing any breach or failing to comply with any legislation prohibiting or regulating unfair trading practices which may from time to time be in force in the Territory or any other area in which the Distributor sells the Products provided that the Principal shall have served notice requiring the Distributor to cease such practice and the Distributor shall have failed to do so within [thirty] days of receipt of such notice.

6.13.9 If the Distributor contends that termination has been effected under cl.6.13.2 in bad faith or that the Distributor has not in fact ceased to comply with the relevant Distributor Requirement as alleged the Distributor shall have the right to appeal the termination of this Agreement by submitting the matter for resolution by an [arbitrator] [expert] in accordance with cl. [ ] and in the event of such an appeal the notice shall be suspended pending its outcome and immediately upon the giving of the decision by the [arbitrator] [expert] the notice shall thereupon be cancelled or have immediate effect depending upon whether the appeal is allowed or disallowed respectively. 6–132

6.13.10 No termination shall take effect under cl.6.13.8, if the Distributor contests the same unless, and until a court of competent jurisdiction rules (upon the application of the Principal or otherwise) that the Distributor has in fact carried on the unfair trading practice in question and upon the giving of a ruling to this effect this Agreement shall thereupon automatically terminate. 6–133

The provisions for termination with or without notice always received considerable attention from the Commission. The object of the Commission is to prevent termination or the threat of termination of the agreement being used to enforce disguised restrictions on competition. This is particularly possible where termination by notice can be given without pointing to any particular reason for giving it. The provisions therefore have to be seen to work in a fair and objective manner. Clauses 6.12 and 6.13 are designed to achieve this effect, and are based upon Commission decisions.

In *Re SABA (No.2)* [1984] 1 C.M.L.R. 677 the Commission held that provisions for termination and expulsion from the network similar to cll.6.12 and 6.13 were not objectionable as they were not open to abuse. The only power of unconditional termination that remained to the principal was in the event that all the dealership arrangements were terminated. Termination for breach or failure to meet selection criteria was permitted, but if the dealer disputed SABA's decision a final expulsion was possible only after a decision by a court. A breach of the national law against unfair competition prevailing in the relevant dealer's territory (*e.g.* selling as a loss leader) 6–134 does not place the distribution system in jeopardy and SABA could therefore terminate the arrangement only if the dealer did not dispute the matter, or if the breach had been proved in court. In this way the danger of a subjective finding of a breach of the law against unfair competition and of arbitrary expulsion from the network is prevented. Furthermore the reference to the applicability of the appropriate national competition law ensures that a dealer can be penalised only on account of actions which are considered unfair under relevant national regulations.

6–135 The same types of clauses relating to termination were contained in the agreements set up by Grundig, and these were approved by the Commission in *Re Grundig AG*. It is not entirely clear that such arrangements for termination are always necessary. In *Yves St Laurent SA*, the agreements were for a set period of one year. In *Parfums Givenchy SA*, the agreements were also for one year, but in the absence of breach they were renewable by tacit agreement. One possible explanation for the Commission's benign view of the termination provisions, was that an existing retailer did not have to requalify as an authorised retailer on the expiry of his agreement, so that renewal was automatic (certainly in the case of Givenchy) under the acceptance procedure.

6–136 Clauses 6.13.6 and 6.13.7 need to be approached with caution. Their operation in a selective distribution system which is open to all those who satisfy the criteria for an authorised distributor or retailer is limited, because the new owner of the business can always apply to join the system, and will, at least after a waiting period (see Chapter 6.18 below) become a member if he complies with the relevant criteria. In both *Yves St Laurent SA* and *Parfums Givenchy SA*, the agreements provided that, where there was a change of control of the retailer or a sale of the business to a new owner, the new owner could take on the agreement provided he continued to qualify under the criteria contained in the agreement.

6–137 It is a question whether such detailed and complicated provisions are required. In a sense, these provisions are only express safeguards which ensure that the principal will not exercise rights of termination in an abusive or discriminatory manner which will amount to an indirect hardcore restraint (for instance by using the threat of arbitrary termination to enforce resale price maintenance). Clearly nothing in Reg.2790/99 requires the inclusion of such provisions. Nor do these provisions of themselves affect any competition law assessment under Art.81(3). There it would be the question of the principal's actual conduct in relation to termination that would be called into account, rather than clauses which prevented a potential abuse. However, as will be seen in Chapter 6.23, similar provisions are required under Reg.1400/2002 relating to selective distribution in the motor vehicle sector. Regulation 1400/2002, in fact goes farther than these provisions and also covers many more issues than simply abusive termination. Where Reg.2790/99 does not apply, given that the market share of the principal will therefore exceed 30 per cent, and significant competition law concerns will always be present, particularly if the principal is in a dominant position, it seems a good idea to use provisions of this nature (or perhaps even equivalent to those contained in Reg.1400/2002) to demonstrate and guarantee the legitimacy of the principal's operation of the selective distribution system.

The same question can be raised in relation to the discussion on the right to refuse to supply (Chapter 6.8.2) or policing provisions (Chapter 6.9), but the difference is that these clauses regulate continuing activity under the agreement during the life of the agreement, and therefore are more likely to be used as a disguised rendition than the one-off threat of termination. Thus, with these clauses the need to demonstrate the "purity" of the principal's intentions is much greater, even where Reg.2799/90 applies, and certainly where it does not.

6.14 Effects of termination

See cl.4.17. **6–138**

The comments in Chapter 5.17 apply to selective distribution systems as well as other distribution arrangements within the EC. However, the very nature of a selective distribution system means that the treatment of the clause in a selective distribution agreement is somewhat different. Firstly, a distributor who is no longer part of the system will not be able to sell off his stock to other persons within the system. Since he is not part of the system they will not be able to buy from him. Secondly, if he is a retailer, although he will be able to sell to end users, he may well no longer have access to the technical arrangements and facilities which he needs to go on servicing the products he has sold under the selective distribution arrangement. It may even be that his failure to implement or maintain such arrangements led to his termination in the first place. Under these circumstances consumers would certainly not get proper service when buying his remaining stock from him, and the reputation of the products in the market, which it is sought to conserve and enhance by the selective distribution system, would be damaged. These seem good reasons for taking the stock from the distributor or retailer at a fair price, and leaving consumers to go to the newly appointed replacement, or some other authorised dealer in the vicinity. The provisions regarding disclosure of customer lists (cl.4.17.5) for the products by the distributor to the principal are thus to be regarded in the light of the necessity that the principal may well have to contact customers so that they are aware of the new distributor's existence and can contact him for after-sales service.

On the basis of this analysis, it seems that exemption under Art.81(3), or **6–139** avoidance Art.81(1) altogether, is more likely with buy-back clauses in the context of a selective distribution agreement. There is also a powerful argument that, if a distributor who is a wholesaler could be forbidden from selling to unauthorised dealers and to end-users in relation to goods that he purchased during the continuance of the agreement, why should not those obligations survive the termination or expiry of the agreement in relation to such goods. On this basis, the terminated distributor (but not a retailer) could be prevented at the very least from selling his stock except to another authorised dealer. An authorised retailer could, on the same basis, also be prevented from selling stock to an unauthorised dealer, but would have the right to sell to end users.

6.15 Confidentiality

6–140 It is suggested that where the agreement relates to technical products and technical information will be changing hands, the longer forms for the definition of information and the more extended confidentiality clauses in Chapter 1.4 above should be used.

6–141 This type of clause is permitted for the protection of knowhow under the final proviso to Art.5(b) of Reg.2790/99. See the detailed discussion in Chapter 5.18. Protection of knowhow is clearly of much more importance in a selective distribution system where the technical training of the distributor is essential to enable him to supply proper sales advice and also after sales service and maintenance. Here the relationship has some resemblance to a franchise agreement and it may be appropriate to impose not only a confidentiality clause, but also the one year post-termination non-compete clause permitted by Art.5(b) for the purpose of protecting knowhow (see the discussion in Chapter 5.18)

6–142 Under Art.1(f) of Reg.2790/99 knowhow is defined (as in the Technology Transfer Block Exemption Reg.240/96) as "a package of non-patented practical information, resulting from experience and testing by the supplier, which is secret, substantial and identified; in this context "secret" means that the knowhow, as a body or precise configuration and assembly of its components, is not generally known or easily accessible; "substantial" means that the knowhow includes information which is indispensable to the buyer for the use, sale or resale of the contract goods or services; "identified" means that the knowhow must be described in a sufficiently comprehensive manner so as to make it possible to verify that it fulfils the criteria of secrecy and substantiality.

6.16 Transmission of rights

6–142A See cl.4.19.

6.17 Technical support for distributor

6–143 6.17 The Principal undertakes to provide the knowhow and technical support and training in accordance with Sch.4 to the Distributor to enable it to market sell service and maintain the Products and the Distributor undertakes to accept implement and make full use of the same in order to market sell service and maintain the Products likewise in accordance with Sch.4.

This provision and Sch.4 are of course only for products of a technical nature. They would be omitted if one were dealing with luxury goods. The sort of provisions that would be required then would be purely concerned with assistance by way of marketing and sales promotion which are dealt with in Chapter 6.22.

6.18 Appointment of authorised retailers

6.18.1 Both the Principal and the Distributor shall be free to appoint Authorised Retailers in the Territory [but in each case the appointing party shall consider whether the area in which the relevant Authorised Retailer is situated has sufficient sales potential to support a further retail outlet and shall consult with the other party prior to such appointment to obtain any relevant information to assist in the determination of the matter]. **6–144**

The section of the clause in square brackets relates to what the Commission calls "quantitative criteria". These have been discussed in various cases. In general they are regarded with suspicion and permitted only where they aid in the implementation of qualitative criteria (by giving those who are lucky enough to be appointed a high turnover to keep them interested in providing a proper service and concentrating on the sale of the products) and also where the market is in luxury, rather than necessary, goods and is largely fragmented.

In *Re Omega Watches* [1970] C.M.L.R. D49 the permitted use of quantitative criteria is explained. Omega of Switzerland appointed five exclusive distributors who each had a defined area of the EC as their territory. Each distributor could not sell outside his territory and had to obtain his supplies from Omega only. Each distributor had the right to sell on his goods obtained from Omega only to certain retailers in his territory appointed by Omega. There was thus a two-tier system in existence, as in this precedent. Each distributor had to use a standard form of agreement with the approved retailers which prevented his retailers from obtaining supplies other than from the relevant distributor, and from exporting goods outside that retailer's territory. **6–145**

Article 81(1) was contravened by the arrangement as a whole, but the Commission granted an exemption under Art.81(3) to that part of the arrangement controlling the number of retailers appointed by the distributors in their territories. This was because the quantitative restriction applied by Omega was justified as necessary to ensure that each retailer had a sufficient level of business to support his operations, and would therefore be able to employ proper staff both to promote sales and to provide customer service. **6–146**

In the Perfume Decisions (*Christian Dior* and *Lancome* [1973] Fourth Report on Competition Policy), the Commission looked at a fragmented market in luxury goods. Each of the companies had the same arrangement, which consisted of a network of exclusive distributors each having a defined area of the EC. Each distributor could sell only to retailers approved by the **6–147** company and had to impose the following restrictions on each retailer: to sell only to consumers; to buy supplies only from the distributor for its territory and to comply with fixed retail prices. The Commission required the removal of all these restrictions so that, as in *Re Omega*, cross-border trading at freely determined prices was permitted. Thus any retailer could buy from and sell to any other retailer or distributor in the EC, at any price he could obtain. The Commission then went on to say that it had now no grounds to intervene under Art.81(1) even though the principal company still had the right to approve retailers, and no approved retailer or distributor, could sell to a retailer who was not approved. The Commission took the view that it need not intervene against the mere restrictive selection of trading points (even though this was partly quantitative) in view of the characteristics of the market for perfumes and beauty and toiletry products in the EC which consisted of many competing firms of similar size, each holding a fairly small share of the market.

6–148 However, it reserved the right to carry out checks to see that the selection of retailers was made on reasonable grounds (*e.g.* a reasonable number of high class retailers in the perfume business) and not to punish retailers who engaged in cross-border trading or price cutting. By 1975, the whole perfume industry in the EC had become regulated more or less along these lines (see [1975] Fifth Report on Competition Policy paras 57 to 59) without any formal applications for negative clearance or exemption.

6–149 Nevertheless, the Commission has gradually moved away from the implicit acceptance of quota restrictions in this area. In *Société d'Hygiène Dermatologique de Vichy v Commission* the European Court of First Instance upheld a Commission Decision that a selective distribution system which allowed only dispensing chemists to sell the relevant skin-care products infringed Art.81(1) and would not be granted an exemption under Art.81(3). The requirement did not apply to the technical qualifications of trained sales staff, (*i.e.* that they should have a pharmacist's diploma), which would have been an objective qualitative criterion, but to the type of outlet. The Commission and the Court were not convinced by Vichy's arguments as to why it was necessary to sell through a pharmacy, with a dispensing chemist, rather than through any outlet with one or more of the sales staff holding a pharmacist's diploma.

6–150 Since Vichy could not demonstrate a qualitative reason for sale through a pharmacy, the requirement was in fact a quota, since it restricted the potential number of outlets (who could have employed sales staff with a pharmacist's diploma) without a reason based upon an objective qualitative criterion. Furthermore "the effects on competition were accentuated by the fact that, by reason of the intake quota and constraints of professional ethics imposed on dispensing chemists in most of the Member States concerned, it was well known that competition between dispensing chemists was restricted".

6–151 This type of thinking has continued into the three leading cases, of *Re Yves St Laurent SA*, *Re Parfums Givenchy SA* and *Re Grundig AG*, where the selective distribution networks operated no quota system at all, in the sense that all of the distributors or retailers who could comply with the relevant acceptance criteria were to be admitted into the system.

In general the Commission has always realised the need for quantitative restrictions in selective distribution for technically sophisticated products, where servicing is important, and the staff premises and equipment needed to carry out servicing properly requires a large investment. **6–152**

In *Re Bayerische Moterenwerke* [1975] 1 C.M.L.R. D44 BMW appointed in Western Germany exclusive distributors which had fairly large defined areas of the country as their exclusive territory. Each such distributor could appoint (subject to BMW's approval) further subdistributors within his exclusive territory, each of whom would have an exclusive sales area. BMW undertook not to supply third parties direct, and the distributors and sub-distributors undertook not to obtain supplies other than from authorised distributors and subdistributors elsewhere in Western Germany or the rest of the EC. BMW thus imposed both quantitative and qualitative criteria for the selection of distributors and subdistributors. **6–153**

The qualitative criteria related to the adequacy of business facilities (particularly technical capability and expertise) and secondly the willingness of the distributor or subdistributor to comply with the restrictions confining sales and purchases to the authorised network, and to comply with BMW's sales and marketing policy. **6–154**

As regards the quantitative criteria, BMW took care to appoint only sufficient distributors and subdistributors to ensure that each had a level of sales high enough to support his business. **6–155**

The Commission held that the arrangements as a whole did contravene Art.81(1) because no third parties outside the network could (except for a few rare exceptions) buy directly from BMW, and many dealers who could meet the qualitative criteria were still excluded from the network by the quantitative criteria. Thus trade within the EC as a whole was affected, even though the network covered only Western Germany. **6–156**

However, the Commission granted an exemption under Art.81(3) again following *Re Omega*, on the grounds that where one is dealing with high-quality and expensive products like BMW cars, it is important for reasons of technical expertise, after-sales service and maintenance, and sufficient inventory, that there be only a restricted number of suitable dealers. The qualitative criteria that BMW imposed were necessary to ensure that the right sort of dealer was appointed to handle their products, and the quantitative criteria enabled each such approved dealer to maintain a sufficiently high level of turnover to ensure that he had both the economic means and the incentive to comply with the qualitative criteria. In addition it was felt that such a streamlined distribution network would in general result in an improved service to customers at a lower cost, so that in addition to the quality of service, customers would also have a share in the economic benefits produced by the system. **6–157**

In fact the criteria applied by the Commission to BMW's network were applied by it to other automobile manufacturers and this culminated in the block exemption for selective distribution systems in the motor trade, **6–158**

(Reg.123/85, renewed as Reg.1475/95.) It should however be noted that the Commission has changed its stance on quantitative restrictions in the motor vehicle sector in the interests of promoting greater competition. The new position is reflected in the latest block exemption (Reg.1400/2002) which is discussed later in the chapter at 6.26.

6–159 The current position under Reg.2790/99 is that quantitative restrictions are exempted where the regulation applies, even if combined with other non-hardcore restraints such as non-compete or exclusive distribution (see the Guidelines para.186).

6–160 Quantitative restrictions lead to loss of or a reduction in intra-brand competition, so that, where the regulation does not apply, the assessment of the market power of the supplier and his competitors is of prime importance. The Commission comments that:

> "Another important factor is the number of selective distribution networks present in the same market. Where selective distribution is applied by only one supplier in the market which is not a dominant undertaking, quantitative selective distribution does not normally create net negative effects provided that the contract goods, having regard to their nature, require the use of a selective distribution system and on condition that the selection criteria are necessary to ensure sufficient distribution of the goods in question. The reality however seems to be that selective distribution is often applied by a number of suppliers in a given market."

6–161 It can be seen from this quotation that, as in the case of most issues with selective distribution systems, the determining factor for either the withdrawal of exemption under Reg.2790/99, or the failure of Art.81(3) otherwise to exempt the arrangements, is bound up in the problem of the cumulative effect of numbers of selective distribution systems covering the relevant market.

6–162 6.18.2 The appointment shall in each case be made by the signature by the appointing party and the relevant retailer of a copy of the Retailer Agreement.

The appointment is made on a uniform basis under the Authorised Retailer Agreement.

6–163 6.18.3 Within one month after such appointment, the appointing party shall notify the other party of such appointment by sending a notice thereof together with a copy of the relevant signed and dated Retailer Agreement.

This provision has a practical use in that both parties will then know of the retailer so that they can supply him. However, it also enables the principal to object to and require the distributor to terminate the appointment of a retailer made by the distributor where the retailer does not in fact comply with the Retailer Requirements. It will also have application if quantitative criteria (either by way of quota system or exclusive areas of operation) are applied to the appointment of retailers and it is necessary to monitor the number and location of appointments made.

> 6.18.4 The Principal undertakes to reply to all applications by Authorised Retailers within one month of receipt, and failing such reply the Principal undertakes to sign on request with such retailer an authorised Retailer agreement. **6–164**

Again this type of requirement is intended to make sure the principal does not use unjustified delay in ruling on an application as a means of disguised restriction on "undesirable" retailers. It can be argued (as in the case of termination in Chapter 6.13) that this provision goes more towards demonstrating non-discriminatory behaviour rather than having, of itself, a direct effect on competition. As in Chapter 6.13, there are therefore some arguments for not including this provision, except where Reg.2790/99 does not apply, because of the principal's large market share, and it is therefore helpful to demonstrate the "purity" of the principal's intentions.

The comments in Chapter 6.18.1 about quantitative criteria for the selection of retailers of course apply in the same way to the selection of distributors or wholesalers on a quantitative basis. Thus again, Reg.2790/99, where it applies, would exempt selective distribution systems where quantitative selection criteria are applied at the distributor or wholesaler level. **6–165**

6.19 Appointment of authorised distributors

> 6.19.1 The Distributor may nominate to the Principal persons whom the Distributor considers comply with the Distributor Requirements and request the Principal to appoint them as Authorised Distributor in any area outside the Territory. Failing an adverse reply from the Principal within two months of receipt of such nomination the Principal shall be obliged to sign an Authorised Distributor Agreement with the relevant person in respect of the relevant area. **6–166**

This clause is also intended to make appointment of authorised distributors easier, and to prevent unjustified delay by the principal in ruling on such appointments.

> 6.19.2 The Principal undertakes to the Distributor that in all cases where an Authorised Distributor is appointed for the Network, the Principal will sign with the distributor concerned an Authorised Distributor Agreement in identical terms to this Agreement. **6–167**

This clause, like cl.6.8.2, is designed to ensure that the whole of the system will run on uniform standard agreements at both levels of distribution.

The precedents in cll.6.18 and 6.19 are based upon the arrangements in the Commission Decisions *Re SABA (No.2)*, *Re IBM PC* and *Re Grundig AG*. In this connection it is also interesting to look at the elaborate and somewhat specialised provisions for admission contained in *Re Yves St Laurent SA* and *Re Parfums Givenchy SA*, and to consider the Commission's comments on them in those Decisions. However, this precedent, being for **6–168** more general use, is not based upon those two Decisions.

6–169 In *Re SABA (No.2)* [1984] 1 C.M.L.R. 677, under the original arrangements for selecting outlets SABA alone decided who met the criteria, and had an unlimited time to take a decision. The Commission said that "On past experience of such systems the Commission considers that a system giving the manufacturer the sole and unrestricted right of admission opens the door to discriminatory application of the admission criteria". The danger of discrimination was felt to arise largely at the retail level where there were a large number of outlets. SABA has eliminated the danger by undertaking that if it does not reply to an application for admission in four weeks it is obliged to sign an agreement with the applicant. All wholesalers in the system are permitted to admit retailers and sign agreements with them on their own authority. They are obliged to notify SABA of the appointment, and SABA is entitled to check that the appointee complies with the criteria and to expel him if there has been an error in admission.

6–170 In *Re the IBM Personal Computer* [1984] 2 C.M.L.R. 342, the Commission approved the provisions in the selective distribution arrangements whereby dealers could nominate other dealers. Wholesalers (second-tier distributors), could notify IBM of nomination for dealership, and the dealer would be automatically appointed if IBM did not act within two months. In the case of IBM's arrangements, dealers corresponded to authorised retailers, and second-tier distributors to the authorised distributors, in this precedent.

6–171 In *Re Grundig AG*, retailers and distributors were to be given a Decision on their application within four weeks, and if, at the end of that time, no Decision had been taken expressly, they were admitted automatically. Grundig is however entitled to use the four-week period to check on whether a candidate does satisfy the criteria for admission.

6–172 Once again, this system enables the necessary monitoring control not only to provide standardisation of agreements and a simple non-discriminatory procedure for appointment, but it also gives the principal the opportunity to monitor the qualifications of proposed distributors and, if necessary, to consider the application of any quantitative criteria.

6–173 Again, it can be argued (as in the case of termination in Chapter 6.13 and in relation to cl.6.18) that likewise this provision acts as a guarantee of non-discriminatory behaviour rather than having, of itself, a direct effect on competition. Thus, as stated before, this type of provision need not be included, except where Reg.2790/99 does not apply, because of the principal's large market share, and it is therefore helpful to give an assurance of non-discriminatory behaviour.

6.20 Interpretation clauses and signature

6–174 The clauses in Chapter 1 should be selected as appropriate.

6.21 Schedule 1—definitions

The definitions needed in this schedule are as follows: the Products, the Territory, the Trade mark, the Information, the Knowhow and the EC. 6–175

These should be taken from Chapter 1 as required. It should be noted that the Territory may well not be a whole Member State of the EC, but only a part of it. Care should also be taken with the definitions of the Information and the Knowhow. The very wide definition of the Information in Chapter 1 goes beyond Knowhow, since it embraces commercial and business information as well. This is correct since the definition of the Information is purposely wide for confidentiality purposes. It would be useful to add the defined term Knowhow as one of the items within the definition of Information. This is not strictly necessary, but it makes the definition clearer. 6–176

The definition of Knowhow needs to be thought about carefully. It will be seen below in Sch.4 that the Knowhow is split up into certain classes but this is satisfactory only if the preliminary definition of the Knowhow covers all that the parties intend it should cover. The definition of the classes will not be able to make up any defects in the basic definition. Care should be taken to ensure that the definition of knowhow is made with sufficient precision to comply with the definition in Reg.2790/99 Art.1(g), where applicable, particularly with regard to the requirement that the knowhow within that definition be "identified". 6–177

6.22 Schedule 2—distributor requirements

Schedule 2—Part 1 6–178

6.22.1 The Distributor shall carry on business as [an electrical and electronic equipment wholesaler] or shall have a separate and substantial division of its operations carrying on such business and such business shall be carried on from separate premises having suitable facilities for the storage, handling and sale of the Products on a wholesale basis.

This clause defines the qualifying business that the distributor must carry on. The phrase in square brackets is by way of example only. It must also be considered whether it is possible to limit the operation of the distributor to one set of authorised premises, in the way that the proviso to Art.4(c) states is permitted in relation to retailers. This issue is discussed in Chapter 6.7, and based on the analysis there, such a limitation would be exempt under Reg.2790/99. In effect it would amount to a type of quantitative restriction.

6.22.2 The Distributor will employ a sufficient number of technically trained staff to enable all demand for the Products to be satisfied and shall establish and maintain [whether directly or through subcontractors] service facilities plant and equipment at one or more locations suitable for the satisfactory care maintenance and repair of the Products (whether or not under warranty) and of a sufficient capacity to satisfy the requirements of end-users of the Products in the Territory for such service. 6–179

This clause is couched in general terms, as is cl.6.22.1. In appropriate cases, where this can be done, it may be possible to specify the requirements in more detail. The problem with this approach, however, is that the agreement then ceases to be a standard form, and the principal also loses some flexibility in exercising his judgment as to just which distributors actually have the qualifications. Some examples more specific to particular businesses can be studied in the discussion of the Decisions and cases coming below, after cl.6.22.3.

6–180 6.22.3 The Principal will provide advice to the Distributor on special tools and special test equipment recommended to support the Products. The Principal will upon request sell to the Distributor all such tools and equipment at reasonable prices and in reasonable quantities, and the Distributor undertakes to purchase a sufficient quantity thereof (either from the Principal or any other suitable source) to enable him to carry out his obligations under cl.6.22.2.

The provisions relating to knowhow in Sch.4 deal with the matters covered by cl.6.22.3 to some extent, but they are sufficiently important to require special mention as a qualification. If the distributor does not comply with this clause he will not be able to service the products.

6–181 The criteria in Pt 1 of this schedule are what are known as objective qualitative criteria, *i.e.* matters with which any person who wishes to perform a proper job of marketing and selling the products concerned would have to comply. It would be unreasonable for a manufacturer to appoint a wholesale greengrocer to distribute television sets or expensive French perfumes, and his refusal to appoint could hardly be considered as restrictive of competition or against the interest of consumers.

6–182 This reaction of the Commission to the need to approve the type of outlet suitable for the sale of the relevant products can be seen in the Decision of *Re Omega* discussed above. Omega imposed qualitative restrictions in that it only approved jewellers or watchmakers as retailers, but this did not require exemption under Art.81(3). In deciding this the Commission followed its Decision in the earliest of the selective distribution Decisions, *Re Kodak* [1970] C.M.L.R. D19 where the Commission permitted restriction of the appointment of Kodak camera film retail outlets to photographic film retailers who possessed suitable premises and suitable storage and display facilities with trained sales personnel.

6–183 However, in a two-tier system the qualifications of the distributor or wholesaler are less important in many areas than those of the retailers. The only products where particular expertise is required at the wholesale level are those which require special handling and storage, or complex technical support from large and expensive dedicated service facilities. Because of this the objective qualitative criteria for the distributor or wholesaler are usually fairly succinct.

6–184 The Commission Decision in the case of *Junghans* [1977] O.J. L30/10 shows the way the Commission approaches these cases, in some detail. Junghans was a manufacturer of watches and clocks based in Western Germany. It had a significant but not very large share of the market for clocks and watches in the EC. It operated by means of a network of wholesalers and sole distributors, and approved retailers. Standard form agreements were signed by it with each wholesaler, distributor and retailer.

The wholesalers and retailers signed identical agreements except that the sole distributors had special exclusive dealing arrangements. They were permitted to sell to any approved retailer, or to any other wholesaler or sole distributor who had an agreement to pass on a similar obligation as to sale, with the exception that the retailer was also permitted, of course, to sell to consumers. They could not export outside the EC, nor market actively within the EC (except for wholesalers who were permitted to do so in Germany, Belgium, Denmark, Italy or Luxembourg). Sole distributors with exclusivity rights for a territory could not in general handle competing products without Junghans' consent. Apart from the above restrictions, Junghans applied no particular criteria for choosing wholesalers and distributors. The selection took place at the retail level. An approved retailer had to: **6–185**

- have properly qualified technical staff;
- have premises suitable for the sale of watches and clocks;
- sell in a specialised department, if a department store, or in a shop separate from the proprietor's house, with its own sales area and display windows;
- stock a representative range;
- provide proper repairs service; and
- if a department store, ensure adjoining goods did not adversely affect the specialist department or its display.

In addition, retailers could supply only to persons within the network, other than for sales for consumers, and could not export outside the EC. Neither retailers wholesalers nor distributors were subject to any form of price control.

Junghans reserved the right to check up on the performance of all the above obligations by any dealer, as well as to require information about sales performance from wholesalers in Belgium, and the Danish sole distributor. Any dealer who contravened his obligations could have his supplies of the products cut off. **6–186**

Basically therefore the Junghans network provided for free movement of goods within the network, with no control of prices. The only problem was the acceptability of the criteria used by Junghans to set up the system. **6–187**

The Commission said that all of the arrangements had to be looked at as a whole, since they formed an integrated system. **6–188**

In so far as the selective aspect of the network was concerned this did not contravene Art.81. Junghans had no criteria for choosing wholesalers and distributors and the criteria it applied to approve retailers were all objective **6–189** ones, of a qualitative nature, of a kind with which anyone who wanted to sell clocks and watches properly to consumers would have to comply anyway. Furthermore Junghans operated no quantitative restrictions. It appointed any retailer who complied with its requirements. Therefore the only criteria governing the selectivity of the system were objective technical ones. Given this, the fact that, apart from sales to consumers, sales were restricted to persons in the system, did not constitute a contravention of Art.81. Because of this it followed that the obligations to give information so that Junghans could police the system, and cut off supplies if it were not complied with, could not contravene Art.81 either. At that particular time, the Commission considered that a ban on export outside the EC was not caught under Art.81(1) either. Furthermore since the retailers' agreement contained no restrictions other than the above, they could not, as separate agreements, contravene Art.81(1) either.

6–190 The restrictions on active marketing in certain areas of the EC, and the prohibitions on handling competitive goods, which were additionally contained in the wholesalers' and distributors' agreements did contravene Art.81(1). However, in so far as these were contained in exclusive distribution agreements they were exempt under the block exemption (then Reg.67/67). Where these obligations were in wholesaler or distributor agreements which were not covered by the regulation, the Commission decided on the merits that an Art.81(3) exemption should be granted, because these restrictions in fact operated to concentrate the efforts of the dealers concerned in their own home areas, thus contributing to the overall efficiency of the system, with resulting benefits in the standard of service, and also producing cost-savings which, because of the considerable competition in the watch and clock industry would be passed on to the consumer in lower prices. In other words this was a sort of extension of the ideas behind Reg.67/67.

6–191 The parts of this Decision concerning limitations on active selling outside the territory need some caution when considered in the light of Art.4 of Reg.2790/99 (see Chapter 6.7.4). The best way of reconciling the two approaches is to regard the Junghans system as a mixed system, partly a selective distribution system, at the retail level, and an exclusive distribution system with assigned territories at the wholesale level. The specific rules on active and passive sales in relation to exclusive distribution would then apply to the wholesalers and distributors, and the specific rules for selective distribution systems would then apply at the retail level. This split approach would still seem to be possible under Reg.2790/99, although, as in Junghans it is still necessary to take account of the effect of the system as a whole at both the wholesale and retail level.

6–192 This view taken in *Junghans* by the Commission was confirmed by the European Court in *Salonia v Poidomani* [1981] E.C.R. 1563. An Italian court referred to the European Court various questions for ruling upon as preliminary points, to decide to what extent a selective distribution system covering the sale of newspapers contravened Art.81(1). Under a national agreement then in force in Italy, press distribution agencies licensed newspaper and magazine retailers, and refused to supply retailers who were not licensed under the system. The court was concerned as to whether these arrangements which solely affected national trade, could cause Art.81 to have any application at all. The European Court said that this was not impossible, since a closed distribution system could have effects on similar systems in other Member States, and, in any case, favoured nationals of Italy, who were the only ones who could get the necessary licences to become retailers. It was for the local court to decide this question upon the particular facts of the case.

The European Court was also asked whether the licensing system itself was contrary to Art.81. The Court replied that selective distribution systems with objective qualitative criteria applied in a uniform manner were not a contravention of Art.81, but it was for the national court to decide on the facts as to whether these were the sort of criteria applied in this particular arrangement. The Court also made the point that this arrangement could not benefit from the block exemption regulation for exclusive distributorship agreements, as it was an arrangement between more than two persons. The multi-party nature of selective distribution systems taken as a whole often rendered the individual agreements incapable of exemption under Reg.67/67, but this was not always the case (see *Re Junghans*). **6–193**

The Commission gave an important Decision concerning the application of qualitative criteria in relation to IBM's selective distribution system for its personal computer range, in *Re the IBM Personal Computer* [1984] 2 C.M.L.R. 342. IBM considered that customers who purchased the larger and more expensive microcomputers for business or professional use were often inexperienced users who purchased from outlets that could not give them proper advice as to exactly the combination of computer, software and peripherals that was appropriate to their needs. This was leading to loss of sales and a decline of the reputation of the personal computer because of the disappointment of such purchasers who were obtaining equipment not suited for their requirements. IBM wished to establish a chain of expert dealers who would give proper advice, and provide proper after-sales service and maintenance. The distribution network was based on objective criteria only, and IBM stated that its object was to appoint as many qualified dealers as it possibly could. **6–194**

The criteria for appointment were: **6–195**

- experienced sales staff, or those willing to and having undergone IBM training;
- proper space for demonstration and display and willingness to keep at least one demonstration model;
- ability to provide customers with technical support and training;
- service facilities with experienced staff trained in IBM requirements;
- ability to run a microcomputer sales business;

- favourable bank reference and credit rating;
- no previous commitments;
- willingness to accept IBM terms and conditions of sale; and
- willingness to comply with the law and with IBM's code of professional conduct, which prohibited false claims for IBM or disparaging or false statements about other products.

6–196 The Commission made it clear that its exemption under Art.81(3) was "based on the present situation in this market in which new highly technical products are being sold mainly to inexperienced users who have not enjoyed the education in computers that is now being offered in many schools and colleges ... The criteria for the selection of the dealers were objective and 'go no further than may reasonably be thought necessary for the distribution of the products in question". In particular the evidence was that there would be no effort to maintain resale prices for the products.

6–197 The thrust of *Re IBM PC* is that the borderline between objective qualitative criteria (discussed above) and subject qualitative criteria (discussed below) changes not only between industries, but also in the same industry with time. It is noteworthy that today most personal computers are sold as quite simple consumer goods, often over the internet, and almost never through selective distribution systems.

6–198 An example of the differing requirements between industries can be found in *Société d'Hygiène Dermatologique de Vichy v Commission*, where the Commission refused to accept that it was technically necessary for certain skin-care products to be sold only through a pharmacy by a practising pharmacist. *Re Grundig AG* is a further interesting example of the way requirements can differ in the same industry over time.

6–199 Grundig's selective distribution system was originally exempted by the Commission under Art.81(3) in the 1985 Commission Decision [1985] O.J. L404. It re-applied for an extension of the approval in 1990. In *Re Grundig AG*, the Commission noted that the market for consumer electronics had changed from the early 1980 with the growth of the discount cash and carry outlet, and a decline in the market share of European manufacturers because of competition from the Far East. The Commission noted that the changes in the industry resulted in consumers losing the advantage of obtaining good technical advice and proper service for the products that they bought, since the cash and carry outlets offered low prices and no real service. Yet this advice and service from expert staff "was becoming increasingly important for many consumers in the face of constant technological innovation". Grundig required the members of its network:

- to have specialised outlets (or departments in such outlets);
- to employ technically trained staff who could offer advice;
- to provide (in the case of retailers) after sales service;

- not to supply any dealer unless he was a member of the network;
- not to advertise products at cash and carry or take away prices; and
- not (in the case of wholesalers) to supply end users.

The Commission found that all of these qualitative criteria were applied objectively and thus fell within the definition of objective qualitative criteria applied without discrimination. The Commission stated that "All the above clauses for ensuring selective distribution by professionally trained wholesalers and retailers who are willing and able to provide advisory and after-sales services, are, given the present market structure and the present competition situation in the consumer electronics sector, not liable to have an appreciable effect on competition between manufacturers or dealers, but are integral parts of a form of distribution that is compatible with Art.81(1)". **6–200**

Schedule 2—Part 2

Here the provisions of cll.4.8, 4.9 and 4.10 should be reproduced with any necessary adaptation. Clause 6.9.6 (no price control) should be remembered as well as the discussion in Chapter 5.9.1 above about the omission of the obligation placed upon the distributor to disclose pricing information to the principal. Together with these clauses should be added, if desired, a purchase target provision based on cll.4.3.5 and 4.24. Here reference should be made to the discussion in Chapter 5.3.5 above on quantity forcing as one of the single branding group of vertical restraints. **6–201**

Finally, it is useful to add a clause along the following lines: **6–202**

> Nothing in this Agreement (including without limitation the provisions of this part of this schedule shall oblige the Distributor to obtain approval or accept directions or give notifications in respect of matters relating to pricing of the Products.

The line of authority in the *SABA* cases shows well the Commission's thinking on what it terms subjective qualitative criteria. These are matters which go beyond the objective requirement to serve purchasers properly. Nevertheless they are qualifications which the principal genuinely wishes his distributors to comply with. He is thus not operating a disguised restriction but is willing to accept into the network any person who agrees to comply. However, they are criteria which not everyone who fulfils the objective qualitative criteria may be willing to comply with, and to this extent they rule out of the network some people who satisfy the objective qualitative criteria and could thus do a proper job of selling the products to customers. They normally relate to adherence to targets, undertaking of sales promotion programmes, or maintenance of specified stock levels or ranges.

In *Re SABA* [1978] 1 C.M.L.R. D61, the German subsidiary of a US corporation manufactured consumer electronics such as radios, televisions **6–203** and hi-fi. Throughout the EC, it operated a two-tier distribution network, consisting of a wholesaler/distributor and retailers. It entered into standard form contracts with dealers of both levels, covering the conditions on which a dealer could be approved as a SABA dealer, and governing the distribution channels to be followed. Once again a dealer had to comply with qualitative criteria (*e.g.* being in the consumer electronics business, provision of proper customer and after-sales service) which related to the technical side of the business, but in addition dealers had to agree to conduct sales promotion activities, stock a complete range of the SABA products and attain certain set sales targets.

6–204 The dealers who bought direct from SABA also had to agree to do so on the basis of six monthly bulk orders, which would be called-off in agreed quantities at agreed dates. In addition, all SABA dealers were restricted to selling only to other dealers within the network (unless they were of course retailers, who could sell to consumers). SABA in its turn agreed not to supply parties outside the network.

6–205 The Commission held that the arrangement contravened Art.81(1) because many dealers who could comply with the criteria relating to the technical side of the business could not, or were unwilling to, comply with the criteria relating to sales promotion and sales targets. Nevertheless, once again, the Commission gave an exemption under Art.81(3) on the grounds that such a streamlined distribution network not only operated more economically, so that the customer paid less for the SABA products, but he also got a better standard of service. In addition the customer benefited from the more accurate sales and production planning which SABA could institute because of its close connection with and control of its network. This increased availability of supplies, choice of models, and gave cost-savings as well.

6–206 In *Metro SB-Grossmarkte v Commission* [1977] E.C.R. 1875, Metro applied to the European Court complaining about the Commission's Decision in SABA. Metro was a wholesale cash and carry firm operating through a number of outlets in Germany. It had been refused supplies by SABA, and it was the complaint of Metro which had initiated the Commission's Decision in *Re SABA*. The Court broadly upheld the Commission's Decision and rejected Metro's application.

6–207 The basis of Metro's application was that, as a cash and carry wholesaler, it could not comply with the various requirements that SABA put upon its dealers, and that these requirements were not such that firms carrying on business like Metro could comply with them. In addition it complained that the SABA system prevented price competition in goods of the same brand.

6–208 The Court held firstly that a selective distribution system is not *per se* a contravention of Art.81(1). This is still so, even if the existence of the system leads to a certain degree of rigidity in pricing, where there is no obligation to maintain fixed prices, and where the product is such that other brands of the same type of merchandise exist in sufficient numbers to provide an adequate stimulus for competition. The Court held that this was particularly so in the present case, where the goods concerned were costly complicated products, for which customer service formed as important a part of the aspects of competition as did pricing. Article 81(1) is concerned with the concept of reasonable competition ("workable competition") taking into account the market and the goods, not absolute competition with no limits at all.

Going on to consider the details of the arrangements the Court held that **6–209** the imposition of objective qualitative criteria which are applied without discrimination are not sufficient to cause the arrangements to contravene Art.81(1). Here it placed the requirements relating to the technical qualifications of the dealer and his staff, the suitability of trading premises, and even the obligation in the case of non-specialist dealers, to open a special department for goods of the SABA type. The other obligations relating to sales targets, bulk purchases and promotions were held by the Court to contravene Art.81(1) but it stated that in appropriate conditions these could be given an exemption under Art.81(3) and that this was an appropriate case, as the Commission had already found. They were not, in addition, conditions with which a large wholesale cash and carry operator like Metro could not have complied if it had wished to do so, even though the requirements were somewhat out of its line of business. Finally the court affirmed that agreements establishing forecasts for supplies over a reasonable period are suitable for exemption under Art.81(3) because they constitute a stabilising influence over employment, thus improving conditions for production, particularly when the market is unfavourable.

In general this Decision can be taken as a justification of the Commis- **6–210** sion's policy of approving selective distribution systems subject to reasonable conditions, and provided that such systems do not eliminate competition in respect of a substantial part of the goods concerned.

The Commission re-examined the SABA arrangements when the original **6–211** exemption was up for renewal and gave a further favourable Decision in *Re SABA (No.2)* [1984] 1 C.M.L.R. 677. The SABA selective distribution arrangements had changed somewhat from the time of the previous Decision, but the Commission was still satisfied that generally the arrangements were either not in contravention of Art.8‘(1) or else deserved exemption under Art.81(3).

The Commission confirmed that objective qualitative criteria regarding **6–212** professional qualifications of dealers, specialist knowledge of staff, quality of trading premises, after sales service, and storage facilities, including a requirement that specialist staff be continually in attendance while the premises were open, did not contravene Art.81(1). "Consumer electronic products ... are exactly the type of valuable consumer durable the Court had in mind in the *Metro* case when it found that selective distribution systems based on qualitative standards could be legitimate".

However, the obligations to be willing and able to order and sell SABA **6–213** products regularly, and to stock the whole range, and, in some cases to agree annual sales targets, went beyond the objective selection criteria, and required to be considered for exemption under Art.81(3). Once again the Commission found that Art.81(3) would apply to exempt the restrictions that contravened Art.81(1). Metro challenged the Commission's Decision—

again unsuccessfully—in Case C-75/84 *Metro SB Grossmarkte GmbH & Co KG v European Commission* [1987] 1 C.M.L.R. 118 where the European Court once more approved the Commission's stance on selective distribution criteria.

6–214 The distinction drawn between objective and subjective qualitative criteria continued to be used in *Re Grundig AG*, where the Commission found that the obligation to stock a full range of Grundig's products (space permitting in the case of retailers), meant that dealers had to undertake sales promotion activities which restricted their commercial independence and went beyond what was necessary for an appropriate distribution of the products. However, this requirement was granted exemption under Art.81(3) on the basis that it enabled Grundig to rely upon a comprehensive network of selected dealers who were "prepared to make a particular effort to distribute Grundig products, thus promoting sales".

6–215 The same distinction is drawn in *Re Yves St Laurent SA* and *Re Parfums Givenchy SA*. In these cases the objective qualitative criteria relating to staff and outlets were more to do with preserving the up-market or luxury nature of the perfume products. Thus the need for technical advice and assistance in the proper surroundings, where the products were displayed to advantage, was held to be important. Similarly, in both cases the subjective qualitative criterion of a minimum purchase commitment was imposed on retailers. For example in *Re Yves St Laurent SA*, it was set for each retailer at 40 per cent of the average sales per retailer throughout the network in the previous year. The Commission stated that such commitments ensured that only retailers interested in promoting the products would take up appointments and enabled the manufacturer to "concentrate distribution on the cost effective retail outlets". They would therefore be granted an exemption under Art.81(3) as promoting the proper distribution of the products.

6–216 Finally a word of caution about the use of the requirements for the distributor to observe the principal's sales and marketing policies as initially as set out in cl.4.9.1. This clause was deliberately omitted from the precedent for the ordinary distributor agreement for use within the EC set out in Chapter 5 above. However, given the nature of selective distribution its imposition is more appropriate in this precedent. Nevertheless its inclusion can cause problems, despite the final clause recommended above to ensure that at least formally the distributor does not have to take account of illegal instructions under the guise of policy directives. Again, everything depends not upon what the parties write down but on what they actually do.

6–217 In *Hasselblad (GB) Ltd v EC Commission* [1984] 1 C.M.L.R. 559 Hasselblad had deleted at the request of the Commission a clause requiring its distributors to take account of the manufacturer's recommendations regarding sales policy, prices and discounts. Obligations were then imposed to require a distributor to submit advertising for approval, and the European Court held that this would contravene Art.81 if it was used in truth to check and control the distributor's pricing.

6–218 It is the current approach of the Commission to qualitative and quantitative selection criteria and to the assessment in general of the effects of selective distribution systems is set out in paras 184 to 198 of the Guidelines.

The Commission confirms (para.185) the previous case law that "Purely qualitative selective distribution is in general considered to fall entirely outside Art.81(1) for lack of anticompetitive effects, provided that three conditions are satisfied". These are that the nature of the product requires a selective distribution system to preserve quality and ensure proper use. Second the criteria must be truly objective and not applied in a discriminatory manner. Third the criteria laid down must not go beyond what is necessary. "Quantitative selective distribution adds further criteria for selection that more directly limit the potential number of dealers by, for instance requiring minimum or maximum sales, or by fixing the number of dealers etc". **6–219**

It can be seen that the Commission has redefined the categories of qualitative and quantitative criteria, by regarding only objective qualitative criteria as qualitative criteria, and including in the definition of quantitative criteria those criteria which were usually described as subjective qualitative criteria in the previous cases. However, since both quantitative and subjective qualitative criteria infringe Art.81(1), the difference in definition is not material. **6–220**

Absent the hardcore restrictions under Art.4, already discussed above, qualitative and quantitative selective distribution is exempted by Reg.2790/90 if the 30 per cent market share is not exceeded (para.186). The regulation exempts selective distribution systems even if they relate to a product which, by its nature, does not require selective distribution. However, in such cases, the selective distribution system does not generally bring sufficient efficiency to outweigh the reduction in intra-brand competition, and therefore the benefit of the exemption is likely to be withdrawn under Art.6 or 7 of Reg.2790/99 if there are significant anticompetitive effects (para.186). **6–221**

Where the regulation does not apply, the Commission has provided guidance as to the way the parties should assess the system for potential exemption under Art.81(3). The anticompetitive effects to be considered are reductions in intra-brand competition, and, especially in case of cumulative effect, foreclosure of certain types of distributors and facilitation of collusion between suppliers or buyers (para.185). In this connection, the Decisions and judgments analysed above should also be consulted, as they provide a good basis for understanding and applying the principles set out in the Guidelines. **6–222**

The most important factors to consider are the market position of the supplier and his competitors and the number of selective distribution networks present on the relevant market. The stronger the position of the supplier the greater the reduction in intra-brand competition (para.187). The reduction in intra-brand competition may be off-set by inter-brand competition from powerful competitors, but the presence of a number of powerful competitors may, conversely, mean that the relevant market is actually covered by a number of strong selective distribution networks which create a cumulative foreclosure effect (para.188). The Commission **6–223** states: "The risk of foreclosure ... has always been greater with selective distribution than with exclusive distribution, given the restriction on sales to non-authorised dealers ... This is designed to give selective distribution a closed system making it impossible for non-authorised dealers to obtain supplies. This makes selective distribution particularly well-suited to avoid pressure by price discounters ..." (*ibid*).

6–224 The biggest concern of the Commission, even if Reg.2790/99 *prima facie* applies is the question of cumulative effect. Where the cumulative effect on competition of a number of selective distribution networks becomes appreciable, the Commission will withdraw the benefit of the regulation under Art.6 or perhaps (if sufficiently serious) under Art.8 of the regulation. The principles relating to cumulative effect as regards selective distribution agreements are set out in para.189 and are broadly similar to, but somewhat more strict than, those relating to exclusive distribution:

- No cumulative effect is likely where the share of the market covered by selective distribution systems is below 50 per cent.
- Even where that share does exceed 50 per cent, no problem should arise if the share of the five largest suppliers is below 50 per cent.
- Where the 50 per cent share is exceeded and the five largest suppliers also have more than 50 per cent of the market, the decisive factor is the extent to which the five suppliers apply selective distribution.
    - The stronger the competitors not applying selective distribution the less likely there is to be foreclosure.
    - If all of the five largest suppliers apply selective distribution, competition concerns will arise
        - particularly if quantitative criteria limiting the number of authorised dealers directly are applied as this will limit the number of new dealers capable of adequately selling the products in question, especially price discounters;
        - but more indirect quantitative selective distribution (*e.g.* objective qualitative criteria with subjective qualitative criteria such as purchasing targets) are less likely to produce net negative effects if such an amount (set as the target) does not represent a significant amount of the dealer's turnover in products of the relevant type.
- As regards individual contributions, as usual, a supplier with less than a 5 per cent market share is not considered to contribute significantly to a cumulative effect.

6–225 It is also possible for buying power to have an anticompetitive effect, for instance where a strong dealer organisation imposes selection criteria on the supplier aimed at limiting distribution to the advantage of its members (para.191)

It will be recalled (see Chapter 6.5.5.) that Art.5(c) prevents suppliers imposing a restriction against selling competing brands of named suppliers as opposed to all competing suppliers. This is to prevent the creation of an exclusive branding club which contributes to the foreclosure of other brands from the market. "This kind of obligation is unlikely to be exemptable when the five largest suppliers have a market share equal to or above 50% unless none of the suppliers imposing such an obligation is one of those five" (para.192) **6–226**

Foreclosure of markets to competing suppliers is more likely to occur when a selective distribution system is combined with one or more of the single branding group of restrictions (particularly non-compete clauses). In that case the principles relating to the assessment of single branding apply. These are set out and discussed in Chapter 5.3.6. Particular attention should be paid to the principles set out in para.146 of the Guidelines concerning the cumulative effect of networks of agreements with single branding restraints. **6–227**

Where the selective distribution system combines objective qualitative criteria with additional obligations (amounting to subjective qualitative criteria) such as a duty to reserve a minimum shelf space or to achieve minimum sales targets, problems are unlikely to occur if the share of the market covered by selective distribution networks is less than 50 per cent, or, where this ratio is exceeded, if the market share of the five largest suppliers is below 50 per cent (para.193) **6–228**

The more mature the market the more likely there is to be loss of intra-brand competition and possible foreclosure of suppliers (para.194). **6–229**

Selective distribution can lead to saving in logistics costs due to economies of scale, irrespective of the nature of the product, but this is usually only a marginal efficiency in selective distribution systems. The case is stronger for new products, complex products, experience products and credence products (para.195) **6–230**

The combination of selective and exclusive distribution is likely to infringe Art.81(1) if it is applied by a supplier whose market share exceeds 30 per cent or in the case of cumulative effects, even if active sales between territories remain free. "Such a combination may exceptionally fulfil the conditions of Art.81(3) if it is indispensable to protect substantial and relationship-specific investments made by authorised dealers" (para.195). **6–231**

Finally, the parties should always test whether there is another way of achieving the desired efficiencies without imposing restraints on competition. For instance, can a contractual obligation to provide a certain level of service be as effective as incentivising a dealer to concentrate on providing adequate service by reducing the surrounding level of competition. "To ensure that the least anti-competitive restraint is chosen, it is relevant to see whether the same efficiencies can be obtained at a comparable cost by, for instance, service requirements alone". (para.196). **6–232**

6.23 Schedule 3—retailer requirements

6–233 6.23.1 The retailer shall have premises suitable for the retail sale of [luxury perfume toiletry and beauty products] [electrical and electronic equipment] and where the premises are not solely dedicated to the sale of such or related [products] [equipment] the retailer shall sell such [products] [equipment] in a specialised department if carrying on business as a department store or other outlet carrying and selling different types of products.

6–234 6.23.2 The retailer shall not carry on business from a dwelling house unless from a part thereof set up as a retail shop with a separate customer entrance and with its own sales area and display windows looking out onto the street.

6–235 6.23.3 The retailer shall not exhibit or sell any item whose trade mark or brand name might give rise to confusion with the Trade Mark.

6–236 6.23.4 The retailer shall carry stocks of all of the Products so that he shall at all times have a full range of the Products from which customers may satisfy their needs for any of the Products.

6–237 6.23.5 The retailer will employ a sufficient number of [technically] trained sales staff on duty at all times during business hours while the retailer's outlet is open for business to enable all demand for the Products to be satisfied [and shall provide at its retail outlet facilities tools and test equipment for routine adjustment commissioning and first-line maintenance and repair of the Products].

6–238 6.23.6 The retailer shall at reasonably frequent intervals mount exhibits of the Products in prominent and appropriate positions in both external shop windows and interior show cases and shall in general at all times display the Products in such a way that their sale appears an essential part of the retailer's commercial activitics.

6–239 6.23.7 The retailer shall use best endeavours to assist all publicity campaigns applicable to the retailer in relation to the Products.

This schedule covers the same ground as the distributor qualifications in Sch.2. The precedent is based on the authorities discussed under Sch.2, but taking account of the differences between retail and wholesale outlets, which mainly concern the premises from which the products are sold. In this schedule the distinction between objective and subjective qualitative criteria is not specifically set out, but in practice only cll.6.23.4 and 6.23.7 are subjective. The position with cl.6.23.6 is not so clear cut, as on the one hand it relates to proper methods of display, and on the other to sales promotion. It is probably, while just on the borderline, an objective criterion, at least in the area of luxury goods based upon statements of the Commission in *Re Yves St Laurent SA* and *Re Parfums Givenchy SA*.

6–240 The phrases in square brackets in cl.6.23.5 are appropriate only for technical products. The second such phrase may not be necessary or may require adaptation. For a discussion of first-line maintenance see Chapter 6.24.12.

Where Reg.2790/99 applies there would be nothing to prevent limiting the activities of the retailer to one set or a number of authorised premises, and, even if Reg.2790/99 did not apply, this would seem to be a provision particularly likely in the case of a retailer to be suitable for exemption under Art.81(3), given the need to require the retailer to concentrate limited resources on serving his customers properly. **6–241**

The general discussion on the impact of quantitative and qualitative criteria (and also the discussion on the impact of cumulative effect) as set out in Chapter 6.22 in relation to distributors also applies in relation to the appointment of authorised retailers. **6–242**

6.24 Schedule 4—technical support

6.24.1 Classification of knowhow

> 6.24.1 For the purposes of this schedule Knowhow shall be divided into the following classes, and the term "Complete Knowhow" shall mean all of these classes in the aggregate: **6–243**

It is necessary first to define the totality of the knowhow with which the schedule is concerned. The schedule is based upon the primary definition of knowhow contained in Sch.1 (see cl.6.21) and proceeds to split the knowhow into various classes, to enable the schedule to treat it in different ways as agreed by the parties. This schedule is based upon the premise that the distributor will take over responsibility in his territory for all repairs and maintenance of the products, including warranty work, and advice and liaison on technical matters with retailers.

> 6.24.1.1 All of the Knowhow necessary to test commission adjust service repair and maintain the Products (in this schedule specifically referred to as "Service Knowhow"); **6–244**

This is the bare minimum of information which the Distributor needs if he is to service the products and sell them properly.

> 6.24.1.2 All of the Knowhow necessary to manufacture each of the Products without further significant development in relation to design, industrial engineering and quality control (in this schedule specifically referred to as "Manufacturing Knowhow"); **6–245**

It is necessary to define the manufacturing information separately as this will not be handed over directly to the distributor upon signature of the agreement, but will be the subject of an escrow agreement (see Chapter 10) only to be handed over to the distributor in the event that the principal is no longer willing or able to give technical support and supply spare parts to the distributor.

> 6.24.1.3 All of the Knowhow necessary fully to understand and exploit the **6–246**

possibilities and potentialities for the application, enhancement, evolution and adaptation of each of the Products (in this schedule specifically referred to as "Development Knowhow"); and

This type of information will be given to a technically qualified distributor who is going to have to adapt products to the requirements of local customers. It will probably have to be given straight away without an escrow agreement, and this precedent proceeds upon that basis, but in suitable cases it might be the subject of the escrow agreement along with manufacturing information, and, in this case, this precedent would have to be adapted accordingly, and use would be made of the definition as a separate item subject to escrow.

6–247 6.24.1.4 All of the Knowhow consisting of and relating to software programs (in this schedule specifically referred to as "Software").

Provision is made for the separate definition of software, given that in most cases it is advisable for its protection that the principal license its use separately on a non-exclusive basis to the distributor. An example of the type of non-exclusive licence required, its detailed provisions and its relationship to the distribution agreement are set out in Chapter 11. Provision for the execution of the relevant licence prior to the handing over of the software appears in cl.6.24.3.

6.24.2 Form of knowhow

6–248 6.24.2 All of the Knowhow shall be in such material form as shall reasonably be required by the Distributor and (where relating to the written or spoken word) solely in the English language, save and except that the Distributor shall have the right to translate the same into any other language at its own expense, without the Principal assuming any liability for the accuracy of the said translation.

This is a reasonably flexible clause giving the benefit of the doubt to the distributor, but it can be made more specific as to the forms in which the information is given if this is appropriate.

6.24.3 Delivery of knowhow

6–249 6.24.3 Upon execution of this Agreement the Principal shall forthwith deliver to the Distributor in accordance with cl.6.24.2 the Complete Knowhow [including the Software (provided that the parties will have previously entered into a written non-exclusive licence for the use of such Software)] other than the Manufacturing Knowhow and the Distributor shall thereupon be entitled to use the same for the purposes of this Agreement subject (in the case of the Software) to the terms and conditions of the aforesaid non-exclusive licence. At the time of such handing over, and thereafter in accordance with any agreed programme, the Principal shall give to the Distributor all such training as may be included within the definition of Knowhow set out in Sch.1.

It should be noted that the wording of this paragraph, tying back to the definitions in cl.6.24.1 does not affect the point that the information to be the subject of the escrow agreement must be detailed fully (see cl.10.2.4). Under this agreement it is supposed that the distributor still has the chance to ask the principal for more information in any class, if it is necessary, and if the principal has it available. The triggering of delivery under the escrow agreement, however, will not usually take place until it is too late to ask the principal to provide further information.

6.24.4 Escrow agreement for manufacturing knowhow

6.24.4 Upon the execution of this Agreement and (if relevant) subsequently in accordance with cl.6.24.5 the Principal shall enter into an Escrow Agreement with the Distributor and an escrow agent [reasonably acceptable to the distributor] [to be appointed by the President of the time being of the Institute of Electrical Engineers in London] [ ] of [ ] (hereinafter called the "Escrow Agent") which shall be in the form set out in Appendix A hereto and shall deposit the Manufacturing Knowhow in accordance with the terms of that Escrow Agreement with the Escrow Agent. **6–250**

Given that an escrow arrangement is required (see Chapter 10) it is not sufficient to execute the agreement itself. The principal and the distributor also have to agree amongst themselves as to the time for execution, and the way in which the escrow arrangement will operate, so that both parties have direct contractual rights against the other to enforce the proper operation of the escrow arrangement. Provision for the escrow arrangement is thus best achieved as part of the overall provisions for the principal to deliver to the distributor the necessary information to enable him to operate as a distributor of the products concerned.

This clause provides for examples of alternative ways in which the escrow agent might be identified if he has not been agreed upon by the parties at the date of signing the distribution agreement. The escrow arrangement is expressed to apply only to Manufacturing Knowhow, and this should be altered as necessary if it is also to apply to other classes of information, such as Development Knowhow or Software. In some cases it may be necessary to split the definition of Software into source codes and materials and object codes, with only the former being held in escrow. The definitions in Chapter 11.3 can be used for this purpose, and a discussion of the distinctions between the various types of software will also be found in that chapter. **6–251**

6.24.5 Additional knowhow

6.24.5 The provisions of this schedule shall apply also to all modifications improvements and alterations to the Knowhow and to all items which relate to further products which become Products under this Agreement after its commencement and which would have been items within the definition of Knowhow had the said products been Products at the said date of commencement and the **6–252**

Principal shall transmit to the Distributor or (as the case may be) deposit such modifications improvements alterations and items in accordance with cl.6.24.3 or 6.24.4 respectively immediately upon their generation or upon a product becoming a Product as aforesaid (as the case may be) and upon such transmission or deposit the same shall become Knowhow and (if relevant) Manufacturing Knowhow for all the purposes of this clause.

This clause provides for a continuing situation. It is not sufficient to impose an obligation to deposit the information in escrow, or to provide the information at the start of the agreement. As new products are added to the agreement, or as improvements are made, the information relating to these must also be communicated and deposited.

6.24.6 Use of manufacturing knowhow

6–253 6.24.6 Upon its acquisition of Manufacturing Knowhow the Distributor shall be entitled to use the same for the purposes of making and having made Products in the Territory for sale and use anywhere in the EC notwithstanding the ownership by the Principal of any intellectual or industrial property rights relating to the Knowhow and the Principal undertakes irrevocably not to exercise such rights in any way so as to prevent or hinder the Distributor from enjoying the rights granted to it under this clause.

This clause enables the distributor to use the manufacturing information once he has acquired it. Given the special situation of the escrow arrangement, it is not usual to require a continuing payment by way of royalty for the use of the information, nor to grant a specific licence as opposed to an undertaking to refrain from exercising relevant industrial property rights. This type of clause would not contravene Art.81(1). It is not usual to restrict the grant of the licence given that by the time the escrow agreement is triggered the principal has presumably lost interest in the products. Nor is the arrangement usually on an exclusive basis, since the principal may well have given the information under the escrow arrangement to other distributors whose rights would conflict if one had been given an exclusive licence.

6.24.7 No modification of products

6–254 6.24.7 During the continuance of this Agreement the Distributor shall not modify or alter the Products in any way without the Principal's prior written consent (such consent not to be unreasonably withheld) save and except that the Distributor shall at all times have the right to add to the Products at its own risk and expense such accessories or interfaces as shall be required to link the Products to any end-user's equipment or to enable the Products to be used together with or incorporated in any other equipment of an end-user.

This restriction is reasonable if one is dealing with a distributor of the products only, or even a manufacturer under licence on a normal basis with a royalty. However, once the escrow agreement is triggered the distributor is on his own, and it would be unreasonable for the principal to continue to exercise this control over his activities. Accordingly the clause specifically relates only to the period whilst the distribution agreement is in existence. It is presumed that in most cases the event that triggers the escrow agreement will also put an end to the distribution agreement.

6.24.8 No warranty as to accuracy of knowhow

6.24.8 The Principal will make reasonable efforts to confirm the accuracy and efficiency of the Knowhow but it makes no warranty or representation that the Distributor can successfully manufacture the Products through use of the Knowhow. **6–255**

This paragraph is appropriate given that the Manufacturing Knowhow will be coming to the distributor through the escrow arrangement, free of charge, without payment of a royalty.

6.24.9 No warranty on infringement

6.24.9 It is understood and agreed that there is no warranty either express or implied on the part of the Principal that the Distributor can make use or sell the Products free from any infringement of the industrial or intellectual property rights of third parties. **6–256**

This provision is inserted for the same reason as cl.6.24.8. If it is desired to insert full warranties on the part of the principal against infringement, then the precedents from Chapter 7 should be used.

6.24.10 Spares

6.24.10 In order to facilitate the proper support and maintenance of the Products by the Distributor the Principal will supply to the Distributor without any additional charge spare parts from the list of approved spare parts for the Products ("Spares"). Under this arrangement the Principal shall upon acceptance of each individual order from the Distributor for the Products be obliged to include with the shipment in respect of each of the Products such items of Spares as the Principal shall consider appropriate, to the value (calculated at the Principal's current list price for the Spares) of the percentage of the order price for that Product which is specified under the definition of that Product contained in Sched 1 as the Free Issue Percentage for that Product. **6–257**

Given that the distributor will be responsible for warranty claims and maintenance he requires an allowance of free spare parts to undertake this work. The principal will select the correct mix of spares based on his experience in maintaining the products.

6.24.11 Epidemic failure

6–258 6.24.11 In addition to cl.6.24.10 the Principal agrees that in the event that a failure caused by a persistent and identical design or manufacturing defect occurs in a large number of Products of the same type, as distinct from random component failure, the Principal will, at its expense, supply to the Distributor any replacement parts necessary to correct the defect in respect of each such Product which has been delivered within twelve months prior to the date that that Product fails by reason of such defect, together with such technical advice and guidance as the Distributor and the Principal shall mutually agree is appropriate. The Distributor will notify the Principal in writing as soon as reasonably practicable of any occurrence of the type described in this paragraph.

This clause deals with what is often called epidemic failure. This can arise either because of a design defect, because there has been a specific batch of faulty components of one type used by the principal to manufacture a particular shipment of the products, or because the principal's manufacturing process is faulty and giving rise to a particular defect on a continuing basis. It is reasonable that the principal should take the responsibility for remedying such matters, since they fall outside the usual warranty arrangements, and indicate that the principal has fallen down fundamentally on his obligations to supply saleable products. The distributor has less expertise than the principal (or may have none at all) to solve such problems, and it is commercially unreasonable for the distributor to bear the expense of remedying them.

6.24.12 Distributor to service warranties

6–259 6.24.12.1 In return for the undertakings given by the Principal in cll.6.24.10 and 6.24.11 the Distributor shall grant to all end-users of the Products sold by the Distributor a [twelve] month warranty [running from the date of purchase by the end-user] against defective workmanship material and design (covering repair or at the option of the Distributor replacement of the faulty Product in both cases free of charge) and shall provide services under such warranty (and under any identical warranty given by any other Authorised Distributor or Authorised Retailer in the Network) to end-users free of charge, and at the expense of the Distributor to the entire exclusion of the Principal.

6–260 6.24.12.2 The Distributor undertakes to liaise with all Authorised Retailers in the Territory to ensure that they implement a system for notifying their customers of such warranty and for dealing with complaints under it and under any of the said identical warranties by replacing the relevant Products with new ones and returning the faulty Products to the Distributor or by sending the faulty Products to the Distributor for repair [or by repairing the faulty Products themselves where this can be achieved by first-line maintenance (as defined in the Service Know-how)] all as the Distributor may direct them. The Distributor shall provide such Authorised Retailers with all necessary training to enable them to implement the system [and to provide such first-line maintenance].

6–261 6.24.12.3 Nothing in cl.6.24.12 shall prevent the Distributor from offering to its customers (at the expense of the Distributor) longer warranty periods or warranties of a wider scope than those provided for in cl.6.24.12.1.

In return for the allowance of spare parts, and the epidemic failure warranty the distributor takes on the warranty liability. He services the warranty through authorised retailers in his territory who will collect the faulty goods from customers and send them back to the distributor. Alternatively the retailer may conduct simple tests and repairs (mainly by replacing plug-in components) or dealing with fuses and wiring (this is known generally as first-line maintenance), while the distributor would be responsible for the more detailed repairs (sometimes known as second-line maintenance). The provisions relating to retailer repairs are in square brackets, because it may well be that the retailers will only exchange faulty products for new ones and send the faulty ones back to the distributor.

The warranty covers not only goods sold by the distributor, but also **6–262** goods sold by other members of the network. The Commission considers that setting up a system which encourages or requires the members not to honour warranties given by other members of the network contravenes Art.81(1). This is discussed below after cl.6.24.14. The distributor will of course recover his costs for these warranty services (apart from the principal's contribution by way of free spare parts) in his selling prices to the authorised retailers, who will recover them, and any costs that they in their turn incur, in implementing the system or making repairs themselves, in the sale price to end-users.

The provisions of cl.6.24.12.3 should be added since they prevent any **6–263** restriction on the distributor's ability to provide additional value to his customers by way of extended warranty, and thus avoid what (by restricting the terms of warranty) might in effect be regarded as some kind of resale price maintenance (although probably not the imposition of minimum prices). Further discussion on this point of the requirement for a minimum level of uniformity for guarantees across the EC can be found in Chapter 6.24.14.

6.24.13 Distributor to provide after-sales service

6.24.13 The Distributor undertakes, either itself, or through Authorised Retailers [or specialist subcontractors] to provide a service at fair and reasonable prices **6–264** to all end-users of the Products (irrespective of whether the Product was first put upon the market by the Distributor or the Principal or another Authorised Distributor and irrespective of whether or not the Product was purchased by that end-user in the Territory or elsewhere in the EC) for the maintenance servicing and repair of the Products which are no longer under or not covered by warranty as detailed in cl.6.24.12.

6.24.14 Quality control in servicing

6–265 6.24.14 The Distributor shall carry out all work under cll.6.24.12 and 6.24.13 or ensure that it is carried out (as the case may be) strictly in accordance with the Service Knowhow.

In the selective distribution cases, since these normally involve manufactured products with a brand name the question of guarantee service has always been very important. In the *BMW, Omega, SABA* and *Grundig* Decisions the Commission required that where a guarantee is given it be honoured in any state by any member of the network, and that each member of the network service products even though they were not sold by him, and even if they were purchased outside of the Member State in which he carried on business. This is intended to prevent the principal using the refusal to give such guarantee service to prevent parallel imports or to prevent a consumer importing products from another Member State.

6–266 Different technical requirements for safety legislation between Member States have sometimes been used to justify such barriers, but the Commission does not accept this on the whole (see Chapter 5.1.1.4.3). This has been reaffirmed by the European Court in four recent cases, Case C-194/94 *CIA Security International SA v Signalson SA and Securitel SPRL* [1996] All E.R. (EC) 557; Case C-5/94 *R v Minister of Agriculture, Fisheries and Food Ex p. Hedley Lomas (Ireland) Ltd* [1996] 2 C.M.L.R. 391; Case C-293/94 *Criminal Proceedings against Jacqueline Brandsma* [1996] All E.R. (EC) 837; and Case C-226/97 *Criminal Proceedings against Lemmens* [1998] All E.R. (EC) 604.

6–267 In *Re the Guarantee by Industrie A Zanussi SpA* [1979] 1 C.M.L.R. 81 the Commission emphasised that a consumer must be entitled to have the guarantee honoured by any Zanussi dealer irrespective of where the product was bought. Zanussi complied with this requirement, by providing that in future after-sales and warranty service would be available through the Zanussi dealer in the country of use, with no reference to the country of purchase. This effectively removed a ban by indirect means on parallel imports.

6–268 The Commission further ruled on guarantees in relation to Moulinex and Bauknecht. Both firms now give an EC wide guarantee in both cases subject only to the condition imposed by the manufacturer that the appliance in question is brought into line with the technical safety standards in force in the country where the guarantee is relied upon. The cost of any necessary adaptation is to be borne by the purchaser of the appliance (see also Case 31/85 *ETA Fabriques D'Ebauches v DK Investment* [1986] 2 C.M.L.R. 674, which related to guarantees for watches).

6–269 The Commission made a general statement of policy on November 5, 1986 concerning consumer guarantees, re-emphasising its position that after-sales guarantees must be valid throughout the EC irrespective of the Member State in which a product is purchased. It recalled both its own and European Court Decisions on selective distribution networks which supported the policy. The Commission also warned that, at the instance of the

European Bureau of Consumers' Unions, it was investigating complaints that certain networks were not honouring this policy.

It should be noted, however, that in *Hasselblad (GB) Ltd v EC Commission* [1984] 1 C.M.L.R. 559 the European Court held (contrary to the Commission's original Decision) that where parallel imports were serviced on the basis of the standard warranty accorded to products sold by the network throughout the EC, but one distributor chose to give an even higher standard of service, and an extended warranty, for the products he himself sold, this did not amount to an attempt to prevent parallel imports (see cl.6.24.12.2)

In the Commission Decision *Re SA D'ieteren NV* ([1992] 4 C.M.L.R. 399), D'ieteren was an authorised distributor for Volkswagen cars. It had appointed a network of dealers, and the arrangements were all covered by the then current block exemption on selective distribution in the motor vehicle trade (Reg.123/1985). D'ieteren sent a circular letter to its dealers recommending them to use only certain motor oils when servicing Volkswagen or Audi vehicles, and telling them to reduce service charges if they used cheaper oils. The letter did not prevent dealers buying, stocking or selling other oils or using them for servicing Volkswagen or Audi vehicles. Motor Oils were not covered by the block exemption, and neither D'ieteren nor the manufacturers manufactured or dealt in motor oils. The dealers had a strong incentive to use the recommended oils as the Volkswagen warranty did not cover damage by unauthorised oils. The Commission held that the first part of the letter was not restrictive on competition as it was based on objective criteria of a technical nature. In any event Art.4(1)(i)(e) of the block exemption permitted the imposition of minimum standards for service and Art.3(4) the imposition of minimum quality standards for spare parts. As for the second part of the letter, an obligation to pass on the benefit of using cheaper oil to consumers whose cars were serviced was clearly not restrictive of competition. **6–270**

BMW v Commission, discussed in Chapter 6.1, is a further example of the Commission's insistence on community-wide guarantee service. **6–271**

There are, however, some limits to the Commission's insistence that manufacturers provide community-wide guarantees. In Case C-376/92 *Metro SB-Grossmarkte v Cartier* [1994] 5 C.M.L.R. 331), Metro complained because Cartier refused to honour guarantees on Cartier watches sold by Metro in Germany which had been obtained outside the EC on the "grey market". Cartier refused on the grounds that within the EC it would honour only guarantees on watches sold by its authorised distributors. **6–272**

Under the German law concept of "imperviousness", the enforceability of a selective distribution system could be attacked on the grounds that it was possible for goods to be sold outside the system so that both authorised and unauthorised resellers were selling the goods in the same market. The Court held that the concept of "imperviousness" had no place in EC law, and that it would be strange if a tighter and more inflexible selective distribution network was treated more favourably under Art.81 than "distribution systems which were more flexible and open to parallel transactions". Thus a **6–273** selective distribution system within the EC which otherwise satisfies the criteria laid down in Art.81 cannot be "denied recognition on the grounds that in countries outside the EC a selective distribution system ... does not (fully) exist so that goods which in the EC are covered by that distribution system can be freely obtained there by persons outside the system and lawfully brought on to the common market".

6–274 The Court then ruled that if the selective distribution itself was lawful, it was also lawful for Cartier to refuse to honour its guarantee unless the watches had been obtained from an authorised reseller.

6–275 For a further case on "imperviousness" in German competition law see Case C-41/96 *VAG-Handlerbeirat eV v SYD-Consult* [1997] C.E.C. 1226 discussed in Chapter 6.1.2.

6–276 Although the operation of the warranty system described in cl.6.24.12.1, throughout the selective distribution network, would prevent disparate warranty provisions indirectly creating a hardcore restriction under Art.4(b) of Reg.2790/99, it is useful, as provided in cl.6.24.12.2 above, to permit the distributor to provide more generous warranty terms, at his own expense, since these would presumably be a competitive element in the sales of the products, along the lines of *Hasselblad*. However, it would not be commercially feasible to require other members of the network to honour those more generous terms. That should be a matter for each distributor in relation to its direct customers only.

6.24.15 Principal to supply spares

6–277 6.24.15 The Principal undertakes during the term of this Agreement and for a period of five years after its termination to maintain adequate stocks of service and replacement parts for the Products and to make them available to the Distributor and its customers for reasonable periods and at reasonable prices to be determined in relation to the different Products and the reasonable life expectancy of the respective Products and or the components and parts thereof.

The supply of spare parts is a delicate issue. The Commission has attacked this in two ways.

6–278 First when approving a selective distribution system it normally requires that spare parts must be freely available to anyone who wants them (see also Art.4(a)(iii), Art.4(i) and Art.4(j) of Reg.1400/2002 discussed in Chapter 6.26 and Art.4(e) of Reg.2790/99 discussed above). The Commission comments in para.56 of the Guidelines on Vertical Restraints on Art.4(e) of Reg.2790/99: "an agreement between a manufacturer of spare parts and a buyer who incorporates those parts into his own products (OEM) may not, either directly or indirectly prevent or restrict sales by the manufacturer of these spare parts to end users, independent repairers or service providers. Indirect restrictions may arise in particular when the supplier of the spare parts is restricted in supplying technical information and special equipment which are necessary for the use of spare parts ... However, the agreement may place restrictions on the supply of spare parts to the repairers or service providers entrusted by the OEM with the repair or servicing of his own goods. In other words the OEM may require his own repair and service network to buy the spare parts from it [*sic; presumably* 'him']".

The consequence of this paragraph is that it would be possible for the manufacturer to impose an obligation on other members of the selective distribution network to obtain spare parts only from (a) the principal himself, or (b) from a source designated by the principal, or (c) (taking into account the wording of Art.4(e) which would also cover spare parts) from other members of the network. This in effect means that authorised members of the network could, under Reg.2790/99, be required only to use "authorised" spare parts, without falling foul of any hardcore restrictions under Art.4. This is not the case with Reg.1400/2002 (see Chapter 6.26) and it would also presumably be correspondingly harder to justify directly under Art.81(3) where Reg.2790/99 did not apply. There is also clearly potential for the benefit of the Regulation to be withdrawn if the manufacturer implements some anticompetitive policy in relation to spare parts such as excessive pricing or restriction of supply along the lines of the dicta in the *Renault* and *Volvo* cases. **6–279**

However, this discussion presupposes that the principal (or its sub-contractor) is the only source of supply of spare parts. If there are other independent manufacturers of spare parts of equivalent quality on the market, then an obligation to purchase only spares originating from the manufacturer of the finished product would amount to a non-compete clause (a quantity forcing clause of 100 per cent of the requirement for spare parts – see Chapter 5.3.5) under Art.5(a). In this case, if the clause were to be exempted under Reg.2790/99, it would have to comply with the particular conditions surrounding non-compete clauses permitted under the exceptions in Art.5(a), or else the parties would have to consider that it was justified directly under Art.81(3). Where Reg.2790/99 did not apply at all the justification under Art.81(3) is of course more difficult. Reference should be made to the discussion on non-compete clauses in Chapter 5.3.6 for the criteria upon which such decisions should be made. **6–280**

Second, the Commission has invoked Art.82 in relation to the supply of spare parts. It has made the statement that any manufacturer has a dominant position in the market relating to the supply of his own spare parts for the equipment he manufactures (at any rate where substitutes made by third parties cannot be freely used) and that any refusal to supply those parts freely may amount to an abuse of his dominant position. This was taken to the European Court in *Hugin Kassaregister AB v EC Commission* [1979] 3 C.M.L.R. 345 where the Court took the view that in theory there could be an abuse of a dominant position by a manufacturer in relation to the market in spare parts for the equipment he manufactured, although the appeal was allowed upon the particular facts of the case because the effect of the abuse on cross-border trade had not been proved, and there was also some doubt as to whether there had actually been an abuse at all. **6–281**

It is an oversimplification to speak of an abuse of a dominant position in the market for spare parts for the machines to be manufactured by the **6–282** enterprise concerned. If the enterprise makes it difficult to maintain its machines then future buyers will become aware of this and refuse to buy those machines, or at least have the option of choosing another type of machine to fulfil their requirements where no such problem exists. The problem really arises, as in the *Hugin* case, for those who have already bought the machines and thus have no choice but to suffer the situation. It could be said that the abuse of the dominant position thus takes place in relation to the market for spare parts of machines of the manufacturer which have already been sold. This line of reasoning is supported by dicta in the *Volvo* and *Renault* cases discussed below.

6–283 In this connection the statement in the Guidelines on Vertical Restraints at para.94 is relevant: "where a supplier produces both original equipment and the repair or replacement parts for this equipment. The supplier will often be the only or the major supplier on the after-market for the repair and replacement parts. This may also arise where the OEM supplier sub-contracts the manufacturing of the repair or replacement parts. The relevant market for the application of [Reg.2790/99] may be the original equipment market including the spare parts or a separate original equipment market and after-market depending on the circumstances of the case, such as the effects of the restrictions involved, the lifetime of the equipment and the importance of the repair or replacement costs".

6–284 The Commission made good use of the precedent in *Hugin* in its Decision *Re Brass Band Instruments Ltd/Boosey and Hawkes Ltd* [1988] 4 C.M.L.R. 67. In this case, ex-employees of Boosey and Hawkes joined together with a firm, which had a large business repairing musical instruments manufactured by Boosey and Hawkes, to manufacture similar instruments in competition. Boosey and Hawkes had an overwhelmingly dominant market position in the particular sector of musical instruments concerned (brass band wind instruments), and reacted vigorously to the threat by refusing, amongst other things, to supply their new competitor with vital spare parts. Without this supply, for which there was no alternative source, the repair business could not continue. Since it was the operation generating the funds which would support the launch of the new competitive manufacturing enterprise, its failure would cause the failure of the manufacturing enterprise and leave Boosey and Hawkes without competition.

6–285 The Commission called the withholding of spare parts an abuse of Boosey and Hawkes' dominant position, and made an order for compulsory supply on fair and reasonable terms. It was referring to the dominant position in spare parts for Boosey and Hawkes' instruments, which arose not because Boosey and Hawkes had a dominant position in the supply of brass band instruments (although this was of course the case) but because the dominant position in the supply of instruments had resulted in a situation where no one other than Boosey and Hawkes was interested in the manufacture and supply of spare parts for those instruments, which, as a business separate from the manufacture and supply of the instruments concerned, was not a viable proposition.

6–286 Two European Court cases on spare parts which are of considerable importance are Case C-238/87 *Volvo AB v Erik Veng (UK) Ltd* [1989] 4 C.M.L.R. 122 and *Consorzio Italiano Delia Componentistica Di Ricambio Per Autoveicoli* and Case 53/87 *Maxicar v Regie Nationale Des Usines Renault* [1989] 4 C.M.L.R. 265. In the former, Volvo refused to give a licence under a UK registered design to Veng to enable it to manufacture body panels to be used as replacement parts for certain models of Volvo cars. There was no question that Volvo was being difficult or unfair in the way it was supplying these spare parts to the market, and the case turned upon whether or not the mere refusal to grant a licence upon fair and reasonable terms under an intellectual property right could be an abuse of a dominant position. The Court held that:

> "Since the right of a proprietor of a protected design to prevent third parties from manufacturing, selling or importing products incorporating the design without his consent constitutes the very subject matter of his exclusive right, an obligation imposed upon him to grant third parties a licence for the supply of such products would lead him to be deprived of the substance of his exclusive right, even in return for a reasonable royalty, and a refusal to grant such a licence cannot in itself constitute an abuse of a dominant position."

The Court went on to explain that the exercise of an intellectual property right reinforces or establishes the dominant position of the proprietor, but is not in itself an abuse of that dominant position. The test is to examine the way in which the proprietor conducts his business, given that he enjoys a dominant position by virtue of the relevant intellectual property right. Here Volvo were behaving properly by supplying spare body panels freely and at reasonable prices to all comers. Thus there was no abuse under Art.82. However, it is quite clear that a manufacturer protected by relevant intellectual property rights—like Volvo—does enjoy a dominant position in the market for the relevant spare parts for his products. If such a manufacturer exercises unfair practices in the supply of such products (such as discrimination in supply, excessive pricing or discontinuing supply while a large number of models are still in circulation) then an abuse of his dominant position would occur. In this event it was suggested that the Commission could impose a compulsory licence if it thought that were the best way of ending the abuse. **6–287**

The *Renault* Decision turned upon the same kind of facts and came to the same result, although here it was not the refusal of the grant of a licence but the mere application to obtain design right protection (thus giving rise to an exclusive right to the design on the part of Renault) which was contended to be the abuse of the dominant position. **6–288**

The Commission was quick to move after these Decisions first became known, and issued a statement on October 12, 1988 accepting that the mere refusal to grant a licence to manufacture spare parts was not a contravention of Art.82, but warning that it would act upon the Court's suggestions that proprietors of such rights who used them so as to be able to **6–289** indulge in abusive behaviour were in contravention of Art.82. The Commission also made it clear that it was investigating the supply of spare parts in the motor industry to see if it could find evidence of such abuse.

6–290 These cases show that (as discussed in Chapter 4.3.7 in relation to *British Armstrong v Leyland*) a mere contractual prohibition upon a distributor not to copy or reproduce aspects or parts of the products (which are unprotected by intellectual property rights) is open to attack under Art.82 (and probably also Art.81) if this is one of the methods by which a principal tries to restrict and control the market in spare parts for the distributed products. Such prohibitions may be justifiable on grounds of the need to maintain technical, quality or safety standards, for the benefit of users, but should always be approached with care. They also reinforce the arguments in Chapter 4.3.7 that the principles in *British Leyland v Armstrong* are still good law and could be extended to apply to spare parts protected by intellectual property rights in situations where action under Art.82 was not appropriate.

6–291 Next there is a Commission Decision *Re Tetra-Pak Rousing SA* [1988] O.J. L272 which goes further than *Renault* and *Volvo* in suggesting that where an undertaking in a dominant position acquires a company which holds an exclusive patent licence, that undertaking could be abusing the dominant position by exercising the rights under the patent licence acquired along with the company. The Decision is an extension of the old principle in the *Continental Can* case, and it was approved by the European Court of First Instance (Case T-51/89 [1991] 4 C.M.L.R. 334).

6–292 A series of very important cases on refusal to grant a licence is known collectively as *Magill*. These cases were a series of judgments at the European Court of First Instance (see Case T-76/89 *Independent Television Publications Ltd v Commission (Magill TV Guide Ltd intervening)* [1991] 4 C.M.L.R. 745), which were confirmed by the European Court (Case C-241/91 [1995] 4 C.M.L.R. 718). The Commission had held that the applicant publisher had infringed Art.82 in so far as it prevented the publication and sale of comprehensive weekly TV Guides in Ireland and Northern Ireland by refusing to grant licences for the reproduction of the advance weekly programme listing of independent television broadcasters in the UK, who had assigned the copyright in lists to it. The Commission ordered it to make available those listings on request, together with permission to publish, under terms approved by the Commission.

6–293 The Court held that the relevant product markets were those for weekly programme listings and television magazines in which they were published, that the applicant was dominant in those markets since potential competitors were dependent on it making available the weekly listings for publication, that although the programme listings were protected by copyright under national law, Community law precluded its use to prevent competition from a new product and to secure a monopoly position.

6–294 This case is important not only in relation to the question of refusal to grant a licence, but also on the question of the principles of "existence versus exercise" of a right. The case relied on *Keurkoop BV v Nancy Kean Gifts BV*

[1983] 2 C.M.L.R. 47, discussed in Chapter 5.5.3, and is a good example of the fact that the question of "justification", discussed previously, is really a value judgment or a matter of public policy. The Court stressed that Art.30 emphasises that:

> "the reconciliation between the requirements of the free movement of goods and the respect to which intellectual property rights are entitled must be achieved in such a way as to protect the legitimate exercise of such rights, which alone is justified within the meaning of that Article, and to preclude any improper exercise thereof likely to create artificial partitions within the market or pervert the rules governing competition within the Community. The exercise of intellectual property rights conferred by national legislation must consequently be restricted as far as is necessary for that reconciliation. Thus, while it is plain that the exercise of the exclusive right to reproduce a work protected by copyright is part of the actual substance of that right and not in itself an abuse of a dominant position, that does not apply when, in the light of the details of each individual case, it is apparent that that right is exercised in such ways and circumstances as in fact to pursue an aim manifestly contrary to the objectives of Article 82. The use of copyright for the purpose of preventing the production and marketing of a new product for which there is potential consumer demand and thereby excluding all competition from the market solely in order to secure the owner's monopoly clearly goes beyond what is necessary to fulfil the essential function of the copyright as permitted in Community law."

There has been much discussion of the extent to which the principles in *Magill* should be applied and exactly how far the judgment can be taken to have extended the law in relation to abuse of a dominant position through refusal to grant a licence of intellectual property right. **6–295**

It is clear that, as mentioned in *Magill*, it is only where "extraordinary circumstances" exist that such a refusal will be considered an abuse of a dominant position. Later cases have thrown some light on this problem, but the matter is still not completely clarified. **6–296**

Before considering the later cases, there are two general reasons why *Magill* may not have such far-reaching effects as was first considered, particularly in the area of refusal to grant a copyright licence in relation to a computer program. First, the question of abuse in relation to refusal to grant rights to copy a software product has already been thoroughly debated and dealt with in the process of introducing the Software Directive. The Commission and the Court would find it difficult to go further without public debate and a further directive. Second, *Magill* was concerned with a very particular form of copyright. The copyright work for which protection was claimed in *Magill* related to a list of items. Now, copyright cannot subsist in a list of items under the copyright law in force in most of the jurisdictions within the EC. The ability of the compiler of a list to claim copyright in it is a peculiarity of the law on copyright in force in the UK and Ireland. **6–297**

6–298 Thus, the Court was being asked to protect what most of the judges involved in the case regarded as an "inferior" form of intellectual property, not worthy of protection in most of the EC. For instance, they talked of the basic function of copyright as being to protect the moral rights in the work and ensuring a reward for creative effort. This is the continental basis for copyright protection rather than the common law basis of the exclusive right of reproduction. This is why the compilation of a list receives protection only at common law. From reading the reported decisions there seems little doubt that the Court, both at first instance and on appeal, treated the case more as one concerned with an attempt to prevent the use of information (see for instance, "the Appellants by their conduct were using their *de facto* monopoly over programming information . . .") which was not confidential, rather than as a refusal to grant a licence of a copyright work. It was then quite possible, whether implicitly or explicitly, to make the value judgment under Art.30 that the protection of this particular type of copyright was, under the circumstances, less important than the promotion of competition, so that its protection was not held to be "justified".

6–299 This approach would contrast sharply with the approach that a court in the UK would take, and this has, perhaps created some of the alarm and despondency surrounding the decision, but *Magill* is not necessarily a precedent in the area of the much more "important" type of copyright protecting a computer program where the promotion of competition has already been dealt with in the Software Directive. Here, the value judgement under Art.30 is much more likely to come down in favour of the protection of the copyright in the program than it did in *Magill*, since the Software Directive has, in effect, already said what exercise of his copyright by the rightholder is justified and where, in the interests of competition, those rights must be overridden.

6–300 In this context it is instructive to compare the very different approaches to the protection of computer programs as copyright works in the US and the UK.

6–301 In the US decision of *Computer Associates International v Altai Inc* (982 F rd 693 (2d Circuit) 1992) a three stage test was applied to the granting of copyright protection to elements of a computer program. First comes "abstraction"—analysing the program's structure and isolating each level of abstraction in it. Next comes "filtration"—examining the structural components at each level to see if they were protectable under the law of copyright at all. Finally comes "comparison"—has there been copying of those elements of the program which survived the filtration test? A reading of the many US cases on the subject of the protection of computer programs leaves little doubt that there is a tension between protection of such programs under copyright law and the desire to promote competition under anti-trust law. To some extent these tensions are reconciled in the filtration process, where some value judgments can be made which would, in the interests of competition, deny certain elements of the program protection under the law of copyright.

6–302 In the English decision of *IBCOS Computers Ltd* v *Barclays Mercantile*

Finance Ltd [1994] F.S.R. 275, Jacob J. ignored *Computer Associates v Altai* and stated a simple test for copyright infringement—what are the works in which the plaintiff claims copyright; are the works "original" as that term is understood under copyright law in the UK; was there copying from that work; and if there was copying, has a substantial part of that work been produced?

Looking at the facts in *Magill*, it can be seen that the copyright in the lists **6–303**
would never have survived the filtration process in *Computer Associates v Altai*, but would certainly have received protection under *IBCOS*. Copyright law in the UK thus has no need of the value judgment implicit in Art.30 or the filtration process to grant or deny protection to a copyright work, but the decision in *Magill* cannot really be understood except on this basis. It can by no means be assumed that the Commission or the Court would in future come to a similar decision in relation to a computer program without the very clear and manifest evidence of abuse which was stated as requirement in *Renault* and *Volvo*.

The use of various design rights or copyright under national law to pre- **6–304**
vent the import of copied spare parts from outside the relevant territory is discussed in Chapter 5.1.1.4.1. The new rights granted in the UK to unregistered designs and their effect on the market in spare parts are discussed in Chapter 4.3.7.

It is now appropriate to consider the various cases in which *Magill* has **6–305**
since considered or applied. The first case to consider *Magill* correctly concentrated on the fact the abuse found there was not actually a refusal to grant a licence, but the use of a dominant position in an upstream market (the control of the copyright in programme listings) to prevent competition in a downstream market (the publication a competing magazine which included those listings). This concept of prevention of competition on a down stream market by an upstream supplier was applied in *Donovan v Electricity Supply Board* ([1998] Eu L.R. 212, Supreme Court (Ireland)) but not in relation to refusal to grant a licence of intellectual property rights.

In 1992, ESB, the sole producer of electric power in Ireland, altered its **6–306**
conditions of supply to require a completion certificate from an RECI inspector or RECI registered contractor, RECI being a limited company set up to promote the safety and interests of the public as users of electrical services. Non members of RECI claimed this was an abuse of ESB's dominant position, contrary to the Competition Act 1991, s.5 (Ireland) and in 1992 issued plenary proceedings and obtained an interlocutory injunction to restrain implementation of the new scheme. In the plenary proceedings the High Court held that ESB had unintentionally abused its dominant position contrary to s.5, and awarded damages arising from the abuse. ESB appealed, arguing that the trial judge had failed correctly to identify the market in which it was alleged to be dominant, ESB not being a serious competitor for low voltage electrical installation market where the abuse had occurred, and that as the abuse had been unintentional, damages were inappropriate.

The Court dismissed the appeal. It held that ESB was able to make its will **6–307** prevail in the low voltage sub market (the downstream market) by virtue of its total dominance in the market for the supply of energy (the upstream market), but was not entitled to do so. The Court applied *Magill.* The Court further held that there was no analogy between a fine imposed by the Commission of European Communities and an action for damages under the 1991 Act, which was for compensation irrespective of the motives of the party in default unless a question of exemplary damages arose which it did not here.

6–308 Case T-198/98 *Micro Leader Business v Commission* [2000] 4 C.M.L.R. 886 considered *Magill* in relation to the supply of software. This case was therefore far more closely connected with the refusal to grant a licence of intellectual property. MLB, supplied wholesale office and computer equipment which included computer software products manufactured by an American company, MC. MLB imported copies of the French language version of MC's Canadian software into France. The software was identical to the product sold in France by MC's subsidiary, MF, but lower in price. MF took steps to prevent the sale of any French language versions of the Canadian product to anyone other than an approved MF distributor thus effectively preventing MLB from importing copies of the Canadian software. MLB made a complaint to the European Commission, contending that the activities of MF and MC breached the EC Treaty Arts 81 and 253).

6–309 The Commission dismissed the complaint. MLB then instituted proceedings in the European Court seeking annulment of the Commission's decision. MLB contended that MC and MF were engaged in concerted practices designed to keep prices on the French market high, and that MC and MF had abused their dominant position in the French market by fixing prices at an artificially high level.

6–310 The Court held that the Commission had been correct in their conclusion that MC and MF could not have been guilty of concerted practices since they formed a single economic entity and that by virtue of Council Directive 91/250 (the so-called Software Directive—see Chapter 11), rights of distribution into the common market had not been exhausted following sale of a software package into Canada and therefore unauthorised importation of the Canadian product into France did amount to an unlawful infringement of MC's copyright.

6–311 The Commission's conclusion that the prohibition in question amounted to lawful enforcement of copyright pursuant to Council Directive 91/250 and that there had been insufficient evidence provided to substantiate the assertion of abuse of dominant market position in France was, however, flawed. Although normally enforcement under copyright was lawful, such enforcement could amount to abuse in exceptional circumstances. The Court referred to *Magill.* Evidence had been provided of alleged abusive conduct and such evidence should not have been dismissed out of hand without an investigation into whether the conduct complained of had been abusive in line with the findings in *Magill.*

6–312 In *HM Stationery Office v Automobile Association Ltd* [2001] E.C.C. 34, Ch D, in proceedings for infringement of copyright commenced by HMSO, the AA alleged that HMSO were abusing their dominant position concerning information about new roads in breach of the EC Treaty Art.82. The AA maintained that the breach arose from the fact that HMSO had requested a royalty fee pursuant to the grant of a licence, and that other users of the information such as Ordnance Survey did not pay for the use of the information.

The Court considered *Magill* and held that no copyright holder was obliged to grant a licence for a nil royalty The evidence in relation to other users lacked substance and was misconceived in so far as it related to the Ordnance Survey, which was itself part of the Crown. The fact that one part of the Crown did not charge another part for use of Crown copyright could not amount to discrimination between the Crown itself and third parties. **6–313**

In *Intel Corp v VIA Technologies Inc* [2002] E.U. L.R. 502, Ch D, the Court applied the basic principle that refusal to grant a licence of an intellectual property right was not an abuse of a dominant position, and found no exceptional circumstances of the sort found in *Magill*. **6–314**

Intel applied for summary judgment in its favour on VIA's competition law defence and counterclaim to its patent infringement action. In its defence and counterclaim, VIA contended that Intel's refusal to grant a patent licence was an abuse of dominant position and therefore in contravention of Art.82 and s.18 of the Competition Act 1998. **6–315**

The Court granted summary judgment for Intel. It applied *Volvo AB v Erik Veng (UK) Ltd*, and considered *British Leyland Motor Corp Ltd v TI Silencers Ltd* and *Magill*. Whilst it admitted that there was a tension between the rights conferred upon a patent holder and the rules regulating and promoting competition, in general, the holder of an intellectual property right was entitled to refuse to allow others to make use of that right. The Court also held that there was no merit in VIA's argument that if a patent holder offered a licence on terms which breached Art.81, then the offeree was entitled to a licence on its own terms if it rejected the offer. **6–316**

The most important case to consider *Magill* to date is Case T-184/01 *IMS Health Inc v Commission (No.2)* [2002] 4 C.M.L.R. 2, although not yet a final judgment, it has concentrated on just when the "exceptional circumstances" spoken of in *Magill* can be said to arise. **6–317**

IMS, through a subsidiary, provided data report services in Germany to the pharmaceutical industry. It had devised a system, (the "brick system") under which Germany was artificially divided into a number of areas so as to monitor sales of pharmaceuticals in those areas. IMS sued competitors, P (later purchased by N) and A, for breach of copyright for their use of the brick system in providing a competing data report service essentially similar to IMS's, and based upon the brick system. **6–318**

IMS sought a definitive injunction restraining the alleged breach of copyright, but the proceedings were stayed pending a reference to the European Court so that N and A were able to use the brick system pending a final decision by the national court. IMS refused requests from both N and A for licences to use the brick sytem. N complained to the Commission of the European Union that this refusal by IMS constituted a breach of Art.82. **6–319**

The Commission issued an interim decision requiring IMS to licence the brick system to N. IMS appealed to the European Court of First Instance against the Commission's decision, seeking its interim suspension pending the delivery of the national court's decision.

6–320 The Court of First Instance allowed IMS's appeal partly on the criteria of the balance of convenience, but also because there was a serious issue to be tried as to the soundness of the legal reason upon which the Commission's decision had been based, namely whether the principle in *Magill* had been correctly applied. This, on its face, justified the interim relief sought.

6–321 The President of the Court commented on *Magill* as follows:

> "It is clear from the reasoning ... in the *Magill* case that there are a number of potentially important differences ... the approach of the Commission would provisionally appear, in large measure, to depend upon the notion of exceptional circumstances to which the Court refers [in *Magill*] ... the applicant has made out a provisional prima facie case that the Commission has misconstrued the scope of the principles set out in *Magill* by finding that ... the applicant's refusal to grant a copyright licence to N, among others, so that the latter could provide ***essentially the same information services***, based in large part on freely available data, on the ***same market*** and to the ***same potential consumers*** as the services currently provided by the former amounts to a prima facie abuse of its dominant position ..."

6–322 The issue in this case is of course that while in *Magill* a dominant position in an upstream market was used to prevent competition in a downstream market, here the Commission has extended the principle to use of a dominant position by way of refusal to grant a licence of a copyright to prevent competitors coming into the same market on which the right holder is already actively using the copyright work (see the phrases emphasised in the passage above). It remains to be seen just how the substantive decision will be made in this case, (although an appeal against this interim decision of the Court of First Instance was dismissed by the European Court later in 2002 under reference C-481/01 P (R) 1), but there is a clear indication that the Court of First Instance believes the Commission has gone too far in its application of *Magill* and that the "exceptional circumstances" in *Magill* can only be said to arise where the upstream/downstream dichotomy is present. If so, this would bring *Magill* into line with all of the other cases in this area, (particularly *Renault* and *Volvo*) which hold that the simple refusal to grant a licence of an intellectual property right can never of itself be an abuse of a dominant position.

6–323 The position in relation to refusal to licence intellectual property rights (including knowhow) under UK competition law is not dissimilar from the position under EC competition law discussed above. The current position under UK competition law is set out in a draft Guideline (OFT 418 of November 2001: Intellectual Property Rights). This Guideline is discussed in Chapter 8.1.2 in relation to its treatment of licences of intellectual property under the Chapter I Prohibition of the Competition Act 1998. The Guideline will remain in draft until the Commission has finalised its position on the reform of the technology transfer block exemption (Reg.240/96) (see Chapter 8.28) The Guideline refers to intellectual property rights (including knowhow) as "IPR".

So far as the Chapter II Prohibition is concerned, the Director General takes the view that ownership of an IPR will not necessarily create a dominant position. Whether or not dominance results from ownership of an IPR will depend upon the extent to which there are substitutes for the product, process or work to which the IPR relates. Factors to be taken into account include the market shares of the undertaking in question as well as barriers to entry into the relevant market. Other constraints on the undertaking such as buyer power or government regulation are also relevant. (OFT 418 para.3.3.) A persistently high market share may indicate no more than persistently successful innovation. The Director General will therefore make his assessment on a case by case basis (para.3.4) **6–324**

The important issue is whether the dominant undertaking is using its dominant position in an abusive way (para.3.6) **6–325**

Paragraph 3.7 states that a refusal to licence by a dominant holder is not in itself an abuse. It may however be that in certain situations refusing to licence the IPR may infringe the Chapter II Prohibition if there is no objective justification for that refusal. This may be the case in particular where the IPR: **6–326**

- relates to a product or service which is essential for the activity in question because there is no real or potential substitute; or
- relates to a new product or service whose introduction might be prevented, despite specific, constant and regular potential demand on the part of consumers.

The principles laid down here are supposedly based upon the EC cases but do not seem to be so clearly expressed. The first point appears to relate to the "essential facilities" principle, and the second to principles set out in *Magill*, in relation to abuse of an upstream dominant position to prevent competition in a down stream product or service. So far as the second point is concerned, it does not seem to distinguish clearly between upstream and downstream markets. This would reflect the Commission thinking discussed in *IMS Health v Commission*, where the European Court has already cast doubt, in its interim decision, on the Commission's approach. The final judgment in this case will clearly be of decisive importance in clarifying this issue. **6–327**

Tying or bundling may be an abuse and therefore infringe the Chapter II Prohibition when imposed by an undertaking in a dominant position, unless such provisions are necessary for a satisfactory exploitation of the licensed IPR or for ensuring that the licensee conforms to quality standards (para.3.8) **6–328**

6–329 Provisions which would infringe the Chapter I Prohibition (even if they are exempted under Reg.2790/99 or the Vertical Restraints Order) would infringe the Chapter II Prohibition if imposed by an undertaking in a dominant position (para.3.9)

6–330 Innovation will naturally lead to an undertaking earning post-innovation profits significantly higher than its competitors (para.3.10) There therefore will not necessarily be an infringement of the Chapter II Prohibition where a proprietor of IPR holds a dominant position and charges a higher selling price or royalty rate for a product, process or work protected by its IPR as compared with a product, process or work not protected by an IPR (para.3.11).

6–331 There is no power to grant exclusions from the Chapter II Prohibition, and the benefit of a block exemption does not prevent the undertaking's behaviour from being an abuse under the Chapter II Prohibition. However, if the agreement has an individual exemption granted by the Director General (in relation to the Chapter I Prohibition) it cannot be looked at again under the Chapter II Prohibition in the absence of any change of circumstances. The same position applies if the agreement has a parallel exemption by way of an individual exemption under Art.81(3), under the old regulatory framework (para.3.15).

6–332 Finally, it should be noted that the Commission has been much concerned with the issue of the extent to which registered and unregistered design rights through the EC are an obstacle to third party suppliers manufacturing and selling spare parts. The intention is to exclude so far as possible spare parts from any design right protection, except to the extent that they have an aesthetic aspect (in terms of their novelty and individual character) and this aspect remains visible after they have been incorporated in the relevant product. The current position and the impact of Council Directives 71/98 (on the harmonisation of the legal protection for registered designs) and 6/2002 (on the creation of a Community Design) are discussed in Chapter 4.3.7.

6.24.16 No other warranties from principal

6–333 6.24.16 Save as expressly provided in this schedule or elsewhere in this Agreement the Principal gives no warranty to the Distributor and shall be under no liability in respect of the Products (including without limitation in relation to any defects in their design, workmanship or materials) and gives no warranty as to their function suitability for any purpose or as to their performance specifications except as specifically set out or referred to in Sch.1, and all other warranties express or implied by law legislation or otherwise howsoever are hereby expressly excluded.

This clause cuts across the terms of supply of the principal set out in Chapter 4.26 (see cl.4.26.2.9) and referred to in cl.6.8.2. It is however more suitable for the technically sophisticated product for which the distributor has taken warranty responsibility, and should be used when this schedule is adopted. Otherwise the specific provisions of cll.6.24.10, 6.24.11 and 6.24.12 will be undermined by general law and by the provisions of cl.4.26.2.9 so that the warranty arrangements will become unworkable, with the residual liability still falling on the principal contrary to the intention of the parties as set out in this schedule. The schedule in Chapter 4.26 can be used for terms of supply, but cl.4.26.2.9 should be amended accordingly (see Chapter 6.8.2 for the suggested alternative wording).

6.25 Schedule 5—authorised retailer agreement

6.25.1 Parties

6.25.1 The parties will be the authorised retailer (the "Retailer") and either the distributor or the principal (the "Appointor"). **6–334**

6.25.2 Scope and purpose

6.25.2.1 The products detailed in Sch.1 (the "Products") are manufactured by [ ] (the "Principal") and marketed, distributed and sold in the EC through a network of distributors and retailers authorised and appointed for this purpose (the "Network" "Authorised Distributors" and "Authorised Retailers" respectively). **6–335**

6.25.2.2 Each Authorised Retailer fulfils the qualifications and has undertaken the obligations set out in Sch.2 ("Retailer Requirements") under an agreement made with the Principal or an Authorised Distributor in terms identical to this Agreement. **6–336**

6.25.2.3 The Retailer wishes to be appointed an Authorised Retailer and the Appointor wishes to appoint the Retailer as such upon the terms of this Agreement. **6–337**

These provisions reproduce with appropriate alterations the provisions of cl.6.2 covering Authorised Distributors.

6.25.3 Appointment as authorised retailer

6.25.3 The Appointor hereby appoints the Retailer as an Authorised Retailer in the Network for the sale of the Products in accordance with and subject to the terms of this Agreement and the Retailer hereby accepts such appointment. **6–338**

6.25.4 Compliance with the retailer requirements

6.25.4 The Retailer undertakes that he will fulfil and comply with the Retailer Requirements during the continuance of this Agreement. **6–339**

6.25.5 Supply of the products

6–340 6.25.5.1 The Retailer may obtain supplies of the Products from the Appointor but may also purchase the Products from any other Authorised Retailer or Authorised Distributor in the EC or from the manufacturer.

6–341 6.25.5.2 Except as provided in cl.6.25.5.1 the Retailer shall not resort to other sources of supply for the Products.

6–342 6.25.5.3 The Retailer shall retain for at least one year duplicate copies of invoices relating to all purchases of the Products and the Appointor shall have the right to inspect the said invoices on demand.

6–343 6.25.5.4 The Appointor will accept orders for the Products placed with it by the Retailer provided it has sufficient stock of the Products to do so and will make all reasonable efforts to execute such orders in accordance with the terms of the relevant order.

6–344 6.25.5.5 All orders for the Products placed by the Retailer upon the Appointor shall be upon the current standard terms and conditions of sale of the Appointor.

6–345 6.25.5.6 The Appointor and the Retailer each undertake to the other not to sell Products to persons who are not Authorised Retailers Authorised Distributors or end-users of the Products.

6–346 6.25.5.7 The Retailer shall retain for at least one year duplicate copies of invoices or other supporting vouchers relating to sales of the Products by it and the Appointor shall have the right to inspect the same on demand.

6–347 6.25.5.8 Nothing in this clause or elsewhere in this Agreement shall entitle the Appointor to pay regard to or monitor the prices at which the Retailer sells the Products.

These clauses are largely based on the equivalent provisions for the Authorised Distributor, but somewhat simplified for use with a retailer who will operate from one or at most a small number of outlets.

6.25.6 Sales assistance

6–348 6.25.6.1 The Appointor undertakes to assist the Retailer to increase sales by providing him with appropriate publicity material.

6–349 6.25.6.2 The Appointor will supply to the Retailer reasonable quantities of available sales promotion and technical literature, catalogues and maintenance manuals and data appropriate to the Products free of charge. Such literature and data shall be in the English language.

6–350 6.25.6.3 The Appointor will train the Retailer's service and technical sales staff in accordance with an agreed training programme, free of charge to the Retailer, and in particular will explain and assist the Retailer to implement a system of warranty service for the Products in accordance with the policy laid down from time to time by the Principal.

6.25.6.4 The Appointor will provide the Retailer with further technical assistance and support by the issue of regular bulletins advising the Retailer of support service developments and technical advances. **6–351**

6.25.6.5 Technical channels of communication will be established so that the Retailer's staff can rapidly obtain technical advice and support from the Appointor. Such advice and support will be promptly provided by the Appointor to the Retailer free of charge. **6–352**

6.25.6.6 The Retailer undertakes to observe the technical instructions and operate the system of warranty service [and repair] for the Products as communicated to it under cl.6.25.6.3. **6–353**

6.25.6.7 The Appointor may fulfil its obligations to the Retailer under this clause either itself or through third parties appointed by it for this purpose. **6–354**

This clause allows the distributor to pass on as necessary to the retailer the warranty service and repair obligations imposed on the distributor by the principal, and obliges the retailer to observe them. Clause 6.25.6.7 covers the situation where the retailer is appointed by the principal and the principal passes on training obligations to the distributor rather than fulfilling them direct.

6.25.7 Assignment

See cl.4.19. **6–355**

6.25.8 Death of retailer

6.25.8 This Agreement shall terminate automatically upon the death of the Retailer (where the Retailer is a natural person) or upon the death of one of the partners in the Retailer (where the Retailer is a partnership). A surviving partner spouse or adult child of the Retailer carrying on the Retailer's business shall however have the right to enter into an Agreement with the Appointor upon terms identical to this Agreement. **6–356**

This clause covers the likely situation of the retailer running as a sole proprietor or a partnership.

6.25.9 Commencement and term

6.25.10 Termination

6.25.11 Effect of termination

For the three cll.6.25.9 to 6.25.11 use cll.6.12, 6.13 and 6.14 replacing "Authorised Distributor" with "Retailer". **6–357**

6.25.12 General undertakings by retailer

6–358 These clauses can be reproduced from cl.6.5 replacing the term "Authorised Distributor" with the term "Retailer". They may be considered rather "heavy" for a retailer relationship and if so they can be tailored, reduced or omitted. In practice, except for the due diligence provision, they are unlikely to be commercially very important in the case of a retailer.

6.25.13 Industrial property rights

6–359 See cl.4.13. Again in most cases this clause could be omitted without much practical risk, where one is dealing with a retailer.

6.25.14 Confidentiality

6–360 A short form clause like cl.4.18 would be appropriate here.

6.25.15 Interpretation clauses and signature

6–361 The clauses in Chapter 1 should be selected as appropriate.

6.25.16 Schedule 1—the products

6.25.17 Schedule 2—the retailer requirements

6–362 These should be reproduced from cl.6.23.

6.26 Selective distribution in the motor vehicle sector

6–363 The Commission has always been particularly concerned with impediments to the creation of a free market within the EC for motor vehicles, caused by the varying technical specifications for such vehicles in different Member States, and the need to create an expensive and technically sophisticated network of dealers to supply and (more important) maintain them. Motor vehicles are usually the most expensive consumer durables purchased by consumers, and the most expensive purchase that most consumers ever make, with the exception of real property. For this reason, the motor vehicle sector has always received special attention from the Commission.

6–364 Apart from the various BMW cases already mentioned earlier in this chapter, reference should be made to the Commission's concern about obstacles to the sale of right-hand drive cars on the continent to UK purchasers. This was considered in the Decision *Re Ford Werke* [1983] O.J. L327/83 and again in the Commission Notice ([1985] 1 C.M.L.R. 481) concerning difficulties experienced by customers wishing to buy Alfa Romeo cars with right-hand drive.

The latter problem related particularly to delivery dates and availability and mainly concerned UK nationals buying in Belgium and Luxembourg. Following Commission intervention, Alfa Romeo circularised its distributors emphasising that obstacles to delivery must be avoided. Prices and delivery dates should take reasonable account of the specific costs and circumstances of supplying such vehicles. All contractual obligations concerning guarantee and after-sales service should be applicable to right-hand drive cars. Finally, where a customer did not buy personally a third party should be permitted to buy on his behalf with a signed authorisation and a copy of the customer's signed passport or identity card. **6–365**

The Commission regularised the situation with regard to selective distribution systems in the motor vehicle distribution and servicing trade by the block exemption under Reg.123/85 which embodied most of the principles it had developed over the previous 15 years or so in the area of selective distribution arrangements, adapted to the particular circumstances of this trade. It was renewed in 1995 by Reg.1475/95 which has now been replaced, upon its expiry, by the current Reg.1400/2002). **6–366**

Regulation 123/85 was intended to be the first of a series of block exemptions for selective distribution arrangements in different industries, but so far no others have been forthcoming, and the idea appears to have been dropped after the general attention to selective distribution agreements in the Block Exemption on Vertical Agreements (Reg.2790/99). **6–367**

Regulation 123/85 permitted the imposition by a manufacturer of restrictions preventing a dealer from selling vehicles or parts from another manufacturer, actively seeking business outside his territory, subcontracting distribution servicing or repairs without consent, and selling new vehicles or spares to dealers outside the network. **6–368**

However, the system could not be so restrictive that dealers became so dependent upon the manufacturer that their freedom to compete was impaired. Spare parts supplied by third parties, provided they were of the same quality as the manufacturer's official spare parts, could also be sold by dealers within the network. The manufacturer's warranty must permit warranty service to be given in any Member State of the EC, regardless of in which state the car was purchased. Finally, consumers must be able to order cars with the specifications required for the state where they are to be registered from any dealer within the network in any other Member State. **6–369**

One of the first Decisions under this regulation was *Re Automobiles Peugeot SA* [1986] O.J. L295. Peugeot had notified to the Commission a reasonably standard type of selective distribution network, but its theoretically beneficial aspects for consumers were outweighed in the Commission's view, by Peugeot limiting the sale of right hand drive vehicles in such a way that dealers in left hand drive Member States could not satisfy orders for new cars with right hand drive from customers in other Member States. **6–370**

In effect this prevented British customers purchasing from dealers in continental Europe. The Peugeot arrangements were refused exemption, and held not to come under the regulation until these restrictions were removed.

6–371 In Case C-3232/93P *Automobiles Peugeot SA v Commission* [1994] E.C.R. I–2727) the Court upheld the decision of the Court of First Instance and of the Commission, (Commission Decision [1992] O.J. L66), that a company which carries on the business of acting on behalf of consumers in the purchase of motor vehicles from a manufacturer or his authorised dealers is to be regarded as an agent or intermediary for the purposes of Reg.123/85. The regulation permitted, *inter alia*, individual consumers to purchase a new vehicle in a Member State other than their own, and to use the services of a purchasing agent to help them do this (see Art.3(11) of the regulation). Eco System SA supplied such services as a purchasing agent (or "intermediary" as it is called in the regulation) on a professional basis for all comers, and advertised and promoted its activities widely.

6–372 Peugeot refused to supply Eco System SA, told its authorised dealers not to do so either, and sought to distinguish Eco System on a number of grounds from an intermediary within the meaning of Art.3(11), and to characterise it as an independent contractor. This would have meant that it would have been justified in refusing to supply cars to Eco System under the regulation because it would then have been an unauthorised dealer. Peugeot first contested that Eco System bore the risks that the customer would withdraw from the sale and leave the car on Eco System's hands, the risk of damage while the car was in storage, the risk of the customer not being able to pay for the car and the exchange rate risk. The Commission rejected this on the grounds that the car never belonged to Eco System but always to its customer and that none of the risks mentioned were borne by Eco System as an inherent part of the transactions, since they could only occur by accident and not as the normal consequence of the transaction taking place as planned. In any event such risks could only arise, if at all, for a short period between collection of a vehicle by Eco System and delivery to the customer. Peugeot also suggested Eco System obtained discounts and other benefits from dealers which it did not pass on to customer, and thus was trading in its own right. The Commission held that this was factually incorrect. Eco System accounted for such matters strictly to the customer and was remunerated only by way of commission on the net purchase of the car. Finally, Peugeot claimed the scale of Eco System's activities and its promotional activities were inconsistent with an intermediary. The Commission rejected this contention, since Eco System undertook each transaction on the basis of a proper authorisation from the would-be purchaser, and was free to promote itself to the extent it thought appropriate provided this was through legal means.

6–373 The European Court of Justice concluded "It had to be recognised that the exercise on a professional basis of the activity of intermediary could involve promotion to the public, the possibility of concentrating efforts on certain brands of vehicles, and furthermore the acceptance of risks inherent in any *undertaking* offering services. That was the case with Eco System;

after a thorough analysis of its activity ... [it] could not be regarded as assuming any legal or economic risk characteristic of the activity of purchase and sale but on the contrary had to be regarded as acting in the capacity of a duly authorised intermediary".

Later cases on the regulation attempted to use it as a sword rather than a shield. Authorised distributors of certain makes of motor vehicles applied to the French courts to complain of the activities of unauthorised dealers who had imported the same makes of motor vehicles into France on the grey market and were selling them in competition with the authorised distributors. They asked the French courts to rule that since their authorised selective distribution networks were protected by the regulation, and the grey market resellers were acting as distributors of the relevant products without authorisation, the Regulation would apply to prevent grey market activity of the kind complained of. The French courts referred the matter to the European Court which, not surprisingly, ruled that block exemptions deal with "the relations between suppliers and their approved distributors" and confined themselves to "stating what the parties to such agreements may or may not undertake" but do not "seek to regulate the activities of third parties themselves who operate in the market outside the framework of distribution agreements" (see Case C-226/94 *Grand Garage Albigeois SA v Garage Massol SARL* ([1996] E.C.R. I-651); Case C-309/94 *Nissan France SA v Dupasquier* [1996] C.E.C. 503; Case C-128/95 *Fontaine SA v Aqueducs Automobiles SARL* ([1997] 5 C.M.L.R. 39); Case C-41/96 *AG-Handlerbeirat eV v SYD-Consult* [1997] C.E.C. 1226 is based partly on the application of these principles, but this time in Germany) **6–374**

Other cases in which the Commission considered the Regulation, and which are discussed in this chapter are the Commission Decision *Ford New Holland Ltd*, and the European Court decisions in *BMW v Commission* and *Bundeskartellamt v Volkswagen AG/VAG Leasing GmbH*. **6–375**

The previous block exemptions covering the motor vehicle sector (Reg.123/85 and Reg.1475/95) largely failed in their purpose, in that consumers have not enjoyed a fair share of the alleged efficiencies generated by the restraints exempted under the regulations. This is largely because the cumulative effect of the many distribution networks covering the sector have led to a significant reduction in both intra-brand and inter-brand competition. Part of the problem was also caused by the fact that the previous regulations allowed a combination of selective and exclusive distribution arrangements with territorial limitations on active sales outside allocated territories which, in effect, created a type of exclusive customer allocation (including a prohibition on setting up branches or operations outside the territory—the "location clause"). As the Commission stated in the Guidelines on Vertical Restraints para.179: "A combination of exclusive customer allocation and selective distribution is normally hardcore, as active selling to end-users by the appointed distributor is usually not left free". **6–376**

The new regulation (Reg.1400/2002) aims to increase competition in the sale of new vehicles at all levels of distribution, but also in vehicle servicing and repair. Given the observed anticompetitive effects of the current dis- **6–377** tribution networks in the motor vehicle sector, the Commission felt that exemption under Reg.2790/99 would still allow the possibility of too great restraints on competition in this sector, and so considered it appropriate to continue to apply a specific block exemption which, while more flexible than the previous regulations, also contained stricter conditions for exemption than those contained in Reg.2790/99.

6–378 Regulation 1400/2002 is based on the same principles as Reg.2790/99. Unlike Reg.123/85 and Reg.1475/95, it does not prescribe a rigid model for motor vehicle distribution with which the parties must comply in order to enjoy exemption. Instead it leaves a wide amount of choice, so that, provided the basic conditions for the application of the regulation are met, and no hardcore restrictions are present, many different business models could enjoy exemption. However, despite this flexibility, the regulation is much stricter than the previous ones when it comes to ensuring effective competition.

6–379 Article 2 of the regulation is broadly similar to Art.2 of Reg.2790/99 except that the exemption covers "vertical agreements where they relate to the conditions under which the parties may purchase, sell or resell new motor vehicles, spare parts for motor vehicles or repair and maintenance services for motor vehicles". Article 1(n) defines "motor vehicle" as "a self propelled vehicle intended for use on public roads and having three or more wheels". Thus the regulation does not cover agricultural or construction vehicles such as tractors, bulldozers or excavators; nor does it cover two wheeled vehicles such as motor cycles. Distribution arrangements relating to these vehicles would be covered by Reg.2790/99.

6–380 Article 3.1 provides that the exemption in Art.2 shall apply subject to certain market share tests (as in the case of Reg.2790/99). In general the exemption applies where the supplier's market share on the relevant market does not exceed 30 per cent. However, if the supplier operates a quantitative selective distribution system for the sale of new motor vehicles, the market share threshold in respect of that system is increased to 40 per cent. Where the supplier operates only a qualitative distribution system (whether for new motor vehicles, spare parts for motor vehicles or repair and maintenance services) then no threshold applies at all.

6–381 Article 1(f) defines a selective distribution system in the same way as Art.1(d) of Reg.2790/99, but adds a proviso that no selective distribution system will fall within the definition and hence be covered by the regulation and enjoy the benefit of exemption unless restrictions on supply to unauthorised dealers do not prevent (a) the distributors or repairers in the system having the "ability to sell spare parts to independent repairers" (see Art.4.1(i)) and (b) the supplier from fulfilling his obligation to provide independent operators with all technical information, diagnostic equipment, tools and training required for the repair and maintenance of motor vehicles or for the implementation of environmental protection measures". (see Art.4.2).

6–382 Article 1(g) defines a quantitative selective distribution system as one "where the supplier uses criteria for the selection of distributors or repairers which directly limit their number". Article 1(h) defines a qualitative distribution system as one "where the supplier uses criteria for the selection of distributors or repairers which are only qualitative in nature, are required by the nature of the contract goods or services, are laid down uniformly for all distributors or repairers applying to join the system, are not applied in a discriminatory manner, and do not directly limit the number of distributors or repairers". These definitions are the same as those applied by the Commission to general selective distribution systems. Thus the quantitative system includes not only quota systems but also the so-called subjective qualitative criteria, such as requiring minimum or maximum sales. The qualitative system is limited to the so-called purely qualitative or objective qualitative criteria (see the discussion under the section relating to Sch.2 Pt 2 above and para.185 of the Guidelines on Vertical Restraints).

Article 3.2 contains the 30 per cent market share test for the buyer in relation to exclusive supply agreements, in the same way as Reg.2790/99. **6–383**

The rest of Art.3 contains certain provisions which the relevant agreement must contain if it is to qualify for exemption under the regulation. First, any agreement concluded with a distributor or repairer must be freely transferable to another distributor or repairer within the system (Art.3.3). This allows distributors or repairers to buy and sell their businesses freely without the requirement for consent from the supplier. The hope is that larger distribution or repair organisations (operating across borders) will arise, which can act as a counterbalance to the power of the manufacturers. **6–384**

Each agreement concluded with a distributor or repairer must only be terminable by notice in writing giving "detailed, objective and transparent reasons for the termination" (Art.3.4). Each such agreement must either be for a fixed term of at least five years, with a provision that either party must give at least six months prior notice of an intention not to renew, or be for an indefinite period with a provision normally requiring two years' notice of termination by either side which is reduced to at least one year, where the supplier is obliged to pay "appropriate" compensation on termination or where the termination is necessary to reorganise the whole or a substantial part of the network (Art.3.5) The purpose of this provision is to prevent discriminatory terminations, or the threat of them, as a weapon to enforce anticompetitive practices. This is a similar approach to that taken by the Commission in its Decisions *Re Saba (No.2)* and *Re Grundig* (see the discussion and the precedent in Chapter 6.13). **6–385**

Article 3.6 provides that each party (without prejudice to their right of resort to court) shall have the right to submit disputes concerning fulfilment of contractual obligations to an independent expert or arbitrator. The disputes covered are: supply obligations, setting or attainment of sales targets, implementation of stock requirements, implementation of an obligation to provide or use demonstration vehicles, conditions for the sale of different brands, the issue whether the prohibition to operate out of an unauthorised place of establishment limits the ability of the distributor of motor vehicles other than passenger cars or light commercial vehicles to expand its business, whether termination of an agreement is justified by the reasons given in **6–386** the notice. Similar provisions, but only in relation to termination, were approved by the Commission in the Decisions *Re Saba (No.2)* and *Re Grundig* (see the discussion and the precedent in Chapter 6.13).

6–387 Article 4 lists the relevant hardcore restrictions. These are similar to Art.4 of Reg.2790/99 but rather stricter. Article 4.1(a) deals with resale price maintenance in the same terms as Reg.2790/99 Art.4(a) (see Chapter 5.9.1). Art 4.1(b) deals with restrictions on the territories in which or the customers to whom the distributor or repairer may sell. This is broadly similar to Art.4(b) of Reg.2790/99 except that the prohibition on authorised members of a selective distribution system selling to unauthorised distributors cannot apply to the sale of spare parts to independent repairers who use them for the repair and maintenance of a motor vehicle. The prohibition of the restriction on cross-supplies within a selective distribution system under Art.4.1(c) is the same as Art.4(d) of Reg.2790/99. The prohibition of the restriction on active or passive sales by retailers in a selective distribution system in Art.4(c) of Reg.2790/99 is mirrored in Art.4.1(d) and (e) of the regulation, but is much expanded (see the discussion of these issues in relation to general selective distribution agreements in Chapter 6.7).

6–388 In the case of retailers within a selective distribution system covered by Reg.1400/2002, retailers must be free to sell new passenger cars or light commercial vehicles (as defined in Art.1(o) and (p)) and spare parts for any motor vehicle or repair and maintenance services for any motor vehicle to any end user, with no restriction on active or passive sales. However, a restriction on sales from an unauthorised place of establishment is permitted, subject to Art.5.2(b) which excludes from the benefit of the regulation any obligation which directly or indirectly limits the retailer's ability to establish additional sales or delivery outlets for passenger cars or light commercial vehicles at other locations within the EC where selective distribution is applied. This last proviso effectively excludes the location clause discussed above from the benefit of the exemption, in respect of the specific activities to which it relates, although it does not come into effectuntil October 1, 2005 (see Art.5(2)(b) and Art 12.2)). So far as sales of new motor vehicles other than passenger cars or light commercial vehicles are concerned, there is the same prohibition on restrictions of active or passive selling to end users, but here the supplier may prohibit sale from an unauthorised place of establishment and in this case there is no proviso relating to location clauses, as Art.5(2)(b) only applies to passenger cars and light commercial vehicles. Thus the location clause is preserved for the sale of motor vehicles not falling within these two categories.

6–389 It can be seen that, so far, the regulation has given suppliers considerable flexibility, in that they can either set up an exclusive distribution network where dealers are allocated a given territory and are free to sell to operators that are not members of the official network, or a selective distribution network where dealers are not allocated a sales territory and are not free to sell to unauthorised operators. If a selective system is chosen the manufacturer may apply a combination of qualitative and quantitative criteria (subject to market share) or he may select dealers according to purely qualitative criteria, with no ceiling on the number of dealers (not subject to market share). In all selective distribution networks the manufacturer can prohibit sales other than to members of the network and to end users.

So far the regulation, with some necessary adaptation, has imposed a choice of regimes very similar to those available under Reg.2790/99. However, Art.4 also imposes a number specific prohibitions on hardcore restrictions designed to deal with specific anticompetitive practices in the motor vehicle sector. **6–390**

Hardcore restrictions on the distributor only concerning the sale of new motor vehicles are as follows: **6–391**

- Restrictions on the right to sell any new motor vehicle corresponding to a model within the contract range (Art.4.1(f)).
- Restrictions on the right to subcontract repair and maintenance services to authorised repairers, without prejudice to the supplier's ability to require the distributor (before sale) to disclose the name and address of the subcontractor, and its distance from the sales outlet, to prospective purchasers, provided the supplier also imposes such obligations on dealers whose repair facilities are not on the same premises as their sales outlet (Art.4.1(g)).

Previously suppliers were able to oblige dealers to provide maintenance and repair services as opposed to subcontracting them. The proviso to this provision is to deal with the argument from suppliers that dealers may subcontract to distant repairers which will cause buyers of their vehicles inconvenience. **6–392**

There are then a number of hardcore restrictions only concerning the sale of repair and maintenance services and spare parts: **6–393**

- Restrictions on the authorised repairer's ability to limit its activities to repair and maintenance and distribution of spare parts (previously suppliers could require authorised repairers to sell new vehicles as well) (Art.4.1(h)).
- Restrictions on the sale of spare parts by members of a selective distribution system to independent repairers (Art.4.1(i)).
- Restriction agreed between a supplier, of original spare parts or spare parts of matching quality, or of repair tools, diagnostic or other equipment, and a manufacturer of motor vehicles limiting the supplier's ability to sell these goods or services to authorised or independent distributors or authorised or independent repairers or end users (Art.4.1(j)).
- Restrictions on a distributor's or authorised repairer's ability to acquire original spare parts or spare parts of matching quality from third parties of its choice and to use them for repair or maintenance of motor vehicles, without prejudice to the ability of a supplier of new

motor vehicles to require the use of original spare parts supplied by it for warranty, free servicing and vehicle recall work (Art.4.1(k)).

- Restriction agreed between a manufacturer of motor vehicles and a supplier of components used in initial assembly of motor vehicles preventing the supplier placing its trade mark or logo effectively and in an easily visible manner on the components supplied or on spare parts.

6–394 It can be seen that the prohibition of these restrictions is designed to make it easy for independent repairers and third party spare part manufacturers to compete, in the market for repair and maintenance services and the supply of spare parts, with the traditional authorised dealers and authorised repairers. The Commission states that the cost of repair and maintenance is in many cases as high as the purchase price of a new vehicle. While this may be an exaggeration for effect, it is true that in many cases the margins on repair and maintenance are much higher than on the sale of new vehicles, and thus offer an opportunity for reduction through competition.

6–395 It is also important that independent repairers or distributors of spare parts are truly able to compete effectively. They must therefore be given proper access to technical information, diagnostic and other equipment, and tools, including any relevant software, and training required for the repair and maintenance of the relevant manufacturer's motor vehicles. The exemption under the regulation therefore does not apply to any agreements of a manufacturer who refuses or hinders such access (Art.4.2). In particular if the relevant item is covered by an intellectual property right or constitutes knowhow, access shall not be withheld in any abusive manner (*cf. Volvo AB v Erik Veng (UK) Ltd* and *Consorzio Italiano Delia Componentistica Di Ricambio Per Autoveicoli and Maxicar v Regie Nationale Des Usines Renault*).

6–396 Article 5 covers (like Art.5 of Reg.2790/99) certain specific obligations which are not exempted under the regulation. As with Reg.2790/99, the rest of the agreement can take advantage of the regulation and the parties must then consider whether to drop the particular clause or whether it can take advantage of exemption under Art.81(3) in the special circumstances of the case in question.

6–397 Article 5.1(a) provides that as regards the sale of new motor vehicles, repair and maintenance services or spare parts, the exemption does not apply to any direct or indirect non-compete obligation. The definition of a non-compete obligation and the way this prohibition operates is broadly the same as the equivalent provisions under Art.1(b) and 5(a) of Reg.2790/99 (see the general discussion in Chapter 5.3.6). There are, however, three important differences.

6–398 First, Art.1(b) of the regulation defines "non-compete obligation" so that it excludes an obligation that the distributor be obliged to sell motor vehicles from other suppliers in separate areas of the showroom in order to avoid confusion between the makes. Thus an obligation to provide "brand-specific" areas in the showroom (but not separate premises) is exempt under the regulation. The definition in Art.1(b) also excludes an obligation that the distributor have brand-specific sales personnel for different brands of motor vehicles, but in this instance, only if the distributor decides to have brand-specific personnel and the supplier pays all the additional costs involved.

The second difference is that the quantity forcing provision is set at 30 per cent of the dealer's turnover rather than 80 per cent. Thirdly, there is no special treatment for a non-compete obligation for a fixed term of up to five years. The result is that any non-compete obligation of any length must be considered directly under Art.81(3) on the special circumstances of the case in question. **6–399**

Article 5.1(b) provides that the exemption under the regulation does not apply to any direct or indirect obligation limiting the ability of an authorised repairer to repair and maintain vehicles from competing suppliers. This provision again promotes competition on the repair market. **6–400**

Art 5.1(c) provides that the exemption under the regulation does not apply to any direct or indirect obligation causing members of a distribution system not to sell motor vehicles or spare parts of particular competing suppliers or not to maintain motor vehicles of particular competing suppliers. This provision is analogous to Art.5(c) of Reg.2790/99 and deals with the issue of boycotting certain suppliers (see Chapter 6.5.5). **6–401**

Article 5.1(d) excludes any post-termination non-compete obligation from exemption under the regulation. This is unlike Art.5(b) of Reg.2790/99 where at least a one year obligation is permitted if required to protect knowhow. One would have considered that the protection of knowhow is probably more important under arrangements for the distribution repair and maintenance of motor vehicles (see Art.4.2 of the regulation in particular), but at least there is nothing in the regulation which prohibits the protection of knowhow under suitable confidentiality obligations.) **6–402**

Article 5.2(a) provides that there is no exemption under the regulation for any direct or indirect obligation causing a retailer not to sell leasing services relating to the contract goods or to corresponding goods. This is to prevent the manufacturers requiring the use of their own tied leasing companies, and also to prevent them prohibiting the retailer from offering leasing services for competing products. **6–403**

Article 5.2(b) excludes the location clause from the exemption so far as regards passenger cars and light commercial vehicles. However, the fact that the provision is located in art 5 does mean that it would be possible, in theory, to justify the imposition of this obligation under Art.81(3) in the special circumstances of any particular case. In any event it should be remembered that this provision does not come into force until October 1, 2005 (Art.12.2) so that both existing and new location clauses for the distribution of passenger cars and light commercial vehicles will be able to take advantage of exemption under the regulation until that date. **6–404**

Article 5.3 provides that as regards repair and maintenance or the sale of spare parts, the regulation grants no exemption to any direct or indirect obligation as to the place of establishment of an authorised repairer in a selective distribution system. This means that there is no longer any **6–405** exemption under the regulation for location clauses relating to the activities of repair and maintenance and the supply of spare parts. Unlike Art.5.2, this provision came in with immediate effect from October 1, 2002. Again, such a clause, not being a hardcore restriction does not prevent the rest of the agreement from benefiting from exemption under the regulation, and the clause itself could, in appropriate cases be considered for exemption under Art.81(3).

6–406 Articles 6 and 7 contain withdrawal and non-application provisions similar in principle to Arts 6, 7 and 8 of Reg.2790/99. The only difference is that the grounds for withdrawal under Art.6 of the regulation are more specific and designed to deal with what the Commission sees as particular anticompetitive issues in the motor vehicle sector. Thus withdrawal can occur not only on the general ground of effects incompatible with Art.81(3) but in particular:

- where access to relevant markets or competition therein is significantly restricted by the cumulative effect of parallel networks of vertical restraints set up by competing suppliers or buyers, or
- where competition is restricted on a market where one supplier is not exposed to effective competition from other suppliers, or
- where prices or conditions for supply differ substantially between geographic markets, or
- where discriminatory prices or sales conditions are applied within a geographic market.

6–407 Finally, Arts 8 and 9 cover the guidelines for calculation of market share and turnover respectively, and do not differ substantially from Arts 9 and 10 of Reg.2790/99. Article 11 obliges the Commission to monitor the operation of the regulation (with particular regard to its effect on competition in motor vehicle retailing and after sales servicing and the structure and concentration of motor vehicle distribution and any resulting effect on competition) and to draw up a report by May 31, 2008. Article 12 provides that the regulation enters into force on October 1, 2002 and expires on May 31, 2010 (the same date as Reg.2790/99 so that renewal for both regulations can be reviewed together). Article 10 provides for a transitional period to September 30, 2003 for agreements in force on October 1, 2002 which were exempt under Reg.1475/95.

6.27 Franchise agreements

6–408 Finally, note should be taken of developments in the field of franchise agreements. It is not within the scope of this book to deal with franchise agreements, but the law on the subject somewhat resembles that relating to selective distribution agreements, and is also helpful in this area in that the position of the franchisee is almost analogous to that of the authorised retailer in a selective distribution system. Some note should therefore be taken of the relevant law.

Franchising is subject to the ordinary rules of competition law under Art.81, but in Case 161/84 *Pronuptia de Paris GmbH v Pronuptia de Paris Irmgard Schillgalis* [1986] 1 C.M.L.R. 414) the European Court stated, rather along the lines of the selective distribution cases, that franchise agreements are not themselves illegal under Art.81, but that their status depends upon the individual circumstances and provisions of each arrangement. **6–409**

Under the arrangements Pronuptia (the franchisor) granted to Mrs Schillgalis (the franchisee) a franchise granting the exclusive right to use the "Pronuptia de Paris" trade name for sales and advertising purposes, undertook to open no other Pronuptia shops in the franchisee's area, and undertook to assist and train the franchisee and her staff to set up and run her business and advertise in accordance with Pronuptia standards methods and techniques. In return the franchisee undertook to buy 80 per cent of her wedding dresses and a percentage of other dresses, to be agreed, from the franchisor, and the balance exclusively from approved suppliers, to pay an entry fee and a royalty on turnover, consider the franchisor's recommended prices without obligation to follow them, to advertise only with the franchisor's approval, to set as the principal objective of the business the sale of wedding dresses, not to compete with Pronuptia shops and not to open another competing shop herself, and not to assign the franchise without consent. **6–410**

The proceedings arose from a claim by Pronuptia for arrears of royalty which the franchisee met by a claim that the agreement was void as it contravened Art.81(1). Various arguments were put forward before the national courts in support of this, and the matter was referred to the European Court for a preliminary decision. **6–411**

The Court noted that this was the first time it had ruled on a franchise contract. It distinguished three main types of franchise: **6–412**

> "Contracts for the franchising of services by virtue of which a franchisee offers a service under the trade name, trade mark and brand name of the franchisor and in the manner provided for by him, and complies with the latter's instructions; contracts for the franchising of production by virtue of which the franchisee himself manufactures products according to the instructions of the franchisor, which he then sells under the latter's brand name; and finally franchise contracts in respect of distribution by virtue of which the franchisee merely sells certain products in a shop which carries the franchisor's name."

The Court did not rule on the third type of franchise, but considered and advised on the first two types only. It seems that by this third type of franchise the Court intended to refer to franchises where the franchisor sold no goods to the franchisee, and the franchisee obtained the goods to be sold **6–413** from some other source. The Pronuptia arrangement would thus fall under the first type of franchise agreement mentioned by the Court. The Court then, rather confusingly, in the rest of the judgment, refers to the first two types of franchise agreement collectively as "franchise agreements for distribution" or "franchise agreements for the distribution of goods".

6–414 The Court distinguished franchise contracts in respect of distribution from those contracts conferring a sales concession or those linking dealers in a selective distribution network since the latter two do not involve use of the same name, application of uniform commercial methods or the payment of a licence fee in consideration of the advantages accorded.

6–415 Similarly Reg.83/83 (then 67/67) could not apply to such franchise agreements,

> "since the category of agreements covered by the regulation is defined with reference to obligations to deliver and purchase and not in regard to factors such as use of the same brand name, application of uniform commercial methods and payment of a licence fee ... which are the characteristics of franchise contracts in respect of distribution."

6–416 In any case obligations other than those permitted by the regulation were imposed both on the franchisor and the franchisee.

6–417 The Court held that:

> "the compatibility of franchise agreements for the distribution of goods with Article 81(1) depends on the provisions contained therein and their economic context;
>
> provisions which are strictly necessary in order to ensure that knowhow and assistance provided by the franchisor do not benefit competitors do not constitute restrictions of competition for the purposes of Article 81(1);
>
> provisions which establish the control strictly necessary for maintaining the identity and reputation of the network identified by the common name or sign do not constitute restrictions of competition for the purposes of Art 81(1);
>
> provisions which share markets between the franchisor and the franchisee constitute restrictions of competition for the purposes of Art 81(1);
>
> the fact that the franchisor makes price recommendations to the franchisee does not constitute a restriction on competition so long as there is no concerted practice between the franchisor and the franchisees or between the franchisees themselves for the actual application of such prices; and
>
> franchise agreements for the distribution of goods which contain provisions sharing markets between the franchisor and the franchisees or between franchisees are capable of affecting trade between Member States."

6–418 A series of further Decisions by the Commission on franchising followed, based on this judgment—*Re Pronuptia* [1987] O.J. L13, *Re Yves Rocher*

[1987] O.J. L8, *Re Computerland Europe* [1987] O.J. L222, *Re Servicemaster* [1989] 4 C.M.L.R. 581 and *Re Charles Jourdan* [1989] O.J. L35.

The Commission, with the above experience was able to formulate a block exemption for franchise agreements relating to distribution and service franchises (Reg.4087/88). The Regulation came into force on February 1, 1989. Broadly, it permitted the grant of franchises exclusive to a particular territory and restrictions on the franchisee to exploit the franchise only from his contract premises, not to canvass actively for business outside the franchise territory and not to sell competing goods. Obligations of an objective nature to ensure the quality of the franchisee's provision of goods or services could be imposed as well as obligations of confidentiality and other restrictions to protect the franchisor's trade secrets and intellectual property rights. **6–419**

The regulation has now been superseded by Reg.2970/99, although that regulation now provides very little specific provisions relating to franchises. The most pertinent is Art.2.3 which provides for the licence or assignment of intellectual property rights to the buyer provided that those provisions do not constitute the primary object of such agreements and are directly related to the sale or resale of goods or services by the buyer or its customers. This clearly covers franchises, including soft drink bottling franchises where the franchisor supplies concentrated extract for the buyer to dilute and bottle (see para.35 of the Guidelines on Vertical Restraints). Franchises which are primarily concerned with the licensing of intellectual property rights and knowhow as opposed to the supply of goods and services are not covered by the Regulation, but para.43 of the Guidelines on Vertical Restraints states they will be treated in a similar way to those franchise agreements which are covered by the regulation (some discussion of these different types of franchise agreements can be found in Chapter 8.1). Article 5(b), providing for a limited post-termination non-compete obligation if necessary to protect knowhow, is also relevant to franchises. **6–420**

This approach is made possible because most of the provisions commonly included in franchise agreements as discussed above are either not caught by Art.81 at all (basically in relation to the protection of knowhow) or are all permitted by the regulation as non-hardcore restrictions. **6–421**

The Guidelines on Vertical Restraints discuss franchising agreements in paras 43 to 44 and paras 199 to 201, and provide a useful summary of the previous case law and the current Commission thinking. **6–422**

Paragraph 44 of the Guidelines lists obligations which are considered necessary to protect the franchisor's intellectual property rights: **6–423**

- not to engage, directly or indirectly, in any similar business;
- not to invest in a competing undertaking to an extent which gives the franchisee power to influence its economic conduct;
- not to disclose knowhow not in the public domain to third parties;
- to communicate experience gained in exploiting the franchise and

grant the franchisor and other franchisees a non-exclusive licence to use the relevant knowhow;

- to inform the franchisor of infringements of licensed intellectual property rights and assist him in any legal action against the infringers;
- not to use licensed knowhow for purposes other than exploiting the franchise;
- not to assign the franchise without the franchisor's consent.

6–424 So far as the other restraints on the franchisee are concerned, para.200 of the Guidelines states that:

> "As for the vertical restraints on the purchase, sale and resale of goods and services within a franchising agreement, such as selective distribution, non-compete or exclusive distribution, the Block Exemption Regulation applies up to the 30% market share threshold for the franchisor or the supplier designated by the franchisor. The guidance provided earlier in respect of these types of restraints applies also to franchising subject to the following specific remarks:
>
> 1) . . . the more important the transfer of knowhow, the more easily the vertical restraints fulfil the requirement for exemption
> 2) A non-compete obligation on the goods or services purchased by the franchisee falls outside Art 81(1) when the obligation is necessary to maintain the common identity and reputation of the franchised network. In such cases, the duration of the non-compete obligation is also irrelevant under Art 81(1), as long as it does not exceed the duration of the franchise agreement itself."

Chapter 7

Manufacturing Agreements Outside the EC

Contents

7.1 Commercial and legal background

This chapter looks at the way in which rights and obligations to manu- **7–01**
facture products can be linked into and form part of a distribution agree-

ment. If looked at in terms of the extent to which the principal can distance himself from the operation relating to his products in a particular territory, this type of relationship is the farthest that he can move from his initial position of running a local operation himself, through a branch or subsidiary company. Now he has delegated not only representation and marketing (an agency arrangement) and the risk in the sale of products in the territory (a distribution arrangement) but also their manufacture as well.

7–02 It should be stressed that this chapter is not primarily concerned with the licensing of technologically complex products where the more detailed provisions of full-length licensing agreements are perhaps more appropriate, since the transaction can be considered on its own merits separately from distribution arrangements. The precedents here have developed in an evolutionary mode from an original distribution agreement (where relatively simple consumer products have been distributed for some years, on the basis of purchase of fully finished ready-packaged product obtained from the principal), in response to pressures both from the distributor and from the market place for a greater participation by the distributor in the operations of the principal, particularly in the area of manufacture.

7–03 As a rule of thumb, the income that a principal derives from a distribution agreement covering the simple sort of consumer products is likely to be more (per unit of product) than that from a licensing agreement. This is normally the case even when taking into account the additional direct costs that the principal incurs by manufacturing these products. With products of this type, which can be sold both on the home and (without much adaptation) on the export market as well, his export sales are regarded as an additional volume of marginal business which, apart from any net profit that he actually receives from them, in fact gives him a contribution, that he would not otherwise receive, towards the fixed overheads that he has to bear (irrespective of whether he makes exports or not) in order to service his home market. For a principal in this position, exports can either provide a useful means of overhead recovery (if he has to export at lower prices than those prevailing in his home market in order to meet international competition) or, if prices are firm, (so that he can sell at the same levels as in his home market), a very high margin of gross profit providing both overhead recovery and good net profit levels as well.

7–04 Thus, in these cases, the principal is unlikely to want to change from the position of servicing the export market by manufacturing the products himself, and selling them locally through a distributor, unless some outside factors force him to do so. So far as the distributor is concerned, he may well have the desire to take a greater part of the gross margin on the products, so that he is willing to undertake the costs and risks of manufacture himself, to avoid having, as it were, to subsidise, by the level of his buying price, the principal's fixed overheads on his home market business. Alternatively, he may feel that local manufacture will enable him to sell more cheaply, which will give him a greater volume, and economies of scale, which in the end will return him a higher net profit overall.

7–05 The pressure for this change in favour of the distributor is likely to come once the distributor has sold well and become established in the market for a number of years, so that he not only has the resources and capital to take on the investment of setting up in manufacture, but also has sufficient goodwill and local knowledge of the territory, that the principal cannot afford to stop dealing with him, even on a less profitable basis. Once this situation arises, the distributor is thus in a strong position to dictate the terms of their future relationship.

Market forces also influence the decision as to whether or not to manufacture locally. In many countries, particularly, but by no means exclusively, developing countries, an imported product will often carry a premium price, compared with an identical product manufactured locally by a licensee, because consumers are prepared to pay more for what they regard (rightly or wrongly) as a superior quality of product, perhaps from a country that has an international reputation for the manufacture of that class of goods (such as Italian shoes, or French perfumes). A local licensee is thus often forced to put his locally manufactured version on the market cheaper than competing imported products in order to get a reasonable share of the market. It therefore requires fine judgment in each case for the principal dealing with this type of goods to decide whether exploitation of the product in the territory will best be achieved by taking a royalty on a greater volume of sales at a cheaper price, or continuing to receive a higher margin (but on lower volumes) from the sale price of the products he manufactures himself. **7–06**

On the other hand, in some countries, where labour costs are low, particularly where dealing with products that are labour rather than capital intensive, it may genuinely be possible to manufacture a product as good as or even better than that made by the principal himself, and at a lower cost, particularly if one takes into account the various subsidies and assistance which are often available in developing countries to encourage the formation of local manufacturing industries. In this case, particularly where the local manufacturer can exploit the good will attached to a particularly well-known trade mark, by affixing it to low-cost, locally made products, this may be the best way to maximise sales of the product in the territory. In this case both parties gain more by the arrangement and the principal is compensated for the lower margin generated through a royalty by taking it on the larger volume of sales thus created. **7–07**

In some cases, as electronic equipment manufacturers are now discovering, it may well pay to set up such operations not only to service a local market, but to provide a supply service for exports elsewhere as well, perhaps even for the principal to sell in his home territory. **7–08**

In some territories, government intervention in the market place also produces an effect on the arrangements between the distributor and the principal. In many countries, particularly developing ones, governmental bodies are of course aware of the economics involved in local manufacture as opposed to importation. Where they wish to tip the scales in favour of local manufacture they can do this easily enough by imposing a system of import licences and quotas to regulate, and in some cases to prohibit, the import of certain types of products. Alternatively high customs duties are **7–09** imposed, and sometimes even additional luxury taxes, upon certain classes of products as a means of discouraging their import. The reason for this is sometimes a desire to protect local manufacturers of similar products (this is often achieved by imposing tariff barriers on imported goods, to make them uncompetitive with local equivalents, rather than by outright bans). More often, however, it is motivated by the need to prevent the depletion of scarce foreign exchange reserves, required to pay for the importation of items vital to the country's development, on goods that are regarded as non-essential, or for which adequate substitutes can be obtained locally. In these situations the only way that certain products can make an impact on the market at all is by way of local manufacture, and the principal, and, indeed the distributor, have no choice but to agree to this mode of exploitation.

7–10 There is, finally, one situation in which the principal often desires to licence local manufacture, and this is where he has a product which has become obsolete in his home market, but which still has a potential in the export territory that he is dealing with. In this case he cannot justify the setting up or continuation of the manufacturing facilities in his own country, because of the low volume of sales that will result, particularly if he is located in a country where manufacturing costs are high. In this case, it pays him to license off the products that he no longer makes himself, since he is getting an income (even if the royalty is at a low level) from products which he can exploit in no other way. In most cases, there will be almost no costs that he will have to set against the royalty, except those of supervising the operation of the agreement and of the administration relating to the collection of the royalty. Even his initial research and development costs related to the product (if there were any) will presumably have long ago been recovered against sales made before the product ceased to be manufactured by him, or else written off. The only other cost associated with the transaction will be the initial costs of transferring the manufacturing information, helping the local manufacturer to set up his production facility, and training the local staff. This is usually recovered immediately by a lump sum payment from the local manufacturer at the start of the agreement. Once this has been made, the local manufacturer is often left to his own resources almost entirely, and connection with him, except for collection of the royalty, is minimal.

7–11 The precedent in this chapter concentrates upon the manufacture of consumable items like prepared foods and drinks, dietary products, cosmetics, over the counter pharmaceutical products, and products which, due to technical progress, are now regarded as based on obsolete or at the least obsolescent technology. The factor which most of these products have in common is that the technical information relating to them is very often purely knowhow covering matters such as formulae and manufacturing methods, for which there is no patent protection, or where the relevant patents have already expired. Another common factor is that for many of these products the trade mark under which they are sold, and the good will attached to it, is the most important piece of relevant industrial property, and the factor that really determines whether the product will sell successfully or not. This precedent is not concerned with EC law relating to the licensing of technology, nor does it deal with the impact of the new competition regime in the UK under the Competition Act 1998. Both of these matters are dealt with in detail in Chapter 8. Instead it attempts to set out provisions that are suitable for territories where neither of these regimes applies.

Of course, just as in the case of the precedent in Chapter 4, nothing discussed above would prevent a licensor based in one of the Member States, including the UK, from entering into an agreement in this form with a licensee outside the EU (subject to certain caveats around the possibility of reimportation of goods sold by the distributor into the EU – see the discussion in Chapter 5.5.2) and applying the national law of the relevant Member State as the governing law of the agreement. It should, however, be realised that, quite apart from EC law or the national law of a Member State of the EU (including the UK) on the subject, local transfer of technology laws has particular relevance to these agreements, and examples of this will also be given during the analysis of the precedent. No licence agreement should be contemplated for any territory, particularly a developing country, without considering the existence and possible impact of transfer of technology legislation on the arrangements. **7–12**

7.2 Licence

7.2 The Principal hereby grants the Licensee an [exclusive] [non-exclusive] licence to make and have made and/or distribute and sell the Products under the Trade Mark in the Territory during the continuance of this Agreement using for this purpose [the Patents] [and] [the Knowhow]. **7–13**

This clause is a simple licence grant, and the phrases in square brackets provide for the various alternatives possible, although such licences are usually granted on an exclusive basis, given that the licensee will not want to invest in the necessary set-up costs for local manufacture unless he can be assured of at least an initial period without competition from other licensees of the same technology.

7.3 Licensee's general undertakings

7.3.1 Due diligence

7.3.1 The Licensee shall during the continuance of this Agreement use its best endeavours to manufacture and market the Products and exploit the [Patents] [Knowhow] [Knowhow and the Patents] in accordance with the terms of this Agreement. **7–14**

This provision serves the same purpose as the rather longer obligations imposed on a distributor under cl.4.3.1.

7.3.2 No interference with sales of products

7–15 7.3.2 The Licensee shall not do anything that may prevent the sale or interfere with the development of sales of the Products in the Territory.

This provision mirrors cl.4.3.2, and serves the same purpose.

7.3.3 Conforming to local legislation

7–16 7.3.3 The Licensee will ensure that it conforms with all legislation rules regulations and statutory requirements existing in the Territory from time to time in relation to the manufacture marketing distribution and sales of the Products.

This is a similar provision to cl.4.3.3 and inserted for the same purpose, but adapted to include the fact of manufacture.

7.3.4 Proper storage of products

7–17 7.3.4 The Licensee undertakes to store the Products and ingredients raw materials and packaging therefor under conditions that will prevent deterioration and also where necessary and at the request of the Principal store particular items under special conditions and in accordance with special procedures such as may be appropriate to their requirements including without limitation the observation of proper rotation of stock for items used in the manufacture of the Products so that all such items are used in such manufacture before the expiry of the specified shelf-life or (if none) of the period during which it is reasonable to expect that they can be stored without deterioration. Where the Licensee is responsible for clearing items through customs and other import formalities into the Territory it shall exercise its best endeavours to ensure that such clearance is carried out as quickly as possible and that pending such clearance the items are stored as aforesaid. The Licensee agrees to allow the Principal or its authorised representative to inspect the Products and any other such items when in storage under the control of the Licensee from time to time upon reasonable notice.

This provision is similar to cl.4.3.4 but again adapted to include manufacture. This clause is particularly important where the licensee purchases special ingredients from the principal, and they must be stored and used under specified conditions and within specified time limits.

7.3.5 Targets

7–18 7.3.5 The Licensee undertakes to achieve targets in relation to the Products in accordance with Sch.2.

This provision is a usual one in most licence agreements, since it is in the interest of the licensor to ensure by some type of underpinning that the licensee will exploit the licensed products as vigorously as possible.

7.3.6 Non-competition clause

> 7.3.6 The Licensee undertakes during the continuance of this Agreement not to manufacture or sell in the Territory any goods competitive with the Products or be interested directly or indirectly in the importation into the Territory of any such goods without the Principal's prior written consent. This provision shall not apply to those goods (if any) listed in Sch.3. **7–19**

This is a normal type of provision to find in licensing agreements. However, it must be remembered that many local manufacturers have a variety of products in their portfolios some of which may compete with each other. Because of this fact, it is often necessary to compromise and to permit the manufacture of at least some specified competing products. These can be listed in Sch.3.

7.3.7 Patent and trade mark notices

> 7.3.7 The Licensee shall leave in position and not cover or erase any notices or other marks (including without limitation details of patents or notices that a trade mark design or copyright relating to the Products is owned by the Principal or a third party) which the Principal may place on or affix to the Products [to any component part of the Products, or] to any item relating to the Products or their packaging supplied by the Principal. **7–20**

This is a similar provision to cl.4.3.8 and serves a similar purpose. Since the principal may well be supplying some products in finished form or packaging material, or containers, this clause is still of potential use in a manufacturing situation. The phrase in square brackets could be used for mechanical or electrical products, for instance, where the principal supplies components to the licensee.

7.3.8 Indemnity

> 7.3.8 The Licensee undertakes that it will indemnify the Principal against all proceedings costs liabilities injury loss or damage arising out of the breach or negligent performance by the Licensee of the terms of this Agreement. The Licensee undertakes that it will maintain product liability insurance (in an amount and upon terms satisfactory to the licensor) in respect of all Products manufactured and sold by it. Upon demand the Licensee shall from time to time furnish the Licensor with evidence (satisfactory to the Licensor) of the existence and the extent of the coverage of such insurance. **7–21**

This provision is a general indemnity similar to cl.4.3.10. In addition it makes the Licensee responsible for product liability insurance for the products he manufactures. This is important, because in some jurisdictions, particularly if the damage is caused by defective design, formulation, or process instructions provided by the principal, or in respect of which the principal is required under the agreement to exercise some supervision, there could be a question of liability for the damage being traced back to him.

7–22 If it could be clearly established that the damage were caused solely by a neglect of the principal, the licensee would have a right of action against him, which, by subrogation, the licensee's insurers would exercise against the principal. This issue can be dealt with by getting the insurers to waive their subrogation rights. However, in practice, it is best dealt with by ensuring that the licensee has no right of action against the licensee in the first place. For instance, in this case, an exclusion clause should be inserted elsewhere in the agreement providing that the licensor has no liability to the licensee in the event that the licensed knowhow is incomplete or defective, and thus, when applied by the licensee, results in the manufacture of defective products (for examples see cll.6.24.8 and 6.24.9 and the disclaimers and warranties set out in cl.7.25.10). However, such a clause would have to be notified to and accepted by the licensee's product liability insurers, because it is a waiver of the rights which the licensee would otherwise have at law against the licensor. For the insurers, acceptance of such a clause is tantamount to a waiver of their subrogation rights under the policy.

7–23 Even in the absence of clauses dealing with subrogation rights in one way or another, in most instances, unless there is the clearest evidence of fault on the part of the principal, the insurers are likely to settle the claim rather than attempt difficult and expensive litigation against the principal, who will often not reside in the same country as the insurers in any case.

7.4 Enquiries

7–24 7.4 The Principal shall during the continuance of this Agreement refer all enquiries received by it for sale of the Products in the Territory to the Licensee. The Licensee shall during the continuance of this Agreement refer to the Principal all enquiries it receives for the Products for sale outside or export from the Territory [other than in the case of Products sold within the Territory as ship's or aircraft's stores for use sale or consumption on such ship or aircraft outside the Territory or for ultimate sale in a duty-free shop in the Territory].

This is the standard clause for use when the principal wishes to ring-fence the licensee's territory and prevent export from the territory by the licensee.

7.5 Extra-territorial activities

7–25 7.5 During the continuance of this Agreement the Licensee shall not sell outside or export or assist in or be a party to the export of the Products from the Territory unless the prior consent of the Principal has been obtained [provided that this clause shall not prevent the sale of the Products by the Licensee as ship's or aircraft's stores or to duty-free shops as referred to in cl.7.4].

This clause should be considered in conjunction with cl.7.4.

7–26 In many territories outside the EC there is no legislation which restricts the imposition of export bans, and the wording will be sufficient as it stands. There are however countries which have special transfer of technology legislation which to varying degrees regulates the imposition of bans on export outside of the country concerned. In the case, for instance, of India, it is not possible to impose a ban on an Indian licensee which will prevent him from exporting licensed products manufactured in India outside of India. There have even been instances of requiring the principal to actively promote the Indian licensee and put export business his way. In other countries the requirement may be to permit the licensee to export to any country where the principal has not got a prior commitment to a third party which would be breached by such export.

As part of his enquiry into local transfer of technology legislation, the principal must therefore ascertain if and to what extent he can impose an export ban. To the extent that he cannot, he must then consider whether in practice the licensee will really be able to export either at all, or at any rate into markets which might concern the principal, taking into account the size of the licensee's local market, and his capacity to satisfy it. **7–27**

7.6 Supply of the products

7.6.1 Options to manufacture or purchase

7.6.1 The Licensee shall be entitled to exercise any or all of the following options: **7–28**

7.6.1.1 to manufacture the Products;

7.6.1.2 to purchase semi-finished Products and finish and pack the same;

7.6.1.3 to purchase the Products in bulk and pack the same; and

7.6.1.4 to purchase finished Products ready packaged.

The options in this clause allow the licensee the freedom to set his operation either at a particular period in time, or, in relation to any one of the products, at any stage between that of distributor and full manufacturer. Depending upon the technical competence of the distributor, it is not unusual for him to start off as a packer from bulk, work up to finishing operations and end as a full manufacturer.

7.6.2 Subcontracting

7.6.2 The Licensee may subcontract the activities of manufacture packaging and finishing referred to in cl.7.6.1 but always subject to cl.7.19. **7–29**

This is a normal provision, as often the distributor himself does not have the manufacturing resources required.

7.6.3 Purchase from principal of components and ingredients

7–30 7.6.3 In the exercise of the options contained in cl.7.6.1 the Licensee shall as relevant purchase from the Principal those components raw materials and packaging (if any) listed in Sch.4 and all finished and semi-finished Products unless in any instance the Principal in relation to any or all of the aforesaid items otherwise directs in writing.

This clause must be used with care. This is another sensitive area in the control of technology transfer legislation of some countries. For instance, such a provision is not permitted in India, and licensees in that country must be left free to procure components and materials from any source that can supply them satisfactorily. One reason why these provisions are so closely controlled is that many of the countries concerned have required local manufacturing, rather than distribution arrangements, to cut down on imports and save foreign exchange. They also control the level of royalty under the licence agreement for the same reason. If an obligation were to be imposed that parts or ingredients for the products were to be obtained only from the principal, then the import of these items would at least partly defeat the intention of requiring a local manufacturing arrangement in the first place. There is also the point that the principal may well find it tempting to charge higher prices than are strictly justified on these components to enable him to recover revenue from the territory at a higher rate than has been set under the local laws for the level of royalty.

7–31 Many highly successful local manufacturing operations are based upon the supply by the principal of a vital ingredient. Most soft drink manufacturers, for instance, work under a licence from the originator of the drink, under which they undertake to manufacture the soft drink locally, according to thc originator's instructions, using the originator's trade mark, and purchasing all the ingredients and packaging wherever is most economical, except for the concentrate which contains the flavour for and is the basis of the drink. This is produced only by the originator, and is purchased by the licensee solely from the originator or his designated supply source. This on the one hand ensures uniformity and good quality of the licensed product, and on the other provides a satisfactory way for the originator to collect revenue in proportion to sales actually made by the licensee. The originator is remunerated from the purchase price of the concentrate, without the need of having to charge a separate royalty, or to investigate sales, and calculate what is due to him, or to rely on the local manufacturer to send him returns of sales for this purpose. He also collects the "royalty" in advance of sales being made, which is of obvious assistance for his cash flow. In addition, the aspect of confidentiality is fully safeguarded, since the licensee never has to learn of the ingredients and method of manufacture of the concentrate.

7–32 Such operations are perhaps more strictly called franchising operations rather than manufacturing operations. In most territories such arrangements are permitted, because the tie in of the requirement to purchase the necessary ingredient is indispensable for the success of the local operation.

7.6.4 Quality control

7.6.4 The Licensee shall undertake the obligations in relation to quality control and related matters set out in Sch.5. 7–33

This is a standard provision in most licences, although it may not be necessary in cases where the licensee does not sell under a trade mark of the principal, so that the principal is less concerned about the reputation which the manufactured products have in the market. However, even in such cases it is unwise for the principal to leave the licensee totally to his own devices. In the last analysis, the principal may become liable if a substandard product is manufactured by the licensee, either through ignorance or intention.

7.6.5 Terms and conditions of supply of licensor

7.6.5 The parties hereto agree that orders placed by the Licensee with the Principal for items cl.7.6.3 shall be on the terms set out in Sch.6. 7–34

7.6.6 Royalty

7.6.6 The Licensee shall pay a royalty to the Principal in respect of the Licensee's activities under this Agreement in accordance with Sch.7. 7–35

This is the provision that triggers the payment of royalty. The specific provisions relating to royalties will be dealt with in the relevant schedule.

7.7 Licensee's records

7.7 The Licensee shall keep proper books of account and records together with copies of invoices and other relevant papers showing all orders placed and executed and shall allow the Principal or its authorised representative access to the said accounts records invoices and papers for the purpose of checking any information given by the Licensee to the Principal or of obtaining any information or data relevant to the performance of the rights and duties of the Licensee under this Agreement at all reasonable times (whether this Agreement be terminated or not) until all duties and obligations of the Licensee to the Principal have been performed and discharged in full. 7–36

This provision is necessary to enable the principal to ascertain if royalty returns are being made properly, and if other provisions of the agreement, such as export restrictions, are being observed. Note that the obligation survives the termination of the agreement, to enable the principal to ascertain the situation in the event of a dispute which leads to termination of the agreement.

7.8 Advertising and merchandising

7–37 7.8.1 The Licensee shall expend upon advertisements point of sale promotion merchandising and publicity material for the Products (hereinafter called "Advertising") during each consecutive period of twelve months of the currency of this Agreement (other than the first such period which commences upon the date hereof) not less than a sum equal to [ ] per cent of the actual proceeds of sale of the Products in the Territory during the preceding such period. The said proceeds shall be calculated on the same basis as that provided in para.2 of Sch.7 save that there shall be included the actual proceeds of sale of finished Products likewise calculated on the said basis. For the first period of twelve months aforesaid the Licensee shall expend upon Advertising not less than the sum of [ ].

It is in the interest of the principal to ensure that the level of advertising expenditure, for which the licensee will be responsible, is agreed at the outset and set down in the agreement by way of a fixed sum for the first year, and thereafter as a percentage of sales. The licensee may well regard the need to keep on with advertising expenditure as unnecessary or dispensable in years when sales are few, and costs up. However, it is in just these circumstances that the principal will want to see added sales revenue generated by increased advertising, since the principal's return on the arrangement is geared to the overall sales volume. Sales of the finished product are also included in this calculation, unlike the calculation for royalty where the principal makes his money on his sale price to the licensee.

7–38 7.8.2 All Advertising shall be subject before issue by the Licensee to the prior written approval of the Principal of the form manner extent and wording thereof.

7–39 7.8.3 All sales promotion activities for the Products of whatever nature must receive the prior written approval of the Principal which reserves the right to veto the same entirely at its discretion.

7–40 7.8.4 The cost of all Advertising and sales promotion activities shall unless otherwise decided be borne by the Licensee.

7–41 7.8.5 The cost of all merchandising returns from customers relating to the Products shall (unless otherwise agreed in writing) be borne by the Licensee.

Clauses 7.8.3 to 7.8.5 are identical to cll.4.8.2 to 4.8.4 and serve the same purpose.

7.9 Sales and marketing policies

7–42 7.9.1 The Licensee shall conform to the general sales and marketing policies philosophies and principles of the Principal and the Principal reserves the right to issue directions from time to time to the Licensee to ensure such conformity.

This provision is useful, in territories where it is enforceable.

7.9.2 Selling prices for the sale of the Products in the Territory by the Licensee shall be established and may be revised from time to time by the Licensee [after consultation with and approval by the Licensor] [and the same and all changes in the same shall be promptly notified by the Licensee to the Principal prior to being put into effect]. **7–43**

In some territories it is still possible for the principal to control the selling price, although this is not often the case. Where it is possible, the first phrase in square brackets can be used. The second phrase in square brackets containing the requirement as to notification is a restriction on the licensee's right to change prices, but not such a severe one. It may be a compromise position in territories which do not permit price fixing by the licensor, but are not so strict as to prevent him having a say in the matter at all. In any case, such provisions should not be included in a licence without a careful check on the position under the local law in force in the relevant territory.

7.9.3 The Licensee undertakes [not to alter any of the Products (or their packaging) nor to offer them for sale in a group package and] to apply the Trade Mark to all Products manufactured and or sold by the Licensee, and not to present any such Products for sale otherwise than with the Trade Mark affixed thereto and in accordance with the get-up required by the Principal. **7–44**

This is a provision which mirrors that for distribution agreements in cl.4.9.3.

7.9.4 The Licensee undertakes not to apply the Trade Mark to any item not one of the Products nor to distribute or sell any such items with the Trade Mark so applied or engage in any other practice or activity likely to mislead potential purchasers into believing that an item is one of the Products when in fact it is not. **7–45**

This merely sets out the position under the general law, that no licensee of a trade mark can use it in ways not authorised by the licence, and mirrors the provision in cl.4.9.4.

7.9.5 The Licensee shall be permitted to identify itself upon the packaging of the Products as the manufacturer thereof, and shall, in any event indicate on the packaging of that Product that the Product is manufactured under licence from the Principal. **7–46**

This is a provision which is normal in licence agreements, both to preserve the rights of the principal, but also to ensure that in the event of defective manufacture of a product it is clear who the manufacturer is.

7.10 Stock of the products

7.10 The Licensee shall at all times during the continuance of this Agreement carry at least [three months stock] of the Products (in a finished state) and at least [one months] stock of all the relevant raw materials components ingredients and packaging for the Products so that all orders received by the Licensee can be supplied without undue delay and shall supply such reports as to stock levels and movements as the Principal may from time to time request. **7–47**

This provision is still necessary in a licence agreement. It is in both sides' interests that production is carried on at a sufficient rate to ensure that the licensee keeps a reasonable buffer stock of finished products to enable demand to be satisfied. It is also desirable that the licensee keeps sufficient stock of raw materials to keep his production line fully fed. The details of this clause would have to be adapted considerably depending on the nature of the products, the delivery times for raw materials, the rate of stock turnover, and product shelf-life.

7.11 Licensee's staff

7–48 7.11 The Licensee shall maintain during the continuance of this Agreement sufficient staff to manufacture distribute sell and promote the sale of the Products throughout the Territory and perform in a timely and satisfactory manner the Licensee's obligations under this Agreement and in particular shall create and maintain a sales force of sufficient size from time to time to fulfil the Licensee's obligations under this Agreement in relation to the sale and marketing of the Products.

A standard provision, adapted from that for a distributor, but extended to cover manufacture as well as all the other marketing activities.

7.12 Monthly reports

7–49 A standard monthly reporting provision should be inserted. Clause 4.12 is suitable.

7.13 Industrial property rights

7–50 Clauses 4.13.1, 4.13.2 and 4.13.3 should be adapted and inserted as 7.13.1, 7.13.2 and 7.13.3 respectively.

7.14 No joint venture or partnership

7–51 See Chapter 1.9.

7.15 Commencement and term of agreement

7–52 7.15.1 This Agreement shall commence upon [ ] and continue in force for a period of [three years] from that date subject to earlier termination as herein provided.

This is the usual provision for commencement and duration.

7.15.2 The Licensee shall obtain at its own expense all necessary permissions consents and licences (including but without limitation governmental health authority licences if required) to enable the Licensee to manufacture market distribute and sell the Products in the Territory and obtain any other governmental permission consent or licence necessary for the full and legal operation of this Agreement including (if necessary) registration of this Agreement with the relevant governmental authority to enable remittance in accordance with this Agreement of the royalty payable to the Principal hereunder. **7–53**

This is a particularly important clause in territories where there is either control of technology transfer legislation and or exchange controls. In some countries the relevant technology transfer authorities are concerned to approve the terms of the licence in order to make sure that the obligations imposed upon the licensee are in accordance with its policy. Some of the matters that they are concerned with, although details differ, are the presence of export bans, tied-in sales of related or unrelated products, and the amount of any up-front payment, which is generally regarded as intended to cover the costs of transfer, but not to yield an excessive profit. The obligations to give complete training and also to pass on and licence improvements to the licensed technology during the life of the agreement are also regarded as important (see Chapter 1.2.11). Lastly the level of the royalty will be considered. Luxury or non-essential products, or products which have local substitutes are likely to be permitted only low royalties, often in the region of one or two per cent. Technologically essential products may get a royalty as high as five or six per cent, but except in very special cases, countries which control the level of royalty that can be charged rarely permit rates much above six per cent.

Leaving aside the question of approval of the agreement from the point of view of technology transfer, there is also the question of exchange control. This is normally carried out by a separate government department, and the fact that the licence has been approved from the point of view of technology transfer does not mean that exchange control for remitting the whole, or any part of the royalty will be given automatically. In many cases, application has to be made initially for a consent in principle, and then on a piecemeal basis for every remittance of the royalty out of the territory. In any event, even where permission to remit is granted, the royalty is more often than not subject to a withholding tax, which must be deducted before payment. **7–54**

Finally there are all of the other permissions, such as medical or safety that must be obtained before the products can be marketed, for which the same considerations apply as in the case of a distributor. **7–55**

7.15.3 See cl.4.15.3. **7–56**

7.15.4 See cl.4.15.4. **7–57**

7.16 Termination

The clauses set out as 4.16.1 to 4.16.7 inclusive can be reproduced here. **7–58**

It should be noted that licensees are not normally protected by local laws **7–59** or granted compensation for termination by due notice or expiry of an agreement by effluxion of time. In some territories, however, certain rights continue to be enjoyed by the licensee even after the agreement has been terminated. This arises as a rule under the control of transfer of technology legislation in a territory. For instance a licensee might under the local law be granted on a compulsory basis a royalty free fully paid up licence which is irrevocable and perpetual, after a period of due performance of the agreement, and payment of a certain total sum by way of royalties. The possibility of this should always be part of the enquiry made when looking into local technology transfer legislation.

7.17 Effects of termination

7–60 7.17.1 Upon termination of this Agreement from any cause whatsoever (including but without limitation expiry by effluxion of time) other than the operation of cl.7.16.1 the Principal shall subject to the remainder of cl.7.17 be obliged to repurchase at manufactured or landed cost as the case may be the following items (hereinafter collectively called the "Stock"):

7.17.1.1 the quantity of each finished Product held by or on behalf of the Licensee at the date of termination up to a maximum equal to the quantity of the relevant Product sold during the [six] month period prior to the date of termination; and

7.17.1.2 the quantity of each raw material packaging material or component and semi-finished Product held by or on behalf of the Licensee at the date of termination up to a maximum equal to that necessary to manufacture the quantity of the relevant finished Product sold during the [six] months period prior to the date of termination.

7–61 7.17.2 Upon receipt of payment for the Stock the Licensee shall return or procure the return to the Principal or the Principal's nominated recipient or recipients in the Territory of the Stock and of the following items (collectively the "Items"): all samples patterns instruction books technical pamphlets catalogues specifications formulae and manufacturing instructions for the Products and of all advertising materials and other documents and papers whatsoever sent to the Licensee and relating to the business of the Principal (other than correspondence between the Licensee and the Principal which does not relate to technical matters) together with any copies thereof which may be in the possession or under the control of the Licensee.

7–62 7.17.3 Any Items or Stock which the Principal does not choose to have returned under cl.7.17.2 shall (subject in the case of Stock to the receipt by the Licensee of payment therefor) be destroyed forthwith by the Licensee in the presence of the Principal or the authorised representative of the Principal.

7–63 7.17.4 Notwithstanding the foregoing the Principal may but shall be under no obligation to take over any Stock which is unmerchantable obsolete illegal damaged deteriorated defective or otherwise unfit for sale or (where any item has a shelf-life) with more than half of its shelf-life expired.

7.17.5 The Licensee shall destroy in accordance with the procedure provided in cl.7.17.3 at its own expense and without making any charge on the Principal all finished Products or packaging material not taken over by the Principal which are obsolete illegal damaged deteriorated defective or otherwise unfit for sale or (where relevant) with more than half of their shelf-life expired, irrespective of whether they form part of the Stock or not. **7–64**

7.17.6 Upon termination of this Agreement under cl.7.16.1 the Principal shall have an option but not the obligation to purchase the Stock. Should the Principal decide not to exercise the option the Licensee shall be obliged to act immediately upon the said termination: **7–65**

7.17.6.1 in relation to Items in accordance with cll.7.17.2, 7.17.3 and/or 7.17.5 as relevant; and

7.17.6.2 in relation to the Stock in accordance with cl.7.17.5.

7.17.7 Upon termination of this Agreement from any cause whatsoever (including expiry by effluxion of time) the Licensee shall have no further rights to use the Trade Mark in any way whatsoever and in particular but without prejudice to the generality of the foregoing shall cease to use the Trade Mark on its letterheads packaging vehicle liveries or elsewhere and shall sell any stocks of the Products not disposed of under the previous clauses of 7.17 in packaging which bears neither the Trade Mark nor the name of the Principal. **7–66**

7.17.8 Upon such termination the Licensee shall (if so required) supply the Principal with a list of the Licensee's customers for the Products. **7–67**

7.17.9 Upon such termination the Licensee shall (if legally possible) assign to the Principal free of charge all permissions consents and licences (if any) relating to the manufacture and or marketing and or distribution and or sale of the Products and execute all documents and do all things necessary to ensure that the Principal shall enjoy the benefit of the said permissions consents and licences after the said termination to the entire exclusion of the Licensee. **7–68**

7.17.10(a) Upon such termination the Licensee shall cease to use in any way whatsoever the Patents and all information and knowhow relating to the Products including but without limitation all knowhow and information disclosed to the Licensee by the Principal under para.1 of Sch.5. **7–69**

AND/OR

7.17.10(b) Upon such termination the Licensee shall cease to have any right to exploit the Knowhow, and shall procure the return to the Principal of all material embodiments of the Knowhow, whether or not readable by the human eye, including without limitation all patterns, instruction books, technical pamphlets, specifications, formulae, manufacturing instructions, and drawings relating to the Products which are not public knowledge.

This clause is analogous to cl.4.17, and the principal has the same motivations for requiring its inclusion as a principal under a distribution agreement.

7.18 Confidentiality

7–70 The long form clauses in Chapter 1.4 coupled with the definition of Information in Chapter 1.2.10 should be used here.

7.19 Transmission of rights

7–71 7.19 The benefit of the rights granted to the Licensee by this Agreement shall be personal to the Licensee who shall not without the prior consent in writing of the Principal mortgage or charge the same to any third party nor subcontract or assign the same or part with any of its rights or obligations hereunder save that the foregoing shall not prevent:

7–72 7.19.1 the Licensee from factoring or mortgaging or in any way creating a charge or security over Products the title in which shall have passed to it or book-debts created by the sale of such Products; and

7–73 7.19.2 the Licensee from subcontracting the activities of manufacture packaging or finishing of the Products to a third party [or carrying on the same through a connected person] under cl.7.6.2 provided that such subcontracting shall not be taken to relieve it from any of its duties or obligations under this Agreement in relation to such activities including but without limitation those set out in cl.7.18 and in Sch.5. All obligations undertaken by the Licensee under this Agreement in relation to manufacture including but without limitation those set out in cl.7.18 and Sch.5 shall be imposed upon such subcontractors by the Licensee by means of a written agreement between the Licensee and each such subcontractor in a form approved in writing prior to signature by the Principal. Upon the signature of each such agreement a copy thereof shall forthwith be supplied to the Principal by the Licensee.

It is normal to impose restrictions on assignment, and sublicensing, but to permit in certain cases the manufacture, or distribution of the products by subcontractors who are under the control of the licensee, and carry out defined duties upon his behalf only.

7–74 The clause as drafted does not permit true sublicensing, where the licensee can in his turn sublicence the benefit of the agreement to a third party in return for a royalty. This is really equivalent to assignment, and robs the principal of the direct control that he requires over the operations carried out under the licence agreement. Such sublicensing arrangements are normally appropriate only where the licensee's grant covers a very large state (*e.g.* the USA or Canada) and it might be appropriate for him to subdivide operations to various sublicensees in different areas, and in effect supervise them on behalf of the principal.

7–75 Many companies, as a matter of policy however, do not permit such sublicences, on the ground that it removes the direct relationship and control that they would have over a direct licensee. In some cases, they do however, insert an option in the agreement that enables a licensee to ask them to licence certain parts of the industrial property direct to customers of the licensee. This is often done in licences which include an element of software and hardware together. The matter is discussed and dealt with in connection with software in Chapter 11.

7.20 Interpretation clauses and signature

7.21 Schedule 1—definitions

This Schedule should include, in separate parts the appropriate definitions of the Products, the Territory, the Trade Mark, the Patents, and the Know-how. **7–76**

7.22 Schedule 2—targets

> The Licensee undertakes to achieve during each consecutive period of twelve months of the currency of this Agreement (subject to prior termination in accordance with cl.7.15) the first such period to commence upon the date of commencement of this Agreement, sales targets for the Products during the relevant period as follows: **7–77**
>
> Period Target

OR

> The Licensee undertakes to pay during each consecutive period of twelve months of the currency of this Agreement (subject to prior termination in accordance with cl.7.15) the first such period to commence upon the date of commencement of this Agreement, royalties in respect of sales of the Products during the relevant period calculated in accordance with Sch.7 or the relevant one of the following sums of money whichever is the greater:
>
> Period Pounds Sterling

The most usual imposition is minimum sales targets where the licensee acts as both a distributor and a local manufacturer. Minimum royalties are most common where the licensee acts as only a local manufacturer and on an exclusive basis.

If it is intended to deal with an obligation to produce a minimum quantity the royalty provisions in Sch.7 would have to be redrafted completely. Minimum production obligations are more usual in process patent licences, where the royalty can more easily be linked to a unit sum per item produced by the use of the process. **7–78**

Royalties for the manufacture of licensed products generally function more easily on the basis of a percentage of net sales, which makes a minimum production quantity obligation of no value to the principal. It is true that the result of the minimum sales target is to achieve at least a minimum **7–79** level of royalty but the result of failure to achieve a sales target under cl.7.16 is the possible termination of the agreement rather than the payment of a minimum royalty.

7.23 Schedule 3—exceptions to any restrictions upon the licensee dealing with competitive goods

7–80 This is where any permitted dealings with competitive goods should be listed. Where one is using standard form agreements the wording of the heading makes it possible to leave the schedule in and mark it "vacant" or "none" in order to avoid throwing out the numbering of the other schedules and their cross-referencing, if this is desired.

7.24 Schedule 4–items to be purchased from principal

7–81 This is where the items (if any) specified in cl.7.6.3 should be listed.

7.25 Schedule 5—specifications, production methods and quality standards

7–82 7.25.1 The Principal shall upon the date of signature of this Agreement supply the Knowhow to the Licensee.

This is a short form clause. More elaborate provisions, including in relation to training programmes, may be necessary, and these can be taken from the extended clauses on knowhow provision in Chapter 6.24.

7–83 7.25.2 The Licensee shall (unless otherwise specifically permitted by the prior written approval of the Principal) comply fully with all those requirements contained in the Knowhow for the quality of materials and workmanship used in the manufacture finishing and packing of each of the Products and for the appearance design and get-up of each of the Products and its packaging.

This is the basic obligation to comply with required quality standards.

7–84 7.25.3 The Licensee shall not put on the market any Products or packaging in respect of which it has not achieved full compliance with the said requirements.

This clause is the other side of the coin from cl.7.25.2. If the licensee does make substandard products, he must not be allowed to put them on the market.

7–85 7.25.4 The Licensee shall send (at its expense) two samples packaged for retail sale from the first batch of each Product to be manufactured or finished by or for it after the commencement of this Agreement to a quality control laboratory nominated by the Principal and no sale or distribution of that Product shall take place until the Principal signifies its written agreement that the sample in question complies fully with its requirements as aforesaid.

The approval before commencement of production is essential so that the principal can see that in practice the licensee has understood how to manufacture the product.

7.25.5 Each year on the anniversary of the date of signature of this Agreement the Licensee shall despatch (at its own expense) to a quality control laboratory nominated by the Principal two finished samples packaged for retail sale chosen at random of each Product manufactured finished or packed by or for it during the preceding year. **7–86**

With some products this is done much more frequently, often, as is the case with most soft drinks, once a month. This again permits control and verification of the extent to which the licensee is manufacturing products properly.

7.25.6 The Principal shall have the right on reasonable notice during business hours by its authorised representatives to visit any places (under the control of the Licensee or its subcontractors) where the Products or raw materials or packaging for the Products are manufactured finished packed or stored and to inspect and to take samples to ascertain to what extent the Licensee is complying with the aforesaid requirements. **7–87**

Apart from sampling the principal must have the right to verify compliance by inspection.

7.25.7 If any law or governmental regulation in the Territory prevents the Licensee from full compliance with the requirements as aforesaid the Licensee shall notify the Principal of this in writing stating in what way the requirements will have to be amended to conform to such law or regulation and requesting the Principal to approve such amendment. The Principal shall not unreasonably withhold such approval and shall in any case reply in writing within [thirty] days of receipt of such a request. The Licensee shall be responsible for and bear the expense of ascertaining the aforesaid amendments and all consequent necessary reformulations or changes in components design manufacturing or packaging materials or methods for the relevant Product. **7–88**

This provision is necessary to take into account particular matters like permitted ingredients, which may change from time to time, and in different ways. The same comments apply largely to safety and electrical connection requirements and so on.

7.25.8 The Principal warrants that neither the sale nor use of the Products nor the use of the Knowhow in accordance with this clause shall cause the Licensee to infringe any intellectual or industrial property rights owned or controlled by a third party and the Principal shall indemnify the Licensee against any and all actions costs claims demands expenses and liabilities whatsoever resulting from any actual or alleged infringement as aforesaid [other than damages or expenses of a consequential nature or in respect of loss of contracts or loss of revenue or **7–89** profits] and at its own expense the Principal will defend any proceedings which may be brought in that connection provided that this clause shall not apply unless:

7.25.8.1 the Licensee shall promptly notify the Principal in writing of any allegation of infringements; and

7.25.8.2 the Licensee shall make no admissions without the Principal's consent; and

7.25.8.3 the Licensee shall allow the Principal to conduct and or settle all negotiations and litigation and shall give the Principal all reasonable assistance in relation thereto (all the costs incurred or recovered in such negotiations and litigation being for the Principal's account); and

7.25.8.4 the Principal shall be under no liability under this indemnity in respect of any infringement or alleged infringement as aforesaid occasioned by the use of a design or specification originated by the Licensee as a result of the carrying out of work in order to adapt any of the Products to its customers' requirements.

This clause gives a wide indemnity to the licensee over the use of the knowhow for all the licensed purposes. The problem of to what extent the principal can be persuaded to give such a warranty depends of course upon the relative bargaining powers of the two parties. More limited warranties and exclusion clauses are discussed in Chapter 6.24.8 and 6.24.9 with particular relation to manufacturing knowhow delivered under an escrow arrangement (see Chapter 10). The phrase in square brackets in the body of the clause will, if inserted, exempt the principal from liability for more than the direct costs and awards or settlements relating to infringement claims.

7–90 7.25.9 Any and all intellectual and industrial property rights throughout the world resulting from any work carried out by the Licensee in order to adapt the Products to its customers' requirements [or relating to an improvement to the Products generated by the Licensee] shall vest exclusively in [the Licensee] [and be assigned upon demand by the Licensee to the Licensor]. [The Licensee undertakes that it will grant [[a non-exclusive] [a sole] licence of such rights upon fair and reasonable terms, to be agreed, including as to duration, royalty and territory, to the Principal] [a royalty-free, fully paid-up, worldwide and irrevocable [sole] [non-exclusive] licence (with power to sublicence) of such rights without limit of time to the Principal]].

This grant-back clause provides either for all rights in improvements and adaptations to the licensed products made by the licensee to vest in and be assigned to the licensor, or else for them to vest in the licensee, but subject to a grant back licence in favour of the licensor. The grant-back licence may either be of the widest nature (and free of charge) or, if the licensee's bargaining position is strong enough, then it may be only upon terms to be agreed. It should be remembered that a clause on terms to be agreed is not normally enforceable under the common law, as being only an agreement to agree, but that there are civil law countries where such clauses impose, at the very least, an obligation to negotiate in good faith, and not capriciously to refuse to grant a licence at all.

7.25.10(a) The Licensor will make reasonable efforts to confirm the accuracy and efficiency of the Knowhow but it makes no representation or warranty that the Licensee can successfully manufacture the Products through use of the Knowhow. **7–91**

OR

7.25.10(b) The Licensor hereby warrants that the Knowhow and Intellectual Property furnished to the Licensee hereunder will enable a Person skilled in the manufacture of [RF and digital telecommunications equipment] to manufacture use and sell [the Product] [products which conform to the specifications set out in Schedule].

OR

7.25.10(c) The Licensor hereby warrants that by utilising the Knowhow and Intellectual Property furnished to the Licensee hereunder, the Licensor is able to manufacture the Products in the Licensor's own factory at [ ], but the Licensor makes no representation or warranty that the Licensee can successfully manufacture the Products.

These clauses provide for the status of the knowhow licensed under the agreement. Version (a) excludes liability for the efficacy of the licensed technology and would be used in conjunction with the full wording in the indemnity clause discussed in cl.7.3.8 above. Version (b) undertakes some liability in that it measures the efficacy of the licensed technology by reference to an objective standard. Even if the licensor is not able to use the licensed technology properly, at least someone skilled in the general type of manufacture concerned would be able to do so. Finally, version (c) provides at least some comfort for the licensee, in that he knows the licensed technology is successfully applied by the licensor himself. It should be noted that under versions (b) and (c) above, the implication is that the knowhow and intellectual property is of itself complete and accurate and therefore sufficient to achieve the stated purpose if the licensee is competent to use it. Such warranties impose quite onerous obligations and are not to be undertaken lightly.

7.26 Schedule 6—terms of supply of principal

The provisions of cl.4.26 can be used here. **7–92**

7.27 Schedule 7—royalty

7.27.1 The Licensee shall pay the Principal during the continuance of this Agreement a royalty of [ ] per cent upon sales as hereinafter defined. **7–93**

7–94 7.27.2 The said royalty shall be calculated on the actual proceeds of sales made by the Licensee of all the Products which have been manufactured finished and or packed by or for the Licensee under cl.7.6.1 and less all discounts and allowances provided that:

7.27.2.1 as respects any and every sale or other disposition made on terms allowing to the purchaser or other recipient a discount or allowance greater than normal trade discounts or allowances in the Territory such discount or allowance in so far as it is greater than a normal trade discount or allowance shall be ignored and added back in calculating the royalty in respect of each and every such sale or disposition.

This is a simple form of royalty clause, although more elaborate ones are available. One point which always needs consideration, is whether all transactions in the products manufactured are at a commercial value. If one takes a royalty upon actual proceeds of sale, all discounts and inter-company transactions at lower than commercial value, or free samples or reduced price bargains, will reduce the actual royalty collected. These matters will usually be in the control of the Licensee, who can thus force the principal to contribute his share towards these expenses by the reduction in his royalty. Clause 7.27.2.1 permits these matters to be taken into account in a relatively straightforward way.

7–95 7.27.3 The royalty payment to the Principal under this schedule shall be due on 31 March, 30 June, 30 September and 31 December in each year on the said sales of the Products made in the three calendar months preceding each date and each such payment shall be remitted in full free of all charges and deductions other than withholding taxes to the Principal in London within thirty days of the due date in pounds sterling at the closing middle market rate of exchange on that day on the London money markets between pounds sterling and the currency in which the relevant sales were made. Together with each such remittance the licensee shall provide the licensor with a certificate (in a form satisfactory to the licensor) detailing the amount of withholding tax deducted in respect of the relevant remittance.

This is a standard type of clause for the accounting and payment of royalty. One of the problems will be the obtaining of exchange control permission in some territories, and the onus for this is put upon the licensee. Withholding tax is expressed to be borne by the licensor and deducted by the licensee. This is the standard practice, and The principal should take advantage of any double-taxation convention between his country of residence and the territory, which will permit him to set-off the withholding tax against the tax which he would otherwise pay in his country of residence on the royalty received by him. This is of course not possible between countries where there is no double taxation convention in force, but, in many such countries, as in the UK, in practice the principal is permitted to set-off the withholding tax against the royalty as an expense allowable in any case.

Chapter 8

Manufacturing Agreements Inside the EC

Contents

8.1 Commercial and legal background

8.1.1 Current position under EC competition law

8–01 Chapter 7 considered licensing agreements outside the EC. This chapter looks at the way licensing agreements require adaptation to deal with the specific issues raised by EC competition law, and provides amendments to the precedent contained in Chapter 7 which will achieve this result.

8–02 The position under EC law changed in the direction of greater simplification, upon the coming into force of Commission Regulation 240/96 (in this chapter referred to as the "Regulation") on the application of Art.81(3) of the Treaty to certain categories of technology transfer agreements. Previously under EC law, one had to take account of four situations:

- patent licences and patent licences coupled with a licence of related knowhow covered by the Block Exemption on Patent Licences (Reg.2349/84) (the "Patent Block Exemption");
- knowhow licences and mixed knowhow and patent licences, covered by the Block Exemption on Knowhow Licences (Reg.556/89) (the "Knowhow Block Exemption");
- knowhow and patent licences of various types which for various reasons fell outside the relevant block exemptions; and
- licences which were chiefly concerned with other types of intellectual property rights, such as trade marks, design rights, or copyright.

8–03 The current situation is that the Regulation replaced the Patent Block Exemption and the Knowhow Block Exemption with effect from April 1, 1996. However, it specifically provides that the agreements which were exempt under the old block exemptions on March 31, 1996 are now granted exemption under the Regulation (Art.11(3)), which applies until March 31, 2006 (Art.11(2)). The Regulation was intended by the Commission to be clearer and more understandable to the practitioner, to provide greater legal certainty and to apply the same rules to as many different categories of licence agreements as possible to avoid disparity of treatment. At the same time it relaxed some of the requirements contained in the old block exemptions.

8–04 It should also be noted that the situation is by no means settled. This section describes the present position under EC competition law, but the Commission has embarked upon an exercise to amend the Regulation, or replace it with a new regulation, in line with the more modern thinking on competition law embodied in Reg.2790/99. The prospects for the future are discussed in Chapter 8.28 below.

8.1.1.1 Licences covered by the technology transfer block exemption (Reg.240/96)

Under Art.1 the Regulation applies to "pure" patent licensing agreements, "pure" knowhow licensing agreements, and "mixed" licensing agreements for both patents and knowhow, including both licences where the knowhow is ancillary to the patents or independent of them (see recital 5). It is also extended to cover licences falling within any of the foregoing categories which also contain licences of other intellectual property rights where they contribute "to the achievement of the objects of the licensed technology" (see recital 6) and contain "no restrictive provisions other than those also attached to the licensed knowhow or patents and exempted under the Regulation" (Art.10(15)). This means that out of the four categories listed above, probably the only licences of intellectual property rights which fall outside of the Regulation are those relating to pure licences of intellectual property rights (such as copyright licences, particularly software licences) or licences where, although knowhow or patents are part of the bundle of rights in the licence, they are ancillary to the main purpose of the agreement. The most likely area where this can occur is in relation to trade mark licences or franchise agreements. **8–05**

For instance, *Re Moosehead Breweries Ltd/Whitbread and Company plc* [1991] 4 C.M.L.R. 391 was a mixed knowhow and trade mark licence covering the production and sale of beer. Although exemption was granted under Art.81(3) it was held that the Knowhow Regulation could not apply as "in the present case the principal interest of the parties lies in the exploitation of the trade mark rather than of the knowhow. The parties view the Canadian origin of the mark as crucial to the success of the marketing campaign". Interestingly enough this decision also shows that much franchising of production (where often the trade mark is a crucial element—see, *e.g.* most soft drink franchises) could probably not have taken advantage of the Knowhow Block Exemption either. It is a subject of some discussion as to whether the different wording of the Regulation would apply to a case like *Re Moosehead/Whitbread*, but a reading of recital 6 and Art.5(4) would suggest that this was not what was intended by the Commission, even though the detailed drafting of Arts 1(1) and 10(15) could perhaps be construed rather more widely. **8–06**

The best view is that the Regulation will be unlikely to apply to such arrangements (which fall rather within the sphere of franchising than simple manufacturing licences). Franchise agreements are discussed in detail in Chapter 6.27, particularly as to their treatment under Reg.2790/99. However, for the purposes of this chapter, the most important characteristic of franchising agreements to be kept in mind is that they contain a trade mark licence, since the essence of the arrangement is that the franchisee carries on business on the basis of a common methodolgy, or with the assistance of knowhow, provided by the franchisor under the franchisor's trade mark. Thus *Moosehead* is best thought of as an instance of an industrial franchise, or what is sometimes called a franchise of production. **8–07**

8–08 The Franchising Block Exemption (Reg.4087/88) provided no assistance in cases like *Moosehead* since it covered only franchising of distribution. Nor, because of the mixed nature of the arrangement, could such franchises come under Reg.83/83 either (see Chapter 8.6).

8.1.1.2 The demarcation between Reg.240/96 and Reg.2790/99

8–09 The position is somewhat clearer after the passing of the block exemption for vertical agreements (Reg.2790/99) which replaced both Reg.4087/88 and Reg.83/83). Article 2(5) of Reg.2790/99 provides that it has no application to vertical agreements covered by, *inter alia*, Reg.240/96. The demarcation between the two regulations is to be found by looking at the primary purpose of the vertical agreement. Regulation 2790/99 can only apply if the primary purpose of the vertical agreement relates to the use sale or resale of goods or services. If the primary purpose of the vertical agreement is the licensing of intellectual property rights, then Reg.2790/99 cannot apply and Reg.240/96 may apply depending upon the type of intellectual property licensed.

8–10 Article 2(3) of Reg.2790/99 provides that the block exemption applies to "vertical agreements containing provisions which relate to the assignment to the buyer or use by the buyer of intellectual property rights, provided that those provisions do not constitute the primary object of such agreements and are directly related to the use sale or resale of goods or services by the buyer or its customers". The Guidelines on Vertical Restraints comment on this provision in more detail in para.30:

- The IPR provisions must be part of an agreement under which the parties may purchase sell or resell certain goods or services.
- The IPRs must be assigned to or for use by the buyer.
- The IPR provisions must not constitute the primary object of the agreement.
- The IPR provisions must be directly related to the use sale or resale of goods or services by the buyer or his customer (In the case of franchising where marketing forms the object of the exploitation of the IPRs, the goods or services are distributed by the master franchisee or franchisees).
- The IPR provisions in relation to the contract goods or services, must not contain restrictions of competition having the same object or effect as vertical restraints which are not exempted under the Block Exemption Regulation.

8–11 Paragraph 31 of the Guidelines sums up the matter as follows: "These conditions ensure that the Block Exemption Regulation applies to vertical agreements where the use, sale or resale of goods or services can be performed more effectively because IPRs are assigned to or transferred for use by the buyer. In other words restrictions concerning the assignment or use of IPRs can be covered when the main object of the agreement is the purchase or distribution of goods or services".

Regulation 2790/99 can thus apply in two quite different situations. The first is where under some general distribution agreement, the principal licences ancillary intellectual property to the distributor to enable the distributor to sell or service the contract goods more efficiently. This is common, for instance in selective distribution networks for technical goods where the distributor provides after sales service (see Chapter 6.24). The second is where intellectual property is licensed under those types of franchise agreement which relate to the use sale or resale of goods or services. **8–12**

Thus paragraph 35 of the Guidelines states: "The IPR provisions will normally concern the marketing of goods or services. This is for instance the case in a franchise agreement where the franchisor sells to the franchisee goods for resale and in addition licences the franchisee to use his trade mark and knowhow to market the goods. Also covered is the case where the supplier of a concentrated extract licences the buyer to dilute and bottle the extract before selling it as a drink". **8–13**

Paragraph 43 states: "Licensing in franchise agreements is covered by the Block Exemption Regulation if all five conditions listed in para 30 are fulfilled. This is usually the case, as under most franchise agreements, including master franchise agreements, the franchisor provides goods and/or services, to the franchisee. The IPRs help the franchisee to resell the products supplied by the franchisor or by a supplier designated by the franchisor or to use those products and to sell the resulting goods or services". **8–14**

Thus, for the purposes of Reg.2790/99, provisions relating to IPR must be supportive of the main purpose of the agreement, namely to sell or provide goods and/or services. Some examples will assist to illustrate these principles. **8–15**

First, in a fast food franchise, the franchisee will obtain the ingredients or uncooked items from the franchisor or a source designated by the franchisor, will prepare and sell them using instructions, methods and procedures explained to him by the franchisor (knowhow) under the franchisor's trade marks, from the franchised premises which will have been laid out and constructed in the fashion prescribed by the franchisor (knowhow) using staff trained in the franchisor's sales and marketing procedures (knowhow). **8–16**

Second, a soft drinks franchisee will purchase concentrated extract from the franchisee, add sugar water and carbon dioxide in his bottling plant, according to prescribed procedures and recipes (knowhow), bottle the resulting drinks in bottles bearing the franchisor's trade mark and then market and sell the finished product using the marketing and sales techniques (knowhow) and advertising copy (copyright) that the franchisor provides him with. **8–17**

Third, a franchisor will provide steam-cleaning equipment and detergents and other cleaning fluids to a franchisee for the purpose of providing the service of cleaning carpets and curtains in commercial and domestic pre- **8–18** mises. The franchisee will be provided with technical training and assistance (knowhow) so that he is capable of operating the equipment properly and providing an efficient service. He will then provide the service under the franchisor's trade mark using the franchisor's marketing and sales techniques (knowhow) to find customers.

8–19 In terms of the discussion on franchising in Chapter 6.27, Reg.2790/99 thus covers franchising of distribution where the aim is to enable the franchisor to sell goods or provide services, reselling goods and/or using equipment supplied by the franchisor and with the benefit of the use of the franchisor's knowhow, copyright and/or trade mark.

8–20 However, Reg.2790/99 would not cover the situation where the primary aim of the franchise is the exploitation of intellectual property rights on their own. Paragraph 43 of the Guidelines continues: "Where the franchise agreement only or primarily concerns licensing of IPRs such an agreement is not covered by the Block Exemption Regulation, but it will be treated in a way similar to those franchise agreements which are covered by the Block Exemption Regulation".

8–21 For instance, in the case of *Moosehead* discussed above, just as the situation could not fall within the Knowhow Block Exemption (because the primary aim was the exploitation of the trade mark not the knowhow) so it could not fall within Reg.2790/99 since no goods (such as concentrated extract or other ingredients) or services were supplied to Whitbread by Moosehead, merely a recipe for the lager and a right to use the trade mark on finished product. Thus *Moosehead* can be regarded as a franchise agreement, but not a franchise of distribution covered by Reg.2790/99. See para.32 of the Guidelines.)

8–22 When dealing with licences of intellectual property there are, therefore, a number of possibilities in relation to EC competition law:

- Where Reg.2790/99 is in general applicable it will cover franchising agreements where the primary aim is the use sale or resale of goods or services.
- Treatment similar to Reg.2790/99 will apply to franchise agreements which only or primarily concern licensing of IPRs.
- Reg.240/96 applies where the primary aim is the licensing of a patent or knowhow or both a patent and knowhow.
- All other licences of intellectual property will (including franchising agreements where the primary aim is the use sale or resale of goods or services and where Reg.2790/99 does not apply) fall to be considered as to whether in the circumstances of the particular case they infringe Art.81(1) and, if so, whether they are exempt under Art.81(3).

8–23 In addition to the *Moosehead* situation, para.32 of the Guidelines also lists a number of other licences of intellectual property that are not covered by Reg.2790/99:

- Agreements under which one party provides another party with a mould or master copy and licences the other party to produce and distribute copies.
- The pure licence of a trade mark or sign for the purposes of merchandising.
- Sponsorship contracts concerning the right to advertise oneself as being an official sponsor of an event.
- Copyright licensing such as broadcasting contracts concerning the right to record and/or the right to broadcast an event.

Thus, for the purposes of this Chapter, it is necessary to distinguish between the true manufacturing licence and the industrial franchise or the franchise of production as typified by *Moosehead.* **8–24**

Since the industrial franchise cannot take advantage of Reg.2790/99, as explained above, any such arrangement will now have to be considered by the parties under the new regulatory framework for EC Competition law (see Chapter 5.1.1.2) to decide whether its terms infringe Art.81(1) and, if so, whether an exemption under Art.81(3) is justified. **8–25**

In the past such arrangements have been notified and have obtained exemption under Art.81(3), as it is unreasonable to expect a licensee to undertake the investment involved unless he is given an exclusive area of manufacture, even though some cross-border trade must be permitted. In the *Pronuptia* case (for full details see Chapter 6.27) "franchising of production" was mentioned only briefly but, if one were to apply the guidelines given in that case to franchising of production, they appear mostly in line with the general law on the grant of manufacturing licences within the EC. There seems no reason why a properly worded franchise of production, using the guidelines in the Regulation, should not enjoy the benefit of exemption under Art.81(3). **8–26**

None of the versions of the grant of licence discussed in this section provide for the licensing of any other industrial or intellectual property rights necessary for the manufacture of the products except the use of an associated trade mark to apply to the products manufactured under the agreement as specifically permitted by the Regulation. However, in the event that any other right (such as a registered design or a copyright) is involved, a defined term (*e.g.* the Registered Design) should be introduced, with reference if necessary to more detail in Sch.1. The right can then be included within the scope of the licence granted by the relevant version of cl.8.2. **8–27**

8.1.1.3 The market share test under Reg.240/96

Drafts of the Regulation contained a provision excluding the application of the Regulation in situations where the licensee had a market share of greater than 40 per cent. The Commission justified this on the grounds that the new **8–28** block exemption would focus on the economic strength of the licensee. Weaker players were hampered by the extensive blacklist in the old block exemptions, but their very weakness meant their activities had no real effect on competition. On the other hand, dominant undertakings would still affect competition even if they complied with the requirements in the old block exemptions. On this basis, the Commission was prepared to relax the list of prohibited restrictions, in return for preventing dominant undertakings from taking advantage of the block exemption at all.

8–29 This proposal produced such fierce opposition that the Commission, although it believed in the importance of the measure, dropped the market share requirement as a condition for application of the Regulation, and compromised by including in Art.7(1) a provision which enabled it to withdraw the benefit of the exemption where the effect of the agreement was "to prevent the licensed products from being exposed to effective competition ... which may in particular occur where the licensee's market share exceeds 40 per cent". The licensee's market share is defined in Art.10(9) as "the proportion which the licensed products and other goods or services provided by the licensee which are considered ... interchangeable or substitutable for the licensed products ... represent [of] the entire market for the licensed products and all other interchangeable or substitutable goods and services in the common market or a substantial part of it".

8–30 This market share test applies at the date the Commission is making its enquiry, not at the date the licence is granted, and the test can be applied only if the Commission investigates. Thus, even if an undertaking has a market share of greater than 40 per cent it will not lose the benefit of the block exemption automatically, but only as a result of a Commission Decision to withdraw the exemption following investigation. Nor does the undertaking have any obligation to check if its market share is greater than 40 per cent either at the time the licence is granted or at any time thereafter, although the Commission does suggest (see recital 27 of the Regulation) that an undertaking which believes it has a market share of greater than 40 per cent can notify any agreement for exemption if it wishes to do so, even if the agreement appears to comply in all respects with the Regulation.

8–31 In any investigation, the Commission will take into account market dynamics over a reasonable period of time, rather than taking a snapshot of the market at one instant. It can be said that, although the application of the test at some indeterminate point after the grant of the licence may militate against legal certainty, the Commission always has the power (under any block exemption) to withdraw exemption at any time if it considers competition is unduly restricted by the arrangement (see Case T-7/93 *Scholler Lebensmittel GmbH & Co KG v Commission European* and *Langnese-Iglo v Commission* [1995] E.C.R. II-1713.) The addition of the market share test here specifies only one particular instance when it might do this. Also the benefit of an exemption is not lightly withdrawn, and the parties to the agreement are entitled to a proper hearing before the Commission, and to make representations, before this measure can be taken.

8.1.1.4 The Commission's approach to knowhow licences

In order to understand the provisions of the Regulation it is first necessary to understand the background to the Commission's views on the effect on competition of licences of knowhow and intellectual property rights, and how these views found expression first in the Patent Block Exemption and the Knowhow Block Exemption and how they have been modified in the Regulation. **8–32**

Knowhow, although it is sometimes referred to loosely as an industrial or intellectual property right, is not in the true sense a right against all the world, conferring a monopoly in relation to a particular territory, in the way that trade marks, patents, copyright or registered designs do. This being so, the considerations discussed in Chapter 5.1.1.4 relating to Arts 28 and 30 of the EC Treaty, and the use of parallel industrial property rights to prevent free movement of goods within the EC cannot apply. There are no industrial property rights in knowhow which exist objectively and can be exercised in parallel. Rights in knowhow arise *in personam* rather than *in rem*. They can be based upon the general law of confidentiality (in some Member States of the EC such as the UK) which forbids a person who has had information disclosed to him in confidence to use or disclose it otherwise than for the purposes for which it was disclosed. Otherwise they arise solely from agreement between the parties, whereby one party delivers information to the other, and the party to whom information is disclosed binds himself to the discloser as to the use which he will make of the information, and the price that he will pay for the disclosure, whether by way of royalty or lump sum. **8–33**

The Commission thus does not regard what is often called a knowhow licence, as in truth a licence at all, but only an agreement to hand over information upon certain conditions, because, apart from the agreement, there is no way in which the party who discloses the information can control the use of it by the party to whom it has been disclosed. Except for the imposition of an obligation to keep the information confidential, the Commission has made it clear that it does not consider that the party making the disclosure has any other right that can be seen as arising independently of the agreement so as to qualify for consideration as to whether its protection is "justified" under Art.30 in derogation of the principles of free movement of goods contained in Art.28 of the EC Treaty. Thus every provision under the licence, including the binding by the discloser of his own right to use the information (*e.g.* by the grant of an "exclusive" knowhow licence) will be a potential contravention of Art.81(1), and each case must be considered on its merits by the parties for exemption under Art.81(3), unless it falls within the Regulation. **8–34**

Thus the Commission will always regard an exclusive knowhow licence to be in contravention of Art.81(1), so that if the parties desire exclusivity they must either justify the imposition of the restriction under Art.81(3), or claim the benefit of the Regulation. **8–35**

8–36 Where a knowhow licence is non-exclusive and does not impose other restrictions which would be caught under Art.81(1) the Commission has stated that the licence is not caught merely because obligations are imposed to keep the knowhow confidential. Care must however be taken in these cases to ensure that the knowhow licence is not regarded as only a part of the arrangements, so that, while the licence itself receives negative clearance some ancillary agreement is caught.

8–37 In the Commission Decision *Re The Agreements Between Schlegel Corporation and Compagnie Des Produits Industriels De l'Ouest SA* [1984] 2 C.M.L.R. 179 the Commission confirmed that a knowhow agreement on a non-exclusive basis, granting the right to use knowhow to make the product in any Member State of the EC and to sell it throughout the world was not a contravention of Art.81(1). However, this was coupled with an agreement by the licensee to use and to purchase exclusively from the licensor a particular component for the product for a period of five years. This agreement was held to contravene Art.81(1) since it was too long for a normal long-term sale agreement.

8–38 Originally, one looked to various Commission decisions to give pointers as to the way in which knowhow licences should be drafted so as to avoid Art.81(1) or so as to be most likely to obtain exemption under Art.81(3). This ceased to be necessary for the most part once the Knowhow Block Exemption was created. Now, under the Regulation, most knowhow licences will be able to claim exemption. Even those which do not automatically fall under the Regulation will, currently, be able to take advantage of the accelerated opposition procedure discussed below, and the provisions of the Regulation give a sufficient guide in most cases to the terms in the agreements that the Commission finds acceptable or unacceptable.

8.1.1.5 The previous block exemption for patent licences

8–39 When one turns to licences of true intellectual property rights such as patents or trade marks where rights arise *in rem* independently of the agreement, the Commission still considered, for many years, that an exclusive licence of such a right automatically entailed restrictions (purely by reason of the exclusive nature of the grant) which in principle contravened Art.81(1), thus requiring an application for exemption under Art.81(3), and giving the Commission the power, in theory, to scrutinise every exclusive licence of industrial property rights in the EC, and exercise a discretion in considering whether it was in the public interest.

8–40 When the first draft of the Patent Block Exemption was published the Commission still maintained this view. However, the European Court decision in the so-called "*Maize Seed*" case (*LC Nungesser KG and Kurt Eisele v EC Commission* [1983] 1 C.M.L.R. 278) required the Commission to change that view.

8–41 First of all the Court held that plant breeders' rights, which are rights created by statute under national laws, analogous to, but not the same as, patents, should be treated the same as other industrial and commercial property rights for the purposes of Arts 30 and 81 of the EC Treaty. The case, which is concerned with licences of those rights, can thus be taken as an authority for licences of all industrial property rights generally.

The German and British governments intervened in the proceedings and submitted that the basis of the Commission Decision which was being contested was misconceived in that the Commission regarded every exclusive licence of an industrial or commercial property right, whatever its nature, as an agreement prohibited by Art.81(1) so that in all cases the Commission had the right to consider whether it should be granted exemption under Art.81(3). **8–42**

The Court however distinguished two types of exclusive licence. There was the "open exclusive" licence where the licensor undertook to the licensee not to grant "other licences in respect of the same territory and not to compete himself with the licensee in that territory". The other type of exclusive licence was one where there was an "assignment or licence with absolute territorial protection, under which the parties to the contract propose, as regards the products and the territory in question, to eliminate all competition from third parties, such as parallel importers or licensees for other territories". **8–43**

The Court concluded that, at least in the present situation, the "grant of an open exclusive licence, that is to say a licence which does not affect the position of third parties such as parallel importers and licensees for other territories, is not itself incompatible with Art 81(1)". **8–44**

However, the restrictions in this case went on to attempt to prevent parallel imports and imports from other licensees, and "the Court has consistently held that absolute territorial protection granted to a licensee in order to enable parallel imports to be controlled and prevented results in artificial maintenance of separate national markets contrary to the Treaty". Thus these restrictions were subject to Art.81(1) and it was within the discretion of the Commission as to whether or not the facts of the case justified the grant of exemption to those arrangements under Art.81(3). **8–45**

It was in the light of the distinction between the open exclusive licence and the licence with absolute territorial protection that the Commission then proceeded to review, and to relax, the wording of the Patent Block Exemption to the form in which it came into force. **8–46**

Since knowhow is not regarded as an industrial property right by the Commission, and the *Maize Seed* case applied only to industrial property rights with no mention of knowhow, the Commission was not required to change its view of exclusive licences relating only to knowhow, and, despite representations to the contrary, did not at that stage regard them as suitable subjects for inclusion in the block exemption granted by the Patent Block Exemption. The inclusion within the Patent Block Exemption of a licence covering patents and knowhow associated with the licensed patents was as far as the Commission was then prepared to go. **8–47**

Therefore the Patent Block Exemption applied to a transfer of knowhow only where the agreement combined "the licensing of patents and the **8–48** communication of knowhow". Nevertheless the knowhow still had to have some relation to the patent, even if it were more important to the realisation of the invention than the patent. It was not possible to bring a knowhow licence within the Patent Regulation by combining it with a licence of a patent, if the knowhow had no relation to the patent. This is now specifically permitted in the case of a mixed licence under the Regulation (see recital 5).

8.1.1.6 The previous block exemption for knowhow licences

8–49 It is now necessary to consider the history of the Knowhow Block Exemption which came into effect from July 1 1989. Following many representations from industrial and other interested parties, the Commission approved the need for a block exemption, similar to the Patent Block Exemption, to apply to certain classes of knowhow licences. The Commission stated (Preamble (1) to the Knowhow Regulation):

> "The increasing importance of non-patented technical information ... commonly termed "knowhow", the large number of agreements currently being concluded by undertakings ... solely for the exploitation of such information ... and the fact that the transfer of knowhow is, in practice, frequently irreversible, make it necessary to provide greater legal certainty with regard to the status of such agreements under the competition rules, thus encouraging the dissemination of technical knowledge in the Community. In the light of experience so far it is possible to define a category of such knowhow licensing agreements covering all or part of the common market which are capable of falling within the scope of Article 81(1) but which can normally be regarded as satisfying the conditions laid down in Article 81(3)..."

Some of its preliminary thinking on the subject can be seen in the Commission Decision *Re Jus-Rol* [1988] O.J. L69.

8–50 The Knowhow Regulation applied not only to licences of knowhow ("pure knowhow licensing agreements") but also to two categories of mixed knowhow and patent licensing agreements. The first category comprised of agreements which were not exempted under the Patent Block Exemption (*i.e.* mixed agreements which included the licence of patents which were not necessary for the achievement of the objects of the licensed technology, but where the licensed technology contained both patented and non-patented elements). The second category comprised of agreements which (whether or not the patents licensed with the knowhow were necessary for the exploitation of the knowhow) contained obligations which restricted the exploitation of the relevant technology by the licensor in Member States without patent protection in so far as and as long as such obligations were based in whole or in part on the exploitation of the licensed knowhow and fulfilled the other conditions set out in the Knowhow Block Exemption.

8.1.1.7 The provisions of Reg.240/96

It is now possible to see how the Regulation combined and improved upon the old block exemptions. The Regulation follows the same pattern as the old block exemptions, and it is convenient to summarise its provisions here. Licences covered by the Regulation may contain the restrictions listed in Art.1 relating to exclusivity, but must not contain the restrictions listed in Art.3 (the "black list") which are generally considered to be restrictive of competition. Obligations listed in Art.2 (the "white list") may be imposed, as they are not generally considered restrictive of competition, and ought to be exempted even if, under the special circumstances of a particular case, they happen *prima facie* to be caught by Art.81(1). The black list is shorter than in the old block exemptions, and the white list, although many of its provisions follow the old block exemptions, has been redrafted and simplified, and some new provisions have been added to it. **8–51**

The provisions of Art.1 will be dealt with at a later stage in this chapter, but it will again be useful to summarise briefly the provisions of Arts 2 and 3. **8–52**

Under Art.2, the following obligations are not considered restrictive of competition: **8–53**

- Confidentiality restrictions covering the licensed knowhow, even after termination of the agreement.
- Prohibitions on sublicensing or assigning.
- Restrictions on exploitation of the licensed knowhow or patents after the termination of the licence, in so far and so long as the knowhow still remains secret and the patents remain in force.
- An obligation on the licensee to grant a licence to the licensor over improvements generated by the licensee provided that to the extent the improvement is severable from the licensed knowhow, the licence is non-exclusive so that the licensee can exploit the improvement as he wishes, (provided this does not involve disclosure of the licensor's confidential knowhow) and that the licensor has undertaken a reciprocal obligation (either exclusive or non-exclusive) to license improvements generated by the licensor.
- Obligations on the licensee to adhere to minimum quality standards or to procure from the licensee goods and services, (in so far as such adherence or procurement is necessary for a technically proper exploitation of the licensed technology, or conforms to minimum quality standards respected by the licensor and its other licensees), and to permit the licensor to carry out related checks.
- Obligations on the licensee to inform the licensor of misappropriation of the knowhow or infringement of the licensed patents, or to take or assist the licensor in taking legal proceedings related to such matters.

- Obligations to continue paying royalties
  - for the periods and according to the methods freely determined by the parties where the knowhow becomes public without the act of the licensor, (without prejudice to the right of the licensor to claim damages if the knowhow was disclosed by the licensee in breach of the agreement); and
  - over a period beyond the duration of the licensed patents in order to facilitate payment.
- Obligations restricting the field of use of the licensed knowhow and patents.
- Minimum royalty obligations.
- A "most favoured nation clause" binding upon the licensor.
- Obligations for the licensee to mark the product manufactured under the licence with the licensor's name.
- An obligation on the licensee not to use the licensed technology to construct facilities for third parties, provided such obligation is without prejudice to the licensee's right to expand his own facilities or set up additional facilities on normal commercial terms including payment of additional royalty.
- An obligation on the licensee to supply only a limited quantity of the licensed product to a particular customer where the licence was granted to give that customer a second source of supply (this also applies where it is the customer himself who is the licensee).
- Reservation by the licensor of the right to exercise rights conferred by a patent to oppose exploitation of the technology by the licensee outside the territory.
- A reservation by the licensor of the right to terminate the licence if the licensee contests the validity of the patents or the secrecy of the knowhow.
- A reservation by the licensor of the right to terminate a patent licence if the licensee contends that the patents are not necessary.
- An obligation on the licensee to use best endeavours to manufacture and market the licensed product.
- Reservation by the licensor of the right to terminate the exclusivity of a licence and to cease to licence improvements if the licensee starts to compete with the licensor in the EC and a right to require the licensee to prove that he is not using licensed knowhow to do this.

8–54 Under Art.3 the following restrictions must not be contained in the licence if it is to fall within the Regulation:

- Restrictions on the pricing of the licensed products.
- Restrictions between the parties on competition in research and development, or production use or distribution of competing products, without prejudice to the provisions on the white list which oblige the licensee to use best endeavours, and give the licensor the right to alter an exclusive licence to a non-exclusive one if the licensee does start competing.
- One or both parties are required to refuse, without objective reason, to meet demand for the products, or make it difficult for users or resellers to obtain the products from other resellers in the common market, in particular by the exercise of intellectual property rights.
- Restrictions within a field of use to particular groups of customers or specific market segments, for the purpose of market sharing between the parties.
- Quantity restrictions on the licensee's production using the licensed technology, except those restrictions specifically permitted under Art.2 and Art.1(8).
- Obligations on the part of the licensee to assign improvements generated by the licensee to the licensor in whole or part.
- A requirement on the licensor not to license other undertakings to exploit the licensed technology in the licensed territory for periods exceeding those set out in Art.1(2) and (3), and a requirement on either party not to exploit the licensed technology in the territory of the other party or of other licensees for a period exceeding that referred to in Arts 1(2)(3) or (4).

The Regulation contains an opposition procedure in Art.4 which provides **8–55**
that the exemption under the Regulation shall also apply to agreements containing obligations restrictive of competition (provided that they contain no restrictions on the black list) if they are notified under Art.81(3) of the EC Treaty and the Commission does not oppose the exemption within four months. The opposition period under the old block exemptions was six months. Another new feature is the so-called "grey list". These are provisions where the opposition procedure is expressly stated to apply; namely to the following restrictions:

- The imposition on the licensee of the obligation to adhere to quality standards, or procure goods and services, which are not necessary for a technically proper exploitation of the licensed product, or not necessary for adherence to generally respected quality standards.
- No-challenge clauses binding on the licensee.

These clauses were previously on the black list under the old block exemptions. Application under the opposition procedure is to be made using a short form A/B with a minimum amount of information (see recital 25 of the Regulation).

8–56 Here it should be noted the short form non-opposition procedure will become inapplicable once the new regulatory framework under Reg.1/2003 comes into effect on May 1, 2004 (see Chapter 5.1.1.2 and the Commission's remarks set out in Chapter 8.28). After that date, the presence of a provision from the grey list will prevent the Regulation applying at all, but the parties will not be able to notify the relevant agreement to the Commission, to take advantage of the non-opposition procedure. Instead, they will themselves have to decide whether Art.81(3) applies to exempt the whole agreement. Presumably, if the agreement otherwise complies with the Regulation, and given the status of the grey list in the Regulation, this will be easier to do than in the case of the inclusion of a provision on the black list.

8–57 It should be noted that there are analogous provisions to those in the old block exemptions which enable the Regulation to apply to licences which are non-exclusive, or less restrictive than is possible under Art.1, even if they contain any of the obligations contained in Art.2, or any similar obligations but more limited in scope (see Arts 1(5), 2(3) and 2(4)).

8–58 Article 5 states that the Regulation does not apply to certain types of agreements. Patent pools are excluded. So (in the case of a joint venture) are licensing agreements between the partners, or between any of the partners and the joint venture, unless the participating parties together have less than a 20 per cent market share where the licence covers production only, or less than a 10 per cent market share where it covers production and distribution. Licensing agreements between competitors are excluded unless the parties are not subject to any territorial restrictions within the EC. Agreements whose main purpose is the licensing of intellectual property rights other than patents, and agreements entered into solely for the purposes of sale (ie franchise agreements) are also excluded.

8–59 Article 6 applies the Regulation to sublicences, assignments subject to earn-out royalties and agreements where the rights and obligations of the licensor or the licensee are assumed by connected undertakings.

8–60 Article 8 has a wide definition of patents, which includes plant breeders certificates, semiconductor topographies and supplementary protection certificates for medicinal products. The definition also includes applications for such rights. Article 8(3) makes it clear that the Regulation also applies to licensing agreements which are automatically prolonged by the inclusion of improvements, provided that the licensee has the right to refuse such improvements or each party can terminate on the expiry of the initial term and at least every three years thereafter.

8–61 There are several definitions which need to be dealt with. Article 10 contains a number of useful definitions. Article 10(1) defines knowhow as technical information which is secret, substantial and identified. This means that the Regulation does not cover commercial or marketing knowhow, so that, for instance, a franchise agreement relating to distribution could not fall within the Regulation (see Art.5(5)). Article 10(2) defines "secret" quite broadly as something which is not "generally known or easily accessible". Article 10(3) defines "substantial" as "useful", that is capable of improving the competitive position of the licensee. Article 10(4) defines "identified" as described or recorded (in such a manner as to make it possible to verify that the knowhow fulfils the criteria of secrecy and substantiality and that the licensee is not unduly restricted in the exploitation of his own technology) by being set out either in the licence agreement or in a separate document or other appropriate form at the latest when the knowhow is transferred.

Thus, for the Regulation to apply to a knowhow licence, the knowhow **8–62** must in summary relate to technical matter and be important, and identifiable. This has obvious implications for the way knowhow is defined in the licence agreement or actually transferred. The draftsman who wishes to obtain the advantage of the regulation will have to define the relevant knowhow very precisely. None of the definitions in Chapter 1.2.11 would do by themselves. Versions (b) and (d) in that section come closest to it, but only because these refer to documents that have to be handed over, and will presumably be identifiable at the latest at the date of transfer. Detailed reference to manuals, drawings and specifications in a schedule will probably be necessary.

This definition of knowhow has now become standard in the Commis- **8–63** sion's practice and is widely applied. For instance a similar definition is used in Reg.2790/99 and in Reg.1400/2002.

8.1.1.8 Licences of intellectual property not covered by Reg.240/96 or Reg.2790/99

Finally, there are still licences of intellectual property rights which remain **8–64** outside the Regulation, but are not covered by Reg.2790/99 because they constitute the primary purpose of the agreement and are not "directly related to the use, sale or resale of goods or services by the buyer or its customers".

How are these to be dealt with? This situation will occur where a patent **8–65** and/or knowhow licence would fall under the Regulation, except for the fact that it also contains a licence of another intellectual property right which is of too much importance to be regarded as "ancillary" (see the discussion on *Re Moosehead/Whitbread* above). Similarly a pure licence of intellectual property rights other than patents would also fall outside the Regulation.

However, the Commission equates licences of copyright and design rights **8–66** to patent licences. In its Twelfth Report on Competition Policy (para.88) in referring to its 1982 Decisions *Re STEMRA* and *Re Neilson-Hordell/Richmark* it said:

> "The Commission has already indicated in several cases its views on the application of the competition rules to export restrictions in licences having as their object the manufacture and sale of products protected by copyright. In such cases the attitude taken by the Commission is generally the same as that adopted towards patent licensing agreements."

8–67 In both Decisions the Commission had prohibited contractual export bans, a no-challenge clause, a non-competition clause, an obligation to transfer title to copyright in improvements to the licensor, and a clause requiring payment of royalties on products not protected by copyright. This view of the Commission has now been confirmed by the Decision in the *Maize Seed* case. Thus, although the Regulation cannot apply to licences of copyright or design rights, there is little doubt that licences of such rights which follow the guidelines of the Regulations (in so far as they are applicable) would currently receive exemption under Art.81(3) fairly easily in most cases. Similarly under the new regulatory framework (see Chapter 5.1.1.2) where the parties base their licence on the provisions of the Regulation, they should have less concerns about the applicability of Art.81(3).

8–68 It should therefore be possible to use this precedent for such licences, with some confidence as to the applicability of Art.81(3). It would also be possible, as in the case of patent licences, by relying on the *Maize Seed* case decision, to draft an open exclusive licence of such rights, imposing only the obligations mentioned in Art.2 of the Regulation as not generally restrictive of competition. In the absence of other restrictions the licence would not in this case contravene Art.81(1) at all.

8–69 Trade mark licences which are unconnected with a distribution, manufacturing or franchise agreement are not common. The trade mark licence discussed in Chapter 12 is meant to act as an ancillary agreement for the distribution and manufacturing agreements in this book, and its status under Art.81 is discussed in that chapter. For the purposes of this book the most important type of copyright licence is that relating to software licences. These are discussed in Chapter 11.

8–70 Finally it should be noted that in this precedent, unlike Chapter 7, reference is made not to the "Principal" but to the "Licensor". This has been done deliberately because the Regulation speaks consistently of the "Licensor", and it was felt that complete substitution of this term with the "Principal" would become too confusing. However, when drafting a specific agreement using this precedent there is no legal reason why the licensor cannot be referred to as the "Principal" if so desired.

8.1.2 Current position under UK competition law

8–71 The current position under UK competition law is based upon the principles set out in the Competiton Act 1998 and is described in a draft Guideline from the Office of Fair Trading (OFT 418 November 2001: Intellectual Property Rights). The OFT does not intend to finalise and issue the Guidelines until the Commission has resolved upon the final form of the replacement for the Technology Transfer Block Exemption (Reg.240/96) (see Chapter 8. 28 below) but the current draft of the Guideline provides a useful summary of the current position under UK competition law. As would be expected (see s.60 of the 1998 Act) the position does not differ substantially from that already described under EC competition law.

There follows a summary of the main points of the Guidelines in relation to licensing of intellectual property ("IPR"). For the purposes of the Guidelines it should be noted that the term "IPR" includes knowhow. **8–72**

Initially OFT 418 fixes upon certain differences between the approach of EC and UK competition law in relation to IPR. At the EC level there is a tension between national systems of IPR protection and the Community single market objective. In certain circumstances, the "exercise" of IPRs under national laws may operate to compartmentalise the single market. As a result, much of the EC case law dealing with IPRs has been driven by the single market objective. The Director intends to follow the principles developed in EC case law in relation to IPRs, but in practice will do this only where they are relevant in a domestic context (para.1.8) **8–73**

The mere existence of an IPR will not be anti-competitive. There may however be circumstances where the exercise of an IPR is anticompetitive (para.1.9). **8–74**

Under the Chapter I Prohibition, many agreements which include IPR provisions are likely to benefit from an exclusion or exemption (para.2.5). Agreements that do not are subject to the Chapter I Prohibition, but do not fall within its scope, unless they have an appreciable effect on competition (para.2.6) (here the usual provisions as to "appreciable effect" apply—namely parties' combined share on relevant market not to exceed 25 per cent, no price fixing or market sharing and no impact by way of cumulative effect—see para.2.15 and compare the equivalent provisions in the Guideline OFT 401: The Chapter I Prohibition). **8–75**

The most relevant exclusion is The Competition Act (Land and Vertical Agreements Exclusion) Order 2000 (SI 2000/310). This excludes vertical agreements relating to the sale or purchase of goods and services and covers the same ground as Reg.2790/99, except the former excludes all such vertical agreements from the scope of the Chapter I Prohibition, (unless they fix prices) while the latter only excludes such agreements from the scope of Art.81(1) where the market share of the supplier or (where relevant the buyer) does not exceed 30 per cent, and subject to certain hardcore restraints and other anticompetitive conditions in addition to price fixing. **8–76**

The Order treats licences of IPR contained in such agreements in the same way as Art.2(3) of the regulation. The main effect of this would be to exclude the usual provisions of franchise agreements and distribution agreements coupled with trade mark licences from the scope of the Chapter I Prohibition, just as Reg.2790/99 does in relation to Art.81(1) (see the discussion in Chapter 8.1). **8–77**

Since Reg.2790/99 is also a parallel exemption for the purposes of the Chapter I Prohibition (see s.10(2) of the 1998 Act), there is considerable overlap between the regulation and the Order, and the UK government has given consideration as to whether it would be sensible to repeal the Order so far as it relates to vertical agreements and rely on the parallel exemption under Reg.2790/99. To date the Order still remains in force. **8–78**

So far as parallel exemptions are concerned, in addition to Reg.2790/99, Reg.240/96 (technology transfer block exemption), Reg.2658/00 (speciali- **8–79** sation agreements) and Reg.2659/00 (research and development agreements) are also relevant, although the latter two may not always be relevant given that they contain market share thresholds at or below the 25 per cent level, and at this level the appreciable effect threshold of 25 per cent under the Chapter I Prohibition will apply in any event (para.2.13). In practice there are many agreements which include IPR provisions that are likely to benefit from a parallel exemption by virtue of one of these block exemptions (para.2.14).

8–80 The general approach to the most common forms of restrictions in agreements which include IPR provisions is set out in paras 2.17 to 2.27. In addition to price fixing and market sharing the main competition concerns will be any provisions which foreclose the market (para.2.18). In these situations it is unlikely that exclusions or parallel exemptions will apply to exclude the agreement in question. The main restraints to be considered which are likely to infringe the Chapter I Prohibition are:

- Any provisions in an IPR licence which directly or indirectly impose minimum resale prices (para.2.19).
- Any provision for an exclusive grant back licence to the licensor of improvements made by the licensee (para.2.23).
- Post-term use bans exceeding the lifetime of the IPR, or a requirement to continue paying royalties after the IPR has expired (para.2.24).

8–81 The following provisions are unlikely to infringe the Chapter I Prohibition:

- Grants of exclusive rights to manufacture and sell goods in a particular territory and/or the grant of a particular field of exploitation are unlikely to infringe the Chapter I Prohibition unless they have a foreclosure effect (para.2.21).
- Provisions preventing sublicensing or assignment (para.2.23).
- Quality control provisions (para.2.25).
- Tying provisions may infringe the Chapter I Prohibition where they have a foreclosure effect unless they are necessary for quality control (para.2.26).
- Minimum quantity provisions will not infringe the chapter I Prohibition unless they have the effect of preventing the licensee from using other IPR to compete with products made using the licensed IPR, and, as a result, they have an appreciable effect on competition through a foreclosure of the market (para.2.27).

8–82 Finally, it should be noted that s.70 of the Competition Act, 1998 repealed ss.44 and 45 of the Patents Act 1977. Section 44 made void certain anticompetitive conditions in patent licences, particularly tying provisions. Section 45 established conditions for termination or variation of a patent licence once the patent(s) to which it related had ceased to be in force. These sections were repealed because the prohibitions in the 1998 Act provide adequate safeguards against anticompetitive provisions in relation to those matters, in respect of patent licences made on or after March 1, 2000. These sections continue to apply to patent licences made before that date (paras 4.1. to 4.3)

For all practical purposes the current position under UK competition law in relation to the licences of intellectual property is the same as that under EC competition law, given the application of Reg.240/96 as a parallel exemption under s.10(2) of the 1998 Act. On this basis the discussion of the precedent in the remainder of this chapter proceeds upon the basis of EC competition law alone. The many detailed provisions relating to cross-border trade and demarcation of territories are in practice unlikely to be of any significance in the event that a licence applies only to the UK and has no effect on trade between Member States. However, it is of course possible to partition the UK up into separate territories in such a way that the partitioning would have an effect on trade within the UK (*e.g.* three licences with territorial limitations to England and Wales, Scotland and Northern Ireland respectively). In this case, the territorial provisions in the precedent could be usefully adapted so as to impose territorial restraints and at the same time take advantage of the parallel exemption available under s.10(2) of the Act in relation to Reg.240/96. **8–83**

8.2 Licence

In this Agreement the following terms shall have the following meanings: **8–84**

"Licensed Technology" means the Knowhow [and the Patents] and includes improvements subsequently made thereto irrespective of whether and to what extent such improvements are Exploited by the parties to this agreement or by other licensees of the Licensor.

"Licensed Products" means goods or services the production or provision of which requires the use of the Licensed Technology and includes the Products.

"Exploit" means any use of the Licensed Technology, in particular (a) in the production of Licensed Products or (b) in the active or passive sales in a territory of Licensed Products, even if not coupled with manufacture of Licensed Products in that territory, or (c) the leasing of Licensed Products; and "Exploitation" shall be construed accordingly.

"First Date" means the date when the relevant Licensed Product [is] [was] first put on the market within the EC by a licensee (including the Licensee) under a licence of the Licensed Technology granted by the Licensor. [For the avoidance of doubt the parties agree that the date as aforesaid was . . .]

"Necessary Patents", "Territory of the Licensor", "Parallel Patents" and "Connected Undertaking" shall bear the meanings assigned thereto in Art.10(5), (12), (13) and (14) respectively of Commission Regulation 240/96.

Before drafting clauses which deal with the licence grant, some extra definitions in addition to the usual ones relating to the Knowhow, the Patents, the Territory and the Products are necessary, and will be referred to in various places in the precedent as required. These definitions are based on Art.10 of the Regulation, with some adaptation and interpretation except in the case of the last four definitions which are simply incorporated by reference. In order to avoid disrupting the numbering system it is possible to place them in Sch.1 along with the usual definitions mentioned in this paragraph.

8–85 The definition of licensed technology is somewhat shorter than that provided in the Regulation, but it does include improvements as required by the Regulation. This is because it is assumed that the knowhow and or patents licensed under the agreement comply as a matter of fact with the detailed definitions of Art.10(5) and (7). If this were not the case, the Regulation could be inapplicable anyway, unless some knowhow or patents qualified, and the remainder could be treated as "ancillary". The draftsman should always satisfy himself as to the qualifying nature of the knowhow and patents before concluding that the Regulation applies.

8–86 It should be noted that the definition of licensed products (products which *require* the use of the licensed technology—see Art.10(8)) is always at least co-extensive with the Products, and in some cases can be wider.

8–87 The First Date definition is important as it is the baseline from which various periods of restriction permitted by the Regulation commence to run. The problem with such a definition is that it leaves open for argument what the date actually is. Wherever possible, if the product has already been put on the market, the draftsman should ascertain the facts. Once this has been done it is possible to substitute a simple date for this definition, or to include the general definition but using the phrase in square brackets. In any event use of the definition will be no protection if the date does not match the true facts. The date under the definition can of course be a date in the future, after the signature of the relevant agreement, if the product is a new one that has not yet been put on the market at all. This is important if the licensee has to go through a period of set-up of manufacturing facilities, or the procedures for product registration or clinical trials before he can commence manufacture and sale.

8–88 With the aid of these definitions it is now possible to set out a licence grant which complies with the Regulation.

8–89 8.2.1 The Licensor hereby grants the Licensee a licence under the [Knowhow] [Patents] [Patents and Knowhow] to make [or have made by way of a subcontractor or a Connected Undertaking] the Products in the Territory.

8–90 8.2.2 The Licensor hereby grants the Licensee a licence to distribute and sell the Products manufactured pursuant to cl.8.2.1 under the Trade Mark within the EC (subject to cl.8.5).

8–91 8.2.3(a) The Licensor undertakes that (subject to the continuance of this Agreement) to the extent that and for so long as the Licensed Technology continues to be protected by one or more of the Patents licensed by it under cl.8.2.1 it will neither license a third party to Exploit the Licensed Technology in the Territory, nor Exploit the Licensed Technology in the Territory itself.

OR

8.2.3(b) The Licensor undertakes that (subject to the continuance of this Agreement) for a period expiring ten years from the First Date or when the Knowhow ceases to be "secret" or "substantial" within the meaning of Art.10(2) and (3) of Commission Regulation 240/96, whichever first occurs, it will neither license a third party to Exploit the Licensed Technology in the Territory, nor Exploit the Licensed Technology in the Territory itself.

OR

8.2.3(c) The Licensor undertakes that (subject to the continuance of this Agreement) for the Confidential Period or the Necessary Patent Period (whichever is the longer) it will neither license a third party to Exploit the Licensed Technology in the Territory, nor Exploit the Licensed Technology in the Territory itself. For the purposes of this clause (a) the "Confidential Period" shall mean a period expiring ten years from the First Date or when the Knowhow ceases to be "secret" or "substantial" within the meaning of Art.10(2) and (3) of Commission Regulation 240/96 whichever first occurs, and (b) the "Necessary Patent Period" shall mean the period during which a Necessary Patent licensed by it as one of the Patents under cl.8.2.1 remains in force in the Territory.

Clauses 8.2.1 and 8.2.2 provide the basic grant of the licence, and are self-explanatory. It should be remembered that the definition of licensed technology includes improvements. While this is important for the purposes of the Regulation, it may not be the intention of the parties to licence improvements under the agreement at all. It is thus necessary to deal with this specifically in the definitions of the knowhow and of the patents in detail in Sch.1, rather than to permit improvements to be swept in indiscriminately by using the term "Licensed Technology" in this clause. It should also be remembered that where improvements are included automatically, and thereby prolong the duration of the periods of protection granted under Art.1 by refreshing the licensed technology, there must be inserted in the termination provisions under cl.8.16 an option to permit the licensee to refuse such improvements or (in the absence of such a right) an option to terminate the licence on the expiry of the initial term and at least every three years thereafter (see Art.8(3)).

Next, returning to the point that the licensed technology may be capable **8–92**
of use for more products than those which are subject to the grant of the licence in the specific agreement, the wording of cl.8.2.1 can be a field of use restriction as it stands. This is permitted under Art.2(1)(8) of the Regulation. The Regulation also permits additional restrictions on the licence granted which go beyond the field of use. Under Art.2(1)(12) the licensee can be restricted from using the licensed technology to construct "facilities" for third parties (*e.g.* production lines), but cannot be restricted from increasing the capacity of his own "facilities" or setting up additional "facilities" for

himself, provided he pays the proper royalty and otherwise agrees normal commercial terms. Under Art.2(1)(13), he can be restricted to providing product as a second source of supply, and, under Art.1(1)(8), to producing a product for own use only, although in this latter case the restriction can apply only for the same limited periods as apply to cl.8.9.3.

8–93 Clause 8.2.3, however, needs some consideration. Version (a) is for pure patent licences. Version (b) is for pure knowhow licences. Version (c) is for mixed knowhow and patent licences. They comply with Arts 1(1)(1) and (2), and Art.1(2), (3) and (4) respectively.

8–94 The drafting of version (a) causes some particular problems. The limitations on the restrictions imposed by this version must be based on the wording of Art.1(2), covering pure patent licenses. However, Art.1(2), somewhat confusingly, contains various limitations on the length of the restrictions permitted under Art.1(1) in one omnibus clause, providing limitations "to the extent that and for as long as the licensed product is protected by parallel patents, in the territories respectively of the licensee (points (1), (2), (7) and (8)), the licensor (point (3)) and other licensees (Points (4) and (5))".

8–95 If one reads Art.10(13) and Art.1(2) literally, the patents licensed to the licensee in question can be "Parallel Patents", but only where there are also true parallel patents in existence in other areas outside the licensed territory which are the equivalent of the licensed patent in the licensee's territory. This is because otherwise there would no patents for the licensed patent (being the parallel patent in the licensee's territory) to be parallel to within the terms of the definition in Art.10(13) ("patents which . . . protect the *same* invention in *various* Member States"). This is clearly illogical, since it would mean that where there were no patents parallel to the licensed patent, the restrictions in points (1), (2), (7) and (8) could never be imposed at all. This cannot be what the Regulation intended, and seems to be an unintended effect of the omnibus drafting of Art.1(2). For instance, recital 12 simply states that the obligations detailed in Art.1 "may be permitted . . . in respect of territories where the licensed product is protected by patents as long as these remain in force". Similarly, recital 16 contains the phrase "so long as the patents remain in force". Both of these recitals are clearly concerned only with whether there is patent protection, in the relevant territory where the restriction bites, on a stand alone basis without any concern as to the existence of parallel patents. In cases where this is not the licensee's territory, the patent concerned will, of necessity, be a patent parallel to that licensed to the licensee, and this is what the definition in Art.10(13) is really getting at. However, there is no such necessity when dealing with the licensee's territory, when only the duration and extent of the protection granted by the licensed patent is relevant.

8–96 On the basis of the above discussion, version (a) has thus been drafted so as to limit the restrictions on the licensee in relation to the protection provided by the licensed patent in the licensee's territory. The defined term "Patents" is used, and the confusion caused in relation to the precise definition of "Parallel Patents" is avoided by not using that definition at all.

Version (b) causes no particular problems. The reference to the ten-year limitation period is clear enough, provided that one uses the definition of the "First Date" as set out above. However, the use of this period in version (c), together with the qualification of these periods by reference to the life of "Necessary Patents" as defined in Art.10(5) does cause some problems. **8–97**

Article 10(5) defines "necessary" as "necessary for the putting into effect of the licensed technology in so far as, in the absence of such a licence, the realisation of the licensed technology would not be possible or would be possible to a lesser extent or in more difficult or costly conditions". The article concludes "Such patents must therefore be of technical legal or economic interest to the licensee". Thus, a value judgment is required as to which patents qualify as "necessary", although if a licensee is prepared to pay for their use, *prima facie* they would seem to be of interest to him. These points cannot be covered by drafting into cl.8.2.3 phrases about "necessary" patents. If one deems the licensed patents "necessary", the Commission, in applying the Regulation, will simply look at the facts as to what is necessary and ignore the wording. On the other hand, if one uses the wording in Art.1(4), one is simply postponing the decision as to what patents, if any, are "necessary", and leaving the matter unclear until either the parties have an argument or the Commission intervenes. **8–98**

A statement by the licensee that he agrees and accepts that the patents are necessary is not strictly a no-challenge clause. The grey-list provision on no-challenge clauses, Art.(4)(2)(b), does not cover a challenge as to whether a patent is necessary. However, such a statement could well be an "obligation restrictive of competition" not covered by the Regulation, which would prevent reliance on the Regulation and would currently necessitate a reference of the agreement to the Commission under the opposition procedure in Art.4. (In this connection, it should also be remembered that Art.2(1)(16) permits a licensor to insert a provision terminating the licence if the licensee raises a claim that a patent is not necessary.) **8–99**

It should also be noted here that the periods mentioned in cl.8.2.3 could fall outside the limit on the validity of the block exemption under the Regulation, since the Regulation is valid only until the end of 2006. The assumption is that licences granted with ten-year periods which run beyond 2006 will be protected by transitional provisions in whatever block exemption replaces the current Regulation. This was what happened in 1996, but, of course, it is hard to be certain whether this will occur again in 2006. It is, of course, possible to impose these restrictions for a period of less than ten years (for knowhow) or for a period less than the life of the patent in question if the parties so desire (see Art.1(5)). **8–100**

Finally, care must be taken with any difference between the extent of the grant under cll.8.2.1 and 8.2.2, and the extent of the restrictions under cl.8.2.3. The version of these clauses in this precedent proceeds on the basis that there is no such difference. In this case, the licensor simply binds himself not to do in the territory what he has licensed the licensee to do. However, since cll.8.2.1 and 8.2.2 use the definitions of the "Patents", and/or "Know-how" and the "Products", while cl.8.2.3. relates to the "Licensed Tech- **8–101** nology", this may not always be the case. First the term "Licensed Technology" includes improvements. The "Patents" and/or the "Knowhow" may not do so. Second, cl.8.2.3 refers to "Exploitation of the Licensed Technology". This may well be far wider than making or having made and distributing the Products. As discussed above, the definition of the "Products" can be a field of use restriction covering only some of the products or uses to which the licensed technology can be put. Also, the term "exploit" includes sublicensing, which clearly is not permitted by the versions of cll.8.2.1 and 8.2.2 in this precedent.

8–102 Since Art.1(5) permits restrictions of the types set out in Art.1(1) but of "a lesser scope", it is possible for the licensor to cut down the extent of the restrictions in cl.8.2.3 to match a limited licence grant under cll.8.2.1 and 8.2.2. For instance, if the licensed technology can be used for products A and B, the licensor could licence the licensee under cll.8.2.1 and 8.2.2 only for Product A and bind himself under cl.8.2.3 only in respect of product A, leaving himself free to exploit the licensed technology in the licensee's territory in relation to Product B. Commercially, the licensor would clearly be wise to consider matching the restrictions to the extent of his grant wherever he wished to preserve his freedom to exploit the technology in the licensee's territory in other ways. However, there does not seem to be any requirement under the Regulation to match the restrictions to the grant as a matter of course in order to take advantage of the Regulation.

8–103 The only problem that might arise would be where the grant was so narrow, and the restriction so wide that the purpose of the licence was really some kind of disguised market sharing, which was aimed at preventing the licensor from exploiting his technology in a particular territory, even though the grant to the licensee was so narrow that, for all practical purposes, the licensee was in fact not really exploiting it either. Since these are the sort of arrangements that are likely to be entered into between competitors, Art.5(1),(2) or (3) may apply to exclude the arrangement from the Regulation, or the arrangement may later have the benefit of the Regulation withdrawn by the Commission for anti-competitive behaviour under Art.7.

8.3 Licensee's general undertakings

8.3.1 Due diligence

8–104 8.3.1 The Licensee shall during the continuance of this Agreement use its best endeavours to manufacture and market the Products and Exploit the [Patents] [Knowhow] [Knowhow and the Patents] in accordance with the terms of this Agreement.

This provision as it stands, is in the terms permitted by Art.2(1)(17) of the Regulation so far as the first part is concerned. The second part relating to exploitation is also acceptable since its scope is defined by the terms of the agreement. If the agreement is exempt under the Regulation this provision must, *ipso facto*, be unobjectionable.

8.3.2 Conforming to local legislation

8.3.2 See cl.4.3.3. **8–105**

8.3.3 Proper storage of products

See cl.7.3.4. **8–106**

8.3.4 Targets

8.3.4 The Licensee undertakes to achieve targets in relation to the Products in accordance with Sch.2. **8–107**

The Regulation provides that "obligations to pay a minimum royalty or to produce a minimum quantity of the licensed product or to carry out a minimum number of operations exploiting the licensed invention" may be imposed (Art.2(1),(9)). This point is dealt with in more detail in Sch.2.

8.3.5 Non-competition clause

8.3.5(a) The Licensee undertakes during the continuance of this Agreement not to manufacture or sell in the Territory any goods competitive with the Products or be interested directly or indirectly in the importation into the Territory of any such goods without the Licensor's prior written consent. This provision shall not apply to those goods (if any) listed in Sch.3. **8–108**

OR

8.3.5(b) If Licensee during the continuance of this Agreement enters into competition within the EC with the Licensor (including with a Connected Undertaking of the Licensor), in respect of research and development, production, use or distribution of products or services competing with the Products, then the Licensor shall have the right to serve a notice upon the Licensee requiring the Licensee to cease such competing activity within thirty days of service of such notice, and, if the Licensee does not cease such competing activity within thirty days of such service, immediately on the expiry of the said period of thirty days cl.8.2.3 [and cl.8.25.9] shall be deemed to be deleted from this Agreement so that the licences granted by this Agreement become non-exclusive [and neither party shall have any further rights in respect of improvements generated by the other after the date of such amendment] [and the Licensee shall furnish proof to the Licensor that the Licensee is not using the Licensed Technology in connection with such competing activity].

Version (a) is a normal type of provision to find in licensing agreements. However, the treatment of such prohibitions in relation to the EC is such that they are regarded as requiring exemption under Art.81(3). In several decisions the Commission has held that, both in the field of patent licences and of knowhow agreements, such a provision is acceptable and has granted exemption to it. However, the Regulation does not permit the imposition of such a sweeping restriction on competition. Those who wish to take advantage of the Regulation must confine themselves to imposing a requirement for best endeavours to exploit in terms of cl.8.3.1 without a specific ban on dealing in competing goods. However, Art.2(1)(18) of the Regulation permits the licensor in the event of such competing activity, to make an exclusive licence non-exclusive, to cease communicating improvements, and to require the licensee to prove that he is not using the licensor's technology to make competing products. A suggested clause is set out in version (b). The position needs to be considered carefully together with the possibility of the application of Art.81(3) if it is wished to impose a full restriction on competing activity. It is hard to see why a licensee would willingly accept the obligation, in the last phrase in square brackets, to prove that he is not using the licensor's technology in the competing activity. It is hard to prove a negative, except perhaps if he can demonstrate a clean room approach to the competing activity (*i.e.* carried on by persons who have had no access to the licensor's technology). Most licensees would, at least, want to qualify this phrase with the concept of proof which is reasonably satisfactory or reasonably conclusive.

8.3.6 Patent and trade mark notices

8–109 See cl.7.3.7.

8.3.7 Indemnity

8–110 See cl.7.3.8.

8.4 Enquiries

8–111 8.4 The Licensee shall during the continuance of this Agreement refer to the Licensor all enquiries it receives for the Products for sale or ultimate delivery outside the EC.

This is a provision which (except in special circumstances) has long since been regarded as not in contravention of Art.81(1) (see *EMI v CBS* and *Polydor v Harlequin* discussed in Chapter 5.5). However, the European Court has already ruled that arrangements relating to imports from outside the EC into only one Member State may in fact affect trade between Member States (see *Javico AG v Yves Saint Laurent Parfums SA* discussed in Chapter 5.5 and see also *EMI v CBS, Polydor v Harlequin* and *Bureau Europeen des Unions de Consommateurs v Commission* discussed in Chapter 5.1.1.4.1). In this last case the Court stated that it is *prima facie* not impossible that the agreement whose objective is to restrict imports from a non-member country into one of the Member States, falls within the scope of Art.81(1) or Art.82.) In the circumstances of the new single market after 1992, such clauses, even though they relate to exports from a Member State, not imports into it, should be viewed with more caution, and avoided unless felt to be commercially essential. In cases of real doubt (for instance where the restriction could affect states bordering the EC, and thus indirectly affect trade within the EC by hindering export to and reimport to the EC from that state), it will be necessary to consider whether Art.81(3) can apply.

8.5 Extra-territorial activities

8.5.1(a) The Licensee shall not during the continuance of this Agreement carry on the following activities in any area within the EC which is outside the Territory in respect of (a) any territory (a "reserved territory") or (b) any customer group (a "reserved customer group") which has in the case of either (a) or (b) been reserved to the Principal or allocated by the Licensor to another licensee: **8–112**

8.5.1.1 actively approach individual customers in a reserved territory or a reserved customer group for orders for the Products (including without limitation by way of direct mail or personal visits); or

8.5.1.2 actively approach a reserved customer group or a specific group of customers in a reserved territory through advertisements in media or other promotions specifically targeted at that reserved customer group or at customers in that reserved territory; or

8.5.1.3 open branches for the sale of the Products in a reserved territory, or establish a distribution outlet or warehouse for the Products in a reserved territory.

8.5.2 Notwithstanding the provisions of this clause, the Licensee shall be entitled to carry out general advertising or promotions in media or on the internet that reach customers in a reserved territory or a reserved customer group provided that such advertising and promotion is primarily intended to reach customers (including without limitation customers in the Territory) who are outside any reserved territory and do not form part of any reserved customer group ("general customers") and that such advertising and promotion is a reasonable way to reach such general customers. **8–113**

8.5.3 The reserved territories and the reserved customer groups in existence at the date of this agreement are set out in Sch.1. Upon a territory becoming or ceasing to be a reserved territory or upon a group of customers becoming or ceasing to be a reserved customer group, the Principal shall notify the Distributor of this occurrence and thereupon Sch.1 shall be deemed to have been amended accordingly. **8–114**

8.5.4 The Licensee shall not (during the continuance of this Agreement sell the Products outside the EC [except into areas from which it is reasonably likely that reimportation of the Products into the EC would occur]. **8–115**

8.5.5 The Licensor shall impose on any other distributor or agent appointed by it **8–116** for areas of the EC outside the Territory obligations identical to those imposed upon the Licensee under cll.8.4 and 8.5 including cl.8.5.3

OR

8.5.1(b) The Licensee shall not (subject to the continuance of this Agreement) for a period expiring ten years from the First Date or when the Knowhow ceases to be "secret" or "substantial" within the meaning of Art.10(2) and (3) of Commission Regulation 240/96, whichever first occurs Exploit the Knowhow in each of the areas comprised within the Territory of the Licensor, namely:

8–117 8.5.2 The Licensee shall not (subject to the continuance of this Agreement) for a period expiring ten years from the First Date or when the Knowhow ceases to be "secret" or "substantial" within the meaning of Art.10(2) and (3) of Commission Regulation 240/96, whichever first occurs manufacture or use Licensed Products in each of the following areas within the EC being areas outside the Territory other than those detailed in cl.8.5.1 in which the Licensor has granted a licence of the Knowhow to a third party on terms similar to this Agreement, namely:

8–118 8.5.3 The Licensee shall not (subject to the continuance of this Agreement) for a period expiring ten years from the First Date or when the Knowhow ceases to be "secret" or "substantial" within the meaning of Art.10(2) and (3) of Commission Regulation 240/96, whichever first occurs, in the areas detailed in cl.8.5.2:

8.5.3.1 advertise Licensed Products or canvass or solicit orders for Licensed Products; or

8.5.3.2 open branches for the sale of Licensed Products; or

8.5.3.3 maintain distribution depots for Licensed Products.

8–119 8.5.4 Without prejudice to the generality of cl.8.5.3 the Licensee shall not put Licensed Products on the market in response to unsolicited orders in any of the areas detailed in cl.8.5.2 (subject to the continuance of this Agreement) for a period expiring five years from the First Date or when the Knowhow ceases to be "secret" or "substantial" within the meaning of Art.10(2) and (3) of Commission Regulation 240/96, whichever first occurs.

8–120 8.5.5 The Licensee shall not during the continuance of this Agreement sell Licensed Products outside the EC [except into areas from which it is reasonably likely that reimportation of Licensed Products into the EC would occur].

8–121 8.5.6 The Licensor shall impose on any other licensee licensed by it to Exploit the Knowhow in any areas of the EC outside the Territory obligations identical to those imposed upon the Licensee under cll.8.4 and 8.5, including cl.8.5.6.

8–122 8.5.7 Upon an area ceasing or commencing to fall under cll.8.5.1 or 8.5.2 or upon an area ceasing to fall under one of the said clauses and commencing to fall under the other of the said clauses, the Licensor shall notify the Licensee of this occurrence, and thereupon the list under cl.8.5.1 and/or cl.8.5.2 as the case may be shall be deemed to have been amended accordingly.

8–123 8.5.8 Notwithstanding the provisions of this clause, the Licensee shall be entitled to carry out general advertising or promotions in media or on the internet that reach customers in areas falling under cll.8.5.1 or 8.5.2 ("reserved areas") provided that such advertising and promotion is primarily intended to reach customers (including without limitation customers in the Territory) who are outside any reserved areas ("general customers") and that such advertising and promotion is a reasonable way to reach general customers.

OR

8.5.1(c) The Licensee shall not (subject to the continuance of this Agreement) for the Confidential Period or the Necessary Patent Period (whichever is the longer): **8–124**

8.5.1.1 Exploit the Knowhow and the Patents in each of the areas comprised within the Territory of the Licensor, namely:

8.5.1.2 manufacture or use Licensed Products in each of the following areas within the EC being areas outside the Territory other than those detailed in cl.8.5.1 in which the Licensor has granted a licence of [the Knowhow] [the Knowhow and the Patents] to a third party on terms similar to this agreement, namely:

8.5.1.3 in the areas detailed in cl.8.5.1.2:

8.5.1.3.1 advertise Licensed Products or canvass or solicit orders for Licensed Products; or

8.5.1.3.2 open branches for the sale of Licensed Products; or

8.5.1.3.3 maintain distribution depots for Licensed Products.

8.5.2 Without prejudice to the generality of cl.8.5.1 the Licensee shall not put Licensed Products on the market in response to unsolicited orders in any of the areas detailed in cl.8.5.2 (subject to the continuance of this Agreement) until the expiry of the Confidential Period or the Necessary Patent Period as defined in cl.8.5.1, whichever first occurs. **8–125**

8.5.3 For the purposes of this cl.8.5(a) in respect of cl.8.5.1, the "Confidential Period" shall mean a period expiring ten years from the First Date or when the Knowhow ceases to "secret" or "substantial" within the meaning of Art.10(2) and (3) of Commission Regulation 240/96 whichever first occurs, (b) in respect of cl.8.5.2, the "Confidential Period" shall mean a period expiring five years from the First Date or when the Knowhow ceases to be "secret" or "substantial" as aforesaid whichever first occurs, and (c) in respect of both cll.8.5.1 and 8.5.2 the "Necessary Patent Period" shall mean the period during which a Necessary Patent licensed by it as one of the Patents under cl.8.2.1 remains in force in the relevant area of the Territory of the Licensor. **8–126**

8.5.4 The Licensee shall not (during the continuance of this Agreement) sell Licensed Products outside the EC [except into areas from which it is reasonably likely that reimportation of Licensed Products into the EC would occur]. **8–127**

8.5.5 The Licensor shall impose on any other licensee licensed by it to Exploit the Knowhow and the Patents in any areas of the EC outside the Territory obligations identical to those imposed upon the Licensee under cll.8.4 and 8.5, including cl.8.5.6. **8–128**

8–129 8.5.6 Upon an area ceasing or commencing to fall under cll.8.5.1 or 8.5.2 or upon an area ceasing to fall under one of the said clauses and commencing to fall under the other of the said clauses, the Licensor shall notify the Licensee of this occurrence, and thereupon the list under cl.8.5.1 and/or cl.8.5.2 as the case may be shall be deemed to have been amended accordingly.

8–130 8.5.7 Notwithstanding the provisions of this clause, the Licensee shall be entitled to carry out general advertising or promotions in media or on the internet that reach customers in areas falling under cll.8.5.1 or 8.5.2 ("reserved areas") provided that such advertising and promotion is primarily intended to reach customers (including without limitation customers in the Territory) who are outside any reserved areas ("general customers") and that such advertising and promotion is a reasonable way to reach general customers.

OR

8–131 8.5.1(d) The Licensee shall not during the continuance of this Agreement for so long as and to the extent that a Parallel Patent protecting a Licensed Product remains in force in the relevant area Exploit the Licensed Technology in each of the areas comprised within the Territory of the Licensor, namely:

8–132 8.5.2 The Licensee shall not during the continuance of this agreement for so long as and to the extent that a Parallel Patent protecting a Licensed Product remains in force in the relevant area manufacture or use that Licensed Product in each of the following areas within the EC being areas outside the Territory other than those detailed in cl.8.5.1 in which the Licensor has granted a licence of the Patents to a third party on terms similar to this agreement, namely:

8–133 8.5.3 The Licensee shall not during the continuance of this Agreement in each of the areas detailed in cl.8.5.2 for so long as and to the extent that a Parallel Patent protecting a Licensed Product remains in force in the relevant area:

8.5.3.1 advertise that Licensed Product or canvass or solicit orders for that Licensed Product; or

8.5.3.2 open branches for the sale of that Licensed Product; or

8.5.3.3 maintain distribution depots for that Licensed Product.

8–134 8.5.4 Without prejudice to the generality of cl.8.5.3 the Licensee shall be prevented from putting a Licensed Product on the market in response to unsolicited orders in any of the areas detailed in cl.8.5.2 during the continuance of this Agreement for so long as and to the extent that a Parallel Patent protecting that Licensed Product remains in force in the relevant area or for a period of five years from the First Date, whichever is the shorter.

8–135 8.5.5 The Licensee shall not (during the continuance of this Agreement) sell Licensed Products outside the EC [except into areas from which it is reasonably likely that reimportation of Licensed Products into the EC would occur].

8–136 8.5.6 The Licensor shall impose on any other licensee licensed by it to Exploit the Patents in any areas of the EC outside the Territory obligations identical to those imposed upon the Licensee under cll.8.4 and 8.5, including cl.8.5.6.

8.5.7 Upon an area ceasing or commencing to fall under cl.8.5.1 or cl.8.5.2 or upon an area ceasing to fall under one of the said clauses and commencing to fall under the other of the said clauses, the Licensor shall notify the Licensee of this occurrence, and there upon the list under cl.8.5.1 and/or cl.8.5.2 as the case may be shall be deemed to have been amended accordingly. **8–137**

8.5.8 Notwithstanding the provisions of this clause, the Licensee shall be entitled to carry out general advertising or promotions in media or on the internet that reach customers in areas falling under cll.8.5.1 or 8.5.2 ("reserved areas") provided that such advertising and promotion is primarily intended to reach customers (including without limitation customers in the Territory) who are outside any reserved areas ("general customers") and that such advertising and promotion is a reasonable way to reach general customers. **8–138**

Version (a) of cl.8.5 is for use in the EC, together with cl.8.4, but only in situations where the Regulation does not apply (refer to Chapter 8.4 for the point about imports from outside the EC in cl.8.5.2.) If the licence is exclusive, then exemption under Art.81(3) should in most cases be possible, given that the wording is modelled upon the block exemption for vertical agreements (Reg.2790/99). Versions (b), (c) and (d) are based upon Art.1 of the Regulation. Version (b) is for use with a pure knowhow licence, version (c) for use with a mixed knowhow and patent licence and version (d) for use with a pure patent licence. It should be noted that in the treatment of version (d) the term "Parallel Patents" is now used, since, in this case, where the restrictions relate to territories outside the licensed territory, it is easily and correctly applied, and none of the problems discussed in relation to version (a) of cl.8.2.3 above can arise here. Note also that, despite the discussion in Chapter 8.2 on the possibility or desirability of limiting the restrictions on the licensor to the extent of the grant to the licensee, this course has not been followed here. The restrictions imposed on the licensee are by way of the definition "Licensed Products" not the "Products". This makes them as wide as possible. This is consistent with the Regulation, since, to the extent the definition "Licensed Products" covers more than the "Products", the licensee will have received no grant at all under cl.8.2 in relation to the wider definition. Thus, irrespective of the contractual restrictions in the licence, the limited grant of the licence will preclude the licensee from carrying on such extra-territorial activities anyway.

Leaving aside licences covered by the Regulations, licences of other industrial property rights, including trade marks, copyright and registered designs have to be dealt with under general principles of law, in the light of particular cases and decisions. The *Maize Seed* case shows that generally open exclusive licences of any of these rights (which of course does not include agreements relating to pure knowhow) will not contravene Art.81(1) so that, in general, providing the restrictions on extra-territorial activity follow the pattern in version (a) of cl.8.5 the licence should not be caught under Art.81(1). If versions (b) or (c) of cl.8.5 are used for licences not covered by the Regulations then consideration must be given to the application of Art.81(3), and in many cases exemption would presumably be appropriate. **8–139**

8–140 Finally, if the parties so agree, the restrictions in these clauses can be imposed for periods of less than five or ten years, or of the life of the parties in question (see Art.2(4) and (5).

8–141 All versions carry a suitable version of the "internet" clause discussed in Chapter 5.5)

8.6 Supply of the products

8.6.1 Options to manufacture or purchase

8–142 8.6.1 The Licensee shall be entitled to exercise any or all of the following options:

8.6.1.1 to manufacture the Products;

8.6.1.2 to purchase semi-finished Products and finish and pack the same;

8.6.1.3 to purchase the Products in bulk and pack the same; and

8.6.1.4 to purchase finished Products ready packaged.

The options in this clause allow the licensee the freedom to set his operation either at a particular period in time, or, in relation to any one of the products, at any stage between that of distributor and full manufacturer. Depending upon the technical competence of the distributor, it is not unusual for him to start off as a packer from bulk, work up to finishing operations and end as a full manufacturer.

8–143 When considering arrangements within the EC, there is no reason why the options stated above should not be combined in one agreement. However, it does not seem likely that if this is done the agreement will be able to take advantage of the block exemption either for vertical agreements (Reg.2790/99) or of the Regulation, even supposing it fell under the latter if one left aside the options relating to purchase of finished product. If this is the case, where it is wished and possible to take advantage of the Regulation, the options for purchase of finished, bulk and (depending upon what stage the patent applies) semi-finished products should be removed either entirely, or put into a separate agreement, and cast in the form which would permit Reg.2790/99 to apply to it. There is a useful discussion of the points that arise in cases like this in the Commission Decision *Re DDD Ltd/Delta Chemie* [1988] O.J. L309. This was a mixed exclusive distribution agreement and knowhow licence, but the case was, in any event, decided before the Knowhow Regulation came into force.

8.6.2 Subcontracting

8–144 8.6.2 The Licensee may subcontract [or carry out through a Connected Undertaking] the activities of manufacture packaging and finishing referred to in cl.8.6.1 but always subject to cl.8.19.

In so far as the EC is concerned, this provision is not objectionable, and indeed the Regulation expressly permits the licensee either to manufacture himself, or to subcontract the manufacture, or to have the manufacture carried on by a "connected person" (see Art.6(3) of the Regulation). In particular it is important to note that when sublicensing the subcontractor, sufficient restrictions can be imposed upon him to make sure that he is not set up as another licensee of the products, with all the rights of a licensee in connection with cross-border trade, supply to third parties and so on. For further discussion and some details on subcontracting arrangements in the EC see Chapter 5.1.1.3.13. It should also be remembered that the Regulation applies in situations where the licensee wishes (and is bound) only to manufacture for his own use, either directly or through a subcontractor (see Art.1(1)(8)), but, in this latter case, subject to the restrictions on the term of the licence required by Art.1(2), (3) or (4) which are identical to the restrictions set out in cl.8.9.3 below.

8.6.3 Purchase from licensor of components and ingredients

8.6.3 In the exercise of the options contained in cl.8.6.1 the Licensee shall only procure from the Licensor or any other source previously approved in writing by the Licensor those goods and services (if any) listed in Sch.4 the same being necessary [for a technically proper Exploitation of [the Knowhow] [the Patent] [the Knowhow and the Patent] in accordance with Sch.5] [for ensuring that the Products conform to the minimum quality specifications that are applicable to the Licensor and its other Licensees]. **8–145**

This clause complies with Art.2(1),(5). The two alternatives in square brackets are set out in the article. It is not entirely clear whether both can be used in the same agreement as a justification for purchasing necessary goods from the licensor, but the wording of the article does not seem to preclude it. The standard for goods to qualify as necessary is quite a high one. Mere assertions of the need to keep up quality or safety standards will not be sufficient unless such standards are objectively verifiable and specified in advance (*Windsurfing International Inc v EC Commission* [1986] E.C.R. 611 ECJ.) However, under the Regulation it is possible to include a tying requirement relating to "unnecessary goods" but this is a grey-list provision (see Art.4(2)) which currently will require the licence to be notified under the opposition procedure in Art.4, and after May 1, 2004 will require the parties to consider the application of Art.81(3) directly.

8.6.4 Quality control

8.6.4 The Licensee shall undertake the obligations in relation to quality control and related matters set out in Sch.5. **8–146**

This clause is not regarded as anti-competitive, and is specifically stated not to be an obligation restrictive of competition in Art.2(1)(5) of the Regulation. This sort of provision is also not regarded as restrictive of competition in other types of licence agreements. For instance, in its Decision *Re Carlsberg Beers* [1985] 1 C.M.L.R. 735 the Commission gave negative clearance and exemption to a licensing agreement for the production of Carlsberg lager in the UK. Although the Commission considered that for other reasons the arrangements as a whole required exemption under Art.81(3) the important point of the Decision is the confirmation that certain obligations relating to quality standards and control are regarded as not contravening Art.81(1). These were:

- An Obligation by the licensor to provide information necessary for analysis and quality control, and for the licensee to abide by the licensor's product standards and specifications;
- An undertaking that if the licensor licensed other companies to brew the beer in the UK it would apply the same quality standards specifications and technical requirements to them; and
- An obligation for each party to transmit to the other information about improvements.

8.6.5 Terms and conditions of supply of licensor

8–147 See cl.7.6.5.

8.6.6 Royalty

8–148 See cl.7.6.6.

8.7 Licensee's records

8–149 See cl.7.7.

Such clauses are not held to be restrictive of competition since they merely reinforce and police the primary obligations under the agreement. If these primary obligations are not anti-competitive, the policing provisions cannot be so either (see *Re SABA (No. 2)* [1984] 1 C.M.L.R. 677 and the discussion in Chapter 6.9.6).

8.8 Advertising and merchandising

8–150 **8.8.1** See cl.7.8.1.

8.8.2 See cl.7.8.2.

8.8.3 See cl.7.8.3.

8.8.4 See cl.7.8.4.

8.8.5 See cl.7.8.5.

These clauses are permissible within the EC provided that they are not used by the licensor for controlling the licensee's pricing policy, or imposing other disguised restrictions on competition with the excuse of giving policy directives. For instance in *Re Carlsberg*, discussed in Chapter 8.6.4, there was permitted an agreement that the licensor and licensee share UK marketing expenses, consult on the setting of advertising and marketing objectives, and set up a consultative committee to monitor the agreement and seek to settle disputes amicably, failing which they would be referred to an arbitrator. This point has also been considered in the selective distribution cases, discussed in Chapter 6.9.6 and Chapter 6.22.5.

8.9 Sales and marketing policies

8.9.1 See cl.7.9.1. **8–151**

Care should be taken as to the operation and use of this clause in the EC. Its purpose may be relatively harmless but it can be regarded as an obligation restrictive of competition in that it could be used to give directions to the licensee about matters which would take the licence outside the Regulation and perhaps cause it to contravene Art.81(1). Examples would be instructions not to sell to certain classes of customers, or not to give priority to export sales. A clause which seeks to deal with the problem, covering both cll.8.8 and 8.9 is set out for use within the EC as cl.8.9.6.

> 8.9.2 Selling prices for the sale of the Products in the Territory by the Licensee shall be established and may be revised from time to time by the Licensee. **8–152**

In the EC selling prices must be determined by the licensee. Under the Regulation, restrictions on the "determination of prices, components of prices or discounts" are on the black list (Art.3(1)).

> 8.9.3 The Licensee undertakes to apply the Trade Mark to all Products manufactured and or sold by the Licensee, and not to present any such Products for sale otherwise than with the Trade Mark affixed thereto and in accordance with the get-up required by the Licensor **8–153**
>
> PROVIDED THAT
>
> the Licensee shall be bound by this obligation only for so long as [the Knowhow remains "secret" and "substantial" within the meaning of Art.10(2) and (3) of Commission Regulation 240/96/EC] [the Licensor is bound by its undertaking under cl.8.2.3].

This is a provision which is generally enforceable within the EC. It is covered specifically in the Regulation in Art.1(7). The proviso deals with the limitation on this period required by the Regulation. The phrase in the first set of square brackets applies to a pure knowhow licence. The phrase in the second set of square brackets can be used for a pure patent licence or a mixed knowhow and patent licence, as, in these cases, the period is identical to the period for the licensor's undertaking under the relevant versions of cl.8.2.3 (see Art.1(2), first para, Art.1(3) third para, and Art.1(4) fourth para). The same limitation as in cl.8.9.3 applies to a licence restricted to manufacture by the licensee for his own use under Art.1(1)(8).

8–154 **8.9.4** See cl.7.9.4.

This merely sets out the position under the general law, that no licensee of a trade mark can use it in ways not authorised by the licence. This being the case, there should normally be no objection to its use within the EC.

8–155 8.9.5 The Licensee shall mark the Products with an indication they are manufactured under licence from the Licensor [and with an indication of the Patent].

This provision is unobjectionable within the EC. Indeed the Regulation specifically states this as one of the permitted obligations in Art.2(11).

8–156 8.9.6 Nothing in this Agreement (including without limitation cll.8.8 and 8.9) shall oblige the Licensee to obtain approval or accept directions or give notifications in respect of matters relating to pricing of the Products or (except as expressly provided for in this Agreement) as to the persons to whom the Products shall be sold by the Licensee or the areas in which and the purposes for which the Products shall be used or sold.

This clause sets out some of the more obvious ways in which disguised restrictions can operate under the cover of cll.8.8 and 8.9. It must be emphasised however that if in fact the parties are operating such disguised restrictions then the inclusion of the clause will not save them from action by the Commission.

8.10 Stocks of the products

8–157 See cl.7.10.

8.11 Licensee's staff

8–158 See cl.7.11.

8.12 Monthly reports

A standard monthly reporting provision should be inserted. Clause 4.12 is suitable. **8–159**

8.13 Industrial property rights

Clauses 4.13.1, 4.13.2 and 4.13.3 should be adapted and inserted as 8.13.1, 8.13.2 and 8.13.3 respectively. **8–160**

> 8.13.4 No provision in cl.8.13 or in any agreements or documents executed pursuant to cl.8.13 or elsewhere in this Agreement shall have effect so as to prejudice or hinder the right of the Licensee to challenge the validity of the Patents, the Trade Mark, or any other intellectual or industrial property rights belonging to the Licensor [or the secrecy or substantiality of the Knowhow as defined in Art.10(2) and (3) respectively of Commission Regulation 240/96]. **8–161**

If this clause is not inserted, then the question arises as to whether the licensee can have the right to challenge the licensor's intellectual property. If there are provisions anywhere in the agreement which amount to a no-challenge clause then the agreement will not automatically qualify for exemption under the Regulation (see Art.4(2)(3)), but will have to be submitted under the opposition procedure in Art.4 for a special scrutiny by the Commission.

It has been confirmed in many cases that no-challenge clauses or delimitation agreements are contrary to Art.81(1). This is discussed more fully in relation to distribution agreements under Chapter 5.13 but mention should be made in connection with licences of the Commission Decision *IMA AG/Windsurfing International Inc (WSI)* [1984] 1 C.M.L.R. 1 where the Commission considered various licence provisions in this area that it regarded as contrary to Art.81(1). These were: **8–162**

- an obligation to affix to all boards in the range of the licensee a notice that the boards were licensed by WSI, even though it was only one component (the rigs) that were so licensed;
- an obligation on the licensee to acknowledge certain word and design marks as valid trade marks;
- a right on the part of the licensor to terminate the agreement if the licensee started production in a territory not covered by a patent; and
- no-challenge clauses.

This Decision was confirmed and commented on in *Windsurfing International Inc v Commission* [1986] E.C.R. 611 when the European Court confirmed the Commission's stand. However, it should be noted that Art.2(15) **8–163** and (16) of the Regulation does permit the licensor to terminate the agreement in the event of a challenge by a licensee (see cl.8.16.8).

8–164 The *Maize Seed* case also contained a relevant finding in this area. The Court confirmed that a settlement of legal proceedings related to an industrial or commercial property right remains subject to Art.81. It may not be declared void in order to permit the legal proceedings to be reopened, but it does prevent the operation by either party of any restrictions in it relating to competition.

8–165 A further decision of the European Court, Case 65/86 *Bayer AG and Maschinenfabrik Hennecke GmbH v Sullhofer* [1990] F.S.R. 300, stated that while no-challenge clauses may fall under Art.81(1) as a rule such a clause would have no restriction on competition if the licence is a free one or, even if not free, it relates to a technically outdated procedure not used by the undertaking which accepted the no-challenge obligation. While interesting for the purpose of licences granted to settle disputes and therefore perhaps a gloss on the ruling in the *Maize Seed* case the decision obviously has little relevance for commercial licences.

8.14 No joint venture or partnership

8–166 See cl.1.9.

8.15 Commencement and term of agreement

8–167 See cl.7.15.

8.16 Termination

8–168 The clauses set out as 4.16.1 to 4.16.7 inclusive can be reproduced here.

Additionally, it should be noted that although a licence which contains a no challenge clause cannot take advantage of the Regulation, but must currently be submitted for clearance under the opposition procedure in Art.4 (see Chapter 8.13) it is possible to provide that the licence shall terminate in the event of a challenge as to the validity of the licensed patents or as to the secret or substantial nature of the licensed knowhow (Art.2(1),(15)) or as to whether one of the patents continues to be a "necessary patent" (Art.2(1),(16)). Such a clause can be inserted as cl.8.16.8 where required using something along the following lines:

8–169 8.16.8 In the event that the Licensee contests in or by way of any legal proceedings [or in any other way whatsoever] [the validity of any of the Patents] [or] [the secrecy or substantial nature of the Knowhow] [or] [that any of the Patents has ceased to be a Necessary Patent] the Licensor may [terminate this Agreement with immediate effect, by service of notice upon the Licensee] [serve notice on the

Licensee requesting him to cease such contest immediately and, if the Licensee does not cease such contest within seven days of receipt of such notice, this Agreement shall thereupon automatically terminate].

8.17 Effects of termination

See cl.7.17. **8–170**

This clause is analogous to cl.4.17, and the licensor has the same motivations for requiring its inclusion as a licensor under a distribution agreement. The problem of the use of cl.7.17 in the EC is again bound up with the restrictions upon competition it imposes by preventing the licensee from disposing of his own property (stocks and products) freely after the termination of the agreement. This problem has been discussed in relation to distribution agreements in Chapter 5.17 and in relation to selective distribution agreements in Chapter 6.17. The same considerations apply in the case of licence agreements. However, with regard to licences, as opposed to distribution agreements, one must consider the effect of its inclusion upon the operation of the Regulation.

8–171 Once the clause is included the Regulation can no longer apply. This is certainly a restriction other than one of the permitted restrictions in Arts 1 and 2 of the Regulations. In this case it will currently be possible to use the opposition procedure for submission for special exemption under Art.4. Given the difficulties with this clause it is better to omit it or to make it an option that can only be exercised by mutual agreement. One important point is that, to the extent the licensee pays royalties on sales, the clause should make it clear that a royalty will be paid on stocks of the products sold after the termination of the licence if they are not purchased by the licensor under some version of cl.7.17.

8–172 It should however be noted that both versions of cl.7.17.10 comply with the Regulation. Version (a) relating to patents is covered by Art.2(1)(3) which permits a post-termination ban on exploiting the licensed patents so long as they remain in force. Version (b) imposing a similar ban in relation to knowhow is likewise covered by the Regulation.

8–173 Prior to the issue of the Knowhow Regulation the general drift of Commission decisions was that once knowhow had been communicated it was not possible to restrict its use after the termination of the agreement, although it was possible to continue to restrict its disclosure in breach of a confidentiality obligation. This follows logically from the Commission's view that no rights exist in knowhow independently of agreement except (perhaps) confidentiality. Once the agreement has been terminated there is no legal mechanism for preserving and enforcing the restriction, unless a clause in the contract is to be given perpetual force. Such a clause obviously contravenes Art.81(1).

8–174 The Regulation, however, now goes further and permits the imposition not only of a confidentiality obligation both during and after the expiry of the agreement (Art.2(1)(1)), but also a post-use ban in so far and so long as the knowhow is still secret (Art.2(1),(3)). This means that the old Commission decisions which permit the licensee to carry on using knowhow after termination of the agreement, provided the knowhow remained secret and the licensee continued paying a royalty, no longer seem applicable. The choice is now between an agreement that goes for a defined term (or until terminated by notice) with thereafter a post-use ban, if the knowhow is still secret, and an agreement that carries on indefinitely, with royalties being paid until the knowhow becomes public, with certain special provisions depending upon the reason for the publication (which are best dealt with in relation to the provision for payment of royalties). Even if the Regulation does not apply, version (b) would presumably be the subject of exemption under Art.81(3).

8.18 Confidentiality

8–175 See cl.7.18.

The clauses cause no problems under EC law, and are permissible under the Regulation (see Art.2(1)(1) and (3).

8.19 Transmission of rights

8–176 See cl.7.19.

As far as the Regulation is concerned, the provision as drafted above is acceptable. Article 2(1)(2) permits a ban on assignment and sublicensing. This provision with its limited raising of this restriction to permit manufacture by a subcontractor falls within the "restrictions of a lesser scope" in Art.2(3). The extension of the licence agreement by inserting a right to sublicence, rather than just subcontract, is also permitted on the basis of the same reasoning. So far as manufacture by a connected person is concerned this is covered by Art.6(3).

8.20 Interpretation clauses and signature

8.21 Schedule 1—definitions

8–177 This schedule should include, in separate parts the appropriate definitions of the Products, the Territory, the Trade Mark, the Patents, the Knowhow, and the special definitions (in the case of licences intended to fall within the Regulation—see Chapter 8.2). This device makes it possible to use uniform numbering for the rest of the schedules. If applicable it should also contain lists of reserved territories and reserved customer groups under version (a) of cl.8.5.1.

8.22 Schedule 2—targets

8.22 The Licensee undertakes to pay during each consecutive period of twelve months of the currency of this Agreement (subject to prior termination in accordance with cl.8.15) the first such period to commence upon the date of commencement of this Agreement, royalties in respect of sales of the Products during the relevant period calculated in accordance with Sch.7 or the relevant one of the following sums of money whichever is the greater]: **8–178**

Period	Pounds sterling

While sales targets are sometimes imposed, and such obligations are recognised in the EC, but require exemption under Art.81(3), the wording of the Regulation would not permit such a provision. Article 2(1)(9) permits "an obligation on the licensee to pay a minimum royalty or to produce a minimum quantity or to carry out a minimum number of operations".

If it is intended to deal with an obligation to produce a minimum quantity or carry out a minimum number of operations the royalty provisions in Sch.7 would have to be redrafted completely. Such obligations are more usual in process patent licences, where the royalty can more easily be linked to a unit sum per item produced by the use of the process. **8–179**

8.23 Schedule 3—exceptions to any restrictions upon the licensee dealing with competitive goods

A restriction upon a licensee not to deal in competing goods can apply only within the EC, where it has been the subject of specific exemption under Art.81(3) (see the discussion in Chapter 8.3.5.) **8–180**

8.24 Schedule 4—items to be purchased from licensor

It will be recalled that, within the EC, and particularly under the Regulation, this schedule should normally only contain items which must be purchased from the licensor in order to achieve a technically proper exploitation of the licensed technology (see cl.8.6.3). **8–181**

8.25 Schedule 5—specifications, production methods and quality standards

See cll.7.25.1–7.25.7. **8–182**

These clauses comply largely with EC law and the Regulation. The only concern under the Regulation is that the requirements imposed must be to observe minimum quality specifications, including technical specifications, to ensure that the licensed product conforms to the minimum quality specifications applicable to the licensor and other licensees (see Art.2(1)(5)). The requirements set out in the schedule should not go beyond this or the agreement will currently have to be notified under the Art.4 opposition procedure (see Art.4(2)(a)).

8–183 See cl.7.25.8.

The provisions of this clause are unobjectionable under EC law and are contemplated, in so far as relates to the assistance required from the licensee, by Art.2(1),(6).

8–184 8.25.9(a) Any and all intellectual and industrial property rights throughout the world resulting from any work carried out by the Licensee in order to adapt the Products to its customers' requirements or relating to an improvement to the Products generated by the Licensee shall vest exclusively in the Licensee. The Licensee undertakes that it will grant to the Licensor [a non-exclusive licence [(with power to sublicence)] of such rights upon fair and reasonable terms to be agreed, including, without limitation, as to duration, user, royalty and licensed territory] [a royalty-free, fully paid-up, worldwide and irrevocable non-exclusive licence [(with power to sublicence)] of such rights without limit of time to use for all purposes] [a sole licence [(with power to sublicence)] of such rights upon fair and reasonable terms to be agreed, including without limitation as to duration, user, royalty and licensed territory] [a royalty-free, fully paid-up, worldwide and irrevocable sole licence [(with power to sublicence)] of such rights without limit of time for all purposes].

OR

8.25.9(b) To the extent that either party generates improvements in or new applications for the Licensed Technology, all intellectual and industrial property rights throughout the world in such improvements or applications shall vest in the party originating the same. Each party shall grant to the other in respect of such intellectual and industrial property rights a royalty-free, fully paid-up, worldwide and irrevocable non-exclusive licence [(with power to sublicence)] without limit of time, for all purposes.

OR

8.25.9(c) The parties shall communicate [on a non-exclusive basis] regularly to each other the existence of any experience gained in Exploiting the [Licensed Products] [the Knowhow] [The Knowhow and the Patents] and the existence of any improvements in or new applications of the same. Upon request each party shall negotiate with the other for the grant to the other of a licence upon terms to be agreed covering any of the aforesaid experience, improvements or applications, or any intellectual or industrial property rights relating thereto. All intellectual and industrial property rights throughout the world in such experience inventions or applications shall vest in the party originating the same.

EC law would in general seem to regard version (a) of this clause as being in contravention of Art.81(1) but likely to receive an exemption if the phrases in the first or second set of square brackets were used. The phrases in the third and fourth set of square brackets are less likely to receive exemption. It should be noted that any clause requiring the licensee to give an exclusive grant-back or to assign the relevant intellectual property rights to the licensor certainly contravenes Art.81(1) and is highly unlikely to be able to justify exemption under Art.81(3).

The position with grant back clauses is considerably more complicated under the Regulation, since it requires a certain amount of reciprocity. It should be remembered that none of the definitions of patents or knowhow in Chapter 1.2 covers improvements, except cl.1.2.11.4 in version (b) of cl.1.2.11 in relation to knowhow, and that, from the licensor's point of view, the obligation to communicate improvements is an onerous and unwelcome one. In effect, if the licensee wants a licence on subsequent technology he has to negotiate with the licensor again as to the terms on which he will receive it. **8–185**

Thus version (a) of cl.8.25.9 would fail under the Regulation because of lack of reciprocity even if the first or second phrase in square brackets were used (*i.e.* a non-exclusive licence). Article 3(6) of the Regulation prohibits a clause where "the licensee is obliged to assign in whole or in part to the licensor rights to improvements to or new applications of the licensed technology". Arguably a sole licence (*i.e.* one where the owner of the technology can continue to use it himself, but cannot licence to anyone except the sole licensee) does not fall within this provision, since such a licence is not an assignment. On this basis, it would be possible, whatever the combination of phrases chosen from version (a), for so long as it applies (*i.e.* until May 1, 2004) to use the short form procedure under Art.4 of the Regulation to receive what would hopefully be a quick clearance. Otherwise the parties would have, themselves, to consider the possibility of exemption under Art.81(3). **8–186**

Under the Regulation, Art.2(1)(4) provides that an obligation to grant back a licence on his own improvements to, or his new applications of, the licensed technology, may be imposed on the licensee. This is subject to the proviso that, where the improvements are severable, (*i.e.* can be used on their own without a licence of the basic licensed technology) such a licence must not be exclusive, so that the licensee is free to use such improvements himself or licence them to third parties, provided he does not rely on or license the basic licensed technology when doing this. **8–187**

This causes some problems when dealing with new applications and non-severable improvements. Here, the licence granted back may be an exclusive one. However, it is, in general, possible only to make sense of such a grant if it is exclusive in respect of all the world except the licensed territory of the licensee under the original licence, because the grant of an exclusive worldwide licence would mean the licensee could no longer use the improvement or new application himself. This would be equivalent to an assignment which would be black listed under Art.3(6). **8–188**

However, because the non-severable improvement or new application could (by definition) not be used without a licence of the basic licensed technology, the licensee's ownership of the intellectual property in, and any reservation by the licensee of the right to use, the non-severable improve- **8–189** ment or new application will be of only limited practical use. First, on the basis that the grant-back licence cannot prevent at least some use by the licensee, or it becomes an assignment, he will be able to use the non-severable improvement or new application free of charge himself, in the original licensed territory, for so long as he continues to have a licence of the basic licensed technology. Second, if the grant-back licence is royalty bearing, then he will enjoy some income from the exploitation of the non-severable improvement or new application by the original licensor. Third, to the extent that the grant-back licence does not cover all of the world, or does not provide rights to sublicence, then he may be able to use his ownership of intellectual property rights in the non-severable improvement or new application to bargain with the original licensor and grant him further licences to exploit the non-severable improvement or new application in return for further royalties.

8–190 The reciprocal obligation on the licensor is to grant an exclusive or nonexclusive license of his own improvements (but not new applications) of the licensed technology. However, there is no distinction here, as in the case of the licensee, between severable and non-severable improvements. Common sense suggests that the licensor would satisfy the reciprocity requirement by, at a minimum, merely adding the improvements to the grant of the original licence, so that they were useable by the licensee for the duration of and upon the same terms as the original licensed technology. Presumably there is also nothing in principle that would prevent the licensor from imposing a further royalty for such a use.

8–191 The final problem under the Regulation is that it does not address new applications developed by the licensee of the licensed technology where there is a field of use restriction on the licensed technology which would prevent the licensee from exploiting them. If the licence were silent upon the issue of grant-back in these circumstances, the licensee might own such new applications, but would be unable to use them for lack of a right to use the basic licensed technology. In principle, therefore, there seems no reason why it would not be possible to draft the grant-back clause to cover such new applications even if the licensee could not use them himself, and still fall within the Regulation, provided the licensor accepted the reciprocal obligation so far as related to improvements.

8–192 Version (b) provides a simple example of reciprocal grant-back, on the basis discussed above, which would satisfy Art.2(1)(4). However, version (b) should be used very cautiously, since the grant of the licence is very wide, and the licensor is undertaking a considerable obligation in terms of improvements.

8–193 Given the complexities of the matters concerned, once one goes beyond version (b) it is very difficult to draft a general precedent that is worth consideration. The best advice seems to be either to ignore improvements altogether, with at most the use of a clause spelling out an intention to negotiate further licences as required, as set out in version (c) of cl.8.25.9 above, or else to use the guidelines discussed above and spell out in precise detail, and probably in a separate schedule, exactly what the rights in improvements and new applications are to be in the particular case, after detailed negotiation on the subject. Even if they do not fall precisely within Art.2(1)(4), there seems no reason why the opposition procedure under Art.4 should not be used, so long as it is applicable, (*i.e.* until May 1, 2004) provided no assignment obligation falling under the blacklist of Art.3(6) is included. Otherwise the parties will, themselves, have to consider exemption under Art.81(3).

Lastly, it should be remembered to include a termination option of the type referred to in Art.8(3) if version (b) is used to bring improvements automatically within the term of the licence. Version (c) should cause no problems in this respect since the fact that the parties have to agree on the details of the grant in each case, as well as whether there will in fact be a grant at all, provides the licensee with the necessary option to refuse. **8–194**

8.26 Schedule 6—terms of supply of licensor

The provisions of cl.4.26 can be used here. Reference should be made to the subject of apportionment and quotas in time of shortage of supply discussed in Chapter 5.27. **8–195**

8.27 Schedule 7—royalty

8.27.1 See cl.7.27.1. **8–196**

8.27.2 See cl.7.27.2.

8.27.3 See cl.7.27.3.

8.27.4 In so far as the royalty under this schedule is paid for the use of the Knowhow the said royalty is only paid in respect of use of the Knowhow in accordance with this Agreement and a further royalty for any use of the Knowhow other than for the manufacture of the Products under this Agreement and or for any use whatsoever of the Knowhow (including such manufacture) after the expiry of this Agreement shall be payable by the Licensee to the Licensor upon terms and conditions and at rates to be agreed. **8–197**

8.27.5 Nothing in this schedule or elsewhere in this Agreement shall oblige the Licensee to pay any royalty (whether during the currency of or after the termination of this Agreement) in respect of any Knowhow which comes into the public domain by the action of the Licensor. **8–198**

8.27.6 In the event that the Knowhow becomes public other than by the action of the Licensor the Licensee shall continue to pay royalties during the term of this Agreement in accordance with this schedule. The obligation contained in this clause shall subsist notwithstanding anything else contained in this Agreement, and shall be without prejudice to the payment of any additional damages in the event of the Knowhow becoming publicly known by the action of the Licensee in breach of this Agreement. **8–199**

Clause 8.27.4 represents the older EC decisions relating to field of use restrictions in Knowhow licences. It is still valid, although perhaps unnecessary under the Regulation. Clauses 8.27.5 and 8.27.6 comply with Art.2(1)(7)(a) of the Regulation, and are compatible with the various provisions in the agreement (see for example cl.8.2.3) which may cease if the knowhow becomes public knowledge. These other obligations may terminate of themselves, but the agreement is still left in existence. Article 2(1)(7)(b) permits royalties to spread over a period longer than the duration of the agreement "in order to facilitate payment", in respect of licensed patents, but this is clearly an exceptional provision which is more appropriate to the concept of the "earn-out assignment" referred to in Art.6(2) of the Regulation. If the licensor wishes to impose such an obligation it must be clearly drafted to show that it relates to a requirement to facilitate payment, otherwise it will require notification under the opposition procedure of Art.4, and, in the absence of a desire to facilitate payment, it is hard to see what grounds the Commission would have for approving such a provision.

8.28 Future developments in the field of licensing under EC competition law

8–200 The approach of the Commission to the assessment of the anticompetitive effects of various agreements has changed over the last few years in that a greater emphasis is now placed on the market power of the undertakings that are parties to the relevant agreement. Previously the practice was to prescribe in detail in a regulation the permitted form of agreement and the provisions it should and should not contain if it were to take advantage of exemption under the relevant regulation. This approach can be seen in the old regulations relating to block exemption for distribution and purchasing agreements (Reg.83/83 and 84/83) and to selective distribution in the motor vehicle sector (Reg.123/85 and Reg.1475/95).

8–201 This approach has currently been abandoned in favour of block exemptions which provide for freedom of contract for undertakings with low market shares provided they avoid specified hardcore restrictions. The most striking examples are Reg.2790/99 covering vertical agreements in general, discussed in Chapter 5 and the current block exemption for the motor vehicle sector, Reg.1400/2002 discussed in Chapter 6. Other instances can be found in Reg.2658/2000, the block exemption for specialisation agreements, Reg.2659/2000, the block exemption for research and development, and the Notice on Agreements of Minor Importance 2001, all discussed in Chapter 5.

8–202 The Regulation thus seems to be the only survivor of the old prescriptive approach. It is also to a further degree rendered obsolescent by the abandonment of the procedure for notification to the Commission for exemption under Art.81(3), which will come into effect on May 1, 2004 once the new regulatory framework pursuant to Reg.1/2003 comes into force.

Thus it is not surprising that the Commission has decided to replace the Regulation to bring it into line with current thinking before its expiry in 2006. **8–203**

The Commission published an Evaluation Report on the Regulation in December 2001 in which it proposed replacing the Regulation with a less prescriptive regulation covering a wider range of licensing agreements and conforming to the general scheme and principles of Reg.2790/99. Comments were sought by April 2002. The Report and copies of the comments from interested parties can be found on the Commission's section of the Europa web site. In June 2003 the Commission published a draft regulation accompanied by a draft set of guidelines. Again these are available from the Europa website. The Commission's intuition is that a new block exemption regulation should come into force by May 1, 2004, on the same date as the new regulatory framework under Reg.1/2003. **8–204**

The Commission published a statement adopting the Evaluation Report and setting out its general position on January 7, 2002 (IP/02/14). The Conclusions set out in the Evaluation Report can be summarised as follows: **8–205**

- The Regulation is considered overly formalistic and complex and is too narrow in scope. It does not cover a number licensing agreements that do not pose great risks to competition.

- The Regulation does not place sufficient weight on inter-brand issues and does not follow a consistent approach as regards the competitive relationship between licensors and licensees. It may thereby cover certain licensing agreements that do not deserve coverage because they are anticompetitive in effect.

- The Regulation is out line with recent reforms concerning vertical (Regs 2790/99 and 1400/2002) and horizontal (Regs 2658/2000 and 2659/2000) agreements, which affects the coherence of Community competition policy and the predictability of the rules.

- A new regulation could take the form of a wide, umbrella-type block exemption regulation in combination with a set of Guidelines. It will need to cover a wider array of patent and knowhow licences than the Regulation, but it will also be necessary to investigate the appropriateness of including other IPR agreements, particularly copyright licences.

- Alignment will be sought with the new type of regulations by concentrating on a limited hardcore list.

- It will also be necessary to consider to what extent such a wide block exemption should be limited by reference to market share thresholds or some other threshold in order to effectively protect competition and innovation.

- So far as market power is concerned:

- Market share thresholds are more appropriate for restraints that do not relate to the exploitation of the licensed IPR.
- As regards restraints relating to licensed IPR it is more appropriate to work with market share thresholds where the licence is between competitors.
- It is not appropriate to cover licensing by dominant companies by a block exemption as anticompetitive agreements of dominant companies can in principle not be exempted.

- To the extent that the regulation had no application guidelines would have to clarify competition policy with appropriate references to the Guidelines on Horizontal Cooperation and the Guidelines on Vertical Restraints.

The terms of the draft regulation published in June 2003 are closely based on the principles set out in the Evaluation.

8–206 Recital 5 of the draft makes it clear that the regulation only applies to licensing agreements "where the licensor permits the licensee to exploit the licensed technology for the manufacture or provision of goods or services. It should not deal with licensing agreements for the purpose of doing research or development. It should also not deal with licensing agreements to set up patent pools."

8–207 Recital 19 makes it clear that the regulation covers technology transfer agreements "even if the conditions are stipulated for more than one level of trade, by for instance requiring the licensee to set up a particular distribution system and specifying the obligations the licensee must or may impose on resellers of the products produced under the licence. However, such conditions and obligations must comply with the competition rules applicable to supply and distribution agreements. Supply and distribution agreements concluded between a licensee and its buyers are not exempted by this Regulation. These agreements are only exempted if covered by a block exemption regulation for supply and distribution agreements."

8–208 Finally, recital 20 makes the point that the regulation is without prejudice to the application of Art.82. As the Evaluation Report stated, it is not appropriate for a block exemption to cover agreements made by an undertaking in a dominant position.

8–209 Article 1 extends the scope of the regulation beyond that of Reg.240/96, but not to the extent that some interested parties would have desired, by including some software licences. The regulation now provides that the definition of "technology transfer agreement" covers agreements for patent licences, knowhow licences, software copyright licences and mixed patent, knowhow or software copyright licences. The regulation also permits, the licensing of what, under Reg.240/96, were known as "ancillary rights", by extending this definition to include such agreements which contain "provisions which relate to the sale and purchase of products [see the reference to supply terms and conditions in recital 19] or which relate to the licensing of other intellectual property rights or the assignment of intellectual property rights, provided that those provisions do not constitute the primary object of the agreement and are directly related to the manufacture or provision of the contract products."

This extension would cover the licence of, for instance a registered or unregistered design relating to a product to be manufactured using a process protected by licensed patents. It would also relate to an ancillary trade mark licence. However, once again, it would not cover the franchise of production, in terms of *Moosehead* (see the discussion in Chapter 8.1.1.1 and 8.1.1.2 above.) Thus the current demarcation between Reg.240/96 and Reg.2790/99 will still be preserved. **8–210**

The definition of knowhow is substantially similar to that contained in Reg.240/96 and in Regs 2790/99 and 1400/2002. That is, the "knowhow" must be "secret, substantial and identified" if a licence of it is to be covered by the regulation. It should be noted that the definition of "substantial" "means that the knowhow includes information which is indispensable for the manufacture or provision of the contract products." This definition (by the use of the word "includes") does not exclude other types of knowhow (*e.g.* marketing knowhow) from coming under the licence as part of the package of licensed knowhow, provided it is "secret" and "identified", but it will not cover a licence of such knowhow on its own. A licence of this type of knowhow is appropriate for exemption, if at all, in relation to a franchise of distribution covered by Reg.2790/99 (see the discussion in Chapter 6.27). **8–211**

Article 2 provides (like Reg.2790/99 and 1400/2002) that Art.81(1) shall, subject to the provisions of the regulation, have no application to "technology transfer agreements entered into between two undertakings for the manufacture or provision of contract products." It should be noted that the limitation to "two undertakings" excludes patent pools (see recital 5) and that the phrase "manufacture or provision of contract products" limits the regulation to agreements entered into for the purpose of manufacture or provision of products only. (By the definition in Art.1, "products" means goods and services.) Thus (see recital 5) this excludes licences for purposes of research and development and other bare licences of intellectual property. It also excludes primary licences of intellectual property other than patents and software copyright (*e.g.* registered designs) even if for the purpose of the manufacture of goods or the supply of services. **8–212**

Harking back to the time limits on the imposition of restrictions permitted under Reg.240/96, the second paragraph of Art.2 provides that this exemption only applies (to the extent that the relevant agreement contains restrictions of competition falling within the scope of Art.81(1)) "for as long as the licensed property right has not expired or been declared invalid, or, in the case of knowhow, remains secret, except in the case where the knowhow becomes public by the action of the licensee, in which case the exemption shall apply for the duration of the agreement." **8–213**

Following the principles laid down in the Evaluation, the benefit of the regulation is only available, where the parties to the agreement are competing undertakings, if the combined market share of the parties does not exceed 20 per cent on the relevant technology and on the relevant product **8–214** markets. Where the parties are not competitors, the test does not relate to combined market share. Here the parties can only take the benefit of the regulation if the market share of *each party* on the relevant technology and the relevant product market does not exceed 30 per cent.

8–215 It is important to realise that the two market tests are cumulative. This has two consequences.

8–216 First, the parties will be "competing undertakings" if they compete on the relevant technology market and/or the relevant product market. Article 1(h) of the regulation states that:

- "undertakings compete on the relevant technology market if they licence competing technologies (actual competitors)."
- "undertakings compete on the relevant product market if the undertakings are both active on the relevant product and geographic market(s) on which the contract products are sold or which will be replaced by the contract products (actual competitors on the product market) or would, on realistic grounds, undertake the necessary additional investments or necessary switching costs so that they could enter the(se) relevant product and geographic markets(s) in response to a small and permanent increase in relative prices (potential competitors on the product market).

8–217 It should be noted that the regulation does not apply a test for potential competition on the relevant technology market, but it does apply such a test on the relevant product market.

8–218 Second, the market share test applies cumulatively to both the relevant technology and the relevant product markets. In order to pass the test, the threshold must not be exceeded on either the relevant product or the relevant technology market. (See para.61 of the draft Guidelines.) Article 3.3 of the regulation attempts to supplement these general rules by specifying that "the market share of a party on the relevant technology market is defined in terms of the presence of the licensed technology on the relevant product market(s): a licensor's market share on the relevant technology market(s) shall be the combined market share on the relevant product market of the contract products manufactured or provided by the licensor and its licensees."

8–219 This provision is amplified by the draft guidelines, paras 62 and 63:

- "In the case of technology markets, the licensor's market share is to be calculated on the basis of all sales by the licensor, the licensee and other licensees of products incorporating the licensor's technology, and this for each market separately. Where the parties are competitors on the technology market, sales of products incorporating the licensee's technology must be added to the sales of the products incorporating the licensed technology [this is because here the test of *combined* market share applies]. In the case of new technologies that have not yet generated any sales, a zero market share is assigned. When sales commence the technology will start accumulating market share."

- "In the case of product markets, the licensee's market share is to be calculated on the basis of the licensee's sales of products incorporating the licensed technology and competing products (*i.e.* the global sales of the licensee on the product market in question). Where the licensor is also a supplier of products on the relevant market, the licensor's sales on the product market in question must also be taken into account [again applying the *combined* market share test for competing undertakings]. In the calculation of product market shares, however, sales made by other licensees are not taken into account when calculating the licensee's or the licensor's market share."

Article 4 then deals with hardcore restrictions in the same way as Reg.2790/99 and 1400/2002.

Where the parties are competing undertakings, the hardcore restrictions are:

- restriction of the parties' ability to determine their prices when selling to third parties;
- limitation of output or sales, except where limitation on the output of contract products is imposed on the licensee in a non-reciprocal agreement;
- allocation of markets or customers except a restriction on the licensee to own-use manufacture or provision of the contract products provided this does not prevent sale of the contract products as spare parts;
- restrictions on licensee to exploit his own technology or restrictions on the parties carrying out research and development, unless this latter restriction is indispensable to prevent disclosure of licensed knowhow to third parties.

This list is less complex and shorter than the equivalent list in Reg.240/96, but its implications are more far-reaching, particularly in the area of exclusive licences or licences with territorial exclusivity or field of use restrictions, when entered into between competitors with more than the combined market share. **8–220**

Where the parties are not competing undertakings the hardcore restrictions are similar to those in Reg.2790/99, namely: **8–221**

- Restrictions on the territory in which or of the customers to whom the licensee may sell the contract products, *except*:
    - restrictions of sales into the exclusive territory or to an exclusive customer group reserved for sales by the licensor;

  - restriction of active sales into the exclusive territory or to an exclusive customer group allocated by the licensor to another licensee;
  - restriction to manufacture or provide the contract products only for own use by the licensee including sale of contract products as spare parts for his own products;
  - restriction of sales to end users by a licensee operating at the wholesale level of trade;
  - restriction of sales to unauthorised distributors by members of a selective distribution system.
- The restriction of active or passive sales to end users by licensees who are members of a selective distribution system which operate at the retail level, without prejudice to the possibility of prohibiting a member of the system from operating out of an unauthorised place of establishment;
- The restriction of the ability of the parties to the agreement to carry out research and development, unless such restriction is indispensable to prevent the disclosure of the licensed knowhow.

8–222 It is also important to realise that undertakings which commence a relationship of technology transfer may not be competitors at the outset, but may become so during the course of their association. In this case, the hardcore list for competing undertakings would then apply to them (as would the 20 per cent threshold) rather than the less stringent provisions of the hardcore list for non-competitors.

8–223 Article 5 contains, like Art.5 of Reg.2790/99, a number of obligations which cannot benefit from exemption under the regulation, but do not prevent the rest of the agreement (absent any hardcore restrictions) from taking that benefit. Any Art.5 obligation must be considered by the parties specifically to decide if, under the circumstances of the case, it can benefit from exemption under Art.81(3). The obligations are mainly based around the old "grey-list" of Reg.240/96, so that the scrutiny and decision by the parties themselves as to whether they can take direct advantage of Art.81(3) in any particular case, replaces the non-opposition procedure of Reg.240/96. These obligations are as follows:

- Any direct or indirect obligation on the licensee to grant an exclusive licence to the licensor or a third party designated by the licensor in respect of his own severable improvements to or his new application of the licensed technology;
- Any direct or indirect obligation on the licensee to assign in whole to the licensor or to a third party designated by the licensor rights to improvements [*NB. Here there is no mention of severable improvements*

so presumably non-severable improvements are covered as well] to or new applications of the licensed technology;

- Any direct or indirect no challenge clause, without prejudice to the ability of the licensor to terminate the agreement in the event of such a challenge;
- Any direct or indirect obligation limiting the output of contract products by the licensee in a non-reciprocal technology transfer undertaking between competing undertakings.

Article 6 contains the usual provisions permitting the Commission, and local competition law authorities in respect of areas within their jurisdiction, to withdraw the benefit of the regulation (pursuant to Art.29 of Reg.1/2003) in respect of any agreement which nevertheless has effects incompatible with the conditions laid down in Art.813). **8–224**

Article 7 contains the usual cumulative effect provisions so that the Commission may declare the regulation non-applicable to any market where more than 50 per cent of that market is covered by parallel networks of similar technology transfer agreements. **8–225**

Article 8 specifies rules for calculating market shares. Again the market share test has to be applied every year, with a five per cent tolerance margin permitted over the relevant threshold (provided this does not continue for more than two consecutive years) and further permission to exceed even this five per cent tolerance margin for one year, provided that the two permissions cannot be combined so as to give a period of exemption where the market share is in excess of the relevant threshold for more than two consecutive years. **8–226**

Article 9 repeals Reg.240/96 with effect from May 1, 2004, but provides for a transitional period until October 31, 2005 for agreements in force on April 30, 2004 provided that on that date they satisfied the conditions for exemption under Reg.240/96. **8–227**

Article 10 provides that the regulation comes into force on May 1, 2004 and expires on March 31, 2014.

The draft regulation and guidelines will doubtless receive scrutiny from all interested parties and may well change in matters of detail before their final implementation. In particular, the range of the intellectual property covered by the regulation and the levels of market share thresholds are likely to be the subject of some criticism and further debate. However, the broad thrust of the regulation is unlikely to be changed. **8–228**

The one area where it appears that the regulation would most benefit from further scrutiny is in the definitions of competing undertaking and of relevant product and technology markets, the way that market shares are calculated on each market, and whether there should be separate and cumulative tests for both the relevant product and the relevant technology market. Certainly the guidelines and the regulation could at least benefit from some further clarification in this area. **8–229**

8–230 So far as drafting is concerned, clearly where the regulation applies, there will be greater freedom as to the drafting of technology transfer agreements, but some of the more restrictive provisions relating to territorial and customer exclusivity, which Reg.240/96 permitted, will not be exempt under the new regulation and will now require to be considered specifically for exemption by the parties under Art.81(3). So far as drafting agreements which can take the benefit of the regulation is concerned, a better starting point in many cases would seem to be the distribution agreement set out in Chapter 5, to which could be added the necessary licence grants as provided for in Chapter 8. However, it would be premature to finalise detailed new precedents (particularly where the parties cannot take advantage of the regulation, and above all where they are competitors who cannot take advantage of the regulation) until the final form of the regulation and the guidelines is available.

Chapter 9

Consultancy Agreements

Contents

9.1 Commercial and legal background

9.1.1 General commercial issues

Apart from conventional distribution or agency arrangements it is often useful to appoint a consultant who will act as an auxiliary to an agent or, more usually, to a distributor. In this chapter, for convenience, the term "distributor" may be taken to include "agent". The consultant may exercise an independent monitoring function for the principal, or provide specialist marketing or technical skills. Above all he is able to act as an extension of the principal in the territory, and to carry out for the principal many tasks **9–01** which would otherwise require visits of the principal's own staff. The consultant is not only cost-effective (particularly in the more distant territories), but also provides a constant presence for the principal in the territory. In territories where the distributor who is preferred for commercial reasons may have language difficulties in communicating with the principal, or, for one reason or another, may lack the necessary staff or the enthusiasm to deal with administrative matters or to communicate regularly on all the matters of interest to the principal in the territory, the use of a consultant who can provide such services can sometimes be an acceptable compromise. A consultant can also be used to provide specialist services to help in the introduction of products to a new territory such as carrying out clinical tests for pharmaceutical products or assisting in the obtaining of licences from local regulatory authorities (see cll.9.3.4 and 9.6.2). It is difficult to produce as a precedent one reasonably standard consultancy agreement with simply some alternatives for certain clauses. Therefore the approach adopted in this chapter is to discuss more generally the possible types of consultancy agreements, and to suggest clauses that may be combined in various ways to meet particular needs.

9–02 It should be noted that most such consultants are not to be regarded as agents in the sense that agency relationships are considered in Chapters 2 and 3. In particular most of the consultancy relationships discussed in this chapter would fall below the "negotiating threshold" that a commercial agent is required to exceed before he can claim protection under the Council Directive 86/653 of December 18, 1986 on the Coordination of the laws of the Member States relating to self-employed Commercial Agents (see Chapter 3.2). However care should be taken to consider whether, in some exceptional cases consultants covered in this chapter might actually be regarded as fully-fledged agents (see Chapter 9.18).

9.1.2 Competition law considerations

9–03 Competition law has little impact on consultancy agreements of the type dealt with in this chapter. This is mostly because they have no provisions in them which attract the attention of competition law authorities.

9–04 Where a consultancy agreement is entered into and implemented for legitimate purposes there should be no problem with either EC or UK competition law. The only two possible areas restrictive of competition would be if the consultant were appointed on an exclusive basis in respect of a particular territory or customer group (not provided for in this precedent) or where the consultant is (as provided for in cll.9.10 and 9.11) prevented from working for a competitor of the principal for the duration of the agreement.

9–05 So far as EC competition law is concerned, a consultancy agreement, unlike an agency agreement, is an agreement between two undertakings who are economically independent of each other. The consultant is an independent contractor supplying certain defined services to the principal in return for his fee or commission. Thus a consultancy agreement can be scrutinised under Art.81, subject of course to the doctrines of appreciable effect either on competition or on trade between Member States, (see Chapter 5.1.1.3.7) which in most cases will rule out the application of Art.81(1) in any event.

However, a consultancy agreement is a vertical agreement for the supply of services, and, as such, in relation to EC competition law, leaving aside the question of appreciable effect, it is necessary to consider the impact of Reg.2790/99. *Prima facie* the regulation applies to consultancy agreements (unless they are entered into between competitors and no exemption is applicable under Art.2.4(c)), and since consultancy agreements of the type in this chapter have no hardcore restrictions under Art.4 of the regulation, it is only necessary to consider the applicable market share provisions and any non-compete obligations caught under Art.5. **9–06**

Since it is the consultant who is supplying the services, and the principal who is purchasing them, the market share test will apply to the consultant and not the principal. It is therefore most unlikely that consultants of the type referred to in this chapter will have a market share, in the relevant market for consultancy services of the relevant type, sufficiently large to put the agreement outside the regulation, unless the consultant is actually an employee of or partner in one of the large international consulting houses. **9–07**

The only other possible cause for non-application of the regulation would be if the consultancy agreement amounted to an exclusive supply obligation. This is defined as "any direct or indirect obligation causing the supplier [*i.e.* the consultant] to sell the ... services specified in the agreement only to one buyer [*i.e.* the principal] inside the Community" (see Art.1(c) of the regulation). In this case, the market share of the principal has to be considered, but it is the market share "of the relevant market on which it purchases the contract ... services" (see Art.3.2 of the regulation). Again, it seems highly unlikely that, even if the consultant is obliged only to supply the principal within the EC, that the principal (who is after all concerned with the manufacture and sale of goods and wants the consultant to assist in this) will be purchasing such a large amount of consultancy services that it will be purchasing more than 30 per cent of the consultancy services in the relevant market. **9–08**

The conclusion must therefore be that, except in extraordinary situations, consultancy agreements of the type dealt with in this chapter will fall within the scope of Reg.2790/99, even if they have, in fact, an appreciable effect which brings them within Art.81(1) in the first place. If there are any vertical restraints in the agreement which would otherwise be subject to Art.81(1), they will be exempt under the regulation, provided that (if they are non-compete clauses) they comply with the conditions in Art.5, and that they are not hardcore restrictions under Art.4 (none of which restrictions, in any event are really relevant to consultancy agreements of the type covered in this chapter). **9–09**

An exclusive appointment of the consultant would (even if it did contravene Art.81(1)) thus be granted exemption under the regulation. How- **9–10** ever, such a clause amounts to a non-compete obligation, within the definition contained in Art.1(b) of the regulation, since the principal (the buyer of the services) is, in effect, undertaking that he will not buy competing services from other consultants. Thus, the consultancy agreement should be for a fixed term of five years or less, or the exclusivity period should only last for such a term, even if the agreement itself thereafter continues for a further fixed term or indefinitely. (See the discussion on non-compete clauses within Art.5 of the regulation in Chapter 5.3.6).

9–11 Where this is commercially impractical, the best course it to provide that the agreement should expire automatically at the end of a fixed term not exceeding five years, but that either party may terminate it prior to such expiry by serving due notice. Since most consultancy agreements are unlikely to last for more than five years, this achieves, from a practical point of view, the same object as an agreement with an indefinite term. Alternatively, the parties can consider whether the agreement has an appreciable effect which brings it within Art.81(1) anyway, and simply ignore the impact of EC competition law if they feel that that this is not the case. Alternatively, they might consider exemption under Art.81(3).

9–12 The only other provisions to consider in this chapter would be cll.9.10 and 9.11. These are non-compete obligations (certainly in the case of cl.9.10 and arguably in the case of cl.9.11) but they do not fall within the scope of the definition of "non-compete" obligation in Art.1(b) of the regulation. This definition relates to non-compete obligations imposed on the buyer of the goods or services (*i.e.* the principal) not the supplier (*i.e.* the consultant). Thus, although cl.9.10 does create an exclusive supply obligation within the terms of Art.1(c) of the regulation, unless the principal holds more than the 30 per cent market share in the purchase of the relevant consultancy services on the relevant market, cll.9.10 and 9.11 will enjoy exemption under the regulation as will the rest of the agreement.

9–13 One way to make sure of this issue and to remove any doubt in relation to the operation of an exclusive supply obligation is to provide that cl.9.10 is restricted to a competitor of the principal in relation to the territory and the products only. Thus, at least in theory, the consultant will be able to sell his services to more than one buyer within the EC.

9–14 So far as UK competition law is concerned The Competition Act 1998 (Land and Vertical Agreements Exclusion) Order 2000 (SI 2000/310) (the "Vertical Restraints Order") will in practice exclude consultancy agreements from the scope of the Chapter I Prohibition (even if they fall within it in the first place) in the same way as discussed above in relation to EC law and Reg.2790/99.

9–15 The only remaining question relates to consultancy agreements which are used for the purpose of monitoring the distributor's pricing and sales policies, in order to assist in attempts to prevent exports or to impose resale price maintenance. Such purposes are clearly anti-competitive under either EC or UK competition law, or, indeed, the local competition law of other states, particularly other Member States of the EC. If they are discovered by the relevant competition law authorities, this will result in the withdrawal of the benefit of Reg.2790/99 or of the Vertical Restraints Order. In this case, the parties will *prima facie* infringe Art.81(1) or the Chapter I Prohibition, since the agreement clearly has an anti-competitive object. The only thing that can then save them is to plead that the agreement had no appreciable effect. Given that the object of the agreement is anti-competitive this will be difficult to achieve (see the discussion in Chapter 5.1.1.3.6).

9.2 Parties

For the purposes of this chapter, the company appointing the consultant will be referred to as usual as the Principal, and the consultant as the Consultant. It should be noted that although the term "consultant" has no precise legal definition it tends to connote in English law, at least, an independent contractor, rather than an employee. That is someone who exercises his particular skills for a defined purpose and for the remuneration laid down in a contract, but who is free to exercise those skills in the way that he considers best, without detailed supervision, in order to achieve that purpose. In the situations with which this chapter is concerned there is thus a contractual relationship (defined by the specific ends that the principal wishes to achieve) between the consultant and the principal who engages him, but the consultant will normally have no contractual relationship with the distributor or agent also acting in the territory. He will have no power to bind the principal by representations made on his behalf, nor to conclude contracts for or act as agent in relation to the sale of the products which are the subject of the distribution or agency agreement. **9–16**

A consultant is often a convenient aid to sales in areas where a company does not wish to appoint an agent or distributor, and also does not wish to open a local office from which to trade since this could make him subject to local taxation legislation or registration requirements with which it might be difficult or onerous to comply. It is true that many countries have legislation which permits a company to open a non-trading branch office for purposes of sales promotion and marketing assistance only, provided all sales contracts are concluded by the company from its country of residence, so that the branch office takes no part in the formation of the contract. This arrangement often provides exemption from liability to tax, on the basis that the company is not trading in the country concerned. Hong Kong, for instance, has legislation to this effect, which provides a short and relatively simple procedure for registration. However, not all countries have such simple procedures. A consultant who operates in the same way as a non-trading branch and provides the same range of duties avoids this problem entirely, both as to registration requirements, and as to the necessity to consider in borderline cases whether the company actually is trading within the territory or not. **9–17**

9.3 Purposes

9.3.1 Marketing assistance to distributor

9–18 9.3.1 The Principal at present sells the Products in the Territory under an agreement made with [ ] of [ ] dated [ ] (referred to respectively as the "Distributor Agreement" and the "Distributor"). It is the intention of the Principal to employ the Consultant to assist with the marketing of the Products in the Territory through the Distributor in the manner and on the terms set out below.

OR

9.3.2 Product introduction

9–19 9.3.2 It is the intention of the Principal to make use of the services of the Consultant to assist with the marketing of the Products in the Territory in the manner and on the terms set out below to all governmental departments and statutory or state corporations in the Territory (collectively the "customer").

OR

9.3.3 Finding a distributor

9–20 9.3.3 The Principal wishes to market the Products in the Territory and requires the services of a consultant to identify a suitable distributor (the "Distributor") for this purpose and (after the conclusion of an agreement between the Principal and the Distributor) to assist with the marketing of the Products in the Territory through the Distributor in the manner and on the terms set out below.

OR

9.3.4 Licences to market the products

9–21 9.3.4 The Principal wishes to market the Products in the Territory and requires the services of a consultant to [perform clinical tests and] assist the Principal [and its duly authorised distributor for the Territory (the "Distributor")] to undertake the execution of all [other] necessary formalities to obtain the grant of a licence for the sale of the Products in the Territory from all relevant local governmental or other regulatory bodies.

This clause should sufficiently set out the purposes for which a consultant might be appointed. Clause 9.3.1 would apply in the case where there is an existing distributor in the territory who requires support or monitoring. Clause 9.3.2 would be suitable where help is required in introducing a customer to the products, and in giving him sufficient assistance so that after introduction, the customer can conclude direct purchasing contracts on his own without the intervention of a distributor. This type of arrangement is more often required for technically sophisticated products sold to large organisations who are likely to become regular purchasers of standardised ranges of products, and are capable of supporting themselves once they have become familiar with the products. Clause 9.3.3 applies to the case where assistance is required in the appointment of a distributor coupled with continuing monitoring afterwards.

Clause 9.3.4 applies only to the specialised case of assistance with product registration and should be adapted as necessary for specific purposes. It can be combined with any of the other purpose clauses as required. Clinical tests are required before a licence can be obtained to market pharmaceuticals in most countries, and in some countries cosmetic products require licences as well. These tests require specialised facilities and often can be carried out only by licensed laboratories. Another instance of the need for registration is in the area of telecommunications products. Before items such as telephone handsets, modems, telex or fax machines or PABX equipment can be sold and connected to the network in a territory various permissions have to be obtained. In territories where the telecommunications authority has a monopoly of the sale of such equipment no distributor will be required but the equipment has to be approved by the authority before it will adopt it as an item for sale and connection to its network. In territories such as the UK or the US where sale and installation of such equipment is liberalised, an independent regulatory body has the power to test the equipment and grant a licence for its sale and connection to the network. Again the obtaining of the approval and, in some cases the carrying out of the tests, requires technical expertise which a distributor may not have. In appropriate cases cll.9.3.2 and 9.3.4 can be used together. **9–22**

Where a distributor exists or is to be appointed the duty to obtain the licence itself is more usually imposed upon the distributor who will ultimately sell the products, with the consultant acting in an advisory capacity. However, caution should be exercised lest by asking a consultant to carry out tests and assist in a registration he is inadvertently given sufficient powers to register the product and obtain a licence in his own name. In some countries, for instance most South American countries, the licence is not transferable and only the person to whom the licence is granted can act as distributor. The grantee of the licence is thus considered to have been so appointed and can register himself as such. It is then not possible to dismiss him without payment of compensation. The combination of the personal licence and the right to compensation can put such a "consultant" in a very strong bargaining position against the principal. Any requests for powers of attorney or other authorities which are said to be required before the consultant can act need therefore to be considered very carefully to decide just what authority is being conferred, particularly where they require translation before the principal's personnel can understand them. In cases like this it is advisable to consult local lawyers before giving such authorisations (for further consideration of the personal nature of product licences see Chapter 4.17.6). **9–23**

9–24 It should be noted that these clauses do not provide for an exclusive appointment, and such consultancy agreements are rarely exclusive. However, where this is required an additional clause should be added to cl.9.3 as follows:

> The Principal agrees that during the continuance of this Agreement he will appoint no other consultant to carry out the same activities in the Territory in relation to the Products as specified in this Agreement to be carried out by the Consultant.

Where the appointment is exclusive care should be taken in relation to the competition issues discussed in Chapter 9.1.2. In particular it may be prudent, for the reasons discussed there, to use version (b) of cl.9.4.2 where the appointment is on an exclusive basis.

9.4 Date and term

9–25 9.4.1 This Agreement shall take effect upon [ ] (the "Effective Date").

9–26 9.4.2(a) Subject to cll.9.4.3 and 9.17 this Agreement shall continue [for a fixed period of twelve months from the Effective Date and thereafter] until terminated by three months notice by one party to the other.

OR

9.4.2(b) Subject to cll.9.4.3 and 9.17 and the proviso to this clause this Agreement shall continue until terminated by three months notice by one party to the other PROVIDED THAT this Agreement shall in any event, if not already terminated, terminate automatically without notice upon the expiry of a period of [five years] from the date of its signature.

9–27 9.4.3 This Agreement may be terminated by the Principal by immediate notice upon the termination for any reason of the Distributor Agreement].

Version (b) of cl.9.4.2 should be used within the EC where the consultancy agreement is entered into on an exclusive basis. (See the discussion on competition issues in Chapter 9.1.2.)

9–28 Consideration should be given as to whether to couple the term of the consultancy agreement to the term of any relevant distribution agreement where one exists, and cl.9.4.3 can be added for this purpose. Where the consultant is to act in the introduction of products without a distributor, or to identify and assist in the appointment of a distributor, he will often require an initial fixed term, and this can be provided as in cl.9.4.2 as desired. Care should be taken to decide whether notice can be given so as to expire upon the termination of the fixed period or whether it can only be given once the fixed period has expired, thus effectively prolonging the stated fixed period by the period of notice.

9.5 Supervision and assistance

9.5.1 Liaison with distributor

The Consultant shall: **9–29**

9.5.1 visit the Distributor regularly (not less than [once a month]) and otherwise make regular and frequent contact with the Distributor by telephone telex or letter in order to supervise and assist in the performance by the Distributor of its obligations under the Distributor Agreement and to use best endeavours to assist and encourage the Distributor to adopt policies and practices (consistent with the terms of the Distributor Agreement) for purchasing stocking and marketing the Products that are calculated not only to meet current demands for the Products in the Territory but also to promote and increase the same.

OR

9.5.2 Technical advice

9.5.2 render to the Distributor all necessary technical advice and assistance in relation to the obtaining of all approvals required for the marketing sale and use of the Products in the Territory. **9–30**

OR

9.5.3 Sampling

9.5.3 take samples of the Products from the market in the Territory and send them to the Principal if he encounters items which in his reasonable opinion do not appear to be of merchantable quality or have been repackaged or otherwise tampered with or modified contrary to the provisions of the Distributor Agreement. **9–31**

OR

9.5.4 Market research

9.5.4 conduct in the Territory market research relating to the products covering in particular such matters as market shares pricing policies activities of competition any relevant changes of government policy or new legislation and local patterns of consumption. **9–32**

OR

9.5.5 Marketing advice

9–33 9.5.5 advise the Principal on all aspects of marketing the Products in the Territory including without limitation advertising and sales promotion.

OR

9.5.6 Infringement watch

9–34 9.5.6 keep a regular watch for any infringement in the Territory of any of the Principal's intellectual and industrial property rights.

AND (in all cases)

9.5.7 Reports

9–35 9.5.7 The Consultant shall issue regular quarterly reports to the Principal not later than ten days after the end of each calendar quarter on all the above activities as well as any special reports or studies as and when requested by the Principal or as and when he shall come across a matter in respect of which it is desirable that the Principal be notified at once.

This clause sets out the more usual duties of the consultant where there is an existing distributor. It will be noted that cll.9.5.1 to 9.5.3 are concerned with direct supervision of and assistance to the distributor. It will be necessary therefore for the consultant to be aware of relevant provisions of the distribution agreement (if not the whole document), and to provide, either in the distribution agreement, or by way of a separate authority constituting the consultant the authorised representative of the principal, for the distributor to accept the direction of and work with the consultant in these areas. The remaining paragraphs are concerned with ancillary activities which the distributor may either not have the skill, the staff or the willingness to carry out himself. Selection should be made as appropriate from cll.9.5.1 to 9.5.6 but cl.9.5.7 should always be included.

9.6 Product introduction

9.6.1 Sales promotion

9–36 9.6.1 The Consultant shall promote the Products with the customer and help the customer to plan for their introduction by giving technical advice in relation to all matters concerning the Products.

OR

9.6.2 Clinical tests

9.6.2.1 The Consultant shall carry out [clinical] tests in accordance with the regulations current in the Territory [and in all other necessary ways advise and assist the Distributor] [the Principal] to enable the granting by the relevant governmental authorities in the Territory of a licence to [the Distributor] [the Principal] to sell the Products in the Territory. **9–37**

AND

9.6.2.2 The tests shall be carried out [and all advice and assistance given] with all due despatch and in accordance with the highest standards of established current practice in the Territory and in compliance with the requirements of the relevant legislation. [In particular the Consultant shall ensure that all necessary consents are obtained from all human subjects taking part in clinical tests and their parents or guardians if necessary and that all laws in the territory relating to the use of animals for such tests are complied with]. The Consultant shall furnish with all reasonable promptness to the Principal written progress reports on the tests as and when requested and provide a detailed report upon their completion. **9–38**

Clause 9.6.1 is intended to be coupled with cl.9.3.2. It would then be usual to add all or most of the duties set out in cl.9.5, other than cll.9.5.1–3. Clause 9.6.2 is intended to be coupled with cl.9.3.4 and to be adapted as necessary depending upon whether clinical tests or other types of tests are required. It is then necessary to consider what continuing role the consultant will have within the territory, and to add other duties from cl.9.5 if appropriate.

9.7 Identifying a distributor

The Consultant shall: **9–39**

9.7.1 assist the Principal to find a [new] distributor for the Products in the Territory.

9.7.2 cooperate with the Principal so as to facilitate the sale of the Products through such distributor [and generally assist in a smooth takeover by such distributor from the existing distributor]. **9–40**

9.7.3 assist the Principal and such distributor with his experience and knowledge relating to the Territory and to the marketing of the Products in it. **9–41**

This clause may be applied in a situation where there is no distributor, or where an existing distributor must be replaced and a new distributor appointed. In the latter case it is not unknown to appoint the existing distributor as the consultant to find a new distributor. This is useful not only in cases where the existing distributor wishes to retire or to discontinue, but it may also be used to ease the transition where the principal is dissatisfied with the current distributor, but wishes the termination to be as amicable as possible. In these situations where remuneration is to be by way of commission (see cl.9.8.1) then the agreement should obviously be for a fairly short fixed term. Alternatively a fixed fee (see cl.9.8.2) should be used, and provisions inserted for payment of all or part of the fee only after an agreement with an acceptable distributor has been signed, and the distributor has performed satisfactorily for an initial period. If, on the other hand, a continuing relationship is contemplated, the clauses in cl.9.5 can be added as necessary and cl.9.7.3 may well therefore be superfluous.

9.8 Remuneration

9.8.1 Commission on distributors purchases

9–42 9.8.1 In consideration of the performance by the Consultant of his obligations under this Agreement the Consultant shall be paid by the Principal a commission of [ ] per cent of the net invoice price before any value added or sales taxes or other taxes or duties [FOB port of shipment] [Ex Works of the Principal] (as defined in the edition of Incoterms from time to time current) of each order for the Products placed by the Distributor. Such commission to be paid to the Consultant within thirty days after the end of the calendar quarter in which full payment for the relevant invoice is received by the Principal from the Distributor.

OR

9.8.2 Commission on customer's purchases

9–43 9.8.2 In consideration for the performance by the Consultant of his obligations under this Agreement the Consultant shall be paid by the Principal a commission at an agreed percentage net invoice price before any value added or sales taxes or other taxes or duties [FOB port of shipment] [Ex Works of the Principal] (as defined in the edition of Incoterms from time to time current) of each contract for the purchase of the Products placed by the customer for use in the Territory. Such commission to be paid to the Consultant within thirty days after the end of the month in which full payment is received by the Principal from the customer for the contract in question. The percentage rate for each such contract shall be mutually agreed between the Principal and the Consultant and may vary from contract to contract. The Consultant shall notify the Principal whenever he considers that it is likely that a contract for the Products may be placed in order that the percentage rate for that contract may be agreed. In default of such notification or agreement the percentage rate for a contract shall be [ ]. The Principal and the Consultant also agree that in no case shall the percentage rate be less than [ ] per cent or more than [ ] per cent.

OR

9.8.3 Fixed sum for product introduction

9–44 9.8.3 The Consultant shall be paid a fixed sum of [ ] upon the completion of the tests and the delivery of the report referred to in cl.9.6.2 of this Agreement.

OR

9.8.4 Fixed sum for identifying distributor

9.8.4 The Consultant shall be paid a fixed sum of [ ] within thirty days of the signature of a distribution agreement by the Principal and a distributor introduced by the Consultant to the Principal, and the fixed sum of [ ] at the expiry of a period of [twelve] months from the date upon which such distributor first puts the Products generally on the market (other than for the purposes of test marketing) in the Territory, provided that at the expiry of such period the distribution agreement between the Principal and the distributor remains in force, no notice of termination has been or is likely to be served thereunder, and the distributor has during such period performed his obligations under that distribution agreement to the reasonable satisfaction of the Principal. **9–45**

OR

9.8.5 Hourly rate

9.8.5 The Consultant shall be paid for his services at the rate of [ ] for each hour (excluding travelling time) for which he is engaged on the duties provided for in this Agreement. The Consultant shall invoice the Principal on the last day of each calendar month for services rendered under this Agreement at the said rate detailing the number of hours spent and the duties performed. Each invoice will be paid by the Principal within thirty days of its receipt. **9–46**

These clauses provide a variety of ways of remuneration. Clause 9.8.1 is probably the most usual method where a distributor is to be or has been appointed. Clause 9.8.2 is more suited to the case where the consultant is working direct with a customer to assist the introduction of products. Clause 9.8.3 is useful where only limited and defined tasks are to be performed. Clause 9.8.4 is tailored for the special task of finding a distributor. It should be noted here that the second payment should not run from the date of signature given that there will usually be a period between signature and the first sale by the distributor, not only to allow him to get in a stock of the products but also to complete any registration formalities. The exception relating to test marketing ensures that the preliminary period, when the distributor may be trying the acceptability of the products before committing himself fully to the agreement, is not taken into account. Clause 9.8.5 is an alternative clause that can be used where the tasks the consultant has to perform are not closely linked to concrete results or the sales volume eventually achieved by a product in the relevant territory. Clinical tests or other registration formalities (see cl.9.6.2) or general market research or monitoring not particularly connected with the activities of a distributor could, in many cases, appropriately be paid for in this way, although there are obvious difficulties in monitoring the time charges of a consultant who is operating on his own in a territory far away from the Principal.

9.9 Expenses

9–47 9.9.1 The Consultant shall not be entitled to claim travelling and other expenses incurred by him in the performance of his duties under this Agreement since the same are allowed for in setting the level of remuneration under cl.9.8.

OR

9–48 9.9.2 The Consultant shall be paid by the Principal reasonable travelling and other expenses incurred by him in the performance of his duties under this Agreement provided that all expenditure in excess of [ ] per calendar month shall be subject to the prior written approval of the Principal. The Consultant shall claim all such expenses by sending an invoice to the Principal at the end of each calendar month showing full details of and with supporting vouchers for each item of expenditure and the Principal shall make payment within [ ] days of the date on which the invoice is received.

Depending upon the arrangement reached either cl.9.9.1 or cl.9.9.2 should be used to cover the question of expenses. Where cl.9.9.2 is used in conjunction with cl.9.8.4 it is often convenient to line up the dates and payment times for invoices under the two clauses.

9.10 Warranty on conflict of interest

9–49 9.10(a) The Consultant warrants that he is not at the commencement of this Agreement retained by a competitor of the Principal (whether or not in relation to the Territory or the Products) and that during the existence of this Agreement he will not accept instructions from any competitor or potential competitor of the Principal either directly or indirectly nor do any other act or thing which may give rise to a conflict of interest.

OR

9.10(b) The Consultant warrants that he is not at the commencement of this Agreement retained by any person who competes with the Principal in the Territory in relation to the Products, and that during the existence of this Agreement he will not accept instructions from any such person.

9.11 Notification of conflict of interest

9–50 9.11 The Consultant shall notify the Principal if at any time during the existence of this Agreement he becomes aware of the likelihood of his taking on a consultancy which could cause a conflict of interest between his duties to the Principal and those to a third party.

Although it is not usual to appoint a Consultant on an exclusive basis in a territory, and the precedents in this chapter do not therefore provide for this, for obvious reasons the provision of services to a competitor or the carrying on of a competing activity should be precluded wherever possible. This may well not be acceptable where the Consultant is providing the clinical test services (see cl.9.6.2) or only specialised market survey services are required. Version (a) is more stringent than version (b), and the latter is more likely to be generally acceptable to consultants, unless the term of the agreement is very short. If neither version is acceptable, it may, as a fall-back position, be possible to gain acceptance of only cl.9.11, dispensing with cl.9.10. However in these cases the confidentiality clause (see cl.9.13) should be replaced by the much more stringent clauses set out in Chapter 1.4. Also in extreme cases it might be possible and necessary to bind the consultant with the obligations against competing activities in cl.1.5.

When dealing with these issues within the EC, even if it were possible to persuade the consultant to agree to version (a) of cl.9.10, it is probably wise to restrict the operation of cl.9.10 to the territory and the products by using version (b). The issues raised in relation to competition law in Chapter 9.1 should be studied before a final decision is taken on the way to proceed. Certainly cl.1.5 should not be used in these circumstances without a thorough consideration of the competition law issues. **9–51**

9.12 Due diligence

9.12 During the continuance of this Agreement the Consultant shall devote such of his time attention and abilities to his duties hereunder as may be necessary for their exercise. **9–52**

Although clauses such as this are notoriously difficult to enforce, particularly in borderline cases, they do serve a practical purpose of stating the parties' intentions in this area. They can often be used to give a good reason for termination with notice even where a clear breach cannot be demonstrated.

9.13 Confidentiality

9.13 The Consultant shall not (except in so far as necessary for the proper performance of his duties) during or at any time after the termination of this Agreement disclose to any person any information relating to the Products or to the Principal or Distributor or to the business affairs or trade secrets of either of them which have or shall after the commencement of this agreement become known to him. **9–53**

This is a short-form confidentiality clause suitable for most consultancy situations. Where confidentiality is regarded as particularly important the more elaborate clauses suggested in Chapter 1 should be used.

9.14 Good business practice

9–54 The Consultant undertakes and warrants to the Principal:

9.14.1 that the laws of the Territory the laws of the country in which the Consultant is resident (the "Consultant's country of residence") and the laws of the country specified in cl. [ ] as governing this Agreement (the "proper law") do not prohibit the Consultant or the Principal from entering into this Agreement nor do they render any provision of this Agreement unlawful.

9–55 9.14.2 that the Consultant will not (in contravention of the laws of the Territory or of the Consultant's country of residence or of the proper law) give or agree to give or offer any gift loan fee reward advantage or other valuable consideration of any kind to government officials customer representatives or any other persons (whether or not out of the remuneration paid to him under cl.9.8 or by way of expenses claimed under cl.9.9 or from any other source) for the purpose of furthering the sale of the Products in the Territory.

9–56 9.14.3 that the Consultant is not connected directly or indirectly with either government officials customer representatives or any other persons who are in a position to benefit from or influence or further the sale of the Products in the Territory.

9–57 9.14.4 that at any time during the existence of this Agreement the Consultant will on request give to the Principal a written confirmation that the undertakings and warranties in cll.9.14.1, 9.14.2 and 9.14.3 remain unbreached.

The true purpose of consultancy agreements is sometimes called into question. They can obviously be used to put a semblance of legality upon many doubtful transactions, from assisting a consultant to violate the exchange control or taxation laws of his country, or providing an inducement to an official to commit his organisation to purchasing products from a principal for which he acts as consultant, to putting a consultant in sufficient funds to enable him to offer bribes to such officials. This type of arrangement may not only be illegal under the laws of the consultant's country of residence, but also illegal under the laws of the country where the principal is resident. There are thus serious consequences, both at civil and under criminal law, where the arrangement is illegal under one or more of the relevant legal systems, not only for the consultant but also for the principal.

9–58 In the US, for instance, under the Prevention of Foreign Corruption Act, severe criminal penalties are imposed upon companies and their officers who further the sale of their products overseas by means of such arrangements. The SEC has even taken the position that where a principal resident in the US either directly or through a subsidiary or affiliate principal overseas conspires with a consultant to violate the exchange control or taxation legislation of any foreign country, it has itself committed an act which is probably unlawful, and which must be disclosed publicly in its relevant SEC filings.

9–59 In the UK there are various common law and statutory criminal offences relating to bribery. The giving to or the receiving of bribes by a public officer concerning the discharge of his public duties is an indictable offence at common law. The definition of public duty is very widely construed, and has been described as "any duty in the discharge of which the public is interested" (see *R. v Whittaker* [1914] 3 K.B. 1283, CCA in which an army officer was found guilty of the offence for taking bribes which influenced him in the award of a catering contract for his regiment). A recent instance was the case of *R. v Garner* [1988] 10 Cr.App.R. (S) 445, where the accused bribed prison officers to take luxury goods into prison for the benefit of prisoners.

In the Public Bodies Corrupt Practices Act 1899, s.1 it is provided that **9–60** every person who is a "member officer or servant of a public body" who shall "corruptly solicit or receive ... any gift loan fee reward or advantage ... for doing or forbearing to do anything in respect of any matter or transaction whatsoever ..." and "every person who corruptly gives promises or offers ... any gift loan fee reward or advantage" to a public official for the same purpose is guilty of a criminal offence. By s.7 of the Act a public body is basically defined as any local authority in the UK. The consent of the Director of Public Prosecutions is required to bring proceedings under the Act.

The Prevention of Corruption Act 1906 extends this type of offence into **9–61** the general field of commercial dealings. Section 1(1) provides that any agent who "corruptly accepts or obtains ... from any person ... any gift or consideration as an inducement or reward for doing or forbearing to do ... any act in relation to his principal's affairs or business ..." is guilty of an offence; similarly any person who "corruptly gives or agrees to give or offers any gift or consideration to any agent as an inducement or reward for doing or forbearing to do any act in relation to his principal's affairs and business ..." is likewise guilty of an offence. Section 1(2) provides that "for the purposes of the Act 'consideration' includes valuable consideration of any kind; the expression 'agent' includes any person employed by or acting for another; the expression 'principal' includes an employer". By s.1(3) employees of the Crown, or of any local authority are deemed to be agents of their employer. Once again the consent of the Director of Public Prosecutions is required to bring proceedings under the Act.

In the recent case of *R. v Natji* [2002] 1 W.L.R. 2337, where the accused **9–62** bribed immigration officers employed by the Home Office, it was confirmed that the definition of public body in s.7 of the 1889 Act does not include the Crown. Therefore in cases relating to servants of the Crown, the correct procedure is to apply to the Director of Public Prosecutions for leave to prosecute under s.1 of the 1906 Act.

The Prevention of Corruption Act 1916 further extended the previous two **9–63** Acts. By s.2 it is provided that where "any money gift or other consideration has been paid or given to or received by a person in the employment of His Majesty or any Government Department or public body by or from any person or agent of a person holding or seeking to obtain a contract from ..." that person "... any money gift or other consideration shall be deemed to have been paid or given corruptly unless the contrary is proved". This puts a heavy onus on contractors and the officials that they deal with where a payment of this sort has been made, and it is often provided in central government or local authority contracts for the contractor expressly to warrant that no corrupt payments have been made in order to obtain the contract.

9–64 The 1916 Act extended the definition of "public body" for the purposes of the 1899 and 1906 Acts so that the term now means local and public authorities of all descriptions and any person serving under such a body is deemed to be serving as its agent within the 1906 Act.

9–65 Although in practice these Acts have not been widely invoked they do have a considerable scope in the area of commercial transactions which is not often realised. The case of *Morgan v DPP* [1970] 3 All E.R. 1053 shows this strikingly. Morgan was employed as an inspector of cars, and was also a shop steward. He caused his union to black a subcontractor to his employer. He then offered to the subcontractor to arrange with the union to take him off the black list in return for a bribe. The Court held that the phrase in the 1906 Act "in relation to his principal's affairs" was to be construed widely, that Morgan was an agent of his employer for the purposes of the 1906 Act, and that his activities were caught within the phrase, even though they related directly to his union and only indirectly to his employer.

9–66 It can thus be seen that where UK law applies to a questionable consultancy contract there are a variety of possible offences. A principal which employs an employee of a customer as a consultant, because that employee can influence the customer in the placing of the contract with the principal, is guilty of an offence, in that the principal has made a corrupt arrangement with an agent of the customer (*i.e.* the customer's employee). Similarly the consultant has committed an offence by benefiting from the corrupt arrangement as an agent of his employer. If a consultant and a principal enter into a consultancy arrangement to enable the consultant to make corrupt payments to third parties the principal and the consultant will be guilty of having made the corrupt payments to agents of the customer, or to public officials, and the employees of the customer will be guilty as agents of their employer, or as public officials, for accepting them.

9–67 The question of the liability of an agent to account to his principal for moneys received on the principal's behalf is dealt with in Chapter 2.3.13 and 2.14. In connection with consultancy, it is enough to note that as regards the civil law, where an employee receives a bribe in relation to his employer's business he has a civil liability to account for the bribe to his employer (see *Boston Deep Sea Fishing and Ice Co v Ansell* (1888) 39 Ch. D. 339 CA; *Logicrose Ltd v Southend United Football Club Ltd* [1988] 1 W.L.R. 1256 and *Fyffes Group Ltd v Templeman* [2000] 2 Lloyd's Rep. 643).

9–68 There is also in some cases a right of action for the employer against the person who has given the bribe. The court presumes that in a contract of sale which has been obtained by bribery the price has been increased by the amount necessary to fund the bribe, and that the buyer can therefore claim as damages the amount of the "excess" price from the seller as well as the actual bribe from his fraudulent employee, thus in fact recovering twice over (see *Industries and General Mortgage Co Ltd v Lewis* [1949] 2 All E.R. 573).

When considering consultancy agreements with a foreign element under the laws in force in the UK, it is now necessary to take account of the effect of Pt 12 (Bribery and Corruption) of the Anti-terrorism, Crime and Security Act 2001. This legislation has amended the position under the common law and the subsisting legislation in the UK discussed above, to bring it more or less in line with the approach taken in the US. **9–69**

Section 108(1) of the Act provides that for the purposes of the common law offence of bribery it is immaterial if the functions of the person who receives or is offered a reward have no connection with the UK and are carried out in a country or territory outside the UK. **9–70**

Section 108(2) amends s.1 of the Prevention of Corruption Act 1906, by providing that for the purposes of that section it is immaterial if (a) the principal's affairs and business have no connection with the UK and are conducted in a country or territory outside the UK and (b) the agent's functions have no connection with the UK and are carried out in a country or territory outside the UK. **9–71**

Section 108(3) amends s.7 of the Public Bodies Corrupt Practices Act 1889 to include within the definition of public body "any body which exists in a country or territory outside the United Kingdom and is equivalent to any" UK public body described in the section. **9–72**

Section 108(4) of the Act amends s.4(2) of the Prevention of Corruption Act 1916 to include within the description of local and public authorities covered by that section authorities existing in a country or territory outside the UK. **9–73**

Section 109 creates new offences relating to bribery and corruption committed outside the UK. The section applies if a national of the UK or a body incorporated under the law of the UK does anything in a country or territory outside the UK and the act would (if done in the UK) constitute a corruption offence as defined in the section. In that case the act constitutes the offence concerned and proceedings may be taken in the UK. Corruption offences are defined as any common law offence of bribery, the offences under s.1 of the 1889 Act, and the first two offences under s.1 of the 1906 Act (bribes obtained by or given to agents). **9–74**

Finally s.110 provides that the presumption of corruption in certain cases under s.2 of the 1916 Act is not to apply to anything that would not be an offence apart from s.108 or s.109 of the 2001 Act. **9–75**

These amendments, taken as whole, effectively prevent UK nationals or legal entities incorporated in the UK from committing acts outside the UK which, if committed within the UK in relation to persons or bodies in the UK, would amount to an offence relating to bribery and corruption. To date there have been no reported prosecutions under the 2001 Act. **9–76**

Where, however, more important and difficult questions are raised in the area of international consultancy agreements is to what extent their illegality under the various relevant systems of law can make them unenforceable at civil law. The effect of the 2001 Act is to make such agreements illegal **9–77** contracts, in so far as they relate to international bribery and corruption. In this case, just as in the case where such an arrangement was wholly within the UK, it would, of course, be an illegal contract which was unenforceable in all respects at civil law.

However, an international consultancy agreement may still be entered into for purposes which would be illegal under the law of a foreign jurisdiction (*e.g.* to avoid local taxation or exchange control legislation) but which did not constitute an offence under the 2001 Act.

9–78 Where there is an agreement for these purposes between a UK principal and an overseas consultant, if a UK court has jurisdiction in the matter, according to the ordinary principles of private international law, it will proceed by applying three rules to the situation.

9–79 First, a UK court will not take notice of provisions of a foreign law which it regards as contrary to public policy (*i.e.* to the basic guiding principles of UK law). In *Kahler v Midland Bank Ltd* [1950] A.C. 24 Lord Simmonds pointed out that the court will disregard foreign laws where they are of a "penal and confiscatory nature".

9–80 Second, a UK court will refuse to enforce a contract, although legal under UK law, the performance of which would directly or indirectly violate the laws of the place of performance. The principle is based upon grounds of public policy. A contract is held to be void which is opposed to British interests and in particular which is apt to jeopardise friendly relations between the British government and any other government with which this country is at peace. As an example, in *Foster v Driscoll* [1929] 1 K.B. 470 it was held that a contract to import whisky into the US during Prohibition was not enforceable. It was stated that the court would not enforce a contract "made between parties to further an adventure to break the laws of a foreign state" and that the "object to be attained by this agreement being a breach of international comity, the agreement was contrary to public policy and void".

9–81 Third, UK courts do not enforce foreign revenue or penal laws but they will take notice of them in "those cases where as one of the terms of that law contracts are rendered invalid by the foreign law" (*per* Maguire C.J. in *Peter Buchanan Ltd v McVey* [1955] A.C. 516 in which arrangements made to avoid paying tax in Scotland, which were illegal under Scots law but not Irish law, were declared invalid by an Irish court).

9–82 Some recent cases which have dealt with such issues (before the passing of the 2001 Act) are *Arab Monetary Fund v Hashim (No.9)* [1993] 1 Lloyd's Rep. 543; *Petrotrade Inc v Smith* [2000] 1 Lloyd's Rep. 486; and *Konameni v Rolls Royce Industrial Power (India) Ltd* [2002] 1 W.L.R. 1269 in which the English court refused to hear a case concerning allegations of bribery and corruption in India on the grounds of *forum non conveniens.*

9–83 When these principles are applied to international consultancy agreements entered into either for the purposes of tax or exchange control evasion it will readily be seen that (given the illegality is not caused by a foreign law which is "penal or discriminatory") a UK court which has jurisdiction because the proper law of the contract is for example English law, will not enforce the contract, even though it is legal under English law, if it is illegal under the foreign law of the place of performance. To the extent necessary for this purpose it will take note of the relevant foreign criminal or revenue laws. Further, supposing the agreement were illegal under the proper law (English law) of the contract the court would still refuse to enforce it even if it were legal under the foreign law of the place of performance. Lastly, in the remote case where a UK court had jurisdiction over a contract with a foreign proper law and a foreign place of performance, it would determine the legality of the contract according to the relevant foreign law, and ignore UK law for this purpose. However, since these principles of private international law are in fact applied in the same way by the courts of most jurisdictions throughout the world, and even in countries where bribery is an accepted part of business life it is not usually legalised, the end result for a contract contemplating bribery or tax or exchange control evasion would be the same. The consequences are that a consultant under an illegal arrangement will be unable to sue for his commission and the principal will be unable to enforce any of the consultant's obligations.

The clauses set out above are thus designed to make clear the position of the principal with regard to undue influence, bribery, and tax or exchange control evasion. While it is of course not sufficient to insert the clauses and close one's eyes to obvious violations, these clauses should, if conscientiously enforced in situations where it is known or reasonably suspected that the consultant intends to commit illegal acts, provide sufficient protection in most jurisdictions against criminal liability being imposed upon the principal even if the consultant does in fact breach them. **9–84**

9.15 Disclosure and registration

9.15.1 Principal may disclose agreement

9.15.1 The Principal shall have the right to disclose the existence of this Agreement and its contents to any governmental authority either in the Territory or in the countries in which the Principal and the Consultant are resident for the purpose of registration or for any other purpose. **9–85**

9.15.2 Consultant to register agreement

9.15.2 If required by the law of the Territory or (if different) of the country in which he is resident the Consultant shall at his own expense forthwith register this Agreement with any relevant governmental authority and take all other necessary actions at his own expense to render the operation of this Agreement lawful. **9–86**

Coupled with the business ethics clause in cl.9.14 it is useful to provide for a right on the part of the principal to disclose the agreement to appropriate authorities. It is often useful for the principal to do this in circumstances where he is negotiating for a large contract and is uncertain whether the consultancy agreement is permitted under the particular circumstances or if its existence, if later discovered, will disqualify him from tendering, or result in the cancellation of the contract if obtained. For instance, in tendering for US defence contracts it is common practice to use *bona fide* consultancies as advisers on strategy for the bid, but their existence is usually disclosed and the consultant's fees are not normally allowable costs under US Department of Defence cost-investigated contracts. In many countries, for instance in most Middle Eastern states, such agreements are required to be declared and put upon a public register to prevent their use for illegal purposes. Clause 9.15.2 provides for this eventuality.

9.16 Indemnity for breach

9–87 9.16 The Consultant shall indemnify the Principal for any loss or damage suffered by the Principal as a result of any breach by the Consultant of the terms of this Agreement.

This standard clause should be inserted although the complete indemnity may well be commercially unacceptable to a consultant.

9.17 Termination without notice

9–88 9.17.1 If the Consultant shall neglect or fail or refuse or become unable for any reason to carry out his obligations under this Agreement or commit any serious breach of these obligations or become insolvent or enter into any arrangement with his creditors the Principal shall be entitled to terminate this Agreement immediately by notice given to the Consultant.

9–89 9.17.2 If the Consultant acts in any way which in the reasonable opinion of the Principal tends to the prejudice of the sales of the Products in the Territory including without limitation any involvement whether directly or indirectly in the sale or marketing in the Territory of goods which are competitive with any of the Products the Principal shall be entitled to terminate this Agreement immediately by notice given to the Consultant.

These standard clauses should be inserted. Note particularly that cl.9.17.2 complements and reinforces the undertaking not to engage in competing activities (see cl.9.10). It should also be noted that there is normally no provision excusing the consultant from the performance of his duties because of events of "force majeure" or other happenings beyond his reasonable control. Although some consultants would contest this, it is generally accepted that a consultant should not be entitled to suspend his activities for such events but that the principal should be entitled to cancel the agreement and move on to another consultant, who can act, if he can find one.

9.18 No compensation on termination

9.18 Termination of this Agreement for any reason shall not entitle the Consultant to compensation and shall be without prejudice to the rights of both parties accrued before the date of such termination. **9–90**

This clause should be inserted as a matter of standard practice, but it must be remembered that in some countries a consultant may be entitled by law to compensation for termination, so that this clause may be overruled. This could occur either because the position of a consultant is expressly protected under local law (which is rare) or else because his duties in a particular case are such as to bring him within the definition of an agent and so entitle him to the protection of local laws providing compensation to agents upon termination, which are much more widespread. It would be almost certain, that a consultant who is appointed to introduce a product to a customer (see cl.9.3.2) approaches very closely to an agent, and may well be indistinguishable so far as the laws of some countries are concerned (see Chapters 2.7 and 3.2 for a full discussion of this question in relation to agents).

9.19 Return of documents

9.19 The Consultant or his personal representatives shall upon the termination of this agreement immediately return to the Principal free of charge all correspondence specifications brochures or other documents or records (including tapes discs or other media used for storing computerised records) which relate to the Products or the Principal or the Distributor and which are in his possession or otherwise under his control. **9–91**

This clause ties back to the confidentiality clause (see cl.9.13).

9.20 Payments

9.20 All payments under this Agreement shall be made to the Consultant in [Sterling] in [the Territory] and the Consultant agrees that he will pay all taxes levied on these payments (including without limitation value added or similar taxes and income tax payable by him in [the Territory]). **9–92**

This clause is vital to cover the question of currency fluctuation risk and exchange control requirements. It is also a reasonably polite way of pointing out to the consultant his duties in the matter of complying with exchange control and taxation law, in relation to his commission, and thus fits in with cl.9.14 and to cl.9.14.1 in particular. The effect of agreements violating English or foreign revenue or exchange control laws has been discussed in cl.9.14.

9.21 Interpretation clauses and signature

9–93 Standard clauses from Chapter 1 should be adapted as necessary. In most cases a clause on notice and proper law are the most important. The other standard clauses are unlikely to add a significant measure of legal protection in most cases, and on balance are probably to be avoided in the interests of a shorter and more commercially acceptable document, except in cases where the draftsman foresees that there are specific areas of risk to be covered.

Chapter 10

Escrow Agreements

Contents

10.1 Commercial and legal background

Escrow agreements have developed from the old practice of requiring some **10–01** third party to hold a valuable item until the fulfilment of certain conditions, and then to deliver it, automatically, upon the fulfilment of those conditions, to a designated person. The item was said to be held in escrow. It was often the practice to hold an executed deed in escrow, and then to perfect its operation by delivery to the beneficiary named in the deed, when certain conditions had been fulfilled. This practice is still common today in England in conveyancing transactions. Another very common practice in conveyancing transactions which has some of the elements of holding in escrow, but not all, is the solicitor who acts as stakeholder when he holds a deposit, paid over upon the exchange of contracts, pending completion (see *Vincent v Primo Enterprises Ltd* [1969] 2 Q.B. 609, CA; *Kingston v Ambrian Investment Co Ltd* [1975] 1 All E.R. 120, CA)

The escrow arrangement has however been developed to particular **10–02** importance in the field of technology transfer and licences for the use of computer programs.

In the area of technologically sophisticated products a distributor may **10–03** commence an arrangement where he sells finished products of his principal, and has to receive a certain amount of technical information to enable him to market the product intelligently, and to provide maintenance and warranty services. This is often confined to functional and testing specifications and related information, coupled with a maintenance manual, so that he can explain to his customers what the product does, and can test, adjust and maintain it, if it is not functioning properly. However, this limited level of knowledge held by the distributor implies that the principal is able and willing to back up the distributor with the detailed knowledge which he uses to manufacture the product, and develop it further, and that the principal will be in a position to provide all the necessary support by way of advice and spare parts, and also to manufacture replacement products and parts as required.

10–04 The distributor will be concerned as to his position, particularly in the light of continuing contractual obligations that he undertakes to his customers, over the repair and replacement of the products he sells. Further, quite apart from contractual obligations, a distributor may well need to give his customers assurances about long-term support and maintenance if he is to sell the products successfully. If the principal goes out of business or ceases to be interested in the particular products concerned, the distributor will not be able to fulfil these obligations or expectations, with the level of information he has, and any distributor would therefore be unwise to undertake them, unless he had access to the whole of the information and knowhow necessary to enable him to become a manufacturer of the products himself, to turn out spare parts, and to give support to the same extent that the principal can.

10–05 The problem of the distributor could be met by the principal handing over to him on the start of the agreement all of the necessary information, subject to a contractually binding obligation on the part of the distributor not to use it, except in the happening of certain events. Understandably, however, a principal may not be willing to provide the distributor with this level of information at the start of a pure distribution arrangement. Not only is the distributor not paying for this amount of information, but it may well be that the most valuable aspects of the information are knowhow, which can be protected only by confidentiality undertakings, and that the principal, irrespective of compensation, may not wish to disclose this, even with secrecy undertakings. He may well fear a breach of the contractual obligations by the distributor, or a successor in title to the distributor, or a liquidator, so that the information is used to set up in manufacture in breach of the obligation, or disclosed, whether or not inadvertently, to customers or competitors.

10–06 On the other hand, the distributor's needs are not met by contractual undertakings from the principal. The principal may undertake to support the product and supply spare parts for a long period of time (in some capital goods industries where the product does not develop very quickly 20 years is sometimes used, although in high technology products, which evolve more rapidly, five years is often regarded as normal). However, if the principal goes out of business through insolvency, or is acquired by another organisation, the distributor may not be able to enforce these obligations by obtaining a court order for specific performance nor to obtain compensation by way of damages. In any case, the distributor is concerned not so much with obtaining compensation, as having the necessary information to support the products.

Nor will the insertion of a contractual provision to hand over information upon ceasing to do business in the products, be wholly satisfactory. The distributor will have practical problems in locating the actual information, persuading the principal to put it into a form to be handed over, and actually getting the principal to give it to him, and any liquidator who is appointed may refuse to honour the obligations, and leave the distributor to prove in the liquidation as an unsecured creditor for the breach of contract. The distributor cannot obtain specific performance of the obligation as against the liquidator. **10–07**

The concept of the holding of manufacturing information in escrow has developed to satisfy the conflicting needs of the distributor for information, (which he can require to be handed over to him against the will of the principal and his liquidator, if necessary), and the desire of the principal to protect the secrecy of his information and not to be required to disclose it unless he wishes to do so. **10–08**

The information is irrevocably placed in the hands of a third party, who has the absolute obligation to hand it over to the distributor upon the happening of certain events. In the simplest case, this would be when the principal goes into liquidation, or ceases to carry on business in the products. Another instance would be if the principal were to make a definite default in the support of the products, and the distributor has to rely on his own resources to support the product. A third possibility is the desire of the distributor to have an option to convert his distribution agreement into a manufacturing licence upon the payment of a licence fee. In this case, he could well have a distribution agreement in force and active, a signed licence agreement which is in suspense, but can be activated upon a down payment, and an escrow agreement which will ensure that, upon the down payment, the necessary information to enable the distributor to operate under the licence agreement will be transferred without argument. **10–09**

Another area in which the escrow arrangement is very important is that of the software licence. The distributor, or indeed a user, of software, is usually provided only with what is known as the object code of a computer program. This enables the distributor to sell and the user to use the actual program by loading it into his computer. Object codes are written in machine code (the lowest level of computer language—basically strings of binary numbers). However, such object codes are created, by the programmers who write the software in the first place, from what is known as the source code. Source codes are written in higher level languages (which are easier for computer programmers to work with) such as COBOL, FORTRAN or C+ + or 4GL, but have to be "translated" into object codes to enable them to be run quickly and efficiently on the computer. The source code is converted into the actual object code by means of what are known as either assembler or compiler programs. Although one can operate the program perfectly successfully with the object code, if it is necessary to **10–10** correct an error in the program, or to modify it in any way, this cannot usually be done without access to the source code, assemblers and compilers, and often to the working papers (such as flow charts) of the programmers who wrote the program.

10–11 Again the principal is understandably reluctant to release this information to the distributor, since it will enable him to reproduce and modify the program himself, and to set up in business on his own, without further reference to the principal. Nevertheless, in this area, more than any other, the source materials are vital to support the program and its users, and, without this information, the distributor will, in the absence of the principal, be unable to do this. Again the escrow arrangement provides a safe way of identifying and looking after the information until it is necessary for it to be handed over to the distributor.

10–12 The precedent set out below is a document which is entered into as a tripartite agreement between the principal, the escrow agent and the distributor. It attempts to deal with most of the issues raised above, but it should be remembered that many professional escrow agents have their own standard forms, from which they are loathe to depart. It is important to remember that this is only one half of the escrow arrangements—the part that provides for the mechanics of the escrow. The rights to use the information in escrow and the triggering events which apply to it are detailed in the licence or distribution agreement between the principal and the distributor or licensee. An example of these arrangements, and a discussion to the relevant issues, is set out in Chapter 6.24.

10.2 Definitions

10–13 10.2.1 "The Principal" means [ ] whose registered office is situated at [ ].

10.2.2 "The Escrow Agent" means [ ] of [ ].

Any person firm or company that possesses the legal capacity to enter into contracts may be an escrow agent. One would normally not choose an individual who was a minor, or otherwise unqualified to enter into a contract, and, in practice, the most likely escrow agent is a solicitor or a bank. Another possibility is a company which has been specifically set up to act for this purpose in relation to technological information. Such companies are usually found to have extended their activities into the escrow field from a primary business of offering safe storage facilities for archival information.

10–14 Such companies operate particularly in the area of backup storage of computer records for security purposes. These records need special storage facilities, with controlled temperatures and humidity, and screening from magnetic fields, and particularly careful handling, so that these companies are therefore well suited to the holding of information related to escrow arrangements for computer programs, since most of this information will be in the form of computer records (such as magnetic tape, or disks) which will in itself require these special storage facilities. However in some cases the increasing use of cd-rom as a storage device has meant that much less specialised storage facilities are required.

> 10.2.3 "The Place of Deposit" means [ ] or such other place as the Escrow Agent may notify to the Distributor and Principal. **10–15**

Here the actual place of deposit will be specified. It is normal to provide that the actual place will not be changed by the escrow agent without first notifying this to both the principal and the distributor, since for obvious administrative reasons both the principal and the distributor need to know where the information is deposited at all times.

> 10.2.4 "The Package" means the [master disk, software listings, source code and associated documentation] [the drawings, manufacturing information and other knowhow], all as detailed in and in the form described in Sch.1 hereto, and including all updates to and replacements thereof supplied from time to time by the Principal pursuant to cl.10.2.2. **10–16**

The phrases in square brackets are suggested illustrations. The important part of the definition is the reference to the description and detail in Sch.1. The purpose of the escrow arrangement is to enable the distributor to get into his possession specified information, deposited in a particular place in a particular form. General descriptions such as "all the knowhow necessary to manufacture the products" will be useless. It is up to the distributor to agree with the principal at the time of deposit exactly what is to be deposited and in what form, and to satisfy himself that this is adequate for his requirements. This information, and the form in which it is to be provided, must be described in detail in the schedule.

If, after the distributor gets possession of the information, he finds that it is insufficient for his purposes, the existence of contractual remedies will normally be of no assistance since the principal will either have gone out of business or be in dispute with the distributor. The distributor does not require the right to institute legal proceedings, and often cannot wait until they have been completed. He needs immediate access to the information to enable him to service his customers for the products. **10–17**

It will be difficult for the distributor to verify at the time of deposit that the principal has actually complied with his deposit obligations under the schedule. The whole purpose of the arrangement is that the distributor is not to have access to the information at that time. He will either have to rely on the good faith of the principal, or hire an independent expert to carry out a verification and issue a certificate that the principal has complied with his obligations. The principal will have to give his consent to this arrangement, and will probably require the expert to enter into a confidentiality undertaking before the expert is given access. Nowadays, it is quite common for escrow companies in high technology fields (particularly software) to provide an inspection and verification service as part of their escrow service. A suggested clause for this is set out below as version (a) of cl.10.3.2. **10–18**

10–19 10.2.5 "The Distributor" means [ ] having its registered office at [ ];

10.2.6 The Charges' means the charges of the Escrow Agent as detailed in Sch.2 hereto.

This escrow agent normally acts for a fee, and the precedent as drafted is contractually binding upon the escrow agent because of the consideration created by the promise of the principal to pay the charges. The distributor takes the benefit of the agreement, and can enforce it against the escrow agent, as well as the principal, because he is a party to the agreement, even though he himself provides no consideration to the escrow agent.

10–20 Where the distributor was not a party to the escrow agreement, it would in many cases be possible in the UK for him to enforce his rights under it pursuant to the Contracts (Rights of Third Parties) Act 1999 (see Chapter 1.10), but this is clearly not such a satisfactory position, and the distributor should in all circumstances make sure he is party to the escrow agreement. Failing this, there should be a clear expression of his rights to enforce the provisions for his benefit pursuant to the Act. Here the relevant precedent from Chapter 1.10 could be applied, suitably adapted.

10.3 Scope and purpose

10–21 10.3.1 In consideration of the payment of the Charges by the Principal to the Escrow Agent the Escrow Agent agrees and undertakes both to the Principal and the Distributor jointly and severally to hold the Package as trustee thereof, upon and subject to the terms and conditions of this Agreement and the trusts hereinafter appearing.

This agreement, supported by consideration, as described in cl.10.2.6, creates a trust of the package in which the principal is the settlor, the escrow agent the trustee and the distributor the beneficiary. The trust concept is vital to the proper functioning of the arrangement. The settlement of the physical items contained in the package is a trust of personal (as opposed to real) property which puts the package out of the reach of both the principal and any of his successors in title, a liquidator, or receiver. The escrow agent has the duty to fulfil his trust in favour of the distributor, and the settlement cannot be revoked by the principal or any of the other persons mentioned, so that the distributor is safeguarded from any events involving the principal subsequent to the creation of the trust which might cause the principal or any third party to try to regain control of the package (see *Windsor Refrigerator Co Ltd v Brands Nominees Ltd* [1960] 2 All E.R. 568; *Gleasing v Green* [1975] 2 All E.R. 696, CA; and *Terrapin International Ltd v Inland Revenue* [1976] W.L.R. 665).

10–22 10.3.2(a) The Escrow Agent shall carry out such tests and make such inspection as is [considered by it to be reasonably required] [listed in Sch.1] to verify that the Principal has complied with its obligations under this Agreement to deposit with the Escrow Agent all of the materials and documents which are contained in the details of the Package listed in Sch.1, including updates to the Package pursuant to and in accordance with cl.10.4.3.2. [The Escrow Agent shall in particular carry out such tests and make such inspection as is [considered by it to be reasonably required] [listed in Sch.1] to ascertain that the Package contains true, accurate and functioning versions of the source code described in Schedule 1 as part of the Package including any updates to such source code made pursuant to cl.10.4.3.2.] The Escrow Agent shall carry out such tests and inspection promptly upon receipt of the Package and of any update thereto pursuant to cl.10.4.3.2, and shall notify both the Principal and the Distributor in writing of the results of such tests and inspection immediately upon completion thereof.

OR

10.3.2(b) The Escrow Agent takes no responsibility and disclaims all liability as to whether the items comprised within the Package deposited by the Principal comprise all or any of the materials and documents which are contained in the details of the Package listed in Schedule 1 or whether the Principal has complied with its obligations to update the Package pursuant to and in accordance with cl.10.4.3.2. It is the responsibility of the Principal and the Distributor to ascertain all such matters, and to institute whatever procedures between themselves or third parties they may deem appropriate for such purpose.

Version (a) of this clause provides for a verification service by the escrow agent. The alternative, version (b), disclaims all liability for the contents of the Package. The two are obviously mutually exclusive.

10.4 The trusts

10.4.1 The Principal shall on [ ] deliver the Package to the authorised representatives of the Escrow Agent at the Place of Deposit. **10–23**

10.4.2 The Escrow Agent shall upon such delivery provide to the Principal a signed acknowledgement of receipt, and shall send a copy thereof to the Distributor. **10–24**

Clauses 10.4.1 and 10.4.2 provide the administrative framework for delivery. It may be that the escrow agent is not prepared to send copies of the receipt to the distributor, in which case cl.10.4.2 should be redrafted to impose this obligation upon the principal.

10.4.3 Upon such delivery title to the Package shall vest in the Escrow Agent, and the Escrow Agent shall hold the same as trustee upon the following trusts: **10–25**

It is important that the legal title in the package passes upon delivery from the principal to the escrow agent. Thus delivery actually triggers the existence of the trust, and removes the package from the control and ownership of the principal, and of course, his successors in title. A receiver of the principal's assets under a charge would not be able to take the package, since the package ceases upon delivery to be one of the assets of the principal. A liquidator or trustee in bankruptcy would have the same difficulty, and, in addition, a liquidator or trustee in bankruptcy would not be able to raise the various provisions as to conveyances in fraud of creditors, or transactions at an undervalue, at least in cases where the escrow agreement was properly entered into in good faith, and as a result of the existence of a distribution agreement.

10–26 The precedent for an escrow agreement in this chapter is drafted on the basis of English law, so that the concepts of trust property, and the comments about avoidance of transactions in fraud of creditors upon insolvency, are made in the light of English law. It is of course possible to have an escrow agreement under the law in most jurisdictions. The concept of escrow is a common law one, and most common law jurisdictions usually recognise both the concept of escrow and the concept of the trust. Under English law it is considered a question of fact whether or not the arrangement entered into constitutes a true escrow agreement (*Thompson v McCullough* [1947] 1 All E.R. 265, CA). The escrow arrangement is, for instance, freely used in the US and Canada.

10–27 Most of the jurisdictions based upon civil codes have somewhat similar concepts stemming, in many cases, from Roman law concepts such as "mandate". They would not use the same wording relating to trusts, but would impose the same obligations and use the language as to transfer of title and delivery of the package. However, care should always be taken to ascertain that the local law in fact permits the escrow type of arrangement and that, if it does, any particular formalities by way of execution, witnessing, payment of stamp duty, and, perhaps, registration of the agreement are complied with. If in any doubt, a distributor who is dealing with a principal outside a common law jurisdiction could use one of the jurisdictions where the escrow agreement is a generally recognised concept, such as England or one of the states of the US, probably New York. There is no particular reason, except convenience, why the distributor or the principal should be resident in the same jurisdiction as the escrow agent.

10–28 10.4.3.1 To deliver the Package to the Distributor, and to vest title to the same in the Distributor, upon the Distributor producing to the Escrow Agent a certificate in the form set out in Sch.3 signed by [the Distributor] [a solicitor in private practice acting on behalf of the Distributor] [a notary public];

As a matter of practice, escrow agents, particularly bankers, do not want to go into the rights or wrongs of any situation, and to decide upon their own initiative whether they should hand over the package in any particular case. They require something obvious and unambiguous. The difficulty with providing an ascertainable event that is immediately and without doubt obvious to the escrow agent is that the events upon which the distributor wishes to take delivery of the package are not like this. The insolvency of the principal can only be evidenced after a search in one or more public registers or after receiving a copy of a court order. The existence of a default or a dispute that justifies the handing over is similarly a matter which requires judgment. Further it is no use providing that the escrow agent should hand over the package on the direction of the principal or upon the direction of the distributor, since the aim is to keep the package out of the control of both principal and distributor until the circumstances themselves objectively justify delivery.

The usual way around this problem is to provide for the certification of the happening of a particular event as set out in this clause. The certification should either be by the distributor (if the principal and the escrow agent will both accept this), or by some third party on behalf of the distributor, whom both the escrow agent and the principal can accept as responsible and impartial. The drafting of the certificate in alternative forms is dealt with the schedule. The phrases in square brackets suggest possible alternatives for a certifying authority. **10–29**

The idea of the distributor himself signing the certificate is not as unreasonable as it may seem at first sight. Given that the distributor is a reputable firm, and of reasonable substance (or presumably the principal would not have appointed him as distributor in the first place), and given that the distributor will normally wish to exercise the right to receive the package while still in business, and in order to carry on in business, the principal would still be able to exercise remedies against the distributor, either for breach of undertakings in the distribution agreement, or the escrow agreement, or under the general law, to restrain the use by the distributor of the information in the package, if it were obtained by a false or incorrect certification. After all the purpose of the escrow agreement is to keep the distributor in business, and it seems likely that in most cases a distributor who is about to go out of business would not trigger the agreement. **10–30**

An alternative would be to provide that the package should be delivered upon the distributor producing a copy of a court order from a court of competent jurisdiction evidencing the insolvency of the principal, or, for instance, certified copies of entries from a public register showing the appointment of a receiver or the fact that the principal had been wound up or ceased to do business. These types of evidence, except in the most clear cut cases, suffer either from the fact that the escrow agent still has to make some value judgment upon them, or that they may take a long time to obtain (particularly if there has to be a court hearing before the order can be made and a copy obtained), and the distributor may well wish to obtain the package much more quickly. **10–31**

It is the practice in some agreements to require that, instead of a certificate, a statutory declaration or its local equivalent be used. This can be appropriate in that it adds a degree of formality and weight to the certification. Some agreements also provide for a copy of the certificate to be served upon the principal, and for an opportunity for the principal to serve a counter-notice, in which event the escrow agent has no liability to release the package until some dispute resolution procedure is gone through. The problem with this is the length of time it takes for this procedure. Although an expert clause could be used if the dispute were over a question of fact, most of the events which trigger an escrow relate to questions of law (*e.g.* is **10–32** the principal insolvent or did he commit a breach?) or at least questions of mixed law and fact. At least under English law, these questions cannot be submitted to an expert for a final and binding decision in a short space of time. Simple expert clauses which submit questions of law or mixed law and fact to the binding decision of an expert are, under English law, normally void. They are regarded as against public policy because they oust the jurisdiction of the court (see Chapter 1.6.2). The best that can be done here is to try to provide for a short form arbitration procedure, under the Aribtration Act 1966, where the arbitrator is not required to give reasons for his award. Such an award, for all practical purposes cannot be the subject of an appeal the court. However, even here, time will be taken before the escrow can be finally triggered.

10–33 10.4.3.2 To permit the Principal (or any third party nominated by the Principal) access to the Package upon reasonable notice, for inspection, for the deposit of additional items (which shall thereupon become part of the Package), [and for the removal of items from the Package provided that each item is replaced with a new or updated version of such item (which shall thereupon become part of the Package) and that title to each such item removed shall thereupon vest again in the Principal];

These provisions are necessary if the package contains information of a type which requires updating. The most usual example of this is information relating to a computer program, where the program itself may be refined, corrected and improved by the principal, and new editions of it issued on a regular basis. Even with other types of products modifications and improvements may be necessary from time to time.

10–34 Some problems may arise where the escrow agent is required to police the replacement by the principal of old items by new versions, as provided for in the phrase in square brackets. On the other hand, the continued adding of items to the package, without the removal of obsolete ones, may in practice make it too large for proper handling or storage. In some cases this is solved by providing for the termination of the existing escrow arrangement, and the starting of a new arrangement, with only updated and relevant items in it, whenever the package gets too large to handle conveniently. As stated above, it is becoming increasingly the practice for escrow companies to be willing to provide these verification and supervisory services (see version (a) of cl.10.3.2) for a fee.

10–35 10.4.3.3 To deliver the Package to the Principal, and to vest title to the same in the Principal, upon receipt of a certificate in the form set out in Sch.4 hereto signed by [the Principal] [a solicitor in private practice acting on behalf of the Principal] [a notary public].

If the distribution agreement has been terminated by the principal for just cause or by proper notice, then the escrow agreement also needs to fall away. The same problems apply to ascertainment by the escrow agent of the right of the principal to require redelivery and revesting of title as apply to the ascertainment of the right of the distributor to take delivery. The remarks made upon cl.10.4.3.2 therefore apply here as well. Here, however, the distributor is concerned that the principal does not trigger redelivery in circumstances where the termination of the distribution agreement by the principal is not justified. There is also the point that even termination of the distribution agreement may not release the distributor from the support obligations he has undertaken to his customers. He may still need the backup from the principal, or require the principal to take over those obligations. In some situations the escrow agreement may therefore need to continue, and the principal should not be permitted to take back the package under these circumstances.

Again, as in the case where the distributor gives the certificate, if the principal wrongfully obtains the redelivery of the package, the principal will in most cases still be in existence and solvent so that the distributor stands a reasonable chance of successfully bringing legal proceedings to remedy the matter. **10–36**

[10.4.3.4 To permit any third party nominated jointly by the Principal and the Distributor to have access to the Package for the purpose of carrying out the procedures referred to in cl.10.3.2.] **10–37**

This clause should only be inserted when version (b) of cl.10.3.2 is used.

10.5 Safekeeping

10.5.1 The Escrow Agent shall not use deliver up or deal with the Package otherwise than in accordance with the terms of this Agreement and its responsibilities hereunder as trustee of the Package. **10–38**

This clause is inserted simply to clarify the responsibilities of the escrow agent. The escrow agent is a trustee, and he has responsibilities to discharge his duties under the trust properly. He would not only be liable to the principal as settlor, but also to the distributor as beneficiary, in the event of a breach of trust.

10.5.2 The Escrow Agent shall not be entitled to exercise any banker's lien or other lien charge security or right of retention whatsoever in order to justify refusal to deliver up and vest title to the Package in either the Distributor or the Principal in accordance with cl.10.3. **10–39**

This clause is inserted as a precautionary measure to cover the situation where the escrow agent is banker or otherwise acts in a professional capacity for one or the other of the parties. If that party owes the escrow agent for services rendered in that professional capacity, or, in the case of a bank, is due to repay the bank a loan made to him by the bank, the escrow agent may be able to exercise under the general law a right of retention or lien over items in his possession which he would otherwise be obliged to hand over to that party. Thus the escrow agent might refuse to deliver the package to the distributor until the distributor agreed (for instance) to repay a bank loan (then due for repayment) made to the distributor by the escrow agent in his capacity as the distributor's banker. The law on such liens, and in particular the question of the property over which they can be exercised, is not always clear. To avoid controversy it is better to spell out the exclusion clearly in the escrow agreement.

10–40 10.5.3 The Escrow Agent shall exercise reasonable care in the safekeeping of the Package, in particular by storing it at the Place of Deposit, in a secure area [suitable for the storage of magnetic computer media].

This merely recites the ordinary duty of care which the escrow agent would probably have imposed upon him as an implied term of the agreement in any event. The last phrase in square brackets is designed for computer programs held in escrow. Unless the escrow agent is a specialist in storing such items, he will probably not agree to this type of provision. The importance of correct storage is however obvious, as it is no use the distributor obtaining the package in due course and finding that it has deteriorated so as to be unusable.

10–41 10.5.4 The Escrow Agent shall not (except in so far as necessary for the proper performance of his duties) during or at any time after the termination of this Agreement disclose to any person any information relating to the Package which has or shall after the commencement of this Agreement become known to the Escrow Agent.

It is desirable to impose a confidentiality obligation on the escrow agent in relation to the escrow material. More detailed obligations can be imposed, based on those in Chapter 1.4, and perhaps set out in a special agreement if desired, particularly in the case where the escrow agent has any duties relating to inspection or verification of the escrow material.

10.6 Term and termination

10–42 10.6.1 This Agreement shall terminate only in the following events:

10.6.1.1 Upon the expiry of a period of thirty days after the Escrow Agent has served notice to the Principal and to the Distributor that the Principal has failed to pay any of the Charges due at the date such notice is served, provided that during such period of thirty days neither the Principal nor the Distributor has paid the said charges;

Although it is quite reasonable for the escrow agent not to have to continue with an arrangement if his charges for doing so are not paid by the principal, it would be too easy for the principal to avoid the whole arrangement by refusing to pay the charges. The remedy is either as here to give the distributor an opportunity to pay the charges himself (and then claim them back under a provision inserted in his distribution agreement) or else to provide that, in the event of termination for non-payment of charges, after notice has been given to the principal and he has still not paid, the package should be delivered to the distributor. In many cases the escrow fee will be a lump sum paid up front when the escrow is set up. This is obviously most desirable from the distributor's point of view, but may be impractical in cases where the escrow package must be updated from time to time.

10.6.1.2 Upon notice to the Escrow Agent in writing, delivered to the Place of Deposit and signed by the Principal and the Distributor; **10–43**

It is sensible for both parties to be able to terminate the arrangement, either because they wish to substitute a new package, or because the distribution agreement has been terminated amicably, or varied in such a way that there is now no need for the escrow agreement.

10.6.1.3 Upon delivery up to either the Distributor (under cl.10.4.3.1) or to the Principal (under cl.10.4.3.3). **10–44**

This clause provides for the termination of the agreement and the discharge of the escrow agent's responsibilities once the package has been properly delivered under the terms of the trust.

10.6.2 Upon termination of this Agreement under cll.10.6.1.1 or 10.6.1.2 the Escrow Agent shall deliver the Package to the Principal, and title thereto shall thereupon vest in the Principal. **10–45**

Once the agreement has been terminated in terms of cl.10.6 it makes sense for the package to be delivered back to the principal, who will not want the escrow agent simply to destroy it. However, the comments about the possibility of delivery up to the distributor in the event of the agreement being terminated under cl.10.6.1.1 should be noted.

10.7 Interpretation clauses and signature

Suitable clauses from Chapter 1 should be included as appropriate. **10–46**

10.8 Schedule 1—the package

10.9 Schedule 2—the charges

10.10 Schedule 3—the distributor's certificate

10.10 To [the Escrow Agent] **10–47**

I [ ] of [ ] being a solicitor in private practice acting for the Distributor [ ] whose registered office is at [ ] hereby certify as follows:

(a) Having made due enquiry at [the Companies Registry] I have determined that [a liquidator] [a receiver] of the Principal [ ] whose registered office is situated at [ ] was appointed on [ ].

(b) Having made due enquiry of my clients and of the Directors of the Principal, I am satisfied that the Distribution Agreement between the two parties made on [ ] has terminated by reason of the appointment of the said [liquidator] [receiver], and that no person firm or company reasonably satisfactory to my clients has offered to my clients to assume the obligations of the Principal under that agreement although my clients have made requests to that effect.

signed [ ]
Solicitor
Dated [ ]

This provides a simple form of certificate relating to the insolvency of a principal which is a limited company. Paragraph (b) provides for the possibility of a liquidation for amalgamation or reconstruction, where a new entity would take over the Principal's backup obligations to the distributor and would offer, if not the continuation of the agreement, at least the necessary support.

10–48 Set out below are alternative versions of paras (a) and (b) to illustrate other possible situations that the certificate could cover.

10–49 10.10(a) I attach hereto a certified copy of [a receiving order in bankruptcy made by the court on [ ] appointing a trustee in bankruptcy of the assets of [ ] of [ ] the Principal] [a certified copy of a court order made on [ ] for the compulsory winding-up of [ ] of [ ] the Principal] [a certified copy of a court order made on [ ] giving judgment in favour of [ ] of [ ] the Distributor against [ ] of [ ] the Principal for a breach of the Distribution Agreement made between the Distributor and the Principal on [ ] justifying termination thereof by the Distributor]

(b) I certify that by reason of the events leading to the making of the said order, and by reason of the granting of the said order by the court, the Distribution Agreement made between the Distributor and the Principal on [ ] was lawfully terminated [by the Distributor] on [ ].

OR

(a) I certify that cl [ ] of the Distribution Agreement between [ ] of [ ] the Distributor and [ ] of [ ] the Principal made on [ ] provides that the Distributor is entitled to receive the Package (as defined in the Escrow Agreement between yourself and the Principal dated [ ] upon payment to the Principal by the Distributor to the Principal of the sum of [ ].

(b) I certify that the said sum of [ ] was paid to the Principal by the Distributor on [ ] and I attach hereto a certified copy of the Principal's acknowledgement of receipt to the Distributor for the payment of the said sum.

These different versions of the certificate can be adapted slightly for use by a notary public. The notary public will not act on behalf of the distributor, but will certify to the existence of a particular state of affairs or as to the validity of certain documents. Thus any of the suggested versions above could be certified by a notary public. It is prudent where a notary public in a particular country is to be used to enquire in advance as to the form that the certificate should take, so that there is no difficulty later on in obtaining a properly executed certificate. In all cases the escrow agent will be entitled to demand a certificate exactly in the form set out in the schedule before he acts, so that failure to obtain a certificate precisely in the form required would cause problems.

The certificates would have to be adapted again if they were to be given by **10–50** the distributor himself.

10.11 Schedule 4—the principal's certificate

10.11 I [ ] of [ ] being a solicitor in private practice acting for [ ] of **10–51** [ ] the Principal, hereby certify that the Distribution Agreement made on [ ] between my clients and [ ] of [ ] the Distributor was terminated on [ ] [by notice duly served by the Principal upon the Distributor under clause [ ] thereof] [by expiry by effluxion of time] [by the appointment of a liquidator/receiver of the Distributor] [by the Distributor ceasing to carry on business for more than thirty consecutive days] [by the Principal having obtained judgment against the Distributor for a breach of the Distribution Agreement which justifies termination thereof by the Principal, and I attach a certified copy of the relevant court order].

signed [ ]
Solicitor
Dated [ ]

This certificate will need adaptation to suit the particular circumstances of the distribution agreement. It should be approached with caution by a draftsman acting on behalf of a distributor, because too much latitude in its terms will entitle the principal to get redelivery of the package in circumstances where this is not justified. It is probably wise to confine its operation to the events suggested. There is, in particular, no real need for the principal to get the package back quickly so that immediately upon termination for breach he needs to serve notice upon the escrow agent without waiting to take proceedings. He already knows what the information is, and is only concerned with the safe custody of the package, which presumably can remain with the escrow agent pending resolution of the dispute.

Chapter 11

Software Distribution Licences

Contents

11.1 Commercial and legal background

Where the products to be distributed are driven by software it is usual to require a separate set of licensing arrangements to cover and protect the use of the software. This involves a licence from the principal, who originates the software, to the distributor who sells the products concerned, and a sublicence from the distributor to the purchaser of the products to allow him to use the software to operate the products he has bought. In cases where the software is particularly sensitive, and where the end-users are few, the principal imposes upon the distributor an obligation to require the end-user to enter into a licence for the software direct with the principal. **11–01**

In many countries the exact legal status of software was for many years in doubt, particularly as to whether it was covered by the local laws relating to copyright or not. Courts in different countries have held that software is entitled in varying degrees to the protection of local copyright law. An example is the early Australian case *Apple Computer Inc v Computer Edge Pty Ltd* [1984] F.S.R. 246, which held that software was not protected by copyright (this decision is now no longer good law. See, for an example of the current approach in Australia based on copyright protection, *Trumpet Software Pty Ltd v OzEmail Pty Ltd* [1997–8] Inf. T.L.R. 451, Fed Ct (Aus).) **11–02**

In the UK there has always been some doubt about the situation and this was corrected to some extent by the Copyright (Computer Software) **11–03**

Amendment Act 1985.

11–04 The current position in the UK is now settled under Pt 1 of the Copyright, Designs and Patents Act 1988. Section 3(1)(b) includes computer programs within the definition of "literary works", so that computer programs now enjoy copyright protection in the UK as literary works. Under s.9(3) the author of a computer-generated work is deemed to be the person by whom the arrangements necessary for the creation of the work were undertaken, but, other than this, normal rules as to the attribution of authorship apply to computer programs as they do to other literary works. A computer program with a human author under the Act thus originally enjoyed protection for the life of the author plus 50 years, while a computer-generated program enjoyed protection for 50 years only from the date of generation (s.12(3)). However, following the passing of the Duration of Copyright and Rights in Performances Regulations 1995 (SI 1995/3297) implementing Council Directive 987/93, which harmonised the term of protection of copyright and related rights within the EC and the EEA, the first of these periods only has been extended from 50 years to 70 years. It should be noted that this extension applies only in respect of those works whose country of origin is one of the Member States of the EEA or the EC.

11–05 The copyright owner has the exclusive right to copy, issue copies, broadcast, perform or adapt a work (s.16). In so far as these rights are relevant they apply to computer programs, but, in particular, under s.17(2) copying includes storing the work in any medium by electronic means. Since a computer program is usually loaded into the computer's memory and in any event parts of it are stored in changing areas of the computer's memory as the program runs, all these operations amount to copying and thus no one can lawfully run a computer program without the express or implied permission of the copyright owner. Nor can a person make any changes to a program for which he has obtained a licence to run, without further express or implied permission (s.21(1) and (4)). Section 56 in effect enables a distinction to be made between computer programs "bought over the counter" and all other types. Section 56(1) provides that the section applies where a copy of a work in electronic form has been purchased on terms which expressly or impliedly or by virtue of operation of any rule of law allow the purchaser to copy the work or adapt it or make copies of an adaptation in connection with his use of it.

11–06 Under s.56(2), if there are no express terms:

- preventing transfer of the copy by the purchaser,
- imposing obligations which continue after a transfer,
- prohibiting the assignment of any licence or terminating any licence on a transfer, or
- providing for the terms on which a transferee may do the things which the purchaser was permitted to do,

the transferee may do anything that the purchaser was permitted to do, but the purchaser loses all rights with respect to any copy of the work which he retains.

An example will make the operation of this clear in relation to computer programs. Where a purchaser goes into a computer retailer and purchases a word-processing program for his home computer, he obviously has the implied consent of the author to load it into his computer and run it (which amounts to copying) and probably also to make a backup copy in case the original disk becomes damaged. There may also be some options in the program (such as setting up special functions on user-defined keys) which enable him to tailor the copy of the program to his own requirements. He will have an implied licence to make these adaptations as well. He obviously has no right to make copies of the program to give to his friend. However, he can sell the original disk, or indeed the backup disk (s.56(3)) to his friend who thereupon enjoys the same rights to run and to make backup copies and to adapt as the original purchaser did. If the original purchaser has a copy of the disk left, he must destroy it, as it is now an infringing copy. **11–07**

The European Commission was much concerned with the legal status of software in the late 1980s and their concern resulted in the passing, after a great deal of discussion and lobbying from many different interests, of the so-called Software Directive (Council Directive on the legal protection of computer programs 250/91). This Directive was implemented in the UK by the Copyright (Computer Programs) Regulations 1992 (SI 1992/3233). The basic concept of the Directive was harmonisation to ensure that all Member States treated software under their local laws as a literary work subject to the Berne Convention. This objective has been achieved, and a great many of the provisions in the Directive reflect the provisions in the Copyright Designs and Patents Act 1988, which, as will be seen below, required comparatively little amendment to comply with the Directive. **11–08**

The problem which caused most controversy and delayed the finalisation of the Directive, was the extent to which there should be derogation from the rights of the holder of copyright in a program to prevent it being copied in the sense of being run on a computer (not in the sense of replicating further copies of the program for unlawful exploitation) to enable the user of the program to study the way in which the program worked. The debate ranged around whether such a derogation should go so far as to permit decompiling or disassembling a program (so-called reverse engineering) or should be limited merely to observing the function of the program. A further debate was the extent to which such derogation, however extensive it was, should be allowed only for the purpose of determining the interfaces between the program being studied and other relevant programs or hardware, or whether there should be permission for more general purposes, or even for any purpose at all. There was also a question as to whether the UK concept of fair-dealing allowed any or all of these acts without the permission of the copyright holder anyway. **11–09**

The proponents of these derogations held that without them it was not practically possible to produce a competitive environment in which many different compatible programs and peripheral hardware products with the **11–10** same function can be offered to users. They accepted that copying (in the sense of replicating) existing programs was obviously an infringement, and pointed out that the so-called process of reverse engineering is so expensive and time-consuming that in practice a pirate would not bother with it, but would merely copy disks and sell them. On the contrary, the study of existing programs enabled programmers to understand techniques and to see how programs interface with each other, so that they could produce a greater variety of compatible but original programs of their own. Their opponents took the view that any derogation from the laws of copyright would be disastrous, and would rob the authors of programs of the rights to exploit their copyright in them as they wish.

11–11 There were obvious public policy issues in this area, particularly in the area of competition law, which transcended the question of how the laws of copyright should apply. In the end, the solution adopted was a compromise which did not entirely please either side in the debate. Article 6 of the Directive contains provisions which permit copying (in the sense of loading and running a program) for the purposes of reverse engineering in the very restricted circumstances where the acts are "indispensable to obtain the information necessary to achieve the interoperability of an independently created computer program with other programs" provided that the acts are performed by a lawful licensee of the program (or someone acting on his behalf), the information has not previously been readily available, and the acts are confined to those parts of the program necessary to achieve interoperability. The information obtained cannot be used for other purposes, or in a manner which "unreasonably prejudices the right holder's legitimate interests or conflicts with a normal exploitation of the computer program". The drafting is convoluted, and not always understandable, as one would expect where the provision has been subject to intensive lobbying and final compromises. The aim, however, is clear. Either the producers of computer programs will make the interface information available or their licensees can get it for themselves by reverse engineering.

11–12 The Statutory Instrument which implemented the Directive in the UK has made some changes to the 1988 Act to bring it into line with the Directive, and in particular to deal with the common law concept of fair dealing. Article 6 of the Directive is implemented verbatim by a new s.50B, which also attempts a definition of "decompilation". A new s.29(4) is then inserted to provide that decompilation within the meaning of s.50B is not fair dealing. This means that the avenue open to someone in the UK who wants to decompile is to follow the strict provisions of Art.6 as implemented by s.50B. No other form of decompilation can be carried out under the protection of the right to fair dealing.

11–13 The Statutory Instrument also implements the other provisions of the Directive which necessitated changes to the 1988 Act. Section 50A now makes it clear that a lawful user of a computer program can copy it for back up purposes (Art.5(2)). Section 50C permits a lawful user of a program to copy or adapt it as necessary for its lawful use, including the correction of errors (Art.5(1)), unless otherwise provided by contract, and s.296A(1)(c) permits the study of a program by its lawful user while it is running to "understand the ideas and principles which underlie any element of the program" (Art.5(3)). These rights are overriding under the Directive and the 1988 Act, so that it is not possible to exclude them by contract (see s.296A(1) and Art.9(1)), except for the right to copy and adapt under Art.5(1). This right can be "prohibited under any term or condition of an agreement regulating the circumstances in which [the user's] use is lawful" (see s.50C(1)(b) and Art.5(1)), which would clearly include a software licence.

Saphena Computing Ltd v Allied Collection Agencies Ltd [1995] F.S.R. 616, CA (where the events which were the subject of the litigation occurred in 1985 and 1986) contains a useful discussion of the implied right to correct errors that may or may not have existed under English law prior to the passing of both the 1988 Act and the Statutory Instrument. The point is made that if a licensee has lawful possession of source code then there is also an implied right to use it to correct any errors in the object code of the program licensed to him. However, it is doubtful that this would extend to a right to decompile object code and correct errors in it, if the licensee had no lawful access to the relevant source code. Further the right was strictly limited to error correction and did not extend to any other adaptations or improvements. It is doubtful whether this aspect of the case has survived the Software Directive. Article 5(1) is broad enough to allow decompilation of object code for both error correction and adaptation if this is "necessary for the use of the computer program by the lawful acquirer in accordance with its intended purpose". However, Art.5(1) can be excluded by specific contractual provisions, and these would presumably be sufficient to exclude any implied right under the doctrine in *Saphena* as well. **11–14**

It should also be noted that where this right exists, the action of repairing or correcting the program ("debugging") has been held to be more akin to that of a proof reader than an author, so that the repairer does not acquire any copyright over either the program itself or the actual changes made to it (*Fylde Microsystems Ltd v Key Radio Systems Ltd* [1998] F.S.R. 449, Ch D). **11–15**

The question of the right to correct errors in computer programs is only one of the special instances relating to the common law "right to repair" which is discussed in general terms in Chapter 4.3.7 and is based upon the House of Lords decision in *British Leyland Motor Co Ltd v Armstrong Patents Co Ltd* [1986] A.C. 577, as applied in *Saphena*. Reference should be made to that section for a fuller discussion and analysis of the relevant cases. Although the matter has now been settled for areas within the EC by the Software Directive, so far as computer programs are concerned, these principles do still have useful application in common law jurisdictions outside the EC. **11–16**

Finally, it should be remembered that, following the *Volvo* and *Renault cases*, and despite the ruling in *Magill*, it is clear that now the rights of a copyright holder are defined under the Directive, albeit somewhat circumscribed by and subject to Arts 5 and 6 of the Directive, it will not be easy to make him grant a licence under them on the grounds of an abuse of a dominant position (see Chapter 5.23). The Copyright, Designs and Patents **11–17**

Act does have a provision (s.144) that permits the cancellation or modification of terms of copyright licences, or the grant of compulsory licences in a situation where a Monopolies and Mergers Commission Report has stated that such terms, or the refusal to grant a licence, operate, may be expected to operate, or have operated against the public interest. After the passing of the Competition Act 1998, the Competition Commission has taken over this function upon the dissolution of the Monopolies and Mergers Commission. (see s.45(2) and (3) of the Act). The European Court in *Volvo* has also given encouragement to the Commission to work along these lines, and the results of this can be seen in *Magill*, but the remedy is obviously a slow one, and not very useful in the fast-changing world of computer programs.

11–18 The Software Directive and the 1988 Act, as amended, have stood the test of time and the pressures of technological innovation. Council Directive 29/2001 on the harmonisation of certain aspects of copyright and related rights in the information society, specifically states in recital 50:

> "Such a harmonised legal protection [under the Directive] does not affect the specific provisions on protection provided for by [the Software Directive]. In particular it should not apply to the protection of technological measures used in connection with computer programs, which is exclusively addressed in that Directive. It should neither inhibit nor prevent the development or use of any means of circumventing a technological measure that is necessary to enable acts to be undertaken in accordance with the terms of art 5(3) or art 6 of [the Software Directive]. Articles 5 and 6 of that Directive exclusively determine exceptions to the exclusive rights applicable to computer programs."

11–19 Software licences are imposed mainly in two ways. The first is the negotiation and signature of a specific software licence prior to, and as a condition of the supply of the relevant program. The second is by way of the so-called "shrink wrap" licences (*i.e.* licences enclosed in the package with the copy of the software).

11–20 There is some doubt as to whether a shrink wrap licence is enforceable if the terms come to the notice of the purchaser after the contract has been concluded. On this basis they could not form part of the contract (see, for instance, *Olley v Marlborough Court Ltd* [1949] 1 K.B. 532). However, the use of such licences is widespread in the industry. The practice has now also extended to the Internet, where those who wish to purchase a copy of a program are often invited to consent to licence terms as part of the process of actually downloading the software. On any theory of contract law, provided the terms have actually come to the attention of the purchaser before the contract is concluded, there is no problem with their incorporation. This could occur in a number of ways, including incorporation by reference. One example would be if the licence terms were visible on the package itself and the user saw the package before acquiring the program. However, the question arises as to what happens when the program is acquired before the terms are seen, and the acquirer is then invited to accept the terms or reject them, return the copy and get his money back.

This was considered in *Beta Computers (Europe) Ltd v Adobe Systems (Europe) Ltd* (1996) S.L.T. 604, decided under Scots law. In this case a program was supplied to an order made over the phone, and when it was supplied the package contained a shrink-wrapped licence. The package was never opened, and the acquirer sought to return it on the grounds that no contract for the supply had been concluded because they had never opened the package and accepted the terms of the licence. The court decided that a contract for the supply of software was one in which the supplier undertook to make both the medium and the right of access to and use of the program available to the acquirer. This required that the conditions of the right of access and use be settled before the contract could be concluded. Since those conditions were contained in the shrink wrapped licence, the contract could not be concluded until the acquirer had opened the package and accepted them. **11–21**

This case does not however appear to have been referred to in later decisions, nor, in fact, have there been later decisions in the UK which were concerned with the validity of shrink wrapped licences. The current general approach thus appears to be that when a purchaser of a shrink wrapped product opens the package, he is bound by the terms of the licence if they were visible before opening. If they were not so visible, then he has the choice, once the package is opened and he has read, or been invited to read, the terms (often during the process of installing the program), of keeping the product, and thus accepting the licence, or returning the product for a refund. To some extent, the issue has become less important in the EC because of the prescriptive nature of the Software Directive, which deals with most of the issues that a purchaser of a shrink wrapped licence would be concerned with (*i.e.* the rights to use, to make back up copies and to resell it). **11–22**

Although shrink wrapped licences are used for "mass-market" software, whatever the doubts about their enforceability, it is not the way in which most producers of business or industrial software deal with software of any significance or value. They derive their revenues by a controlled licensing of each copy of their program, and also rely on this control to ensure the proper maintenance and functioning of both the relevant program, and, often, the associated hardware. Similarly, giving indiscriminate rights to adapt such programs to many people results in the end in a loss of uniformity between different copies of the programs, and a consequent deterioration in the performance and maintenance of the program, and, often, in the user community's perception of its quality. Article 5(1) of the Directive (and s.56(2) of the 1988 Act) preserves the right to the copyright owner to continue to license individual copies of his program on this personalised basis, on the terms that he considers desirable, subject only to the overriding provisions of Art.5(2) and (3) and Art.6 discussed above. **11–23**

However, it must be asked what is the purpose of such licences, or indeed the terms included in shrink wrapped licences, given the detailed terms of the **11–24**

Directive and the 1988 Act. The provisions of the legislation will give the lawful acquirer the right to use the program he acquires, and prevent him from replicating it and distributing copies to third parties, whether or not free of charge or for commercial gain. Reverse engineering for interface information (Art.6), making of backup copies (Art.5(2)) and study of the program while running (Art.5(3)) cannot be prohibited by the licence terms. However, Art.5(1) and s.56 are flexible enough to allow the licensor to control the rights the user would otherwise have to adapt or correct the program, and, above all, to control as the licensor wishes the question of transfer by the licensee of his copy of the program to a third party.

11–25 This precedent therefore provides a licence which can be used to control those matters which can be controlled under the Directive and the 1988 Act, but also takes account of the mandatory provisions of that legislation. It is thus drafted for use within the EC, and proceeds on the basis that copyright can and does subsist in computer programs. However, since it also expressly sets out the restrictions permitted and expressly grants the rights required by the legislation, it can be used in other territories, where there is no analogous legislation or where (although this is now increasingly rare) copyright protection is not accorded to software. The web of contractual licences between principal, distributor and end-users should thus have the same effect as protection through a statute expressly extending the protection of copyright law to software. Clearly, outside the EC, reference should be made to the local law on protection of computer programs, and this would be particularly true in the US, where the law surrounding the protection of computer programs as copyright works is very complex, and rather different to that prevailing in the EC. However, in most jurisdictions the provisions of the licence should be acceptable, after some adaptation to remove references to the Software Directive or the 1988 Act. The biggest difference is likely to be that in most jurisdictions outside the EC the extent to which reverse engineering can be prohibited by an express term in the licence is much greater. This is particularly true in the US.

Software licence

11–26 11.2 Preamble

11.2.1 The parties hereto have executed a Distribution Agreement (the "Distribution Agreement") on [ ] relating to [a range of microprocessors and other computer equipment] as detailed therein (the "Products").

The licence starts by reciting the existence of the associated distribution agreement. The preamble should be sufficiently full to identify the agreement and the products it relates to.

11–27 11.2.2 The Distributor acknowledges that the software programs necessary for the operation of the Products and the source material upon which such programs are based are the exclusive property of the Principal and the Distributor desires to obtain a non-exclusive licence in respect of the same.

This clause covers the object codes which are used to operate the products and also the source codes and associated material which are used to generate the object codes (for a fuller discussion of the distinction see Chapter 10.1). The basic principle of the licence arrangement is stated here. All of the software remains in the ownership of the principal and all rights to it are granted under licence only. Even apart from the particular problems of s.56 of the Copyright, Designs and Patents Act, software should never be sold along with a product, if one is concerned to protect it, in any jurisdiction where there is the slightest doubt as to the extent of copyright protection granted to software under the local law.

With source material it is not so much the copying that one is concerned **11–28** with (as in the case of object codes) but the preservation and restriction of the use of the ideas contained in it which might be used (without infringement of copyright) to produce new object codes that performed the same functions as those originally generated from the source material, but which were produced without making copies either of the original object codes or the source material.

11.2.3 In consideration of the foregoing purposes and the mutual promises of the **11–29** parties each to the other contained herein, the parties agree with each other as hereinafter appears.

In common law jurisdictions, where the concept exists, this clause provides the necessary consideration to make the agreement enforceable. Other options are to pay a licence fee, even if a nominal sum, or, in jurisdictions such as the UK which recognise the concept, to execute as a deed. Another method giving rise to consideration would be the promise of the distributor to execute the distribution agreement in return for the grant of the licence agreement by the principal. In this case the distribution agreement would have to be executed after the licence agreement and cl.11.2.1 would have to be amended to reflect this. In certain jurisdictions an agreement does not need to be supported by consideration in which case cl.11.2.3 could well be omitted.

11.3 Definitions

11.3.1 The "Program" shall mean the software object codes in machine readable **11–30** form necessary to operate the Products including all modifications and enhancements to such codes.

The core of the definitions is the definition of the program which will be licensed to end-users. This is the object code that will actually operate the products.

11–31 11.3.2 The "Source Material" shall mean the source code software listings flow charts and all available associated documentation and information relevant to the Program including all data and software relevant to the said source code and to the compilation or assembly and application thereof, an inventory of which is set out in Appendix A hereto, including all modifications and enhancements thereto.

The definition of the program is then used to define the source code and associated material including compiler or assembly software (see Chapter 10.1). It is desirable for the sake of certainty that the source material be defined by reference to an actual list attached as an appendix. It should be noted that both cll.11.3.1 and 11.3.2 include modifications and enhancements in the scope of their definitions. Software products normally go through a number of editions, each designed to correct errors in and improve upon the performance of the previous one, as weak points are revealed through actual operation of the earlier editions.

11.4 Licence for source material

11–32 11.4.1 The Principal hereby grants to the Distributor the personal nonexclusive non-assignable right to use the Source Material in conjunction with its exploitation of the licence conferred upon it by the Distribution Agreement.

The licence of the source codes and object codes are for different purposes, and upon different terms. The licence for the source code is only to enable the distributor to understand, copy and test the object codes and to service and test the products which they operate. The licence is, as is usually the case, a nonexclusive one. Any territorial protection or exclusivity which the distributor enjoys will arise through the provisions of the distribution agreement in relation to the products covered by it. Given that the licence is non-exclusive, and does not contain territorial restrictions, and that it is not part of a larger arrangement designed overall to restrict competition, Art.81 of the Treaty of Rome will have no application to licences granted to distributors within the EEC.

11–33 The Block Exemption for Vertical Agreements (Reg.2790/99) extends to "vertical agreements containing provisions which relate to . . . the use by the buyer of intellectual property rights provided that those provisions do not constitute the primary object of such agreements and are directly related to the use sale or resale of goods or services by the buyer or its customers" (Art.2(3)). The provisions of this software licence, given that the software is ancillary to the purposes of the main distribution agreement, should be covered by the regulation. The only issue is that the wording of Art.2(3) implies that that would only be one vertical agreement (*i.e.* the distribution agreement) with the licensing provisions incorporated within it. Although the Commission is not likely to take such a formalistic point, it might be better, in circumstances where the regulation is to be relied upon, if the precedent in this chapter were incorporated in the relevant distribution agreement, perhaps in an attached schedule made an integral part of the agreement.

The Guidelines on Vertical Restraints also give further guidance in connection with such licences of software: **11–34**

> "Resellers of goods covered by copyright (books software etc) may be obliged by the copyright holder only to resell under the condition that the buyer, whether another reseller or the end user, shall not infringe the copyright. Such obligations on the reseller, to the extent that they fall under art 81(1) at all, are covered by the Block Exemption Regulation." (para.39)
>
> "Buyers of hardware incorporating software protected by copyright may be obliged by the copyright holder not to infringe the copyright, for example not to make copies and resell the software or not to make copies and use the software in combination with other hardware. Such restrictions, to the extent that they fall within art 81(1) at all, are covered by the Block Exemption Regulation." (para.41)

Again, where the regulation does not apply, the parties will under the new regulatory framework have to consider the application of Art.81(3) in regard to the specific possibilities of such provisions, but, if the main distribution agreement itself can take specific advantage of Art.81(3), it is most likely that the ancillary licence for software will be able to do likewise as well. **11–35**

Mention should also be made of the position under the Technology Transfer Block exemption (Reg.240/96) discussed in Chapter 8. This block exemption also extends to cover licences of knowhow or patents or of patents and knowhow which also contain licences of other intellectual property rights where they contribute "to the achievement of the objects of the licensed technology" (see recital 6) and contain "no restrictive provisions other than those also attached to the licensed knowhow or patents and exempted under the Regulation" (Art.10(15)). This issue is discussed in Chapter 8.1. The licence of software which falls within this classification could be effected by the use of licence terms very similar to the ones in this precedent. Again, given the wording of the regulation, it is better to include the licence terms for the software in the technology transfer agreement itself, rather than have a separate agreement. This is probably more important in relation to Reg.240/96 than it is for Reg.2790/99 as the former is more formalistic in design and content than the latter. **11–36**

> 11.4.2 The Distributor hereby acknowledges having received from the Principal a copy of the Source Material. **11–37**

This licence presupposes that the distributor will require to use the source codes during the normal operation of the distribution of the products, and that he will not rely upon the principal for backup. In Chapter 10.1 the alternative possibility is discussed of leaving the source material in escrow, relying on the principal for backup, and taking a licence only of the object codes. If this were the case this agreement could be adapted accordingly by removing any reference to the source code, incorporating the relevant parts of the technical support Schedule from Chapter 5.24 in the distribution agreement with suitable modifications, and executing an escrow agreement along the lines of the precedent in Chapter 10.

11–38 11.4.3 The Distributor shall only use the Source Material in pursuance of and in order to enjoy fully its rights under the Distribution Agreement and shall not use the Source Material or any derivative or part thereof other than in accordance with the terms of the present nonexclusive licence.

This is simply an express restriction to the purposes of the licence, and is inserted for the avoidance of doubt to make the position absolutely clear to the distributor.

11–39 11.4.4 Nothing in this Agreement shall confer any right upon the Distributor to:

11.4.4.1 modify or alter the Source Material without the prior consent of the Principal or market or install any Program under the terms of the Distribution Agreement utilising any such modification or alteration without the prior consent of the Principal; or

The licence controls here the modification of the object codes by the distributor with the use of the source code. The possession of the source material will enable him to make modifications, but the principal who is concerned for the proper operation of his software should not allow this without prior approval, to make sure the modifications have been carried out properly, and that his software, in so far as this is a requirement, operates in a uniform manner for all customers.

11–40 Here the impact of the Software Directive needs to be considered. Clearly the decompilation right has no application to source code, as it is already decompiled. Nor does the right to study the program while functioning, since the whole purpose of source code is that it can be studied in documentary form. It is possible to contract out of the adaptation right, and this has been done in cl.11.4.4.1. The question of the extent to which the Distributor could make use of interface information in the source code is considered in Chapter 11.4.4.2.

11–41 11.4.4.2 sell lease sublicence or otherwise dispose of or disclose the Source Material other than to the Principal whether for consideration or otherwise.

The source code is for the use of the distributor only. There is thus a need to impose on him an obligation not in any way to dispose of it to third parties. It is not part of the arrangements that he should pass it on to his customers. If this were required in any particular, and very special, situation, the principal would probably be wise to require the end-user to enter into a licence covering the source materials direct with the principal. It is also quite usual to enter into a separate confidentiality agreement covering use and disclosure of the source code, and this can be achieved using the clauses in Chapter 1.4.

11–42 It is a question as to the extent that a confidentiality agreement can restrict the right to use interface information granted by Art.6, supposing that the distributor also carries on business as a software developer, and needs this interface information for his own programs. The interface information in this case comes not from decompilation, but from studying the source code documentation. This interface information is clearly not "readily available" since it is protected by the confidentiality restriction. However, Art.6 provides a right of decompilation followed by a right to use the interface information obtained by such decompilation for certain purposes. This Article can have no application to interface information obtained in another way—*i.e.* by studying source code documentation. Thus, despite Art.9(1), the provisions of the confidentiality agreement should lawfully be able to restrict the use of the interface information obtained by studying the source code. It would of course be open to the distributor to start from scratch and decompile a copy of the object code, thus taking advantage of Art.6, but he would have to use a scrupulous and well-documented clean room approach to discharge the very heavy burden of proof that he had not in fact merely taken advantage of the information obtained by studying the source code.

11.5 Licence for program

The Principal hereby grants to the Distributor the personal nonexclusive non-assignable right to copy market and sublicence the Program in conjunction with its exploitation of the rights conferred upon it by the Distribution Agreement in accordance with which the Distributor shall be entitled to: **11–43**

11.5.1 produce copies (in each case modified by the addition of the relevant user's name and licence number) of the Program; and

The distributor must be permitted to produce copies of the object codes to pass on to his customers for the products.

11.5.2 produce copies of the relevant manual for the operation of the Program and the Products (the "Manual") for use by sublicensees of the Program only; and **11–44**

In some cases, principally where the software is application software for use on a computer system that performs a function such as accounting or word-processing, or electronic mail, a manual will be necessary to operate the whole system. The distributor needs the right to make copies of the manual, as this is simply a book governed by the ordinary laws of copyright. For the same reason the licensing provisions which apply to the software, in particular in relation to end-users, need not apply to the manual. The manual will merely be an item sold by the distributor to the end-user along with the products.

11.5.3 grant sublicences (identified by user name and licence number) of the Program to purchasers of the Products (either directly or through dealers or **11–45** agents) to use the Program with the Products and to copy the Program for backup and for no other purposes.

This clause gives the right to the distributor to sublicence his end-users to use the program with the products. It is necessary to include the reference to dealers or agents, as the distributor may be a wholesaler, who will pass on the products and software object codes to retailers. In this case the retailers will have to conclude the sublicence on behalf of the distributor with their customers. The wording recognises the rights to make backup copies which would be mandatory under the Software Directive (Art.5(2)).

11.6 Terms of sublicence

11–46 11.6 Each sublicence of the Program granted pursuant to cl.11.5.3 by the Distributor shall be contained in a written document signed by the Distributor and the sublicensee [a copy of which shall be sent to the Principal immediately upon execution] and shall be in the following terms:

It is necessary to specify the terms of the sublicence if the principal is adequately to control the arrangements. The clauses used here merely say what the terms should be and leave the distributor to turn them into a proper sublicence. If preferred these clauses can be used as the basis of a sublicence document which is then attached as a Schedule to this agreement, so that the form of the sublicence is absolutely fixed at the outset.

11–47 11.6.1 As between the sublicensee and the Distributor all copies of the Program supplied in order to operate Products sold by the Distributor to the sublicensee shall be the property of the Distributor and except as provided by the sublicence (and s.296A of the Copyright Designs and Patents Act 1988) the sublicensee shall have no rights to copy or adapt the program, or to use, sell, dispose of or transfer the Program or any copies thereof in the possession of the sublicensee.

This clause leaves open the question of who actually is the owner of the copy of the program concerned, but makes it clear that it is not the sublicensee. Again the restrictions on adapting the program are included as permitted by Art.5(1) of the Software Directive, but here the limited rights to decompile and study could have application to someone who has the object code only, and s.296A, or whatever is the relevant implementation of the Software Directive under the particular governing law, should be inserted. The danger with not inserting reference to this provision is that the clause as it stood without the exception could be regarded as illegal, and, since there is no possibility of severance as it is drafted, it could be held completely unenforceable.

11–48 11.6.2 The Distributor hereby grants the sublicensee a royalty-free fully paid-up licence without limit of time to use the Program for the purpose of operating the Products and [to copy] [to make one copy of] the Program for backup

> purposes only [provided that this licence shall not (subject to cl.11.1) give the sublicensee any rights to copy and or use the Program other than for the Products in relation to which it was supplied and on the sublicensee's site for which the relevant Products were originally supplied].

The basic sublicence is the right to use only. It is then a question of whether the right to copy for backup or security purposes should be given. This is of course required by the Software Directive Art.5(2), but, in any event, in practice it is possible to copy most forms of software and it is likely that this right will be exercised, probably quite innocently, even if it is not specifically granted. Sometimes the number of backup copies that can be made is also controlled. Further possible restrictions relate to the use only on a designated piece of equipment or only at a designated site. These restrictions are more usual in licences where a royalty is charged, to prevent the overuse of one copy of the program, and to encourage the taking out of licences on additional copies for which further royalties can be charged. The reference to cl.11.1 is necessary to carry over the point about s.296A (or other relevant local implementation) of the Software Directive discussed in Chapter 11.1.

This particular sublicence is expressed to be royalty-free because the **11–49** software is here considered merely as an adjunct to the product. Both the principal and the distributor are in fact recovering the cost of the software, and taking a profit on it, out of the selling price of the products. This is possible where each product sold needs a copy of the program, and programs are not meant to be disposed of independently of products.

Where programs are sold independently, a proper software distribution **11–50** agreement covering the products would have to be executed. Space forbids the reproduction of such an agreement in this book, but in fact the distribution agreements together with clauses adapted from this licence to cover source material and object codes could be integrated into one agreement. The main question to consider would be whether the software would be distributed under the shrink wrap licence system or whether the distributor would conclude individual sublicences as in this agreement.

Where application software programs are disposed of independently of **11–51** hardware, the tendency is greater to use shrink wrap licences rather than licence them under specific individual sublicences, particularly if they are supplied on a large scale to ordinary members of the public. An example here would be software packages for personal computers. Here, however, the problems of s.56 of the Copyright, Design and Patents Act, and the problems connected with the enforceability of shrink wrapped licences need to be borne in mind. All of these issues are discussed in Chapter 11.1.

It should be noted that where the shrink wrap option is adopted, for the **11–52** purposes of EC competition law, the sale of the software packages is regarded as a sale of goods, so that a distribution agreement covering such products would be able to advantage of the Block Exemption for Vertical Agreements (Reg.2790/99). Para 40 of the Guidelines on Vertical Restraints states:

"Agreements under which hard copies of software are supplied for resale and where the reseller does not acquire a licence to any rights over the software but only has the right to resell the hard copies, are to be regarded as agreements for the supply of goods for resale for the purpose of the Block Exemption Regulation. Under this form of distribution the licence of software only takes place between the copyright owner and the user of the software. This may take the form of a 'shrink wrap' licence, ie a set of conditions included in the package of the hard copy which the end user is deemed to accept by opening the package."

11–53 Once this stage is reached the distribution agreement is not markedly different from one for any other product provided that the principal provides the copies of the program to the distributor for onward sale.

11–54 Where the distributor will produce copies of the program himself (perhaps because they will be pre-installed on hardware before sale of the hardware) the grant of the licence to the distributor to produce copies of the program will be necessary, as well as a system for remunerating the principal by way of royalty for each copy made by the distributor. In this case, the agreement approaches very closely to a manufacturing licence, and the precedent for a manufacturing licence, with some adaptation of the licence clause guided by this chapter, could be used.

11–55 In the case of particularly valuable software, it still remains the case that where it is disposed of separately from hardware the tendency is to do so by way of a licence, and perhaps, sublicence system, in return for a royalty. In some cases the royalty is a lump sum up-front payment only, to cut down on costs of collection.

11–56 11.6.3 The sublicensee shall keep confidential and shall not be entitled to disclose the Program to any third party. All copies of the Program shall remain the property of the Distributor and upon the sublicensee ceasing to use the Products in respect of which the said copies were made the sublicensee shall return to the Distributor the said copies. For the avoidance of doubt the sublicensee shall not be entitled to sell, loan or in any other way dispose of the said copies to third parties.

This is the confidentiality clause which, coupled with the duty to return, safeguards the software. It should be noted that the distributor will have the duty to return to the principal the copies returned to him under this clause only if the main licence agreement is terminated as between the principal and the distributor.

11–57 [11.6.4 All software licensed hereunder is in an "as is" state. No warranty or indemnity of any kind whatsoever is given by the Distributor in respect of the Program and all conditions and warranties express or implied by law or statute or otherwise are hereby expressly excluded.]

This clause is one which requires consideration. The distributor may wish to give a warranty for commercial reasons, but whether it is sensible for him to do that depends very much on the skill he possesses to make use of the software source material to correct errors in the program. If he has to rely in practice on the principal for this service, even if he has the source materials, then the principal may well be able to insist upon this clause, whatever the distributor wishes, or at any rate to permit the distributor to give only a restricted warranty. Most software warranties are of a restricted nature, usually limited to replacement of defective copies and to best endeavours to correct errors which come to light. The "as is" warranty is however by no means unusual. For a discussion on the question of the legality of excluding liability in this way see Chapter 11.11.1.3.

> [11.6.5 Upon notification by the Principal to the sublicensee that this Agreement between the Principal and the Distributor has been terminated, the Distributor's rights and obligations under the sublicence shall automatically be assigned forthwith to the Principal who shall thereupon be deemed a party to the sublicence and all rights and obligations thereunder shall be directly enforceable by or against the Principal as the case may be.] **11–58**

This clause provides a possible way, coupled with the provision of copies of each sublicence as it is executed, for the principal to step into the distributor's shoes and service and control sublicensees directly if the distributor goes out of business or breaks the agreement.

11.7 Copyright notice and disclaimer

> 11.7 The Distributor shall ensure that all copies of the Program and of the Manual made by the Distributor will incorporate a notice in the form set out in the Schedule hereto indicating that copyright in the Program and the Manual is vested in the Principal and in the case of the Manual containing a disclaimer. **11–59**

This clause deals with marking the copies of the object codes and the manual (if relevant) that circulate to end-users. The details of the provisions are discussed in the comments on the relevant Schedule entries.

11.8 Term and termination

> 11.8.1 Subject to cl.11.8.2 this Agreement shall come into force on the date hereof and shall remain in force [without limit of time notwithstanding the termination of the Distribution Agreement] [until the termination of the Distribution Agreement, when it shall automatically expire]. **11–60**

The licence agreement can survive the distribution agreement to enable the distributor to carry on servicing the copies of the programs that he has already disposed of to end-users (see *Harbinger UK Ltd v GE Information Services Ltd* [1999] Masons C.L.R. 335). An alternative is for the agreement to terminate at that time and for the principal to take over these obligations. Whether or not the agreement terminates with the Distribution Agreement, the question of what happens if the distributor goes out of business or breaches the agreement has to be addressed. Even if the agreement does not terminate automatically with the distribution agreement, the agreement should terminate upon the occurrence of these events and the provisions of cl.11.6.5 be invoked.

11–61 11.8.2 The Principal may terminate this Agreement immediately by notice to the Distributor:

11.8.2.1 In the event that the Distributor shall breach any of the provisions of this Agreement and such breach is not remedied within [sixty days] of receipt by the Distributor of a request from the Principal to remedy the same;

11–62 **11.8.2.2** Insert cl.4.16.3.

11.8.2.3 Insert cl.4.16.4.

11.8.2.4 Insert cl.4.16.5.

11.8.2.5 Insert cl.4.16.6.

11.8.2.6 Insert cl.4.16.7.

11–63 11.8.3 Upon termination under cl.11.8.2 the Distributor shall immediately thereafter return the Source Material and all copies of the Program in its possession to the Principal and pay all sums (if any) due to the Principal from the Distributor under the Distribution Agreement.

This provides for termination for breach. The source codes must be returned, and there is no need for the distributor to keep any copies of the object codes that he has not disposed of to end-users.

11–64 11.8.4 Subject to cl.11.6.5 termination under cl.11.8.2 shall not affect sublicences already granted by the Distributor under cl.11.6 and irrespective of such termination the Distributor shall be obliged to return to the Principal all copies of the Program returned to it after the date of such termination pursuant to cl.11.6.3.

11–65 11.8.5 Clauses 11.8.2, 11.8.3 and 11.8.4 shall survive the termination of this Agreement.

Even after termination the distributor must retain the obligation to return any copies of the program returned to him, but other than this, the termination of the main licence cannot be allowed to affect the sublicences already properly granted to end-users prior to the termination of the agreement. The only exception would be if the Principal has decided to use the provisions of cl.11.6.5 to take over the licence himself.

11.9 No warranty

11–66 No warranty of any nature whatsoever whether expressed or implied shall be deemed to have been created by this Agreement. In the event that the Distributor

> in any way alters or modifies the Program other than with the prior consent of the Principal any warranty provision expressed or implied with respect to Products incorporating the whole or any part of such modified or altered Program shall lapse.

Just as no warranty may be given by the distributor to end-users, so the principal may give no warranty to the distributor. The same considerations as to the grant of a software warranty apply as discussed in cl.11.6.4 above. Questions of exclusion of liability are discussed in Chapter 11.11.1.3 below.

11.10 Interpretation clauses and signature

Selections from Chapter 1 should be made as appropriate. **11–67**

11.11 Schedule—copyright notices and disclaimer

11.11.1 Copyright Notice—Manual

The following Notice and Notes shall appear on the [first page of the] Manual: **11–68**

"(c) [ ] [1990]"

"Issue Number [ ] Date [ ]"

"Note: This manual and the accompanying program are copyright. Copies of the program may be made solely for the personal use of the original end-purchaser with the products to which it relates. Duplicating for any other purpose, copying selling or otherwise distributing the program or the manual is forbidden."

This is a warning which may deter copying that is unauthorised, and does have the merit of clearly stating the law on the subject, and the rights of the purchaser of the products. If this was a separate disposal of software with no associated hardware, the notice would have to be adapted to remove the reference to the products.

"Note: Although programs are tested before release no claim is made regarding the accuracy of the program. The copyright owner and its distributors cannot assume liability or responsibility for any consequential loss or damage, however caused, or for loss of contracts, business interruption or loss of profits, arising from the use of the program, or any defect in it. Programs are licensed only on the basis of this understanding. [Although this program is designed [to fit the statutory and other usual accounting needs of most typical small to medium-sized companies], it may not be suitable for all companies' requirements, and individual applications should be thoroughly tested before implementation.]" **11–69**

This is a suggested disclaimer. It would not prevent the end-users from asking for a new copy of a program which they received in a damaged state, but that would be the limit of liability, if the clause were held to be enforceable. It is unlikely that the clause would be wholly enforceable in consumer sales in most jurisdictions where consumer sales are specially protected. For instance, the EC Directive on Unfair Terms in Consumer Contracts (13/93) would probably prevent reliance on such a clause in all Member States of the EC. So far as business sales are concerned, it is probably possible at least to attempt to contract out of liability in most jurisdictions. This is possible in the US. In the UK the situation is complicated by the question of the precise scope of the application of the Unfair Contract Terms Act 1997 (UCTA) to licences of intellectual property, and questions as to the legal status of software. These issues have already been touched upon briefly in relation to licences of intellectual property in general in Chapter 1.3.5 where reference is also made to the relevant case law (*Saphena Computing Ltd v Allied Collection Agencies Ltd* [1995] F.S.R. 616, CA; *The Salvage Association v Cap Financial Services Ltd* [1995] F.S.R. 654 and *St Albans City and District Council v International Computers Ltd* (reported at first instance [1995] F.S.R. 686 and on appeal at [1996] 4 All E.R. 481).

11–70 To summarise the relevant discussion in Chapter 1.3.5, under the laws of the UK (other than Scotland) Sch.1 of UCTA excludes UCTA from applying to any contract "so far as [the contract] relates to the creation or transfer of a right or interest" in intellectual property or knowhow. The same thing is achieved in relation to the law of Scotland by the wording of s.15. For further details reference should be made to Chapter 1.3.5. Here the argument will concentrate, for convenience, upon the wording in Sch.1, but the outcome would not be any different under the law of Scotland.

11–71 The *St Albans* case, although it did not discuss Sch.1, does provide an approach which would shed some light on the problem. The case concerned a contract for the development and supply of a computer program to collect a local tax to be levied by the St Albans City and District Council, known in the UK as "community charge". The court at first instance found that International Computers Ltd (ICL) were in breach of their contractual obligations through the supply of a faulty program which significantly overstated the relevant population under their jurisdiction and thus caused them to suffer a loss of revenue.

11–72 On appeal, the Court confirmed that, in their view, on the basis of the findings of fact at first instance, ICL was obliged to provide software which would be fit for its purpose and that it was in breach of that obligation. The next question was whether UCTA applied to the contract at all. The Court of Appeal found that, on the basis of the facts found at first instance, the parties were dealing on ICL's written standard terms and that hence s.3 of UCTA applied to the contract. Thus ICL's exclusions and limitations of liability for breach of contract could be enforceable only if they passed the reasonableness test in s.11 of UCTA. The court at first instance had held that the clauses in question did not pass this test, and the Court of Appeal refused to disturb the judge's finding of fact in regard to this issue. Thus the remaining question was as to the measure of damages, and in this case, the Court of Appeal found certain reasons in law (not relevant to this particular discussion) substantially to reduce the damages which had been awarded at first instance.

The question to be considered is how to marry the decision in *St Albans* as to the application of UCTA with the exclusion in Sch.1, discussed above, in relation to licences of intellectual property. At first instance, the judgment contained *obiter dicta* suggesting that software was goods. If this were the case a licence of software would be a supply of goods, and there would then be a conflict between the application of ss.6 and 7 of UCTA (applying it to contracts for the supply and sale of goods) and Sch.1 excluding its operation in relation to a licence of an intellectual property right (namely a copyright licence relating to the software). **11–73**

The first part of the answer to the problem can be found in Glidewell L.J.'s judgment. He first noted that during the hearing of the case there had been "discussion of a more general question, namely, is software goods?". He then made the point that the program itself consists of "intangible instructions or commands" but that "in order that the program should be encoded into the computer itself it was necessarily first recorded on a disc, from which it could be transferred to the computer. During the course of the hearing the word 'software' was used to include both the (tangible) disc ... and the (intangible) program itself. In order to answer the question it is necessary to distinguish between the program and the disc carrying the program. In both the Sale of Goods Act 1979 s.61 and the Supply of Goods and Services Act 1982 s.18 the definition of 'goods' 'includes all personal chattels other than things in action and money ...'. Clearly a disc is within this definition. Equally clearly, a program, of itself is not". **11–74**

If one applies Glidewell L.J.'s dicta to shrink wrapped software then the sale of shrink wrapped software over the counter is clearly a sale of goods (the discs and the manual) but the right to use the program is conveyed through the shrink-wrapped licence or, by implication, under the Software Directive. This would not be inconsistent with *Beta Computers (Europe) Ltd v Adobe Systems (Europe) Ltd*, discussed above, although in that case the matter was approached somewhat differently. For the purposes of English law, the supply of shrink wrapped software to an end-user could be expressed as an agreement for sale of goods (the medium and the manual) which is subject to a condition precedent—agreement as to the terms of the relevant licence—before it is perfected and title passes. As another instance, the sale of a complete computer system, software and hardware would also be a sale of goods. In this connection Glidewell L.J. quoted and approved the Australian case *Toby Construction Ltd v Computa Bar (Sales) Pty Ltd* [1983] 2 N.S.W.J.R. 48. On the same principle sale of a machine which has software embedded in a microprocessor which controls its functions would also be a sale of goods. The analogy is clearly very close to the sale of any other tangible embodiment of a copyright work such as a book or a video tape. **11–75**

So far one conclusion that can be drawn from this is that an agent who deals in tangible embodiments of software programs can be regarded as an agent for the supply of goods, in just the same way as an agent who deals in **11–76** books or video tapes. Such agents will obviously thus be caught under the Council Directive 653/86 of December 18, 1986 on the Coordination of the laws of the Member States relating to self-employed Commercial Agents (see the discussion in Chapter 3.2).

11–77 The next question Glidewell L.J. considered was the question of liability if a faulty program is supplied on a disc:

> "Is this a defect in the disc ... would the seller or hirer of the disc be in breach of the terms as to quality and fitness for purpose implied by s 14 of the Sale of Goods Act and s.9 of the Act of 1982? [counsel for the appellants] argues that they would not. He submits that the defective program in my example would be distinct from the tangible disc, and thus that the 'goods'—the disc—would not be defective."

11–78 The learned Lord Justice found no authority to guide him ("In expressing an opinion I am therefore venturing where others have, no doubt wisely, not trodden"), but he came to the conclusion that a defect in the program was a defect in the disc. He gave the example of an instruction manual (a book or video) for repairing a car. Suppose the instructions in it were wrong, and anyone who followed them caused serious damage to the car: "In my view the instructions are an integral part of the manual. The manual ... including the instructions would in my opinion be 'goods' ... and the defective instructions would result in a breach of the implied terms in s.14 [of the Sale of Goods Act 1979]". He then equated a disc with a defective program to a manual with defective instructions: "If the disc is sold or hired by the computer manufacturer, but the program is defective, in my opinion there would *prima facie* be a breach of the terms as to quality and fitness for purpose implied by the Sale of Goods Act or the Act of 1982".

11–79 If the learned Lord Justice's view is correct, it provides a convincing way of reconciling the application of UCTA to the supply of goods with the exclusion of UCTA in relation to licences of intellectual property. The supply of software on a tangible medium is a mixed contract for the supply of goods and a licence of a right to use the copyright work recorded on them. Since Sch.1 excludes the application of UCTA only "so far as [the contract] relates" to a licence of intellectual property, the terms of the licence cannot be scrutinised under UCTA. However, the defect in the program is regarded as a defect in the tangible goods supplied under the contract, and nothing in Sch.1 prevents UCTA applying to that part of the contract relating to the supply of goods. It may be asked what is the status of a clause in the licence itself excluding liability for defects in the program. The answer is that, on this argument, such a clause would be regarded as an exclusion relating to goods and not to intellectual property at all, so that UCTA would still apply to it. Nor would it be possible to include a clause along the lines that one condition of the grant of a licence would be a waiver by the licensee of the right to complain of defects in the program. This would be presumably simply be regarded as another variety of exclusion clause, perhaps falling under s.13 of UCTA.

Glidewell L.J. then commented that, in the case in question, the program had been downloaded by ICL direct into the computer of St Albans, and no disc on which the program was recorded was transferred to St Albans. **11–80**

> "As I have already said, the program itself is not 'goods' within the statutory definition. Thus a transfer of the program in the way I have described does not, in my view, constitute a transfer of goods. It follows that in such circumstances there is no statutory implication of terms as to quality or fitness for purpose."

The learned Lord Justice, however, then went on to find that such terms would be implied by common law: **11–81**

> "In the absence of any express term as to quality or fitness for purpose, or of any term to the contrary, such a contract is subject to an implied term that the program will be reasonably fit for ie reasonably capable of achieving the intended purpose."

He referred to *Trollope & Colls Ltd v NW Metropolitan RHB* [1973] 1 W.C.R. 600 as authority for this proposition. Incidentally this opinion can be reconciled with the finding in *Saphena* that no supplier can be expected to provide software that is bug free, by the proposition that even programs that are reasonably fit for their purpose may contain bugs, but that it is always a question of degree and materiality. The program will cease to be reasonably fit for purpose if the incidence of the bugs rises to a level which prevents the program discharging that purpose to a reasonable extent. Below that level bugs can be tolerated. **11–82**

If one looks at Glidewell L.J.'s opinion in the context of the application of Sch.1, the issues are again easily reconcilable. The contract was not just for the supply of a software program. It covered the supply of hardware, and the development of the software, as well as associated installation. Taken as a whole the contract was thus clearly one for the supply of goods and services, including the development of the program (*i.e.* the supply of a solution), with express terms covering fitness for purpose of the end product. The licence of the finally developed software program was only one element of this. Thus Sch.1 could not prevent UCTA applying to all the elements of the contract except the narrow terms of the licence permitting St Albans to use the developed program. The contract with St Albans thus becomes simply one of the mixed contracts for the licence of intellectual property together with the supply of goods and other services, discussed in Chapter 1.3.5. **11–83**

What conclusions can be drawn from the above? First, if the learned Lord Justice is correct when he equates defects in a program with defects in the medium on which it is supplied, then any exclusion of liability for defects in software supplied on a tangible medium will be subject to scrutiny under UCTA. Second, if the contract is for the development and supply of software, then any exclusion of liability for defects in the developed software, **11–84** will be subject to scrutiny under UCTA irrespective of whether or not the developed product is supplied on a tangible medium. UCTA will bite on the development aspect of the contract (*i.e.* the supply of a service) whether or not it can also look at the supply of the developed program in the context of a supply of goods.

11–85 However, if the contract is purely for the supply of a developed piece of software, which is supplied by some form of downloading with no tangible medium involved, it seems hard to see how anything is involved but a pure licence of the program in question. On the basis of Glidewell L.J.'s opinion the "intangible program" is not goods, and no development is involved in the contract. If this is the case, to what does the contract relate except the "creation or transfer of a right or interest" in intellectual property? Unless some other element is present, there seems no reason why Sch.1 should not operate to exclude UCTA entirely from any scrutiny of the contract, including any terms excluding liability for defects in the program. If this view is correct, it is clearly important since more and more programs are supplied by downloading in this way, for instance over the Internet. Those who wish to exclude liability in relation to the supply of software products (other than in the case where the contract is one of development and supply) would thus be advised, at least on the above analysis, and in the present state of the law, to make sure that the contract is purely for the supply of the program, and that the program is either supplied electronically over a network or that the supplier retains possession and ownership of the relevant medium and downloads the program on to the user's computer himself. Arguably, then, any exclusions of liability for defects in the program should thus be excluded from the scrutiny of UCTA by the operation of Sch.1.

11–86 It should be noted that none of the opinions of the learned Lord Justice, in relation to the status of software, were necessary for the decision of the appeal. Indeed he expressly stated these views were no more than an expression of opinion. They would thus be regarded as *obiter dicta*. First of all the Court found that there were express terms in the contract which covered these issues. Second, according to the court, the default arose out of the failure to develop a solution which was reasonably fit for its purpose. This would go to the way in which the development was carried out and the way in which the provisions of the contract were implemented generally. As discussed above, there is no question but that UCTA would apply to a mixed contract of this nature, irrespective of any element of it relating to licensing intellectual property which alone would be excluded by Sch.1. There was thus no real need to consider whether software (whether or not embodied on a tangible medium) was goods, nor whether (if it were so embodied) a defect in the program amounted to a defect in the medium.

11–87 Nevertheless the expressions of the learned Lord Justice's views on the subject are particularly useful to shed light on a very difficult area. The initial opinion that the program is not goods, but that the medium on which it is recorded is, seems likely to be accepted in future cases where the issues turn on this point. The analysis above of the scope of Sch.1 in relation to software contracts, (whether for development and supply or purely for supply), where no physical medium is involved in its transfer, are based only upon this initial opinion and thus can also be considered very persuasive, even if not completely definitive. Similarly the status of shrink-wrapped software as goods, based as it is on this initial opinion, seems also reasonably certain. Nor would one doubt the learned Lord Justice's conclusion that in the absence of a provision to the contrary there is an implied term in any contract for the supply of software that it be reasonably fit for its intended purpose.

It is, however, respectfully submitted that the learned Lord Justice's other **11–88** finding which equates defects in the program with defects in the medium on which it is recorded, is more controversial. This is based on the analogy of a manual containing defective instructions. There is, however, no authority quoted for assuming that the supply of a manual containing defective instructions is a breach of s.14 of the Sale of Goods Act. The defect could equally well be considered under the branch of the law relating to liability for negligent misstatements. Nevertheless, there are two authorities that would support this view. In *Cox v Riley* [1988] 88 Cr.App.R. 54, the defendant was held to have maliciously damaged a machine where he erased the program which controlled it. Similarly in *R. v Whitely* [1991] 93 Cr.App.R. 25, a hacker was held to have maliciously damaged a disc because he reduced its value by tampering with and amending programs stored on it. These cases would, by analogy, suggest that a defect in the program stored on a disc constitutes a defect on the disc itself, because the manifestation of the defect is to be found in the arrangement of the magnetic particles on the disc. These particles are arranged in a way which causes the computer (controlled by the program) to produce a result which is not the one contracted for, or indeed, if the defect is serious enough, no result at all.

In conclusion, the *St Albans* case has provided some very interesting and **11–89** helpful guidelines as to the status of software and the liability for defects in it, but it still leaves many questions unanswered in this area. Decisions in cases which are directly on these points are required before the matter can be cleared up fully, but in the meantime the prudent draftsman should take account of the views expressed by Glidewell L.J. in *St Albans*, and the tentative conclusions of the present writer in relation to them, in order to minimise liability for clients who are responsible for the supply of software.

Glidewell L.J.'s approach has been followed in *Holman Group Limited v* **11–90** *Sherwood International Limited* [2000] Masons C.L.R. 72. Havery J. believed that on the facts of the case the software was not "goods" within the meaning of ss.6 and 7 of UCTA because of the wording of the contract which defined Sherwood's obligations in terms not of delivering a tangible copy of the software but in terms of delivering and installing object code. He was, however, satisfied that in this case a common law implied term of suitability for purpose would be applicable.

The approach is also consistent with the view of the Commission on the **11–91** status of shrink wrapped software as goods, set out in para.40 of the Guidelines on Vertical Restraints discussed in Chapter 11.6.2.

11–92 11.11.2 Copyright Notice—Programs

The following Notice and Notes shall appear on the [second screen] of the Program:

"[Title of Program]
(c) [ ] [1990]
Issue Number [ ] Date [ ]
Licence Number [ ]
All unauthorised reproduction prohibited
Refer to accompanying manual before use
Press Space Bar to Continue."

This is a provision which can be used to incorporate a copyright notice in the program itself, so that whenever the program is run on the computer the frame showing the notice will be displayed initially. Such a provision is not useful where the software runs a machine other than a computer with a visual display unit. In some cases it is technically possible to incorporate such notices in operating software in such a way that the notice is printed out first of all when any printed output is generated by the program. As a last resort the notice can be put on the outside of the magnetic disc or tape reel on which the program is stored.

11–93 "Note: Where modifications and enhancements are made to the Program and/or the Manual in accordance with this Agreement the Distributor shall, when reissuing the Program or the Manual as the case may be, amend the relevant Notices by the use of the new issue number, and the relevant date of reissue, in the place of the current issue number and date."

This provides for updating of the manual and the program with a method of keeping track of alterations by edition numbers and dates. This is useful, since it enables the distributor and the principal to know in each case what edition of the program an end-user has got if he requires advice on any aspect of it, for instance a particular error which is known to occur in only a given edition.

Chapter 12

Trade Mark Licences

Contents

12.1 Commercial and legal background

The distribution agreements in Chapters 4, 5 and 6 and the manufacturing licences in Chapters 7 and 8 all contemplate, in varying degrees, the marketing of the relevant products under trade marks belonging to the principal, and they all contain certain provisions relating to the use of those trade marks. Although these agreements do not really need a separate trade mark licence to stand alongside them, there are occasions when it is useful to have a separate trade mark licence, particularly if it is necessary to register it in a particular territory. Accordingly this precedent, although it contains nothing radically different from the detailed trade mark provisions in the chapters mentioned above, does bring together conveniently in one place the provisions relating to the licensing of a trade mark in connection with one of those agreements. It can be seen that the precedent works on the basis that the trade mark licence agreement will be referred to in the manufacturing or distribution agreement to which it relates and that the relevant definitions of trade mark, territory and products and required quality standards will all be found in that other agreement. Care will therefore have to be taken, when this approach is followed, to adapt the other precedent accordingly and remove from it all references to trade marks except the definitions and a clause setting out the obligation to grant a separate licence. An example of such a clause which would, for instance, replace the licence grant in cl.7.2 discussed in Chapter 7.2, is set out below: **12–01**

12–02 The Principal hereby grants the Licensee an [exclusive] [non-exclusive] licence to [make and have made and/or] distribute and sell the Products in the Territory during the continuance of this Agreement [using for this purpose [the Patents] [and] [the Knowhow]], under the Trade Mark which shall be licensed to the Licensee pursuant to a formal trade mark licence to be executed between the parties on the same date as this agreement.

By way of illustration, if this approach were followed for the precedent set out in Chapter 7, the following changes would be required, in addition to this clause:

- clause 7.13—amend to remove references to trade marks as one of the intellectual property rights covered by these provisions;
- clause 7.17.7—delete;
- clause 7.25.4 and 5—delete; and
- clause 7.24.8—amend by excluding trade marks as one of the intellectual property rights covered by these provisions.

12–03 One of the main purposes of the separate trade mark licence is to have it registered in the relevant trade mark registry of the territory concerned, without having to disclose details of the associated manufacturing or distribution agreement. This registration confers various rights upon the licensee and the licensor which vary depending upon the governing law of the territory of registration. In some jurisdictions, agreements must be drafted in a formal way to comply with the requirements for registration in the territory as a "registered user". The main purpose of this is to ensure that the trade mark owner's rights are protected and that he cannot lose control of the mark to the licensee or a third party. Here the key requirement is usually that the licensor must show he can exercise proper control over the way the licensee can use the trade mark, and in particular over the quality of the products or services put on the market by the licensee and in connection with which the licensee is allowed to use the trade mark. This licence does not necessarily comply with all of these requirements, and its suitability will need to be investigated in the light of the relevant local law. It is a licence which is designed to comply with the law in relation to trade marks in force in the UK under the new regime of the Trade Marks Act 1994, and as such no longer has to consider the strict requirements of registered user.

12–04 The Trade Marks Act 1994 has abandoned the old registered user system, under which the registrar would consider any registered user agreement for the proper element of control over the licensee before he would register it. Licensors and licensees are free to agree to the terms of the licences between them and any written licence as so agreed is effective once it is signed by the grantor. Either party may apply to register a written licence, and the registrar will be obliged to register it without objection or scrutiny. However, this is not to suggest that licensors will be wise to abandon any system of control over their licensees. Controls are still as important as ever to maintain the good reputation of the mark, and, subject to competition law, to restrict the territory in which, and the products or services in connection with which, the licensee can use the mark.

Registration is voluntary, but is still important under the Act. The licensee's licence is not effective against a third party, who purchases the mark or takes an exclusive licence, unless it is registered. Nor, until the licence is registered can the licensee take any action against infringers or require the licensor to do so. Finally, a delay in registration of more than six months from the date of grant will prevent the licensee from obtaining any damages for infringement occurring between the date of grant and date of registration. **12–05**

The Act also provides for the rights of a licensee to be protected by his licensor from third party infringers. Under a non-exclusive licence grant, unless the trade mark licence provides otherwise, and provided the licence has been registered, the licensee has the right to call upon the licensor to proceed against third party infringers, and may do so himself, if the licensor refuses or does not do so within two months, in which case the licensor must be joined as a third party. Since these arrangements apply to licences in existence at the time of the coming into force of the Act, and since the Act applies unless the licence expressly provides to the contrary, there are many licences that, provided they have been registered, could be affected by this new regime. Under an exclusive licence grant, the licensor may choose to put the licensee in the same position as if he were an assignee and allow him to proceed directly against infringers in his own name without reference to the trade mark owner. These rights under the Act will, however, apply only if the parties expressly adopt them. They do not apply by implication just because the licence has been granted on an exclusive basis. If they are not expressly adopted the treatment of the licence in relation to infringement is as if it had been a non-exclusive licence. **12–06**

Finally, although the precedent does not allow for this, the Act recognises bare licences of trade marks which are unconnected with a distribution or manufacturing licence covering the licensor's products or services. Under the old law the registrar was obliged to refuse to register such licences, which were said to be no more than "trafficking" in trade marks (*i.e.* treating them as a separate commodity as opposed to an identifying mark for other goods or services). This coupled with the fact that the Act now, for the first time, also recognises sublicences of trade marks, has greatly expanded the possibility for franchising trade marks. **12–07**

12.2 Preamble

12.2.1 The parties hereto have executed a [manufacturing agreement] [distribution agreement] on [ ] (the "Agreement") relating to [a range of healthcare and dietary products] as detailed therein (the "Products"). **12–08**

12–09 12.2.2 The Agreement provides for the Licensee to [make and have made and/or] distribute the Products under certain trade marks as therein defined ("the Trade Marks") in certain countries as therein defined (the "Territory"). The parties now wish to enter into this formal Trade Mark Licence to permit the Licensee to use the Trade Marks in connection with the [manufacture and] distribution of the Products under the Agreement.

As described in Chapter 12.1, these clauses set out the purpose of the licence and link it in to the agreement covering the products to which the trade marks are to be affixed.

12.3 Grant of rights

12–10 12.3 The Licensor hereby grants the Licensee a [non-exclusive] [exclusive] licence subject to the terms and conditions of this Agreement to use the Trade Marks in the Territory in relation to the Products.

This is a standard form of grant, and causes no particular issues for areas outside the EC. So far as EC law is concerned, an agreement which licences a trade mark whether alone or in conjunction with other intellectual property rights can contravene Art.81(1) (see *Sirena Srl v Eda Srl* [1971] 2 C.M.L.R. 260 and *Re Moosehead Breweries Ltd/Whitbread and Company plc* [1990] O.J. L100.) However whether it does so or not depends upon the particular restrictions contained in the licence agreement (see Case C-161/84 *Pronuptia de Paris GmbH v Pronuptia de Paris Irmgard Schillgalis* [1986] 1 C.M.L.R. 414). An open exclusive licence of the type described in relation to plant breeders rights in the *Maize Seed* case (*LC Nungesser KG and Kurt Eisele v EC Commission* [1983] 1 C.M.L.R. 278) would not *prima facie* therefore appear to offend Art.81(1) (see the discussion on trade marks in relation to this case in Chapter 8.1).

12–11 When the trade mark licence is associated with a manufacturing agreement for which exemption is claimed under the block exemption for technology transfer agreements (Commission Regulation 240/1996 on the application of Art.81(3) of the Treaty to certain categories of technology transfer agreements—see Chapter 8), the licence of the trade mark, at least when granted under the manufacturing agreement is also exempt provided that no restrictions other than those permitted in respect of the licensed technology are imposed in respect of the trade mark. There is nothing in the wording of the Regulation to suggest that the trade mark cannot be licensed in a separate agreement provided no additional restrictions are imposed, but this will require very careful drafting, and it is easier and safer in most cases to combine the grant of the trade mark with the grant of the other licensed technology in one agreement as is done in Chapter 8, unless there are very pressing reasons to the contrary.

12–12 Where the parties wish to take advantage of exemption for a distribution agreement under the block exemption for vertical agreements (Reg.2790/99) care does have to be taken in relation to Art.2(3) of the regulation. This permits vertical agreements, such as distribution agreements, to contain licences of intellectual property granted by the supplier in relation to the contract goods or services provided that the provisions relating to the relevant intellectual property do not contain "restrictions of competition having the same object or effect as vertical restraints which are not exempted by [Reg.2790/99]" (see the discussion on this point in Chapter 5.2).

The only issue is that strict compliance with the wording of Art.2(3) would require that there only be one vertical agreement (*i.e.* the distribution agreement) with the licensing provisions incorporated within it, perhaps by way of a schedule. As discussed above, the position is probably the same under the Technology Transfer Block exemption (Reg.240/96) discussed in Chapter 8, to the extent that it can still apply if a trade mark licence is coupled with the relevant licences of knowhow or patents or of patents and knowhow (see Chapter 8.1.). (For a further discussion of this issue in relation to ancillary software licences see Chapter 11.4.1.) **12–13**

It should be said that, as it stands, this trade mark licence is probably not of itself in contravention of Art.81(1), in any event, but, since it is dependent upon another distribution or manufacturing agreement, it will fall to be considered as part of the whole package of arrangements between the parties, and in this case the status of the distribution or manufacturing agreement under Art.81(1) is the deciding factor. **12–14**

12.4 Specifications, production methods and quality standards

12.4.1 The Licensee undertakes not to use the Trade Marks in relation to any products or services other than the Products and to use the Trade Mark in relation to Products only where such Products comply with the specifications, production methods and quality standards set out in [Sch.[5] of the Agreement] (the "Required Quality Standards"). **12–15**

12.4.2 The Licensee will, on reasonable notice, permit the Licensor to enter into all premises under the Licensee's control for the purpose of inspecting the character and quality of the Products (and all packaging, ingredients and components thereof) provided under the Trade Marks in order to ascertain their compliance with the Required Quality Standards. The Licensee will on request provide samples of all Products supplied to third parties, including customers of the Licensee, that bear or refer to any of the Trade Marks. **12–16**

12.4.3 The Licensee shall use the Trade Marks only in accordance with the Licensor's corporate manual relating to the Trade Marks entitled [ ] dated [ ] and with issue number [ ], a copy of which has been issued by the Licensor to the Licensee prior to execution of this Agreement and receipt whereof the Licensee hereby acknowledges. [The Licensor shall promptly forward to the Licensee copies of all updates to or new issues of such manual, and the Licensee shall comply with the same immediately upon receipt thereof.] **12–17**

These provisions are standard quality control provisions. Clause 12.4.2 could be used in combination with the relevant provisions in cll.7.25.4 and 7.25.5, referred to in Chapter 12.1, or those clauses could be used here instead. Attention is drawn to the sentence in square brackets at the end of cl.12.4.3. Compliance with this provision could cause the licensee considerable expense in changing his get-up and packaging without notice. Many licensees will therefore require some notice and a transitional period before they have to implement new trade mark usages.

12.5 Term

12–18 12.5.1 The licence granted by this Agreement shall commence on the date that the Agreement comes into force and shall continue for so long as the Agreement remains in force

PROVIDED THAT:

12.5.1.1 in the event the Licensor has reasonable grounds for believing that in any country comprised within the Territory one of the Trade Marks infringes a trade mark or trade name of a third party (whether or not registered in such country) the Licensor may terminate this Agreement in respect of that trade mark in that country by notice with immediate effect;

12.5.1.2 in the event in any country comprised within the Territory one of the Trade Marks cannot be licensed under this agreement until governmental approval or permission has been obtained, the parties will cooperate with all reasonable expedition to apply for such approval or permission at the Licensee's expense, and the grant of the licence in respect of that Trade Mark shall become effective only when and if such approval or permission has been obtained.

12–19 12.5.2 Upon termination of this agreement in whole from any cause whatsoever (including expiry by effluxion of time) the Licensee shall have no further rights to use the Trade Marks in any way whatsoever

PROVIDED THAT:

in the case of a termination of this agreement in part pursuant to cl.12.5.1.1 in respect of one of the Trade Marks in relation to any country comprised within the Territory the Licensee shall only be obliged to cease to use the relevant one of the Trade Marks in the relevant country,

AND PROVIDED FURTHER THAT:

the Licensee shall, in particular but without prejudice to the generality of the foregoing cease (in the case of a termination in whole) in respect of the Trade Marks and (in the case of a termination in part) in respect of the relevant one of the Trade Marks in the relevant country to use the Trade Marks or the relevant one of the Trade Marks (as the case may be) on its letterheads packaging vehicle liveries or elsewhere and shall sell any stocks of the Products remaining in its ownership and possession upon the date of such termination in packaging which does not bear the Trade Marks or the relevant one of the Trade Marks (as the case may be) nor the name of the Principal.

The trade mark licence is dependent upon the relevant manufacturing or distribution agreement, and therefore cl.12.5.1 provides that it is to be coterminous with it. The trade mark licence is expressed to commence when the main agreement comes into force because the main agreement may not come into force on signature, if any relevant governmental or other consents are necessary for its complete operation. However, the approach taken by this book is generally to provide for the agreement to come into force on signature and to terminate within a fixed short period if such consents are not then obtained (see for example the discussion in Chapter 4.15.2 and 4.15.3 on these points). Clauses 12.5.1.1 and 12.5.1.2 provide for partial commencement or termination of the licence in respect of specific parts of the territory.

Clause 12.5.2, which is rendered somewhat complicated by the need to cater for whole and partial termination, makes the usual provisions for the licensor to stop using the trade marks after termination. **12–20**

12.6 Trade mark rights

See cl.4.13. **12–21**

12.7 No warranty

12.7 It is understood and agreed that: **12–22**

12.7.1 there is no warranty either express or implied on the part of the Licensor that any of the Trade Marks can be used by the Licensee pursuant to this agreement and/or the Agreement free from any infringement of any intellectual or industrial property rights of any nature whatsoever (including without limitation both registered and unregistered trade marks and brand names) of third parties; and

12.7.2 notwithstanding anything contained in this agreement or the Agreement the Licensor has no obligation to the Licensee to bring or prosecute suits or actions against third parties for infringements of the Trade Marks. **12–23**

It is most unusual to give a warranty against infringement in a trade mark licence, and there seems to be nothing in either EC law or the Unfair Contract Terms Act 1977 that would require this (see the discussion on the exclusion of the Act in relation to licences of intellectual property in Chapter 11.9). Clause 12.7.2 is a common provision in trade mark licences and, where the Trade Mark Act 1994 applies, it also serves to disapply the obligations otherwise imposed upon the licensor by the Act in favour of the licensee to take action over third party infringement. It would be equally effective for this purpose whether the licence were an exclusive or a non-exclusive one (see the discussion of these obligations in Chapter 12.1 above).

12.8 Assignment and subcontracting

12–24 See cl.7.19.

12.9 Notices

12–25 See cl.1.11.

12.10 Interpretation clauses and signature

12–26 The appropriate clauses should be selected from Chapter 1 as required.

Chapter 13

Australia*

Contents

13.1 Introduction 13-01

13–01 Australia is a common law country, and accordingly a good deal of the discussion of English law in the principal text is applicable. However, there are two main factors to keep in mind in relation to Australia when considering the application of the various agreements.

13–02 First, the Commonwealth of Australia is a federation of six states (Victoria, New South Wales, Queensland, South Australia, Western Australia and Tasmania) and two self-governing territories (Northern Territory and Australian Capital Territory) with a federal parliament. While there is a growing recognition in each jurisdiction of the value of uniform laws, there are still differences. Care should be taken in structuring any transaction to take into account the laws of all relevant states and territories, and legal advice will be required in relation to all jurisdictions in which an agreement is to take effect.

13–03 Second, the most significant legislative code affecting agreements of the kind under consideration is the Trade Practices Act 1974 (Cwlth) (TPA). The TPA drew heavily on US anti-trust law and the initial Act and subsequent amendments have also resulted in an extensive code of consumer protection law. It established the Trade Practices Commission, now known as the Australian Competition and Consumer Commission (ACCC). The ACCC is the regulatory body and watchdog; it has adopted a highly interventionist approach and is particularly rigorous in relation to transactions which may appear to have an anti-competitive purpose or effect and

* This chapter was updated by Cheng Lim, Partner, with the assistance of Stephen Rebikoff, Solicitor, both of Mallesons Stephen Jaques, Melbourne. The contributions of Robin Vague and Miles Standish, previously of Mallesons Stephen Jaques, in writing the original chapter, are acknowledged.

in relation to conduct which it considers misleading. Part IV of the TPA proscribes certain "restrictive trade practices", essentially anti-competitive behaviour. Provisions in agreements which will bear particular scrutiny are those which relate to third line forcing, resale price maintenance and price fixing. It should also be noted in this context that there is no Australian equivalent to the EU procedure for block exemptions, however authorisation on a case-by-case basis is available for certain conduct which might otherwise breach provisions of Pt IV. Part IVA of the TPA proscribes unconscionable conduct. Its provisions are aimed at preventing a stronger party in a transaction taking advantage of its position by behaving unconscionably, and apply to consumer transactions and to transactions involving small business. Part V of the TPA deals with consumer protection. It proscribes misleading and deceptive conduct and implies a number of terms, conditions and warranties into consumer transactions for the supply of goods or services. Part VA of the TPA establishes a limited code of liability in respect of defective goods. The implied terms, and a manufacturer's liability for defective goods, may not be excluded. However, in some circumstances relating to the supply of non-consumer goods and services, liability under the implied terms may be limited by agreement of the parties.

13–04 The TPA overrides parties' choice of law.

13.2 Agency agreements

13.2.1 General relationship

13–05 There are no significant differences between Australian law in relation to the relationship between agent and principal and English law. However, there is no legislation equivalent to EC Council Directive 653/86 governing the general relationship of principal and agent: the concept has been developed in Australia by the common law. In Australia, an agent has the power to bind a principal within the scope of the agent's actual or ostensible authority.

13.2.2 Carrying on business in Australia

13–06 If an agent has authority only to solicit orders which will be transmitted to the overseas principal—and become contractually binding only when accepted by the principal—the principal will generally be considered to be operating a "representative office" in Australia, rather than carrying on business. However, this always depends on the particular circumstances.

13–07 Conversely, if an agent has authority to enter into contracts and bind the principal, the principal will generally be considered to be carrying on business in Australia. A foreign principal carrying on business in Australia through a local agent must:

- register a company or business name in each state and territory in which business will be carried on;
- establish a registered office within Australia (normally, the principal place of business of the agent); and
- if a corporation, register as a foreign corporation with the Australian Securities and Investments Commission.

If the agent is to act as a debt collector for the principal, the agent may be required in some Australian jurisdictions to register as a commercial agent. Agents may also be required, or find it advantageous, to register for goods and services tax (GST) (see Chapter 13.2.3). **13–08**

13.2.3 Permanent establishment

Normally, if an Australian agent has, and regularly exercises, the power to enter into contracts binding the principal, the principal will generally be considered, for taxation purposes, to be a non-resident taxpayer carrying on business at or through a permanent establishment (PE) in Australia. If the agent's authority is confined to activities preparatory to the conclusion of a binding contract, the principal will generally not be carrying on business through a PE. **13–09**

A non-resident taxpayer carrying on business through a PE is required to pay tax on assessable income derived from Australian sources. Assessable income includes gross income according to ordinary concepts and net capital gains made on the disposal of assets. Expenses necessarily incurred in gaining assessable income or in carrying on a business are generally deductible. Outgoings of a capital, private or domestic nature are not deductible. Capital losses also accrue on the disposal of assets. Capital losses cannot be offset against most ordinary income, only against capital gains. The principal is not required to pay Australian tax on any income which is not derived from Australian sources. **13–10**

If the principal is not carrying on business in Australia through a PE and there is a double taxation treaty between Australia and the country in which the principal is resident, generally no Australian taxation is payable on Australian source income and that income will be taxed exclusively by the country in which the principal is resident (subject to Australian withholding tax, discussed below). Double taxation treaties exist between Australia and many countries, including most EU countries. **13–11**

Australian withholding tax may be imposed on payments of interest, dividends and royalties from residents to non-residents. **13–12**

Australia also has a 10 per cent (GST) which is payable by the supplier on the supply of most goods, services and rights supplied in or in connection with Australia. The supplier will normally seek to pass on this cost to the recipient of the supply. A supply will be GST-free in some circumstances if it is to a non-resident who is not in Australia when the thing supplied is done. **13–13**

However, it is possible that if a non-resident carries on business through an Australian agent with a fixed and definite place of business in Australia then the non-resident will be deemed to be in Australia and the supplier will be liable for GST on supplies made to that non-resident. Entities which are liable to pay GST can be registered for GST, allowing them to claim input tax credits for any GST included in the price of GST items they acquire. This allows the GST liability to be passed through to the end consumer. An entity must register for GST if its current or projected annual turnover is A$50,000 or more. Other entities may choose to register for GST.

13–14 Despite recent efforts at simplification, Australia's taxation legislation is voluminous and complex. In the course of structuring a proposed relationship, expert tax advice should be sought from an Australian lawyer.

13.2.4 Specific product legislation

13–15 There is a wide range of Australian legislation relating to goods and their marketing within Australia. Significant obligations in respect of packaging, labelling and safety are applied, in particular, to goods in the food and pharmaceutical industries. Regulatory approval is also required in relation to telecommunication products. Some imported goods must be labelled with their place of manufacture.

13.2.5 Power to bind

13–16 An agent may bind a principal to third parties only within the scope of the agent's actual or ostensible authority. As under English law, in Australia ostensible authority arises on the basis of a representation, made by the principal to third parties, that the agent has the authority to bind the principal. Independent actions or representations made by the agent will not put the agent in a position of ostensible authority.

13.2.6 Guarantees

13–17 A guarantee made by the agent to the principal should be in writing; however, no special formalities of wording or execution are required.

13–18 Generally, under Australian law, any variation or waiver of the primary contract between the principal and the customer will result in the guarantee being unenforceable, unless there is an express term in the contract of guarantee that it is not affected by any such variation or waiver. It is usual to include such a term. It is also a usual, and desirable, practice to obtain both a guarantee and an indemnity in relation to debts and other obligations. Increasingly in Australia, courts are requiring evidence that a guarantor has obtained independent legal advice prior to entering into the guarantee.

13.2.7 Trade marks—authorised users

Since the introduction of the Trade Marks Act 1995 (Cwlth), the concept of "registered user" no longer applies to trade marks registered in Australia, but the Act contemplates "authorised users" who are not registered. It is most desirable that a formal licence agreement is entered into between the principal and the agent in relation to trade marks, outlining precisely what the agent is permitted to do in relation to the trade marks and the principal's control in relation to the agent's use. The licence should expressly negate the rights of an authorised user which are provided under the Act. In the absence of a contrary agreement, the Act permits an authorised user to exercise many of the powers of the owner of the registered mark, including bringing an action for infringement, objecting to the importation of infringing goods, and even sublicensing. **13–19**

13.2.8 Termination and compensation

If there is proper termination of the agreement by the principal due to the agent's breach, the agent would not normally be entitled to any compensation. It is usual, and desirable, to specify in the agency agreement the events which will give rise to a right to terminate, such as material breach of the agreement which is not remedied, insolvency and criminal acts. **13–20**

Of course, if the agent terminates due to the principal's breach, the agent is entitled to damages for breach of contract. **13–21**

As discussed in Chapter 3.4, there is no legislation which entitles the agent to compensation where the agreement is terminated by notice, properly given under the agreement, or expires due to the effluxion of time. However, Australian courts have developed an equitable cause of action based on equitable estoppel. The leading High Court case is *Waltons Stores (Interstate) Ltd v Maher* (1988) 164 C.L.R. 387, where it was held that equitable estoppel may be used as a "sword" as well as a "shield". Care should be taken to ensure that a principal does not represent to an agent (or encourage an agent to believe) that an agency agreement will be renewed. If the principal makes such a representation (or encourages such a belief) and the agent relies on that representation to the agent's detriment, it may be unconscionable for the principal to resile from the representation. In those circumstances, the agent will have a cause of action and may be awarded damages or, in appropriate cases, injunctive relief. Similar remedies might be available under the TPA in respect of any false representations in relation to the agency, including representations as to renewal or continuation of the agency. In certain cases, termination may give rise to a claim of unconscionable conduct under the TPA (see Chapter 13.3.5). **13–22**

If an agreement is terminated in breach of the agreement or for breach of the agreement, damages are awarded to the affected party in accordance with the general principles relating to damages for breach of contract; that **13–23** is, damages are awarded to compensate the plaintiff for losses following naturally from the breach of the agreement. There is no special law relating to agents.

13.2.9 Secret commissions and gifts

13–24 The giving and taking of secret commissions and corrupt gifts by an agent is covered in Australia by the general law and by statute (including criminal law and, in some jurisdictions, specific secret commissions legislation). Under the general law, an agent may be liable for breach of fiduciary duty if the agent acquires any profit apart from that intended by the principal at the time the agreement was entered into. Under the criminal law, an agent will be liable to a fine and/or (if a natural person) imprisonment, if convicted. Offences include receiving or soliciting a secret commission and giving or receiving a false or misleading receipt or account. Gifts to members of the agent's family may also be deemed to be gifts to the agent.

13.2.10 Formalities

13–25 No registration or government approval is necessary for an agency agreement. Where a party is a corporation, it is preferable that it executes the agreement by affixing its common seal. In some Australian jurisdictions, stamp duty is levied on the execution of an agency agreement.

13.2.11 Exchange control and withholding tax

13–26 Generally, no exchange control permission is required to remit funds overseas from Australia. Currency (both Australian and foreign) may be freely brought in and out of the country. A person remitting an amount of more than A$10,000 out of Australia may be required to report the transaction to the Australian Transaction Reports and Analysis Centre. This is not an exchange control mechanism—the requirement is aimed at tax evasion and money laundering. Generally, money remitted by an agent in Australia to an overseas principal will not be subject to Australian withholding tax unless it is in the nature of interest, dividends or royalties (see also Chapter 13.4.8).

13.2.12 Ownership issues

13–27 In the event of the insolvency of the agent, as a general principle, property held by the agent on behalf of the principal will not form part of the estate of the agent and will not be available to creditors.

13–28 If the agent has dishonestly disposed of the principal's property to a third party, the principal's ability to assert rights of ownership will depend on whether or not the third party took the property with actual or constructive knowledge of the rights of the principal to the property. Generally, where the third party is a *bona fide* purchaser without (actual or constructive) notice, the third party may acquire title to the property.

If a sale of property has been authorised by the principal, the principal has a right to recover the proceeds. Difficulties associated with tracing proceeds when agent's and principal's funds are mixed, mean that the preferable course is to require the proceeds to be paid into a separate trust account. The agreement should also confirm that debts in respect of the sale are debts owed to the principal. The same principles will probably also apply if the sale has not been authorised by the principal. By virtue of the fiduciary relationship between an agent and a principal, both the proceeds and the debt would usually be held on trust for the principal. The agreement should confirm that. However, if the proceeds are not paid into a separate trust account (which would be expected if the agent acted without authority), tracing the proceeds will be extremely difficult. There are no formalities required before a principal may attempt to preserve the rights discussed in relation to property wrongfully dealt with by its agent. **13–29**

Ownership issues may also arise in circumstances where one enters into a supply contract and includes in it a retention of title clause, sometimes referred to as a "Romalpa" clause. Such clauses allow the supplier to retain title in or create a trust in relation to the goods or proceeds of re-supply where those goods are used in a manufacturing process. Romalpa clauses need to be structured carefully to ensure enforceability. **13–30**

13.3 Distribution agreements

13.3.1 General relationship

There is no specific Australian legislation dealing with distributors, whether exclusive or non-exclusive. There is no legislation equivalent to EC Commission Regulation 2790/99 which covers vertical agreements generally. However, competition law principles such as those contained in the TPA will be applicable to vertical arrangements (see Chapter 13.3.4). A distributor will generally be an independent contractor who acquires the goods from the principal and resells them. A distributor will not generally have authority to bind the principal. **13–31**

13.3.2 Carrying on business or permanent establishment in Australia

In the absence of any other relationship, it is most unlikely that an overseas principal who appoints an Australian distributor will be considered to be carrying on business in Australia. However, if for some reason a principal **13–32** with an Australian distributor is considered to be carrying on business in Australia, it will need to attend to the registration requirements (discussed at Chapter 13.2.2). It is also unlikely that an overseas principal who appoints an Australian distributor will be required to pay Australian taxes as the principal will not generally be carrying on business through a PE in Australia. This is because a distributor is an independent contractor who is not able to bind the principal. However, in certain circumstances, if the distributor is a subsidiary of the principal, the principal may be treated as having a PE in Australia in which case the discussion of taxation of the Australian-source income of non-residents (discussed at Chapter 13.2.3) will apply.

13.3.3 Intellectual property rights

13–33 Copyright subsists in original works, which may be literary, dramatic, artistic or musical. Copyright also subsists in "subject matter other than works", for example, sound recordings, cinematograph films, radio and television broadcasts, and published editions of works. Computer programs are protected as literary works. In most cases, copyright subsists for the life of the author of the work plus 50 years. No registration is required for copyright to subsist.

13–34 The Copyright Act 1968 (Cwlth) contains a number of provisions relating to parallel importation. A copyright owner has extensive rights against unlicensed importers of copies of works, even if no copyright laws were breached in the place where the copies were acquired. These rights can enable an overseas copyright owner to establish exclusive distribution networks in respect of copyright material. Under the legislation, exceptions currently exist which permit parallel importation in relation to books and sound recordings. Copyright in labels and packaging (where the underlying goods are not subject to copyright) cannot be used to prevent parallel imports. There is a bill currently before Parliament which proposes to extend the exceptions to permit parallel importation of software (including interactive computer games), periodicals and sheet music. Australian trade marks legislation does not restrict parallel importing.

13–35 In 2000, significant amendments were made to the Copyright Act, which were designed to deal with developments in digital and communications technologies (in relation to software, see Chapter 13.5.3). One important amendment aimed at making copyright protection technology-neutral was the addition of a "right to communicate the work to the public" to the list of exclusive rights of copyright owners. There have also been amendments to include the protection of authors' moral rights. Under the Copyright Act, authors have a right of attribution of authorship, and protection against the false attribution of authorship and derogatory treatment of their work. Moral rights only accrue to individuals and are not assignable. An author may give consent to uses which would otherwise be an infringement of their moral rights.

Registrable designs may be registered under the Designs Act 1906 (Cwlth). A registered design is protected for an initial term of 12 months. Total maximum protection available for registered designs is 16 years, if the appropriate extensions are obtained. **13–36**

Complex provisions in the Copyright Act relate to the overlap of copyright and design protection. Generally, the provisions have the effect that copyright protection is not available for most registrable designs. That is, reproducing a design in three dimensions will not infringe copyright subsisting in the original design as an artistic work. These provisions do not apply to designs consisting solely of two-dimensional patterns applicable to the surface of an article (for example, a screen-print applied to a T-shirt). The copyright/design provisions have been controversial and are currently the subject of review, which may result in amendments to the legislation. **13–37**

Additional protection for intellectual property rights exists in respect of patents (Patents Act 1990 (Cwlth)), trade marks (Trade Marks Act 1995 (Cwlth)), plant variety rights or breeder's rights (Plant Breeder's Rights Act 1994 (Cwlth)) and circuit layouts or "EL rights" (Circuit Layouts Act 1989 (Cwlth)). In all cases, except circuit layouts, registration is required. **13–38**

The legislation relating to intellectual property rights is federal legislation. Registration, where required as a prerequisite to protection, will confer protection throughout Australia without additional formalities. **13–39**

13.3.4 Trade Practices Act

The introduction to this chapter stresses the significance of the TPA in relation to all the agreements discussed in the text. Part IV of the TPA which deals with anti-competitive conduct is particularly relevant to vertical arrangements such as distribution agreements. The main issues likely to arise in respect of which the TPA should be taken into account are discussed below (see also Chapter 13.3.5,13.3.12 and 13.3.13). **13–40**

First, the principal is free to charge different prices and contract upon different terms with two or more of its distributors (whether within the one territory or in separate, defined territories), but since the TPA proscribes anti-competitive conduct, the likely effect of the arrangements on competition must always be considered. **13–41**

Second, whether the grant of exclusivity in respect of a particular territory is permitted under the TPA is sometimes an issue. A grant of exclusivity would amount to "exclusive dealing" under the TPA, but is prohibited only if the conduct has the purpose or effect of substantially lessening competition in a market. In most cases, particularly where there are a number of competitive products in the market, the grant of exclusivity would not substantially reduce competition in the market. If however, the products are unique and there are no substitutes for them, then this would need to be looked at carefully. Exclusivity in relation to customers also requires careful consideration as the issues are similar. **13–42**

Third, a refusal to grant a distributorship (*e.g.* to protect the grant of an **13–43** exclusive distributorship) could constitute a prohibited "taking advantage" of market power for an anti-competitive purpose under s.46 of the TPA. However, on the basis of the recent High Court decision in *Melway Publishing Pty Ltd v Robert Hicks Pty Ltd* (2001) 205 C.L.R. 1, s.46 of the TPA would not be contravened by such a refusal where the structure of the exclusive distributorship system which is being protected has a reasonable commercial basis and is intended to secure business advantages which would exist in a competitive environment.

13–44 Fourth, the TPA prohibits "exclusionary provisions" (collective boycotts), whatever the effect on competition. In general terms, an exclusionary provision is an agreement between two or more competitors (including those who would be in competition but for an agreement) which has the purpose of preventing, restricting or limiting the supply of goods or services to particular persons or classes of persons. The provisions prohibiting collective boycotts have been interpreted broadly. At the very least, distributorships of this kind should sound a note of caution. Secondary boycotts may also contravene the TPA, depending on their purpose and effect. This prohibition is particularly relevant in the context of industrial action.

13–45 The fifth important area is that the practice of resale price maintenance is proscribed by the TPA, regardless of its effect on competition. Generally, a principal will breach the resale price maintenance provisions if it specifies a price (or minimum price) at which the goods must be resold or services resupplied by the distributor. The price specified need not be a specific figure: for example, a specification that the price charged must not be less than that charged by other retailers in the industry will breach the provisions. Where a price is stated to be a "recommended" price, the principal will not be taken to have breached the provisions simply because it has stated a recommended price; however, other factors will be taken into consideration and the result will depend on all the circumstances. A principal may determine a maximum price at which goods or services may be resold. However, it should always be kept in mind that agreements or arrangements between competitors which have the effect or purpose of fixing prices for goods or services in a relevant market will breach the TPA. Thus whilst recommended prices and maximum prices are permitted, if they turn out to be the actual prices charged by a distributor or all distributors, that increases the risk that not much more is required before there is a prohibited price fixing arrangement, either between the principal and distributors or between distributors. (The position of a distributor is to be contrasted with the position of an agent. For an agent, the principal is entitled to set prices, for they are the principal's own prices.)

13–46 The sixth area where the TPA is relevant is in relation to the imposition of an obligation to deal exclusively with the principal (practices which are sometimes referred to as "full line forcing" or "first line forcing") and an obligation to acquire goods or services from a third party nominated by the principal (referred to as "third line forcing"). The principal is free to impose upon a distributor an obligation to purchase and keep stocks of the products which are the subject of the distribution agreement, if the required source of supply is not designated. A requirement to purchase products from the principal is permitted if there is no substantial lessening of competition. However, a requirement to purchase products from a third party (third line forcing), even if the third party is a related corporation of the principal, is prohibited outright, regardless of the effect on competition.

13.3.5 Unfair trading practices

Clearly, a principal can prohibit a distributor from engaging in unfair practices. Again, the important Australian legislation in relation to unfair practices, with emphasis on consumer protection and protection of small business, is the TPA. The main consumer protection provisions of the TPA are echoed in state legislation. **13–47**

Unfair practices which are proscribed by the TPA in relation to consumer transactions include: misleading and deceptive conduct; false representations; claiming payment for unsolicited goods or services; offering prizes or gifts without intention to supply; bait advertising; pyramid selling; referral selling; and supply of goods not complying with safety standards or product information standards. **13–48**

The TPA also sets out specific prohibitions on unconscionable conduct in consumer transactions and certain business transactions. Consumer transactions are those where a corporation supplies goods or services to a person for their personal or domestic use. Business transactions are transactions under A$3,000,000 involving the supply to or acquisition of goods or services by a person or a corporation, other than a listed public company. The TPA contains a non-exhaustive list of factors to which a court may have regard in determining if a person has engaged in unconscionable conduct. These factors include the relative bargaining strengths of the parties and the extent to which the stronger party used unfair tactics or undue pressure. **13–49**

The TPA is particularly relevant to agency and distribution arrangements that take place via a franchise system. As there is often an imbalance of bargaining power between the franchisor and franchisee, the provisions prohibiting unconscionable conduct are often invoked in the context of franchise arrangements. Further, a mandatory industry code exists that regulates the conduct of participants in franchising. Breaches of this code give rise to remedies under the TPA. The code does not apply where the franchisor is a foreign entity and grants only one franchise or master franchise in Australia. The code requires franchisors to provide and maintain disclosure documents, the purpose of which is to enable prospective and current franchisees to make informed decisions about whether to enter into or renew a franchise arrangement. The code also regulates cooling off periods, transfer and termination of franchises and establishes a dispute resolution procedure with an emphasis on mediation. **13–50**

Where parties enter into a contract, arrangement or collateral arrangement which leads directly to a person performing work in an industry in New South Wales, the "unfair contract" provisions of the Industrial Rela- **13–51** tions Act 1996 (NSW) may apply. Agency, distribution and licensing (particularly involving franchising) are areas in which, provided there is a sufficient connection to New South Wales, the provisions will often apply. The provisions operate in addition to the principles of unconscionable conduct.

13–52 The unfair contract provisions vest in the New South Wales Industrial Relations Commission a very broad power to declare void or vary agreements on the grounds that they are unfair, harsh or unconscionable, or against the public interest. The Commission also has a broad discretion in relation to remedies.

13–53 The Commission has deliberately avoided defining the term "unfair" with any precision. Instead, the Commission takes what it describes as a "common sense" view in the circumstances of each individual case. Importantly, contracts which may have been "fair" at formation, may be subsequently found to be "unfair" due to the manner of their operation (including the influence of subsequent external factors) or the circumstances of their termination.

13.3.6 Damages for non-performance

13–54 Liquidated damages clauses are enforceable in Australia, provided the amount represents a genuine pre-estimate of loss. It is, therefore, possible to provide for payment of liquidated damages for delay or failure to perform. In practical terms, however, in an ongoing distribution agreement where there are different products being supplied, in different volumes and at different prices, it may be difficult to pre-estimate damages.

13–55 It is possible to contract out of liability for failure to perform obligations, except in respect of those conditions, terms and warranties which are implied by statute (particularly by the TPA) and are non-excludable. Generally, terms implied by statute relate to warranties as to title and quiet possession, quality, fitness for purpose, and due skill and care.

13–56 It is not uncommon to exclude liability for failure to deliver products on time.

13–57 The Vienna Convention on Contracts for the International Sale of Goods has been implemented into Australian domestic law in all jurisdictions and regulates certain international sale contracts. No terms are implied under the Convention, however, the seller is required to deliver goods which are of the quantity, quality and description required by the contract. The Convention defines circumstances in which the goods do not conform with the contract, namely fitness for purpose and quality, but the parties may exclude these provisions.

13.3.7 Specific product legislation

13–58 As discussed in Chapter 13.2.4 in the context of agency, there are wide-ranging legislative provisions in Australia regulating sale, composition, ingredients, packaging and advertising of products. Accordingly, it is important to oblige the distributor to comply with the regulatory process, to obtain the necessary consents or licences and to comply with labelling and advertising requirements in the territory.

13.3.8 Power to bind

A distributor may bind a principal to third parties only if the distributor has express or ostensible authority to do so. In most genuine distributorships, a distributor will have no such authority and as a result will have no power to bind a principal. **13–59**

13.3.9 Trade marks—authorised users

The desirability of an authorised user agreement in relation to an agent is discussed in Chapter 13.2.7. It is probably more desirable in relation to a distributor. The principal's rights to the marks should be acknowledged, and the limits on the distributor's rights to use them specified. **13–60**

13.3.10 Compensation

The rights of a distributor to compensation on termination or expiry of an agreement are determined by the provisions of the agreement and the general law. The position is the same as agency agreements, discussed in Chapter 13.2.8. There is no specific legislation providing for compensation to distributors. **13–61**

13.3.11 Formalities, exchange control, withholding tax

There are no formal requirements or exchange controls in relation to a distribution agreement (see Chapter 13.2.10 and 13.2.11 in relation to agency). **13–62**

Payments from the distributor to the principal will generally not be in the nature of interest, dividends or royalties and will not therefore be subject to Australian withholding tax. If the distributor is a subsidiary of the principal, profits may be remitted in the form of dividends, in which case a liability to pay Australian withholding tax may arise, depending upon whether the dividend is franked or unfranked. **13–63**

13.3.12 Exclusion of liability

There are extensive limits on the ability of a principal to exclude liability for the supply of defective products, particularly consumer products. **13–64**

13–65 As already foreshadowed, the TPA prescribes certain warranties and conditions in respect of contracts for the supply of goods. The TPA prohibits modification or exclusion of the prescribed terms. Under the TPA, manufacturers are also liable directly to consumers for goods which do not correspond with their description, are of unmerchantable quality, do not conform to sample, are unfit for a stated purpose, or do not comply with an express warranty. In addition, the TPA provides an extensive code in relation to the liability of manufacturers for defective goods. Similarly, liability may not be excluded or modified by contract. There is a statutory indemnity from the manufacturer to the supplier, in respect of any liability to a consumer.

13–66 Where the principal does not have a place of business in Australia, the distributor (as the importer of the goods) is deemed to be the manufacturer under these provisions of the TPA. Therefore, both the distributor and the principal (the actual manufacturer) will be liable under these provisions.

13–67 In these circumstances, it will not generally be possible for an overseas manufacturer to exclude liability to an Australian distributor in respect of liability under the TPA for consumer products or defective products. An approach often taken is to insert a provision excluding any liability apart from statutory liability, but given the extensive scope of the statutory liability, at least in the context of consumer products, there is little room for the provision to operate effectively.

13–68 The issue always requires careful analysis in the context of the particular products being distributed.

13.3.13 Selective distribution systems

13–69 It is possible to set up a selective distribution system in Australia. However, many critical aspects of the structure must be analysed for compliance with the TPA. The most important are discussed in Chapter 13.3.4. Territory and customer exclusivity must be examined for competitive effect. Effective price controls will probably have to be abandoned (because of the prospect of resale price maintenance and price fixing). Third line forcing is always an issue. For example, an agreement between the principal and an authorised retailer to acquire product only from authorised distributors, is outlawed. On the other hand, an obligation to obtain product only from the person granting the rights (full or first line forcing) is usually acceptable (subject to the overall competitive effect), so that if the authorised retailer agreement is not with the principal, but an authorised distributor, the agreement can generally require acquisition of product from that authorised distributor. (It should be noted that the use of the term full or first line forcing does not necessarily connote an obligation to acquire the full range of items in a particular product line, as it does, for instance, in the UK.)

13–70 Refusal to supply distributors may be able to be justified, but again the purpose and likely competitive effect must be examined. See the discussion in Chapter 13.3.4. An example of a prohibited refusal is where the reason for the refusal is the distributor's price cutting. A principal can generally refuse to supply for genuine commercial reasons associated with the quality of the distributors and the number and location of distributors required for a commercially viable distribution system.

13.4 Manufacturing agreements

13.4.1 Legislative controls

There is no Australian legislation specifically controlling transfers of technology. Of the generally applicable legislation, the most important to consider in relation to the structure of a manufacturing agreement is the tax legislation, particularly transfer pricing and withholding tax (discussed in Chapter 13.4.8), and the TPA. **13–71**

13.4.2 Trade Practices Act

Many of the issues mentioned in the context of distribution agreements (see Chapter 13.3.4) are relevant to manufacturing agreements. In particular, the TPA contains a number of provisions relating to product liability which are likely to impact on manufacturers (see Chapter 13.3.12). **13–72**

Exclusivity issues must be considered in the context of their competitive effect. The principal is generally free to differentiate between licensees in imposing differing scales of royalties or payment terms, subject to the likely competitive effect. The principal is not free to set prices charged for licensed products sold by the manufacturer. **13–73**

A significant commercial issue is invariably the extent to which the principal can require the manufacturer to purchase ingredients, components or packaging from specified sources. The manufacturer may be required to purchase these from the principal (full or first line forcing), subject always to the competitive effect, but may not be required to purchase them from other named suppliers (third line forcing). It is possible, however, to impose genuine quality controls in relation to items used in manufacture and to require the principal's approval for items purchased and the source of supply, provided that the licensee's choice of suppliers is effectively preserved and that the approval process is genuinely directed to quality aspects. **13–74**

In this context, ss.144–146 of the Patents Act 1990 (Cwlth) should be kept in mind when drafting a manufacturing licence for Australia. In general terms, if a condition of a patent licence has the effect of prohibiting or restricting a licensee from using a third person's product or process, or requiring the licensee to acquire a product not protected by the patent from the principal, the condition may be void. There are, however, a number of limitations in the application of the sections which should be considered in each case. For example, they apply to prohibitions or restrictions on the use **13–75** of a product or process, not sale. There is also a specific exception in relation to the supply of spare parts.

13–76 Another issue which often arises is the extent to which the principal can restrict the export of products by the licensee outside the licensed territory. Here, under the TPA one looks at the competitive effect in the Australian market. Restrictions on export outside Australia are generally acceptable. Restrictions on sale from one distributor's territory within Australia to any other part of Australia require closer examination, however.

13.4.3 Intellectual property rights

13–77 The subject of manufacturing agreements is generally patents and knowhow. Both are protected in Australia, patents by registration under the Patents Act 1990 (Cwlth) and knowhow under the law relating to obligations of confidence. A patent may be registered in respect of a new manner of manufacture. A standard patent term is 20 years. Recent amendments provide for "innovation patents", which essentially replace the old "petty patents" system. The innovation patent has a term of eight years and cannot be extended. Innovation patents have a lower threshold of novelty or inventiveness than standard patents and are intended to be cheaper and easier to obtain. They are not substantively examined prior to registration, but cannot be enforced against third parties until such examination has occurred. The protection for other important intellectual property rights is discussed in Chapter 13.3.3.

13.4.5 Trade marks—authorised users

13–78 If the manufacturer is to use the principal's trade marks in relation to licensed products, a trade mark licence or authorised user agreement (see Chapter 13.2.7) is essential.

13.4.6 Upfront fees

13–79 The principal is entitled to require payment of an up-front sum for transfer of the technology to the licensee. There are no restrictions expressly controlling this, unless the law relating to unconscionability is invoked by the conduct of the principal in the circumstances of the case.

13.4.7 Other general issues

13–80 Many of the issues mentioned in relation to distribution or agency agreements are also relevant to manufacturing agreements. These include unfair trading practices (see Chapter 13.3.5), damages for non-performance (see

Chapter 13.3.6) specific product legislation (see Chapter 13.2.4 and 13.3.7), compensation on termination or expiry (see Chapter 13.2.8 and 13.2.10) and formalities (see Chapter 13.2.10 and 13.3.11).

The position in relation to the licensee's power to bind the principal is also the same (see Chapter 13.2.5 and 13.3.8). In most cases, a manufacturer would not have power to bind the principal. **13–81**

13.4.8 Payments

Generally, no exchange control permissions are required to remit licensee payments (such as lump sums, royalties, or payments for items purchased) to an overseas principal (see Chapter 13.2.11). **13–82**

There are tax issues, however, in relation to the treatment of royalties (and in this regard "royalties" can include amounts expressed as "lump sums"). If the principal's remuneration under the licence agreement is in the nature of royalties, those royalties will be subject to Australian witholding tax. If the principal is not carrying on business through a PE in Australia, royalties will be subject to withholding tax of 30 per cent if the principal is a resident of a country with which Australia does not have a double taxation agreement. Where a double taxation treaty exists between Australia and the country of residence of the principal, the rate of withholding tax is that agreed in the treaty. Commonly, in treaties made by Australia, the rate is 10 per cent or 15 per cent. **13–83**

Where the principal is carrying on business through a PE in Australia, the royalties will be liable to tax at the full company rate on the net amount, *i.e.* after deductions. **13–84**

There are also transfer pricing provisions in the Australian tax legislation and applicable double tax treaties, and these will apply if the parties are not dealing at arm's length in relation to the transfer of technology. Particular care must be taken where, for example, the licensee is a related entity of the principal. **13–85**

Whilst these tax considerations will often be the main driving force for the way in which the licensee's payments are structured, the parties are generally able to provide for the method of payment and the term of payment without legislative interference. For example, there are no controls in Australia on the total amount of royalties which may be charged by the principal. Nor does a licensee have any right under Australian law to a free, paid-up licence after the expiration of a certain period of time, or the payment of a certain total amount of royalties. Further, there are no rules under Australian law determining how a royalty is to be calculated. However, there are taxes and duties, including customs duty payable on imported goods, and GST payable on the supply of most goods, services and rights, which should be taken into account. Where a royalty is payable it may form part of the total consideration upon which GST is calculated. **13–86**

Unlike the position in the EU, Australia does not have any specific legislative prohibition on the payment of royalties after a patent has expired. A **13–87** provision requiring continued payment of royalties would not, of itself, be void under ss.144–146 of the Patents Act 1990 (Cwlth) (see Chapter 13.3.2). However, expiration of a patent results in a statutory right of either party to terminate the licence on three months' notice. That does not prevent imposing royalties in respect of the ongoing use of knowhow. Moreover, in respect of knowhow, there is no reason under Australian law why a principal could not negotiate an entitlement to royalties despite the knowhow entering the public domain. Commercially, of course, a licensee would not be likely to agree to this.

13.4.9 Liability

13–88 There is greater scope for the principal to exclude liability to its licensee in respect of the technology and services provided than is the case with exclusion of liability to a distributor. The principal generally will not be either a manufacturer or supplier of products, so that the non-excludable provisions of the TPA will generally not apply.

13.5 Miscellaneous

13–89 There are a number of general issues discussed in earlier chapters which are common to all or some of the agreements.

13.5.1 Confidentiality

13–90 Australian law relating to confidential information is substantially the same as the law in England. Confidential information is protected by the general law, separate from any contractual obligation of confidence, so that an express confidentiality agreement is not required. Nevertheless express confidentiality provisions are generally considered to be desirable. They usually spell out in detail what uses and disclosures of the confidential information are permitted and not permitted. It is also possible that a party may by express agreement impose greater obligations of confidence than those under the general law. The issue is largely untested, although in the recent decision of *Maggbury Pty Ltd v Hafele Australia Pty* Ltd [2001] H.C.A. 70 the High Court made it clear that a confidentiality obligation which is not limited in time is not enforceable (being a restraint of trade) where the relevant information has entered the public domain.

13.5.2 Restrictive covenants

13–91 Restrictive covenants are permitted, but always require careful consideration. Potentially, covenants preventing competing activities may be wider during the term of an agreement than after it. Subject to the provisions of the TPA, it is generally acceptable to restrict competition during the life of the agreement. The TPA may proscribe such a restriction where the effect is a substantial lessening of competition.

The validity of a restraint upon competition following the termination or expiration of the agreement will depend upon whether it is reasonable in all the circumstances of the case. The geographical and temporal extent of the restraint, together with the nature of the products and services restrained, will be significant factors to be considered in determining this question. **13–92**

13.5.3 Software

Amendments made in 1984 to the Copyright Act 1968 (Cwlth) made it clear that, in Australia, computer software (both source code and object code) is a literary work in which copyright may subsist. No registration is required to prove subsistence and/or ownership of copyright in Australia. Amendments made in 2000 under the "Digital Agenda" reforms saw the addition of detailed provisions clarifying the copyright protection of computer programs and permissible uses. For example, copies made as an incident of running, backing up and maintaining the computer program are specifically permitted, as is reverse engineering for interoperability. **13–93**

Eligible layout (EL) rights in circuit layouts are protected under the Circuit Layouts Act 1989 (Cwlth). Since a 1991 decision of the Federal Court of Australia (*IBM v Commissioner of Patents* (1991) 33 F.C.R. 218) computer software (particularly systems software) is patentable. Consistent with what is happening overseas, there is also a trend in Australia to patent business processes, particularly when implemented by the use of computer systems. **13–94**

Software may be subject to obligations of confidentiality. It may also be the subject of contractual restrictions expressly agreed between the principal and its licensee. **13–95**

13.5.4 Escrow agreements

Australian law recognises the concept of escrow. In Australia, escrow agents are commonly used in agreements for the development of software, where a complete copy of source code listings will often be held by the escrow agent to be handed to the licensee in the event of, for example, the insolvency or winding-up of the software developer. Generally, where an escrow agreement is supported by consideration it is irrevocable. No special formalities are required to make an escrow agreement enforceable. The agreement should be in writing. Any party which is a corporation should execute the agreement under its common seal. Each party to the underlying transaction and the escrow agent should all be parties to the escrow agreement. **13–96**

13.5.5 Powers of attorney

13–97 Generally, no formality is required for the valid appointment of an agent. However, in certain circumstances the appointment must be in writing. The most relevant circumstance in the present context is that in several jurisdictions the appointment must be in writing where the agency, distributorship or licence is intended to continue for over 12 months.

13–98 Appointment of an agent by deed, or an instrument executed under the common seal of a corporation, is generally required in order to empower the agent to execute a deed. Presently, in all States of Australia except Victoria, the power must be registered and in some jurisdictions a nominal amount of stamp duty is payable.

13–99 Generally, unless contrary to its express terms, a power of attorney is revocable. Where the agent does not have notice of revocation and acts under the power, the agent is entitled to rely on the power against the principal.

13.5.6 Whole agreement clauses

13–100 Australian law permits the use of "whole agreement" clauses. Generally, the use of such a clause is most desirable, although, obviously, care should be taken to ensure that there are not, in fact, extraneous documents that the parties intend to form part of the agreement.

13–101 The use of a "whole agreement" clause will not be a defence to a claim for misleading and deceptive conduct or false representation in breach of the TPA, or a cause of action in estoppel.

13.5.7 Arbitration

13–102 Uniform commercial arbitration legislation exists in all Australian jurisdictions. The legislation prescribes a model for structured arbitration for parties seeking an alternative to the courts. The legislation recognises arbitration agreements made by parties to commercial transactions.

13–103 As the intention of the legislation is to provide a genuine alternative to the judicial process, the courts do not have a strong regulatory role. However, the court has extensive general procedural powers, including the power to:

- set aside an award and remove the arbitrator where there has been misconduct on the part of the arbitrator;
- make interlocutory orders in relation to an arbitration.

13–104 Parties to an arbitration have a general right to seek leave to appeal to the court on any question of law arising out of an award. However, the court may grant leave only where the question in dispute could substantially affect the rights of a party and there is either manifest error of law on the face of the record or strong evidence that the arbitrator made an error of law and that the determination of the question may add substantially to the certainty of commercial law. With the consent of the parties, the court may determine any preliminary question of law.

The parties to an international agreement may agree to exclude the jurisdiction of the court to grant leave to hear an appeal from an award, or to determine a preliminary question of law (an exclusion agreement). Any other clauses in an agreement purporting to otherwise prohibit or restrict access to the court, or to limit the jurisdiction of the court, are void. **13–105**

An award made under an Australian arbitration subject to Australian law may, by leave of the court, be enforced in the same manner as a judgment or order of the court and, where leave is given, judgment may be entered in the terms of the award. Costs, unless agreed otherwise by the parties, are in the discretion of the arbitrator. **13–106**

The UNCITRAL Model Law on International Commercial Arbitration, adopted by the UN Commission on International Trade Law in 1985, has the force of domestic law in Australia by virtue of the International Arbitration Act 1974 (Cwlth). Where parties to an arbitration agreement are each resident in a country which is a signatory to the 1958 UN Convention on the Recognition and Enforcement of Foreign Arbitral Awards, the Convention may be invoked in the enforcement of an award. Under the International Arbitration Act, such an award is binding for all purposes on the parties to the arbitration agreement, and may be enforced in Australian courts as if the award had been made in Australia. **13–107**

Generally, the arbitrator is bound to decide the issue in accordance with legal principles. However, if the parties agree, the arbitrator may determine any issue by reference to considerations of general justice and fairness. An award made by an arbitrator in this way is no different from any other arbitral award and may be enforced accordingly. The court's power to intervene is unaffected in relation to procedural issues; however, leave to appeal will not be granted on a question of law arising out of the award. **13–108**

There is an increasing tendency in Australia to provide for alternative dispute resolution, through mediation rather than arbitration, as a precondition to litigation. **13–109**

13.5.8 Force majeure

As under other common law jurisdictions, there is no precise definition of the phrase "*force majeure*" in Australian law. Accordingly, it is desirable to spell out in the agreement the events which constitute "*force majeure*" and the consequences of the occurrence of *force majeure* events. **13–110**

In the absence of a *force majeure* clause, the parties would be thrown back to the doctrine of frustration and all the uncertainties associated with the general nature of that doctrine. In Australia, this is generally the common law doctrine, although some jurisdictions of Australia have legislation **13–111** dealing with frustrated contracts, for example, the Frustrated Contracts Act 1978 (NSW).

13–112 The High Court of Australia has approved of the approach of Lord Reid and Lord Radcliffe to the doctrine of frustration in *Davis Contractors Ltd v Fareham UDC* [1956] A.C. 696 outlined in Chapter 1 above.

13.5.9 Environmental laws

13–113 Australia has over 300 Acts (with numerous regulations under those Acts) relating to environmental matters and more than 80 agencies or authorities at both Federal and State level. Generally matters of national environmental significance are regulated under federal legislation leaving other matters to be regulated by laws of the relevant states.

13–114 Generally, environmental legislation impacts on businesses in two principal areas: pollution control and waste disposal, and land use and planning.

13.5.9.1 Pollution control and waste disposal

13–115 All States have passed legislation establishing a National Environment Protection Council (now the Environment Protection and Heritage Council) which is charged with making national environment protection measures. These measures must relate to ambient air quality, ambient water quality, hazardous substances, recycling of materials, motor vehicle noise and emissions, contaminated sites and the protection of amenity in relation to noise.

13–116 All states and territories have legislation which addresses the pollution of land, waters and air. In each jurisdiction regulations cover the emission of effluent, the emission of pollutants, the emission of noise or odours, the generation of waste, the transport or deposit of waste and the storage, handling, use or transport of dangerous goods.

13–117 The legislation seeks to prevent environmental harm through a range of regulatory mechanisms including licences, environment protection policies and environment management and best practice. The principle of ecologically sustainable development is a major object of the environment protection legislation.

13–118 Generally, the legislation in each jurisdiction provides for certain offences. These include breaching a licence or other regulatory mechanism, conducting certain activities without a licence or authority or failing to carry out an environmental audit.

13.5.9.2 Land use planning

13–119 The responsibility for land use planning is generally shared between the local councils, government departments and the Minister administering the planning legislation with the local councils playing a predominant role. For larger developments, the responsibility may be passed to the State Minister.

Under these planning instruments land is classified into particular zones (*e.g.* residential, commercial, light industrial, rural and public purposes) on which certain activities are grouped together. Environmental impact assessments also play an important role in this regard. These are regulated by state and federal legislative provisions but are frequently carried out at the behest of local government bodies to ensure that developers take primary responsibility for environmental protection from the effects of their proposal. **13–120**

Other legislative controls exist which aim to conserve natural, urban, historical and cultural resources by giving them special protected status. **13–121**

13.5.10 Electronic transactions

The Electronic Transactions Act 1999 (Cwlth) (which is mirrored by legislation in the States and Territories) governs electronic transactions and provides for contracts transacted electronically to be as legally enforceable as written contracts. In general terms, it only applies to transactions with governmental authorities unless there is specific agreement between the parties to the relevant transaction. **13–122**

13.5.11 Privacy

The Privacy Act 1988 (Cwlth) has long governed the practices of Government bodies in relation to protecting individuals' privacy. In December 2001 the Act was amended to apply to private sector organisations with an annual turnover of greater than A$3 million. **13–123**

Under the Privacy Act, private sector organisations must comply with the "National Privacy Principles" or "NPPs" governing how they collect, use, store and disclose personal information, such as customer information. For example, businesses conducting direct marketing campaigns—whether by mail or email—must obtain peoples' consent before collecting their contact and personal details and must provide them with a mechanism for opting out of receiving further direct marketing material.

The NPPs also prohibit the transfer of personal information outside of Australia unless certain conditions are met. These conditions aim to ensure that the recipient of the information is bound under contract or law to protect the privacy of the personal information to substantially the same extent as the NPPs. **13–124**

Chapter 14

Hong Kong*

Contents

One of the main reasons why manufacturers and suppliers enter into agency, distribution or licensing agreements is that they wish to expand into a new product market but are unfamiliar with that market. They may wish to minimise some of the risks of expansion by relying on the local knowledge and resources of the agent, distributor or licensee. Hong Kong is almost entirely dependent on imported resources and is therefore an important market in its own right. In addition, it is often chosen as a base for sales in the South-East Asia region. The main reasons for this are: **14–01**

- a favourable geographical position;
- a well-established business community;
- English is widely used in commercial and financial circles;
- an excellent communications network;
- one of the lowest tax jurisdictions in the world;
- strong links with China and other countries in the South-East Asia region;
- the absence of exchange controls;
- a common law system; and
- an independent judiciary and a highly stable legal system.

Despite the concerns of some, these perceived advantages have not been affected by Hong Kong's return to Chinese sovereignty on July 1, 1997 after **14–02**

* The 2002 revision to this chapter was written by Derek Roth-Biester LLB, Solicitor England and Wales and Senior Associate at Masons, Hong Kong. The original chapter was written by Richard Bates in 1996.

150 years of British rule. This in large part stems from the policies declared by the Chinese government in the Joint Declaration Treaty concluded with the United Kingdom in 1984, one of which was that the laws in force in Hong Kong as at June 30, 1997 would remain basically unchanged after the territory became a Special Administrative Region (hence HKSAR) of the PRC on July 1, 1997. Indeed, these policies were enshrined in the Basic Law promulgated by the National People's Congress of the PRC which acts as the constitution of the HKSAR, and specifically states that the common law and rules of equity apply to Hong Kong so far as they are applicable to the circumstances of Hong Kong or its inhabitants subject to:

- any laws which contravene the Basic Law; and
- any amendment by the legislature of the HKSAR.

14–03 The post-handover form of government has been referred to as "One Country: Two Systems", reflecting the guarantee from the PRC that Hong Kong will be granted the special status of a capitalist, autonomous and common law jurisdiction for at least 50 years, during which time the common law system will continue in place and reference will still be made to UK case law and to case law from other common law jurisdictions, although appeals to the Privy Council have ceased and are instead made to the Court of Final Appeal in Hong Kong.

14–04 Given Hong Kong's background as a colony of the UK, therefore, it is not surprising that many of its own statutes (called "Ordinances") are, for the most part, restatements of English laws. Hong Kong law, is then, similar to the law of England and Wales (UK law) but not identical, since the provisions of the relevant Ordinance may not be quite the same as the comparable UK Act and the common law is often interpreted or applied in a slightly different way. Probably the most significant difference is the fact that the European Union and UK regulatory controls and anti-competitive agreements which were in force in the UK at the time of the handover clearly do not apply to Hong Kong. In fact, Hong Kong currently has no anti-competition legislation and very few regulatory controls or consumer protection laws, although the government is constantly looking at ways to improve competition in the Hong Kong market. In 1996, the Consumer Council called for the establishment of a competition authority and the introduction of US and European-style competition laws in Hong Kong, but their proposals received little support from the business community. As a result, the Government formed the Competition Policy Advisory Group ("COMPAG") in 1997 with a view to formulating an official Statement on Competition Policy. In its 2001 annual report, COMPAG stated that the Government would not interfere with market forces simply on the basis of the number of operators, scale of operations, or normal commercial constraints faced by new entrants. Action would be taken only when market imperfections or distortions limit market accessibility or market contestability, and impair economic efficiency or free trade, to the detriment of the overall interest of Hong Kong. This has therefore left open the possibility for anti-competitive legislation in the future.

The purpose of this chapter is to highlight the principal areas of Hong Kong law relevant to drafting agency, distribution or licensing agreements for the sale and/or manufacture of goods in Hong Kong, and to state the major implications of agreeing that any such agreement will be governed by Hong Kong law. Note that the law is stated as at November 2002. **14–05**

14.1 Agency agreements

14.1.1 Definition

The general definition of an agent under Hong Kong law is the same as that at common law. However, there are statutory provisions governing specific types of agent, such as dealers in securities/commodities, barristers and solicitors, estate agents and insurance brokers, etc. with the common law applying to other, more generic types of agents in a slightly different way. Just as in the UK, the term "agency" is used indiscriminately in Hong Kong to describe a wide range of different business relationships, some of which would more correctly be described as direct sale, distribution or licensing agreements. **14–06**

14.1.2 Carrying on business in Hong Kong

As a general rule, the appointment of a local agent by a foreign principal will mean that the principal will be deemed to carry on business in Hong Kong. The question of whether or not a "non-resident" is carrying on business in Hong Kong most often arises in the context of determining if Hong Kong profits tax is payable by the non-resident. Profits tax is payable only if the Inland Revenue can establish that the non-resident "is carrying on a trade, profession or business in Hong Kong". The comparable test in the UK is whether the non-resident is carrying on a "trade, profession or vocation". The two tests are similar enough for decisions of the UK courts (in cases such as *Werle & Co v Colquhoun* (1888) 2 T.C. 402, CA; *Grainger & Son v Gough* (1896) 3 T.C. 462, HL; *MacPherson & Co v Moore* (1912) 6 T.C. 107; *Jabbour v Custodian of Israeli Absentee Property* [1954] 1 W.L.R. 139; and *Adams v Cape Industries Plc* [1990] 1 Ch. 433) to be considered persuasive, although "business" would seem to be slightly wider in scope encompassing most activities of a commercial nature. **14–07**

The classic distinction is between trading in Hong Kong and trading with Hong Kong. Unlike other jurisdictions, there is no requirement that a foreign entity has to have a permanent establishment before it will be subject to local profits tax—simply carrying on business in Hong Kong will suffice. The concept of permanent establishment is recognised under Hong Kong **14–08** law although, rather confusingly, this is defined in the rules for calculating the amount of assessable profits rather than in the legislation for determining whether profits tax is actually payable. The setting up of a permanent establishment is not, then, a prerequisite for the payment of profits tax but it will mean that profits tax is payable.

14–09 The appointment of an agent can, in certain circumstances, lead to the principal being considered as having a permanent establishment, although the Inland Revenue Rules state that this will not be the case unless the agent:

- has, and habitually exercises, a general authority to negotiate and conclude contracts on behalf of his principal; or
- has a stock of merchandise from which he regularly fills orders on behalf of his principal.

14–10 The main determining factor is whether or not the agent has the right to negotiate and enter into contracts on behalf of the principal. If the agent has this right, the principal will be deemed to have a permanent establishment in Hong Kong and will be subject to Hong Kong profits tax. If the agent does not have this right (but is, for example, a marketing or introductory agent who simply introduces customers to the principal or acts as a liaison officer between customer and principal) the principal is not likely to be deemed to be carrying on a business in Hong Kong.

14–11 An agent who has no general authority to negotiate contracts on behalf of his principal, but who maintains a stock of products from which he fulfils orders, is commonly termed a "consignment agent". The appointment of a consignment agent will mean that the principal will be deemed to have a permanent establishment in Hong Kong and therefore will be carrying on business in Hong Kong. However, in *Sulley v AG* (1860) 2 T.C. 149 the court held that the appointment of an agent in Hong Kong to purchase goods on behalf of a principal for shipment outside Hong Kong did not mean that the principal was carrying on business in Hong Kong.

14–12 In addition to being chargeable to profits tax, a foreign principal carrying on business in Hong Kong:

- will have to apply for and maintain a business registration certificate; and
- may have to register with the Registrar of Companies in Hong Kong as an oversea company.

14.1.3 Business registration certificate

14–13 All persons carrying on business in Hong Kong are required to apply for a business registration certificate. Although the Business Registration Ordinance (Cap 310) ("BRO") does not define "carrying on a business", an application under the BRO is made to the Commissioner of Inland Revenue and it is therefore likely that the Commissioner will apply the "taxation test". The provisions of the BRO apply even if the foreign principal does not have a "place of business" in Hong Kong and is, therefore, not required to register as an "oversea company" in Hong Kong. If the principal considers that it will be deemed to be carrying on business in Hong Kong, it should include a term in the agency agreement requiring the agent to obtain a business registration certificate on its behalf, to maintain the certificate during the continuance of the agency and to provide it with a copy of the certificate, and of each renewal.

14.1.4 Registration as an overseas company

A company incorporated outside Hong Kong which establishes a place of business in Hong Kong is required to register as an oversea company with the Registrar of Companies. The relevant test is not whether the oversea company is carrying on business, but whether it establishes a place of business in Hong Kong. The Companies Ordinance (Cap 32) defines place of business as including "... any place used for the manufacture or warehousing of goods, but does not include a place not used by the company to transact any business which creates legal relations ...". The double negative is confusing, but it is suggested that if the principal appoints an agent with the authority to negotiate and conclude contracts in Hong Kong and the agent commonly does so, the safest course of action would be to treat the agent's office as a place of business of the principal in Hong Kong—since it would be "used by the company to transact business which creates legal relations"—and for the principal to register in Hong Kong as an oversea company. If registration is required, particulars of the principal's constitution, officers and accounts must be delivered to the Registrar within one month of the establishment of the place of business and the principal will have to nominate one or more persons resident in Hong Kong to accept service on its behalf. **14–14**

14.1.5 Taxation

Under the Inland Revenue Ordinance (Cap 112) ("IRO"), companies carrying on business in Hong Kong are liable to profits tax in respect of profits arising in or derived from Hong Kong. Profits tax is the equivalent of corporation tax in the UK and is currently charged at the standard rate of 16 per cent. Only Hong Kong source income is generally subject to profits tax—the principal is not required to pay Hong Kong tax on profits earned outside Hong Kong. By virtue of s.2(1) of the IRO "profits arising in or derived from Hong Kong" are deemed to include all profits from business transacted in Hong Kong through an agent. Profits are calculated in accordance with generally accepted accounting principles in Hong Kong, which are similar to those in the UK, as adjusted to comply with the specific **14–15** requirements of the IRO. Certain receipts, such as dividends and profits arising from the sale of capital assets are specifically excluded from the charge to profits tax. Hong Kong has no capital gains tax.

14–16 Once the Revenue determines that the principal has a permanent establishment in Hong Kong, it is entitled to assess the principal to profits tax. The assessment can be made by the Revenue on the basis of:

- the amount of profits shown by the principal in its accounts as being attributable to Hong Kong; or
- Hong Kong profits and world-wide profits on the basis of the percentage that Hong Kong turnover bears to the world-wide turnover (if there are no accounts or if the Revenue considers that such accounts do not show the true amount of profits); or
- on the basis of a fair percentage of Hong Kong turnover (where it would be impractical or unfair to use either of the methods set out above).

14–17 The appointment of a consignment agent has two implications as far as taxation is concerned. First, the principal will be liable to Hong Kong profits tax on his assessable profits calculated on one of the bases set out above. Second, the proceeds of sale of such products will give rise to an immediate tax liability, sometimes referred to as "consignment tax", which is treated as an advance payment of profits tax. A consignment agent is required to:

- file quarterly returns with the Commissioner, showing the gross proceeds from such sales; and (at the same time)
- pay to the Commissioner a sum equal to 1 per cent of such proceeds or such lesser sum as may be agreed by the Commissioner (in practice the Commissioner usually agrees to accept 0.5 per cent of gross proceeds).

14–18 Although the Revenue is entitled to assess the principal on the basis of its actual profits—whilst giving credit for the consignment tax already paid by the consignment agent—it usually accepts the consignment tax as the ultimate tax liability. In theory, if the principal considers that its tax liability is less than the amount of the consignment tax, it could elect to be taxed on the basis of its actual profits. The IRO contains provisions (similar to s.126 of the UK Finance Act 1995) which allow the Inland Revenue to assess the principal for profits tax:

- directly; or
- in the name of the agent

and to recover the tax from the agent whether or not the agent has received such profits.

As only income arising in or derived from Hong Kong is subject to tax, there is usually no need to consider double taxation relief. If the principal is not considered to be carrying on business in Hong Kong, any Hong Kong source income will not be taxed in Hong Kong but will be taxed exclusively in the jurisdiction in which the principal is resident. However, non-residents who receive royalties or licence fees in return for the use of certain industrial or intellectual property are liable to profits tax on such receipts (see Chapter 14.3.3). **14–19**

14.1.6 Specific product legislation

There is no specific legislation in Hong Kong regulating the international sale of goods, with much of the domestic sale of goods legislation therefore applying to the international sale of goods. The Sale of Goods Ordinance (Cap 26) (based on the UK Sale of Goods Act 1893) contains the usual terms relating to risk, property and title in goods and implies terms relating to fitness for purpose and merchantable quality, etc. In practice, buyers and sellers usually adopt one of the international forms such as CIF or FOB Incoterms (2000) produced by the International Chamber of Commerce. **14–20**

The categories set out below detail the main types of goods which are subject to licensing, labelling or packaging requirements for their import into and/or sale in Hong Kong: **14–21**

- dangerous goods;
- dutiable commodities (alcohol, tobacco, oil and certain cosmetic products);
- foodstuffs;
- pesticides and chemicals;
- pharmaceutical products;
- telecommunications equipment;
- textiles.

By way of example, all foodstuffs sold in Hong Kong must comply with legislation regulating their labelling and colouring and their harmful additives and preservatives content. The sale of pharmaceutical products is carefully controlled and there are also restrictions on how these products are advertised for sale. Apart from the categories of goods set out above there are few requirements for the labelling of goods on sale in Hong Kong. Note however that under the Consumer Goods Safety Regulations, where consumer goods are marked with any warning or caution with respect to their safe-keeping, use, consumption or disposal, the warning or caution must be in both English and Chinese. Furthermore, the Trade Descriptions Ordinance (Cap 362) prohibits the application of false trade descriptions or false **14–22** trade marks to goods. "Trade description" is widely defined and includes any indication of the quantity, size or gauge, method of manufacture, composition, fitness for purpose, physical characteristics or place or date of manufacture.

14–23 Historically, there have been few safety requirements for goods sold in Hong Kong, but there are now two safety-specific Ordinances in force which impose minimum safety standards.

14–24 The Toys and Children's Products Safety Ordinance (Cap 424) prohibits the manufacture, import or supply of toys or children's products unless these comply with specified international, European or American standards for the safety of such products. Furthermore, the Consumer Goods Safety Ordinance (Cap 456) contains a more general requirement that consumer goods be reasonably safe and comply with the appropriate safety standard or safety specification determined by the Hong Kong Secretary for Trade and Industry. Unlike the UK legislation, which covers only suppliers, the Hong Kong legislation also extends to manufacturers and importers. The Commissioner of Customs and Excise is given extensive powers under both Ordinances to test goods, to warn manufacturers, importers and suppliers that their goods do not meet the appropriate safety standards and to prohibit their manufacture, import or supply, or require their withdrawal from sale in Hong Kong. Customs and Excise are also empowered to inspect and seize offending goods. Offences under both Ordinances are punishable by fines of up to HK$100,000 and one year's imprisonment (for the first offence) and HK$500,000 and two years' imprisonment (subsequent offences).

14–25 There is no specific product liability legislation equivalent to, say, the UK Consumer Protection Act 1987. Detailed advice should always be sought with regard to specific products.

14.1.7 Authority of agent to bind principal

14–26 The UK legal concepts of actual and apparent or ostensible authority apply in Hong Kong. Thus a principal will be bound by the acts of its agent only if the agency agreement gives the agent actual authority, either expressly or impliedly, to bind the principal, or if the agent has apparent authority to act on the principal's behalf. As in the UK, apparent authority depends on a representation by the principal to the third party that the agent has the ability to bind the principal. To succeed in a claim against the principal the third party must establish that a representation of this type has been made and that it has acted on the representation. Unless the principal makes such representations to third parties it will not be bound by the unauthorised acts of its agent.

14.1.8 Del credere guarantee

It is not common for agents in Hong Kong to guarantee the payment of sums due from third parties under contracts entered into by the agent on behalf of the principal (a so called "del credere agent"). Hong Kong agents asked to accept such liability would certainly require additional commission. No specific formalities or documentation are required for a guarantee of this type. The UK Statute of Frauds 1677 has been repealed in Hong Kong and therefore guarantees need not be in writing and may be proved in the same way as any other contract. As a guarantee is simply a form of contract, albeit a rather specialised one, the usual rules apply. It must: **14–27**

- either have consideration or be under seal;
- be executed by the guarantor; and
- identify the parties and all material terms.

The guarantee should also contain the usual clauses:

- extending the guarantee to any variation or amendment of the underlying agreement;
- preventing the guarantor from claiming against the third party until the principal has received all sums due from the third party or the guarantor; and
- stating that the guarantee will not be discharged by the winding up or liquidation of the debtor.

It would be to the principal's advantage to include a term stating that the certificate of the principal as to the amount of the sums due from the third parties would be deemed to be conclusive and binding on the guarantor. Since a guarantee of a void debt is itself void it might also be preferable for the principal to obtain an indemnity in this regard. **14–28**

14.1.9 Intellectual property protection—trade mark

Trade marks are registrable in Hong Kong. Registration is currently governed by the Trade Marks Ordinance (Cap 43) ("TMO") which is similar to the UK Trade Marks Act 1938. This Ordinance was due to be repealed by the Trade Marks Ordinance (Cap 559), which was approved by Hong Kong's Legislative Council in 2000 but which is not in operation as at the date of this publication. The new Ordinance would bring Hong Kong's trade mark law in line with the UK Trade Marks Act 1994 and, *inter alia*, permit the registration of shapes, sounds and smells. **14–29**

Companies intending to carry on business in Hong Kong should first register their trade marks, as registration facilitates and speeds the enfor- **14–30** cement of such trade marks. Section 27(1) of the TMO provides that registration confers the exclusive right to use the trade mark and that such a right will be infringed by any unauthorised use in the course of trade of a mark identical to or so nearly resembling the registered trade mark as to be likely to deceive or cause confusion. For exceptionally well known and distinctive marks, it may be possible to register a defensive trade mark, even if the owner does not intend to use the trade mark in respect of the class of goods/services in which the application is made. Unless an application for a defensive mark is to be made, the application must designate a particular class of goods or services. There are two types of registration: Part A and Part B, the basic difference being that the requirements for registration under Part A are more onerous and that the holder of a Part B registration may not be entitled to an injunction or other relief in an action for infringement where the defendant establishes that the use of the trade mark of which the plaintiff complains is not likely to deceive or cause confusion. The new Trade Marks Ordinance (Cap 559) will do away with the distinctions between Part A and Part B. On acceptance of an application a certificate is issued and backdated to the date of the application. Registration lasts for seven years and is renewable for periods of 14 years. Note that an application to register the trade mark in any country which is a member of the Paris Convention will give the applicant priority back to the date of such application in respect of any application to register in Hong Kong.

14–31 There are no restrictions on the licensing of trade marks in Hong Kong. However, where the agent or distributor will be using the principal's trade mark under licence, it is advisable to register the agent as a registered user. This is to set out the rights of, and restrictions on, the agent with regard to the use of the trade mark and to ensure that the use by the agent of the trade mark is considered to be use by the owner. Use by the agent will then mean that the owner, rather than the agent, will acquire rights through such use of the trade mark. The goods and/or the packaging should be labelled with the universal trade mark symbol, to indicate that they carry a trade mark, and should state the owner of the trade mark. This will help to establish not only that an infringer knew of the existence of the trade mark, and that the copying of that trade mark would lead to confusion, but also that the trade mark belongs to the owner and not the licensee. A registered user agreement cannot be registered until the trade mark itself is registered. This is another reason why owners should give serious consideration to the registration of their trade marks in Hong Kong before the appointment of a local agent or distributor who intends to make use of such marks.

14.1.10 Termination and compensation

14–32 An agency agreement can be terminated either by agreement between the parties or by operation of law. The parties are entitled to agree the provisions relating to termination in the agreement, but in the absence of such provisions the agreement will be terminable by the principal on reasonable notice. The events of breach giving rise to a right to terminate under Hong Kong law are the same as in the UK—breach of confidence, breach of the duty of loyalty, etc. If the agent terminates the agreement due to the breach of the principal, the agent is entitled to damages for breach of contract and these are calculated on the usual basis. It is always preferable to set out the grounds for, and effects of, termination in the agreement itself.

There is no equivalent of the Commercial Agents (Council Directive) Regulations 1993 in Hong Kong. No compensation will be payable to the agent if the agency agreement terminates by agreement, expiry, performance, frustration or the insolvency of either the agent or the principal. **14–33**

14.1.11 Corrupt gifts and secret commissions

Hong Kong has an unfortunate reputation for unethical business practices including the giving of corrupt gifts and the payment of secret commissions. The Hong Kong government recognises this fact and has taken a number of steps to improve Hong Kong's image. These steps include the establishment of the Independent Commission Against Corruption ("ICAC") and the passing of the Prevention of Bribery Ordinance (Cap 201) ("PBO"). **14–34**

The ICAC was established in 1974 in response to growing fears regarding corrupt practices in Hong Kong. It is an independent body reporting directly to the Chief Executive and is, among other things, charged with considering and investigating complaints alleging corruption, as well as suspected offences under the following Ordinances: **14–35**

- the ICAC Ordinance (Cap 204);
- the Elections (Corrupt and Illegal Conduct) Ordinance (Cap 554);
- the PBO.

The ICAC has wide-ranging investigative powers, including powers to detain and question suspects, to search premises, to seize accounts and other documents and to require suspects to declare their assets and income specifying how, when and where such assets were obtained. **14–36**

An agent in Hong Kong owes his principal the usual duties to avoid conflicts of interest, to disclose interests in contracts etc, but these common law rules have been supplemented by the criminal sanctions set out in s.9 of the PBO which deals with corrupt transactions with agents. The main offence is set out at subsection (1) below: **14–37**

> "Any agent who, without lawful authority or reasonable excuse, solicits or accepts any advantage as an inducement to or reward for or otherwise on account of his—
>
> (a) doing or forbearing to do, or having done or forborne to do, any act in relation to his principal's affairs or business; or

(b) showing or forbearing to show, or having shown or forborne to show, favour or disfavour to any person in relation to his principal's affairs or business,

shall be guilty of an offence."

14–38 Section 9 is rather inelegantly drafted and is difficult to interpret. The ICAC has published a statement which, although not legally binding, sets out its view on what it considers to be the main provisions of the Ordinance:

> "In simple terms, the Law makes it an offence for an agent to solicit or accept without his principal's permission an advantage as an inducement to or reward for doing something in relation to the principal's business."

14–39 "Advantage" is widely defined and covers any gift, loan, fee, reward or commission in money or other terms, any office, employment or contract, any payment, release or discharge of a loan, obligation or other liability or any other service or favour. Subject to a general requirement of reasonableness, it does not apply to providing food, drink or other entertainment for clients or potential customers. Given the wide definition it is possible for almost anything to constitute an advantage but note that the agent will not commit an offence if he accepts such an advantage with the principal's consent. In short, s.9 does not prevent the receipt of commissions by an agent provided the principal is aware of these and has given his consent. In this way, lawful commissions are distinguished from secret payments or bribes made to agents at the expense of their principal, for example, in return for the agent placing orders with particular customers.

14.1.12 Formalities

14–40 There are no special formalities for the execution or witnessing of agency agreements. No governmental approval is required and there are no registration requirements. No stamp duty is payable on the execution of such agreements. If the agent is a company, it is prudent for the principal to require a board minute of the agent approving the agency agreement and authorising the signatory to sign the agreement on behalf of the agent. While an agency agreement does not have to be under seal, it can be if the parties so require. There is no equivalent to s.36A of the UK Companies Act 1985 providing that companies may dispense with their common seal. Companies incorporated in Hong Kong are required by s.16(2) of the Companies Ordinance to have a common seal which must be affixed to deeds in accordance with their articles of association (s.32(1)(a)).

14.1.13 Exchange controls—withholding tax

There are no foreign exchange controls in Hong Kong. Apart from the consignment tax described in Chapter 14.1.5 above and the withholding tax payable in respect of royalties or licence fees for the use of foreign industrial or intellectual property rights (described in Chapter 14.3.6) the agent is generally free to remit out of Hong Kong all moneys collected on behalf of the principal. **14–41**

14.1.14 Ownership issues—tracing

It is important for the agreement to make it clear that the agent holds all stocks of the product as bailee for the principal. This is to ensure, as far as possible, that the principal can establish ownership of the goods, and so will be entitled to assert its rights of ownership over the goods against third parties, including a receiver, liquidator or trustee in bankruptcy in the event of the insolvency of the agent. To facilitate identification of goods belonging to the principal, these should be appropriately marked and, if possible, stored separately from any goods belonging to the agent. Hong Kong's Factors Ordinance (Cap 48) is identical in all material respects to the UK Factors Act 1889. This means that it is essential for the agreement to extend the principal's ownership to any proceeds of sale and book debts in respect of such goods. This is because, under the Factors Ordinance, a third party purchaser for value who is not aware that the goods are owned by the principal will obtain good title to the goods irrespective of whether or not the principal has consented to the sale, provided that the agent is in possession of such goods with the consent of the principal. The ability of the principal to trace its claim to the proceeds of sale depends on the same factors as in the UK. To facilitate tracing, the agreement should: **14–42**

- state that the agent holds any proceeds of sale on trust for the principal; and
- require all such proceeds to be paid into a separate trust account in the name of the agent as trustee for the principal.

There are no formalities, legal procedures or registration requirements necessary for the principal to obtain or preserve any of its rights to the goods.

14.2 Distribution agreements

14.2.1 Definition

14–43 As in the UK, the term "distributor" is used to refer to an independent operator who purchases goods on its own account for resale to third parties at its own risk. Consequently, there is no contractual relationship between the principal and the distributor's customers. Distribution agreements are very common in Hong Kong. One reason for this is that people in Hong Kong resent any attempts by outsiders, particularly foreigners, to control their business activities. They prefer the freedom that a distribution agreement gives them to trade on their own terms, arguing that they are in the best position to judge the market as a result of their local knowledge and contracts.

14.2.2 Carrying on business in Hong Kong

14–44 As a general rule, the appointment of a local distributor will not result in the foreign principal being deemed to carry on business in Hong Kong. The relevant test is set out in Chapter 14.1.2. The principal must be "carrying on a trade, profession or business in Hong Kong". Where all the principal does is to sell goods to a Hong Kong distributor it will, in the absence of any other trading activity in Hong Kong, be deemed to be trading *with* Hong Kong, with no attendant registration requirements. However, if the principal opens a sales office in Hong Kong or even simply uses a warehouse to store goods prior to sale, it may be deemed to be trading *in* Hong Kong. If so, the registration requirements set out in Chapter 14.1.3 and 14.1.4 will apply.

14.2.3 Taxation—withholding tax

14–45 Profits tax is payable only if the principal carries on business in Hong Kong. It will not be payable as a result of the appointment of a local distributor unless the principal is otherwise deemed to be carrying on business in Hong Kong. If so, the Hong Kong source income of the principal will be subject to profits tax as set out in Chapter 14.1.5. Only Hong Kong source income is taxable.

14–46 Despite the fact that the principal is not carrying on business in Hong Kong certain receipts, such as royalties or licence fees for the use of industrial or intellectual property in Hong Kong, are, by virtue of s.15(1)(b) of the IRO, deemed to constitute Hong Kong source receipts of a business carried on in Hong Kong. It is not common for distributors to purchase goods and to make separate payments for the use of the intellectual property rights relating to such goods, but if payments of this nature are made, either to the principal or to a third party who holds such rights, the recipient will be taxed on these receipts even if it is not otherwise carrying on business in Hong Kong. Assessable profits are deemed to be 10 per cent of the gross amount of such payments. A Hong Kong distributor who uses foreign industrial or intellectual property rights and who pays a non-resident a royalty or licence fee is required to withhold 10 per cent of the gross amount of such royalty or licence fee and to retain this until the Revenue requires payment (see also Chapter 14.3.6).

14.2.4 Intellectual property rights

Many countries, the US in particular, have been critical of Hong Kong's record on the protection of intellectual property rights. The reality is that Hong Kong has a well structured and comprehensive set of intellectual property laws and is in the process of upgrading these in line with its international commitments, such as those under the Agreement on Trade Related Aspects of Intellectual Property Rights (a subsidiary agreement to the agreement establishing the World Trade Organisation (WTO)), usually referred to by its acronym "TRIPS". Rather than a lack of law, the problem is one of enforcement. **14–47**

For a number of years Hong Kong has been flooded with pirated software and music from the PRC which, according to the Hong Kong government, has swamped local law enforcement efforts. Counterfeit software, DVDs, VCDs and music CDs together accounted for over 90 per cent of the cases handled by Customs and Excise in Hong Kong in 2001. Counterfeit watches, leather goods and clothing are also a common problem. According to Customs and Excise, one of their major problems is establishing the subsistence of copyright and who owns such copyright. This is particularly difficult where copyright vests in a foreign owner who does not have an agent or distributor in Hong Kong charged with monitoring infringement and assisting in the protection and enforcement of such rights, or where the owner's intellectual property rights are not protected by one of the representative bodies such as the Business Software Alliance (computer software) or the International Federation of the Phonographic Industry (sound recordings). **14–48**

The following statutory provisions regulate the protection of intellectual property in Hong Kong: **14–49**

- Copyright Ordinance (Cap 528);
- Layout-Design (Topography) of Integrated Circuits Ordinance (Cap 445);
- Patents Ordinance (Cap 514);
- Trade Descriptions Ordinance (Cap 362);

- Trade Marks Ordinance (Cap 43);
- Registered Designs Ordinance (Cap 522);
- Prevention of Copyright Piracy Ordinance (Cap 544).

14–50 Trade marks have already been considered in Chapter 14.1.9. Similar considerations apply if a distributor is to use any of the principal's trade marks, particularly the requirement that such trade mark(s) should be registered in Hong Kong and that the distributor should enter into a registered user agreement. Copyright and design rights are considered in Chapter 14.2.4.1 and 14.2.4.2 and patents are discussed in Chapter 14.3.3.

14.2.4.1 Copyright

14–51 Although copyright law in Hong Kong is similar to that in the UK, it is not identical. One reason for this is that, although the Copyright Ordinance was amended in 1997 to bring it in line with most of the copyright provisions of the UK Copyright Designs and Patents Act 1988, some elements from the UK Copyright Act 1956 (on which the Copyright Ordinance was originally based) have remained. Furthermore, in an effort to enhance the protection of copyright against piracy, the Hong Kong Government passed the Intellectual Property (Miscellaneous Amendments) Ordinance ("IPMAO") in 2000 which broadened the Copyright Ordinance's definition of activities which could constitute infringement of copyright, particularly in relation to the bootlegging of movies and the corporate use of infringing copyright works. The legislation was so broadly drafted, however, that it criminalised certain activities which hitherto came within the scope of fair use. The government was pressured into passing the Copyright (Suspension of Amendments) Ordinance in 2001, under which the effects of the IPMAO were suspended (currently until the end of July 2003) save in relation to four specific categories of works, namely films, television drama, sound and visual recordings of musical works and computer software.

14–52 Save for these differences, the position under Hong Kong law is broadly similar to the UK law. There is no registration procedure. Copyright subsists automatically in all literary, dramatic, musical and artistic works; television and sound broadcasts; sound recordings; cinematograph films; and the published editions of literary, dramatic or musical works provided that such works are original. Copyright normally subsists for the life of the author plus 50 years (in the case of computer-generated works, the 50-year period runs from the end of the calendar year in which the work was made), but where the artistic work is *applied industrially* and a corresponding design is registered or capable of registration (under the Registered Designs Ordinance) the copyright period is reduced to 15 years from the date of first publication.

14–53 Pursuant to s.22(2) of the Copyright Ordinance, copyright is infringed if any person without the licence of the copyright owner does, or authorises another to do, any of the acts restricted by the copyright. The restricted acts are categorised either as (presumably direct) infringement or secondary infringement. Thus, reproducing the work in any material form will be a direct infringement but the import, export, possession of or dealing with (or providing the means for making infringing copies) of a copyright work will be only a secondary infringement. The importance of the categories lies in the fact that, to bring successful proceedings for secondary infringement, the party alleging secondary infringement of copyright must establish that the alleged infringer knew or had reason to believe that they were importing, exporting, in possession of, dealing with or providing the means for making such infringing copies.

The Copyright Ordinance sets out a number of criminal offences in relation to the infringement of copyright, but the recent revisions to the Copyright Ordinance mean that the offence depends on the type of work being infringed. Generally speaking, any person who possesses, for the purposes of a trade or business, an infringing copy of a work, or other subject matter in which copyright subsists, is guilty of a criminal offence, although it is a defence if the person accused did not know or have reason to believe that it was an infringing copy. However, in relation to the four specified categories of works (films, television drama, sound and visual recordings of musical works and computer software), there is a much broader requirement of possession "for the purpose of, or in the course of" any trade or business. The additional words "in the course of" were added so as to dispense with the common perception that the original wording of the section ("for the purpose of") applied only to those whose business purpose was trading in infringing copies.

Regardless of the type of work being infringed, goods should be labelled **14–54** to indicate that copyright subsists in them. This can be done by including a statement to this effect on the goods themselves or the packaging for the goods and by the use of the universal copyright symbol. Labelling will assist in establishing that the infringer knew that the unauthorised goods breached the copyright belonging to someone else and improve the chances of success of any criminal proceedings or civil proceedings for secondary infringement. The Copyright Ordinance allows the copyright owner to swear an affidavit claiming ownership of copyright and to exhibit a true copy of the copyright work. This affidavit is admissible in evidence to prove ownership of copyright without further proof.

14.2.4.2 Design rights

Industrial drawings and designs are protectable under both the general **14–55** copyright law (the copyright in an industrial design drawing will be infringed if the product of such design is reproduced without the consent of the copyright owner) and under the legislation relating to registered designs. Since 1997 Hong Kong has had its own independent system for the registration of designs under the Registered Designs Ordinance (Cap 522)

("RDO"), which replaced the colonial regime under which designs which were registered in the UK under the Registered Designs Act 1949 were enforceable in Hong Kong under the old UK Designs (Protection) Ordinance.

14–56 The old law is still relevant, as the validity of designs either registered or applied for in the UK prior to the date on which the RDO came into force (June 27, 1997) is determined in accordance with the UK's Registered Designs Act 1949 (as amended by the Copyright, Designs and Patents Act 1988). The RDO is based on the 1949 Act as amended, save for one significant difference—the RDO assesses novelty on a world-wide basis, whereas the 1949 legislation as amended considers novelty on the basis of designs published only in the UK (and, by extension to its then-territory, Hong Kong).

14–57 In relation to new designs, a person who has filed an application for registration of a design in a country which is a signatory to the Paris Convention or a WTO member will gain priority for a period of six months from the date of the original application to register the same design under the RDO. Once registered, designs are protected for an initial period of five years, and renewable for successive five-year periods up to a maximum of 25 years.

14–58 There are two methods of enforcement of intellectual property rights in Hong Kong: criminal and civil. If a complaint is made to Customs and Excise they may be prepared to raid premises, seize goods and take criminal proceedings for infringement of intellectual property rights. The owner of the intellectual property rights is also entitled to bring civil proceedings against the infringer.

14.2.5 Terms of appointment

14–59 The main difference between a UK based distribution agreement and a distribution agreement for use in Hong Kong will be the absence of any provisions necessary to comply with UK or European anti-competitive or regulatory controls. Hong Kong currently has no anti-competitive legislation or restrictive trade practices legislation (although see the introduction to this Chapter regarding Hong Kong's efforts in this regard), leaving the principal free to contract with distributors on whatever terms it considers fit. There are no restrictions on the principal charging one or more distributors different prices whether or not such distributors are appointed for the whole Territory or separately defined areas within Hong Kong. Subject to the common law rules on restraint of trade discussed below, the principal is free to dictate resale prices, to restrict the distributor from selling in particular areas or to particular clients and to require the distributor to maintain whatever stocks of the product the principal deems appropriate.

14.2.6 Unfair practices

The principal is also free to prohibit the distributor from engaging in any activity which the principal considers to be "unfair". The law relating to consumer protection in Hong Kong is less well developed than that in the UK, but there are a small number of consumer protection Ordinances, most of which are modelled on UK legislation. Examples include: **14–60**

- the Sale of Goods Ordinance (Cap 26) (based on the UK Sale of Goods Acts) which prohibits exclusion of the implied terms as to the seller's right to sell, merchantable quality and fitness for purpose when selling to consumers; and
- the Control of Exemption Clauses Ordinance (Cap 71) (discussed in Chapter 14.2.13).

The Unconscionable Contracts Ordinance ("UCO") (Cap 458) is another piece of consumer protection legislation which is specifically aimed at unfair practices. It applies only to consumer contracts. If the court finds the contract or any part of the contract to have been unconscionable it may: **14–61**

- refuse to enforce the contract;
- enforce the remainder of the contract without the unconscionable term; or
- limit the application of, or revise or alter any unconscionable part so as to avoid any unconscionable result.

The Ordinance does not define the word "unconscionable", although it does provide a non-exhaustive list of the matters to be considered by the court in determining whether or not a clause is unconscionable. The intention behind the legislation may have been to enable the courts to censor misleading or deceptive behaviour in a similar way to legislation in other countries, such as s.52 of the Australian Trade Practice Rules. The Ordinance does not specifically require there to have been misleading or deceptive conduct, but it is likely that any such conduct will now render certain terms in a contract entered into as a result, unconscionable. In the limited number of cases (primarily covering credit card contracts) concerning the UCO since its introduction, the Hong Kong Courts have interpreted the UCO as granting the Courts new powers, unshackled by the traditional theories of contract law, to do justice in consumer contracts particularly where the bargaining power is unequal and the consumer has no choice over terms contained in standard form contracts. **14–62**

14.2.7 Liquidated damages—contracting out

14–63 The rules governing liquidated damages in Hong Kong are the same as in the UK. Liquidated damages clauses are acceptable provided that the payment for delay or non-performance represents a genuine pre-estimate of loss. Where such clauses impose payments which bear no relation to the loss caused by the breach in question, they are open to challenge on the basis that they constitute a penalty. If the court finds a term to be a penalty it will be ineffective and the party alleging breach will be left to rely on the court to assess damages on the normal contractual basis.

14–64 There is nothing to prevent the principal from stipulating that it will not be liable to the distributor for the failure to meet delivery dates or from refusing to agree to fixed delivery dates at all. Indeed, it is also possible for the principal to contract out of the implied terms relating to fitness for purpose, merchantable quality, etc. Terms excluding liability for special, indirect and consequential loss (including loss of profits or economic loss) are very common and have been upheld by the Hong Kong courts.

14.2.8 Specific product legislation

14–65 These are discussed in Chapter 14.1.6. It is usual for the principal to require the distributor to comply with all applicable legislation with regard to the importation, storage, packaging, labelling, advertising and sale of products in Hong Kong and to indemnify the principal against any claim by a third party in that regard.

14.2.9 Authority of distributor to bind principal

14–66 Unless the distributor is given express or ostensible authority to bind the principal, it will not be entitled to do so under Hong Kong law. It is advisable to set out not only that the distributor is not entitled to bind the principal, but also that the distributor must always describe itself as an "authorised" distributor.

14.2.10 Compensation

14–67 The right to compensation on the termination or expiry of an agency agreement is discussed in Chapter 14.1.10. The same rules apply to the termination or expiry of distribution agreements. Distributors have no statutory right to compensation. The rights of a distributor in this regard will be determined by the agreement itself or the general law.

14.2.11 Formalities

There are no specific formalities with regard to the execution or witnessing of distribution agreements. No stamp duty is payable in respect of such agreements and no prior governmental approval is necessary. **14–68**

14.2.12 Exchange controls

Hong Kong has no exchange controls. **14–69**

14.2.13 Exclusion of liability for defective goods or services

The Control of Exemption Clauses Ordinance (Cap 71) ("CECO") is based on the UK Unfair Contract Terms Act 1977 and in the same way prohibits any attempt to exclude liability for death or personal injury in business or consumer contracts. In its contract with the distributor, the principal can exclude or restrict liability for negligence and the implied terms as to merchantability and fitness for purpose only to the extent that it satisfies the "reasonableness" test. The same will apply for the distributor's contracts with its customers, save for those that are consumers, in which case the implied warranties may not be excluded at all. **14–70**

14.2.14 Selective distribution systems

There are currently no regulatory controls or anti-competitive legislation in Hong Kong which would prevent a principal establishing a selective distribution system. **14–71**

14.3 Manufacturing agreements

Hong Kong is one of the leading manufacturing centres in the world, although much of the actual manufacturing has now moved to factories in Southern China to take advantage of lower labour costs and tax incentives in the PRC. **14–72**

14.3.1 Technology transfer

There is no legislation controlling the transfer of technology to a licensee in Hong Kong. Parties are free to agree whatever terms they consider appropriate. The Hong Kong government encourages technology transfer through an inward investment programme and in fact formed the Hong **14–73**

Kong Science & Technology Parks Corporation in May 2001 to establish purpose-built environments with a view to facilitating the promotion of technological innovation and the application of new technologies in Hong Kong. Furthermore, the government's Digital 21 initiative has been the centrepiece of its efforts to encourage Hong Kong's development as a high tech centre, and has seen the government taking steps to deregulate the telecommunications industry and promote broadband internet connectivity throughout the region.

14.3.2 Terms of trade

14–74 Manufacturing agreements in Hong Kong tend to be much simpler than those for use in the EC, the main reason being that it is not currently necessary to ensure that the agreement complies with EC and/or UK anti-competitive legislation. There are no mandatory terms or terms which must be excluded from such agreements. It is possible to impose an export ban on the licensee during the term of the licence agreement. There is no equivalent of the EC Technology Transfer Block Exemption (Reg.240/96). Subject to the common law requirements relating to restraint of trade, there is nothing currently to prevent licensors from requiring licensees to purchase ingredients, components or packaging either from specified suppliers or from the principal, irrespective of whether or not these are technically vital for the proper manufacture of the products. A principal is free to impose different scales of royalties and different terms on one or more licensees who may be assigned exclusive areas within Hong Kong and to impose restrictions on to whom they may sell the products and at what price.

14.3.3 Intellectual property protection—patents

14–75 Hong Kong has a reputation for reacting swiftly to new or innovative products. In addition to Hong Kong's increased ties to China resulting from its return to Chinese sovereignty, it is close to and has strong connections with many other countries in South-East Asia, all of which have low labour costs. The combination of these two factors has meant that it is not uncommon to find a copy product on sale in Hong Kong within days of the launch of the original product in the UK or Europe. New products can be protected in a number of ways. Trade marks have already been considered in relation to agency agreements at Chapter 14.1.9. In the case of manufacturing agreements similar considerations will apply if the licensee is to be entitled to use the principal's trade marks, particularly the requirements that trade marks should be registered in Hong Kong and that the licensee should enter into a registered user agreement in respect of such marks. Copyright and design rights are considered in Chapter 14.2.4.1 and 14.2.4.2 and apply equally to manufacturing agreements. It is particularly important when entering into manufacturing agreements with Hong Kong licensees to ensure that design rights are protected. New or innovative products may also be capable of patent protection.

Prior to 1997, patent protection in Hong Kong was based on the UK system and allowed the registration in Hong Kong of British and European Patents. However, an action for infringement of a patent in Hong Kong was not possible until the patent had been registered in Hong Kong. Under the old Registration of Patents (Hong Kong) Ordinance ("RPHKO"), the proprietor of a Hong Kong registered patent was granted the same rights—including a right of action for infringement of that patent in Hong Kong with the court being free to grant such relief as would be available to the plaintiff in the UK—as if the patent had been granted in the UK and extended to Hong Kong. **14–76**

However, Hong Kong got its own patent law upon its return to Chinese sovereignty. The Patents Ordinance (Cap 514) introduced a two-tier system for patent registration which was based on the old legislation with regard to standard patents (in so far as registration as a standard patent depends on patent registration elsewhere) but which also created a new, Hong Kong short-term patent. Note that the old legislation is still relevant in Hong Kong, as it applies to any infringements prior to the coming into force of the Patents Ordinance (June 27, 1997) and to applications for registration pending under the old legislation as at that date. **14–77**

The Patents Ordinance now provides for two forms of patent protection: **14–78**

- a standard patent—with a 20-year term;
- a short-term patent—with an eight year term.

Registration of standard patents will be based on the registration in Hong Kong of patents granted by a "designated patent office". Currently, only the UK Patent Office, the European Patent Office (in turn designating the UK) and the PRC's State Intellectual Property Office ("SIPO") are "designated patented offices". There is a two-stage application process for standard patents. First, within six months of the publication of the application for the patent to the designated patent office, the applicant must request that the Registrar of Patents records that designated patent application (called a "request to record"). The Registrar will check that an application for the patent has been made in a designated patent office and, provided the formalities have been complied with (such as the contents of the application and the due payment of filing and advertisement fees), must then record the application for the Hong Kong patent. Second, within six months of the later of the grant of the patent by the designated patent office and the publication of the request to record, the applicant must apply to the Registrar of Patents to request that the patent is registered in Hong Kong. After checking both that the patent has been granted by the designated patent office and that the request to record has been published, and provided the formalities regarding contents of the application and the due payment of filing and advertisement fees have been complied with, the Registrar must **14–79** register the patent in Hong Kong, grant a standard patent, issue a certificate and publish the patent specification. Once granted, the Hong Kong standard patent is independent of the patent granted in the designated patent office, save that the duration of the patent is 20 years from the date of filing the application in the designated patent office.

14–80 Since registration is little more than a formality and is not expensive, there is little excuse for failure to register a standard patent. Owners of British or European patents would be well advised to register their patents as a protective measure even if they have no current intention of selling their products in Hong Kong. As with trade marks and copyright, it is advisable to advertise registered patents in Hong Kong, giving details of the registration number, and for the patent registration details to be marked on the goods and/or their packaging.

14–81 The short-term patent, which can be registered independently of any application in a designated patent office, is designed to protect inventions with a short-term commercial life. Short-term patents are different from standard patents in that they are obtainable without the need to conduct a full search and have a maximum duration of eight years. Two types of application are also available—those which originate in Hong Kong and those which are based on international applications for utility models which designate China.

14–82 Where the application originates in Hong Kong, the applicant files with the Registrar of Patents a request for grant, a specification, an abstract and a prior art search report (which has to be conducted by one of the designated patent offices (the same as for standard patents) or the designated international searching authorities, which currently comprise the patent offices of Austria, Australia, Japan, Russia, Sweden and the USA as well as the European Patent Office). The Registrar considers the application to determine if the usual formalities have been complied with, but at no point does he consider substantive patent questions such as patentability. If the formalities are complied with, the Registrar must grant a short-term patent, although he may refuse a grant where he considers that the publication or working of the invention would be contrary to public order or morality.

14–83 An application based on an international application for a utility model patent designating China may apply for a short-term patent in Hong Kong. The application must be made within six months either of the application entering the national phase in China or of the date of issuance of the National Application Notification by the Chinese Patent Office, and must be accompanied by the prescribed documentation such as photocopies of the international search report and the translation of the international application published by the SIPO.

14–84 Note that the transitional provisions of s.3(1) of the Patents Ordinance provide that an existing registered patent (*i.e.* a UK or European registered patent) which was registered in Hong Kong under the old legislation is deemed to be a standard patent with effect from the date on which the Patents Ordinance came into force. In respect of any applications which were outstanding as at such date, the RPHKO continues to apply and, on grant, a certificate of registration is treated as issued on the day before the Patent Ordinance's commencement date and is then deemed to be a standard patent pursuant to s.3(1).

14.3.4 Technology transfer payments

The principal may require a licensee to pay an upfront fee for the transfer of technology rights to the licensee. There are no controls on such fees. The taxation of upfront fees is discussed in Chapter 14.2.3. 14–85

14.3.5 General issues

A number of the issues discussed above in relation to agency and distribution agreements also apply to manufacturing agreements. These are: 14–86

- specific product legislation—see Chapter 14.2.8;
- compensation on termination or expiry—see Chapter 14.1.10;
- formalities—see Chapter 14.2.11;
- restrictions on "unfair" trading practices—see Chapter 14.2.6;
- liquidated damages and penalties—see Chapter 14.2.7;
- authority to bind a principal—see Chapter 14.2.9; and
- exchange controls—see Chapter 14.2.12.

14.3.6 Taxation

The taxation of royalties is discussed in Chapter 14.2.3. Section 15(1)(b) of the IRO deems the following sums to be Hong Kong business receipts: 14–87

> "sums ... received by or accrued to a person for the use of or right to use in Hong Kong a patent, design, trade mark, copyright material or secret process or formula or other property of a similar nature, or for imparting or undertaking to impart knowledge directly or indirectly connected with the use in Hong Kong of any such patent, design, trade mark, copyright, secret process or formula or other property."

This section applies irrespective of whether or not the payments are made to a person who is resident in Hong Kong. The assessable profits of non-residents receiving such payments are deemed to be 10 per cent of the sums received.

Section 20B of the IRO allows the Revenue to assess Hong Kong residents directly for the profits tax if they pay to non-residents copyright 14–88 royalties or other payments for the use of intellectual property rights as set out in s.15(1)(b). Anyone liable to receive an assessment under s.20B is required to retain an amount out of such payments sufficient to pay the tax and is indemnified against the non-resident in respect of any sums so withheld. The legislation applies to a one-off or lump sum payment, provided such payment is made for the use of, or right to use, the intellectual property right in question. Payments for the outright sale of such rights will not be taxable. In short, there is a 10 per cent withholding tax on any payments to non-residents for the use of intellectual property rights in Hong Kong.

14.3.7 Royalties

14–89 There is no equivalent in Hong Kong of the EC Technology Transfer Block Exemption (Reg.240/96) and, therefore, nothing to prevent the licensor requiring a licensee to pay royalties even after the expiry of a patent or after knowhow has come into the public domain. There are no restrictions on the level or amount of royalty that a licensor may charge. The licensee has no right under Hong Kong law to a royalty free licence after a certain period of time, or after the payment of a certain amount of royalties.

14.3.8 Import requirements

14–90 Hong Kong is a free port. Import and export licensing requirements are therefore kept to a minimum. Only a small number of products require an import/export licence. In the main these are products of the type set out in Chapter 14.1.6 where it is necessary to regulate the importation of these on grounds of health, safety, protection of the environment, security or to prevent smuggling. Hong Kong is also a signatory to a number of bilateral agreements restricting the import and export of textile products. This means that a licence is required for the import or export of certain types of this product and that quotas are imposed on the export of textiles but not on their import.

14–91 Under the Dutiable Commodities Ordinance (Cap 109) the import or manufacture of the following products are also subject to duty:

- alcoholic beverages;
- cosmetics;
- methyl alcohol;
- petrol, fuel and oil; and
- tobacco.

14–92 Although not strictly import duties, there are a number of other charges relating to the import of certain products into Hong Kong. Anyone importing a motor vehicle into Hong Kong is required to register the vehicle, which will then be subject to first registration tax. There is a trade declaration tax of HK$0.5 for imports and exports of up to HK$10,000 in value and thereafter this tax is levied at the rate of HK$0.25 for each additional HK$1,000 of value.

14.4 Miscellaneous

14.4.1 Confidentiality

The law relating to confidentiality in Hong Kong is the same in all material respects as that in the UK. In the absence of any express agreement, the common law applies. It is possible, and indeed preferable, for the parties to expressly agree their respective obligations of confidentiality and for these obligations to impose more onerous restrictions than those implied under the common law. There are no particular formalities for an agreement of this nature. If anything, the current lack of any anti-competitive legislation in Hong Kong means that it may be possible to impose more onerous restrictions than in the UK. For instance, restrictions on the use or disclosure of information in the public domain are currently not expressly prohibited in Hong Kong as they are in the EC under Art.81 of the EC Treaty, although, as in the UK, they may be deemed void as an unreasonable restraint of trade. The same is true of restrictions on the disclosure of confidential information after the termination of the relevant agreement. Such obligations will be enforced only to the extent that they are reasonably necessary to protect the interests of the party seeking to prohibit disclosure and do not constitute an unreasonable restraint of trade. **14–93**

14.4.2 Restrictive covenants

Again, the current absence of any anti-competitive legislation means that there is generally more scope for imposing restrictions on competition in Hong Kong. The competing activity clause set out in Chapter 1.5 would be appropriate for use during the life of not only agency agreements but also distribution and licensing agreements. If possible, such restrictions should be limited geographically to Hong Kong. **14–94**

The considerations which apply to restrictions on competition after the expiry or termination of the relevant agreement are the same as those in the UK. Such restrictions are *prima facie* void as being an unreasonable restraint of trade, but may be enforceable if the party seeking to rely on the restriction can establish that the restraint is reasonable and is no wider than is necessary to protect the commercial interests of such party. These restrictions commonly include a "blue-pencil" clause which seeks to limit **14–95** the extent of such restrictions to that which is reasonable in terms of the area, period and nature of the business protected. Rather than relying on clauses of this type it is preferable to draft the restrictions from the outset on the basis of what is the minimum necessary to protect the commercial interests of the relevant party.

14.4.3 Computer software

14–96 The recent legislative efforts to bolster copyright protection under the Copyright Ordinance (as to which see Chapter 14.2.4.1) have helped Hong Kong start to move away from its former status as a major centre for the commercial copying and marketing of unlicensed computer software, yet software piracy remains a problem. This perhaps has less to do with the ineffectiveness of such amendments (indeed, 2001 saw the number of prosecutions brought by Customs and Excise under the Copyright Ordinance more than double those brought in 2000) than with other factors. Hong Kong has relatively open borders and is in close proximity to other nations with inadequate copyright protection—China, Indonesia, the Philippines and Taiwan are all on the United States' Trade Representative's Special 301 Priority Watch List, which identifies those countries which deny adequate or effective protection of intellectual property rights (although note that Hong Kong was removed from the list in 1999). These factors combine to present software pirates with a potentially lucrative and easily accessible market.

14–97 Furthermore, Hong Kong's well-deserved reputation as a marketplace for inexpensive electronics means that the equipment needed to mass produce pirated software discs can be bought relatively cheaply, making software piracy financially attractive. This problem was somewhat alleviated by the passing in 1998 of the Prevention of Copyright Piracy Ordinance (Cap 544) ("PCPO"), which created a licensing regime for manufacturers of "optical discs" (which definition includes CD-ROMs) and provided for stiff criminal penalties for offences under the PCPO. The Customs and Excise is taking its responsibilities under the PCPO seriously—almost 40 per cent of the 9 million copyright infringing optical discs seized in 2001 were CD-ROMs.

14–98 Nevertheless, because of these factors it is vital that software producers closely control and monitor the licensing of their software. The precedent for a software distribution licence set out in Chapter 11 is appropriate for use in Hong Kong and needs little amendment, since it imposes the necessary restrictions and grants the necessary rights on the basis of contract rather than the provisions of any particular statute. The requirement for the licensee to include a copyright notice is particularly important for the distribution of computer software in Hong Kong. As discussed in Chapter 14.2.4, one of the major difficulties faced by Customs and Excise in Hong Kong is proving the subsistence and ownership of copyright in computer software, particularly where copyright is held by a foreign owner who does not have a local representative in Hong Kong. A copyright notice will not only establish that an infringer knew that copyright for the product belongs to someone else, but will also assist Customs and Excise in identifying the copyright owner and contacting them in connection with a criminal prosecution against any infringer.

14.4.4 Escrow

Hong Kong recognises the concept of escrow whereby an independent party agrees to hold documents, goods or other items to the order of a third party with instructions to release them on the happening of certain events. There is no requirement that an agreement of this type be under seal, but it is important to clearly set out in writing the escrow instructions and, in particular, the conditions for release. A deed delivered in escrow will not take effect until the escrow conditions have been satisfied. It cannot be recalled by the parties and once the conditions are satisfied it will be deemed to be effective—and therefore should be dated—on the date of delivery. **14–99**

As in the UK, such agreements are used in the computer software industry, and although they are less common in Hong Kong they are being used with increasing regularity. Licensors of software programs sometimes enter into a source code deposit agreement with the licensee and an escrow agent pursuant to which the licensor agrees to deposit the source code for licensed computer programs with the escrow agent and the agent undertakes to release this to the licensee upon the occurrence of certain events. Such events usually include the insolvency of the licensor and the breach by the licensor of any material term of the licence. A number of clearing banks in Hong Kong offer escrow services, although our experience has been that they are unwilling to accept obligations to update software held in their care, with the result that software escrow agents for Hong Kong licences are commonly based in the UK, such as the National Computing Centre and the Information Technology Telecommunications and Electronics Association (Intellect). **14–100**

14.4.5 Powers of attorney

The law relating to powers of attorney is governed by the Powers of Attorney Ordinance which is identical in all material respects to the UK Powers of Attorney Act 1971. The formalities required are therefore the same as in the UK. The instrument creating a power of attorney must be signed and sealed by, or by direction and in the presence of, the donor of the power. However, there is no equivalent of the Law of Property (Miscellaneous Provisions) Act 1989 and so deeds must still fulfil the three essential requirements of being written on paper, sealed and delivered. As stated in Chapter 14.1.12 there is no equivalent of s.36A of the UK Companies Act 1985 and Hong Kong companies must therefore have a common seal. **14–101**

Powers of attorney are generally revocable by: **14–102**

- agreement between the principal and attorney;
- notice from the principal to the attorney (whether or not accepted by the attorney);
- notice from the attorney to the principal (there is some dispute as to whether or not this requires the consent of the principal); and
- breach or repudiation of the power of attorney by the attorney.

14–103 Hong Kong law also provides for the creation of enduring powers of attorney (which are not revoked by the mental incapacity of the donor) through the Enduring Powers of Attorney Ordinance (Cap 501), which is substantially the same as the UK Enduring Powers of Attorney Act 1985. This Ordinance provides that enduring powers of attorney must be in the form and executed in the manner both as prescribed under the subsidiary Enduring Powers of Attorney (Prescribed Forms) Regulations (Cap 501A).

14.4.6 Whole agreement clauses

14–104 The law relating to whole agreement clauses is the same as in the UK. See Chapter 1.8.

14.4.7 Arbitration

14.4.7.1 General outline

14–105 Arbitration in Hong Kong is complicated by the fact that the governing legislation, the Arbitration Ordinance (Cap 341), provides for two distinct regimes:

- domestic arbitration—originally based on the UK Arbitration Acts 1950–1979 and recently updated to incorporate some of the amendments effected by the UK Arbitration Act 1996; and
- international arbitration—following the UNCITRAL Model Law.

14–106 The UNCITRAL Model Law provides that if the parties have their place of business in different countries, any arbitration will be deemed to be an international arbitration. However, there is nothing to prevent parties to an international arbitration from agreeing to adopt the domestic regime, either in the arbitration agreement or after the dispute arises—indeed, there may be certain advantages in doing so. Whichever regime is adopted it is important to state this clearly in the agreement.

14–107 The Arbitration Ordinance is similar to the UK Arbitration Act 1996 in many respects, but there are still a number of differences. A detailed comparison of domestic and international arbitration is beyond the scope of this chapter, but we have set out below some of the major differences with particular reference to where arbitration in Hong Kong differs from arbitration in the UK. A comprehensive comparison of the international and domestic regimes is set out in volume 1 of *Halsbury's Laws of Hong Kong*.

1 Domestic and international

Conciliation Non-adversarial methods of dispute resolution are common in Asian culture. The settlement of disputes by conciliation is specifically provided for under the Arbitration Ordinance. If the parties agree to refer disputes to conciliation the Ordinance provides that, if the parties cannot agree on the identity of the conciliator, the court may appoint the conciliator. Although there is no provision for the conciliator to give a legally binding determination capable of enforcement (this would be contrary to the spirit of conciliation) the Ordinance does provide that, if the parties agree, a written conciliation agreement can be enforced in the same way as an arbitration award. The Ordinance also provides that if someone has acted as conciliator, this will not prevent them from acting as an arbitrator. **14–108**

Hearings in camera Court proceedings arising out of arbitration are held *in camera*. **14–109**

Freedom of representation There is no requirement that advocates or arbitrators must be admitted as lawyers in Hong Kong. The parties are free to select both the arbitrators and the counsel of their own choice. **14–110**

2 Domestic

Single arbitrator Domestic arbitrations are referred to a single arbitrator unless the parties otherwise agree. **14–111**

Majority decision If the parties decide that they wish to appoint three arbitrators there is a possibility that one or more of their decisions will differ. The Ordinance provides that a majority decision will be binding, and in the event that all three arbitrators differ, the decision of the Chairman will be final. **14–112**

Consolidation The ability of the Hong Kong courts to consolidate a number of arbitrations is often seen as a major advantage to arbitration under the domestic regime. In other jurisdictions the consolidation of a number of multi-party arbitrations requires the consent of all the parties, but in Hong Kong the court has a discretion to order a consolidation where there are common questions of law or fact, where the rights arise out of the same transaction or series of transactions, or if for some other reason they consider it is desirable to consolidate the arbitrations. **14–113**

The Hong Kong International Arbitration Centre (HKIAC)

14–114 The HKIAC is a non-profit-making independent organisation established in 1985 as a forum for arbitration and other forms of dispute resolution in Hong Kong. In addition to providing facilities for hearing disputes, the HKIAC will act as the appointing and/or administering body. Irrespective of whether or not it is nominated as the appointing authority, it will also assist in the selection and appointment of arbitrators from the panel of qualified arbitrators it maintains. The HKIAC has its own rules for domestic arbitration—the HKIAC Domestic Arbitration Rules—and for international arbitrations has adopted the UNCITRAL Rules for International Arbitration. It also has a number of model arbitration clauses. Its model clause for international arbitration pursuant to the UNCITRAL rules is set out below.

14–115 International Arbitration Agreement

Any dispute, controversy or claim arising out of or relating to this contract, or the breach termination or invalidity thereof, shall be settled by arbitration in accordance with UNCITRAL Arbitration Rules as at present in force and as may be amended by the rest of this clause.

The appointing authority shall be Hong Kong International Arbitration Centre.

The place of arbitration shall be in Hong Kong at Hong Kong International Arbitration Centre (HKIAC).

There shall be only one arbitrator.[1]

Any such arbitration shall be administered by HKIAC in accordance with HKIAC Procedures for Arbitration in force at the date of this contract including such additions to the UNCITRAL Arbitration Rules as are therein contained.[2]

[1] *This sentence must be amended if a panel of three arbitrators is required.*

[2] *This sentence may be deleted if administration by HKIAC is not required. If it is retained the Centre will then act as a clearing house for communications between the parties and the arbitral tribunal and will liaise with the arbitral tribunal and the parties on timing of meetings etc, will hold deposits from the parties and assist the tribunal with any other matters required.*

The HKIAC also suggests a clause whereby parties to an international arbitration may opt out of the UNCITRAL Model Law and instead adopt the domestic regime. This is set out below.

14–116 Opt out agreement

The parties to this agreement hereby agree that this agreement is or is to be treated as a domestic arbitration agreement notwithstanding the provisions of the Arbitration Ordinance, Chapter 341 of the Laws of Hong Kong. The parties further agree that all or any dispute that may arise under the terms of this agreement are to be arbitrated as a domestic arbitration.

14.4.7.2 Judicial intervention

Judicial intervention in arbitration is minimal, but again the position in Hong Kong differs depending upon whether the arbitration is proceeding under the domestic or international regime. **14–117**

Under the domestic regime in general the courts in Hong Kong have similar powers to the UK courts. They are able to appoint and remove arbitrators, make a number of interlocutory orders (issue subpoenas, examine witnesses on oath, etc.), grant "interim measures of protection" and, in certain circumstances, set aside the award. **14–118**

The major difference between international and domestic arbitration is that there is no right of appeal from an award in an international arbitration but it is possible to appeal against a domestic award. Having said this, the circumstances in which a domestic award may be appealed are limited. The position in Hong Kong is almost identical to that in the UK. The court will intervene only on the application of one of the parties to the arbitration, and then only on certain limited grounds. The courts are not entitled to review the arbitrator's finding of facts. Appeals on questions of law are allowed, but the courts in Hong Kong are unwilling to interfere unless all of the parties to the arbitration consent to judicial review or unless the court is prepared to give leave to appeal on other grounds. In *AG v Technic Construction Co Ltd* [1986] H.K.L.R. 541 the Hong Kong Court of Appeal held that the guidelines laid down in the UK case of *Pioneer Shipping Ltd v BTP Tioxide Ltd (The Nema)* [1982] A.C. 724 (the so-called "Nema Guidelines") applied to domestic arbitration in Hong Kong, so restricting the circumstances in which leave to appeal will be granted. The Nema Guidelines set out a number of different categories of cases although, in the light of subsequent case law, these should now be viewed as a spectrum of possible cases. There is generally a presumption of finality of the arbitration award and against granting leave to appeal, and a judge will not give leave to appeal unless there is a strong *prima facie* case that the arbitrator was wrong in his construction of the contract. Leave is not often granted, although the presumption against grant is lessened where the question of law is of general applicability (*e.g.* on a point arising from a standard form of contract in general use in Hong Kong). It is also possible for the parties to "contract out" and exclude any judicial review of the award. The HKIAC suggest the model clause set out below: **14–119**

Exclusion agreement **14–120**

In relation to all matters referred to arbitration by this agreement the right of appeal under section 23 of the Arbitration Ordinance Chapter 341 of the Laws of Hong Kong and the right to make an application under Sect 23A thereof are hereby excluded.

If the parties contract out of the right to appeal, the only circumstances in which the award could be referred to the courts are where there is evidence of bias, corruption or misconduct etc on the part of the arbitrator(s).

14.4.7.3 Enforcement

14–121 Although it is possible to sue on an arbitration award itself, most applicants take advantage of s.2H of the Arbitration Ordinance which enables both domestic and international awards to be enforced as judgments, provided the leave of the court is first obtained. Both Hong Kong and the PRC are parties to the New York Convention on the Recognition and Enforcement of Foreign Arbitral Awards ("the New York Convention"). Unless one of the grounds for refusal is established, Hong Kong courts must recognise and enforce foreign arbitration awards made in countries which are also signatories to the New York Convention. The grounds for refusal are taken from Art.V of the New York Convention. Awards made in countries which are not signatories to the Convention are enforceable under the Ordinance in the same manner as domestic awards.

14–122 A special problem was created by the Chinese resumption of sovereignty over Hong Kong. The New York Convention no longer applied to Hong Kong/PRC cross-border awards because Hong Kong was now a part of the PRC, meaning awards in Hong Kong were not "foreign" to the PRC and vice versa. By the same token, Hong Kong's special status under the "one country, two systems" policy meant that the awards could not be considered to be domestic either. The situation was resolved in February 2000 by the Arbitration (Amendment) Ordinance (and in the PRC by a Notice and Judicial Interpretation issued by the Supreme People's Court in January 2000) and now the position is the same as prior to handover. Cross-border awards can be summarily enforced under the New York Convention by a simple application to the relevant court for leave to enter judgment in terms of the award.

14.4.7.4 Amiable composition

14–123 The effect of a clause requiring an arbitrator to decide a reference on the basis of what he thinks is fair and reasonable, rather than on the principles of the laws of Hong Kong or another jurisdiction (referred to as "amiable composition") is unclear under Hong Kong law. To date there has been no Hong Kong case on this point. This uncertainty is compounded by the fact that the Model Law specifically allows a tribunal to decide a reference as *amiable compositeur* if the parties have expressly authorised it to do so. Certainly, if the parties wish the tribunal to resolve the dispute by amiable composition they will need to expressly say so in the agreement.

14.4.7.5 Which regime?

Parties to an agency, distribution or licensing agreement in Hong Kong are almost certain to fall within the international regime. In what circumstances should they opt out of the Model Law? The possibility of appeal from a domestic award is often seen as the main reason to opt for international arbitration, but the circumstances in which the court will grant leave to appeal in domestic arbitrations are very limited. The misconception that international arbitrations have to have three arbitrators (and are consequently more cumbersome and costly than reference to a single arbitrator under the domestic regime) is often cited as a reason for choosing domestic arbitration, but in fact it is possible to agree to submit disputes to a single arbitrator. In view of the flexibility of both regimes, there is little to choose between the two. The more important question is whether to arbitrate or to litigate. In our view the major advantage of arbitration lies in the enforceability of Hong Kong arbitration awards outside Hong Kong. Enforcing an arbitration award under the New York Convention is usually less problematic than attempting to enforce a judgment. Far more countries are signatories to the Convention than have agreements for the reciprocal enforcement of judgments and arbitral awards made in Hong Kong can be enforced in more than 120 other jurisdictions. **14–124**

14.4.8 Force majeure

Force Majeure is not defined under Hong Kong law but, as in the UK this term is used to refer to circumstances beyond the control of the parties which, if they occur entitle the party affected to delay performance of its obligations until such circumstances cease to apply. The parties are free to determine for themselves what events, if any, will be deemed to constitute events of *force majeure*, although after the outbreak of SARS it is now common to include epidemics within the definition. *Force majeure* clauses commonly provide that if the relevant event continues for a certain period of time, then the contract can be terminated whilst preserving the rights of the parties which have accrued prior to such event. There is no concept of "hardship" under Hong Kong law and the common law doctrine of frustration applies. **14–125**

Chapter 15

Japan*

Contents

15.1 Introduction

This chapter examines particular aspects of Japanese law which should be considered by the practitioner who is preparing an agency, distribution or licensing agreement with a Japanese party. Where possible, the authors have refrained from restating the general principles elaborated upon in earlier chapters of the book and discuss only those key issues relating to Japanese law at the time of writing in February 2003. Where considerable changes were necessary to conform clauses presented in earlier chapters to Japanese law, they have been restated using the identical numbering system. **15–01**

For the sake of convenience, this chapter assumes that the agreement will be governed by Japanese law. This assumption presents some difficulties because agreements will often be governed by the law of another jurisdiction. However, although in nearly all cases the choice of a foreign governing law will be valid, issues of conflicts of laws and public policy in Japan may restrict the ability of a foreign party to enforce the terms of such an agreement in Japan (see Chapter 15.2.1). As the scope of this chapter is insufficient to deal with issues of conflict of laws issues and public policy in Japan comprehensively, two general suggestions are offered to the practitioner drafting a commercially significant agreement which is to be subject to a governing law other than that of Japan. First, so far as commercially reasonable, the agreement should be drafted to conform to Japanese law in order to avoid potential conflict of laws issues; and second, in cases of **15–02**

* This chapter was written by Keiji Matsumoto of Mori Hamada & Matsumoto, Tokyo. The author gratefully acknowledges the research and writing assistance of Jason J. Kee, participant in the University of Toronto's Work in Japan Programme.

uncertainty the practitioner should seek competent advice from qualified Japanese legal counsel.

15–03 The key sources of law which impact on international agency, distribution and licensing agreements are regulatory statutes, such as anti-monopoly and intellectual property legislation, the Commercial Code and the Civil Code. As a general rule, the application of regulatory statutes is mandatory, and as a result the parties are not permitted to opt out of such provisions by contractual agreement. For example, the parties to a contract are not able to contract around most regulatory statutes by selecting a more lenient jurisdiction for the governing law. On the other hand, most provisions of the Commercial Code and the Civil Code are discretionary, leaving the parties considerable leeway in terms of freedom of contract. As a result, the detailed general provisions of the precedent require only minor modifications in order to conform to Japanese law, while other substantive provisions relating to the agency, distributorship or licence may require considerable changes.

15.2 General provisions

15.2.1 Governing law and court jurisdiction

15–04 The choice of a foreign law as the governing law of an agreement is generally enforceable in Japan, with some important exceptions. As in most other jurisdictions, these exceptions generally relate to public policy concerns and to domestic law in areas such as trade, foreign exchange control and the prevention of monopolies. Thus, for example, a foreign governing law clause will not, as a general rule, allow the parties to escape from anti-monopoly legislation relating to such things as the prohibition of resale price maintenance.

15–05 A foreign judgment can be recognised for the purpose of enforcement in Japan if:

- the judgment is final and in accordance with the provisions of the relevant agreement and the governing law;
- the jurisdiction of the foreign court is not denied under Japanese law (at present the jurisdiction of nearly all Western countries is accepted);
- the defendant has received service of process otherwise than by public notice or has appeared before the foreign court;
- the judgment is not repugnant to public policy in Japan; and
- there exists reciprocity as to the recognition by such foreign court of a final judgment obtained in Japan.

15–06 The parties are also generally free to designate in which courts disputes will be settled, and where a Japanese court is to given jurisdiction the District Court of Tokyo is often designated.

15.2.2 Arbitration

The arbitration and amiable composition clauses provided for in the provision are valid under Japanese law and both domestic and foreign arbitration awards are enforceable in Japan if the countries to which the parties belong are signatories to the New York Convention on the Recognition of Foreign Arbitral Awards of 1958 or other bilateral or unilateral international treaties. When arbitration is to be conducted in Japan, for a domestic agreement the rules of the Japan Commercial Arbitration Association are most often designated while for an international agreement the rules of the International Chamber of Commerce or UNCITRAL are commonly used. In order to discourage unnecessary arbitration proceedings, Japanese parties to international contracts often insist that the place and rules of arbitration be determined by the location of the party against whom arbitration is demanded. It is also common for parties to designate a particular language, most often English, as the language to be used in the proceedings. A revised cl.1.6.1(b) (discussed in Chapter 1 above) might read as follows: **15–07**

> 1.6.1(b) Any dispute or claim arising out of this Agreement shall be finally settled by arbitration conducted in [English] (i) in [Tokyo] pursuant to the rules of [the Japanese Commercial Arbitration Association] if initiated by the Principal or (ii) in [New York] pursuant to the rules of [the American Arbitration Association] if initiated by the Distributor, by which rules each party agrees to be bound. **15–08**

15.2.3 Stamp duties

A stamp duty of ¥4,000 is payable on a master contract for continuing transactions such as an agency, licensing and distribution agreement. Stamp duties may also be payable in Japan in connection with the transfer of certain real estate and intellectual property rights generally depending on the value of the transaction. It should be noted, however, that in the case of agreements signed outside Japan, even if they are to be performed in Japan, no stamp duties are payable in Japan. **15–09**

15.2.4 Competing activity

15.2.4.1 Prior to termination

Agency The Commercial Code prohibits an agent from engaging in competitive activities with its principal except with the permission of the principal and cl.1.5.1 restricting involvement with competing activities during **15–10** the term of the agreement is acceptable. However, Japanese courts generally consider that a principal grants an agent an implied permission to continue dealing in competitive products which the agent was already selling at the time of the agreement. It should be noted, however, that if the agreement is made conditional on the agent ceasing to deal in competing products which it is already selling, the agreement is likely to run foul of anti-monopoly legislation as an unfair business practice. Consequently, it may be necessary to modify cl.1.5.1 in certain circumstances.

15–11 *Distributor* As with agents, it may not be permissible to require a distributor to cease trading in goods with which it has previously dealt and thus the appropriateness of cll.1.5.1 and 4.3.6 will have to be considered if a distributor is already dealing in competitive products. Even if the distributor is not already dealing in competitive goods, such restrictions are also likely to be illegal if the supplier is in a dominant position in the industry and competing suppliers will be adversely affected.

15–12 *Licensee* Depending on market conditions (*i.e.* if there is an adverse effect on competition in a market, or competing companies will be deprived of licensees for their technology or the opportunity of doing business), restrictions on the handling of competing products or the use of competing technology by a licensee may not be allowed and, therefore, cll.1.5.1 and 8.3.5 may need to be deleted or modified. However, one important exception is that a licensee who is granted an exclusive licence may be restricted from using competitive technology where the licensee was not already using such technology at the time of entering into the agreement, the rationale being that the restriction on the use of competitive technology will encourage the exclusive licensee to fully exploit the licensed technology.

15.2.4.2 After termination

15–13 Restrictions on competitive activity following termination present greater difficulties. However, the restrictions provided in cll.1.5.2(a) and 1.5.2(b) are generally acceptable under Japanese law provided that:

- the time period of the restriction is reasonable under the circumstances; and
- the termination is related to the fault of the agent, distributor or licensee, as the case may be.

15–14 For example, in the case of an exclusive import distributorship agreement the restriction would not be enforceable if the principal were to give advance notice of termination pursuant to cl.4.16.1. As a result, the principal should ensure that the grounds for termination are as specific as possible and relate to the failure of the agent, distributor or licensee, as the case may be, to meet its obligations.

In the case of exclusive import distributorship agreements, the Japanese Fair Trade Commission (the "FTC"), the body responsible for enforcing anti-monopoly legislation, has indicated that restrictions on competitive activity following termination are permissible if the principal can show justifiable reason, for example the need to prevent the misuse of confidential information such as marketing knowhow which has been disclosed to the distributor. However, such restrictions must be limited to the minimum extent necessary to protect the principal's interests. With respect to licence agreements, the FTC generally considers that prohibitions on the use of competitive knowhow following termination are permissible insofar as it is difficult to prove whether the licensee has acquired new knowhow from another source or is continuing to use the principal's knowhow. However, this is only permissible for a short period after the expiration or termination of the licensing agreement to, and only the extent necessary to prevent unauthorised exploitation of the licensed know-how. Furthermore, as the unlawful use of patents can normally be identified easily, restrictions on the use of competitive patents following termination require specific justification, and any post-expiration restrictions on the use of competitive patents will be a *prima facie* unfair trade practice. **15–15**

15.2.5 Power of attorney and escrow agreement

Japanese law would recognise the validity of the power of attorney provided for in cl.1.6.7 without any particular formalities, but the provision making such power of attorney irrevocable would not be enforceable. Although only rarely, an escrow agreement similar to the one provided for in Chapter 10 would also be permissible in Japan. **15–16**

15.2.6 Product liability

The new Product Liability Law came into effect in Japan on July 1, 1995 and requires manufacturers to pay consequential damages for losses of human life and property due to defects in manufactured products. Defects are defined as a lack of safety, which such products should normally have, in view of the characteristics of such products, including foreseeable method of use at the time of delivery. Both manufacturers and importers can be held liable under the law. In addition, a party which applies its trade mark or trade name to a product in such a manner as to lead consumers to believe that the product was manufactured by that party can be held liable. Defences permitted on the part of manufacturers are limited to: **15–17**

- the impossibility of recognising such defects under technology levels available at the time of delivery; and

- the defects being attributable to the manner of assembly of the components instructed by such manufacturer and there being no negligence on its part.

Claims are limited to the period ending on the earlier of two years after damages are recognised and 10 years after delivery.

15–18 Although the statute will generally not apply to agents, distributors and licensees may be at considerable risk of liability. In the case of certain classes of products, whether the principal or the distributor (or licensee) will ultimately bear any such risk and procure necessary insurance will be an important matter of discussion.

15.3 Agency agreements

15–19 The concept of agency under Japanese law does not differ substantially from that of most other jurisdictions. An agent is permitted to make a declaration of intention on behalf of a principal and it is the principal who is directly charged with meeting any obligations arising out of such declaration. The regulation of the principal-agent relationship is generally more lenient than for the principal-distributor relationship, particularly with regard to anti-monopoly legislation. In addition, since the sale of products under an agency agreement constitutes a direct sale from the principal to the customer, there is no "resale" and so the restrictions on resale price maintenance do not apply.

15–20 However, it should be noted that it is the substance and not the form of the agreement in question which will determine whether it is characterised as an agency or a distribution agreement and an attempt to characterise what is effectively a distribution agreement as an agency agreement will not succeed in exempting the agreement from anti-monopoly legislation. The following will tend to result in a relationship being characterised as one of agency:

- the products are sold in the name of the principal;
- the principal bears the risk of loss of the goods prior to delivery to the ultimate purchaser and the risk that the products will not be sold;
- the principal retains title to the products;
- the income of the agent is based upon a commission; and
- the principal retains control over the goods.

15.3.1 Termination

15–21 Due to the fact that, unlike distributors, sales agents generally do not make substantial investments in promoting the principal's products, there are generally no judicially imposed restrictions on the parties agreeing to exclude compensation on termination, as provided for in cl.2.7.3(b).

15.3.2 Ostensible authority

There are three cases in which a principal can be held liable for the unauthorised acts of his agent or apparent agent: **15–22**

- although the apparent agent has not been formally appointed by the principal, the principal has authorised the apparent agent to use the principal's trade name or has indicated to third parties that the apparent agent is his agent;
- the agent engages in activities in excess of its authority and a third party can show justifiable reason for concluding that the agent had authority to engage in such activity; and
- a third party acting in good faith executes a contract with an agent without knowing that the agent's authority has been terminated.

In general, the provisions of the precedent should suffice to protect the interests of the principal against an allegation by a third party that the principal is liable for the unauthorised acts of its agent.

15.3.3 Collections and bailee

Under the provisions of the Commercial Code, if an agency is characterised as a commission agency (*i.e.* the agent holds the inventory of the products as bailee for the principal and sells them in the agent's own name but for the account of the principal) and unless the parties or commercial practice provide otherwise, the commission agent will be liable for the default of customers. The version of Sch.4 relating to consignment stock set out in Chapter 2.14 makes the commission agent so liable. Consequently, in a situation where the agent is acting as a commission agent and it is not intended that the agent be liable for the failure of customers to perform, the parties should use the version of Sch.4 relating to holding consignment stock set out in Chapter 3.14, and should substitute the following for cl.2.3.14: **15–23**

> 2.3.14 The Agent does not guarantee to the Principal the due performance by any customer or customers of contracts which they have entered into with the Principal as a result of the Agent's activities under this Agreement. **15–24**

Where the original cl.2.3.14 is to be included, there are no particular formalities relating to the granting of a guarantee under Japanese law.

The legal relationship between a bailee and principal does not differ substantially from most other jurisdictions and the use of a bailee will **15–25** generally not result in the principal being deemed to be conducting business in Japan for tax purposes.

15.3.4 Trade mark registration

15–26 Although an exclusive licensee of a trade mark may register its use at the Patent Office, such registration is not required for the licence to be effective. However, if an agent does wish to register a trade mark (for example in order to be able to take action directly against third party infringers without the involvement of the principal), cl.8.2.1.1 (see Chapter 15.5.1 below) should be appropriately modified and included.

15.4 Distribution agreements

15–27 Unlike agency agreements, distribution agreements are subject to considerable scrutiny under regulatory statutes, in particular anti-monopoly legislation with respect to resale price maintenance. Because of concerns over resale price maintenance, the scrutiny is especially strong when it comes to international agreements which grant sole import distribution rights for a product in Japan.

15.4.1 Exclusivity

15–28 While exclusive distributor contracts are not prohibited, if they are characterised as unfair business practices under anti-monopoly legislation they may become illegal. The FTC considers that the use of exclusive dealing by a company with a dominant position in an industry is often an impediment to fair competition, the most important factor in determining whether a company is dominant being high market share. The FTC also normally views the granting of exclusivity to a single distributor to be a less serious restraint of competition than restrictions on multiple distributors from dealing in competitive products. This is because in the case of the granting of exclusivity to a single distributor other distributors can normally obtain alternative products from competing suppliers, while a restriction on multiple distributors from dealing in competitive products will severely limit the available distribution channels for competing suppliers. However, an exclusive distributor arrangement may become illegal if a single distributor becomes an exclusive distributor for many suppliers and thereby makes it difficult for competing distributors to obtain products.

15.4.2 Parallel imports

15–29 The requirement in cl.4.6.1 that the distributor purchase all its supplies of the distributed products from the principal is enforceable under Japanese law. However, in the case of an exclusive import distributorship, the parties should be aware that the exclusive grant to the distributor will not ensure that the importation of genuine products (*i.e.* products which are manufactured by the principal or under licence from the principal) by third parties will be prohibited and action to prevent such parallel importation by way of the exercise of trade mark or similar rights will not be allowed. Such prohibition will, however, be permitted if there is a justifiable reason, such as the need to protect consumers who are being misled into believing that products with different specifications are the same.

15.4.3 Lowest prices to distributor

The requirement that the principal provide the distributor with its lowest sales price under cl.4.6.3 is valid under Japanese law. **15–30**

15.4.4 Selling prices and sales restrictions

Resale price maintenance is explicitly prohibited by anti-monopoly legislation, except for a narrow range of copyrighted products such as books, magazines and music, for which the approval of the FTC is required. The restriction on resale price maintenance applies irrespective of whether the principal is in a dominant position in the industry. There are a number of exceptions to the above, the most important being that a principal can impose resale price restrictions on a distributor which is a wholly owned subsidiary of the principal. Restrictions on sales territory, customers and sales methods are likely to be illegal if the principal has a dominant position in the industry and if the effect of such restrictions is to maintain a higher price level. Otherwise, the principal is normally free to restrict the distributor from actively engaging in sales outside a designated territory or customer group so long as the prohibition is not absolute, for example by permitting the distributor to fill unsolicited orders from customers outside the designated territory or customer group. **15–31**

15.4.5 Stock of the products

Full-line forcing is usually illegal under anti-monopoly legislation. As a result, if the combined effect of the definition of products in cl.1.2.1 and the minimum stock level requirements of cl.4.10 is to impose on the distributor an excessive burden for carrying a full-line of the principal's products, such provisions may be illegal. **15–32**

15.4.6 Termination

15–33 Although the termination with notice provisions of cl.4.15.1 are generally enforceable, Japanese courts have occasionally used the principles of abuse of right, equity and good faith to refuse to enforce similar provisions, particularly in the case of the termination of exclusive distributor agreements on short notice. The courts may examine the efforts and investment of the distributor to develop business, the amount of time it will take for the distributor to change to an alternative product line and the percentage of the distributor's business that the discontinued line of products comprises in determining a reasonable period of notice, although for most product categories a period of six months would seem to be commercially reasonable assuming the above-mentioned efforts and investment are not substantial.

15–34 In the case of termination for cause, courts generally require that a breach be serious enough to justify the disadvantage of termination on the distributor. As a result, the inclusion of the second series of square brackets referring to a material breach in cl.4.16.1 is preferable, although whenever possible it is best to set out the grounds for termination as concretely as possible. In the case of a failure to meet sales targets, the courts may be willing to enforce a provision converting an exclusive agreement into a non-exclusive one, but if commercial circumstances make this unreasonable then cl.4.16.2 should be acceptable provided that the targets are reasonable in the circumstances.

15.4.7 No compensation on termination

15–35 A clause excluding any compensation to the distributor for termination is enforceable. However, it will be effective only if the termination itself is valid. A principal concerned about the possibility of the distributor attempting to claim compensation for valid termination should consider substituting a more explicit version of cl.4.15.4:

15–36 4.15.4 The Distributor shall not be entitled to any compensation on the termination of this agreement under cll.4.15 or 4.16 for any cause whatsoever [including but without limitation expiry by effluxion of time]. Without limiting the generality of the foregoing the Distributor acknowledges that

(i) the Distributor has no expectation and has received no assurances that its business relationship with the Principal will continue beyond the initial or subsequent term of this agreement or its earlier termination under cll.4.15 or 4.16

(ii) any investment by the Distributor in the promotion of the Products is expected to be recovered or recouped by the Distributor from anticipated profits obtained from the sale of the Products during the term of this agreement and

(iii) the Distributor shall not have or acquire by virtue of this Agreement or otherwise any vested, proprietary or other right in the promotion of the Products or in any goodwill created by its efforts hereunder.

15.4.8 Duty to supply

Although even in the absence of a specific provision the courts generally recognise the right of a principal to refuse to supply goods if the distributor has failed to pay for previous deliveries, the principal should carefully consider the rights which it may have short of termination in such cases. For example, in one case a Tokyo court held that a principal did not have the right to refuse delivery of goods when a distributor had paid for goods but had failed to pay associated freight charges. As a consequence, cl.4.26.2.3 might be rewritten to explicitly give the principal the right to withhold supply if the distributor has defaulted on its payment obligations: **15–37**

> 4.26.2.3 Delivery dates or periods specified in orders accepted by the Principal are firm provided that the Principal is in possession of all information and documents necessary to permit the Principal to proceed to fill such order in a timely manner and without interruption and further provided that without prejudice to any other remedies it may have under this Agreement the Principal shall be entitled to extend such delivery date or periods or cancel such orders if the Distributor shall have failed to make any payments under cl.4.26.2.8. **15–38**

15.4.9 Security interest

Although the principal will automatically have a statutory security interest in the goods sold to the distributor, in the case of default the principal will have to foreclose on the goods in accordance with relevant laws. However, as this statutory security interest is not in itself an ownership interest, the principal may not recover the full amount possible if conflicting security interests exist or if the goods are sold and the proceeds paid to other creditors prior to foreclosure by the principal. Consequently, the preferred alternative is to provide that the principal shall retain title to all transferred goods until payment has been received by the principal. Although the distributor is free to sell such goods to a third party (who acquires full title), the retention of title has the advantage of avoiding the need for any formal foreclosure proceedings while giving the principal priority over other creditors. If there are concerns about the distributor's financial strength and if the agreement is to be governed by Japanese law, the following clause, which does not require any formal registration in order to be valid, may be included: **15–39**

> 4.26.2.8.1 Title to any goods shall pass from the Principal to the Distributor only upon payment for such goods being made as specified under cl.4.26.2.8 provided that the Distributor shall be entitled to transfer the title for any such goods to a *bona fide* third party purchaser whether or not the title for such goods has passed to the Distributor. **15–40**

15.5 Licensing agreements

As with distribution agreements, licensing agreements are subject to a number of regulatory statutes, in particular anti-monopoly and intellectual **15–41** property legislation. The practitioner who is drafting a licensing agreement will want to be especially careful to ensure that the agreement does not violate the anti-monopoly guidelines of the FTC.

15.5.1 Licence and registration

15–42 An exclusive licence for an issued patent, a registered utility model or design or a registered trade mark is, if registered, generally referred to as a *sen'yo* exclusive licence under Japanese intellectual property statutes. Although a *sen'yo* exclusive licence takes effect upon signing, until it is registered with the Patent Office the licensee will have no right independent of the principal to exclude others from using the licensed right. The system is based upon one of constructive notice, and so the first licensee to register a *sen'yo* exclusive licence is able to exclude any other licensee from exercising a similar contractual right registered subsequently. Applications for registration of a *sen'yo* exclusive licence must be filed jointly by the principal and the licensee and the courts generally consider that the principal has an obligation to cooperate in the registration procedure. As a result, in cases where the licensee intends to register any of the intellectual property rights granted by the licence, the following cl.8.2.1.1 should clarify the obligations of the parties:

15–43 8.2.1.1 The registered exclusive licence shall be deemed to be a *sen'yo* exclusive licence as defined in relevant Japanese statutes. Upon request of the exclusive Licensee, the Principal shall fully cooperate in registering the *sen'yo* exclusive licence at the Patent Office in the name of the exclusive Licensee. Any expenses for such registration shall be borne by the exclusive Licensee.

The registration procedure will normally take several months and basic terms of the licence, including the scope, duration, territory and amount of royalty, will be noted in the registration, which may be inspected by the public.

15.5.2 FTC Guidelines

15–44 The FTC has established new guidelines with respect to both patent and knowhow licensing agreements as to what types of provisions may violate anti-monopoly legislation (see Chapter 15.5.16). The guidelines have broad application, indicating that while FTC enforcement policy under the guidelines is "not directly applicable" to matters beyond patent and know-how licensing restraints, it will nevertheless be applied "*mutatis mutandis* to other forms of intellectual property to the extent possible on the basis of the nature of these rights". Moreover, the guidelines expressly apply FTC enforcement policy to licensing restraints constituting unreasonable restraints of trade, monopolization and unfair trade practices, and sets forth the FTC's analysis of the these types of conduct.

15.5.2.1 Unreasonable Restraints of Trade

Under the rubric of unreasonable restraints of trade, the guidelines proscribe licensing arrangements among actual or potential competitors, such as certain cross-licenses, "multiple" licenses and patent pools, that substantially restrict competition in a relevant market. Specifically prohibited are licensing agreements imposing "mutual restrictions" regarding: (a) sale price; (b) sales volume; (c) manufacturing volume; (d) sales outlets; (e) sales territories; (f) fields of research and development; (g) licensing third parties; or (h) technology to be used by the parties, where the effect of such restrictions is substantially to reduce competition. **15–45**

15.5.2.2 Monopolization

The guidelines condemn as unlawful private monopolization licensing conduct that "exclude[s] or control[s] the business activities of other firms, and substantially restrict[s] competition in a market for particular products or particular technologies". Liability for monopolization may arise from patent pooling, cross-licensing, "concentrations" of patents, or other exclusionary licensing conduct employing unfair trade practices. The FTC's principal articulated concern in this context is with refusals to license by a dominant firm, or dominant combination of firms, that effectively exclude new entrants or substantially impede the functioning of existing competitors. **15–46**

15.5.2.3 Unfair Trade Practices

With respect to unfair trade practices, the guidelines, in essence, establish four classifications for contractual provisions: **15–47**

- restrictions which are generally permitted (the "white" classification), including minimum or maximum volume and/or use requirements, "best efforts" obligations, field of use/technology restrictions, restrictions on duration (within patent life), territorial restraints (within Japan), obligations to protect the secrecy of know-how (for the duration of the license), and non-exclusive or "appropriate price" grant-backs;
- restrictions which may or may not be permitted depending on market conditions (the "gray" classification), including maximum volume and/or use restrictions, package licensing, restrictions regarding customers to whom the licensee can sell or on use of competing products,

quality or supply restrictions, obligations to use a trade mark, "no challenge" clauses or obligations not to assert patent rights, royalties not based on production or use of licensed intellectual property, and unilateral termination clauses;

- restrictions which may or may not be permitted depending on market conditions, but which are highly likely to impede competition and not be permitted except with justifiable reason (a subset of the "gray" classification, sometimes referred to as the "dark gray" classification), including restrictions on R & D, exclusive grant-backs, and restrictions on use of competing products or payment of royalties after patent expires; and

- restrictions which are not permitted except with justifiable reason (the "black" classification), including clauses restricting sale prices (horizontal price fixing) and resale price maintenance.

15–48 These classifications signal the likelihood that a restraint will be found to violate the anti-monopoly law, as well as how the FTC will analyze the conduct. "White" list restraints are exempted exercises of intellectual property rights that "*do not, in principle*", violate the anti-monopoly law "because they are considered to have a negligible effect on competition in a market". The legality of "gray" list restraints are determined on a case-by-case basis, by inquiry into each restraint's competitive effects. As a general proposition, if a "gray" list licensing arrangement substantially impedes or restricts competition in a relevant market, it is unlawful. "Dark gray" list restraints are subject to the same inquiry, but the FTC presumes that it will be highly likely to find the restraint impedes competition upon completion of their analysis, and hence be unlawful. "Black" list restraints violate the anti-monopoly law "*in principle* . . . because of the great adverse effect they have on competition", and thus the anticompetitive effect of "black" list restraints is presumed.

15–49 As this summary may suggest, the guidelines are quite detailed, covering a wide range of conduct and including a list of defined terms, an interpretation of the scope and nature of the anti-monopoly legislative exemption for the "exercise of [intellectual property] rights", and examples (some hypothetical, others based on FTC cases) illustrating types of licensing conduct that may raise competitive concerns. Accordingly, it is advisable for the practitioner drafting a licensing agreement to refer to the full text of the guidelines. However, it should be noted that greater detail does not necessarily assure greater clarity, and the guidelines remain sufficiently vague to make it often difficult to know whether a specific provision will be acceptable. Consequently, in the event of uncertainty, it may be advisable to submit a draft licensing agreement to the FTC's prior consultation system for review prior to execution (see Chapter 15.5.16 below).

15–50 In the case of a single agreement which licenses a patent and knowhow, both sets of guidelines apply.

15.5.3 Export restrictions

In the light of Japanese anti-monopoly legislation, cl.8.4 relating to the handling of enquiries from outside of the licensed territory and cl.8.5 restricting exports out of the licensed territory need to be carefully considered. In particular, the FTC considers that such restrictions may, depending on market conditions, constitute an unjustifiable restraint of trade. In making this determination, the FTC gives consideration to such factors as whether the licensor has registered the patent rights for the patented products in the area for export, whether the licensor itself is engaged in continuous marketing activities with respect to patented products there or whether the licensor has assigned the export areas as the exclusive sales territory of third parties, etc. The following revised cll.8.4 and 8.5.1(a) will in almost all cases satisfy the guidelines established by the FTC for export restrictions: **15–51**

8.4 The Principal shall during the continuance of this Agreement refer all enquiries received by it for the sale of the Products in the Territory to the Licensee. The Licensee shall during the continuance of this Agreement refer to the Principal all enquiries it receives for Products for sale outside or export from the Territory to any territory in which **15–52**

(i) the Principal has registered its Patents on the Products; or
(ii) the Principal has been conducting continuous marketing activity of the Products; or
(iii) the Principal has assigned an exclusive sales territory to a third party [other than in the case of Products sold within the Territory as ship's or aircraft's stores for use sale or consumption on such ship or aircraft outside the Territory or for ultimate sale in a duty-free shop in the Territory].

The Licensee acknowledges that the territories identified in the foregoing (i) (ii) and (iii) include those territories listed from time in Sch.1 as "reserved territories".

Cl.8.5.1(a) should be amended as follows: **15–53**

8.5.1(a) The Licensee shall not during the continuance of this Agreement carry on or be party to the following activities in any area outside the Territory that is (a) a territory identified in para.(i) (ii) or (iii) of cl.8.4 (a "reserved territory") or (b) a customer group within the scope of para.(ii) or (iii) of cl.8.4 (a "reserved customer group") unless the prior written consent of the Principal has been obtained (provided that this clause shall not prevent the sale of the Products by the Licensee as ship's stores or aircraft's stores or to duty-free shops as referred to in cl.8.4]:

It is then possible to use cll.8.5.1.1 to 8.5.13 inclusive and cll.8.5.2 and 8.5.3 as printed in Chapter 8. Clauses 8.5.4 and 8.5.5 should be deleted.

15.5.4 Quality standards and supply of materials

15–54 Clause 8.6.3 and Sch.4 should be handled with care as the FTC considers that unless there is justifiable reason, the obligation of a licensee to purchase raw materials or components from the principal or a person designated by the principal may be illegal under anti-monopoly legislation. However, such restrictions are permissible in cases where the imposition of quality standards is insufficient to:

- guarantee the effectiveness of the licensed patent or knowhow where the principal has guaranteed the effectiveness of such licensed patent or knowhow; or
- maintain the goodwill of a trade mark in the case that a trade mark is licensed in addition to the relevant patent or knowhow.

15–55 Similarly, as licensing terms setting quality requirements for manufactured products are viewed similarly, in many cases the quality control obligations imposed on the licensee under cl.8.6.4 and Sch.5 will be permissible only if they are required in order to meet the objectives outlined above.

15.5.5 Grant-back of improvements

15–56 The grant-back of improvements made by the licensee to the principal under cl.8.25.9(a) will often have to be modified. In some cases the FTC views a lack of reciprocity in such a provision to be an unfair trade practice under anti-monopoly legislation, especially if the licence granted back to the principal is on an exclusive basis. As a result, it will sometimes be preferable to use cl.8.25.9(b) or to redraft cl.8.25.9(a) in order to make the obligations reciprocal, for example by requiring the parties to licence and/or communicate any improvements to each other on a non-exclusive basis for the duration of the agreement. If non-reciprocal exclusivity is required, then it is advisable to modify the phrase "upon fair and reasonable terms to be agreed" in cl.8.25.9(a) to "upon fair and reasonable terms, and for such appropriate price, to be agreed", as the FTC considers that such an arrangement will not constitute an unfair trade practice if the licensor is deemed to have paid "an appropriate price" for the exclusive rights to the improvement.

15.5.6 Terms of supply

15–57 In cases when Sch.6 is to be included to provide for the supply of materials by the principal to the licensee, it may be prudent to include revisions relating to the response of the principal in the case of a default in payment by the licensee (see Chapter 15.4.8) or the protection of the principal in case of the insolvency of the licensee (see Chapter 15.4.9).

15.5.7 Royalty payments

As the FTC considers that obligations to pay a royalty on knowhow after such knowhow has come into the public domain is highly likely to be deemed an unfair business practice (unless it is an installment payment or a deferred payment of royalty), cl.8.27.5 should be included. The FTC does not recognise an exception to this general position in cases where the knowhow has come into the public domain other than by the fault of the principal or the licensee, unless the royalty is only to be paid for a "short period" thereafter that is within the term of the licensing agreement. Accordingly, the first phrase in brackets in cl.8.27.5 should be used, and cl.8.27.6 should either not be included, or modified to limit the term of royalty payments to a short period after the knowhow has entered the public domain, and within the term of the licensing agreement. **15–58**

Although the charging of different royalty rates to different non-exclusive licensees without justifiable reason might constitute an unfair business practice under anti-monopoly legislation, there are no court decisions on the point. **15–59**

15.5.8 Restrictions on marketing

The requirement under cll.8.8.2 and 8.8.3 that advertising and sales promotion be approved in advance by the principal, will generally not violate Japanese anti-monopoly legislation provided that: **15–60**

- there is justifiable reason for the restrictions (for example in order to protect the goodwill of a trade mark); and
- the effect is not to maintain higher prices in the licensed territory or otherwise violate anti-monopoly legislation (see also Chapter 15.4.4).

Restrictions on sales and marketing policies under cl.8.9.1 and on customers are viewed in a similar fashion.

15.5.9 Selling prices

Although anti-monopoly legislation generally prohibits resale price maintenance, there is no problem with requiring the licensee to notify the principal of its selling prices for licensed products, so long as the purpose of such notification is solely for the purpose of market research or the calculation of royalties. As a result, the phrase in square brackets in cl.7.9.2 requiring such notification can usually be included without any difficulty. Nevertheless, the inclusion of cl.8.9.6 serves as a useful reminder that the principal cannot regulate resale prices of the products by indirect means. **15–61**

15.5.10 Trade marks

15–62 Clause 8.9.3 requiring that the licensee apply the trade mark to all products manufactured by the licensee should also be carefully considered in light of anti-monopoly regulations. The FTC sometimes considers it an unfair trade practice to require a licensee to use a trade mark designated by a principal for goods manufactured under the patent or knowhow of the principal, especially after termination of such patent or knowhow. Such restriction will be viewed as an unfair business practice if the licensee is deprived of the freedom to select a trade mark of its own, particularly where the principal is in a dominant position in the market.

15.5.11 Stock of the products

15–63 Although it is generally permissible to require the licensee to maintain minimum stock levels, as in the case of distribution agreements such requirements may become illegal if the result is to impose an excessive inventory burden on the licensee for products it does not wish to carry (see Chapter 15.4.5).

15–64 Conversely, restrictions imposed upon the licensee's stock levels or sales volume is sometimes regarded as an unfair trade practice under the anti-monopoly legislation.

15.5.12 Intellectual property rights

15–65 A requirement that the licensee not challenge the validity of the licensed patent or the secrecy of the licensed knowhow, or that a licensee not assert patent rights against a licensor, is sometimes viewed as an unfair trade practice under anti-monopoly legislation. Although the FTC has not explicitly indicated that this also applies to trade marks, it has implicitly done so, and in cases where it is necessary to expressly recognise such a right of challenge cl.8.13.4 should be reproduced as written.

15–66 However, it is permissible that the principal be granted the right to terminate the agreement if the licensee challenges the validity of a licensed patent (and presumably a licensed trade mark) or the secrecy of the licensed knowhow. Thus, in appropriate cases, the opening four lines of cl.8.16.8 may be revised as follows to provide such a right of termination:

15–67 8.16.8 On the Licensee challenging the validity of the Patents, the Trade Mark, or any other intellectual or industrial property rights belonging to the Principal [or the secrecy of the Knowhow] the Licensor may [terminate this Agreement ...]

15.5.13 Other registrations

In quite exceptional cases where an agreement relates to national interest, international licensing agreements relating to the export of technology into Japan are subject to advance reporting under the Foreign Exchange and Foreign Trade Act, with submission through the Bank of Japan to the Ministry of Finance and to the ministry having jurisdiction over the particular industry. **15–68**

15.5.14 Royalty withholding tax

The withholding tax on patent and knowhow licence royalties is 20 per cent, but principals from many industrialised countries which have tax treaties with Japan, including the US, UK, France and Germany, qualify for a reduced rate. **15–69**

15.5.15 Termination

Although the precedent proposes a fixed term in cl.8.15.1, in some cases the parties may prefer to provide for a structure similar to cl.4.15.1 whereby the agreement will automatically extend following the initial period and be terminable by either party with advance notice. In such cases, in order not to fall foul of anti-monopoly legislation the advance notice period will have to be reasonable, although for most product categories a period of six months would seem to be acceptable assuming the efforts and investment of the licensee have not been substantial. Also, an especially long initial term may be illegal as an unfair business practice if the result is to restrict the business activities of the licensee after the licensed patent or knowhow has ceased to have substantial commercial value. **15–70**

15.5.16 FTC review

Prior to June 18, 1997, the FTC maintained a mandatory notification system unique to Japanese Anti-monopoly legislation. This system required that designated types of agreements between Japanese and foreign parties, including certain distribution and licensing agreements, be filed with the FTC within 30 days of signing (domestic agreements were exempted from this requirement). The FTC would then review such agreements, and recommend any changes necessary to bring such agreements into line with anti-monopoly legislation, in particular to ensure that the agreements did not contain provisions which constitute unreasonable restraints of trade or unfair business practices. If the parties failed to implement changes **15–71** recommended by the FTC, the FTC was empowered to request that all or part of the agreement be invalidated.

15–72 While the FTC remains empowered to take appropriate action against unreasonable restraints of trade, monopolization and unfair business practices, this notification system was repealed in 1997, effectively ending differential treatment of international and domestic distribution and licensing agreements by the FTC, and bringing Japanese Anti-monopoly legislation enforcement according to the FTC's new and more concrete guidelines more in line with US and EU Competition law practice.

15–73 Furthermore, the FTC started to offer a prior consultation system whereby a company may request prior written clearance by the FTC of proposed contractual provisions or conduct. As with the old notification system, the FTC reviews such agreements and recommends any changes necessary to bring such agreements into line with anti-monopoly legislation and FTC guidelines. However, unlike the old reporting (and the still older prior approval) system, the prior consultation system is entirely voluntary.

15–74 In determining whether a contract is likely to substantially lessen competition, the FTC will consider a variety of factors, including such things as the market share of the products covered by the agreement, the overall business capability of the supplier and the presence of substitutes for the product in question. For example, the FTC takes the position that a contract between a distributor ranked first and with 25 per cent or higher market share and a supplier in competition with the distributor is highly likely to constitute restraint of trade. A number of exceptions apply, in particular where the supplier is producing a product under licence from the distributor or for contracts of less than five years for selling a new product into the domestic market.

15–75 In general, agreements between parent and subsidiary companies are not regulated by the anti-monopoly statutes and regulations as such transactions are viewed as being essentially equivalent to intra-company transactions.

Chapter 16

Singapore*

Contents

16.1 Agency and distribution agreements

Singapore is one of the least restrictive countries to invest in and operate from with regard to any form of business venture. There are minimal restrictions on the import and export of goods. There are also minimal restrictions on foreign investments generally. The operation of the Exchange Control Act (Cap 99), as announced in a circular dated May 25, 1978 issued by the Monetary Authority of Singapore (the "MAS"), has been suspended since 1978, and there is effectively no foreign exchange control in Singapore. There is also currently no generic anti-trust legislation in Singapore, although the Entrepreneurship and Internationalisation Sub-committee of the Economic Review Committee (established in October 2001), in its report issued on May 30, 2002, has recommended the enactment of generic competition law that prohibits cartel activities and abuse of dominance by significant market players, and reviews mergers and acquisitions for all sectors of the economy. **16–01**

Singapore's central location within South East Asia, as well as Asia, as a **16–02**

* This chapter was originally written by Vemala Rajamanickam of Allen & Gledhill, Singapore, together with Kala Anandarajah and Phuak Hoon Leng, then also of Allen & Gledhill, and later revised by the first-mentioned, with the assistance of Elizabeth Wong and Jocelyn Chew, also of Allen & Gledhill.

whole is another attractive factor for distributors to operate in the country. It also has an excellent infrastructure and a strong financial and banking arena. Over the years, Singapore has also developed into an international air-sea cargo centre, with a duty-free port.

16–03 There are no restrictions as to who may be appointed as an agent or distributor in Singapore. An individual carrying on business in Singapore as a sole proprietor or in partnership registered under the Business Registration Act (Cap 32), or a corporate entity incorporated or registered under the Companies Act (Cap 50) may thus be appointed.

16–04 An important advantage of using an agent or distributor in Singapore is the certainty in the application of the laws of this country and the fast and efficient court system available for the resolution of disputes. Dispute resolution may also be by way of arbitration or mediation. Further, Singapore law, which includes English common law, is well developed and sophisticated enough to deal with the complexities of modern commerce.

16–05 The taxation laws in Singapore are continually reviewed and revised to encourage business development in Singapore. The corporate tax rates are favourable and numerous tax allowances and incentives are available.

16–06 Finally, the different languages and cultures thriving within Singapore ensure easier access into the surrounding fast developing countries, including China, Vietnam and India.

16.2 Distributor and agent distinguished

16–07 There is no legislation governing the appointment of an agent or distributor. The relationship is governed to an extent by English common law principles but these principles are modified by the courts in Singapore. Thus, as in England, the distributor is, in law, the buyer of the products from the manufacturer or supplier. The distributor is essentially a customer of the manufacturer or supplier who then sells the products to third parties who are his own customers. As the distributor acts as a kind of middleman in distributing the manufacturer's or supplier's products, the nature of his relationship with the manufacturer or supplier is often confused as being that of an agent-principal. In reality, he buys the products as principal on his own account from the manufacturer or supplier and resells these products in the designated territory. He does not act as a channel of communication between the manufacturer or supplier and the third party and does not create a contractual relationship between the manufacturer or supplier and the end customers. The distributor's earnings are represented by the profit made from the margin of difference between the purchase and the sale price.

16–08 An agent, in contrast, acts on behalf of, or represents, another person, called the principal, in such a way as to be able to affect the principal's legal position in respect of third parties by the making of contracts or the disposition of property. In short, with respect to the outside world, an agent can acquire rights for his principal and subject his principal to liabilities.

The agency relationship can arise by mutual agreement (*i.e.* by contract) or by the operation of law, and is usually independent of any contract that may exist between the principal and the third party. Where there is a contract, the nature and extent of the agency relationship will be spelt out. The agent's earnings are usually represented by a commission payment from his principal. **16–09**

Whether an agent or distributor is to be appointed in a given situation depends on a number of commercial factors including the nature of the products and the market as well as the particular needs of the principal or the supplier. **16–10**

16.3 The law applicable to an agency or distribution arrangement

There are no specific statutory enactments dealing generally with agency or distribution arrangements in Singapore, save that the Factors Act (Cap 386) governs agents who in the ordinary course of their business have authority to sell goods on behalf of their principals. The Factors Act is a reproduction of the United Kingdom Factors Act 1889, which is made applicable in Singapore in its entirety (except in one respect) by virtue of the Application of English Law Act (Cap 7A). **16–11**

Insofar as agency or distribution arrangements are contractual arrangements, English common law principles of contract law will govern the relationship between the parties concerned. The common law of England is applicable in Singapore by virtue of the Second Charter of Justice 1826 subject to such modifications as the circumstances of Singapore and its inhabitants may require. The Application of English Law Act further confirms the applicability of English common law in Singapore. In addition, there are two statutes which apply generally to contracts, namely, the Unfair Contract Terms Act (Cap 396) and the Misrepresentation Act (Cap 390). Both these Acts are reproductions of English statutory enactments and are made applicable in Singapore (the former made applicable with a few modifications) by virtue of the Application of English Law Act. **16–12**

Although an agency or distribution agreement is not in itself a contract of sale of goods and is therefore not governed by the law relating to the sale of goods, individual contracts of sale entered into pursuant to the agency or distribution agreement are so governed. In this regard, reference must be made to two statutes in force in Singapore, namely, the Sale of Goods Act (Cap 393) and the Sale of Goods (United Nations Convention) Act (Cap 283A). The former is a reproduction of the United Kingdom Sale of Goods Act 1979 which is made applicable in Singapore in its entirety (save for certain provisions) by the Application of English Law Act. The latter came into force on March 1, 1996 and gives effect to the UN Convention on Contracts for the International Sale of Goods. **16–13**

Certain products are subject to control or expressly prohibited by legislation. The Sale of Food Act (Cap 283) and the Food Regulations (Reg.1) provide measures to ensure the quality, purity and accurate labelling of **16–14** food. The Sale of Drugs Act (Cap 282), the Medicines Act (Cap 176) and the Medicines (Advertisement and Sale) Act (Cap 177) control the licensing and labelling of drugs and medicines. The Medicines Act in particular requires all medicinal products sold in Singapore to be licenced with the Centre for Pharmaceutical Administration of the Health Sciences Authority in Singapore. The Drug Registration Branch of the Product Evaluation and Registration Division is responsible for the registration of medicines and the continual review of approved medical products. In respect of the supply of specified categories of goods, the Consumer Protection (Trade Descriptions and Safety Requirements) Act (Cap 53) and the Consumer Protection (Safety Requirements) Regulations 2002 make it mandatory to comply with the prescribed safety requirements for those goods.

16–15 With regard to imports of products, the Regulation of Imports and Exports Act (Cap 272A) provides for the registration, regulation and control of imports and exports. An example of a product which has been banned from import into Singapore is chewing gum. This was effected pursuant to the Regulation of Imports and Exports (Chewing Gum) Regulations (Reg.4). There are also other statutes which regulate and control imports of particular products. For example, the Arms and Explosives Act (Cap 13) and subsidiary legislation made thereunder require a licence to be obtained for the import, manufacture and sale of arms and explosives.

16–16 As for import taxes or duties, the Customs (Duties) Order (Ord.4) sets out the custom duties payable, but the categories of products affected are very limited, which reflects Singapore's status as a free and open port. The Order, however, does specify that Goods and Services Tax at the rate of four per cent, levied in accordance with s.16 of the Goods and Services Tax Act (Cap 117A), is payable on imports. This rate will be increased to 5 per cent, with effect from January 1, 2004. There is also legislation dealing with the imposition of countervailing and anti-dumping duties, namely, the Countervailing and Anti-dumping Duties Act (Cap 65B).

16–17 Singapore is active in enacting laws to preserve the environment. A number of environmental laws have been enacted, some of which have an impact on the licensing, storage and labelling requirements for the import of products into Singapore. For instance, the Environmental Pollution Control Act (Cap 94A) provides that no person shall import or sell any hazardous substance unless he holds a requisite licence for such purpose. Further, no person shall possess for sale, sell or offer for sale any hazardous substance unless the container of the hazardous substance is labelled in the manner prescribed and approved.

16–18 The Hazardous Waste (Control of Export, Import and Transit) Act (Cap 122A) prohibits the import of hazardous or other waste unless the importer is the holder of a requisite import permit or the import has been ordered/authorised pursuant to Article 11 of the Basel Convention on the Control of Transboundary Movements of Hazardous Wastes and their Disposal.

16.4 Fiscal incentives

There are free trade zones in Singapore, namely, zones where goods in transit may be warehoused or packaged pending their transmission to respective destinations. There are five free trade zones for seaborne cargo and one for air cargo. Free trade zones provide facilities for the storage and re-export of dutiable and controlled goods. Goods in transit can be repacked or processed in free trade zones without incurring customs duties. **16–19**

In 1990, the Approved International Traders (AIT) Scheme was introduced to boost international trading activities through Singapore and to provide incentives for international trading activities conducted from Singapore. The scheme is administered by the International Enterprise Singapore (formerly the Trade Development Board of Singapore), also known as IE Singapore. **16–20**

International trading companies with worldwide networks and good track records qualify for the scheme and are granted a concessionary tax rate of 10 per cent on qualifying trading income with effect from the year of assessment 1991. To qualify under the scheme, the trading company must buy and sell from third countries. Approval for AIT status is granted on a case by case basis for both the type of commodities and the minimum turnover required. The approved commodities under the scheme include agricultural commodities and bulk edible products, industrial commodities, mineral commodities, building materials and machinery components. The list of approved commodities for tax concessions is reviewed and extended periodically. **16–21**

From June 1, 2001, the AIT Scheme and the Approved Oil Traders (AOT) Scheme were merged and administered as the Global Trader Programme (GTP). The specific conditions of the AIT Scheme remain unchanged. **16–22**

As far as taxation of income is concerned, Singapore has signed agreements for the avoidance of double taxation with 44 countries. All of Singapore's arrangements for the avoidance of double taxation provide for tax credit structures. The current tax rates (for the year of assessment 2002) are 24.5 per cent for corporations and a range between 3 per cent to 26 per cent for individuals. For the year of assessment 2003, the tax rates will be revised to 22 per cent for corporations and a range between 4 per cent to 22 per cent for individuals. **16–23**

16.5 Types of agency and distribution arrangements

There are three main types of distribution arrangements: **16–24**

- an exclusive distribution arrangement;
- a sole distribution arrangement; and
- a non-exclusive distribution arrangement.

The distribution arrangement usually defines the territory within which the distributor is to operate, and may even restrict the distributor's right to sell to certain classes of customers or to deal in certain lines of products which may compete with products of the principal.

16–25 The term used to describe the relationship between the parties is, however, not conclusive. In the final analysis, the precise nature and scope of a distribution arrangement and the rights and obligations of the parties must be ascertained from the express or implied terms of the agreement.

16–26 There are no restrictions under Singapore law as to the type of distribution arrangement the parties may enter into. This is left to the parties to determine depending on their commercial objectives and needs.

16–27 With regard to agents, although there are various common classifications of agents such as estate agents, insurance agents and forwarding agents, in the context of the sale of goods, the agency would generally be a special agency arrangement on a sole or exclusive or non-exclusive basis.

16–28 Regardless of whether a distribution or agency arrangement is to be entered into, one must be careful not to engage in pyramid selling which is illegal in Singapore under the Multi-Level Marketing and Pyramid Selling (Prohibition) Act (Cap 190). This Act defines a pyramid selling scheme or arrangement as any scheme or arrangement for the distribution or the purported distribution of a commodity whereby:

> "(a) a person may in any manner acquire a commodity or a right or a licence to acquire the commodity for sale, lease, licence or other distribution;
>
> (b) that person receives any benefit, directly or indirectly, as a result of—
>
> (i) the recruitment, acquisition, action or performance of one or more additional participants in the scheme or arrangement; or
>
> (ii) the sale, lease, licence or other distribution of the commodity by one or more additional participants in the scheme or arrangement; and
>
> (c) any benefit is or may be received by any other person who promotes, or participates in, the scheme or arrangement (other than a person referred to in paragraph (a) or an additional participant referred to in paragraph (b))."

16–29 The Minister for Law has the power, by order, to exclude certain schemes or arrangements from the definition of "pyramid selling scheme or arrangement". This power has been exercised by the enactment of the Multi-Level Marketing and Pyramid Selling (Excluded Schemes and Arrangements) Order (O 1).

16.6 Elements of a good agency or distribution agreement

As with any contract, the mark of a good agency or distribution agreement is one which is succinct, clear and comprehensive. All the rights, duties, obligations and liabilities of the parties should be spelt out with precision. These elements are especially important since such agreements frequently transcend different jurisdictions. Essential clauses to be incorporated in an agreement are discussed here on the assumption that the agreement is to be governed by Singapore law, which should, of course, be expressly provided for in the agreement. **16–30**

Clauses which are relevant both to an agency agreement and to a distribution agreement include, but are not limited to the clauses set out below. **16–31**

16.6.1 Definition of territory

The geographical definition of the territory within which the distributor is to distribute the goods, or within which the agent can act, must be defined clearly. In view of the relatively small market within Singapore, a distributor or an agent appointed in Singapore may be required to distribute the products to, or operate in and around, the surrounding countries, and in particular the ASEAN and other Asian countries. In such a situation, the agreement should contain provision to ensure that it is subject to such regulatory approvals as may be necessary and compliance with all applicable legislation and rules in the jurisdictions concerned. **16–32**

16.6.2 Advertising and market information

The supplier or principal, as the case may be, generally wishes to see a demand created and built up in the designated territory for his products and to have his trade mark advertised if the products are distributed under that mark. To this end, a clause requiring the distributor or the agent to undertake obligations to promote the sale of the products in the manner prescribed in the agreement, for example, by personal visits to customers or by advertising, would normally be included. **16–33**

16.6.3 Protection of intellectual property rights

The supplier or principal would wish to ensure that his intellectual property rights are protected. Intellectual property rights in Singapore are comprised of rights relating to patents, registered designs, copyright and related rights, trade marks, geographical indications and layout designs of integrated circuits. **16–34**

In the case of trade marks, where goods are sold under a particular trade **16–35** mark, a clause that the distributor or agent will not tamper with the mark and will be vigilant in drawing to the attention of the supplier or principal any infringement or improper or wrongful use of the mark in the territories concerned, should be included.

16–36 In the case of other intellectual property rights, the supplier or principal would similarly wish to ensure that his intellectual property rights are not infringed by third parties operating in the designated territory. As the distributor or agent would be in a better position to identify such infringements the supplier or principal may impose a term that the distributor or agent will assist in protecting the intellectual property rights of the supplier or principal from infringement by third parties.

16–37 Apart from the obligations imposed under the agreement on the distributor or agent, registration of the supplier's or principal's patents and trade marks in Singapore and other territories where the products are to be marketed or sold ought to be considered. Legislation is in force in Singapore for the registration and protection of trade marks. This is the Trade Marks Act (Cap 332). In the case of patents, the Patents Act (Cap 221) provides a system for direct registration of patents in Singapore. This Act is based on the UK Patents Act 1977.

16–38 A supplier or principal is also able to protect copyright in his subsisting works. The law governing copyright in Singapore is the Copyright Act (Cap 63) passed in 1987 and based on the Australian Copyright Act 1968. Computer programs fall within the definition of "literary work" as defined in the Copyright Act (Cap 63) and thus are entitled to copyright protection.

16–39 Another issue to consider is the law on parallel imports. In Singapore, parallel imports are goods which are manufactured outside Singapore by or with the consent of the copyright owner in the place of manufacture and are imported into Singapore, but not necessarily with the consent of the Singapore copyright owner. By virtue of a recent amendment to the Copyright Act, parallel imports into Singapore are permissible without the consent of the Singapore copyright owner. Consent of the Singapore copyright owner is required only where there is no copyright owner in the country of manufacture.

16–40 There is also legislation in force in Singapore for the protection of registered designs, layout designs of integrated circuits and geographical indications.

16–41 The Registered Designs Act (Cap 266) came into operation on November 13, 2000 and repealed the UK Designs (Protection) Act 1985 (Cap 339). The Registered Designs Act provides for the lodgment in Singapore of applications for registration of designs. Previously, such applications had to be lodged in the UK. All designs registered in the UK before November 13, 2000 are still protected in Singapore, but after this date, UK registered design owners will have to renew their UK designs in Singapore if they wish to continue registering their designs in Singapore.

16–42 The Layout-designs of Integrated Circuits Act (Cap 159A) provides statutory protection for original lay-out designs that are created after the commencement of the Act (*i.e.* February 15, 1999).

The Geographical Indications Act (Cap 117B) which came into effect on January 15, 1999 is new piece of legislation protecting geographical indicators which had to be previously protected under the Consumer Protection (Trade Descriptions and Safety Requirements) Act (Cap 53), the Trade Marks Act (Cap 332) and/or the general common law of passing off. **16–43**

16.6.4 Exclusion of liability for breach

It is relevant to consider whether either party to the distribution or agency agreement can insert a clause to exclude liability for breach of the agreement. It is generally possible to exclude liability for breach of contract where both parties enter into the contract in the course of their business. Where the contract is a standard form contract, the Unfair Contract Terms Act requires the exclusion clause to satisfy the criteria of reasonableness. A standard form contract is one in which the terms have been formulated by one party to be used in a recurring business enterprise so as to save costs and time, and which thus has not been the subject of a true negotiation between parties. **16–44**

16.6.5 Confidentiality and restraint of trade

A confidentiality provision in an agency/distribution agreement is of considerable importance to prevent the agent/distributor from divulging or using confidential information for purposes other than the discharge of the agency/distribution functions. Provision may also be made for a continuation of the confidentiality obligation for a period of time after the termination or expiration of the agreement. **16–45**

In addition to preserving confidentiality, the supplier or principal may also wish to ensure that the distributor or agent is restrained from dealing in the products after the termination of the agreement. If he so desires, this must be expressly spelt out in the agreement. **16–46**

The common law principle that all restraint of trade clauses are *prima facie* void unless reasonable in the interest of the parties concerned as well as in the interest of the public, applies in Singapore. **16–47**

16.6.6 Contracts (Rights Of Third Parties) Act (Cap 53B)

When drafting the distributorship or agency agreement, it is important to keep in mind the effect of the Contracts (Rights of Third Parties) Act (Cap 53B). **16–48**

The Contracts (Rights Of Third Parties) Act came into force on January 1, 2002 and reformed the common law position with regard to privity of contract. It is based on the UK Contracts (Rights of Third Parties) Act 1999 (see the discussion of this Act in Chapter 1.10). It confers upon third parties, **16–49** in certain circumstances, the right to enforce benefits conferred upon them in contracts to which they are not a party. Parties who do not intend for third parties to have rights in accordance with the Contracts (Rights Of Third Parties) Act will have to provide for this expressly in the contract.

16.6.7 Government and other statutory approvals

16–50 Legislative restrictions, as well as those imposed by the applicable regulatory authority, have to be considered for the sale of particular products. For instance, for the sale of food, the Sale of Food Act and the Food Regulations have to be considered. These, among others, provide measures to ensure the quality and accurate labelling of food. The Medicines Act and the regulations made thereunder control both the type of medicinal products that may be imported into the country and the labelling requirements for these products.

16–51 There is also environmental legislation which requires approvals to be obtained before certain products may be imported into the country. In particular, there is legislation governing the importation, sale, transit, storage, use and dealing of hazardous substances namely, the Environmental Pollution Control Act and the Hazardous Waste (Control of Export, Import and Transit) Act.

16.6.8 Termination clauses

16–52 The agreement would usually prescribe the period for which it is to remain in force. It is also common practice to define the initial term of the agreement and to provide that thereafter the agreement shall continue in force either indefinitely or from year to year unless terminated by written notice of the length prescribed in the agreement. Where there is a continuation of the agreement from year to year, the agreement would usually require the notice to be given before the expiration of each yearly period.

16–53 The agreement may further provide for the immediate termination of the agreement on the occurrence of stipulated events, for example, a breach of the agreement, the cessation of business, a change in the constitution of a contracting party or the insolvency or liquidation of a contracting party. Certain of these stipulated events may not involve the default of a contracting party (for instance a change in constitution). In such cases, the agreement may also cover the subject of compensation payable in the event of a premature termination of the agreement not due to the distributor's or agent's default. The agreement may also include a force majeure clause to excuse a party from performing the contract due to unavoidable causes.

16–54 Where the termination concerned is occasioned by reason of a breach of contract, the recovery of damages would be governed by common law principles. Such damages are also, of course, recoverable by the innocent party in the event of any breach of the contract, even if it does not result in the termination of the contract.

16.6.9 Dispute resolution, choice of law and jurisdiction

Provisions on dispute resolution, choice of law and jurisdiction are important provisions in agency or distribution agreements, particularly those relating to cross-border agreements. With regard to choice of law, the parties are generally free to expressly agree on the applicable law governing an agreement. The Singapore courts will give effect to the parties' express choice of law if their choice is *bona fide* and legal and does not contravene public policy. In a similar vein, the parties to an agreement can agree to submit all disputes regarding the agreement to the exclusive jurisdiction of the courts of a particular country. The Singapore courts will generally hold the parties to an exclusive jurisdiction clause in the agreement, as seen in the recent Singapore case of *The Hung Vuong-2; Owners of the Ship or Vessel "Hung Vuong-2" v Owners of Cargo Lately Laden on Board the Ship or Vessel "Hung Vuong-3"* [2001] 3 S.L.R. 146 at 151, where it was held that a party seeking to bring an action in a Singapore court in breach of a jurisdiction clause must show "strong cause". **16–55**

Careful thought must be given to the types of resolution methods that may be employed in the event of a dispute between the parties. There are a number of methods regularly used to resolve disputes in international commercial transactions. Examples are renegotiation, mediation/conciliation, arbitration and litigation. **16–56**

In a cross-border agency or distribution agreement, it is most common to find a dispute resolution clause which provides for arbitration of any dispute that may arise under the agreement. Arbitration is favoured as a dispute resolution device of choice because a major advantage of arbitration lies in the fact that an international treaty, the United Nations Convention on the Recognition and Enforcement of Foreign Arbitral Awards (New York, June 10, 1958), permits the enforcement of arbitral awards rendered in one Convention country in another Convention country. 132 countries, including Singapore, have ratified or acceded to this Convention (as per the status update on the United Nations Commission on International Trade Law (UNCITRAL) website, updated as at October 28, 2002). Accordingly, a Singapore arbitral award would be enforceable in any of the other Convention countries. In contrast to arbitration, there is no parallel international treaty for the enforcement of court judgments. **16–57**

A further advantage of arbitration lies in the fact that it is possible to appoint an expert in the relevant field to hear and resolve the dispute. Arbitration also makes it easier to preserve the confidentiality of sensitive and proprietary information. This may not always be possible with litigation. **16–58**

The Singapore government has been active in promoting Singapore as a centre for arbitration and has provided the necessary infrastructure by establishing the Singapore International Arbitration Centre (the SIAC) in **16–59**

1991. The SIAC provides free information and advice on dispute resolution in Singapore and will, on request, administer arbitrations from the onset of dispute up to the making of the award. The SIAC also maintains a Panel of Accredited Arbitrators consisting of local and international experts from which parties may appoint the arbitrators for their dispute.

16–60 Singapore's arbitration laws also enhance Singapore's suitability as an international arbitration forum. For example, the International Arbitration Act (Cap 143A) was amended in 2002 to clarify that the rules of arbitration adopted by the parties will apply and be given effect, to the extent that such rules are not inconsistent with a provision of the UNITRAL model law or Part II of the International Arbitration Act. Essentially, this amendment serves to give as much effect as possible to the parties' choice of arbitral procedure.

16–61 Should the parties prefer litigation as a means of resolving disputes arising under the agreement, it is noteworthy that due to the reorganisation and revisions of the court system and rules, litigation has become a much quicker and efficient process. Thus, a suit filed in the High Court of Singapore can now be heard within a period of six months. An appeal from a decision delivered by a lower court is usually heard within six months from the date of appeal.

16.6.10 Clauses relevant to distribution agreements only

16.6.10.1 Appointment

16–62 The right of the distributor to purchase the products for resale in the territory defined in the agreement will be granted on a sole, exclusive or non-exclusive basis and this must be specified in the agreement. It is important that a distribution agreement puts it beyond doubt that the distributor is acting as a principal in his own right in buying from the supplier and reselling to customers in the designated territory, and that the distributor has no authority or power to bind the supplier, or to contract in the name of and create a liability against the supplier.

16.6.10.2 Supply of products

16–63 Under a distribution agreement, the distributor may give an undertaking to place orders of a fixed quantity or amount with the supplier at regular intervals or within a fixed period. In this regard, the distribution agreement may give the supplier an option of giving notice of termination if the orders placed by the distributor do not represent the stipulated quantity or value. Alternatively, a distribution agreement may require the distributor to place orders with the supplier only if and when the distributor receives such orders from customers in the designated territory.

16.6.10.3 Conditions of purchase and resale

A distribution agreement is not in itself a contract of sale of goods. It merely lays down the general terms on which later individual contracts of sale will be concluded. In this respect, it is usual to find a clause in the distribution agreement providing for the distributor to be bound by the supplier's conditions of sale, as are from time to time in force, in making its purchases from the supplier. **16–64**

The distribution agreement may also require the distributor, in reselling the goods it buys from the supplier, to do so on like terms to the conditions of sale of the supplier. In particular, if the supplier seeks to limit the warranties it gives with respect to the products, the supplier may require the distributor not to give any greater warranties with respect to the products than those that the supplier is prepared to give to the distributor. It is pertinent to note in this context the application of the Sale of Goods Act, which incorporates provisions with respect to the formation of the contract. These include the implied conditions and warranties that are applicable, the effects of a contract for the sale of goods, the performance of the contract, the rights of unpaid sellers against the goods and actions for breach of contract. **16–65**

It is also pertinent to mention that there is no legislation specifically governing product liability. Thus, liability for injury arising from defective products would be determinable according to common law principles. **16–66**

16.6.10.4 Time of payment and passing of title

As the distributor deals as a principal in relation to the supplier, the latter would wish payment to be made immediately upon the supply being made. This is particularly pronounced in an exclusive or sole distributorship arrangement. The distributor, however, would wish to pay the supplier for the goods with the proceeds arising from the sale of the products. Thus, the distributor would prefer to make payment on a credit basis. **16–67**

Where payment is on credit terms, the supplier may require title to the products to continue to remain with him until full payment has been received from the distributor. To achieve this, a retention of title clause may be inserted into the distributorship agreement. If the distributor is a company registered under the Companies Act and the retention of title clause has the effect of providing the supplier with a security interest over the products and/or their proceeds, so as to constitute a charge, the obligation to register the charge under the Companies Act should be noted. Where there is a failure to register a charge that is registrable, apart from the consequences under the Companies Act for the distributor, the security interest of the supplier would be void as against the liquidator in the event of the insolvency of the distributor, and against any creditor of the company. **16–68**

16.6.11 Clauses relevant to agency agreements only

16.6.11.1 Agent's authority

16–69 The agreement would normally authorise the agent to promote the sale of the products, but not necessarily to enter into any contract with a customer on behalf of the principal. This is significant, as the act of the agent in concluding contracts on behalf of the principal (where the principal is a foreign corporation) in the territory may give rise to the implication that the principal is carrying on business in the territory. Consequently, this would expose the principal to tax implications and registration obligations under the Companies Act.

16.6.11.2 Remuneration

16–70 The agent's right to remuneration or commission would be specified in the agreement. The remuneration of an agent is normally in the form of commission on sales, which may include commission (albeit at a lower rate) in respect of sales concluded by the principal directly with customers in the territory.

16.6.11.3 Accounting to principal

16–71 An agency agreement would usually impose an obligation on the agent to keep proper accounts and records of all agency transactions and to produce these to the principal in accordance with the terms of the agreement or upon request by the principal. The agent would be required to keep the records of such accounts, money and property of the principal separate from his own. Where an agent is authorised to receive monies on behalf of the principal, the agreement should impose on the agent the obligation to account for and to pay to the principal all such monies.

16.7 Manufacturing agreements

16–72 The following sections (Chapter 16.8–16.10) discuss issues relating to the transfer of technology in the context of manufacturing agreements.

16.8 Technology transfer

16–73 A transfer of technology may be effected in any of the following forms:

- the licensing of the use or exploitation of trade marks;

- the assignment or licensing of the use or exploitation of patents for inventions, improvements, industrial models and drawings;
- the furnishing of technical knowhow and information by plans, diagrams, models etc, or
- technical consultancy services and assistance in whatever form it may be furnished.

In Singapore, there is no legislation in force controlling the transfer of technology, save for provisions contained in the Patents Act (s.55), the Copyright Act (Pt VI) and the Layout-Designs of Integrated Circuits Act (Pt V) dealing with compulsory licences of patents, copyrights and layout-designs of integrated circuits respectively. Neither is there any need to obtain government approvals for the transfer of technology. Technology transfer is therefore largely a matter of contract between the supplier and the acquirer of the technology. For example, a licensor of technology is free to license his technology upon different terms, such as different scales of royalties, to two or more licensees, each of whom has a separate and defined exclusive area of operation in a particular territory, or each of whom is appointed on a non-exclusive basis for that territory. The common law principles of contract law would be applicable in this regard. **16–74**

16.9 Protection of intellectual property rights

Given that a transfer of technology in a manufacturing agreement would principally involve intellectual property as the subject matter, it is relevant to consider the protection of intellectual property rights under Singapore law. **16–75**

Under the Patents Act, applicants for patent protection are able to register patents in Singapore and thus secure privileges and rights similar in all material aspects to those accorded to patentees whose patents are registered in the UK under the United Kingdom Patents Act 1977. An applicant desiring patent protection in Singapore may, instead of making an application under the Patents Act, file an international application for a patent under the Patent Cooperation Treaty (signed at Washington on June 19, 1970). Singapore is a signatory to the Treaty. Under the Patents Act, an international application under the Patent Cooperation Treaty is treated as an application under the Act. **16–76**

With the registration of a patent for an invention under the Patents Act, the patentee is entitled to an absolute monopoly in respect of the invention for a period of 20 years from the date of filing his patent application or such other date as may be prescribed. This monopoly right allows him to prevent others from exploiting his invention. **16–77**

Under the Copyright Act, the owner of the copyright in a work or other subject matter is given a bundle of exclusive rights to do certain acts. These acts would include reproduction in any material form, broadcasting, per- **16–78** formance in public and the making of an adaptation. The nature of the exclusive rights granted by the Act vary according to the category of work or subject matter. There is no registration process under the Act to enjoy the rights accorded by the Act. Copyright accrues automatically and immediately on the creation of a work or other subject matter. It should be noted that there is no violation of copyright if another person independently creates a work which happens to be substantially similar to the copyright work.

16–79 In so far as trade marks or service marks are concerned, the Trade Marks Act confers a statutory monopoly for the use of the mark in relation to the goods or services for which it is registered. The period of protection for a mark is 10 years but registration can be renewed for further periods of 10 years each. The registration of a mark under the Trade Marks Act, whilst according protection to the mark under the Act, does not prevent the trade mark holder from pursuing an action for passing-off in respect of an unauthorised user of the mark.

16–80 Under the Registered Designs Act, a registered design in Singapore may be protected for a maximum of 15 years. The initial period of registration is five years from the date of registration but may be extended for up to two further periods of five years each after the initial period. A design refers to features of shape, configuration, pattern or ornament applied to an article via an industrial process. The registration of a design under the Registered Designs Act gives the owner the exclusive right to make or import the design into Singapore, for sale, hire or use for the purposes of trade or business. It also gives the owner the right to sell, hire and offer or expose for sale or hire, any article in respect of which the design is registered. The right in the registered design is infringed by any person who uses the design without the consent of the registered owner.

16–81 A layout-design of an integrated circuit is essentially a three-dimensional disposition of the elements and interconnections making up an integrated circuit (which is an electronic circuit in which the elements of the circuit are integrated into some medium and function as a unit). Such layout-designs are protected under the Layout-designs of Integrated Circuits Act. A layout-design which qualifies for protection under this Act is protected automatically as there is no requirement for registration or deposit of the layout-design. The duration of protection is either 10 years after the first commercial exploitation, if the exploitation takes place within five years after the year it is created, or in any other case, 15 years after the year it is created.

16–82 In the case of geographical indications, these are indications which identify a particular good as originating from a place where a given quality, reputation or other characteristic of the good is essentially attributable to its geographical origin, for example, "Champagne" and "Bordeaux". Protection under the Geographical Indications Act is limited only to geographical indications of a country/territory which is a member of the World Trade Organisation, a party to the Paris Convention for the Protection of Industrial Property, or one designated in the Government Gazette by the Minister as a qualifying country. Like copyright, protection for geographical indications arise automatically. If, however, the geographical indication meets the registrability requirements under the Trade Marks Act, it may be registered as a trade mark, collective mark or certification mark.

Apart from statutory protection, intellectual property is also protected by the law (common law) of confidence which protects confidential information. This is particularly significant in the context of commercial trade secrets. In addition, goodwill attached to a business is protected by the tort of passing-off at common law. **16–83**

16.10 Critical contractual terms

16.10.1 Restrictive terms and conditions

Contractual restrictions are commonly imposed by a supplier of technology on the party acquiring it. Examples are a ban on exports, a restriction as to the customers the licensee may serve, a resale price maintenance provision and a tying clause. The question may arise as to whether such restrictions are enforceable in the light of the common law doctrine of restraint of trade which is applicable in Singapore. Under this doctrine, contractual provisions in restraint of trade are *prima facie* void unless they are reasonable in the interests of the parties concerned as well as in the interest of the public. Additionally, where licensing of a patent is involved, the Patents Act must be considered, as the Act renders void certain restrictive terms in a patent licence. **16–84**

A licensing arrangement is a typical example of technology transfer in a manufacturing agreement. The licensee may be given the exclusive right to manufacture and sell the products using the licensed technology in the contract territory. To protect the interests of the licensor or other licensees, the licensing agreement would prohibit the licensee from exploiting the licensed technology or selling the products manufactured therewith outside the contract territory. Such a ban on exports is in reality a limit on the rights granted by the licensor to the licensee. The licensor is merely exercising his rights as the owner of the relevant intellectual property and the licensee is not being asked to give up a freedom which he would otherwise have had. Consequently, a prohibition of exports in this regard is not a restraint of trade and the doctrine of restraint of trade does not apply. The licensor is therefore at liberty to restrict the licensee from exporting products manufactured with the licensed technology outside the territory for which he is licensed. **16–85**

In a similar vein, the licensor is equally at liberty to set resale prices for products manufactured by the licensee using the licensed technology and to impose restrictions on the classes of customers to whom the licensee may sell these products. Such restrictions are limits on the rights granted by the licensor to the licensee. **16–86**

A tying clause, in contrast, is subject to the doctrine of restraint of trade **16–87** and its reasonableness must be examined. Under a tying clause, the licensee is required to obtain products or services exclusively from the licensor or his nominee. The licensee is therefore restrained from doing what he would otherwise have been free to do. Where the tied products or services are necessary for the proper exploitation of the licensed technology, it is unlikely that the courts in Singapore would hold the tying clause to be unreasonable. On the other hand, where the tied products or services are outside the scope of the licensed technology, the tying clause may be considered as being unreasonable and consequently unenforceable.

16–88 With respect to a tying clause contained in a licence to work a patented invention, the Patents Act must be considered. The Act declares it unlawful for a patentee to grant a licence to work a patented invention which is conditional on the licensee also acquiring other goods from the patentee or his nominee, or conditional on the licensee not acquiring articles or patented processes not supplied or owned by the patentee or his nominee. A tying clause of this nature is void under the Act. Neither the Act, nor the regulations made under it, provide that a tying clause in a licence to work a patented invention is permitted on the ground that the items subjected to the tying clause are technically necessary for the proper realisation of the patented invention. This is designed to control attempts by a patentee to extend his monopoly rights under his patent to items which are not the subject of the patent.

16–89 The existence of a tying clause caught by the Act in a licence granted by the patentee can effectively nullify the patent. A defendant in any proceedings for infringement of a patent has an absolute defence if he is able to prove that at the time of the alleged infringement such a tying clause relating to the patent in suit was in force. This is the case even though the defendant is a stranger to the contract containing the offending clause.

16–90 An important exception to the foregoing must be noted. A tying obligation in a patent licence is permitted under the Act if the patentee offered to grant a licence on reasonable alternative terms, which does not include a tying clause prohibited under the Act, and the licensee can relieve himself of the tying obligation by giving three months' written notice and paying such compensation as may be determined by an arbitrator.

16.10.2 Royalty terms

16–91 The obligation to pay royalties, the period for which such royalties are payable and the quantum of royalties are matters purely of contract as there is no legislation governing such payments. In particular, there is nothing to prevent the parties from agreeing that the party acquiring technology is obliged to continue paying royalties after the technology enters the public domain. An obligation to pay a minimum royalty is permissible and it is up to the parties to determine how the royalty payable is to be calculated. Again, there is no legislation giving a licensee of technology the right to a free paid-up licence after a certain period of time, or after payment of a certain amount of royalty. It is up to the parties to provide for it expressly in their contract.

As the operation of the Exchange Control Act (Cap 99) (as announced in the MAS circular dated May 25, 1978) has been suspended since 1978, the remittance of royalties and other payments under a licence agreement to or from Singapore may be made freely, save that where a royalty is paid by a party in Singapore to a non-resident person, there is a liability to withhold tax payable on the royalty at the rate of 15 per cent under the Income Tax Act (Cap 134). Notice of the withholding must be given to the Comptroller of Income Tax within 10 days of the withholding. The tax withheld must be paid to the Comptroller within 10 days of payment of the royalty. A Goods and Services Tax at four per cent is also payable on the royalty if the licensor is a registered person under the Goods and Services Tax Act (Cap 117A). With effect from January 1, 2004, the Goods and Services Tax will be raised to 5 per cent. **16–92**

16.10.3 Exclusion of liability for breach

The only statute applicable in Singapore which deals with exclusion of liability clauses is the Unfair Contract Terms Act, which in effect is a reproduction of the UK Unfair Contract Terms Act 1977. Under this Act, a party in breach may not seek to exempt itself from liability by contract unless the contractual term satisfies the requirement of reasonableness. This, however, applies only to exemption clauses incorporated in a contract entered into upon the defaulting party's written standard terms of business. The Unfair Contract Terms Act is not applicable to exemption clauses incorporated in negotiated contracts entered into by the parties. The enforcement of an exemption clause in a negotiated contract will be determined in accordance with common law principles. In particular, when in doubt, the courts applying the *contra proferentem* rule will be inclined to construe an exemption clause against the party relying on it. **16–93**

16.10.4 Termination

An agreement providing for the transfer of technology, such as a licensing agreement, would usually incorporate a provision entitling the licensor to terminate the agreement forthwith on the occurrence of certain events, for example a breach of the agreement by the licensee, the insolvency or liquidation of the licensee, non-payment of royalties payable under the agreement and the improper use of the licence. The agreement is also likely to contain a provision giving either party the right to terminate the agreement by giving a specified period of notice. **16–94**

Quite apart from an express termination clause, a party to a contract is entitled to terminate the contract forthwith at common law if the other party commits a breach of a condition or otherwise repudiates the contract. **16–95**

If the term breached is not a condition, it could be an innominate term, the breach of which gives rise to a right to terminate the contract if the nature and consequences of the breach are so serious as to deprive the innocent party of substantially the whole benefit which he is to derive from the contract.

16–96 In addition, under the Patents Act, a statutory right is given to either party to a patent licence to terminate the licence (to the extent that the licence relates to the product/invention) on giving three months' written notice at any time after the patent, which is the subject matter of the licence, has ceased to be in force. This statutory right of termination prevails over any contrary provision in the patent licence.

16.10.5 Compensation on termination

16–97 Where a licensing agreement is terminated by the licensor, whether by virtue of a termination clause or under common law, on the ground of a breach on the part of the licensee, the licensee, being the defaulting party, will not have any right to compensation under the general law relating to breach of contract, there being no specific law applying purely to licensees or acquirers of technology. In such a situation, it is the licensor as the aggrieved party who is entitled to compensation. He may claim damages at common law against the defaulting party by commencing legal action.

16–98 Alternatively, the licensor as the aggrieved party may claim the agreed amount of compensation stipulated in the agreement. Under Singapore law, it is possible to include a clause imposing an obligation to pay a specified amount of money by way of liquidated damages for breach of contract, including delay or failure to perform the contract. The amount of liquidated damages must be a genuine pre-estimate by the parties of the loss that the non-defaulting party is likely to suffer in the circumstances. If the sum is in the nature of a penalty, the courts will not uphold the term of the contract. The local law on this subject is based on English common law.

16–99 Where the agreement is terminated by the licensor without notice in accordance with the termination clause and other than for breach of contract, the licensee does not have any legal entitlement to compensation in the absence of any provision in the agreement according such right. Similarly, the licensee has no legal right to compensation if the licensor terminates the agreement by giving the contractual period of notice or the agreement expires by effluxion of time, unless the agreement provides otherwise.

16.10.6 Formalities

16–100 There are no prescribed formalities to the execution of an agreement relating to technology transfer. The agreement may be executed under hand or under seal. It should also be noted that under the Electronic Transactions Act (Cap 88) (which came into force on July 10, 1998), unless otherwise agreed by the parties, an offer and the acceptance of an offer may be expressed by means of electronic records. An "electronic record" is defined in the same Act as "a record generated, communicated, received or stored by electronic, magnetic, optical or other means in an information systems or for transmission from one information system to another".

Where a licensee is granted a right to use a registered mark, it is advisable to secure the right to such user in an agreement and to ensure that the appropriate application for registration of the licensee as a registered user of the mark is made under the Trade Marks Act. Until the licence agreement is registered, it is ineffective as against a person acquiring a conflicting interest in or under the registered trade mark in ignorance of it. **16–101**

A licence or assignment of a patent granted under the Patents Act should also be registered under that Act. Registration enables a licensee's claim to the property in a patent or application for a patent to prevail over conflicting claims in the circumstances specified in the Act. **16–102**

Applications for the record of assignment, mortgage or license of a registered design under the Registered Designs Act should also be made at the Registry of Designs. Unless and until such an application is made, the registrable transaction is ineffective as against a person acquiring a conflicting interest in the registered design in ignorance of it. **16–103**

16.11 Laws relating to unfair trade practices

There is currently no legislation in Singapore dealing with unfair trade practices or unfair competition. However, Singapore law does provide for fair competition in certain areas. In respect of registered trade and service marks, the Trade Marks Act gives statutory recognition to fair competition by protecting such marks. At common law, the tort of passing-off protects goodwill in marks, whether registered or not, names and get-up in connection with goods or services, by prohibiting any person from misrepresenting his goods or services as those of another. In addition, the Consumer Protection (Trade Descriptions and Safety Requirements) Act (Cap 53) makes it an offence to make a false trade description of goods. **16–104**

The Singapore Ministry of Trade and Industry has conducted a public consultation on a draft Consumer Protection (Fair Trading) Bill. The proposed Bill is designed to protect consumers (being defined as individuals only) against unfair practices. The Bill does not apply to, *inter alia*, transactions and proposed transactions where the value of the transaction exceeds S$20,000, or where the amount of compensation payable by the consumer exceeds S$20,000. The proposed Bill gives a consumer who has suffered loss as a result of an unfair practice by a supplier the right to bring an action in a court to obtain compensation from the supplier. Under the Bill, it will be an unfair practice to do or say anything (or omit to do or say anything), if as a result a consumer might reasonably be deceived or misled, to make a false claim, or to take advantage of a consumer if the person knows (or should reasonably be expected to know) that the consumer is not **16–105** in a position to protect his own interests or is not reasonably able to understand the effect of the transaction in question.

16–106 The common law tort of injurious falsehood is of importance in the area of comparative advertising. To establish a case of injurious falsehood, there must be proof of a false and malicious disparagement by the defendant of the goods, business or services of the plaintiff. The disparagement must be such that a reasonable and sensible person would take it to be a serious claim and specific claim that, in comparison with the defendant's good, the plaintiff's products are materially defective (see *Clark & Lindsell on Torts*, 18th ed. (2000), para.23–20).

16–107 The Singapore Code of Advertising Practice, which is non-statutory in nature, regulates and controls advertising in Singapore by providing guidelines to advertisers, advertising agencies, media and individuals on what is and/or is not acceptable. The Code provides, among other things, that advertisements should not unfairly attack or discredit other products or advertisements and should not take unfair advantage of the goodwill attached to the trade mark or symbol of another firm or its products or the goodwill acquired by the other firm's advertising campaign.

16–108 The current Code was published in 1976, and has remained unchanged since. However, the Code is expected to be updated in the near future.

16.12 Other relevant considerations

16–109 There is legislation in Singapore governing quality, licensing, labelling and safety requirements for products. There is also legislation providing for the regulation and control of imports, as well as imposing taxes or duties on imports, see Chapter 16.3.

Chapter 17

The United States[1]

Contents

17.1 Introduction

Due to its large consumer market and the extensive demand for innovative technology, the United States is an extremely attractive market for many licensors, distributors and manufacturers. This chapter provides a general overview of the relevant US regulatory environment and identifies selected key issues which non-US licensors, distributors and manufacturers should consider prior to entering into agency, distributorship or licensing transactions in the United States or with US persons. This chapter then outlines certain contract issues that could be of particular importance to a lawyer representing a non-US party to an agency, distribution or licensing agreement that is either subject to US law or with a US counterparty. **17–01**

There are a number of general and specific matters that are likely to be relevant to a non-US entity commencing or continuing to do business in the United States, including general tax planning concerns and strategies, the appropriate form in which to operate a business in the United States (branch versus subsidiary) and a thorough review of the scope and applicability of laws, regulations and administrative and judicial decisions that may affect a particular transaction. Such matters are beyond the scope of this chapter, but could significantly affect the success of a particular transaction. **17–02**

[1] A number of lawyers at Mayer, Brown, Rowe & Maw LLP and its associated US limited partnership Mayer, Brown, Rowe & Maw LLP, have contributed to this chapter. For further information contact: (i) Mark R. Uhrynuk or Sterling M. Dorish, a partner and associate resident in the London office of Mayer, Brown, Rowe & Maw LLP (+44 (0)20 728 4282) or (ii) Michael E Bieniek or Deborah Schavey Ruff, partners resident in the Chicago office of Mayer, Brown, Rowe & Maw LLP (+1 312 782 0600). *The material contained in this Chapter was prepared as of November, 2002. This material is not a comprehensive treatment of the subject matter discussed herein and is not intended to provide legal advice.*

17.2 Regulatory overview

17–03 The US legal system consists of (i) federal laws, statutes and administrative and judicial rulings of general applicability throughout the United States and (ii) state and local laws, statutes and administrative and judicial rulings that apply solely to activities in a particular state or locality (or to a subsidiary incorporated in such state).

17–04 These two basic levels of regulation are supported by separate court systems. The federal level consists of federal district courts located in each state or similar jurisdiction. Appeals from those courts may be taken to a court of appeals, with final appeals taken to the US Supreme Court. Each state has a similar court system with the court of first instance being the state district or county courts (or magistrates, in certain instances), with appeals taken in most cases to a state court of appeals and then to a state supreme court. Federal courts are courts of limited subject matter jurisdiction. A dispute must involve a question of federal law or must be between parties of different domicile to be heard in federal court. In some circumstances, a suit filed in state court that could have originally been filed in federal court may be "removed" to federal court.

17–05 The effect of the US's dual system is that US federal laws almost always apply to contractual relationships (even if the agreement expressly purports to be governed by the laws of a particular US state) and that the laws of one or more states may apply to a specific contractual relationship, depending on the location and scope of the underlying business activities. As a general matter, most purely contractual issues are governed by state law, while federal law governs antitrust matters and interstate commerce as well as most issues relating to intellectual property rights (with the notable exception of trade secrets/knowhow). It is generally necessary to comply with both federal and state laws, although federal law may (but does not always) pre-empt inconsistent state laws.

17.2.1 US federal laws

17–06 At the federal level, laws particularly relevant to agency, distribution and licensing arrangements will include those relating to intellectual property rights, competition/antitrust matters, international trade and taxation.

17.2.1.1 Intellectual property rights

17–07 In the United States, there are generally four types of intellectual property rights that are protected by law; namely, patents, trade marks and service marks, copyrights and trade secrets. With the exception of trade secrets, these intellectual property rights are primarily regulated at the federal level. Applicable federal statutes in this area are (i) the Patent Act of 1952, (ii) the

Copyright Act and (iii) the Lanham Act (as amended by the Trademark Law Revision Act of 1986). A brief description of the protections provided by these statutes is contained in Chapter 17.3.1 below.

17.2.1.2 Competition/antitrust

The principal federal competition/antitrust statutes in the United States are (i) the Sherman Act, (ii) the Clayton Act (as amended by the Robinson-Patman Price Discrimination Act) and (ii) the Federal Trade Commission Act. The Sherman Act deals primarily with issues involving restraint of trade and monopolisation. The Clayton Act deals primarily with mergers, price discrimination, tying arrangements and other arrangements that could lessen competition. The Federal Trade Commission Act generally prohibits unfair competition and unfair or deceptive practices affecting US commerce. In addition, the federal agencies responsible for antitrust enforcement released the 1995 Antitrust Guidelines for the Licensing of Intellectual Property. The common law doctrine of unfair competition is also relevant at the federal level. Aspects of these laws that are most significant to agency, distribution and licensing agreements are discussed in greater detail in Section III.B below. **17–08**

17.2.1.3 International trade law

US international trade law includes a wide range of laws affecting international trade in goods, services, technology and capital. Among the most important of these laws are: **17–09**

- the trade remedies laws, including the antidumping and countervailing duty laws and safeguard laws, which provide tariff and related remedies against unfairly priced, unfairly subsidized and injurious imports of goods;
- the customs laws, which establish requirements and rules for the classification, valuation and marking of imported merchandise;
- the laws implementing multilateral and bilateral trade agreements, including the WTO, NAFTA, and the free-trade agreements between the United States and such countries as Israel, Jordan and Chile, which set special rules for importation, investment and services trade;
- the embargo laws, which prohibit almost all business dealings between US companies and such countries as Cuba, Iran, Iraq, Libya, Sudan and others, as well as nationals of such countries and thousands of "specially designated nationals";
- the export control laws, which restrict the use, the user, and the destination of certain goods and technologies originating in the United States;

- the anti-boycott laws, which bar US companies from participating in, or providing information in support of, international boycotts that conflict with US foreign policy;
- the anti-bribery laws, which bar US companies, directly or indirectly, from offering or paying anything of value to foreign government officials, foreign political parties or candidates, or officials of public international organisations, in order to obtain or retain business or to secure any improper advantage; and
- the national security laws, which require that foreign investors obtain approval from the US government prior to concluding the acquisition of US companies involved in defence, intelligence, or other national security businesses.

An analysis of these laws, which are quite complex and that are enforced by the imposition of substantial sanctions, is beyond the scope of this chapter.

17.2.1.4 Taxation

17–10 In the United States, taxes may be imposed at the federal, state and local level. Although analysis of US taxation is beyond the scope of this chapter, it is important that any non-US entity entering into agency, distribution or licensing arrangements in the United States determine the extent to which such activity could subject such entity to US taxation.

17–11 Under US income tax law there is a distinction between (i) passive US source income, which is generally subject to withholding tax at a flat rate of 30 per cent (unless reduced by an applicable treaty) and (ii) income effectively connected with a US trade or business (and a US "permanent establishment" if certain treaties apply), which is taxed at US domestic rates for that income and, in the case of a non-US corporation, potentially subject to a further branch profit tax of 30 per cent (unless reduced by an applicable treaty). Whether income arising out of an agency, distribution or licensing arrangement gives rise to a US trade or business depends on a variety of factors, including the existence of a US office and the activities of US employees and agents. The test to determine whether such income connected with a US trade or business is US-sourced is dependent on (i) whether the income arises out of assets used or held for the use and the conduct of a trade or business within the United States or (ii) whether the activities of such a US trade or business are a material factor in the realisation of the income. If a non-US company maintains a US office or other fixed place of business, certain foreign source income attributable to the office also is considered connected with the US business.

17–12 In addition, in the case of agency, distribution or licensing arrangements with related persons, a non-US party should ensure that any potential transfer pricing issues are in order and that inter-company royalty rates comply with the applicable provisions of the US Internal Revenue Code of 1986 and the Internal Revenue Service thereunder.

17.2.1.5 Other areas of federal regulations

There are a number of industry-specific federal laws that may affect the distribution of certain types of products, such as the distribution of automobiles (the Automobile Dealer Suits Against Manufacturers Act), distribution of fuel (the Federal Petroleum Practices Act) and food and pharmaceutical products (the Food and Drug Act). An analysis of these and other areas of federal regulation is beyond the scope of this Chapter. **17–13**

17.2.2 US state law

In establishing agency, distribution and licensing relationships, a non-US party entering the US market is well advised to consider the United States as a group of 50 separate markets. Areas of regulation at the state level that will be particularly relevant to consider include: (i) the Uniform Commercial Code (the "UCC"), which governs, *inter alia*, the sale of goods within a particular state; (ii) the Uniform Computer Information Transactions Act (the "UCITA"), which governs, *inter alia*, contract law that applies to computer software, multimedia products, computer data and databases, and online information; (iii) sales representatives laws, which generally protect the right of a sales representative or agent to receive a commission; (iv) state franchise and business opportunity laws, which regulate the treatment of franchisees and the offer and sale of "business opportunities"; (v) state "doing business" laws, which require the registration of entities doing business in a particular state; and (vi) trade secret laws. Certain aspects of these laws and regulations are discussed in Chapter 17.3 and 17.4 below. **17–14**

Contracts entered into with respect to activities in a particular state or purported to be governed by the laws of a US state will be subject to state statutory and common law. For example, the implied covenant of good faith and fair dealing, which arises in most states through adoption of the UCC or by state court decision, serves to protect the interests of agents and distributors in their contractual relationship with suppliers. In addition, there may be specific state regulation over a particular type of industry. This may include, for example, car, farm equipment and fuel dealers and the distribution of alcohol and food. **17–15**

While applicable state law (as well as local regulations and case law) should be reviewed in detail prior to entering into an important contractual relationship governed by the laws of a particular US state, there are often "Uniform" or "Model" laws that have been passed in one form or another in many or most states, depending on the area of law involved. This chapter is necessarily limited to a discussion of generally applicable state law. For important commercial relationships, it would be prudent to obtain advice from knowledgeable US counsel, since local law, decisions or practice may vary substantially. **17–16**

17.2.3 International conventions

17–17 The United States is a party to the UN Convention on Contracts for the International Sale of Goods ("CISG Convention"). The CISG Convention will undoubtedly be known to international manufacturers and suppliers of goods, however, a non-US party selling goods in the United States should consider the application of the UCC and the UCITA (described in Chapter 17.3.3 and 17.3.4 below). The United States is also a party to the U.N. Convention on the Recognition and Enforcement of Foreign Arbitral Awards (the "New York Convention"). The application of the New York Convention to the contractual relationships covered by this Chapter is discussed at Chapter 17.3.10 below.

17.3 Selected issues

17.3.1 Intellectual property rights: patents, trade marks, copyrights and trade secrets

17.3.1.1 Patents

17–18 A United States patent gives an inventor the right, for a limited time period, to exclude all others from making, using, selling, offering for sale, or importing the invention. The statutory guidelines for obtaining a patent in the United States are governed by the Patent Act. Patents are granted by the US government in a document called a "Letters Patent" issued by the US Patent and Trade mark Office. The issued patent discloses and defines the invention and establishes the inventor's rights.[2]

17–19 Once an application for a patent has been filed in the US Patent and Trade mark Office, the applicant may mark products embodying the invention with the designation "Patent Pending" or the abbreviation "Pat. Pend.". These expressions mean an application has been filed that has been neither abandoned nor issued as a patent. Since the patent application is kept in secrecy by the US Patent and Trade mark Office during its pendency, a "Patent Pending" notice is a way to deter competitors that cannot determine the extent of patent protection available or even when a patent might issue.

17–20 When a patent ultimately issues, patented products must be marked with the word "Patent" or the abbreviation "Pat." and the US patent number. The purpose of this marking requirement is to inform the public that an article is protected by a US patent. If a patented article is sold without such notice and the patent is subsequently infringed, the patent owner's recovery of damages may be severely limited. If a patent owner has sold unmarked

[2] It is beyond the scope of this Chapter to discuss the various requirements to obtaining a US patent and the procedures involved.

patented products, damages cannot be recovered for any infringing acts occurring before the alleged infringer received actual notice of the patent.

A US patent may be owned by more than one entity such as joint inventors or multiple assignees. In the absence of any agreement to the contrary, each of the joint owners of the patent may exploit the patented invention without the consent of the other owners and without an accounting to any of the other owners for any profits received from assigning or licensing the patent. Any interest in the US patent or patent application is assignable by written instrument. Assignments affecting title to US patents should be recorded in the US Patent and Trade Mark Office to provide priority protection against subsequent assignments in the patent. The Patent Act provides that an assignment should be recorded in the US Patent and Trade Mark Office within three months of the date of the transfer, or prior to the subsequent assignment, in order to provide protection against another purchaser who acquires rights in the patent. **17–21**

While grant of a patent gives the patent owner (either the original inventor or an assignee) the right to exclude others from making, using, selling, offering for sale or importing the invention into the United States, a patent owner may license others to make, use or sell the invention. A patent owner may license all or part of the patent rights under a wide variety of terms. A patent may be licensed for a limited period or for the entire life of the patent. A license may either be exclusive or nonexclusive, and may be limited to a field of use or to a geographic area. In addition to pure intellectual property considerations, patent licenses are governed by general state contract law, as well as other US law, such as antitrust limitations. A patent may be licensed for a lump sum royalty, a continuing royalty, or a combination of both. Royalties can be payable on dollar volume of goods produced, unit volume, or any other arrangement which can be agreed upon by the parties. The parties may also wish to consider terms such as minimum annual royalties and the incorporation of any patented improvement to the licensed technology. Royalty rates may also be tiered such that a lower royalty rate is in place while a patent application is pending, with a higher royalty rate being initiated once the US patent issues. One important provision to note under the US patent laws is that only an exclusive licensee has the standing to bring an action for patent infringement. Additionally, under US antitrust laws, a license provision that prohibits a licensee from challenging the validity of the licensed patent is unenforceable. **17–22**

A company seeking to take a license, such as for a invention involving biotechnology, from a non-profit institution, should be aware of special statutory rules applicable to federally funded projects of institutional licensors. The Bayh-Dole Act was enacted by the US Congress in 1980 (and amended in 1984). The purpose of this statute is to enable non-profit institutions, such as universities, to take title to their federally funded patented inventions and to grant exclusive licenses to those inventions for commercial purposes. It appears from the statutory provisions of the Bayh-Dole Act, however, that Congress intended a federally funded licensor institution to have the ability to grant exclusive licenses to make, use and sell **17–23** products commercially while simultaneously offering non-exclusive research licenses to make and use, but not sell, the invention.

17–24 The Bayh-Dole Act requires the exclusive licensee of a federally funded invention to reduce the teaching of the patent to "practical application". This has been interpreted to mean actual manufacture in the case of a composition or product. Under the Bayh-Dole Act, the invention must be utilised and the benefits of the invention made available to the public on reasonable terms. When an exclusive licensee has not taken, or is not expected to take within a reasonable time, steps to achieve practical application of the invention, then the Bayh-Dole Act provides that the US government retains the right to grant non-exclusive research licenses, that is licenses to make and use the invention for research purposes, but not to sell the invention—even though the invention has already been exclusively licensed for commercial purposes. Potential licensees should be aware when entering negotiations with US non-profit or academic institutions that, if the patents to be licensed involve federally funded technology, the Bayh-Dole Act provides for contemporaneous exclusive commercial licensing and non-exclusive research licensing. In 1987, all relevant provisions of the Bayh-Dole Act, as amended, the US Office of Management and Budget issued circular and the Presidential Memorandum on government patent policy were finalized and consolidated into what amounts to an operating manual for technology transfers on a national basis that specifies the rights and obligations of all parties involved.

17.3.1.2 Trade marks

17–25 In the United States, a trade mark can be any word, phrase, design, symbol, sound, colour, scent, or virtually anything, which is used in commerce by an entity to identify their particular goods or services and distinguish them from those of competitors. Protection for trade marks in the United States is provided by a federal trade mark statute, known as the Lanham Act.

17–26 In the United States, rights in a trade mark arise through use of the mark in commerce. While not mandatory in the United States, a federal trade mark registration does provide many important advantages.[3] The registration of a trade mark with the US Patent and Trade mark Office provides nationwide constructive notice to third parties of the owner's exclusive right to use the particular trade mark in conjunction with the goods or services for which it has been registered. A US federal trade mark registration also provides the trade mark owner with access to the US federal court system

[3] Because rights in a trade mark arise through use of the mark, even without a Federal registration, a mark may still be protected under US common law. However, common law rights in a trade mark will only exist in those specific geographic areas where the mark has actually been used. Additionally, all 50 states in the United States provide for the state registration of a trade mark. However, with state registrations, the trade mark rights may only extend to the actual areas of geographic use or at most, the actual state where registration has been obtained. It is beyond the scope of this Chapter to outline the US trade mark registration process and the protection afforded by such registrations.

and other procedural advantages in the event that the trade mark is infringed and requires enforcement of rights through a civil action. In addition, the Lanham Act allows for an owner of a registered trade mark to record the trade mark with the US Custom Service to prevent importation of infringing goods from foreign countries. If a trade mark is registered, intentional use of an identical or substantial indistinguishable trade mark on similar goods can amount to counterfeiting, which may give rise to heavy civil damages and/or criminal penalties. Finally, another benefit to securing a US federal trade mark registration is that such a registration may serve as the basis for obtaining similar registrations of the trade mark in foreign countries.

In order to give notice to others that a trade mark is protected by a federal trade mark registration, the symbol "®" should be used. Where a trade mark is not yet federally registered, the symbol "TM" can be used to provide notice to others that the mark is considered the trade mark of a particular company. It is important to note that the Lanham Act prohibits using the registration symbol "®" on any trade mark which is not federally registered. **17–27**

The owner of a trade mark may license or assign the trade mark to others. An assignment of a trade mark results in the actual change in the ownership of the mark. Unlike many foreign countries, in the United States a trade mark can only be assigned with the goodwill of the business to which the mark pertains. A trade mark will be considered assigned "in gross" when it is assigned alone without a corresponding sale of the business or assignment of the associated goodwill. An assignment of a trade mark "in gross" can result in the abandonment of the trade mark. While trade mark applications based upon use are assignable, intent to use applications are generally not assignable prior to establishing use of the mark, except to a successor to the business or portion thereof to which the mark pertains. As with patent assignments, trade mark assignments should be recorded in the US Patent and Trade mark Office within three months of the date of the assignment to be effective against subsequent transferees without notice. **17–28**

The owner of a trade mark may also license the mark to others. With a license, the trade mark owner retains ownership of the trade mark and merely grants the right to use the trade mark to another. In this respect, it is important that the trade mark owner maintain control over the use of the trade mark, as well as the nature and quality of the goods or services which are offered in conjunction with the mark as it is used by the licensee. Where the trade mark owner does not retain control over the quality and nature of the products and services or the use of the trade mark by the licensee, the license is deemed to be a "naked license" and may result in the abandonment of the trade mark. As with patent licenses, only an exclusive licensee has standing to bring an action for trade mark infringement. **17–29**

Assignees and licensees of US trade marks should also be aware of regulations of various US government agencies which impact the use of trade marks on packaging, labelling and advertising in certain industries. US government agencies such as, the Food and Drug Administration, the **17–30**

Bureau of Alcohol, Tobacco and Firearms, the Environmental Protection Agency, the Federal Trade Commission and International Trade Commission all have specific regulations regarding packaging and labelling requirements with which an assignee or licensee must comply.

17.3.1.3 Copyright

17–31 Copyrights are the ownership rights of authors in the works they create. In the United States, copyrights arise automatically when the work is created. Registration is not necessary to secure a copyright. The Copyright Act is the federal statute in the United States that embodies the statutory protection for copyrights. Under the Copyright Act authors receive exclusive rights in their works for certain periods of time, after which the works are dedicated to the public. While copyrights can be obtained in a variety of types of works, copyright protection is not available under the Copyright Act for ideas, processes, concepts, discoveries, typefaces, ingredients, blank forms, or slogans.[4]

17–32 While a copyright notice is not required by the Copyright Act, use of such a notice is advisable to place third parties on notice that proprietary rights are claimed in the work. The recommended notice includes the symbol "©", the year, name of the author and the phrase "all rights reserved". The terminology "all rights reserved" is included in the notice to strengthen copyright protection in certain Latin American countries.

17–33 The owner of a US copyright receives five exclusive rights: (i) the right to reproduce the work; (ii) the right to produce derivative works based from the original work; (iii) the right to publicly distribute the work; (iv) the right to publicly perform the work; and (v) the right to publicly display the work. Each of these rights may be transferred or licensed by the copyright owner. Great flexibility is available in transactions involving copyrights. Some of the above rights may be transferred or licensed separately, while others retained. Additionally, the degree to which each right may be licensed is nearly limitless. A copyright owner may, for example, decide to divide the distribution rights among several licensees according to geographic areas or various media restrictions. For example, a licensor may decide to license the right to distribute an educational video to one licensee in California and another in Colorado, or a licensee may only acquire the right to distribute the educational video program to schools or educational institutions, and may be precluded from distributing the educational program in any other market. Thus, unless the granting provisions of a license agreement are clearly and specifically drafted, a licensee may be precluded from obtaining full benefit of the licensed right.

17–34 One important area in copyright licensing relates to technological advancements. Where an advance in technology makes it possible to exploit

[4] A review of the requirements for applying and obtaining copyright protection in the United States is beyond the scope of this Chapter.

the work in a manner not possible when the license was first executed, this raises the question of whether the new use falls within the scope of the license granted. To minimise disputes in this area, the language of the license grant should include broad, unrestricted language to allow the licensee to exploit any technological advance. In any license negotiations involving copyrights it is important for both the licensor and licensee to determine whether they have retained or acquired all rights in the licensed work which may be necessary to achieve their business objectives.

Because the rights in a copyrighted work can be divided so specifically, one of the most contested areas in copyright licensing involves ambiguous terminology used in drafting the grant of the various rights in the copyrighted work. Issues relating to ambiguities in licenses are construed in accordance with accepted principles of contract law. Because contract law in the United States varies among each of the particular states, the state law under which a copyright license is construed may be critical. Therefore, it is imperative that the choice of law provision in any copyright license be carefully considered. **17–35**

When contracting to obtain rights, either by assignment or license, to a copyrighted work that is owned by more than one party, one should remember that joint owners of a copyright may exploit their rights without consent of the other owner. However, unlike joint owners of patents, the joint owners of a copyright must account to the other owner for any profits received from licensing or transfer of the copyrighted work. **17–36**

Finally, it is possible under the Copyright Act for authors to terminate any transfers of their rights after 35 years. There is a five year time period within which revocation of the transfer may be elected under the Copyright Act. The rationale behind the revocation is that many times the true value of a work is unknown at the time of the initial transfer. The right to revoke a copyright transfer allows for the author to negotiate fairer compensation for the work. The right to revoke, however, does not attach to works made for hire. Although much debate has surrounded the right to revoke copyright transfers, with the pace of technology, this right may have little impact outside of artistic or literary works. The Digital Millennium Copyright Act of 1998 amended the Copyright Act to add several provisions that deal with the unique concerns of copyright owners and Internet Service Providers in the digital age. Additionally, the Sonny Bono Act of 1998 extended the copyright term to life of the author plus 70 years. **17–37**

17.3.1.4 Trade secrets

In the United States the term "trade secrets" applies to a wide range of technical and business information. Precisely defining a trade secret is difficult as there is no federal statute which protects trade secret information. Trade secrets are protected by individual state statutes in the United States. The majority of US states, however, have adopted, with some modification, the Uniform Trade Secrets Act. Under the Uniform Trade Secrets Act, a **17–38** trade secret is defined as "information that derives economic value, actual or potential, from not being generally known to, or readily ascertainable by, other persons who could obtain value from its disclosure or use, so long as reasonable efforts have been made to maintain its secrecy". Thus, a trade secret can be any information, not known publicly that provides business advantage over competitors. Trade secrets can also consist of a combination of publicly known information, where the combination of information is unique and has not been publicly disclosed. "Knowhow" may constitute a trade secret, but such know-how must be information that is not generally known in the industry, as opposed to general technical information known in a particular industry.

17–39 Unlike patents, trade marks or copyright, trade secret protection lasts forever, so long as the information is maintained in secret. While there are no statutory guidelines established as to how much secrecy is necessary to protect a trade secret, US courts have indicated that "reasonable" security measures are required to protect trade secret information. While absolute secrecy is not required, what constitutes "reasonable" security measures will necessarily vary dependent upon the type of information to be protected and the business environment in which the trade secret information is to be used.

17–40 Even if the trade secret protection measures are in place within a company, such measures will be useless unless the security measures are consistently and routinely enforced. Once a trade secret is disclosed, the owner's right to legal protection is lost. Trade secret protection, however, only extends to the prevention of others obtaining the trade secrets through improper means. Trade secret law will not protect against another party obtaining the information by fair means, such as by independent discovery, reverse-engineering, or accidental disclosure.

17–41 Trade secret information can be assigned or licensed. Because "trade secrets" are often difficult to define, and since trade secret information has a potentially infinite life span, there are several difficult issues raised in most trade secret licensing arrangements. These include the duration of a trade secret license, how long secrecy or confidentiality restrictions can be imposed on the licensee, the length of time royalty payments are required and what happens to the information once the license is terminated.

17–42 Since the value of trade secret information is dependent upon the information remaining secret, it is imperative in the licensing of trade secret information that appropriate safeguards are in place, both physically as well as contractually, to protect the confidential nature of the information and that these safeguards are enforced by the licensor. At a minimum, a licensor should require a licensee to have at least the following procedures in place to ensure that the licensed information remains secret:

- Anyone to whom the trade secret will be disclosed should, before the actual disclosure, sign an agreement to maintain its confidentiality.
- All trade secret information should be stamped with proprietary legends.

- Security measures should be specifically defined to ensure restricted access to the trade secret information.
- Employees to whom the trade secrets are disclosed, or who will be developing trade secrets, should sign non-disclosure agreements, and consideration given as to whether their employment contracts should include a reasonable covenant not to compete.
- Disclosure of trade secrets to employees should be on a "need to know" basis.
- All departing employees should be debriefed at an exit interview concerning their obligations of confidentiality.

17.3.2 US antitrust restrictions

US federal antitrust laws must be reviewed in connection with most business transactions in the United States. While these laws have potential application to certain activities outside the territory of the United States, this discussion will focus on activities within the United States. The critical application of these laws for purposes of this chapter will most likely be in connection with the license of intellectual property rights, but some general principles will help place that discussion in context. **17–43**

There is a long history under US antitrust laws of distinguishing certain competitive behaviour as *per se* illegal. Such treatment is applied to restraints the nature and effect of which are "plainly anticompetitive". This means that the particular effects on a market are not studied to determine if such behaviour has a negative impact on competition. Most economic behaviour occurring in the United States, however, is instead increasingly analysed under a *rule of reason* analysis, which examines activities in the context of existing and potential markets and the effect on competition within such markets. The *per se* rule has been used less and less over the years, and generally only to such actions as horizontal price fixing, market division among horizontal competitors, group boycotts, output restraints and resale price maintenance. This distinction, and competition law in general in the United States, depends on the ever evolving views of the courts and the current administration's view on the role of competition policy. **17–44**

The current US enforcement policy in respect of licensing of intellectual property rights is set forth by the US Federal Trade Commission and the US Department of Justice in the 1995 Antitrust Guidelines for the Licensing of Intellectual Property (the "IP Guidelines"). The IP Guidelines apply to intellectual property protected by patent, copyright and trade secret law, and to know how. The IP Guidelines do not apply to trade marks. While some of the policies embodied in the IP Guidelines are similar to the recent initiatives in connection with changes to the EC Technology Transfer Block Exemption (Reg.240/96/EC) discussed in Chapter 8, there are important **17–45** differences. Also, the IP Guidelines are not considered to be part of US antitrust law such that they would bind courts, but rather reflect the views of the US administration in implementing US antitrust policy. However, the IP Guidelines form a useful evaluation of antitrust law as applied to intellectual property licensing and may be considered persuasive authority by some courts.

17.3.2.1 Assessing relevant markets

17–46 The IP Guidelines continue to use the *per se* versus *rule of reason* distinction. In analysing the competitive effects of a licensing arrangement, however, the enforcement agencies will look at three different markets. If the effect on licensing arrangements can be adequately assessed within the relevant markets for the goods affected by the arrangements, the agencies will look at the markets for the goods covered by the license, including both the markets for final goods and for intermediate goods. Where the competitive effects are not so readily assessable, the agencies may look at "technology markets" and "innovation markets". Technology markets consist of the licensed technology and close substitutes that could significantly restrain the exercise of market power with respect to the licensed technology. The innovation market is perhaps the most significant development in the IP Guidelines, and calls for review of "research and development directed to particular new or improved goods or processes, and the close substitutes for that research and development". Thus, in determining the competitive effect of a licensing transaction using this approach, the effect of a restraint on research and development activities and the effect on the market in a next generation of technology would have to be examined.

17.3.2.2 Specific provisions

17–47 The following summarises the effect of the IP Guidelines and US antitrust law in general on particular types of provisions.

- *Territorial Restrictions:* Territorial as well as field of use restrictions are generally lawful, and are explicitly permitted in connection with patent licenses. Antitrust concerns may occur where one party has a significant market share, or where competitors horizontally divide a market, the latter of which is *per se* illegal.

- *Cross-License Agreements and Pooling Arrangements:* Typically these restraints are legal and analysed under the *rule of reason* approach. Cross-licensing of blocking patents and pooling of licenses with one or more parties is also generally permitted, especially if done in connection with the settlement of infringement disputes. The effect of these arrangements on the innovation market must be analysed. If few other companies will have the capability to compete against the contracting parties' research and development capacity, future markets may be considered to be significantly restrained. This is particularly likely if the parties have monopoly power or are actual or potential competitors. "Packaging" arrangements are generally permissible if reasonable. For example, in approving a compulsory blanket license of songs, the authorities cited the resulting efficiency created by this arrangement. At a minimum, absent compelling reasons, a licensor should generally make available (or at least be open to requests for) licenses for only a portion of the package at a price related to the value of the less extensive license. Arrangements such as packaging and pooling, however, can also be viewed as "tying".

- *Tying:* Historically, tying of one product license with another obligation has been viewed as *per se* illegal if the seller is able to use market power in the tying product to force purchases of the tied product. The IP Guidelines, however, call for the restraints to be analysed under the *rule of reason*. As a general rule, tying should be avoided unless there is a compelling business reason. Even then, if the party seeking to tie has significant market power, utmost caution should be used. Tying can also include required maintenance contracts and "branded" spare part purchasing requirements. It also may include "tying out" arrangements in which a licensee is contractually prohibited from dealing with the licensor's competitors.
- *Exclusivity:* Exclusive licenses are generally permitted and, in any event, are analysed under the *rule of reason*. While also analysed under the *rule of reason*, exclusive dealing arrangements can raise antitrust concerns, and the benefit to the licensor should at a minimum outweigh any limits to actual or potential competing technologies. Non-exclusive grants should not arouse any antitrust concerns.
- *Resale Price Restrictions:* While there is some case law to the contrary, resale price provisions should be avoided. The IP Guidelines generally conclude that they are *per se* illegal.
- *Grant-Back Provisions:* Non-exclusive grantbacks requiring the payment of a reasonable license fee are generally permitted under the IP Guidelines. Exclusive grantbacks, especially among significant market competitors that could threaten actual or potential markets, are suspect and should be avoided.
- *Sub-Licenses:* If the licensee is given the right to grant sublicenses, an antitrust concern can be raised if the licensor is permitted to approve sub-licensees and both parties to the license have significant market power.
- *Royalties:* Royalty provisions are generally left to the discretion of the contracting parties. The most frequent problems in this area arise when royalties are based upon sales of products that do not incor-

porate the licensed intellectual property, require payment beyond the duration of such rights, or are otherwise coerced. This can also give rise to "patent abuse". Review of royalty payments and other potential restraints will be analysed under the US antitrust laws based on the complete business relationship, and not only the contract at issue.

- *Litigation:* Lawsuits to enforce intellectual property rights are generally immune from antitrust scrutiny unless they are merely a "sham". Although the test varies, sham litigation may be found where the plaintiff's legal claim was objectively baseless.

17.3.2.3 Safety zone

17–48 Restraints meeting certain criteria that indicate they are unlikely to result in any anticompetitive effect may qualify for the "safety zone" contained in the IP Guidelines. Restraints falling in the "safety zone" will not be challenged absent extraordinary circumstances. In determining whether an arrangement is within the safety zone, the IP Guidelines look only to the goods market, unless the licensing arrangement has a significant effect on competing technologies or on research and development. In any event, the first criterion is that the restraint cannot be of the type generally described as *per se* illegal. If the restraint is not *per se* illegal and the goods market is the appropriate market, the arrangement will be within the safety zone so long as the licensor and its licensees have less than a 20 per cent market share in each significantly affected market. If the technology market must also be addressed, and market share data is scarce, the restraint will be "safe" if there are at least four other independently controlled technologies which are substitutable by users at comparable cost. If the innovation market is addressed, the IP Guidelines require at least four independent entities which have the incentive and means to engage in research and development which would constitute a close substitute to the licensed rights for the restraint to fall within the safety zone. It is unclear how important this safety zone will be since the IP Guidelines generally will not condemn a license which does not threaten actual or potential competition, as analysed through the market for final and for intermediate goods, the licensed rights and close substitutes, as well as the market for new and improved goods or processes, including research and development activities.

17.3.3 Uniform commercial code

17–49 Article Two of the UCC addresses the sale of goods and may be relevant to a non-US party that is selling or distributing goods in connection with an agency, distribution or other relationship in the United States. The UCC, which is one of the "uniform" laws endorsed by the American Law Institute and the National Conference of Commissioners on Uniform State laws, has been adopted in various versions in each of the 50 states. Under the UCC, with certain exceptions, the parties to a contract can select the law of the state they wish to govern their agreement, so long as the transaction bears a reasonable relationship to the chosen jurisdiction.[5]

Article Two of the UCC applies to "goods", which are all things (including specially manufactured goods) that are movable at the time they are identified in the contract for sale, other than the money in which the price is to be paid, investment securities and things in action.[6] There are two approaches for determining whether Article Two of the UCC applies to a contract involving both goods and non-goods (such as services). Most courts will apply the UCC to such a contract only if the "predominant" purpose of the contract, viewed in its entirety, was for the sale of goods. If a contract meets this test, those courts will apply the UCC to the entire contract. A minority of courts will apply the UCC only to the portions of a mixed contract that involve goods. **17–50**

Article Two of the UCC sets forth rules pertaining to contract formation, interpretation, performance, breach, repudiation and remedies. Differing rules may apply, depending on whether the parties are "merchants" (*e.g.* persons who deal in such goods as well as most other persons engaged in business, as opposed to consumers or other inexperienced buyers). **17–51**

Article Two of the UCC contains two primary traps for the unwary. First, the UCC rejects the "mirror-image" principle, which requires that the acceptance and offer must perfectly "mirror" one another before a contract is formed, as well as other contract formalities. Rather, "[a] contract for the sale of goods may be made in any manner sufficient to show agreement, including conduct by both parties which recognises the existence of such a contract".[7] A contract normally will not fail even if the parties do not agree on all the terms. Under the UCC, therefore, a contract may be formed under circumstances far short of the formalities usually expected by non-US practitioners. There need not be an actual contractual instrument; virtually any writing, such as purchase orders, invoices or letters, or conduct by the parties reflecting the existence of a contract, will suffice. Indeed, if the parties intended to make a contract such that the quantity of goods involved can be ascertained, a court usually will find a contract exists. **17–52**

Second, Article Two of the UCC establishes rules and default contract terms if the parties' agreement either has omitted terms or includes conflicting terms. For example, between merchants, terms in an acceptance that are additional to or different from those offered or agreed upon become part of the contract unless (i) the offer expressly limits acceptance to the terms of the offer, (ii) the additional or differing terms "materially" alter the contract or (iii) the other party objects within a reasonable time to those terms.[8] **17–53**

[5] UCC §1–105. A proposed revision to this section would expand the parties' ability to choose the governing law without regard to the relationship to the chosen jurisdiction.
[6] UCC §2–105(1).
[7] UCC §2–204(1).
[8] UCC §2–309(1).

17–54 If the agreement as broadly defined is silent as to certain terms, the UCC may supply "gap-filling" provisions. For instance, if the parties fail to include a time for delivery, delivery of the goods must be within a "reasonable time" as viewed under all the circumstances.[9] If there is no provision for the place of delivery, delivery generally will be at the seller's place of business. If the goods are to be shipped but risk of loss is not specified, then risk of loss usually passes from the seller to the buyer at the point of shipment. The UCC presumes that contracts for goods are shipment contracts unless otherwise agreed. If the seller is required to deliver the goods at a particular destination (*e.g.* FOB New York), however, the presumption is overcome and risk passes to the buyer upon the seller's tender of the goods at the destination. Unless the agreement otherwise states, payment is due at the time and place at which the buyer is to receive the goods even where the place of shipment is the place of delivery. If the parties have not agreed upon the price of the goods, then price is set at "a reasonable price at the time of delivery".[10]

17–55 Article Nine of the UCC covers the granting and maintenance of a "security interest" in personal property and fixtures. If properly obtained and maintained, a security interest provides the secured party with certain priorities in the event of a bankruptcy proceeding involving the debtor. In certain circumstances, an Article Nine security interest could be used by a non-US manufacturer or supplier to protect its goods from other creditors of a US agent, distributor or licensee. US bankruptcy proceedings are discussed in greater detail in Chapter 17.3.11 below.

17.3.4 Uniform computer information transaction act

17–56 Like the UCC, the UCITA was developed to promote uniform contract principles to be applied to transactions that relate to computer software, databases and related products. Because the development of UCITA was completed recently, the UCITA has not yet been widely adopted by the states.

17–57 The UCITA is generally viewed as a licensor-friendly set of laws for interpreting contracts. Like the UCC, the UCITA establishes rules and default contract terms if the parties agreement omits such terms or contains conflicting terms. Additionally, the UCITA resolves issues about contract formation, offer and acceptance relating to shrink-wrap licenses.

17–58 Licensees should be wary of several provisions in the UCITA First, the UCITA permits licensors to unilaterally amend certain of their agreements with licensees. Second, the UCITA permits licensors to incorporate "automatic restraint" and "electronic self-help" codes into their products, so that licensees are at risk that the licensor can disable a product then in use by the licensee. Third, various rules regarding the "first sale doctrine" under

[9] UCC §2–308.
[10] UCC §2–305.

intellectual property laws are modified by the UCITA, making it uncertain whether the rightful owner of a copy of computer software may loan that copy to others in the absence of an express prohibition.

17.3.5 Sales representative laws

Over half the states in the United States have adopted laws which govern the rights of sales representatives or agents. As a general matter, these laws apply to principals who sell their products through sales representatives or agents who solicit orders for these products and are compensated by commission. Dealers and distributors who purchase goods for resale generally are not covered by such statutes. The laws typically apply whether or not a principal has a place of business in a particular state and, in such cases, deem the principal to be doing business in such state for purposes of personal jurisdiction. These laws vary from state to state but primarily operate to protect the agent's right to receive a commission for its services and impose penalties on principals who fail to make commission payments to a sales representative. Such penalties could include actual damages plus fines (in some cases, with treble damages) and attorneys' fees and costs. The legislative intent behind these laws is to protect the interests of sales representatives who spend considerable time developing their territory to be in a position to properly market their products. With a few exceptions, these laws do not generally impose "good" or "just" cause standards in terminating agency relationships, but the treble damage and attorney fee-shifting features of such laws make it important to carefully review any termination of such relationships. In addition to the typical requirement to timely pay commissions, these laws often include other requirements, such as a requirement that the agreement be in writing, that the agent's compensation is set out in the agreement, that the supplier provide a copy of the agreement to the agent and obtain written evidence of the agent's receipt of such agreement. In certain states, such as California, the law expressly treats any waiver of these requirements as contrary to public policy and thus void. **17–59**

17.3.6 State franchising and business opportunity laws

The effect of franchising laws in the United States must be considered by a prospective trade mark licensor and, to a lesser extent, every supplier of branded goods or services for distribution in the United States. Many US states have enacted laws that require sellers of "franchises" and "business opportunities" (as defined by each such state) to disclose certain information to potential franchisees and business opportunity buyers, and register and/or post bonds with the state. A particular state's law applies if a distributor or a licensee is located or has operations in that state. Also, state laws may impose restrictions on the substantive relationship between the franchiser and the franchisee, such as limitations on terminations, which are **17–60** meant to protect the franchisee who has invested in a certain brand and built up goodwill and a market. While these laws generally would not apply to most agency arrangements because they do not, for example, include payment of a "franchise fee", it is important to review each business relationship in light of these laws to avoid their inadvertent application. Such laws have been found to apply to distribution and manufacturing agreements which incorporate trade mark licenses. In any event, a review of such laws will help avoid unnecessary problems when a licensor desires to terminate or alter its distribution methods in the United States. The US Federal Trade Commission also has issued a rule requiring sellers of "franchises" and "business opportunities" (as defined by the rule) to make specific disclosures. Although compliance with these mandatory disclosure and registration requirements is often cumbersome and expensive, franchisers and business opportunity sellers that fail to comply (and their individual officers, directors and employees) may be subject to substantial civil and criminal liability.

17.3.6.1 Franchises

17–61 Most state franchise laws provide that a contractual relationship constitutes a "franchise" if each of the following elements are satisfied:

- *Trade Mark or Brand Identification:* The operation of the business of the sale of goods or services is substantially associated with the supplier's trade mark or service mark, or the dealer or distributor is licensed to use the trade mark;
- *Marketing or Operations Plan:* Either (i) the supplier prescribes or suggests a marketing plan or (ii) the parties share a community of interest in the marketing of the goods or services; and
- *Franchise Fee:* The dealer or distributor is required to pay a franchise fee, often in excess of a specified amount, usually $500.

17–62 If any one of these elements does not exist, there often is no franchise relationship. However, in New York, a franchise relationship will be deemed to exist if there is a franchise fee and either the trade mark or the marketing component. Similarly, New Jersey does not require the franchise fee element in order to find a franchise relationship. Nonetheless, to avoid the inadvertent application of these statutes it is necessary to ensure that at least one of three elements does not exist.[11]

- *Franchise Fee:* It may be easiest to avoid the franchise fee element.

[11] It is possible that these elements could exist in all three types of franchise relationships discussed in Chapter 6.27 and Chapter 8.1 namely, franchise of services, franchise of production or a distribution franchise. While such distinctions are obviously important in organising business relationships, they are not generally distinguished for purposes of state franchise laws.

While such fees are typically broadly defined to include all types of payments, there is an exception for the *bona fide* wholesale price of goods. Minimum purchase requirements may also be franchise fees, thus reasonable sales quotas should be used instead. Any other fee, deposit, payment (including discounts that benefit the supplier) can constitute franchise fees. Reasonable security deposits to ensure, for example, any failure to service products sold may not constitute a franchise fee.

- *Trade mark:* The trade mark element of a franchise is more difficult to avoid. In some states, the existence of an authorised distributor of branded goods or services would satisfy this element but in other states, it may be easier to avoid. As a general matter, to avoid this component of the franchise test it is best to limit to the greatest extent possible the permitted uses of the mark by the licensee and to prohibit the distributor from using the mark as of a part of its business name or in identifying its business to customers.
- *Marketing:* The marketing plan element is also difficult to avoid. This element may be met merely by suggesting marketing strategies, making promotional materials available or even because of a supplier's overall marketing plan whereby the supplier grants exclusive dealerships, depending in each case on the particular state's provisions. To minimise the possibility of satisfying this element, compliance with any marketing advice should be made truly voluntary. Moreover, quality control could be "limited to actually maintaining the quality of a product" instead of dictating marketing methods, product presentation or operation of the dealership. Finally, it is best to deal with distributors that have other lines of business, so that they are not economically dependent on a continuing relationship with the supplier.

It may be possible to avoid the inadvertent application of the state franchise laws by organising activities from a state that does not have a franchise law. It is possible that a court will apply that state's laws if chosen as the governing law of the contract. Arbitration provisions may assist in this process. However, it is important to keep in mind that a state may, irrespective of the state of organisation and any governing law provision, apply the law of another state depending upon the interests of the parties involved. **17–63**

If a relationship is treated as a franchise under applicable state law, the law will impose limitations on the parties ability to terminate the relationship by dictating notice requirements and, in many states, requiring "good cause" for termination and providing the breaching party with an opportunity to cure. Accordingly, a non-US supplier or manufacturer should attempt to define "good cause" in light of a particular state's definition. A well thought through, reasonable clause, such as one which covers failure to meet required performance standards, is often enforceable. In addition to termination issues, franchise laws may allow the franchisee to assign the **17–64** agreement despite contractual restrictions against assignment and may invalidate clauses requiring purchases of goods and supplies from a particular source. Unfortunately, these critical issues are very state specific, and each state's laws, regulations and decisions must be reviewed. In addition, waiver of these rights is usually unenforceable.

17.3.6.2 Business opportunities

17–65 In addition to the regulation of franchises, many US states also regulate "business opportunities" and impose disclosure and/or registration requirements, and possibly require the posting of a bond. These relationships are usually defined as involving the sale or lease of any products, equipment, supplies or services for the purpose of enabling the purchaser to start a business and, in connection with which, the seller makes certain representations, including location assistance, indications that seller will purchase resulting products, guarantees and/or buy-back or refund offers and marketing and/or earning claims. In some cases, the mere representation by the seller that there is a market for the product or services may be enough.

17–66 There are two principal exceptions to the application of these statutes.

- *Licensed Distributors:* Suppliers who, in conjunction with the sale of goods to dealers or distributors, license the dealers or distributors to use a federal or state registered trade mark, are exempt. Accordingly, it may be advantageous for non-US manufacturers or suppliers to include in their distribution agreements a limited license for the distributors to use such trade marks in connection with product sales. This exemption is limited and extreme care is required to limit representations to potential distributors.

- *No Initial Payment:* Manufacturers or suppliers that do not require any "initial payments" are exempt. Typically, this would include any payments made within the first six months of establishing a distributorship. If it was likely that these laws might otherwise apply, it would be sensible, where possible, to avoid any payments for inventory until after the distributor receives payment from its customer, at a minimum for the first six months. There are several other minor exemptions that might apply in a given state, such as where the seller has a net worth of from $1 million to $15 million depending on the state involved.

17.3.6.3 Strategies to avoid application

17–67 In summary form, the following "top ten" ways to avoid being a franchise or business opportunity are as follows:

- Do not require dealers to pay a direct or indirect franchise fee;
- Establish sales quotas at levels a reasonable business person could meet instead of requiring dealers to make minimum purchases;
- Sell inventory to dealers at bona fide wholesale prices;
- Do not impose minimum required sales quotas or purchase amounts during the first six months of a new dealership;
- License dealers to use the mark for the limited use of selling products;
- Prohibit dealers from using the mark to identify their company, and police this prohibition;
- Never make promises or other express representations regarding a potential dealer's prospects;
- Require new dealers to acknowledge in writing that no guarantees or express promises were made to them;
- Never represent the company as a "franchise"; and
- Where possible, avoid making any earnings claims or marketing plan representations

In addition, it may be helpful to allow dealers within the first six months of their business to delay paying the licensor for inventory until the dealers receive orders and payments from customers to strengthen the argument that this is not a business opportunity in states with no applicable trade mark exception. **17–68**

17.3.7 State "doing business" regulations

Each US state has a separate statute which governs the amount and type of business that an entity can carry on in such state before it must be registered to do business in that state. Both US and non-US companies must consider whether they are "doing business" and must be registered with the relevant authority in a particular state. Even if activities in a particular state do not require registration in that state, the activities may subject a party to taxation and service of process and suit in that state. While virtually any activity could give rise to taxation, most states require more persistent activity before registration to do business is required. Although there is no general federal "registration" to do business, certain activities can require reporting to various federal agencies. **17–69**

Most states have adopted a version of the Model Business Corporation Act that excludes certain activities from registration; even if an exclusion seems to apply, it is important to look at the totality of the business relationships within a particular state. For example, an otherwise exempt activity may require registration depending on the degree of control exer- **17–70** cised over the local activities.

17–71 The most helpful exclusion for agency relationships is one that applies when a non-US principal approves outside the United States all contracts entered into by an agent on the principal's behalf. In such circumstances, registration may not be required in the state where such contracts are entered into. If relying on this exemption, however, the non-US contracting party should ensure that by contract and in the course of dealing, the local agent has no authority to bind the non-US corporation, even if this authority is rarely used.

17–72 If a non-US party has established a US subsidiary to carry out operations in a particular US state, it is permitted without further action to carry out business in the state of its incorporation. Accordingly, if all contracts are approved through the US subsidiary in the state of incorporation or outside the US, no further registration should be required. Conducting business through a US subsidiary may render the foreign parent company itself amenable to suit in some jurisdictions under some circumstances.

17–73 Another exclusion from the state registration requirements may exist if the non-US party sells into the state through an independent contractor. Whether a contractual relation qualifies as one with an "independent contractor" depends on a number of factors, often focusing on the autonomy of the agent or distributor. Even if sales in a particular state take place through independent contractors or distributors, registration may be required if the non-US contracting party provides after sale services, regularly visits accounts, promotes business or has an office in the state. In certain states, even when this exemption applies, a certificate which names a resident agent to receive process in the state on behalf of the non-US party may have to be filed.

17–74 Many states also have exemptions for:

- *Isolated transactions:* To qualify these transactions must be completed within a certain period of time, typically 30 days, and not be in the course of a number of repeated transactions;
- *Secondary corporate activities:* Activities such as advertising, opening and maintaining bank accounts, holding shareholder or director meetings in a state or preliminary acts (*e.g.* activities carried out to determine if there is a sufficient market or suitable agents to sell a product in a particular state); however, these activities taken together could constitute doing business in a state;
- *Extending credit:* The extension of credit (including obtaining security on such credit) and the collection of debts, if registration is not otherwise required; and
- *Leasing:* Personal property leases in connection with a distributorship, although if a number of leasing transactions are carried out, qualification may be required; consigning goods to an independent agent, absent control, is also generally permitted without qualification.

If an entity is required to register to do business in a particular state but fails to do so, most states will not let the entity enforce contracts in that state. Other consequences for failure to register include monetary penalties and even personal fines imposed on individuals acting for the noncomplying entity. Agents can also be subject to fines for wrongfully doing business. **17–75**

In any event, given the state by state variation of these rules, it is best to first identify those states in which a contracting party will have any contact, whether through agents, promotional visits, or otherwise, and confirm what activities in that state will either require registration or give rise to taxation. With this knowledge, activities in the various states can be organised in the most efficient manner and with assurance that a contracting party can file suit to enforce its rights. **17–76**

17.3.8 Products liability

Any non-US company that produces or markets its products in the United States will be subject to US products liability laws. In this context, "market" is broadly defined to include purposeful cultivation of the US market (*e.g.* sales to a non-US distributor by a non-US manufacturer knowing that the distributor would sell the products into the United States may subject the manufacturer to the jurisdiction of the US courts). The jurisdictional reach of US federal and state courts is significant. Whether or not the non-US manufacturer will be subject to the jurisdiction of a US court will depend, in large part, on the particular state involved and whether such state has a "long-arm" statute that extends its jurisdiction to the extent allowed under the US constitution. While establishing such jurisdiction may only require certain "minimum contacts", as a general matter, there has to be more than the mere placing of products into the stream of commence outside the United States. **17–77**

While a review of US product liability regulation is beyond the scope of this Chapter, non-US manufacturers and suppliers should be aware of the issues presented by the US legal environment in this area. While many similarities may exist between US products liability laws and those of other countries, there are significant differences both in the substance of the laws and the procedures involved. The key differences are primarily in the areas of procedure (wide ranging discovery rules), standing (the ability to bring class action suits), fee arrangements (existence of contingency fees), damage awards (most of the 50 US states allow punitive damages in addition to compensatory damages) and the jury process (in the United States, juries are used both for criminal and civil trials). There also are some cases in the United States that hold a trade mark licensor liable for injuries caused by the branded product, even if the licensor did not design, manufacture or market the product. It may be prudent to explore purchasing insurance against products liability claims in the United States or to require that the foreign party be named as an insured on the US party's products liability insurance if it has such a policy. Unlike in many other parts of the world, such insurance is commonly available in the United States. **17–78**

17.3.9 Packaging, labelling, contents, safety and other standards

17–79 There are laws and regulations at both the federal and state level which, due often to some particular public or national interest, may effect the process or means by which products are manufactured, marketed or delivered. If a non-US contracting party's knowledge of these requirements and the US market in a particular product is negligible, a US-based agent can generally be contractually required to either assist in or fully organise compliance with such laws. The applicable laws will vary widely with a particular product. For example, machinery may be subject to both federal and state safety laws as well as both government and industry standards. Warnings of potentially dangerous conditions must be given. If food is being sold, there is a great concern for proper packaging and labelling, as well as compliance with health standards. If the product is instead computer software, typically most of these laws are not applicable, except perhaps if dealing with consumers. Even with software, there are packaging concerns, such as the provision of a "shrink wrap" license to the purchaser, which attempts to bind the purchaser to, for example, limitations on the liability of the seller. As in many other countries, the enforceability of a such a license is at best doubtful, but still widely used.

17.3.10 Governing law; enforcement; arbitration

17.3.10.1 Governing law and consent to jurisdiction

17–80 Any contract involving agency, distribution or licensing activities in the United States should specify both the governing law of the contract and the designated forum for dispute resolution. There is no US federal law covering contracts generally. A US-based contracting party will invariably request that the law of the state with which it is more familiar govern the relationship. This presents some difficulty for the non-US contracting party, because it may not want to engage counsel familiar with a particular state's law. Typically, for a state's law to apply to a particular contract, there must be a reasonable relationship or nexus between the activities governed by the contract and the relevant state. The State of New York, however, allows parties to a contract involving a transaction worth at least $250,000 to agree that New York law shall govern the contract whether or not such contract "bears a reasonable relationship" to New York. In addition, US courts generally tend to enforce governing law clauses unless it would be unreasonable under the circumstances, for example due to fraud or undue influence or to apply the law of a particular jurisdiction would be against US public policy. Some states, however, have tended not to give effect to choice-of-law clauses.

17–81 In addition to selecting the governing law, the contracting parties may agree to allow disputes to be decided by the courts most familiar with the governing law. While the non-US party may not desire to have the relationship governed by the "home" state courts of its US counterparty, a "third" state such as New York may be acceptable to both. The selection of an "exclusive" or "non-exclusive" jurisdiction of a particular states court may be considered. (*i.e.* "Any dispute arising under this Agreement or the relationship between the parties shall be determined exclusively by the courts of New York"). Some courts have held forum selection clauses to be "non-exclusive" unless the clauses expressly say that they are "exclusive". Depending on the nature of the relationship, the US party may request the non-US party to specifically submit to the jurisdiction of the courts of the state in which it is agreed that disputes would be heard and to appoint an agent for service of process within that state.

No matter what forum is selected in the contract, a designated US court **17–82** may refuse to hear the suit under the doctrine of *forum non conveniens*. This discretionary doctrine may be applied where, for example, all of the witnesses to the events in dispute are in a state or country other than the selected forum. Waivers of the right to assert *forum non conveniens* are helpful, although not always given affect. In New York, the doctrine of *forum non conveniens* is inapplicable if the transaction involves at least $1 million, the defendant has consented in the contract to submit to the jurisdiction of New York courts and the contract specifies the application of New York law. A handful of states, however, afford little or no effect to forum selection clauses.

17.3.10.2 Enforcement

Under US law, every judgment of a court of another state is, in one sense, a **17–83** "foreign judgment" that cannot be enforced directly but must be made subject to another action. Under US law, however, the judgments of any court within the United States shall have the same "full faith and credit" given them in every court within the United States as they may have by law or usage in the courts of the state where they are rendered. Typically, a final judgment issued by a foreign-country court can be recognised and enforced by a simple action against another party, usually by motion or by summary judgment. It should be noted, however, that no federal law governs the enforcement of foreign-country judgments and that even in US federal courts it is state law rather than federal law that applies to this subject.

There are certain grounds for refusal of recognition of foreign judgments. **17–84** First, the US court (whether state or federal) may not recognise a judgment of a foreign court rendered under a judicial system that does not provide impartial tribunals or procedures compatible with the due process of law. In addition, a US court may not recognise a foreign judgment if the court that rendered the judgment did not have jurisdiction over the defendant in accordance with the law of the state rendering the judgment as well as the international rules of jurisdiction. Second, there are a number of discretionary grounds for non-recognition including (i) lack of subject-matter jurisdiction, (ii) inadequate notice, (iii) fraud, (iv) public policy and (v) conflict or inconsistency.

17–85 There is no uniform procedure for the enforcement of foreign country judgments, and no provision for the registration in order to enforce the foreign judgment. It is necessary to bring an action against the third party and therefore to acquire jurisdiction over such party. In the United States, judgments are rendered only in US dollars and a judgment denominated in a foreign currency will be converted into dollars as the date of the judgment granting enforcement. Interest on a foreign money judgment from the date of that judgment until entry of the judgment of a court in the United States can normally be claimed as it would be on any other fixed obligation.

17.3.10.3 Arbitration

17–86 Contracting parties often consider providing for arbitration or alternative dispute resolution procedures. There may be many reasons for parties to keep their dispute away from the courts, the most relevant being the protection of the sensitive and confidential nature of the subject matter (particularly, where the licensing of innovative technology or know how is involved) and the perceived need for expert decision-makers which may not be available through the court system. Arbitration also has certain limitations because it will only be binding on the contracting parties and therefore important non-parties to the agreement may not be joined to the arbitral proceedings. Further, a party's ability to obtain interim relief, such as a preliminary injunction, may be hindered.

17–87 Arbitration provisions are typically recognised in the United States, even when the subject matter of the dispute is intellectual property rights, and courts typically will dismiss or stay lawsuits brought in violation of such clauses. Arbitral awards generally do not come within the law of recognition of foreign judgments since they are governed by the New York Convention, of which the United States and over 100 countries are members, and federal legislation implementing the convention. Accordingly, arbitral decisions may be easier to enforce in a foreign country than a US court award. Notwithstanding the terms of a particular contract, some subject matters which involve a US public interest, such as certain antitrust issues, may not be arbitrable and may have to be pursued (or defended) in the US courts. Recent US case law suggests, however, that US courts will not interfere with a non-US arbitration body hearing a claim involving a US antitrust matter unless the non-US arbitration has decided the issue in a manner that is contrary to US public policy. If a US contracting party's statutory rights are not fully recognised by the arbitrator's decision, the US party may request a US federal court to determine whether the resulting arbitration award violates US public policy. However, the ability of a party to set aside an award on the basis that the statutory rights of such party were not fully recognised is extremely limited.

17.3.11 Insolvency and bankruptcy issues

In the United States, insolvency proceedings are principally governed by federal law, which typically differentiates between secured and unsecured creditors. Unsecured creditors include all companies that have not gone through the special procedures to obtain a perfected security interest as discussed in Chapter 17.3.3 above (*e.g.* typically signing a security agreement and filing a UCC-1 financing statement in each relevant jurisdiction). In a bankruptcy proceeding, unsecured creditors are given a *pro rata* portion of the available assets after payment of certain expenses and satisfying the claims of secured creditors. Even if there are specific assets that the principal or supplier provided to the agent or distributor and the contract provides for return of these assets upon the agent's insolvency, an unsecured principal may be left empty handed. **17–88**

As a practical matter, a principal can avoid some of the risk of agent insolvency if payments for the sale of a product by an agent go directly to the principal. If this is not possible, there is little protection given to the principal. Even if the sale was not authorised, the principal will only be able to make a general claim against the remaining assets of the insolvent agent. If the other party knew or had reason to know that the transaction was unauthorised, the most likely result is that the overall assets of the insolvent agent can be increased, but not necessarily with any special rights accruing to the principal. **17–89**

Under the US Bankruptcy Code of 1978, once bankruptcy proceedings are initiated an "automatic stay" goes into effect. The effect of the automatic stay is that all actions involving the bankrupt's assets (including the commencement of the legal actions, enforcement of claims, security interests and judgments, and any setoff action) are blocked by the bankruptcy court. A creditor can petition the court to seek relief from this stay but, in the absence of such relief, all claims involving the bankrupt estate are under the administration of the bankruptcy trustee (who may be the bankrupt). **17–90**

The US Bankruptcy Code also contains complex provisions regarding the treatment of "executory contracts" (contracts in which the obligations of both parties remain unperformed to the extent that the failure to perform such obligations would constitute a material breach of the contract entitling the non-breaching party to terminate). Accordingly, a provision in an executory contract providing for immediate termination upon an event of bankruptcy may not have any operative effect. **17–91**

In the context of an intellectual property license, immediate termination for the licensee's insolvency would allow the licensor to reject the license agreement and put the licensee at risk of infringing the intellectual property rights of the licensor or a third party. In 1985, the US Bankruptcy Code was amended to permit certain licensees to either (i) treat the license as terminated due to the breach of contract and to have a claim against the licensor as an unsecured creditor, or (ii) elect to keep the license in effect (in such event, the licensee will be obliged to make royalty payments under the terms **17–92** of the license agreement) but the licensor will be relieved of certain obligations such as the obligation for maintenance, upgrades and other support. In addition, the licensee will be deemed to waive any claim for setoff. Importantly, these 1985 amendments did not cover trade mark and trade name licenses and a trade mark licensee remains at risk of losing its license if the agreement qualifies as an executory contract that is properly rejected in the exercise of its business judgement.

17–93 In the event that a licensee is bankrupt, there is no special relief for a licensor and the general rules of rejection or assumption of an executory contact will apply. A licensor may seek to avoid the situation where a bankrupt licensee is in a position to assume a license agreement by seeking to terminate the agreement prior to bankruptcy (which may not be practical) or by taking a security interest in the license agreement itself.

17–94 US bankruptcy courts also may void or transfer the contractual obligations or rights of the insolvent party notwithstanding the terms of the contract. That is, bankruptcy courts generally are free to ignore contractual restrictions and to assign or transfer a contract to a third-party even when the contract states that it is non-assignable, non-transferable or terminated by insolvency or bankruptcy of one of the parties. There are some limitations on this power. For example, if the agreement is an executory contract, most bankruptcy courts will uphold a non-contractual restriction on assignability under applicable non-bankruptcy law, such as a state law restriction on the assignment of "personal" contracts. In general, a contract may be considered personal where the obligations to be performed involve such a relationship of personal confidence that is must have been intended that the contract rights would be exercised and obligations performed by that particular party or where the parties' relationship was formed as a result of one party's confidence in the skills, abilities or judgment of the other party. Non-exclusive patent and copyright licenses are considered personal and cannot be transferred without the explicit authorization of the licensor. As a result, a bankruptcy court cannot transfer an insolvent party's patent or copyright license without the licensor's express consent. Although the authority is less extensive, this rule also applies to trade mark licenses.

17.4 Contract issue checklist

17–95 The following is a brief drafting checklist to assist non-US parties who are considering entering into agency, distributorship or licensing agreements.

17.4.1 Main terms

17.4.1.1 Recitals

17–96 A typical US agreement may include clauses that discuss the major commercial purposes of the transaction, and perhaps the principal purposes for entering into the agreement. These clauses are often referred to as "Recitals" or "Whereas" clauses and always appear at the beginning of the agreement. If there is some legal issue that is important to the parties, such as sharing certain information that could be interpreted as anticompetitive, these clauses can also explain the parties' intent, and why the particular business transaction should or should not be viewed in a particular manner. Additionally, these clauses are occasionally used to resolve ambiguities in the interpretation of the other clauses in the agreement.

17.4.1.2 Definitions

Most of the definitions described in Chapter 1 are also appropriate in the US (*e.g.* definition of licensed products or services, methods of marketing, territory, etc.). Trade secrets and know-how are often defined separately from patents and other federally protected intellectual property rights because of the differing requirements of the relevant laws and because the parties may wish to expressly include or exclude specific information from the clauses that apply to trade secrets and know how. **17–97**

17.4.1.3 Grant

The key issues here are often exclusivity and whether the licensor is allowed to sell competing products in the territory. Territorial restrictions are judged by a rule of reason standard and are typically upheld by US courts so long as there is reasonable commercial justification for their imposition. If sub-licenses are permitted, there could be antitrust implications if the licensor has the right to approve potential sub-licensees. Often specific accounts, such as existing accounts or international accounts, are carved out. **17–98**

17.4.1.4 Compensation/royalties

The main issues here are defining with precision the manner in which royalties will be calculated and analysing the application of US antitrust law to the compensation/royalty provisions. For purposes of US antitrust law, in the case of non-exclusive licensees or distributors, royalty and other compensation arrangements should be identical or at least similar. Any variations should be supported by sound business reasons. For example, discounted rates given for larger volumes of sales should be justifiable by volume-related cost savings. **17–99**

17.4.1.5 Warranties, covenants and indemnities

Typically, the supplier or licensor will state either that it has good title to the licensed property or that it has no knowledge that it does not have good title **17–100** and that it otherwise has the right to enter into the agreement. Licensors and suppliers may also state that no infringement claims have been made or are pending. A supplier or licensor may request certain warranties and covenants regarding the financial condition of the agent, distributor or licensee. The supplier or licensor may also indemnify the licensee or distributor for any infringement claims by third parties. Note that infringement warranties and indemnities may be provided together or independently, and that they provide different protections to the licensor or distributor. Licensors may perform indemnity obligations without breaching the agreement, but an untrue infringement warranty is a breach of the agreement. The licensee or distributor usually is required to comply with all applicable laws in connection with products or services it provides. Agreements usually disclaim "all other warranties, express or implied, including but not limited to implied warranties of merchantability and fitness for a particular purpose and any statutory warranty or non-infringement". In addition to such disclaimers, there is often a limitation of liability as follows: "In no event shall [licensor/supplier] be liable or responsible for any loss of profit or any other commercial damage, including but not limited to any special, incidental, indirect, consequential or punitive damages to [dealer/licensee] or its customers pursuant to any cause of action arising out of or relating to this agreement". This limit may be coupled with a provision limiting any damages to the amounts earned by the licensor/supplier under the agreement. Finally, there may be specific limits on any performance or other criteria set forth in the agreement. Certain states require that disclaimers of this nature are printed in capital letters in bold typeface. If no disclaimer is included, the various state laws will often imply a fairly full warranty, including that the product is fit for the particular purpose. It is also helpful to require that the licensee maintain insurance which names the licensor as an additional insured.

17.4.1.6 Dispute resolution and governing law

17–101 The contract should contain a clause indicating which state law is to govern, and whether disputes will be heard, exclusively or non-exclusively, in a particular state's courts or by arbitration. If the law of a particular US state is to govern the relationship, the contract will typically specify that "This Agreement in all respects shall be governed by and construed in accordance with the internal laws of the State of [New York]". The word "internal", or the phrase "without regard to that state's conflicts-of-law rules", is added to avoid application of such state's conflicts of law principles, which may dictate that another forum's substantive laws should be applied to the dispute at issue. To the extent possible under local law, non-US parties to US agency, distributorship or licensing contracts should seek a waiver of the US counterparties right to a jury trial. Again, a disclaimer of this nature is usually capitalised and in bold type face.

17.4.1.7 Term and termination

A distinct US issue in this area is the potential effect of the state franchising and business opportunity laws discussed above in Chapter 17.3.6 above. These laws could restrict termination rights and may require registration of the agreement itself. Furthermore, state sales representative laws and other state laws of general application may be implicated, such as the implied covenant of good faith and fair dealing laws. There is no similar concept to the Council Directive 653/86 of December 18, 1986, on the Coordination of the laws of the Member States relating to self-employed Commercial Agents, in the United States, and absent special relationships or expectations, contracts are freely terminable without payment for developed territories or customers. Obviously, more definite contract termination provisions are preferred. Typical clauses permit termination for breach of any material term (with notice and opportunity to cure, if appropriate), failure to meet quotas or commence sales and upon bankruptcy or insolvency. These last events may not be effective in a bankruptcy scenario, but are still widely used. Typically, to be enforceable a breach must involve a material aspect of performance. For this reason, a party should keep a record of warnings or notices delivered to the other party to support a claim of substantial non-performance. A party terminating a contract in other circumstances may run the risk of being sued for a violation of the implied covenant of good faith and fair dealing or the laws governing relationships with agents or sales representatives. "Evergreen" agreements are generally permitted. While they may be a convenient commercial arrangement for the parties, contracting parties should consider identifying an initial term, which may be helpful in establishing that a subsequent termination of the agreement was reasonable. For example, in the case of an agreement for an undefined term, where an agent or distributor has invested time and effort building up the market for the principal's products, the termination of a contract could result in liability (or at least a claim for liability) for breach of the implied covenant of good faith and fair dealing. **17–102**

17.4.2 Related concepts

17.4.2.1 Statute of frauds

All contracts entered into with US parties should be in writing. Most states have enacted a so-called "Statute of Frauds" pursuant to which agreements to sell goods valued at over $500 or which last for over one year are not enforceable unless in writing. The laws governing sales representatives in certain US states also require contracts to be in written form. **17–103**

17.4.2.2 Resale pricing

17–104 Pricing arrangements can raise legal issues and should be avoided. As a general matter, manufacturers should refrain from discussing with distributors the pricing practices or policies of other distributors.

17.4.2.3 Independent contractor

17–105 There is typically language stating that the licensee or distributor is an "independent contractor". This seeks to avoid the application of agency principles and to prevent the licensee or distributor from being able to bind the licensor or supplier. If dealing with an individual, it can also help avoid any income tax withholding issues and social security payments.

17.4.2.4 UCC

17–106 To the extent that a contract for the sale of goods does not cover a certain contractual term, the relevant state UCC (or, in the case of software and databases, the UCITA) will have "gap filling" terms which will dictate the parties' relationship to the extent it is not set forth in the contract. In addition, under §2–306 of the UCC, an exclusive dealing arrangement means that a manufacturer must use its best effort to supply the goods and the distributor must use its best efforts to sell them.

17.4.2.5 Post termination covenants not to compete

17–107 Enforceability of non-competition agreements will depend upon the state and the nature of the services involved. In many states, non-competition agreements will be enforced by the courts if the terms are found to be commercially reasonable. Generally, courts will not enforce a non-competition agreement if (i) the geographical scope exceeds the territory in which the agent or distributor was authorised or licensed to act, (ii) the prohibited activities are broader than necessary or (iii) the duration is too long. Local state advice is recommended to address particular state law variations and enforceability.

17.4.3 Sample provisions/boilerplate[12]

17.4.3.1 Grant of license

17–108 As discussed in Chapter 17.4.1.3 above, the parties will need to consider issues such as exclusivity as well as appropriate limitations on duration, field

[12] Sample provisions provided in this section are for purposes of illustration only and may not be suitable in concept, scope or terms for a particular transaction or in a particular jur-

of use, territory and sub-licensing. The following is a broadly drafted licensee favourable sample provision for a software license.

Sample Provision: **17–109**

"For the term of this Agreement, Licensor hereby grants to Licensee an exclusive right and license to use for any commercial or noncommercial purpose, reproduce, market, distribute, modify, adapt, create derivative works of, license and sub-license, throughout the Territory and in any and all media known and unknown, the object code and source code versions of the computer programs further described in *Exhibit A* attached hereto and incorporated by reference herein, as such computer programs may be updated, supplemented or modified from time to time including, without limitation, derivative products thereof (the '*Software*') and user documentation associated therewith (the '*Documentation*'; and together with the Software, collectively, the '*Software Package*')."

17.4.3.2 License support/technical assistance

Typically, a license will be accompanied by provisions dealing with initial and ongoing assistance and identifying which party will be responsible for costs associated such technical support and assistance. The following is a sample "pro-licensee" provision. **17–110**

Sample Provision: **17–111**

"Licensor agrees to support, debug and maintain the Software Package, at Licensor's sole expense and without cost to Licensee, on a prompt and on-going basis. Such support by Licensor shall include (without limitation) telephone, facsimile, e-mail and on-line support to Licensee or its licensees. Such maintenance shall include (without limitation) installation and configuration of and training with respect to the Software Package for Licensee and such other licensees as Licensee requests. In addition, [at Licensor's sole expense and without cost to Licensee,] Licensor agrees to arrange for the engagement of third parties to provide maintenance if requested by Licensee and shall cooperate with and assist such third parties."

17.4.3.3. Modifications/enhancements

The parties to an arrangement involving a software license should address the issue of responsibility for and procedures relating to modifications and/or enhancements. The funding and ownership rights to such modifications/enhancements will be a matter of negotiation between the parties and will depend, in part, on whether the modification/enhancement is a general upgrade or unique to the licensee and which party funds or undertakes the modification/enhancement. Provisions dealing with this issue will vary in complexity, the following is a basic provision drafted from the licensee's perspective. **17–112**

17–113 Sample Provision:

"(a) Licensor agrees to update, supplement or modify the performance, operation, function, platform and any other characteristics of the Software Package or any component thereof and to create new versions, releases and translations (each a '*Modification*') on an on-going basis as requested by Licensee.

(b) Within [insert number] days of receipt of a written request from Licensee attaching written specifications for a Modification of the Software Package, the Licensor shall develop a plan, including a schedule and draft work statement, for completing the Modification. Licensor shall not commence any Modification unless such is approved in writing by Licensee."

17.4.3.4 Ownership

17–114 A licensor will want the license to clearly state that ownership of the technology/product remains with it. Issues could arise with respect to ownership rights to enhancements to the extent these are funded or developed by the licensee.[13]

Sample Provision:

"Except for the Licences and as otherwise set forth in this Agreement, Licensor shall retain all rights, title and interest in the Software Package [and all Modifications]. [Licensor acknowledges and agrees that Licensee shall own jointly with Licensor an undivided interest in the whole of, but with no duty to account for profits in connection with, all rights, title and interest in Modifications and related documentation created by Licensor; *provided, however*, that Licensee shall have all rights, title and interest in Modifications created by Licensee or paid for by Licensee.]"

17.4.3.5 Third party claims

17–115 A licensor may be prepared to give a limited indemnity for third party claims arising as a result of infringement of third party intellectual property rights that do not relate to any default on the part of the licensee. Related issues that would need to be resolved include identifying the party which will have responsibility for defending the claim and related procedures.

Sample Provision:

"Licensor shall indemnify Licensee against, and agrees to hold it harmless from, any and all losses, costs, liabilities and expenses (including attorney's fees and

[13] In the event a licensee develops an enhancement to a particular technology/product, the licensor will want to have access to the improvements. From a US antitrust perspective, a licensor should not expect more than a non-exclusive, worldwide license for the enhancement itself. Moreover, for US antitrust purposes, such a "grant back" provision typically requires the licensor to pay a reasonable royalty for the use of the enhanced technology/product.

expenses [and the costs of litigation and investigation]) incurred or suffered by Licensee arising out of, relating to or concerning in any way any claims alleging that the Software Package infringes the copyright, patent, trade mark, trade secret or other intellectual property right of a third party. Without limiting the foregoing, and in addition to Licensee's remedies hereunder and at law and in equity, should the possibility arise that Licensee may lose, or have declared invalid or void, any right, title or interest in the Software Package or any right to use or sublicense the Software Package, then [at Licensee's option] Licensor shall[, at its sole expense,] promptly either (i) modify the Software Package, without materially diminishing its functional capabilities, to make it noninfringing or (ii) acquire or purchase for Licensee's benefit hereunder such rights as are necessary to allow and vest in Licensee the rights to use the Software Package in the manner contemplated by the Agreement."

17.4.3.6 Disclaimers

The parties to a agreement may wish to limit liability by disclaiming any warranties implied by law and limiting a party's rights and remedies to breaches of the representations and warranties actually set out in the agreement. **17–116**

Sample Provision: **17–117**

"EXCEPT AS OTHERWISE SET FORTH HEREIN, NEITHER PARTY MAKES ANY REPRESENTATIONS OR WARRANTIES OF ANY KIND, EXPRESS OR IMPLIED, WITH RESPECT TO THE SOFTWARE PACKAGE, OR THE FUNCTIONALITY, PERFORMANCE OR RESULTS OF USE THEREOF. NEITHER PARTY GIVES ANY IMPLIED WARRANTY OF MERCHANTABILITY, IMPLIED WARRANTY OF FITNESS FOR ANY PARTICULAR PURPOSE, OR IMPLIED WARRANTY ARISING BY USAGE OF TRADE, COURSE OF DEALING OR COURSE OF PERFORMANCE."

17.4.3.7 Limitations on liability

Typically, the licensor (or, depending on the agreement, both parties) will want to limit liability for consequential and indirect damages. Also, a party may request a cap on any liability relating to direct damages. **17–118**

Sample Provision:

"IN NO EVENT SHALL [THE LICENSOR] [A PARTY] HAVE ANY LIABILITY OR RESPONSIBILITY FOR ANY SPECIAL, INDIRECT, INCIDENTAL, CONSEQUENTIAL OR EXEMPLARY DAMAGES OR FOR INTERRUPTED COMMUNICATIONS, LOST DATA OR LOST PROFITS, ARISING OUT OF OR IN CONNECTION WITH THIS AGREEMENT, THE TRANSACTIONS CONTEMPLATED HEREBY, THE SOFTWARE PACKAGE OR THE USE OF THE SOFTWARE PACKAGE, EVEN IF SUCH PARTY HAS BEEN ADVISED OF (OR KNOWS OR SHOULD KNOW OF) THE POSSIBILITY OF SUCH DAMAGES. [IN THE EVENT THAT [THE

LICENSOR] [A PARTY] IS FOUND TO BE LIABLE FOR DIRECT DAMAGES, SUCH LIABILITY AND RESPONSIBILITY SHALL, IN THE AGGREGATE, BE LIMITED TO AND SHALL NOT EXCEED THE TOTAL AMOUNTS PAID OR TO BE PAID HEREUNDER.]"

17.4.3.8 Miscellaneous

17–119 There are other provisions of a general nature that are typically covered in a US contract:

- "Royalty/Payment Provisions": Issues to the considered may include determining the relevant royalty base, net sales price, minimum royalties, revaluation issues and taxes. Any required withholding taxes should be required to be deducted before payment. The currency, location and means of payments should be included.
- "Sale and Delivery Terms": Terms like "FOB" should be defined in the distribution agreement or reference made to a specified body of rules (such as the UCC or Incoterms) as the meaning of these terms can vary from state to state and from any generally accepted international standards.
- "Best efforts" provisions are widely seen. They put a burden on the agent, licensee or distributor to apply himself. (See discussion above regarding §2–306 of the UCC).

17–120 Sample Provision:

"Representative shall devote sufficient time and exercise its best efforts as required to vigorously solicit and obtain orders for the Product so as to maximize distribution throughout the Territory. In accordance with this obligation, Representative shall (without limitation): (1) maintain a professional, competent and trained sales force of at least [insert number] full-time employees who have successfully completed training by the Company in the Product and who will spend no less than a majority of their time soliciting customers and potential customers of the Product in the Territory; (2) devote its exclusive efforts to the Company's Product and not distribute or solicit orders of any similar or competing product within the Territory during the term of this Agreement and for [insert number] years after its conclusion; (3) satisfy a minimum sales requirement of at least [insert dollar amount] during each [insert time period]; (4) expend, at Representative's sole cost, at least [insert dollar amount] in each calendar year for the purpose of advertising the Product within the Territory; and (5) produce and distribute, at Representative's sole cost, sales brochures regarding the Product, provided that each such sales brochure has been submitted to the Company for prior approval and such prior approval is granted in writing."

- "*Force Majeure*" clauses, excusing performance during certain catastrophes, are widely used and enforceable. The United States often has a broad definition of this term so specific language set forth in the agreement is preferable.

Sample Provision: 17–121

"Neither party shall be liable for failure to comply with any of the terms of this Agreement to the extent that such failure has been caused solely by fire, any attack on, outbreak or escalation of hostilities or act of terrorism involving the United States, any declaration of war by Congress, insurrection, government restrictions, force majeure or other causes beyond such party's reasonable control; provided that the effects of any such cause could not have been reasonably avoided by the non-performing party, and provided further that the non-performing party shall promptly give notice to the other party and shall exercise all reasonable efforts to resume performance as soon as possible."

- "Assignments" should be restricted, as contracts are otherwise generally assignable without consent in the US (as explained above, however, such clauses may be disregarded in bankruptcy proceedings).

Sample provision: 17–122

"This Agreement may not be assigned (voluntarily, by operation of law or otherwise) by any party without prior written consent of the other party."

- "Entire agreement clauses" are widely used to attempt to keep the business relationship to what was finally signed and agreed and avoid reference to discussions and negotiations leading up to the final contract.

Sample Provision: 17–123

"This Agreement supersedes and merges all prior proposals, understandings and all other agreements, oral and written, between the parties relating to the subject matter of this Agreement. There have been no representations or statements, oral or written, that have been relied on by any party hereto, except those expressly set forth in this Agreement. This Agreement may not be modified, altered or amended except by written instrument duly executed by both parties."

Chapter 18

Cyprus*

Contents

18.1 Introduction

Cyprus has been an independent and sovereign republic with a presidential system of government since 1960, when it gained its independence. Until that time it had been a British colony. The Cypriot legal system followed English law until 1960, and since then it has been closely modelled on its English counterpart. **18–01**

Cyprus has adopted the Anglo-Saxon legal system, which allows most English cases to be cited in Cypriot courts. Under certain conditions, the cases are treated as binding, but in most instances they are used as guidelines.[1] **18–02**

In examining agency and distribution in the context of Cyprus law it should always be borne in mind that both legal terms are relatively new concepts to the Cypriot legal system. The continuous development of the Cyprus economy coupled with Cyprus application for European Union membership indicate that this area of the law is becoming very significant. **18–03**

The main principles of agency and distribution law are laid out in ss.142–149 of the Cypriot Contract Law[2] and essentially reflect their common law principles. English Common Law principles apply where no express statutory provisions are made and offer much guidance in interpreting the provisions of the Cypriot Contract Law. **18–04**

Additionally, various pieces of legislation have recently been enacted, the most important of which relate to commercial agents; namely: **18–05**

* This chapter was written by Panayiotis Neocleous LL.B. (Bristol), Barrister-at-Law, Partner with Andreas Neocleous & Co, of Limassol, Cyprus.

[1] *Katina Hajitheodosiou v Petros Koulia* (1970) 1 C.L.R. 310; *Constandinides v Pitsillos* (1980) 2 J.S.C. 279.

[2] Contract Law, Cap 149.

- Commercial Agents Law[3] (the "1986 Law");
- Regulations of Relations between Commercial Agents and Principals Law[4] (the "1992 Law"); and
- Commercial Agents (Amendment) Law[5] (the "1994 Law").

18.2 Agency agreements

18.2.1 General relationship

18–06 In general at common law, the term "agency" is used to describe the body of general rules under which one person, the agent, has the power to change the legal relations of another, the principal.[6]

18–07 Contract law and property law are the most important areas of the law where the power of the agent to bind the principal are analysed. An agent may have power to bind his principal by contract and by acts connected with the performance of a contract, or he may have power to receive property for his principal or make a valid disposition of his principal's property. Similar considerations may appear in areas such as torts.

18–08 The legal doctrines which are applicable can be divided into the following two broad categories:

- the first category relates to the agent's power to bind his principal and is important with respect to third party dealing with such agents (the "external aspects of agency"); and
- the second category relates to the rights and liabilities of the agent and principal *inter se* and to the fiduciary duties of the agent as well as to the agent's remuneration and compensation (the "internal aspects of agency").

18–09 Where the agent's authority emanates from a manifestation of consent, whether implied or express, to act or represent the principal made by the principal to the agent himself the authority is called actual or implied consent. Where, however, the agent's authority results from a manifestation of consent made by the principal to a third party then the authority is called apparent authority. In addition, implied authority may be inferred from the circumstances of each particular case[7]; any written or oral evidence may be considered by the Cypriot courts in determining the circumstances of the

[3] Law 76 of 1986.
[4] Law 51(1) of 1992.
[5] Law 21(1) of 1994.
[6] Section 142 of Cap 149 provides that an agent is "... a person employed to do any act for another, the principal, or to represent the principal in dealings with third parties".
[7] Section 147 of Cap 149.

case.[8] Finally the consent my be granted subsequently by the principal by virtue of ratification of the agent's acts.

Under Cypriot Law there the following main categories of agents: **18–10**

- *General agent.* A general agent has the authority to act for his principal in all matters concerning a particular trade or business, or to do some act in the ordinary course of his trade, profession, or business.
- *Special agent.* A special agent is an agent who has authority only to do some particular act or to represent his principal in some particular transaction not being in the ordinary course of his trade, profession or business as an agent.
- *Sub-agent.* Section 151 of Cap 149 provides that a sub-agent is "... a person competent to contract, employed by and acting under the control of the original agent in the business of the agency". Section 152 further provides that as long as the sub-agent is properly appointed, the principal is, as far as third parties are concerned, represented by the sub-agent and is bound by and accountable for his acts as if he were an agent originally appointed by the principal. The agent is responsible to the principal for the acts of the sub-agent and the sub-agent is responsible for his acts to the agent and not to the principal.[9] It should also be noted that s.154 provides that where an agent appoints without authority a person to act as a sub-agent, the agent is liable for his acts both to the principal as well as to third parties. The principal is not represented by or liable for the acts of the sub-agent; nor is the sub-agent liable to the principal.
- *Mercantile agent.* The definition of a mercantile agent is set out in s.2(1) of the Sale of Goods Law.[10] He is a person who has, in the customary course of his business as such agent, authority to sell goods, to consign goods for the purpose of sale, to buy goods, or to raise money on the security of goods. The significance of a mercantile agent has been greatly reduced nowadays.
- *Canvassing agents.* A canvassing agent is a person who often represents others, such as estate agents or insurance agents. The function of a canvassing agent is generally to introduce business. They are not agents in the strict meaning but are covered by certain doctrines established by the law of agency and especially those relating to the fiduciary obligations owed by the agent to the principal.
- *Distributors and franchisees.* Franchise holders and distributors of particular products are often referred to as agents. Although it is possible that such persons are agents in the sense that their obligations

[8] It may be inferred from the above that the agreement between the agent and the principal may not be contractual as, for example, an agent can act gratuitously.
[9] Except in the case of fraud or wilful wrong.
[10] Law 19(1) of 1994.

to their principal are those of an agent, even though they deal with the outside world in their own names, such persons are regarded at Common Law as purchasers for resale and agency principles are not strictly applicable.

- *Commercial agents.* A commercial agent is defined by s.2 of the 1986 Law as follows: "Every legal or natural person who, by his capacity as independent intermediary, has the permanent authority to negotiate on behalf of another person, the principal, the sale or purchase of goods or negotiate and conclude such actions in the name and on behalf of the principal".

18.2.2 Carrying on business in Cyprus

18–11 Cyprus has a free-market, open economy. The authorities have implemented simple administrative procedures to expedite matters concerning especially foreign entrepreneurs, reflecting the importance Cyprus attaches to the development of its potential as an international and regional business centre. The attraction of foreign capital has always been the primary objective of the island's development policy.

18–12 The Constitution guarantees the right of private property and does not discriminate between Cypriots and non-Cypriots. Nationalisation has never been part of the government's policy, nor is it contemplated in any way in the future. Furthermore, Cyprus is a signatory to the Convention for the Settlement of Disputes between States and Nationals of other States and the Multilateral Investment Guarantee Agency Agreement.

18–13 The 1986 Law and subsequent pieces of legislation were enacted to bring domestic law into line with European Union Law. The 1986 Law contains provisions similar to those of the European Community Council Directive 653/86 (the "1986 EC Directive").

18–14 Section 3 of the 1986 Law sets up a council responsible for the registration of commercial agents as well as the conditions applicable for such registration.[11] The abovementioned council has wide powers, including the power to remove a commercial agent from its register,[12] as well as the power to issue regulations. Breach of any of the provisions of the 1986 Law constitutes an offence punishable by six months imprisonment or a maximum fine of £300, or both.

18–15 In addition to the 1986 Law the 1992 Law is a further attempt to bring domestic law in line with EU legislation. It covers the duties of the agent towards his principal and vice versa, remuneration, commission, termination of the agency contract, rights to indemnity and compensation on such termination and restraint of trade.

18–16 It has not yet been ascertained whether the above two pieces of legislation are compatible or reconcilable with Common Law principles. However,

[11] Under s.4 of the 1986 Law a register of commercial agents is established.
[12] Section 5 of the 1986 Law.

bearing in mind the fact that both pieces of legislation incorporate verbatim the exact text of the 1986 EC Directive on the coordination of the laws of Member States relating to self employed commercial agents, any interpretation given by the European Court of Justice on this issue is of the essence and is most likely to be followed by Cypriot courts.

The Cypriot National Committee of the International Chamber of Commerce (the "ICC") has implemented a firm policy of educating Cypriot businessmen on issues relating to the smooth conduct of international trade. The ICC has further prepared a model form of international commercial agency contract as well as a model distributorship contract in order to assist Cypriots engaged in international trade. It should be noted that the above two model contracts have been prepared on the assumption that they will apply only on international contracts with self-employed commercial agents or distributors for the sale of goods. **18–17**

Finally, in its efforts to liberalise further its economy and attract foreign capital, in February 1997, the government relaxed the rules and regulations applicable to inward investment. Under the new regime, administrative procedures have become simpler and it is now possible for foreign legal and physical persons to own up to 100 per cent of local corporations.[13] **18–18**

18.2.3 Permanent establishment

In principle where a Cypriot agent exercises his power to enter into agency contracts binding the principal, the principal will be considered for taxation purposes as carrying on business through a permanent establishment in Cyprus.[14] **18–19**

A non-resident principal carrying on business through a Cypriot permanent establishment will be taxed on all his taxable income derived from Cypriot sources. However, it should always be borne in mind that Cyprus has an extensive network of double tax treaties which should be considered in deriving the tax burden of the principal.[15] **18–20**

18.2.4 Specific product legislation

The Trade Description Law of 1987[16] was enacted to protect consumers from inaccurate or misleading trade descriptions. The Law prohibits any person carrying on a trade, business or profession from applying an inaccurate trade description to goods or supplying or offering to supply goods to which an inaccurate trade description applies. **18–21**

[13] Provided that such investment does not impose any national or environmental risks.

[14] This principle is not applicable where the agent is only doing mere preparatory work for the conclusion of a contract.

[15] *Introduction to Cyprus Law*, by Andreas Neocleous *et al.*: Chapter 7 provides an extensive analysis on the taxation laws of Cyprus.

[16] Law 5 of 1987.

18–22 Section 5 of Law 5 of 1987 prohibits the importation or supply within Cyprus of any goods which are not labelled in an obvious and clear manner with an indication of the country of production or manufacture.

18–23 Law 5 of 1987 was amended in 1992 by the Trade Description (Amendment) Law of 1992.[17] The said law provides that an offence is committed by a person who, during the execution of a trade, business or profession provides consumers with any misleading indication as to the price of any product or services.

18–24 The Safety of Consumers Products Law[18] introduces and implements the European standards for the safety of products. The above law provides that buyers must be informed of any dangers resulting from incorrect use of products. By virtue of Law 99(I) of 1997, Law 74(I) of 1994 was amended to the effect that every producer, importer, seller and deliverer of consumer products is under a duty to give to the Consumer Protection Authority any information of which he acquires knowledge which could lead to the conclusion that any consumer product might endanger the safety or health of consumers or is in any way defective.

18–25 The Defective Products (Civil Liability) Law[19] renders the producer/manufacturer of defective goods strictly liable for any damage caused by such products and bring the legislation in this area into line with European legislation. Law 105(I) of 1995 implements all European Directives in the area of product liability, including the 574/85 Directive.

18.2.5 Power to bind

18–26 An agent who is appointed by virtue of a contract is bound to act within the scope of the terms of the contract and most important of all not to exceed his authority. The authority of the agent may be actual (express or implied) or apparent. Actual authority is the authority which the principal has given the agent wholly or in part by means of words or writing or is regarded by the law as having been given to him because of either the legal interpretation or the relationship and dealings of the two parties. Actual authority is a legal relationship between principal and agent created by a consensual agreement to which they alone are parties. Its scope is to be ascertained by applying the ordinary principles of construction of contracts, including any proper inferences from the express words used, the usage of the trade, or the course of the business or trade.

18–27 Apparent authority involves the assumption that there is no authority at all. Under this doctrine, where a principal represents that another person has authority, he may be bound as against a third party by the acts of that person within the authority which that person appears to have; in such a

[17] Law 3 of 1992.
[18] Law 74(1) of 1994.
[19] Law 105(I) of 1995.

case the principal may be bound although he has not given that person such authority.

If an agent deals on his own account in the business of the agency without obtaining the prior consent of his principal the principal may repudiate the transaction where any material fact has been dishonestly concealed from him by the agent or the dealings of the agent have been disadvantageous to him. The principal is also entitled under these circumstances to claim from the agent any benefit that may have resulted to the agent from the transaction. **18–28**

Contracts entered into through an agent and obligations arising from acts done by an agent may be enforced in the same manner and will have the same legal consequences as if the contracts have been entered into and the acts done by the principal. In addition any notice given or information obtained by the agent in the course of the business transacted by him for the principal will have the same legal consequences as between the principal and third parties.[20] **18–29**

If an agent exceeds his authority and the authorised and unauthorised part of his actions can be separated from each other then the authorised part will be binding on the principal and the principal will then have the choice to affirm or reject the unauthorised part. Where, however, the unauthorised part cannot be separated from the authorised part the principal is entitled not to recognise the transaction. **18–30**

Unless it is a term of any contract an agent cannot personally enforce contracts entered into by him on behalf of his principal, nor do such contracts personally bind him. Such a term will be presumed where: **18–31**

- the contract is made by an agent for the sale or purchase of goods to or from a merchant who is residing abroad;
- the agent does not disclose the name of his principal; and
- the principal, though disclosed, cannot be sued.[21]

Where an agent, acting without the authority of his principal, assumes obligations on behalf of his principal against third parties the principal is bound by such acts or obligations if he had by his words or conduct induced third parties to believe that such acts and obligations were within the agent's scope of authority. **18–32**

Similarly, representations made or fraud committed by an agent, acting in the course of his principal's business, have the same effect on agreements made by such an agent as if such misrepresentations or frauds have been made or committed by the principal.[22] **18–33**

The difference between a disclosed from an undisclosed principal should also be addressed at this point. A disclosed principal is a principal, whether **18–34**

[20] Section 190 of Cap 149.
[21] Section 190 of Cap 149.
[22] However, this principle does not apply where the agent has made representations or committed fraud in matters which do not fall within his authority.

identified or unidentified, whose existence as principal is known at the time of the transaction to the person dealing with the agent. An undisclosed principal is a principal whose existence as principal is not known at the time of the transaction to the person dealing with the agent. It is a well established principle that an undisclosed principal can sue or be sued on the contract of his agent.

18–35 Finally, it should be noted that by virtue of s.159 of Cap 149 where one person does act on behalf of another without his knowledge or authority, the other may elect to ratify or disown such acts. If he ratifies them the same effects will follow as if they had been performed with his authority.

18–36 Ratification may be express or implied by the conduct of the person on whose behalf the acts are done, but there can be no valid ratification by a person whose knowledge of the facts of the case is materially defective.[23] Moreover, an authorised act done by one person on behalf of another which, if done with authority, would have the effect of subjecting a third person to damage or of terminating any right or interest of a third person, cannot by ratification be made to have such effect.

18.2.6 Termination and compensation

18–37 Section 161 of Cap 149 provides that an agency is terminated by the following:

- revocation of the agent's authority by the principal;
- renunciation of the business of the agency by the agent;
- completion of the business of the agency;
- death or unsoundness of mind of either the principal or the agent; or
- adjudication of the principal as bankrupt or insolvent under the provisions of any law relating to bankruptcy or insolvency.

18–38 In addition to the above the authority of the agent may be revoked in the following circumstances:

- by agreement between the parties;
- expiration of an agency for an agreed period or after a certain time has elapsed which is reasonable in all the circumstances;
- occurrence of an event which by agreement between the parties will determine the authority or on the occurrence of which the agent may reasonably infer that the principal does not or would not wish the authority to continue;

[23] Sections 157 and 158 of Cap 149.

- destruction of the subject matter of the agency; and
- happening of any event rendering the agency or its objects unlawful, impossible or otherwise frustrating the agency or its objects.

Furthermore, section 162 of Cap 149 provides that where the agent has himself an interest in the property which forms the subject matter of the agency, the agency cannot, in the absence of an express contract, be terminated to the prejudice of such interest. Subject to this provision, the principal may revoke the agent's authority at any time before the authority has been exercised so as to bind the principal. If the agent's authority has been partially exercised the principal cannot revoke the agent's authority concerning actions and obligations arising from acts already undertaken by the agent. **18–39**

Cap 149 further provides that where there is an express or implied contract that the agency should continue for any particular period of time, the parties must compensate each other, as the case may be, for any earlier revocation or renunciation of the agency without sufficient cause. The parties are obliged to give reasonable notice of such revocation or renunciation to each other and, unless they do so, any resulting damage must be made good to the one by the other.[24] The termination of the agent's authority does not take effect before it becomes known to him and before it becomes known to third parties. It should be noted that when the agent's authority is terminated the authority of all sub-agents by him is also terminated. **18–40**

Part IV of the 1992 Law makes provisions for the execution and expiration of a commercial agency agreement. It imposes an obligation on both parties to contract and sign a written agreement which determines the terms of the commercial agency agreement and any other subsequent terms to be agreed. It should be noted that where the parties continue to execute a fixed term commercial agency agreement after its expiration, it is considered to have become a commercial agreement of indefinite duration. **18–41**

If a commercial agency agreement is of an indefinite period, either party may terminate it on the basis of the other party failing to perform the whole or part of its obligations by giving a written notice to this effect. The period of this notice shall be the same for both parties and is specified in the 1992 Law.[25] **18–42**

Subject to the above every agent has a right against his principal to be indemnified against all losses and liabilities incurred by him in the execution of his authority. In *G G Kazinos & Co v Letraset (Export) Ltd of London*, the plaintiff claimed more that £50,000 against the defendant as damages for breach of an agency agreement. The plaintiff carried on business as a commission agent and the defendant was an exporter of graphic products. **18–43**

[24] *G G Kazinos & Co v Letraset (Export) Ltd of London* (1982) 2 J.S.C. 443.

[25] One month for the first year of the agreement, two months for the second year, three months for the third year, four months for the fourth year, five months for the fifth year and six months for the sixth and subsequent years.

The issue was whether the agency agreement could be terminated, and if so, the appropriate notice that it should have been given under the circumstances. The contract made no provision for termination, and the court concluded that the agreement was terminable on reasonable notice. The court emphasised that the question of the length of the notice depended on the facts existing at the date such notice was given. A factor that the court further considered was the expenses incurred in setting up and running the agency. On the basis of the abovementioned factors the court held that the reasonable notice for that case was nine months and as a result the defendant was entitled to damages on the basis of the amount it would have earned if reasonable notice had been given.[26]

18–44 In *Pipis v Constandinidou*[27] the court held that reasonable notice must be given of the revocation or renunciation of authority; otherwise, the damage caused to the principal or agent must be made good. It was held that damage may be recovered if it flows naturally from the breach of the agency contract or it is of a type that could reasonably be said to have been within the contemplation of the parties as likely to result if either party is in breach. In this case the court assessed the damage suffered by the aggrieved party by using as a measure the market value of the property under examination at the date of the breach. The object of the judgement as to the amount of the damages was to restore the plaintiff to the position in which he would have been had the agency contract been performed.

18–45 In *Yiannis Panayides Limited v Costa Karatsi Limited*[28] held that the criteria to be applied in considering the level of damages to be awarded included the duration of the agency agreement, the volume of work involved, and whether the agent, according to the agreement, had incurred expenses introducing the principal's product in the market.

18–46 *Goodwill.* An agent has the right to be indemnified if the contract expires or is terminated for reasons other than his own default. Such indemnity may be construed as compensation for the goodwill created by the agent which accrued to the principal after the end of the contract or as compensation for the loss suffered by the agent as a consequence of the expiration or termination of the contract.

18–47 Goodwill is one of the criteria taken into consideration by the court in assessing the amount of indemnity on the expiration of the contract or on its termination for reasons other than the agent's fault.

18–48 Under s.18 of the 1992 Law, the commercial agent is entitled to such as an indemnity if and to the extent that:

- he has introduced new customers to the principal or has significantly increased the volume of business with existing customers and the principal continues to derive substantial benefits from the business with such customers; and

[26] It should be noted that the court held also that the pecuniary loss caused to the plaintiff as a result of the loss of the goodwill of one particular client was too remote and thus irrecoverable.
[27] (1982) 1 J.S.C. 170.
[28] Judgements of Cypriot Courts, Nicosia Bar Association (1993) volume 6, at p. 505.

- the payment of this indemnity is fair and equitable, having regard to all the circumstances and in particular the commissions lost by the commercial agent on the business transacted with such customers.

It is important to note that the agent's right to claim indemnity is lost if he does not notify the principal within one year following termination of his intentions to pursue his claim. **18–49**

The 1992 Law does not allow the parties to agree to a deviation from these provisions to the detriment of the commercial agent. The 1992 Law[29] also sets out the circumstances in which damages are not due; in particular, where: **18–50**

- the principal terminates the commercial agency agreement due to the agent's fault which would justify, according to the law, an immediate termination;
- the commercial agent terminates the commercial agency agreement on the basis of its duration having lapsed, or due to ailment of the agent or due to physical fitness, as a result of which it is not possible reasonably to request the agent to continue his activities; and
- after entering into an agreement with the principal by virtue of which the commercial agent assigns to a third party the rights and obligations which he has undertaken pursuant to the commercial agency agreement.

Commission on post-termination sales. In all cases the applicable test is whether, as a matter of construction of the commercial agency agreement, the parties intended that the agent should be paid commission after termination. **18–51**

The older authorities support the view that the words used in the contract must be clear and unequivocal so as to entitle the agent to such a commission. However, this view has been questioned and it now seems that the normal rules as regards implying terms into a contract should be applied. **18–52**

Section 9 of the 1992 Law provides that, if an agency agreement falls within the scope of this law, the commercial agent is entitled to receive commission for commercial transactions concluded after the termination of the agreement if: **18–53**

- the transaction is mainly attributable to the commercial agent's efforts during the period covered by the agency agreement and the transaction was entered into within a reasonable period after the expiration of the agreement; or
- the order of the third party was placed either with the commercial agent or with the principal before the expiration of the agency agreement.

[29] Section 19.

18–54 *Return of documents*. The principal is entitled to have delivered up to him at the termination of the agency all documents concerning his affairs that have been prepared by the agent. In every case it is necessary to decide whether the document in question came into existence for the purpose of the agency relationship or for some other purpose.

18–55 The 1992 Law and the Cyprus Contract Law do not contain any specific provisions on this issue.

18–56 *Agent's rights in principal's bankruptcy*. The Contract Law provides that an agency may be terminated where the principal is declared bankrupt or insolvent under the provisions of any bankruptcy or insolvency law. The question whether the authority of an agent is revoked by the bankruptcy of the principal depends on the nature and terms of his employment, but in principle the agency will rank *pari passu* with all other unsecured creditors.

18–57 *Principal's property held by agent and agent's bankruptcy*. An agent's bankruptcy will not necessarily end the relationship. This will much depend on the agency agreement and the particular circumstances of each case.

18.2.7 Commissions on sales

18–58 It is the principal's duty to pay his agent commission. Where there is an express term as to payment, the remuneration and the amount will depend on the term. There is an implied agreement to pay remuneration whenever a person is employed to act as an agent in circumstances which raise the presumption that he would, to the knowledge of his principal, have expected to be paid.

18–59 In *Tsamkooshoglou Trading Company v Cytechno Ltd*[30] it was held that an agent is entitled to his commission at the time he earns it. An agent has earned his commission when the agent has brought about the event on which commission is to be paid.

18–60 An agent is entitled to remuneration for his services as agent, if either expressly or impliedly the agency contract so provides. Where the contract contains express terms as to remuneration, the agent cannot claim remuneration other than in accordance with those terms. In the absence of express terms, the right to claim any remuneration and the amount and terms of payment are determined by such terms as may be implied. In determining what the implied terms are, the court must consider all the circumstances of the case, the nature and length of the services, the express terms of the contract, and the customs and usage of the particular trade.

18–61 In cases of remuneration in the form of a commission, the 1992 Law sets out the circumstances in which a commercial agent is entitled to a commission for commercial transactions contracted after the expiration of the agreement. An agent is entitled to commission during the agreement if (a) the transaction was secured by the mediation of the commercial agent, (b) the transaction was contracted with a third party whom the commercial

[30] (1974) 11 J.S.C. 1124.

agent had secured earlier as a client for transactions of a similar type, or (c) the agent was appointed to cover a particular geographical area and/or particular group of people, and the transaction was contracted within the same geographical area, or a person who belongs to that group even if, for the transaction, negotiations were carried out by a person other than the commercial agent or a different agreement was contracted by the commercial agent.

18.2.8 Formalities

In principle an agency may be created by: **18–62**

- express appointment;
- implication of law from the conduct or situation of the parties or from the necessity of the case; or
- subsequent ratification by the principal.

As explained previously the actual relationship of the parties is determined by all the circumstances of the case and not merely from the use of the word "agent" or "agency" in an agreement. The relationship of principal and agent can be established only by the consent of both parties and an agency relationship usually arises by way of an agreement but this need not be in writing. **18–63**

Section 143 of Cap 149 provides that any person may appoint an agent provided that he himself has the capacity to contract.[31] **18–64**

Under Cypriot law it is the duty of the agent to conduct the business of his principal in accordance with the directions given by the principal.[32] In the absence of such directions the agent is bound to conduct the business in accordance with the prevailing trading customs of the particular business at the place where the agent conducts such business. If the agent does not act in accordance with such directions and any loss or damage arises, the agent is under a duty to compensate the principal. If any profit, on the other hand accrues, the agent must account to the principal for it. **18–65**

An agent must exercise reasonable duty in the execution of his duties. What is reasonable will depend on the circumstances of each case as well as the trading customs applicable. If direct and foreseeable losses arise from the agent's negligence, want of skill or misconduct, the agent must compensate the principal to this effect.[33] **18–66**

The necessary requirements for a person to become a commercial agent are the following[34]: **18–67**

[31] Section 11 of Cap 149 provides that any person of sound mind whose capacity to contract is not restricted by reason of any other law has capacity to contract.
[32] Section 171 of Cap 149.
[33] However, the agent is not responsible if the damage is not foreseeable or too remote.
[34] Section 3 of the 1994 Law, which amended s.4 of the 1986 Law.

- was not convicted within the last 10 years preceding the date of the submission of the application to become a commercial agent of any offence under the Exchange Control Law or the Customs and Consumption Taxes Law, or any other offence which entails immorality or dishonesty;
- has never been declared bankrupt; and
- is a high school graduate.

18–68 Moreover, s.3 of the 1992 Law places a commercial agent under a general duty to act according to the law and in good faith towards the principal and in the best interests of the principal. Specifically, every commercial agent is under a duty to make every possible effort to negotiate or conclude the transactions entrusted to him and pass to the principal all information he has acquired.

18–69 A principal is under a duty to indemnify the agent against the consequences of every legal act of the latter within the authority conferred on him.[35] The principal must indemnify the agent for the consequences of any act performed under his instructions by the agent in good faith, even if such acts are harmful to third parties. However, the principal is not liable to indemnify his agent for any act whatsoever which entails criminal liability, even if performed pursuant to the principal's instructions.

18–70 The principal has the right to terminate the agency contract if the agent, in the course of conducting the agency, transacts for his own benefit and without the principal's consent, provided that it is obvious either that the agent dishonestly failed to disclose to the principal any material fact or that the transactions of the agent have caused damage and losses to the principal. In such a case the principal may claim for the agent any profit the latter has acquired from such transactions.

18–71 The authority of the agent may be express or implied. If there is an express agreement, whether contractual or not, between principal and agent this agreement will regulate the relationship between principal and agent. The scope of the agreement is determined by applying the ordinary principles of the construction of contracts, including any proper inferences from an express words used, trading customs and the course of business between the parties.

18–72 The agreement may be contractual in which case the relations between the agent and the principal are regulated by the law of contract. However, an agency may be implied where each party has acted in a way in which it would be reasonable for the other to infer from his conduct that they have consented to an agency relationship.

18–73 In a contract entered into through an agent any obligations arising from the acts of the agent may be enforced in the same manner and will have the same legal consequences as if the contract had been entered into and the acts done by the principal in person.

[35] Section 182 of Cap 149.

An agent having authority to do an act has authority to do every lawful thing that is necessary to complete such an act. An agent having authority to carry on a business has authority to do every lawful thing necessary for the purpose, or usually done in the course of conducting such business. **18–74**

If an agent appoints and delegates the execution of acts and duties to a sub-agent without express or implied authority to do so the agent is liable for the sub-agent's acts both to the principal and to third persons. **18–75**

The principal is not represented by the sub-agent nor is he responsible for the acts of the sub-agent; nor is the sub-agent accountable or liable to the principal. Where an agent has express or implied authority to appoint a person to act for the principal in the business of the agency such a person is not a sub-agent but an agent for the principal for such part of the business of the agency as is entrusted to him by the principal. **18–76**

It is important to note that s.14 of the 1992 Law provides that the parties to a commercial agency agreement must conclude and sign a written contract which will determine the terms of the agreement. **18–77**

18.2.9 Exchange control and withholding tax

The impact of exchange control restrictions on agency agreements should be considered in the light of the Exchange Control Law, as amended by Law 53 of 1972. Section 35(1) of the Exchange Control Law provides that "it shall be an implied condition in any contract that, where, by virtue of this Law, the permission or consent of the Central Bank of Cyprus is at the time of the contract required for the performance of any term thereof that term shall not be performed except insofar as the consent or permission is given or not required". **18–78**

In *Neoptolemos-Spyropoulos v Transvania Holland NV Amsterdam*[36] the Supreme Court stated that the failure to make express reference to the obtaining of a consent or permission of the Central Bank does not render a contract void or illegal but merely suspends the performance of a term until such consent or permission is obtained. Section 35(1), however, would invalidate a contract where the parties are shown to have contemplated the performance of the term violating the law, despite the provision. **18–79**

It should be stressed that it is always advisable to sign an agency agreement following consultation with the Central Bank of Cyprus and to insert a contract term which envisages the Central Bank's powers by carefully specifying their effect on the life of the contract and stating where liabilities would lie. **18–80**

It should be noted that an individual or a corporation violating the provisions of the Exchange Control Law may incur penal sanctions in the form of imprisonment or a fine. **18–81**

At present and due to the forthcoming accession of Cyprus into the **18–82**

[36] (1979) 1 C.L.R. 421.

European Union there are steps towards partially liberalisation of the exchange control rules and regulations of Cyprus.

18.2.10 Litigation issues—principal's exposure to local jurisdiction

18–83 Order 5, r.8, of the Civil Procedure Rules provides that, where a contract has been entered into in Cyprus by or through an agent residing or carrying on business in Cyprus on behalf of a principal residing or carrying on business outside Cyprus, a writ of summons in an action relating to or arising out of such a contract may, by leave of the court or a judge given before the determination of such agent's authority or of his business relations with the principal, be served on such agent. Notice of the order giving such leave and an office copy thereof and of the writ of summons will forthwith be sent by prepaid, double-registered letter post to the defendants at his address out of the jurisdiction.

18–84 It is the agent's duty under s.189 of Cap 149 and under the common law to communicate all relevant information to his principal and he will be deemed to have done so.

18–85 In addition an agent is entitled to initiate proceedings against third parties on behalf of the principal. However, the usual practice is that such proceedings are usually initiated by both the agent and the principal.

18.3 Distribution agreements—manufacturing agreements

18–86 There are no statutory provisions governing distribution or manufacturing agreements and often the legislation does not make any distinction between agent and distributor or manufacturer. The principles discussed in the previous parts of this chapter as well as the general principles of common law would *prima facie* apply to distributors and manufacturers.

18–87 It should be noted, however, that in the area of competition law, the Exclusive Distribution Agreements (Block Exemption) Order of 1995 applies. Lawyers should always draft exclusive distribution agreements consistent with its main principles and, wherever it is not possible to do so, to tailor the agreement as closely as possible to the provisions of the 1995 Order so that the Cyprus Competition Committee will more readily grant an individual exemption.

18–88 The Order sets out a number of obligations which may be imposed on the supplier of an exclusive distribution agreement and which may be imposed on the distributor. The Order is not applicable to agreements entered into for the resale of drinks in premises used for the sale and consumption of beer or for the resale of oil products in gas stations.

18.4 Miscellaneous

18.4.1. Confidentiality

Cyprus Law follows the same legal principles with English law with respect to confidential information. In principle an express confidentiality agreement is not required and confidential information is generally protected under common law. However, express confidentiality provisions in a contract are considered to be desirable for additional and clear protection of the interests of the parties. **18–89**

It should always be borne in mind, however, that once an agreement is terminated all confidentiality terms will be tested on the basis of whether they impose on the parties an unreasonable restraint of trade. In determining what is an unreasonable restraint of trade the Cypriot courts will always examine the facts of each particular case. **18–90**

18.4.2 Restrictive covenants

A restrictive covenant can always be interpreted as a clause or a covenant in restraint of trade whereby a party agrees to restrict his trade or to conduct his profession or business in a particular locality or for a specified period of time. If such clauses are deemed to be unreasonable then they will be held by the Cyprus Courts to be void and thus unenforceable. In this category there are two types; the first is a covenant by an employee not to compete with his employer either during or after the termination of his employment and the second is a covenant by a seller not to carry on a business which will compete with the business of the purchaser. **18–91**

18.4.3 Escrow agreements

Cyprus law recognises the concept of an escrow agent. Escrow agents are commonly used in agreements tangible or intangible assets will be held by the escrow agent to be handed over to a party pending completion of a contract. The general principles of Cyprus contract law apply to escrow agreements and it should always by borne in mind that an escrow agency agreement must be for good and valuable consideration. **18–92**

18.4.4 Powers of attorney

It is usually common for a power of attorney to be issued in favour of an agent enabling him to execute certain documents for and on behalf of his principal. A power of attorney need not be registered but it is advisable if it **18–93** was duly certified and supported by the relevant corporate resolution of the company authorising the issue of such a power of attorney.

18.4.5 Arbitration

18–94 Arbitration awards are enforceable on the basis of the Cypriot Law on International Arbitration[37] and the Convention of the Recognition and Enforcement of Foreign Arbitral Awards of the United Nations of 1958 (the New York Convention). As a contracting party to the New York Convention Cyprus is bound to enforce awards made in foreign states which are contracting parties to that Convention.

18.4.6 Force majeure

18–95 There is no express definition of "*force majeure*" under Cyprus law. The general principles of common law apply with the result that unless the events which constitute "*force majeure*" are listed in the agreement then the doctrine of frustration and all the uncertainties associated with it might apply.

[37] Law 101 of 1979.

Chapter 19

International Agency, Distribution and Licensing Agreements in the Czech Republic*

Contents

19.1 Introduction

The Czech Republic has a statute based legal system and consists of a single jurisdiction. The legislation is strictly in a written form and is contained in acts and other legal regulations mainly adopted by the bicameral legislative body of Parliament (in Czech called "Parlament České republiky"). The main body of commercial legislation is the comprehensive Act No.513/1991 Coll., as amended, (the "Commercial Code") which went into effect in January 1992 and to a certain extent, relevant provisions of the Act No.40/1964 Coll. As amended, (the "Civil Code"). This Commercial Code also attempts to bring Czech commercial law into line with most of the European Union commercial legislation. Harmonisation is still a continuing process in the Czech Republic as its aim is to become a full member of the European Union in 2004. The following text reflects the valid legislation only as of November 4, 2002. **19–01**

* Jan Kotík, Lukáš Vondryska and Martin Bourgeault: Associates DEWEY BALLANTINE, v.o.s., Prague.

19.2 Agency agreements

19.2.1 General relationship

19–02 Agency agreements are regulated by the mandatory provisions of the Commercial Code on contract on commercial representation (in Czech "Smlouva o obchodním zastoupení"; ss.652–672a) ("agency agreements").

19–03 In an agency agreement, an agent or "commercial representative" (in Czech "obchodní zástupce"), undertakes activities for the purpose of identifying third parties interested in doing business with the principal or concluding agreements with a third party on behalf and on the account of the principal. The principal undertakes to pay a commission to the agent. The agent may conclude such any agreement on behalf of the principal only on the basis of a valid power of attorney issued by the principal. The agent is only entitled to reimbursement of its costs incurred while carrying out its obligations if the contract so expressly provides. The rights and obligations of agents are mainly governed by the Commercial Code with the exception of some specialised activities, such as, *e.g.* agents dealing with certain legal matters relating to intellectual property. The relevant provisions of the Commercial Code regarding agency agreements do not apply to agents who are not paid for their services and to brokers working, *e.g.* at either the Prague Stock Exchange or the Czech commodity exchanges. The definition of commercial agent set out in the Commercial Code is in compliance with the relevant provisions of the EC Council Directive 653/86. There are two types of commercial representations under the Commercial Code, exclusive and non-exclusive.

19.2.2 Carrying on business in the Czech Republic

19–04 The concept of agency in Czech law is based on the idea of representation. The agency agreement is a contract in which the principal gives to another person, the agent, the power to act for and on behalf of the principal.

19–05–07 A principal, *i.e.* an entity with its registered office or permanent address outside the territory of the Czech Republic, appointing an agent with the authority to solicit orders and transmit enquiries to prospective clients, or with delegated power to conclude contracts agreements on behalf and on the account of the principal, will not be considered to carry on business in the Czech Republic. A principal appointing an agent to sell goods owned by the principal, stored in the territory and held by the agent on behalf of the principal, will equally not be considered to carry on business in the Czech Republic.

A principal would be deemed to carry on business in the Czech Republic if it has an enterprise or a branch located in the territory of the Czech Republic (the "Entity"). Under the Commercial Code, an enterprise is the aggregate of tangible and intangible components relating to a specific business activity. Legal obligations under the Commercial Code relating to carrying on business include the obligation for the principal to legally establish a company or a branch and register it in the Commercial Register.

19.2.3 Tax status

The Czech tax system covers both personal income tax and corporate income tax, depending on the status of the tax payer. For agents having authority to enter into agreements binding the principal, the principal will generally be considered as a non-resident for taxation purposes and therefore he will be subject to taxation in the Czech Republic only on his Czech income. **19–08**

A legal entity that has its registered seat in the Czech Republic and/or is managed or controlled from the Czech Republic is a tax resident in the Czech Republic. If a principal is a tax resident in the Czech Republic, then he will be subject to taxation in the Czech Republic on his global income. **19–09**

In addition foreign principals with a permanent establishment[1] in the Czech Republic may benefit from a double taxation treaty between the Czech Republic and the principal's country of residence. The Czech Republic has entered into double taxation treaties with more than 50 countries (including all EU Member States, most other European states and the USA). **19–10**

19.2.4 Specific product legislation

There are many specific legal regulations relating to the sale, composition, ingredients, packaging, labelling and other such product-related issues in the Czech Republic (*i.e.* Act on protection of consumers, and others) which are in the process of being amended to be in compliance with EU legislation. Most of the regulations are aimed at protecting the rights of the consumer in connection with quality and safety and other requirements, especially important in certain industries, such as the pharmaceutical and food industries. **19–11**

19.2.5 Agent's power to bind

An agent without a valid power of attorney from the principal may not legally or contractually bind the principal to a third party. **19–12**

[1] The Act No.586/1992 Coll., the Income Tax Act, as amended defines "permanent establishment" for the tax purposes as a place where the business activity is generally conducted for more than 6 consecutive months within any 12 month period. (*e.g.* workroom, office, place of outlet, storage, etc.).

19.2.6 Guarantees

19–13 It is possible for the agent to provide a guarantee to the principal, guaranteeing the payment of debts of customers to the principle. Under Czech law there are only two legal requirements to provide such a guarantee: (i) it must be in writing, and (ii) the agent will receive a special commission for such purpose. Please note that such commission is not defined in the Commercial Code. Usually such guarantee is included in the agency agreement. There are no other legal requirements regarding the form or wording of such a guarantee.

19.2.7 Trade marks

19–14 There are various industrial property rights and regulations in the Czech Republic (for example patents, trade marks or registered designs). In particular, trade marks are mainly regulated and protected under the Act No.137/1995 Coll., as amended, the Trade Marks Act. In the Czech Republic, a principal may directly register a trade mark or may ask his agent to register the trade mark in the name of the principal. If the principal registers a trade mark in the Czech Republic, the agent is only authorised to use the rights attached to this trade mark on the basis of a formal licence agreement which should be registered with the Czech Trademark office. The principal, as owner of the trade mark, can exercise his powers to protect the trade mark, including actions for infringement, etc. Such ownership is effective against third parties as of the date of registration in the register kept by the Industrial Property Office. In some cases the principal registers his trade mark in favour of his agent to allow him to use the trade mark in the territory. In case of conflict between the principal and the agent, it is possible for the principal to register the same trade mark under its name by submitting a claim to the relevant Czech court. Finally, it is recommended that the principal specifies in the agency agreement the exact use of such trade mark and in which territory it may be used, within the provisions of the agency agreement.

19.2.8 Termination and compensation

19–15 In the event of termination of the agency agreement due to the breach of such agreement by the agent, the agent has no right to compensation under Czech law. In the event of termination not caused by breach of the agreement by the agent, the agent shall be entitled to compensation under certain conditions as set forth in the Commercial Code. It must be noted that generally the Commercial Code sets forth that the amount of compensation shall not exceed the annual average commission received by the agent.

19.2.9 Corrupt gifts and commissions

The agent is generally obliged to fulfil his duties in accordance with the terms and conditions as set out in the agency agreement. However, the Commercial Code does not expressly regulate issues concerning corrupt gifts or secret commissions. If the agent participates in or is intentionally involved in such activity, he may face a financial penalty or even be imprisoned for a period of eight years under certain circumstances. Bribes or corrupt practices in connection with the management of the principal's assets constitute criminal infractions under ss.160 or 225 of the Czech Criminal Code. **19–16**

19.2.10 Formalities

There are no formal requirements necessary to ensure the validity and binding nature of agency agreements. **19–17**

19.2.11 Exchange control and withholding tax

The Czech agent transferring money to a principle outside of the Czech Republic based on an agency agreement is generally not subject to any exchange control permission. In addition, such money transfer will not be subject to withholding tax in the territory of the Czech Republic except in certain cases relating to dividends, interest and intellectual property royalties. **19–18**

19.2.12 Principals' rights against third parties

The sole fact that the agent holds stock or money for the principal does not imply the acquisition of any part of the principal's property. Therefore, in the event of the insolvency of the agent, the creditors of the agent are not authorised to satisfy their claims against the agent through property belonging to the principal. On the other hand, in the event that the agent has dishonestly disposed of the principal's property to third parties, such disposition would only be valid if the third party acquired the principal's property in a "bona fide" manner *e.g.* the third party was not aware of the agent's inability to dispose of such property. **19–19**

In the event that any part of the property belonging to the principal becomes part of the assets taken from the agent for any insolvency proceedings against the agent, the principal may file a special action (*actio exscidere*; in Czech called "excinda, ní, aloba") to the relevant court to exclude such property from the insolvency proceedings. **19–20**

Regarding the aforementioned "bona fides" acquisition of the property, **19–21** the principal may recover damages caused by the agent dishonestly disposing of its property to third parties, whether the sale was authorised by the principal or not, by filing a court action against the agent. In such a case the principal would firstly have to prove to the court his ownership of the property, and then the dishonest disposition of such property (especially if previously authorised by him). It is highly recommended for the principal to precisely specify the use of his property together with other rights and liabilities of the agent in the agency agreement. Despite the Czech court system being improved to be in harmonisation with the EU legislation, courts proceedings are quite lengthy and are a less effective option for the principal to recover such damages from the agent. The principal may consider the issue of incorporating an arbitration clause in the agency agreement to settle such disputes in a more efficient manner.

19.3 Distribution agreements

19.3.1 General relationship

19–22 Generally, there is no special regulations covering distribution agreements and the relationship between distributor and principal in the Czech Republic. Therefore general provisions of the Commercial Code on the sale of goods apply to such a relationship.

19.3.2 Carrying on business

19–23 A principal would not be regarded as carrying on business or having a permanent establishment in the Czech Republic if he has a distributor in such territory.

19.3.3 Intellectual property

19–24 Czech intellectual property law provides various forms of protection based on the specifications of individual products. The following discussion will only focus on its main features.

19–25 Copyright[2] applies to literary, artistic or scientific work (including software or databases as described below in Chapter 19.5.3) expressed in a form perceivable to another person as the result of an author's individual creative activity. Copyright automatically attaches to the work, without any registration requirements. These protected works include audio and video tracks (*e.g.* songs and movies), software, etc. The Czech copyright regulations are divided into two sections—protection of the moral rights of the author and of the material rights. The duration of the author's moral rights protection

[2] Reg. under Act No.121/2000 Coll., as amended, on copyrights and other related rights.

lasts for the period of the author's life. Protection of the author's material rights is also for the author's life plus 70 years after death. In addition, there is no need for registration there.

Design rights[3] consist mainly of the protection of the whole or part of a product, taking into consideration colour, shape, special features or any other specifications. The new and unique character of such product is a condition to be fulfilled if the product is to be registered with the Industrial Property Office. The design rights protection is valid for five-year periods and is renewable for a maximum duration of 25 years. **19–26**

A trade mark[4] is an identification sign of each product or service for the purposes of differentiating and distinguishing it from other products or services. The Industrial Property Office will register such trade mark after the fulfilment of certain legal requirements. These requirements include, for example, specific representation of the product or service, sufficient differences from other products or registered trade marks. The duration of such protection is valid for 10-year periods and may be renewed for an unlimited number of years. **19–27**

In regard to patents,[5] the Industrial Property Office may only register a patent on an invention which is new, capable of industrial application, and which presents "inventive progress" in the technical solution of some problem. There are some exemptions which include scientific theories or mathematical methods, which can not be registered. The duration of patent protection is 20 years. **19–28**

Licence agreement. Industrial Property rights (*e.g.* patents, trade marks, designs, etc.) are transferable by virtue of a formal written licence agreement concluded between a licensor and a licensee pursuant to the Commercial Code. Such an agreement must then be registered with the respective register administrated by the Czech Industrial Property Office. The licensee is authorised to exercise such intangible rights to the extent and in the territory specified in such licence agreement. On the other side, the licensee is obliged to make payments or to provide other material values (payment in kind) in return. The licensee is also bound to exercise such respective rights, if required under relevant law (for example in case of trade marks, etc.). The licensor may continue to exercise the rights which are the object of the licence agreement and may also grant them to other persons. However, the licensee may not allow other persons to exercise these rights. Following the conclusion of a licence agreement, the licensor is bound, without any undue delay, to make available to the licensee all the documentation and information required for the exercise of its rights under the licence agreement. After termination of the licence agreement, the licensee must return all the documentation made available to him and keep relevant information confidential until it becomes known in the public domain. If the licensee is restricted in the exercise of his rights by certain persons, or if he ascertains

[3] Reg. under Act No.207/2000 Coll., as amended, on industry designs protection.
[4] Reg. under Act No.137/1995 Coll., as amended, on trade marks.
[5] Reg. under Act No.527/1990 Coll., as amended, on inventions and rationalisation proposals, and see n.4.

that certain persons are violating these rights, he has the obligation to report it to the licensor without undue delay. The licensor shall, again without undue delay, take all necessary legal steps to protect and allow the licensee to exercise his rights. When the licensor takes such steps, the licensee is bound to co-operate with him to the extent necessary. If the licence agreement is not concluded for a definite period, it may be terminated by notice. Unless the licence agreement sets forth a different period of notice, the given notice takes effect one year from the end of the month in which it is delivered to the other party.

19.3.4 Anti-competition

19–29 Problems regarding the issue of price, personal or other limitations or exclusions in relation to the product, set by the principal, are usually dealt with and specified in the relevant agreement. The principal may specify some obligations for the distributor regarding price or other terms. Generally, the principal is free to agree on different terms and conditions including price, with two or more distributors, unless of course there is an exclusive relationship. The principal and distributor must be cautious in concluding such agreements so as not to infringe or breach any Czech competition law pertaining to competition issues. Distribution agreements that impose restrictions on competition are generally void and prohibited, unless certain exemptions apply, such as horizontal. However, the relevant legislation[6] does not apply to horizontal agreements (agreements concluded at the same level on the relevant market) between competitors that do not affect more than 5 per cent of the specified "relevant" market, nor to vertical agreements between non-competitors, where the limit is set at 10 per cent. The relevant Act also sets forth some other conditions and also the possibility for the competitors to seek some individual exclusions to be granted by the Antimonopoly Office.

19.3.5 Unfair trading practices

19–30 The Czech Republic has generally harmonised its unfair trading practices legislation with EU law. Therefore, there are defined specific and general examples of such behaviour, mainly in the Commercial Code.[7] According to the Commercial Code, "unfair competition" means conduct in economic competition which breaches accepted practices of competition and which may be detrimental to other competitors or customers. The Commercial Code specifies some individual cases of unfair competition practices, such as misleading advertising, misleading marketing of goods or services, bribery

[6] Act No.143/2001 Coll., as amended, on economic competition protection; and other relevant regulations.

[7] Other regulation is to be found in the Act on customer protection, or in the advertising legislation.

and violation of trade secrets. Even if the principal did not prohibit such behaviour, the distributor's business activities would have to comply with such legislation.

19.3.6 Damages for non-performance

Any damage for non-performance shall be set out in the agreement. If not, general terms and conditions set out under the Commercial Code apply. Under these, should a distributor or principal fail or omit to fulfil any of their obligations under the distribution agreement, they shall be liable for the damage caused by such failure or omission. In addition, the principal or the distributor may, under Czech law, impose a contractual penalty clause for non-performance, and therefore limit their liability in the event of non-performance, except those which are statutory and can not be excluded by agreement. The Czech law does not permit one of the contracting parties to waive its right to claim damages prior to the occurrence of such damages. At the same time the law does not explicitly exclude agreements to limit claims for damages (including claims for compensation for loss of profit) to a pre-ascertained amount, such amount being in full and final settlement of all liability for non-performance under a contract. However, such pre-ascertained amount must not be only a symbolic, negligible amount but needs to truly reflect the value of the relevant contractual performance and the anticipated magnitude of the potential damage. Failing to determine such a "realistic" cap might cause a potential challenge to the agreement on the basis of circumventing the law. **19–31**

19.3.7 Specific product regulation

See Chapter 19.2.4 (specific product legislation) in relation to the Agency agreement. This section fully applies to the principal-distributor relationship. **19–32**

19.3.8 Distributor's power to bind

Generally, a distributor may not bind the principal to third parties. This could only be possible if the principal provided the distributor with a power of attorney authorising the distributor to act on his behalf in relation to specific transactions in respect of which the principal would then be obliged to assume some degree of liability. **19–33**

19.3.9 Trade marks

See Chapter 19.2.7 and 19.3.3. **19–34**

19.3.10 Compensation on termination

19–35 As mentioned above in the general section on distribution agreements, there is no specific law covering distribution agreements, and in particular no law covering compensation to distributors. So, the termination and related compensation, and certainly other relevant issues, would be subject to the general law if there is no provision in the agreement regarding the same. We would like to point out some general issues relating to the termination of the agreement under general Czech law, if the parties do not specify otherwise in the agreement. The distributor is not entitled to any specific compensation in the event of a breach of the distribution agreement and any liability for the breaching party will be determined in accordance with the Commercial Code. This sets out the terms and conditions under which it is possible to terminate such an agreement, including related liabilities for the distributor or principal (for example termination of the agreement in case of the occurrence of a material breach as specified in the Commercial Code, etc.).

19.3.11 Formalities, exchange control, withholding tax

19–36 There is no special formal requirements in connection with the execution of a distribution agreement including exchange control permission. The payments from the distributor to the principal will not generally be subject to withholding tax in the territory of the Czech Republic, except under certain circumstances (as described in Chapter 19.2.11).

19.3.12 Exclusion of liability

19–37 Generally, the principal has to supply the distributor with products of the specified quality and quantity. If there is no specific provision on liability in the agreement, the provisions of the Commercial Code will prevail. Under Czech law the distributor is obliged to inspect the quality and quantity of goods supplied. If there is no failure or non-performance, the distributor is obliged to pay for the goods. It further implies that once such inspection has been made and the distributor accepts the goods, the principal has satisfied his contractual obligations and the distributor may not raise a complaint of non-conformity in relation to the quality, quantity or specified other criteria at a later date (except for latent defects, discrepancies or faults that may be claimed at a later date). Notwithstanding the following, the distributor in co-operation with the principal is generally liable for the products being in compliance with Czech law and regulations regarding packaging, health, sanitation and any other issues as stated under the relevant laws and regulations. However the exclusion or limit of the principal's liability is not possible with respect to actual damage caused by the fault of the principal.

19.3.13 Selective distribution system

In general, a selective distribution system is possible in the Czech Republic. However, it needs to comply with the Czech Anti-monopoly legislation. Selective distribution systems deal with a situation whereby the principal restricts the sale of goods to a specific group of distributors, who satisfy certain criteria, such as ensuring satisfaction of technical selling conditions or further service (especially in the case of luxury goods, etc.). The most relevant thing regarding Anti-monopoly laws in such situations is whether the principal imposes upon the distributors' qualitative or quantitative (quota) requirements. In general, the qualitative are not contrary to the law, while quota restrictions may result in a breach of Anti-monopoly law. Selective distribution systems based on quantitative criteria, acceptable under the relevant law must in particular ensure that such criteria are reasonable and justified for the specified goods. There are, in practice, two types of selective distribution systems based either on quantitative criteria: (i) the number of distributors is limited in connection with the extent of the distribution area or distance between distributors; or (ii) principal demands certain quantity limits on the distributed goods or services (such as a minimum limit of goods to be distributed within a certain period of time, etc.). Both above-mentioned quantitative criteria are contrary to the law, unless they are permitted under an exemption granted by the Anti-monopoly office. **19–38**

19.4 Manufacturing agreements

19.4.1 General relationship

There are no specific regulations covering the control of the transfer of technology to a licensee in the territory in the Czech Republic. There would be some similar issues as discussed in previous sections of this text. We refer especially to the taxation and intellectual property rights as discussed in Chapter 19.2 and 19.3. **19–39**

19.5 Miscellaneous

19.5.1 Confidentiality

One of the objectives which were harmonised in the past was the protection of confidential information and the protection of trade or business secrets under Czech law. General law, therefore, excluding the necessity to set forth any such provisions in an agreement protects both rights. **19–40**

Firstly, information that is considered to be of a confidential nature is information which is disclosed to a party during some form of representa- **19–41** tion or negotiation with the intention that it not be disclosed to third parties but to secure it within the framework of the said relationship (with some exceptions for cases of disclosure requested by the court or some other governmental office). Such confidential information is usually protected even if the contract is not concluded. A party that discloses or uses confidential information in breach of the terms and conditions of the agreement is liable for any damage caused to the other party by the breach. A party that is concerned that its business secrets might be used or disclosed may seek a court injunction prohibiting such use or disclosure.

19–42 There are no defined validity periods for such rights and it would therefore depend on each individual situation. It is possible to agree to a greater obligation of confidentiality than the general law requires. Except for the agreed terms and conditions of such use of the confidential information, there are no other formal requirements. In addition, the definition "confidential information" used in the agreement may also include information which is generally known or is in the public domain. If the recipient has received such information, it would be possible to restrict him to using it under certain circumstance. However, in the event of a dispute; the protection is much more likely to be enforced if an agreement restricting the use of such "confidential information" exists.

19.5.2 Restrictive covenants

19–43 It is generally possible to restrict an agent, distributor, licensee or any other party (other than an employee) with whom a contract to provide services is made, from competing with the other party to the agreement during or after the life of the agreement. There are no specific legal provisions regarding the extent of such restrictions under Czech law, whether during the life of the agreement or even after its termination. However, such restrictions have to be made in compliance with the relevant law on economic competition. See Chapters 19.3.4 and 9.3.13.

19.5.3 Software

19–44 Conditions for the protection of software generally appear to be in compliance with EU legislation. Software is considered to be a work protected under the Act on copyrights and related rights. This Act also sets forth the terms and conditions for such protection, including the period of the protection of the author's rights, possible transfer of such rights and other related conditions. Software is protected in the territory of the Czech Republic and rules are set out on how to use, copy or disclose it. One of the general exemptions valid specifically and only for software is that the Act limits the extent of the author's rights for the software. For example it is possible to make a copy of software for personal use and purposes if required. The Act also regulates the so called "employees' works" (in Czech "zaměstnanecká díla"). These works, which have been done in connection with or on the basis of an employment contract may be used distributed or otherwise retained by the employer (except for the non-transferrable personal rights of the author).

19.5.4 Escrow agreements

There are no specific Czech regulations covering the concept of an independent party who holds documents, goods or other items with a mandate to hand them to another party upon the occurrence of a certain event. However the concept of contractual freedom as set forth in the Commercial Code in s.269 enables the conclusion of such agreements generally governed by the Commercial Code, which are not specified as a particular type of contract. Such contract must however satisfy the general requirement as set out in the Commercial Code, which is *inter alia* to adequately identify the object of their obligations. If the parties fail to do so, such a contract is not considered to have been concluded. **19–45**

19.5.5 Power of attorney

There are not many requirements regarding the form, execution or content of a power of attorney under Czech law except for some statutory provisions under the Commercial Code and the Civil Code (Act No.40/1964 Coll., as amended). **19–46**

A power of attorney must be in writing, except for some minor exceptions. A power of attorney would have to clearly specify the powers to be granted and for what purpose it was submitted, and must be signed by the person granting the power of attorney. The power of attorney is generally deemed to be terminated when: (i) the purpose for which it was submitted has been finalised, if the power of attorney does not provide otherwise, (ii) it is revoked by the principal, (iii) it is terminated by the agent, (iv) if an agent dies, or (v) in the event that the principal dies, unless the power of attorney provides otherwise. The power of attorney also terminates under certain circumstances, such as expiration of the specified time given in the power of attorney, or mutually agreed termination. If the principal revokes the power of attorney, the agent must be provided with such notice. If the agent is not aware of the termination he may act as if the power of attorney were to be effective and bind the principal against third parties, provided that the third party was not aware of the termination. There is also a special regulation revoking the power of attorney in the event of insolvency proceedings under the Czech Bankruptcy Act. The Czech law does not acknowledge the concept of an irrevocable power of attorney. **19–47**

19.5.6 Whole agreement clauses

19–48 There are basically no obstacles to using such clauses in agreements under Czech law. Conversely, this is a commonly used provision and forms a part of many agreements. Such clauses mostly state that the agreement constitutes the entire understanding of the parties to the agreement on the subject matter thereof and supersede all prior negotiations and understandings between them, whether written or oral. It is also common to incorporate in such clauses a sentence ensuring that any future amendments are to be made in writing and signed by all parties to the agreement.

19.5.7 Arbitration

19–49 As discussed above, court proceedings in the Czech Republic sometimes constitute very lengthy and uncertain processes for a party to satisfy its claims. Arbitration proceedings have some advantages, *e.g.* there is only one level of court (first instance), rapidity, informality and wide scope of enforceability of arbitration award. Most of the relevant legislation on Arbitration proceedings and the enforceability of awards is contained in Act No.216/1994 Coll., as amended. There is one Arbitration Court attached to the Economic Chamber of the Czech Republic and Agricultural Chamber of the Czech Republic which is the only permanent arbitration court with the general sphere of activity relevant for the determination of property disputes in conformity with the above-mentioned Act. Arbitration proceedings before such arbitration courts are usually conducted in accordance with its rules, published in the official Trade Gazette (in Czech "Obchodní věstník") unless the parties to the dispute have agreed otherwise. Such rules as well as other information are at the disposal of disputing parties and other persons involved or interested in the proceedings free of charge, at the seat of the Court or the regional court branches, or on its web address www.arbcourt.cz. Arbitration awards are enforceable abroad (pursuant to the New York Treaty on recognition and enforcement of foreign arbitration awards date June 10, 1958) as well as in the Czech Republic.

19–50 Courts may intervene in arbitration proceedings under certain circumstances as set forth in the Act. Firstly, the court may remove an arbitrator if he was biased and did not resign. Consequently, the court may also derogate from the arbitration award on the proposal or appeal of any party to the arbitration proceedings if: (i) an award was issued in a case where it is not allowed, (ii) the arbitration (provision of the) clause was void, (iii) there was an irresponsible or unauthorised arbitrator, (iv) the arbitrators have not decided by majority, (v) any party was not provided with sufficient opportunity to plead, during the proceedings, (vi) the award is for something that was not requested by the successful party, or (vii) there are reasons for special remedy under the Act on Civil Procedure.

In deciding on the case, the arbitrators shall proceed according to the law applicable to the dispute; they may however decide the dispute according to principles of equity if they have been explicitly entrusted therewith by the parties. 19–51

19.5.8 Force majeure

Force majeure" is one of the possible reasons under which a liability for damage or non-performance is excluded or limited. A provision specifying individual situations to be deemed as "*force majeure*" is always preferable because the Czech law does not have a specific definition of a "*force majeure*" event. However, the Commercial Code has a provision setting forth circumstances in which liability can be excluded and which appears to be somewhat similar to the concept of "*force majeure*". This states that such circumstances will constitute an event excluding liability for non-performance if they arise independently of the obligor's will, preventing the obligor from performing his obligation and could not have been averted nor their consequences overcome, provided that occurrence of such an event was unpredictable at the time when the obligor undertook to perform such obligation. It is a common, and highly recommended, practice to include a detailed definition of "*force majeure*" clauses in a contract to avoid any further disagreement about the nature of an event, which should constitute a "*force majeure*" event. 19–52

If there is not such a provision and any dispute occurs in connection with non-performance in relation to the agreement, the court will consider each individual situation and decides if such non-performance was caused by "*force majeure*" or otherwise.

Chapter 20

Hungary*

Contents

Introduction

Hungary is not a common law country, and in relation to its legal system two main factors have to be emphasised. First, Hungary's legal system belongs to the so-called continental law family and has a strong Roman law and German-Austrian law basis. Furthermore, these basic elements were influenced by the Austrian legal system during the era of the Austro–Hungarian Empire. **20–01**

Second, Hungary is an EU accession state. Therefore, intensive legal harmonisation of "*acquis communitaire*" has been and is taking place taking into consideration of the planned accession date of May 1, 2004. **20–02**

20.1 Agency agreements

20.1.1 General relationship between agent and principal

The Hungarian legal regulation on agency agreements basically follows Directive 653/86 of the European Union when it states that "a commercial agent is a person who—upon a permanent commission, for remuneration—intermediates contracts concerning purchase or other agreements on goods, including the case when the agent is entitled to conclude the contract either in the name and on behalf of the principal or in his own name in favour of the principal". **20–03**

It is also important to emphasise that a commercial agent can be con- **20–04**

* This chapter was written by Dr Tamás Gödölle Attorney at Law, Partner (Budapest), with the assistance of Dr Alexandra Molnár (Budapest) both of Bogsch & Partners of Budapest.

sidered as independent only if he is not employed by the principal. In addition, a person whose representation right is based on any legal provisions (such as the director of a company, a partner in a partnership, a liquidator or receiver) cannot be considered as a commercial agent.

20–05 The subject of the agency agreement might cover not only goods, but also services, valuable rights and securities.

20.1.2 Carrying on business in Hungary (when the principal appoints an agent to seek out orders and transmit enquiries or with delegated power to conclude contracts on behalf of the principal)

20–06 In this case the principal is regarded as carrying business in Hungary and considered to have a permanent establishment (branch office) in Hungary if *inter alia*:

- it has permanent business premises, equipment, or machinery in Hungary that are partly or wholly used for business purposes; or
- it commissions a third party to conclude contracts in Hungary in the principal's name and on its behalf or the third party stores the goods of the principal and delivers them regularly to buyers in the name and on behalf of the principal, except, if *inter alia*:
    - the business premises are only used for storing or presentation of goods,
    - the storing of the principal's goods is only for storing and presentation purposes or the stored goods are raw materials to be assembled or manufactured by a third party,
    - the agent commissioned by the principal is an independent representative.

20–07 The agent is regarded to be independent if:

- he is economically and legally independent from the principal,
- the representation of the principal belongs to his regular business and activities,
- the principal has no right to directly instruct or inspect the agent, and
- the business risk is undertaken by the agent.

20.1.3 Carrying on business in Hungary (when the principal appoints an agent to sell goods owned by the principal, stored in the territory)

20–08 For details please see Chapter 20.1.2.

20.1.4 Formalities of carrying on business in Hungary

In order to establish an individual undertaking or firm a so-called undertaking permit is required. In order to carry out any activities in the form of a corporation, the establishment of the respective corporation (business association, Hungarian branch office, business representation office) is required. **20–09**

20.1.5 Taxation

The principal is to pay corporate tax upon: **20–10**

- the revenue generated by the permanent establishment (branch office); and
- the other revenues generated from sources in Hungary (interest, royalties, dividend, etc.)

Permanent establishment: The balance sheet profit/loss of the permanent establishment has to be determined. Then this profit/loss is required to be adjusted in order to determine a profit/loss that is proportionate to the revenues of the permanent establishment compared with the worldwide revenues of the principal. This adjusted profit/loss, but at least a minimum of 12 per cent of the total expenses of the permanent establishment will be the tax base, and after this base, 18 per cent of corporate tax is to be paid. **20–11**

Other revenues from Hungary: All revenues from interest or royalties are taxed at 18 per cent, with the exception of (i) interest paid on Hungarian government bonds, (ii) interest paid by Hungarian banks, (iii) delay interest and (iv) the interest and royalties paid by a Hungarian party under agreements signed after January 1, 2001, if the interest (royalty) rate does not exceed the regular interest rate (royalty) applied on the Hungarian market by independent parties. **20–12**

20.1.6 Specific product legislation

For the information of consumers the Hungarian Consumers Protection Act provides a general definition of labelling, packaging and safety requirements. However, specific provisions are also applicable for different kinds of products (such as pharmaceutical, tobacco and dairy products). **20–13**

Basically only safe products can be marketed, *i.e.* those that do not endanger the life, health or physical integrity of the consumers during the proper or reasonably expected usage of the product. **20–14**

Besides the above, the packaging or the labelling of the goods shall contain all relevant data (*i.e.* precise indication of the name of the product, name and address of the producer, distributor, place of manufacture) **20–15** necessary to keep the consumer properly informed in a legible and unambiguous way in the Hungarian language.

20–16 Furthermore, the label also has to contain—depending on the character and function of the product—the size, net weight of the product, its ingredients (quality and quantity composition thereof), its expiry date and basic technical features.

20–17 Certain products can only be marketed with instructions and handling guides (*i.e.* garment products) and in the case of imported products a Hungarian handling guide shall also be attached to the product that is identical with the one enclosed in the foreign language.

20–18 The product shall be packaged in such a way as to protect the quality of the product and facilitate the transport of the product without any detrimental effect on the product. Furthermore it should meet the requirements of health and safety at work.

20.1.7 Power to bind

20–19 Should the independent commercial agent be entitled to conclude the contract in the name and on behalf of the principal according to the agency agreement concluded between them, any declarations by third parties addressed to the agent concerning the conclusion of the agreement shall be effective with regard to the principal upon their declaration to the agent.

20–20 Where, the agent is not entitled to conclude the contract, any declarations by third parties are considered to be not effective with regard to the principal if they are only made to the agent.

20.1.8 Del credere guarantee

20–21 A guarantee by agent of the fulfilment of the obligations of third parties may be stipulated in the agency agreement and it is also possible to stipulate a special commission for this responsibility (so-called "del credere" commission).

20–22 Both the stipulation of the above guarantee and the amount of the commission depend on the parties' mutual agreement. Should the parties make such provisions, the del credere commission shall be due upon the conclusion of the contract.

20.1.9 Trade marks and other industrial property rights—authorised use

20–23 It is of great importance to conclude a licence agreement so as to be entitled to utilise any industrial property rights (trade marks, patents, designs) held by the principal, in which it is expressly determined by the parties which rights the agent is entitled to utilise, and to what extent, since the permission of the principal—as rightholder—is essential for the lawful use of these rights.

The Hungarian Patent Office has jurisdiction over the recording/registration of a licence agreement. However, there is no obligation to file such a request for registration with the Office. Nevertheless it is advisable to register the agreement since it might facilitate the assertion of rights (through authorisation of the registered user/licensee). **20–24**

20.1.10 Compensation on termination of the agreement

Where the principal terminates the agency agreement because of the agent's fundamental breach of the agreement with immediate effect, the agent is not entitled to compensation. The law does not define a "fundamental breach of contract" therefore it is advisable to specify in the agency agreement the events which would give the principal the right to terminate the agreement with immediate effect. **20–25**

The agent is not entitled to compensation if the agreement has been terminated by him, unless he has terminated it because of age, physical disability or illness or because of conduct on the part of the principal which is of such a nature that the agent cannot be expected to continue the agency activity. **20–26**

In the case of ordinary termination by the principal without cause the agent can demand compensation only by meeting the following two requirements jointly: 1) the agent has obtained new clients and the principal gains significant benefit on the basis of business relations with clients obtained by the agent after the termination of the agreement; and 2) the payment of the compensation is fair and reasonable (considering the lapse of the agent's right for commission). **20–27**

The amount of the compensation may not exceed the average amount of one year's commission calculated over the previous five years. Where the contract has lasted for less than five years it may not exceed the yearly average commission received by the agent during the term of the agreement. **20–28**

20.1.11 Corrupt gifts and secret commissions

The agent cannot accept any remuneration from third parties without the approval of the principal. In addition general criminal laws (*e.g.* corruption) are applicable concerning illegal advantages given or promised by the agent to third parties for signing a contract; or concerning given or promised presents/benefits to the agent with the same aim. **20–29**

20.1.12 Formalities of the agreement

Any agency agreement can be concluded validly only in writing. However registration or government approval is not necessary for an agency agreement. **20–30**

20–31 As a minimum requirement the written agreement shall contain the exact details of the contracting parties, the subject of the agreement and the signature of the parties.

20–32 A written document is accepted in any legal dispute as proof of evidence if it is witnessed by two persons (also giving the address of the witnesses) or where the signatures of the parties are legalised by a notary public or the document is countersigned by an attorney at law.

20–33 These rules are also applicable for private deeds concluded abroad, however it is necessary to get them legalised by the relevant Hungarian embassy or consulate.

20.1.13 Exchange control permissions

20–34 There are no exchange control permissions required for the remitting of the money collected by the agent on behalf of the principal.

20.1.14 Withholding taxes

20–35 Corporate taxes are to be paid by the principal either as a withholding tax or by direct payment to the Tax Authority. Withholding tax is applied if the principal receives revenue from a company business or business entrepreneur in Hungary.

20–36 If the revenue is interest or royalty, then the Hungarian party shall determine and pay the corporate taxes to the Tax Authority (withholding tax) at the latest by the twelfth day of the month after the month of payment.

20–37 If the revenue is other income, then the principal is to determine and pay the corporate taxes to the Tax Authority (no withholding tax) within 30 days counted from the receipt of the revenue.

20–38 If there is a double taxation treaty between Hungary and the country of the principal, then the rules of the treaty are to be applied.

20–39 However if the taxes are paid by the Hungarian party, then any surplus tax paid may be reclaimed by the principal after payment (the tax rate under the treaty may only be directly applied upon the permission of the Tax Authority), whereas if the taxes are paid by the principal, it may directly apply the tax rate of the treaty, no additional reclaiming is necessary.

20.1.15 Ownership of the principal's property (questions 20.1.15 to 20.1.17)

20–40 In the event of the insolvency of the agent he has no power to dispose of assets not belonging to him and the creditors of the agent cannot assert any rights over such property. In the course of the execution procedure on such property the principal has the right to declare that the assets put in execution do not belong to the agent.

In the event that the agent dishonestly disposes of the property remitted to him to any third parties: 1) in the course of commercial trade, then the affected third party acquires ownership rights on the property (breach of rule "nemo plus iuris"); 2) not in the course of commercial trade, only third parties acting in good faith acquire ownership rights upon payment of the purchase price. **20–41**

The principal can enforce his ownership rights through litigation and can request the court to declare its ownership rights over the property. **20–42**

20.2 Distribution agreements

20.2.1 General definition

There is no specific legal regulation concerning this type of agreement in Hungary, the general contractual rules are applicable. A distributor is a person who purchases the principal's goods for resale and sells them to different third parties. **20–43**

The so-called vertical agreements, in which the participating undertakings operate at different levels of distribution do not fall under the prohibition of restriction of competition if the total annual turnover of the parties and their related undertakings does not exceed HUF 4 billion. **20–44**

Thus, in general, the grant of exclusivity or non-exclusivity is exempt from the prohibition on restriction of competition. However the exemption does not apply to vertical agreements which impose exclusivity on the supplier, if the buyer's market share on the relevant market exceeds 30 per cent. **20–45**

20.2.2 Carrying in business in Hungary

See the answer under Chapter 20.1.2. **20–46**

20.2.3 Formalities

General rules concerning the formalities of a written agreement are applicable. **20–47**

20.2.4 Taxation

See the answer under Chapter 20.1.4. **20–48**

20.2.5 Intellectual property protection

20–49 All individual and original works—creations of literature, science or art—may fall under copyright protection. The copyright protection of works originates from their creation, no registration is necessary to obtain such protection. Copyright protection shall be provided during the lifetime of the author and for 70 years following the author's death (Act LXXVI of 1999).

20–50 Design protection can be obtained for any new designs that are of individual and original character by way of an application for registration. Design protection lasts for five years from the date of application and upon request it can be renewed for further five-year periods for four times at the most (Act No.XLVIII of 2001).

20–51 It cannot be excluded that a design might qualify as a copyright work as well, and parallel protection may be applied (*i.e.* under certain circumstances an element of a trade mark mark could also qualify as copyright work).

20–52 Furthermore, there are specific legal regulations concerning trade marks (Act No.XI of 1997), patents (Act No.XXXIII of 1995) and topography protection of microchips (Act No.XXIX of 1991).

20.2.6 Appointment of different distributors in Hungary

20–53 The principal is free to conclude any agreements regarding the number of distributors and the terms and conditions of the contracts. However the principal must meet the general competition law requirements. For example the exemption from restriction of competition shall not apply to agreements which directly or indirectly, or under certain circumstances restrict the buyer in fixing or determining the purchase prices.

20.2.7 Restrictive trading practices

20–54 Any agreements that restrict economic competition are prohibited under the Act on prohibition of unfair and restrictive market practices. This prohibition applies in particular to those agreements that fix directly or indirectly purchase or sale prices. It is also prohibited to conclude an agreement which restricts or controls the distribution of goods. Therefore a provision according to which the distributor may sell the products only to certain classes of customers falls foul of this prohibition.

20–55 An agreement shall not be prohibited if it is of minor importance, that is agreements where the total joint market share of the contracting parties does not exceed 10 per cent of the market concerned. However this exception shall not apply to agreements setting prices.

20–56 Agreements concluded between related undertakings (*i.e.* one controls the other) do not fall within the application of the prohibition.

The Office of Economic Competition may be requested to declare that an agreement (or a planned agreement) does not fall under prohibition. **20–57**

20.2.8 Principal's powers to impose different obligations upon the distributor

If such a binding order qualifies as abuse of a dominant position, it is illegal and invalid. **20–58**

20.2.9 Unfair trading practices

In general it is prohibited to conduct economic activities in an unfair manner, in particular in a manner violating or jeopardising the lawful interests of competitors and consumers. Furthermore, slavish copying and the violation and jeopardising of the reputation and the credit-worthiness of competitors are also prohibited. Interference with the integrity of tendering and any misuse of business secrets (for details please see Chapter 20.4.1) is also prohibited. **20–59**

It is prohibited to mislead consumers (*i.e.* in respect of the price, essential characters of the products, or information influencing the consumers' choice), and further to apply methods restricting consumers' freedom of choice (*i.e.* to make the objective comparison of goods more difficult). **20–60**

20.2.10 Limitation of liability

Liability for the breach of contract cannot be excluded validly. Limitation of liability is only possible if it fulfils the requirements below: **20–61**

- Liability for breach of a contract caused deliberately, or by culpable negligence or by a criminal act, or liability for damages as a result of death, physical injury or damage to health cannot be excluded. Limitation or exclusion of other types of liability is possible, but only if the disadvantages caused by such limitation are balanced by any other *advantages* given to the adversely affected party.
- There is no noteworthy published judicial decision on this matter. However it should be mentioned that any discount of the purchase price itself cannot be considered as an *advantage* that could serve as a basis for limitation of liability.

20.2.11 Specific product legislation

Please see the answer under Chapter 20.1.6. **20–62**

20.2.12 Power to bind

20–63 The distributor is entitled to undertake obligations to third parties in the name and on behalf of the principal, if there is a respective authorisation in the distribution agreement concluded between the principal and the distributor.

20.2.13 Trade marks and other industrial property rights—authorised use

20–64 Please see the answer under Chapter 20.1.9.

20.2.14 Termination because of breach of contract

20–65 It is possible to terminate the contract because of breach of contract or any other reason, only in accordance with the terms of the contract and on the basis of the general rules of contractual law. For example in case of a delay the other party may terminate the contract in case his contractual interest has ceased provided that he can prove this fact.

20.2.15 Termination without notice

20–66 The above are applicable to termination of the contract with immediate effect.

20.2.16 Formalities, exchange control permissions, withholding taxes

20–67 See the respective answers written above concerning agency agreements, especially under Chapter 20.1.14.

20.2.17 Limitation of liability between distributor and principal for defective products

20–68 According to the Hungarian Act on product liability—that fully corresponds to the rules of the European Union—the manufacturer of a product is liable for damages caused by the defective product. In the case of an imported product this rule shall also apply to the importer of the product. However, this does not influence the importer's enforceable claims towards the manufacturer.

20–69 Where the manufacturer or the importer of the product is unknown, all known distributors of the product shall be considered as manufacturers of the product until the distributor identifies the manufacturer or the dis-

tributor, from whom he purchased and the product that he sold to the consumer.
Any limitation or exclusion of liability towards the consumers shall be deemed as null and void. Product liability devolves upon the manufacturer for ten years from the date of first distribution of the product.

20.2.18 Selective distribution system

Where the aim of the agreement is to restrict competition, (*i.e.* to impose a conditions upon the distributor as to from whom he may purchase or to restrict the number of the purchases that the members of the distribution system can make), this will be in conflict with the effective rules on competition and will be considered invalid. **20–70**

20.3 Manufacturing agreements

20.3.1 Control of technology transfer and its details

Government Regulation No.86 of 1999 lists the exemptions from prohibition of restrictive market practices concerning technology transfer agreements in Hungary, according to which the prohibition shall not apply to patent licensing agreements, to knowhow licensing agreements and to mixed patent and knowhow licensing agreements (hereinafter referred to as "mixed licensing agreements"), and furthermore to sub-licensing agreements. **20–71**

The fact that the agreement includes an obligation on the licensor (a) not to exploit the licensed technology in the territory himself or (b) not to license other undertakings to exploit the licensed technology does not exclude the applicability of the exemption. **20–72**

The exemption is only granted if the agreement concluded between one patentee (or in the case of a joint patent, several patentees) and one licensee. **20–73**

The exemption shall not apply where—for example—the contracting parties had been competing manufacturers before concluding the agreement concerning the licensed product or patented process and upon the agreement either of them is restricted as to the customers he may serve or the joint market share of parties exceeds 30 per cent of the relevant type of products. Furthermore, the exemption shall not apply to those agreements that include determination of prices of the licensed product. **20–74**

For the purposes of the regulation "knowhow" means all valuable economic, technical, organising knowledge and information. "Patent" means patent applications, utility models, utility model applications, microelectronic topographies and applications. **20–75**

20.3.2 Industrial property legislation

20–76 Please see the sections concerning distribution agreements.

20.3.3 Setting of resale prices

20–77 Setting of minimum prices, or fixing prices is prohibited as restrictive of competition and is considered null and void.

20.3.4 Unfair trading practices, Limitation of liability, specific product legislation, trade marks and other industrial property rights, formalities, exchange control permissions, power to bind, termination of the agreement

20–78 For these questions see the sections concerning agency and distribution agreements.

20.4 Miscellaneous questions

20.4.1 Confidentiality

20–79 In general according to the Hungarian Civil Code any person who discloses or misuses any business secrets commits a breach of the law.

20–80 Beside the above the Act on the prohibition of unfair and restrictive market practices also states that "it is prohibited to gain access to or to use business secrets in an unfair manner, furthermore, to disclose such secrets or to publish them".

20–81 It is considered to be gaining access to business secrets in an unfair manner where the access has been gained without the approval of the entitled person through a party who has a confidential or business relationship with the entitled person.

20–82 Business secrets are all facts, information, solutions or data in connection with which the entitled person has a lawful and justified interest in keeping secret, provided that the entitled person has taken all necessary steps to keep them secret. The term "confidential relationship" covers employment relationships, other work-related relationships and membership relationships. The term "business relationship" means a relationship in which information is disclosed in business negotiations or in offers made prior to the conclusion of a transaction. It is immaterial if the negotiations or offers are not followed by the conclusion of the contract.

20–83 Taking into consideration the fact that the parties are free to stipulate the terms and conditions of the agreement (within the framework of the mandatory legal provisions) they may also stipulate sanctions and the extent of liability for breach of confidentiality.

20.4.2 Restrictive covenants

As a general rule it is not possible to restrict an agent/distributor, etc. with whom a contract to provide services is made from competing with the other party to the agreement during the existence of the agreement. However the Act on agency agreements contains certain exceptions to these rules: restrictive covenants can be concluded validly in writing, for a maximum period of two years after termination of the agreement, only in consideration of remuneration and providing it only applies to identical activity. To the other two types of agreements—in the absence of any specific rules—the general regulations are applicable. **20–84**

20.4.3 Software

Under the Hungarian copyright Act computer programs and their related documentation (hereinafter referred to as "software") shall fall under copyright protection whether fixed by source code or object code or any other form, including user application programs and operation systems. Copyright protection shall also be provided to the adaptation of the original program language to a different program language. **20–85**

Economic rights (right of exploitation) on software can be transferred. On the basis of a licensing agreement authorisation to use software can also be obtained. **20–86**

Unless otherwise concluded, the author's exclusive rights shall not cover reproduction, alteration, adaptation, translation or any other modification of the software—including the correction of mistakes—as well as reproduction of the achievements of these activities in so far as these activities are carried out by the person authorised to acquire the software in compliance with the intended purpose of the software. No provisions in the licensing agreement shall prohibit the user from making back-up copies of the software provided that it is necessary for that use. Any person entitled to use a copy of the software shall be entitled—without the author's further authorisation—to observe and study the operation of the software during the process of its loading, display, running, transmission or storage in order to get to know the ideas or principles that are the basis for any software element. **20–87**

No authorisation from the author is required for the reproduction or translation of the code that is indispensable for the acquisition of the interface information necessary for the combined operation of independently created software, provided that (a) these acts of use are performed by the entitled user; (b) the information necessary for the combined operation has not been easy to access; and (c) these acts of use are limited to those parts of the software that are necessary for combined operation. **20–88**

Licensing agreements shall be concluded in written form. However, when software copies are commercially distributed it is not obligatory to conclude a written agreement. **20–89**

20.4.4 Escrow agreements

20–90 Hungarian law does recognise the concept of escrow agreements. Basically the contract has to stipulate who the parties are, what the subject of the escrow is, for how long the contract lasts and upon what events the party holding in escrow is obliged to hand over the items held in escrow to the other party.

20–91 Such an agreement cannot be irrevocable. As to its formalities see those concerning the agency agreement.

20.4.5 Powers of attorney

20–92 In commercial matters the power of attorney has to contain the name (firm name), address (seat) of the principal, the name and seat of the attorney or attorneys at law, the signatures of the parties, the date and place of signature, the matter concerned. In taxation matters a power of attorney with special formalities required by the taxation authorities is necessary. A power of attorney can be revoked at any time.

20.4.6 Whole agreement clauses

20–93 The current Hungarian Civil Code does not contain any provisions concerning whole agreement clauses. However, it does not prohibit them either. Therefore the application of such clauses depends upon the contractual will of the contracting parties.

20–94 The draft proposals for the new Hungarian Civil Code do contain a statement that the new Civil Code should provide that, where a clause in the parties' written agreement declares that the written agreement shall be deemed to be the whole agreement between the parties, the consequence is that all previous negotiations not included in the agreement shall not form a part of the agreement.

20.4.7 Arbitration

20–95 According to the Hungarian Civil Code "the parties may stipulate arbitration instead of judicial litigation procedure for their disputes if at least one of the parties is a person who carries out business activity professionally, the dispute has arisen in connection with this activity and the parties are free to dispose of the subject of the procedure".

20–96 The Act on business associations makes is possible for the parties, in accordance with the provisions of Act LXXI of 1994 on arbitration, to stipulate a permanent or contingent arbitration procedure in the articles of association (deed of foundation) with regard to corporate legal disputes.

Legal disputes arising in relation to the articles of association or to the operation of the business association between the business association and its members (shareholders), including former members excluded from or otherwise withdrawing from the business association, or among the members (shareholders) *inter se* shall qualify as corporate legal disputes. **20–97**

The competence of the ordinary courts to intervene in the arbitration, which the parties cannot exclude by expressed terms in their agreement, is as follows: **20–98**

- The court in front of which a suit has been initiated in a matter that is the subject of the arbitration agreement may reject the claim without any summons or may terminate the lawsuit upon the request of any of the parties.
- Should any of the parties fail to appoint his own arbitrator or should two arbitrators not agree on the appointment of the third arbitrator, the missing arbitrator will be appointed by the court upon the request of any of the parties.
- Where an arbitration court is to consist of only one arbitrator and the parties cannot agree on the appointment of the arbitrator, the ordinary courts will appoint the arbitrator, upon the request of any of the parties. Furthermore ordinary courts decide on petitions concerning the expulsion of arbitrators.
- Ordinary courts provide legal aid concerning the performance of the procedures for the collection and delivery of evidence through the issue of appropriate court orders.
- Ordinary courts have competence to nullify the arbitration awards in specified cases.

The arbitration award has the same effect as a legally binding judicial decision. The general judicial enforcement provisions are applicable to the enforcement of the arbitration award. As a general rule, arbitration awards made abroad can be enforced if they meet the requirements which must be considered as "acknowledged" on the basis of Hungarian law. The acknowledgement does not require a separate procedure. Should the award be acknowledged, the general judicial enforcement provisions are applicable. **20–99**

20.4.8 Force majeure (vis maior)

The Hungarian Civil Code determines "vis maior" only in a very general manner according to which "vis maior" means all unavoidable external events that occurred outside of the control of the parties, for which a party is not liable. Examples would be an earthquake, or the cancellation of a lease because the leased premises have been burned down through arson not **20–100** attributable to the lessor or the lessee. Furthermore, the parties are entitled to stipulate those events which shall be deemed as "vis maior".

20–101 Should the performance of the contract become impossible for any reason, for which none of the parties is responsible, the contract will terminate. However, the party becoming aware of the impossibility of the performance is obliged to advise the other party of this without delay. For any damages occurring due to lack of such notification the party obliged to give such advice is liable.

20–102 In general, the Hungarian Civil Code provides for the possibility of the court modifying a contract only and exclusively if any circumstances have occurred in the long-term legal relationship of the parties after the conclusion of the contract and, as a result, the contract has become harmful to the significant interests of any of the parties. In addition, in the case of certain contract types (basically those which consist of an agreement to perform a further contractual obligation at a later date, for instance an agreement to sell shares in a company, with the purchase to be completed at some time after the purchase agreement is signed) it is sometimes possible for the party to be absolved from the relevant obligation under the contract. A party may be relieved from performance of the relevant obligation, should he prove that due to a circumstance that occurred after the conclusion of the preliminary contract he is not able to execute the contract by performing the obligation, or, in the case of this circumstance, the terms of the contract themselves would require the other party not to insist on performance of the relevant obligation.

Chapter 21

Poland

Contents

21.1. Agency agreements

21.1.1 Definition

Polish legislation on agency agreements is regulated under the Civil Code, which states that under an agency contract an agent conducts on-going intermediation in accordance with its corporate purpose and for consideration, in the conclusion of contracts with clients for the benefit of the principal or on behalf of a principal. This means that an agent is able to act for the benefit of the principal, and either in its own name or on the principal's behalf. There are no significant differences between Polish and EC law (EC Directive 653/86) in relation to agent/principal relationships. **21–01**

21.1.2 Conducting business in Poland

Generally, the determination of whether a principal who appoints an agent in the territory of Poland will be regarded as carrying on business in Poland always depends on particular circumstances. It can be assumed that if an agent is vested with authorisation to conclude contracts on behalf of a principal then the principal will be deemed as conducting business in Poland. On the other hand, it may be assumed that if an agent has the sole authority to solicit orders and transmit enquiries, then the principal may not be deemed as conducting business in Poland. In such cases there will be no obligation for the principal to register its activity in Poland. In both cases, final determination will depend on the scope of the principal's activity, agency relationship, organisation and continuity of the activity. **21–02**

The establishment of commercial activity in Poland by foreign companies **21–03** is based on the principle of reciprocity, unless international agreements provide otherwise. A number of corporate vehicles are available to foreign investors who wish to establish a presence in Poland as principals. The final choice depends on whether the principle of reciprocity is recognised in the principal's country of origin with regard to Polish companies.

21–04 The available vehicles include: registered partnerships, professional partnerships, limited partnerships, limited joint-stock partnerships, limited liability companies, joint stock companies, branches (where the commercial activity is restricted to within the scope of business of the "parent" entity), representative offices (where activities are restricted to the promotion of the "parent" entity) and sole trader.

21–05 A foreign principal carrying on business in Poland through a local agent being one of the above vehicles must:

- register its activity in the National Court Register (or in the case of representative offices the Register kept by the Economy Minister);
- register its activity for tax and statistical purposes;
- make and receive payments through bank account under particular circumstances;
- obtain a license if he intends to carry on certain kinds of business activities (such as prospecting for or surveying mineral deposits, extracting minerals; manufacturing and trading in explosives, arms and ammunition; manufacturing and trading in fuel and energy; protection of persons and property; air transport; construction and running of toll motorways; management of railways and provision of railway transport; broadcasting radio and TV programmes).

21.1.3 Taxation

21–06 Taxation depends on whether the agent will act on behalf of the principal or whether it will act as an independent agent. Despite recent efforts at simplification, Polish tax legislation is complex. In the course of structuring any agency relationship, expert tax advice should be sought from a Polish lawyer.

21.1.3.1 Agent acting on behalf of a principal

21–07 If the agent has, and regularly exercises the power to enter into contracts binding the principal then the principal will generally be considered, for taxation purposes, to be a non-resident taxpayer carrying on business at or through a permanent establishment (PE) in Poland.

21–08 A non-resident taxpayer carrying on business through a PE is required to pay tax on assessable income derived from Polish sources. Assessable income includes gross income according to ordinary concepts and net capital gains made on the disposal of assets. Expenses necessarily incurred in gaining assessable income or in carrying on business are generally deductible.

21.1.3.2 Independent agent

If business will be carried out by an independent agent who conducts his own activity then the principal will not be deemed to be carrying on business in Poland through a PE. Under this structure generally no Polish taxes are payable on Polish source income and that income will be taxed exclusively by the country in which the principal is resident. Please note however, that the independence of the agent may be questioned by tax authorities when the agent performs activities which belong to the sphere of the principal rather than to that of its own business operations. The mentioned risk may arise when the agent not only sells the goods or merchandise of the enterprise but also acts as a permanent agent having the authority to conclude contracts on behalf of the principal. **21–08A**

21.1.3.3 VAT issue

VAT consequences also depend on the factual form of the agent's activity. **21–09** Under the first contemplated option (see Chapter 21.1.3.1) the agent conducts his activity on the account of and in the name of the principal. In fact the agent role is to connect the final consumer with principal. The sale agreement is concluded between the principal and the final consumer. The final consumer is the importer of the goods and is obliged to pay customs duty (if applicable) and import VAT. The agent will be entitled to receive the agreed commission from the principal. Commission will be subject to VAT and will be invoiced by the agent to the principal. The principal has two possibilities for deducting Polish VAT paid on agent commission. The first possibility is the application of a direct refund from the Polish tax authorities (Polish regulations provide for the possibility of obtaining a VAT refund for non-Polish taxpayers, however, to obtain this refund certain conditions must be satisfied) and the second possibility is that the principal becomes a Polish registered VAT taxpayer. According to the second option, (see Chapter 21.1.3.2) unless the agent also has a right to conclude contracts on behalf of the principal, the agent will be deemed an importer of goods and will be obliged to pay customs duty (if applicable) and import VAT. The principal also has two means of recovering Polish VAT paid on agent commission; these are presented above.

If the agent's authority is confined to preparatory activities related to the **21–10** conclusion of a contract, the principal will generally not be carrying on its business through a PE.

21.1.4 Specific product legislation

21–11 There are a wide range of specific Polish regulations relating to goods, their marketing or sale in Poland. The most significant relate to advertising, labelling, packaging, and their safety and waste disposal. There are specific registration and supervision procedures for technical devices or other goods that may threaten human life or health, under which regulatory approval is required. Specific regulations relate to pharmaceuticals and food.

21.1.5 Power to bind

21–12 An agent is authorised to conclude contracts on behalf of a principal and to receive declarations for him where he holds authorisation to do so. If the agent does not have express authority from the principal to bind him or if he exceeds its scope, the validity of any contract concluded without such authorisation by the agent depends on its confirmation by the principal (*negotium claudicans*). It is important to emphasise the existence of legal presumption in respect of confirmation made by the principal, unless the principal notifies the third party that he does not confirm the contract concluded by the agent, which should be done immediately after the principal receives information on its conclusion. The principal's explicit refusal to confirm the contract will result in the contract being invalid.

21.1.6 Guarantee

21–13 A guarantee made by an agent to a principal that the agent will be liable for the performance of the obligation by the client should be made in writing with no specific formalities concerning the wording or execution being required in this respect. The guarantee will specify the agreed scope of the agent's liability and remuneration (*del credere commission*). It is of significance that the agent's liability may relate only to a specified contract or to contracts with a specified client that were concluded through the intermediation of the agent or by the agent on the principal's behalf.

21.1.7 Intellectual property rights

21–14 Generally any use of the principal's industrial property rights by the agent, including trade marks, patents, industrial designs and utility models, requires a licence in writing between the parties. It is desirable for the parties to outline precisely what the agent is permitted to do in relation to a trade mark, patent, industrial design or utility model and the principal's control over the agent's use. The agent would have a right to grant a further licence only with the principal's prior consent. The licence could be recorded in the respective Patent Office's Register. This would allow the agent to actively protect the principal's industrial property. If the principal grants an exclusive licence to the agent and this is registered in the appropriate register, then the agent may, to the same extent as the principal, enforce his claims in the event of an infringement, unless the licence stipulates otherwise.

As far as copyright licences are considered, only exclusive copyright licences require written form. Principals who are copyright owners shall specify fields of exploitation, scope, territory and the period of such use. The agent would then not have the right to grant further licences unless it is stipulated otherwise. If the parties conclude an exclusive licence, then the agent may, to the same extent as the principal, enforce his claims in the event of infringements, unless the licence stipulates otherwise. There is no need to register copyright licence agreements. **21–15**

21.1.8 Termination and compensation

An agency contract that was concluded for a fixed period and continues to be performed by both parties after that period has expired is deemed to be concluded for an indefinite period. **21–16**

An agency contract may be terminated by either party with immediate effect, regardless of its duration (for fixed or indefinite periods) because of the failure of one party to carry out all or part of his obligations, or where exceptional circumstances arise. **21–17**

Only where agency contracts are concluded for indefinite periods may either party terminate such by notice without stipulating cause. The notice period is one month for the first year of the contract, two months for the second year commenced, and three months for the third year commenced and subsequent years. The parties may not agree to shorter notice periods but they may agree on longer periods. In such cases the notice period to be observed by the principal must not be shorter than that to be observed by the agent. **21–18**

In the event of the termination of the contract by service of due notice or by expiry of time the agent is entitled to compensation to the extent that he has brought the principal new customers or has significantly increased the volume of business with existing customers and the principal continues to derive substantial benefits from the business with such customers. The agent may exercise this claim if payment of the indemnity is equitable having regard to all the circumstances and, in particular, the commission lost by the agent on the business transacted with such customers. The amount of the compensation may not exceed a figure equivalent to the agent's remuneration for one year calculated from the agent's average annual remuneration over the preceding five years. If the contract goes back less than five years the compensation shall be calculated on the average during the subject period. The payment of such indemnity will not prevent the agent from seeking damages under general rules. **21–19**

If due termination of the contract by the principal takes place, whereby he **21–20** terminates the contract because of a default attributable to the agent which justifies immediate termination of the agency contract, then the agent would not entitled to any compensation.

21.1.9 Secret commissions and gifts

21–21 There are no specific legislations dealing with taking of secret commissions and corrupt gifts by an agent. These acts are generally prohibited under the Criminal Code of 1997 and the Law on Counteracting Unfair Competition of 1993 only with respect of public officers, who are prohibited from taking corrupt gifts. However the parties can regulate this issue in the agency agreement and impose on the agent a contractual liability in this regard.

21.1.10 Formalities

21–22 No formalities are necessary for an agency contract to be regarded as legally valid and enforceable under Polish law. Specific regulations apply to the authorisation (power of attorney) in the event that such authorisation to act on behalf of the principal is given to the agent. These requirements are described in Chapter 21.4.5.

21.1.11 Exchange control and withholding tax

21.1.11.1 Exchange control

21–23 The Foreign Exchange Law, which came into force on October 1, 2002, focuses on liberalisation of foreign exchange transactions. In order to adjust foreign exchange regulations to EU requirements, the Act does not provide for any limitations in the flow of capital and payments between Poland and EU Member States.

21–24 In addition, because of the solution applied in the Foreign Exchange Law, foreign exchange transactions with countries that belong to the following organisations will be completely free: (i) European Economic Area (EEA), (namely the EU Member States and Iceland, Norway and Liechtenstein); and (ii) Organisation of Economic Co-operation and Development (OECD).

21–25 With respect to the foreign exchange law, these countries have been treated on equal terms with EU Member States and, thus, limitations in foreign exchange transactions with third party states will not apply to those countries.

21–26 The Foreign Exchange Law provides for few restrictions in respect of the liberalisation of foreign exchange dealings. One of the restrictions stemming from the act may generally apply to agents which collect cash funds for the benefit of the principal. Therefore, not only do they relate to transactions carried out with third party states, but also dealings with EU Member States (and other states within the EEA and OECD). In accordance with this restriction it will be necessary to obtain a foreign exchange permit in order to assess and accept, from non-residents, receivables in currencies other than convertible or Polish currency. The latter restriction, which refers to the terms and conditions on which foreign exchange dealings may be performed abroad, does not limit its freedom to perform them or effect related payments.

Bearing in mind the limitations which may result from other Acts, the limitation provided for in the Foreign Exchange Law may be abolished by way of an individual foreign exchange permit. Individual foreign exchange permits will be required in cases concerning a waiver of limitations and obligations stipulated in the Act, if these are not covered by general permits, or if the conditions for waiver set out in the relevant general permit are inapplicable to the particular circumstances of the case. **21–27**

21.1.11.2 Withholding tax

Polish withholding tax may be imposed on payments of interest, dividends and royalties from residents to non-residents. Generally, where the funds collected by the agent only relate to goods sold by the principal there will be no withholding tax. However, if payments made by the principal's clients may even be partly treated as interest on credit sales, then such interest may be subject to withholding tax on the interest under relevant double tax treaties. **21–28**

21.1.12 Ownership issues

In the event of an agent's insolvency, property belonging to a principal and only held by the agent on its behalf will not form a part of the agent's estate and therefore will not be available to its creditors. **21–29**

If the agent has dishonestly transferred and disposed of the principal's property to a third party, the principal's ability to assert its ownership rights will depend on whether or not the third party took the property in bad faith. Where the third party purchaser is a bona fide purchaser, he may acquire title to the property. This does not prevent the principal from seeking damages under the contractual relationship from the agent. **21–30**

If an agent has been authorised to act in the name of the principal, the proceeds should automatically be included in the principal's assets. In the event the agent conceals these proceeds, the principal is entitled to seek a return of the proceeds and damages under general contractual terms. Therefore, the parties should specify the agent's obligations in detail, in particular, in respect of the proceeds that are to be transferred to the principal. There are no formalities to be observed before a principal may **21–31** attempt to protect his rights in relation to property wrongfully dealt by its agent. The agent will be obliged to repay the proceeds and damage unless his non-performance is attributable to circumstances for which he is not liable.

21.2 Distribution agreements

21.2.1 Definition

21–32 Under Polish law a definition of a distribution agreement exists under the Law on the Protection of Competition and Consumers of 2000. A distributionship means an agreement entered into by business entities operating at different levels of trade with the object of purchasing goods for re-sale. Specifically, distribution agreements are regulated in the Ordinance of the Council of Ministers which implements *inter alia* provisions of Commission Regulation (EC) 2790/99, and regulates exclusive supply obligations, exclusive purchase obligations, selective distributorships and franchise distributorships.

21.2.2 Conducting business in Poland

21–33 Determination whether a principal who appoints a local distributor in Poland will be regarded as carrying on business in Poland depends on the particular circumstances. In the absence of any additional relationship between the parties of a distribution agreement, in a large majority of cases where a distributor acts on its own account and on its own behalf a foreign principal will not be deemed to be carrying on business in Poland. If for any reasons the principal will commence business in Poland, then he will need to attend to certain registration requirements as defined in Chapter 21.1.2 above.

21.2.3 Exchange control and withholding tax

21–34 If under the distribution agreement a distributor is recognised as a dependent agent of the principal (non-resident taxpayer) then the principal will have a Permanent Establishment and will be required to pay tax on assessable income derived from Polish sources. Assessable income includes gross income according to ordinary concepts and net capital gains made on the disposal of assets. Expenses necessarily incurred in gaining assessable income or in carrying on business are generally deductible. However, the above mentioned tax risk is remote as the distributor will purchase the principal's goods and re-sell them to customers.

21–35 Generally, there will be no requirement to obtain a foreign exchange permit (see general remarks presented above where agent agreements are discussed).

There will be no withholding tax under the presented factual circumstances described here in relation to payments made by the distributor. 21–36

21.2.4 Design rights, copyright and other intellectual property rights

Polish legislation on industrial design protection complies with EC Directive 71/98. Under the Industrial Property Law of 2000 an industrial design may be registered by the Polish Patent Office if it is new and holds individual character. Design under this Law means the external appearance of a entirety or part of a product resulting from its features. A registered design may be protected for one or more periods up to a total term of 25 years. 21–37

It is important to note that a design protected by a registered design right is also eligible for protection as a trade mark and under copyright law. This additional and parallel protection depends on fulfilment of its protection prerequisites as specified under appropriate laws. It is also clearly stated that copyright protection is not available for those products that are manufactured by means of an industrial design after the lapse of the design right deriving from its registration. 21–38

According to the Law on Copyright and Neighbouring Rights of 1994 a copyright subsists in any manifestation of creative works of an individual nature, established in any form, irrespective of its value, designation or manner of expression. In particular, the copyright may subsist in: literary, journalistic, scientific and cartographic works; artistic works; photographic works; industrial designs; musical or textual and musical works; audiovisual works; collections or data bases. Computer programs are protected as literary works. No registration is required for copyright to subsist. In general copyrights expire 70 years after the author's death. 21–39

According to the Industrial Property Law any sign represented or capable of being represented graphically may be deemed a trade mark, provided that it is capable of distinguishing the goods. The term of the trade mark protection right is 10 years from the date of filing its application with the Patent Office. This term can be extended for subsequent 10-year periods. 21–40

General rules on the use of intellectual property rights are discussed in Chapter 21.1.7 above. In respect of distribution agreements the same rules apply. Generally, the parties should specify licensed rights in detail and a right to grant a possible sublicense if such need arises, to avoid any future disputes in this respect. In practical terms, in a standard distribution agreement the parties would organise the entire sale system as a franchise distribution agreement. 21–41

21.2.5 Law on the protection of competition and consumers

Determination of whether a distribution agreement or a particular distribution clause infringes the rules on fair protection of competition and consumers is made upon two major pieces of local legislation: the Law on 21–42 the Protection of Competition and Consumers of 2000 and the Law on Counteracting Unfair Competition of 1993. This chapter provides only a general overview and focuses on the main issues that may arise. Any legal assessment in this regard will depend on the particular circumstances of each case.

21–43 Polish law generally prohibits any agreements that seek to or result in eliminating, stifling or otherwise distorting competition and also cites examples of illegal arrangements. However this general prohibition does not apply to arrangements entered into by business entities operating at different levels of trade, whose combined market share in the preceding calendar year was not higher than 10 per cent. Significantly, some vertical agreements and clauses are in general excluded from this prohibition. The exclusions cover exclusive purchase obligations, exclusive supply obligations, selective distributorships and franchise distributorships. Below we present the major exclusions in this regard. However it is of significance that these exemptions apply only on the condition that the market share held by the principal does not exceed 30 per cent of the relevant market on which it sells the goods or services under contract. In the event of exclusive supply obligations the market share held by the distributor should not exceed 30 per cent of the relevant market on which it purchases the goods or services under contract. Furthermore these exclusions do not apply to vertical distribution agreements in the motor vehicle sector.

21–44 Firstly, in general the principal is not free to charge prices and apply contracts upon different terms with two or more distributors whether within the one territory or in separate, defined territories. Under local legislation application, in similar contracts with third parties, of onerous or disparate contract conditions is prohibited. Additionally, distribution agreements should not manifest factually unjustified differential treatment of certain distributors, under the Law on Counteracting Unfair Competition. In this way parties would obstruct market access for other parties and could be subject to legal actions brought by those parties. This means that only rational economic reasons would allow a principal to charge different prices and apply contracts upon different terms, which should be carefully examined before their inclusion in the distribution agreement.

21–45 Secondly, whether it is acceptable under local law to grant exclusivity in respect of particular territory or the imposition of customer categories to whom a distributor may sell products may become an issue. In practice in several cases in this regard this depends on the impact on competition and possible justification. In general restricting the territory into which, or of the customers to whom the distributor may sell the goods or services under contract is prohibited, with the exception of the following practices:

- restriction of active sales in exclusive territory or to an exclusive customer group reserved to the principal or allocated to another distributor where such restriction does not restrict sales by the customers of the distributor;

- restriction of sales to end users by a distributor operating at the wholesale level of trade;
- restriction of sales to unauthorised distributors by members of a selective distribution system; and
- restriction of the distributor's ability to sell components, supplied for the purposes of incorporation, to customers who would use them to manufacture the same type of goods as those produced by the principal.

Additionally, it is permissible under local law to restrict the territorial activity of a distributor being a franchisee under a franchise distribution agreement upon certain conditions. **21–46**

Thirdly, as far as resale prices are considered, a principal is not permitted to set them freely. In general, any arrangements that reduce competition by fixing, whether directly or indirectly, prices and other conditions of the purchase or sale of goods are prohibited. In particular the principal cannot restrict the distributor's ability to determine its sale prices, however, without prejudice to the possibility of the principal imposing a maximum price or recommending a sale price. This means that the parties cannot agree on minimum prices or fixed prices that would be used by the distributor, however they can specify maximum and recommended sale prices. **21–47**

Fourthly, under local law a principal is generally free to impose an obligation upon a distributor to purchase and keep a full stock of the products which are the subject of the distribution agreement. This follows from the general exception under the prohibition regarding vertical agreements that include an exclusive purchase obligation under the condition that the market share held by the principal does not exceed 30 per cent, as indicated above. In other cases, where the share exceeds this amount this would have to be carefully scrutinised and depends specific cases. Furthermore, it is permissible to impose an obligation on the distributor to purchase a certain minimum number of products or a certain range of products. **21–48**

21.2.6 Unfair trading practices

Appropriate Polish legislation in relation to unfair trading practices emphasizes consumer protection and the protection of fair trading practices among business entities. The Law on Counteracting Unfair Competition contains the following major unfair trading practices that are illegal and may constitute the subject of legal action: misleading designation of the business entity, false or fraudulent designation of the geographical origin of goods or services, misleading designation of goods or services, breaches of business confidentiality, encouraging others to terminate or not to perform a contract, counterfeiting products, obstructing market access, bribery of public officers, dishonest or prohibited advertising. In addition to the enumerated unfair trading practices this local law sets out a general clause, **21–49** whereby an unfair practice is any activity which violates the law or good practice, if it threatens or impairs the interests of another business entity or consumer. This allows to bring an action against other, non-defined unfair trading practices.

21.2.7 Liquidated damages and contracting out liability

21–50 Polish law permits the inclusion of a liquidated damages clause in a contract but only with regard to non-pecuniary obligations. Parties may therefore stipulate that the redress of damage resulting from a failure or delay in performance of a non-pecuniary obligation will take place by payment of a specified sum. In respect of pecuniary obligations, either party may demand statutory interest or—if stipulated—contractual interest for delays. In practice it may be difficult to pre-estimate damages that might arise during the life cycle of a distributionship.

21–51 It is acceptable under local law to contract out of liability for failures to perform obligations. However parties to such agreements cannot exclude liability for damage that another might intentionally cause. Such stipulations would be deemed invalid.

21.2.8 Specific product legislation

21–52 There are a wide range of specific Polish regulations relating to goods and their marketing in Poland that will apply both to agency and distribution agreements (as described in Chapter 21.1.4). The most significant relate to advertising, labelling, packaging, safety and waste disposal. Consequently, obliging the distributor to comply with all applicable regulations is recommended.

21.2.9 Power to bind

21–53 A distributor may bind a principal to third parties only if the distributor has the authority to act on behalf of the principal. Under the most common distributorships, a distributor will not have the authorization of the principal and will not be empowered to bind him. Should it transpire that the distributor acts as an attorney, where he has no authorisation or exceeds its scope, then the validity of any contract concluded in the name of the principal will depend on the principal's approval of the contract. The absence of such approval will cause the invalidity of the contract.

21.2.10 Termination and compensation

21–54 Rights of a distributor to compensation on termination of the distribution agreement are determined under general provisions of civil law. It is recommended that the parties specify in detail the rules on termination, right to compensation and events of breach. In general, under Polish law the applied rules depend on whether it is a delay or material breach. Compensation due depends on the damage, contribution of the other party, responsibility for the default and other individual circumstances that the court will take into account.

21.2.11 Formalities

No formalities are necessary for a distribution contract to be regarded as legally valid and enforceable under Polish law. On account of potential disputes it is recommended to conclude a distribution agreement in a written form. **21–55**

21.2.12 Exclusion of liability

Principles on liability for defective goods are covered by the Civil Code. It is possible to modify the rules, even to exclude liability under the principle for defective goods only if both parties are professional entities (not customers). However such modification will be invalid if the principal has concealed the defects. A new and separate Act on the specific Terms of Sale of Consumer Goods of 2002 regulates the rules on liability for defective goods with respect to sale to consumers. **21–56**

21.2.13 Selective distribution systems

In general, vertical selective distribution systems are acceptable under local law upon the same condition as described above in Chapter 21.2.5, which relates to the market share as held by the principal (30 per cent). In other cases, whether such systems do not obstruct competition should be carefully examined. Permissible selective distributorships are defined as systems where a principal undertakes to sell goods or services under contract only to selected, according to defined criteria, distributors, and where these distributors are not permitted to sell such goods or services to unauthorised distributors. However, these agreements should be scrutinised as to whether they contain any terms or clauses that may seem not to be permitted. This particularly applies to territory or customer exclusivity. This also applies to criteria other than quality as used by the principal, *e.g.* quantity. In certain industries, such as the operation of pharmacies, there are also limitations as to the number of pharmacies that can be owned by one business entity. **21–57**

Refusal to supply unsuitably qualified distributors is also generally acceptable under local law. A principal may impose certain restrictions on the sales of its products in outlets that do not comply with the general criteria specified in the distribution agreement in this regard. **21–58**

21.3 Manufacturing agreement

21.3.1 Definition

21–59 There is no Polish legislation that deals specifically with transfer of technology to a licensee. The only piece of legislation of any interest in this regard is the Industrial Property Law of 2000 which regulates, *inter alia*, transferring and licensing of patents, trade marks, utility models and industrial designs. It is significant to note that the new Ordinance of the Council of Ministers of 2002 on technology transfer agreements which in general implements the provisions of the Commission Regulation (EC) No.240/96.

21.3.2 General issues

21–60 Many of the important issues discussed above are also relevant in relation to manufacturing agreements. These include unfair competition (see Chapter 21.2.6), liquidated damages and contracting out of liability for damages (see Chapter 21.2.7), specific product legislation (see Chapter 21.2.7), power to bind the principal (see Chapter 21.1.5 and 21.2.9), compensation on termination and expiry (see Chapter 21.2.10), formalities (see Chapter 21.2.11) and intellectual property rights and their licensing (see Chapter 21.1.7 and 21.2.4). For this reason they are not discussed below in detail, but only where such need arises.

21.3.3 Law on the protection of competition and consumers

21–61 Determining whether a manufacturing agreement infringes the rules on fair protection of competition and consumers is made upon the same local legislation as indicated above in Chapter 21.2.5, *i.e.*: the Law on the Protection of Competition and Consumers of 2000 and the Law on Counteracting Unfair Competition of 1993. Many of the issues that are usually governed by manufacturing agreements will fall under the restrictions described above in relation to the distributorships. Therefore the above comments on distributorships could be relevant in this context. It is important to note the significance of the Ordinance of the Council of Ministers of 2002 on technology transfer agreements which generally complies with the requirements of Commission Regulation (EC) No.240/96.

21–62 The Ordinance excludes from under this general prohibition those industrial property and know-how agreements that are concluded between two business entities and which fulfil specific requirements included thereof. However, this exclusion will not apply if an agreement seeks to or results in distorting competition on the relevant market for the licensed products, and in particular, if the market share held by both parties exceeds 30 per cent of the relevant market. This chapter provides only a general overview and focuses on the main issues which may arise. Since the rules in the Ordinance are described in a very detailed manner, any legal assessment in this regard will depend on the particular circumstances of each case.

The extent to which a principal may impose on a manufacturer an obligation excluding the export of manufactured products is a significant issue inherently associated with manufacturing agreements. There is no explicit rule in this regard. However, there is a clear prohibition of clauses restricting the parties from competing with the other in respect of distribution, research, development or similar. On the other hand imposing on a licensee an obligation not to pursue an active policy of putting the licensed product on the market in the territories which are licensed to other licensees is clearly permitted, and in particular not to engage in advertising aimed at those territories. With respect to exclusivity issues they have to be considered in the context of their competitive effect and there are also specific provisions in this regard. **21–63**

Another important issue that will arise in manufacturing agreements is the possibility to impose an obligation to use specific ingredients or components. Generally a manufacturer may be obliged to follow a genuine manufacturing process criteria and quality control requirements. It is also permissible to require the principal's approval for items purchased and the source of supply or even to procure goods or services from the principal or from a business entity designated by the principal, in so far as these quality specifications or ingredients are necessary for the proper manufacture of the products. **21–64**

In general a principal will not have total freedom in differentiating the level of royalties and other terms in respect of different licensees, subject to the restrictions imposed by the two above mentioned pieces of local legislation: the Law on the Protection of Competition and Consumers and the Law on Counteracting Unfair Competition as described above (see Chapter 21.2.5). In particular such clauses should not manifest factually unjustified differential treatment of certain licensees that would run contrary to the local law. **21–65**

On the other hand a principal cannot impose a restriction on a licensee in respect of determining prices, prices of components or discounts for the licensed products. It is also clearly prohibited to restrict a licensee's access to the customers he may serve, in particular by being prohibited from supplying certain classes of user or employing certain forms of distribution. This, however, does not prohibit the parties from imposing on the licensee a restriction to supply only a limited quantity of the licensed product to a particular customer, where the licence was granted so that the customer could have a second source of supply inside the licensed territory. **21–66**

It would be unacceptable to require a licensee to pay extra royalties after the lapse of the exclusive patent or trade mark rights of the principal. However it is permissible to pay over a period going beyond the duration of the licence agreement in order to facilitate its payment. It is also permissible **21–67** to continue paying the royalties until the end of the agreement in the event of the know-how becoming publicly known other than by the action of the principal. The parties cannot exclude the possibility to bring a legal action against the principal for damages in the event of the know-how becoming publicly known by actions of the principal, which are in breach of the agreement.

21.3.4 Industrial property rights

21–68 The subject of most manufacturing agreements includes patents and kno-whow. Patents are protected in Poland upon their registration under the Industrial Property Law of 2000. They are granted for any inventions which are new, involve an inventive step and are applicable for industrial use. The term of protection is 20 years.

21–69 There is no specific legislation in respect of protection and transfer of typical knowhow. However know-how can be protected as confidential information under the Law on Counteracting Unfair Competition that is described below in Chapter 21.4.1.

21–70 It is essential for the parties to a manufacturing agreement to use the principal's trade marks in relation to licensed products. It is permissible to impose on the licensee an obligation to use specific trade marks.

21–71 It is necessary that the parties conclude a written patent or trade mark licence in accordance with the requirements mentioned in Chapter 21.1.7 above. The same applies to other intellectual property rights. For the sake of effective protection of intellectual property rights in Poland it may be practical to register licences with the appropriate Polish Patent Office's register. A holder of an exclusive licence registered with the appropriate register can, to the same extent as the principal, enforce his claims in the event of infringements, unless the licence stipulates otherwise.

21.3.5 Exchange control, withholding tax and other tax issues

21.3.5.1 Exchange control

21–72 Generally, there will be no requirement to obtain a foreign exchange permit (see general remarks presented above where agency agreements are discussed).

21.3.5.2 Withholding tax

21–73 In principle, royalties in respect of licences to use patents and similar property and similar payments are income to the recipient. The general tax rate is 20 per cent of the royalties, however, due to double taxation treaties the 20 per cent tax rate can be lowered.

21.3.5.3 Taxation of intangible services from abroad

If the principal is recognised as a non Polish resident and additionally he originates from a country with which Poland has not concluded a treaty on the avoidance of double taxation, the regulations presented below could apply. From January 1, 2003, the CIT Act catalogue of earnings received in Poland by non-resident taxpayers (*i.e.* those who do not have their registered office or management board in Poland) and which are subject to flat-rate income tax "at source" has been expanded by "other earnings" for "intangible services". The CIT regulations provide a specific sample list of such services (advisory services, market research, management and supervision and guarantees and pledge), and payments for these services are subject to 20 per cent tax rate. **21–74**

21.3.5.4 VAT issues

VAT regulations recognise following operations as being subject to Polish VAT: (i) granting licenses or authorising use of a license and transferring the author's copyright within the meaning of copyright law in respect of computer programs; (ii) selling rights or granting licenses and sub-licenses within the meaning of the industrial property law; (iii) transferring a joint trade mark or a joint guarantee trade mark for use within the meaning of the Industrial Property Law. **21–75**

The VAT law uses the "place of supply" rules in respect of granting licenses and transferring intellectual property rights. These regulations implicitly indicate who is liable for VAT (service provider vs. service recipient) and on what operations. Where: **21–76**

- the service provider is a foreign entity while the service recipient is a Polish entity, the service is deemed to have been supplied in Poland (for the service recipient the transaction will be classified as an import of services taxable at the 22 per cent rate);
- both the service provider and the service recipient are Polish entities (based or resident in the territory of Poland), the service is deemed to have been provided in Poland (for the service provider this will be classified as domestic sales taxable at the 22 per cent rate);
- the service provider is a Polish entity while the service recipient is a foreign entity, the service is generally deemed to have been provided abroad (for the service provider the transaction will be classified as an export of services taxable at a 0 per cent rate);

- the service provider is a Polish entity and the foreign service recipient is a VAT payer in Poland, the service is deemed to have been supplied where the purchaser carries on business related to that service.

21–77 Taxation arises in respect of services for granting licenses and transferring intellectual property rights when the payment is received (or made in the case of imported services) in whole or in part, and not later than the payment deadline.

21–78 VAT law also has provisions governing transactions effected through agents (such as distributors). Pursuant to this provision, distributors will purchase and provide the above services (*i.e.* granting licenses) themselves irrespective of the fact that they are not parties to the license agreements.

21–79 VAT on the importation of services will not be deductible where the payment is made to an entity whose residence, registered office or place of management is located in the territory of a country conducting harmful tax practices. This restriction does not apply to countries other than those listed in the attachment to the VAT act. The list includes 41 countries (including Monaco and Liechtenstein) none which are EU Member States.

21.4 Miscellaneous

21.4.1 Confidentiality

21–80 Generally, confidential information is treated under Polish law as a business secret and is protected under the Law on Combating Unfair Competition and additionally under Art.39 of TRIPS if: (i) it has some commercial value, and (ii) the business entity has undertaken appropriate measures to preserve the information's confidentiality. A business secret is defined as technical, technological trade, organisational or any other information concerning the business and possessing commercial value that is not disclosed to the public. A legal assessment would depend on the nature of the data, *i.e.* whether it is highly detailed information or of a more general nature which may be accessible on the Internet or available from other sources and on the measures in respect of protection as taken by the business entity. Disclosure or use by unauthorised persons of a business secret would be treated as an unfair practice and could result in legal action if it endangers or infringes the business entitiy's interests.

21–81 There is no need to conclude a confidentiality agreement to obtain protection. However express confidentiality provisions are desirable. They should define what the parties treat as confidential information and what uses or disclosures are permitted and which are not permitted. This would allow a determination of the scope of the confidential information and avoid any further disputes in this respect. This could also impose greater obligations on confidentiality than those imposed under general provisions of law. There are no formalities in respect of the form of the confidentiality agreement. However, even if the parties to an agency, distribution or manufacturing agreement do not conclude a confidentiality agreement, such information remains protected.

Clauses that impose an obligation to treat as confidential knowhow or other information after such information becomes publicly known may be deemed as restricting competition. This would depend on its impact on competition and possible justification of such practices. Insofar as confidential information has not entered the public domain, parties are obliged to treat it as confidential, even if the confidentiality agreement has expired. **21–82**

Unauthorised use endangering or infringing upon the interests of the business entity would expose the infringer both to civil and criminal liability. Specifically, this may occur if such use would infringe upon the entity's business situation or if the data holds very high economic value. The court could order in such situation: a redress of damage, return of unjust benefits, a fine in an appropriate amount designated for a specific public purpose, the making of a public statement by the infringer with appropriate content. In criminal law individuals who disclose or use such protected secret information could be liable to a fine, restriction of liberty or deprivation of liberty for up to two years. **21–83**

21.4.2 Restrictive covenants

Restrictive covenants restricting an agent, distributor or a licensee from competing with the principal are permitted and recommended under agency, distributorships or under manufacturing agreements, but they always require careful consideration. Generally parties are free in imposing restrictive measures during the life of the agreement and after its termination or expiration if these measures do not restrict competition. **21–84**

Potentially, restrictions upon the parties after the term of the agreement should be examined in more detail. The validity of the restrictive covenant would depend on whether it is reasonable to use it under the circumstances of the case. Any geographical indications with regard to the parties' exclusivity may be deemed as anti-competitive and therefore prohibited. **21–85**

21.4.3 Software

Computer software is treated as a literary work in which copyright subsists and is protected under the Law on Copyright and Neighbouring Rights of 1994. Polish provisions on the protection of software comply with the EEC Directive 250/91. This means that its protection depends on the same conditions as with literary works as defined in Chapter 21.2.3. This protection does not cover ideas and principles which underline any element of the software. There is no need to register copyright. **21–86**

Both a software licence and a software transfer agreement need to be **21–87** executed in written form otherwise being invalid. A licensee cannot grant a software sub-licence unless otherwise specified in the software agreement.

21–88 Parties to a software licence agreement or any similar agreement may limit the use of the software subject to the provisions on permissible use contained in the law on Copyright and Neighbouring Rights. This means that the copyright holder cannot prevent the person having a right to use it: making a back-up copy; observing, studying and testing the functioning of the software in order to determine the ideas and principles which underlie any element of it if he does so while performing loading, displaying, running, transmitting or storing the program which he is entitled to do. Additionally, it seems that the parties to a software licence cannot restrict decompilation (reverse engineering) of the software which is permitted upon certain conditions.

21.4.4 Escrow agreements

21–89 Although Polish law does not recognise the concept of escrow agreements, in practice they are construed if such need arises. They are used in agreements for development of software, whereby an independent escrow agent holds a complete back-up copy that will be handed to the licensee in the event of insolvency of the software licensor. The parties are free to structure their obligations under the escrow agreement. No special formalities are required to make an escrow agreement enforceable. Having such agreement in writing is recommended.

21.4.5 Powers of attorney

21–90 Specific regulations apply to powers of attorney in the event such authorisation to act in the name of the principal is given to the agent, distributor, manufacturer or other. According to general rules in Poland, if the validity of an act in law that the agent is supposed to perform requires a specific form, then the authorisation for its performance is granted in the same form. However, if the principal is a foreign person, then it shall suffice that the form required by the law of the state where the authorisation is being given has been observed. A power of attorney needs a PLN 15 stamp in order to be legally binding.

21–91 In the event of a transfer of immovable property located in Poland, a notarial deed embodying the authorisation would be required. This deed will be legalised by a Polish consulate or the consul itself may draft the deed.

21–92 The power of attorney may be revoked for any reason at any time unless the principal has renounced its revocation for reasons justified by the nature of the legal relationship on which the power of attorney is granted. The authorisation expires on the death of the principal or the attorney unless specified otherwise. The attorney may appoint other attorneys for the principal only if such authorisation follows from the contents of his power of attorney, statutory law or from the legal relationship on which the power is based.

21.4.6 Whole agreement clauses

Polish law permits the use of "whole agreement" clauses whereby the parties agree that prior negotiations, representations and statements shall not form a part of the agreement. **21–93**

In general, contractual intentions of the parties are interpreted in the light of the circumstances in which they were made. In the case of agreements the intention of the parties and the purpose of the agreement should be established rather than sole reliance on its literal wording. **21–94**

21.4.7 Arbitration

Polish law recognises arbitration clauses and the parties may appoint arbitration courts in disputes over property rights. Such clause or agreement should be executed in writing and signed by both parties. It is important that such arbitration clause should specify the subject of the dispute or relationship under which such dispute may arise. The parties may also determine the artbitrators, the method of their appointment and the method of proceedings. **21–95**

Since the intention of the legislation on arbitration is to provide alternative dispute resolution, in practice there have to be strong grounds to overturn arbitration court awards. Polish law provides for the grounds to overturn a final arbitration award and generally it does not otherwise empower courts to intervene in arbitration proceedings. Polish Code of Civil Procedure determines the sole grounds for overturning an arbitration court's award, which include, *inter alia*: (i) invalidity or expiration of the arbitration clause; (ii) deprivation of the ability for a party to provide a defence during the arbitration proceedings; (iii) infringement of the stated arbitration rules; (iv) contradiction of the arbitration award with the law; (v) incomprehensibility of the award. Following the above, Polish courts interpret these grounds in a very strict manner, rather narrowing its jurisdiction than widening it. **21–96**

In order to enforce an award the interested party firstly files the award with the civil court in order to receive a decision on its enforceability. A civil court will refuse to grant such decision if this award is contrary to the principles of social coexistence or the rules of law. Secondly, this award should be enforced in the same manner as a civil court judgment and, where leave is granted, this award may enter into force. **21–97**

Poland is a party to the New York Convention on the Recognition and Enforcement of Foreign Arbitral Awards of 1958 and awards granted in the contracting states may be enforced in a similar manner as described above. **21–98**

21.4.8 Force majeure

21–99 Polish law does not provide for a *force majeure* motion but it includes in general civil law rules a similar concept known as *rebus sic stantibus*. According to the Civil Code, if, following an extraordinary change of circumstances, the performance of an agreement would be faced with excessive difficulties or threaten one of the parties with a substantial loss, which the parties did not foresee when concluding the contract, the court may, after considering the interests of the parties, define the mode of performing the obligations and the degree of performance and even decide upon termination of the contract. This applies only to extraordinary circumstances and is an exemption from the general rule: *pacta sunt servanda*. Additionally, the parties may specify the scope of *force majeure* in an appropriate agreement, defining both its scope and consequences.

Chapter 22

Romania*

Contents

22.1 Introduction

Private law in Romania benefits from a long and rich tradition inspired by French law. Both systems of law belong to the same family of the Roman law system. The Romanian Civil Code and Commercial Code have enjoyed a remarkable longevity and still have a vast relevance and impact in trade relations. **22–01**

Nevertheless, recent political developments have generated economic changes aimed at the establishment of an open market economy. The complex process of privatisation of all the state-owned companies required a new commercial legal framework. Thus new laws have been passed in rapid succession, the result being a mass of amendments, supplements and repealings of trade legislation. The most important regulations reflecting these changes are Law 31/1990 on Trade Companies, as amended to date and republished, Government Emergency Ordinance 88/1997 on Companies Privatisation amended and supplemented to date by Law 99/1999 regarding **22–02**

* General provisions by Dominic Morega, LLB (Bucharest), Partner with the assistance of Ioana Popescu, LLB (Bucharest), LLM (Bucharest, Sorbonne).

Agency by Nicolae Tanasoiu, LLB (Bucharest), LLM (London) with the assistance of Bogdan Scotnitchi, LLB (Bucharest).

Distribution by Gelu Titus Maravela, LLB (Bucharest), LLM (Warwick), Associate with the assistance of Dorin Costin Coza, LLB (Iasi).

Licensing by Gelu Titus Maravela, LLB (Bucharest), LLM (Warwick), Associate with the assistance of Ioana Popescu, LLB (Bucharest), LLM (Bucharest, Sorbonne).

Some Measures for the Acceleration of Economic Reform and Law 137/2002 regarding Some Measures for the Acceleration of Privatisation.

22–03 Another political objective with an important impact on the legal framework for trade was the application made by Romania for integration into the European Union. Important steps have been taken in order to harmonise the national legal framework with the legal framework of the European Union, including corporate law, competition law, fiscal law, environmental law, etc.

22–04 Despite the growth of laws in various areas of trade during the last decade, up until now only the agency agreement has received specific and express regulation, but this regulation can be criticised for the excessive imposition of mandatory terms and conditions. Neither the distribution agreement nor the licensing agreement have any specific legal framework, a situation which has often created difficulties in practice where such contracts are in frequent use. Disparate legal provisions focused on agency and distribution or licensing agreements are included in competition regulations, modified recently in order to increase harmonisation with the related legislation at European Union level. The Competition Council adopted and completed important regulations regarding the chains of exclusive and selective distribution, the commercial relations in agency and the transfer of technology. Nonetheless, the complexity of each of the agreements make necessary specific regulations establishing restricted clauses, forbidden acts or facts, exemptions, etc.

22–05 The present status quo of the private legal framework, characterised by permanent fluctuations, lack of harmonisation, and novelty, makes life rather difficult for small, medium-sized or even large companies, and for Romanian or foreign investors, who are confronted with a strong risk of unpredictability in their day to day actions. To these factors, we must also add the lack of specific legal provisions in areas of great interest such as agency, distribution or licensing agreements. Bearing in mind all these shortcomings, in order to secure for oneself the greatest chance of success in business, the best lawyer's advice at this moment would be the following old saying: "*At sunrise, in the savannah, the deer is already running for its fresh grass; at sunrise, in the savannah, the lion is already running after the deer. Whether one is a deer or a lion, the sunrise in the savannah must find one running*".

22.2 General provisions

22.2.1 Restrictive covenants

22–06 In the field of agency, distribution, and licensing contracts, restrictive covenants with regard to the contracting partner or other third parties, in general, have to be in accordance with the mandatory statutory provisions of Law 21/1996 on Competition and, in particular, with the specific regulations and rules made by the Competition Council.

Article 5 of Law 21/1996 forbids agreements and practices between traders aimed at limiting and taking over control of distribution, restraining or hindering access to the free market and free competition for all the other companies, or preliminary agreements entered into in order to prevent buying from or selling to a certain company. **22–07**

The prohibition of such practices can be lifted by the Competition Council which may allow such restrictive covenants by issuing a decision excluding them, based on the interested party's request, from the relevant category of prohibited practices, if some specific conditions are met. Furthermore, it can exempt any agreements or individual practices from other legal prohibitions and limitations if such preliminary requirements are also fulfilled. **22–08**

The exemptions allowed by the Competition Council depend on several objective factors, such as the existence of the restrictive covenants only for the duration of the contract, the nature of the commercial transactions, the products or services which are the object of the restrictions, geographic area, relevant market, etc. **22–09**

22.2.2 Confidentiality

The Romanian legal framework does not regulate the protection of confidential information as such. Thus in the absence of any specific clause in a contract, the general legal provisions should be applied. However, there are several specific regulations about the protection of certain categories of confidential information in the fields of banking, securities, public investment funds, media, telecommunications and personal data processing, which must be respected by certain entities specified by the relevant law. **22–10**

Law 11/1991 on Unfair Competition, as amended and supplemented to date, provides that all information which can be considered as commercial secrets should not be disclosed or even used by any trader or any of his employees, without permission from the legal holder of that secret or against fair commercial use. The act of giving away or of using any commercial secret which can be considered as unfair competition can be punished as a minor offence or, even as criminal offence. **22–11**

The lack of a specific legal framework concerning the legal protection of information, and the need for avoiding the difficulties posed by Law 11/1991 in defining unfair competition practices, forces the contracting parties to settle confidentiality issues amongst themselves by inserting confidentiality clauses into their concluded agreements. **22–12**

Consequently, the contracting parties may establish which information is confidential, to whom it cannot be given away, the period for ensuring confidentiality, even after termination of the contract, or the specific sanctions for breaching of the confidentiality obligation. In complex contracts concerning the transfer of technology, licenses or distribution, it is highly recommended to insert express and detailed clauses regarding confidentiality. **22–13**

The contracting parties can agree upon confidentiality clauses no matter **22–14** how restrictive these may be, so long as these clauses do not encroach upon public order, moral or mandatory provisions.

22.2.3 Software

22–15 The general protection of software is regulated by Law 8/1996 on Copyrights and Allied Rights. This law establishes the moral and proprietary-rights of any author with regard to a literary, artistic or scientific intellectual creation. This law contains special provisions in respect of the exclusive rights belonging to the software's author. These are the right to create and authorise (i) the permanent or temporary reproduction of a program, in whole or in part, through any means and any form; (ii) the translation, adaptation or any other transformation to which the software is subject; and (iii) spreading or disseminating the original software in any possible way.

22–16 Foreign citizens, who are copyright owners, benefit from the protection of conventions or international treaties that Romania has ratified or, in their absence they benefit from equal treatment with Romanian citizens, under the condition of reciprocal treatment based on the bilateral and/or multilateral conventions to which Romania is a signatory party.

22–17 In order to streamline and strengthen the measures against piracy in the software field, the legal framework has recently been enriched by a special enactment, namely the Government Ordinance 124/2000 on the Completion of the Legal Framework regarding Copyrights and Allied Rights with Measures for Fighting Piracy in the Field of Audio, Video and Software Programs, as amended to date by Law 213/2002. This enactment defines some specific terms (*e.g.* software license, unauthorised market, distinguishing mark, etc.) and establishes express obligations for the traders who produce, distribute, commercialise or lease software to register the software program with the Romanian Office for Copyright Protection. In this respect, all documents and information about software will be mentioned in a special register called the Software Register, which is administered by the Romanian Office for Copyright Protection.

22.2.4 Escrow agreements

22–18 Romanian law does not recognise expressly the general concept of escrow, as "independent party who holds documents goods or other items with a mandate to hand them to another party upon the happening of a certain event". The law defines and applies only to the concept of an escrow account, *i.e.* an account generally opened at banks by public institutions, on the grounds of an agreement between two or more parties. These accounts are used for depositing monies which are available to the owner's account within a fixed limit and based on special conditions.

22–19 Although there is no specific legislation in respect of escrow agreements, theoretically, based on the freedom to contract, the parties may enter into an escrow agreement which is an agreement for depositing money at a party's disposal using specific clauses to settle rights and obligations. The only problem when entering into such arrangements is related to the establishment of the escrow agent (other than a bank and for operations other than payments), as this agent must have the legal capacity for performing escrow operations.

Because the escrow activity does not benefit from a legal definition or a legal classification, companies (excepting the banks that are empowered to open escrow accounts) do not have the legal capacity for being appointed as escrow agents by the contracting parties. However, it is possible to conclude an escrow arrangement in which the contracting parties may nominate as escrow agent a private person, and also the specific conditions for enforcing the escrow agreement. **22–20**

If such a contract is about to be signed, it is subject to all the formal conditions required for any other contract. **22–21**

22.2.5 Powers of attorney (POA)

In commercial law, the conditions of POA are regulated by the Commercial Code that supplements, as the case may be, the provisions of the Civil Code. **22–22**

The commercial mandate can be characterised as an onerous contract (*i.e.* it is not presumed as being gratuitous—Art.374 of Commercial Code) by which a person gives power to another to negotiate and conclude for and on his behalf one or several business transactions. **22–23**

POA can be a unilateral act, which contains the rights and duties of the mandatary, or a bilateral contract containing the mutual rights and duties of the contracting parties. This contract must fulfil the same formalities as any other contract. For *ad probationem* purposes it is required to be in written form while for the purposes of enforcement against third parties it is recommended that unilateral POA (especially, the ones given by private persons, who can not stamp their documents) should be authenticated by the public notary. **22–24**

In principle, POA may be revoked by the mandator notifying the mandatary and, in specific cases third parties as well. If a POA does not declare expressly the conditions for revoking/ending the mandate, according to the law, the mandate ends in case of death, interdiction, insolvency or bankruptcy of the principal or of the mandatary. Pursuant to Art.391 of the Commercial Code, the principal or the mandatary who, without a legitimate cause, by his revocation or renunciation interrupts the execution of a mandate, is liable for the damages that he caused based on this unreasonable interruption. **22–25**

22.2.6 Whole agreement clauses

Romanian law recognises the whole agreement clause. Although the Romanian legal framework presumes that the last agreement of the con- **22–26** tracting parties demonstrates the real contractual will of the parties and substitutes for previous understandings, for security and clarity, it is recommended to insert such a clause in all contracts. The presence of such a clause in an agreement may avoid any misinterpretation of various previous and extraneous written protocols and/or disparate clauses that may be considered part of the relevant agreement and can keep at bay any confusion in respect of the real meaning of the contracting parties' will. Article 977 of the Civil Code stipulates that "the agreement has to be interpreted according to the will of the parties and not the strict meaning of the terms used in the agreement".

22.2.7 Arbitration

22–27 The institution of private arbitration has been settled since 1865, when the first form of the Civil Procedure Code was adopted. The law relating to arbitration is now set out in the Fourth Book of the Civil Procedure Code (Arts 340–370), the new form of this code being much influenced by the UNCITRAL statutory provisions.

22–28 The Civil Procedure Code settles different forms of arbitration namely ad-hoc arbitration and institutional arbitration, arbitration in law *stricto juris* and arbitration in equity *ex aequo et bono*, as well as national arbitration or international arbitration. Arbitration occurs with regard to pecuniary claims between persons who have the capacity to exercise their rights, but cannot apply to litigation concerning rights that are not subject to contract such as civil rights, status rights, rights regarding citizenship, etc. In Romania, the most common arbitration is organised by arbitration courts organised within the counties' chamber of commerce or by commercial arbitration courts organised within the Romanian Chamber of Commerce and Industry.

22–29 The contracting parties may enter into arbitration agreements which settle the basic rules of arbitration or they may merely insert arbitration clauses into an underlying agreement signed before the dispute. However, they may enter into an arbitration agreement even after litigation has begun in order to regulate that litigation.

22–30 Arbitration agreements regulate the object of the arbitration, the settling procedure, the name or the way the arbitrators will be appointed, and also the setting up of the arbitration panel, the conditions for revoking the appointment of the arbitrators, time and place for arbitration, the procedure provisions for settling the litigation, the court fee, etc. According to the law, arbitral agreements or clauses must be written, if not they are void.

22–31 The decision rendered by the appointed arbitrators is irrevocable, binding and can be enforced as a writ of execution. The only appeal against this decision is action to cancel the arbitral award, which can be initiated for specific reasons, expressly and restrictively enumerated by the law. The action for cancellation is adjudicated by the Romanian court that would have been competent to solve the litigation in the absence of the arbitration agreement or clause.

The Romanian courts have competence, besides cancelling an arbitral award, to enforce it as a writ of execution or to decide upon the recognition and enforcement of a foreign arbitral award. **22–32**

The conditions for recognising and enforcing a foreign arbitral award are stipulated expressly by Law 105/1992 on the Private International Law. This law assimilates the statutory provisions of New York Convention of 1958 on the Recognition and Enforcement of the Foreign Arbitration Award, ratified by Romania since 1961. It is worth noting that the Romanian courts cannot adjudicate upon the merits of the foreign arbitral award or amend it. **22–33**

After the competent Romanian court recognises the foreign arbitral award, the interested party may obtain its enforcement if the following cumulative conditions are met, namely: (i) the arbitral award is binding and mandatory according to the law of the arbitration court which pronounced it; (ii) the right to ask for compulsory execution is not prescribed according to Romanian law; and (iii) there are no reasons concerning public order which may deny its enforcement. **22–34**

Finally, under Romanian law, the contracting parties may consent to an arbitration whereby the arbitrator would judge *ex aequo et bono*, without the application of any specific statutory provisions or legal principles, national or international, this clause being perfectly valid. However, careful attention should be given to such types of foreign arbitral awards as other real difficulties may occur when recognising and enforcing them. The Romanian court will verify the irrevocable character of the ruling, or the existence of any fraud committed during the procedures under the law of the state where the decision has been made and consider if the public order is respected. **22–35**

22.2.8 Force majeure

There is no legal definition of *force majeure*. However, doctrine and the case law accept that *force majeure* is an extraneous, unpredictable and unavoidable event that objectively and without any party's fault prevents the implementation of a contractual obligation assumed by the contracting parties. **22–36**

In principle, *force majeure*, once established, constitutes a cause for exoneration of the party involved. **22–37**

On the issue of liability, *force majeure* produces two effects: one extinctive and one suspensive. In this respect, when the contractual debtor is stopped from the completion of his duties because of the interference of any *force majeure* event, according to Art.1083 of the Civil Code, his obligation of implementation will no longer exist. **22–38**

However, it is worth pointing out that in the case of agreements with successive execution only those obligations whose execution became impossible in that period of time will end and consequently, after the end of the event of *force majeure*, the debtor must carry on with the obligations stipulated in the agreement, except where he can prove that the *force* **22–39** *majeure* event made the further carrying out of the agreement absolutely impossible. In addition, in the case of an agreement with successive execution, the obligations of the parties are suspended as long as the *force majeure* exists, and no party may ask for the execution of these obligations or sue for damages, except in those cases whereby a party had been formally served notice to perform the agreement and the *force majeure* event occurred after the formal notice.

22–40 *Force majeure* has effect by virtue of law, even if it is not inserted in an agreement. Romanian law does not expressly stipulate the possibility of adjusting the conditions of a contract when the completion of an obligation becomes too onerous for one of the contracting parties because of a substantial change in the circumstances under which the contract was signed (the so-called hardship clause). Article 969 the Civil Code stipulates the rigid legal principle *pacta sunt servanda* meaning that the contracting parties should comply with all the terms and conditions of their agreement. Romanian law also stipulates the principle of fair agreement performance under Art.970 of Civil Code, meaning that the agreement obliges not only compliance with its expressly stated terms and conditions, but also with all that equity, custom and law impose.

22–41 The contracting parties are free to agree relating to clauses concerning *force majeure* and hardship, and they can increase or decrease the liability as they wish. For these reasons, the contracting parties may agree what constitutes an event of *force majeure* and its legal effects, and also the specific conditions of the agreement for implementation or liability, in the case of a *force majeure* event beyond the reasonable control of one of the contracting parties.

22.3 Agency

22.3.1 Definition and general conditions

22–42 The Romanian law regulating the contractual relationship between agent and principal is Law 509/2002 on Permanent Commercial Agents. According to the provisions of Law 509/2002, "permanent commercial agent" means the trader, individual or legal entity empowered to carry on the following activities: (i) to negotiate business for another individual or legal entity, called the principal; or (ii) to negotiate and to conclude business for and on behalf of the principal. The agent carries out the specific service as an onerous activity. In conclusion, the agent has the power to bind a principal within the scope of the agent's ostensible authority.

22.3.2 Carrying on business in the territory

22–43 According to Romanian law, if the principal concludes with the agent an agency agreement, the agent represents the principal's interests and negotiates business in the name of the principal or concludes contracts on behalf of the principal within the limits of the ostensible authority given by the principal to the agent.

If the agent's activity is limited to obtaining orders or seeking commercial offers for the principal, the contract is to be concluded directly between the principal and the potential commercial partner. **22–44**

If the agent has representation powers conferred by the principal in order to negotiate and carry out commercial operations on behalf of the principal, the operations will be effected in the name of the principal, but the agent will be mentioned in the commercial contract to be concluding as representative of the principal. However, from the perspective of the legal transactions concluded, Romanian law considers the principal as carrying on business in the territory. **22–45**

22.3.3 Guarantees

Under the agency agreement, the agent can assume expressly the obligation that the third party will honour the contract with the principal. However, if this is not expressly agreed in the agency agreement, the agent is not obliged to guarantee to the principal that the third party will execute his obligations. **22–46**

Also, the principal can conclude with the agent a security agreement by which the agent undertakes himself to execute the obligation assumed by the third party in case the latter does not do so. There is no special preliminary formality in order to render the security agreement valid. **22–47**

22.3.4 Corrupt gifts and secret commissions

The act of giving and/or taking corrupt gifts and secret commissions by an agent is punished by the Romanian Criminal Code as crimes of accepting undeserved benefits or accepting/offering bribes. Moreover, there are special laws covering other fraudulent activities related to these, *e.g.* Law 78/2000 on Preventing, Finding and Sanctioning Corruption Deeds and Law 161 on Certain Measures for Ensuring Transparency when Carrying Out Dignitary and Public Duties and Preventing and Fighting Corruption, etc. Under the criminal law, a guilty agent who is a natural person will be liable to imprisonment and the corrupt gifts or secret commissions will be confiscated. **22–48**

22.3.5 Ownership issues

If the agent holds stock, money or other property belonging to the principal, and the agent becomes insolvent, the goods that are the property of the principal will not be included in the agent's estate and will not be available for creditors. **22–49**

22–50 If the agent has been dishonest in administering the property of the principal and sold these goods to a third party, the principal will be able to assert ownership rights depending on the third party's representations about his state of knowledge concerning the property at the purchase date. If the third party acted in good faith thinking that the agent was the real owner of the goods, he will remain the owner of the purchased goods and the agent should provide compensation for the principal's damage. If the third party knew at the purchase date that the agent was not the owner of the respective goods, then the nullity of the ownership title of the agent implies the cancellation of the sale-purchase agreement, so that the principal would assert and regain his property.

22–51 If the sale was authorised by the principal, the agent is obliged to send the amount received to the principal; following this operation, the commission due to the agent should be paid to the agent. Therefore, the principal has the right to recover the proceeds from the agent in the case of an authorised sale when the agent does not comply with his obligation, and the amounts due to the principal and used by the agent for his own benefit will bear interest for overdue payment.

22–52 If the sale was not authorised by the principal, he can trace into the agent's patrimony (estate) in order to recover the price obtained by the latter from the sale of the principal's goods.

22–53 There are no specific formalities or legal procedures required before the principal may attempt to preserve his ownership rights in relation to property wrongfully and/or dishonestly dealt by his agent. In order to regain his property, when it is possible in view of the above-mentioned legal conditions, the principal should sue the agent and the third party.

22.4 Distribution

22.4.1 General considerations and related legislation

22–54 Under the Romanian legal framework there is no express definition of the distribution agreement. It seems to be a form of the sale agreement, but it is governed by general rules of law and not by those provisions of the Romanian Civil Code and the Romanian Commercial Code regarding the sale agreement. According to Romanian Government Ordinance 21/1992 on Consumers Protection, a distributor is a company that is part of the distribution chain. That ordinance also stipulates several obligations for the distributor, such as: (i) to assure himself that the products offered for sale are safe and that the prescribed or declared conditions are respected; (ii) not to sell any product on which the distributor considers to be dangerous and to announce to the competent public authorities and also the manufacturer the presence on the market of a dangerous product as soon as the distributor becomes aware of that matter; (iii) to recall from sale those products which the authorities qualified by law ascertained that they did not fulfil the prescribed or declared characteristics, if this is the only way to eliminate those deficiencies; (iv) and to keep all stocks of products held in hygienic and sanitary conditions appropriate for their transport, handling, storage and sale and respecting the technical conditions specified by the producer.

22.4.2 Carrying on business in the territory

As discussed in Chapter 22.3.2 above, in order to be considered as carrying on business in Romania the principal has various options upon which to base his contractual relation with the distributor. **22–55**

22.4.3 Competition terms related to prices and other imposed obligations

According to the Romanian legal framework regarding the protection, maintenance and stimulation of competition, it is considered as being an anti-competitive practice, and therefore forbidden, to apply unequal conditions for equivalent transactions which prevent or hinder competition. Agreements that respect the following conditions (which are cumulative) are exempted: (i) include enough positive effects as compared to the negative ones, in order to compensate for the restraint on competition; (ii) the beneficiaries or the consumers also enjoy an advantage from those agreements; (iii) the competition restraints are indispensable for obtaining those advantages; (iv) those agreements do not allow in any way the principal and the distributor to eliminate competition from a substantial part of the market concerning products like the distributed ones; (v) those agreements significantly contribute or could contribute to at least one of the following conditions: improving the product distribution, promoting technical or economical progress, improving the product's quality, reinforcing the competition positions of small and medium size enterprises on the internal market, increasing the competitiveness of Romanian products abroad, working for long-term lower prices for consumers. **22–56**

Law 21/1996 on Competition states that the product's prices are to be determined in a free manner by competition, based on supply and demand. The principal can recommend a certain or a minimum sale price, but he cannot, directly or indirectly, impose that price upon the distributor. Usually, the law forbids restraint of the territory or the classes of customers to whom the distributor may sell the products. However, the Romanian Competition Council established some exceptions: (i) the principal may restrict its direct distributors to resell the products in a territory or to those classes of customers that are exclusively reserved for himself or other distributors, but all the distributors are allowed to use the Internet or catalogues for passive resale; (ii) the wholesale distributor may be restrained from resale to final consumers; (iii) in a selective distribution system the principal may prohibit the distributor from reselling to non-authorised distributors. **22–57**

Based on the freedom to contract rule, the principal may impose upon the **22–58** distributor an obligation to purchase and keep at all times a full stock of each one of the products that comprise the range of products which are the subject of the distribution agreement, if that does not minimise competition.

22.4.4 Exclusion of liability for defective goods

22–59 According to Romanian law the seller is responsible for selling or supplying defective goods or services to consumers and he cannot escape his liability. Nonetheless, the principal will be free to exclude his pecuniary liability for such sales to the distributor, if the distributor agrees to it. In order for the liability exclusion clause to be effective, it is necessary that the principal act in good faith, meaning that the principal did not know that the relevant goods were defective. The principal can fully exclude his liability for supplying defective goods or services, or just diminish it. For example, the principal can undertake obligations only to supply spare parts or only to make the necessary repairs.

22.4.5 Selective distribution systems

22–60 The Romanian Competition Council regulations define the selective distribution system as the distribution system in which the principal decides to sell, directly or indirectly, the products or services stipulated in the agreement only to the distributors selected based on pre-established criteria, while the distributors agree not to resell those products or services to non-authorised distributors. The principal is allowed to forbid the members of the selective distribution system to sell to non-authorised distributors. The retailers who are members of such a system may not be restrained from reselling the products to end-users, but notwithstanding this requirement the principal may impose restrictions regarding the location from which they carry on their activities. The retailers are free to advertise and resell using the Internet. Selective distribution can be joined with exclusive distribution only if active and passive sales are not restrained.

22–61 Within a selective distribution system it is forbidden to restrict the cross-supplies between different distributors who are members of the system, including those that operate on different levels of the system. So, selective distribution cannot be combined with the distributors' obligation to purchase the products stipulated in the agreement from a single entity, for example an exclusive purchase clause. The principal cannot require the wholesale distributors to refuse to supply to designated retail companies. The principal is also not allowed to directly or indirectly impose on the system's members an obligation not to sell the products of competitors.

22–62 Agreements or contractual clauses that breach the competition regulations are considered null and void. Infringements of these rules are punished either as conduct in contravention of law, or as crimes.

22.5 Licensing

22.5.1 Legal framework

A licensing agreement mediating technology transfer is not the subject of any specific Romanian legislation, in spite of the increasing number of business transactions operating on such a basis. The absence of a specific legal framework makes the general contractual provisions applicable. However, general rules regarding licensing agreements are established by the intellectual property legal framework or competition regulations. It is arguable that the licensing agreement is ultimately a construction of the doctrine and of the practice that completes a contractual arrangement by relying on certain provisions of laws having other objects. **22–63**

22.5.2 Clauses including permitted or forbidden competition restrictions

The possibility of restricting the licensee from exporting products outside the licensed territory is settled by competition rules establishing the validity of such clauses under certain conditions. The degree of restrictions allowed varies between (i) the licensee's obligation of abstention from production or utilisation of the licensed product in the territories of other licensees; (ii) the licensee's obligation of not engaging in active policies of marketing promotion or publicity regarding the licensed product in the territories of other licensees and the obligation of not creating any subsidiary or distribution warehouse in the specified territories; (iii) the licensee's obligation of not selling the licensed product in the territory attributed to other licensees, in response to offers to purchase coming from those territories. Depending on the type of licence agreement (patent licence, knowhow licence or mixed patent and knowhow licence) and on the type of restrictive clause included in the agreement, the period of time during which the restriction is valid varies, but not exceeding the limits of five years or of ten years from the date the licensed product is sold for the first time on the Romanian market by one of the licensees. **22–64**

However, the principal cannot forbid the licensee to reject offers to buy coming from users or re-sellers within the licensee's territory who wish to resell the products in other territories than the one reserved to the licensee in question on the Romanian market. **22–65**

Competition regulations allow contractual clauses containing the licensee's obligation to purchase products or services from the principal or from a supplier nominated by the principal. However, this is allowed as long as the specified products or services are necessary for the appropriate technical exploitation of the licensed technology or in order to attest that the licensed product observes the minimum quality requirements that apply to the principal and to other licensees and in order to enable the principal to make the proper checks. **22–66**

22–67 According to competition regulations, a clause that may restrict the licensee's freedom to establish the prices for the licensed products is regarded in itself as restrictive of competition and therefore excluded from the benefit of exemption. Furthermore, the general rule is to prohibit any agreement that has as its object the direct or indirect concerted fixing of selling prices, of tariffs, rebates, supplements or of any other inequitable commercial condition.

22–68 The competition rules also prohibit agreements that include obligations not to sell to certain economic agents without a reasonable justification. The law excludes from exemption and considers restrictive of competition the clauses of agreements whose parties were already competitors as producers before the award of the licence. The forbidden restriction consists of preventing one of the parties, in the same technical field of utilisation of on the same market of the product, from free selection of its customers especially by imposing a prohibition on supplying certain classes of users.

22.5.3 Royalty terms

22–69 Regardless of the type of the license agreement (exclusive or non-exclusive licence), it is prohibited for the principal to apply in relation to his business partners, dissimilar conditions for equivalent transactions. The prohibition is applicable only if this difference of treatment between the business partners creates for one of them a disadvantage in his competitive position on the market.

22–70 However, the principal may agree to apply a "most-favoured nation" clause for the benefit of the licensee.

22–71 There is no specific prohibition regarding an up-front payment by way of a lump sum, therefore the principal can impose such an obligation. In respect of the control of the amount of such payment the relevant legislation does not include specific provisions. The parties are free to establish by negotiations the amount of the up-front payment taking into consideration the nature and the object of the agreement.

22–72 Competition regulations allow the principal to impose on the licensee the obligation of continuing to pay the royalty until the end of the contract, in the amounts, and for the periods of time established in the agreement, even if the knowhow has come into the public domain in any other way than by the principal's action, without affecting the payment of any supplementary damages, where the knowhow has become public by an action of the licensee that breaches the contractual provisions. The same obligation of continuing to pay the royalties is allowed for a certain period after the licensed patents have expired in order to assist in payment by instalments.

22–73 There are no specific regulations imposing a maximum or minimum level for the royalties and the general rule is that the parties' are at liberty to establish the price of the agreement in accordance with the nature and the object of the agreement. However, the majority of the licensing agreements are concluded with a clause of *minimum guarantee* consisting of a minimum amount that is owed by the licensee regardless the profits he may obtain. Such a clause is included by competition regulations in the category of clauses that, in general, are not restrictive of competition and therefore exempt under the block exemption.

Although the right to a free paid-up licence is not set out in any express legal provision, the basic rule of the parties' liberty to establish according to their own wishes the conditions of the agreement allows such a clause. **22–74**

The parties are at liberty to establish the way the royalty is going to be calculated based upon the sales value obtained by the licensee. There is no legal prescription imposing a specific calculation rule in this respect. **22–75**

22.5.4 Import conditions

The Customs Code and Romanian Import Custom Tariff establish the legal framework for imported goods. The import custom taxes are determined based upon the Romanian Import Custom Tariff that establishes the classified list of goods subject to taxation. The custom tax is expressed in a percentage amount applied to the goods' customs value based upon the declaration made by the importer. Invoices and other documents justifying the payment of the merchandise must accompany the declaration. Some categories of goods, depending on their destination or nature, may benefit from exemption or deduction in relation to customs taxes. There are certain categories of goods that require for their import a special authorisation or license. Unless they are accompanied by such a document they are prohibited from import. The import licence is personal and therefore its transfer with any title is null and void. **22–76**

The competition regulations prohibit a license agreement containing a clause that allows the exercise of intellectual property rights or the adoption of certain measures in order to prevent users or re-sellers from obtaining by way of import, and from selling on the market of the licensed territory, goods that have been legally put into circulation by the principal or with his approval. **22–77**

22.6 Common elements of agency, distribution and licensing agreements

22.6.1 Formalities related to carrying on business in the territory

If the principal is not resident in Romania, in order to sell his products in Romania he has three options: (i) to set up a company in Romania, on the conditions settled by Law 31/1990 on the Trade Companies; (ii) to open a representative office observing the conditions imposed by Decree-Law 122/1990 on the Authorisation and Functioning in Romania of the Representative Offices of the Foreign Companies and Economic Entities; and (iii) **22–78** to sell the products directly to a Romanian distribution agent for resale purposes. In the last mentioned case the principal should not be regarded as carrying on business in Romania, because the distribution agent acts as an independent entity.

22–79 For the first two situations above mentioned, the principal should fulfil the requirements imposed by Romanian law. The principal will have to register the new company or representative with the trade registry office and obtain the appropriate authorisations or approvals from the competent authority depending on the company's object of activity.

22.6.2 Taxation

22–80 According with the provisions of Law 414/2002 on Profit Tax, foreign companies that carry on activities within a permanent headquarters located in Romania are compelled to pay profit tax, but only for the taxable profit due for the permanent headquarters. The expression "permanent headquarters" includes management places, branches, offices, secondary headquarters, factories, works, plants, stores, shops, etc., but does not include (i) the utilisation of installations with a purpose to store or display products or commodities; (ii) the maintenance of stocks of products or commodities in order to exhibit them at a commercial fair and that can be sold when the fair or the exhibition is finished; (iii) a fixed business office intended to collect information; and (iv) the maintenance of a fixed business office with the purpose to carry on activities having a preparatory or auxiliary nature, but only if the entire activity of that office has a preparatory or auxiliary nature.

22.6.3 Specific product legislation

22–81 A large number of legal provisions issued recently cover the matter of products' manufacture, production, sale, composition, ingredients, quality, storage, packaging, labelling, safety or technical standards. The main products that these legal provisions refer to are food, medicinal or dietary products, textiles and electric devices. There are some requirements for electric devices regarding their energy efficiency. For some products (*e.g.* new food, medicinal or dietary products) the trade on the market requires an approval issued by the Romanian Ministry of Health. Infringements of these rules are punished either as conduct in contravention of the law, or as the crimes of fraud concerning the quality of the merchandise, sale of counterfeit products, falsification of food, medicinal or dietary products or other products.

22–82 The consumer must be informed on the product name; manufacturer's name or trade marks and address; quantity and, after care, guarantee and/or validity term; minimal duration of product life; main technical and qualitative characteristics; compositions; used additives; potential predictable risks; methods of utilisation, handling, storing, conserving and keeping;

contraindications; nutritive value; and the country where the relevant products proceed from.

All information regarding the products offered to the consumer, attached documents and contracts must be written in the Romanian language. **22–83**

22.6.4 Intellectual property rights

According to Law 64/1991 on Patents, the rights over an invention are recognised and protected in Romanian territory by the award of a patent by the State Office for Inventions and Trademarks (SOIT). The patent application containing the identity of the petitioner and the description of the invention, as well as the protection claims, must be registered at SOIT. A patent has protection for a duration of 20 years from the date the patent application was registered. The patent grants to the inventor the exclusive exploitation right over the invention for the entire duration of protection of the patent. However, a temporary protection including the same exclusive exploitation rights is granted for the period between the publication of the patent request and the final issue of the patent. A notice about the issuing of the patent is published in the Official Bulletin of Industrial Property and will represent the issue date of the patent. All patents are registered in the Patents National Registry. The owner of the patent has the obligation to pay the taxes for the patent's maintenance in force during the entire period of validity of the patent. If the taxes are not paid, the owner will be deprived of his exclusive exploitation rights. **22–84**

Law 129/1992 regarding the Protection of Design Rights, as recently amended, establishes that the rights over design rights are recognised and protected by issue of a protection title by the SOIT. The protection title consists of the design right registration certificate that awards to its owner the right of exclusive exploitation on the Romanian territory. In order to obtain the registration certificate an application containing the identification data of the petitioner and of the author, the indication of the product or products in which the design right is going to be incorporated and a short description of the design right characteristic elements must be deposited with the SOIT. The registration certificate is valid for five years from the deposit of the registration certificate application and the validity can be renewed for two successive periods of five years each. On the entire period of validity, the owner of the registration certificate must pay the taxes for the maintenance in force of the certificate in order to prevent the deprivation of the exclusive exploitation rights. **22–85**

The copyright over a literary, artistic or scientific work or over intellectual creations of this kind is recognised and guaranteed in the conditions of Law 8/1996 on Copyright and Allied Rights. It is important to mention that intellectual creation is recognised and protected independently from its public acknowledgement, by the simple fact of its existence, even if it is unfinished or not published or not registered. The protection is not conditioned by the public acknowledgement of the creation or by its registration **27–86** at any public or private authority. The existence of various legal entities charged with the collection, management and administration of pecuniary rights belonging to authors from the same field of creation (*e.g.* theatrical or musical artists) does not prejudice or qualify in any way the protection of the authors' creations. The same logic applies to the role and attributions of the Romanian Office for Copyright Protection entitled to take notice and to supervise the correct enforcement of the copyright and allied rights legal framework.

22.6.5 Trade marks and authorised users

22–87 The principal may authorise the agent, distributor or licensee to use his trade mark based on an exclusive or non-exclusive trade mark licence. The agent, distributor or licensee has the obligation to use the statement *under licence* near the trade mark applied to the products and to use for those products only the trade mark that is the object of the trade mark license agreement. Based upon the license, the principal can object to the other party's conduct breaching the clauses relating to the duration of the trade mark use, the appearance of the trade mark and the nature of the products and services for which the licence was granted, the territory in which the trade mark can be used, the quality of the products and services delivered by the licensee under the trade mark for which the license agreement was concluded. The trade mark licence is enforceable against third parties from the date it is registered at the National Trademarks Registry and published in the Official Bulletin of Industrial Property. The agent, distributor or licensee is not allowed to bring an action for infringement without the principal's express approval, unless the trade mark license agreement stipulates the contrary.

22–88 Even if a trade mark licence is not concluded, the owner of a registered trade mark cannot prohibit other persons from selling products carrying this trade mark if the owner himself has already brought these products on the market or the products were already circulating on the market with the owner's approval.

22.6.6 Unfair trading practices

22–89 Law 11/1991 prohibits as unfair trading any act or situation contrary to honest usage in industrial and trade activities, works execution activities as well as in services. The last amendment of the law restricted the scope of the situations that may be regarded as unfair trade. Some categories of unfair practices are considered as in contravention of the law while other categories are considered crimes. The main forbidden unfair practices include: misleading and deceptive conduct, false representation, denigration, bait advertising, violation of trade secrets, boycott, referral selling, pyramid selling, etc.

22.6.7 Power to bind

Where there is express authority from the principal—which is named *mandate* in the Romanian law, part of the Roman law system—the agent, distributor or licensee can bind the principal to third parties in relation to all the acts necessary for the execution of the mandate, even if these acts are not expressly mentioned by the principal. 22–90

If the agent, distributor or licensee exceeds the powers of his mandate, his acts will not bind the principal unless the principal ratifies them, either expressly or tacitly. The excessive acts that are not ratified may bind the principal only if the conditions of *negotiorum gestio* (the management of the affairs of another) are satisfied. The main condition is that this management proves itself useful for the principal. Also, the principal should have not expressly forbidden the agent to exceed the powers included in the mandate. Even if the conditions for *negotiorum gestio* cannot be satisified, the principal may find himself bound to third parties on the grounds of unjust enrichment. 22–91

Finally, however, doctrine and practice have admitted the existence of the apparent mandate, meaning that the principal may be bound to third parties even in the absence of his consent in this respect, if the third parties contracted with the legitimate and reasonable belief that the agent had power of representation from the principal for the conclusion of such types of acts. 22–92

22.6.8 Liquidated damages and contracting out

Under Romanian law there are two different legal institutions: (i) *penal clause*, or liquidated damages, that represent an anticipatory conventional evaluation of the loss or damage; and (ii) conventions regarding contractual liability. 22–93

The Romanian Civil Code establishes the possibility for the contracting parties of including in their agreement a penal clause allowing the limitation of damages for delay or failure to perform to a pre-ascertained amount. The parties are free to negotiate the pre-ascertained amount as compensating the loss of profit or business and the courts have no power to modify the amount established in the penal clause. Such a clause may represent the full and final settlement of the debtor's liability in case of delay or non-execution of his obligations but it cannot create an option for the debtor of choosing between carrying out his obligations and paying the penal clause. The debtor cannot refuse to execute the agreement by offering to his creditor the penal clause. 22–94

If the parties wish to contract out altogether from liability for failing to perform their contractual obligations, a convention for liability exoneration should be concluded. The validity of such a convention is conditional upon the fact that the debtor's fault in non-executing the agreement is granted exoneration only if it has the form of negligence or imprudence. Intentional 22–95 fault excludes liability exoneration. The parties must conclude the liability exoneration convention before the creation of the damage. The parties can also agree to diminish their liability, in the same way.

22.6.9 Termination and compensation

22–96 The termination of the agreement because of the agent's, distributor's or licensee's breach can be either judicial when it is obtained in court, or established by the parties' agreement to stipulate a termination clause, which can be of various degrees, from I to IV depending on the severity of the effects of the breach. In both cases, the termination presumes a culpable non-execution of one or several contractual obligations by one of the parties and a notification sent to the party in breach to honour his obligation (the notification is not necessary if a IV degree termination clause is stipulated). In order for the termination to take place by reason of the fault of the agent, distributor or licensee the contractual breach must concern important and relevant obligations, such as the obligation to negotiate in a proper manner and in the interest of the principal the conditions of the business with the third party, to respect the principal's reasonable indications when dealing with business transactions and the obligation to pay the royalties or to exploit the licensed invention or knowhow in accordance with the limits established in the license agreement.

22–97 The agent, distributor or licensee guilty of contractual breach must compensate for the damage suffered by the principal by reason of the non-execution of his obligations. Generally, the termination of the agreement caused by the agent's, distributor's or licensee's contractual breach does not entitle the agent to any compensation.

22–98 The agent, distributor or licensee may have the right to the fees for the transactions concluded between the principal and the third party after the termination of the agency agreement if the business achievement date is close to the termination date of the agency agreement and the accomplishment of the business is mostly due to the activity carried out by the agent.

22–99 In the case of termination by proper notice of the principal, the agent, distributor or licensee is not entitled to compensation unless he proves that he suffered damage produced by the principal's decision to end the agreement or the agreement includes a clause stipulating such compensation. There is also the possibility, for each or both contracting parties, to terminate the agreement without prior notice because of exceptional circumstances, other than *force majeure*, which render impossible the continuation of the contractual relations between the principal and the agent, distributor, or licensee. In this case, the party that declares the termination of the agreement without prior notice must compensate for the damage suffered by the other contracting party.

22–100 The expiry of the agreement by elapse of time without renewal does not suppose any compensation to be paid to the agent.

In the event of termination of the agreement without prior notice, thus causing damage to one of the parties, the compensation should reflect the proportion of the damage caused by such termination. If the parties have anticipated, by the form of a penal clause, the amount of the damages, the compensation will be equivalent to this amount. The parties may also agree upon the amount of the damages at the termination date of the agreement without notice. In the most frequent cases when the parties disagree about the existence or the proportions of the damage, the competent courts will make the evaluation. Under the Romanian Civil Code, the result of this judicial evaluation must lead to compensation including both the actual damage and the loss of potential gain. Only the damage that could be predicted at the moment of the conclusion of the contract will be taken into consideration for the compensation, unless the damage was caused intentionally, and in this case the compensation must also include the payments for the damages that could not have been predicted at the beginning of the agreement. Only direct damage is subject to compensation, meaning the damage that is the direct effect of the event that generated the non-execution of the agreement. **22–101**

In the specific case of a distribution agreement (a provision) stating that orders would be accepted by the principal only at his absolute discretion could represent a condition depending only on the principal's wish, a condition that is expressly forbidden by Art.1010 of the Romanian Civil Code. **22–102**

22.6.10 Execution, witnessing, stamping, registration formalities

Romanian law does not establish any special form or conditions for the validity of the agency, distribution or licensing agreement. However, the complex and detailed clauses of such agreements necessitate the conclusion of the agreement in a written form. **22–103**

Between the contracting parties the agreement is valid and binding regardless of its registration and publicity. The agreement must be concluded in a number of copies reflecting the number of contracting parties. Since companies are the entities most frequently concluding agency agreements, the legal framework regulating the witnessing of documents permits testimonial proof if the court approves it. **22–104**

Business precautions render advisable the authentication of the agreement by a public notary, as authenticated acts benefit from a legal presumption of authenticity and validity that can be rejected only by the actual proof of a false declaration. **22–105**

The signatures of the parties must be written down on the agreement-paper. Usually, under the Romanian law, the contracting parties' stamps are also required. If the agreement gives rise to an economic concentration, the approval of the Romanian Competition Council must be obtained. **22–106**

22.6.11 Exchange control permissions and withholding taxes

22–107 Generally, no exchange control permissions are required to remit funds abroad. Residents are free to conduct such operations involving currency and they do not face any particular restrictions. When an external transfer of available currency takes place, residents have the obligation of proving with supporting documents the nature of the operation involving currency and an external payment order for currency should be filed in this respect. The non-residing persons or entities may also transfer abroad without restrictions the available currency placed in bank accounts. In order to prevent money laundering, the operations regarding cash deposit or withdrawal of currency amounts exceeding Euro 10,000 must be reported to the National Office for Preventing and Fighting Money Laundering. If sums up to this amount are transferred from bank accounts, the operation should be reported only if suspicions regarding money laundering arise.

22–108 For the specific situation when the principal is a person or a legal entity non-resident in Romania and the agent is a Romanian person or legal entity, the law establishes a profit tax rate that represents 25 per cent of the profit obtained from the activities. These taxes owed by the non-resident principal for the incomes obtained in Romania are calculated and withheld by the agent.

22–109 The tax should be paid to the state budget in quarterly instalments, by the 25th day of the month following the quarter's end. If the tax is not paid in due time, delay penalties are applicable. However, where a double taxation treaty exists between Romania and a foreign country, the provisions of the treaty will prevail if the principal presents to the Romanian fiscal authorities a certificate of fiscal residence attesting that the provisions of the double taxation treaty are applicable.

22–110 If by way of a distribution agreement the distributor undertakes to pay to the principal any royalties or commissions for using or concession of a certain right, a 15 per cent tax, calculated from the gross income paid to the principal, must be withheld and paid to the state budget by the distributor before remitting them to the principal.

22–111 For the specific situation when the principal is a person or a legal entity non-resident in Romania and the licensee is a Romanian person or legal entity, the law establishes a tax on royalties that represents 15 per cent of the income resulting from the payment of royalties. This tax owed by the non-resident principal for the incomes obtained in Romania is calculated and withheld by the licensee. The tax should be paid to the state budget the same day the payment of the taxable income, in the form of royalties, is made to the principal.

Chapter 23

Choosing between Agents, Distributors and Licensees—practical guidelines

Contents

23.1 Commercial and legal background

In this concluding chapter an attempt will be made to summarise the various commercial and legal considerations, as well as to provide some practical guidelines which a principal should take into account when trying to decide which one or more of the contractual relationships covered in this book is the appropriate channel for the particular type of business carried on by him. The various options open to a principal can be summarised as follows: **23–01**

- vertical integration (use of own branch or subsidiary);
- demonstrators or showrooms;
- marketing consultants;
- distribution franchisees;
- production franchisees;
- licensees;
- commercial agents; or
- distributors.

23.2 Vertical integration

23–02 From a commercial point of view the advantages of vertical integration spring from the absolute degree of control which the principal (or, in this case, parent company) has over the integrated levels in the supply chain. To the extent that his supply chain is vertically integrated, he is in complete control of, and enjoys all of the margin generated by, the distribution between the various levels of the integrated chain. He also controls the prices and terms of trade between the various levels, and the terms of trade with third parties at the level at which the product finally leaves the integrated supply chain. In theory a manufacturer could carry vertical integration from the factory to the retail outlet and have total control over the supply chain for his product all the way to the end user, and enjoy all the margin generated by the sale to that end user.

23–03 However, from a commercial point of view the disadvantages of vertical integration are also caused by this same element of control. True, the principal has freedom in his terms of trade and avoids sharing with a third party the margin that the integrated levels in the supply chain generate. However, this means there is no external third party, such as an independent distributor, with whom any part of the business risk or costs (including capital investment) can be shared in return for a share in the margin. Furthermore, where levels in a supply chain are part of a corporate group there is seldom the true incentive to take risks and win business which drives an independent distributor, who has assumed both the risk and the chance for reward, out of his activities. Corporate employee incentive schemes may, to some extent, lessen the problem, but in most cases, cannot replace the motivation of a distributor who knows he will go out of business if he makes the wrong decisions or fails to generate enough sales. Finally, it should not always be assumed that vertical integration is the most cost-effective method of distribution, just because all costs are controlled by the principal and he enjoys the whole of the margin. Lack of expertise at a particular level of distribution coupled with the need to absorb corporate overheads generated by the requirement to control and police the integrated system may outweigh the benefit of enjoying all of the margin. The more cost-effective way may well be to let a third party with more expertise run the particular level in the chain, and to trade part of the margin for reduced risk less capital investment and a lower cost method of distribution.

23–04 From a legal point of view, as well, there are advantages and disadvantages to vertical integration. These arise mainly in the areas of competition law and taxation.

23–05 A vertically integrated supply chain is largely unaffected by competition law. In the absence of some abuse of a dominant position, the arrangements between the levels of a vertically integrated supply chain cannot be scrutinised by competition law authorities (whether EC or domestic), and the terms of trade between the various wholly owned levels in the supply chain will be solely a matter for the principal (see Chapter 4.1).

However, vertical integration can bring its own legal problems in the area of taxation. First of all the use of branches or subsidiaries will expose at least part of the profits generated by the vertically integrated supply chain to taxation in jurisdictions outside that in which the principal is resident. In the absence of efficient double taxation treaties this may well result in additional and unnecessary charges to tax. Second, the use of a branch in a foreign country will often (in these cases) also expose the principal itself to taxation under the relevant foreign jurisdiction. Third, most taxation authorities scrutinise very closely the transfer prices between the different members of a vertically integrated supply chain. The various authorities will be concerned to establish that the transfer prices are set on an arm's length basis and fairly reflect the value of the product transferred, so that profits are not artificially shifted from one jurisdiction to another. Very often the rules used by such authorities to establish this fair value are complicated and bear little resemblance to commercial realities. Many manufacturers are deterred from extensive vertical integration of their supply chains by the difficulties with setting and justifying transfer prices, and the dangers of retrospective investigations resulting in the levying of large additional charges to tax, even in cases of quite honest attempts at setting transfer prices, which do not in fact comply with the relevant authority's rules. In conclusion, a principal should not even consider vertical integration without a thorough investigation of the taxation problems involved, and, in particular, without checking that his terms of trade between levels in the chain cause no problems because of transfer pricing issues. **23–06**

Even if these matters are resolved satisfactorily, in general, a principal would be wise not to consider vertical integration of his supply chain for too many levels. The further down the supply chain from the factory that the integration reaches, the less the principal is likely to have any particular expertise, and the less cost-effective the supply chain is likely to be. This will start to outweigh the advantages gained by control and enjoyment of the whole margin. Lack of expertise and the need to increase incentives and reduce capital investment and the risk and cost of distribution will lead to a point at which the principal finds it advantageous to stop the vertical integration and to contract with third parties. It must be said that while even ten years ago vertical integration was quite popular, the trend is now for businesses to specialise in the level (or sometimes levels) of the supply chain in which they have real expertise and can add real value. Vertically integrated supply chains are often quite short, and, in many industries, non-existent. Thus, manufacturers will often cease their activities at the factory gates, and turn their products over to specialist wholesalers or distributors, who in their turn will supply specialist resellers or retailers. A good example of this is the motor trade (discussed in Chapter 6) with its different levels of specialised distributors. **23–07**

23.3 Demonstrators or showrooms

23–08 These types of operations act only as a "shop window" for the producer's goods, and are thus rather ancillaries to the supply chain than a part of it. They can assist in marketing efforts by bringing the relevant products to the notice of potential customers, but, once this has been done, their only role is to channel sales prospects through to the principal himself who will then deal with the negotiation and conclusion of any resulting orders.

23–09 As discussed in Chapter 3.2 such operations fall below the "negotiating threshold" and thus would not be subject to the provisions of the Council Directive 653/86 of December 18, 1986 on the Coordination of the laws of the Member States relating to self-employed Commercial Agents. However, because of this, they can be of little help in closing orders and are an expensive means of marketing products in relation to their contribution to the sales effort.

23–10 In most cases, such operations are most efficiently used not on a regular basis, but from time to time, either to assist in the launch of new products, or to generate sales leads at exhibitions and trade shows.

23.4 Marketing consultants

23–11 The type of relationship envisaged here is embodied in the agreement discussed in Chapter 9. Like the demonstrators or showrooms operations the purpose of marketing consultants is to act as auxiliaries in the sales process by providing general advice and assistance to the sales effort in a particular territory, or for a particular opportunity. They can also be used to collect general market intelligence and to supervise local agents or distributors in their sales activities. By the nature of their activities marketing consultants, even when paid on some kind of commission basis in relation to sales made in their territories, do not carry on the activities of negotiating or negotiating and concluding those sales, and thus are below (or perhaps, better, outside) the negotiating threshold referred to in Chapter 3.2.

23–12 Marketing consultants are clearly an added expense which contributes only indirectly to the sales effort, and therefore their use is not often justifiable in terms of the value they add. Their best use is in relation to large capital projects in special markets. For instance it is quite common to retain such consultants, who may also act as lobbyists, when bidding for large US defence contracts. The other use is to enable a principal to contract out the job of policing his agents or distributors in unfamiliar territories. For instance, if, in a territory with a very different culture to that of the principal, the best distributor is a local firm, with no international experience and no language in common with the principal in which they can communicate easily, the most efficient course for the principal may very well be to choose as a "go-between" a marketing consultant who, although himself not suitable as a distributor, is more cosmopolitan, and who can communicate with both sides thereby bridging the difference between the two cultures.

23.5 Distribution franchisees

Some discussion of the definition of franchisees of distribution can be found in Chapter 6.27. Such franchisees normally exist at the retail level, in relation to consumer goods and services, and they tend to have a restricted area of operation, often only a single set of retail premises. Examples of such operations are the various franchised fast food chains or photocopying and printing services. **23–13**

Franchising of distribution is not really intended to act as a channel for the sale of goods. Any goods supplied (such as, in the case of fast food, the items of food themselves) are often supplied only to ensure that the franchisee supplies items to the required quality standard. The franchisor is primarily interested in obtaining a return by way of a royalty or other fee for the use of his trade mark, brand and get-up in the operation which distributes the goods in question. This is why franchise operations for the supply of services are also not only possible but popular. **23–14**

Although distribution franchise operations require little capital investment, the cost of running them is considerable, since the franchisor must train, monitor and support all of his franchisees on a continuing basis. He must also carry on advertising to support and promote the franchised brand. This means that the franchisor needs to obtain a commensurate level of return from the fees and royalties which his franchisees pay him. A successful franchise operation can therefore work only if the franchisor has a strong brand, continually reinforced by his promotional activities, which will attract franchisees who are willing to pay well for its use. These conditions will mean that franchising of distribution is unlikely to be a common method of exploitation for most principals. **23–15**

23.6 Production franchises

Production franchising is discussed briefly in Chapter 6.27 and in Chapter 8.1.1.1 AND 8.1.1.2. In essence the proprietor of a product will franchise a manufacturer to produce and distribute that product, in accordance with the prescribed formulae and processes owned by the proprietor, to defined quality standards, and then to market and sell that product under the proprietor's trade mark, brand and get-up. **23–16**

The same points arise in relation to distribution agreements, discussed above. The only difference is that since this is a franchising of production it takes place at the level of the manufacturer who may also (perhaps) act as a distributor or wholesaler, but not usually as a seller to the end user or as a retailer. Again the primary purpose of the parties is the exploitation of the franchisor's brand. This means that, since the franchisee has to incur the heavy capital investment of setting up in production for the relevant product, he is unlikely to take this risk unless he feels that the brand concerned is very strong indeed. Thus franchising of production is limited, as a rule, to a handful of brands which can be regarded as household names in the **23–17** relevant areas where the franchise is granted. The franchising of the production of soft drinks and beer are probably the best examples of such operations.

23.7 Licensing

23–18 Where the proprietor does not have a strong brand, but has attractive and desirable technology, a simple licence agreement (with or without the use of an associated trade mark or brand name) is a possible alternative to distribution either by vertical integration or through an agent or distributor.

23–19 This type of relationship is at the opposite end of the spectrum of control to vertical integration. Here, except, probably for quality control and monitoring, the licensor has very little control over the licensee's operation. In return for this ceding of control, the licensor has off-loaded almost all of the risk and cost and all of the required capital investment, and placed the maximum incentive on the licensee. However, the licensor will also have traded away most of the margin, and keep only a royalty which, in most cases, will be fairly low. Although rates vary with different industries, territories and products, it is unlikely that a product will command a royalty of more than 10 per cent, unless it is of outstanding technical importance. In many cases, royalties will in fact more likely tend to be something around 5 per cent, or even less.

23–20 However, it must be said that such royalties (which are often accompanied by upfront payments to cover technology transfer and start-up training) have very little ongoing cost associated with them, so that they can be more of a benefit to the licensor's bottom line than a larger margin generated by the sale of a product to a distributor. The picture can be made even more attractive for the licensor if he is prepared to grant an exclusive licence, since, in most cases, in return for this, he will be able to require a minimum royalty commitment from the licensee which will shift even more risk on to the licensee and create an even greater incentive for increasing sales.

23–21 Where the licensor lacks capital to expand his own operations or cannot export economically to a particular territory, where local regulations require domestic manufacture or impose quotas on exports, or where the licensor has ceased to market the relevant product in his home territory, licensing can be a most attractive way of exploiting technology to generate income. Such income may be at a relatively modest level, however it is incremental revenue which has little cost associated with it, and therefore generates a significant net profit, as opposed to a gross margin.

23.8 Commercial agents

23–22 The use of a commercial agent is the closest the principal can come to vertical integration without using a wholly owned subsidiary or a branch.

Since the agent acts on behalf of the principal, the principal still retains most of the margin and a very substantial degree of control over the agent's activities. Nonetheless, the principal has shifted at least some of the business risk on to the agent, and provided him with a considerable incentive to increase sales, since the agent is rewarded by a commission on the sales which his activities generate.

From a legal point of view the use of an agent of itself does not give rise to major taxation issues; nor is a principal usually regarded as doing business in a territory in which he has appointed an agent, except in the case where the agent can conclude contracts in the territory on behalf of the principal and (in some cases) even if he cannot actually conclude such contracts, he holds a consignment stock from which he fills orders accepted by the principal and on the direction of the principal (see Chapter 2.14.1). Needless to say if the agent both concludes contracts on behalf of the principal in the territory and then satisfies those contracts out a stock of consignment goods, the principal will in almost all cases be regarded as doing business in the territory. **23–23**

Further the relationship between principal and agent is not governed to any significant extent in most cases by competition law (see Chapter 4.1). However, the choice of an agent will mean that the principal must have regard to Council Directive 653/86. This will, in particular, impose on the principal the duty to act in good faith towards the agent and to pay him compensation on termination of the agency relationship other than by reason of the agent's default (see Chapter 3). **23–24**

23.9 Distributors

The use of a distributor lies, in a sense, mid way between the alternatives of vertical integration and licensing. The principal has ceded a significant degree of control and a large share of his margin in return for the assumption of a larger part of the capital investment and the cost and risk of doing business. Such an assumption, of course, gives the distributor a much greater incentive to increase the sales. **23–25**

From a legal point of view the appointment of a distributor does not give rise to particular taxation issues, since the principal is doing business with a third party. Further, distributors are by definition not subject to the protection of Council Directive 653/86, although in some cases they may be protected by the domestic law of the jurisdiction in which they are carrying on business. However, the relationship between principal and distributor is closely controlled by competition law (see Chapter 4.1 and 5.1) and for this reason, the principal has little freedom to control the distributor's activities (*e.g.* by setting resale prices or terms of trade for resale, or by controlling too closely which customers the distributor can deal with). **23–26**

23.10 Comparison between agent and distributor

23–27 When deciding whether to appoint an agent or a distributor, there are a number of factors which should always be taken into account, and it is now useful to summarise these.

23.10.1 Control over the goods to be sold

23–28 Where the principal wishes to exercise close control over the goods to be sold, before they reach the end user, an agent is the better choice. The agent does not take title to the goods and (except in the case of an agent with consignment stock) does not even take possession of them. In both legal and practical terms, the agent thus has very little opportunity to modify, mistreat or tamper with the goods, and has no opportunity to build up excessive or unsaleable inventory. On the other hand, the distributor takes both title and, in most cases, possession of the goods. He is thus responsible for handling, storage and distribution of the goods, and, even if he is not given the legal right, will certainly have the practical opportunity to modify, adapt or repack the goods. Finally, the distributor can build up excessive inventory, or inventory which has become unsaleable due to his poor handling. As discussed in Chapter 4.17.4, this is likely to become a problem for the principal upon termination of the agreement, if not before.

23.10.2 Control of customer base

23–29 The principal who wishes to retain control of the customer base is more likely to succeed with the appointment of an agent than a distributor. As a "value added" reseller, the distributor has a direct relationship with the customer base. They are his customers, rather than the principal's customers. The principal may even not know who all of the distributor's customers are. The distributor therefore looks after his customers and knows their requirements, while the principal does not. Thus, the distributor, with his superior knowledge, can often dictate the product and marketing strategies for his territory. The agent, however, has a less central role in the customer relationship, since the principal has a direct contract with each customer. Here the customers are the customers of the principal rather than of the agent.

23–30 It can thus be said that the distributor by his activities builds up his own good will in his own customer base, while the agent builds up the principal's good will in what is, in effect, the principal's customer base. Because of this the agent is less able to hold the principal to ransom than a distributor if there is a dispute between them or upon the termination of the contract. However, equally, this is the reason why agents in many jurisdictions enjoy special protection on termination of the agency agreement, whereas distributors do not.

23.10.3 Control of pricing and contractual terms

A principal who wishes to set the end user price will clearly have to use an agent rather than a distributor. The distributor buys from the principal in bulk on a volume related discount and must be free to set his own prices for each resale in nearly all jurisdictions. On the other hand, the agent has to work off the principal's list prices, and can (unless specifically authorised) permit volume discounts authorised by the principal only in relation to each individual transaction. Similarly, the distributor is substantially free to set his own contract terms for resale of the goods he purchases from the principal. An agent may well have no more power than to negotiate proposals, or even just to pass on offers to the principal, which the principal can reserve the right finally to accept or reject, upon contractual terms that he finds satisfactory. Even where the agent has power to negotiate and conclude a contract, this will be within well-defined limits of authority that enable the principal to control the terms upon which the relevant contract is finally concluded. **23–31**

23.10.4 Monitoring of performance

The monitoring of a distributor, because he has made his own investment in the business, has assumed more risk and cost and thus demands, and is granted, greater freedom of action, is much more burdensome and costly than the monitoring of an agent. In the case of a distributor, the principal must monitor the sales performance, financial status, level of customer service, volume of purchases from the principal and technical competence. However, in the case of an agent, the only thing that needs to be monitored is the agent's performance in gathering orders. All of the other functions carried out by the distributor are, in this case, carried out by the principal himself. **23–32**

23.10.5 Financial control

More principals have lost money, or even gone out of business altogether, through lack of proper credit control over their distributors than for any other reason. Most, if not all, distributors look to the principal to finance their operations by long credit terms. A distributor will, in preference, buy from the principal on, for example, 90 days payment terms, and resell on, *e.g.* 30 days payment terms to his customers. This means that if the customers are prompt payers, and the distributor does not build up too much inventory, the distributor will be able to repay the principal out of the resale proceeds. He is thus using the principal as a source of interest free finance. Many principals accept this, and build the financing charge into their prices (often providing a special discount for early payment), but the result of this **23–33** arrangement is that the principal is taking the credit risk on all of the distributor's customers, without having any control over the extent of the risk which the distributor takes. Thus, using a distributor in effect "bundles" the credit risk for a whole territory into the question of the solvency of the distributor, and it must not be forgotten that even if the distributor's customers pay on time there are additional business risks (*e.g.* lack of sales or litigation) which cause the distributor to become insolvent anyway. On the other hand, the use of an agent leaves the credit risk in a territory at the level of each separate customer with whom the principal chooses to deal. Thus not only can the principal control the extent of that risk himself, but the risk instead of being "bundled" is spread out across the individual deals as they are transacted.

23.10.6 Type of industry and goods sold

23–34 Given the above analysis, it would appear that it is nearly always preferable for a principal to use an agent rather than a distributor. However, this leaves aside the question of the type of industry and goods involved.

23–35 In many cases it will not be practical for the principal to act through an agent. Where the goods are of a type which require a presence in the territory for technical support and after-sales service, and/or extensive and varied inventory, an agency operation is not suitable, since, in most cases, the agent's commission will not be sufficient to fund the investment required. If the principal chooses to use an agent he will have to set up such an operation himself. In this case he might as well go all the way to vertical integration and hire salesmen in the territory. Where this option is not feasible (it may be too expensive, at least if the principal has to do this in a number of territories, or the territory may be one in which the principal cannot effectively do business) then he must find a local operator who will undertake the investment to provide a full-service local operation. In return for this investment the local operator will almost always require to be appointed as distributor with a sufficient share of the margin to compensate him for the risk and capital investment undertaken. Examples of goods falling within this class are motor vehicles, small and medium sized plant and machinery, and consumer durables such as televisions or washing machines.

23–36 However, where one is concerned with a large one off sale of capital goods, such as aircraft, ships, or large industrial plant and machinery, with a high capital value, the use of an agent is indicated. The principal will have arrangements in place for after-sales service and support (often from his home base by travelling engineers). The complexity of such items requires the use of expert service unlikely to be found in a local distributor, and their high price provides sufficient margin to enable the principal to provide this service himself.

23–37 Where one is concerned with commodities such as grain or sugar, raw materials or components, or items with a small unit value such as low value consumer goods like cosmetics or confectionery, the choice between an agent or distributor is much harder to make. It may well depend upon the remoteness of the territory and whether it is feasible to satisfy orders from wholesalers direct by import into the territory (in which case an agent would be suitable) or whether there are a large number of small transactions which have to be settled out of a local inventory. In the latter case, although the use of an agent with consignment stock is possible, principals tend to prefer that, in situations where they cannot readily monitor and control the consignment stock, the local operator should take the control of and risk in the stock, and thus be appointed as distributor. This will obviously be particularly important in the case of fragile or perishable goods, or of goods with a short shelf life.

23.11 Conclusions

It can be seen that the choice between the various relationships described in this book, and summarised in this chapter, comes down to a choice for the principal between retaining control, risk and margin and trading out control and margin in varying degrees in return for the increased assumption of risk, capital investment and cost by the other party to the relationship. The reasons for such a trade may be the desire to avoid risk and cost, shortage of capital, a policy decision to increase the incentive of the other party to make sales, or the need (because of the nature of the goods or industry concerned) to persuade the other party to set up a local operation in a territory where the principal finds it too costly or otherwise impractical to do this. Of course, the principal's reasons may be a mixture of more than one or of all of these reasons. **23–38**

When making such a choice, the principal should first of all analyse and understand the impact of the issues in the preceding paragraph and then design and adopt the relationship which is most commercially sensible and is most likely to make his business succeed. Once this has been done, the principal can decide with his lawyers how best to deal with any legal or regulatory issues which arise. It cannot, however, be emphasised too much that the decision should be driven from a business viewpoint and not with a view to worrying first about legal issues. It would, for instance, be entirely wrong to choose an agent because one wanted to avoid competition law problems, when the business in question demanded a distributor. It would be equally wrong to choose a distributor, when an agent was necessary, just to avoid Council Directive 653/86. Once the business decision has been properly taken it is the task of the lawyer, hopefully with the help of the suggestions in this book, to embody the desired relationship in an agreement which is both legal and has practical business efficacy. **23–39**

Appendix 1

Specimen Questionnaires for Local Lawyers

This appendix contains a set of specimen questionnaires which can be used to seek advice from local lawyers as to the particular effect of local law on the various agreements contained in this book. The foreign chapters in this book have largely been prepared using these questionnaires as a basis. **A1–01**

Questionnaire 1 relates to Agency Agreements. Questionnaire 2 relates to Distribution Agreements, including selective distribution, and Questionnaire 3 to Manufacturing Agreements. Questionnaire 4 contains a variety of materials relating to Chapters 1, 6, 8 and 9, which is of more general interest, and can be used in combination with one or more of the other questionnaires as required. Where a mixed licence and distribution agreement is concerned (see Chapter 7.6) a combination of Questionnaires 2 and 3 should be used. **A1–02**

References in the questionnaires to "local law", "territory", and "products" should either be replaced by specific terms, or be defined in the covering letter. Care should be taken to give sufficient information about the products to ensure that the lawyer replying to the questionnaire has his mind directed to all relevant legislation. These questionnaires are not intended to be exhaustive, and consideration should always be given to additional questions that may be required in particular cases. However, the questionnaires do form a skeleton that should, in most cases, provide sufficient preliminary information so that, coupled with the precedents and commentary, intelligent advice and a first draft can be prepared for comment by the client. **A1–03**

As details of the proposed arrangements become clearer, supplementary questions may need to be asked of the local lawyer, and even advice on details of drafting be sought. **A1–04**

It is of course possible to draft an agreement without reference to local law, and send it to a local lawyer for detailed comment. In practice this tends to waste more time in detailed drafting discussions, and often leaves one still uncertain as to exactly what the local law is on particular points. Time is probably in fact more often saved by careful structured preliminary research and enquiry. **A1–05**

No questions relate to EC law, since it is assumed that the enquirer will (based on the material in the body of this book) have a general idea of the **A1–06** problems to be faced. Any further enquiries can be made on the basis of study of the many excellent standard reference works available in most of the languages spoken within the EEC.

1 Agency agreements

A1–07 **1.1** What is the general definition of the relationship between agent and principal under local law?

1.2 Is a principal who appoints an agent in the territory to seek out orders and transmit enquiries, or with delegated power to conclude contracts on behalf of the principal, regarded in either or both cases under local law as carrying on business in the territory?

1.3 Is a principal who appoints an agent to sell goods owned by the principal, stored in the territory, and held by the agent on behalf of the principal, regarded as carrying on business in the territory?

1.4 If the answer to 1.2 or 1.3 is yes, what formalities, if any, does the principal have to carry out, by way of registration or otherwise, in order to be able so to carry on business in the territory?

1.5 What taxation will a principal under 1.2 and 1.3 be required to pay in the territory upon the revenue of the business which he is regarded as carrying on in the territory, or upon the revenue of any other business which he carries on outside the territory?

1.6 Are there any specific laws relating to sale, composition, ingredients, packaging, labelling, safety or technical standards, or registration, or otherwise in relation to the products and their marketing in the territory? If so, please give details.

1.7 How far can an agent bind his principal to third parties under the laws of the territory, when he does not have express authority from the principal so to bind the principal?

1.8 Where the agent is required by the principal to enter into a guarantee of the debts to the principal of customers whom he finds for the principal, ("del credere guarantee") or with whom he concludes contracts on behalf of the principal, what formalities and documentation are required to ensure that that guarantee is legally binding? Is any special set of words required for such a guarantee?

1.9 Is it necessary for the agent to execute a registered user agreement or other documentation to ensure that he can use the principal's industrial property rights, particularly trade marks, without acquiring ownership in them, or jeopardising the principal's ownership in them as against third parties?

1.10.1 What rights has the agent to compensation on termination of the agency agreement:

1.10.1.1 in the event of termination because of the agent's breach of the agreement (please specify what events of breach will be regarded in practice under local law as justifying such termination); and

1.10.1.2 in the event of termination by proper notice, or by expiry by effluxion of time, without renewal?

1.10.2 In the event that the agreement is terminated without notice, and compensation is payable, either under the general law relating to breach of contract, or under a specific law providing for agents, what is the way in which the compensation for such termination is measured?

1.11 What is the local law in force regarding corrupt gifts and secret commissions?

1.12 What formalities are necessary by way of execution, witnessing, stamping, or registration or governmental approval so that an agency agreement can be regarded as legally valid and enforceable for all purposes under the local law? Please give details.

1.13 What exchange control permissions, if any, are required for the remitting by the agent to the principal of money collected in the territory on behalf of the principal? Please give details.

1.14 Are any withholding or other taxes levied in the territory on moneys referred to in 1.13 which must be settled whether or not prior to remitting them, and whether or not by the principal or the agent? Please give details.

1.15 Where the agent holds stock or money or other property belonging to the principal, can the principal assert his rights of ownership against third parties:

1.15.1 in the event of the insolvency of the agent; and

1.15.2 in the event that the agent has dishonestly disposed of them to third parties?

1.16 To what extent do the rights of the principal if any under 1.15 extend to enable him to take the proceeds of sale of that property disposed of by the agent:

1.16.1 where the sale was authorised by the principal; and

1.16.2 where the sale was not authorised by the principal?

1.17 In order to obtain or preserve any rights given to the principal under local law, under 1.15 and 1.16, what formalities or legal procedures, particularly in regard to registration, if any, are required under local law? Please give details.

2 Distribution agreements

A1–08 **2.1** What is the general definition under local law of the relationship between principal and distributor (*i.e.* an independent operator who purchases goods on his own account for resale to third parties, at his own risk)?

2.2 Is a principal who appoints a distributor in the territory regarded as carrying on business in the territory?

2.3 If the answer to 2.2 is yes, what formalities, if any, does the principal have to carry out, by way of registration or otherwise, in order to be able so to carry on business in the territory?

2.4 What taxation will a principal under 2.2 be required to pay in the territory upon the revenue of the business which he is regarded as carrying on in the territory, or upon the revenue of any other business which he carries on outside the territory?

2.5 What protection is given under the local law to design rights or copyright in the products, and is registration necessary to obtain such protection?

2.6 How far is the principal free to charge different scales of prices and contract upon different terms for two or more distributors, appointed either both for the whole of the territory on a non-exclusive basis, or each of whom have a separate and defined exclusive area of operation in the territory?

2.7 How far is the principal free to set resale prices and otherwise impose restrictions upon the distributor as to the classes of customers to whom the distributor may sell the products?

2.8 Is the principal free to impose upon the distributor an obligation to purchase and keep at all times a full stock of each one of the products that compose the range of products which are the subject of the distribution agreement?

2.9 Is there a local law relating to unfair trading practices, and if so, what practices are regarded as unfair so that the principal can prohibit the distributor from carrying them out?

2.10 Is it possible under the local law to impose a clause providing that damages for delay or failure to perform may be limited to a pre-ascertained amount, and that payment of such amount shall be in full and final settlement of all liability for such delay or failure, including liability for compensation for loss of profit, or business? How far is it possible to contract out altogether under the local law from liability for failure to perform obligations under a contract, particularly obligations to deliver goods?

2.11 Are there any specific laws relating to sale, composition, ingredients, packaging, labelling, safety or technical standards, or registration, or otherwise in relation to the products and their marketing in the territory? If so, please give details.

2.12 How far can a distributor bind his principal to third parties under the laws of the territory, when he does not have express authority from the principal so to bind the principal?

2.13 Is it necessary for the distributor to execute a registered user agreement or other documentation to ensure that he can use the principal's industrial property rights, particularly trade marks, without acquiring ownership in them, or jeopardising the principal's ownership in them as against third parties?

2.14 What rights has the distributor to compensation on termination of the distribution agreement:

2.14.1 in the event of termination because of the distributor's breach of the agreement (please specify what events of breach will be regarded in practice under local law as justifying such termination); and

2.14.2 in the event of termination by proper notice, or by expiry by effluxion of time, without renewal?

2.15 In the event that the agreement is terminated without notice, and compensation is payable, either under the general law relating to breach of contract, or under a specific law providing for distributors, what is the way in which the compensation for such termination is measured, and what effect, if any, on the measurement, would be caused by a provision in the agreement stating that orders would be accepted by the principal only at his absolute discretion?

2.16 What formalities are necessary by way of execution, witnessing, stamping, or registration or governmental approval so that a distribution agreement can be regarded as legally valid and enforceable for all purposes under the local law? Please give details.

2.17 What exchange control permissions, if any, are required for the remitting by the distributor to the principal of payment for consignments of the products? Please give details.

2.18 Are any withholding or other taxes levied in the territory on monies referred to in 2.17 which must be settled whether or not prior to remitting them, and whether or not by the principal or the distributor? Please give details.

2.19 To what extent under local law is it possible to exclude liability as between the distributor and the principal for the supply of defective goods or services?

2.20 Is there any local law which regulates a system of distribution which controls and restricts the number of outlets through which the products are distributed, at all levels, from the distributor to the retailer? (selective distribution system). In particular is there any law which makes refusal to supply a breach of civil or criminal law, and, if so, what, if any, are the circumstances in which a refusal to supply is justified?

3 Manufacturing agreements

A1–09 **3.1** Is there any legislation in force controlling the transfer of technology to a licensee within the territory?

3.2 If the answer to 3.1 is yes, please give full details of the legislation, and in particular any mandatory terms that must be included in licence agreements, what terms must be excluded, and what terms, if any, are optional.

3.3 In particular, to what extent is it possible under the local law to restrict the licensee from exporting products outside the territory for which he is licensed?

3.4 Is it possible under local law to require the licensee to purchase ingredients, components or packaging for the products, either only from specified suppliers, or only from the principal? Can the obligation be imposed for any items, or must it be only for items technically vital for the proper manufacture of the products?

3.5 What protection is given under the local law to patents design rights or copyright in the products, and is registration necessary to obtain such protection? Please give details.

3.6 How far is the principal free to impose different scales of royalties upon and licence upon different terms to two or more licensees, each of whom have a separate and defined exclusive area of operation in the territory, or each of whom are both appointed on a non-exclusive basis for the whole of the territory?

3.7 How far is the principal free to set resale prices for products manufactured by the licensee and otherwise impose restrictions upon the licensee as to the classes of customers to whom the licensee may sell the products?

3.8 Can the requirement be imposed on the licensee to pay an up-front payment by way of a lump sum, to cover costs of transfer of technology, and is the amount of this payment controlled in any way?

3.9 Is there a local law relating to unfair trading practices, and if so, what practices are regarded as unfair so that the principal can prohibit the licensee from carrying them out?

3.10 Is it possible under the local law to impose a clause providing that damages for delay or failure to perform may be limited to a preascertained amount, and that payment of such amount shall be in full and final settlement of all liability for such delay or failure, including liability for compensation for loss of profit, or business? Is it possible to contract out altogether from liability for failure to perform obligations under a contract, particularly for failure to deliver goods?

3.11 Are there any specific laws relating to sale, composition, ingredients, packaging, labelling, safety or technical standards, or registration, or otherwise in relation to the products and their marketing in the territory?

3.12 How far can a licensee bind his principal under the laws of the territory to third parties, when he does not have express authority from the principal so to bind the principal?

3.13 Is it necessary for the licensee to execute a registered user agreement or other documentation to ensure that he can use the principal's industrial property rights, particularly trade marks, without acquiring ownership in them, or jeopardising the principal's ownership in them as against third parties?

3.14 What rights has the licensee to compensation on termination of the licence agreement:

> **3.14.1** in the event of termination because of the licensee's breach of the agreement (please specify what events of breach will be regarded in practice under local law as justifying such termination); and
>
> **3.14.2** in the event of termination by proper notice, or by expiry by effluxion of time, without renewal?

3.15 In the event that the agreement is terminated without notice, and compensation is payable, either under the general law relating to breach of contract, or under a specific law providing for licensees, what is the way in which the compensation for such termination is measured?

3.16 What formalities are necessary by way of execution, witnessing, stamping, or registration or governmental approval so that a licence agreement can be regarded as legally valid and enforceable for all purposes under the local law? Please give details.

3.17 What exchange control permissions, if any, are required for the remitting by the licensee to the principal of payments for items purchased, and for payment of royalties? Please give details.

3.18 Are any withholding or other taxes levied in the territory on monies referred to in 3.17 which must be settled whether or not prior to remitting them, and whether or not by the principal or the licensee? Please give details.

3.19 To what extent under local law, if at all, can the principal impose an obligation to continue to pay royalty after licensed patents have expired, or licensed knowhow has come into the public domain?

3.20 Are there controls under the local law as to the level and or the total amount of royalty which may be charged by the principal?

3.21 Does the licensee have a right under local law to a free paid-up licence after a certain period of time, or after payment of a certain amount of royalty?

3.22 Are there particular rules under local law as to the way in which the sales value, on which royalty is to be levied, is to be calculated (*e.g.* exclusion of the value of components purchased by the licensee from manufacturers within the territory)?

3.23 Please specify any import quotas imposed, import licences required, and the level of customs and other import taxes levied, for imported goods of the same class as the products.

4 Miscellaneous questionnaire

4.1 Confidentiality:

A1–10 **4.1.1** What are the provisions of the local law relating to the protection of confidential information? Is protection granted in any circumstances without the execution of an express confidentiality agreement or undertaking? If so, please give details.

4.1.2 Is it possible to impose by an express agreement or undertaking greater obligations of confidentiality than those imposed under the general law relating to confidentiality? If so, please state if the express agreement has to be in any particular form and whether particular formalities of execution stamping or registration have to be observed. Please give details.

4.1.3 Where an express confidentiality agreement is permitted under the general law, are there any restrictions as to the obligations that can be imposed by that agreement? In particular, is it possible to restrict the rights of the recipient of information to use it, even though the information has come into the public domain?

4.2 Restrictive covenants:

4.2.1 To what extent is it possible to restrict an agent, distributor, licensee and any other party (other than an employee) with whom a contract to provide services is made, from competing with the other party to the agreement during the life of the agreement? **A1–11**

4.2.2 To what extent is it possible to continue the restrictions mentioned in 4.2.1. after the agreement has expired? In particular to what extent in this situation does the geographical extent and or the length of time of the restriction affect its enforceability?

4.3 Software:

4.3.1 Please specify what protection, if any, is given to software under the local law. **A1–12**

4.3.2 Irrespective of the answer to 4.31, to what extent can software be protected in the territory by restrictions upon its use, copying, or disclosure, made in an express agreement?

4.4 Escrow agreements:

4.4.1 Does the local law recognise the concept of an independent party who holds documents goods or other items with a mandate to hand them to another party upon the happening of a certain event (escrow arrangement)? **A1–13**

4.4.2 If the answer to 4.4.1 is yes, can such an arrangement be made irrevocable, so that the original owner of the goods documents or other items, who has given them to the independent party, cannot revoke his mandate, and require them to be returned to him?

4.4.3 Where such arrangements are recognised under the local law, what formalities by way of agreements, execution, registration, and stamping are required to make the arrangement legally enforceable?

4.5 Powers of attorney:

A1–14 Please give details of the law relating to powers of attorney in commercial matters. In particular, what formalities are required by way of form, execution, witnessing, stamping, and registration, and in what circumstances can a power of attorney be revoked, other than in accordance with any express terms contained in the document constituting the power of attorney?

4.6 Whole agreement clauses:

A1–15 Does the local law permit a clause in an agreement providing that the written agreement shall be deemed to be the whole agreement between the parties, and that all previous negotiations, representations and statements, whether written or oral, shall not form part of the agreement, and shall have no legal effect?

4.7 Arbitration:

A1–16 **4.7.1** Please give a general outline of the local law governing arbitration.

4.7.2 Please specify to what extent the courts can intervene in the arbitration, to regulate the appointment of the arbitrator, and the procedure to be followed in the arbitration, and to hear appeals as to questions of law or questions of fact, arising during the course of the arbitration, or relating to the award that is made by the arbitrator. To what extent can the parties exclude the intervention of the court by express terms contained in the arbitration agreement?

4.7.3 What is the procedure under the local law for enforcing an arbitration award made under a local arbitration subject to the local law?

4.7.4 What is the procedure under the local law for enforcing an arbitration award made outside the territory under a foreign law?

4.7.5 What is the effect of a clause requiring the arbitrator to decide a reference on the basis of what he thinks is fair and reasonable, and not upon the principles of any law, local or foreign? (amiable composition). If such a clause is valid under the local law, to what extent will the courts enforce any award made in pursuance of it, and to what extent can the courts intervene to regulate the procedure followed in the arbitration?

4.8 Force majeure:

4.8.1 What definition if any is given under the local law to the term "force majeure"? **A1–17**

4.8.2 What are the consequences upon a contract of a happening of "force majeure" as so defined?

4.8.3 Does the local law give any relief to a contracting party in the event of a happening which is not force majeure, but which makes the contract more onerous to perform than that party had contemplated when he entered into the contract? (Hardship)

4.8.4 To what extent may the parties provide by an express term of a contract for relief from delay or failure to perform contractual obligations by reason of the occurrence of events of force majeure, hardship, or any other event beyond the reasonable control of the party affected?

[illegible] force majeure [illegible] [illegible] [illegible] [illegible] [illegible] of the party affected?

Appendix 2

Questionnaire on the Local Implementation of Council Directive 653/86 on the Coordination of the Laws of the Member States Relating to Self-Employed Commercial Agents

1 Implementation

Please describe the local legislation used to implement the Directive, including reference and date it came into force. All agency agreements covered, including those in existence on the date the local legislation came into force? **A2–01**

Austria Commercial Agents Act ("Handelsvertretergesetz—BGBL 1993/88)—Legal Gazette 1993 No.88. Implemented March 1, 1993 for both then existing and all new contracts.

Belgium Law on Commercial Agents adopted April 13, 1995—Belgian Official Gazette of June 2, 1995. Implemented June 12, 1995 for all then existing and new contracts.

Denmark Danish Act on Commercial Agents and Travelling Salesmen (Lov om handelsagenter og handelrejsende) Law No.272 of May 2, 1990. From January 1, 1992 covering both existing and new contracts.

Finland Law for Commercial Representatives and Salesmen (Laki Kauppaedustajista ja Myyntimiehista) 417 of August 5, 1993 (based on Government Proposal 201/1991). Came into force November 1, 1992 and applying to both then existing and new contracts from January 1, 1994.

France Law 91–593 (June 25, 1991) and Decree 92–506 (June 10, 1992) which modified the previous legislation on commercial agents (Decree 58–1345 of December 23, 1958) to bring it into line with the Directive. Came into force June 27, 1991 applying to both existing and new contracts from January 1, 1994.

Germany Law for Implementation of the EC Directive on the Coordination of the Law Relating to Self-Employed Agents (October 23, 1989—BGB1, 1910) amending Art.84 of the German Commercial Code. Came into force January 1, 1990 for new contracts and covers all existing contracts from January 1, 1994.

Greece Presidential Decrees 219/3.5.1991, 249/28.6.1993, and 88/22.4.1994 culminating in a consolidating Decree 312/22.8.1995 containing the Codification of the Laws of Commercial Agents. The Codification applies to all new contracts and retroactively to all contracts in existence on January 1, 1994.

Iceland Act Respecting Commission Sales Transactions No.103/1992. Came into force for new agreements on January 1, 1993, and for existing agreements from January 1, 1994.

Ireland European Communities (Commercial Agents) Regulations 1994 (SI 33/1994). From January 1, 1994 applying to all existing and new contracts. Amended by the European Communities (Commercial Agents) Regulations 1997 (SI 31/1997).

Italy Legislative Decree of the President of the Republic dated September 10, 1991. Certain transitional provisions relating to implementation of the indemnity having now expired, the Law now fully covers all existing and new contracts.

Liechtenstein The Council Directive itself was published in the Liechtenstein Law Gazette GBL. 1995 Nr.68. It appears that in many cases Liechtenstein implements EC legislation merely by publishing the original EC directive in the Law Gazette. However, in 2001 (by publication in the Law Gazette (LGBL 2001 Nr.171) the Liechtenstein legislation on commercial agents was more specifically amended to bring it into line with the Directive. The current legislation is thus contained in Title 8 of the Commercial Code—Handelsvertreter (Agent)—Arts 87–109.

Luxembourg Law dated June 3, 1994 (published July 6, 1994). From January 1, 1994 applying to all new contracts and to all contracts existing at that date.

Netherlands Law of July 5, 1989 (Stb 1989 312). Came into force November 1, 1989 applying to all existing and new agreements.

Norway Act of Commercial Agents of June 19, 1992 No.56 (Lov om handelsagenter og handelsreisende). Came into force January 1, 1993, both new and existing agreements were covered from January 1, 1994.

Portugal Decree 118/93 of April 13, 1993 amended the existing Decree relating to agency agreements (178/86 of July 3, 1986) to bring it into line with the Directive. From January 1, 1994, existing and new agreements are covered by the amended Decree.

Spain Law 12/1992 dated September 27, 1992. From January 1, 1994 both existing and new agreements are covered.

Sweden The Act on Commercial Agents (1991:351). Implemented January 1, 1992 and applying to all existing and new agreements from January 1, 1994.

2 Art.2(2)—secondary agents

Member States have the option to exclude "secondary agents" from local implementation. Has this option been taken up, and, if so, how are "secondary agents" defined? **A2–02**

Austria Secondary agents are not excluded.

Belgium Secondary agents are not excluded, but unpaid agents are.

Denmark Secondary agents are not excluded.

Finland Secondary agents are not excluded.

France The term is not used, but all agents whose activities are regulated by special statutory regimes are excluded. Also where the parties have entered into a general agreement whose main purpose is something other than an agency relationship (*e.g.* distributorship) but which provides for an agency relationship as a subsidiary activity, the parties may exclude the operation of the Directive in relation to this subsidiary activity.

Germany The Law excludes part-time agents but does not define them. This is a question of fact to be decided in each case.

Greece Secondary agents are not excluded.

Iceland Provision has been made to exclude certain categories of secondary agents by ministerial regulation.

Ireland Secondary agents are defined as consumer credit agents and mail order agents, and their activities are excluded.

Italy Secondary agents is not a term understood in Italian law, and they have therefore not been excluded.

Liechtenstein The legislation does not deal with secondary agents.

Luxembourg The law specifically states that secondary agents are included.

Netherlands Secondary agents are excluded but there is no definition in the Law.

Norway Secondary agents are not excluded.

Portugal Secondary agents are not excluded.

Spain Secondary agents are not excluded. However, trade union representatives and stock market agents (brokers) are specifically excluded.

Sweden Secondary agents are not excluded.

3 Art.7(2)—commission

A2–03 *The local implementation must specify that an agent shall also be entitled to commission on transactions entered into by the principal either direct or through another agent either:*

(a) *where he is entrusted with a specific geographical area or specific group of customers; or*

(b) *where he has an exclusive right to such specific area or specific group with a customer in such area or group.*

Which alternative has been adopted?

Austria First alternative, (a).

Belgium First alternative, (a).

Denmark First alternative, (a).

Finland First alternative, (a).

France First alternative, (a).

Germany First alternative, (a).

Greece First alternative, (a).

Iceland First Alternative, (a).

Ireland Second alternative, (b).

Italy Italy has not simply implemented either alternative. The Law provides that unless the parties expressly agree otherwise the agent is entitled to commissions on transactions directly entered into by the principal in the area entrusted to the agent (whether on an exclusive or non-exclusive basis). Additionally, under general law, if a grant is made on an exclusive basis, the agent is (unless the parties expressly provide other wise) entitled to commissions on businesses transacted by the principal either directly or indirectly through third parties.

Liechtenstein First alternative (a)

Luxembourg First alternative, (a), but this rule does not apply if a provision of the contract expressly states that the agent is not entitled to exclusive rights to the relevant area or customers. (Presumably entitlement thus also arises where the grant is expressly made on an exclusive basis.)

Netherlands First alternative, (a).

Norway First alternative, (a).

Portugal Second alternative, (b).

Spain Second alternative, (b).

Sweden First alternative, (a).

4 Art.13(2)—agreements to be evidenced in writing

Member States have the option to provide that an agency agreement shall not be enforceable unless evidenced in writing. Has this option been adopted, and, if so, is there any special requirement as to what is sufficient "evidence in writing"? For instance is an agreement signed by both parties required, or is an exchange of correspondence or even a letter of appointment signed by the principal, enough? **A2–04**

Austria Option not adopted.

Belgium Option not adopted.

Denmark Option not adopted.

Finland Option not adopted, however a post-termination restraint of trade clause is not enforceable unless it is in writing.

France Option not adopted. Commercial courts have also decided that the existence of a commercial agency can be evidenced orally or by any documents whether or not they amount to a formal agreement.

Germany Option not adopted, but covenants not to compete and the undertaking by the agent of del credere obligations must be in writing.

Greece Option adopted. The contract must either be a formal agreement in one document signed by both parties, or an exchange of correspondence reflecting the proposal by the principal with all of its terms and the acceptance of all the terms by the agent. A letter of appointment from the principal is insufficient unless accompanied by a written acceptance from the agent.

Iceland Option adopted. The provision simply states: "Commission sales agreements shall be in writing".

Ireland Option adopted, but no specific guidance as to what "evidenced in writing" means.

Italy Option not adopted.

Liechtenstein Option not adopted.

Luxembourg The law requires a formal agreement in writing signed by both parties, in two originals, one for each party. If there is no such agreement the *agent* can prove the existence of the relationship by any oral or documentary evidence available to him.

Netherlands Option not adopted.

Norway Option not adopted.

Portugal Option not adopted, but the concession to the agent of an exclusive right to a specific area or specific customer group requires a written agreement of the parties to be enforceable.

Spain Option not adopted.

Sweden Option not adopted.

5 Art.15(3)—notice to terminate

A2–05 *Member States have the option to extend the mandatory periods of notice to terminate an agency agreement up to six months for agreements in existence for six years or more. Has this option been adopted?*

Austria Option adopted.

Belgium Option adopted.

Denmark Option adopted.

Finland Option adopted, but (as permitted in Directive) the parties can agree that the notice required to be given by the agent need not be greater than three months.

France Option not adopted.

Germany Option adopted.

Greece Option adopted.

Iceland Option adopted.

Ireland Option not adopted.

Italy Option adopted.

Netherlands Option not adopted

Liechtenstein Option not adopted.

Luxembourg Option adopted.

Norway Option adopted, but (as permitted in Directive) the parties can agree that the notice required to be given by the agent need not be greater than three months.

Portugal Option not adopted.

Spain Option adopted.

Sweden Option adopted, but (as permitted in Directive) the parties can agree that the notice required to be given by the agent need not be greater than three months.

6 Art.16 (*b*)—termination in exceptional circumstances

The Directive is stated not to affect any law of a Member State which provides for immediate termination "where exceptional circumstances arise". What would be exceptional circumstances for the purposes of the local law? **A2–06**

Austria Either party entitled to terminate for a serious reason ("wichtiger Grund"). Examples entitling principal to terminate are: agent becoming incapable of carrying out his obligations; agent behaving in a way rendering him unworthy of principal's confidence (taking bribes, transmitting orders where not required, deceiving principal in important commercial matters); material breach by agent; agent committing assault or battery against principal; and agent becoming insolvent. Examples entitling agent to terminate are: agent becoming incapable of carrying out his obligations; if principal improperly reduces or withholds agent's remuneration or is otherwise in material breach of the agreement; principal commits assault or battery against agent; and principal closes down branch of his company where agent had main field of activity. (Note: The term "wichtiger Grund" is a general concept used in the law of contracts, which has generated considerable and complex case law in its interpretation. The examples given above are not exhaustive. Additionally the parties may agree other less serious grounds for immediate termination provided that this does not create a relationship which unfairly prejudices either the agent or the principal.)

Belgium Either party may terminate where exceptional circumstances make any business cooperation between the parties definitely impossible or where the other party is in material breach of the agreement. Termination is effected by service of a seven day notice specifying the fault and confirming that its severity justified immediate termination.

Denmark Exceptional circumstances are interpreted as any substantial breach of contract, and any economic circumstances (*e.g.* insolvency) which have the result that the agent cannot conduct his activities in an acceptable manner.

Finland Exceptional circumstances are defined as "such neglect or other behaviour by one contracting party that the other party could not reasonably be required to continue the contractual relation ship". Examples would be material misrepresentation; an act which severely prejudices the other party's interest or which severely undermines the other party's trust and confidence in the party committing such act; and a material breach of contract. Any rights to terminate are lost unless the aggrieved party acts to terminate the contract without undue delay upon becoming aware that such cause for termination has arisen.

France Exceptional circumstances are defined as substantial breach or force majeure.

Germany The contract can be terminated without notice for "wichtiger Grund" (see Austria above).

Greece Under Greek law in general the courts have the power to decide whether the event in question justifies immediate termination depending upon the circumstances of each case. Force majeure which continues for an unreasonably long period of time would be one example.

Iceland It is permissible to terminate an agreement without advance notice if either party does not in some respect abide by the provisions of the agreement. It is also permitted to terminate an agreement without notice in the case of unforeseeable circumstances which affect either party and which considerably change the basis of the agreement so that it is obviously unfair that the party concerned should be required to abide by the original agreement.

Ireland The Regulations do not define "exceptional circumstances" but it is assumed they would include force majeure.

Italy No mention is made of Art.16(2) in the Law, but likely examples would be material breach of contract or a serious breach of trust by the agent.

Netherlands Exceptional circumstances are defined as circumstances of such a nature that the terminating party cannot reasonably be expected to continue the agreement.

Liechtenstein The contract can be terminated without notice for "wichtiger Grund" (see Austria above).

Luxembourg Exceptional circumstances are breach or circumstances that definitively make it impossible for the parties to continue their relationship.

Norway Exceptional circumstances are interpreted as material breach.

Portugal Exceptional circumstances are defined as circumstances that render impossible, or seriously prejudice, the performance of the agency agreement for the purposes for which the parties entered into it. They are based on objective elements and correspond to the idea of a "fair cause" for the termination of the agreement. An example would be loss of the market for the goods covered by the agency agreement for reasons not attributable to the default of either party.

Spain Exceptional circumstances are limited to breach or insolvency.

Sweden In the preamble to the law force majeure and serious long-term illness (where the agent is a natural person) are mentioned as examples of exceptional circumstances, otherwise the court will determine this on a case by case basis.

7 Art.17(1)—indemnity or compensation?

A2–07 *Member States must provide for the remedy of indemnity (Art.17(2)) OR compensation (Art.17(3)) upon termination of the agency agreement except by reason of the agent's breach, or voluntary resignation or assignment (Art.18). Which alternative has been adopted? What guidelines (if any) are in existence either in the local implementation or through judicial precedent as to the way in which the amount of awards under the adopted remedy (compensation or indemnity as the case may) are calculated. Is it possible to say roughly on the average how much such awards usually are?*

Austria Indemnity calculated by considering expansion of business produced by agent, benefits enjoyed by principal after termination, agent's loss of commission as a result of termination. Awards tend towards upper limit.

Belgium Indemnity calculated by considering the prejudice caused to the agent by the loss of new customers he has found or existing customers whose business he has increased, and the benefit the principal enjoys from them after the termination.

Denmark Indemnity. In the court cases that have been brought, the court has tended to award the maximum compensation permitted by the Directive.

Finland Indemnity.

France Compensation. In fact this remedy in the Directive was based upon the remedy of compensation already granted to agents under French law (see detailed discussion in Chapter 3.7.)

Germany Indemnity. This remedy has been available under German law since the late 1950s. There is considerable case law as to the precise method of calculation. The indemnity remedy in the Directive was in fact copied from the original German Law (see detailed discussion in Chapter 3.7.)

Greece Indemnity. Greek law in general requires strict proof of damage so that any claim is decided on its particular facts, depending upon the evidence brought by the agent, but subject to the maximum permitted by the Directive.

Iceland The enabling legislation appears to be based on the option for indemnity, although it uses terminology rather akin to damages for breach of contract. In any event the limitations specified for the remedy of indemnity clearly apply to the calculation.

Ireland Originally there was some doubt as to which remedy the 1993 Regulations implemented, or whether in fact neither remedy at all was properly provided for. The Commission considered Ireland had not properly implemented the Directive, and the amending Regulations in 1997 were therefore brought in to clarify that the adopted remedy was compensation. Since the Irish authorities considered that they had adopted the remedy of compensation in the original 1993 Regulations, the 1997 Regulations merely clarify the issue for the avoidance of doubt. Thus, the effective date for the implementation of the remedy is still January 1, 1993, and not the date the 1997 Regulations came into effect.

Italy Indemnity. The Law appears to permit payment of the indemnity EITHER where the agent has brought new customers or developed the principal's business OR where it is equitable—whereas the Directive requires that BOTH these conditions be satisfied, and the Commission has commenced infraction proceedings to require an amendment. In Italy there were National Collective Agreements between associations of principals and associations of agents, dated June 20, 1956 and October 13, 1958, which by law apply to all agency agreements. These provide for levels of payment on termination. By a further collective agreement (the Ensarco Agreement of October 30, 1992) principals and agents agreed they would continue to apply the old guidelines under the collective Agreements to calculating the amount of indemnity. This has been upheld in court on the basis that the Directive provides no guidelines for calculating amounts but only a maximum cap. Awards calculated under these guidelines are usually considerably less than the maximum.

Netherlands In effect the option of indemnity has been adopted, as the provisions of Art.17(2) are embodied in the Law, although the Law refers to the remedy as "client compensation".

Liechtenstein Indemnity. It appears that Liechtenstein does not permit payment of indemnity to the agent in the case of death, but it does permit such payment if the agent can no longer carry out his duties due to age or illness.

Luxembourg Indemnity. (There is some doubt whether the implementing legislation is entirely correct since it seems to permit payment of the indemnity EITHER where the agent has brought new customers to, or developed, the principal's business OR where it is equitable—whereas the Directive requires that BOTH these conditions be satisfied.)

Norway Indemnity.

Portugal Indemnity.

Spain Indemnity. Awards are at the judge's discretion and not usually published. In practice it can be inferred that the maximum amount will generally be the rule.

Sweden Indemnity. The preamble to the Law lists certain factors to be taken into account: the reduction or elimination of the agent's costs after termination, duration of the contractual relationship, size of promotion and marketing costs, agent's sales efforts and the agent's success in the market.

8 Art.17(2)(a)—restraint of trade clause

A2–08 *In calculating the indemnity (where this remedy has been adopted) the Member States may specify that one of the circumstances to be taken into account is whether or not there is a restraint of trade clause binding the agent after termination. If the local implementation has adopted the alternative of indemnity, does it deal specifically with this point?*

Austria Not applicable as such clauses are void under Austrian law.

Belgium If there is such a clause it raises a presumption (which the principal may rebut) that the agent has created and increased business and that the principal has benefited substantially from this.

Denmark No specific mention is made in the implementing legislation.

Finland No mention is made in the Law, but the court would be likely to take account of the presence or absence of such a clause in calculating the indemnity.

France No mention is made in the Law, and the presence or absence of the clause would make no difference to the calculation of compensation.

Germany The implementation does not include a reference to a restraint of trade clause.

Greece The Law provides that the presence or absence of a restraint of trade clause is one factor specifically to be taken into account.

Iceland A post-termination non-compete clause is one of the factors to be taken into account in calculating the indemnity.

Ireland Not applicable.

Italy No mention is made of a restraint of trade clause.

Luxembourg The Law provides that loss of business or revenues by reason of the presence of a restraint of trade clause is one of the circumstances to be taken into account when determining whether the payment of the indemnity is equitable.

Liechtenstein No mention is made of a restraint of trade clause.

Netherlands No specific mention is made, but this is one of the factors that would be taken into account in calculating the "client compensation".

Norway No mention is made of a restraint of trade clause.

Portugal There is a separate provision under Portuguese law which entitles the agent to additional compensation (besides the indemnity) if he is bound by a post-termination restraint of trade clause.

Spain The Law provides that the existence of a restraint of trade clause should be taken into account in calculating the indemnity, but no further guidelines are given.

Sweden The preamble to the Act states that the existence of a restraint of trade clause could be a circumstance to take into account when calculating the indemnity.

9 Art.17(2)(c)—damages

Where the remedy specified is indemnity, a claim for indemnity shall not prevent the agent from "seeking damages". How is this provision interpreted, and what sort of things could the agent seek damages for? **A2–09**

Austria The agent can in addition to indemnity claim damages under general principles of Austrian law (*e.g.* premature termination by principal, payment of commissions owed by principal, damages for principal's misrepresentation, etc).

Belgium Damages can be claimed at law for premature termination with out justification calculated on the unexpired portion of the contract and the current remuneration at the date of termination.

Denmark The agent can seek damages at law for such matters as premature termination of the contract, or for the cost of investment made on behalf of the principal in the expectation that the contract would continue in existence.

Finland Damages for breach of contract can be claimed. Additionally, where the agent has made capital investments which are greater than "customary" he would be entitled to compensation for these in addition to the indemnity.

France Not applicable as the remedy is compensation. However, in addition to the remedy of compensation a claim can be raised for damages at law for premature termination of the contract (see Chapter 3.7.)

Germany Damages at law for breach of contract or misrepresentation are freely available in addition to the indemnity.

Greece Damages (direct, indirect and consequential) in addition to the indemnity are freely available under the general law (subject to proof of *quantum*).

Iceland Rather confusingly the enabling legislation appears to equate the remedy under indemnity with breach of contract and then to also allow a further remedy in relation to damages for the "financial loss" that the agent sustains due to the termination of the agency agreement. This financial loss principally constitutes lost commission which the agent would have earned by due performance of the agreement, and any capital investment which is still not amortised at the date of termination.

Ireland Not applicable.

Italy A concurrent claim for damages for breach of contract can be made.

Liechtenstein No specific mention is made of Art.17(2)(c).

Luxembourg Liquidated damages can be claimed for premature termination or serious breach of contract. Such damages are specified in the implementing legislation as a sum equal to the remuneration that would have been received for the period between the breach and the normal termination of the contract. The court must calculate this by looking at previous remuneration and other relevant circumstances, and has a discretion to reduce the sum if it considers it too high.

Netherlands A concurrent claim for damages for breach of contract is available.

Norway A concurrent claim for damages for breach of contract is provided under the Law.

Portugal A concurrent claim for damages for breach of contract is available under the general law.

Spain A specific provision in the Law provides for an additional compensation where the principal terminates an agreement of indefinite length in circumstances where the agent has not been able to amortise the costs and expenses that he had incurred for the performance of the agency contract on the principal's advice. This remedy is not available if the contract is a fixed term contract which expired by effluxion of time, although in this case the agent can still claim the indemnity. The calculation of such compensation is again basically in the discretion of the judge and there are no published decisions or guidelines. It is unclear to what extent other damages can be claimed but presumably other losses due to breach of contract (*e.g.* failure to pay commissions when due) might also be claimable under the general law.

Sweden A concurrent claim for damages can be made under the Act. The claim can be made as a result of any breach of the agent's rights under the agreement, and can cover all costs and losses, including indirect damages and loss of profit.

10 Art.20(4)—reasonable restraint of trade

Is a two year post-termination restraint of trade clause generally regarded as reasonable. **A2–10**

Austria All such clauses are void under Austrian law.

Belgium A restraint of trade clause must not be longer than six months.

Denmark A two year restraint of trade clause is generally considered to be reasonable.

Finland The Law permits restraint of trade clauses of up to a maximum of two years, but each clause has to be examined to see whether it is reasonable in all the circumstances of the case, so that no general rule as to what is a reasonable period can be given.

France The Law permits restraint of trade clauses for up to two years, and these would normally be considered reasonable.

Germany A restraint of trade clause up to two years is permitted by the Law. This was already incorporated in the German legislation from 1953.

Greece The Decree provides for only a one year restraint of trade clause.

Iceland A two year restraint of trade clause is permitted provided it is in writing and is linited to the area or group of customers and to the goods or sevrices to which the agency related.

Ireland A two year restraint of trade clause is likely to be reasonable as a general rule, but it does depend upon the circumstances of the particular case.

Italy A restraint of trade clause of up to two years is permitted.

Liechtenstein two year restraint of clause is allowed, but only if the agent receives an equitable compensation for accepting it.

Luxembourg A restraint of trade clause is permitted for only 12 months after termination. In Luxembourg such clauses often have a sum specified in them as liquidated damages payable by the covenantor if he breaches the clause. The Law permits the court to reduce the period of time or the level of the liquidated damages if (after taking account of the interest of the principal) he finds that the consequences of the period are inequitable for the agent, or that the amount is unreasonable.

Netherlands A two year restraint of trade clause would be considered reasonable.

Norway The Law permits a restraint of trade clause for up to two years provided it is in writing. A period of two years is generally considered reasonable, but the Norwegian Contract Act, s.38 provides that any restraint of trade clause is not binding if it unreasonably restricts the agent's possibilities to make a living and is regarded as more extensive than what is necessary to protect against competition.

Portugal A restraint of trade clause for a period of two years is regarded as reasonable.

Spain A two year restraint of trade clause is in general likely to be reasonable.

Sweden A two year restraint of trade clause is likely to be reasonable, but the courts have a jurisdiction to modify such a clause (what ever its duration) if they consider it to be more extensive than is reasonable in any particular case.

11 Additional comments

A2–11 *Are there any additional issues not covered in the items listed above which are worthy of mention?*

Austria None.

Belgium The legislation in Belgium applies not only to agents dealing in goods (those covered by the Directive) but to agents "entrusted in a permanent way and for valuable consideration...with the negotiation of business deals...". Thus agents for services are also covered, except such agents regulated by specific statutes such as insurance and credit agents.

Denmark None.

Finland There is a general statute which gives the court the power to amend unreasonable contractual provisions and the enabling legislation for the Directive specifically applies this statute to agency agreements. This power could be used, for instance, to shorten the period of a restraint of trade clause.

France The legislation in France also applies to agents for services as well as goods.

Germany None.

Greece None.

Iceland The legislation applies not only to agencies for the supply of goods but also to agencies for the supply of services.

Ireland None.

Italy In addition to the Directive many aspects of agency agreements are, by law, governed by the National Collective Agreements referred to above. Italian case law shows that agents who are natural persons tend to be treated more favourably than legal entities. Additionally, under s.409 of the Civil Code, in many respects the status of natural persons who are agents is equated with that of employees.

Liechtenstein None.

Luxembourg None.

Netherlands Agents for services as well as goods are covered. Agents covered by statutory regimes (such as insurance agents) are excluded.

Norway None.

Portugal None.

Spain The legislation in Spain covers agents who negotiate and/or conclude "commercial operations" which covers not only trade in goods but also services.

Sweden None.

12 Other relevant jurisdictions

A2–12 The position of the implementation of the Directive in the UK is covered in detail in Chapter 3.

Appendix 3

Flow Chart 1
EC and UK Competition Law Jurisdictions

A3–01

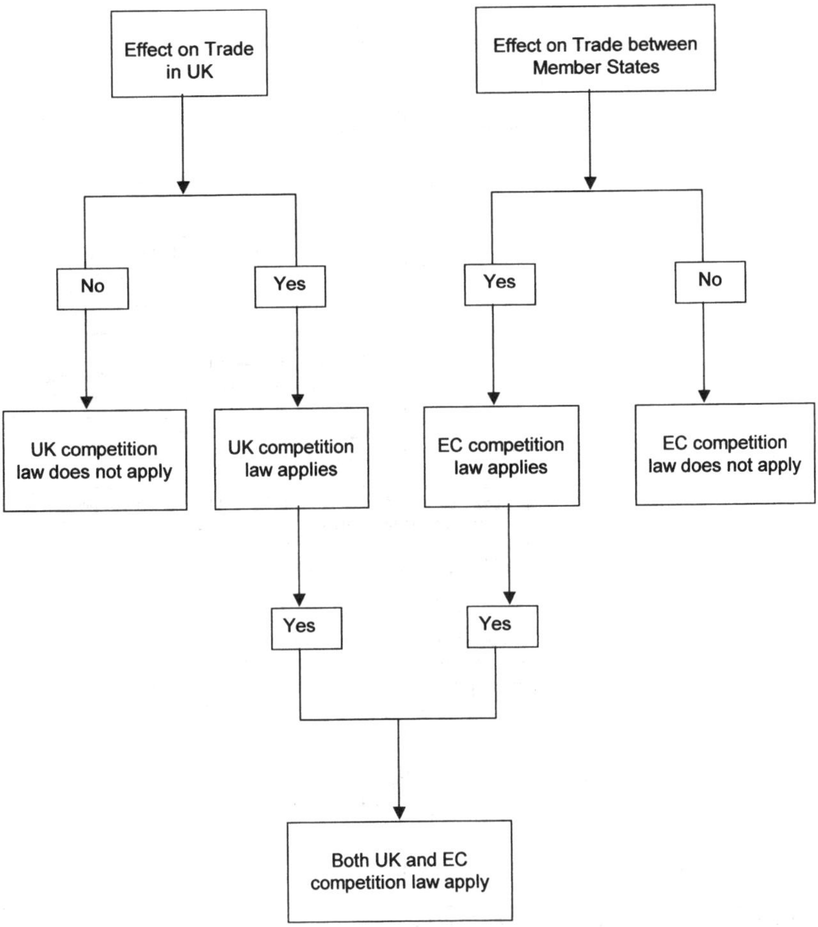

Flow Chart 2
Art.81—General Application

A3–02

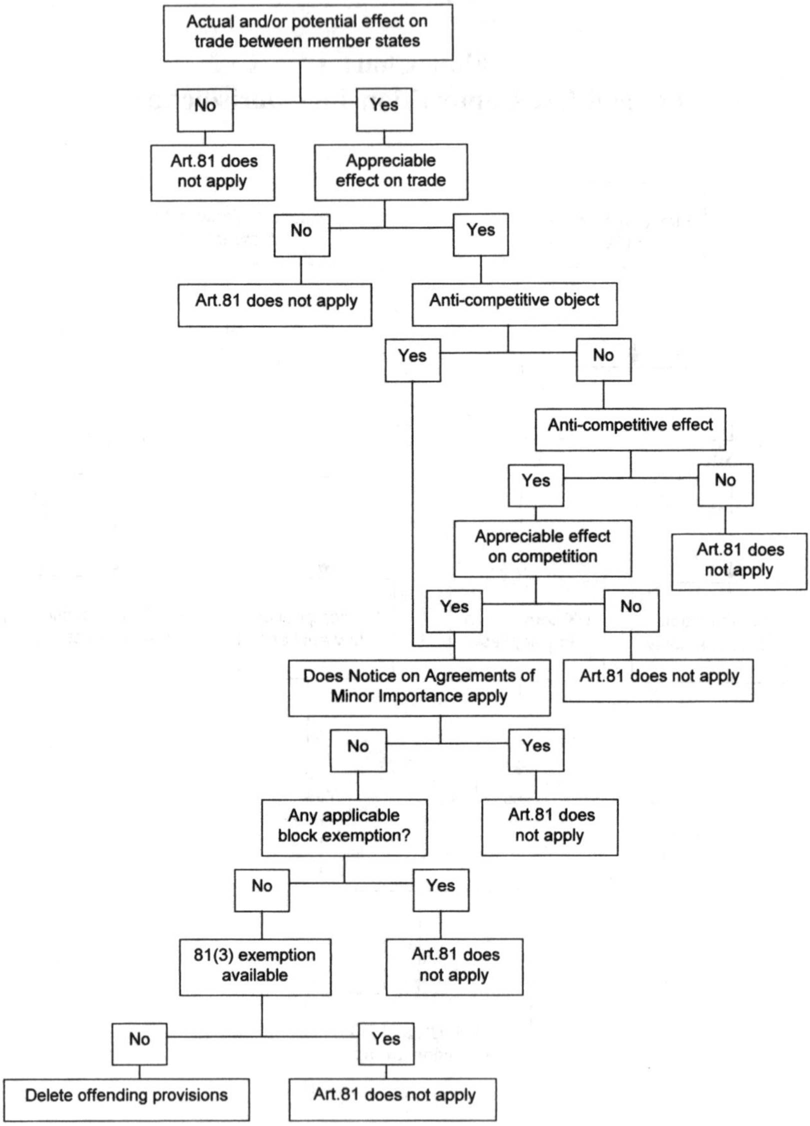

Flow Chart 3
Vertical Restraints under EC Competition Law

A3–03

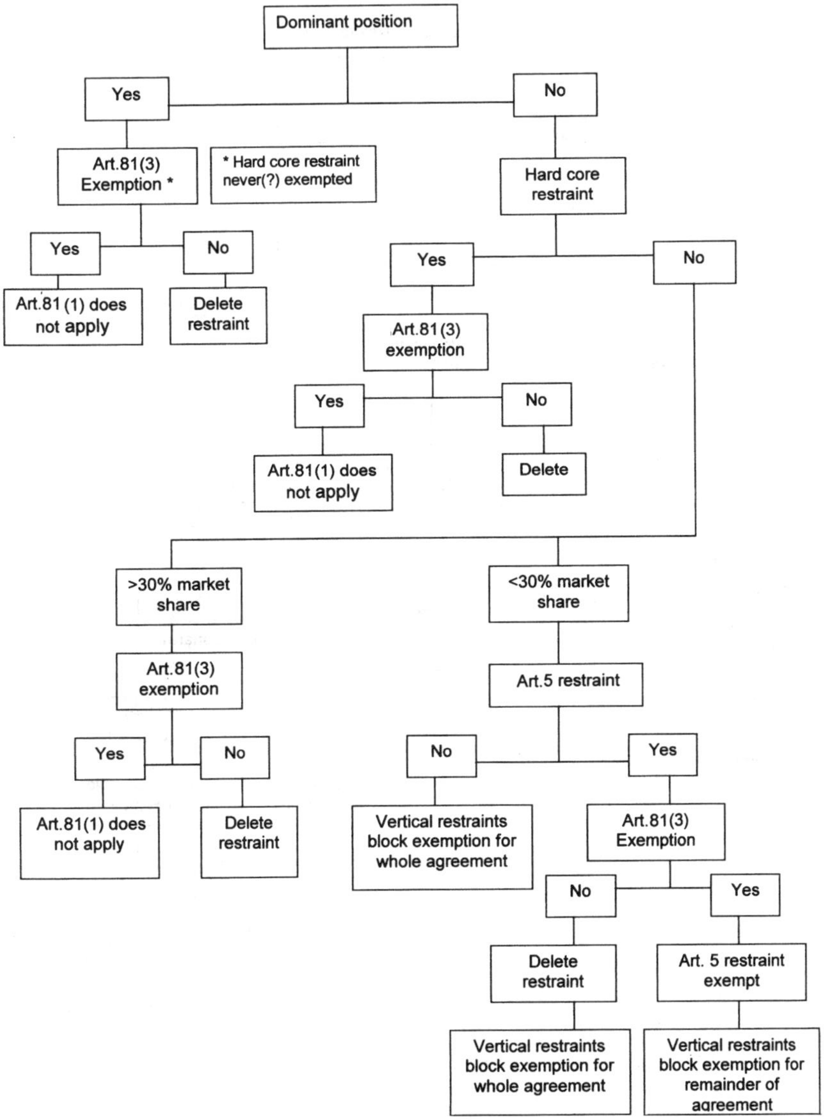

Flow Chart 4
Vertical and Horizontal Restraints under UK Competition Law

A3–04

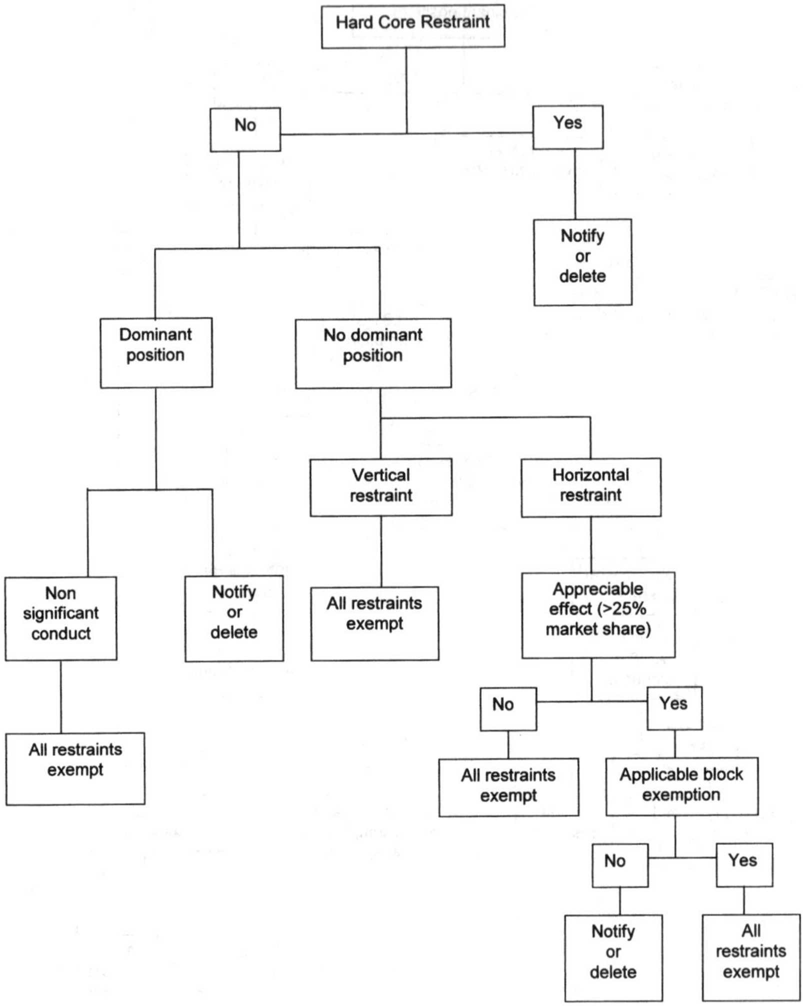

Appendix 4

Web Sites for EU and UK Legislation

1. The home page for the European Union can be found at: **A4–01**

http://europa.eu.int/index_en.htm

Within that site:

- The home page for competition issues can be found at: http://europa.eu.int/comm/competition/index_en.html
- EU competition law legislation and notices can be found at: http://europa.eu.int/comm/competition/antitrust/legislation/entente3_en.html
- Reports of many EU competition law cases can be found at: http://europa.eu.int/comm/competition/antitrust/cases/

2. The following site which is a link from the Europa web site also contains useful case reports and copies of notices and legislation relating to EC competition law issues: **A4–02**

http://europa.eu.int/eur-lex/en/index.html

3. All relevant UK legislation can be found through the following site: **A4–03**

http://www.hmso.gov.uk

4. The home page of the UK Office of Fair Trading web site can be found at: **A4–04**

http://www.oft.gov.uk/default.htm

This contains links to relevant information on competition law for both businesses and consumers. The OFT guidelines and commentary referred to in this book can be found through accessing the business section of the site at:

http://www.oft.gov.uk/Business/default.htm

Index

Instruction for use of the companion disc

Introduction

These notes are provided for guidance only. They should be read and interpreted in the context of your own computer system and operational procedures. It is assumed that you have a basic knowledge of WINDOWS. However, if there is any problem please contact our help line on 020 7393 7266 who will be happy to help you.

CD Format and Contents

To run this CD you need at least:

IBM compatible PC
CD-ROM drive
Microsoft Word 6.0/95

The CD contains data files of the clauses in this book. It does not contain software or commentary.

Installation

The following instructions make the assumption that you will copy the data files to a single directory on your hard disk (e.g. C:\International Agency).

Open your **CD Rom drive**, select and double click on **setup.exe** and follow the instructions. The files will be unzipped to your **C drive** and you will be able to open them from the new **C:\International Agency** folder there.

LICENCE AGREEMENT

Definitions

1. The following terms will have the following meanings: "The PUBLISHERS" means Sweet & Maxwell of 100 Avenue Road, London NW3 3PF (which expression shall, where the context admits, include the PUBLISHERS' assigns or successors in business as the case may be) of the other part on behalf of Thomson Books Limited of Cheriton House, North Way, Andover SP10 5BE.
"The LICENSEE" means the purchaser of the title containing the Licensed Material.
"Licensed Material" means the data included on the disk;
"Licence" means a single user licence;
"Computer" means an IBM-PC compatible computer.

Grant of Licence; Back up copies

2. (1) The PUBLISHERS hereby grant to the LICENSEE, a non-exclusive, non-transferable licence to use the Licensed Material in accordance with these terms and conditions.

(2) The LICENSEE may install the Licensed Material for use on one computer only at any one time.

(3) The LICENSEE may make one back-up copy of the Licensed Material only, to be kept in the LICENSEE's control and possession.

Proprietary Rights

3. (1) All rights not expressly granted herein are reserved.

(2) The Licensed Material is not sold to the LICENSEE who shall not acquire any right, title or interest in the Licensed Material or in the media upon which the Licensed Material is supplied.

(3) The LICENSEE shall not erase, remove, deface or cover any trademark, copyright notice, guarantee or other statement on any media containing the Licensed Material.

(4) The LICENSEE shall only use the Licensed Material in the normal course of its business and shall not use the Licensed Material for the purpose of operating a bureau or similar service or any online service whatsoever.

(5) Permission is hereby granted to LICENSEES who are members of the legal profession (which expression does not include individuals or organisations engaged in the supply of services to the legal profession) to reproduce, transmit and store small quantities of text for the purpose of enabling them to provide legal advice to or to draft documents or conduct proceedings on behalf of their clients.

(6) The LICENSEE shall not sublicense the Licensed Material to others and this Licence Agreement may not be transferred, sublicensed, assigned or otherwise disposed of in whole or in part.

(7) The LICENSEE shall inform the PUBLISHERS on becoming aware of any unauthorised use of the Licensed Material.

Warranties

4. (1) The PUBLISHERS warrant that they have obtained all necessary rights to grant this licence.

(2) Whilst reasonable care is taken to ensure the accuracy and completeness of the Licensed Material supplied, the PUBLISHERS make no representations or warranties, express or implied, that the Licensed Material is free from errors or omissions.

(3) The Licensed Material is supplied to the LICENSEE on an "as is" basis and has not been supplied to meet the LICENSEE'S individual requirements. It is the sole responsibility of the LICENSEE to satisfy itself prior to entering this Licence Agreement that the Licensed Material will meet the LICENSEE's requirements and be compatible with the LICENSEE's hardware/software configuration. No failure of any part of the Licensed Material to be suitable for the LICENSEE's requirements will give rise to any claim against the PUBLISHERS.

(4) In the event of any material inherent defects in the physical media on which the licensed material may be supplied, other than caused by accident abuse or misuse by the LICENSEE, the PUBLISHERS will replace the defective original media free of charge provided it is retumed to the place of purchase within 90 days of the purchase date. The PUBLISHERS' enure liability and the LICENSEE's exclusive remedy shall be the replacement of such defective media.

(5) Whilst all reasonable care has been taken to exclude computer viruses, no warranty is made that the Licensed Material is virus free. The LICENSEE shall be responsible to ensure that no virus is introduced to any computer or network and shall not hold the PUBLISHERS responsible.

(6) The warranties set out herein are exclusive of and in lieu of all other conditions and warranties, either express or implied, statutory or otherwise.

(7) All other conditions and warranties, either express or implied, statutory or otherwise, which relate in the condition and fitness for any purpose of the Licensed Material are hereby excluded and the PUBLISHERS' shall not be liable in contract or in tort for any loss of any kind suffered by reason of any defect in the Licensed Material (whether or not caused by the negligence of the PUBLISHERS).

Limitation of Liability and Indemnity

5. (1) The LICENSEE shall accept sole responsibility for and the PUBLISHERS shall not be liable for the use of the Licensed Material by the LICENSEE, its agents and employees and the LICENSEE shall hold the PUBLISHERS harmless and fully indemnified against any claims, costs, damages, loss and liabilities arising out of any such use.

(2) The PUBLISHERS shall not be liable for any indirect or consequential loss suffered by the LICENSEE (including without limitation loss of profits, goodwill or data) in connection with the Licensed Material howsoever arising.

(3) The PUBLISHERS will have no liability whatsoever for any liability of the LICENSEE or any third party which might arise.

(4) The LICENSEE hereby agrees that

(a) the LICENSEE is best placed to foresee and evaluate any loss that might be suffered in connection with this Licence Agreement;

(b) that the cost of supply of the Licensed Material has been calculated on the basis of the limitations and exclusions contained herein; and

(c) the LICENSEE will effect such insurance as is suitable having regard to the LICENSEE's circumstances.

(5) The aggregate maximum liability of the PUBLISHERS in respect of any direct loss or any other loss (to the extent that such loss is not excluded by this Licence Agreement or otherwise) whether such a claim arises in contract or tort shall not exceed a sum equal to that paid as the price for the title containing the Licensed Material.

Termination

6. (1) In the event of any breach of this Agreement including any violation of any copyright in the Licensed Material, whether held by the PUBLISHERS or others in the Licensed Material, the Licence Agreement shall automatically terminate immediately, without notice and without prejudice to any claim which the PUBLISHERS may have either for moneys due and/or damages and/or otherwise.

(2) Clauses 3 to S shall survive the termination for whatsoever reason of this Licence Agreement.

(3) In the event of termination of this Licence Agreement the LICENSEE will remove the Licensed Material.

Miscellaneous

7. (1) Any delay or forbearance by the PUBLISHERS in enforcing any provisions of this Licence Agreement shall not be construed as a waiver of such provision or an agreement thereafter not to enforce the said provision.

(2) This Licence Agreement shall be governed by the laws of England and Wales, If any difference shall arise between the Parties touching the meaning of this Licence Agreement or the rights and liabilities of the parties thereto, the same shall be referred to arbitration in accordance with the provisions of the Arbitration Act 1996, or any amending or substituting statute for the time being in force.